Mathematics
UNLIMITED
Teacher's Edition

WHAT TEACHERS ARE SAYING ABOUT MATHEMATICS UNLIMITED

"Introductory activities are useful, well explained, and good for all children."

"Like the variety of activities to challenge top students."

"Offers concrete examples."

"The variety of problem-solving formats teaches students to think."

"It has everything I want."

"Clear—everything you could ask for."

"Very motivating."

"Easy to use."

"Good introduction to the concept."

"A logical progression of how to think out problems."

"A lot of support for teachers."

"Thorough and concise."

"Sequencing of skills is meaningful."

"Progression is good and easy to follow."

"Would appeal to my kids."

"Good mental math sessions."

"Very good thought involvement."

"Especially like the estimation."

"It's geared to all pupils and very relevant."

"Geared to developing good mathematical reasoning. Excellent problem-solving and critical thinking examples."

"Like the multiple choice (common error 'Checkpoint') as practice for standardized tests."

"Challenges the students."

"Much more helpful than other Teacher's Editions."

"Format is easy to follow."

"Everything needed is there."

"Challenging activities."

"Excellent problem solving."

"Illustrations are motivating."

"Great teaching suggestions."

"Well-developed sequential stages."

"Lots of good teacher support activities."

"Problem solving is an integral part of every lesson."

"Presentation is complete."

"Fits the needs of children on many levels."

"Follow-up is helpful, especially mental math."

"Includes activities for everyone."

"Teacher's Edition directions are in intelligent, appropriate language."

"Well-organized, well-marked, well-numbered pages."

"Provides much support for teachers."

"The 'common errors' chart is great."

"The most complete Teacher's Edition."

"A lot of help for the teacher."

"Explains procedures for teaching in an organized manner. Does not talk down to the teacher. Also like the remediation for specific errors."

 **Harcourt Brace Jovanovich, Inc.**

Holt, Rinehart and Winston, Inc.

Orlando · Austin · San Diego · Chicago · Dallas · Toronto

GRADE 8

Mathematics
UNLIMITED

TABLE OF CONTENTS

AUTHORS

FRANCIS "SKIP" FENNELL   **BARBARA J. REYS**   **ROBERT E. REYS**   **ARNOLD W. WEBB**

CREDITS

BULLETIN BOARD ART BY PHIL CARVER N' FRIENDS

TECHNICAL ART BY VANTAGE ART, INC.

MEET THE AUTHORS

OF MATHEMATICS UNLIMITED

Francis "Skip" Fennell   Barbara J. Reys   Robert E. Reys   Arnold W. Webb

An exceptional author team whose expertise reflects the latest thinking in the teaching of mathematics, a wealth of curriculum and subject area specialists, and the contributions of over 1,000 elementary teachers—from schools all across the country—have helped make MATHEMATICS UNLIMITED uniquely responsive to the realities of today's classroom.

AUTHORS

FRANCIS "SKIP" FENNELL, Ph.D.,

Pennsylvania State University, has over 20 years' classroom experience and is currently Associate Professor of Education at Western Maryland College. He is the author of numerous articles, textbooks and research papers, is a widely respected speaker and consultant in the field of math education and a member of the editorial board of Arithmetic Teacher.

BARBARA J. REYS, Ph.D.,

University of Missouri at Columbia, is currently Assistant Professor of Mathematics Education there. She brings a wide range of teaching experience to the development of MATHEMATICS UNLIMITED—from a small Missouri-Arkansas district to inner city and suburban schools to courses at the college level. She has extensive publishing credentials, has coordinated the preparation of lessons and materials incorporating fresh ideas and teaching methods, and has served as mathematics consultant for Instructor since 1982.

ROBERT E. REYS, Ed.D.,

University of Missouri at Columbia, is an internationally recognized expert on estimation and mental mathematics. He has been Professor of Mathematics Education at UMC since 1967 and has an impressive record of presentations and publications. He serves as referee for The Arithmetic Teacher, The Mathematics Teacher, Journal for Research in Math Education, and other prestigious national journals.

ARNOLD W. WEBB, Ph.D.,

New York University, is Senior Research Associate/Director of Higher Education at Research for Better Schools. Former Assistant Commissioner for Education Programs with the New Jersey State Department of Education, he has also served as Dean of the School of Education at the City University of New York. He has worked in several capacities with the New York City Board of Education.

SENIOR CONSULTANTS

Michael C. Hynes
Professor of Education
University of Central Florida
Orlando, Florida

S. Stuart Flanagan
Professor of Mathematics Education
College of William and Mary
Williamsburg, Virginia

Robert D. Postman
Professor of Mathematics Education
Mercy College
Dobbs Ferry, New York

CONSULTING EDUCATORS

Edward C. Beardslee
Associate Professor of Mathematics and Computer Science
Millersville University of Pennsylvania
Millersville, Pennsylvania

Grace Burton, Associate Professor, Department of Curriculum
University of North Carolina at Wilmington
Wilmington, North Carolina

Jack A. Hope
Department of Curriculum Studies
University of Saskatchewan
Saskatoon, Saskatchewan

Henrietta Pesce
Educational Consultant
Moorestown, New Jersey

Marilyn Rehwald
Assistant Principal
Los Angeles United School District
Los Angeles, California

Yolanda Rodriguez
Mathematics Teacher
Agassiz School
Cambridge, Massachusetts

MEET THE TEACHER CONSULTANTS

ON MATHEMATICS UNLIMITED K-8

TEACHER CONSULTANTS

Martha Accordino
St. Virgilius School
Broad Channel, New York

Don Ackert
Williamsburg-James City County
Schools
Williamsburg, Virginia

Dolly Adams
Union County Elementary School
Blairsville, Georgia

LaVerne Amick
Tempe, Arizona

DeVere L. Anderson
Cajun Valley Junior High School
El Cajun, California

Tina Angelini
Academy Street School
Glassboro, New Jersey

Beth H. Applegate
Central School
Tooele, Utah

Thomas Aucone
Edwards School
Beverly, Massachusetts

Janice Austin
Glen Forest Elementary School
Falls Church, Virginia

Blaine D. Bendixon
Brockbank Junior High School
Magna, Utah

Sylvia Benson
Syracuse School
Layton, Utah

Virginia Anne Beyerle
A. H. Shaw Elementary School
Phoenix, Arizona

Lucille Binz
Capri School
Campbell, California

Susan Bizorik
Kansas City School District
Kansas City, Missouri

Claudia Blackwell
Peter Marshall School
Anaheim, California

Bertha Bonner
Lafayette School
Chicago, Illinois

Candice Bradley
Union County Elementary School
Blairsville, Georgia

Eden E. Bright
Dana Hills High School
Dana Point, California

T. C. Broberg
Danbrook Elementary School
Anaheim, California

Judy T. Brown
Woodbury Elementary School
Garden Grove, California

Mary Brown
Winston-Salem, North Carolina

Vivian Brown
Detroit, Michigan

Douglas Brumbaugh
University of Central Florida
Orlando, Florida

Norma L. Bull
Riner Elementary School
Riner, Virginia

Cynthia L. Burson
Garfield School
Phoenix, Arizona

David Capaldi
Winman Junior High School
Warwick, Rhode Island

Frank Caputa
Ann Street School
Newark, New Jersey

Lynn Carr
Churchville Elementary School
Churchville, Maryland

Neil Carrigan
Morgan Middle School
Morgan, Utah

Anne Clifford
White Plains School
White Plains, New York

Beverly Collins
Elmwood School
Stockton, California

Glenn Coltharp
Tomahawk Elementary School
Olathe, Kansas

Jan Colwill
Longfellow School
Sioux Falls, South Dakota

Terry E. Crites
William Wood College
Fulton, Missouri

Jane Decker
Columbus Academy
Columbus, Ohio

Henry Diehl
Allentown School District
Allentown, Pennsylvania

Karen Doherty
Westchester Day School
Mamaroneck, New York

Barry Doran
DeKalb County Schools
Decatur, Georgia

Christine Eastmond
Brooklyn, New York

Cynthia Eckenrode
Robert Morton Elementary School
Westminster, Maryland

Vivian Eilebrecht
Truth or Consequences Middle
School
Truth or Consequences, New Mexico

Carol Ellis
Spartanburg City Schools
Spartanburg, South Carolina

Sharon G. Ellis
Mt. Logan Middle School
Logan, Utah

Barbara A. Everhart
Buies Creek School
Buies Creek, North Carolina

Kathy Farris
Christianburg Primary School
Christianburg, Virginia

Nancy Fenney
Normandy School District
St. Louis, Missouri

Bronna Flanagan
South Calloway Public Schools
South Calloway, Missouri

Tom Foley
George Moscone School
San Francisco, California

Roger A. Fowles
Morgan School
Morgan, Utah

Elizabeth B. Frazier
Wilson County Schools
Wilson, North Carolina

Cindy Frogge
Havencroft Elementary School
Olathe, Kansas

Kathleen Furey
Stearne School
Philadelphia, Pennsylvania

John George
Frederick County Schools
Frederick, Maryland

Patrick A. Gillan
Jenks Elementary School
Philadelphia, Pennsylvania

Charlotte Goie
Daniel Street School
Lindenhurst, New York

Bonnie Graney
Sensory Road Elementary School
Winchester, Virginia

Sylvia Green
John F. Kennedy Elementary School
Madison, Wisconsin

Neva Griffin
Anniston City Schools
Anniston, Alabama

Ruth Harbin
Educational Center
Olathe, Kansas

Elaine C. Harvey
Monterey School District
Monterey, California

Kathleen Hauser
Terraset Elementary School
Reston, Virginia

Bonnie Worley Havens
Ashlawn Elementary School
Arlington, Virginia

Larry Hawkins
Zia Junior High School
Las Cruces, New Mexico

Kathleen Hayden
PS 114
Belle Harbor, New York

Ruth A. Hempen
Ashlawn Elementary School
Arlington, Virginia

Nina Hennigh
Pojoaque Elementary School
Santa Fe, New Mexico

Susan Hood
Riner Elementary School
Riner, Virginia

Sister Karen Hopkins
St. Patrick School
Portland, Maine

Larry L. Houser
Carroll County Public Schools
Westminster, Maryland

Lindsey Howell
Spring Creek School
Seven Springs, North Carolina

Don Hruska
Merrymen School
Marinette, Wisconsin

Maureen Hughes
Brooklyn, New York

Alma Hunter
Detroit, Michigan

Carolyn Hutson
Union County Elementary School
Blairsville, Georgia

Judy B. Jones
Berkeley Elementary School
Williamsburg, Virginia

Mary Beth Judd
North Summit School
Coalville, Utah

Loretta Karbach
Immaculate Conception School
Jenkintown, Pennsylvania

Mary Kay Karl
Schaumberg Elementary Schools
Schaumberg, Illinois

John Katzel
Hough Street School
Barrington, Illinois

Michael Kay
Westlake Elementary School
Westlake Village, California

Jerri Kazmierczak
Los Alamitos School
San Jose, California

David Kearney
Tomahawk Elementary School
Olathe, Kansas

Virgie I. Keith
Pulaski County Schools
Pulaski, Virginia

John Kelley
Brockton Public Schools
Brockton, Massachusetts

Mary Kepple
Hampstead Elementary School
Hampstead, Maryland

Iras Kidwell
Brawley Elementary Schools
Brawley, California

Luther Kirk
Riner Elementary School
Riner, Virginia

Judy Knapp
Twinsburg Elementary School
Twinsburg, Ohio

Elmer Koch
Minneapolis Public Schools
Minneapolis, Minnesota

Steve Leinwand
Connecticut Department of
   Education
Hartford, Connecticut

Roberto R. Lemus
Horace Mann Junior High School
San Francisco, California

Agnes Leonardich
Monterey Diocese
Monterey, California

Gordon Lewis
Washington, D.C., Public Schools
Washington, D.C.

Renee Lindenman
Forest Hill School
San Jose, California

Christine M. Lockhart
Robert Morton Elementary School
Westminster, Maryland

Vicki Lunceford
Brawley Elementary Schools
Brawley, California

Kim MacLean-Blevins
Winfield Elementary School
Westminster, Maryland

Cathy Maples
Robeson County Schools
Lumberton, North Carolina

Harry B. Marcopolos
Calvert School
Baltimore, Maryland

Sam Maroon
Boxford-Topsfield Schools
Topsfield, Massachusetts

Gary Marshall
Williamson Central School District
Sodus, New York

Linda Martin
Mt. Olivet Elementary School
Martinsville, Virginia

Benito Martinez
Pojoaque Elementary School
Sante Fe, New Mexico

Maureen McAnarney
Washington Elementary School
Olathe, Kansas

Sister Kathleen McKernan
Our Lady of Mercy Convent
Winston-Salem, North Carolina

Shirley McMinn
East Petersberg Elementary School
East Petersberg, Pennsylvania

Donna McPartland
Taneytown Elementary School
Taneytown, Maryland

Kevin Mecklin
Cathedral Grammar School
Portland, Maine

Oscar Mendez-Reinlin
New York City Schools
New York, New York

Sandra Mervine
Lurgan Elementary School
Lurgan, Pennsylvania

Zita Michalski
Acacia Elementary School
Fullerton, California

Kathy Mick
Swegel Elementary School
Salem, Oregon

Diane Miller
Louisiana State University
Baton Rouge, Louisiana

Sue Miyabara-McCaskey
Taylor School
San Jose, California

Lee Moeller
Rose Avenue School
Modesto, California

Janice Mort
Tarrant Elementary School
Hampton, Virginia

Peter O. Mortenson
Eisenhower Junior High School
Salt Lake, Utah

Richard Neilsen
Fall Mountain Regional Schools
Alstead, New Hampshire

Diane Nunnaley
Framingham Public Schools
Framingham, Massachusetts

Suzanne O'Brien
Kimball School
Concord, New Hampshire

Cathy Panetti
Parkway School District
St. Louis, Missouri

Donna Parish
Zia Junior High School
Las Cruces, New Mexico

Carol Perkins
Black Bob Elementary School
Olathe, Kansas

Nancy Petersen
Phoenix, Arizona

Sharon Piazza
Taylor School
San Jose, California

Beatrice Pitta
Ann Street School
Newark, New Jersey

Ginger Porter
Havencroft Elementary School
Olathe, Kansas

Elizabeth Postman
Hillsdale Schools
Hillsdale, New Jersey

Ann Radford
Princeton School
Princeton, North Carolina

Kevin M. Reich
East Hampton Middle School
East Hampton, Connecticut

Nancy Fox Ring
Ancillae-Assumpta Academy
Wyncote, Pennsylvania

Barbara L. Roberts
Springfield, Oregon

George A. Rogers
O. Wright School
Modesto, California

Robert Ross
De Vargas School
San Jose, California

Don W. Scheuer, Jr.
Bucks County Community College
Jenkintown, Pennsylvania

Howard Schremp
Camden Middle School
Camden, New York

Anthony Serpe
Elkhorn Avenue School District
Elkhorn, Wisconsin

Bill Setzer
Roanoke County Schools
Salem, Virginia

Diane E. Shearer
Lowell School
San Jose, California

Wilbur M. Simon
Normandy School District
St. Louis, Missouri

Deborah B. Simpkins
Riner Elementary School
Riner, Virginia

Louise M. Smith
Charleston County Schools
Charleston, South Carolina

Kathy Stackhouse
Academy Street School
Glassboro, New Jersey

Fred R. Stewart
Neshaminy School District
Richboro, Pennsylvania

Becky Stone
Union County Elementary School
Blairsville, Georgia

Harry D. Stratigos
School District of Lancaster
Lancaster, Pennsylvania

Al Tarras
Hastings Junior High School
Hastings, Minnesota

Jennifer Zack Taylor
Flora Vista School
Encinitas, California

Joyce Taylor
West Valley School
Sunnyvale, California

Ethel H. Thurman
Kansas City, Missouri

Frank Tippett
West Middle School
Westminster, Maryland

Esther Ujifusa
Taft Elementary School
Orange, California

Lin Viavada
Greenfield Junior High School
El Cajun, California

Sue Volger
San Marcos Junior High School
San Marcos, California

Jane Wagner
Ladd Elementary School
Waynesboro, Virginia

Sharon Waicus
Buies Creek Elementary School
Buies Creek, North Carolina

Helen Ward
Houston TSD
Houston, Texas

Joy Ward
Hope Middle School
Chicago, Illinois

Blanchard Watson
Williamson Central School District
East Williamson, New York

Marjorie R. White
La Presa Elementary School
Spring Valley, California

Allan Wojtach
Cary Middle School
Cary, Illinois

Gloria Woolfolk
Farraday School
Chicago, Illinois

J. Wendell Wyatt
South East Missouri State University
Cape Girardeau, Missouri

Lucy Mirisciotti Young
Canon-McMillan School District
Canonsburg, Pennsylvania

Barbara S. Yurick
Whittier School
Phoenix, Arizona

PACING CHART

This chart includes material for three courses of study—Basic, Average, and Extended. It shows one approach to providing for individual differences in assigning the year's work. The Pacing Chart is just a suggested plan. The flexibility of the instructional approach of MATHEMATICS UNLIMITED enables you to develop plans to meet your students' needs.

The lessons suggested for omission from the Basic course of study are those extending content covered previously in the Basic course of study. Before presenting lessons suggested as optional in the Average course of study, you may wish to evaluate the developmental readiness of your students. These suggestions are provided to help you plan for each student a balanced course of study that will provide a solid foundation for the content presented at the next grade level.

CHAPTER	PAGES	BASIC	AVERAGE	EXTENDED
1 ADDITION AND SUBTRACTION OF WHOLE NUMBERS AND DECIMALS	2–40	17 days	15 days	13 days
2 MULTIPLICATION AND DIVISION OF WHOLE NUMBERS AND DECIMALS	42–78	15 days (omit 76–77)	14 days	12 days
3 NUMBER THEORY, EXPRESSIONS, AND EQUATIONS	80–118	18 days	17 days	15 days
CUMULATIVE TEST 1–3		1 day	1 day	1 day
4 FRACTIONS	120–164	18 days (omit 162–163)	17 days	16 days
5 MEASUREMENT	166–198	14 days	12 days	11 days
6 RATIO, PROPORTION, AND PERCENT	200–238	16 days (omit 226–227, 236–237)	16 days	15 days
CUMULATIVE TEST 4–6		1 day	1 day	1 day
7 INTEGERS, RATIONALS, AND REALS	240–278	17 days	16 days	17 days
8 EQUATIONS AND INEQUALITIES IN ONE VARIABLE	280–312	10 days (omit 298–301, 310–311)	11 days (optional 298–299, 310–311)	14 days
9 STATISTICS AND PROBABILITY	314–352	11 days (omit 320–321, 330–333, 338–339)	15 days (optional 320–321, 330–333)	15 days
CUMULATIVE TEST 7–9		1 day	1 day	1 day
10 GEOMETRY	354–396	14 days (omit 394–395)	14 days (optional 394–395)	16 days
11 PERIMETER, AREA AND VOLUME	398–436	12 days (omit 402–403)	13 days (optional 402–403)	14 days
12 EQUATIONS AND INEQUALITIES IN TWO VARIABLES	438–468	8 days (omit 452–453, 466–467)	10 days (optional 452–453)	12 days
FINAL TEST		2 days	2 days	2 days
TOTAL		175 days	175 days	175 days

MEASUREMENT OBJECTIVES

PTER 1: Addition and ubtraction (Whole umbers and Decimals)

- write short word names for whole numbers d decimals expressed as standard numerals d vice versa, through 15 digits
- write expanded numerals for whole numbers d decimals expressed as standard numerals d vice versa, through 10 digits
- identify the value of a digit in whole numbers d decimals, through 13 digits
- compare and order whole numbers, money ounts, or decimals
- round whole numbers, money amounts, or cimals
- add and subtract whole numbers, money ounts, or decimals
- estimate sums and differences of whole mbers, money amounts, or decimals
- use information from a double bar graph with roken scale to solve problems

PTER 2: Multiplication nd Division (Whole umbers and Decimals)

- multiply or divide a whole number or money ount by a whole number
- multiply or divide a decimal by powers of 10
- multiply or divide a decimal by a whole number
- multiply or divide a decimal by a decimal
- estimate products and quotients of whole mbers
- estimate products of decimals
- identify extra or needed information in a oblem and solve
- choose the operation to solve problems
- identify subgoals and solve multistep problems

PTER 3: Number Theory, pressions, and Equations

- determine if a number is divisible by 2, 3, 4, 5, 8, 9, or 10
- find square roots of perfect square numbers
- write standard numerals in scientific notation d vice versa
- find the LCM or GCF of up to 3 numbers by ime factorization, with exponents
- find the value of numerical expressions using e rules for the order of operations
- solve 1-step and 2-step equations
- check that an answer is reasonable
- use information from a table to solve problems
- choose the operation and write a number ntence to solve a problem

PTER 4: Fractions

- find a fraction equivalent to a given fraction
- compare and order fractions and mixed mbers
- write a fraction as a whole or mixed number d vice versa
- add or subtract fractions and mixed numbers
- multiply or divide fractions and mixed numbers
- write a fraction as a decimal and vice versa
- solve 1-step and 2-step equations involving ctions
- estimate sums, differences, products, and otients of fractions and mixed numbers
- use information from a pictograph to solve oblems
- write a simpler problem as a strategy for lving problems
- interpret the quotient and the remainder

CHAPTER 5: Measurement

A To choose the appropriate metric or customary unit of length, mass, or capacity

B To change between measures of length, mass, volume, or capacity in the metric and customary system

C To add and subtract, with regrouping, in the customary system

D To find temperature changes (Fahrenheit and Celsius)

E To add, subtract, or change between units of time

F To find elapsed time across time zones

G To formulate sensible questions

H To use the formula $d=rt$ to solve problems

I To use information from a road map to solve problems

CHAPTER 6: Ratio, Proportion, Percent

A To solve proportions

B To find actual measure given scale and scale measurement and vice versa

C To write a decimal or a fraction as a percent and vice versa

D To find the percent of a number

E To find what percent a number is of a given number

F To find the number given the percent of it

G To find the percent of increase or decrease

H To write a proportion to solve problems

I To make an organized list to solve a problem

J To use the formula $i=prt$ to solve problems

K To use information from a circle graph to solve problems

CHAPTER 7: Integers, Rationals, Reals

A To compare and order integers

B To add or subtract integers

C To multiply or divide integers

D To write a decimal in scientific notation using negative exponents

E To compare and order rational numbers

F To add or subtract rational numbers

G To multiply or divide rational numbers

H To name or locate an ordered pair in a coordinate plane

I To use information from a graph with a scale above and below zero to solve problems

J To check that the solution answers the question

K To identify subgoals and solve multistep problems

CHAPTER 8: Equations and Inequalities (One Variable)

A To evaluate algebraic expressions

B To solve 1-step and 2-step equations involving rational numbers

C To solve 1-step inequalities

D To solve 2-step inequalities

E To graph an equation or inequality

F To write an equation for a problem and solve

G To use a guess-and-check strategy to solve problems

H To organize information in a table to find a pattern to solve problems

I To use information from a schedule to solve problems

CHAPTER 9: Statistics and Probability

A To collect and record data by making a table, bar graph, histogram, broken-line graph, circle graph, or pictograph

B To find the mean, median, mode, and range

C To find all possible permutations of a set of objects

D To find all possible combinations of a set of objects

E To list the elements of a sample space for an experiment

F To find the probability of a simple event

G To find the probability of independent events

H To find the probability of dependent events

I To compute the expectation of an event for a given number of trials

J To select appropriate notation to aid in solving problems

K To interpret information from graphs and statistics

CHAPTER 10: Geometry

A To name points, lines, line segments, and rays and to identify parallel and perpendicular lines

B To name, measure, and classify angles and to find the complement or supplement of an angle

C To construct an angle or segment congruent to a given angle or segment and to construct the bisector of a line segment or an angle

D To find the measures of vertical, alternate interior, and corresponding angles

E To construct perpendicular or parallel lines

F To classify triangles according to the measures of their angles or sides and to find the measure of an angle given the measures of the other two angles

G To identify and name polygons and to find the measure of an angle given the measures of the other interior angles

H To identify the parts of a circle

I To identify congruent figures and lines of symmetry

J To solve problems involving corresponding parts of similar polygons

K To identify translations, rotations, or reflections

L To use working backward as a strategy to solve problems

M To draw a picture to solve a problem

CHAPTER 11: Perimeter, Area, Volume

A To find the perimeter of polygons and the circumference of circles

B To find the area of squares, rectangles, parallelograms, triangles, trapezoids, and circles

C To find the length of the side of a right triangle by using the Pythagorean Rule

D To find the length of a side of a right triangle using sine, cosine, and tangent ratios

E To find the surface area of prisms, pyramids, cones, and cylinders

F To find the volume of prisms, pyramids, cones, and cylinders

G To identify subgoals and solve multistep problems

H To use information from a picture to solve problems

I To choose a formula to solve a problem

CHAPTER 12: Equations and Inequalities (Two Variables)

A To write, solve, or graph the solutions of equations in two variables

B To graph a pair of equations

C To write, solve, or graph the solutions of inequalities in two variables

D To draw a diagram to solve a problem

6

PROBLEM SOLVING

Using an organized approach, pp. 8-9, 122-123, 174-175, 316-317, 388-389, 418-419
Analyzing problems
  identifying relationships, sequencing, prioritizing, and questioning, pp. 31, 42-43, 48-49, 113, 122, 174, 388, 418-419
  discriminating relevant from irrelevant information, pp. 16-17, 58-59, 122-123
  observing patterns, pp. 330-331, 384-385, 388-389, 418-419
Communicating understanding, pp. 84-85, 92-93, 170-171, 240-241, 272-273, 288-289, 320-321, 376-377, 392-393, 410-411
Strategies
  acting it out, p. 48, 113, 122-123, 135, 174-175, 388-389, 418-419
  making a model, pp. 18-19, 78-79, 240, 242, 421, 429, 430
  drawing a picture, pp. 312-313, 316-317, 319, 325, 364-365, 388-389, 418, 428
  guessing and checking, pp. 98-99, 111, 122, 174, 316, 388, 418
  making/using a diagram, chart, or graph, p. 178, 256, 278, 316-317, 361, 364, 371, 388-389, 394, 418-419, 428
  finding a pattern, p. 85, 330-331, 384-385, 388-389, 418-419, 427
  using a simpler problem, pp. 196-197, 316-317, 388-389, 418-419
  working backward, p. 235, 270-271, 316-317, 388-389, 418-419
  choosing a formula, pp. 356-357, 388-389
Choosing an appropriate strategy, pp. 122-123
  justifying the choice, pp. 26-27, 86-87, 126-127, 236-237
Selecting appropriate materials and methods, pp. 174-175, 316-317, 388-389, 418-419
  choosing the operation
    add or subtract, pp. 56-57
    add, subtract, multiply, or divide, pp. 76-77, 122-123, 164-165, 174-175
  estimating
    or using an exact answer, pp. 26-27, 122-123, 174-175, 236-237, 316-317
    closer to the actual value, pp. 86-87
    overestimating and underestimating, pp. 126-127
  using information, pp. 16-17, 178-179, 256-257, 278-279, 292-293, 294-295, 316-317, 344-345, 389, 414-415
  making
    a plan to solve two-step problems, pp. 90-91, 123, 174-175, 316-317
    a plan to solve multistep problems, p. 174, 220-221, 222, 316-317, 388-389
    a tree diagram, pp. 364-365, 394
  checking
    for a reasonable answer, pp. 42-43, 58-59, 86-87, 236-237, 357, 390-392
    that the solution answers the question, pp. 390-391
  interpreting the remainder, pp. 144-145, 244-245
  reasoning, pp. 39C, 41
Demonstrating fluency, pp. 31, 61, 101, 147, 181, 223, 259, 333, 355, 367, 397, 428
Writing
  an equation, pp. 76-77, 122-123, 168-169, 174
  generating and extending problems, p. 1, 5, 11, 37, 92-93, 96-97, 129, 143, 153, 163, 170-171, 181, 229, 235, 240-241, 242-243, 258, 272-273, 316, 325, 338-339, 350-351, 361, 375, 376-377, 389, 403
  a simpler problem, pp. 196-197, 316-317, 388-389, 418
  a proportion, pp. 274-275, 317
  questions, p. 317, 350-351, 388-389
Chapter Openers
  planning, p. 1, 37, 69, 109, 229
  spending money, p. 153, 189, 265
  research, p. 305, 403
  preparing a description, p. 341
  conducting a survey, p. 375, 397, 427

7

PROBLEM SOLVING

Using an organized approach, pp. 18-19
Patterns, p. 55, 318-319, H232
Choosing the operation
  add, subtract, or multiply, pp. 64-65, 97, 100-101, 147, 149, 151
Writing
  Generate and extend problems, p. 9, 37, 73, 75, 81, 104-105, 107, 111, 161, 189, 193, 199, 201, 227, 235, 237, 263, 269, 276, 277, 301, 309, 333, 339, 351, 359, 374, 375, 385, 387, 398, 399, 433, 457
  an equation, pp. 150-151, 178, 444-445, 438
  an inequality, pp. 444-445
  a recipe, p. 465
  a simpler problem, pp. 190-191, 242
  a proportion, pp. 272-277, 290-291, 294-295, 297-298, 313, 317, 324, 333, 348
Estimating
  to solve problems, p. 9, 90-91, 134-135, 400-401
  overestimating and underestimating, pp. 58-59
  or using an exact answer, pp. 96-97, 178
  with decimals and percents, p. 278, 285, 287
Using information
  from the Infobank, pp. 26-27
  from a map, pp. 108-109
  from a graph, pp. 34-35, 128-129, 134-135, 179, 450-451
  from a pictograph, pp. 142-143, 242
  from a recipe, pp. 218-219, 243
  from a picture or a model, pp. 342-343
  from a scattergram, pp. 394-395
  from a train schedule, pp. 260-261
  from a circle graph, pp. 298-299, 325
  from a box-and-whisker graph, p. 391, 468
  from a histogram, pp. 392-393
  from a stem-and-leaf plot, p. 390, 468
Identifying
  needed information, pp. 52-53, 135, 324, 439
Making
  a picture or diagram, p. 167, 277, 344, 355, 357, 368-369, 377, 432-433, 449
  a model with concrete materials, p. 69, 104, 139, 146, 148, 153, 359, 367, 432, 465, H210
  graphs, tables, charts, pp. 108-109, 128, 142-143, 152, 167, 193, 218-219, 227, 260-261, 277, 298-299, 319, 342, 355, 357, 368-369, 377, 432, 449, 453-455, 457
  an organized list, pp. 180-181, 432
  a plan to solve 2-step problems, pp. 70-71, 179
  a plan to solve multistep problems, pp. 244-245, 360-361
  inferences, p. 466
Checking
  that the solution answers the question, pp. 170-171
Using formulas
  distance, ($d = rt$), pp. 252-253, 438
  interest, ($I = prt$), pp. 292-293, 325
Act it out, p. 69, 153, 193, 315, H222
Guess and check, p. 13, 110, 125, 157, 281, 364-365, 432
Selected notation, pp. 214-215, 432
Working backward, pp. 334-335
Using a simpler problem, pp. 190-191, 242, 407, 413
Interpreting the remainder, pp. 224-225, 438
Commission—fixed amount using percent, pp. 286-287
Choosing a formula, pp. 374-375, 439
Misinterpreting information from a graph, pp. 408-409
Chapter Openers
  Decision making, p. 1
  Experiment, p. 43, 117, 235
  Planning, p. 81, 199, 309, 351, 423
  Spending money, p. 161
  Conducting a survey, p. 269, 385
Projects, p. 37, 73, 111, 153, 193, 227, 263, 301, 345, 377, 417, 457

8

PROBLEM SOLVING

A 4-step plan, pp. 16-17
Analyzing the problem, pp. 16-17, 84-85, 105, 109, 113, 117, H212, H218
Developing an organized approach, p. 1, 9, 16-17, 35, 48, 110-111, 144-145, 214-215, 362-363
Choosing the operation, pp. 62-63, 102-103, 178, H210
Selecting materials and methods, p. 1, 16-17, 41, 99, 165, 337, 431, 447
Patterns, relations, and functions, p. 75, 109, 117, 250-251, 296-297, 444-447, 450-453, 458, 465, 469, H209, H216, H221, H229
Generating and extending problems, p. 11, 41, 45, 77, 81, 109, 163, 183, 236, 301, 431, 461
Writing
  an equation, pp. 110-111, 178-179, 256-257, 288-289, 370
  a simpler problem, pp. 144-145, 346, 423, 472
  a proportion, pp. 204-205, 371, 449
Estimating
  to solve problems, p. 9, 54-55, 136-137, 179, 256-257, 370-371, 448-449, 458-459
  overestimating and underestimating, pp. 54-55, H207
  or using an exact answer, pp. 136-137
Using information
  from the Infobank, pp. 24-25, 386-387
  from a graph, pp. 32-33, 126-127, 228-229, 248-249, 320-321, 344-345, 371, H223
  from a road map, pp. 190-191, 257
  from a picture, pp. 414-415
  from a schedule, pp. 302-303
  from samples, pp. 326-327, 370-371
  from a table, pp. 16-17, 71, 96-97, 157, 296-297, 314-315, 386, 449
Identifying and recording needed information, pp. 48-49, 170-171, 257
Making
  a model, pp. 416-417, 472
  a plan to solve multi-step problems, pp. 68-69, 178-179, 256, 270-271, 406-407, 448-449, 458-459
  an organized list, pp. 214-215
Acting it out, p. 13, 170-171, 214-215, 342-343, 351, 472, H215
Drawing a picture, p. 13, 181, 378-379, 442-443, 458-459, 470, H228
Checking
  for a reasonable answer, pp. 86-87, 178, 256
  that the solution answers the question, pp. 262-263
  for hidden assumptions, pp. 422-423
Using formulas, pp. 184-185, 222-223, 257, H227, H228
Guessing and checking, pp. 290-291, 370-371, 448-449, 458-459, H208, H209, H210, H212
Selecting notation, pp. 338-339, 458-459
Interpreting information from a graph, pp. 344-345
Interpreting the remainder, pp. 154-155, 178-179, 256-257, 370-371, 448-449, 458-459
Working backward, pp. 68-69, 362-363, 448-449, 458-459
Formulating a sensible question, pp. 172-173
Choosing a formula, pp. 185, 223, 428-429, 448-449
Choosing a strategy or method, p. 99, 178-179, 256-257, 337, 370-371, 448-449, 458-459
Chapter Openers
  Research, p. 1, 79
  Decision making, p. 41
  Planning, p. 119, 239, 353, 437
  Spending money, p. 165, 199, 279
  Conducting a survey, p. 313
  Measurement applications, p. 397
Projects, p. 35, 71, 113, 157, 193, 231, 273, 305, 347, 389, 431, 461

6

PROBLEM SOLVING (cont.)

Projects, pp. 31, 61, 101, 147, 181, 233, 259, 267, 297, 333, 399, 425

NUMBER SENSE: ESTIMATION AND MENTAL MATH

ESTIMATION

Rounding whole numbers
  through nearest 10,000, pp. 14-15, 74-75, H195
  through nearest 1,000,000, pp. 14-15
Rounding decimals
  nearest whole number, tenth, hundredth, thousandth, and ten-thousandth, pp. 46-47, 50-51, 94-95, 166-167, 202-203
Rounding fractions and mixed numbers, pp. 207-209, 211, 235
Rounding money
  nearest **$1,000,** $10, $1, **$0.10,** $0.01, pp. 14-15, 26-27, 96-97, 166-167, 386
Rounding decimal quotients, pp. 166-167, 202-203.
Rounding data for use in graphing, pp. 380-383, 386-387
Estimating
  area, pp. 355, 357
  sums by clustering, p. H199
  sums by front digits, pp. 12-13
  sums by rounding, pp. 14-15, 50-51
  differences by rounding, pp. 14-15, 50-51
  products by front digits, p. 73
  products by rounding, pp. 74-75, 94-95
  quotients, pp. 116-117, 161, H201
  with fractions, pp. 207-209, 211, 234-235
  with mixed numbers, pp. 208-209
  with measures, p. 171, 247, 309
  with money, pp. 14-15
  or using an exact answer, pp. 26-27, 122-123, 174-175, 236-237, 316-317
  closer to the actual value, pp. 86-87
  overestimating and underestimating, pp. 126-127
Problem solving, pp. 26-27, 86-87, 122-123, 126-127, 174-175, 236-237, 316-317

MENTAL MATH

Numeration and number theory, p. 3
Whole numbers
  addition, p. 19, 393
  subtraction, p. 23
  multiplication, p. 79, 81, 129, 201A, 393
  division, p. 119, 129, 133
Decimals, p. 55, 163
Fractions, p. 215, 233, 235, 239
Time, money, measurement, p. 353
Geometry, p. 353
Probability and statistics, p. 393
Ratio, proportion, percent, p. 283, 287
Equations and inequalities, p. 201

7

PROBLEM SOLVING (cont.)

Analyzing problems, p. 73, 107, 468
Select appropriate materials and methods, p. 1, 2, 5, 9, 26, 27, 43, 55-57, 70-71, 83, 104-107, 111, 134-135, 147-149, 178-181, 193, 199, 213-215, 218-219, 222-223, 227, 235, 254-255, 257, 260-261, 263, 269, 271, 276-277, 289, 301, 309, 333, 339, 351, 359, 374-375, 384, 387, 398-399, 433, 457

NUMBER SENSE: ESTIMATION AND MENTAL MATH

ESTIMATION

Rounding whole numbers
  through nearest million, pp. 8-14, 25, 45C, 48-50, 396-397, H213
  through nearest billion, pp. 392-393, 396, 449C
Rounding decimals
  nearest whole number, tenth, hundredth, thousandth, ten-thousandth, pp. 24-25, 28-29, 60-61, 106-107, H227
Rounding fractions and mixed numbers, pp. 172-173, 206-207
Rounding money
  nearest $0.01, $1, $10, pp. 10-11, 24-25, 48-49, 60-63, 69, 106-107, 211, 400-401
Rounding decimal quotients, pp. 106-107
Rounding data for use in graphing, pp. 392-393, 396
Estimating
  sums by front digits, pp. 10-11
  sums by rounding, pp. 10-11, 14-15, 28-29
  differences by front digits, pp. 12-13
  differences by rounding, pp. 12-13, 28-29
  products by rounding, pp. 48-50, 60-61, H212
  quotients, pp. 86-87, 94, 103
  with fractions and mixed numbers, p. 167, 172-173, 175, 206-207
  with measures, pp. 236-237
  with percents, p. 285
  to solve problems, p. 9, 90-91, 134-135
  overestimating and underestimating, pp. 58-59
  or using an exact answer, pp. 96-97, 400-401
Problem solving, p. 9, 58-59, 90-91, 96-97, 134-135, 178, 400-401

MENTAL MATH

Numeration and number theory, p. 123, 133, 137
Whole numbers
  addition, p. 15
  multiplication, p. 63, 123, 133, 203, 209, 435
  division, p. 85, 93
Decimals, p. 55
Fractions, p. 203, 209
Time, money, measurement, p. 249, 353
Geometry, p. 353
Ratio, proportion, percent, p. 285, 289
Integers, rationals, reals, p. 427, 433, 435

8

NUMBER SENSE: ESTIMATION AND MENTAL MATH

ESTIMATION

Rounding whole numbers
  through nearest million, p. 8, 10-11, 46-47, 299, H207
Rounding decimals
  nearest whole number, tenth, hundredth, thousandth, ten-thousandth, and **hundred-thousandth,** pp. 22-23, 58-59, 64-67, 150-151, 405, 411-413, 424-427, H207
Rounding fractions and mixed numbers, pp. 128-129, 140-141
Rounding money
  nearest $1,000, **$100,** $1, $0.10, $0.01, pp. 10-13, 22-23, 26-27, 46-47, 60-61, 64-67
Rounding decimal quotients, pp. 64-67
Estimating
  sums, pp. 10-11, 14, 26-27
  differences, pp. 12-13, 14, 26-27
  products, pp. 46-47, 50-51, 58-59, 299
  quotients, pp. 46-47
  with decimals, pp. 23, 26-27, 28-29
  with fractions and mixed numbers, pp. 128-129, 140-141
  with money, pp. 10-13, 26-27, 46-47, 60-61, 64-67
  square roots, p. 83
  to solve problems, p. 9, 179
  overestimating and underestimating, pp. 54-55
  or using an exact answer, pp. 136-137
Problem solving, p. 9, 54-55, 136-137, 179, 256-257, 370-371, 448-449, 458-459

MENTAL MATH

Whole numbers
  addition, p. 153, 175, 283, H207
  subtraction, p. 153, 283
  multiplication, p. 51, 153, 283
  division, p. 65, 153, 283, 285
Decimals, p. 65
Fractions, p. 153, 209
Time, money, measurement, p. 167, 175, 196R
Ratio, proportion, percent, p. 209, 219
Equations and inequalities, p. 153, 283
Integers, rationals, reals, p. 261, 283, 455

6

NUMERATION AND NUMBER THEORY

NUMERATION

WHOLE NUMBERS
Reading and writing numbers
  through 999,999, pp. 2-3, 437
  through 999,999,999,999, pp. 4-5
  through quadrillion, p. 5C
Place value
  through hundred thousands, pp. 2-3, 437
  through hundred billions, pp. 4-5, 15C
  through quintillions, p. 5C
  expanded form, pp. 2-3, 437
Comparing and ordering
  using symbols, pp. 6-7, 21M, 47A, 437
  least to greatest, pp. 6-7, 21M, 437
  greatest to least, pp. 6-7, 437
Rounding
  through nearest 10,000, pp. 14-15, 74-75, 438
  through nearest 1,000,000, pp. 14-15, 26-27, 96-97, 166-167, 386, 438
  nearest $1,000, $10, $1, $0.01, pp. 14-15
Powers and exponents
  meaning, pp. 84-85, 139A, 194-195, 427
  scientific notation, p. 226E
Order of operations, pp. 112-113, 121M, 143C, 157A, 443
Estimation, p. 15
Roman numerals, p. 35E
Greek numeration system, p. 3C

DECIMALS
Tenths and hundredths
  reading and writing, pp. 38-39
  related to fractions, pp. 38-39, 202-203
  related to mixed numbers, pp. 38-39
Thousandths, **ten-thousandths, and hundred-thousandths**
  reading and writing, pp. 40-41, 439
Place value, pp. 38-41, 439
Comparing and ordering
  on a number line, pp. 44-45
  using symbols, pp. 44-45, 51M, 64R, 93A, 95, 439
  least to greatest, pp. 44-45, 439
  greatest to least, pp. 44-45, 439
Equivalent decimals, pp. 44-45
Rounding
  nearest whole number, tenth, hundredth, **thousandth, and ten-thousandth,** pp. 46-47, 50-51, 94-95, 166-167, 202-203, 439
  nearest **$1,000,** $10, $1, **$0.10,** $0.01, pp. 14-15, 96-97, 166-167, 386
Writing decimals for percents, pp. 282-283
Patterns, p. 53C

NUMBER THEORY
Divisibility by 2, 3, 5, **6,** 9, 10, p. 115
Multiples, pp. 190-191, 447
Common multiples, pp. 190-191, 222, 427
Least common multiple, pp. 190-191, 222, 427, 447
  using prime factorization, p. 427
Factors and common factors, pp. 192-193, 427
  using prime factorization, p. 195, 427
Greatest common factor, pp. 192-193, 200-201, 427
  using prime factorization, p. 427
Prime and composite numbers, pp. 194-195
Prime factorization, pp. 194-195, 249A, 427
Factor tree, pp. 194-195
Twin primes, p. 195C
Square root, p. 100
Using a calculator, p. 13C, 100, 146, 222
Mental math, p. 3
Problem solving, p. 7C, 26-27, 98-99, 191C

7

NUMERATION AND NUMBER THEORY

NUMERATION

WHOLE NUMBERS
Reading and writing numbers
  through hundred trillions, pp. 2-3, H193
Place value
  through hundred trillions, pp. 2-3, 51A, H193
  expanded form, pp. 2-3, 77E, H193
Comparing and ordering
  using symbols, pp. 4-5, 11, 13, 49, 197E, H193
  least to greatest, pp. 4-5, 197E, H193
  greatest to least, pp. 4-5
  1 less than, 1 greater than, pp. 4-5
Rounding
  on a number line, p. 8
  through nearest million, pp. 8-14, 25, 45C, 48-50, 396-397, 398
  through nearest billion, pp. 392-393, 449C
  nearest $0.01, $1, $10, pp. 10-11, 24-25, 48-49, 60-63, 69, 106-107, 211, 400-401
Powers and exponents
  meaning, pp. 120-121
  using exponents, pp. 120-121, 126-127, 169, 212, 271A, H212
  first power, zero power, pp. 120-121
  scientific notation, pp. 122-123, 131M, H196
  negative exponents, p. 453C
  expanded form, p. 77E
Order of operations, pp. 136-137, 169A, 387A
  multiplication dot (·) symbol, pp. 136-137, 145A
Egyptian numeration system, p. 41E
Mayan numeration system, p. 5C
Number patterns, p. 7C, 115E
Fibonacci sequence, p. 21C

DECIMALS
Reading and writing decimals, pp. 20-21
Place value through millionths, pp. 20-21
  expanded form, pp. 20-21
Comparing and ordering,
  using symbols, pp. 22-23, 29, 197E
  least to greatest, pp. 22-23, 197E
  greatest to least, pp. 22-23
Equivalent decimals, pp. 20-21
Rounding
  nearest whole number, tenth, hundredth, thousandth, and ten-thousandth, pp. 24-25, 28-29, 60-61, 106-107
  nearest $0.01, $1, $10, pp. 10-11, 24-25, 48-49, 60-63, 106-107, 211
Writing decimals for fractions, pp. 216-217, 220-221, 230R, 280-281, 283
Writing decimals for percents, pp. 280-281, 283M, 304R

NUMBER THEORY
Divisibility, by 2, 3, **4,** 5, 6, **8,** 9, 10, pp. 118-119, 131M, 431A
Even numbers, p. 118
Multiples, pp. 132-133, 478
Common multiples, pp. 132-133
Least common multiple, pp. 132-133, 156R, H196
Factors and common factors, pp. 130-131
Greatest common factor, pp. 130-131, 156R, H196
Odd numbers, p. 118
Pascal's Triangle, p. H210
Prime and composite numbers, pp. 124-125
Sieve of Eratosthenes, p. 125
Prime factorization, pp. 126-127, 131M, 132-133
Relatively prime, pp. 130-131
Unity, p. 124
Abundant numbers, p. 127C, 157E
Deficient numbers, p. 127C, 157E
Perfect number, p. 127C, 157E
Factor tree, pp. 126-127
Square, pp. 120-121
Square root, pp. 120-121, 131M
Perfect Square, pp. 120-121
Goldbach's Theory, p. 125C
Base-five, p. 141C
Using a calculator, p. 139, 149
Mental math, p. 123, 133, 137
Reasoning, p. 13
Problem solving, pp. 364-365, 400-401

8

NUMERATION AND NUMBER THEORY

NUMERATION

WHOLE NUMBERS
Reading and writing numbers
  through hundred trillions, pp. 2-3, 479
  through sextillions, p. 5
Place value
  through hundred trillions, pp. 2-3, 19M, 479
  expanded form, pp. 2-3, 479
Comparing and ordering
  using symbols, pp. 4-5, 11, 13
  least to greatest, pp. 4-5, 479
  greatest to least, pp. 4-5
Rounding
  on a number line, p. 8
  through nearest million, p. 8, 10-11, 46-47
  nearest **$1,000, $100,** $1, $0.10, $0.01, pp. 10-13, 22-23, 26-27, 46-47, 60-61, 64-65
Powers and exponents
  meaning, pp. 82-83
  using exponents, pp. 82-83, 95M, 98-99, 116R, 189A, H212
  first power, zero power, pp. 82-83
  scientific notation, pp. 84-85, 95M, 139A, 235R, 254-255, 470-471
  negative exponents, p. 235R, 254-255, 471
  operating with exponents, p. 85, 235R, 254-255, 470-471
  quadratic equations, p. 309E
Order of operations, pp. 98-99, 116R, H212
Sequences, p. 117E, 469, H209, H220, H221, H229
Number patterns, p. 75E, 109C, 117E, 133C, 469
Egyptian, **Babylonian,** Roman, and Hindu number systems, p. 39E, 469

DECIMALS
Reading and writing decimals, pp. 18-19
Place value through millionths, pp. 18-19
  expanded form, pp. 18-19
Comparing and ordering
  using symbols, pp. 20-21, 27, 453A
  least to greatest, pp. 20-21
  greatest to least, pp. 20-21, 29A
  decimals and fractions, p. 151, H214
Equivalent decimals, p. 18
Rounding
  nearest whole number, tenth, hundredth, thousandth, ten-thousandth, and **hundred-thousandth,** pp. 22-23, 58-59, 64-67, 150-151, 405, 411-413, 424-427, H207
  nearest $1,000, **$100,** $1, $0.10, $0.01, pp. 10-13, 22-23, 26-27, 46-47, 60-61, 64-65
Writing decimals for fractions, pp. 150-151
Writing decimals for percents, pp. 210-211, 217M, 234R

RATIONAL AND IRRATIONAL NUMBERS
Reading and writing, pp. 258-259, 266-267
Comparing and ordering, pp. 258-259
Investigating with calculator, pp. 266-267

NUMBER THEORY
Divisibility, pp. 80-81, 95M
Multiples, pp. 94-95, H211
Least common multiple, pp. 94-95, 201A, H211
Factors, pp. 88-89
Greatest common factor, pp. 92-93, 95M, 120-121, 201A, 481, H211
Prime and composite numbers, pp. 88-89, 95M, H211
Relatively prime, pp. 92-93
Prime factorization, pp. 90-91, 92-93, 149A, 189A, 249, 481, H211
Factor tree, pp. 90-91, 149A
Square and square root, pp. 82-83, 95M, 266-267, 309E, 400-401, H211
Cube root, p. 91C, H211
Perfect square, pp. 82-83
Radical expressions, p. 277E
Sieve of Eratosthenes, p. 89
Venn diagram, p. 105
Using a calculator, p. 83, 112, 267
Reasoning, p. 5, 105
Problem solving, pp. 290-291, 459

6

ADDITION: WHOLE NUMBERS

Basic facts to 18, pp. 10-11
Properties
  commutative, pp. 10-11, 437, H195
  zero, pp. 10-11, 437
  associative, pp. 10-11, 437, H195
Inverse operations
  adding to check subtraction, pp. 22-25, H196
Adding 2-digit numbers through 6-digit numbers, pp. 18-19, 21M
Column addition, pp. 20-21, 438
Adding money, pp. 18-21, 52-53, 90-91, 126-127, 438
Adding units of time, pp. 252-253
Adding customary units of length with regrouping, pp. 248-249
Estimating sums, pp. 12-15, 21M, 86-87, 126-127, 438, H199
Order of operations, pp. 112-113
Solving equations, pp. 28-29, 34R, H204, H206
Solving inequalities, p. 65E
Using a calculator, p. 30, 146
Mental math, p. 19, 393
Reasoning, p. 41
Problem solving, pp. 26-27, 56-57, 76-77, 86-87, 90-91, 126-127, 164-165, 174-175

SUBTRACTION: WHOLE NUMBERS

Basic facts to 18, pp. 10-11, 437
Properties
  zero, pp. 10-11
Inverse operations
  adding to check subtraction, pp. 22-25
Subtracting 2-digit numbers through 6-digit numbers, pp. 22-25, 438
Subtracting across zeros, pp. 24-25, 438
Subtracting money, pp. 22-25, 55, 90-91, 126-127, 389, 438
Subtracting units of time, pp. 252-253
Estimating differences, pp. 12-15, 86-87, 126-127, 438
Order of operations, pp. 112-113
Subtracting customary units of length with regrouping, pp. 248-249
Solving equations, pp. 28-29, 34R
Solving inequalities, p. 65E
Using a calculator, p. 30, 146
Mental math, p. 23
Reasoning, p. 39C, 41, H196
Problem solving, p. 25C, 26-27, 39C, 56-57, 76-77, 86-87, 90-91, 126-127, 164-165, 174-175, 389

7

ADDITION: WHOLE NUMBERS

Properties
  commutative, pp. 6-7
  order, pp. 6-7
  associative, pp. 6-7
  identity, pp. 6-7
Inverse operations
  adding to check subtraction, pp. 6-7
Adding 2-digit numbers through **7-digit** numbers, pp. 14-15, 17M
Column addition, pp. 14-15
Adding money, pp. 14-15, 30-31, 33A
Adding customary units of length, pp. 246-247
Adding temperature, pp. 256-257
Estimating sums, pp. 10-11, 14-15, 58-59
Order of operations, pp. 136-137
Addition expressions, pp. 138-139
Solving equations, pp. 138-141, 221A, 479
  two-step, pp. 148-149, 479
Palindrome, p. 31C
Using a calculator, p. 139
Mental math, p. 15
Problem solving, pp. 58-59, 64-65, 70-71, 100-101
Reasoning, pp. H209, H218, H231

SUBTRACTION: WHOLE NUMBERS

Subtracting zero, pp. 6-7
Inverse operations
  adding to check subtraction, pp. 6-7, 16
Subtracting 2-digit numbers through **7-digit** numbers, pp. 16-17, 119A
Subtracting across zeros, pp. 16-17
Subtracting money, pp. 16-17, 32-33
Subtracting customary units of length, pp. 246-247
Subtracting temperature, pp. 256-257, 430-431
Estimating differences, pp. 12-13, 58-59
Order of operations, pp. 136-137
Subtraction expressions, pp. 138-139
Solving equations, pp. 138-141, 221A, 479
  two-step, pp. 148-149, 479
Reasoning, p. 13, H209, H231
Problem solving, pp. 58-59, 64-65, 70-71, 100-101

8

ADDITION: WHOLE NUMBERS

Properties
  commutative, pp. 6-7, 23A, H207
  associative, pp. 6-7, 23A, H207
  identity, pp. 6-7, 23A
Inverse operations
  adding to check subtraction, pp. 6-7, 14
Adding through 7-digit numbers, pp. 14-15, 19M, 469, H207
Adding money, pp. 10-11, 14-15, 26-27, 28-29, 38R
Adding units of time, pp. 182-183
Adding customary units
  of length, pp. 174-175
  of weight, pp. 176-177
  of capacity, pp. 176-177
Estimating sums, pp. 10-11, 14
Order of operations, pp. 98-99, H212
Addition expressions, pp. 280-281, 295C, 361A, 469-470
Solving equations, pp. 100-101, 104-105, 108-109, 221A, 481
  two-step, pp. 108-109, 284-285
Solving inequalities, pp. 292-295
  two-step, pp. 298-299
Adding with radicals, p. 277E
Writing equations, pp. 110-111
Using a calculator, p. 34, 272
Mental math, p. 153, 175, 283
Problem solving, pp. 48-49, 54-55, 62-63, 68-69, 102-103, 110-111, 178-179, 406-407

SUBTRACTION: WHOLE NUMBERS

Properties
  zero, pp. 6-7
Inverse operations
  adding to check subtraction, pp. 6-7, 14
Subtracting through 7-digit numbers, pp. 14-15, 19M
Subtracting across zeros, pp. 14-15
Subtracting money, pp. 12-15, 26-27, 30-31, 38R
Subtracting units of time, pp. 182-183
Subtracting customary units
  of length, pp. 174-175
  of weight, pp. 176-177
  of capacity, pp. 176-177
Estimating differences, pp. 12-13
Order of operations, pp. 98-99, H212
Subtraction expressions, pp. 280-281, 361A
Solving equations, pp. 100-101, 104-105
  two-step, pp. 108-109, 284-285, H197
Solving inequalities, pp. 292-295
  two-step, pp. 298-299
Writing equations, pp. 110-111
Subtracting with radicals, p. 277E
Using a calculator, p. 34, 272
Mental math, p. 153, 283
Problem solving, pp. 48-49, 54-55, 62-63, 68-69, 102-103, 110-111, 178-179, 406-407

6

MULTIPLICATION: WHOLE NUMBERS

Relating addition and multiplication, pp. 70-71
Basic facts, pp. 70-71
Properties of multiplication
  commutative, pp. 70-71
  associative, pp. 70-71
  identity, pp. 70-71
  zero, pp. 70-71
  distributive, pp. 70-71, 81
Three factors, p. 79, 81
Inverse operations
  multiplying to check division, p. 114, 118,
    120, 130, 136, 140
Multiplying by multiples of 10, pp. 72-73, 89M,
  441
Estimating products, pp. 73-75, 86-87,
  126-127, 441
Multiplying 2-digit through 6-digit numbers by
  a 1-digit number, pp. 78-79, 89M
Using concrete materials, pp. 78-79
Multiplying a 2-, 3-, or 4-digit number by a
  2-digit number, pp. 80-81, 89M, 125A, 441,
  H199
Multiplying a 3- or 4-digit number by a 3-digit
  number, pp. 82-83, 89M, 105R, 125A, 441
Multiplying money, pp. 78-83, 88, 90-91,
  96-97, 105R, 126-127, 441
Order of operations, pp. 112-113
Lattice multiplication, p. 104E
Exponents, pp. 84-85, 194-195, 427, 441
Solving equations, p. 111, 142-143, 168-169,
  444
Using a calculator, p. 85, 104E, 146
Mental math, p. 79, 81, 129, 201A, 393
Problem solving, p. 83C, 86-87, 90-91,
  126-127, 164-165, 168-169, 174-175

DIVISION: WHOLE NUMBERS

Meaning of division, p. 110
Basic facts, pp. 110-111, 121M
Properties, pp. 110-111
Related sentences, pp. 110-111
Using concrete materials, p. 110
Inverse operations
  multiplying to check division, p. 114, 118,
    120, 130, 136, 140
Estimating quotients, pp. 116-117, H201
Dividing by 1-digit divisors
  with remainders, p. 114, 121M
  using concrete materials, p. 114
  2-digit quotients, pp. 118-119
  3- and 4-digit quotients, pp. 120-121
  zeros in quotient, pp. 120-121
  short division, pp. 124-125
Dividing by multiples of 10, pp. 128-129, 443
Dividing by 2-digit divisors
  1- and 2-digit quotients, pp. 130-135, 444,
    H202
  3-digit quotients, pp 134-135, 444
  4- and 5-digit quotients, pp. 136-137
  correcting estimates, pp. 132-139, 151R
  zeros in quotient, pp. 138-139, 151R
Dividing by 3-digit divisors, pp. 140-141
Interpreting the remainder, pp. 144-145,
  244-245
Patterns, p. 128, 158, H202, H203
Average (mean), pp. 378-379, 381M, 389, 427
Dividing money, pp. 118-121, 124-125,
  130-131, 134-141, 151R, 154-161, 443
Short division, pp. 124-125, 443
Order of operations, pp. 112-113, 142-143,
  146
Solving equations, p. 111, 142-143, 168-169,
  444
Using a calculator, p. 141, 146, 177
Mental math, p. 119, 129, 133
Reasoning, p. 135
Problem solving, p. 111C, 117C, 131C, 137C,
  144-145, 164-165, 168-169, 174-175,
  244-245, 389

7

MULTIPLICATION: WHOLE NUMBERS

Properties
  commutative, pp. 44-45, 57M
  associative, pp. 44-45, 57M
  identity, pp. 44-45, 57M
  zero, pp. 44-45, 57M
  distributive, pp. 44-45, 57M, 63
Inverse operations
  multiplying to check division, pp. 82-83, 88,
    92
Multiplying by multiples of 10, pp. 46-47, 57M
Estimating products, pp. 48-50, 58-59
Multiplying 2-digit through 6-digit numbers by
  a 1-digit number, pp. 50-51, 57M, 187A
Multiplying 2-digit through **6-digit** numbers by
  a 2-digit number, pp. 54-55, 57M, 83CTM
Multiplying larger numbers, pp. 56-57, 187A,
  H194
Multiplying money, pp. 48-51, 54-55, 56-57,
  62-63, 66-67, H194
Scientific notation, pp. 122-123, 131M, H196
Order of operations, pp. 136-137, 145, 169A
Multiplication expressions, pp. 144-145
Solving equations, pp. 146-147, 221A, H197
  two-step, pp. 148-149, H197
Using a calculator, p. 47, 149
Mental math, p. 63, 123, 133, 203, 209
Problem solving, pp. 58-59, 64-65, 70-71,
  100-101
Reasoning, pp. H213, H215, H220, H223

DIVISION: WHOLE NUMBERS

Properties, pp. 82-83
Related sentences, pp. 82-83
Inverse operations
  multiplying to check division, pp. 82-83, 88,
    92
Estimating quotients, pp. 86-87, 94, H195
Dividing by 1-digit divisors, pp. 88-89, 95M
  short division, pp. 88-89
Dividing by multiples of 10, pp. 84-85, 95M
Dividing by 2-digit divisors, pp. 92-93, 95M
Dividing by 3-digit divisors, pp. 94-95
Interpreting the remainder, pp. 224-225, 438
Dividing money, pp. 84-89, 92-95, 98-99,
  102-103, 106-107, 237A
Short division, pp. 88-89
Order of operations, pp. 136-137, 145, 169A
Division expressions, pp. 144-145
Solving equations, pp. 146-147, 221A, 479
  two-step, pp. 148-149, H197
Mental math, p. 85, 93
Reasoning, pp. 99, H213, H214, H215, H220
Problem solving, pp. 100-101, 224-225, 438

8

MULTIPLICATION: WHOLE NUMBERS

Properties
  commutative, pp. 42-43, 53M
  associative, pp. 42-43, 53M
  identity, pp. 42-43, 53M
  zero, pp. 42-43
  distributive, pp. 42-43, 53M, 295C
Inverse operations
  multiplying to check division, pp. 42-43, 52
Multiplying by multiples of 10, pp. 44-45, 53M
Estimating products, pp. 46-47, 50-51, 299
Multiplying 2-digit through 6-digit numbers by
  a 1-, 2-, or 3-digit number, pp. 50-51, 61A
Multiplying money, pp. 46-47, 50-51, 53M,
  60-61
Scientific notation, pp. 84-85, 95M, 139A,
Order of operations, pp. 98-99, H212
Multiplication expressions, pp. 280-281
Solving equations, pp. 100-101, 106-107, 481,
  H212
  two-step, pp. 108-109, 284-285, 482
Solving inequalities, pp. 292-295
  two-step, pp. 298-299
Patterns, p. 109C
Using a calculator, p. 83, 85, 112
Mental math, p. 51, 153, 283
Problem solving, pp. 48-49, 54-55, 62-63,
  68-69, 102-103, 178-179, 406-407

DIVISION: WHOLE NUMBERS

Properties, pp. 42-43
Inverse operations
  multiplying to check division, pp. 42-43, 52
Dividing by multiples of 10, pp. 44-45
Estimating quotients, pp. 46-47
Compatible numbers, pp. 46-47
Dividing by 1-, 2-, and 3-digit divisors,
  pp. 52-53, H209-H210
Dividing money, pp. 46-47, 52-53, 64-67, 74R,
  89A
Short division, p. 65
Scientific notation, p. 85
Order of operations, pp. 98-99
Interpreting the remainder, pp. 154-155
Division expressions, pp. 280-281, 361A
Solving equations, pp. 106-107, 481, H212
  two-step, pp. 108-109, 284-285, 482
Solving inequalities, pp. 292-295
  two-step, pp. 298-299
Using a calculator, p. 85
Mental math, p. 65, 153, 283, 285
Problem solving, pp. 54-55, 68-69, 102-103,
  154-155, 178-179, 406-407

6

DECIMALS

7

DECIMALS

8

DECIMALS

6

FRACTIONS

Equal parts, pp. 198-199
Parts of whole, pp. 198-199
Parts of set, pp. 198-199
Writing fractions, pp. 198-199
Equivalent fractions
  using multiplication, pp. 198-199, 205M, 447
  using cross products, pp. 198-199, 447
  using division, pp. 200-201
Greatest common factor, pp. 192-193, 200-201
Simplest form, pp. 200-201, 205M, 428, H205, H207
Comparing and ordering
  on a number line, p. 206
  fractions using symbols, pp. 206-207, 209, 407A
  mixed numbers using symbols, pp. 206-207, 209
  least to greatest, pp. 206-207
  greatest to least, pp. 206-207
Changing fractions to whole or mixed numbers, pp. 204-205, 447
Changing whole and mixed numbers to an improper fraction, pp. 204-205, 447
Writing decimals for fractions, pp. 202-203, 222, H197, H210
Fractions as percents, pp. 284-285, 428, H210

ADDITION
Adding
  like fractions, pp. 210-211, 448, H206, H207
  unlike fractions, pp. 210-211, 428, 448
  like mixed numbers, pp. 214-215, 227R
  unlike mixed numbers, pp. 214-215, 218-219, 227R, 448
  three addends, p. 211, 214-215

SUBTRACTION
Subtracting
  like fractions, pp. 212-213, 448
  unlike fractions, pp. 212-213, 448
  like mixed numbers, pp. 216-217, 289A, H206
  unlike mixed numbers, pp. 216-217, 289A
  with renaming, pp. 218-219, 227R, 289A, 448

MULTIPLICATION
Multiplying
  fractions, pp. 230-231, 243M, 349A
  cancellation, pp. 230-233, 449
  fractions and whole numbers, pp. 232-233, 243M, 267A, 349A, 428, H208
  three factors, p. 231, 233, 449
  fractions and mixed numbers, pp. 238-239, 349A, 449
  mixed numbers, pp. 238-239, 243M, 263R, 267A, 349A, 449
  using models, pp. 230-231, 232-233, 238-239

DIVISION
Reciprocal, pp. 242-243
Dividing
  whole numbers and fractions, pp. 240-241, 243M, 321A, 377A, 449
  using models, pp. 240, 242
  fractions and mixed numbers, pp. 242-243, 263R, 321A, 377A, 450
Estimating with fractions and mixed numbers, pp. 207-209, 211, 234-235
Patterns, p. 231
Solving equations, p. 213, 233
Distributive property, p. 239
Unit fractions, p. 233
Using a calculator, p. 203, 222, 241
Mental math, p. 215, 233, 235, 239
Problem solving, pp. 196-197, 220-221, 294-295, 388-389, 428

7

FRACTIONS

Meaning, pp. 162-163, H217
Equivalent fractions using multiplication or division, pp. 164-165, H217
Simplest form, pp. 164-165, 177M
Greatest common factor, pp. 130-131, 164-165
Comparing and ordering
  fractions using symbols, pp. 168-169, 197E, H218
  mixed numbers using symbols, pp. 168-169, 173, 197A, 207
  least to greatest, pp. 168-169, 197E, H218
  greatest to least, pp. 168-169, H218
  using cross products, pp. 168-169
Estimating, p. 167
Changing fractions to whole or mixed numbers, pp. 166-167, H198
Changing whole or mixed numbers to improper fractions, pp. 166-167, H198
Writing decimals for fractions, pp. 216-217, 220-221, 230R, 231E, 280-281, 283M, H200
Writing fractions as decimals, pp. 220-221, H200
Fractions and percents, pp. 278-279, 282-283, 304R

ADDITION
Adding
  like and unlike fractions, pp. 174-175, 177M, H218
  like and unlike mixed numbers, pp. 182-183, 183CTM, 196R, 247A, H280
Estimating sums, pp. 172-173, 175
Three addends, pp. 174-175, 182-183
Magic square, p. 183
Solving equations, pp. 188-189, H199

SUBTRACTION
Subtracting
  like and unlike fractions, pp. 176-177, 247A
  like and unlike mixed numbers, pp. 184-185, 196R, 247A
  with renaming, pp. 186-187, 247A, 480
Estimating differences, pp. 172-173
Solving equations, pp. 188-189, H199

MULTIPLICATION
Multiplying
  fractions, pp. 200-203, 213M, 273A, H219
  cancellation, pp. 202-203
  fractions and whole numbers, pp. 208-209, 213M
  fractions and mixed numbers, pp. 208-209, 213M
  mixed numbers, pp. 208-209, 213M, 481
  three factors, pp. 200-203, 208-209, 213M, 273A
Solving equations, pp. 222-223, 482
Estimating products, pp. 206-207

DIVISION
Reciprocal, pp. 210-211
Dividing
  fractions by a fraction, pp. 210-211
  whole numbers by a fraction, pp. 210-211
  fractions by a whole number, pp. 210-211
  mixed numbers, pp. 212-213, A81-H199
Solving equations, pp. 222-223, H200
Interpreting the remainder, p. 224, 225
Patterns, p. 189C
Unit fraction, p. 165
Density, p. 163C
Mean, p. 391
Using a calculator, p. 201
Mental math, p. 203, 209
Problem solving, p. 179, 190-191, 218-219, 224-225, 334-335

8

FRACTIONS

Meaning, pp. 120-121
Equivalent fractions using multiplication or division, pp. 120-121
  using cross products, pp. 120-121
Simplest form, pp. 120-121
Greatest common factor, pp. 92-93, 95M, 120-121, 201A, H213
Least common denominator, pp. 124-125, 201A
Comparing and ordering
  on a number line, pp. 124-125
  fractions using symbols, pp. 124-125, 128-129, 140-141
  mixed numbers using symbols, pp. 124-125, 128-129, 140-141
  least to greatest, pp. 124-125
  greatest to least, pp. 124-125
  decimals and fractions, p. 151
Changing fractions to whole or mixed numbers, pp. 122-123
Changing mixed numbers to improper fractions, pp. 122-123
Writing decimals for fractions, pp. 150-151, H214
Writing fractions as decimals, pp. 150-151, 234R, H214
Fractions and percents, pp. 208-209, 212-213, 217M, 234R, H217

ADDITION
Adding
  like and unlike fractions, pp. 130-131, 135M, H213
  like and unlike mixed numbers, pp. 130-131, 135M, 160R
Estimating sums, pp. 128-129
Three addends, pp. 130-131
Solving equations, pp. 152-153, H198, H199, H214
  two-step, pp. 284-285
Solving inequalities, pp. 298-299
  two-step, pp. 298-299

SUBTRACTION
Subtracting
  like and unlike fractions, pp. 132-133, 482
  like and unlike mixed numbers, pp. 132-138, 160R, H198
  with renaming, pp. 134-135, 160R
Estimating differences, pp. 128-129
Solving equations, pp. 152-153, H198, H199, H214
  two-step, pp. 284-285
Solving inequalities, pp. 298-299
  two-step, pp. 298-299

MULTIPLICATION
Multiplying
  fractions, pp. 138-139, 323A
  cancellation, pp. 138-139
  fractions, whole numbers, and mixed numbers, pp. 142-143, H198, H213
  three factors, pp. 138-139, 142-143, H213
Estimating products, pp. 140-141
Solving equations, pp. 152-153, 482-483, H214
  two-step, pp. 284-285
Solving inequalities, pp. 298-299
  two-step, pp. 298-299

DIVISION
Reciprocal, pp. 146-147
Dividing
  fractions by a fraction, pp. 146-147, 213A
  fractions, whole numbers, and mixed numbers, pp. 148-149, H198-H199
Estimating quotients, pp. 140-141
Solving equations, pp. 152-153, 482
  two-step, pp. 284-285
Solving inequalities, pp. 298-299
  two-step, pp. 298-299
Patterns, p. 133C, 470
Mean, **median, mode,** p. 317, H223
Using a calculator, p. 125, 151
Complex fractions, p. 161E
Mental math, p. 153, 209
Problem solving, pp. 96-97, 136-137, 144-145, 154-155, 288-289, 362-363, 370, 448

6

TIME, MONEY

TIME
Equivalent units of time, pp. 252-253
Adding and subtracting units of time,
  pp. 252-253
Fractions and time, p. 215, 217
Ratios and time, pp. 272-273
Reading 24 hour time, p. 184E
Time card, p. 253C
Time zones, pp. 256-257
Problem solving, pp. 236-237, 256-257

MONEY
Counting bills, p. 193
Rounding to nearest **$1,000,** $10, $1, **$0.10,**
  $0.01, pp. 14-15, 96-97, 166-167, 386
Estimating, pp. 12-15, 86-87, 96-97, 166-167,
  386
Adding, pp. 18-21, 52-53, 126-127
Subtracting, pp. 22-24, 55, 126-127, 389
Multiplying, pp. 78-83, 88, 93, 96-97
Dividing, pp. 118-121, 124-125, 130-131,
  134-141, 154-161, H203
Unit pricing, p. 131C
  better buy, p. 131, 177, 291, H203
Percents, pp. 288-289
Writing and solving equations, pp. 168-169
Using a calculator, p. 85, 177, 291
Problem solving, pp. 86-87, 126-127, 168-169,
  196-197, 236-237, 389

7

TIME, MONEY

TIME
Equivalent units of time, pp. 250-251
Adding and subtracting units of time,
  pp. 250-251
Elapsed time, pp. 250-251
Time zones, pp. 254-255
Fractions and time, p. 187, 203, 209, 213, 223
Median times, p. 389
Schedules, pp. 260-261, 439
Using a calculator, p. 251
Problem solving, pp. 90-91, 96-97, 260-261,
  325, 439

MONEY
Rounding to nearest $0.01, and dollar,
  pp. 10-11, 24-25, 48-49, 60-63, 69, 106-107,
  211, 400-401
Estimating, pp. 10-11, 24-25, 48-49, 58-59,
  60-63, 69, 106-107, 211, 400-401
Adding, pp. 14-15, 30-31, 33A, H193
Subtracting, pp. 16-17, 32-33, H193
Multiplying, pp. 50-51, 54-55, 56-57, 62-63,
  66-67, H194
Dividing, pp. 84-85, 88-89, 92-95, 98-99,
  102-103, 106-107, 237A
Unit pricing, p. 107, 217, 249, 279
Percents, pp. 284-285
Percent increase, percent decrease,
  pp. 296-297, 485
Range, mean, median, mode, p. 389, 391,
  H207
Commission, pp. 286-287
Interest, pp. 292-293, 325
Using a calculator, p. 279, 344
Problem solving, pp. 58-59, 96-97, 100-101,
  286-287, 292-293, 318-319, 400-401,
  450-451

8

TIME, MONEY

TIME
Equivalent units of time, pp. 182-183
Adding and subtracting units of time,
  pp. 182-183, H216
Elapsed time, p. 169C, 182-183, H216
Time zones, pp. 186-187
Fractions and time, p. 149, 153
Using a plane schedule, pp. 302-303
Problem solving, p. 257, 302-303, 414-415

MONEY
Rounding to nearest **$1,000,** $100, $1, $0.10,
  $0.01, pp. 10-13, 22-23, 26-27, 46-47,
  60-61, 64-67
Estimating, pp. 10-13, 22-23, 26-27, 46-47,
  60-61, 64-67
Adding, pp. 10-11, 14-15, 26-29, 38R, 475
Subtracting, pp. 12-15, 26-27, 30-31, 38R, 480
Multiplying, pp. 46-47, 50-51, 53M, 60-61
Dividing, p. 46-47, 52-53, 64-67, 74R, 89A
Fractions and money, p. 123C, 293A
Percents, p. 218, 220-221, 224-225, H201
Percent increase, percent decrease,
  pp. 226-227
Mean, median, mode, p. 317
Interest formula, pp. 222-223, 257
Reasoning, p. 227
Problem solving, p. 9, 54-55, 62-63, 68-69,
  96-97, 178-179, 222-223, 257, 296-297,
  449, 459

6

MEASUREMENT

Length
  metric units: millimeter, centimeter, meter, kilometer, pp. 170-173, measuring to the nearest mm and cm, pp. 170-171
    equivalent measures, pp. 170-173
    choosing the appropriate unit, pp. 170-171, 446
  customary units: inch, half-inch, quarter-inch, eighth-inch, sixteenth-inch, foot, yard, mile, pp. 246-247
    measuring to the nearest inch, half-inch, quarter-inch, sixteenth-inch, pp. 246-247
    equivalent measures, pp. 248-249, 450
    choosing the appropriate unit, pp. 246-247
    adding and subtracting units of measure, pp. 248-249, H208
Perimeter
  metric units:
    of polygons by adding, pp. 342-343, 347, 359M, 455
    using formulas, pp. 342-343, 353, 359M, 455
  customary units, pp. 342-343, 455
Circumference, pp. 346-347, 359M
Pi, pp. 346-347, 354-355, 359M, 371R
Area formulas
  metric units:
    rectangles, pp. 348-349, 355C, 359M, 455
    parallelograms and triangles, pp. 352-353, 355C, 359M, 428
    circle, pp. 354-355, 359M, 371R
  customary units, pp. 348-349, 352-355, 359M, 455
Surface area
  metric units:
    rectangular prism, pp. 360-361, 456
    cylinder, pp. 360-361, 456
  customary units, pp. 360-361, 456
  approximate area of irregular figures, pp. 349, 355
Volume formulas
  metric units:
    rectangular prism, pp. 362-363, 456
  customary units, pp. 362-363, 456
Capacity
  metric units: milliliter, liter, **kiloliter,** pp. 176-177
    equivalent measures, pp. 176-177, 446
  customary units: **fluid ounce,** cup, pint, quart, gallon, pp. 250-251, H208
    equivalent measures, pp. 250-251, 450
    choosing the appropriate unit, pp. 250-251, 450
Mass/Weight
  metric units: gram, kilogram, milligram, p. 137C, 176-177
    equivalent measures, pp. 176-177, 446
  customary units: ounce, pound, ton, pp. 250-251
    equivalent measures, pp. 250-251
    choosing the appropriate unit, pp. 250-251
Temperature
  degrees Celsius, p. 255, 414-415
  degrees Fahrenheit, p. 254, 410, 413
Estimating measures
  metric units:
    length, p. 171
  customary units:
    length, p. 247
Determining the degree of accuracy required, pp. 170-171, 172-173, 176-177, 246-247, 250-251, 252-253
Operating with measures, p. 159C, 248-249
Indirect measurement, p. 370E
Using a calculator, p. 258, 363
Mental math, p. 353
Reasoning, p. 173C, 343, 355
Problem solving, pp. 312-313, 356-357, 388-389, 414-415

7

MEASUREMENT

Length
  metric units: millimeter, centimeter, decimeter, meter, dekameter, hectometer, kilometer, pp. 236-237
    measuring to the nearest mm and cm, pp. 236-237
    equivalent measures, pp. 238-239, 241M, 266R, H201
    choosing the appropriate unit, pp. 236-237, 241M
    comparing lengths, p. 239
  customary units: inch, sixteenth-inch, foot, yard, mile, pp. 246-247
    equivalent measures, pp. 246-247, H201
    choosing the appropriate unit, pp. 246-247
    adding and subtracting units, pp. 246-247
Perimeter
  metric units, pp. 352-353
    using formulas, pp. 352-353, 363M
  customary units, pp. 352-353
Circumference, pp. 354-355, 355C, 363M, 380R, 429A
Pi, pp. 354-355, 380R
Area formulas
  metric units:
    square, rectangle, parallelogram, pp. 356-357, 363M
    triangles, trapezoids, quadrilaterals, pp. 358-359
    circle, pp. 362-363, 371C, 380R, 429A
  customary units, pp. 356-359, 362-363
Surface area
  metric units:
    rectangular prism, **cylinder, square pyramid,** pp. 370-371
    lateral area, p. 370
  customary units: pp. 370-371
Volume formulas
  metric units:
    rectangular prism, **cube, triangular prism, cylinder,** pp. 372-373, 468, H221, H228
  customary units, pp. 372-373, 468
Capacity
  metric units: milliliter, **centiliter, deciliter,** liter, **dekaliter, hectoliter,** kiloliter, pp. 240-241
    equivalent measures, pp. 240-241, 259C
    choosing the appropriate unit, pp. 240-241
  customary units: fluid ounce, cup, pint, quart, gallon, pp. 248-249, H222
    equivalent measures, pp. 248-249, 484
    choosing the appropriate unit, pp. 248-249
Mass/Weight
  metric units: milligram, **centigram, decigram,** gram, **dekagram, hectogram,** kilogram, pp. 240-241
    equivalent measures, pp. 240-241, 259C, 483
    choosing the appropriate unit, pp. 240-241
  customary units: ounce, pound, ton, pp. 248-249
    equivalent measures, pp. 248-249
    choosing the appropriate unit, pp. 248-249
Temperature
  average temperature, p. 257, 437
  degrees Celsius, pp. 149, 256-257, 425
  degrees Fahrenheit, pp. 149, 256-257, 430-431, 435, 444-445
  choosing appropriate temperatures, pp. 256-257
  adding and subtracting temperatures, pp. 256-267, 430-431
Estimating measures
  metric units: length, pp. 236-237
Operating with measures, pp. 246-247
Precision in measurement, pp. 258-259
Greatest possible error, p. 267E
Using a calculator, p. 251, 262
Mental math, p. 249, 353
Problem solving, pp. 242-245, 342-343, 360-361, 364-365, 368-369, 374-375, 439, 444-445

8

MEASUREMENT

Length
  metric units: millimeter, centimeter, decimeter, meter, dekameter, hectometer, kilometer, pp. 166-167
    measuring to nearest mm and cm, pp. 166-167
    equivalent measures, pp. 166-167, 177M, 196R, H215
    choosing the appropriate unit, pp. 166-167
  customary units: inch, foot, yard, mile, pp. 174-175
    equivalent measures, pp. 174-175, 177M, 484
    choosing the appropriate unit, pp. 174-175
    adding and subtracting units, pp. 174-175
Perimeter
  metric units, pp. 398-399
  customary units, pp. 398-399
Circumference, pp. 404-405, H204
Pi, pp. 404-405
Pythagorean rule, pp. 400-401
Area formulas
  metric units: square, rectangle, parallelograms, pp. 408-409, H205
    triangles and trapezoids, pp. 410-411, H205
    circle, pp. 412-413
  customary units, pp. 408-413
    hectare, pp. 183C
Surface area
  metric units:
    prisms and pyramids, p. 147C, 418-419
    cylinders and **cones,** pp. 420-421, H205
Volume formulas
  metric units:
    prism and **pyramids,** p. 147C, 424-425, H206
    cylinders and **cones,** pp. 426-427
    sphere, p. 435E
  customary units, pp. 424-427
Capacity
  metric units: milliliter, liter, kiloliter, pp. 168-169
    equivalent measures, pp. 168-169, 177M
    choosing the appropriate unit, pp. 168-169
    comparing capacity, p. 169
    relating capacity and volume, pp. 170-171, 471, H199
  customary units: fluid ounce, cup, pint, quart, gallon, pp. 176-177
    equivalent measures, pp. 176-177
    choosing the appropriate unit, pp. 176-177
    adding and subtracting units, pp. 176-177
Mass/Weight
  metric units: milligram, centigram, gram, kilogram, pp. 168-169
    equivalent measures, pp. 168-169, 177M
    choosing the appropriate unit, pp. 168-169
    comparing mass, p. 169
    relating mass to volume, pp. 170-171, 471, H199
  customary units: ounce, pound, ton, pp. 176-177
    equivalent measures, pp. 176-177
    choosing the appropriate unit, pp. 176-177
    adding and subtracting units, pp. 176-177
Temperature
  degrees Celsius, pp. 188-189, 246-247, H216
  degrees Fahrenheit, pp. 188-189, 246-249, H216
  choosing appropriate temperatures, pp. 188-189
  changes in temperature, pp. 188-189, 247
Greatest possible error, pp. 180-181, H200
Significant digits and accuracy, p. 197E, 430
Operating with measures, pp. 174-177, H215
Using a calculator, p. 192, 457
Mental math, p. 167, 175, 196R
Reasoning, p. 227
Problem solving, pp. 248-249, 270-271, 378-379, 406-407, 414-415, 428-429, 442-443, 448, 459

6

GEOMETRY

7

GEOMETRY

8

GEOMETRY

6

PROBABILITY AND STATISTICS

PROBABILITY
Predicting events, pp. 392-393
Possible outcomes, pp. 392-393, 401R
Favorable outcomes, pp. 392-393, 401R
Probability
 as a fraction, pp. 392-393, 401R, 457
 of 1, pp. 392-393
 of 0, pp. 392-393, 457
Combinations, pp. 48-49, 364-365, 394-395, 418-419, 458
Tree diagrams, pp. 364-365, 458
Independent events, pp. 394-395, H216

STATISTICS
Survey, p. 397, 427
Sample Population, p. 141, 379, 397, 427, H215
Tally, pp. 376-377, 397, 427
Collecting, organizing, and interpreting data, pp. 376-377, 378-379, 397, H215
Tables
 reading, p. 7C, 45, 53, 126-127, 217C, 219C, 253C, 254, 255, 273, 349
 making, p. 353, 363, 376-377, 381M, 384-385, 407
Mean, median, mode, range, pp. 378-379, 381M, 405A, 427, 457, H215
Interpreting statistics, p. 397, 400E, 427

GRAPHING
Bar graphs
 reading, pp. 344-345
 making, pp. 382-383, 457, H215
Pictographs
 making, pp. 380-381
Line graphs
 reading, pp. 344-345, H213
 making, pp. 386-387, H216
Double line graphs
 reading, pp. 414-415
Circle graphs
 reading, pp. 292-293, 316-317, 389
 constructing and interpreting, pp. 292-293, 316-317, 327, 428
Graphing ordered pairs of integers, pp. 416-417, 417C, 430, H218
Latitude and longitude, p. 262E
Using a calculator, p. 363
Using concrete models, pp. 392-393, 394-395
Mental math, p. 393
Problem solving, pp. 48-49, 126-127, 292-293, 316-317, 344-345, 364-365, 379, 384-385, 389, 414-415, 418-419

7

PROBABILITY AND STATISTICS

PROBABILITY
Predicting events, pp. 402-403, 413C
Possible outcomes, pp. 402-405
Favorable outcomes, pp. 402-403
Random choices, pp. 402-403
Probability
 as a fraction, pp. 402-403
 of 1, pp. 402-403
 of 0, pp. 402-403
Combinations, pp. 180-181, 214-215, 404-405, 412-413, 432-433
Tree diagrams, pp. 404-405, H207
Sample space, pp. 404-407
Independent events, pp. 410-411, 447C
Dependent events, pp. 412-413
Empirical probability, p. 421E

STATISTICS
Tallies, pp. 386-387
Tables
 reading, p. 23, 29, 386-389, 392-393, 396-399
 making, pp. 318-319, 432
 making a frequency table, pp. 386-387, 399M, 403C
 relative frequency, pp. 386-387
Measures of central tendency, pp. 388-389, 420R
 mean, median, mode, pp. 388-391, 399M, 420R, H206
 Range, p. 388

GRAPHING
Bar graphs
 reading, p. 408, 450-451
 making, pp. 392-393
Box-and-whisker graphs
 reading, pp. 391, 468
 making, pp. 391, 468
Double bar graphs
 reading, pp. 34-35, 128-129, 134-135
 making, pp. 392-393, 417
Histogram
 reading, pp. 392-393
 making, pp. 392-393
Pictographs
 reading, pp. 142-143, 242
 making, pp. 392-393, 465
Broken-line graphs
 reading, pp. 128-129, 179, 409, 450-451
 making, pp. 396-397, 399M, 417
Double line graphs
 making, p. 397
Scattergram, pp. 394-395
Stem-and-leaf plot
 reading, p. 390, 468
 making, p. 390, 468
Circle graphs
 reading, pp. 298-299, 325
 making, pp. 398-399, 417, 466
Graphing
 ordered pairs of integers, pp. 448-449
 equations, pp. 446-447
 equations in two variables, pp. 454-455
 inequalities, pp. 446-447
 reflections, translations, and rotations, pp. 338-341
Using a calculator, p. 416
Problem solving, pp. 128-129, 134-135, 142-143, 179, 180-181, 214-215, 242, 298-299, 318-319, 325, 394-395, 408-409, 432-433

8

PROBABILITY AND STATISTICS

PROBABILITY
Predicting events, pp. 342-343
Possible outcomes, pp. 328-329, H223
Random choice, pp. 334-335, H224
Probability
 as a fraction, pp. 334-335, H224
 of 1, pp. 334-335
 of 0, pp. 334-335
Combinations, pp. 214-215, 330-333, 338-339, 459, H204
Tree diagrams, pp. 328-329
Sample space, pp. 328-329
Permutations, pp. 330-333, H224
Factorials, p. 333, H224
Independent events, pp. 336-337, H224
Dependent events, pp. 340-341, H224

STATISTICS
Tally, pp. 314-315
Tables
 reading, p. 11, 317, 449
 making a frequency table, pp. 314-315, 318-319, 325M, 342-343
 relative frequency, pp. 314-315
Measures of central tendency, pp. 316-317, 325M, H223
Mean, median, mode, range, pp. 314-317, 325M, 350R, 471, 472, H204, H223
Normal distribution, p. 351E
Samples, pp. 326-327, 370-371
Evaluating arguments, pp. 150-151, 327, 330-331
Investigating bias, pp. 313, 327, H134

GRAPHING
Bar graphs
 reading, pp. 248-249
 making, pp. 318-319
Double bar graphs
 reading, pp. 32-33, 179
 making, pp. 318-319
Histogram
 reading, pp. 318-319
 making, pp. 318-319
Pictographs
 reading, pp. 126-127
Line graph
 reading, pp. 246-247, 371
 making, pp. 322-323, 325M, H223
Double line graphs
 reading, pp. 322-323
 making, pp. 322-323
Scattergram, pp. 320-321
Circle graphs
 reading, pp. 228-229, 371
 making, pp. 324-325
Stem-and-leaf plot, p. 471
 reading, p 471
 making, p. 471
Box-and-whisker graph, p. 472
 reading, p. 472
 making, p. 472
Selecting appropriate format, pp. 325, H132
Correctly interpreting information from a graph, pp. 344-345, H223
Graphing
 ordered pairs of integers, pp. 382-383, 446-447
 reflections, pp. 382-383, H226, H229
 translations and rotations, pp. 384-385
 equations, pp. 300-301
 equations in two variables, pp. 450-451, H229
 systems of equations, pp. 452-453, 465E
 inequalities, pp. 300-301, 454-457
 parallel lines, p. 465E, H229
Using a calculator, p. 337, 346
Problem solving, pp. 32-33, 126-127, 214-215, 228-229, 248-249, 320-321, 326-327, 338-339, 344-345, 370-371, 449-459

6

RATIO, PROPORTION, PERCENT

RATIO
Meaning of, pp. 266-267
Application problems, pp. 38-39, 40-41, 282-283, 284-285, 286-287, 288-289, 290-291, 301
Writing fractions, pp. 266-267
As a rate, pp. 266-267
Equal ratios, pp. 268-269, 281M, 370E
Similar figures, pp. 324-325, 370E
Indirect measurement, p. 370E
Using to solve probability problems, pp. 392-393, 394-395
Pi, pp. 346-347, 354-355, 359M, 371R

PROPORTION
Cross products, pp. 268-269, 272-273, 281M, 370E, 451
Scale drawing, pp. 276-279
Rates, pp. 266-267
Writing proportions, pp. 274-275, 388-389

PERCENT
Meaning, notation, pp. 280-281, 451
  using concrete models, pp. 280-281, 292, 316-317
Decimals as percents, pp. 280-283, 451
Fractions as percents, pp. 280-283, 451
Percents for fractions, pp. 284-285, 451, H209, H210
Percent of a number, pp. 286-287, 292-293, 301R, 395A, 452
Percent one number is of another, pp. 288-289, 301R, 395A, 452
Finding a number when a percent of it is known, pp. 288-289, 395A, 452
Estimating with percents, pp. 290-291
Sales tax, p. 452
Discount, pp. 286-289, 452
Circle graphs, pp. 292-293, 316-317
Commission, p. 300E
Using a calculator, p. 291
Mental math, p. 283, 287
Problem solving, p. 269C, 274-275, 278-279, 285C, 292-293, 316-317, 388-389

7

RATIO, PROPORTION, PERCENT

RATIO
Meaning of, pp. 270-271
Writing fractions, pp. 270-271, H223
As a rate, pp. 270-271
Unit rate, pp. 270-271
Equal ratios, pp. 272-273, H202
Similar figures, pp. 330, 333, 348R
Pi, pp. 354-355
Golden ratio, p. 305E

PROPORTION
Cross products, pp. 272-273, 283M, 317A, 332-333, 484
Using models, p. 465
Scale drawing, pp. 276-277
Writing proportions, pp. 273-275, 324, 332-333
For percents, pp. 294-295
Distance formula, pp. 252-253, 438

PERCENT
Meaning, notation, pp. 278-279
Decimals as percents, pp. 278-281, 283M, 304R, H203
Fractions as percents, pp. 278-279, 282-283, 304R
Percents for fractions, pp. 282-283, 304R, H203
Percent of a number, pp. 284-285, 313A, H203
Estimating with percents, p. 285
Percent one number is of another, pp. 288-289, 313A, H203
Finding a number when a percent of it is known, pp. 290-291, 313A, H203
Using proportions, pp. 294-295
Percent of increase and decrease, pp. 296-297, H204
Circle graphs, pp. 298-299, 325, 398-399
Commission, pp. 286-287
Interest, pp. 292-293
Using a calculator, p. 279
Mental math, p. 285, 289
Problem solving, pp. 252-253, 274-275, 286-287, 292-293, 298-299, 313, 317, 324-325, 333, 348, 439, H224

8

RATIO, PROPORTION, PERCENT

RATIO
Meaning, pp. 200-201
Writing fractions, pp. 200-201, H217
As a rate, pp. 200-201
Unit rate, pp. 200-201
Equal ratios, pp. 200-201
Similar figures, pp. 380-381
Pi, pp. 404-405
Trigonometric ratios, pp. 402-403, 413M
As a percent, pp. 208-209

PROPORTIONS
Cross products, pp. 202-203
Scale drawing, pp. 206-207
Writing proportions, pp. 202-205, 371, 449
For percents, pp. 224-225, 485
Distance formula, pp. 184-185, 235R, 257
Inverse proportions, p. 235R

PERCENT
Meaning notation, pp. 208-209
Decimals as percents, pp. 210-211, 217M, 234R, H201
Fractions as percents, pp. 208-209, 217M, 234R, H201, H217
Percents for fractions, pp. 208-209, 212-213, 217M, H217
Percent of a number, pp. 216-217, 265A, H201, H218
Percent one number is of another, pp. 218-219, 265A, H201
Finding a number when a percent of it is known, pp. 220-221, H218
Using a proportion, pp. 224-225
Percent of increase and decrease, pp. 226-227, H201, H218
Circle graphs, pp. 228-229, 324-325, 371
Interest formula, pp. 222-223, 257
Sample, pp. 326-327, 370-371, 449
Mental math, p. 209, 219
Problem solving, pp. 184-185, 204-205, 222-223, 228-229, 257, 326-327, 370-371, 449

6

EQUATIONS AND INEQUALITIES

Solving equations
addition, pp. 28-29, 34R, 53
subtraction, pp. 28-29, 34R, 55, H196, H204, H206
multiplication, pp. 110-111, 142-143, H207
division, pp. 110-111, 142-143
with fractions, p. 213, 233
with ratios, pp. 268-269
with decimals, p. 53, 55, 76-77, 168-169
involving proportions, pp. 272-277
with percents, pp. 288-291
with integers, p. 409, 413
Writing equations, pp. 28-29, 76-77, 122-123, 142-143, 168-169, 174-175, 288-291, 388-389
Order of operation, pp. 112-113, 121M, 143C, 157A, 443
Inequality readiness
whole numbers, pp. 6-7, 21M, 47A, 113C
decimals, pp. 44-45, 50-51, 64R, 93, 95
fractions, pp. 206-207, 209
mixed numbers, pp. 206-207, 209
integers, pp. 406-407
Solving inequalities, p. 65E
Mental math, p. 201
Problem solving, pp. 76-77, 168-169

PATTERNS, RELATIONS, AND FUNCTIONS

Exploring other numeration systems, p. 3, 35
Exploring patterns of exponents, pp. 84-85, 227
Writing expressions, pp. 28-29, 76-77, 142-143, 168, 274, 286, 294, 356, 428
Ordered pairs
on a coordinate grid using a computer where appropriate, pp. 416-417, 430
Number patterns, p. 53C, 231C, 159C
Problem solving, pp. 330-331
Building functions
using concrete models, p. 417, 430
generating a rule, p. 417, 430

7

EQUATIONS AND INEQUALITIES

Expressions
addition, pp. 138-139
subtraction, pp. 138-139
multiplication, pp. 144-145
division, pp. 144-145
with decimals, pp. 138-139
simplify, pp. 77, 110, 120-121, 123, 167
Solving equations
addition, pp. 138-141, 221A
subtraction, pp. 138-141, 221A
multiplication, pp. 146-147, 221A
using models, pp. 146-147
division, pp. 146-147, 221A
with fractions, pp. 188-189, 222-223
with ratios, pp. 270-271
with decimals, pp. 140-141, 146-147, 221A
involving proportions, pp. 272-273, 276-277, 283M, 294-295
with percents, pp. 284-285, 288-291, 296-297
with integers, pp. 440-441
Solving two-step equations
addition, pp. 148-149
subtraction, pp. 148-149
multiplication, pp. 148-149
using models, pp. 148-149
division, pp. 148-149
with integers, pp. 452-453
Writing equations, pp. 150-151, 178, 284-285, 296-297, 290-291, 334-335, 438, 444-445
Order of operation, pp. 136-137, 169A, 387A
Solving inequalities
addition, pp. 442-443
subtraction, pp. 442-443
multiplication, pp. 442-443
division, pp. 442-443
Writing inequalities, pp. 444-445
Graphing
inequalities, pp. 446-447
equations, pp. 446-447
equations in two variables, pp. 454-455
ordered pairs, pp. 448-449
Problem solving, pp. 150-151, 178, 334-335, 438, 444-445

PATTERNS, RELATIONS, AND FUNCTIONS

Ordered pairs
on a coordinate grid, pp. 448-449
Solving equations
table of values, pp. 452-454
Graphing
reflections, translations, rotations, pp. 338-341
Number patterns, p. 5, 7C, 13, 21C, 31, 55, 87, 115E, 125, 165, 189C, 192, 221, 281, 318, 330-331, 355, 407, 427, 455C, H210, H211, H217, H232

8

EQUATIONS AND INEQUALITIES

Expressions
addition, pp. 280-281, 295C, 361A, H221
subtraction, pp. 280-281, 361A, H221
multiplication, pp. 280-281, 361A
division, pp. 280-281, 361A
with integers, pp. 280-281, 287M, 361A
Radical expressions, p. 277E
Solving equations
addition, pp. 100-101, 104-105, 108-109, 221A
subtraction, pp. 100-101, 104-105, H212
multiplication, pp. 106-107, H212
division, pp. 106-107, H212
with fractions, pp. 152-153
with decimals, pp. 100-101, 104-107, 470
with percents, pp. 216-221, 226-227
with integers, pp. 245C, 282-283, H221
with real numbers, pp. 282-283, H221
Solving two-step equations
addition, pp. 108-109, 284-285
subtraction, pp. 108-109, 284-285
multiplication, pp. 108-109, 284-285, H221
division, pp. 108-109, 284-285
with decimals, pp. 108-109, 284-285
with fractions, pp. 284-285
with integers, pp. 284-285, 308R
with real numbers, pp. 284-285, 308R, H221
Solving equations in two variables, pp. 438-441, 464R, 447M, H206, H221
Writing equations, pp. 110-111, 216-221, 285, 288-289, 299, 441A
Word problems from equations, pp. 286-287
Order of operations, pp. 98-99
Quadratic equations, p. 309E
Solving inequalities
addition, pp. 292-295, 487
subtraction, pp. 292-295, 487
multiplication, pp. 292-295, 487
division, pp. 292-295, 487
Solving two-step inequalities
addition, pp. 298-299, 487
subtraction, pp. 298-299, 487
multiplication, pp. 298-299, 487
division, pp. 298-299, 487
with decimals, pp. 298-299
with fractions, pp. 298-299
with integers, pp. 298-299
with real numbers, pp. 298-299
Solving inequalities in two variables, pp. 454-455
Writing inequalities, p. 299
Graphing
real numbers, pp. 268-269, 446-447, H220
inequalities, pp. 300-301, H222
inequalities in two variables, pp. 456-457
equations, pp. 300-301
equations in two variables, pp. 450-451, 464R
a system of equations, pp. 452-453, 465E
parallel lines, p. 465E
Using a calculator, p. 430
Mental math, p. 153, 283
Problem solving, pp. 110-111, 288-289, 370

RELATIONS AND FUNCTIONS

Ordered pairs
on a coordinate grid, pp. 268-269, 382-385, 446-447, 450-457
Solving equations using table of values
pp. 440-441, 444-445, 450-453, 464R, H206
Graphing
reflections, translations, rotations, pp. 382-385, H229
equations, pp. 300-301
equations with two variables, pp. 450-451, 465E, H229
systems of equations, pp. 452-453, 465E, H230
parallel lines, p. 465E, H229
Relations and functions, pp. 444-445, 446-447, H206
Number patterns and sequences, p. 75E, 109C, 117E, 133C, 318-319

6

CALCULATOR

Using a calculator to
display greater numbers, p. 13
check products, p. 104E
to add and subtract, p. 30
complete a sales slip, p. 85
find square roots, p. 100
divide, pp. 140-141
compare prices, p. 177, 291
mixed operations with parentheses, p. 146
find a repeating decimal, p. 203
divide a whole number by a fraction, p. 241
find common multiples and least common
multiples, p. 222
find a decimal for a fraction, p. 222
find equivalent customary measures, p. 258
find digits with a line of symmetry, p. 329
complete a table of volumes, p. 363
find the volume of a cube, p. 363, 420
compute with integers, p. 413
complete a table with percents, p. 428
solve multistep problems, pp. 146, 222
compare decimals, p. H197
write decimals and percents for fractions,
p. H210
Choosing the method
mixed operations with whole numbers,
p. 191

CONSUMER

Handling money
making change, p. 25C, 90-91, 174-175
completing a sales slip, p. 185
savings, p. 119, 291
sales tax, pp. 90-91, 286-287, 291
discount, pp. 286-287
rate of discount, pp. 288-289
Spending money
total cost, p. 21, 81, 90-91, 93, 97, 174-175
estimating costs, p. 15, 174-175
utilities, p. 97
better buy, p. 131C, 177, 291, H203
average amount, p. 141, 155
enough money, pp. 90-91
using a price list, pp. 174-175
budget, pp. 292-293, 316-317
Earning money
wages, p. 83, 119, 196-197
time cards, p. 253C
profit, pp. 196-197, 221
allowance, p. 293
Food
using a menu, pp. 26-27
using a recipe, pp. 294-295
Travel
determining costs, p. 159
foreign exchange, p. 167
budget, pp. 168-169
different time zones, pp. 256-257
Investing
stocks, p. 193, 196-197, 201, 207, 217C,
219C
Using a calculator, p. 85, 177, 291
Problem solving, pp. 26-27, 90-91, 168-169,
174-175, 196-197, 220-221, 256-257,
274-275, 292-293, 294-295, 316-317

7

CALCULATOR

Using a calculator to
review rounding skills, p. 36
relate addition and multiplication, p. 47
find next digit on a calculator with 8-digit
display, p. 110
find sums, p. 139
solve multiplication equations, p. 149
find cubes and cube roots, p. 192
multiply fractions, p. 201
solve time problems, p. 251
solve time-consuming problems, p. 262
find the unit price, p. 279
find discounted prices and prices with sales
tax, p. 344
interpret circle graphs, p. 416
Choosing the method
multiplication of whole numbers, p. 83CTM,
139
addition of mixed numbers, p. 183CTM
skills applications, pp. 2-3, 104-105,
106-107, 139, 146-147, 148-149, 296-297,
330-331, 332-333, 358-359, 416, H212,
H217, H223, H227

CONSUMER

Handling money
making change, pp. 134-135, 249
sales tax, p. 285, 344
Spending money
comparison shopping, p. 23
utilities, p. 31, 33A
total cost, p. 33, 67, 211, 213, 285
unit price, p. 107, 217, 249, 279
budget, p. 9, 201, 291, 295, 450-451
magazine subscription, p. 281
postage expenses, p. 29, 389
expenses, p. 429, 441
using a price list, pp. 400-401
computing discounted prices, p. 344
Earning money
yearly sales, p. 15, 17, 142-143
wages, p. 99, 165, 169
profit, p. 191, 221, 389, 429
net income, p. 441
commission, pp. 286-287
Food
reading a label, p. 249
using a recipe, pp. 218-219, 243
Travel
determining costs, p. 69, 134-135, 400-401
time zones, pp. 254-255
Investing
stocks, p. 189
Borrowing money
interest formula, pp. 292-293, 325
Using a calculator, p. 279, 344
Problem solving, p. 9, 134-135, 142-143, 191,
218-219, 243, 286-287, 292-293, 325,
400-401, 450-451

8

CALCULATOR

Using a calculator to
add and subtract decimals, p. 34, H208
estimate square roots, p. 83
explore order of operations, pp. 88-89
multiply larger numbers, p. 112
find equivalent fractions, p. 125
rename customary measurements, p. 192
find the volume of solid figures, p. 457
investigate irrational numbers, pp. 266-267
add and subtract integers, p. 272
find the prime factorization, p. 243
compare square roots, p. 293
find the mean, p. 346
work with the Pythagorean rule, p. 401
solve an equation, p. 430
apply the concept of significant digits,
p. 430
compare rational numbers, p. H220
Choosing the method
division with whole numbers and decimals,
p. 99CTM
multiplication with whole numbers and
decimals, p. 337CTM

CONSUMER

Handling money
making change, p. 15, 62-63, 68-69
saving, p. 299
Spending money
comparison shopping, p. 53, 227
total cost, p. 61, 68, 69, 169, 177
budget, p. 61A, 221, 294
unit price, p. 65, 67
using postal rate table, pp. 96-97
enough money, p. 179
cost of advertising, pp. 296-297, 458
renting a car, p. 459
Earning money
yearly sales, p. 143A
wages, p. 217, 221, 225, 227, 235E, 295
profit or **loss,** p. 178, 225, 286
Food
using a recipe, pp. 204-205
Travel
fuel economy, p. 67
determining costs, p. 9, 54-55, 68-69,
190-191
reading a map, pp. 190-191, 257
using a plane schedule, pp. 302-303
Investing
rate of interest, p. 235E
Borrowing money
installment payments, pp. 222-223, 257,
287, H218
Problem solving, p. 9, 54-55, 62-63, 68-69,
96-97, 178-179, 190-191, 204-205, 222-223,
257, 296-297, 302-303, 458-459

6

TECHNOLOGY

Program commands
LOGO, pp. 66-67
BASIC, pp. 106-107, 186-187, 372-373
Writing a program
for multiplication, p. 187
Applications
geometry, pp. 66-67, 302-303
percents, pp. 106-107
sales tax, pp. 186-187
computation, pp. 186-187, 373
measurement, pp. 302-303

LOGICAL REASONING

Writing a logical statement **and its negation,**
p. 60
Identifying valid and invalid conclusions,
p. 296, 315C
Conclusions using *some, none, all,* p. 315C
Using Venn diagrams, p. 366
Problem solving, p. 39C, 41, 273, H201, H202,
H203, H204, H205, H206, H207, H211,
H213, H214, H215, H216

7

TECHNOLOGY

BASIC
programs, pp. 232-233, 306-307, 382-383
commands, pp. 232-233, 306-307, 382-383
IF/THEN comparisons, pp. 306-307
spaghetti programs, p. 385
addition of decimal numbers, pp. 232-233
LOGO
programs, pp. 78-79, 158-159, 462-463
commands, pp. 78-79, 158, 462-463
repeating procedures, pp. 158-159
use of coordinates, pp. 462-463

LOGICAL REASONING

Subsets, p. 152
Venn diagrams, p. 152
Equivalent statements, p. 300
Compound statements, p. 300
And, p. 300
Or, p. 300
Valid conclusions, p. 456
Invalid conclusions, p. 456
Problem solving, pp. 25, 45, 99, 127, 152,
295, 300, 441, 456, H209, H210, H213,
H214, H215, H216, H220, H221, H226,
H227, H228, H229, H230

8

TECHNOLOGY

BASIC
programs, pp. 76-77, 162-163, 236-237,
310-311
commands, pp. 76-77, 162-163, 236-237,
310-311
IF/THEN comparisons, pp. 76-77
renaming fractions as decimals, p. 162
use of semi-colon to connect statements,
p. 163
**use of INTEGER FUNCTION to round
numbers,** pp. 236-237
exponents, pp. 310-311
scientific notation, pp. 310-311
order of operations, p. 311
LOGO
programs, pp. 394-395, 466-467
commands, pp. 394-395, 466-467
to draw figures, pp. 394-395
to draw polygons, pp. 466-467

LOGICAL REASONING

Sets, p. 156
Subsets, p. 156
Disjoint sets, p. 156
Venn diagrams, p. 156
Equivalent statements, p. 304
Conditional statements, p. 304
Converse statements, p. 304
Truth tables, p. 304
Valid conclusions, p. 460
Invalid conclusions, p. 460
Conclusions using *all, some, none,* p. 460
Problem solving, p. 13R, 227R, H210, H214,
H216, H218
Logic tables, p. 469
Properties, p. H207
Estimation, p. H207
Using a calculator, p. H208
Adding decimals, p. H208
Patterns, p. H209, H221, H229
Multiplying decimals, p. H209
Prime numbers, p. H211
GCF and LCM, p. H211
Order of operations, p. H212
Integers, p. H219
Rational numbers, p. H220
Equations, p. H221
Inequalities, p. H222, H230
Mean, median, and mode, p. H223
Probability, p. H224
Geometry, p. H225
Volume, p. H228

Mathematics
UNLIMITED

 Harcourt Brace Jovanovich, Inc.
Holt, Rinehart and Winston, Inc.

Orlando · Austin · San Diego · Chicago · Dallas · Toronto

AUTHORS

Francis "Skip" Fennell
Associate Professor of Education
Western Maryland College
Westminster, Maryland

Barbara J. Reys
Assistant Professor of Curriculum
and Instruction
University of Missouri, Columbia, Missouri
Formerly Junior High Mathematics Teacher
Oakland Junior High, Columbia, Missouri

Robert E. Reys
Professor of Mathematics Education
University of Missouri
Columbia, Missouri

Arnold W. Webb
Senior Research Associate
Research for Better Schools
Philadelphia, Pennsylvania
Formerly Asst. Commissioner of Education
New Jersey State Education Department

ILLUSTRATION

Anthony Accardo: pp. 56, 57, 82, 280, 281 • Bob Aiese: pp. 168, 169 • Beth Baum: pp. 250, 254, 255, 331, 332, 333, 343 • Ron Becker: pp. 71, 305 • Robin Brickman: pp. 246-247, 260, 460 • Brad Clark: pp. 14, 108, 130, 131, 418 • Laura Cornell: pp. 22, 23 • Jack Davis: p. 193 • Jack Freas: pp. 44, 45, 200 • Mark Giglio: pp. 166, 167 • Deirdre Newman Griffin: p. 18 • Meryl Henderson: p. 182 • Debora Kaplan: p. 242 • Linda Miyamoto: pp. 4, 5, 90, 100, 101, 113, 132, 133, 134, 210, 220, 221, 328 • Jim Owens: pp. 230, 272, 346, 460 • Rosanne Percivalle: pp. 30, 142, 187, 209, 226 • Tom Powers: pp. 52, 53, 120, 121, 148, 149, 176, 216, 217, 316, 336, 347, 412, 420, 454, 455 • David Reinbold: p. 46 • Beverly Rich: p. 272 • Claudia Sargent: pp. 70, 156, 273, 338, 366, 382, 383, 389, 426 • Joel Snyder: pp. 310, 460 • Krystyna Stasiak: pp. 104, 105 • Jane Sterrett: pp. 258, 259, 440 • Arthur Thompson: pp. 431, 461 • Debbie Tilley: pp. 106, 107, 295 • Vantage Art Inc.: p. 245 • Nina Wallace: pp. 58, 59, 174, 322, 438 • Debora Whitehouse: pp. 89, 124, 125, 138, 188, 206, 207, 254, 255, 325, 384, 398, 446, 447 • Nina Winter: pp. 134, 152, 153, 284, 344 • Paul Yalowitz: pp. 28, 29, 35, 231, 246, 247, 260, 261 • Mark Yankus: pp. 6, 7 • M. O'Reilly: pp. H212, H215, H227. **Chapter Opener Illustrations:** Joe Lapinsky: pp. 1, 41, 79, 119, 165, 199, 239, 279, 313, 353, 397, 437. **Cover Illustration:** Jeannette Adams.

PHOTOGRAPHY

Animals, Animals/Richard Kollar: p. 54; Patti Murray: pp. 136, 137 • AP/World Wide Photos: p. 374 • Art Resource: p. 110 • David Bartruff: p. 404 • Black Star/Andy Levin: p. 378; Steve Northrup: p. 13; Doug Wilson: p. 12 • R. J. Dufour, Rice University, courtesy Hansen Planetarium, Salt Lake City: p. 85 • Earth Scenes/Charles Palek: p. 270 top • Focus West/John Biever: p. 344; Lee Mason: p. 48 • Granger Collection: p. 102 • Michal Heron: pp. 128, 141, 228, 262, 326-327 • HRW Photo/Richard Haynes: pp. 84, 170, 330, 342; William Hubbell: p. 150 • Image Bank/John Banagan: p. 24; A. Broccaccio: p. 372; Louis Castaneda: p. 62; Gary Cralle: p. 9; Arthur d'Arazien: p. 386; Geoffrey Gove: p. 144; D. W. Hamilton: p. 190; Terry Madison: p. 127; David Miser: p. 443; O'Rourke: p. 184 • Lawrence Migdale 1983: p. 76 • Museum of Modern Art (Gift of Robert W. deForest, 1925): p. 154 • Odyssey Productions/Walter Frerck: p. 68 • Omni-Photo Communications, Inc./Ken Karp: pp. 18-19, 20-21, 60-61, 94-95, 96, 146-147, 186, 204, 224-225, 286-287, 358-359, 376-377, 452-453; John Lei: pp. 98, 120-121, 122-123, 138-139, 282-283, 298, 338, 444-445 • Photo Researchers/Russ Kinne: p. 2; Helen Marcus: pp. 290-291; Tom McHugh: p. 372; Gerard Vandystadt: p. 181; Daniel Zirinsky 1981: p. 173 • Rainbow/Linda K. Moore: p. 414; Bill Pierce: p. 102 • Shostal Associates: p. 33 • Sports Illustrated/Neil Leifer: p. 314 • Stock Market/Mark Ferri: p. 222; Kasz Macaig: p. 47; Ted Mahve: p. 378; Louis Portnoy: p. 68; Robert Semenuik: pp. 27, 406; Christopher Springmann: p. 288 • Woodfin Camp & Associates/Craig Aurness: pp. 296-297; Jonathan Blair: p. 86; Jim Brandenburg: p. 16; David Cupp: p. 270 bottom; Dick Durrance: p. 386; Timothy Eagan: p. 215; George Hall: pp. 302, 458; Michal Heron; pp. 32, 172, 212, 236; Roland & Sabrina Michaud: p. 108 • Mike Yamashita: p. 428 • Leo de Wys/E. Johnson: p. 269; Richard Laird: p. 50. Page H207, Steve Satushek/The Image Bank; H208, HBJ Photo/Earl Kogler; H209, HBJ Photo/Earl Kogler; H210, Roy Morsch/The Stock Market; H211, Mary Kate Denny/PhotoEdit; H214, Robert Everts/ Tony Stone Worldwide; H216, Eric Hayman/Tony Stone Worldwide; H218, HBJ Photo/Earl Kogler; H219, John V.A.F. Neal/Photo Researchers; H220, Tony Freeman/PhotoEdit; H221, Maurits Cornelis Escher, DEPTH, 1955/Art Resource; H222, Tony Freeman/PhotoEdit; H224, HBJ Photo/Earl Kogler; H225, HBJ Photo/Earl Kogler; H230, Jeffry W. Myers/The Stock Market.

Printed in the United States of America

ISBN 0-15-351569-4

CONTENTS

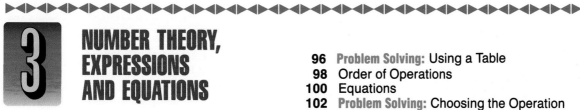

7 INTEGERS, RATIONALS, REALS

8 EQUATIONS AND INEQUALITIES
One Variable

9 STATISTICS AND PROBABILITY

10 GEOMETRY

11 PERIMETER, AREA, VOLUME

12 EQUATIONS AND INEQUALITIES
Two Variables

STUDENT HANDBOOK

CHAPTER 1 OVERVIEW

ADDITION AND SUBTRACTION WHOLE NUMBERS AND DECIMALS

SUMMARY

Chapter 1 deals with whole number and decimal numeration, focusing on place value from the hundred trillions place to the millionths place. Included is a review of addition and subtraction, as well as ordering, comparing, and rounding whole numbers and decimals. This chapter also contains lessons about estimating sums and differences of whole numbers and decimals.

LESSON SEQUENCE

PROFESSIONAL BACKGROUND

The research that shows that many students develop number skills without a deep understanding of number concepts, makes some review and diagnostic work advisable. In one recent study, about 30% of the 12-year olds could not name a whole number between 4,100 and 4,200. To help students understand, provide practice in the naming of numbers between given numbers, especially large numbers. Calculators can be useful here.

Research also points to computational facility with powers of ten as a clear prerequisite for the development of estimation skills and also shows estimation strategies as powerful aids in the development of number understanding and problem-solving skills.

However, estimation should not be introduced and used primarily as a computation-checking device. Studies also show that good estimators use related strategies that are not used by less successful estimators. For instance, they have facility with "front-end strategies" and rounding. As students become more familiar with techniques of estimation, discuss situations from everyday life to help students develop a sense of when to estimate and when an estimate is reasonable.

Resources: Reys, Robert E, et al., "Processes Used by Good Computational Estimators," *Journal for Research in Mathematical Education,* vol. 13 (1982): 183–201.

Ashlock, R. B. *Error Patterns in Computation.* Columbus, Ohio: Charles E. Merrill, 1972.

Hart, K. M., ed., 1981. *Children's Understanding of Mathematics: 11–16.* London, England: John Murray, Ltd.

MATERIALS

place-value blocks
number cards 0 through 9
coffee cans
marbles (4 different colors)
number cubes
calculators
index cards
newspaper ads

VOCABULARY

period (p. 2)
expanded form (p. 2)
trillion (p. 2)
properties of addition (p. 6)
  Commutative
  Associative
  Identity
inverse operations (p. 6)
millionths (p. 18)
astronomical unit (p. 30)

ABOUT THE CHAPTER

This chapter reviews what students have learned about place value and about rounding, ordering, adding and subtracting whole numbers and decimals. For most students, this will be their first encounter with mathematics since classes recessed for the summer. They will need to review these concepts and skills to prepare to learn much of what is taught in the rest of the text.

In Chapter One, students add and subtract whole numbers and decimals to millions.

All the work that students do with numbers requires that they understand the place-value system of numeration. Be alert for students who are having difficulty, and provide additional help now to avoid problems in the future. Review the concept that the place to the left of the decimal point is the ones place, but the place to the right of the decimal point is not the "oneths" place, but the tenths place. Expanded notation will often help students grasp this idea.

The estimation strategies presented in this chapter will help students overcome errors in addition and subtraction which are caused by misaligned decimal points or place value. Ask students to first estimate the answer to an addition or subtraction problem, and then carry out the actual computation.

Four problem-solving lessons are presented in this chapter. These lessons focus on developing an organized approach to problem solving, estimation, using outside sources including the Infobank, and finding and using information from a double-bar graph.

The Group Project builds on the lessons in this chapter and asks students to help plan the purchase of a "Hikers' Hut." The project involves students actively and gives them an opportunity to apply problem solving and other mathematics concepts and skills.

The Enrichment lesson introduces students to the different number systems used by the Egyptians, the Babylonians, and the Romans. The Egyptians and Romans used a numeration system that was not built on place value. The Babylonians had a place-value system based on the number 60.

The Assignment Guide for each lesson lists suggested exercises and special feature assignments for your student groupings. The abbreviations *o* and *e* are used to indicate odd-numbered

exercises and even-numbered exercises, respectively. The features on the pupil's page are indicated by the following abbreviations:

Chlg for *Challenge*
NS for *Number Sense*
F for *Focus*
Calc for *Calculator*
AL for *Another Look*
MCR for *Midchapter Review*
CTM for *Choosing the Method*

Challenge features are conceptually challenging enrichment features suitable for all students. They are not computationally more difficult than the lesson. Number Sense features are activities involving mental computation and estimation. Focus activities highlight reasoning. Calculator features instruct students in using the calculator to perform a skill related to the chapter content. Another Look features are maintenance activities reviewing skills taught earlier in the text. Midchapter Review features provide more practice of concepts presented earlier in the chapter.

USING THE CHAPTER OPENER

The Chapter Opener page and the companion Making Math Work ancillary pages present a situational approach to the chapter. The artwork on the pupil page can be used to stimulate class discussion regarding the problem that is presented. The Making Math Work work sheets provide a focus for the Chapter Opener. Each Chapter Opener presents situational problem-solving activities that can be used to motivate the skills taught throughout the chapter. The work sheets can be used by individuals, small groups, or the whole class, depending on the needs of the class.

In the Chapter Opener activities, students will explore the motions of the earth and sun through direct observation and through research. Students will also make broken-line graphs to record the times at which the sun sets throughout the year.

PROBLEM SOLVING

Mathematics Unlimited provides a valuable problem-solving tool, the 4-Step Plan, for your students. The 4-Step Plan, found on pages 16–17 of the text, provides an organized approach to problem solving that may help students solve problems that are difficult for them. The 4-Step Plan is divided into four parts: Questions, Tools, Solutions, and Checks. Each part addresses one of the four problematic areas for students trying to solve math problems. The 4-Step Plan gives students a systematic foundation from which to approach problem solving.

All students have difficulty with math problems at some time or another. They may not have the same kind of difficulty with every problem. Therefore, students should learn that getting stuck on a problem is natural, and that staying stuck is unnecessary. They should understand that there are many different ways to solve most problems, and any hint that helps them solve a problem is a good one.

The Estimation problem-solving lessons in *Mathematics Unlimited* encourage students to think about a problem before deciding how to solve it. The Estimation lesson in this chapter focuses on whether students should underestimate or overestimate to solve a problem. Encourage any student improvisations that increase their estimating skills. Math problems, as well as real-life problems, are sometimes not accompanied by all of the necessary data. the lessons entitled Using Outside Sources Including the Infobank instruct students in the use of a data source when looking elsewhere for needed information. Lack of familiarity with the data source and how to read it may present difficulties to the students. This lesson provides a situation in which students can develop data-source skills in an easily-monitored classroom setting. Lessons of this type also lend themselves to small group work. Using a Graph is another lesson in using information from an outside source. Graphs are often used in math and in real-life situations, and students should be comfortable reading them.

Most of the problem-solving lessons in *Mathematics Unlimited* lend themselves to small group work. Students can brainstorm and discuss various ways to solve problems.

BULLETIN BOARD

"Our Solar System"

Materials: paper to cover bulletin board, lettering, 10 sheets construction paper, assorted colors, felt-tip pens, scissors, 10 sheets 8-½ × 11″ white paper for Fact Sheets, stapler, books on astronomy

Preparation: Cover board and arrange lettering. Cut ten circles for the ten heavenly bodies in relative scale sizes as shown. Label and attach planets to board and affix a blank Fact Sheet below each one. Assign pairs of students to do research on one of the ten heavenly bodies. Have them collect information about their planet (e.g., circumference, diameter, mean distance, length of year, period of rotation, density, mass) and print their findings neatly on appropriate Fact Sheet.

After pp. 4-5: Have class take same information about each planet (e.g., circumference), and order all ten heavenly bodies from least to greatest accordingly. Ask class to select a different category, such as density, and order all ten bodies again from greatest to least.

After pp. 30-31: Ask students to compare the densities, or other category of information given in decimals, of any two planets by subtraction of decimals.

COMMON ERRORS

Students might have difficulty subtracting a decimal from a whole number. Remind students that enough 0's must be written so that the whole number has as many places as the decimal.

Another error students might make when they subtract a decimal from a whole number is that when they regroup, they might forget to regroup one or more of the place values to the left of the ultra right place value. To correct this error, explain to students that in this type of subtraction, two regroupings are required.

Many lessons in the text contain a Checkpoint feature designed to help you assess students' understanding of the concept being taught and to provide experience for test-taking in the multiple-choice format. Each incorrect multiple-choice response in the Checkpoint is keyed to a common error that students might be making. Remediation suggestions are provided for the possible errors identified. □ indicates a Reteach Master. ■ indicates the teacher-directed remediation provided. ○ indicates a lesson Follow-Up activity. △ indicates review of a previous lesson.

SPECIAL NEEDS

Use base-ten blocks or a labeled place-value chart and counters to review place value and regrouping of whole numbers and decimals for students experiencing difficulty with these concepts. Remind students that 10 of any place value is equal to 1 of the next larger place value. Conversely, 1 of any place value equals 10 of the next smaller place value. Have students read, write, and order numbers that are represented concretely. In preparation for estimation, have students round numbers, reminding them that 5 or more in a particular place value means that the number is rounded "up." Particular attention should be paid to decimals. Stress that a tenth is greater than a hundredth or a thousandth. Use base-ten blocks to show these comparisons concretely.

Have students work with addition and subtraction concretely at first, estimating their answers by rounding. Have them explain each step. Be sure they show regrouping and explain all exchanges. Only when the manipulations are understood should students begin to work in the abstract. Again, have them verbalize their computations to ensure understanding.

Have students who grasp the concepts quickly study the properties of ancient numeration systems (Roman, Babylonian, Sumerian), and write their own system, denoting its properties.

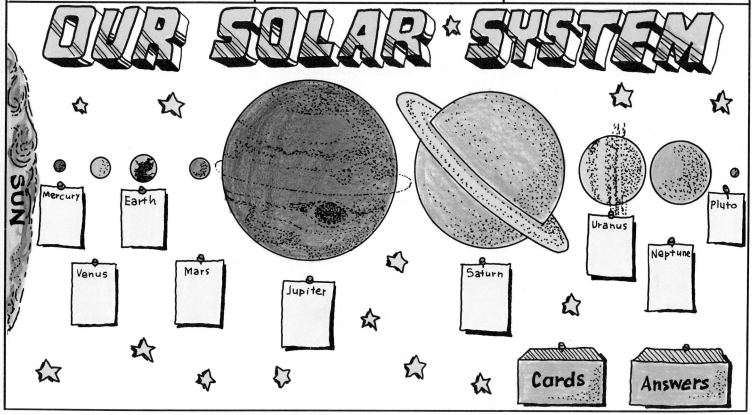

MATH LABS

PUZZLES AND GAMES
Materials: blank cards, felt-tip pen, timer

Write a different decimal on each card. Vary the number of places from card to card. Form groups of four students, each group with a dealer.

Each player decides how many cards he or she can handle at one time. With the timer set for 10 seconds, the dealer picks the cards at random and places them face up on the table. The player then rounds each card to the place value indicated by the dealer within the 10 seconds.

Each player keeps all the cards for which she or he answers correctly, and loses a card for each one missed. The activity ends either when players hold all the cards or at the end of a specified playing time. The winner is the player with the most cards.

MATH CONNECTION (Science)
The Index of Refraction (I) for a substance is a measure of how much light bends while it passes through it. The standard for comparison is air, which has an I_r of 1.00. The greater the I_r for a substance, the more light is refracted when it passes through it.

Have students arrange the following substances in order according to their I_r, from those that bend light least to those that bend it the most.

SUBSTANCE	I_r
carbon disulfide	1.63
water	1.33
salt crystal	1.54
diamond	2.42
ethanol	1.36
glass	1.50

(Water, ethanol, glass, salt crystal, carbon disulfide, diamond.)

CALCULATOR

Students need to understand the processes of addition and subtraction as well as to be able to use paper and pencil algorithms (processes) to solve selected exercises. However, as computations become tedious and time consuming, the calculator should be used in place of the paper and pencil processes. Students still need to learn estimation skills and to be aware of the reasonableness of their results, or they might not recognize an error when it occurs. Also, students must recognize the limitations of the calculator. For example, if the calculator has an 8-digit capacity, then the sum of two 8-digit numbers might not be possible.

Students should have calculators available to work all problem-solving exercises.

Additional Activities: **Drill and Practice:** Use a calculator that has an 8-digit display to add two 10-digit numbers.

$$8,643,721,856$$
$$+\ 5,438,986,735$$

To do this, add the left 4-digit number of each addend (8643 + 5438), then add the right 6-digit number of each addend. (721856 + 986735) Because there is a 1 to regroup from the 6-digit sum, add the 1 to the 4-digit sum.

Exploration: Develop an algorithm similar to the one above to subtract two 10-digit numbers on a calculator that has an 8-digit capacity.

SUBJECT AREA CONNECTIONS

These Subject Area Connections are useful for reinforcing the concepts presented in this chapter.

p. 13-Social Studies: Students estimate to compare the areas of various states.

p. 23-Science: Students round to the nearest whole number the number of days in one year on various planets.

Here are some other activities for presenting these concepts.
- **Social Studies:** Have students research the populations of the five most populous countries, and then order their findings from the greatest to the least.
- **Social Studies:** Have students research and find the difference between the number of people in their home state who voted for George Bush and the number who voted for Michael Dukakis in the 1988 Presidential election.

PLAN AHEAD

You will need restaurant ads from a newspaper for the activity on T.E. p. 23. You will need a computer for the activities on T.E. pp. 5 and 19.

PLANNING CALENDAR
ABBREVIATION KEY

Teacher's Resource Book	*Follow-up Activities*
MMW—Making Math Work	CALC—Calculator
P—Practice	CMP—Computer
R—Reteach	P&G—Puzzles and Games
E—Enrich	MNP—Manipulatives
	MC—Math Connection
	MCM—Math Communication
	NS—Number Sense
	PS—Problem Solving
	RFM—Reinforcement

CHAPTER 1 OVERVIEW

PLANNING CALENDAR

Pages	Lesson Objectives	ASSIGNMENT GUIDE			Class/ Home	More Practice	Math Reasoning	Follow-up	Reteach	Practice	Enrich
		Basic	Average	Extended							
1	Chapter Opener (Use MMW 1,2)	1	1	1							
2,3	To read and write with whole numbers through the hundred trillions.	1-12,13-27o	1-25o,26-27,Chlg	2-24e,26-27,Chlg	H1	H195		MNP	1	1	1
4,5	To compare and order whole numbers	1-21o,23-24,F	1-21o,23-24,F	2-22e,23-24,F	H2	H195		PS CMP	2	2	2
6,7	To identify and use the properties of addition and subtraction	1-18	1-17o,19-24, Chlg	8-18e,19-24, Chlg	H3		H207	NS MM	3	3	3
8	To round whole numbers	1-19o	1-21o	2-22e	H4					4	4
9	To estimate in solving problems	1-4	2-5	2-5	H4					4	4
10,11	To estimate sums of whole numbers using the front-end and rounding methods	2-22e	1-17o,18-23	1-17o,18-23	H5			RFM MC	4	5	5
12,13	To estimate differences of whole numbers using the front-end and rounding methods	1-12,13-23o	1-12e,13-23,F	6-24,F	H6			RFM MC	5	6	6
14,15	To add and subtract whole numbers	1-21,29-31	1-27o,29-32	2-28e,29-32	H7			P&G PS	6	7	7
16,17	To understand the 4-step problem-solving plan	1-6	3-8	5-10	H8			PS, CALC		8	8
18,19	To read and write decimals through millionths	2-18e,20-21,MCR	1-19o,20-22,MCR	2-18e,20-23,MCR	H9			RFM CMP	7	9	9
20,21	To compare and order decimals	1-12,13-23o,25-27, AL	2-24e,25-27,AL	1-23o,25-27,AL	H10			CALC RFM	8	10	10
22,23	To round decimals	1-29o,NS	2-26e,27-29,NS	1-25o,27-29,NS	H11		H207	MC MC	9	11	11
24,25	To use outside sources including the Infobank in problem solving	1-7	2-9	5-12	H12			PS CALC		12	12
26,27	To estimate sums and differences of decimals using the front-end and rounding methods	1-17,26-27	2-24e,26-27	1-25o,26-27	H13		H208	MC NS	10	13	13
28,29	To add decimals	1-12,14-30e,AL	1-12,13-29o,AL	10-30,AL	H14	H195	H208	PS RFM	11	14	14
30,31	To subtract decimals	1-18,24-26,NS	1-17o,24-27,NS	6-14e,16-27,NS	H15	H196	H208	MC CALC	12	15	15
32,33	To use information from a double bar graph	1-6	2-8	3-12	H16			PS NS		16	16
34	Calculator: To add large numbers	34	34	34							
35	Group Project: To calculate costs and time to make a purchase	35	35	35							

36, 37	Chapter Test	39	Enrichment
38	Reteaching	40	Cumulative Review

TESTS

A. To write short word names for whole numbers and decimals expressed as standard numbers and vice versa, through 15 digits

B. To write expanded numbers for whole numbers and decimals expressed as standard numbers and vice versa, through 10 digits

C. To identify the value of a digit in whole numbers and decimals, through 13 digits

D. To compare and order whole numbers, money amounts, or decimals

E. To round whole numbers, money amounts, or decimals

F. To add and subtract whole numbers, money amounts, or decimals

G. To estimate sums and differences of whole numbers, money amounts, or decimals

H. To use information from a double-bar graph, with a broken scale, to solve problems

FAMILY INVOLVEMENT

Family Involvement for Chapter 1 encourages family members to read utility meters and develop measures to conserve the use of electricity, water, and gas or oil in the home. Readings shown on each meter at the beginning of the week are to be recorded on a chart and compared to readings shown and recorded at the end of the week. Families calculate the amount of each resource they used during a week. Then family members are to draw up a list of ideas that contribute to the conservation of each kind of utility. When the list is complete, they are to put their ideas to use. The utility meters are read at the beginning of the week and checked again in a week. Family members are to calculate the amount of each resource they have saved.

Additional activities might include encouraging family members to examine the numerical ranges of several dials or meters around the home, for example, the range, in degrees, of the kitchen oven or thermostat. Have students and their families discuss the range of figures on these dials. Have family members use subtraction to find the range between the lowest and the highest commonly used temperatures.

STUDENT RESOURCES

Bibliography

Haney, Jan P. *Calculators.* Milwaukee: Raintree Publications, Inc., 1985.

Lampert, David. *Rocks & Minerals.* New York: Franklin Watts, 1986.

Silver, Donald M. *Life on Earth.* New York: Random House, Inc., 1983.

Films

Games, Puzzles, and Logic. 13 minutes. Color. 1971. Distributed by Films Incorporated, Wilmette, Ill.

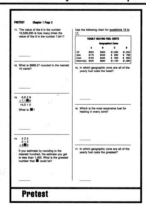

Between the summer solstice and the winter solstice, the days become progressively shorter, and the nights become progressively longer. What would you need to know to determine how much shorter your days will be in a week? in a month? Where would you find the information you need to answer the question?

1 ADDITION AND SUBTRACTION
Whole Numbers and Decimals

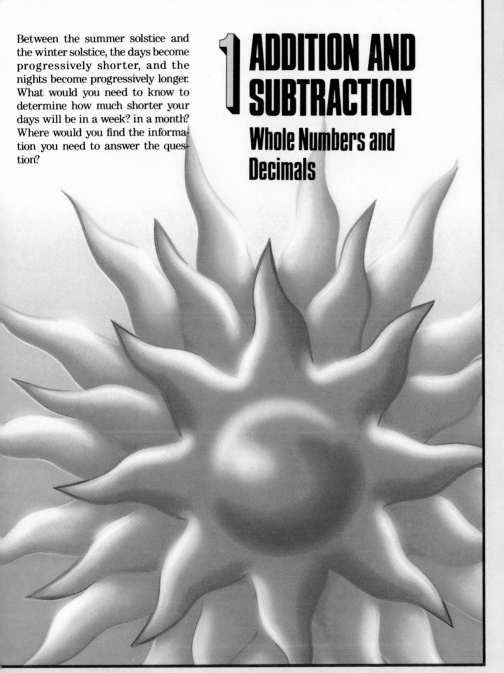

Objective: To explore problems related to length of day

Direct students to look at the picture of the sun. Talk with them about the revolution of the planets around the sun. Tell them that the average distance between Earth and the sun is about 93 million miles. Ask whether any students study astronomy as a hobby. Have them share information about their hobbies with the class.

WHOLE CLASS
Logic
Discuss with students the change in the length of day as the seasons progress. Ask them whether they know the reasons for the changes in the time the sun sets and offer suggestions about where they could find more information about this subject. (encyclopedias, science books, and so on) Discuss the physical conditions that must exist before one can pinpoint the time of the sunset. (a flat area that has an unobstructed horizon.) Ask students why it is not easy to find these conditions and what sources they could consult to find accurate information. (a newspaper or an almanac) Ask how the environment of a mountain or a valley affects the time at which the sun sets. Discuss the reasons for daylight saving time.

INDIVIDUAL
Patterns
Materials: Making Math Work page 1 per student, resource material

Have each student complete Making Math Work page 1 during a two-week period. Suggest that they read a newspaper or listen to a radio to find the necessary information. Have students compare their graphs and discuss any differences. Ask them what source they used to find the time of sunset each day.

SMALL GROUP
Statistics and Probability
Materials: Making Math Work page 2 per student, resource material

Have students work in groups to complete Making Math Work page 2. Suggest that they use almanacs to find the times the sun sets. Ask the groups to compare their graphs. All graphs should contain similar if not the same data. The shape of each graph should be the same. Tell students this graph is known as a *sine curve* and shows a cyclical change. Ask students, "Which day of the year is the longest?" (usually June 21) "Which is the shortest?" (usually December 21)

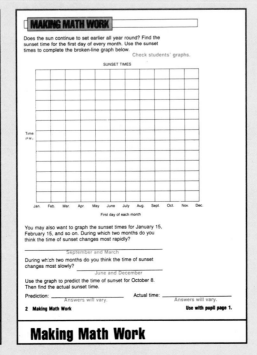

MAKING MATH WORK

In the fall, the sun sets earlier each day. How much earlier does the sun set? Do you think that the sun sets earlier by the same amount of time each day? To explore this question, find the sunset times for 14 days. How will you decide when the sun sets? Do you need to know the sunset time to the nearest minute or to the nearest second? Use your results to complete the broken-line graph below.

Check students' graphs.

SUNSET TIMES

Time (P.M.)

Days 1 2 3 4 5 6 7 8 9 10 11 12 13 14

Use with pupil page 1.   Making Math Work

Making Math Work

MAKING MATH WORK

Does the sun continue to set earlier all year round? Find the sunset time for the first day of every month. Use the sunset times to complete the broken-line graph below.

Check students' graphs.

SUNSET TIMES

Time (P.M.)

First day of each month
Jan. Feb. Mar. Apr. May June July Aug. Sept. Oct. Nov. Dec.

You may also want to graph the sunset times for January 15, February 15, and so on. During which two months do you think the time of sunset changes most rapidly?

September and March

During which two months do you think the time of sunset changes most slowly?

June and December

Use the graph to predict the time of sunset for October 8. Then find the actual sunset time.

Prediction: _____ Answers will vary.   Actual time: _____ Answers will vary.

2 Making Math Work   Use with pupil page 1.

Making Math Work

Objectives: To read and write whole numbers through the hundred trillions

Warm-Up
Dictate the following numbers and have students write them: 19,999; 40,600; 2,430; 6,008; 81,080; 8,008.

GETTING STARTED

Materials: place-value blocks

Use the place-value blocks to show that 10 ones = 1 ten and that 10 tens = 1 hundred. Make clear that each digit in our system has ten times the value of the place to the right.

Explain that the advantage of such a place-value system is that it avoids using a great variety of numbers and that it uses the same numbers many times.

TEACHING THE LESSON

A. Have students separate each of these numbers into periods and then read the number.

154867   27754390   6782345892
(154,867)(27,754,390)(6,782,345,892)

B. Write other large numbers in a place-value chart. Point to various digits, and ask students to state the value of each.

C. Point out that although 0 has a definite place value within a number, it is not necessary to include it in the expanded form.

Checkpoint
The chart lists the common errors students make in determining the place value of whole numbers.

Correct Answers: 1c, 2b

Remediation
- Distribute sets of 10 digit cards, 0 through 9. Have students lay out or "build" large numbers at their desks as you call out each place value.
  - an 8 in the thousands place
  - a 9 in the hundreds place

  Check students' work, and then have them repeat the activity as they work in small groups.

- For these errors, guide students in completing Reteach Master, p. 1.

Whole-Number Place Value

A. The distance that light travels per year is 5,878,496,538,000 miles. How do you read this number?

PERIODS	Trillions			Billions			Millions			Thousands			Ones		
	hundred trillions	ten trillions	trillions	hundred billions	ten billions	billions	hundred millions	ten millions	millions	hundred thousands	ten thousands	thousands	hundreds	tens	ones
			5	8	7	8	4	9	6	5	3	8	0	0	0

Numbers have **commas** that separate every 3 digits into **periods**.

Standard form: 5,878,496,538,000
Short word name: 5 trillion, 878 billion, 496 million, 538 thousand

B. The 6 in the number 362,841,095,002,732 is in the ten trillions place. The **value** of the 6 is $6 \times 10,000,000,000,000$; or $60,000,000,000,000$; or 60 trillion.

C. The **expanded form** of a number shows its value.
$3,060,002,560 =$
$3,000,000,000 + 60,000,000 + 2,000 + 500 + 60$

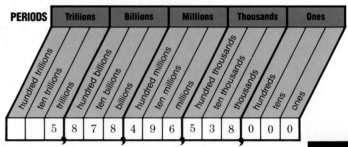

Checkpoint   Write the letter of the correct answer.

1. Find the value of the 8 in 735,680,004,132.

   a. 80 thousand
   b. 8 million
   c. 80 million ◀ (circled)
   d. 80 billion

2. Write the number in standard form for 72 trillion, 900 million, 3.

   a. 72,900,000,003
   b. 72,000,900,000,003 ◀ (circled)
   c. 72,000,000,900,003
   d. 72,000,090,000,003

2

COMMON ERRORS

Answer Choice	Type of Error
☐ 1a, 1d	Chooses incorrect period
■ 1b	Chooses incorrect place within correct period
☐ 2a	Omits billions period
■ 2c	Confuses thousands with millions
■ 2d	Writes number incorrectly within correct period

RETEACH   Whole-Number Place Value

The National Geographic Society recently estimated the population of Asia to be 2,850,567,000. Give the place value of the 8 in this number.

PERIODS	Trillions			Billions			Millions			Thousands			Ones		
PLACE VALUES	hundred trillions	ten trillions	trillions	hundred billions	ten billions	billions	hundred millions	ten millions	millions	hundred thousands	ten thousands	thousands	hundreds	tens	ones
							2	8	5	0	5	6	7	0	0	0

Remember
Commas separate groups of three digits into "periods."

The place value of 8 in 2,850,567,000 is hundred millions.

Here are the estimated populations of the other continents. Write the place value of each underlined digit.

1. Africa   531,000,000   hundred millions
2. North America   395,000,000   ten millions
3. South America   264,000,000   hundred millions
4. Europe   696,433,000   hundred thousands

Write the place value of each underlined digit.

5. 8,988,230   6. 6,696,000   7. 8,348,000
   hundreds   thousands   millions

8. 2,966,850   9. 8,203,000   10. 7,390,000
   ten thousands   millions   ten thousands

11. 7,071,039   12. 6,503,400   13. 5,421,068
    ones   thousands   hundred thousands

Use with pages 2–3.   1

Reteach Worksheet

Write in standard form.

1. 6 million, 200 thousand, 78
6,200,078

2. 300 million, 90 thousand, 800
300,090,800

3. 71 trillion, 8 billion
71,008,000,000,000

4. 245 trillion, 9 million, 106
245,000,009,000,106

5. 304 billion, 29 thousand, 5
304,000,029,005

6. 9 billion, 732 million
9,732,000,000

Write the short word name.

7. 4,360,000
4 million, 360 thousand

8. 28,000,004
28 million, 4

9. 51,000,000,070
51 billion, 70

10. 80,004,000
80 million, 4 thousand

11. 913,000,600,000
913 billion, 600 thousand

12. 7,060,000,002,000
7 trillion, 60 billion
2 thousand

Write the place and the value of the underlined digit.

13. 8,6<u>1</u>3,492
hundreds; 400

14. <u>6</u>3,184,297,351
ten billions; 60 billion

15. 72,18<u>4</u>,005
ten thousands; 80 thousand

16. 9<u>4</u>9,524,625
ten millions; 40 million

17. 6,519,7<u>9</u>3,150,603
billions; 9 billion

18. 7,237,<u>7</u>52,342
hundred thousands;
700 thousand

Write each number in standard form.

19. 80,000,000 + 7,000,000 + 6,000 + 50 + 3   87,006,053

20. 9,000,000,000 + 40,000,000 + 6,000,000 + 2,000 + 80   9,046,002,080

21. 400,000,000 + 2,000,000 + 700   402,000,700

Write each number in expanded form.

22. 50,063
50,000 + 60 + 3

23. 7,000,420
7,000,000 + 400 + 20

24. 82,005,032
80,000,000 + 2,000,000 +
5,000 + 30 + 2

25. 6,000,705,600
6,000,000,000 +
700,000 + 5,000 + 600

Solve.

26. The average rainfall in the United States is 4 trillion, 300 billion gallons per day. Write this number in standard form.   4,300,000,000,000

27. There are about 512,700,000,000 tons of iron ore mined in the world each year. Give the short word name for this number.
512 billion, 700 million

CHALLENGE   **Patterns, Relations, and Functions**

Write the letter of the correct answer.

Which figure comes next in this sequence?

a. **b.** 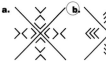 **c.**

Basic: 1–12, 13–27 o

Average: 1–25 o, 26–27, Chlg

Extended: 2–24 e, 26–27, Chlg

Resources
Practice, p. 1   Class/Home, p. H1
Reteach, p. 1   More Practice, p. H195
Enrich, p. 1

Exercise Analysis

1–6	Write standard form for short word name
7–12	Write short word name for standard form
13–18	Determine place and value of a digit
19–21	Write standard for expanded form
22–25	Write expanded for standard form
26–27	Skill applications

You may wish to allow students to use calculators for Exercises 19–21.

Challenge

This feature requires students to find a pattern in a visual sequence.

FOLLOW-UP ACTIVITIES

MANIPULATIVES
Materials: 4 coffee cans, marbles of 4 different colors

Arrange the coffee cans in a row from right to left. Assign a color to each can, as shown below. Each container can hold a maximum of 4 marbles of that color; 5 marbles of a color become 0 marbles of that color and 1 marble of the color in the container to the left.

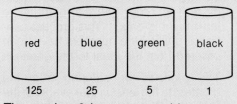

red	blue	green	black
125	25	5	1

The number 9 is represented by 1 green marble and 4 black and is written 14 base five. Similarly, the number 170 is represented by 1 red, 1 blue, and 4 green and is written 1,140 base five. Ask how the number 18 would be shown in this system. (3 green, 3 black)

COMING UP
Ordering numbers around!

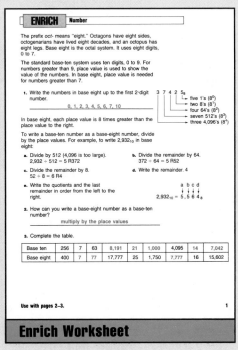

PRACTICE   Whole-Number Place Value

Write the number in standard form.

1. 964 trillion, 200 billion, 701 million, 16 thousand
964,200,701,016,000

2. 18 trillion, 322 million, 941 thousand, 1
18,000,322,941,001

3. one million, thirty thousand, six hundred seventy-eight
1,030,678

Write the short word name for each number.

4. 73,079,937   73 million, 79 thousand, 937

5. 9,251,865,804   9 billion, 251 million, 865 thousand, 804

6. 100,200,600,900,700   100 trillion, 200 billion, 600 million, 900 thousand, 700

Write the value of each underlined digit.

7. 43,5<u>0</u>6,971,384   500 million

8. 6<u>2</u>1,335,954,628,168   20 trillion

Solve.

9. Hector went to visit his sister Luisa at Yale University. He was impressed with the libraries there. Luisa told him that Yale has more than 8,391,707 books. How would Hector write this number in expanded form?
8,000,000 + 300,000 + 90,000 + 1,000 + 700 + 7

Use with pages 2–3.   1

Practice Worksheet

ENRICH   Number

The prefix oct- means "eight." Octagons have eight sides, octogenarians have lived eight decades, and an octopus has eight legs. Base eight is the octal system. It uses eight digits, 0 to 7.

The standard base-ten system uses ten digits, 0 to 9. For numbers greater than 9, place value is used to show the value of the numbers. In base eight, place value is needed for numbers greater than 7.

1. Write the numbers in base eight up to the first 2-digit number.

0, 1, 2, 3, 4, 5, 6, 7, 10

In base eight, each place value is 8 times greater than the place value to the right.

To write a base-ten number as a base-eight number, divide by the place values. For example, to write $2,932_{10}$ in base eight:

a. Divide by 512 (4,096 is too large).
2,932 ÷ 512 = 5 R372

b. Divide the remainder by 64.
372 ÷ 64 = 5 R52

c. Divide the remainder by 8.
52 ÷ 8 = 6 R4

d. Write the remainder. 4

e. Write the quotients and the last remainder in order from the left to the right.
$2,932_{10} = 5,564_8$

2. How can you write a base-eight number as a base-ten number?
multiply by the place values

3. Complete the table.

Base ten	256	7	63	8,191	21	1,000	4,095	14	7,042
Base eight	400	7	77	17,777	25	1,750	7,777	16	15,602

Use with pages 2–3.   1

Enrich Worksheet

3

numbers

Warm-Up

Read aloud groups of numbers such as those shown below. Ask students to state, without using pencil and paper, which number has the digit that has the greatest place value.

2,074; 576,250; 3,000,769; 44,070,101
(44,070,101)

GETTING STARTED

Materials: number cube, 2 sheets of blank paper per pair of students

Have students work in pairs. Tell each student to draw a place-value chart extending from ones to hundred thousands. Have students then take turns rolling the number cube. After each one rolls a digit, he or she should write it in one of the places on the chart. Each student's goal is to try to make the greatest 6-digit number possible with six rolls of the cube. Tell students that once they have chosen a place for a digit, they cannot move the digit to another place, so they should plan their strategy in advance. The student who has the greatest 6-digit number after six rolls is the winner.

TEACHING THE LESSON

A. Remind students that each symbol, < or >, should point to the lesser of the two numbers.

B. Emphasize the fact that when we order numbers from the least to the greatest, we look for the numbers with the fewest digits and order those numbers from the least to the greatest. We then examine the numbers with the next fewest digits and order them also from the least to the greatest. This process continues until all the numbers have been ordered from the least to the greatest.

The process for ordering from the greatest to the least is the reverse of the process just described. Have students order the following numbers from the least to the greatest.

64,876; 9,645; 9,487; 69,387
(9,487; 9,645; 64,876; 69,387)

Comparing and Ordering Whole Numbers

A. The Caribbean Sea covers 971,400 square miles. The Mediterranean Sea covers 969,100 square miles. Which sea is larger?

To compare two numbers, begin by lining up the digits. Then compare digits, beginning at the left.

971,400   9 hundred = 9 hundred
            thousand   thousand
969,100   7 ten thousand > 6 ten thousand

So, 971,400 > 969,100; or 969,100 < 971,400.

> means "is greater than."
< means "is less than."

The Caribbean Sea is larger than the Mediterranean Sea.

B. Order 6,129; 21,434; 20,989; and 21,344 from the least to the greatest.

Compare to find the least.	Compare to find the next greatest.	Compare to find the greatest.
6,129 — 6,129 has no ten thousands.	20,989 < 21,434	21,434 > 21,344
21,434	20,989 < 21,344	
20,989		
21,344		
6,129 is the least.	20,989 is the next greatest.	21,434 is the greatest.

The order from the least to the greatest is 6,129; 20,989; 21,344; 21,434.

Numbers can also be ordered from the greatest to the least. Order 74,349; 72,989; 7,861; and 74,536 from the greatest to the least.

Compare to find the greatest.	Compare to find the next greatest.	Compare to find the least.
74,536 > 74,349	74,349 > 72,989	72,989 > 7,861

The order from the greatest to the least is 74,536; 74,349; 72,989; 7,861.

4

COMMON ERRORS

Some students will think that 169,999 is greater than 175,000 because several digits are greater than those in 175,000.

Remediation

Have students use place-value blocks to compare numbers such as 26 and 8, or 82 and 154. Continue with examples in which both numbers have the same number of digits: 52 and 63, 269 and 280.

Assign Reteach Master, p. 2.

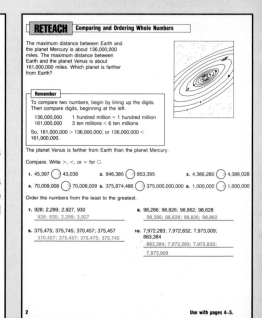

RETEACH Comparing and Ordering Whole Numbers

The maximum distance between Earth and the planet Mercury is about 136,000,000 miles. The maximum distance between Earth and the planet Venus is about 161,000,000 miles. Which planet is farther from Earth?

Remember

To compare two numbers, begin by lining up the digits. Then compare digits, beginning at the left.

136,000,000   1 hundred million = 1 hundred million
161,000,000   3 ten millions < 6 ten millions

So, 161,000,000 > 136,000,000; or 136,000,000 < 161,000,000.

The planet Venus is farther from Earth than the planet Mercury.

Compare. Write >, <, or = for ○.

1. 45,397 ○ 43,038   2. 846,386 ○ 853,395   3. 4,386,280 ○ 4,386,028
4. 70,009,008 ○ 70,008,009   5. 375,874,486 ○ 375,000,000,000   6. 1,000,000 ○ 1,000,000

Order the numbers from the least to the greatest.

7. 928; 2,299; 2,927; 930   8. 98,286; 98,826; 98,862; 98,628
   928; 930; 2,299; 2,927   98,286; 98,628; 98,826; 98,862

9. 375,475; 375,745; 370,457; 375,457   10. 7,972,283; 7,972,832; 7,973,009; 883,384
   370,457; 375,457; 375,475; 375,745   883,384; 7,972,283; 7,972,832; 7,973,009

2   Use with pages 4–5.

Reteach Worksheet

Compare. Write $>$, $<$, or $=$ for ●.

1. 65,286 ● 67,286 $<$
2. 131,842 ● 113,842 $>$
3. 8,505,403 ● 8,505,304 $>$
4. 50,456,100 ● 50,465,100 $<$
5. 684 million ● 684,000,000 $=$
6. 27,684 ● 26,784 $>$
7. 312,666 ● 322,666 $<$
8. 46,012 ● 46,102 $<$
9. 22 million ● 220,000,000 $<$
10. 76,433,334 ● 76,343,334 $>$

Order the numbers from the least to the greatest.

11. 854; 8,540; 850; 8,545
    850; 854; 8,540; 8,545
12. 43,196; 43,169; 43,691; 43,619
    43,169; 43,196; 43,619; 43,691
13. 5,781; 5,871; 5,718; 5,817
    5,718; 5,781; 5,817; 5,871
14. 221,894; 212,894; 212,948; 212,849
    212,849; 212,894; 212,948; 221,894
15. 332; 322; 3,323; 3,233
    322; 332; 3,233; 3,323
16. 76,676; 76,766; 77,677; 76,677
    76,676; 76,677; 76,766; 77,677

Order the numbers from the greatest to the least.

17. 1,623; 163; 1,263; 1,632
    1,632; 1,623; 1,263; 163
18. 934; 9,343; 9,433; 943
    9,433; 9,343; 943; 934
19. 6,892; 6,982; 69,829; 698
    69,829; 6,982; 6,892; 698
20. 823,324; 822,334; 84,264; 832,322
    832,322; 823,324; 822,334; 84,264
21. 465; 4,656; 456; 6,545
    6,545; 4,656; 465; 456
22. 1,423; 1,344; 1,432; 14,243
    14,243; 1,432; 1,423; 1,344

Solve. For Problem 24, use the Infobank.

23. The diameter of Earth at the equator is 7,926 mi. The diameter from pole to pole is 7,899 mi. Which diameter is larger? The diameter at the equator is larger.

24. Use the information on page 473 to solve. List the world's five longest rivers and their lengths, in miles, in order from the longest to the shortest. Nile, 4,180 mi; Amazon, 3,912 mi; Mississippi/Missouri, 3,880 mi; Yangtze, 3,602 mi; Niger, 2,600 mi

FOCUS: REASONING

What is the place-value name of the 6 in the number?

236,452,198,000,000,000,000,000

sextillions quintillions quadrillions trillions

The value of the 6 is 6 *sextillion.*

Give the place-value name of the underlined digit.

1. 32,760,466,378,452,906
    2 quadrillion

2. 746,921,000,000,000,000,000
    700 quintillion

Classwork/Homework, page H2   More Practice, page H195   **5**

ASSIGNMENT GUIDE

Basic: 1–21 o, 23–24, F

Average: 1–21 o, 23–24, F

Extended: 2–22 e, 23–24, F

Resources
Practice, p. 2   Class/Home, p. H2
Reteach, p. 2   More Practice, p. H195
Enrich, p. 2

Exercise Analysis

1–10	Compare using $>$, $<$, and $=$
11–16	Order from the least to the greatest
17–22	Order from the greatest to the least
23	Skill application
24	Data collection and computation

Focus: Reasoning
This feature allows students to apply place-value skills to greater numbers.

FOLLOW-UP ACTIVITIES

PROBLEM SOLVING
The table shows three scores in the same computer game.

Larry	31,276
Matthew	23,480
Marianne	21,925

Who scored the least number of points? (Marianne) Who scored the greatest number of points? (Larry) Have students create and answer similar questions.

COMPUTER
Have each student write a computer program for a guessing game. The computer should pick at random a whole number between 1 and 100.

A possible program:

```
10 RANDOMIZE
20 LET C = INT (RND (0) * 100) + 1
30 PRINT "MAKE A GUESS"
40 INPUT G
50 IF G = C THEN 90
60 IF G < C THEN PRINT "TOO SMALL"
70 IF G > C THEN PRINT "TOO GREAT"
80 GO TO 30
90 PRINT "GOOD WORK"
100 END
```

COMING UP
For rent: Property Studies!

Objectives: To identify and use the properties of addition and subtraction

Warm-Up
Have students find the sums.

$6 + 3 + 4 + 8$ (21) $7 + 3 + 9 + 1$ (20)
$8 + 3 + 0 + 3$ (14) $2 + 5 + 9 + 8$ (24)

GETTING STARTED

Explain to students that letters are often used to stand for numbers. Sometimes, for an equation to be true, a letter can stand for only one number. For example, only if x is 7 will the equation $x = 7$ be true. Sometimes the letter can stand for many numbers, as in $a > 3$. Finally, there are times when the letter can stand for every number, as in the equation $y = y$.

Use the equations below to discuss how many numbers each letter could stand for, while still making the equation true.

$g = g$ $g = 7$ $g > 5$ $g = g + 3$
(all   (one)   (many   (none)
numbers)   but not all)

TEACHING THE LESSON

A. Write the following addition sentence to show a more sophisticated application of the Commutative Property.

$13 + (14 + 16) = (14 + 16) + 13$

B. Point out that the presence of parentheses does not necessarily indicate the Associative Property. In the example above, the position of an entire expression within parentheses has changed.

C. Point out that the Commutative Property does not hold true for subtraction. Demonstrate that $0 - a \neq a - 0$.

D. Emphasize that while $0 - a = a$ is true only if $a = 0$, $a - a = 0$ is true for all numbers.

E. Have students solve for a in such examples as

$12 + 11 - a = 13$ $(a = 10)$
$17 + 9 - a = 26$ $(a = 0)$

Addition and Subtraction

A. Addition is **commutative.** In addition, the *order* of the addends does not change the sum.

$42 + 830 = 830 + 42$

For any numbers a and b,
$a + b = b + a$.

Subtraction is **not commutative.** In subtraction, the order of the numbers may change the difference.

$$13 - 6 \overset{?}{=} 6 - 13$$
$$\downarrow$$
$$7 \quad \neq 6 - 13$$

$\neq$ means "is not equal to."

B. Addition is **associative.** In addition, the *grouping* of the addends does not change the sum.

$94 + (17 + 42) = (94 + 17) + 42$

For any numbers a, b, and c,
$a + (b + c) = (a + b) + c$.

Subtraction is **not associative.** In subtraction, the grouping of the numbers may change the difference.

$$29 - (14 - 7) \overset{?}{=} (29 - 14) - 7$$
$$\downarrow \qquad\qquad \downarrow$$
$$29 - 7 \quad \overset{?}{=} \quad 15 - 7$$
$$22 \neq 8$$

C. Zero is the **identity element** for addition. The sum of a number and zero is the number.

$7 + 0 = 7 \qquad 0 + 16 = 16$

For any number a,
$a + 0 = a \qquad 0 + a = a$.

The difference when zero is subtracted from a number is the number.

$67 - 0 = 67$

For any number a, $a - 0 = a$.

D. When a number is subtracted from itself, the difference is zero.

$89 - 89 = 0$

For any number a, $a - a = 0$.

E. Addition and subtraction are **inverse operations.** They undo each other.

$37 - 12 = 25 \longleftrightarrow 25 + 12 = 37$

For any numbers a, b, and c,

if $c - b = a$, then $a + b = c$.

Math Reasoning, page H207

COMMON ERRORS

Often, students cannot solve for variables in an equation because students do not clearly understand the principle of inverse operations.

Remediation
Students should use inverse operations to rewrite each of the following equations before solving them.

$x + 23 = 40$ $(x = 40 - 23; x = 17)$
$18 + y = 21$ $(y = 21 - 18; y = 3)$

Assign Reteach Master, p. 3.

RETEACH | **Properties of Addition and Subtraction**

The student council operates a supply store at the school. When it opened, the store had 187 pencils in stock. On Monday, 58 pencils were sold; on Tuesday, 19 pencils were sold. Write and solve an expression to show the number of pencils in stock.

Remember
In subtraction, the order of the numbers may change the difference.

The expression that shows the number of pencils in stock is $(187 - 58) - 19 = 110$.

Write and solve an expression to show the number of items remaining in stock.

Item	Opening stock	Monday sales	Tuesday sales	Remaining stock
1. Paper	22	5	7	$(22 - 5) - 7 = 10$
2. Markers	126	26	25	$(126 - 26) - 25 = 75$
3. Pens	204	44	23	$(204 - 44) - 23 = 137$
4. Erasers	62	12	14	$(62 - 12) - 14 = 36$
5. Rulers	81	17	12	$(81 - 17) - 12 = 52$

A florist bought fresh flowers at dawn. Some were sold that morning. Some were sold that afternoon. Write and solve an expression to show the flowers remaining in stock.

Flowers	Bought	Morning sales	Afternoon sales	Remaining stock
6. Carnations	262	95	82	$(262 - 95) - 82 = 85$
7. Roses	206	86	90	$(206 - 86) - 90 = 30$
8. Tulips	172	45	61	$(172 - 45) - 61 = 66$
9. Daffodils	95	22	17	$(95 - 22) - 17 = 56$
10. Lilies	225	46	62	$(225 - 46) - 62 = 117$

Use with pages 6–7.   3

Reteach Worksheet

Complete.

1. $135 + 26 = 26 + \blacksquare$ 135
2. $4,531 - 4,531 = \blacksquare$ 0
3. $(8 + 13) + 62 = 8 + (\blacksquare + 62)$ 13
4. $0 + 92 = \blacksquare$ 92
5. $531 - 0 = \blacksquare$ 531
6. $17 - 9 = 9 - \blacksquare$ 1
7. $3,723 + 1,405 = \blacksquare + 3,723$ 1,405
8. $(9 - 2) - 3 = 9 - (\blacksquare - 3)$ 8
9. $8,732 + (18 + 1) = (\blacksquare + 18) + 1$ 8,732
10. $\blacksquare - 50 = 50 - 35$ 65
11. $7,651 - \blacksquare = 0$ 7,651
12. $(10 - 9) - 1 = \blacksquare - (9 - 1)$ 8
13. $117 + \blacksquare = 117$ 0
14. $65 - \blacksquare = 65$ 0
15. $124 + 282 - \blacksquare = 282$ 124
16. $14 + 31 - 14 = \blacksquare$ 31
17. $78 - 35 = 43$
    $43 + \blacksquare = 78$ 35
18. $199 + 26 = 225$
    $225 - 199 = \blacksquare$ 26
19. $\blacksquare - 0 = a$ a
20. $b + a = a + \blacksquare$ b
21. $c - \blacksquare = 0$ c
22. $a + (b + c) = (a + \blacksquare) + c$ b
23. $a + b - a = \blacksquare$ b
24. $x + 0 = \blacksquare$ x

CHALLENGE

In one large office, 9 editors are arranged as shown. Copy the figure and draw only 2 more squares to give each editor a separate office.

Classwork/Homework, page H3

7

ASSIGNMENT GUIDE

Basic: 1–18

Average: 1–17, o, 19–24, Chlg

Extended: 8–18 e, 19–24, Chlg

Resources
Practice, p. 3   Class/Home, p. H3
Reteach, p. 3   Reasoning, p. H207
Enrich, p. 3

Exercise Analysis
1–18   Apply the properties of addition and subtraction to equations with whole numbers
19–24   Apply the properties of addition and subtraction to equations with variables

Challenge
This nonroutine problem requires students to use their visual-perception skills.

FOLLOW-UP ACTIVITIES

NUMBER SENSE (Mental Math)
Have students use the properties of addition and subtraction to group the terms so that the operations can be performed mentally.

$125 + 379 + 75 = (579)$
$242 + 145 - 100 - 142 = (145)$
$1,027 - 44 + 844 = (1,827)$

MANIPULATIVES
Materials: index cards

Form the class into small groups, and distribute several index cards to each student. Have each student write the name of a property on each card and on the reverse side write an equation that illustrates the property. Have students take turns showing the equations to the others in the group, who are to name and verify the property.

Extend the activity by challenging students to write equations showing two properties.

COMING UP
How to make a whole round!

PRACTICE Addition and Subtraction

Write the missing number.

1. $757 + 468 = 468 + \underline{\ 757\ }$
2. $9,003 - 0 = \underline{\ 9,003\ }$
3. $759 + 0 = \underline{\ 759\ }$
4. $(15 + 47) + 26 = 15 + (\underline{\ 47\ } + 26)$
5. $287 - 287 = \underline{\ 0\ }$
6. $217 + 308 = \underline{\ 308\ } + 217$
7. $94 + (62 + 22) = (94 + 62) + \underline{\ 22\ }$
8. $6,280 + 0 = \underline{\ 6,280\ }$
9. $104 - 0 = \underline{\ 104\ }$
10. $5,091 - 5,091 = \underline{\ 0\ }$
11. $7,462 + 6,186 = \underline{\ 6,186\ } + 7,462$
12. $80 + 246 = 246 + \underline{\ 80\ }$
13. $41,001 + 0 = \underline{\ 41,001\ }$
14. $175 - 0 = \underline{\ 175\ }$
15. $(31 + 91) + 58 = 31 + (\underline{\ 91\ } + 58)$
16. $9 + 0 = \underline{\ 9\ }$
17. $19,539 - 19,539 = \underline{\ 0\ }$
18. $1,763 - 1,763 = \underline{\ 0\ }$
19. $4,891 + 9,746 = 9,746 + \underline{\ 4,891\ }$
20. $39 + (25 + 10) = (39 + 25) + \underline{\ 10\ }$
21. $615 - 0 = \underline{\ 615\ }$
22. $47 + 86 = \underline{\ 86\ } + 47$
23. $16 + (37 + 91) = (16 + 37) + \underline{\ 91\ }$
24. $503 - 0 = \underline{\ 503\ }$
25. $601 - 601 = \underline{\ 0\ }$
26. $999 + 0 = \underline{\ 999\ }$
27. $275 + 353 = \underline{\ 353\ } + 275$
28. $(41 + 19) + 15 = \underline{\ 41\ } + (19 + 15)$
29. $61,580 - 0 = \underline{\ 61,580\ }$
30. $697 - 697 = \underline{\ 0\ }$
31. $(15 + 50) + 54 = 15 + (\underline{\ 50\ } + 54)$
32. $45 - 0 = \underline{\ 45\ }$
33. $6,743 + 0 = \underline{\ 6,743\ }$
34. $27 + (18 + 98) = 27 + (\underline{\ 18\ } + 98)$
35. $9,132 - 9,132 = \underline{\ 0\ }$
36. $413 + 62 = 62 + \underline{\ 413\ }$
37. $397 - 0 = \underline{\ 397\ }$
38. $9,007 + 0 = \underline{\ 9,007\ }$
39. $452 + 810 = 810 + \underline{\ 452\ }$
40. $550 - 550 = \underline{\ 0\ }$

Use with pages 6–7.   3

Practice Worksheet

ENRICH   Number

A **matrix** is a group of numbers organized in rows and columns. The **dimensions** of a matrix are given by the number of rows, by the number of columns, in that order. The dimensions of matrix A are 3 × 2. It is interesting that a matrix can be used in much the same way as individual numbers.

$\begin{bmatrix} 7 & 4 \\ 4 & 1 \\ 5 & 1 \end{bmatrix}$
Matrix A

Matrices (plural of matrix) can be added only when their dimensions are the same. Add each number in one matrix to the numbers in the same position in the other matrices. Each sum is then placed in a new matrix in the same position.

$\begin{bmatrix} 3 & 0 \\ 2 & 4 \end{bmatrix} + \begin{bmatrix} 6 & 2 \\ 5 & 7 \end{bmatrix} = \begin{bmatrix} (3+6) & (0+2) \\ (2+5) & (4+7) \end{bmatrix} = \begin{bmatrix} 9 & 2 \\ 7 & 11 \end{bmatrix}$

Add the following matrices, if possible.

1. $\begin{bmatrix} 11 & 3 \\ 9 & 0 \end{bmatrix} + \begin{bmatrix} 4 & 2 \\ 3 & 8 \end{bmatrix} = \begin{bmatrix} 15 & 5 \\ 12 & 8 \end{bmatrix}$
2. $\begin{bmatrix} ^-2 & 0 \\ 4 & 9 \end{bmatrix} + \begin{bmatrix} ^-3 & 4 \\ 0 & ^-6 \end{bmatrix} = \begin{bmatrix} ^-5 & 4 \\ 4 & 3 \end{bmatrix}$
3. $\begin{bmatrix} 1 \\ 8 \\ 7 \end{bmatrix} + [4 \ 2 \ 3] = $ impossible
4. $\begin{bmatrix} 2 \\ 11 \\ ^-9 \end{bmatrix} + \begin{bmatrix} ^-7 \\ 4 \\ 6 \end{bmatrix} = \begin{bmatrix} ^-5 \\ 15 \\ ^-3 \end{bmatrix}$
5. $\begin{bmatrix} 5 & 16 & 0 \\ ^-10 & 2 & ^-1 \end{bmatrix} + \begin{bmatrix} 4 & 8 & ^-3 \\ 5 & ^-2 & ^-6 \end{bmatrix} + \begin{bmatrix} 0 & ^-4 & ^-6 \\ 1 & 0 & 9 \end{bmatrix} = \begin{bmatrix} 9 & 20 & ^-9 \\ ^-4 & 0 & 2 \end{bmatrix}$
6. Write the value of each letter.
$\begin{bmatrix} 2 & 4 \\ 0 & 9 \end{bmatrix} + \begin{bmatrix} m & n \\ p & q \end{bmatrix} = \begin{bmatrix} ^-1 & 7 \\ 8 & 3 \end{bmatrix}$
$m = ^-3; \ n = 3; \ p = 8; \ q = ^-6$
7. Are the Commutative and Associative Properties of Addition true for matrix addition?   yes
8. Find the missing letter. You will need to use your knowledge of addition and your logic.
$\begin{bmatrix} s & r \\ c & v \end{bmatrix} + \begin{bmatrix} v & w \\ c & r \end{bmatrix} = \begin{bmatrix} c & s \\ c & ^-w \end{bmatrix}$

Use with pages 6–7.   3

Enrich Worksheet

Warm-Up

Have students use < or > to complete.
1. 342 ● 350 (<)
2. 1,020 ● 1,100 (<)
3. 2,484 ● 2,399 (>)
4. 22,548 ● 25,201 (<)

GETTING STARTED

Construct a number line on the chalkboard in increments from 0 to 500.

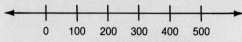

Ask a volunteer to come up and place number 225 on this number line. Have the class discuss the accuracy of the estimate.

Emphasize that 250 is halfway between 200 and 300, and 225 is halfway between 200 and 250. Therefore, a good estimate would be about one-fourth of the distance between 200 and 300.

Have other students model 90, 301, and 450.

TEACHING THE LESSON

A. Point out that if 10,882 were to be rounded to the nearest hundred, a number line could also be used, but the increments would be different.

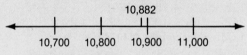

So, 10,882 rounds to 10,900.

B. Test the class to be sure that they know all of the place values. Review, if necessary.

Have students round the following numbers to the place value indicated: 55,993 to the nearest ten thousand (60,000) and 2,064,565 to the nearest hundred thousand. (2,100,000)

Rounding Whole Numbers

A. The greatest ocean depths are found in long, narrow crevices called *trenches*. The Tonga Trench in the Pacific Ocean reaches a depth of 10,882 meters. Round this number to the nearest thousand meters.

10,882 is between 10,000 and 11,000.
10,882 is closer to 11,000.
So, 10,882 rounds to 11,000.

The Tonga Trench is about 11,000 meters in depth.

B. You can also round by using the digit to the right of the place to which you are rounding.

Round 365,747; 641,057; and 56,481 to the nearest hundred thousand.

365,747	641,057	56,481
6 > 5 So, round up.	4 < 5 Round down.	5 = 5 Round up.
365,747 ⟶ 400,000	641,057 ⟶ 600,000	56,481 ⟶ 100,000

Round to the nearest ten thousand.

1. 12,482 10,000
2. 85,555 90,000
3. 310,942 310,000
4. 7,037 10,000
5. 16,051 20,000
6. 279,679 280,000
7. 41,589 40,000
8. 99,843 100,000

Round to the nearest hundred thousand.

9. 327,438 300,000
10. 5,482,525 5,500,000
11. 86,397 100,000
12. 807,831 800,000
13. 987,123 1,000,000
14. 196,001 200,000
15. 7,211,999 7,200,000
★16. 12,889 0

Round to the nearest million.

17. 6,181,313 6 million
18. 18,901,010 19 million
19. 327,039,999 327 million
20. 780,410 1 million
21. 3,822,321 4 million
★22. 97,814 0

8   Math Reasoning, page H207

COMMON ERRORS

Students often round incorrectly by looking at the largest number in a problem instead of paying attention to the place value indicated.

Remediation

Have students circle the place value they are rounding to and then draw a line under the digit next to it. By ignoring the remaining digits and applying the rule of 5, they should learn to round more accurately; for example:

2 ⑦ 5, 6 0 2

to the nearest ten thousand becomes 280,000.

| QUESTIONS | TOOLS | SOLUTIONS | CHECKS |

PROBLEM SOLVING
Estimation

Sometimes you have to estimate to solve a problem.

Zach and Byron are planning a camping trip. They want to spend 2 nights and 2 days camping. They will decide which park they will go to after they decide how much money they can afford to spend on bus fare. They must make campsite reservations 2 weeks in advance. Here is some information:

- To rent a tent costs from $10 to $15 per night.
- Food will cost from $3 to $5 per day for each.
- By the day the trip begins, Zach will have earned $30 to $40 doing yard work.
- By the day the trip begins, Byron will have earned $25 to $45 from baby-sitting.
- Zach has already saved $5, and Byron has $8.

BUS FARES	
(round trip, per person)	
Grey Forest Park	$8.40
Sumac Point	$9.10
Eagle's Neck Park	$15.55
Ropa Canyon	$23.25

Answer each question to help Zach and Byron make their plans. You may have to go back to the plan and revise the numbers as you work.

1. How much money will Zach and Byron have by the time the trip begins? $68 – $98

2. About how much should they plan to spend to rent a tent? $20–$30

3. How much should they plan to spend for food? $12–$20

4. How much money will they have for bus fare? $18 – $66

5. At which park do you think Zach and Byron should make reservations? Explain. Grey Forest; that may be all they can afford.

Classwork/Homework, page H4

ASSIGNMENT GUIDE

Basic: p. 8 1–19 o, p. 9 1–4

Average: p. 8 1–21 o, p. 9 2–5

Extended: p. 8 2–22 e, p. 9 2–5

Resources
Practice, p. 4 Class/Home, p. H4
Enrich, p. 4

GETTING STARTED

Have students discuss trips they have taken with their families. Ask how their families would estimate the amount of spending money they should bring on a trip. Help students conclude that in order to make sure they bring enough money on a trip, they should *overestimate* or round up. Point out that sometimes it is useful to *underestimate* for certain items such as time: for example, if a hotel does not allow guests to check-in before 1:00 P.M., travelers might want to underestimate travel time to make sure they arrive at the hotel after 1:00 P.M.

TEACHING THE LESSON

Before any computation skills are taught, estimation can be introduced as an aid in judging the reasonableness of an answer. Point out that estimation can also be used to find an adequate answer when an exact answer is not necessary or is impossible to obtain. When students read a problem, they must decide

- whether an estimate is sufficient or a precise answer is needed.
- whether to overestimate.
- whether to underestimate.

Questions: In the lesson problem, the range rather than the exact cost of tent rental is given. This information should tell students immediately that an estimate is required. Questions that ask "About how much?" are also answered by estimates.

Tools: In this lesson, estimation involves no rounding, but rather it involves finding the limits of price ranges by overestimating or underestimating. Students must decide whether to use the lower or the higher limit as the best estimate.

Solutions: If students have difficulty with the addition, it may be helpful to work the problem on the board.

Checks: Estimation can be used as a precheck for addition. An estimate should not be checked by finding the exact answer.

COMING UP
"Sum" estimating is a plus!

Objectives: To estimate sums of whole numbers by using the front-end and rounding methods

Warm-Up
Have students add the following numbers mentally.

32 + 55 (87)   21 + 49 (70)
110 + 31 (141)   99 + 84 (183)
17 + 23 + 40 + 60 (140)

GETTING STARTED

Lead the class in a discussion about estimation. Ask the class to define *estimation*. Ask for situations in which students have had to estimate a number. If it is not mentioned, mention the use of estimation when shopping when you want to know the total cost of several items.

Emphasize that estimation is a mental-math technique that is used to achieve an approximation when an exact answer is not needed or when it would be inconvenient to find one.

TEACHING THE LESSON

A. Point out that front-end estimation is a two-step process. The lead digits (the digits *in front*) are added first. That sum is then adjusted by approximating the sum of the remaining digits and adding this second sum to the first sum.

Remind students that to find an estimate they should round the original numbers to numbers that can be added easily mentally.

B. Point out the method used to adjust the estimate. The cents are combined into three groups of approximately $1.00 each. Have students use this method to solve this problem: $4.18 + $3.58 + $7.85 + $5.39. Ask: How did you group the cents? (0.18 + 0.85 ≈ 1.00; 0.58 + 0.39 ≈ 1.00)

Ask: To what place value are the figures in the second column rounded? (dollars)

Estimating Sums of Whole Numbers

A. Astronomers estimate that 12,242 meteorites fall into the oceans annually. Another 448 meteorites fall on the United States, and 6,300 fall over the landmass of the rest of Earth. About how many meteorites hit Earth annually?

Since the data are not exact, an exact answer is not necessary. Find the sum by using front-end estimation or by rounding.

Using front-end estimation

$$\left.\begin{array}{r} 12,242 \\ 448 \\ 6,300 \end{array}\right\} \text{about 1,000}$$

Add the lead digits.
12 + 6 = 18. Use 18,000.

Adjust the sum.
18,000 + 1,000 = 19,000

Estimate: 19,000

Rounding to the nearest thousand

This number is insignificant.

12,242 → 12,000
448 → 0
6,300 → 6,000

Add the rounded numbers.
12,000 + 0 + 6,000 = 18,000

Estimate: 18,000

Both 18,000 and 19,000 are good estimates of the number of meteorites that hit Earth annually.

B. You can also estimate sums of money. Estimate the total cost of the items on the sales receipt.

	Front end	Rounding
$8.98	$8.98 → about $1	$8.98 → $9
4.89	4.89 ⎫ about $1	4.89 → 5
0.15	0.15 ⎭	0.15 → 0
9.49	9.49 ⎫ about $1	9.49 → 9
6.44	6.44 ⎭	6.44 → 6
0.07	0.07	0.07 → 0

Add the lead digits: $27   Add: $29
Adjust: $27 + $3   Estimate: $29.00
Estimate: $30

Both $29 and $30 are reasonable estimates.

10

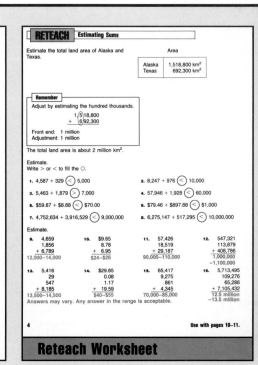

COMMON ERRORS

When addition problems are written horizontally, some students will mistake each number's first digit for a leading digit, without regard for the number's place value.

Remediation
To correct this error, have students rewrite addition problems vertically, aligning the place-value positions correctly. This will help students determine which digits are leading.

Assign Reteach Master, p. 4.

RETEACH Estimating Sums

Estimate the total land area of Alaska and Texas.

Area	
Alaska	1,518,800 km²
Texas	692,300 km²

Remember
Adjust by estimating the hundred thousands.

1,⑤18,800
+ ⑥92,300

Front end: 1 million
Adjustment: 1 million

The total land area is about 2 million km².

Estimate.
Write > or < to fill the ○.

1. 4,587 + 329 ⊘ 5,000   2. 8,247 + 976 ⊘ 10,000
3. 5,463 + 1,879 ⊘ 7,000   4. 57,946 + 1,928 ⊘ 60,000
5. $59.87 + $8.88 ⊘ $70.00   6. $79.46 + $897.88 ⊘ $1,000
7. 4,752,634 + 3,916,529 ⊘ 9,000,000   8. 6,275,147 + 517,295 ⊘ 10,000,000

Estimate.

9.	4,659	10.	$9.65	11.	57,426	12.	547,321
	1,856		8.78		18,519		113,879
	+ 6,789		+ 6.95		+ 29,187		+ 408,786
	12,000–14,000		$24–$26		90,000–110,000		1,000,000
							–1,100,000

13.	5,416	14.	$29.65	15.	65,417	16.	5,713,495
	29		0.08		9,275		109,276
	547		1.17		861		65,286
	+ 8,185		+ 19.59		+ 4,345		+ 7,105,432
	13,500–14,500		$40–$55		70,000–85,000		12.5 million
							–13.5 million

Answers may vary. Any answer in the range is acceptable.

4   Use with pages 10–11.

Reteach Worksheet

Estimate the sum.   Answers may vary. Accept any reasonable estimate.

1.	4,325	2.	50,476	3.	$92.16	4.	682,345
	9,683		47,295		45.27		950,265
	5,085		77,850		1.59		642,817
	+ 3,897		+ 14,948		+ 78.62		+ 17,294

22,000–23,000   180,000–200,000 $200–$220   2,200,000–2,300,000

5. $179.85 + $49.65 + $87.93
$300–$320

6. 72,895 + 57,623 + 136 + 2,571
130,000–140,000

7. $4.36 + $5.98 + $6.65 + $0.89 + $0.32 + $7.56
$25–$26

Estimate. Write > or < for ●.

8. 4,536 + 6,274 + 5,327 ● 15,000   >

9. 6,275 + 2,895 + 9,879 ● 20,000   <

10. 8,886 + 3,127 + 8,527 ● 19,000   >

11. 5,187 + 278 + 5,246 ● 10,000   >

12. 45,265 + 87,867 + 96,845 ● 250,000   <

13. 89,247 + 7,534 + 71,650 ● 160,000   >

14. 562,754 + 695,375 + 87,295 + 43,876 ● 1,500,000   <

15. 4,417,569 + 9,743,417 + 7,195,265 + 3,499,999 ● 21,400,000   >

16. 1,123,754 + 4,256,295 + 172,546 + 1,075,286 ● 7,000,000   <

Choose the letter of the best estimate for the sum.

17. 361,287 + 4,635 + 136,830 + 99,375   c

18. 173,285 + 126,501 + 194,126 + 11,950   b

19. 370,920 + 7,875 + 341,623 + 9,221   d

20. 92,250 + 121,476 + 192,565   a

21. 121,292 + 326,275 + 317,754 + 43,329   e

a. 400,000
b. 500,000
c. 600,000
d. 700,000
e. 800,000

Solve.

22. The diameter of planet Saturn is approximately equal to those of Earth, Mars, Uranus, and Neptune combined. Use the data in the table to estimate the diameter of Saturn.   120,000–122,000 km

23. Use the data in the table at the right to write and solve a word problem.   Check students' problems.

Planet	Average Diameter (km)
Mercury	4,880
Venus	12,100
Earth	12,756
Mars	6,785
Jupiter	142,800
Saturn	
Uranus	51,800
Neptune	49,500
Pluto	3,000 ?

Classwork/Homework, page H5

11

ASSIGNMENT GUIDE

Basic: 2–22 e

Average: 1–17 o, 18–23

Extended: 1–17 o, 18–23

Resources
Practice, p. 5   Class/Home, p. H5
Reteach, p. 4
Enrich, p. 5

Exercise Analysis
1–7   Estimate the sum
8–16   Use < or > to compare estimates
17–21 Match a sum with a reasonable estimate
22   Skill application
23   Problem formulation

FOLLOW-UP ACTIVITIES

REINFORCEMENT
Have students estimate the following sums.
1. 14,233 + 26,708 + 4,835 (46,000)
2. 462,378 + 981,227 + 2,423,811 (3,900,000 or 4,000,000)
3. 666,666 + 3,012 + 288,211 (950,000–1,000,000)
4. 5,388 + 4,001 + 9,777 + 8,418 (27,000–28,000)
5. 74,500 + 98,244 + 81,502 (250,000–300,000)

MATH CONNECTION (Consumer)
When Sam went shopping, he was never sure he had enough money. Have students estimate to determine the approximate cost of each purchase.

Trip 1: $5.22 + $0.49 + $4.79 + $6.50 ($17)

Trip 2: $12.13 + $6.89 + $20.11 + $1.97 ($41)

Trip 3: $2.49 + $3.25 + $1.79 + $5.49 ($12–$13)

Tell students that to avoid embarrassment, Sam wanted to be sure he had enough money. How could he modify his estimation technique to be certain that he didn't underestimate? What would these careful estimates be? (To be sure of having enough, Sam can round each price up to the next highest dollar. The estimates then become $19, $43, and $15.)

COMING UP
What's next? What's the difference?

11

Objectives: To estimate the differences between whole numbers by using the front-end and rounding methods

Warm-Up

Have students estimate the following sums by using the front-end and rounding methods.

			225
		6,281	14,095
	25,446	132	3,460
	+ 8,432	+ 11,920	+ 16,312
(F.E.)	(34,000)	(18,000)	(34,000)
(R.)	(33,000)	(18,000)	(33,000)

GETTING STARTED

Review the first step of the front-end and rounding methods used in the examples above.

Front-end	*Rounding*
25,446	25,000
+ 8,432	+ 8,000
33,000⁺	33,000

Now switch the operation in the above example to subtraction.

$$
\begin{array}{r}
25{,}446 \\
- \ \ 8{,}432 \\
\end{array}
$$

Ask students: Could the same methods used to estimate sums apply to estimation of differences? Draw the following comparison for students.

25,446	25
− 8,432	− 8
17,000	17

With students, move on to the lesson to explore the method for estimating differences more fully.

TEACHING THE LESSON

Extend the lesson by having students use all three methods taught in the skill lesson to estimate these differences.

	49,684	343,481
	− 32,028	− 93,312
(Front-end)	(17,000)	(250,000)
(Rounding, largest place)	(20,000)	(200,000)
(Rounding, second place)	(18,000)	(250,000)

Emphasize that the estimates are checked for reasonableness. Often, a problem will give clues about the accuracy of estimates. Also, because estimation is a mental process, it is a good idea for students to habitually check estimates for reasonableness.

Estimating Differences of Whole Numbers

One estimate indicates that 2,857,000 megawatts of water power are available in the world. Of this supply of potential energy, only about 249,000 megawatts are used. About how many megawatts of water power are not used?

Estimate 2,857,000 − 249,000.

Using front-end estimation

$$
\begin{array}{r}
2{,}857{,}000 \\
- \ \ \ 249{,}000 \\
\end{array}
$$

Look at the smaller number to find the number of lead digits.

Subtract the lead digits. $28 - 2 = 26$. Use 2,600,000.

Adjust the difference. $57{,}000 > 49{,}000$. So, the difference is greater than 2,600,000. Adjust up.
Estimate: More than 2,600,000, or 2,600,000⁺.

Rounding to the largest place

$$
\begin{array}{rcl}
2{,}857{,}000 & \longrightarrow & 3{,}000{,}000 \\
- \ \ \ 249{,}000 & \longrightarrow & 0 \\
\end{array}
$$

Subtract the rounded numbers.
$3{,}000{,}000 - 0 = 3{,}000{,}000$
Estimate: 3,000,000

Rounding to the nearest hundred thousand

$$
\begin{array}{rcl}
2{,}857{,}000 & \longrightarrow & 2{,}900{,}000 \\
- \ \ \ 249{,}000 & \longrightarrow & 200{,}000 \\
\end{array}
$$

Subtract the rounded numbers.
$2{,}900{,}000 - 200{,}000 = 2{,}700{,}000$
Estimate: 2,700,000

An estimate of 3,000,000 megawatts is not reasonable, in this case, because there are less than 2,857,000 megawatts available. Either 2,600,000⁺ or 2,700,000 megawatts is a good estimate for the amount of potential water power that is not used.

Another example:

Estimate $5,726.35 − $2,834.29.

Front-end

$$
\begin{array}{r}
\$5{,}726.35 \\
- \ \ 2{,}834.29 \\
\end{array}
$$

Subtract lead digits. $3,000
Adjust: Since $726.35 < $834.29, adjust down.
Estimate: $3,000⁻

Rounding to the nearest thousand

$$
\begin{array}{rcl}
\$5{,}726.35 & \longrightarrow & \$6{,}000 \\
- \ \ 2{,}834.29 & \longrightarrow & 3{,}000 \\
\end{array}
$$

Subtract: $3,000
Estimate: $3,000

Both $3,000⁻ and $3,000 are reasonable estimates.

12

COMMON ERRORS

Students sometimes round correctly with smaller numbers, but they mistake place value and round incorrectly when working with larger numbers.

Remediation

Encourage students to rewrite larger numbers in an example, such as 43,297 − 12,755, in this form.

43 thousand − 13 thousand

This emphasizes the proper place value and removes unnecessary digits.

Assign Reteach Master, p. 5.

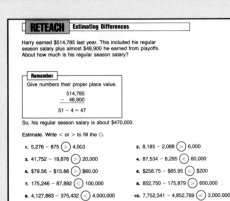

Reteach Worksheet

Estimate the difference. Answers may vary. Accept any reasonable estimate.

1.   6,823
        − 4,454
        2,000⁺

2.   53,916
        − 28,476
        30,000⁻

3.   269,706
        − 178,295
        100,000⁻

4.   8,929,545
        − 5,876,398
        3,000,000⁺

5.   4,728
        − 934
        3,800⁻

6.   26,799
        − 6,893
        20,000⁻

7.   387,562
        − 96,753
        290,000⁺

8.   7,645,213
        − 843,524
        6,800,000⁺

9. $532.23 − $75.00 $460⁻

10. $6,549.92 − $448.39 $6,100⁺

11. 92,835,493 − 4,679,821
      88,000,000⁺

12. 239,586,722 − 89,685,736
      150,000,000⁻

Estimate. Write > or < for ●.

13. 4,023 − 1,289 ● 4,000   <

14. 9,765 − 3,856 ● 7,000   <

15. 11,825 − 7,763 ● 3,000   >

16. 28,378 − 9,243 ● 18,000   >

17. 73,757 − 28,655 ● 50,000   <

18. 247,123 − 105,322 ● 100,000   >

19. 596,338 − 298,317 ● 400,000   <

20. 746,879 − 39,798 ● 710,000   <

21. $829.95 − $35.68 ● $780.00   >

22. $3,411.27 − $825.39 ● $2,700.00   <

23. North America uses about 76,000 megawatts of water power. This continent has 313,000 megawatts of water power available. Estimate the amount of potential water power that is not used.
240,000⁻ megawatts

24. The Grand Coulee Dam in Washington State has a rated capacity of 6,430 megawatts. Its ultimate capacity is over 10,000 megawatts. About how much additional water power should the Grand Coulee Dam eventually generate?
about 4,000 megawatts

FOCUS: REASONING

A plumber, a teacher, and a pilot live in three adjoining houses. The brick house is just to the left of the log cabin. The plumber recently moved from the house on the left. The pilot lives next door to the teacher. The teacher lives in the stucco house. Who lives in the log cabin? (HINT: Draw a picture or act it out.)

For additional activities, see *Connecting Math Ideas,* page 469. the plumber

Classwork/Homework, page H6   **13**

Exercise Analysis
1–12   Estimate the difference between two whole numbers
13–22   Use > or < to compare estimates
23–24   Skill application

Focus: Reasoning
This problem challenges students to organize a complex set of facts and to reason deductively to find the answer.

FOLLOW-UP ACTIVITIES

REINFORCEMENT
Have students determine whether each estimate should be adjusted up or down.
1. 745 − 326 = 400 (up)
2. 918 − 573 = 400 (down)
3. 12,620 − 6,952 = 6,000 (down)
4. 87,426 − 45,393 = 42,000 (up)
5. $463.54 − $179.25 = $300 (down)

MATH CONNECTION
(Social studies)
Have students use the information in the chart to compare the size of different states.

State	Land area (mi²)
Alaska	571,065
California	156,803
Missouri	69,270
Utah	82,346
Vermont	9,278

- Estimate the difference between the area of Utah and the area of California. (70,000 or 80,000 mi²)
- Estimate the difference between the area of Alaska and the area of Missouri. (500,000⁺ mi²)
- Estimate the difference between the combined area of Utah and Vermont and the area of Missouri. (21,000⁺ mi²)

COMING UP
Whole numbers . . . more or less

Name _____ Date _____

PRACTICE Estimating Differences of Whole Numbers

Write > or < for ○.

1. 8,165 − 2,089 ⓞ 6,000
2. 5,896 − 1,547 ⓞ 4,000
3. 6,129 − 387 ⓞ 6,000
4. 19,537 − 5,387 ⓞ 14,000
5. $48.65 − $19.85 ⓞ $20.00
6. $96.37 − $9.55 ⓞ $85.00
7. 26,576 − 19,865 ⓞ 10,000
8. 82,179 − 19,583 ⓞ 60,000
9. 486,925 − 95,467 ⓞ 400,000
10. 689,278 − 417,885 ⓞ 200,000
11. 5,176,429 − 875,265 ⓞ 4,000,000
12. 18,752,469 − 7,895,265 ⓞ 10,000,000

Estimate. Answers will vary. Accept any reasonable estimate.

13. 4,836
    − 978
    3,900⁻

14. 7,234
    − 4,187
    3,000⁺

15. $79.56
    − 15.89
    $60⁻

16. $118.87
    − 79.59
    $40⁻

17. 53,476
    − 8,958
    45,000⁻

18. 81,647
    − 25,879
    60,000⁻

19. 74,529
    − 25,287
    50,000⁺

20. 435,276
    − 89,197
    350,000⁻

Solve.

21. About how many more people attended Thursday than Wednesday?
25,000⁻

22. Did over 25,000 more people attend Friday than attended Thursday?
no

23. About how many more people attended Saturday than Monday?
47,000⁻

24. Did 5,000 more people attend Tuesday than Monday?
no

Date	Attendance
Monday	14,567
Tuesday	18,081
Wednesday	5,869
Thursday	30,287
Friday	54,895
Saturday	61,457

6   Use with pages 12–13.

Practice Worksheet

ENRICH Number

The planet Excalibur proposed a budget of 925 billion grots for colonization of its moon, Tolemac. In order to transport the 230 million colonists, 34 billion grots were to be used.

1. Estimate the amount it costs to transport each of the colonists. Do the calculation mentally.
150 grots

2. Excalibur has a 21-hour day and a 412-day year. Estimate how much is spent to colonize Tolemac each day; each hour.
2.25 billion grots; 100 million grots

The government of Excalibur always spends more money than it has, and must borrow from the planet Nilrem. In the year of the colonization, Excalibur spent 180 billion grots more than it had.

3. If Excalibur already owed Nilrem 1.6 trillion grots, how much did they owe at the end of the year of colonization? Write out the number.
1,780,000,000,000 grots

4. One trillion grots would be a stack of 1,000-grot bills 67 miles high. What is the height of the 1.8-trillion-grot debt in 1,000-grot bills? In 1-grot bills?
120 miles; 120,000 miles

5. The distance from Excalibur to Tolemac is about 240,000 miles. How many 1-grot bills must be stacked to reach this distance?
3.6 trillion

6. If 1.8 trillion 1-grot bills were laid end to end, estimate how many times they would go around the equator of Excalibur, a distance of 31,000 miles. The length of a 1-grot bill is approximately 5 inches.
approximately 6,000 times

NOTE: Accept a reasonable range of answers.

6   Use with pages 12–13.

Enrich Worksheet

13

Warm-Up

Have students mentally compute to find the missing number.

37 = 27 + (10)   89 = (79) + 10
43 = 53 − (10)   75 = (85) − 10
340 = 240 + (100)   685 = 785 − (100)

GETTING STARTED

Materials: place-value blocks

Use place-value blocks to represent two numbers, such as 5,359 and 1,728. Explain that you wish to find the difference between the two quantities. Show how 5,000 must be regrouped as 4,000 + 10 hundreds in order to subtract the hundreds. Then illustrate the example on the chalkboard.

Have pairs of students take turns making up other examples with models and verifying the results by using pencil and paper.

TEACHING THE LESSON

Use the following examples to remind students that column addition is easier if they look for sums of 10 in each column.

```
  46 ⟍        263 ⟍        6,982 ⟍
  35 ⟍ 10     7,049 ⟍ 10     43 ⟍ 10
 124 ⟍ 10      324 ⟍        168 ⟍ 10
+ 85 ⟍       + 57 ⟍       +4,837 ⟍
─────         ─────         ──────
(290)        (7,693)       (12,030)
```

Use the examples above and the example in the text to demonstrate the method of "adding up" to check.

Show that the check step in subtraction makes use of this fact.

If 15,006 − 8,898 = 6,108,
then 6,108 + 8,898 = 15,006.

You may wish to allow students to use calculators for some of these exercises.

Checkpoint

The chart lists the common errors students make in adding and subtracting whole numbers.

Correct Answers: 1b, 2c, 3a, 4b

Remediation

■ Have students write each number in expanded form before attempting to regroup in subtraction.

☐ For these errors, guide the students in completing Reteach Master, p. 6.

Adding and Subtracting Whole Numbers

A. Marjorie climbed a mountain in four days. The table lists how far she climbed each day. How far did she climb in all?

Add 3,268 + 2,849 + 674 + 1,934.

Day 1	3,268 ft
Day 2	2,849 ft
Day 3	674 ft
Day 4	1,934 ft

Estimate the sum before you compute.

```
  3,268 →    3,000
  2,849 →    3,000
    674 →    1,000
+ 1,934 →  + 2,000
─────       ──────
             9,000
```

Add. Regroup if necessary.

```
    2 2 2
  3,268
  2,849
    674
+ 1,934
─────
  8,725
```
The answer is reasonable.

Marjorie climbed 8,725 ft.

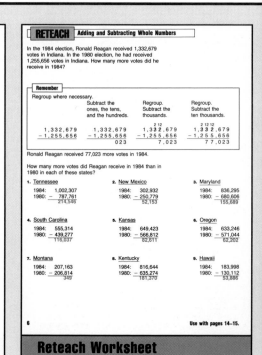

B. You can use addition to check your answer when you subtract.

Find the difference between 15,006 and 8,898.

```
       9 9
   4  10 10 16
  1 5 , 0 0 6
 −    8 , 8 9 8
  ───────────
      6 , 1 0 8
```

Check: 6,108 + 8,898 = 15,006

Find $4,209.10 − $2,110.08.

```
       1 10    0 10
  $ 4 , 2 0 9 . 1 0
 −   2 , 1 1 0 . 0 8
  ─────────────────
  $ 2 , 0 9 9 . 0 2
```

Check: $2,099.02 + $2,110.08 = $4,209.10

Checkpoint Write the letter of the correct answer.

Add or subtract.

1.   53,689
        + 1,492

a. 52,197
b. 55,181
c. 54,071
d. 54,181

2. $494,932.74
       + 16,779.87

a. $478,152.87
b. $500,602.51
c. $511,712.61
d. $400,601.51

3. $845.42
       − 468.95

a. $376.47
b. $423.53
c. $487.57
d. $1,314.37

4.   1,400,603
       − 847,986

a. 2,248,589
b. 552,617
c. 647,383
d. 663,727

14

COMMON ERRORS

Answer Choice	Type of Error
☐ 1a, 2a	Subtracts instead of adds
■ 1c	Fails to regroup
■ 1d	Fails to regroup across period
■ 2b	Fails to regroup completely
■ 3b, 4c	Subtracts the lesser digit from the greater digit regardless of the lesser digit's position
☐ 3c, 4d	Regroups incorrectly
☐ 3d, 4a	Adds instead of subtracts
☐ 2d	Fails to add regrouped numbers to each place value

Add.

1. 3,482 + 1,516 4,998	**2.** 58,142 + 17,964 76,106	**3.** 384,068 + 615,846 999,914	**4.** $31,348.76 + 84,596.72 $115,945.48	**5.** 679,483 + 92,998 772,481
6. 8,167 398 + 1,462 10,027	**7.** 58,672 1,495 + 37,152 97,319	**8.** $ 6.74 19.87 + 356.72 $383.33	**9.** 34,645 8,997 743 + 36,482 80,867	**10.** 748,963 742 68,149 + 436,157 1,254,011

Subtract.

11. 8,846 − 3,415 5,431	**12.** 45,632 − 14,836 30,796	**13.** 446,312 − 24,101 422,211	**14.** $300.07 − 59.19 $240.88	**15.** 8,000,007 − 612,349 7,387,658

Add or subtract.

16. 6,789,123 + 4,713,893 11,503,016

17. $6,740.00 − $367.43 $6,372.57

18. $643,498 − $41,739 $601,759

19. 137,982 + 7,821 + 83 + 999 146,885

20. 31,462 − 1,847 + 298 29,913

21. 77,334 + 1,298 − 53,186 25,446

22. 382 billion + 179 billion 561 billion	**23.** 752 billion − 359 billion 393 billion	**24.** 936 trillion − 354 trillion 582 trillion

Find the missing digits.

★**25.** ■■,■■■ − 26,784 64,871 91,655	★**26.** 2 69■,984 − ■■6,■■■ 486,548 206,436	★**27.** 631,427 843,968 + ■■■,■■■ 2,389,563 914,168	★**28.** 5,632 ■,■■■ + 7,194 18,793 5,967

Solve.

29. One of China's highest mountains, Muztagh Ata, is 7,546 m high. The highest mountain in Pakistan, K–2, is 1,204 m higher. How high is K–2? 8,750 m

30. Look up the altitudes of five other mountains. Draw a table that displays them in order from the greatest elevation to the least elevation. **Answers will vary.**

31. The highest mountain in the world is Mount Everest, at 29,028 ft. The highest mountain in the United States is Mount McKinley, at 20,320 ft. How much higher is Mount Everest? 8,708 ft

★**32.** Mr. Martin bought a camp stove for $39.75, a lantern for $19.92, and a cookware set for $22.84. If the sales tax was $5.78 and he gave the cashier a 100-dollar bill, how much change did he receive? $11.71

Classwork/Homework, page H7

15

ASSIGNMENT GUIDE

Basic: 1–21, 29–31

Average: 1–27 o, 29–32

Extended: 2–28 e, 29–32

Resources
Practice, p. 7   Class/Home, p. H7
Reteach, p. 6
Enrich, p. 7

Exercise Analysis
1–10 Add whole numbers
11–15 Subtract whole numbers
16–21 Mixed practice
22–24 Add and subtract by using short word names
25–28 Use inverse operations to find missing digits
29–32 Skill applications

You may wish to allow students to use calculators for some of these exercises.

FOLLOW-UP ACTIVITIES

PUZZLES AND GAMES
In the examples below, each letter represents a digit. Have students find the digits that will make the additions correct. To help them break the code, tell them that R = 7, T = 2, and H = 8 in the left-hand example and that G = 8 and E = 3 in the right-hand example.

WRONG (37,091)	SEVEN (63,732)
+WRONG +(37,091)	+EIGHT +(39,841)
RIGHT (74,182)	TWELVE (103,573)

PROBLEM SOLVING
The weekly attendance figures at the Good Time Amusement Park are shown below.

Mon.	Tues.	Wed.	Thurs.	Fri.
7,512	11,016	8,175	9,566	10,449

Have students use these data to create and solve problems such as the following.

On Saturday and Sunday, the combined attendance was 57,125. Did more people visit the park during the week or during the weekend? (during the weekend) how many more? (10,407 more)

COMING UP
H is for help!

15

Objective: To understand the 4-step problem-solving plan

Warm-Up
Have students compute the answers.

68 + 85 + 19 (172)
965 + 408 + 148 (1,521)
2,781 + 385 + 48 (3,214)
711 + 245 − 529 (427)

GETTING STARTED

Ask students for suggestions on how to solve the following problem.

You are locked out of your house and have no key. How can you get in?

Have students suggest possible solutions (call a locksmith, crawl in an unlocked window). Point out that to solve a real-life problem, we begin by making sure we know exactly what it is we have to do. Then we collect the tools we need (phone, crowbar) and use them to solve the problem. At the end we look back to make sure that the solution solves the problem. Explain that exactly the same method can be used to solve math problems.

TEACHING THE LESSON

Use the activity in *Getting Started* to help the class see the similarity between solving math problems and solving real-life problems. This will help students feel more at ease with mathematics.

Go over each of the four steps with the class.

Questions: The first question students should ask themselves is: Do I understand the question? Then they should check to make sure that the information they need to solve the problem is available.

Tools: Ask the class to name some additional tools that are not listed here. (operations: subtraction, division; strategies: write an equation, draw a picture; resources: map, another person)

Solutions: Emphasize that students should be careful to get the correct information from a table when solving a problem, especially when the table has more than one kind of information. Ask students to tell which column in the table they would have used if the problem had asked about the age of the parks.

QUESTIONS	TOOLS	SOLUTIONS	CHECKS

PROBLEM SOLVING
4-Step Plan

The key to solving any problem is to proceed in a logical and organized manner. The following 4-step plan will help you to do this. Be sure to complete each step before going on to the next one.

How many acres larger is Yosemite National Park than Sequoia National Park?

OLDEST NATIONAL PARKS

Park	Year	Area (acres)
Yellowstone	1872	2,219,785
Kings Canyon	1890	461,901
Sequoia	1890	402,482
Yosemite	1890	761,170

In this step you get ready to solve the problem.

1. QUESTIONS
Read the problem. Do you understand the *question* being asked? Do you know the vocabulary? Do you have all the information you need? To help you understand the question restate it in your own words.

Find the difference between the areas of the two parks.

In this step you plan your solution.

2. TOOLS
Choose the *tools* you will need to solve the problem. Tools are operations like addition and multiplication, strategies like estimating and finding patterns, and resources like graphs and reference books.

Find the needed information in the table. Use subtraction to find the difference.

In this step you solve the problem.

3. SOLUTIONS
Find the *solution* by applying the tools you have chosen. Use the table to find the areas of Sequoia and Yosemite national parks. Then subtract the areas to find the difference.

```
  761,170 ←Yosemite
− 402,482 ←Sequoia
  358,688
```
Yosemite is 358,688 acres larger.

In this step you check your answer.

4. CHECKS
Check your solution. Does it answer the question? Is it reasonable? Can you solve the problem in a different way to double-check your solution?

Use addition to check.
```
  358,688
+ 402,482
  761,170
```

16

Checks: Make sure that students understand that the solution must answer the question. Since the question asks how many acres larger, the solution, 358,688, answers the question. The answer appears reasonable since an estimate would be close to 360,000. Mention that inverse operations can often be used to check answers. Ask for another example of inverse operations (division is the inverse of multiplication).

Solve each of the following by following the 4-step plan.

- State the problem in your own words.
- Tell which tool you will use to solve the problem.
- Solve the problem.
- Check your solution. Check students' problem statements.

1. The newest national park, Great Basin in Nevada, was established in 1986. How much older than Great Basin is Yellowstone National Park?
subtract; 114 years

2. What is the combined area of the four oldest national parks?
add; 3,845,338 acres

3. The lowest point in Yosemite has an elevation of 610 meters above sea level. How high above that point is the summit of Yosemite's highest mountain, at 3,960 meters above sea level?
subtract; 3,350 meters

4. What is larger, Yellowstone National Park or the combined areas of Kings Canyon, Sequoia, and Yosemite National Parks?
estimate, add, compare; Yellowstone

5. The National Park Service manages 68,234,091 acres of federal land. The U.S. Forest Service manages 189,407,924 acres of land. How much larger is the Forest Service's acreage than that of the Park Service? subtract; 121,173,833 acres

6. Yosemite Falls, the tallest waterfall in the United States, is in Yosemite National Park. It falls in three stages of 1,430 feet, 320 feet, and 675 feet. Find the height of the falls from top to bottom.
add; 2,425 feet

7. The world's tallest sequoia tree is in Sequoia National Park. It is 275 feet tall. The world's tallest Douglas fir tree in Olympic National Park is 221 feet tall. About how much taller is the tallest sequoia tree than the tallest Douglas fir tree?
estimate; about 50 feet

8. Mount Whitney in Sequoia National Park is the highest point in the continental United States. It is 14,494 feet above sea level. Just 60 miles away in Death Valley is the lowest point, 282 feet below sea level. How high above the lowest point is the summit of Mount Whitney?
add; 14,776 feet

9. Acadia National Park was established 44 years after Yellowstone National Park. Redwood National Park was established 52 years after Acadia. In what year was Redwood National Park established?
add twice; 1968

10. The largest national park, Wrangell–St. Elias, has an area 6,725,215 acres larger than the area of Yellowstone National Park. By how much does its area exceed that of Yosemite National Park?
add, subtract; 8,183,830 acres

Classwork/Homework, page H8

ASSIGNMENT GUIDE

Basic:	1–6
Average:	3–8
Extended:	5–10

Resources
Practice, p. 8   Class/Home, p. H8
Enrich, p. 8

Exercise Analysis
Encourage students to estimate answers before solving. This will allow them to decide if an answer is reasonable.

4, 7   Since exact answers are not required, estimates are sufficient.

FOLLOW-UP ACTIVITIES

PROBLEM SOLVING
Copy the following problem on the chalkboard. Tell students that they may need to use a complex plan and several operations in order to solve the problem. The problem can be solved if they tackle it slowly and carefully, one step at a time.

Charlie is 14 years older than Beth. Arnold's age is equal to the sum of Charlie's and Beth's ages. Doris's age is the sum of Arnold's and Charlie's ages. Beth is 19. Find the sum of the ages of all four people. (189)

CALCULATOR
Write the following examples on the chalkboard. Have students use their calculators to check each example and correct the ones that are wrong. Point out that the answer on the calculator does not have to be reentered before students use the inverse operation to check the answer.

- 3,852 − 1,719 = 1,863 (2,133)
- 52,416 + 88,521 = 104,940 (140,937)
- 7,924 − 5,622 = 2,302
- 3,251 + 9,827 = 13,078
- 20,548 − 3,774 = 16,744 (16,774)
- 85,218 + 9,205 = 99,423 (94,423)
- 1,321,005 − 821,022 = 499,983
- 714,000 + 31,718 = 745,718

COMING UP
Every decimal knows its place!

Objectives: To read and write decimals through millionths

Warm-Up
Have students give the value of each underlined digit in the following.

37,854 (800)   562,876 (60,000)

4,025,839 (4,000,000)   859,603 (0)

GETTING STARTED

In 1782, when Congress was debating which monetary system to adopt for the new United States, Thomas Jefferson proposed the decimal system, based on powers of 10, that is still in use.

Jefferson also wanted other aspects of our national life converted to the decimal system; for example, a ten-hour day and a ten-month year. Discuss how our lives would be different if a ten-hour day or a ten-month year had been adopted.

TEACHING THE LESSON

Sometimes, students read decimals incorrectly because they think of the first place to the right of the decimal point—the tenths place—as a counterpart to the ones place. Emphasize the fact that the digits to the right of the decimal point represent only fractional parts of 1. So, another ones place to the right of the decimal point is not possible.

Remind students that the decimal part of any number is always named for the place value of the last digit. Have students read decimals such as 2.309, 0.5567, and 6.009.

Checkpoint
The chart lists the common errors students make in determining decimal place value.

Correct Answers: 1b, 2b

Remediation
■ For these errors, be sure that students understand that the decimal point divides whole numbers from fractional parts of numbers. Any digit to the left of the decimal point may not be counted as a decimal place. All places to the right of the decimal point must be counted through the last nonzero digit.

☐ For these errors, assign Reteach Master, p. 7.

Decimal Place Value

Scientists use **atomic weight** to describe the weight of elements. The atomic weight of aluminum is 26.9815. How do you read this number? The number 26.9815 is a decimal. The place-value chart can be extended to decimals.

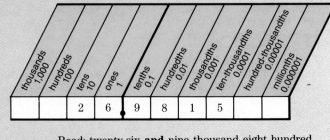

thousands 1,000	hundreds 100	tens 10	ones 1	tenths 0.1	hundredths 0.01	thousandths 0.001	ten-thousandths 0.0001	hundred-thousandths 0.00001	millionths 0.000001
		2	6	9	8	1	5		

Read: twenty-six **and** nine thousand eight hundred fifteen ten-thousandths. This is the word name for the number 26.9815.
The 4 in 2.103462 appears in the ten-thousandths place. The value of the 4 is 4 ten-thousandths, or 0.0004.

You can write zeros to the right of any decimal without affecting the value.

$5.75 = 5.750 = 5.7500$ and $25 = 25.0 = 25.00$

The expanded form of 42.097 is $40 + 2 + 0.09 + 0.007$.

Checkpoint Write the letter of the correct answer.

1. Choose the decimal for sixteen ten-thousandths.

a. 0.00016   **b.** 0.0016
c. 0.016   **d.** 16,000

2. What is the value of 8 in 1.038793?

a. thousandths   **b.** 8 thousandths
c. 8 hundredths   **d.** 8

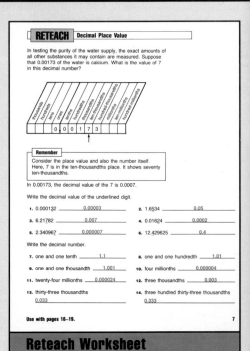

Aluminum is used in airplane construction because it is lightweight.

Iron occurs in the body in the red blood cells.

Because of its beautiful color, Copper is used in ornaments & art work.

COMMON ERRORS

Answer Choice	Type of Error
■ 1a	Uses the same number of zeros as the equivalent whole number
■ 1c	Counts the zero in the ones place
■ 1d	Confuses ten-thousandths with ten thousands
☐ 2a	Uses the place value instead of the digit value
☐ 2c	Uses the incorrect place value
☐ 2d	Uses the digit instead of the place value

Write the decimal.

1. six hundred fifty-five thousandths
0.655
2. one and nine hundred-thousandths
1.00009
3. thirty-five millionths
0.000035
4. two hundred seven thousandths
0.207
5. three thousand eight hundred sixty-one hundred-thousandths   0.03861

Write the word name. **See Answer Key.**

6. 8.543   **7.** 1.000009   **8.** 0.0493   **9.** 1.00163   **10.** 7.03541

Write the value of the underlined digit.

11. 6.05<u>3</u>   **12.** 7.1356<u>2</u>   **13.** 0.15976<u>3</u>   **14.** 3.4352<u>1</u>7
0.003   0.0006   0.000003   0.00001

Write the decimal.

15. 0.04 + 0.005 + 0.0006   0.0456
16. 4 + 0.3 + 0.05   4.35
17. 0.8 + 0.009   0.809
18. 7 + 0.3 + 0.04 + 0.00007   7.34007
19. 30 + 5 + 0.05 + 0.007 + 0.00006 + 0.000003
35.057063

Solve.

20. The atomic weight of argon is 39 + 0.9 + 0.04 + 0.008. Write this as a decimal.   39.948

21. Tellurium was discovered in 1782. Nobelium was discovered in 1957. How many years elapsed between these two discoveries?   175 y

22. Find the atomic weight in decimals for four other elements, and write the word name for each weight.
Answers will vary.

★23. The atomic weight of aluminum is 26.9815. Write this in expanded form using the word name.
See Answer Key.

MIDCHAPTER REVIEW

Write the place and the value of the underlined digit.

1. 752,<u>3</u>21
thousands, 2,000
2. 61,356,90<u>8</u>
tens, 0
3. 0.001<u>4</u>
thousandths, 0.001
4. 17.9<u>3</u>28
hundredths, 0.03

Add or subtract.

5.
  3,154
+ 4,521
  7,675
6.
  19,547
+ 60,428
  79,975
7.
  $342.09
+   65.34
  $407.43
8.
  796,942
+ 81,064
  878,006
9.
  4,628,049
+ 7,247,361
  11,875,410
10.
  6,236
− 4,024
  2,212
11.
  76,581
− 24,377
  52,204
12.
  $565.03
− 248.27
  $316.76
13.
  854,926
− 78,399
  776,527
14.
  6,477,005
− 6,249,183
  227,822

Classwork/Homework, page H9

19

ASSIGNMENT GUIDE

Basic: 2–18 e, 20–21, MCR

Average: 1–19 o, 20–22, MCR

Extended: 2–18 e, 20–23, MCR

Resources
Practice, p. 9   Class/Home, p. H9
Reteach, p. 7
Enrich, p. 9

Exercise Analysis
1–5   Write the standard form for a word name
6–10   Write a word name
11–14   Determine the value of a digit
15–19   Write a decimal for the expanded form
20–21   Skill applications
22   Problem formulation
23   Skill application

You may wish to allow students to use calculators for Exercises 15–21.

Midchapter Review
This review provides an opportunity for you and students to assess their understanding of concepts and skills developed to this point in the chapter.

FOLLOW-UP ACTIVITIES

 REINFORCEMENT

On the chalkboard, write a pair of decimals in which the same digit is used at least once in both decimals; for example, 4.563 and 7.886. Ask which 6 is in the hundredths place. (4.563) Repeat the exercise.

COMPUTER
This program tests students' understanding of place value. On some computers, the program makes mistakes. Have students watch for the mistakes.

```
10 LET A = (INT(RND(0)*10^6))/10^6
20 PRINT "THE NUMBER IS"; A
30 LET B = INT(RND(0)*6) + 1
40 FOR N = 1 TO B
45 LET C = INT (A*10)
50 LET C = INT (A*10)
60 LET A = (A*10) − C
70 NEXT N
80 PRINT "VALUE OF PLACE"; B;
90 INPUT V
100 IF V = C/10^B THEN PRINT "RIGHT!"
110 PRINT "THE VALUE IS"; C/10^B
120 END
```

COMING UP
Specifically, specific gravity!

19

Objectives: To compare and order decimals

Warm-Up
Have students order the following numbers from the greatest to the least.

27,892; 327,892; 27,898; 27,982
(327,892; 27,982; 27,898; 27,892)

GETTING STARTED

Write the following on the chalkboard.

1	2	3	4	5	6	7	8	9
1	2	3	4	5	6	7	8	9

Place a decimal point at random in the top number. Then have students place a decimal point in the bottom number so that the new number is
- equal to the top number.
- greater than the top number.
- less than the top number.

Discuss what will happen to the value of the top number if we move the decimal point one place to the left. (The number becomes smaller.)

TEACHING THE LESSON

A. Point out that *specific gravity* is nothing more than the density of a substance when compared to the density of water. A specific gravity of 2.71 means that a certain volume of calcite is 2.71 times as heavy as an equal volume of water.

B. As an alternative strategy for ordering, have students write in expanded form the decimals they are comparing.

5.51 = 5.00 + 0.5 + 0.01
5.02 = 5.00 + 0.0 + 0.02
0.5 > 0.0   So, 5.51 > 5.02.

C. Remind students that when they compare decimals, they should work from the left to the right. The only digits that have significance for comparison are the first digits that differ in the same place. All digits to the right of that place can be ignored. Thus, 4.678 < 4.801 because 6 < 8, even though 0.078 > 0.001.

Comparing and Ordering Decimals

A. The **specific gravity** of a mineral is found by comparing the weight of a mineral with the weight of an equal volume of water. The specific gravity of calcite is 2.71. The specific gravity of graphite is 2.3. Which mineral has the greater specific gravity?

To compare decimals, align the decimal points. Compare as you would with whole numbers.

2.71   2 = 2
2.3   7 > 3   So, 2.71 > 2.3.

Calcite has the greater specific gravity.

B. Order these decimals from the greatest to the least: 3.04, 3.1, 3.153, 3.0438.

To order decimals, line up the decimal points and compare digits from the left to the right. Write zeros if needed to line up the decimal points.

Compare to find the greatest.

3.0400
3.1000
3.1530   } 3.1530 > 3.100
3.0438

Compare to find the next greatest.

3.1000 > 3.0400

3.1000 > 3.0438

Compare to find the least.

3.0438 > 3.0400

3.153 is the greatest.   3.100 is the next greatest.

The order from the greatest to the least is: 3.153, 3.1, 3.0438, 3.04.

C. Order these decimals from the least to the greatest: 5.110, 5.001, 5.10, 5.01.

Compare to find the least.

5.001 < 5.010

Compare to find the next greatest.

5.01 < 5.10

Compare to find the greatest.

5.100 < 5.110

The order from the least to the greatest is: 5.001, 5.01, 5.10, 5.110.

20

COMMON ERRORS

Some students encounter difficulty when they compare decimals because they fail to align the decimal points correctly.

Remediation
Use examples to emphasize the importance of aligning the decimal points before comparing. Write 79.2 and 9.72. Point to the 7 in 79.2 and the 9 in 9.72 and ask which digit is greater. (9) Then ask which decimal number has the greater value. (79.2) Align the decimal points and compare again. (79.2 > 9.72)

Assign Reteach Master, p. 8.

RETEACH Comparing and Ordering Decimals

The winners of the 400-meter run in the last four Olympic games had times of 44.27 s, 44.6 s, 44.26 s, and 44.66 s. Order these numbers from the least to the greatest.

Remember
To compare decimals, line up the decimal points. Then compare their digits from left to right. Write zeros if necessary.

From the least to the greatest, the decimals are 44.26, 44.27, 44.60, 44.66.

Write the numbers in order from the least to the greatest.

1. 3.05, 3.052, 3.005
   3.005, 3.05, 3.052
2. 4.631, 4.6315, 4.6309
   4.6309, 4.631, 4.6315
3. 0.005, 0.0045, 0.0055
   0.0045, 0.005, 0.0055
4. 3.6032, 3.603, 3.6037
   3.603, 3.6032, 3.6037
5. 1.004, 1.04, 1.4
   1.004, 1.04, 1.4
6. 0.003, 0.03, 0.3
   0.003, 0.03, 0.3
7. 187.1, 187.13, 187.03
   187.03, 187.1, 187.13
8. 2.65, 2.6, 2.065
   2.065, 2.6, 2.65
9. 3.110, 3.001, 3.1, 3.01
   3.001, 3.01, 3.1, 3.110
10. 0.007, 0.07, 0.0071
    0.007, 0.0071, 0.07
11. 3.04, 3.041, 3.41, 3.14
    3.04, 3.041, 3.14, 3.41
12. 0.7382, 0.739, 0.738, 0.7391
    0.738, 0.7382, 0.739, 0.7391
13. 0.1, 0.01, 0.001, 0.011
    0.001, 0.01, 0.011, 0.1
14. 10.1, 10.01, 10.11, 10.101
    10.01, 10.1, 10.101, 10.11
15. 9.345, 9.34, 90.34, 9.034
    9.034, 9.34, 9.345, 90.34
16. 0.0045, 0.045, 0.45, 0.405
    0.0045, 0.045, 0.405, 0.45

8   Use with pages 20–21.

Reteach Worksheet

Compare. Write >, <, or = for ●.

1. 0.43 ● 0.5   <
2. 3.014 ● 3.1   <
3. 3.004 ● 3.04   <
4. 0.6321 ● 0.6312   >
5. 9.1506 ● 9.15060   =
6. 0.304 ● 0.3040   =
7. 0.13642 ● 0.136   >
8. 3.21 ● 3.2047   >
9. 6.047 ● 6.0470   =
10. 1.137624 ● 1.137642   <
11. 0.678 ● 0.678000   =
12. 0.531 ● 0.541362   <

Order the decimals from the greatest to the least.

13. 0.156, 0.1036, 0.019, 0.091
0.156, 0.1036, 0.091, 0.019
14. 9.006, 9.0008, 9.0043, 9.0062
9.0062, 9.006, 9.0043, 9.0008
15. 0.41283, 0.4168, 0.0431, 0.04
0.4168, 0.41283, 0.0431, 0.04
16. 6.39, 6.0342, 6.37, 6.03842
6.39, 6.37, 6.03842, 6.0342
17. 0.074, 0.0704, 0.7044, 0.0074
0.7044, 0.074, 0.0704, 0.0074
18. 22.01, 202.1, 22.10, 221.0
221.0, 202.1, 22.10, 22.01

Order the decimals from the least to the greatest.

19. 4.0362, 4.3182, 4.03
4.03, 4.0362, 4.3182
20. 0.148, 0.0148, 0.1483
0.0148, 0.148, 0.1483
21. 0.8, 0.81362, 0.8163
0.8, 0.81362, 0.8163
22. 3.144263, 3.15, 3.14436, 3.1582
3.144263, 3.14436, 3.15, 3.1582
23. 7.813, 7.8131, 7.1831, 7.0831
7.0831, 7.1831, 7.813, 7.8131
24. 0.732, 0.731, 0.7031, 0.7321
0.7031, 0.731, 0.732, 0.7321

Solve. For Problem 26, use the Infobank.

25. Each year, Australia produces 0.168 million tons of lead ore. Mexico produces 0.162 million tons. Which country produces more lead ore?
Australia

26. Use the information on page 473 to solve. Order the four minerals from the one with the least specific gravity to the one with the greatest.
graphite, olivine, barite

27. The melting point of antimony is 630.74°C, the melting point of germanium is 937.4°C, and the melting point of iodine is 113.5°C. Which mineral has the lowest melting point and which has the highest?   lowest: iodine; highest: germanium

ANOTHER LOOK

Round to the nearest hundred.

1. 671   700
2. 308   300
3. 767   800
4. 941   900
5. 483   500
6. 650   700

Round to the nearest million.

7. 6,217,904   6,000,000
8. 27,415,198   27,000,000
9. 54,521,091   55,000,000
10. 45,500,554   46,000,000

ASSIGNMENT GUIDE

Basic: 1–12, 13–23 o, 25–27, AL
Average: 2–24 e, 25–27, AL
Extended: 1–23 o, 25–27, AL

Resources
Practice, p. 10   Class/Home, p. H10
Reteach, p. 8
Enrich, p. 10

Exercise Analysis
1–12   Compare two decimals
13–18 Order decimals from the greatest to the least
19–24 Order decimals from the least to the greatest
25, 27 Skill applications
26   Data collection and computation

Another Look
This review provides maintenance in the skill of rounding whole numbers to a specified place.

FOLLOW-UP ACTIVITIES

CALCULATOR
Long decimals can be compared easily with a calculator by subtracting one decimal from the other. If the difference is negative, then the number being subtracted is greater. If the difference is positive, then the number being subtracted is less.

REINFORCEMENT
On the chalkboard, write two similar decimal numbers one above the other; for example:

6.4328779
6.4328799

Have a student come to the chalkboard and starting at the left, draw vertical lines through all the digits that are the same in both decimal numbers. When student finds two digits that do not match, ask which is greater. (9 > 7)

COMING UP
Decimal roundup

PRACTICE Comparing and Ordering Decimals

Write >, <, or = for ○.

1. 229.783938 (>) 229.7839348
2. 0.999999 (<) 1
3. 5,674.0123 (<) 5,674.123
4. 6.00002 (>) 6.000002
5. 323,956.987453 (>) 323,956.985753
6. 8.034 (<) 80.34
7. 1.019872 (<) 1.919872
8. 1.00000 (=) 1.00
9. 0.333 (<) 0.3333
10. 10.0 (<) 100.00000
11. 57.345 (=) 57.345
12. 0.99999 (>) 0.1

Write each group of decimals from the least to the greatest.

13. 0.656, 0.565, 0.6565, 0.56565, 0.65
0.565, 0.56565, 0.65, 0.656, 0.6565
14. 0.456789, 0.6789, 0.56789, 0.789, 0.89
0.456789, 0.56789, 0.6789, 0.789, 0.89
15. 0.000666, 0.066006, 0.006066, 0.006606, 0.06606
0.000666, 0.006066, 0.006606, 0.06606, 0.066006
16. 0.53298, 0.52398, 0.54398, 0.54298, 0.534
0.52398, 0.53298, 0.534, 0.54298, 0.54398

Write each group of decimals from the greatest to the least.

17. 0.747447, 0.744774, 0.477447, 0.747474, 0.774774
0.774774, 0.747474, 0.747447, 0.744774, 0.477447
18. 0.9286, 0.9386, 0.8386, 0.9376, 0.928
0.9386, 0.9376, 0.9286, 0.928, 0.8386
19. 0.564897, 0.563997, 0.563897, 0.564997, 0.564887
0.564997, 0.564897, 0.564887, 0.563997, 0.563897
20. 0.000003, 0.003, 0.0003, 0.00003, 0.03
0.03, 0.003, 0.0003, 0.00003, 0.000003

10   Use with pages 20–21.

Practice Worksheet

ENRICH Statistics and Probability

In baseball, a player's batting average (BA) is the number of hits (H) divided by the number of at bats (AB). A player's slugging average (SA) is the total bases divided by (AB). A home run is four bases (4B). Hits include singles, doubles, triples, and home runs.

Complete the chart.

Player	BA	AB	H	2B	3B	HR	SA
Jones	0.270	126	34	4	0	6	0.444
Shipione	0.323	96	31	2	0	2	0.406
Dooley	0.143	14	2	1	1	0	0.357
Moreno	0.284	88	25	5	0	3	0.443

A pitcher's earned run average is the number of earned runs a pitcher has given up for every nine innings pitched.

Complete the chart.

Pitcher	Earned Run Average	Innings	Earned Runs
Garrett	2.45	121	33
DeWitt	3.96	104⅔	46
Gonzales	2.25	4	1
Tasaki	4.29	92⅓	44

Update each player's statistics. Find the amount of change in each player's BA and SA over the week. For each category, order the players from the most change to the least.

Player	This week	New averages BA	New averages SA	Change BA	Change SA	Order BA	Order SA
Jones	10 AB, 2H	0.265	0.426	0.005	0.018	3	4
Shipione	18 AB, 3 H, 1 2B	0.298	0.377	0.025	0.029	2	2
Dooley	21 AB, 9 H, 1 2B, 1 HR	0.314	0.514	0.171	0.157	1	1
Moreno	12 AB, 3 H	0.280	0.420	0.004	0.023	4	3

10   Use with pages 20–21.

Enrich Worksheet

21

Warm-Up

Have students identify the place-value position of the underlined digit in the following examples.

0.8<u>3</u>94
(hundredths)

27.479<u>2</u>7
(ten-thousandths)

3.80<u>3</u>97
(thousandths)

41.<u>0</u>652
(tenths)

0.0008<u>4</u>
(hundred-thousandths)

1<u>7</u>.00634
(ones)

GETTING STARTED

Select two decimals that are separated by a wide interval; for example, 3.1 and 13.1. Have students take turns naming a decimal that is greater than the first but less than the second.

TEACHING THE LESSON

A. Some students may find rounding decimals on a number line easier if equivalent decimals are shown.

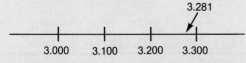

3.281

3.000   3.100   3.200   3.300

Other students may be helped by thinking of the decimal intervals as whole numbers. For example, is 281 closer to 200 or to 300? (closer to 300)

B. Emphasize that in rounding decimals, only the digit to the right of the rounding place is to be considered.

C. Point out that gasoline prices often include 3 digits to the right of the decimal point. Have students round the following gasoline prices to the nearest cent.

$1.295 ($1.30) $1.084 ($1.08)
$1.335 ($1.34) $1.279 ($1.28)

Checkpoint

The chart lists the common errors students make in rounding decimals.

Correct Answers: 1d, 2c, 3d

Remediation

■ Have students round decimals in four steps: Circle the digit of the rounding place; underline the digit to its right; cross out the remaining digits; and then round, using the standard rule.

☐ For these errors, guide students in completing Reteach Master, p. 9.

22

Rounding Decimals

A. You can use a number line to help you round a decimal.

3.281

3.0   3.1   3.2   3.3   3.4

3.281 is between 3.2 and 3.3.
3.281 is nearer to 3.3.

So, rounded to the nearest tenth, 3.281 is 3.3.

B. To round decimals, look at the digit to the right of the rounding place. If the digit is 5 or more, round up. If the digit is less than 5, round down.

Round 57.9129 to the nearest hundredth.
57.9129   2 < 5   So, round down to 57.91.

Rounded to the nearest hundredth, 57.9129 is 57.91.

C. Round $8.479 to the nearest cent.

Rounding to the nearest cent is the same as rounding to the nearest hundredth.

$8.479 rounded to the nearest cent is $8.48.
$8.479 rounded to the nearest ten cents is $8.50.

Checkpoint Write the letter of the correct answer.

1. Round 3.2345 to the nearest thousandth.

a. 3.23   **b.** 3.2   **c.** 3.234   **(d.)** 3.235

2. Round $0.39832 to the nearest cent.

a. $0.30   **b.** $0.39   **(c.)** $0.40   **d.** $0.41

3. Round 0.00834 to the nearest ten-thousandth.

a. 0.008   **b.** 0.01   **c.** 0.0084   **(d.)** 0.0083

22   Math Reasoning, page H207

COMMON ERRORS

Answer Choice	Type of Error
■ 1a, 1b, 3a	Rounds to the incorrect place
☐ 1c, 2b	Drops digits to the right of the rounding place
☐ 2a	Drops digits to the right of the incorrect rounding place
☐ 2d	Rounds money incorrectly
■ 3b, 3c	Rounds down to the incorrect place and rounds down again

---

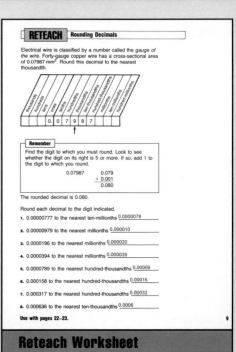

RETEACH   Rounding Decimals

Electrical wire is classified by a number called the *gauge of the wire*. Forty-gauge copper wire has a cross-sectional area of 0.07987 mm². Round this decimal to the nearest thousandth.

0 . 0 7 9 8 7

Remember
Find the digit to which you must round. Look to see whether the digit on its right is 5 or more. If so, add 1 to the digit to which you round.

0.07987   0.079
              + 0.001
                0.080

The rounded decimal is 0.080.

Round each decimal to the digit indicated.

1. 0.00000777 to the nearest ten-millionths 0.0000078

2. 0.00000979 to the nearest millionths 0.000010

3. 0.0000196 to the nearest millionths 0.000020

4. 0.0000394 to the nearest millionths 0.000039

5. 0.0000789 to the nearest hundred-thousandths 0.00008

6. 0.000158 to the nearest hundred-thousandths 0.00016

7. 0.000317 to the nearest hundred-thousandths 0.00032

8. 0.000636 to the nearest ten-thousandths 0.0006

Use with pages 22–23.   9

Reteach Worksheet

Round to the nearest whole number.

1. 0.478
0

2. 136.8
137

3. 4.5455
5

4. 0.864
1

Round to the nearest tenth or to the nearest 10 cents.

5. 7.145
7.1

6. $0.5692
$0.60

7. 8.3512
8.4

8. $9.46052
$9.50

Round to the nearest hundredth or to the nearest cent.

9. $4.285
$4.29

10. 0.01562
0.02

11. 6.8995
6.90

12. $13.899
$13.90

Round to the nearest thousandth.

13. 0.00562
0.006

14. 0.41899
0.419

15. 4.27459
4.275

16. 0.78105
0.781

17. 2.35363
2.354

Round to the nearest ten-thousandth.

18. 1.44883
1.4488

19. 0.96455
0.9646

20. 6.83114
6.8311

21. 6.04593
6.0459

22. 72.998333
72.9983

Round to the nearest hundred-thousandth.

23. 0.007359
0.00736

24. 42.614212
42.61421

25. 0.593004
0.59300

26. 0.000941
0.00094

Solve.

27. The measurement used for water depth in Norway is called a **farn**. Converted to feet, this is 6.176 ft. Round this number to the nearest hundredth. **6.18 ft**

28. The **vadem** is the unit used to measure water depth in the Netherlands. Converted to feet, this is 5.905 ft. Round this number to the nearest hundredth. **5.91 ft**

29. The highest waterfall in the world is Angel Falls in Venezuela, at 3,212 ft. The highest waterfall in the United States is Ribbon Falls, at 1,612 ft. How much higher is Angel Falls than Ribbon Falls?
1,600 ft

NUMBER SENSE

When estimating with decimals, the important digits are right after the decimal point. The other digits are for precision.

Each number in the box is between 0 and 1. Find the three decimals

0.01	0.5027
0.4537	0.49
0.02	0.113
0.976	0.9537
	0.9

1. closest to 1.
0.976; 0.9537; 0.9

2. closest to 0.5.
0.4537; 0.49; 0.5027

3. closest to 0.
0.01; 0.113; 0.02

Classwork/Homework, page H11

23

ASSIGNMENT GUIDE

Basic: 1–29 o, NS

Average: 2–26 e, 27–29, NS

Extended: 1–25 o, 27–29, NS

Resources
Practice, p. 11   Class/Home, p. H11
Reteach, p. 9   Reasoning, p. H207
Enrich, p. 11

Exercise Analysis

1–4   Round to the nearest whole number

5–8   Round to the nearest tenth or the nearest ten cents

9–12   Round to the nearest hundredth or to the nearest cent

13–17   Round to the nearest thousandth

18–22   Round to the nearest ten-thousandth

23–26   Round to the nearest hundred-thousandth

27–29   Skill applications

You may wish to allow students to use calculators for some of these exercises.

Number Sense

These exercises encourage students to estimate decimals by looking at the digit that is right after the decimal point.

FOLLOW-UP ACTIVITIES

 MATH CONNECTION (Science)

The length of a year for any planet in our solar system depends on the time it takes that planet to complete one revolution around the sun. This time is typically measured in Earth days. For each of the planets listed below, have students find the length of its year rounded to the nearest whole number.

Venus 224.70 days (225 d); Earth 365.26 days (365 d); Jupiter 4,332.59 days (4,333 d); Saturn 10,759.2 days (10,759 d)

MATH CONNECTION (Consumer)
Explain to students that they can use rounding to the nearest dollar to estimate the total bill at a store or restaurant. If the bill were $13.75 for a lobster, $1.55 for soup, $1.15 for mineral water, $2.05 for dessert, and $1.32 for tax, a reasonable estimate for the total would be $14 + $2 + $1 + $2 + $1 = $20. Have students write sample bills, exchange them, and then estimate the total amounts.

COMING UP
No standing in line at this bank!

Objective: To use information from the Infobank

Warm-Up

Have students complete the following exercises.

2,716	18,291	91,820	4,519
− 1,845	+ 3,782	− 65,495	+ 992
(871)	(22,073)	(26,325)	(5,511)

GETTING STARTED

For each question below, have students write the source in which they might be able to find the requested information.
1. What is the capital city of Uruguay? (geography book, a map, an atlas, an encyclopedia, geography teacher)
2. What was the closing average of the stock market yesterday? (newspaper, radio or television news broadcast, stockbroker)
3. What are the main ingredients in hollandaise sauce? (a cookbook or a cook)
4. What is the secret ingredient in your Aunt Anna's hollandaise sauce? (Aunt Anna)
5. How tall is the tallest building in the United States? (almanac, record book)

Ask for many different ideas on each piece of requested information. Do not discourage any reasonable suggestion. In particular, do not discourage human sources, particularly knowledgeable ones. Emphasize the importance of using sources that are up to date; for example, an old almanac might not be a good source for Question 5.

TEACHING THE LESSON

The ability to use outside resources to solve problems is a crucial skill.

Students must approach problems with the realization that all needed information may not be supplied. In approaching a problem students must find what is being asked for, determine what information is needed, and then see if that information is supplied. If not, outside sources are needed. This lesson's use of the Infobank familiarizes students with determining needed data and using outside sources to find that data.

Questions: The question in the example will be easily understood by most students. Point out that the question assumes that Dr. Carter prefers the vegetable that has more protein.

Tools: This problem is one of comparison: one amount is being compared to another. Guide students to see that subtraction is the appropriate operation. (To find how much larger one amount is than another, subtract the smaller from the larger.) Re-

---

QUESTIONS	TOOLS	SOLUTIONS	CHECKS

PROBLEM SOLVING
Using Outside Sources, Including the Infobank

Sometimes the information you need to solve a problem is not given in the problem itself. You can often go to books, magazines, newspapers, Infobanks, or other data sources to find the information you need.

> At a restaurant, Dr. Carter can choose peas or broccoli as a side dish. If each serving is 1 cup, which vegetable will provide her with more protein?

You could answer this question if you knew how much protein was contained in 1 cup of each vegetable. Here are the steps you should take to find the information you need.

___ **1.** Find a source that might have the information you need. To answer this question, you might use an almanac, an encyclopedia, or a book about health and nutrition.

___ **2.** To find the page you need, look in the table of contents or in the index.

___ **3.** If the source does not have the information, try another source.

To answer the question, you must know how much protein a cup of each vegetable contains. Look at the Infobank on page 473 to find the information you need.

When you have the information, answer the question.

There are 8.6 grams of protein in a cup of peas.
There are 4.8 grams of protein in a cup of broccoli.
3.8 more grams in 1 cup of peas

$8.6 > 4.8$

Dr. Carter will receive more grams of protein if she orders peas.

24

---

mind students to examine measurements carefully; for example, the protein listing of one food may be given in grams per cup, while another listing may be given in grams per ounce. To make valid comparisons, all measurements must be given in the same units. You may wish to discuss with the class how to read the time lines on page 476 if you are going to assign Exercise 9.

Solutions: Remind students to use care in finding data. Often, similar data is listed side-by-side. Sometimes, data looking like that which is desired may be found, but it may vary in some important way; for example, the Infobank on page 478 lists six of the tallest buildings in the United States, but not *the* six tallest.

Remind students to check carefully that the data they have found is in fact the data they need to solve the problem.

Checks: Since many of these exercises are comparison problems, have students make sure that the larger and the smaller of two quantities have not been confused. Students can also use addition to check subtraction problems and subtraction to check addition problems.

Would you need a reference source to answer each question? Write *yes* or *no*.

1. In a hospital kitchen, the cook prepares two 1-cup servings of corn and three 1-cup servings of okra. What is the total amount of carbohydrates contained in these servings? **yes**

2. Dana has 1 cup of celery and 1 cup of peas. Peas contain 8.6 grams of protein per cup, and celery contains 1.2 grams. How much protein does Dana have? **no**

Solve each problem. Use the Infobank on pages 473–478 if you need additional information.

3. Earl is visiting Australia. He rented a car and drove from Sydney to Dubbo and then to Orange. How many kilometers did he drive? **244 kilometers**

4. The Nile River is the longest river in the world. The Yangtze is 578 miles shorter. How long is the Yangtze River? **3,602 miles**

5. The Gateway Arch in St. Louis is the tallest monument built in the United States. How much shorter is it than the tallest office building with mast in the United States? **929 ft**

6. Eleni buys one pound of fiber rush. She needs 135 feet for a basket she plans to weave and 85 feet for the lid. Will she have enough fiber rush? **yes**

7. Which mineral has the greatest specific gravity: magnesite, olivine, graphite, or barite? **barite**

8. Wilt Chamberlain scored 2,649 points in 1966. How many more points did he score in 1962? **1,380**

9. The city of Geneva was originally settled by soldiers from the Roman Empire. How many years passed between the founding of Rome and the founding of Geneva? **703 years**

10. Ferdinand's minimum daily requirement of protein is 40 grams. His intake so far today has been 10 grams at breakfast and 14 grams at lunch. If he has a serving of Heidi's Hearty Chicken Noodle Soup for dinner, will he meet his minimum requirement? **no**

11. Nina made a special salad for her friends. The salad consisted of broccoli, celery, cauliflower and green beans. Compare and order the vegetables, from the least to the greatest, by the amount of protein. **celery, green beans, cauliflower and broccoli**

12. Dave drove from Coolgardie to Port Augusta in 2 days. Mike drove from Nullarbor to Dubbo in 2 days. Who drove the most kilometers in 2 days? How many more kilometers did he drive? **Mike; 135 more kilometers**

Classwork/Homework, page H12

ASSIGNMENT GUIDE

Basic: 1–7

Average: 2–9

Extended: 5–12

Resources
Practice, p. 12   Class/Home, p. H12
Enrich, p. 12

Exercise Analysis

1–2   Determine whether a reference source is needed to solve a problem

3–12   Use information from the Infobank to solve a problem

FOLLOW-UP ACTIVITIES

PROBLEM SOLVING

Write the following problem on the chalkboard. Have students use the Infobank to solve the problem.

Sally can choose between eating a mixture of vegetables that contains 1 cup of peas and $\frac{1}{2}$ cup of spinach, and eating one serving of Heidi's Hearty Chicken Noodle Soup. Which of these will give Sally more protein? how much more, to the nearest gram? (soup, 1 g more) Which will give Sally more carbohydrates? how much more, to the nearest gram? (vegetables, 11 g more)

CALCULATOR

Materials: 1 calculator per student

Write the following problems on the chalkboard. Have students use a calculator to solve them.

● Between 1947 and 1984 three basketball players were NBA scoring leaders for exactly three years. Which of them scored the most points in his three years as scoring leader, and how many points were scored? (Bob McAdoo; 7,519 points)

● Between 1947 and 1984, four players were scoring leaders for the same number of years. Which of these players scored the fewest points in his years as scoring leader? *Hint:* One of these players changed his name during his career. (Paul Arizin)

● Between 1947 and 1984, only one player was scoring leader exactly four times. Who was this player, and how many points did he score during those years? (George Gervin; 9,733 points)

COMING UP

Sums and differences, from the front

PRACTICE   Using Outside Sources Including the Infobank

The chart below shows some famous ocean voyages, the ships that made them, and the distance and duration of the voyages.

Year	From	To	Ship	Distance (Nautical miles)	Duration
1840	Halifax	Liverpool	*Britannia*	2,610	9 days 21 hours
1854	Liverpool	New York	*Baltic*	3,037	9 days 17 hours
1928	San Pedro	Honolulu	*USS Lexington*	2,226	3 days 1 hour
1944	Halifax	Vancouver	*St. Roch*	7,295	86 days
1950	Japan	San Francisco	*USS Boxer*	5,000	7 days 19 hours
1962	New York	Capetown	*African Comet*	6,786	12 days 16 hours

Do you need the Infobank above to solve the problems? Write *yes* or *no*.

1. The *Brittania* was the first Cunard liner. Cunard was named after Sir Samuel Cunard, who was born in 1787 and died in 1865. How many years did he live? **no**

2. The *St. Roch* was the first vessel to complete the Northwest Passage in one season. How many more miles was its voyage than the voyage of the *Brittania* from Halifax to Liverpool? **yes**

Solve. Use the Infobank above for any additional information you need.

3. In 1846, the *Yorkshire* traveled from Liverpool to New York in 16 days. How much less time did the *Baltic* take for the same voyage? **6 days 7 hours**

4. The *Yorkshire* covered 3,150 miles on its voyage. How many more miles was this than the *Baltic's* voyage between the same places? **113 miles**

5. In 1970 a ship sailed from Capetown to Liverpool via New York, and followed the courses taken by the *African Comet* and the *Baltic.* How many miles was the voyage? **9,823**

6. Write the ships in order from the voyage that took the longest amount of time to the voyage that took the shortest amount of time. **St. Roch, African Comet, Brittania, Baltic, Boxer, Lexington**

7. Is the order for question 6 the same as the order of the ships according to the distance of the voyages? **no**

8. In 1959, Max Conrad flew 5,000 miles solo from Chicago to Rome. It took him 1 day 10 hours. How much longer did it take the *USS Boxer* to cover the same distance? **6 days 9 hours**

12   Use after pages 24–25.

Practice Worksheet

ENRICH   Problem Solving

You have been hired by Dr. Knowitall to supply answers to several questions. Dr. Knowitall has three infobanks: a dictionary, an almanac, and an encyclopedia. You probably have these infobanks in your classroom, too. For each question, tell which infobank you would use, and then use the infobank to answer each question. The answer to a question may be found in more than one infobank.

1. How many more teenagers, 12–17 years old, watch evening situation comedies than watch evening information programs? Use information from the Nielsen ratings. **almanac; 1,600 more**

2. What is the product of the number of syllables in the word *Aristotelian* and the number of syllables in *arithmetically?* **dictionary; 36**

3. What is the difference in altitude between the highest city and the lowest town in the United States? **almanac or encyclopedia; 10,384 feet**

4. What is the cost of sending a 4-pound package via parcel post to U.S. Postal Zone 4? **almanac; answers will vary depending on year; $2.02 (as of '85)**

5. What is the difference between the distance to which the 16-pound shot was thrown by the 1984 Olympic winner and the distance the shot was thrown by the 1920 Olympic winner? **almanac or encyclopedia; 21 ft, 1 7/8 in.**

6. How many months elapsed between the Battle of Montreal and the Battle of Bennington in the Revolutionary War? **encyclopedia or almanac; 21 months**

7. What is the difference in area (square miles) between Kenya and Kentucky? **encyclopedia or almanac; 183.686 mi²**

8. How many words begin with the series *arith?* **dictionary; answers will vary.**

9. Which is the older invention, radio signals or the phonograph? **almanac or encyclopedia; phonograph**

10. How much longer is the Verrazano Bridge than the Golden Gate Bridge? **almanac or encyclopedia; 60 feet**

12   Use with pages 24–25.

Enrich Worksheet

Objectives: To estimate decimal sums and differences by using the front-end and rounding methods

Warm-Up
Have students estimate each sum or difference.
1. $3,248 + 2,442 + 78 + 4,388$ (10,000)
2. $19,472 - 11,853$ $(8,000^-)$
3. $235,691 + 2,778, + 103,885$ (340,000)
4. $87,525 - 32,111$ $(55,000^+)$

GETTING STARTED

Materials: assorted grocery items, price tags, felt-tip pens

On the tags, record the prices of an assortment of grocery items, and attach the tags to the items.

Divide the class into three groups. Assign each group a maximum amount that it can spend; for example, $5, $10, and $15. Members of each group must then decide which items to purchase without exceeding the budget assigned to them and without using paper or calculators. After the decisions have been made, have students discuss the different strategies used to total the prices.

TEACHING THE LESSON

A. Explain that to make correctly adjusted estimates, it is important to look for decimals that group together well.

$$7.89 + 2.39 + 0.13 + 1.58$$

The initial front-end estimate is 10. When adjusting it, point out that when 0.89 and 0.13 are grouped with 0.39 and 0.58, they will make another 2. A good final estimate is 12.

B. Extend the lesson to problems that include both addition and subtraction.

$$\$72.93 + \$5.22 - \$56.28$$

(A good estimate is $22 because the whole numbers total $21 and the decimal parts group to another 1.)

Estimating Sums and Differences of Decimals

A. On Friday, it rained 2.6 inches in Yennemsville. On Saturday, it rained 2.4 inches, and on Sunday, it rained 1.7 inches. On Monday only 0.29 inches of rain fell. Did it rain more than the record of 6 inches in four days in Yennemsville?

You can answer the question without using exact computation. Estimate $2.6 + 2.4 + 1.7 + 0.29$.

Using front-end estimation

Add the whole numbers.
$$2 + 2 + 1 + 0 = 5$$

Adjust the sum.
$$\underbrace{0.6 + 0.4}_{1} + \underbrace{0.7 + 0.29}_{\text{about } 1}$$
$$5 + 1 + 1 = 7$$

Estimate: 7
$$2.6 + 2.4 + 1.7 + 0.29 > 6$$

Yes, it rained more than the record of 6 inches in a four-day period.

Rounding to the nearest whole number

Add: $2.6 + 2.4 + 1.7 + 0.29$
$$\quad\downarrow\quad\ \ \downarrow\quad\ \ \downarrow\quad\ \ \downarrow$$
$$3 + 2 + 2 + 0 = 7$$

B. Estimate $3.2195 - 2.7208$.

Using front-end estimation

Subtract the whole numbers.
$$3 - 2 = 1$$

Adjust the difference.
$0.2195 < 0.7208$. Adjust down.

Estimate: 1^-

Rounding to the nearest whole number

Subtract: $3 - 3 = 0$ ← You need a more exact estimate.

Rounding to the nearest tenth
$$3.2 - 2.7 = 0.5$$

Estimate: 0.5

Other examples:
Estimate $\$14.95 + \$6.53$.

Front end
Add the whole numbers. $\$14 + \$6 = \$20$
Adjust: $\$20 + \$1.50$
Estimate: $\$21.50$

Rounding
Add: $\$15 + \$7 = \$22$, or
$\$15.00 + \$6.50 = \$21.50$
Estimate: $\$22.00$ or $\$21.50$

Estimate $\$95.60 - \$45.75$.
Front end $9 - 4 = 5 \longrightarrow \$50$. Since $\$0.60 < \$0.75$, adjust down. Estimate: $\$50.00^-$
Rounding $\$96 - \$46 = \$50$, or $\$100 - \$50 = \$50$. Estimate: $\$50.00$

26

Math Reasoning, page H208

COMMON ERRORS

Some students make inaccurate estimates of decimal sums and differences because they misunderstand the value of the decimal.

Remediation
Present students with a list of decimals randomly ordered such as 0.92, 0.356, 0.7, 0.89, 0.0754, 0.456, 0.51, 0.052. Have students sort the decimals into 3 sets: close to 1, close to half, close to 0. Have students explain how they made their choices.

Assign Reteach Master, p. 10.

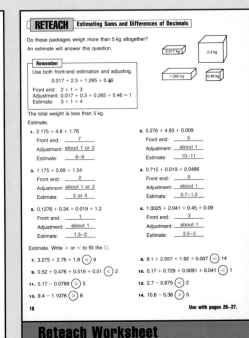

Estimate the sum.   Answers may vary. Accept any reasonable estimate.

1.	4.17 3.82 + 1.49	**2.**	15.27 2.352 + 1.3296	**3.**	0.527 0.075 0.38 + 2.9	**4.**	485.79 3.25 4.98 + 2.175
	9–10		*18–19*		*3.7–4*		*490–500*

5. $5.98 + $0.25 + $0.35 + $0.49
$6.00 – $7.00

6. 29.5 + 10.36 + 12.217
50–52

Estimate the difference.

7.	$56.27 – 43.35	**8.**	$46.95 – 12.78	**9.**	485.2 – 13.54	**10.**	7.892 – 4.7
	$13⁻		*$34⁺*		*470⁺*		*3⁺*

11. 0.3652 − 0.091286   *0.27⁺*   **12.** 9.74 − 2.195   *7⁺*   **13.** 12.0534 − 1.17
11⁻

Estimate. Write > or < for ●.

14. 0.0271 + 0.9 + 0.15 ● 1   *>*

15. 0.0594 + 0.00087 ● 0.1   *<*

16. 4.87 + 4.96 + 3.25 ● 14   *<*

17. 38.8 + 9.887 + 9.789 ● 57   *>*

18. $24.95 + $19.85 ● $46.00   *<*

19. $7.98 + $0.88 + $0.75 ● $9.00   *>*

20. 5.27 − 1.19 ● 3   *>*

21. 8.327 − 5.64 ● 3   *<*

22. 1.475 − 0.39 ● 1   *>*

23. 0.815 − 0.0527 ● 0.5   *>*

24. 0.09 − 0.0856 ● 0.01   *<*

25. $30.65 − $14.89 ● $25.00   *<*

Estimate to solve.

26. On Tuesday, barometric pressure in Yennemsville measured 29.35 in. On Wednesday, it soared to 30.23 in. Was the change in barometric pressure greater than 1 in.?   *no*

27. In Yennemsville, normal precipitation in the month of December is 5.7 inches. In January, precipitation drops to 3.4 inches. In February, 3.2 inches of rain fall. Normal precipitation for those months is 14.4 inches in New Orleans, Louisiana. Is there more or less precipitation in Yennemsville?   *less*

Classwork/Homework, page H13   **27**

ASSIGNMENT GUIDE

Basic:	1–17, 26–27
Average:	2–24 e, 26–27
Extended:	1–25 o, 26–27

Resources
Practice, p. 13   Class/Home, p. H13
Reteach, p. 10   Reasoning, p. H208
Enrich, p. 13

Exercise Analysis

1–6	Estimate a decimal sum
7–13	Estimate a decimal difference
14–25	Use > and < to estimate a decimal sum or difference
26–27	Skill applications

FOLLOW-UP ACTIVITIES

 MATH CONNECTION (Consumer)
Have students determine whether each set of price tags totals more or less than the sum indicated.

1. $4.63 ● $8.79 ● $2.39 ●
more or less than $15? (more)

2. $14.18 ● $7.12 ● $2.99 ●
more or less than $25? (less)

3. $3.56 ● $0.88 ● $1.25 ● $0.49 ●
more or less than $5? (more)

4. $1.99 ● $6.24 ● $2.78 ● $0.59 ●
more or less than $10? (more)

NUMBER SENSE (Mental Math)
Have students estimate each sum or difference mentally.

- 53.81 + 61.47 + 12.76   (126–128)
- 39.683 − 12.76   (27⁻)
- 61.240 − 36.09   (25⁺)
- 4.76 + 3.33 + 2.4 + 5.4593   (15–16)
- $123.34 − $78.65   ($45⁻)
- $6.09 + $64.07 + $7.11   ($77⁺)
- $50.14 − $33.56   ($17⁻)
- $32.33 + $12.78 − $23.41   ($21–$22)

COMING UP
Point by point

PRACTICE   Estimating Sums and Differences of Decimals

The figure shows the progress of a white-water kayak race.

Estimate and write each answer to the nearest whole number.

Note: Answers will vary. Accept any reasonable estimate.

1. How many feet did kayak *A* travel in 40 s?   *90–95 ft*

2. How many feet did kayak *B* travel in 40 s?   *110–120 ft*

3. Which kayak traveled farther in 40 s?   *kayak B*

4. How much farther did kayak *A* travel between the 40-s mark and the 50-s mark than between the 50-s mark and the 1-min mark?   *13–14 ft*

5. How many feet did kayak *B* travel between the 40-s mark and the 1-min mark?   *69–70 ft*

6. How far did kayak *B* travel in the race?   *180–190 ft*

7. How many feet did kayak *A* travel between the 40-s mark and the 1-min mark?   *80–85 ft*

8. How much farther did kayak *B* travel between the 30-s mark and the 40-s mark than between the 10-s mark and the 20-s mark?   *30–35 ft*

9. How far did kayak *A* travel in the race?   *160–180 ft*

10. The direct distance from the start to the finish line is 158.307 ft. How far out of the way did kayak *B* travel?   *25–30 ft*

Use with pages 26–27.   13

Practice Worksheet

ENRICH   Number

Ulf lives in a city that has a steady annual inflation rate of 10%. This year, Ulf has an annual salary of $15,000.00, and he wants to rent a house for $1,500.00 per year. Ulf's boss at the factory offers him two different choices that will cover four years.

Choice #1: The factory will pay Ulf's rent for the next four years, but he will *not* receive a raise in salary.
Choice #2: Ulf will receive a 5% pay raise each year, but he will pay his own rent, which increases 10% each year due to inflation.

Complete the tables below to decide which choice Ulf should take. Ulf's **net total** is the actual amount of money he will be able to spend each year.

Table A: Data for Choice #1

Year	Year 1	Year 2	Year 3	Year 4
Salary	$15,000.00	$15,000.00	$15,000.00	$15,000.00
Minus rent	− 0.00	0.00	0.00	0.00
Net total	$15,000.00	$15,000.00	$15,000.00	$15,000.00

Table B: Data for Choice #2

Year	Year 1	Year 2	Year 3	Year 4
Salary	$15,000.00	$15,750.00	$16,537.50	$17,364.38
Minus rent	− 1,500.00	1,650.00	1,815.00	1,996.50
Net total	$13,500.00	$14,100.00	$14,722.50	$15,367.88

1. List each year in which Ulf's net total is greater under Choice #1 than it is under Choice #2.   *1, 2, 3*

2. Which choice do you think Ulf should take? Explain why.   *Choice #1; it is more profitable to him.*

3. Estimate to find the sum of Ulf's net totals over a period of four years in both Choice #1 and Choice #2.   *$60,000.00; $58,000.00*

Use with pages 26–27.   13

Enrich Worksheet

Objective: To add decimals

Warm-Up

To prepare students for adding decimals, have them practice adding amounts of money.

$2.97	$13.75	$252.67
+ 0.45	+ 10.92	+ 3.99
($3.42)	($24.67)	($256.66)

GETTING STARTED

One technique used by good estimators is that of searching for compatible numbers. For example, in $142 + 33 + 55 + 70 + 290 \approx 600$, the sums of $33 + 70$ and $42 + 55$ and 90 by itself are all close to or compatible with 100.

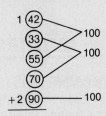

It is then easy to add $100 + 100 + 100$ to the 100 and 200 left in the hundreds place of 142 and 290.

Have students find compatible numbers to estimate the following sums.

$4,285 + 2,725 + 969 + 3,012$ (11,000)
$7,860 + 4,203 + 400 + 6,389$ (19,000)

TEACHING THE LESSON

Relate the Getting Started activity to adding decimals. In the example, $0.35 + 0.31 + 0.48 \approx 1.00$. So, a reasonable estimate of the average snowfall would be $7 + 10 + 5 + 1$ or 23 cm.

Extend the instruction by having students write the following examples in vertical form and find the sum.

$2.6 + 0.034 + 14.83$ (17.464)
$3.856 + 468.2 + 91.0003$ (563.0563)

This exercise should illustrate the importance of aligning the decimal points.

Checkpoint

The chart lists the common errors students make in adding decimal numbers.

Correct Answers: 1a, 2c, 3b

Remediation

■ Students should line up the decimal point in each addend and then write zeros as needed. Encourage students to write a decimal point in the answer before adding.

☐ For these errors, guide students in completing Reteach Master, p. 11.

Adding Decimals

The average monthly snowfall in White Falls for December, January, and February is listed in the chart at the right. What is the total snowfall for these three months?

To add decimals, line up the decimal points, add as for whole numbers, and place the decimal point in the sum.

Month	Average snowfall
December	7.35 cm
January	10.31 cm
February	5.48 cm

Estimate the sum before you compute.

$$
\begin{array}{r}
7.35 \rightarrow \quad 7 \\
10.31 \rightarrow \quad 10 \\
+ \; 5.48 \rightarrow + \; 5 \\
\hline
22
\end{array}
$$

Add. Regroup if necessary.

$$
\begin{array}{r}
1 \; 1 \quad 1 \\
7.35 \\
10.31 \\
+ \; 5.48 \\
\hline
23.14
\end{array}
$$

The total snowfall for these three months is 23.14 cm.

The answer is reasonably close to the estimate.

Other examples:

Add $13 + 1.643 + 0.09 + 3.1006$.

Write zeros in the remaining places to line up decimal places.

$$
\begin{array}{r}
13.0000 \\
1.6430 \\
0.0900 \\
+ \; 3.1006 \\
\hline
17.8336
\end{array}
$$

Write zeros as needed to line up the decimal places.

Add $\$14.29 + \$3.17$.

$$
\begin{array}{r}
\$14.29 \\
+ \; 3.17 \\
\hline
\$17.46
\end{array}
$$

Checkpoint Write the letter of the correct answer.

Add.

1. $0.092 + 2.314 + 3.185$

  a. 5.591   **b.** 6.419   **c.** 14.699   **d.** 5591

2. $0.48 + 1.9 + 0.005 + 2$

  a. 0.74   **b.** 01.585   **c.** 4.385   **d.** 4385

3. $13.6 + 0.08 + 6 + 0.1945$

  a. 14.4745   **b.** 19.8745   **c.** 20.5945   **d.** 198745

Math Reasoning, page H208

COMMON ERRORS

Answer Choice	Type of Error
■ 1b, 1c, 2b, 3a, 3c	Misaligns one addend
☐ 2a	Aligns the digit at the right
■ 1d, 2d, 3d	Omits the decimal point

| RETEACH | Adding Decimals |

The school computer keeps exact records of the amount of time each student works at the terminal. This week, Mary worked at the terminal for 12.35 min, 5.2 min, 10 min, 17.34 min, and 22.6 min. For how many minutes exactly did Mary use the computer this week?

Remember

Before you add decimals, line up their decimal points. Write additional zeros if you need them.

$$
\begin{array}{r}
12.35 \\
5.20 \\
10.00 \\
17.34 \\
+ \; 22.60 \\
\hline
67.49
\end{array}
$$

Mary used the computer for 67.49 minutes this week.

Add.

1. $4.3 + 2.91$ _7.21_   2. $43.6 + 2.95$ _46.55_

3. $168.2 + 4.73$ _172.93_   4. $5.339 + 14.52$ _19.859_

5. $1.454 + 2.98$ _4.434_   6. $18.304 + 76.83$ _95.134_

7. $10.76 + .18 + 4.2654 + 88.005$ _103.2104_   8. $68 + 0.056 + 0.0072 + 3.4$ _71.4632_

9. $8.46 + 5.2 + 0.845 + 0.234$ _14.739_   10. $1.65 + 2.0735 + 0.484$ _4.2075_

11. $1.125 + 0.385 + 1.135 + 0.04$ _2.685_   12. $0.625 + 0.45 + 0.95 + 0.625$ _2.65_

13. $0.3 + 0.04 + 0.005 + 0.0006$ _0.3456_   14. $5 + 5.1 + 5.12 + 5.123$ _20.343_

Solve.

15. In four days, Pedro used the computer for 5 min, 6.2 min, 4.25 min, and 3.175 min. For how many minutes did he use the computer altogether? _18.625_

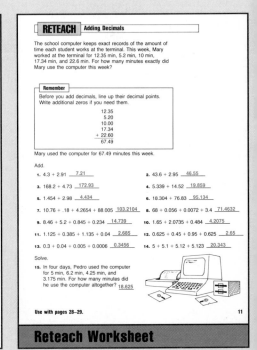

Use with pages 28–29.   11

Reteach Worksheet

Add.

1.	0.62 + 0.27 0.89	**2.**	4.59 + 3.34 7.93	**3.**	65.721 + 28.248 93.969	**4.**	307.924 + 738.018 1,045.942	**5.**	$18,951.36 + 55,008.29 $73,959.65
6.	6.43 + 8.912 15.342	**7.**	38.924 + 6.08 45.004	**8.**	74.21 + 808.4627 882.6727	**9.**	7,412.6 + 99.439 7,512.039	**10.**	$ 890.08 + 4,267.33 $5,157.41
11.	0.361 6.452 + 0.009 6.822	**12.**	35.84 77.6 + 142.096 255.536	**13.**	4.5236 87 + 3.6115 95.1351	**14.**	3.426 9.211 0.904 + 0.270 13.811	**15.**	96.824 3.57 66.9 + 458.023 625.317
16.	11,740 + 692.35 12,432.35	**17.**	$ 32.45 719.80 + 6.34 $758.59	**18.**	$3,430.88 800.91 56.03 + 4,620.74 $8,908.56	**19.**	0.0054 0.02 0.6977 + 44.36 45.0831	**20.**	46,512.3 8.4 4,280 + 27,095.9 77,896.6

21. 67 + 754.8 + 122.094
943.894

22. $768.40 + $7.11 + $0.68 + $12.47
$788.66

23. $42.50 + $9,737 + $64.27
$9,843.77

24. 82,926 + 54.85 + 36.7
83,017.55

25. 0.0239 + 12.3047 + 8.4009
20.7295

26. $31.40 + $0.08 + $779.66 + $11.54
$822.68

Solve.

27. In Perdale, there was a four-day snowstorm. The following daily snow accumulations resulted: 13.25 cm, 14.8 cm, 11.64 cm, and 9.74 cm. How much snow accumulated? 49.43 cm

28. The lowest barometer reading for one day was 756.41 mm. The highest reading for the same day was 2.29 mm more. What was the highest reading for the day?
758.70 mm

29. A hailstone measures 5.34 cm in diameter. Another one measures 3.28 cm in diameter. Round these figures to the nearest centimeter.
5 cm; 3 cm

30. Look in your local newspaper for precipitation figures, and find the total precipitation for one week.
Answers will vary.

ANOTHER LOOK

Write the decimal that has the greatest value.

1. 4.15, 4.296, 4.612 4.612

2. 16.81, 16.9, 16.777 16.9

3. 843.04, 840.43, 843.039 843.04

4. 0.3027, 0.0336, 0.3035 0.3035

Classwork/Homework, page H14   More Practice, page H195 **29**

Classwork/Homework, page H14 · More Practice, page H195

ASSIGNMENT GUIDE

Basic: 1–12, 14–30 e, AL 1–4

Average: 1–12, 13–29 o, AL 1–4

Extended: 10–30, AL 1–4

Resources
Practice, p. 14   Class/Home, p. H14
Reteach, p. 11   More Practice, p. H195
Enrich, p. 14   Reasoning, p. H208

Exercise Analysis
1–10   Add decimals with two addends
11–26   Mixed practice to four addends
27–29   Skill applications
30   Problem formulation

You may wish to allow students to use calculators for some of these exercises.

Another Look
These exercises review comparing and ordering decimals.

FOLLOW-UP ACTIVITIES

PROBLEM SOLVING
A pizza parlor has the following menu.

	Small	Medium	Large
Cheese pizza	$3.89	$5.25	$8.36
Each topping	$0.50	$0.60	$0.90
Thick crust	$0.55	$0.85	$1.50
Deluxe pizza	$6.15	$8.25	$12.95

Refer to the table to find the cost of
• a large pizza with onions. ($9.26)
• a medium pizza with thick crust, sausage, and mushrooms. ($7.30)

Pose related problems such as the following.

A group of students has a total of $13.50 to spend. They want one small deluxe pizza and one thick-crust medium pizza with pepperoni and green peppers. Do they have enough money to buy both? (yes)

REINFORCEMENT
Have each student write a 6-digit decimal to the thousandths place. Then have each student write a 5-digit number with a tenths place and four whole-number places. Have students add and place the decimal point correctly.

COMING UP
AU's!

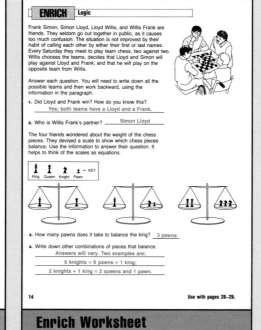

PRACTICE Adding Decimals

Add. Check your answer by estimating.

1.	0.6927 + 0.836 1.5287	**2.**	0.1159 0.5367 + 0.2863 0.9389	**3.**	5.651 89.261 87.2426 + 23.1546 205.3092	**4.**	$70.11 + 25.62 $95.73
5.	0.6966 0.5125 + 0.3957 1.6048	**6.**	45.4789 + 46.2787 91.7576	**7.**	$29.03 76.27 61.58 + 10.42 $177.30	**8.**	0.3978 0.302 0.9564 + 0.48 2.1362
9.	$26.87 + 59.47 $86.34	**10.**	73.468 84.1951 6.1828 + 0.254 164.0999	**11.**	71.8132 20.746 + 61.9367 154.4959	**12.**	0.605 + 0.8183 1.4233
13.	0.143 0.9764 0.7341 + 0.17 2.0235	**14.**	$6,222.03 931.91 + 5.15 $7,159.09	**15.**	0.3156 + 0.7223 1.0379	**16.**	$50.65 5.49 + 0.75 $56.89
17.	63.2108 + 1.367 64.5778	**18.**	8.269 4.8265 87.923 + 3.7442 104.7627	**19.**	0.4727 8.285 + 0.9864 9.7441	**20.**	$531.93 360.28 35.68 + 4.86 $932.75
21.	3.7575 4.7014 + 2.8869 11.3458	**22.**	75.6743 0.8 + 4.62 81.0943	**23.**	$5,794.84 + 885.72 $6,680.56	**24.**	86.3726 69.4605 64.1016 + 94.2732 314.2079

25. 0.9835 + 0.4978 = __1.4813__

26. 0.7452 + 0.6173 = __1.3625__

27. 6.492 + 9.977 = __16.469__

28. 4.394 + 6.5653 = __10.9593__

29. 4.385 + 58.923 = __63.308__

30. 7.4921 + 1.7796 = __9.2717__

14   Use with pages 28–29.

Practice Worksheet

ENRICH Logic

Frank Simon, Simon Lloyd, Lloyd Willis, and Willis Frank are friends. They seldom go out together in public, as it causes too much confusion. The situation is not improved by their habit of calling each other by either their first or last names. Every Saturday they meet to play team chess, two against two. Willis chooses the teams, decides that Lloyd and Simon will play against Lloyd and Frank, and that he will play on the opposite team from Willis.

Answer each question. You will need to write down all the possible teams and then work backward, using the information in the paragraph.

1. Did Lloyd and Frank win? How do you know this?
Yes; both teams have a Lloyd and a Frank.

2. Who is Willis Frank's partner? __Simon Lloyd__

The four friends wondered about the weight of the chess pieces. They devised a scale to show which chess pieces balance. Use the information to answer their question. It helps to think of the scales as equations.

♚ ♛ ♞ ♟ ← KEY
King Queen Knight Pawn

3. How many pawns does it take to balance the king? 3 pawns

4. Write down other combinations of pieces that balance.
Answers will vary. Two examples are:
6 knights = 9 pawns + 1 king;
2 knights + 1 king = 2 queens and 1 pawn.

14   Use with pages 28–29.

Enrich Worksheet

Objective: To subtract decimals

Warm-Up
Have students review subtracting amounts of money.

$12.20	$73.77	$6,627.91
− 8.92	− 15.02	− 1,956.78
($ 3.28)	($58.75)	($4,671.13)

GETTING STARTED

Write the following examples on the chalkboard.

750,000	75,000	7,500	750
− 250,000	− 25,000	− 2,500	− 250
(500,000)	(50,000)	(5,000)	(500)

Have volunteers subtract the four examples. Emphasize the pattern of the differences by pointing out that each difference has decreased by a power of 10.

TEACHING THE LESSON

Students may be interested to know that *astronomical units* are based on the average distance between Earth and the sun: 149.6 million kilometers, or about 93 million miles. The distance from Earth to the sun is 1.000 *AU*. The *AU*'s of all other planets have been calculated on the basis of Earth's distance from the sun.

Emphasize the importance of aligning the decimal points and the need for writing zeros by having students complete the following examples.

8.06	12
− 0.2795	− 0.583
(7.7805)	(11.417)

Checkpoint
The chart lists the common errors students make in subtracting decimals.

Correct Answers: 1d, 2c, 3a

Remediation
■ Have students line up the decimal points before subtracting and then equalize the number of decimal places in both numbers by adding zeros where necessary. Have them locate the decimal point in the answer and then subtract as they would subtract whole numbers.

☐ For these errors, guide the students in completing Reteach Master, p. 12.

Subtracting Decimals

Astronomers use a unit of measure called an **astronomical unit (AU)** to describe the distance of a planet from the sun. The chart lists the distances from the sun to some planets. How much farther away from the sun is Venus than Mercury?

Planet	Distance from Sun (Astronomical units)
Mercury	0.387
Venus	0.723
Mars	1.523
Uranus	19.247
Pluto	39.641

To subtract decimals, line up the decimal points, subtract as for whole numbers, and place the decimal point in the difference. Check by adding.

	Add to check.
0.7 2 3	0.336
− 0.3 8 7	+ 0.387
0.3 3 6	0.723

Venus is 0.336 astronomical units farther away.

Other examples:

Subtract 7.34 − 3.1986.

	Write zeros as needed.
7.3 4 0 0	
− 3.1 9 8 6	
4.1 4 1 4	

Check by estimating.

7.34	→	7
− 3.1986	→	− 3
		4

Subtract $53.84 − $31.78.

$53.84
− 31.78
$22.06

Checkpoint Write the letter of the correct answer.

Subtract.

1. 0.863 − 0.065   **a.** 0.808   **b.** 798   **c.** 0.928   **(d.)** 0.798

2. 5.039 − 0.002432   **a.** 5.037568   **b.** 4.7962   **(c.)** 5.036568   **d.** 5.041432

3. 16 − 3.482   **(a.)** 12.518   **b.** 13.482   **c.** 13.518   **d.** 12.628

30   Math Reasoning, page H208

COMMON ERRORS

Answer Choice	Type of Error
☐ 1a, 2a, 3c, 3d	Fails to regroup correctly
☐ 1c	Adds instead of subtracts
■ 1b	Omits the decimal point
■ 2b	Misaligns the second term
☐ 2d	Adds and subtracts
☐ 3b	Subtracts whole numbers

The class treasury had a balance of $362.58. The decorating committee spent $18.84 for the class party.
How much is left in the class treasury?

Remember
Before you subtract, line up the decimal points of both numbers. Regroup where necessary.

$362.58	$3 6 2 . 5 8
− 18.84	− 1 8 . 8 4
	$3 4 3 . 7 4

There is $343.74 in the class treasury.

Subtract.

1. 85.2	2. 86.33	3. 622.19	4. 3.428
− 14.6	− 17.02	− 111.99	− 1.376
70.6	69.31	510.2	2.052

5. 0.451	6. 8.562	7. 0.304	8. 76.48
− 0.363	− 8.459	− 0.1062	− 12.56
0.088	0.103	0.1978	63.92

Subtract.

9. 562.78 − 156.82 405.96   10. 56 − 22.17 33.83

11. 0.0432 − 0.0351 0.0081   12. 14.7 − 1.835 12.865

13. 14 − 0.063 13.937   14. 1.00452 − 0.0000392 1.0044808

Solve.

15. Michelle had $716.84 in her bank account. She wrote a check for $18.92. How much was left in her account? $697.92

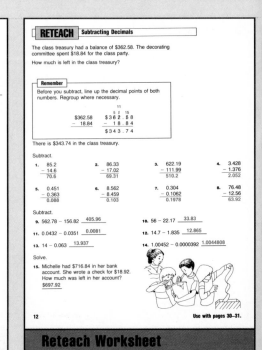

12   Use with pages 30–31.

Reteach Worksheet

Subtract.

1.	57.7 − 16.2 41.5	**2.**	84.32 − 21.28 63.04	**3.**	643.49 − 128.64 514.85	**4.**	0.842 − 0.638 0.204	**5.**	7.4291 − 3.7461 3.6830
6.	0.476 − 0.32 0.156	**7.**	0.9611 − 0.472 0.4891	**8.**	0.3074 − 0.024 0.2834	**9.**	0.53 − 0.498 0.032	**10.**	0.8004 − 0.239 0.5614
11.	41.53 − 33.4 8.13	**12.**	$437.92 − 8.26 $429.66	**13.**	$7,196 − 320.62 $6,875.38	**14.**	18.548 − 9.4726 9.0754	**15.**	3,410.065 − 98.47 3,311.595

16. $486.54 − $329.80
$156.74

17. 6,840 − 329.781
6,510.219

18. 270.006 − 41.293
228.713

19. 671 − 456.082
214.918

20. 0.294 − 0.2507
0.0433

21. $816 − $747.28
$68.72

22. 100.849 − 3.4082 97.4408

23. 1.001826 − 0.000099 1.001727

Solve.

24. Mercury is the closest planet to the sun, and Pluto is the most distant. How much farther away is Pluto? Use the chart on the previous page.
39.254 AU

25. The density of Saturn is 0.619. The density of Jupiter is 0.631 more than Saturn. What is the density of Jupiter? 1.250

26. *Eccentricity* defines the shape of the orbit of a planet. The eccentricity of Mars is 0.093379, and the eccentricity of Venus is 0.006787. What is the difference between their eccentricities?
0.086592

★27. Use the chart on the previous page to solve. Which planet is closer to Venus: Mercury or Mars? How much closer?
Mercury is 0.464 AU closer.

NUMBER SENSE

The decimal point in each number is missing. Insert the decimal point to make the number reasonable.

1. Gerry gets $475 per hour for mowing lawns. $4.75

2. The deposit is $10 on each soda bottle. $0.10

3. It took 1112 gallons of fuel to fill the car's fuel tank. 11.12

4. Carlo weighed 1236 pounds on his 13th birthday.
123.6

Classwork/Homework, page H15 · More Practice, page H196 **31**

ASSIGNMENT GUIDE

Basic:	1–18, 24–26, NS
Average:	1–17 o, 24–27, NS
Extended:	6–14 e, 16–27, NS

Resources
Practice, p. 15 Class/Home, p. H15
Reteach, p. 12 More Practice, p. H196
Enrich, p. 15 Reasoning, p. H208

Exercise Analysis
1–5 Subtract nonragged decimals
6–10 Subtract ragged decimals
11–23 Mixed practice
24–27 Skill applications

You may wish to allow students to use calculators for some of these exercises.

Number Sense
This activity encourages students to make reasonable estimates using their common knowledge of everyday situations.

FOLLOW-UP ACTIVITIES

 MATH CONNECTION (Consumer)
Making change often involves subtracting decimals from whole numbers.

Tell students that they have a $10 bill. Have them determine the amount of change they would receive for each purchase.
- a hammer for $5.79 ($4.21)
- a box of nails for $1.32 ($8.68)
- a saw for $9.37 ($0.63)
- a combination lock for $2.89 ($7.11)
- a roll of tape for $.84 ($9.16)

CALCULATOR
Have students use calculators to solve problems similar to those suggested above. Have them use prices advertised in newspapers. Students should write the problems and the answers and then exchange papers. Encourage them to estimate mentally in order to check one another's work for errors.

COMING UP
Wrapping it up

PRACTICE	Subtracting Decimals

Subtract. Check your answer by estimating.

1.	17.5082 − 12.6201 4.8881	**2.**	28.7988 − 14.1648 14.6340	**3.**	9.5102 − 9.3928 0.1174	**4.**	$39.28 − 5.58 $33.70
5.	74.5897 − 30.5261 44.0636	**6.**	87 − 7.613 79.387	**7.**	$3.98 − 2.10 $1.88	**8.**	67.9105 − 17.0366 50.8739
9.	51.5364 − 5.7 45.8364	**10.**	89.4739 − 51.3134 38.1605	**11.**	65.666 − 8.3425 57.3235	**12.**	99.7057 − 70.7603 28.9454
13.	3.8203 − 1.676 2.1443	**14.**	6.4977 − 1.8483 4.6494	**15.**	44.8889 − 10.0428 34.8461	**16.**	7.059 − 2.6153 4.4437

17. 89.4739 − 51.3134 = _38.1605_

18. 57.5240 − 7 = _50.5240_

What is purple and 5,000 miles long? Subtract. Then write the letter of each problem on the line that has the first two digits of the answer.

A	84.232 − 51.877 32.355	**E**	5 − 2.3614 2.6386	**G**	9.28713 − 7.56349 1.72364	**P**	62.618 − 34.259 28.359
T	12.489 − 5.322 7.167	**O**	9.1 − 6.887 2.213	**F**	4.28951 − 3.64728 0.64223	**N**	114.32 − 73.88 40.44
R	3.99442 − 1.84357 2.15085	**H**	7.22 − 6.1834 1.0366	**I**	6.43892 − 2.56183 3.87709	**W**	55.410 − 14.882 40.528
		L	14.927 − 10.333 4.594	**C**	7.52578 − 5.21953 2.30625		

T H E G R A P E
71 10 26 17 21 32 28 26

W A L L O F C H I N A
40 32 45 45 22 06 23 10 38 40 32

Use with pages 30–31. 15

Practice Worksheet

ENRICH	Patterns

A **magic square** is a set of numbers arranged in a square shape. The sum of the numbers in every row, every column, and every diagonal is the same. This sum is called the **magic sum**.

8	1	6
3	5	7
4	9	2

Magic squares originated in China thousands of years ago. This magic square is from the *I Ching*, a classic Chinese book.

1. What is the magic sum of this square? _15_

Fill in the missing numbers for each square and write the magic sum. (HINT: These magic squares are made from sequences of numbers. A **sequence** is a string of numbers in which consecutive terms are related by a single operation.)

2.

1.6	0.3	0.2	1.3
0.5	1.0	1.1	0.8
0.9	0.6	0.7	1.2
0.4	1.5	1.4	0.1

Magic Sum: ___3.4___

3.

6.4	3.8	3.6	5.8
4.2	5.2	5.4	4.8
5.0	4.4	4.6	5.6
4.0	6.2	6.0	3.4

Magic Sum: ___19.6___

4.

94.7	12.8	6.5	75.8
25.4	56.9	63.2	44.3
50.6	31.7	38.0	69.5
19.1	88.4	82.1	0.2

Magic Sum: ___189.8___

5.

0.215	0.137	0.131	0.197
0.149	0.179	0.185	0.167
0.173	0.155	0.161	0.191
0.143	0.209	0.203	0.125

Magic Sum: ___0.68___

6. All these magic squares follow the same pattern. Make up your own magic square, following this pattern with a number sequence.

sixteenth	third	second	thirteenth
fifth	tenth	eleventh	eighth
ninth	sixth	seventh	twelfth
fourth	fifteenth	fourteenth	first

Answers will vary. All the squares are sequences arranged in the same order. The order of the sequence is given.

Use with pages 30–31. 15

Enrich Worksheet

Objective: To use information from a double-bar graph

Warm-Up

Have students compute the following.

7.6 + 5.8 (13.4)   12.1 − 8.7 (3.4)
14.31 − 8.95 (5.36)   7.6 + 9.51 (17.11)

GETTING STARTED

Sketch a bar graph, a broken-line graph, and a circle graph. Do not worry about scales or values. Have students compare the purposes of the three types of graph. (A *bar graph* is used to compare data, a *line graph* is usually used to show changes in data over time, and a *circle graph* is used to show how a whole is divided up.)

TEACHING THE LESSON

The bar graph is an important information source for students. Bar graphs are frequently used in the news media and advertisements to compare data. A double-bar graph is used to compare two sets of related data. When reading a double-bar graph, it is not as important to find actual numbers as it is to view and compare these numbers side by side, seeing which is larger, which two have the greatest range, and so on. When looking at the graph it is not as important to see that San Juan has 7.0 inches of precipitation in a normal August as it is to see that this amount is considerably more than that of any other city on the graph. It can also be seen from the graph that this is almost three times the amount of precipitation in San Juan in February.

Questions: Students may have difficulty because the question does not contain the information needed to answer it. Suggest that students familiarize themselves with the double-bar graph, its purpose, and the information it contains before looking at the questions.

Tools: Begin by asking students questions about reading graphs. Verify that all students understand what information is given on the graph. Students might copy information from the graph incorrectly. Students also tend to infer that values between those given on the graph can be found by "averaging" the readings on the graph. Remind them that the particular values shown on the graph are the only ones stated. Unless one has other information, one should not draw conclusions about values between those given on the graph.

Solutions: Students are not likely to encounter computational problems in this lesson.

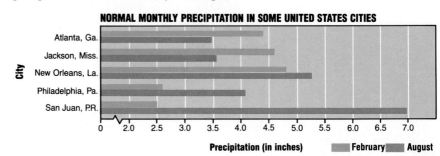

| QUESTIONS | TOOLS | SOLUTIONS | CHECKS |

PROBLEM SOLVING
Using a Graph

A double-bar graph makes it easy to compare two sets of information that are related to each other.

Use the double-bar graph below to answer this question: Which city has the greatest range in precipitation between February and August?

NORMAL MONTHLY PRECIPITATION IN SOME UNITED STATES CITIES

City (vertical axis): Atlanta, Ga.; Jackson, Miss.; New Orleans, La.; Philadelphia, Pa.; San Juan, P.R.

Precipitation (in inches) — scale: 0, 2.0, 2.5, 3.0, 3.5, 4.0, 4.5, 5.0, 5.5, 6.0, 6.5, 7.0

Legend: February | August

- The title tells you that this double-bar graph compares the amount of precipitation for February and August in some United States cities.

- The vertical axis is the line at the left. The horizontal axis is the line at the bottom. The scale along the horizontal axis shows you the amounts of precipitation in inches. The label along the vertical axis shows you the names of the cities.

- The legend tells you that the aqua bar represents the month of February and the orange bar represents the month of August.

  By comparing the two bars for each city, you can see that San Juan, Puerto Rico, has the greatest range in precipitation (2.5 inches and 7.0 inches).

32

Checks: There are several common errors that students make in reading double-bar graphs. Suggest that students check each of the following.
- that they read the numerical scales on the graph correctly and attached the correct units
- that they copied the information correctly
- that they used the legend correctly
- that they checked the reasonableness of their answers (range of numbers, units used, and so on)

Use the double-bar graph on page 32 to answer each question. Write the letter of the correct answer.

1. Which city has the greatest amount of precipitation in February?

a. Jackson
b. New Orleans
c. San Juan

2. Which city has a range in precipitation of 1.5 inches?

a. Atlanta
b. New Orleans
c. Philadelphia

Solve if possible.

3. Which cities are drier in August than in February?
Atlanta and Jackson

4. Which city is the driest during the month of February? San Juan

5. Which city has the smallest range in precipitation between February and August? New Orleans

6. Suppose that, for reasons of health, you needed to live in a city that has dry summers. Which two cities would probably provide the best conditions?
Atlanta and Jackson

7. Which two cities are closest to each other in the amount of precipitation that falls in February and August? Atlanta and Jackson

8. Which cities are wetter in August than in February? New Orleans, Philadelphia, and San Juan

9. Which two cities have a range in precipitation of about 1 inch? Jackson and Atlanta

10. What is the normal amount of precipitation in Atlanta during August? 3.5 inches

11. Which city has the greatest total amount of precipitation for February and August combined?
New Orleans

★12. How much of the precipitation in February in Philadelphia falls as snow? not enough information

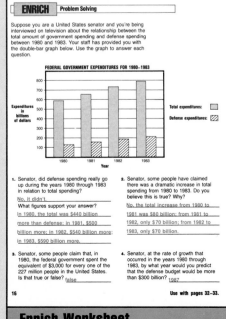

Classwork/Homework, page H16

ASSIGNMENT GUIDE

Basic: 1-6

Average: 2-8

Extended: 3-12

Resources
Practice, p. 16   Class/Home, p. H16
Enrich, p. 16

Exercise Analysis
1-2   Use information from a double-bar graph to choose the correct answer
3-12   Use information from a double-bar graph to solve a problem

FOLLOW-UP ACTIVITIES

PROBLEM SOLVING
Materials: magazines, newspapers per group

Have each group find a table or other source of information in a magazine or newspaper that would be suitable for making a bar graph or a double-bar graph. Have each group present their information to the class and explain why the information could be represented in a bar graph. (Accept any reasonable explanations.)

Give each group a section of the chalkboard and have them draw a bar graph or double-bar graph giving their information. Help them to choose a suitable interval for the graph. Be sure each group has a title and that each axis is labeled and numbered.

NUMBER SENSE (Estimation)
Write the table on the chalkboard. Tell the class that when making a double-bar graph, it is often necessary to round large numbers and to choose numbers to put on the graph scales. Have students choose the numbers they would put on the scale for a double-bar graph for this information. Once they have done this, have them round the numbers accordingly. (Numbers should be rounded to the nearest million or half-million.)

Population of Some Canadian Provinces, 1971 and 1981

Province	1971	1981
Alberta	1,627,874	2,237,724
Manitoba	988,247	1,026,241
Ontario	7,703,106	8,625,107
Quebec	6,027,764	6,438,403

COMING UP
A lesson calculated to please

Objective: To add large numbers on the calculator

Warm-Up

Estimate the sum to the nearest ten.

136.085 + 80.912 = (220)
53.212 + 191.833 = (240)
875.901 + 6.39 = (890)
1,389.723 + 973 = (2,360)

GETTING STARTED

Have students write the following numbers in expanded form.

1. 1.1 (1 + 0.1)
2. 72.45 (70 + 2 + 0.4 + 0.05)
3. 185.6 (100 + 80 + 5 + 0.6)
4. 2.8667   (2 + 0.8 + 0.06 + 0.006 + 0.0007)
5. 16.543 (10 + 6 + 0.5 + 0.04 + 0.003)

TEACHING THE LESSON

Calculator activities in this text are intended to help students explore number relationships, develop new concepts, and assist in computation of very large numbers. It is not recommended that calculators be used to perform simple arithmetic skills or to check answers.

Explain to students that when working with decimals on their calculators, they should estimate the answer, first, because it is easy to misplace the decimal point when entering numbers into their calculators. If each student's answer is not close to the estimate, the computation should be done again. Have students determine how many digits their calculators can display at one time. They should experiment with very large numbers to determine the display capacity of their calculators. When an answer contains more digits than can be displayed, most calculators show only the first part of the answer followed by E, which means "error" and OF, which means "overflow." To add or subtract numbers containing more digits than can be displayed, break up each number into smaller parts. Add the parts independently. Then add those sums to find the sum of the original numbers.

CALCULATOR

When you work with decimals on your calculator, be sure to estimate your answer first. It is easy to press the wrong key or to press an extra 0.

Add: 90.2305 + 35.1902 = ■.

Your estimate should be about 125. If your computed answer is not close to the estimate, work the problem again. The correct answer is 125.4207.

Sometimes it is difficult to compute with very large numbers. Enter this number on your calculator: 872.910289. Does the number appear as you entered it? Most calculators display only eight digits.

Add: 872.910289 + 310.190004 = ■.

To do a problem like this, you should break up both numbers into two or more parts and add the parts separately. Then add the answers without the calculator.

$$872.910289$$
$$+ 310.190004$$

1.100293	← Add the decimal parts.
1182	← Add the whole number parts.
1,183.100293	← Find the sum.

Add. Be sure to estimate first.

1. 473.131262 + 120.970201 **594.101463**		**2.** 445.597211 + 604.300113 **1,049.897324**		**3.** 878.751081 + 389.512446 **1,268.263527**		**4.** 29.6177137 + 10.6121598 **40.2298735**	
5. 417,339,978 + 176,108,415 **593,448,393**		**6.** 600,036,275 + 293,002,004 **893,038,279**		**7.** 771,441,651 + 13,992,013 **785,433,664**		**8.** 896,458,231 + 724,827,001 **1,621,285,232**	
9. 741,986,754 528,459,878 + 287,219,326 **1,557,665,958**		**10.** 845,796,782 147,265,821 + 96,487,099 **1,089,549,702**		**11.** 9,437,821,891 328,946,721 + 79,480,429 **9,846,249,041**		**12.** 2,712,894,875 3,643,754,921 + 6,789,163,587 **13,145,813,383**	

34

GROUP PROJECT

The Inn on the Mountain

The problem: You have a 22-year-old cousin who works in a tourist shop at the foot of a beautiful mountain. She sells paintings of the mountain to visitors. She tells you that her dream is to own and operate a small inn called Hikers' Hut, which is perched on the top of the mountain. She wants to serve those hikers who are hearty enough to arrive there. She says it will take her a year to earn enough money to buy the inn. In response to your questions, she gives you the information provided below. Consider this information, and determine whether her estimate is correct. If it isn't, find out when she will be able to buy Hikers' Hut.

Key Facts
- Hikers' Hut costs $27,550.
- She is paid $23.50 for each painting that she sells.
- She sells an average of 5 paintings each day.
- The tourist shop is open from Monday to Friday.
- Each month that she works at the shop, she spends $75 for rent, $175 for food, and $50 for other expenses.
- She works on her family's farm for 2 months of the year.

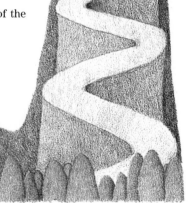

35

Group Project

Group project activities are designed for cooperative learning. Cooperative learning groups allow students to interact, reflect on key questions, and express a group solution to mathematical problems.

The following are general guidelines which you may want to consider for group-project activities.

1. Separate the class into groups with a balance of ability levels and personalities. Groups of four work well for most projects.
2. Present the project to the groups. The amount of review or instruction will vary depending on the level of students' experience working in groups.
3. Encourage students to listen to each other and to respect each other's opinions. Remind them that they are a team and should help one another.
4. Have the groups discuss, analyze, and review their problem. Insure that all students are involved in this process.
5. Have a representative from each group articulate a solution to the problem. Review all viable solutions with the class. (In many cases there will be more than one way to approach and solve the group projects.)
6. Recognize that student involvement and group participation is more important than the end product of a project.

Objectives: To calculate costs and time to make a purchase

USING THE PAGE

Separate the class into groups of three or four. Without using paper and pencil, have each student estimate how much the cousin can save in one year. Then have students present their estimates to the group and explain them.

Have each group agree on a series of steps to find the exact amount the cousin can save in one year. Have one student in the group write down the steps without actually performing any calculations. If students need help, explain that they must first determine how much she earns in a year. When this total is found, then her yearly expenses can be subtracted to find the amount she can save in a year. If the amount is not sufficient, the cost of Hiker's Hut can be divided by the amount saved per year to find the number of years necessary to save enough money. It might be useful for groups to make a table to see the relationship of the variables of cost, earnings, and expenses.

Once each group has outlined a plan, then they can use the numbers given to find the exact amount earned per year ($25,850), her expenses per year ($3,000), the possible amount saved ($22,850), and how long it would take to purchase Hiker's Hut at this rate of savings (about 12 months).

To extend this cooperative learning activity, have each group come up with a plan for the cousin to earn more money so she can buy the hut sooner. Each group can then estimate her new income and expenses, find out the amount saved each year, and determine how long it would now take her to buy Hiker's Hut.

1 CHAPTER TEST

Purpose: The Chapter Test helps to assess students' understanding of the concepts and skills presented in this chapter.

The chart below is designed to help you review the test items by correlating them with the testing objectives that appear in the Chapter Overview.

Item	*Objectives*
1–13	A,B
14–15	C
16–23	D
24–29	E
30–33	G
34–37	F
38–39	H

Bonus

The bonus questions may be used for extra credit, or you may want to assign them to students who complete the test before the rest of the class.

Calculator

You may wish to have students use calculators for the problem-solving portions of the test.

Resources

If you prefer to use this Chapter Test as a review exercise, additional testing materials are available in the Teacher's Resource Book.

CHAPTER TEST

Write each number using short word names and in expanded form. (pages 2–3 and 18–19)
See Answer Key.

1. 621,472 **2.** 7,946,000,310 **3.** 40,000,000,309,436

4. 0.124 **5.** 4.500092 **6.** 91.003906

Write each number in standard form. (pages 2–3 and 18–19)

7. 36 trillion, 519 million, 137
36,000,519,000,137

8. 374 trillion, 9 billion, 7 thousand
374,009,000,007,000

9. 500,000,000 + 50,000,000 + 8,000,000 + 700 + 3
558,000,703

10. 10,000,000,000 + 400,000,000 + 30,000 + 2,000 + 40
10,400,032,040

11. seven hundred fourteen thousand twenty-six millionths
0.714026

12. 0.4 + 0.03 + 0.007 + 0.00008
0.43708

13. 20 + 9 + 0.6 + 0.0008 + 0.00004 + 0.000005
29.600845

Write the value of the underlined digit. (pages 2–3 and 18–19)

14. 204,3<u>1</u>3,940,600
10 million

15. 4.90372<u>4</u>
4 millionths

Compare. Use >, <, or = for ●. (pages 4–5 and 20–21)

16. 9,581,243 ● 9,581,423 <

17. $461,210.93 ● $461,201.96 >

18. 428.0694 ● 428.049 >

19. 0.06238 ● 0.062381 <

Order from the greatest to the least. (pages 4–5 and 20–21)

20. 903,582; 930,582; 903,852
930,582; 903,852; 903,582

21. 7.4921; 4.9217; 7.44902; 4.9172
7.4921; 7.44902; 4.9217; 4.9172

Order from the least to the greatest. (pages 4–5 and 20–21)

22. 89,465; 88,465; 89,456; 89,564
88,465; 89,456; 89,465; 89,564

23. $2,174.05; $2,175.40; $2,157.54
$2,157.54; $2,174.05; $2,175.40

POSTTEST Chapter 1 Page 1

1. What is the standard form for 142 million?

2. What is the value of 9 in 21.00095?

3. What is the standard form for 30 + 2 + 0.05 + 0.006?

4. What is 37,285,012 rounded to the nearest million?

5. LIST
0.04
0.004
0.0004
0.00004
What is the greatest number in the list?

6. What is the standard form for 42 million 6 thousand 16?

7. What is the digit in the hundredths place in the number 700,500.043?

8. What is the standard form for 400,000 + 60,000 + 2,000 + 80 + 3?

9. The average diameter of a human hair is 0.01016 cm. What is this number in words?

10. 60.09 + 403 + 2.0042

Posttest

POSTTEST Chapter 1 Page 2

11. The value of the 5 in the number 54,321 is how many times the value of the 5 in 567?

12. What is $10,008.76 rounded to the nearest 10 dollars?

13.
 4,3 3 7
+5,9■8
10,3 1 5
What is ■?

14.
 4, 6 51
−1,■57
The difference is at least 3,000. What is the greatest number that ■ could be?

Use the following chart for questions 15 to 17.

CHARITY FUND BUDGET

Organization	1st year	2nd year	3rd year	4th year
Forest Scouts	$10,000	$10,000	$12,000	$15,000
Young Farmers	$ 8,000	$10,000	$12,000	$14,000
Youth Center	$20,000	$20,000	$20,000	$20,000
Youth Hot Line	$ 5,000	$ 6,000	$ 5,000	$ 7,000

15. For which organization did the budget increase the most over the four years?

16. Which organization had a decrease from the 2nd to the 3rd years?

17. Which organization had the greatest budget increase from the 3rd to the 4th years?

Posttest

POSTTEST Chapter 1 Page 3

18. Estimate.
24.158
36.426
+10.291

19. A gas station attendant counted the bills in the cash register at closing time. There were 3 hundred-dollar bills, 5 fifties, 8 twenties, 30 tens, and 80 ones. How much money was this?

20. What is the value of the underlined digit in 1,5<u>4</u>3,892?

21. What is 907,184 rounded to the nearest hundred?

22. LIST
0.00045
0.009
0.001
0.0008
What is the least number in the list?

23.
 78.531
−21.467

24. What is the value of the 7 in 538.729?

25. What is the short word name for 700,000,700,700?

Posttest

Round to the nearest hundred million. (page 8)

24. 2,874,207,430,608.5
2,874,200,000,000

25. 459,968,004,897
460,000,000,000

Round to the nearest ten-thousandth. (pages 22–23)

26. 0.87655
0.8766

27. 1.000643
1.0006

Round to the nearest ten cents. (pages 22–23)

28. $523.62
$523.60

29. $1,434.96
$1,435.00

Estimate the sum or the difference. (pages 10–13 and 26–27)   Answers may vary. Accept any reasonable estimate.

30. 2,428,784 + 432 + 572,678
3,000,000

31. 672,087 − 547,491
120,000 $^+$

32. 5.26 + 3.81 + 19.56   27–29

33. 6.93 − 4.32   2$^+$

Add or subtract. (pages 14–15 and 28–31)

34. $5,678.32 + $403.82 $6,082.14

35. 204.07 − 5.072   198.998

36. 49 + 872.3 + 86,870.04 − 0.861
87,790.479

37. 642,811 + 7,410,000 + 3.42 − 11.1
8,052,803.32

Use the double-bar graph to solve. (pages 32–33)

38. Would you expect 1982 energy production to be greater than or less than 65 quadrillion Btu?
greater than

39. What trend can you see in United States energy imports?
They are decreasing.

UNITED STATES ENERGY SUPPLY: 1978–1981

(bar graph: Supply (quadrillion Btu) vs Year 1978, 1979, 1980, 1981)

= total production
= total imports

BONUS

Use the double-bar graph to solve.

In which year was the difference between production and import of energy the least? the greatest? Estimate the difference for each of these years.
1979; 1981; 40 quadrillion Btu; 50 quadrillion Btu

37

For students who have difficulty with written tests, this test can be given orally.

You may wish to test students, orally or in writing, to see if they can explain the steps used in solving selected items. The following summarizes the procedures for solving key test items.

Ex. 16–19

Comparing whole numbers or decimals

To compare whole numbers, line up the digits. Then compare digits beginning at the left. To compare decimals, align the decimal points and compare as with whole numbers.

Ex. 20–23

Ordering whole numbers or decimals from the greatest to the least; from the least to the greatest

To order whole numbers or decimals from the greatest to the least, compare to find the greatest, the next greatest, and the least. To order from the least to the greatest, compare to find the least, the next greatest, and the greatest.

Ex. 24–29

Rounding whole numbers or decimals

To round whole numbers or decimals, look at the digit to the right of the place to which you are rounding. If this digit is 5 or more, round up by adding 1 to the rounding place and changing the digits to the right to zeros. If the digit to the right of the rounding place is less than 5, round down by changing this digit and all digits to the right to zeros. Rounding to the nearest ten cents is the same as rounding to the nearest tenth.

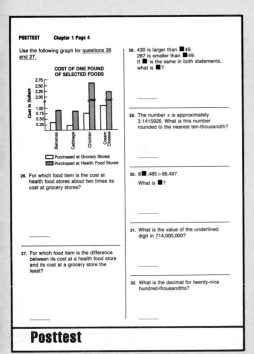

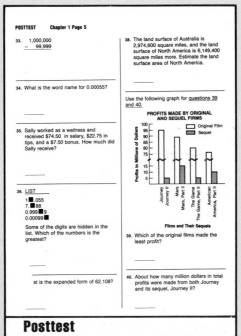

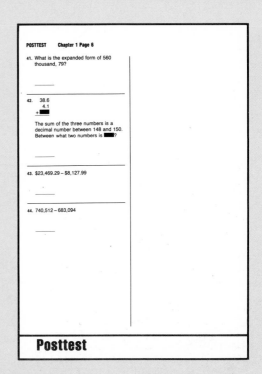

Purpose This Reteaching page provides additional instruction for key concepts in the chapter. It is designed for use by students who have had difficulty with these concepts. It can also be used to provide additional practice for students who require it.

USING THE PAGE

The addition and subtraction of decimals was taught on pages 28–31.

Work through the two examples on the chalkboard. Remind students to be sure to line up the decimal points before adding or subtracting. Point out that zeros can be annexed to any decimal so that each decimal has the same number of digits to the right of the decimal point.

As you work through the examples, review regrouping. Remind students that they should rewrite problems that have been given in horizontal form so that they are in vertical form. Also remind students that they can check each subtraction problem by using addition. Point out that estimation can also be used to check a sum or difference.

Resources

For other practice and activities related to this chapter, see the Teacher's Resource Book.

RETEACHING

To add or subtract decimals, line up the decimal points vertically. Then add or subtract each column as you would for whole numbers. Place the decimal point in the answer directly under the decimal points in the numbers being combined.

Add 0.06 + 1.235 + 46 + 0.078.

```
  0.060  ← Write zeros
  1.235     to line up
 46.000  ← the decimal
+ 0.078     points.
 47.373
```

Subtract $20 − $6.38.

```
 $20.00  ← Write
−  6.38     zeros.
 $13.62
```

Perform the indicated operation.

1.	2.	3.	4.
325.04	8.3502	7.0542	263.12
182.76	10	0.87	13.05
225.35	1.253	8.543	8.6573
+ 490.27	+ 6.4796	+ 1	+ 69
1,223.42	26.0828	17.4672	353.8273

5. 0.47 + 0.1786   0.6486

6. $0.24 + $0.87 $1.11

7. 0.014 + 16 + 13.082   29.096

8. 0.63 + 1.574 + 0.9738   3.1778

9. 43.2 + 0.136 + 6   49.336

10. 1.007 + 0.08 + 10.074 + 7   18.161

11. 231 + 0.8711 + 2.327 + 22.43   256.6281

12. 0.008 + 0.1 + 100 + 14 + 1.047   115.155

13.	14.	15.	16.
0.4684	0.6492	$175.27	4.3
− 0.1679	− 0.4975	− 93.49	− 0.372
0.3005	0.1517	$81.78	3.928

17.	18.	19.	20.
5,986.2	$473	6,342.98	0.368
− 49.379	− 9.88	− 6.399	− 0.0867
5,936.821	$463.12	6,336.581	0.2813

21. 0.16 − 0.07   0.09

22. $16 − $1.49 $14.51

23. 3.73 − 1.965   1.

24. 8 − 1.742   6.258

25. 21 − 0.409   20.591

26. 151 − 0.909   15

27.	28.	29.	30.
965.06	692.04	1,000.04	4,679.13
1.327	− 0.334	9.072	− 62.0197
14	691.706	64	4,617.1103
0.2		0.76	
+ 103.51		+ 5.001	
1,084.097		1,078.873	

38

ENRICHMENT

Ancient Number Systems

Egyptian		∩	9	𝄐	⌐	⌒	𝄐
	1	10	100	1,000	10,000	100,000	1,000,000

The Egyptian number system is called *additive* because the value of a number is found by adding together the values of the symbols for that number.

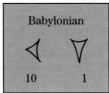 = 21,308

The Babylonian number system was based on the number 60 instead of the number 10. Because the Babylonians had only two symbols, place value is also important. A "10" symbol in the first (ones) place has a value of 10, but in the second (sixties) place, the same symbol has a value of 10 sixties, or 600.

Babylonian

◁ ▽

10   1

Third place	Second place	First place
◁ ▽	◁ ▽ ▽ ◁	◁ ◁ ▽ ▽ ▽ ◁ ◁

11 thirty-six hundreds	22 sixties	33 ones	
$11 \times 3{,}600$ +	22×60 +	33×1	= 40,953

Roman	I	V	X	L	C	D	M
	1	5	10	50	100	500	1,000

The Roman number system is both additive and subtractive. If a symbol has a value greater than or equal to the value of the symbol to its right, then add. If the symbol has a lesser value, then subtract it from the symbol to its right.

MCMLXXXIV = 1,984

Write each number in Egyptian, Babylonian, and Roman numerals.

For additional activities, see *Connecting Math Ideas,* page 469.

See Answer Key.

1. 14   **2.** 683   **3.** 4,342

39

Purpose This Enrichment page provides an additional challenge for those students whose work throughout the chapter and on the Chapter Test shows a thorough understanding of the material. Alternatively, you may wish to use these exercises as a supplementary lesson for the entire class.

USING THE PAGE

As an introduction to the Babylonian system, review with students the Egyptian system of numeration. Explain to them that the value of a number is found by adding up the number of symbols for each place value. Extend this to the Babylonian system. The Babylonians developed the *sexagesimal* systems (based on 60) from which we still take our measurements of time and angles. In their system of numerals, which is based on 60, the first place consists of 1's, the second place of 60's, the third place of 3,600's, the fourth place of 216,000's, and so on. Each place is written in a separate box as shown, with only two symbols—1 and 10. Guide students through the conversion of the introductory problem by computing on the chalkboard: $11 \times 3{,}600 + 22 \times 60 + 33 = 39{,}600 + 1{,}320 + 33 = 40{,}953$. In reviewing the Roman-numeral system, remind students that the number 4 is written IV, 9 is written IX, and so on.

Resources

For additional Enrichment activities, see the Teacher's Resource Book.

Purpose This Cumulative Review page provides an opportunity to reinforce students' understanding of the concepts and skills taught in previous chapters.

The chart below is designed to aid you in reviewing the material by specifying the pages on which various concepts and skills were taught.

Item	Page
1	2–3
2	8
3	18–19
4	10–11
5	14–15
6	18–19
7	22–23
8	26–27
9	2–3
10	30–31
11	24–25
12	12–13

Each Cumulative Review gives students an opportunity to practice taking tests that are written in a multiple-choice, standardized format. Be sure that students understand that if the correct answer is not among the first three given, then they should select the fourth choice—"not given"—as the correct answer. At least one item per test will require students to give this response.

CUMULATIVE REVIEW

Write the letter of the correct answer.

1. What number is 432 trillion, 682?

a. 432,006,082
b. 432,682,000
c. 432,000,000,000,682
d. not given

2. Round 40,785,924 to the nearest ten thousand.

a. 40,786,000
b. 40,790,000
c. 40,800,000
d. not given

3. What number is twenty-eight and one hundred two thousandths?

a. 28.012
b. 28.102
c. 28,120
d. not given

4. Estimate $9,129 + 25,681 + 34,827$.

a. 60,000
b. 70,000
c. 80,000
d. 100,000

5. $48,627,061 - 957,399$

a. 47,669,662
b. 48,679,672
c. 48,779,772
d. not given

6. What number is fifty-two millionths?

a. 0.0052
b. 0.00052
c. 0.000052
d. not given

7. Round $84,976.47 to the nearest dollar.

a. $84,976
b. $84,976.50
c. $84,977
d. not given

8. Estimate $111.57 - 0.653$.

a. 100^-
b. 112^+
c. 110
d. 100

9. What number is five trillion, four billion, seven?

a. 5,004,000,007
b. 5,000,400,000,007
c. 5,400,000,000,007
d. not given

10. $15 - 9.9009$

a. 5.0991
b. 5.1091
c. 6.1001
d. not given

G. COMPANY CAR SALES

Model	This year	Last year
Streak	43,331	50,504
Wave	53,642	39,721
Boreas	51,724	49,837

11. Use the table to find the total number of cars sold this year.

a. 147,687
b. 147,697
c. 148,697
d. not given

12. Use the table to estimate how many more Streaks were sold than Waves last year.

a. 10,000
b. 11,000
c. 12,000
d. not given

40

CHAPTER  OVERVIEW

MULTIPLICATION AND DIVISION WHOLE NUMBERS AND DECIMALS

SUMMARY

Chapter 2 covers the multiplication and division of whole numbers and decimals. Beginning with basic multiplication and division facts, it extends from estimating products and quotients by rounding to multiplication and division of decimals by decimals.

LESSON SEQUENCE

PROFESSIONAL BACKGROUND

While the multiplication and division algorithms for decimals closely resemble their counterparts for whole numbers, there is a subtle but crucial difference that escapes many students. Most students think of multiplication as repeated addition and of division as sharing. While these notions hold for whole numbers, they do not usually hold for decimals. Without any conceptual understanding many students resort to memorizing computational rules for the multiplication and division of decimals.

This situation often leads students to develop misconceived notions such as "multiplication always makes bigger" and "division always makes smaller." To correct this thinking, provide activities that allow students to realize the meaning of multiplication and division. Calculators can be a useful aid here. For example, the following game emphasizes that multiplication does not always result in a product greater than each factor.

Form the class into two teams. The first team displays a number on the calculator. Each team takes turns trying to get the number as close as possible to a target number such as 100, by multiplying each consecutive number by any whole number or decimal they choose.

References: See Reys and Grouws; Driscoll (secondary volume, chapters on calculators and remediation); and Hart.

MATERIALS

centimeter rulers
index cards
felt-tip pen

VOCABULARY

multiplication properties (p. 42)
    Commutative
    Associative
    Distributive
    Identity
powers of 10 (p. 44)

ABOUT THE CHAPTER

Most students will require a brief review of multiplication and a more thorough review of division near the beginning of the school year. Even better students may be rusty after the summer break. This chapter presents the multiplication and division skills that students will need as they work through the rest of the text.

In Chapter Two, students multiply and divide whole numbers and decimals. The chapter also includes lessons about multiplying by powers of 10 and about dividing decimals by decimals.

Students often find the incorrect answer when multiplying because they align the partial products incorrectly. Similar difficulties often lead to errors in division, also. Do not hesitate to give students graph paper to help them keep the columns straight.

The estimation techniques discussed in the chapter will help students to avoid misplacing the decimal point in the quotient or in the product. Have students estimate the product or the quotient and then perform the computation. When the estimate is compared to the answer, the answer should be reasonable. Estimating and comparing is not an absolute check for the correctness of an answer. However, it does help students detect most of the errors that arise from incorrect placement of the decimal point.

In the division algorithm, a decimal divisor must be converted to a whole number before dividing. If students have difficulty with this process, emphasize the process of multiplying both divisor and dividend by powers of 10.

Students should use calculators to multiply and divide whole numbers and decimals. Consumer topics, such as unit pricing, provide a useful way to introduce division on the calculator. Decimal multiplication patterns can be seen very clearly on the calculator. You should be familiar with the way each calculator shows answers too large or too small for display and with the way each calculator shows decimals that continue off the display.

Problem-solving lessons show students how to identify extraneous and unstated information, as well as how to use estimation to solve problems. Other problem-solving lessons in the chapter show students how to solve multi-step problems and how to choose the correct operation.

The Group Project presents students with a Japanese menu that shows prices in yen. Students convert yen to dollars as they order a meal that has a $60 limit. The project involves students actively and gives them an opportunity to apply problem solving and other mathematical concepts.

The Enrichment lesson introduces students to number sequences. Students are asked to apply the mathematical skills learned in previous chapters as they write additional terms for the sequences.

USING THE CHAPTER OPENER

Each Chapter Opener presents situational problem-solving activities that can be used to motivate the skills taught throughout the chapter. The work sheets can be used by individuals, small groups, or the whole class, depending on the needs of the class. Some students might be ready to use the Chapter Opener at the beginning of the chapter; others might first need to develop the skills taught in the chapter.

Students should be encouraged to use the calculator when appropriate. The Chapter Opener focuses on a nonalgorithmic approach to real-life situations relevant to students' experiences. Through an interdisciplinary approach, the Chapter Opener helps students to explore the relationship between mathematics, other areas of the curriculum, and everyday life while developing different strands of mathematics.

In the Chapter Opener activities, students will plan a vacation. Students choose the site of their vacation, plan an itinerary, and budget their time and money accordingly.

PROBLEM SOLVING

Sometimes math problems provide more information than is needed to solve the problem. The lesson Identifying Extra/Needed Information outlines a step-by-step strategy that students can use to evaluate a set of given information. Its purpose is to foster an important life-skill: the ability to distinguish needed information from that which is extraneous.

The Estimation problem-solving lesson in this chapter focuses on whether students should underestimate or overestimate to solve a problem. Although the lesson shows one method for computing these estimates, encourage any student improvisations that increase their estimation skills.

Since almost every math problem requires some kind of computation, the focus of the Choosing the Operation lesson is the skill that students use most often. The Mathematics Unlimited approach is to have students analyze the numbers given in the problem in order to find a solution. This allows students to understand the principal meanings of the operations, to learn the process of taking apart a word problem, and to focus on the relationship between a given set of conditions and a goal.

The lesson Solving Multi-step Problems/Making a Plan focuses on those math problems which cannot be solved until an intermediate operation is performed. The *Mathematics Unlimited* approach to solving these problems is to have students identify which information they need to find before they can solve the problem, and then to have them make a plan listing the intermediate calculations by which the information they need can be obtained from the information they already have.

Most of the problem-solving lessons in *Mathematics Unlimited* lend themselves to small group work. In a comfortable group atmosphere, students can brainstorm and discuss various ways to solve a problem.

BULLETIN BOARD

"Take Math Around the World"

Materials: paper to cover bulletin board, lettering, oaktag for spinner and game pieces, 3 envelopes, push pins, index cards, felt-tip pens

Preparation: Cover board with paper and arrange lettering. Draw game-board as shown. Cut spinner from oaktag and attach near three envelopes as shown. Write ten travel questions for multiplying and dividing whole numbers on index cards, such as "Mr. Orr traveled 64 miles an hour for 12 hours. How many miles did he travel in all?" (768) Write answers on back of cards and place in first envelope. Write ten questions on multiplying decimals and ten questions on dividing decimals by whole numbers and by decimals. Place in second and third envelopes respectively. Make game pieces from oaktag which students can initial to identify as their game pieces.

After pp. 52-53: Allow small groups to go to board and choose cards from first envelope. Have them answer questions, check answers on back, and, if correct, spin the spinner and advance.

After pp. 60-61: Have class play the game with cards in second envelope.

After pp. 66-67: Have students play, answering cards in third envelope. First student to travel around board wins, but everyone should finish.

COMMON ERRORS

A common error that students make in division is to forget to write leading zeros in a decimal quotient. For example:

$$\frac{0.0054}{40)\overline{0.216}}$$

In the above example, students might write 0.54 instead of 0.0054.

To remediate the above error, write several examples on the board for students. At each place value, for example, ask: Does 40 divide into 2? Explain that if it does not, a zero must be written in the quotient. Ask again: Does 40 divide into 21? Then another zero must be written. Finally, ask: Does 40 divide into 216? Now a 5 can be written in the quotient.

Emphasize that the decimal point must be written in the quotient directly above the decimal point in the dividend. Then, each number in the dividend, from left to right, must be examined for divisibility. If the divisor does not divide into the first digit, then a zero must be written above it. If the divisor then does not divide into the first 2 digits, another zero must be written above the second digit, and so on.

SPECIAL NEEDS

Review both basic multiplication facts and basic division facts with students who are having difficulty before proceeding with the algorithm. Use base-ten blocks to reinforce place value and the algorithm, reminding students that when multiplying, for example, 32×9, they are really saying $(30 \times 9) + (2 \times 9)$. When proceeding to the abstract, have students write the problem in expanded notation, and then compute it. Then progress to the "short form" of multiplication, and encourage students to write a zero when multiplying by the tens digit rather than leaving a blank space.

The placement of the decimal point when multiplying decimals might present a problem for some students. Have students show the intersecting portion of the problem on 10×10 grid paper. Relate decimals to fractions. Help students understand the placement of the decimal point rather than having them memorize a rule. Eventually, lead students to the identity property, which will enable them to divide by a whole number.

Use Olympic records as a springboard for having your advanced students work with decimals. For example, in 1980, Sebastian Coe (Great Britain) won the gold medal for running 1,500 meters in 3 minutes 38.4 seconds. What was his average distance run for one minute?

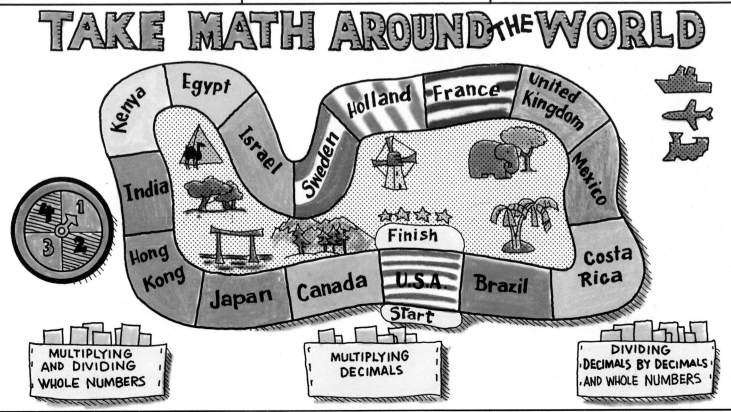

MATH LABS

NUMBER SENSE (Mental Math)

Materials: for each group, 2 cubes with one of the following numbers on each face of each cube: 10, 100, 0, 0.2, 0.25, 0.5; 1 cube with × or ÷ on each face

Three to four students take turns tossing the cubes and performing the appropriate operation mentally. When the operation is division, the divisor should be the lesser number.

NUMBER SENSE (Estimation)

Materials: for each group, a set of 52 index cards, having the numbers 1 through 26 and 0.01 through 0.26 written on them; a set of 10 challenge cards with instructions such as: Estimate the product to the nearest hundred; Estimate the quotient to the nearest tenth; Estimate the range of appropriate quotients.

Three to four students should take turns picking two index cards and one challenge card. In the case of division, the divisor should be the second index card picked. After the student follows the directions on the challenge card, the other students can check that the estimate is reasonable.

NUMBER SENSE (Mental Math)

Materials: for each student, a set of 30 cards, half the cards with numbers between 888,999 and 10,000,000 and the other half with numbers between 0.001 and 0.99, each card with the student's name on the reverse side.

Students should work together in groups of 2 or 3 and combine their cards into one set. One student picks two cards. The next person in turn says a number between the numbers on the two cards, and then picks two cards, and so on. When all the cards have been used, they are returned to the person whose name is on the back, or the cards are shuffled and the activity continues.

CALCULATOR

Multiplication and Division of Whole Numbers and Decimals

The calculator is a useful tool for computations that are tedious and time consuming. However, the calculator is no substitute for thinking or for understanding the process; for example, calculators should be available for problem-solving activities that involve multiplication and division of whole numbers and decimals. But the calculator will not help students to decide which process to perform or which principles to apply.

Students need to know that they will occasionally push buttons incorrectly, which will produce an incorrect answer. Therefore, they need to train themselves to estimate the answer and to verify that the results are reasonable.

Additional Activities: **Drill and Practice:** Use a calculator with an 8-digit display. Multiply two 5-digit numbers. (If you try to multiply directly, your calculator will probably overflow.)

$$96523 \\ \times 74685$$

HINT: Multiply 96523×74 and 96523×685. Then carefully combine the results.

Explorations: Using a calculator with an 8-digit capacity, perform this exercise: $99999999 \div 99999996 = ?$ Is your result 1? If yes, try $55555555 \div 55555554 = ?$ Do you obtain 1 again? Try similar divisions. Can you explain your result?

SUBJECT AREA CONNECTIONS

These Subject Area Connections are useful for reinforcing the concepts presented in this chapter.

p. 57-Social Studies: Students find the actual number of visitors from various countries to the United States in 1984 by multiplying each figure that is represented on a chart as a decimal or as a mixed decimal by 1,000,000.

Here are some other activities for presenting these concepts.

- **Consumer:** From newspapers, have students cut out advertisements for 1 unit of a product at a fixed price. Then have them find the cost of multiple units of each product.
- **Science:** Have students research five airspeed records, and then multiply to find the number of miles each vehicle could cover over various periods of time.
- **Science:** Have students research the number and the average size of farms in various states, and then multiply to find the total farm acreage for each state.

PLAN AHEAD

You will need to prepare index cards for Teaching the Lesson on T.E. p. 50 and for the activity on T.E. p. 67. You will need handouts for the activity on T.E. p. 61.

PLANNING CALENDAR

Pages	Lesson Objectives	ASSIGNMENT GUIDE			Class/ Home	More Practice	Math Reasoning	Follow-up	Reteach	Practice	Enrich
		Basic	Average	Extended							
41	Chapter Opener (Use MMW 3, 4)	41	41	41							
42, 43	To identify the five properties of multiplication and division	1-12, 13-27o	1-12,14-28e	2-22e,23-30	H17			RFM P&G	13	17	17
44, 45	To multiply and divide a whole number by powers of 10	1-33o,AL	2-34e,35-36,AL	10-32e,33-36,AL	H18			NS P&G	14	18	18
46, 47	To estimate products and quotients of whole numbers	1-12,13-31o	3-12,13-31o	4-12,14-30e, 31-32	H19			RFM PS	15	19	19
48, 49	To identify extra/needed information in problem solving	1-4	2-6	3-8	H20			PS RFM		20	20
50, 51	To multiply whole numbers up to 3-digit factors	1-10,11-27o, NS1-6	1-10,12-28e, NS4-9	2-18e,20-29, NS4-9	H21			RFM CMP	16	21	21
52, 53	To divide whole numbers up to 3-digit numbers	1-38o,MCR	2-39e,MCR	4-40e,MCR	H22		H209	RFM P&G	17	22	22
54, 55	To estimate in solving problems	1-4	2-6	3-7	H23			PS CALC		23	23
56, 57	To multiply and divide decimals by powers of 10	1-35o,Chlg	2-36e,Chlg	1-27o,28-37,Chlg	H24		H209	CALC MC	18	24	24
58, 59	To estimate products of decimals	1-37o,38	2-38e	1-27o,29-39	H25			MC NS	19	25	25
60, 61	To multiply decimals	1-12,13-23o,29, AL	5-12,14-28e, 29-30,AL	9-12,14-30,AL	H26	H196	H209	MC PS	20	26	26
62, 63	To choose the correct operation to solve a problem	1-4	2-6	3-8	H27		H210	PS CALC		27	27
64, 65	To divide decimals by whole numbers	1-12,14-38e,NS	1-8,9-41o,NS	6-28e,29-42, NS	H28		H210	NS MC	21	28	28
66, 67	To divide decimals by decimals	1-16,17-39o	1-12,14-40e	2-36e,37-40	H29	H196	H210	P&G NS	22	29	29
68, 69	To make a plan to solve a multi-step problem	1-4	2-6	4-8	H30			PS CALC		30	30
70	Math Communication: To use math vocabulary	70	70	70							
71	Group Project: To plan a meal within a budget; to convert currency	71	71	71							

72,73	Chapter Test
74	Reteaching
75	Enrichment
76,77	Technology
78	Cumulative Review

ABBREVIATION KEY

Teacher's Resource Book
MMW—Making Math Work
P—Practice
R—Reteach
E—Enrich

Follow-up Activities
CALC—Calculator
CMP—Computer
P&G—Puzzles and Games
MNP—Manipulatives

MC—Math Connection
MCM—Math Communication
NS—Number Sense
PS—Problem Solving
RFM—Reinforcement

TESTS

A. To multiply or divide a whole number or a money amount by a whole number
B. To multiply or divide a decimal by powers of 10
C. To multiply or divide a decimal by a whole number
D. To multiply or divide a decimal by a decimal
E. To estimate products and quotients of whole numbers
F. To estimate products of decimals
G. To identify extra or needed information in a problem and solve
H. To choose the operation that is required to solve each problem
I. To identify subgoals and solve multistep problems

FAMILY INVOLVEMENT

Family Involvement for Chapter 2 encourages family members to calculate the calories they use in a month. Students and their families are given a table that shows the number of calories expended per hour during five different activities—sleeping, sitting, standing, walking, and running. Each family member is asked to estimate the time spent per week performing each of the activities listed in the table. They calculate the number of calories they use in one week and then multiply that number by 4 to estimate the number of calories used in one month. Then each family member makes a calendar like the one shown on the lesson page. A record is kept of the number of hours each person devotes to each activity each day. At the end of one month, family members compare their estimated usage to their actual usage.

Additional activities might include having students find out from their parents the average number of miles that they drive or commute each workday. Family members should then calculate the number of miles that the parents drive or commute in one week, in one month, and in one year. Have them display their results on a chart.

STUDENT RESOURCES

Bibliography
Burkes, Joyce M. *The Math Machine Book: Multiplication.* Cockeysville, Md: Liberty Publishing Co., Inc., 1980.

Cisek, James. *Loosening Up: Get Rid of Those Uptight Feelings.* New London, Wisc.: Life Skills Publishing Co., 1981.

Wartski, Maureen C. *A Boat to Nowhere.* Philadelphia: The Westminster Press, 1980.

Films
Powers of Ten. 8 minutes. Color. 1968. Distributed by Pyramid Films, Santa Monica, Calif.

If you could choose the vacation of your dreams, where would you go? You have one week in which to travel on your dream vacation. Decide where you want to go and what you want to do on your trip. Plan and write a budget for the week.

2 MULTIPLICATION AND DIVISION
Whole Numbers and Decimals

Objective: To explore problems related to travel

Direct students to look at the picture of the airplane. Ask students who have traveled by airplane to share their experiences with the class. Different airlines charge varying prices to the same destination. Discuss the importance of checking the prices charged by different companies before drawing up a vacation budget.

WHOLE CLASS
Logic
Materials: Making Math Work page 4 per student

Discuss with students how to go about planning a vacation. Have them choose a few places to which they would like to go and list them in order of preference. Direct students to look at Making Math Work page 4. Have students research their choices to see whether the amount of money they plan to spend for the vacation would be adequate for the place they plan to visit. Have each student write a list of the things he or she will need to do to plan a vacation.

INDIVIDUAL
Number
Materials: Making Math Work page 3 per student

After students have picked a vacation site, have them complete Making Math Work page 3. Emphasize the importance of drawing up an itinerary. Instruct students to list all the things they want to do and organize them chronologically so that they can accomplish all of them. Encourage students to draw up a flexible schedule. Tell them that people often have to change their plans when they travel.

SMALL GROUP

Materials: Making Math Work page 4 per student

Have students who have similar vacation ideas form small groups; for example, those who want to relax in the sun should work together, those who want to tour interesting cities should work together, and so on. Have the groups complete Making Math Work page 4. Some students may want to spend more money on food, whereas others may want to spend more on lodging. Have them compare work sheets and decide who would be good traveling partners. Tell students that when they are traveling with friends, they should make sure that their friends share their goals.

MAKING MATH WORK

Complete each chart. Then compile all the information into an itinerary for your one-week vacation. Remember to include travel time.

Check students' charts.

Vacation event	Length of event

ITINERARY

	Sunday	Monday	Tuesday	Wednesday	Thursday	Friday	Saturday
8 A.M.							
9 A.M.							
10 A.M.							
Noon							
1 P.M.							
2 P.M.							
3 P.M.							
4 P.M.							
5 P.M.							
6 P.M.							
7 P.M.							
8 P.M.							

Use with pupil page 41.　　　Making Math Work　3

Making Math Work

MAKING MATH WORK

Plan a budget for your trip. You have $1,050 to spend. Complete the chart below.
Check students' charts.

Amount allotted per day:	Actual amount per day:
Total allotment for food:	Daily food:
Total allotment for lodging:	Daily lodging:
Total allotment for recreation:	Daily recreation:
Total allotment for transportation:	Daily transportation:
Total allotment for entertainment:	Daily entertainment:

Suppose you traveled to a foreign country. Choose a country that you would like to visit. Find the current rate of exchange. Convert the allotments. Write the conversions below.
Check students' conversions.

Amount allotted for food:	Daily food:
Total allotment for lodging:	Daily lodging:
Total allotment for recreation:	Daily recreation:
Total allotment for transportation:	Daily transportation:
Total allotment for entertainment:	Daily entertainment:

4　Making Math Work　　　Use with pupil page 41.

Making Math Work

Objective: To identify the five properties of multiplication and division

Warm-Up
Give students ten basic multiplication facts and ten basic division facts to complete in less than 30 seconds. Repeat, using different facts.

GETTING STARTED

Write the following on the chalkboard: **1.** Dr. Cooke dressed himself. **2.** Dr. Cooke got out of bed. **3.** Dr. Cooke took a shower.

Ask students to tell in what order Dr. Cooke performed these steps. Is there another order he could have followed? (no) Now write **1.** Dr. Cooke put on his socks. **2.** Dr. Cooke put on his pants. **3.** Dr. Cooke put on his shirt. Ask students to give the order Dr. Cooke performed these steps. Is a second or a third sequence possible? (yes) Discuss why the order of the second set of events is more flexible than that of the first. (The results of the steps are independent; therefore, the steps are interchangeable.)

TEACHING THE LESSON

A. A factor is one of two or more numbers that, when multiplied together, result in a product. 3 and 5 are factors of 15, as are 1 and 15.

B. Write the following on the chalkboard.

$(3 \times 4) \times 5 = 5 \times (3 \times 4)$

Point out that because only the order and not the grouping of factors has been changed, this equation illustrates the Commutative not the Associative Property.

C. Note that the Distributive Property is also Commutative.

$4 \times (3 + 2) = (3 + 2) \times 4$

This property applies because $3 + 2$ is equal to the factor 5. The Distributive Property, however, is not Associative; for example, $4 \times (3 + 2)$ does not equal $(4 \times 3) + 2$.

D. $0 \div 0$ is also undefined because any number makes the equation $y \cdot 0 = 0$ true. It has no unique solution.

E. Remind students to check their answers by performing the inverse operation.

Multiplication and Division

A. Multiplication is **commutative.** The *order* of the factors does not change the product.

$5 \times 7 = 7 \times 5$
For any numbers a and b,
$a \times b = b \times a$.

B. Multiplication is **associative.** The *grouping* of the factors does not change the product.

$(6 \times 3) \times 2 = 6 \times (3 \times 2)$
For any numbers a, b, and c,
$(a \times b) \times c = a \times (b \times c)$.

C. Multiplication is **distributive** over addition. To multiply a sum by a number, you can multiply each addend by the number and then add the products.

$3 \times (5 + 4) = (3 \times 5) + (3 \times 4)$
For any numbers a, b, and c,
$a \times (b + c) = (a \times b) + (a \times c)$.

D. Here are some important facts about 0 and 1.

The product of a number and 1 is the number. For multiplication, 1 is the **identity element.**

$9 \times 1 = 9 \qquad 1 \times 16 = 16$
For any number a,
$a \times 1 = a$ and $1 \times a = a$.

The product of a number and 0 is 0.

$8 \times 0 = 0 \qquad 0 \times 17 = 0$
For any number a,
$a \times 0 = 0$ and $0 \times a = 0$.

If a number other than 0 is divided by itself, the quotient is 1.

$28 \div 28 = 1$
For any number a, if $a \neq 0$, $a \div a = 1$.

If a number is divided by 1, the quotient is that number.

$7 \div 1 = 7$
For any number a, $a \div 1 = a$.

If 0 is divided by any number other than 0, the quotient is 0.

$0 \div 5 = 0 \qquad 0 \div 29 = 0$
For any number a, if $a \neq 0$, $0 \div a = 0$.

You cannot divide by 0. The quotient is undefined.

$8 \div 0$ is undefined because no number n makes $n \times 0 = 8$ true.

E. Multiplication and division are **inverse** operations. They undo each other.

$24 \times 2 = 48 \qquad 56 \div 7 = 8$
$48 \div 2 = 24 \qquad 8 \times 7 = 56$

42

COMMON ERRORS

Students sometimes make the error of ignoring or misinterpreting the use of parentheses.

Remediation
For this error, remind students to complete the operation in parentheses first, and to then complete the rest of the equation.

Assign Reteach Master, p. 13.

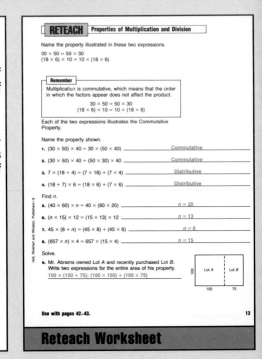

Name the property shown.

1. $37 \times 43 = 43 \times 37$
Commutative

2. $(7 \times 9) \times 2 = 7 \times (9 \times 2)$
Associative

3. $59 \times 1 = 59$
Identity

4. $15 \times (3 + 7) = 15 \times 3 + 15 \times 7$
Distributive

5. $4 \times (12 \times 11) = (4 \times 12) \times 11$
Associative

6. $72 \times 83 = 83 \times 72$
Commutative

Find n.

7. $0 \times 9 = n$ 0

8. $8 \div 8 = n$ 1

9. $843 \div 1 = n$ 843

10. $6 \times (2 + 8) = 6 \times 2 + 6 \times n$ 8

11. $246 \times 0 = n$ 0

12. $3,142 \times 1 = n$ 3,142

13. $75 \times n = 75$ 1

14. $93 \div n = 1$ 93

15. $45 \times n = 0$ 0

16. $72 \times 94 = 94 \times n$ 72

17. $14 \div 1 = n$ 14

18. $9 \times (7 + 2) = n \times 7 + 9 \times 2$ 9

19. $(21 \times 2) \times 9 = n \times (2 \times 9)$ 21

20. $143 \times 79 = 79 \times n$ 143

21. $184 \div 2 = 92$
$92 \times n = 184$ 2

22. $18 \times n = 36$ 2
$36 \div 2 = 18$

Use the properties to compute.

23. $6 \times (12 + 13)$ 150

24. $(52 \times 7) + (52 \times 3)$ 520

25. $(8 \times 1) \times 3$ 24

26. $\frac{1}{2} \times (16 + 24)$ 20

Solve.

27. Does $24 \div 8 = 8 \div 24$?

Is division commutative?
Explain.
No, because $24 \div 8 \neq 8 \div 24$.

★28. Does $(48 \div 24) \div 6 = 48 \div (24 \div 6)$?

Is division associative?
Explain.
No, because $(48 \div 24) \div 6 \neq 48 \div (24 \div 6)$.

★29. Does $(12 + 9) \div 3 = (12 \div 3) + (9 \div 3)$?

Is it true that for any numbers a, b, and c,
$(a + b) \div c = (a \div c) + (b \div c)$?
yes; yes

★30. Does $5 \times (10 - 1) = (5 \times 10) - (5 \times 1)$?

Is it true that for any numbers a, b, and c,
$a \times (b - c) = (a \times b) - (a \times c)$?
yes; yes

Classwork/Homework, page H17

43

ASSIGNMENT GUIDE

Basic: 1–12, 13–27 c

Average: 1–12, 14–28 e

Extended: 2–22 e, 23–30

Resources
Practice, p. 17   Class/Home, p. H17
Reteach, p. 13
Enrich, p. 17

Exercise Analysis
1–6   Name the property shown
7–22   Use the properties to solve for a variable
23–26   Use the properties to compute
27–30   Skill applications

FOLLOW-UP ACTIVITIES

REINFORCEMENT
Have students use the properties of multiplication and division to complete the following table.

X	6	(4)	1	(0)	2
(7)	42	(28)	(7)	(0)	(14)
5	(30)	20	(5)	(0)	(10)
(3)	(18)	(12)	3	(0)	(6)
9	(54)	(36)	(9)	0	(18)
8	(48)	(32)	(8)	(0)	16

PUZZLES AND GAMES
Have students find the product of the following numbers.

$(x - a)(x - b)(x - c) \ldots (x - z)$

Guide students in recognizing the pattern. In each case, x remains the same while the next consecutive letter of the alphabet is subtracted. The three dots indicate that all the letters from a to z are used. In that case, $(x - x)$ will be one of the factors. (Because $(x - x) = 0$ and any number multiplied by 0 is 0, the final answer will also be 0.)

COMING UP
"The powers that be"

Objectives: To multiply and divide a whole number by powers of 10

Warm-Up

Have students identify the property illustrated in each of the following.
$267 \times (30 \times 90) = (30 \times 90) \times 267$
(Commutative); $n \times 1 = n$ (Identity);
$11 \times (3 + 9) = (11 \times 3) + (11 \times 9)$
(Distributive); $(465 \times 37) \times 29 = 465 \times (37 \times 29)$. (Associative)

GETTING STARTED

Write the following example on the chalkboard.

$$\begin{array}{r} 50 \\ \times\ 40 \\ \hline \end{array}$$

Ask volunteers to demonstrate a quick method for finding the product.

TEACHING THE LESSON

A. Remind students that they can also use the Distributive Property in the following example.

$$\begin{aligned} 10 \times 53 &= 10 \times (50 + 3) \\ &= (10 \times 50) + (10 \times 3) \\ &= 500 + 30 \\ &= 530 \end{aligned}$$

Point out that multiplying by 10 leaves a zero in the ones place; multiplying by 100 leaves zeros in the ones and the tens places.

B. A *power* of 10 is the product obtained by using 10 as a factor a number of times. Note that when you divide by a multiple of 10, the divisor and the dividend may each be thought of as having one 10 as a factor; when you divide by a multiple of 100, the divisor and the dividend may be thought of as having two factors of 10, and so on; for example:

$$\frac{600}{200} = \frac{6 \times 10 \times 10}{2 \times 10 \times 10} = 3 \times 1 \times 1 = 3$$

Students should remember that they can check quotients and products by using inverse operations.

Checkpoint

The chart lists the common errors students make in multiplying or dividing whole numbers by a power of 10.

Correct Answers: 1b, 2a, 3c

Remediation

■ For these errors, have students expand the example by writing out all factors of 10 before multiplying or dividing.

☐ For these errors, assign Reteach Master, p. 14.

Multiplying and Dividing by Multiples of 10

A. Powers of 10 are numbers such as 10; 100; and 1,000.

Look at this pattern.

$$10 \times 47 = 470$$
$$100 \times 47 = 4,700$$
$$1,000 \times 47 = 47,000$$

Look at these examples.

$$\begin{aligned} 2 \times 30 &= 60 \\ 20 \times 30 &= 600 \\ 200 \times 30 &= 6,000 \\ 2,000 \times 30 &= 60,000 \end{aligned} \qquad \begin{aligned} 40 \times 5 &= 200 \\ 40 \times 50 &= 2,000 \\ 40 \times 500 &= 20,000 \\ 40 \times 5,000 &= 200,000 \end{aligned}$$

Multiply the two numbers without the zeros. Then write as many zeros as there are in the two factors.

B. To divide by a power of 10, you can change to an easier problem. Use patterns to help you.

$$\begin{aligned} 50 \div 10 &= 5 \\ 470 \div 10 &= 47 \\ 6,000 \div 10 &= 600 \end{aligned} \qquad \begin{aligned} 300 \div 100 &= 3 \\ 2,900 \div 100 &= 29 \\ 64,000 \div 100 &= 640 \end{aligned} \qquad \begin{aligned} 7,000 \div 1,000 &= 7 \\ 80,000 \div 1,000 &= 80 \\ 120,000 \div 1,000 &= 120 \end{aligned}$$

Other examples:

$$\begin{aligned} 60 \div 30 &= 2 \\ 24,000 \div 800 &= 30 \\ 35,000 \div 5,000 &= 7 \\ \$200,000 \div 4,000 &= \$50 \end{aligned} \qquad \begin{aligned} &\text{Think: } 6 \div 3 = 2. \\ &\text{Think: } 240 \div 8 = 30. \\ &\text{Think: } 35 \div 5 = 7. \\ &\text{Think: } 200 \div 4 = 50. \end{aligned}$$

To simplify a division problem, you can remove the same number of zeros from the dividend and the divisor.

Checkpoint Write the letter of the correct answer.

Multiply or divide.

1. 38×100 **a.** 380   **b.** 3,800   **c.** 38,000   **d.** 380,000

2. $6,400 \div 100$ **a.** 64   **b.** 640   **c.** 64,000   **d.** 640,000

3. $3,000 \times 70$ **a.** 43   **b.** 10,000   **c.** 210,000   **d.** 2,100,000

44

COMMON ERRORS

Answer Choice	Type of Error
■ 1a	Uses too few zeros
■ 1c, 1d, 2b, 3d	Uses too many zeros
☐ 2c, 2d	Multiplies instead of divides
☐ 3a	Divides instead of multiplying
■ 3b	Finds correct power of ten; does not multiply

| RETEACH | Multiplying and Dividing by Powers of 10 |

In a period of 100 days, 163,000 immigrants entered the United States. What was the average number of immigrants per day?

Remember

Simplify the division problem before you solve it. Take the same number of zeros away from the ends of the dividend and the divisor.

$$163,000 \div 100$$
$$1630\boxed{00} \div 1\boxed{00} \qquad 1,630 \div 1 = 1,630$$

The average number of immigrants per day was 1,630.

Complete this division table.

	Number	Divide by		
		10	100	1,000
1.	8,000	800	80	8
2.	60,000	6,000	600	60
3.	58,000	5,800	580	58
4.	160,000	16,000	1,600	160

Complete this multiplication table.

	Number	Multiply by		
		10	100	1,000
5.	7	70	700	7,000
6.	80	800	8,000	80,000
7.	32	320	3,200	32,000
8.	150	1,500	15,000	150,000

Solve.

9. In a period of 100 days, the United States admitted 275,000 immigrants from other countries. What was the average number of immigrants admitted per day?

2,750 immigrants

14   Use with pages 44–45.

Reteach Worksheet

Find the product.

1. 8×10
80
2. 13×10
130
3. 10×870
8,700
4. $4,120 \times 10$
41,200

5. 100×5
500
6. $100 \times \$20$
\$2,000
7. 760×100
76,000
8. $1,430 \times 100$
143,000

9. $9 \times 1,000$
9,000
10. $1,000 \times 25$
25,000
11. $508 \times 1,000$
508,000
12. $1,000 \times \$3,300$
\$3,300,000

13. 6×60
360
14. 300×80
24,000
15. $7,000 \times \$50$
\$350,000
16. $600 \times 9,000$
5,400,000

Find the quotient.

17. $10\overline{)90}$
9
18. $10\overline{)\$600}$
\$60
19. $10\overline{)2,000}$
200
20. $10\overline{)10,100}$
1,010

21. $4,000 \div 100$
40
22. $8,500 \div 100$
85
23. $\$13,300 \div 100$
\$133
24. $27,000 \div 100$
270

25. $\dfrac{\$34,000}{1,000}$
\$34
26. $\dfrac{77,000}{1,000}$
77
27. $\dfrac{245,000}{1,000}$
245
28. $\dfrac{407,000}{1,000}$
407

29. $400 \div 20$
20
30. $16,000 \div 400$
40
31. $\$90,000 \div 3,000$
\$30
32. $640,000 \div 8,000$
80

Solve.

33. Arthur rents out his fishing boat for \$50 per day. If he rented it out 20 days last summer, how much money did he earn? **\$1,000**

34. Amy water-skied for a total of 20 hours. If she skied for the same number of hours on each of 10 days, for how many hours did she ski each day? **2 hours**

35. Plan a vacation day for yourself, and schedule the amount of time for each activity. If you were to follow the same schedule for 20 days, how much time would you spend on each activity?
Answers will vary.

36. A corporate plane is flying at an average speed of 120 mph. At that rate, how far would it fly in 1 min? If it did not need refueling, how far could it fly in 10 h?
2 miles; 1,200 miles

ANOTHER LOOK

Add or subtract.

1. $3.9 + 2.2$
6.1
2. $0.43 + 2.07$
2.5
3. $0.08 + 1.12$
1.2
4. $6.39 + 3.61$
10

5. $6.2 - 1.5$
4.7
6. $8.27 + 4.9$
13.17
7. $4.2 + 0.39$
4.59
8. $5.06 - 4.4$
0.66

9. $0.694 + 5.72$
6.414
10. $0.902 - 0.41$
0.492
11. $9.1 + 0.944$
10.044
12. $1.083 - 0.397$
0.686

Classwork/Homework, page H18

45

Exercise Analysis

1–12	Multiply by a power of 10
13–16	Multiply by multiples of 10, 100, 1,000
17–28	Divide by a power of 10
29–32	Divide by a multiple of 10, 100, 1,000
33–34, 36	Skill applications
35	Problem formulation

Another Look
These exercises provide reinforcement in adding and subtracting decimals.

FOLLOW-UP ACTIVITIES

NUMBER SENSE (Mental Math)
Have students perform the following calculations without paper and pencil.

$36 \times 1,000$ (36,000) 100×25 (2,500)
$48,000 \div 1,000$ (48) $1,600 \div 10$ (160)
235×10 (2,350) $6,070 \div 10$ (607)

PUZZLES AND GAMES
Have students find the following words hidden in the puzzle below.

identity; product; quotient; dividend; divisor; commutative; minus; add; subtract; factor; associative; distributive; zero

Words may appear horizontally, vertically, and in reverse.

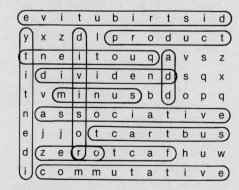

COMING UP
Keep it in your head.

45

Warm-Up
Write the following on the board for students to complete.

389 · 100	4,050 ÷ 10
(38,900)	(405)
1,214 · 1,000	306,330/10,000
(1,214,000)	(30.633)

GETTING STARTED

Have students use > or < to compare mentally.
1. 38 × 103 ● 3,800 (>)
2. 118 × 94 ● 11,800 (<)
3. 741 × 1,024 ● 741,000 (>)
4. 33 × 983 ● 33,000 (<)

Have students explain how they found their answers. Be sure they see that each answer is the product of the first factor and a multiple of 10. The answer is found by comparing the second factor and that power of 10.

TEACHING THE LESSON

A. Students should be alert to the possibility that one number can be rounded up or down, while the other is rounded up; for example:

$$66 \times 73 = 70 \times 70 = 4,900$$

It is more difficult to know whether estimates of this type are overestimates or underestimates. It depends on the size of each factor and how they were rounded.

B. Discuss the fact that the estimated answer is a significant underestimation. Ask students to think of situations in which an underestimate would be appropriate. Suggest those times when one has to have "at least enough," or a minimum amount.

C. Point out that $47.91 ÷ 23 is also about the same as $50 ÷ 25. The answer is still $2. There can be several pairs of compatible numbers for the same problem. Have students use compatible numbers to estimate the following.
1. 91,864 ÷ 41 (90,000 ÷ 45 = 2,000, 94,000 ÷ 47 = 2,000, 100,000 ÷ 50 = 2,000)
2. 79,865 ÷ 241 (80,000 ÷ 200 = 400, 75,000 ÷ 250 = 300)
Both 300 and 400 would be reasonable estimates.

Estimating Products and Quotients of Whole Numbers

A. The Martin family plans a 28-day camping trip along New York State's Seaway Trail. They budget about $75.00 a day for their trip. About how much money do they plan to spend?

The amount of money they will spend will vary somewhat from day to day. So it is reasonable to estimate the product.

Round each factor to its largest place.   Multiply.
28 × $75 $\longrightarrow$ 30 × $80   30 × $80 = $2,400

The Martins plan to spend about $2,400. Since both factors were rounded up, this is an overestimate. The estimated product is $2,400⁻.

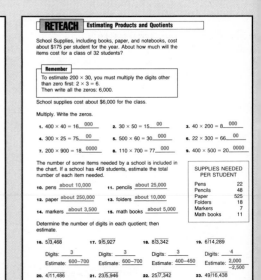

Other examples:

$523.85 $\longrightarrow$	$500	Both factors were rounded down.
× 32 $\longrightarrow$	× 30	
	$15,000⁺	

4,353 $\longrightarrow$	4,000	One factor is rounded up, and one factor is rounded down.
× 897 $\longrightarrow$	× 900	
	3,600,000	

B. You can also adjust when you estimate quotients.
Estimate 25,850 ÷ 15.
Decide on the number of digits in the quotient.

Think: 15)25. Write 1.   Write zeros for the other digits.

$$\begin{array}{r} 1\ ---\ \\ 15\overline{)25,850} \end{array}$$ 15)25,850 $\longrightarrow$ 1,000

Because 15 × 1,000 is 15,000, the estimate is an underestimate. Adjust by writing it as 1,000⁺.

C. Sometimes it is easier to divide with numbers that are close to the divisor and the dividend. Look for numbers that divide with a remainder of 0. These are called **compatible numbers.**

Estimate $47.91 ÷ 23.
Think: $46 ÷ 23 = $2 or $40 ÷ 20 = $2

$47.91 ÷ 23 is about $2.

46

COMMON ERRORS

Some students have difficulty understanding whether their estimated products are overestimates or underestimates.

Remediation
Have students place + or − by the numbers they are rounding to indicate the direction in which they are moving. Tell them that for multiplication, two +'s indicate an overestimate; two −'s indicate an underestimate. A + and a − may mean either. For division, (+) ÷ (−) indicates an overestimate, (−) ÷ (+) an underestimate. The patterns (+) ÷ (+) and (−) ÷ (−) may mean either.

Assign Reteach Master, p. 15.

ASSIGNMENT GUIDE

Basic: 1–12; 13–31 *o*

Average: 3–12; 13–31 *o*

Extended: 4–12; 14–30 *e*, 31–32

Resources
Practice, p. 19   Class/Home, p. H19
Reteach, p. 15
Enrich, p. 19

Exercise Analysis
1–12   Estimate the product
13–18   Estimate to compare numbers
19–30   Estimate the quotient
31–32   Skill applications

FOLLOW-UP ACTIVITIES

REINFORCEMENT
Have students choose which of the following pairs of factors would produce the best estimate for each problem:

1. <u>48 × 51</u>: 40 × 50; 50 × 50; 50 × 60 (50 × 50)
2. <u>342 × 59</u>: 300 × 60; 400 × 60; 350 × 60 (350 × 60)
3. <u>93 × 27</u>: 90 × 30; 100 × 20; 100 × 30 (90 × 30)

PROBLEM SOLVING
A math teacher grades an average of 278 papers per week. What is the total number of papers graded in a school year of 38 weeks? Give an estimate. (An acceptable estimate would be between 11,000 and 12,000 papers per year:

275 × 40 = 11,000
300 × 40 = 12,000)

COMING UP
Multiplying whole numbers

Estimate the product. Answers may vary. Accept any reasonable estimate.

1. 6×49 300⁻   **2.** 8×74 560⁺   **3.** $7 \times \$13.26$ \$70⁺   **4.** $5 \times 3,697$ 20,000⁻

5. 32×84 2,400⁺   **6.** 56×326 18,000   **7.** $48 \times \$3.23$ \$150   **8.** $683 \times \$8.71$ \$6300⁻

9. $876 \times 5,432$ 4,500,000   **10.** $2,463 \times 6,879$ 14,000,000   **11.** $6,345 \times \$18.57$ \$120,000   **12.** $7,689 \times 8,342$ 64,000,000

Estimate. Write > or < for ●.

13. $6,289 \times 72$ ● 420,000 >   **14.** 38×491 ● 12,000 >

15. $30 \times \$49.75$ ● \$1,500 <   **16.** $63 \times 4,856$ ● 250,000 >

17. $283 \times 46,328$ ● 8,000,000 >   **18.** $6,985 \times 9,498$ ● 54,000,000 >

Estimate the quotient. Answers may vary. Accept any reasonable estimate.

19. $63\overline{)37,867}$ 600   **20.** $58\overline{)46,789}$ 800   **21.** $32\overline{)568,345}$ 10,000–20,000   **22.** $49\overline{)\$285.73}$ \$5–\$7

23. $284\overline{)34,556}$ 100   **24.** $793\overline{)94,587}$ 100   **25.** $967\overline{)456,983}$ 400–500   **26.** $653\overline{)\$482.65}$ \$0.70–\$0.80

27. $8,452\overline{)234,673}$ 30   **28.** $5,793\overline{)3,876,452}$ 600–700   **29.** $3,456\overline{)165,679}$ 50   **30.** $4,683\overline{)\$3,432.80}$ \$0.70–\$0.80

Solve.

31. As part of their trip, the Martins camp at the nation's oldest state park, Niagara Reservation. They see Niagara Falls at night and learn that the amount of water flowing over the falls is about 350,000 gallons per second. About how many gallons is that in 2 minutes? 35,000,000–42,000,000 gallons

32. Mrs. Martin's friends have given her money to buy them T-shirts that say, "I Didn't Go Over the Falls in a Barrel, But I Had a Barrel of Fun." She buys 11 shirts that cost a total of \$129.75. About how much does each shirt cost? \$10–\$13

Classwork/Homework, page H19

47

47

Objectives: To identify needed and extra information

Warm-Up
Have students complete the following exercises.

17.2 + 11.7 = ■ (28.9)
1,001 − 110 = ■ (891)
3,000.14 − 268.3 = ■ (2,731.84)

GETTING STARTED

Have students listen carefully to the following word problem.

The Johnson family went on a trip to visit Mr. Johnson's parents. On Monday, they drove 160 miles. On Tuesday, they drove 250 miles. On Wednesday, they drove 75 miles and reached their destination. On Saturday and Sunday, they drove home, covering the same distance they traveled on Monday, Tuesday, and Wednesday. How far did they drive altogether on Saturday and Sunday?

Have students identify the facts needed to solve the problem. (Reread the problem if necessary.) After listing the facts on the board, have students solve the problem. (485 miles; Facts needed: distance traveled on Monday, Tuesday, and Wednesday; that the distance traveled on Saturday and Sunday is the same as the distance traveled on Monday, Tuesday and Wednesday)

TEACHING THE LESSON

Students will often encounter problems in which extra information has been supplied or in which needed information is missing. This situation can be confusing at first. Students may think that they have missed a crucial fact or misunderstood the question. Students must learn to approach these questions systematically and determine what is being asked, what information is needed to find the answer, and whether the needed information is supplied. This lesson encourages students to separate and list the facts that are supplied in the problem and then to determine which facts are relevant. This approach will help to correct a common student impulse to use the first numbers encountered in a problem without determining exactly what the numbers represent.

Questions: Discuss the question in the example. To which leaders does the question refer? (leaders of groups on the Tour of Somerville trail in 1976) What information would you need to solve this question? (the number of leaders)

Tools: The lesson breaks the approach into four steps. Difficulties might arise in

---

PROBLEM SOLVING
Identifying Extra/Needed Information

The *Tour de France* bicycle race covers about 2,500 miles. More than 100 cyclists compete annually. The Tour of Somerville in the United States covers 50 miles. In 1976, a group of bikers led 10,000 other bikers along the trail. How many bikers were there in each leader's group?

A problem may not contain enough information for you to solve it. Sometimes you can supply the information you need. You may also find problems that contain extra information. You have to focus on only the information you need. Follow these steps.

1. Study the question.

   How many bikers were there in each leader's group?

2. List the facts. Cross out the facts that won't help you.

   a. The *Tour de France* is 2,500 miles long.
   b. The Tour of Somerville is 50 miles long.
   c. More than 100 cyclists compete annually in the *Tour de France*.
   d. A total of 10,000 bikers were led in the Tour of Somerville in 1976.
   e. Some bikers led groups of other bikers.
   Cross out *a*, *b*, and *c*.

3. List the facts you need that were not stated in the problem.

   the number of leaders

4. Study the facts you have. If you have all the information you need, or if you know where to find it, solve the problem. If not, write *There is not enough information*.

   There is not enough information to solve this problem.

48

Steps 2 and 3 in listing the needed facts, and identifying extra and missing information. An effective tool for clarifying needed information is to have students write a word equation that describes the facts and the operations needed to find the solution; for example:

$$\text{Number of bikers} \div \text{Number of leaders} = \text{Number of bikers in each group}$$

Breaking the problem down into components like this may help students clarify needed and extra information. Make sure that students realize that in some word problems in which they do not have the necessary information, the information may not be available and so, they cannot solve the problem.

Solutions: Difficulties are not likely to be computational; rather, students might have

difficulty determining the needed quantities and the relationship among them. If needed, have students use the word-equation approach mentioned in the Tools section.

Checks: Students should check any needed information they do not have against their list of facts to be sure that the information was not supplied and crossed out. Alternately, students should read the entire problem through, with the question in mind, to be sure that the information needed to solve the problem is not actually supplied.

Write the letter of the sentence that describes the problem.

1. Almost 100,000 bike riders are members of the League of American Cyclists. They are among the 75 million cyclists in the United States. If 10,000 cyclists live in Pennsylvania, how many live in other states?

   a. There is not enough information to solve the problem.

   (b.) There is more information than you need to solve the problem.

2. The bicycle was introduced in the United States in 1866. By 1897, about 4 million Americans were riding bikes. What was the bike-riding population of California?

   (a.) There is not enough information to solve the problem.

   b. There is more information than you need to solve the problem.

Solve if possible. Identify any needed information.

3. The bicycle was invented in 1790. In 1896, cycling became an official event of the Olympic Games. In how many Olympics has cycling been an event? (HINT: There were no Olympics in 1916, 1940, and 1944.) Depends on the year the book is used.

4. In 1983, Laurent Fignon won the *Tour de France* in a little more than 105 hours. The race was 2,315 miles long. How much faster was his average mile-per-hour speed than the average speed of the racer who finished second? needed information: average speed of the racer who finished second

5. In 1980, people in the United States bought about 7 million bicycles made in their country. They also bought about 2 million imported bicycles. The average foreign-made bike sold for $200. About how much did those people spend on bikes that year? needed information: average price of United States-made bikes

6. A bike shop sells rebuilt 3-speed bikes for $77.50 each. On Monday, 4 people bought rebuilt bikes and 2 people bought new bikes. How much money did the shop receive that day? needed information: price of new bike

7. A biker took a 4-day tour. He biked 35 miles per day. How many miles did he travel? 140 miles

8. A cross-country bike trail covers 4,300 miles. It passes through or near 28 national parks in 10 states. Oregon has 6 of these parks, Idaho has 3, and Montana has 4. How many parks in other states does the trail pass through or near? 15 parks

Classwork/Homework, page H20

Warm-Up

Have students find the missing number.

$252 \times \blacksquare = 252{,}000 \ (1{,}000)$
$\blacksquare \times 100 = 2{,}400 \ (24)$
$9{,}866 \times 10 = \blacksquare \ (98{,}660)$
$350 \times \blacksquare = 35{,}000 \ (100)$

GETTING STARTED

Materials: lined notebook paper, centimeter ruler per student

Have students label the top 13 lines on a sheet of notebook paper from 0 to 12. Tell them that they can multiply 3×5 by placing the 0 end of the ruler on the line marked 0 and turning the ruler until the 3-cm mark lines up with the line marked 1 on the notebook paper. Then students need to find only the place where the line marked 5 intersects the ruler (15 cm) in order to find the desired product (15). Point out that by using millimeters instead of centimeters, they can multiply even larger numbers.

TEACHING THE LESSON

You can provide additional practice in estimation by having students estimate the following products: 44×563 (24,000); 603×478 (300,000); $769 \times 8{,}152$. (6,400,000)

When discussing the Other Examples section, you may want to multiply by the tens in $306 \times 5{,}218$ to demonstrate why the shortcut works.

Checkpoint

The chart lists the common errors students make in multiplying whole numbers.

Correct Answers: 1c, 2c

Remediation

■ For this error, make flashcards that list the basic multiplication facts. Drill students in pairs until they can recall all the basic facts quickly.

☐ For these errors, assign Reteach Master, p. 16.

Multiplying Whole Numbers

Rita is a flight attendant. In the first 10 weeks of the year, she traveled an average of 7,185 miles each week. At that rate, if she works 48 weeks per year, how many miles would she travel per year?

Multiply $48 \times 7{,}185$ to find the number of miles.

You can estimate to see whether your answer is reasonable.

$$
\begin{array}{ccc}
7{,}185 & \rightarrow & 7{,}000 \\
\times \quad 48 & \rightarrow & \times \quad 50 \\
\hline
& & 350{,}000
\end{array}
\qquad
\begin{array}{r}
7{,}185 \\
\times \quad 48 \\
\hline
57\ 480 \\
287\ 400 \\
\hline
344{,}880
\end{array}
$$

Rita travels 344,880 miles per year. The answer is reasonably close to 350,000.

Other examples:

$$
\begin{array}{r}
529 \\
\times\ 476 \\
\hline
3\ 174 \\
37\ 030 \\
211\ 600 \\
\hline
251{,}804
\end{array}
$$
You can omit these zeros.

$$
\begin{array}{r}
5{,}218 \\
\times\ 306 \\
\hline
31\ 308 \\
1\ 565\ 40 \\
\hline
1{,}596{,}708
\end{array}
$$
Write a zero in the tens place and continue to multiply.

$$
\begin{array}{r}
\$49.65 \\
\times\ 27 \\
\hline
347\ 55 \\
993\ 0 \\
\hline
\$1{,}340.55
\end{array}
$$

4×223 million $= 892$ million 13×57 billion $= 741$ billion

Checkpoint Write the letter of the correct answer.

Multiply.

1. $25 \times \$4{,}863$

  a. \$34,041   **b.** \$106,265
  c. \$121,575   **d.** \$133,815

2. $208 \times 7{,}234$

  a. 72,340   **b.** 202,552
  c. 1,504,672   **d.** 1,535,682

COMMON ERRORS

Answer Choice	Type of Error
☐ 1a, 2b	Fails to write zeros in the partial product
■ 1b	Error in a basic fact
☐ 1d, 2d	Adds the regrouped number before multiplying
☐ 2a	Multiplies the greater factor by 10 instead of by the other factor

---

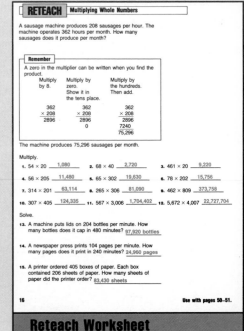

RETEACH Multiplying Whole Numbers

A sausage machine produces 208 sausages per hour. The machine operates 362 hours per month. How many sausages does it produce per month?

Remember
A zero in the multiplier can be written when you find the product.

Multiply by 8.	Multiply by zero. Show it in the tens place.	Multiply by the hundreds. Then add.
362 × 208 2896	362 × 208 2896 0	362 × 208 2896 7240 75,296

The machine produces 75,296 sausages per month.

Multiply.

1. 54×20 __1,080__ 2. 68×40 __2,720__ 3. 461×20 __9,220__

4. 56×205 __11,480__ 5. 65×302 __19,630__ 6. 78×202 __15,756__

7. 314×201 __63,114__ 8. 265×306 __81,090__ 9. 462×809 __373,758__

10. 307×405 __124,335__ 11. $567 \times 3{,}006$ __1,704,402__ 12. $5{,}672 \times 4{,}007$ __22,727,704__

Solve.

13. A machine puts lids on 204 bottles per minute. How many bottles does it cap in 480 minutes? __97,920 bottles__

14. A newspaper press prints 104 pages per minute. How many pages does it print in 240 minutes? __24,960 pages__

15. A printer ordered 405 boxes of paper. Each box contained 206 sheets of paper. How many sheets of paper did the printer order? __83,430 sheets__

16   Use with pages 50–51.

Reteach Worksheet

Multiply.

1. 324 × 2 648	**2.** 3,225 × 3 9,675	**3.** 7,050 × 9 63,450	**4.** 32,156 × 4 128,624	**5.** $4,360.75 × 7 $30,525.25
6. 43 × 27 1,161	**7.** 139 × 62 8,618	**8.** 9,062 × 83 752,146	**9.** $135.22 × 74 $10,006.28	**10.** 761,470 × 14 10,660,580
11. 231 × 145 33,495	**12.** 704 × 352 247,808	**13.** $1,643 × 229 $376,247	**14.** $137.06 × 355 $48,656.30	**15.** 8,937 × 525 4,691,925

16. 27 million × 3 81 million	**17.** 462 billion × 45 20,790 billion	**18.** 64 billion × 326 20,864 billion	**19.** 821 trillion × 249 204,429 trillion

20. 74 × 2,305
170,570

21. 81,432 × 6
488,592

22. 32 × 14,477
463,264

23. 124,872 × 4
499,488

24. 43 × 333,111
14,323,773

25. 426 × 75,193
32,032,218

Solve.

26. Elroy drove an average of 17,740 miles each summer for the last 14 years. What is the total number of miles he drove during the summers? 248,360 miles

27. A Boeing 727 seats 147 passengers, and a Boeing 757 seats 185 passengers. How many more passengers does the 757 seat? 38 passengers

28. Mr. Sorkin made 8 round-trip business flights across the United States last year. It is 2,572 air miles each way. How many air miles did he fly last year? 41,152 air miles

★29. A train from New York to Boston travels 75 mph for 2 h. Then, because of signal problems, it slows to 35 mph for the rest of the trip. If the trip takes 4 h, how many miles does the train travel? 220 miles

NUMBER SENSE

Find an easy way to compute mentally.

Example: $9 \times 5 \times 8 \times 2 = 720$ (with 10 over 5×2, 72 over 9×8)

1. 13 × 5 × 2
130

2. 2 × 58 × 50
5,800

3. 8 × 9 × 5
360

4. 6 × 4 × 1 × 5
120

5. 2 × 7 × 9 × 5
630

6. 5 × 10 × 8 × 2
800

7. 10 × 3 × 50 × 1
1,500

8. 10 × 5 × 4 × 4 × 2
1,600

9. 4 × 10 × 3 × 2 × 5
1,200

Classwork/Homework, page H21

51

ASSIGNMENT GUIDE

Basic: 1–10, 11–27o, NS 1–6

Average: 1–10, 12–28e, NS 4–9

Extended: 2–18 e, 20–29, NS 4–9

Resources
Practice, p. 21   Class/Home, p. H21
Reteach, p. 16
Enrich, p. 21

Exercise Analysis

1–15   Multiply by a 1-, 2-, or 3-digit factor
16–19   Multiply with short word names
20–25   Mixed practice
26–29   Skill applications

You may wish to allow students to use calculators for some of these exercises.

Number Sense

These exercises enable students to regroup factors in a way that makes multiplication easier.

FOLLOW-UP ACTIVITIES

REINFORCEMENT

Have students find the product in the following manner.

261 × 430

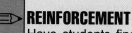

430   430   430
× 1   × 60   × 200
430 + 25,800 + 86,000 = (112,230)

Repeat for similar examples.

COMPUTER

Have students write a program that will instruct the computer to: **1.** Select at random a number from 1 to 100. **2.** Ask the student to select another number from 1 to 100. **3.** Ask the student to multiply both numbers. **4.** Tell the student whether the answer is correct. A sample program is shown below.

```
10 RANDOMIZE
20 INPUT "PICK A NUMBER FROM 1 TO
   100"; N
30 LET C = INT(RND(0)*100) + 1
40 PRINT "WHAT IS THE PRODUCT
   OF"; N; "AND"; C; "?"
50 INPUT P
60 LET D = N*C
70 IF P = D THEN 100
80 INPUT "WRONG. TRY AGAIN."; P
90 GOTO 70
100 PRINT "YOU GOT IT!"
110 END
```

COMING UP

Crossing the Great Divide

51

Warm-Up

Have students multiply 3-digit numbers by 1- and 2-digit numbers.

825 × 9 (7,425) 382 × 65 (24,830)
680 × 7 (4,760) 815 × 64 (52,160)
706 × 9 (6,354) 513 × 39 (20,007)

GETTING STARTED

Demonstrate the usefulness of division in everyday life by relating it to the chapter theme of travel. Write the following three categories on the board: *Before Vacation, During Vacation, After Vacation.*

For each phase, have students think of situations that require division. Make a list; for example, in planning a vacation, you might divide to find the number of times you will wear an outfit, to determine the number of days you will spend in each town, or to find the quantity of gas you will need to reach a certain destination. For each situation listed, have students think of an appropriate problem that requires division to solve.

TEACHING THE LESSON

Use the teaching example on page 52 to review the meaning of *dividend, divisor, quotient,* and *remainder.* Point out that the remainder 35 stands for $\frac{35}{53}$. You may wish to have students use calculators to divide in order to see that $41\frac{35}{53} = \frac{2,208}{53}$. Emphasize the fact that a fraction is another way to show the division of whole numbers. Direct students to the Other Examples section, and call their attention to those examples whose quotients contain zeros. Review the corresponding division as needed.

Dividing Whole Numbers

There were 2,208 passengers on a recent crossing of the *Queen Elizabeth II (QE2).* The list of passengers was printed on computer paper, with 53 names on each sheet. How many full sheets were there? How many names were there on the sheet that was not full?

Divide 53)2,208.
Divide the thousands. Think: 53)2. Not enough thousands.
Divide the hundreds. Think: 53)22. Not enough hundreds.

Divide the tens. **Divide the ones.**
Think: 53)220, or 5)22. **Think: 53)88, or 5)8.**
Estimate 4. **Estimate 1.** Check.

```
      4                        41 R35                  41 ← quotient
53)2,208  Multiply.    53)2,208  Multiply.           × 53 ← divisor
  2 12   Subtract.       2 12↓  Subtract.            ───
  ───    and compare.      ───   and compare.         123
    8                       88                       2 05
                            53                       ─────
                            ──                       2,173
                            35                    +     35 ← remainder
                                                  ───────
                                                  2,208 ← dividend
```

There were 41 full sheets and 1 sheet with 35 names on it.

Other examples:

5,931 ÷ 9   26,879 ÷ 215 $\frac{3,635}{12}$ $42,084 ÷ 7

```
    659              125 R4            302 R11           $6,012
9)5,931         215)26,879         12)3,635         7)$42,084
  5 4              21 5               3 6                42
  ──               ───                ──                 ──
   53               5 37               35                 08
   45               4 30               24                  7
   ──               ────               ──                 ──
    81              1 079              11                  14
    81              1 075                                  14
    ──              ─────                                  ──
     0                  4                                   0
```

Math Reasoning, page H209

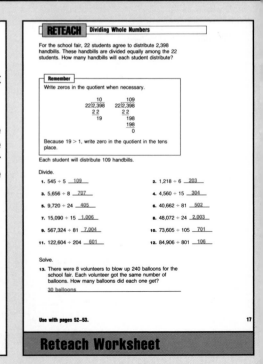

52

COMMON ERRORS

Students often divide correctly but align the quotient incorrectly.

Remediation
Encourage students to estimate the answers before dividing. Then have them check their answers against their estimates to make sure they have placed the quotient correctly.

Assign Reteach Master, p. 17.

RETEACH Dividing Whole Numbers

For the school fair, 22 students agree to distribute 2,398 handbills. These handbills are divided equally among the 22 students. How many handbills will each student distribute?

Remember
Write zeros in the quotient when necessary.

```
    10            109
22)2,398       22)2,398
  2 2             2 2
  ──              ──
   19             198
                  198
                  ───
                    0
```

Because 19 > 1, write zero in the quotient in the tens place.

Each student will distribute 109 handbills.

Divide.

1. 545 ÷ 5 __109__   2. 1,218 ÷ 6 __203__

3. 5,656 ÷ 8 __707__   4. 4,560 ÷ 15 __304__

5. 9,720 ÷ 24 __405__   6. 40,662 ÷ 81 __502__

7. 15,090 ÷ 15 __1,006__   8. 48,072 ÷ 24 __2,003__

9. 567,324 ÷ 81 __7,004__   10. 73,605 ÷ 105 __701__

11. 122,604 ÷ 204 __601__   12. 84,906 ÷ 801 __106__

Solve.

13. There were 8 volunteers to blow up 240 balloons for the school fair. Each volunteer got the same number of balloons. How many balloons did each one get?

__30 balloons__

Use with pages 52–53.   17

Reteach Worksheet

Divide

1. 6)48
   8

2. 8)720
   90

3. 7)143
   20 R3

4. 9)355
   39 R4

5. 24)459
   19 R3

6. 38)789
   20 R29

7. 45)3,095
   68 R35

8. 77)$8,316
   $108

9. 196)5,481
   27 R189

10. 590)19,663
    33 R193

11. 837)67,514
    80 R554

12. 426)130,782
    307

13. 292 ÷ 4
    73

14. 1,587 ÷ 3
    529

15. 3,644 ÷ 7
    520 R4

16. 1,932 ÷ 4
    483

17. 8,049 ÷ 46
    174 R45

18. 78,492 ÷ 93
    844

19. 120,223 ÷ 57
    2,109 R10

20. 13,728 ÷ 15
    915 R3

21. $10,584 ÷ 108
    $98

22. 136,412 ÷ 576
    236 R476

23. 205,833 ÷ 670
    307 R143

24. $927,827 ÷ 393
    $2,360 R347

25. $\frac{763}{7}$ 109

26. $\frac{4,196}{5}$ 839 R1

27. $\frac{32,940}{9}$ 3,660

28. $\frac{6,421}{6}$ 1,070 R1

29. $\frac{75,126}{31}$ 2,423 R13

30. $\frac{105,600}{88}$ 1,200

31. $\frac{50,370}{34}$ 1,481 R16

32. $\frac{723,946}{21}$ 34,473 R13

33. $\frac{262,685}{658}$ 399 R143

34. $\frac{\$1,906,000}{479}$ $3,979 R59

35. $\frac{2,412,954}{318}$ 7,587 R288

36. $\frac{9,918,740}{996}$ 9,958 R572

Solve.

37. If the *QE2* travels at a speed of 32 nautical miles per hour, how many hours will it take to travel 2,752 nautical miles? 86 hours

38. A group of 16 people chartered a boat at a cost of $24,288 for a week. How much did it cost per person? $1,518

39. The cruise ship *South Seas* leaves Los Angeles with 1,263 passengers on board. If another 1,548 passengers board in Panama, how many passengers are there on board? 2,811 passengers

★40. Two advertisements for Scandinavian cruises list different rates. The first rate is $7,450 for 18 days. The second rate is $5,800 for 14 days. Which cruise costs less per day? the 18-day cruise

MIDCHAPTER REVIEW

Name the property.

1. 76 × 1 = 76
   Identity

2. 5 × (6 + 12) = (5 × 6) + (5 × 12)
   Distributive

3. 13 × (3 × 78) = (13 × 3) × 78
   Associative

4. 123 × 87 = 87 × 123
   Commutative

Find the product or the quotient.

5. 70 × 400
   28,000

6. 200 × 600
   120,000

7. $4,673 × 6
   $28,038

8. $456.43 × 74
   $33,775.82

9. 50,200 ÷ 100
   502

10. 4,500 ÷ 90
    50

11. 900)$8,100
    $9

12. 70)$49,000
    $700

Classwork/Homework, page H22

53

ASSIGNMENT GUIDE

Basic:	1–38 o, MCR
Average:	2–39 e, MCR
Extended:	4–40 e, MCR

Resources
Practice, p. 22   Class/Home, p. H22
Reteach, p. 17   Reasoning, p. H209
Enrich, p. 22

Exercise Analysis

1–36 Divide whole numbers in vertical, horizontal, and fraction form, using divisors of from 1 to 3 digits

37–40 Skill applications

You may wish to allow students to use calculators for some of these exercises.

Midchapter Review

This review provides an opportunity for you and students to assess their understanding of the concepts and skills developed to this point in the chapter.

FOLLOW-UP ACTIVITIES

REINFORCEMENT
Write the following on the board.

```
      6,300           129            121 R57
1.  2)1,260  2.  6)759   3.  79)8,216
     12               6                 7 9
     06              15                 1 71
      6              12                 1 58
     00              39                  136
      0              39                   79
      0               0                   57
```

Tell students that there is one error in each example. Have them find the errors and rework each example correctly.
(**1.** misplaces first digit in quotient, and then writes extra zero (630) **2.** divides 39 by 6 incorrectly (126 R3) **3.** subtracts the first partial product incorrectly (104)

PUZZLES AND GAMES
In the following "masked" division example, each digit from 1 to 9 is used exactly once. Have students use the hint provided to find the missing digits.

```
         2xx                297
  x8)x,xxx           18)5,346
```

COMING UP
Getting to the point

53

Objective: To estimate to solve problems

Warm-Up
Have students estimate the following.

114 + 689 (about 800)
1,794 − 205 (about 1,600)
32 × 106 (about 3,200)
4,787 ÷ 398 (about 12)

GETTING STARTED

Tell students that light from the sun travels 299,727 kilometers in 1 second. The distance from the sun to Earth is 149,637,000 kilometers. Ask students about how many seconds it takes for sunlight to reach Earth. (about 500 s) Elicit from students the methods of rounding and estimating they used to find an answer.

TEACHING THE LESSON

Estimation is an essential skill in situations where precision is unnecessary or unobtainable. It should be used to check the reasonableness of a computed answer. Before estimating have students ask:
- Should I estimate or compute an exact answer?
- If I estimate, should I overestimate or underestimate?
- Is my estimate an adequate answer to the question?

In the instructional problems, have students pay particular attention to the reasons for overestimating or underestimating; for example, it would be better to have too much gasoline than to run out on the highway; so, Samantha should *overestimate* the amount she will need. In figuring this amount, she *underestimates* the number of miles her car will travel on 1 gallon.

Questions: Encourage students to think about what *type* of answer the question calls for. In the introductory problem, it is impossible to predict exactly how much gasoline Samantha will need to buy.

Tools: It will be helpful to review both front-end estimation and rounding. Point out that the front-end method results in an underestimate. Encourage students to use their own method of estimating if it is effective.

Solutions: Some of the estimation in this lesson precedes the teaching of the actual computation; for example, multiplication of decimals. In these instances especially, students should use *only* estimation.

Checks: Estimating an answer before computing provides a good check for the reasonableness of an answer. Finding the exact answer should *not* be used as a check on estimation as this would defeat the purpose of estimating.

| QUESTIONS | TOOLS | SOLUTIONS | CHECKS |

PROBLEM SOLVING
Estimation

Sometimes you can solve a problem by estimating. In many cases, you must decide whether you should **overestimate** or **underestimate**.

Samantha is planning to drive to a park about 100 miles away. Her car is almost out of gas. She remembers that gas costs $1.39 per gallon. Her car travels about 25 miles per gallon. How much money will Samantha have to pay for gas? Samantha decides to estimate.

When estimating to find out whether you have enough money, is it usually better to overestimate or to underestimate costs? Samantha overestimates to be sure that she will have enough money.

When estimating how much gasoline she will need, should she round her gas mileage up or down? She rounds down to be sure that she won't use more gas than she has planned to use.

$$25 \rightarrow 20$$

Samantha realizes that since the park is about 100 miles away, the total number of miles for the round trip is about 200 miles. Samantha divides the number of miles by the 20 miles per gallon.

$$200 \div 20 = 10$$

Samantha estimates that she will need about 10 gallons of gas for the round trip. She overestimates the cost per gallon as $1.50 to be on the safe side. She multiplies her estimate of the number of gallons by the estimated price per gallon.

$$10 \times \$1.50 = \$15$$

Samantha decides to take at least $15 to pay for gas.

If you were going to estimate to solve, which amounts in the problems should be overestimated or underestimated? Write the letter of the correct answer.

1. Bobby must be home to meet Claude, who is driving 272 miles to visit him. If Claude leaves at 11:10 A.M. and averages 53 miles per hour, at what time should Bobby plan to be home?

    a. Overestimate the number of miles and underestimate the rate of speed.
    b. Underestimate the number of miles and overestimate the rate of speed.
    c. Underestimate both the number of miles and the rate of speed.

2. Al's car is almost out of gas. He must drive 72 miles to his home. The car travels 33 miles per gallon. How much gas should he buy?

    a. Overestimate the miles per gallon and underestimate the number of miles.
    b. Overestimate both the miles per gallon and the number of miles.
    c. Underestimate the miles per gallon and overestimate the number of miles.

Solve by estimation.

3. Travis has $10. He wants to take a taxi across town. Taxis charge $2.22 for the first mile and $1.46 for each additional mile. His destination is 5 miles away. Does Travis have enough money for a taxi? yes

4. Shelly has $50 to spend on a whale-watch cruise for herself and her sister. Tickets cost $11.60 each, and lunch costs $4.85 per person. Will she have enough money left to buy an $18.99 pair of binoculars? no

5. Shelly and her sister are taking the 12:35 P.M. train. They can walk to the train station in about 22 minutes. They plan to allow 20 minutes to buy their tickets and board the train. At what time should they leave their house? Answers will vary. Times around 11:45 A.M. are good answers.

6. Shelly's sister is paying for the transportation. Round-trip train tickets cost $12.75 per person. A taxi from the train to the harbor costs $5.50. How much will round-trip transportation cost? about $38.00

7. At a cafeteria, prices for adults average about $3.60 for main courses and $0.90 for side dishes. Children's portions are half price. If a family of 2 adults and 2 children each have a main dish and 2 side dishes, how much will the meal cost in all? Answers will vary. Amounts between $15.00 and $20.00 are good answers.

Classwork/Homework, page H23

ASSIGNMENT GUIDE

Basic:	1–4
Average:	2–6
Extended:	3–7

Resources
Practice, p. 23   Class/Home, p. H23
Enrich, p. 23

Exercise Analysis
1–2   Decide whether to overestimate or underestimate
3–7   Estimate to solve

FOLLOW-UP ACTIVITIES

PROBLEM SOLVING
Copy these questions on the chalkboard or provide them as a handout.

1. About how many seconds are there in a year? (about 32,000,000 seconds)
2. The human heart pumps 1 quart of blood in about 10 seconds. About how many quarts does it pump in 75 years? (about 250,000,000 quarts)
3. Lucas scored the following in 9 games of Video Rodeo: 1,396,500; 3,172,000; 2,478,000; 192,500; 1,002,000; 3,954,000; 1,907,500; 706,100; and 2,770,500. About what was his average score? (about 2,000,000)
4. In playing a board game, Felicity started out with $7,500. She lost the following amounts of money: $112; $95; $1,480; $7; $36; $452; and $955. About how much money did she have at the end of the game? ($4,000–$4,400)

Have students estimate the answer to each question and explain how they obtained their estimates.

CALCULATOR
Materials; questions from Problem Solving Follow Up activity (above), calculator per student or group

Have students use their calculators to compute each exact amount in the Problem Solving questions above. (31,536,000 seconds, 236,520,000 quarts, 1,953,233.3 points, $4,363)

COMING UP
This lesson rates a 10.

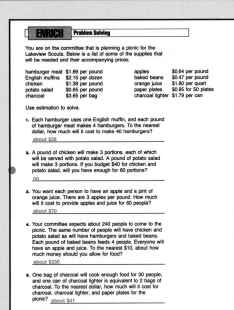

Practice Worksheet

Enrich Worksheet

Objectives: To multiply and divide decimals by powers of 10

Warm-Up
Have students multiply and divide whole numbers by powers of 10, such as:

$731 \times 1,000$ (731,000) $2,590 \div 10$ (259)

GETTING STARTED

Write the following examples on the chalkboard.

5,200	520	52	5.2	0.52
$\times$ 10	$\times$ 10	$\times$ 10	$\times$ 10	$\times$ 10
52,000	5,200	520	(52)	(5.2)

Have students extend the pattern to find the products in the last two examples. Ask them to formulate a rule for multiplying a decimal by 10.

Repeat for division.

TEACHING THE LESSON

A. Remind students that moving the decimal point really consists of altering the place value of the number. Thus, moving the decimal point 1, 2, or 3 places to the right increases the number 10, 100, or 1,000 times.

B. It follows that moving the decimal point to the left reduces a number's value by a power of 10.

Checkpoint
The chart lists the common errors students make in multiplying and dividing decimals by a power of 10.

Correct Answers: 1c, 2c, 3b, 4b

Remediation
■ For these errors, some students might encounter difficulty in remembering in which direction to move the decimal point when multiplying or dividing.

Write 7.0. Guide students in rewriting the number by moving the decimal point 1 place to the right. Have a volunteer read the new number. (70) Ask how many times as great 70 is compared to 7. (10 times)

Write $7 \times 10 = 70$. Continue the exercise by writing 16.0, 82.0, 394.0, 5.7 and 27.86. Emphasize the fact that moving the decimal point 1 place to the right has the same effect as multiplying by 10.

Repeat the activity to show the effect of moving the decimal point 1 place to the left in division.

□ For these errors, guide the students in completing Reteach Master, p. 18.

Decimals and Powers of 10

A. Tara was motorcycling cross-country. At the end of the first day, she had traveled 285.4 miles. If she maintains this rate, how many miles can she travel in 10 days?

To multiply a decimal by a power of 10, move the decimal point one place to the right for each zero in the factor.

Look at the pattern.

$10 \times 285.4 = 2\ 8\ 5\ 4.$	$= 2,854$	one place to the right
$100 \times 285.4 = 2\ 8\ 5\ 4\ 0.$	$= 28,540$	two places
$1,000 \times 285.4 = 2\ 8\ 5\ 4\ 0\ 0. = 285,400$		three places

Tara can travel 2,854 miles in 10 days.

B. Divide 57.24 by 1,000.

To divide a decimal by a power of 10, move the decimal point one place to the left for each zero in the divisor. Write extra zeros if necessary.

Look at the pattern.

$57.24 \div 10 = 5.7\ 2\ 4$	$= 5.724$	one place to the left
$57.24 \div 100 = 0.5\ 7\ 2\ 4$	$= 0.5724$	two places
$57.24 \div 1,000 = 0.0\ 5\ 7.2\ 4 = 0.05724$		three places

Checkpoint Write the letter of the correct answer.

Compute.

1. 83.75×100 **a.** 0.8375   **b.** 83.7500   **c.** 8,375   **d.** 837,500

2. $6.8 \times 1,000$ **a.** 0.0068   **b.** 6.8000   **c.** 6,800   **d.** 6,800,000

3. $7.1 \div 10$ **a.** 0.071   **b.** 0.71   **c.** 07.1   **d.** 71

4. $3.05 \div 1,000$ **a.** 0.000305   **b.** 0.00305   **c.** 0003.05   **d.** 3,050

56   Math Reasoning, page H209

COMMON ERRORS

Answer Choice	Type of Error
■ 1a, 2a	Divides instead of multiplies
□ 1b, 2b, 3c, 4c	Writes zeros but does not move the decimal point
□ 1d, 2d	Writes too many zeros
□ 3a, 4a	Moves the decimal point too many places
■ 3d, 4d	Multiplies instead of divides

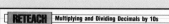

RETEACH **Multiplying and Dividing Decimals by 10s**

The telephone book for Deertown is 1.54 centimeters thick. How high is a stack of 1,000 Deertown phone books? The paper for 1,000 pages costs $4.62. In dollars, how much does each page cost?

Remember

To multiply by 1,000, move the decimal point three spaces to the right.
$1.54 \times 1,000 = 1,54\boxed{0}.$

To divide by 1,000, move the decimal point three spaces to the left.
$4.62 \div 1,000 = 0.\boxed{0}\boxed{0}462$

The stack is 1,540 cm high. One page costs $0.00462.

Complete this multiplication table.

	Number	Multiply by			
		10	100	1,000	10,000
1.	3.6	36	360	3,600	36,000
2.	0.06	0.6	6	60	600
3.	0.367	3.67	36.7	367	3,670
4.	18.43	184.3	1,843	18,430	184,300
5.	0.0052	0.052	0.52	5.2	52

Complete this division table.

	Number	Divide by			
		10	100	1,000	10,000
6.	367.3	36.73	3.673	0.3673	0.03673
7.	45.2	4.52	0.452	0.0452	0.00452
8.	3.6	0.36	0.036	0.0036	0.00036
9.	4,561	456.1	45.61	4.561	0.4561
10.	0.07	0.007	0.0007	0.00007	0.000007

Solve.

11. One sheet of paper weighs 0.001 kilograms. How many kilograms do 1,000 sheets weigh? __1 kilogram__

18   Use with pages 56–57.

Reteach Worksheet

Find the product.

1. 10×7.3
73

2. 10×64.85
648.5

3. 151.32×10
1,513.2

4. 0.45×100
45

5. 100×2.634
263.4

6. 34.219×100
3,421.9

7. $1,000 \times 0.164$
164

8. $39.7 \times 1,000$
39,700

9. $1,000 \times 412.635$
412,635

10. 100×58.951
5,895.1

11. $1,000 \times 8,762.48$
8,762,480

12. 110.06×100
11,006

13. 0.54×10
5.4

14. $1,000 \times 0.0087$
8.7

15. $10 \times 6,459.08$
64,590.8

Find the quotient.

16. $10\overline{)3.7}$
0.37

17. $10\overline{)62.4}$
6.24

18. $10\overline{)521.57}$
52.157

19. $100\overline{)0.023}$
0.00023

20. $100\overline{)784.91}$
7.8491

21. $100\overline{)2,153.6}$
21.536

22. $33.26 \div 1,000$
0.03326

23. $574.394 \div 1,000$
0.574394

24. $8,017.96 \div 1,000$
8.01796

25. $8.653 \div 10$
0.8653

26. $89.53 \div 10$
8.953

27. $787.217 \div 10$
78.7217

28. $\dfrac{90.063}{100}$
0.90063

29. $\dfrac{1,759.32}{100}$
17.5932

30. $\dfrac{41,085.7}{100}$
410.857

31. $\dfrac{748.85}{1,000}$
0.74885

32. $\dfrac{2,196.57}{1,000}$
2.19657

33. $\dfrac{57,430.08}{1,000}$
57.43008

Solve.

34. During a 10-day raft trip, Tara spent a total of 110.5 hours onshore. On average, about how many hours a day did Tara spend onshore?
11.05 h/d

35. In order to join the White-Water Explorer's Club, Lucian had to spend 100 h rafting on the river. If his average speed was 8.45 km/h, how many kilometers did he travel? 845 km

36. In a 1-km race, 4 rafts finished with times of 5.6 min, 8.4 min, 6.5 min, and 5.8 min. What was the difference in time between the fastest raft and the slowest raft?
2.8 min

★37. One team's finishing time in a 100-km white-water marathon was 638.25 min. They finished the last kilometer in 5.73 min. How much faster than their average speed was their speed in the last kilometer?
0.6525 km/min faster

CHALLENGE

If you can recycle 4 aluminum cans into 1 can, into how many cans can you recycle 16 cans? 4

Classwork/Homework, page H24

ASSIGNMENT GUIDE

Basic: 1–35 *o*, Chlg

Average: 2–36 *e*, Chlg

Extended: 1–27 *o*, 28–37, Chlg

Resources
Practice, p. 24   Class/Home, p. H24
Reteach, p. 18   Reasoning, p. H209
Enrich, p. 24

Exercise Analysis

1–15   Multiply a decimal by a power of 10
16–33   Divide a decimal by a power of 10
34–37   Skill applications

Challenge

This problem requires students to see the not so obvious.

FOLLOW-UP ACTIVITIES

CALCULATOR

Have students multiply each of the following decimals by 1,001.

0.628 × 1,001 (628.628)
0.925 × 1,001 (925.925)

Discuss the pattern of the answers. (The digits at both sides of the decimal point are the same. This can be explained by the Distributive Property: 1,001 = 1,000 + 1.) Without using calculators, have students find the following products.

0.777 × 1,001 (777.777)
0.639 × 1,001 (639.639)

MATH CONNECTION (Social Studies)

AIR TRAVELERS TO THE U.S.—1984

Country	Number of Visitors
Japan	1.58 (1,580,000)
England	1.20 (1,200,000)
Mexico	0.8 (800,000)
West Germany	0.51 (510,000)
France	0.31 (310,000)

Tell students that the figure given for air travelers from each country is expressed in millions. Ask them to multiply to find the numbers that each decimal represents.

COMING UP

Product awareness

PRACTICE Decimals and Powers of 10

Compute.

1. 0.006 × 100 = __0.6__
2. 32.58 ÷ 10 = __3.258__
3. 22.88 × 1,000 = __22,880__
4. 30.8 ÷ 10 = __3.08__
5. 0.007 × 100 = __0.7__
6. 1.6 ÷ 10 = __0.16__
7. 0.5 ÷ 1,000 = __0.0005__
8. 476.7 ÷ 10 = __47.67__
9. 0.004 × 1,000 = __4__
10. 0.077 × 10 = __0.77__
11. 10.2761 × 10 = __102.761__
12. 98.95 ÷ 100 = __0.9895__
13. 52.04 ÷ 1,000 = __0.05204__
14. 0.25 × 100 = __25__
15. 2.316 × 10 = __23.16__
16. 0.74 ÷ 10 = __0.074__
17. 189.7 ÷ 1,000 = __0.1897__
18. 5.778 × 100 = __577.8__
19. 5.316 × 100 = __531.6__
20. 16.64 ÷ 10 = __1.664__
21. 0.06 ÷ 1,000 = __0.00006__
22. 68.96 ÷ 10 = __6.896__
23. 0.85 ÷ 1,000 = __0.00085__
24. 32.14 × 100 = __3,214__
25. 38.652 × 10 = __386.52__
26. 21.5 ÷ 10 = __2.15__
27. 0.38 ÷ 100 = __0.0038__
28. 619.5 ÷ 1,000 = __0.6195__
29. 0.01116 × 100 = __1.116__
30. 0.59 ÷ 10 = __5.9__
31. 78.64 ÷ 10 = __7.864__
32. 2,041 ÷ 1,000 = __2.041__
33. 71.3 × 100 = __7,130__
34. 0.2413 × 1,000 = __241.3__
35. 799.8 ÷ 10 = __79.98__
36. 645.8 ÷ 100 = __6.458__
37. 7.8 × 10 = __78__
38. 4.004 × 100 = __400.4__

24   Use with pages 56–57.

Practice Worksheet

ENRICH Number

Per capita income is the average income per person among a group of people. It is one of the most widely used measures of a population's standard of living. Per capita income is calculated by dividing the total income of a population by the number of people in the population.

$$\frac{\text{total income}}{\text{number of people}} = \text{per capita income}$$

1. The United States had a population of 227 million in 1980, and a total income of approximately $2,156 billion. What was the national per capita income that year?
__$9,500__

2. Alaska is a state rich in natural resources. Its per capita income has been the highest of all the states for several years. In 1980, Alaska's total income was about $5.19 billion, and it had 402,000 residents. What was the per capita income? __$12,900__

3. Alaska's total income rose quickly in the early 1980's, following completion of a major oil pipeline. By 1982, the per capita income had risen to $16,300. Assuming that the population remained the same as in 1980, what was the rise in Alaska's total income? __$1.36 billion__

4. In 1980, California had the largest total income of any state. In 1970, total income was about $8.8 billion, and by 1980, it was $25.8 billion. In the same period, California's population grew from 20 million to 23.7 million. Which grew faster, per capita income or population?
__per capita income__

5. Sometimes per capita income can grow rapidly without any increase in standard of living. Why might this happen? (HINT: Fifty years ago an automobile cost $500.) Answers will vary. Possible answers include __inflation, mass production, wages, etc.__

24   Use with pages 56–57.

Enrich Worksheet

Objective: To estimate a decimal product

Warm-Up
Have students estimate each product.

33 × 49 (1,500)   56 × 67 (4,200⁻)
98 × 102 (10,000)   223 × 73 (14,000⁺)

GETTING STARTED

Have students round each decimal to a number that is easy to multiply by.

2.9134 (3)   14.806 (15)
0.339 (0.5)   11.174 (11)
254.276 (250)   0.084 (0.1)

Have students discuss other answers, explaining their reasoning for each.

TEACHING THE LESSON

A. An alternative method for estimating 52 × 46.4 is to rewrite 52 as approximately $\frac{1}{2} \times 100$. Therefore,

$$52 \times 46.4 \approx \frac{1}{2} \times 100 \times 46.4$$
$$\approx \frac{1}{2} \times 4,640$$
$$\approx 2,300$$

B. Have students estimate this product.

38.762 × 49.845
(40 × 50 ≈ 2,000⁻)

C. Extend the lesson to products of three factors.

123.489 × 0.4555 × 3.902

(The factors can be rounded to 125 × 0.5 × 4. Because 0.5 of 4 is 2, and 125 × 2 is 250, a reasonable estimate would be 250⁻.)

Estimating Products of Decimals

A. The average household in the United States has the television set on for 46.4 hours a week. For about how many hours is the television set on during a year?

The amount of time the television is on varies for each week. It is reasonable to estimate the product.

Think: there are 52 weeks in a year.

Round each factor. Then multiply.

$$52 \times 46.4$$
$$\downarrow \quad \downarrow$$
$$50 \times 46 = 2,300$$

> Think: 50 × 46 is half of 100 × 46.

The television set is on for about 2,300 hours during a year.

B. You can estimate products of decimals by rounding each number to its largest place.

Estimate 6.18 × 6.172.
$$\downarrow \quad \downarrow$$
$$6 \times 6 = 36$$

Since both numbers are rounded down, 36 is an underestimate. The adjusted estimate is 36⁺.

C. When you multiply with decimals, look for factors that are close to 1 or close to $\frac{1}{2}$.

Estimate 0.923 × 3.7.
0.923 × 3.7
$$\downarrow \quad \downarrow$$
$$1 \times 3.7 = 3.7$$

The product is 3.7⁻, or slightly less than 3.7.

Estimate 0.5223 × 0.72.
0.5223 × 0.72
$$\downarrow \quad \downarrow$$
$$\frac{1}{2} \times 0.72 = 0.36$$

The product is 0.36⁺, or slightly greater than 0.36.

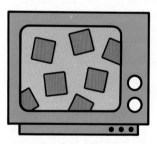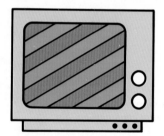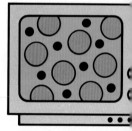

58

COMMON ERRORS

Some students have difficulty estimating decimal products because they round the factors incorrectly.

Remediation
Have students review the rules for rounding, initially with simple examples such as 2.3 and 3.9. Then have them work up to more difficult decimals such as 12.324 and 9.877.

Assign Reteach Master, p. 19

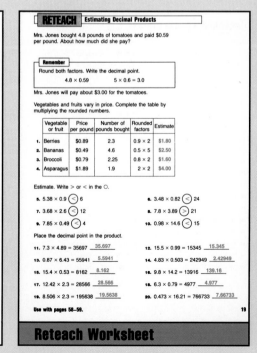

RETEACH Estimating Decimal Products

Mrs. Jones bought 4.8 pounds of tomatoes and paid $0.59 per pound. About how much did she pay?

Remember
Round both factors. Write the decimal point.
4.8 × 0.59   5 × 0.6 = 3.0

Mrs. Jones will pay about $3.00 for the tomatoes.

Vegetables and fruits vary in price. Complete the table by multiplying the rounded numbers.

	Vegetable or fruit	Price per pound	Number of pounds bought	Rounded factors	Estimate
1.	Berries	$0.89	2.3	0.9 × 2	$1.80
2.	Bananas	$0.49	4.6	0.5 × 5	$2.50
3.	Broccoli	$0.79	2.25	0.8 × 2	$1.60
4.	Asparagus	$1.89	1.9	2 × 2	$4.00

Estimate. Write > or < in the ○.

5. 5.38 × 0.9 ⊙ 6
6. 3.48 × 0.82 ⊙ 24
7. 3.68 × 2.6 ⊙ 12
8. 7.8 × 3.89 ⊙ 21
9. 7.85 × 0.49 ⊙ 4
10. 0.98 × 14.6 ⊙ 15

Place the decimal point in the product.

11. 7.3 × 4.89 = 35697   35.697
12. 15.5 × 0.99 = 15345   15.345
13. 0.87 × 6.43 = 55941   5.5941
14. 4.83 × 0.503 = 242949   2.42949
15. 15.4 × 0.53 = 8162   8.162
16. 9.8 × 14.2 = 13916   139.16
17. 12.42 × 2.3 = 28566   28.566
18. 6.3 × 0.79 = 4977   4.977
19. 8.506 × 2.3 = 195638   19.5638
20. 0.473 × 16.21 = 766733   7.66733

Use with pages 58–59.   19

Reteach Worksheet

Estimate by rounding.
Answers may vary. Accept any reasonable estimate.
1. 26×4.57
150
2. 714×6.82
4,900
3. 32.5×28
900
4. 0.81×857
720
5. 7×23.8
140
6. 0.04×92
3.6
7. 317×0.86
270
8. 61.6×18
1,200
9. 4.8×6.8
35
10. 17.8×0.4
8
11. 39.2×0.13
4
12. 2.88×8.8
27
13. 0.056×3.9
0.24
14. 507.4×6.7
3,500
15. 0.009×8.98
0.081
16. 2.003×16.6
40
17. 89×0.046
4.5
18. 313.2×1.9
600
19. 14.9×0.06
.060
20. 0.08×0.37
0.032

In each exercise below, the decimal point has been left out of the product. Estimate to write the correct product.

21. $6.72 \times 8.4 = 56448$
56.448
22. $6.69 \times 2.2 = 14718$
14.718
23. $4.87 \times 0.521 = 253727$
2.53727
24. $0.71 \times 0.513 = 36423$
0.36423
25. $12.1 \times 2.8 = 3388$
33.88
26. $37.6 \times 0.007 = 2632$
0.2632
27. $0.91 \times 68 = 6188$
61.88
28. $0.601 \times 28.61 = 1719461$
17.19461

Estimate. Look for numbers close to 1 or $\frac{1}{2}$.
Answers may vary. Accept any reasonable estimate.
29. 0.91×6.01 6⁻
30. 1.07×88 88⁺
31. 0.509×88.9
44.5
32. 22.2×0.46 11.1⁻
33. 1.4×65 65⁺
34. 0.02×0.94
0.02
35. 617×0.52 308
36. 0.86×328.7 328.7⁻
37. 0.037×0.591
0.019

Solve.

38. A Nielsen rating point represents 849,000 television households. One evening, a popular TV program had a rating of 18.6. Estimate the number of households watching the program. about 16,000,000 households

★39. A solid-state color TV uses an average of 305 kilowatt hours of electricity per year. If a kilowatt of electricity costs 12.3 cents, estimate the yearly cost to operate the TV. about $36

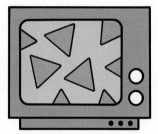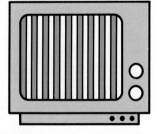

Classwork/Homework, page H25   59

ASSIGNMENT GUIDE

Basic: 1–37 o, 38

Average: 2–38 e

Extended: 1–27 o, 29–39

Resources
Practice, p. 25   Class/Home, p. H25
Reteach, p. 19
Enrich, p. 25

Exercise Analysis

1–20 Estimate a decimal product by rounding each factor to its largest place

21–28 Choose the correct place for the decimal point by estimating the product

29–37 Estimate a decimal product by looking for numbers close to $\frac{1}{2}$ or 1

38–39 Skill applications

FOLLOW-UP ACTIVITIES

 MATH CONNECTION (Consumer)
Tell students that one grocery store sells an average of 89 six-packs of a particular brand of juice each week and that each six-pack costs $2.79. Have them estimate how many dollars' worth of this brand the store sells per year. (The product is equal to $89 \times \$2.79 \times 52$, which students can round to $90 \times \$3 \times 50$. A reasonable estimate would be $13,500.)

NUMBER SENSE (Mental Math)
Have students estimate each product mentally.
- 18.39×7 ($20 \times 7 \approx 140$)
- 5.23×4 ($5 \times 4 \approx 20$)
- 219.5821×6 ($220 \times 6 \approx 1,320$)
- 34.023×3 ($35 \times 3 \approx 105$)
- 4.78×3.02 ($5 \times 3 \approx 15$)
- 43.2×9.23 ($43 \times 10 \approx 430$)
- 5.233×42.2 ($5 \times 42 \approx 210^+$)
- 6.93×24.81 ($7 \times 25 \approx 175^-$)

COMING UP
Point by point

Practice Worksheet

PRACTICE Estimating Products of Decimals

Mark the numbers in the box according to the directions.

1. Draw a circle around the decimals close to but greater than 1.
2. Draw a square around the decimals close to but less than 1.
3. Draw an X over the decimals close to but greater than one half.
4. Draw a ✓ over the decimals close to but less than one half.

0.499 ✓	0.98
0.0099	1.038
0.48236 ✓	0.897
1.109	0.9001
0.49 ✓	0.51

Estimate to find the most sensible answer.
5. 3.17×17.15 a. 5.44 b. 54.37 c. 543.66
6. 0.624×0.482 a. 0.30 b. 3.01 c. 30.08
7. 3.009×2.156 a. 6.49 b. 64.87 c. 648.74
8. 0.98×4.86 a. 0.47628 b. 4.76 c. 47.62
9. 3.68×0.512 a. 0.1884 b. 1.884 c. 18.84
10. 7.38×4.15 a. 3.063 b. 30.62 c. 306.3

Estimate. Adjust by writing + or − where possible.
11. 4.28×5.76 24⁺
12. 1.34×7.8 8
13. 0.98×12.5 12.5⁻
14. 0.489×2.4 1⁻
15. 3.56×1.12 3.5⁺
16. 0.503×4.31 2⁺
17. 3.45×1.1123 3.5⁺
18. 12.4×5.78 72
19. 0.894×3.44 3

Solve.
20. The typical American eats 96.3 pounds of beef each year. If the average price of beef is $2.42 per pound, about how much is spent on beef by each American? $242
21. The typical American eats about 73.5 pounds of hamburger each year. If the average price of hamburger is $1.19, about how much is spent on hamburger? $74

Use with pages 58–59.   25

Enrich Worksheet

ENRICH Measurement

Electric appliances use two components of electricity: voltage and amperage. **Voltage** is the measure of electric force in the circuit. **Amperage** is the measure of the amount of current needed to run the particular appliance.

The product of voltage and amperage is **wattage**. Wattage is the measure of electric power used by an appliance.
$W = A \times V$.

1. Below are some household appliances and their power requirements. Complete the table.

Appliance	Volts	Amperes	Watts
Air conditioner	120	12.5	1,500
Typewriter	120	0.45	54
Desk lamp	120	0.5	60
Washing machine	120	9.0	1,080
Fan	120	0.6	72

Watt hours is the wattage requirement of an appliance multiplied by the number of hours the appliance is used. One **kilowatt hour** is equal to 1,000 watt hours.

2. Fill in the chart to calculate the number of kilowatt hours of electricity used to run each appliance for the month of July. Estimate to check your answer.

Appliance	Hours per day	Watt hours per day	Kilowatt hours per day	Kilowatt hours per month
Air conditioner	12	18,000	18	558
Fan	12	864	0.864	26.784
Washing machine	1	1,080	1.080	33.48
Desk lamp	10	600	0.6	18.6
Typewriter	5	270	0.27	8.37

Total kilowatt hours 645.234

A company that supplies electricity charges a base rate of $15.00 per month, which includes the first 250 kilowatt hours. It charges $0.08 for each additional kilowatt hour.

3. Use the table in example 2 to calculate the bill for electricity for July. $46.62

Use with pages 58–59.   25

59

Objective: To multiply decimals

Warm-Up
Have students multiply and divide by powers of 10.

$36.4 \times 100 (3,640); 8,763.4 \div 10 (876.34);$
$1.819 \times 1,000 (1,819); 3.22 \div 100 (0.0322)$

GETTING STARTED

Write the following examples on the board.

$455 \times 12 = 5,460$
$4.55 \times 12 = 54.6$
$0.455 \times 12 = n \ (5.46)$
$0.0455 \times 12 = n \ (0.546)$

Ask students to find the products in the last two examples. Lead a discussion in which students share their methods of finding the answers.

TEACHING THE LESSON

Remind students that when multiplying, decimal points should not be aligned. Some students may find it easier to understand the correct placement of the decimal point in the product if improper fractions are used; for example:

$1.72 = 1\frac{72}{100} = \frac{172}{100}$ $15.5 = 15\frac{5}{10} = \frac{155}{10}$

Then

$\frac{172}{100} \times \frac{155}{10} = \frac{26,660}{1,000} = 26,660 \div 1,000$

Recall the rule for dividing decimals by a power of 10: The decimal point must be moved 3 places to the left to arrive at 26.660, or 26.66.

Direct students to the Other Examples section, and point out that zeros are written to the right of the decimal point and to the left of the other digits in the product.

Checkpoint
The chart lists the common errors students make in multiplying decimals.

Correct Answers: 1b, 2b, 3b, 4b

Remediation
■ For these errors, review the multiplication algorithm.

□ For these errors, assign Reteach Master, p. 20.

Multiplying Decimals

While visiting London, Karen purchased 15.5 gallons of gasoline for her rented car. The gasoline cost 1.72 pounds sterling (£) per gallon. How much did she spend for gasoline?

Multiply 1.72 by 15.5.

First, estimate the product. $2 \times 16 = 32$

```
    1 . 7  2   ← two places
  × 1  5 . 5   ← one place
      8  6  0
   8  6  0
1  7  2
2  6 . 6  6  0   ← three places
```

Karen spent £26.66 for gasoline. The answer is reasonably close to £32.

Other examples:

```
   0.0018                          $3.72
 ×    2.6                        ×   5.8
    108        Write zeros to     2 976      to the nearest
     36        place the         18 60       cent
  0.00468      decimal point.    $21.576  →  $21.58
```

Checkpoint   Write the letter of the correct answer.

Multiply.

1. $\$36.45 \times 7$ a. $25.515   **b.** $255.15   c. $2,551.50   d. $25,515

2. 0.63×2.7 a. 0.243   **b.** 1.701   c. 17.01   d. 170.1

3. 30.0019×0.06 a. 0.0114   **b.** 1.800114   c. 180.0114   d. 18,001.14

4. $5.12 \times 0.4 \times 0.3$ a. 0.1536   **b.** 0.6144   c. 61.44   d. 6,144

Math Reasoning, page H209

COMMON ERRORS

Answer Choice	Type of Error
□ 1a, 1c, 1d, 2c, 2d, 3c, 3d, 4c, 4d	Misplaces the decimal point
■ 2a	Computes incorrectly
■ 3a, 4a	Fails to multiply by the entire factor

RETEACH Multiplying Decimals

A baby seal weighs 2.5 kilograms. Its mother weighs 8.6 times as much. How much does its mother weigh?

Remember
When both multipliers have one decimal place, there must be two decimal places in the product.

```
    2.5
  × 8.6
   1 5 0
  20 0
  21.50
```

The mother seal weighs 21.50 kilograms.

Multiply.

1. 0.6×0.7 _0.42_   2. 0.35×1.72 _0.602_

3. 3.65×0.07 _0.2555_   4. 4.68×0.05 _0.234_

5. 0.003×0.02 _0.00006_   6. 38.75×0.0012 _0.0465_

Ring the letter of the correct answer.

7. 0.4×0.5 a. 20   b. 2.0   **c.** 0.20   d. 0.020

8. 0.63×1.7 a. 1,071   b. 107.1   c. 10.71   **d.** 1.071

9. 6.8×3.2 **a.** 21.76   b. 2.176   c. 0.2176   d. 0.02176

10. 0.0004×192 a. 768   b. 76.8   c. 7.68   **d.** 0.0768

11. 0.004×3.7 a. 14.80   b. 0.148   **c.** 0.0148   d. 0.00148

Solve.

12. The polar bears in the zoo eat 1.25 pails of fish. The seals are fed 2.4 times as much as the polar bears. How much do the seals eat? _3 pails of fish_

20   Use with pages 60–61.

Reteach Worksheet

Multiply.

1.	3.5 × 6 21	**2.**	12.59 × 0.8 10.072	**3.**	605.14 × 0.3 181.542	**4.**	0.1034 × 9 0.9306
5.	0.471 × 0.32 0.15072	**6.**	2.75 × 72 198	**7.**	483.96 × 3.7 1,790.652	**8.**	0.0025 × 7.8 0.0195
9.	52 × 3.64 189.28	**10.**	740.03 × 0.0468 34.633404	**11.**	22,954.2 × 39.7 911,281.74	**12.**	160.528 × 324 52,011.072

Multiply. Round the product to the nearest cent when necessary.

13.	$37.54 × 32 $1,201.28	**14.**	$8.63 × 4.9 $42.29	**15.**	$71.09 × 0.7 $49.76	**16.**	$452.20 × 1.87 $845.61
17.	$63.38 × 0.008 $0.51	**18.**	$2,196.47 × 47.6 $104,551.97	**19.**	$4,193.51 × 0.0029 $12.16	**20.**	$76,640.07 × 0.438 $33,568.35

21. 0.799 × 783.02
625.63298

22. 5,143.2 × 0.00386
19.852752

23. 55.9234 × 0.4
22.36936

24. 8,912.83 × 0.56
4,991.1848

25. 36.4 × 91.57
3,333.148

26. 0.00462 × 878
4.05636

27. 3.6 × 3 × 0.42
4.536

28. 0.152 × 82,510 × 6.9
86,536.488

Solve. For Problem 29, use the Infobank.

29. Use the information on page 473 to solve. A teen group is going on a 4-week sight-seeing trip around the United States. If they rent one 47-passenger bus and two vans, what is the total cost of the trip?
$23,407

30. Edward paid £3.40 for a visit to Madame Tussaud's wax museum, £3.50 to go to a movie, and £4.20 to go to a concert. How much did this entertainment cost him? £11.10

ANOTHER LOOK

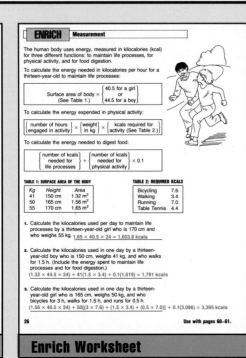

Solve.

1. Tanya visits 47 cities. If she spends an average of 3 days in each city, how long will her trip take?
141 days

2. Bob planned a budget for his 6-week trip. If he budgeted $150 a week for hotels, how much has he budgeted for hotels for the trip? $900

Classwork/Homework, page H26

More Practice, page H196 **61**

ASSIGNMENT GUIDE

Basic: 1–12, 13–23 o, 29, AL

Average: 5–12, 14–28 e, 29–30, AL

Extended: 9–12, 14–30, AL

Resources
Practice, p. 26   Class/Home, p. H26
Reteach, p. 20   More Practice, p. H196
Enrich, p. 26   Reasoning, p. H209

Exercise Analysis

1–12	Multiply a decimal by a whole number or a decimal
13–20	Multiply an amount of money by a decimal
21–26	Mixed practice
27–28	Multiply three factors
29	Data collection and computation
30	Skill application

You may wish to allow students to use calculators for some of these exercises.

Another Look

This review provides maintenance for solving problems that involve multiplying whole numbers.

FOLLOW-UP ACTIVITIES

MATH CONNECTION (Consumer)
The Pokimono Company offers the following supplies to tourists who sign up for hiking trips.

Caps	$9.99	Canteens	$6.55
Visors	$3.25	Bike Rentals	$5.00/h
First-Aid Kits	$19.99	Walking Sticks	$17.50

Have students use this information to answer the following questions.
1. A college student purchases 1 canteen and 2 first-aid kits. How much did she spend? ($46.53)
2. Cindy rents a bike for 4 hours and buys 1 walking stick and a cap. How much did she spend? ($47.49)

PROBLEM SOLVING
What is the largest sum of money that a person can carry without being able to give another person change for a dollar, a half-dollar, a quarter, a dime, or a nickel? ($1.19: a half-dollar, a quarter, 4 dimes, and 4 pennies.)

COMING UP
A "pass" for everybody on this one!

61

Objective. To choose the correct operation to solve a problem

Warm-Up

Have students solve for the missing number.

27 + 195 = ■ (222)   ■ − 111 = 257 (368)
15 × ■ = 180 (12)   20 × ■ = 640 (32)

GETTING STARTED

Write the following information on the chalkboard, and have students fill in the missing operation signs.

66 ■ 18 = 48 (−)   72 ■ 7 = 504 (×)
15 ■ 11 = 165 (×)   37 ■ 12 = 25 (−)
54 ■ 54 = 108 (+)   17 ■ 321 = 338 (+)
79 ■ 58 = 21 (−)   21 ■ 58 = 79 (+)

TEACHING THE LESSON

Choosing the correct operation is probably the most frequent difficulty students encounter in solving problems. In this lesson, students learn that operations are logical links between what they know and what they need to find. By listing given information and information needed, students can usually see which operation(s) they should use. It may be helpful to have students make a list similar to the one in their books.

● If I know (given number)
● And I want to find (total number left)
● Then I can (add, subtract, multiply)

Questions: The question is integral to choosing the operation as it tells students what they need to find. Relate the actual question in the introductory problem (How much did Don spend on the passes?) to its counterpart in the chart below (the total number).

Tools: Have students make a list as shown in the text and outlined above. In the example, explain to students that they know
● that the number in each set is the same.
● the number in each set ($256.45).
● the number of sets (6).

Relate multiplication to extended addition. Review the meanings of the *joining operations* (multiplication and addition). Point out that the critical element that sets off multiplication from addition is that the groups formed must be of the same size.

Solutions: Review the algorithms for multiplication of money and decimals. Emphasize that the number of decimal places in the product is the sum of the number of decimal places in the factors. You may wish to allow students to use calculators for problem solving.

PROBLEM SOLVING
Choosing the Operation

You can find hints in a problem that will help you choose the best operation to use to solve it.

> Don and his family plan to travel by train to several countries in Europe. To save money, Don buys 6 special passes that allow them to travel anywhere they want for a month. Each pass costs $256.45. How much did Don spend on the passes?

Hints:

If you know	and you want to find	you can
● the number in two or more sets	the total number	add.
● the number in one set ● the number taken away	the number that is left	subtract.
● the number in two sets	how much larger one set is than the other	subtract to compare.
● the number in one set ● the number in part of the set	the number in the remaining part of the set	subtract.
● the number in each set is the same ● the number in each set ● the number of sets	the total number	multiply.

You could add to find the total number, but it would be easier to multiply.

the number of sets	×	the number in each set	=	the total number
6	×	$256.45	=	$1,538.70

Don spent $1,538.70 on the passes.

Math Reasoning, page H210

Checks: Have students go back to the list they have made and substitute their answer for the number they wanted to find. Having students use the inverse operation to check should not be encouraged because the wrong operation might have been used initially.

Write the letter of the operation you would use to solve each problem.

1. Roberta's excursion boat carried 87 passengers on the first trip. On the second trip, there were 90 passengers, and on the last trip, there were 107 passengers. How many passengers did the boat carry on the three trips?

   a. addition
   b. subtraction
   c. multiplication

2. The Sea Watch restaurant sells a fish dinner for $7.50. If the cost of preparing the dinner is $3.83, how much of the price is not part of the cost of the dinner?

   a. addition
   b. subtraction
   c. multiplication

Solve.

3. One airline carried 2,346,205 passengers in a year. Another airline carried 846,989 fewer passengers than the first airline. How many passengers did the second airline carry? **1,499,216 passengers**

4. Anita exchanged $425.00 of her $875.32 of spending money for francs. How much money in United States currency did she have left? **$450.32**

5. The Gomez family visited a park that had 5,824 acres. Then they visited another park that had 455,312 more acres than the first park. How large was the second park? **461,136 acres**

★6. At a recreation park, the admission charge is $4.25 for adults and $2.25 for children. Ms. Brown paid for 1 adult and 2 children. She gave the ticket seller a $20 bill. How much change did she receive? **$11.25**

★7. An airline agent checked a bag that weighed 35 pounds, another that weighed 4.5 pounds less than the first, another that weighed 13 pounds less than the second, and a fourth that weighed 7.5 pounds more than the first. How many pounds of baggage did the agent check? **125.5 lb**

★8. In 1984, Chicago's O'Hare Airport had 671,742 takeoffs and landings. This was 28,576 fewer than the San Francisco and Anchorage airports combined. If the Anchorage Airport had 335,509 takeoffs and landings, how many did the San Francisco Airport have? **364,809 takeoffs and landings**

Classwork/Homework, page H27

ASSIGNMENT GUIDE

Basic:	1–4
Average:	2–6
Extended:	3–8

Resources
Practice, p. 27   Class/Home, p. H27
Enrich, p. 27   Reasoning, p. H210

Exercise Analysis
1–2 Choose the correct operation
3–8 Solve

FOLLOW-UP ACTIVITIES

PROBLEM SOLVING
Divide the class into nine groups. Assign each group one of the givens in the *If you know* column on page 62. Have each group use the assigned given to write a problem about a trip. Then have groups exchange and solve problems.

CALCULATOR
Materials: calculator per student

Write the following information on the chalkboard.

456 ■ 789 = 359,784 (×)
456 ■ 789 = 1,245 (+)
73,912 ■ 46,142 = 27,770 (−)
73,912 ■ 46,142 = 120,054 (+)
5,670.8 ■ 33,291 = 38,961.8 (+)
17.5493 ■ 0.15873 = 17.39057 (−)

Have students use calculators to find the operation used to complete each number sentence.

COMING UP
Dividing parts by wholes

Objective: To divide decimals by whole numbers

Warm-Up
Have students multiply the following decimals.

13.72 × 0.88 (12.0736)
235.6 × 32.3 (7,609.88)
0.5659 × 49 (27.7291)
$75.44 × 2.38 ($179.55 to the nearest cent)

GETTING STARTED

$$\begin{array}{c}3.62\\ \textbf{A. } 48\,\overline{\smash{)}1{,}737.6}\end{array} \quad \begin{array}{c}36\,2\\ \textbf{B. } 48\,\overline{\smash{)}1{,}737.6}\end{array} \quad \begin{array}{c}36.2\\ \textbf{C. } 48\,\overline{\smash{)}1{,}737.6}\end{array}$$

Write the above examples on the board. Without figuring, have students identify the example that has the correct answer. (C) Discuss how they arrived at their decisions.

Have students estimate the quotients in the following examples.

$$\begin{array}{c}(40)\\ 8\,\overline{\smash{)}384.8}\end{array} \quad \begin{array}{c}(5)\\ 51\,\overline{\smash{)}292.78}\end{array} \quad \begin{array}{c}(70)\\ 88\,\overline{\smash{)}6{,}372.4}\end{array}$$

TEACHING THE LESSON

A. Remind students that the decimal point serves to separate the whole-number part of the quotient from the decimal or fractional part.

B. Point out that it is sometimes necessary to write zeros in the quotient because there are not enough tenths or hundredths to divide. In the other examples, zeros are written in the dividend in order to divide to the place to the right of the rounding place. Guide students through examples in which they must round to the nearest cent or to the nearest hundredth.

$$\begin{array}{c}(4.13)\\ 6\,\overline{\smash{)}24.75}\end{array} \quad \begin{array}{c}(\$11.69)\\ 18\,\overline{\smash{)}\$210.50}\end{array} \quad \begin{array}{c}(0.33)\\ 8\,\overline{\smash{)}2.67}\end{array}$$

Checkpoint
The chart lists the common errors students make when dividing decimals.

Correct Answers: 1b, 2b

Remediation
■ For these errors, have students correctly place the decimal point in the quotient for each problem before they begin the actual division.

□ For these errors, assign Reteach Master, p. 21.

△ For this error, guide students to the lesson on rounding in the P.E. pp. 22–23.

Dividing Decimals by Whole Numbers

A. Steve went on a 21-day bicycle trip. He traveled 520.8 miles. How many miles per day did he average?

Divide 520.8 by 21.

To divide a decimal by a whole number, place the decimal point in the quotient above the decimal point in the dividend. Then divide as you would with whole numbers.

Steve averaged 24.8 miles per day.

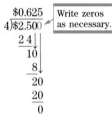

$$\begin{array}{r}24.8\\ 21\,\overline{\smash{)}520.8}\\ \underline{42}\\ 100\\ \underline{84}\\ 16\,8\\ \underline{16\,8}\\ 0\end{array}$$

Estimate to check.

20 × 25 = 500
500 is close to 520.8
So, 24.8 is a reasonable answer.

B. Sometimes you round quotients. Money is usually rounded to the nearest cent.

Divide 0.2352 by 24 and round to the nearest thousandth.

$$\begin{array}{r}0.0098\\ 24\,\overline{\smash{)}0.2352}\\ \underline{216}\\ 192\\ \underline{192}\\ 0\end{array}$$
Sometimes you need to write extra zeros.

0.0098 ⟶ 0.010

Divide $2.50 by 4 and round to the nearest cent.

$$\begin{array}{r}\$0.625\\ 4\,\overline{\smash{)}\$2.500}\\ \underline{2\,4}\\ 10\\ \underline{8}\\ 20\\ \underline{20}\\ 0\end{array}$$
Write zeros as necessary.

$0.625 ⟶ $0.63

Divide 407.55 by 325 and round to the nearest hundredth.

$$\begin{array}{r}1.254\\ 325\,\overline{\smash{)}407.550}\\ \underline{325}\\ 82\,5\\ \underline{65\,0}\\ 17\,55\\ \underline{16\,25}\\ 1\,300\\ \underline{1\,300}\\ 0\end{array}$$

1.254 ⟶ 1.25

Checkpoint Write the letter of the correct answer.
Divide.

1. 1.564 ÷ 34   **a.** 0.0046   **b.** 0.046   **c.** 0.46   **d.** 46

Round to the nearest cent.

2. 8)$17.33   **a.** $2.16   **b.** $2.17   **c.** $21.70   **d.** 217

Math Reasoning, page H210

COMMON ERRORS

Answer Choice	Type of Error
□ 1a	Uses too many zeros
□ 1c	Uses too few zeros
■ 1d, 2d	Omits decimal point
△ 2a	Rounds incorrectly
■ 2c	Misplaces decimal point

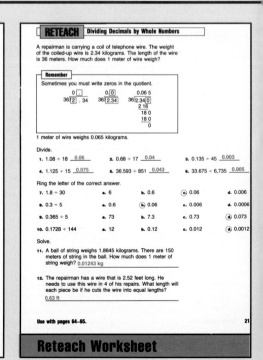

RETEACH Dividing Decimals by Whole Numbers

A repairman is carrying a coil of telephone wire. The weight of the coiled-up wire is 2.34 kilograms. The length of the wire is 36 meters. How much does 1 meter of wire weigh?

Remember
Sometimes you must write zeros in the quotient.

1 meter of wire weighs 0.065 kilograms.

Divide.
1. 1.08 ÷ 18 __0.06__
2. 0.68 ÷ 17 __0.04__
3. 0.135 ÷ 45 __0.003__
4. 1.125 ÷ 15 __0.075__
5. 36.593 ÷ 851 __0.043__
6. 33.675 ÷ 6,735 __0.005__

Ring the letter of the correct answer.
7. 1.8 ÷ 30   a. 6   b. 0.6   c. 0.06   d. 0.006
8. 0.3 ÷ 5   a. 0.6   b. 0.06   c. 0.006   d. 0.0006
9. 0.365 ÷ 5   a. 73   b. 7.3   c. 0.73   d. 0.073
10. 0.1728 ÷ 144   a. 12   b. 0.12   c. 0.012   d. 0.0012

Solve.
11. A ball of string weighs 1.8645 kilograms. There are 150 meters of string in the ball. How much does 1 meter of string weigh? __0.01243 kg__

12. The repairman has a wire that is 2.52 feet long. He needs to use this wire in 4 of his repairs. What length will each piece be if he cuts the wire into equal lengths? __0.63 ft__

Use with pages 64–65.   21

Reteach Worksheet

Divide.

1. 6)22.8
3.8

2. 9)210.6
23.4

3. 7)5.67
0.81

4. 8)$2.16
$0.27

5. 13)50.7
3.9

6. 33)$5.61
$0.17

7. 64)0.768
0.012

8. 28)7.812
0.279

9. 231)1,062.6
4.6

10. 147)79.674
0.542

11. 734)$29.36
$0.04

12. 518)86.3506
0.1667

13. 44.5 ÷ 5
8.9

14. 0.552 ÷ 8
0.069

15. 149.8 ÷ 4
37.45

16. $19.71 ÷ 9
$2.19

17. 3.901 ÷ 83   0.047

18. 9.2512 ÷ 59   0.1568

19. 4.3418 ÷ 34   0.1277

20. 0.864 ÷ 72   0.012

21. $\frac{4.5}{36}$
0.125

22. $\frac{3.486}{83}$
0.042

23. $\frac{\$48.60}{72}$
$0.675, or $0.68

24. $\frac{59.644}{52}$
1.147

25. $\frac{149.144}{412}$
0.362

26. $\frac{29.825}{125}$
0.2386

27. $\frac{437.1312}{561}$
0.7792

28. $\frac{\$4,923.63}{681}$
$7.23

Divide. Round each quotient to the nearest tenth.

29. 6)14.04
2.3

30. 27)172.26
6.4

31. 91)58.24
0.6

32. 337)19,680.8
58.4

Divide. Round each quotient to the nearest cent or the nearest hundredth.

33. 37.583 ÷ 7
5.37

34. $8.70 ÷ 4
$2.18

35. $48.60 ÷ 72
$0.68

36. 21.033 ÷ 246
0.09

Divide. Round each quotient to the nearest thousandth.

37. $\frac{2.4682}{7}$
0.353

38. $\frac{12.4868}{53}$
0.236

39. $\frac{4.4791}{47}$
0.095

40. $\frac{589.2045}{459}$
1.284

Solve.

41. On a trip, 15 teenagers stopped to visit a museum and paid a total of $56.25 for admission. If they all paid the same amount, how much was each admission? $3.75

42. The longest tandem bicycle ever built is 803 in. long. What is its length to the nearest tenth of a foot?   66.9 ft

NUMBER SENSE

You can use short division when the divisor is less than 10. Multiply and subtract mentally. Write each remainder beside the next digit as shown.

$$2,249$$
$$7)15^1,7^34^63$$

Use short division to find the quotient.

1. 4)3,384
846

2. 9)2,212.2
245.8

3. 6)2,522.46
420.41

4. 8)829.344
103.668

Classwork/Homework, page H28

65

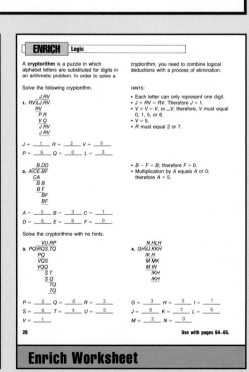

PRACTICE | Dividing Decimals by Whole Numbers

Divide. Round the quotient to the nearest thousandth or to the nearest cent where necessary.

1. 620.1 ÷ 8 ___77.513___

2. 1,863.36 ÷ 288 ___6.47___

3. 8.33 ÷ 2 ___4.165___

4. $\frac{749.331}{783}$ ___0.957___

5. $\frac{14.4}{36}$ ___0.4___

6. $\frac{1.819}{4}$ ___0.455___

7. $196.32 ÷ 64 ___$3.07___

8. 0.1293 ÷ 5 ___0.026___

9. 38.35 ÷ 65 ___0.59___

10. 5.351 ÷ 7 ___0.764___

11. 14.88 ÷ 62 ___0.24___

12. 2.984 ÷ 2 ___1.492___

13. 58.6219 ÷ 328 ___0.179___

14. 6.177 ÷ 71 ___0.087___

15. 206.6 ÷ 4 ___51.65___

16. $\frac{31.80}{32}$ ___0.994___

17. $\frac{3.835}{65}$ ___0.059___

18. $\frac{841.2}{6}$ ___140.2___

19. $215)241.7893 $1.12

20. 47)117.5   2.5

21. 673)58.2614   0.087

22. 22)1.122   0.051

23. 318)$418.71 $1.32

24. 7)535.1   76.443

25. 4)84.12   21.03

26. 55)2.530   0.046

27. 151)23.426   0.155

28   Use with pages 64–65.

Practice Worksheet

ENRICH | Logic

A **cryptorithm** is a puzzle in which alphabet letters are substituted for digits in an arithmetic problem. In order to solve a cryptorithm, you need to combine logical deductions with a process of elimination.

Solve the following cryptorithm.

```
      J.RV
1. RV)J.RV
      RV
      P R
      V Q
      J RV
      J RV
```

J = __1__   R = __2__   V = __5__
P = __6__   Q = __0__   L = __3__

HINTS:
- Each letter can only represent one digit.
- J × RV = RV. Therefore J = 1.
- V × V = V, or _V; therefore, V must equal 0, 1, 5, or 6.
- V = 5.
- R must equal 2 or 7.

```
      B.DD
2. A)CE.BF
      CA
      B B
      B F
      B F
      B F
```

A = __5__   B = __3__   C = __1__
D = __6__   E = __8__   F = __0__

- B − F = B; therefore F = 0.
- Multiplication by A equals A or 0; therefore A = 5.

Solve the cryptorithms with no hints.

```
      VU.RP
3. PQ)RQS.TQ
      PQ
      VQS
      VQS
       S T
       S Q
       TQ
       TQ
```

P = __2__   Q = __0__   R = __3__
S = __6__   T = __4__   U = __5__
V = __1__

```
      N.HLH
4. GH)IJ.KKH
      IK H
      M MK
      M IN
      IKH
      IKH
```

G = __3__   H = __5__   I = __1__
J = __9__   K = __7__   L = __6__
M = __2__   N = __0__

28   Use with pages 64–65.

Enrich Worksheet

ASSIGNMENT GUIDE

Basic: 1–12, 14–38 *e*, NS

Average: 1–8, 9–41 *o*, NS

Extended: 6–28 *e*, 29–42, NS

Resources
Practice, p. 28   Class/Home, p. H28
Reteach, p. 21   Reasoning, p. H210
Enrich, p. 28

Exercise Analysis

1–4   Divide a decimal by a 1-digit whole number

5–8   Divide a decimal by a 2-digit whole number

9–12   Divide a decimal by a 3-digit whole number

13–28 Mixed practice

29–40 Divide, rounding the quotient to the nearest tenth, hundredth, or thousandth

41–42 Skill applications

You may wish to allow students to use calculators for some of these exercises.

Number Sense

These exercises provide an alternative method of dividing a decimal by a whole number.

FOLLOW-UP ACTIVITIES

NUMBER SENSE (Estimation)
331.85 ÷ 32   114.64 ÷ 11
252.037 ÷ 27   83.48 ÷ 8
Of the four division examples shown above, the estimated quotient in three of the four is 10. Find the example in which the estimated quotient is not 10. (252.037 ÷ 27)

MATH CONNECTION (Consumer)
During a recent trip, the Kocik family recorded the following information. Have students use this list to determine the following rates.

miles per day: 1,440.6 miles in 3 days (480.2 miles per day)

cost per gallon: $126.42 for 98 gallons of gas ($1.29 per gallon)

cost per meal: $796.50 for 54 meals ($14.75 per meal)

hours per day: 112.5 hours of sightseeing in 15 days (7.5 h/d)

COMING UP
Watch that decimal point!

65

Warm-Up

Have students find the following quotients.

$0.768 \div 12$ (0.064) $56.4 \div 8$ (7.05)

$\dfrac{1,410.6}{15}$ (94.04) $\dfrac{78.066}{9}$ (8.674)

GETTING STARTED

Write the following on the chalkboard.

$\dfrac{6.66}{3} = 2.22$; $\dfrac{6.66}{2} = 3.33$; $\dfrac{6.66}{1} = 6.66$

Ask students whether they can see a pattern. Point out that the quotient becomes greater as the divisor becomes smaller. Then write the following on the chalkboard.

$\dfrac{1.20}{5} = 0.24$; $\dfrac{1.20}{4} = 0.30$; $\dfrac{1.20}{3} = 0.40$

Ask students what they think will happen if they divide 1.20 by a number between 5 and 4. Guide them to realize that the quotient will be between 0.24 and 0.30.

TEACHING THE LESSON

Explain that moving the decimal point to change the value of both the divisor and the dividend enables students to divide with a whole-number divisor. In this way, it is far simpler to keep track of the place value of digits in the partial products.

Point out that when dividing two decimals, only the divisor needs to be a whole number. Use the following example to show that dividing with two decimals is the *same* as dividing with the multiples of the same power of 10.

$\dfrac{206.4 \times 10}{9.6 \times 10} = \dfrac{2,064}{96} = 21.5$

Use the Other Examples section to show students how to write zeros both before and after the decimal point, when necessary.

Checkpoint

The chart lists the common errors students make in dividing a decimal by another decimal.

Correct Answers: 1c, 2d, 3c, 4d

Remediation

■ For these errors, give students several exercises similar to those on page 67. Have them practice regrouping only the divisor and the dividend.

☐ For these errors, assign Reteach Master, p. 22.

△ For this error, guide students to the P.E. pp. 22–23.

Dividing Decimals by Decimals

Marina drove 206.4 miles during the weekend. Her car used 9.6 gallons of gas. What was the rate of fuel usage in miles per gallon?

Divide $9.6\overline{)206.4}$.

When the divisor is a decimal, multiply both the divisor and the dividend by the smallest power of 10 that will make the divisor a whole number. Place the decimal point in the quotient, and divide as you would with whole numbers.

The rate was 21.5 miles per gallon.

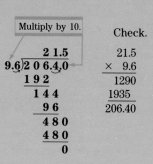
Multiply by 10.

```
        2 1.5
9.6)2 0 6 4.0
    1 9 2
    1 4 4
      9 6
      4 8 0
      4 8 0
          0
```

Check.
```
   21.5
 ×  9.6
   1290
   1935
 206.40
```

Other examples:

```
      $ 2.4 0
9.7 5)$2 3 4 0.0 0
      1950
      3900
      3900
         0
```

```
       7.2 5
3.6 2 4)2 6 2 7 4.0 0
        25368
         9060
         7248
        18120
        18120
            0
```

Find $\dfrac{0.02310}{4.2}$, rounded to the nearest thousandth.

```
     0.0 0 5 5
4.2)0.0 2 3 1 0
      2 1 0
      2 1 0
      2 1 0
          0
```

$0.0055 \longrightarrow 0.006$

Checkpoint Write the letter of the correct answer.

Divide.

1. $3.6\overline{)10.08}$ **a.** 0.028 **b.** 0.28 **(c.)** 2.8 **d.** 28

2. $0.018\overline{)72}$ **a.** 0.004 **b.** 4 **c.** 400 **(d.)** 4,000

3. $0.24\overline{)0.0216}$ **a.** 0.000009 **b.** 0.0009 **(c.)** 0.09 **d.** 0.9

4. Round $0.0887 \div 0.033$ to the nearest tenth.

 a. 2.68 **b.** 2.6 **c.** 2.69 **(d.)** 2.7

66

Math Reasoning, page H210

COMMON ERRORS

Answer Choice	Type of Error
■ 1a, 3a	Uses the total number of decimal places
■ 1b, 3b, 4a	Uses the number of decimal places in the dividend
☐ 1d, 2b	Omits the decimal point
■ 2a	Uses the number of decimal places in the divisor
☐ 2c, 3d	Misplaces the decimal point
△ 4b, 4c	Makes error in rounding

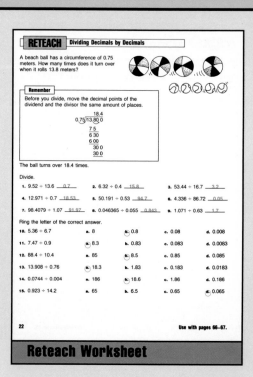

Divide.

1. $0.7\overline{)4.9}$
7

2. $0.6\overline{)0.0228}$
0.038

3. $8\overline{)1.68}$
0.21

4. $0.04\overline{)14.676}$
366.9

5. $9.2\overline{)\$3.22}$
$0.35

6. $0.074\overline{)0.0259}$
0.35

7. $7.5\overline{)\$2.70}$
$0.36

8. $4.8\overline{)96}$
20

9. $2.4 \div 0.12$
20

10. $\$1.47 \div 0.35$
$4.20

11. $10.5 \div 0.0015$
7,000

12. $2.83668 \div 9.21$
0.308

13. $1.71 \div 0.0342$
50

14. $132.3472 \div 457$
0.2896

15. $20.9588 \div 6.04$
3.47

16. $711.5435 \div 0.0863$
8,245

17. $\dfrac{0.02304}{0.64}$
0.036

18. $\dfrac{91}{0.13}$
700

19. $\dfrac{0.46113}{5.7}$
0.0809

20. $\dfrac{29.659}{31.22}$
0.95

21. $\dfrac{32.9346}{42.8}$
0.7695

22. $\dfrac{4.998}{850}$
0.00588

23. $\dfrac{0.002872}{0.0718}$
0.04

24. $\dfrac{71.4974}{1.07}$
66.82

Divide. Round each quotient to the nearest tenth.

25. $0.6\overline{)0.7}$ 1.2

26. $3.6\overline{)1.45}$ 0.4

27. $0.09\overline{)2.75}$ 30.6

28. $0.0458\overline{)2.823}$ 61.6

Divide. Round each quotient to the nearest hundredth
or the nearest cent.

29. $0.426 \div 0.8$
0.53

30. $\$2.96 \div 7.3$
$0.41

31. $\$0.74 \div 0.0632$
$11.71

32. $5.13216 \div 3.52$
1.46

Divide. Round each quotient to the nearest thousandth.

33. $\dfrac{0.2741}{7}$ 0.039

34. $\dfrac{1.7}{0.42}$ 4.048

35. $\dfrac{1.0463}{0.53}$ 1.974

36. $\dfrac{0.381}{10.4}$ 0.037

Solve. For Problem 39, use the Infobank.

37. Natalie drove her car 178.3 miles. If her car gets about 19.5 miles to the gallon, about how many gallons of gas did Natalie use on this trip? Round the answer to the nearest gallon. **about 9 gallons**

38. Jason used 3.6 gallons of gas to drive his economy car 138.7 miles. At what rate in miles per gallon, rounded to the nearest tenth, did his car use gas? **38.5 mi/gal**

39. Use the information on page 473 to solve. A group of 69 people from Chicago want to take a week long trip to Washington, D.C. According to the rental rates, how much would it cost each person to travel the cheapest way to Washington, D.C. by bus? **$84.81 per person**

★40. A speedboat's gas-consumption rate is measured in gallons per hour. The speedboat *Silvershark* uses 18.9 gallons in 2.25 hours. At what rate does the *Silvershark* use gas? If there are 6.3 gallons left in the tank, for how many more hours will the *Silvershark* run? **8.4 gal/h; 0.75 hours**

PRACTICE Dividing Decimals by Decimals

Divide. Round your answer to the nearest thousandth or to the nearest cent where necessary.

1. $\dfrac{1.352}{0.8}$ 1.69

2. $0.016 \div 0.04$ 0.4

3. $\dfrac{0.624}{0.078}$ 8

4. $\dfrac{36.45}{48}$ $0.75

5. $\dfrac{428}{6.4}$ 66.875

6. $7.5 \div 0.15$ 50

7. $5.632 \div 3.2607$ 1.727

8. $\$1.40 \div 2.818$ $0.50

9. $\dfrac{4.346}{0.2173}$ 20

10. $\dfrac{0.87571}{9.218}$ 0.095

11. $8,564 \div 32.54$ 263.184

12. $\dfrac{6.7}{2.264}$ 2.959

13. $7.4\overline{)3,500.8}$ 473.081

14. $0.87\overline{)0.00435}$ 0.005

15. $0.004\overline{)0.00372}$ 0.93

16. $2.818\overline{)1,409}$ 500

17. $5.8\overline{)\$15.95}$ $2.75

18. $8.04\overline{)0.602}$ 0.075

Solve.

19. Mandy is trying to create a liquid that will not evaporate. Her beaker contains 47.5 mL of solution. She wants to put an equal amount of the solution into test tubes by using an eyedropper that holds 0.98 mL. How many times can she fill the eyedropper completely? **48 times**

Use with pages 66–67.   29

Practice Worksheet

ENRICH Logic

A **syllogism** is an argument with two statements and a conclusion. The statements do not need to be true in reality.

> All dogs are animals.
> All animals have 6 legs.
> Therefore, all dogs have 6 legs.

To prove a syllogism to be true or false, you can use Venn diagrams. Let U = all living things, D = dogs, A = animals, and L = 6-legged living things.

If all dogs are animals, then any dogs outside set A do not exist.

If all animals have 6 legs, then any animals outside set L do not exist.

The only dogs remaining are within set L. Thus, all dogs have 6 legs.

All insects are green. No spiders are insects. Therefore, no spiders are green.

Let U = living things
I = insects   G = green things
S = spiders

All insects are green.   No spiders are insects.   There are green spiders.

On another sheet of paper, draw a Venn diagram to prove or disprove each syllogism. Write *true* or *false*.

1. All wrenches are pliers.
No pliers are hammers.
Therefore, no wrenches are hammers. **true**

2. All students are workers.
All workers wear shoes.
Therefore, all students wear shoes. **true**

3. All horses are racers.
All winners are horses.
Therefore, all winners are racers. **false**

4. No kittens are people.
All people are tall.
No kittens are tall. **false**

Use with pages 66–67.   29

Enrich Worksheet

ASSIGNMENT GUIDE

Basic: 1–16, 17–39 *o*

Average: 1–12, 14–40 *e*

Extended: 2–36 *e*, 37–40

Resources
Practice, p. 29   Class/Home, p. H29
Reteach, p. 22   More Practice, p. H196
Enrich, p. 29   Reasoning, p. H210

Exercise Analysis

1–24   Divide a decimal by a decimal or whole numbers by decimals

25–36   Divide by a decimal, rounding the quotient to the nearest tenth, hundredth, cent, or thousandth

37–38, 40   Skill applications

39   Data collection and computation

You may wish to allow students to use calculators for some of these exercises.

FOLLOW-UP ACTIVITIES

PUZZLES AND GAMES
Materials: blank cards; marker

Prepare decks of cards that show one decimal per card and that range from 0.001 to 99.99. Form the class into groups of 4, and give each group a deck of cards. One student from each group will act as the dealer.

Each player is dealt two cards and decides whether to add, subtract, multiply, or divide the decimals on the cards. The object is to obtain an answer that is close to but cannot exceed 21.

A player can ask for additional cards, one at a time, but must use all he or she takes. Players decide the order of operations to be performed on their cards. In the example below, the product of the first two cards is added to the value of the third card.

3.6   5.4   1.2
$(3.6 \times 5.4) + 1.2 = 20.64$

NUMBER SENSE (Mental Math)
Write the following problems on the chalkboard, and have students mentally find the quotients.

$0.8\overline{)560}$ (700) $0.007\overline{)9.1}$ (1,300)

$0.02\overline{)0.005}$ (0.25) $0.09\overline{)0.00054}$ (0.006)

$0.15\overline{)30}$ (200) $0.04\overline{)120}$ (3,000)

$0.05\overline{)16}$ (320) $0.05\overline{)3}$ (60)

COMING UP
Devising divisors

67

Objective. To make a plan to solve a multistep problem

Warm-Up

Have students mentally compute the following multiplication and division chains as you dictate them.

$18 \div 3 \times 6 \div 9$ (4)
$6 \times 4 \div 12 \times 8$ (16)
$3 \times 10 \times 4 \div 6$ (20)
$6 \times 7 \div 2 \div 3$ (7)

GETTING STARTED

Pose this problem to students.

4 children are buying a present for their mother. The present costs $15.00. The children want to know whether they have enough money among them to buy the present.

What is the first thing they must do? (Add the amount of money each child has.) What must they do next? (Compare the amount they have to $15.00.) Summarize the solution process by having students tell
● how many steps they used. (2)
● what operations were used. (addition, subtraction)

Point out that many times in order to find one piece of information, other pieces must be found first.

TEACHING THE LESSON

A *two-step or multistep problem* is one in which students must perform one or more intermediate steps to find the information needed to solve the problem. A useful approach to solving two-step problems is to have students
● identify the information they have.
● identify the information they need.
● use the given information to find the needed information.
● use the derived information to solve the problem.

Some students may benefit from working in small groups on multistep problems.

Questions: The question is direct and easy to comprehend.

Tools: The development of the plan is the crucial strategy in solving multistep problems. Have students write a plan as outlined above. If students have difficulty writing a plan, have them work backward from the final goal. In the lesson problem, they need to find how many boxes of birdseed are needed. What will tell them this? (the number of bags needed) How will they find the number of bags needed? (by determining how many bags are eaten per day and multiplying by 4) How will they determine how many bags are eaten per day? (by multiplying the number of bags eaten per

PROBLEM SOLVING
Solving Multi-step Problems/Making a Plan

You may need to use more than one step to solve a problem. Before you can answer the question that is asked, you may have to find some facts that are not stated. You can use the numbers that are given to find the numbers that you need. Making a plan can help you solve such a problem.

> The Smiths are going on a trip for 4 days. While they are away, a neighbor will feed their 8 parrots. Each parrot eats about 3 bags of birdseed per day. Birdseed is packaged 16 bags to a box. How many boxes of birdseed will be needed for 4 days?

Needed data: bags of birdseed eaten each day
bags of birdseed needed for 4 days

Plan

Step 1: Find the number of bags of birdseed eaten by the 8 parrots each day.

Step 2: Find the number of bags of birdseed needed for 4 days.

Step 3: Find the number of boxes of birdseed needed.

Step 1:
number of bags = number of bags × number of
per day   per parrot   parrots
n =   3 bags   × 8 parrots; So $n = 24$.

Step 2:
bags needed   =   bags per day   ×   number of days
for 4 days
x =   24 bags   ×   4 days; So $x = 96$.

Step 3:
boxes needed = bags needed ÷ number of bags per box
for 4 days
y =   96 bags   ÷   16 bags per box
y =   6

So, 6 boxes of birdseed will be needed for 4 days.

> *Work backward* to find the total number of boxes.

68

day by each parrot by the number of parrots)

Solutions: Computational difficulties will be minor. You may wish to allow students to use calculators in problem solving.

Checks: Most difficulties will arise from setting up situations incorrectly. Have students check their plan backward by substituting their answer for the words in the plan to see if it makes sense.

Complete the plan for each problem by writing the missing steps. **See Answer Key.**

1. Each of the 27 members of the Wilderness Club carries a 30-pound backpack on a camping trip. If nonfood items make up 20 pounds of each person's backpack, what is the total weight of the food supplies carried by all the club members?

—— **1.** Find the amount of food carried by each person.

—— **2.**

2. A camping store stocks 1,000 kerosene lanterns of various sizes. One of every 10 lanterns is large. The store sells large lanterns for $50 each. How much money does the store take in if it sells every large lantern in its stock?

—— **1.** Find the number of large lanterns that the store has in stock.

—— **2.**

Make a plan for each problem. Solve. For some problems, you may find it helpful to work backward. **See Answer Key.**

3. In the last 12 days, 2,400 people have taken the Royal Gorge Ranch raft trip through the rapids. The ranch used 25 rafts each day. On the average, how many people rode in each raft each day?

4. The Thunderama Roller Coaster has 12 cars. Each car holds 5 people. The roller coaster completes 6 rides per hour, 12 hours per day. How many people can ride the Thunderama in a day?

5. An airport checks in an average of 1,500 passengers per hour. Each passenger checks an average of 30 pounds of baggage. How many pounds of baggage are handled in one day?

6. Gail bought a backpack that cost $58.00. The sales tax on $58.00 amounted to $4.35. Gail gave the salesclerk four $20 bills. How much change did Gail receive?

7. A bus goes from the airport to the center of the city and back. The fare is $2.55 each way. The bus can hold 28 passengers. On holidays, the bus is always full. How much money is collected in total fares for 3 round trips on a holiday?

★8. Mr. and Mrs. Coe plan to spend $1,200 for a 10-day trip. It will cost them $47 per day to rent a van. They will spend 2 nights in a hotel that charges $50 per night and the rest of the time at a campsite that charges $2.00 per night. They plan to spend $30 per day for food. How much will they have available to spend per day on other items?

Classwork/Homework, page H30

Exercise Analysis
1–2 Write the missing step to solve each problem
3–8 Make a plan to solve each problem

FOLLOW-UP ACTIVITIES

PROBLEM SOLVING
Write these problems on the chalkboard or provide them as a handout. Have students make a plan and solve each problem.

1. Last weekend the River Ranch rented 26 rafts on both Saturday and Sunday. Each raft holds 8 people. If all the rafts were full, how many people rode the rafts last weekend? (416 people)

2. The Adventurers Club paid $240 to rent 16 rafts. If club members rented all 26 rafts, how much did the club pay? ($390)

3. Smaller rafts rent for $12.50 each. Jane rented 3 small rafts and paid with two $20 bills. How much change will she receive? ($2.50)

CALCULATOR
Materials: calculators

Write these examples on the chalkboard or provide them as a handout.
- $17 \times (84 - 23)$ (1,037)
- $(609 - 21) \div 7$ (84)
- $19 \times (28 + 6)$ (646)
- $622 + \left(\frac{840}{5}\right) + 718$ (1,508)
- $785 + \left(\frac{249}{3}\right) - 418$ (450)
- $\left(\frac{540 \times 45}{15}\right) + 828$ (2,448)
- $\frac{16,250 \div 13}{25} \times 6,321$ (316,050)
- $\left(\frac{17 \times 44}{11} \times \frac{55}{20}\right) + 219$ (406)

Because calculators do only one operation at a time, students cannot solve $2 \times (5 + 3)$ by pressing $2 \times 5 + 3 =$ because 2 would be multiplied by 5 before 3 could be added to it. To solve, students must use the Commutative Property of Multiplication to rearrange the problem: $5 + 3 \times 2 = 16$.

Have students use a calculator to solve each of the multistep problems.

COMING UP
Wrapping it up

Objective: To use math vocabulary

Warm-Up

Write the following on the chalkboard and have students make use of all the digits to write every decimal less than 1. Then have them order the decimals from the least to the greatest.

5, 0, 5, 6

(0.0556; 0.0565; 0.0655; 0.5056; 0.5065; 0.5506; 0.556; 0.5605; 0.565; 0.6055; 0.6505; 0.655)

GETTING STARTED

Have students write these three headings on a piece of paper.

Photography, Music, Cooking

Read the following words aloud, and have students classify and write each word beneath the correct heading.

ingredient	melody	darkroom
lens	recipe	tempo
light meter	casserole	synthesizer
rhythm	shutter	boil

(Photography: darkroom, lens, light meter, shutter)
(Music: melody, tempo, synthesizer, rhythm)
(Cooking: ingredient, recipe, casserole, boil)

TEACHING THE LESSON

Have students discuss why it is important to recognize and to understand math vocabulary terms. (in order to understand what is being asked in a math problem)

Have students complete the exercises on this page. Then have volunteers name math terms that were not listed. As each term is named, have students write on their papers an example that illustrates the term. When this activity is completed, have students share their answers.

(Possible responses might include addend, 2 + 2; sum, 8; factor, 3 × 6; obtuse angle, ∠108°)

MATH COMMUNICATION

Fields as varied as business, science, and recreational handicrafts have their own special vocabularies. Read this paragraph.

When using a pattern to cut a waistcoat in corduroy, lay the pattern with the grain so that the nap will run upward. Cut notches and mark darts, buttonholes, and pockets before removing pattern pieces. When attaching facings, ease underarm and neckline on garment. Trim seam allowances and selvages; then bind seams.

If you were a tailor working with napped fabric, you would know what these words mean. When you work with mathematics, you need to know the meanings of special words and phrases.

Match the word or the phrase with its meaning.

1. Commutative Properties **f**
2. Associative Properties **e**
3. Identity element for addition **d**
4. inverse operations **c**
5. digit **a**
6. Distributive Property **b**

a. a whole number from 0 through 9

b. To multiply a sum by a number, you can multiply each addend by the number and then add the products.

c. two operations that undo each other, such as addition and subtraction

d. 0: when zero is added to a number, the answer is the same as the original number.

e. The grouping of addends or factors does not change the sum or the product.

f. The order of addends or factors does not change the sum or the product.

Name the property or properties that each example illustrates.

7. $(13 \times 4) \times 6 = 13 \times (4 \times 6)$ **Associative**

8. $(7 \times 13) + (7 \times 14) = 7 \times (13 + 14)$ **Distributive**

9. $25 \times 780 = 780 \times 25$ **Commutative**

10. $2(10 + 7) = 2 \times 10 + 2 \times 7$ **Distributive**

70

GROUP PROJECT

Not Just Hamburgers

The problem: You are visiting some friends in Japan. Your parents want you to take your two hosts out to dinner. They have sent you $60 in United States currency for the entire meal. Since you are treating, your hosts ask you to order the meal. Using the menu below, figure out what to order that will not cost more than $80, and add up the bill. 140 yen (¥) equals $1.

KYOTO GARDENS RESTAURANT

Salads		Entrees	
Bean Sprout Salad	¥275	Chicken Teriyaki	¥1,015
Green Salad	¥275	Beef Teriyaki	¥1,070
		Tempura Dinner	¥1,300
Side Orders		Sukiyaki—sliced beef and vegetables	¥1,015
Tempura—fried shrimp and vegetables	¥900	Sushi—raw fillets of fish on rice	¥960
Spring Roll	¥275		
Kara-Age—Japanese-style chicken wings	¥510	Beverages	
		Calpico—Japanese Soft Drink	¥150
Noodles and Rice		American Soft Drinks	¥150
		Tea	¥100
Fried Rice	¥425		
Yakisoba—Japanese noodles	¥425		

71

ASSIGNMENT GUIDE

Basic:	p. 70, p. 71
Average:	p. 70, p. 71
Extended:	p. 70, p. 71

Objectives: To plan a meal within a budget; to convert currency

USING THE PAGE

This project allows students to use a menu to plan a meal for three people. Have students work in groups of three. Each group should plan their meal together. Advise students of these considerations: the tastes of their guests, whether they wish to share any dishes, and which combinations of dishes create a pleasing blend.

Each group should discuss methods of determining whether the cost of the meal is less than $80, and then choose the best method. Tell students that they should find the method that uses the fewest number of actual conversions from dollars to yen.

You may wish to tell students that the number of yen per dollar often changes from day to day, and have them consult a newspaper to find the exchange rate for that day.

To extend this activity, distribute menus from inexpensive to moderately priced local ethnic restaurants, such as Greek, Italian, Chinese, and so on. Have each group of students plan a meal for several people with a total cost under $50 or $75. Have them find out from a bank or newspaper what the exchange rate is between the United States dollar and the currency of the country whose cuisine they are planning to eat.

Have each group then determine the total cost of their dinner and convert it into the currency of that country.

2 CHAPTER TEST

Purpose: The Chapter Test helps to assess students' understanding of the concepts and skills presented in this chapter.

The chart below is designed to help you review the test items by correlating them with the testing objectives that appear in the Chapter Overview.

Item	*Objectives*
1–15	A
16–25	B
26–27	C
28–30	D
31	C
32–33	D
34–35	C
36–39	D
40–41	E
42–43	F
44–45	E
46–47	G
48	H
49	I

Bonus

The bonus question may be used for extra credit, or you may want to assign it to students who complete the test before the rest of the class.

Calculator

You may wish to have students use calculators for the problem-solving portions of the test.

Resources

If you prefer to use this Chapter Test as a review exercise, additional testing materials are available in the Teacher's Resource Book.

CHAPTER TEST

Multiply or divide. (pages 44–45, 50–53, 56–57, 60–61, and 64–67)

1. 326 × 8 — **2,608**
2. 7,184 × 6 — **43,104**
3. 539 × 27 — **14,553**
4. 4,572 × 86 — **393,192**
5. 52,006 × 329 — **17,109,974**
6. 2,782 × 5,014 — **13,948,948**
7. 131 × 258 — **33,798**
8. 7,904 × 176 — **1,391,104**
9. 28,917 × 843 — **24,377,031**
10. $109.52 × 634 — **$69,435.68**
11. $24\overline{)3,168}$ — **132**
12. $273\overline{)\$1,646.19}$ — **$6.03**
13. 434,561 ÷ 702 — **619 R23**
14. 6,792 ÷ 10 — **679.2**
15. 13 × 200 — **2,600**
16. 28.72596 × 1,000 — **28,725.96**
17. 6.24 ÷ 10 — **0.624**
18. 36.518 ÷ 10 — **3.6518**
19. 7.001408 ÷ 1,000 — **0.007001408**
20. 328.741 ÷ 100 — **3.28741**
21. 0.723 ÷ 100 — **0.00723**
22. $\frac{3.21}{100}$ — **0.0321**
23. $\frac{7.954}{100}$ — **0.07954**
24. $\frac{36.5107}{1,000}$ — **0.0365107**
25. $\frac{0.07}{1,000}$ — **0.00007**
26. 4.92 × 78 — **383.76**
27. 0.643 × 246 — **158.178**
28. 12.52 × 0.731 — **9.15212**
29. 4.926 × 3.141 — **15.472566**
30. 0.17692 × 3.4 — **0.601528**
31. 0.0824 × 309 — **25.4616**
32. 9.54 × 2.7 — **25.758**
33. 32.794 × 0.015 — **0.49191**
34. $43\overline{)149.64}$ — **3.48**
35. $319\overline{)4.147}$ — **0.013**
36. $1.9\overline{)15.58}$ — **8.2**
37. $2.015\overline{)0.058435}$ — **0.029**
38. $0.078\overline{)0.500838}$ — **6.421**
39. $4.00027\overline{)772.852164}$ — **193.2**

Estimate the product or the quotient. (pages 46–47 and 58–59)
Answers may vary. Accept any reasonable estimate.

40. 54 × 76 — **4,000**
41. 3,872 × 9,405 — **36,000,000**
42. 0.038 × 0.472 — **0.02**
43. 12.762 × 0.00839 — **0.1**
44. $24\overline{)2,897}$ — **100+**
45. 214,272 ÷ 186 — **1,000+**

72

POSTTEST Chapter 2 Page 1

1. 400 × $300 ____
2. 372.05 × 10 ____
3. 0.00324 ÷ 6 ____
4. Estimate.
   17,507 ÷ 181 ____
5. The entrance fee to a zoo is $2.00 for adults and $1.25 for children. How much did it cost a family of 2 adults and 3 children? ____
6. Barb Barnacle's fish store sold 3 boxes of white fish, 15 boxes of shrimp, and 12 boxes of fish sticks to a local restaurant. If each box weighed 24 oz, how many boxes of seafood were sold?
   Which of the given numbers is not needed to solve the problem?
   a. 3 b. 12
   c. 15 d. 24 ____
7. 50.92 ÷ 100 ____
8. 8 × 49.62 ____
9. $0.07\overline{)0.00056}$
10. Estimate.
    47 × 69 ____
11. Estimate.
    12.001 × 0.099 ____
12. Estimate.
    69.001 × 899.008 ____

Posttest

POSTTEST Chapter 2 Page 2

13. Sid has 32 letters to mail for his boss. Each letter needs 1 stamp and Sid has 4 books of stamps. Does he have enough stamps to mail the letters?
    What additional information is needed to solve the problem?
    a. the cost of a book of stamps
    b. the number of stamps needed for the letters
    c. the number of stamps in a book
    d. the weight of each letter ____
14. On a 4-day trip, a family spends $25 per day on gas, $35 per day on food, and $200 for spending 3 nights in a hotel. How much did the trip cost? ____
15. 0.305 × 0.068
16. $9,373 ÷ 13 ____
17. A national chain of hamburger restaurants has 2,540 stores. The chain advertises that 50 billion hamburgers have been sold. There are 256 million people in the United States. If you were asked to find the average number of hamburgers eaten by each person in the United States, what information would you not need from this problem? ____
18. There are 99.6 million households in the United States. A company wants to advertise on a national evening television news show. What additional information is needed so the company can determine the number of households in which their advertising will be seen? ____
19. It costs $1.25 to buy a weekly magazine. What is the total cost for the year? ____

Posttest

Identify any extra or needed information. Solve if possible. (pages 48–49)

46. Lily is changing her American dollars to francs. She has $128. If there are 6 francs to the dollar, how much is 1 franc worth? **16.7¢; extra information: Lily has $128.**

47. Lucian is visiting Venice. After a trip to St. Mark's Square, he tips the gondolier $3. About how many Italian lire is this? **Needed information: How many lire to a dollar?**

Write the letter of the operation you would use to solve the problem. (pages 62–63)

48. Daryl made a bicycle trip across his state. On the first day he rode 83 miles, 97 miles on the second day, 70 miles on the third day, 102 miles on the fourth day, and 56 miles on the fifth day. How many total miles did he travel?

a. addition   **b.** subtraction   **c.** multiplication

Solve. (pages 68–69)

49. Lucian spends 3 days in Venice, 5 days in Rome, 9 days in Florence, 2 days in Trieste, and 7 days in Naples. He also spends time in Milan and returns home from there. If his entire trip is 30 days and he leaves Milan on August 31, on what day did he arrive in Milan? **August 27**

BONUS

Solve.

Rita's skiing trip was planned for 6 days and 5 nights. Transportation to the ski resort cost $55.70 and her ski lodge cost $35.00 per night. If she had a budget of $620.00, how much would she have left to spend each day for food and entertainment after she paid for transportation and lodging?   **$55.60**

73

For students who have difficulty with written tests, this test can be given orally.

You may wish to test students, orally or in writing, to see if they can explain the steps used in solving selected items. The following table summarizes the procedures for solving key test items.

Ex. 16

Multiplying decimals by powers of 10

To multiply a decimal by a power of 10, move the decimal point one place to the right for each zero in the factor.

Ex. 10, 26–33

Multiplying decimals

To multiply decimals, multiply as with whole numbers. Then count the number of decimal places in both factors and place the decimal point in the product, counting from the right the appropriate number of decimal places. If necessary, add zeros to the front of the product to place the decimal point.

Ex. 34–35

Dividing decimals by whole numbers

To divide a decimal by a whole number, place the decimal point in the quotient above the decimal point in the dividend. If necessary, write zeros in the quotient or dividend. Then divide as with whole numbers.

Ex. 36–39

Dividing decimals by decimals

To divide a decimal by a decimal, multiply both the divisor and the dividend by the smallest power of 10 that will make the divisor a whole number. Then place the decimal point in the quotient above the decimal point in the dividend, and divide as with whole numbers.

Name _____ Date _____

POSTTEST   Chapter 2 Page 3

20. $23\overline{)23{,}391}$

21. $10\overline{)0.01073}$

22. A person drove 180 mi on one day and 250 mi on the next day. How many miles did he drive altogether for the two days?

23. Estimate.
420
×892

24. 6.008
× 100

25. Electricity costs $0.20 per kilowatt hour. If a refrigerator uses 42.5 kilowatt hours per month, what is the yearly cost?

26. Estimate.
5.9098 × 1.0999

27. 6,000 × 30,000

28. $20\overline{)4.026}$

29. Estimate.
32 × 6.93

30. A marching band has 5 players in each of 8 rows, and 3 players in each of the last two rows. How many players are in the band?

Posttest

Name _____ Date _____

POSTTEST   Chapter 2 Page 4

31. 24,401 × 3.02

32. $16.2\overline{)$1.56}$
What is the quotient rounded to the nearest cent?

33. There were 42 members in a stamp club. Fifteen new members joined the club. What is the total number of members now?
What operation should be performed to solve the problem?

34. $5,022.07
×   12.5
Round the product to the nearest cent.

35. The cost of a shirt is $18, and the cost of a pair of slacks is $60. About how many times the cost of a shirt is the cost of the slacks?

36. A menu in a Japanese restaurant has prices listed in yen instead of dollars. A dinner costs 6,780 yen. What is the cost in dollars if 225 yen are equivalent to one dollar?
What operation should be performed to solve the problem?

Posttest

Purpose This Reteaching page provides additional instruction for key concepts in the chapter. It is designed for use by students who have had difficulty with these concepts. It can also be used to provide additional practice for students who require it.

USING THE PAGE

Dividing decimals by decimals was first taught on pages 66–67.

Review the process of making the divisor a whole number by multiplying both the divisor and the dividend by the same power of 10. Also remind students that sometimes it is necessary to write zeros in the dividend, as shown in the second example on this page. While working through the two examples, be sure to give students an opportunity to participate in each step. Encourage students to use estimation in order to check their answers. Be sure to remind students that they can use multiplication to check their answers.

Point out that Exercises 9–16 require students to find quotients to the nearest tenth or hundredth. For these exercises, students should have two or three decimal places in the quotient before rounding.

Resources

For practice and activities related to this chapter, see the Teacher's Resource Book.

RETEACHING

To divide a decimal by a decimal, multiply the divisor and the dividend by the power of 10 that will make the divisor a whole number. Then divide as you would with whole numbers.

Divide $0.12\overline{)0.612}$.

Multiply by 100 (move each decimal point two places to the right).

Place the decimal point in the quotient above the decimal point in the dividend.

Divide as with whole numbers.

$$0.12\overline{)0.612} \qquad 12\overline{)61.2}$$

$$\begin{array}{r} 5.1 \\ 12\overline{)61.2} \\ \underline{6\,0} \\ 1\,2 \\ \underline{1\,2} \\ 0 \end{array}$$

Divide 45 by 16.1. Round to the nearest hundredth.

$$16.1\overline{)45.0}$$

$$\begin{array}{r} 2.795 \to 2.80 \\ 161\overline{)450.000} \\ \underline{322} \\ 128\,0 \\ \underline{112\,7} \\ 15\,30 \\ \underline{14\,49} \\ 810 \\ \underline{805} \\ 5 \end{array}$$

Multiply by 10 (move each decimal point one place to the right). Place the decimal point in the quotient. Write zeros where necessary.

Divide to one place more (thousandths) than the place to which you are rounding.

Divide.

1. $\$0.50\overline{)\$88.50}$
177.00

2. $0.3\overline{)62.628}$
208.76

3. $19.6\overline{)82.32}$
4.2

4. $0.57\overline{)368.79}$
647

5. $0.36\overline{)0.96156}$
2.671

6. $0.035\overline{)0.1365}$
3.9

7. $0.105\overline{)2,452.38}$
23,356

8. $0.263\overline{)789}$
3,000

Find each quotient to the nearest tenth.

9. $1.15\overline{)825}$
717.4

10. $0.061\overline{)14}$
229.5

11. $25.4\overline{)82.25}$
3.2

12. $0.342\overline{)1}$
2.9

Find each quotient to the nearest hundredth.

13. $\$0.49\overline{)\$10.43}$
21.29

14. $1.8\overline{)44.2}$
24.56

15. $0.079\overline{)197}$
2,493.67

16. $\$0.03\overline{)\$4}$
133.33

74

ENRICHMENT

Number Sequences

A set of numbers written in a particular order is called a **sequence.** Each number in the sequence is called a **term.** There are seven terms in the following sequence.

2, 5, 8, 11, 14, 17, 20

If a pattern is obvious, all the terms do not have to be written. Instead, you can use the symbol "...," which means, "and so on."

2, 5, 8, ... , 20

Since the first three terms differ by 3, it is easy to determine that 11, 14, and 17 are the unwritten terms of the sequence.

If a sequence never stops, it is **infinite** and can be written with the "and so on" symbol at the end.

1, 3, 5, 7, 9, ...

Sequences can be formed by using any of the arithmetic operations.

1, 2, 4, 7, 11, 16, ...   57, 52, 47, 42, 37, ...
(+1) (+2) (+3) (+4) (+5)   (−5) (−5) (−5) (−5)

5, 15, 45, 135, 405, ...   720, 144, 36, 12, 6, 6.
(×3) (×3) (×3) (×3)   (÷5) (÷4) (÷3) (÷2) (÷1)

Find the pattern. Write the next three terms in each sequence.

1. 6, 12, 18, ...
24, 30, 36
2. 7, 28, 112, ...
448, 1,792, 7,168
3. 112, 109, 105, 100, ...
94, 87, 79
4. 896, 448, 224, ...
112, 56, 28
5. 1, 4, 9, 16, ...
25, 36, 49
6. 3, 3, 6, 18, 72, ...
360, 2,160, 15,120
7. 6,561, 2,187, 729, ...
243, 81, 27
8. 1, 8, 27, 64, ...
125, 216, 343
9. 1, 1, 2, 3, 5, 8, 13, ...
21, 34, 55
10. 5, 5, 10, 15, 25, 40, ...
65, 105, 170
11. 1, 9, 33, 105, 321, ...
969, 2,913, 8,745
12. 1, 6, 4, 9, 7, 12, 10, 15, ...
13, 18, 16
13. $\frac{1}{2}, \frac{3}{3}, \frac{5}{4}, \frac{7}{5}, \frac{9}{6}, \dots$
$\frac{11}{7}, \frac{13}{8}, \frac{15}{9}$
14. 16.2, 8.1, 4.05, ...
2.025, 1.0125, 0.50625

For additional activities, see *Connecting Math Ideas*, page 469.   **75**

Purpose This Enrichment page provides an additional challenge for those students whose work throughout the chapter and on the Chapter Test shows a thorough understanding of the material. Alternatively, you may wish to use these exercises as a supplementary lesson for the entire class.

USING THE PAGE

Emphasize to students that a number sequence builds upon itself; that is, each term is drawn from the term that precedes it or from its place in the sequence. A sequence can begin with any number. It can end with a particular number or it can continue infinitely.

Discuss with students the meaning of *ellipses* (...) and the concept of *infinity*. A sequence can be built with any mathematical operation or series of operations. Exercise 8 is a sequence of cubes. Exercises 9 and 10 are Fibonacci sequences. Exercise 11 involves two operations ([n + 2] · 3). Tell students that sequences can also be built with fractions, decimals, square roots, and so on.

Resources
For additional Enrichment activities, see the Teacher's Resource Book.

Objectives: To use the BASIC IF...THEN and GOTO statements in computer programming

Warm-Up

Have students solve the following.

$6 \times (210 \div 7) = \blacksquare$ (180)
$(45 \times 7) \div (25 \div 5) = \blacksquare$ (63)
$468 \div (27 \div 3) = \blacksquare$ (52)
$(966 \div 14) \times 50$ (3,450)

GETTING STARTED

Review with students the rules for the order of operations. Have a volunteer write them on the chalkboard by using the *if . . . then* construction. (For example, "If an operation is in parentheses, then solve it before solving operations outside the parentheses. If there are no parentheses, then compute with exponents first, and follow with multiplication, division, addition, and subtraction, in that order." Accept any correct variations of this style.)

TEACHING THE LESSON

Present students with the following rules of the BASIC programming language.

1. The computer will carry out a BASIC statement without a line number as soon as RETURN or ENTER is pressed.
2. A program is a series of numbered statements, usually in multiples of 10.
3. The computer will run a program when the command RUN is entered.
4. The last line of a program should be END, although a program will run without it.
5. The LIST command is used to see the statements that a program contains.
6. The command NEW will clear a computer's memory.
7. The term *command* refers to the words RUN, LIST, and NEW. These words are not used within a program.

Tell students that the terms IF...THEN and GOTO are statements and are used in programs to change the order in which statements are executed. Be certain that students understand that there are many other programming statements in the BASIC language.

TECHNOLOGY

You can use the IF . . . THEN statement in BASIC to compare two numbers or variables.

1. Write the symbol or symbols that will make each statement true.

   IF B ● 10 THEN PRINT "B IS LESS THAN 10"   <
   IF B ● 10 THEN PRINT "B IS LESS THAN OR EQUAL TO 10"   <=
   IF B ● 10 THEN PRINT "B IS NOT EQUAL TO 10"   <>
   IF B ● 10 THEN PRINT "B IS GREATER THAN 10"   >
   IF B ● 10 THEN PRINT "B IS GREATER THAN OR EQUAL TO 10"   >=

You can use the GOTO statement to send the program to another line.

The GOTO statement tells the computer which line to do next. It can tell the computer to jump forward and skip lines or to jump back to a previous line.

2. What does this program print when you RUN it?

   10 PRINT "THE DOG IS"
   20 GOTO 40
   30 PRINT "NOT"
   40 PRINT "A POODLE"   THE DOG IS A POODLE

You can use the GOTO statement with the IF . . . THEN statement. Here is a program that asks for two numbers, and then subtracts the numbers and tells you the difference. In this program, B must be less than A.

10 PRINT "TYPE A NUMBER"
20 INPUT A
30 PRINT "TYPE A NUMBER SMALLER THAN" A
40 INPUT B
50 IF B > A THEN GOTO 30
60 LET C = A − B
70 PRINT "THE DIFFERENCE BETWEEN" A "AND" B "IS" C

76

3. Rewrite the program so that it asks for two numbers and prints the quotient of the first divided by the second. Be sure that the second number is not zero.

60 IF B = 0 THEN GOTO 30
70 LET C = A/B 80 PRINT "THE QUOTIENT OF" A "DIVIDED BY" B "IS" C

Here is a program that asks for two numbers and their product. Notice that you can put two statements on one line by using a colon.

```
10 PRINT "TYPE A NUMBER": INPUT I
20 PRINT "TYPE ANOTHER NUMBER": INPUT J
30 LET K = I*J
40 PRINT "WHAT IS THE PRODUCT OF" I "AND" J: INPUT N
50 IF N = K THEN GOTO 90
60 PRINT "THAT'S NOT RIGHT"
70 PRINT "TRY AGAIN"
80 GOTO 40
90 PRINT "GOOD WORK"
```

4. If you ran this program, typed in 8 and 20, and then typed 170, what would the computer print?

THAT'S NOT RIGHT TRY AGAIN WHAT IS THE PRODUCT OF 8 AND 20?

5. Finish this program. It asks for two numbers and their product. It tests whether your answer is too great, too small, or correct. If your answer is too great or too small, the program goes back and has you try again.

```
10 PRINT "TYPE A NUMBER ";: INPUT I
20 PRINT "TYPE ANOTHER NUMBER ";: INPUT J
30 LET K = I*J
40 PRINT "WHAT IS THE PRODUCT OF" I "AND" J: INPUT N
50 IF N = K THEN GOTO 130
60 IF N > K THEN GOTO ____  100
70 PRINT "_____"  TOO SMALL
80 PRINT "TRY AGAIN"
90 GOTO ____  40
100 PRINT "TOO GREAT"
110 PRINT "TRY AGAIN"
120 GOTO ____  40
130 PRINT "GOOD WORK"
```

77

FOLLOW-UP ACTIVITIES

COMPUTER
Challenge students to write a BASIC program that will determine whether three angles could be the angles of a triangle. Remind them that the sum of the measures of the angles of a triangle must be equal to 180°. Make sure they use the IF...THEN and GOTO statements in their programs.
Sample program:

```
10 PRINT "TYPE THREE MEASURES
   OF ANGLES"
20 INPUT A, B, C
30 LET D = A + B + C
40 IF D = 180 THEN GOTO 80
50 PRINT "THESE ANGLES DO NOT
   FORM A TRIANGLE"
60 PRINT "ENTER THREE OTHER AN-
   GLES"
70 GOTO 20
80 PRINT "THEY ARE THE ANGLES OF
   A TRIANGLE"
90 END
```

COMPUTER
Present students with the following chart that compares standard mathematics symbols for *less than*, *greater than*, or *equal to* with their equivalent BASIC symbols.

Math	BASIC	Meaning
=	=	is equal to
≠	<>	is not equal to
>	>	is greater than
≥	>=	is greater than or equal to
<	<	is less than
≤	<=	is less than or equal to

Challenge students to use these and the IF...THEN, GOTO, and LET commands to write a BASIC program that compares numbers by using inequalities. If you have a computer available, have students check their programs by running them on a computer. (Answers will vary.)

Purpose This Cumulative Review page provides an opportunity to reinforce students' understanding of the concepts and skills taught in previous chapters.

The chart below is designed to aid you in reviewing the material by specifying the pages on which various concepts and skills were taught.

Each Cumulative Review gives students an opportunity to practice taking tests that are written in a multiple-choice, standardized format. Be sure that students understand that if the correct answer is not among the first three given, then they should select the fourth choice—"not given"—as the correct answer. At least one item per test will require students to give this response.

CUMULATIVE REVIEW

Write the letter of the correct answer.

1. Estimate $85{,}835 - 26{,}751$.

a. 20,000   **b.** 59,000
c. 79,000   d. 81,000

2. $49{,}719 + 163{,}321 + 2{,}472{,}857 + 64{,}099$

a. 2,538,877   b. 2,638,996
c. 2,749,997   **d.** not given

3. Estimate $9.341 + 28.6962 + 0.8542$.

a. 30   b. 45
c. 39   d. 50

4. $342 - 43.091$

a. 298.019   **b.** 298.909
c. 299.091   d. not given

5. Order from the greatest to the least: 4.0134, 4.0143, 40.1343.

a. 4.0134, 4.0143, 40.1343
b. 40.1343, 4.0134, 4.0143
c. 40.1343, 4.0143, 4.0134
d. not given

6. $\$6{,}006.93 - \$17.89$

a. $5,098.04   **b.** $5,989.04
c. $5,999.14   d. not given

7. $9.0894 - 0.32908$

a. 8.75996   b. 8.76006
c. 9.75996   **d.** not given

8. $8.932 + 89.32 + 809.2 + 3.9824$

a. 65.780   b. 908.4344
c. 947.276   **d.** not given

9. Round 7,343.02456 to the nearest thousandth.

a. 8,000   b. 7,343.02
c. 7,343.025   d. not given

10. Compare $6{,}987{,}521 \bullet 6{,}985{,}721$.

a. >   b. <
c. =   d. not given

11. What number is $7{,}000{,}000 + 40{,}000 + 4{,}000 + 7$?

a. 7,447   b. 7,404,007
c. 7,044,007   d. not given

12. Use the bar graph to find the food that showed the greatest gain in consumption from 1959 to 1981.

a. eggs   **b.** poultry
c. cheese   d. not given

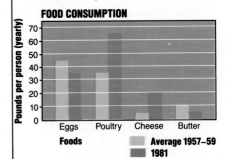

FOOD CONSUMPTION

Pounds per person (yearly) / Foods: Eggs, Poultry, Cheese, Butter

Average 1957–59
1981

13. Use the bar graph to find the food that was consumed the least from 1957 to 1959.

a. eggs   **b.** cheese
c. butter   d. not given

78

CHAPTER  OVERVIEW

NUMBER THEORY, EXPRESSIONS AND EQUATIONS

SUMMARY

Chapter 3 deals with number theory and equations. Divisibility, scientific notation, roots, square root, greatest common factor, and least common multiple are covered. Included are lessons on the ordering of operations and the solving of 1- and 2-step equations containing whole numbers and decimals.

LESSON SEQUENCE

PROFESSIONAL BACKGROUND

Many students will have a weak understanding of large numbers and the place value of their digits. Calculators can be useful diagnostic devices if used with activities that challenge students to produce numbers under particular constraints. For instance, when they begin with 15 on the screen, have students determine the number of successive multiplications needed to arrive at a product between 10,000 and 15,000.

Calculators can also be used to help familiarize students with the results of combinations of operations, and with the order of operations. Write the following expression on the chalkboard.

$$29 \bigcirc 15 \bigcirc 13 = \blacksquare$$

Have students experiment with calculators, and use different combinations of operations and parentheses, so that the right side of the equation will equal each of the following:
57, 5,655; 448; 1; 0.1487179.

Solving equations is a particularly troublesome area for many students because of their often tenuous hold on the concept of an unknown and the concept of equivalence. Research shows that many students find it difficult to understand that to perform the same operation on both sides of an equation does not affect the equivalence of the equation. Thus, some students may compensate incorrectly by rewriting $37 + b = 168$ as $b = 205$. It is important to keep alert for such misconceptions.

References: See Herscovics and Kiernan; Driscoll (secondary volume, chapters on calculators and algebra).

MATERIALS

graph paper
scissors
digit cards
bulletin board or felt board
blocks or tiles
calculators
match sticks
balance scale and weights
index cards

VOCABULARY

divisibility (p. 80)
even numbers (p. 80)
odd numbers (p. 80)
exponent (p. 82)
base (p. 82)
power (p. 82)
square of the number (p. 82)
perfect square (p. 82)
square root (p. 82)
scientific notation (p. 84)
standard form (p. 84)
factor (p. 88)
prime number (p. 88)
composite number (p. 88)
unity (p. 88)
prime factorization (p. 90)
factor tree (p. 90)
greatest common factor (p. 92)
relatively prime (p. 92)
least common multiple (p. 94)
order of operations (p. 98)
equation (p. 100)
equality (p. 100)
variables (p. 100)
algebraic sentences (p. 100)

ABOUT THE CHAPTER

The lessons in this chapter provide eighth-grade students with their first exposure to the principles of algebra. The first part of the chapter develops the skills that students need to successfully solve equations. There are 2 lessons in this chapter in which students are given the opportunity, in problem-solving settings, to work cooperatively. In these lessons students are confronted with real-life situations through which they are encouraged to develop and apply a variety of strategies.

In Chapter 3, students learn about divisibility, powers and roots, factors, prime factorization, greatest common factor, and least common multiple. Students learn to solve equations using replacement and then using addition, subtraction, multiplication, and division. Finally, students learn to solve 2-step equations.

Many of your students will be taking algebra, either in the first or second year of high school. This chapter is the first of several opportunities in this book for students to learn those skills that are fundamental to success in algebra. It is certainly worthwhile to devote additional time now to ensure that students grasp these algebra skills to the limit of their ability.

Stress the importance of the first lessons in the chapter. The skills developed here are essential for solving equations. It is important that students understand that whatever operations are performed on the left side of the equal sign must also be performed on the right side of the equal sign. Students need knowledge of inverse operations to help them solve equations.

Students can check the solution to every equation by substituting the solution in the original equation. Each side of the equation will yield the same result if the solution is correct.

Students should use the calculator to estimate and find square roots. Calculators can also be used to find a number raised to a power. Many calculators use scientific notation to represent numbers too large or too small for the display. Students should be shown this use of scientific notation.

Four problem-solving lessons are presented in this chapter. These lessons focus on checking for a reasonable answer, using a table, choosing the operation needed to solve a problem, and choosing and writing an equation.

The Group Project actively involves students and asks them to devise their own system of measurement. The Enrichment lesson introduces students to sequences and asks them to find the general rule for a term in the sequence.

USING THE CHAPTER OPENER

Each Chapter Opener presents situational problem-solving activities that can be used to explore the skills taught throughout the chapter. The work sheets can be used by individuals, small groups, or the whole class, depending on the needs of the class. The Chapter Opener focuses on a nonalgorithmic approach to mathematics through real-life situations relevant to students' experiences. Through an interdisciplinary approach, the Chapter Opener helps students explore the relationships between mathematics, other areas of the curriculum, and everyday life while developing different strands of mathematics.

In the Chapter Opener activities, students will explore patterns with prime, composite, and Mersenne numbers. Students will also examine the reasons why these patterns work and the difficulties involved in proving or disproving a theory.

PROBLEM SOLVING

The purpose of the lesson Checking for a Reasonable Answer is to teach students to verify that their answer to a problem is a sensible one. Students should recognize that both the size and the assigned units of an answer must be reasonable. The lesson in this chapter focuses on the size of the answer and is good for small-group work.

Obtaining information from an outside source is a necessary skill for solving math problems as well as for addressing real-life problems that confront us every day. In addition to teaching students how to use data not given in a problem, the lesson Using a Table in this chapter discusses the organization of data in tables, and instructs students in a step-by-step method of obtaining needed information from data tables. This lesson also lends itself to small-group work.

Since almost every math problem requires some kind of computation, the focus of the Choosing the Operation lesson is the skill students use most. The *Mathematics Unlimited* approach is to have students analyze the numbers given in the problem in order to find a solution. This helps students to understand the principal meanings of the operations, to learn the process of taking apart a word problem, and to focus on the relationship between a given set of conditions and a goal. The lesson in this chapter extends the lesson from the previous chapter to include division.

The lesson Writing an Equation builds upon the skill of Choosing the Operation. Students will need to decide which operation is indicated by each problem. Rather than suggesting key terms to be read as signals by students, the *Mathematics Unlimited* approach encourages students to reconceptualize the problem in algebraic terms. Because there is often more than one way to write an equation, this lesson is good for small-group work in which students can exchange various solutions to the problem.

Most of the problem solving lessons in *Mathematics Unlimited* lend themselves to small-group work. In a comfortable group atmosphere, students can brainstorm and discuss various ways to solve problems.

BULLETIN BOARD

"Pascal's Triangle"

Materials: paper to cover bulletin board, lettering, envelope, paper strips, felt-tip pen

Preparation: Cover bulletin board with paper and arrange display lettering. Write the numbers in Pascal's triangle as shown. Place the paper strips in the envelope attached below the triangle.

After pp. 82-83: Have students select one of the horizontal rows in Pascal's triangle and add all the numbers in it on a paper strip. Have them express this sum as a power of 2. Ask them if they can do this with all rows. (Yes, in the nth row, the sum of numbers is 2^n.)

After pp. 88-89: Have class list the prime numbers (2, 3, 5, 7) and the composite numbers (4, 6, 10, 15, 20, 21, 35) in the triangle.

After pp. 90-91: Have students choose a row. Ask them if the number of the row they chose is a factor of every number in the row (except the ones)? (If the number of the row is prime, such as 3, 5, or 7, then 3, 5, or 7 will be a factor of every number in the row, with the exception of the ones.)

Extension: Challenge students to discover other patterns in Pascal's triangle. For example, in any row, if the numbers are added and subtracted by turns, the result is always 0. In row 5: $1 - 5 + 10 - 10 + 5 - 1 = 0$.

COMMON ERRORS

Students sometimes have difficulty solving equations with variables because they forget to use all operations needed to solve for the variables on both sides of the equations. For example, students might solve $x + 6 = 42$ as follows:

$$x + 6 - 6 = 42$$
$$x = 42$$

or:

$$x + 6 = 42$$
$$x + 6 - 6 = 42 + 6$$
$$x = 48$$

A useful remediation for these errors is to have students circle each operation that they use on each side of equations. After they do this, they can compare and be sure the same operations were used on both sides of the equations.

Students should also be encouraged to check all their answers when they solve equations. A quick check will show students when they have solved an equation incorrectly. This is done easily by substituting the value found for that variable in the original equation.

SPECIAL NEEDS

Finding factors and multiples and defining the difference between them will be a major source of difficulty for some students. However, prior to working with factors and multiples, students need to know the difference between prime numbers and composite numbers. Have them use color tiles to determine if an array with more than one row or column can be formed. For example, the following arrays can be made with 12 tiles: 3×4, 4×3, 6×2, 2×6, 1×12, 12×1. Therefore, 12 is a composite number. 1, 3, 4, 6, and 12 are factors of 12. Have students use 11 tiles to show a prime number. Only a 1×11 and a 11×1 array can be formed. Therefore, the factors of 11 are 1 and 11. Have each student make and keep a chart that lists all numbers and their factors.

To distinguish between factors and multiples, a mnemonic device might help. There are fewer factors and more multiples of any given number. A factor is smaller than the given number, and a multiple is greater than the given number. Any number is both a factor and a multiple of itself.

Using divisibility rules, challenge advanced students to determine all prime numbers from 200 to 500. Have them use calculators to find multiples of these numbers, as well.

MATH LABS

NUMBER SENSE (Mental Math)
Materials: box with 7 cubes, each cube with one of the following numbers on a face: 1, 2, 2, 3, 5, 7

Three to four students take turns tossing the cubes in the box. The person who tosses the cubes multiplies the numbers on the top face of each cube and tells the other students the product. These students must then factor the product mentally to find the prime numbers on the tops of the cubes.

PUZZLES AND GAMES
Materials: student-made set of 54 index cards, each with different numbers between 1 and 635. The numbers on groups of six cards should be divisible by 2, 3, 4, 5, 6, 7, 9, or 10.

Two to four students are given seven cards each. The remaining cards are put in a pile face down in the center of the table. Students try to get groups of 3 or 4 cards that are divisible by the same number, or that are divisible by consecutive numbers. For instance, 2, 58, 102 are all divisible by 2; while 2, 27, 628 are divisible by 2, 3, and 4 respectively.

Students take turns picking the top card from the pile in the center of the table and discarding a card they do not need. The next student can take the card just discarded or a card from the pile. The activity continues until one student has a group of three and a group of four cards, and that student is the winner.

NUMBER SENSE (Estimation)
Two to four students each write their names on one side of 8 index cards and a two-, three-, four-, or five-digit number on the other side. These sets of cards are combined. Then each student in turn takes a card and estimates the square root. The other students check that the estimate is reasonable. The activity ends when all the cards have been used.

CALCULATOR

Many topics in number theory can be explored by using a calculator. For example: factors, primes, and composites can be investigated by using a calculator. Also, finding the LCM and the GCF may be quicker with a calculator. To use a calculator efficiently to express these concepts, a thorough understanding of the concepts is necessary. Also, manipulating expressions and equations can be enhanced by using the calculator. Problem solving is also enhanced by using a calculator. Hence, students should have calculators available whenever they are working with problem-solving activities.

Additional Activities: **Drill and Practice:** Insert the operation symbols ($+$, $-$, $\times$, $\div$) in the boxes to obtain the desired result. Assume these are calculator codes. Insert ( ) where necessary following the rules for the order of operations.

$$6 \,\square\, 4 \,\square\, 8 \,\square\, 7 = 23$$
$$6 \,\square\, 4 \,\square\, 8 \,\square\, 7 = 73$$
$$6 \,\square\, 4 \,\square\, 8 \,\square\, 7 = 10$$
$$6 \,\square\, 4 \,\square\, 8 \,\square\, 7 = 5$$
$$6 \,\square\, 4 \,\square\, 8 \,\square\, 7 = 112$$

Exploration: $-$ Sums = products: Test these:

$$1.625 + 2.6 \;?\; 1.625 \times 2.6$$
$$101 + 1.01 \;?\; 101 \times 1.01$$
$$4.2 + 1.3125 \;?\; 4.2 \times 1.3125$$

Can you find other pairs of numbers whose sum is their product? Hint: $a + b = a \times b$ or $b = a/a - 1$.

SUBJECT AREA CONNECTIONS

Here are some other activities for presenting these concepts.
- **LANGUAGE ARTS:** Have students research and define the vocabulary terms included in the lesson on powers and roots.
- **SOCIAL STUDIES:** Have students research and discuss professions which use algebraic equations and scientific notation.
- **SCIENCE:** Have students research the maximum depth of the Atlantic ocean and determine a scale to which the depth can be shown on a piece of paper. Have students draw a representation of the ocean depth, and, using the rules of divisibility, mark off depth zones on the paper. Then have them research the depths at which various fish live, and write the name of each in the appropriate zone.

PLAN AHEAD

You will need digit cards for the Getting Started on page T.E. p. 80. You will need blocks or tiles for the activity on T.E. p. 89. You will need calculators for the activity on T.E. p. 99. You will need a balance scale and weights for the Remediation and the activity on T.E. pp. 104 and 105. You will need to prepare call-and-response cards for the activity on T.E. p. 109.

PLANNING CALENDAR
ABBREVIATION KEY

Teacher's Resource Book	Follow-up Activities
MMW—Making Math Work	CALC—Calculator
P—Practice	CMP—Computer
R—Reteach	CNS—Consumer
E—Enrich	P&G—Puzzles and Games
	MNP—Manipulatives
	MC—Math Connection
	MCM—Math Communication
	NS—Number Sense
	PS—Problem Solving
	RFM—Reinforcement

PLANNING CALENDAR

Pages	Lesson Objectives	ASSIGNMENT GUIDE			Class/ Home	More Practice	Math Reasoning	Follow-up	Reteach	Practice	Enrich
		Basic	Average	Extended							
79	Chapter Opener (Use MMW 5,6)	79	79	79							
80,81	To use the rules of divisibility	1-35o,36-38,NS	2-34e,36-38,NS	7-35o,36-39,NS	H31				23	31	31
82,83	To define *base, exponent, root, square* and *square root*	1-24,39,CALC	1-8,9-31o,32-39, CALC	4-24e,25-39, CALC	H32		H211	MCM RFM		32	32
84,85	To explore writing numbers in scientific notation; to use scientific notation to compute	84,85	84,85	84,85	H33			P&G	25	33	33
86,87	To check for a reasonable answer in problem solving	1-4	2-6	3-8	H34			PS CALC		34	34
88,89	To define *factors, prime numbers,* and *composite numbers*	1-15,17-41o,AL	2-40e,41-42,AL	1-15o,24-42,AL	H35		H211	MNP PS	26	35	35
90,91	To find the prime factorization of a number by using a factor tree	1-49o	4-46e,47-49	10-46e,47-50,Chlg	H36			CMP PS	27	36	36
92,93	To find the greatest common factor by the prime factorization method	1-12, 13-27o	5-12,13-31o, 33-34	8-12,14-32e,33-34 Chlg	H37	H197		PS RFM	28	37	37
94,95	To find the least common multiple by the listing method and by the prime factorization method	1-35o,MCR	2-36e,MCR	10-12,14-36e, MCR	H38		H211	MCM	29	38	38
96,97	To use information from a table to solve problems	1-4	2-5	2-6	H39 H40			PS CALC		39-40	
98,99	To discuss the rules for solving numerical expressions	1-9,11-33o,CTM	1-6,8-36e,CTM	2-32e,33-36,CTM	H41		H212	NS P&G	30	41	39
100,101	To define an *algebraic sentence, a variable,* and an *equation*	1-10,11-33o,AL	1-10,12-34e, 38-39,AL	5-10,12-34e,35-39, AL	H42			MNP PS	31	42	40
102,103	To choose the correct operation to solve a problem	1-6	2-8	3-10	H43			CALC PS		43	41
104,105	To solve one-step algebraic equations with addition and subtraction	1-21	1-9,11-31o	13-33,F	H44	H197		MNP P&G	32	44	42
106,107	To solve one-step algebraic equations with multiplication and division	1-24	6-30	13-33,Chlg	H45	H197	H212	MCM PS	33	45	43
108,109	To solve two-step algebraic equations	1-24	10-39	16-39,Chlg	H46	H198		P&G MCM	34	46	44
110,111	To write an equation to solve a problem	1-4	2-6	3-8	H47		H212	PS MNP		47	45
112	Calculator: To determine the least and the greatest products for a given number of digits	112	112	112							
113	Group Project: To set a standard of measurement; to calculate weights based upon it	113	113	113							

114,115	Chapter Test	117	Enrichment
116	Reteaching	118	Cumulative Review

TESTS

A. To determine if a number is divisible by 2, 3, 4, 5, 6, 8, 9, or 10.

B. To find square roots of perfect square numbers

C. To write standard numerals in scientific notation, and vice versa

D. To find the LCM or GCF of up to 3 numbers by prime factorization with exponents

E. To find the value of numerical expressions, using the rules for the order of operations

F. To solve one-step and two-step equations

G. To check that an answer is reasonable

H. To use information from a table to solve problems

I. To choose the operation and write a number sentence to solve a problem

FAMILY INVOLVEMENT

Family Involvement for Chapter 3 encourages family members to learn how to use scientific notation to express the distances of several stars from Earth. Family members examine a chart on stars and locate Sirius. Students and their families are given the distance in light-years of Sirius from Earth, which is expressed in scientific notation. The speed of light in both miles and kilometers and the definition of a light-year are given. Students and their families are asked to write the distances from Earth of the stars Andromeda, Orion, Pleides, and Rigez. In order to write these distances, they must convert light-years to miles expressed in zeros and in scientific notation. Family members are also asked to consult a history book to determine what was happening on Earth when the light began its journey from each star to our planet.

Additional activities might include encouraging family members to measure several long distances in or around their homes. Students and their families should then formulate equations that express the distances they have found. Each equation should be expressed in scientific notation, that is, $30 \text{ ft} = 3 \times 10^1$; $65 \text{ ft} = 6.5 \times 10^1$.

STUDENT RESOURCES

Bibliography

Daniel, Becky. *Math Thinkercises.* Carthage, IL: Good Apple, Inc., 1988.

Fekette, Irene, and Jasmine Denver. *Mathematics: The World of Science.* New York: Facts on File Publications, 1984.

Hershey, Robert L. *How to Think with Numbers.* Los Altos, California: William Kaufman, Inc., 1982.

Films

Mathematical Peep Show. 12 minutes. Color. 1958. Distributed by Encyclopaedia Britannica Educational Corp., Glenview, Ill.

Do you think that there is a prime number that is larger than every other prime number? Mathematicians have answered this question by using logic. Find out whether you can discover a prime number that is greater than 1,000. Do you think that there is a greatest prime? How could you prove your answer?

3 NUMBER THEORY, EXPRESSIONS AND EQUATIONS

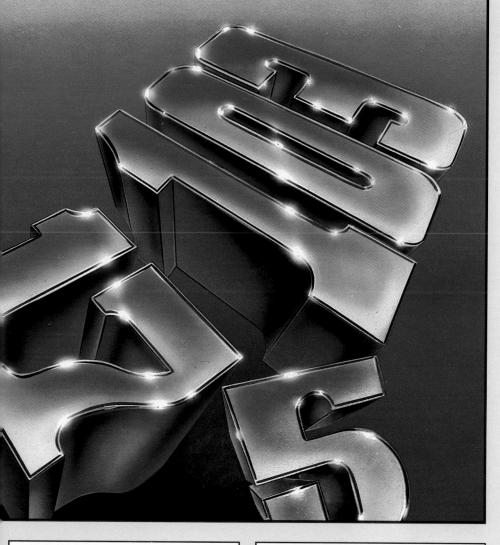

Objective: To explore facts related to numbers

Direct students to look at the picture of the numbers. The numbers 17 and 103 are prime. The number 175 is composite. Ask students whether they can recall the meanings of the terms *prime numbers* and *composite numbers*. (*Prime numbers* have exactly two factors; *composite numbers* have more than two factors.) Large numbers cannot be classified automatically as prime or composite. They need to be subjected to tests to discover in which category the number belongs. Analyzing general rules makes it easy to see number patterns.

INDIVIDUAL
Patterns and Functions
Have students find the pattern that emerges from adding sums of successive odd numbers. Have them add the first two odd numbers. (1 + 3 = 4) Then take the sum (4), and add it to the next successive odd number, 5. (4 + 5 = 9) Have them repeat the step until a conclusion can be drawn from the sums. (9 + 7 = 16, 16 + 9 = 25, 25 + 11 = 36) By examining the sums, students should realize that they are all perfect squares. After they discover the pattern, have them check to see whether their predictions were correct.

SMALL GROUP
Number/Patterns and Functions
Materials: Making Math Work pages 5 and 6

Have students complete Making Math Work pages 5 and 6. Make sure they keep in mind the idea of number patterns as they work. Then have students work in groups to try to come up with their own patterns based on perfect, Mersenne, composite, or prime numbers.

WHOLE CLASS
Logic
Discuss with students how far a pattern must be tested before it can be considered proved.

Can patterns be proved if all possibilities have not been tested? (no) Many patterns that appear to continue indefinitely have remained theories (or conjectures) for a long time because they have not been proved or disproved.

Explain that there is no largest prime number; this fact has been deduced through logical reasoning based on the understanding of numbers. Have the different groups describe the pattern they came up with in the Small Group activity. Challenge class members to disprove the theories.

MAKING MATH WORK

Do you think there are any patterns that tell which odd numbers are prime and which are composite? Here is a pattern for you to explore. You may want to use a calculator. Write your answers in the chart. Check students' charts.

n	Prime?	$2^n - 1$	Prime?
2	yes	$2^2 - 1 = 3$	yes
3	yes	$2^3 - 1 = 7$	yes
4	no	$2^4 - 1 = 15$	no
5	yes	$2^5 - 1 = 31$	yes
6	no	$2^6 - 1 = 63$	no

Numbers of the form $2^n - 1$ are called **Mersenne numbers.**

Do you see a pattern if n is 2, 3, or 4?

To explore the pattern further, you can try other values of n. Is there any easy rule for finding the next value for $2^n - 1$?

Continue to explore the numbers for $2^n - 1$ for values of n to n = 12. Does the pattern of primes continue, or does it change?

What is your guess now as to the pattern of prime and composite numbers for $2^n - 1$?

How could you find out whether your guess is correct or incorrect?

If n is prime, then $2^n - 1$ is prime. Also, if $2^n - 1$ is prime, so is n.

Double the previous value. Then add 1.

The pattern changes. For n = 11, $2^n - 1$ is composite.

If n is composite, so is $2^n - 1$. If n is prime, no conclusion can be made about $2^n - 1$.

Discuss with students.

Use with pupil page 79.　　　　　Making Math Work 5

Making Math Work

MAKING MATH WORK

The mathematician Euclid found that some numbers are equal to the sum of their factors. Here are the first two examples of these numbers that are called **perfect numbers.**

Number	Factors	Sum of factors
6	1, 2, 3	1 + 2 + 3 = 6
28	1, 2, 4, 7, 14	1 + 2 + 4 + 7 + 14 = 28

Here is a pattern for you to explore with perfect numbers.

n	
	$(2^n - 1) \cdot (2^{n-1})$
2	$(2^2 - 1) \cdot (2^1) = 3 \cdot 2 = 6$
3	$(2^3 - 1) \cdot (2^2) = 7 \cdot 4 = 28$

Notice that each of the perfect numbers has a Mersenne number for one of its factors, and a power of 2 for its other factor. Discover whether this pattern produces other perfect numbers.

If n = 4, then $(2^4 - 1) \cdot (2^3) = 15 \cdot 8 = 120$. The factors of 120 are 1, 2, 3, 4, 5, 6, 8, 10, 12, 15, 20, 24, 30, 40, and 60.
1 + 2 + 3 + 4 + 5 + 6 + 8 + 10 + 12 + 15 + 20 + 24 + 30 + 40 + 60 = 240.
So, the pattern does not continue.

Other perfect numbers are 496 and 8,128. Experiment in the space below, and decide whether these numbers have Mersenne numbers as factors. What do you think is true?

If a number is a perfect number, one of its factors is a Mersenne number.

6 Making Math Work　　　　　Use with pupil page 79.

Making Math Work

Objective: To use the rules of divisibility

Warm-Up

Have students add mentally the digits of the following numbers.

409 = (13) 5,884 = (25) 89,102 = (20)
221 = (5) 9,367 = (25) 148,975 = (34)

GETTING STARTED

Materials: graph paper, scissors per pair of students

Have students work in pairs. Have one student choose a number, *x*, between 1 and 10 and a number, *y*, between 20 and 50. Have that student ask a second student whether *x* will divide *y* with no remainder. The second student should be allowed about 2 to 3 seconds to answer. The second student should then cut a strip of graph paper *y* squares long and fold it into segments of *x* squares long. After the strip has been folded as many times as possible, the student can ascertain that if there are no squares left over, *x* divides *y*.

TEACHING THE LESSON

Guide students in testing for divisibility by completing the following chart.

Number	Divisible By							
	2	3	4	5	6	8	9	10
70								
432								
845								
2,160								
59,868								
703,910								
4,769,384								

You may wish to allow students to use calculators while working through this lesson.

Divisibility

If a number is divided by another number and the remainder is zero, the first number is **divisible** by the other number.

A whole number is divisible by

2	if the number ends in 2, 4, 6, 8, or 0. A number that is divisible by 2 is called an **even number.** All other numbers are **odd numbers.**
3	if the sum of its digits is divisible by 3. $651 \rightarrow 6 + 5 + 1 = 12 \rightarrow 12 \div 3 = 4$
4	if the number formed by the last two digits is divisible by 4. $536 \rightarrow 36 \div 4 = 9$ 536 is divisible by 4.
5	if the number ends in 0 or 5. 9,865 is divisible by 5, because it ends in 5.
6	if the number is divisible by 2 and by 3. 114 ends in 4. $114 \rightarrow 1 + 1 + 4 = 6 \rightarrow 6 \div 3 = 2$ 114 is divisible by 2 and by 3. So, it is divisible by 6.
8	if the number formed by the last three digits is divisible by 8. $9,208 \rightarrow 208 \div 8 = 26$
9	if the sum of the digits is divisible by 9. $3,654 \rightarrow 3 + 6 + 5 + 4 = 18 \rightarrow 18 \div 9 = 2$
10	if the ones digit is 0, as in 40; 170; and 5,630.

Is 87,624 divisible by 6?

Since 4 is in the ones place, 87,624 is divisible by 2. Since $8 + 7 + 6 + 2 + 4 = 27$, and 27 is divisible by 3, 87,624 is divisible by 3. So, 87,624 is divisible by 6, because it is divisible by 2 and by 3.

80

COMMON ERRORS

Students often mistake the rules for divisibility by 3 and 9 by looking at the value of the last digit in the number instead of adding up the digits.

Remediation

Have students divide numbers that end in 3 or 9 but are not divisible by them, such as 223 and 259. Then have students apply the tests for divisibility by 3 and by 9 to the following numbers: 9,113; 4,689; 35,643; 276,522.

Assign Reteach Master, p. 23.

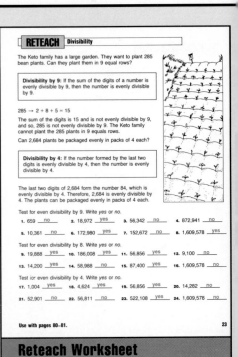

RETEACH Divisibility

The Keto family has a large garden. They want to plant 285 bean plants. Can they plant them in 9 equal rows?

Divisibility by 9: If the sum of the digits of a number is evenly divisible by 9, then the number is evenly divisible by 9.

$285 \rightarrow 2 + 8 + 5 = 15$

The sum of the digits is 15 and is not evenly divisible by 9, and so, 285 is not evenly divisible by 9. The Keto family cannot plant the 285 plants in 9 equals rows.

Can 2,684 plants be packaged evenly in packs of 4 each?

Divisibility by 4: If the number formed by the last two digits is evenly divisible by 4, then the number is evenly divisible by 4.

The last two digits of 2,684 form the number 84, which is evenly divisible by 4. Therefore, 2,684 is evenly divisible by 4. The plants can be packaged evenly in packs of 4 each.

Test for even divisibility by 9. Write yes or no.

1. 659 _no_   2. 18,972 _yes_   3. 56,342 _no_   4. 872,941 _no_

5. 10,361 _no_   6. 172,980 _yes_   7. 152,672 _no_   8. 1,609,578 _yes_

Test for even divisibility by 8. Write yes or no.

9. 19,888 _yes_   10. 186,008 _yes_   11. 56,856 _yes_   12. 9,100 _no_

13. 14,200 _yes_   14. 58,988 _no_   15. 87,400 _yes_   16. 1,609,578 _no_

Test for even divisibility by 4. Write yes or no.

17. 1,004 _yes_   18. 4,624 _yes_   19. 56,856 _yes_   20. 14,282 _no_

21. 52,901 _no_   22. 56,811 _no_   23. 522,108 _yes_   24. 1,609,578 _no_

Use with pages 80–81.   23

Reteach Worksheet

Write *yes* or *no*.

Is the number divisible by 2?

1. 189 no **2.** 83 no **3.** 254 yes **4.** 5,050 yes **5.** 5,095 no

Is the number divisible by 3?

6. 424 no **7.** 120 yes **8.** 5,424 yes **9.** 35,183 no **10.** 3,393 yes

Is the number divisible by 4?

11. 2,460 yes **12.** 1,786 no **13.** 18,604 yes **14.** 2,004 yes **15.** 21,000 yes

Is the number divisible by 5?

16. 255 yes **17.** 112 no **18.** 4,024 no **19.** 21,005 yes **20.** 10,002 no

Is the number divisible by 6?

21. 324 yes **22.** 892 no **23.** 7,166 no **24.** 10,813 no **25.** 10,950 yes

Is the number divisible by 3? by 9? by 10?

26. 1,944 **27.** 2,072 **28.** 32,136 **29.** 11,118 **30.** 39,006
yes; yes; no no; no; no yes; no; no yes; no; no yes; yes; no

31. 2,005 **32.** 3,250 **33.** 4,000 **34.** 10,010 **35.** 25,155
no; no; no no; no; yes no; no; yes no; no; yes yes; yes; no

Solve.

36. Use divisibility rules to write $\frac{4,212}{7,920}$ in simplest form. $\frac{117}{220}$

37. Use divisibility rules to write $\frac{1,728}{10,368}$ in simplest form. $\frac{1}{6}$

38. Write a number that is divisible by 2, 3, 4, and 5. Answers will vary, but 120 is one example.

39. Write a divisibility test to show when a number is divisible by 12. A number is divisible by 12 if it is divisible by both 3 and 4.

NUMBER SENSE

It is easy to multiply by 10, 100, and 1,000. You can use them to estimate quickly.

Example: $\$9.67 \times 15$
Since $\$9.67$ is close to $\$10$, estimate $\$10 \times 15 = \$150$.

Estimate. Use 10, 100, and 1,000 where possible.
Answers may vary. Accept any reasonable estimate.

1. 47×96
4,700–5,000

2. $45 \times \$9.77$
$450–$500

3. 356×981
350,000–356,000

4. $19 \times \$102.53$
$1,900–$2,000

5. $1,037 \times 826$
800,000–826,000

6. $98 \times 4,753$
475,300–500,000

Classwork/Homework, page H31

81

ASSIGNMENT GUIDE

Basic: 1–35 *o*, 36–38, NS

Average: 2–34 *e*, 36–38, NS

Extended: 7–35 *o*, 36–39, NS

Resources
Practice, p. 31 Class/Home, p. H31
Reteach, p. 23
Enrich, p. 31

Exercise Analysis
1–35 Apply the rules of divisibility
36–39 Skill applications

You may wish to allow students to use a calculator for some of these exercises.

Number Sense
This activity provides students with practice in estimating numbers to the nearest ten, hundred, thousand, and dollar using mental computation.

FOLLOW-UP ACTIVITIES

PROBLEM SOLVING
What is the smallest number that is divisible by 2, 3, 4, 5, 6, 7, 8, 9, and 10? (2,520) The trick here is to decide which divisibility tests are accounted for twice. A number divisible by 8 is also divisible by 2 and 4, and a number divisible by 9 can also be divided evenly by 3. The factors of 2 and 3 present in 8 and 9 eliminate 6; 5 and 2 eliminate 10. Therefore, the product of the remaining factors ($5 \times 7 \times 8 \times 9 = 2,520$) accounts for every divisibility test.

REINFORCEMENT
Have students write these numbers.
a. the largest 10-digit number divisible by 6 (9,999,999,996)
b. the largest 10-digit number divisible by 3 (9,999,999,999)
c. the smallest 10-digit number divisible by 6 (1,000,000,002)
d. the smallest 10-digit number divisible by 3 (1,000,000,002)
e. the largest 10-digit number divisible by 5 (9,999,999,995)
f. the largest 10-digit number divisible by 8 (9,999,999,992)

COMING UP
Power is the root of all . . . exponents.

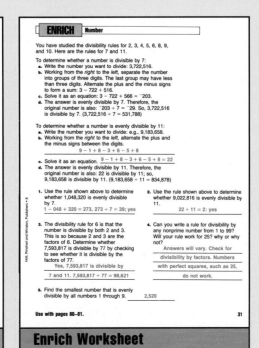

PRACTICE Divisibility

Write *yes* or *no*.

Is the number divisible by 2?

1. 8,356 yes **2.** 53,775 no **3.** 437 no **4.** 29 no
5. 1,274 yes **6.** 322 yes **7.** 2,180 yes **8.** 33,455 no

Is the number divisible by 3?

9. 243 yes **10.** 1,200 yes **11.** 6,801 yes **12.** 11 no
13. 15 yes **14.** 25,006 no **15.** 421 no **16.** 100,005 yes

Is the number divisible by 4?

17. 76,521 no **18.** 390,062 no **19.** 973 no **20.** 48 yes
21. 886 no **22.** 567 no **23.** 2,004 yes **24.** 6,935 no

Is the number divisible by 5?

25. 13 no **26.** 95,215 yes **27.** 3,750 yes **28.** 102,211 no
29. 26 no **30.** 500,909 no **31.** 638 no **32.** 773 no

Is the number divisible by 6?

33. 672 yes **34.** 34 no **35.** 611 no **36.** 48,928 no
37. 199 no **38.** 47,068 no **39.** 21 no **40.** 5,940 yes

Is the number divisible by 9?

41. 155 no **42.** 81 yes **43.** 77 no **44.** 5,001 no
45. 563 no **46.** 4,292 no **47.** 6,885 yes **48.** 19 no

Is the number divisible by 10?

49. 300 yes **50.** 400,000 yes **51.** 6,020 yes **52.** 909 no
53. 25,005 no **54.** 170 yes **55.** 898 no **56.** 50,000 yes

Use with pages 80–81. 31

Practice Worksheet

ENRICH Number

You have studied the divisibility rules for 2, 3, 4, 5, 6, 8, 9, and 10. Here are the rules for 7 and 11.

To determine whether a number is divisible by 7:
a. Write the number you want to divide: 3,722,516.
b. Working from the *right* to the *left*, separate the number into groups of three digits. The last group may have less than three digits. Alternate the plus and the minus signs to form a sum: 3 − 722 + 516.
c. Solve it as an equation: 3 − 722 + 566 = ¯203.
d. The answer is evenly divisible by 7. Therefore, the original number is also: ¯203 ÷ 7 = ¯29. So, 3,722,516 is divisible by 7. (3,722,516 ÷ 7 = 531,788)

To determine whether a number is evenly divisible by 11:
a. Write the number you want to divide: e.g., 9,183,658.
b. Working from the *right* to the *left*, alternate the plus and the minus signs between the digits.
9 − 1 + 8 − 3 + 6 − 5 + 8
c. Solve it as an equation. 9 − 1 + 8 − 3 + 6 − 5 + 8 = 22
d. The answer is evenly divisible by 11. Therefore, the original number is also: 22 is divisible by 11; so, 9,183,658 is divisible by 11. (9,183,658 ÷ 11 = 834,878)

1. Use the rule shown above to determine whether 1,048,320 is evenly divisible by 7.
1 − 048 + 320 = 273, 273 ÷ 7 = 39; yes

2. Use the rule shown above to determine whether 9,022,816 is evenly divisible by 11.
22 ÷ 11 = 2: yes

3. The divisibility rule for 6 is that the number is divisible by both 2 and 3. This is so because 2 and 3 are the factors of 6. Determine whether 7,593,817 is divisible by 77 by checking to see whether it is divisible by the factors of 77.
Yes, 7,593,817 is divisible by 7 and 11. 7,593,817 ÷ 77 = 98,621

4. Can you write a rule for divisibility by any nonprime number from 1 to 99? Will your rule work for 25? why or why not?
Answers will vary. Check for divisibility by factors. Numbers with perfect squares, such as 25, do not work.

5. Find the smallest number that is evenly divisible by all numbers 1 through 9.
2,520

Use with pages 80–81. 31

Enrich Worksheet

Objectives. To define *base*, *exponent*, *root*, *square*, and *square root*

Warm-Up

Have students multiply the following numbers.

$4 \times 4 \times 4$ (64); $2 \times 2 \times 2 \times 2 \times 2$ (32);
12×12 (144); $5 \times 5 \times 5$ (125);
$3 \times 3 \times 3 \times 3$ (81)

GETTING STARTED

Draw the following dot patterns on the chalkboard to represent the first three square numbers.

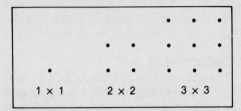

| 1×1 | 2×2 | 3×3 |

Have students draw dot patterns for 4^2, 5^2, 6^2, 7^2, 8^2.

Have them write the corresponding multiplication below each dot pattern.

TEACHING THE LESSON

A. You might expand the definition of *power*: $32 = 2^5 =$ *the fifth power of 2,* or *2 to the fifth power*; similarly, $6^7 =$ *the seventh power of 6,* or *6 to the seventh power.*

Exponents and square-root signs can also be used with decimals. Extend the lesson by having students evaluate the following decimal expressions.

$(1.2)^2$ (1.2×1.2, or 1.44)
$(0.03)^2$ (0.03×0.03, or 0.0009)

$\sqrt{0.64}$ (0.8)
$\sqrt{0.81}$ (0.9)

Any number other than 0 with an exponent of 0 is defined as having a value of 1. (0^0 is undefined.)

You can show how this generally accepted convention leads to some interesting facts.

$1^1 = 1$ and $1^0 = 1$
$0^2 = 0$ and $2^0 = 1$

B. Have students use the table to find the square of 7 and the square root of 7. Use the number 5 to repeat the exercise. You may wish to allow students to use calculators while working through this lesson.

82

Powers and Roots

A. What is the value of 2^5?

In the expression 2^5, 5 is called the **exponent** and 2 is called the **base.**

$$2^{5 \leftarrow \text{exponent}} = \underbrace{2 \times 2 \times 2 \times 2 \times 2}_{5 \text{ factors}} = 32$$

An exponent shows how many times a number or base is used as a factor. So, $2^5 = 32$.

32 is said to be a **power** of 2.

To find the value of the expression 4^2, use the base 4 as a factor 2 times.

$$4^2 = 4 \times 4 = 16$$

Zero can be used as an exponent.

$$8^0 = 1 \qquad 25^0 = 1 \qquad 162^0 = 1$$

Any number multiplied by itself is called the **square of the number.**

Since $4^2 = 16$, you can say that the **square root** of 16 is 4, or $\sqrt{16} = 4$.

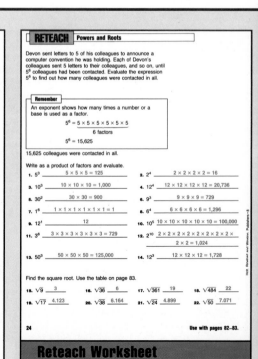

B. A table of squares and square roots is shown at the right. A square of a whole number is called a **perfect square.** If a number is not a perfect square, its square root can not be a whole number. For example, $\sqrt{10}$ is approximately equal to 3.162 (rounded to the nearest thousandth). You can write this as $\sqrt{10} \approx 3.162$.

Number	Square	Square root
1	1	1
2	4	1.414
3	9	1.732
4	16	2
5	25	2.236
6	36	2.449
7	49	2.646
8	64	2.828
9	81	3
10	100	3.162

82

COMMON ERRORS

Students often confuse the exponent of a number with a factor. For example, $2^4 = 2 \times 4$, instead of $2 \times 2 \times 2 \times 2$.

Remediation

Have students practice writing the longhand meaning of each expression before evaluating it.

$3^4 = 3 \times 3 \times 3 \times 3$
$4^3 = 4 \times 4 \times 4$

Assign Reteach Master, p. 24.

RETEACH | Powers and Roots

Devon sent letters to 5 of his colleagues to announce a computer convention he was holding. Each of Devon's colleagues sent 5 letters to their colleagues, and so on, until 5^6 colleagues had been contacted. Evaluate the expression 5^6 to find out how many colleagues were contacted in all.

Remember

An exponent shows how many times a number or a base is used as a factor.

$$5^6 = \underbrace{5 \times 5 \times 5 \times 5 \times 5 \times 5}_{6 \text{ factors}}$$

$$5^6 = 15,625$$

15,625 colleagues were contacted in all.

Write as a product of factors and evaluate.

1. 5^3 ____ $5 \times 5 \times 5 = 125$ 2. 2^4 ____ $2 \times 2 \times 2 \times 2 = 16$
3. 10^3 ____ $10 \times 10 \times 10 = 1,000$ 4. 12^4 ____ $12 \times 12 \times 12 \times 12 = 20,736$
5. 30^2 ____ $30 \times 30 = 900$ 6. 9^3 ____ $9 \times 9 \times 9 = 729$
7. 1^6 ____ $1 \times 1 \times 1 \times 1 \times 1 \times 1 = 1$ 8. 6^4 ____ $6 \times 6 \times 6 \times 6 = 1,296$
9. 12^1 ____ 12 10. 10^5 ____ $10 \times 10 \times 10 \times 10 \times 10 = 100,000$
11. 3^6 ____ $3 \times 3 \times 3 \times 3 \times 3 \times 3 = 729$ 12. 2^{10} ____ $2 \times 2 \times 2 \times 2 \times 2 \times 2 \times 2 \times$ $2 \times 2 = 1,024$
13. 50^3 ____ $50 \times 50 \times 50 = 125,000$ 14. 12^3 ____ $12 \times 12 \times 12 = 1,728$

Find the square root. Use the table on page 83.

15. $\sqrt{9}$ ___ 3   16. $\sqrt{36}$ ___ 6   17. $\sqrt{361}$ ___ 19   18. $\sqrt{484}$ ___ 22
19. $\sqrt{17}$ ___ 4.123   20. $\sqrt{38}$ ___ 6.164   21. $\sqrt{24}$ ___ 4.899   22. $\sqrt{50}$ ___ 7.071

24   Use with pages 82–83.

Reteach Worksheet

82

Write as a product of factors and evaluate.

1. 5^2
$5 \times 5 = 25$

2. 1^3
$1 \times 1 \times 1 = 1$

3. 7^4
$7 \times 7 \times 7 \times 7 = 2,401$

4. 8^1
$8 = 8$

5. 2^3
$2 \times 2 \times 2 = 8$

6. 9^5
$9 \times 9 \times 9 \times 9 \times 9 = 59,049$

7. 6^4
$6 \times 6 \times 6 \times 6 = 1,296$

8. 10^4
$10 \times 10 \times 10 \times 10 = 10,000$

Rewrite and evaluate each. Use exponents.

9. 3×3
$3^2 = 9$

10. $5 \times 5 \times 5 \times 5$
$5^4 = 625$

11. $14 \times 14 \times 14$
$14^3 = 2,744$

12. $2 \times 2 \times 2$
$2^3 = 8$

13. $5 \times 5 \times 5 \times 5 \times 5$
$5^5 = 3,125$

14. 10×10
$10^2 = 100$

15. $10 \times 10 \times 10 \times 10$
$10^4 = 10,000$

16. $6 \times 6 \times 6 \times 6 \times 6$
$6^5 = 7,776$

17. $2 \times 2 \times 3 \times 3$
$2^2 \times 3^2 = 36$

Find the square root. Use the table.

18. $\sqrt{1}$ 1

19. $\sqrt{25}$ 5

20. $\sqrt{64}$ 8

21. $\sqrt{81}$ 9

22. $\sqrt{49}$ 7

23. $\sqrt{144}$ 12

24. $\sqrt{36}$ 6

25. $\sqrt{4}$ 2

26. $\sqrt{100}$ 10

27. $\sqrt{121}$ 11

28. $\sqrt{400}$ 20

29. $\sqrt{225}$ 15

30. $\sqrt{45}$ 6.708

31. $\sqrt{19}$ 4.359

32. $\sqrt{37}$ 6.083

33. $\sqrt{22}$ 4.690

34. $\sqrt{46}$ 6.782

35. $\sqrt{13}$ 3.606

★**36.** $\sqrt{1.44}$ 1.2

★**37.** $\sqrt{9.61}$ 3.1

★**38.** $\sqrt{21.16}$ 4.6

39. Use the information in the Infobank on page 474 to find the cube root of 729.
9

n	n^2	$\sqrt{n}$	n	n^2	$\sqrt{n}$
1	1	1.000	26	676	5.099
2	4	1.414	27	729	5.196
3	9	1.732	28	784	5.292
4	16	2.000	29	841	5.385
5	25	2.236	30	900	5.477
6	36	2.449	31	961	5.568
7	49	2.646	32	1,024	5.657
8	64	2.828	33	1,089	5.745
9	81	3.000	34	1,156	5.831
10	100	3.162	35	1,225	5.916
11	121	3.317	36	1,296	6.000
12	144	3.464	37	1,369	6.083
13	169	3.606	38	1,444	6.164
14	196	3.742	39	1,521	6.245
15	225	3.873	40	1,600	6.325
16	256	4.000	41	1,681	6.403
17	289	4.123	42	1,764	6.481
18	324	4.243	43	1,849	6.557
19	361	4.359	44	1,936	6.633
20	400	4.472	45	2,025	6.708
21	441	4.583	46	2,116	6.782
22	484	4.690	47	2,209	6.856
23	529	4.796	48	2,304	6.928
24	576	4.899	49	2,401	7.000
25	625	5.000	50	2,500	7.071

CALCULATOR

You can use the trial-and-error method to estimate square roots on a calculator.

$\sqrt{12}$ is between $\sqrt{9}$ and $\sqrt{16}$.

$\sqrt{12}$ is between 3 and 4.

Try 3.4. $3.4 \times 3.4 = 11.56$

Try 3.5. $3.5 \times 3.5 = 12.25$

3.5 is the better estimate.

Find the square root on a calculator. Round to the nearest tenth.

1. $\sqrt{17}$
4.1

2. $\sqrt{56}$
7.5

3. $\sqrt{72}$
8.5

4. $\sqrt{88}$
9.4

5. $\sqrt{112}$
10.6

6. $\sqrt{473}$
21.7

Classwork/Homework, page H32

83

Exercise Analysis

1–8   Write exponents as factors and evaluate

9–17   Write factors as exponents and evaluate

18–38   Use a table to find the square root

39   Data collection

You may wish to allow students to use a calculator for some of these exercises.

Calculator
These exercises provide additional practice in finding square roots and in rounding decimals to the place value indicated.

FOLLOW-UP ACTIVITIES

MATH COMMUNICATION
Algebraic expressions can also be evaluated by using exponents. In order not to confuse variables, however, a raised dot (·) is used to indicate multiplication.

Have students write the following as a product of factors.
1. a^5 ($a \cdot a \cdot a \cdot a \cdot a$)
2. x^3 ($x \cdot x \cdot x$)
3. y^6 ($y \cdot y \cdot y \cdot y \cdot y \cdot y$)
4. b^6 ($b \cdot b \cdot b \cdot b \cdot b \cdot b$)
5. c^3 ($c \cdot c \cdot c$)

REINFORCEMENT
Show that the square numbers are the sums of successively added odd numbers.

$1 = 1$ $1 + 3 = 4$
$1 + 3 + 5 = 9$ $1 + 3 + 5 + 7 = 16$

Have students write the sequence for the next four square numbers. ($1 + 3 + 5 + 7 + 9 = 25$; $1 + 3 + 5 + 7 + 9 + 11 = 36$; $1 + 3 + 5 + 7 + 9 + 11 + 13 = 49$; $1 + 3 + 5 + 7 + 9 + 11 + 13 + 15 = 64$)

COMING UP
Scientific notation

Objectives: To explore writing numbers in scientific notation; to use scientific notation to compute

Warm-Up
Have students evaluate.

10^2 $(10 \times 10 = 100)$
10^3 $(10 \times 10 \times 10 = 1,000)$
10^5 $(10 \times 10 \times 10 \times 10 \times 10 = 100,000)$

GETTING STARTED

Write the following multiplication problem on the chalkboard.

$215,000 \times 238,000$ $(51,170,000,000)$

Foster a class discussion about different ways students could use to help them find this product and shortcuts they could take. Ask students how they could find this product on a calculator. (Find 215×238; attach 6 zeros to that product.)

TEACHING THE LESSON

Materials: calculators

There are two approaches that you can use in teaching this lesson: (1) have students work individually through the developmental questions and convene in groups of four to work on Thinking/Working as a Team or (2) have students work through the developmental parts in groups of four and have a class discussion for Thinking/Working as a Team.

A. When computing a number that goes beyond the boundaries of the display, most calculators move the decimal point in the answer n places (8 places on an 8-digit calculator) to the left, but some discussion should be focused on calculators that print only an "E" or a zero to indicate an overload. Students should realize that they can change this display to a number in standard form by moving the decimal point 8 places to the right on an 8-digit calculator (10 or 12 places on calculators that accommodate those numbers of digits). This is equivalent to multiplying the number by 100,000,000, or 10^8. Explain that this is what is indicated to be done when a number is written in scientific notation. Emphasize the convention of making the decimal part of a number a number greater than or equal to 1 but less than 10.

Elicit from students that they can rewrite a number that has been written in scientific notation in standard form by moving the decimal point to the right the number of places indicated in the exponent. Also, make sure that they realize that they can rewrite a number

---

Scientific Notation

A. It is often difficult to compute with very large numbers. Some numbers are even too large for your calculator.

- How many digits will your calculator display? Find out by entering the digits 1, 2, 3, 4, ... until the display is full. **Most 8-digit calculators will read 12345678.**
- What number does your display show? Using pencil and paper, multiply that number by 10.

- Now do this multiplication on your calculator.

- Compare your display with those on your classmates' calculators. Did anyone get a result that is different from yours? How does your display compare to your answer on paper? **Most calculators will read 1.2345678—the correct answer divided by 100,000,000.**
- Did any of the calculators display a decimal between 1 and 10 for the product? If so, could you multiply this number by a power of 10 to get the actual product? **You could multiply by 100,000,000.**

Thinking as a Team

Very large numbers are often written in a shorthand called **scientific notation**. This notation uses a decimal multiplied by a power of 10. The decimal is always greater than or equal to 1 but is less than 10.

In scientific notation the number 40,000,000 is written 4×10^7. 45,000,000 is written 4.5×10^7. How would you write 75,000 in scientific notation? **7.5×10^4**

1. What is a quick way to multiply a decimal by a power of ten?

2. How would you write 5.01×10^5 in standard form? **$5.01000 = 501,000$**

3. How would you write 28,500,000 in scientific notation? **2.85×10^7**

4. How would you write 12,140 in scientific notation? **1.214×10^4**

5. How would you write a power of 10 in scientific notation? **1×10^x—e.g., $1,000 = 1 \times 10^3$**

Answers may vary—you could move the decimal point to the right the same number of places as the exponent.

84

---

that has been written in standard form in scientific notation by first moving the decimal point to the right of the first digit. The number of places the decimal point was moved is then used as the exponent in the power of 10.

B. For question 1 in Working as a Team, students can round 31,536,000 seconds to 32,000,000 seconds. After they have written both factors in scientific notation, students can write the product in scientific notation for questions 2 and 3 by first multiplying the decimal parts and then multiplying the powers of 10. Guide them to realize that when they multiply powers of 10, they can simply add the exponents.

(Continued on p. 85.)

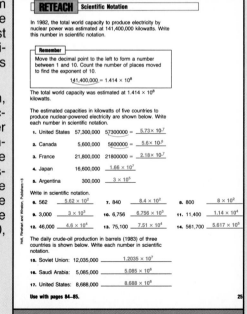

RETEACH | Scientific Notation

In 1982, the total world capacity to produce electricity by nuclear power was estimated at 141,400,000 kilowatts. Write this number in scientific notation.

Remember
Move the decimal point to the left to form a number between 1 and 10. Count the number of places moved to find the exponent of 10.

$141,400,000 = 1.414 \times 10^8$

The total world capacity was estimated at 1.414×10^8 kilowatts.

The estimated capacities in kilowatts of five countries to produce nuclear-powered electricity are shown below. Write each number in scientific notation.

1. United States 57,300,000 $57300000 = \underline{5.73 \times 10^7}$
2. Canada   5,600,000 $5600000 = \underline{5.6 \times 10^5}$
3. France   21,800,000 $21800000 = \underline{2.18 \times 10^7}$
4. Japan   16,600,000 $\underline{1.66 \times 10^7}$
5. Argentina   300,000 $\underline{3 \times 10^5}$

Write in scientific notation.

6. 562 $\underline{5.62 \times 10^2}$ 7. 840 $\underline{8.4 \times 10^2}$ 8. 800 $\underline{8 \times 10^2}$
9. 3,000 $\underline{3 \times 10^3}$ 10. 6,756 $\underline{6.756 \times 10^3}$ 11. 11,400 $\underline{1.14 \times 10^4}$
12. 46,000 $\underline{4.6 \times 10^4}$ 13. 75,100 $\underline{7.51 \times 10^4}$ 14. 561,700 $\underline{5.617 \times 10^5}$

The daily crude-oil production in barrels (1983) of three countries is shown below. Write each number in scientific notation.

15. Soviet Union: 12,035,000 $\underline{1.2035 \times 10^7}$
16. Saudi Arabia: 5,085,000 $\underline{5.085 \times 10^6}$
17. United States: 8,688,000 $\underline{8.688 \times 10^6}$

Use with pages 84–85.   25

Reteach Worksheet

B. A light-year is the distance light travels in one year. Light travels at the rate of approximately 186,000 miles per second. About how many miles in length is a light-year? 5,952,000,000,000 miles

Working as a Team

1. About how many seconds are there in a year? How would you write this number in scientific notation? How would you write the speed of light in scientific notation? about 32,000,000 seconds; 3.2×10^7 seconds; 1.86×10^5 miles per second
2. How could you use your calculator to find the number of miles in a light-year?
Use scientific notation.
3. When you multiply two numbers written in scientific notation, which part is easier to multiply first? What relationship do you see between the exponents in the factors and the exponent in the product?

It is easier to multiply the decimals first; the exponent in the product is the sum of the exponents in the factors.

4. Try multiplying other numbers using scientific notation to see whether this relationship is always true. It is.
5. How does scientific notation help you to multiply large numbers?

It provides an easy way of keeping track of place value.

The average distance from the Sun to Earth is about 93,000,000 miles. How could you use scientific notation and a calculator to find the number of seconds it takes for light from the Sun to reach Earth? What relationship do you see among the exponents of the numbers in this calculation?

You could divide the decimal parts first; the exponent in the quotient is the difference between the exponents in the dividend and the divisor; it takes about 500 seconds for light from the Sun to reach Earth.

Find the volume of a cube whose edge is 2.1×10^3 cm long. Write your answer in scientific notation.
9.261×10^9 cm^3

In which other fields of science might you use scientific notation to express large numbers? Find some examples to share with your classmates.

Two examples are chemistry and physics.

ASSIGNMENT GUIDE

Basic: p. 84, p. 85

Average: p. 84, p. 85

Extended: p. 84, p. 85

Resources
Practice, p. 33   Class/Home, p. H33
Reteach, p. 25
Enrich, p. 33

For question 4 you may wish to have students use calculators to compute the following problems.

$(2.61 \times 10^3) \times (3.7 \times 10^6)$
$[9.657 \times 10^9]$
$(3.4 \times 10^5) \times (7.8 \times 10^8)$
$[2.652 \times 10^{14}]$

Elicit from students that scientific notation is helpful in multiplying large numbers because it provides a convenient method for handling zeros.

Help students realize that when they divide with scientific notation, they should divide the decimal parts first and then *subtract* the exponent in the divisor from the exponent in the dividend. Have them use calculators to compute the following problems.

$(6.82 \times 10^7) \div (2.2 \times 10^4)$ $[3.1 \times 10^3]$
$(1.2 \times 10^{12}) \div (4.8 \times 10^9)$ $[2.5 \times 10^2]$

Foster a class discussion about fields of science, such as chemistry and physics, in which scientific notation is used.

FOLLOW-UP ACTIVITIES

PUZZLES AND GAMES
Play a concentration-like game with groups of 6 to 8. On a bulletin or felt board, set up an array of 36 cards. On the back of the cards, write at random 18 numbers in both standard and scientific notation, 1 number per card. Students take turns picking 2 cards. If the cards have the same number, student keeps the pair. If not, the cards are turned back facedown. Be sure to leave cards in an ordered array. The player who has the most pairs when all cards are gone wins.

COMING UP
This class is prime.

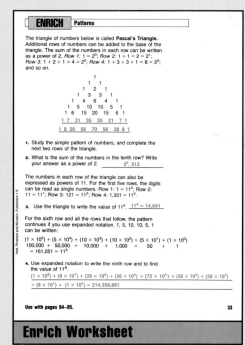

Practice Worksheet

Enrich Worksheet

Objective: To check the reasonableness of an answer

Warm-Up
To prepare the students for this lesson, have them solve the following.

$12 \times \$20 = (\$240)$
$8,190 \div 9 = (910)$
$14^2 = (196)$
$\sqrt{64} = (8)$

TEACHING THE LESSON

Present the following problem to students and discuss how to find a reasonable estimate.

A school buys a chess book for each of the 10 members of the chess team. About what would the total cost of the books be?

Ask students what information would help us to make an estimate. (the price of the books) Since this is unavailable, point out that the best you can do is make a rough estimate based on what you think a chess book might cost. Ask for suggested costs. Point out that the likely cost of all the books is between $50 and $200.

TEACHING THE LESSON

Checking for a reasonable answer involves not only checking the size of the number, but also the units used and the way in which the answer is reported. Often, in their haste to give an answer, students overlook units or other information needed to explain a numerical answer.

Questions: Suggest that, when students arrive at unreasonable answers, they recheck to see that they have used the information provided in the example.

Tools: Suggest to students that estimating a reasonable answer before solving a problem can help them recognize an unreasonable answer. Often, only a rough estimate is needed to rule out a possible answer. Remind students to use the listed choices to gauge their estimates. Often, this is the fastest way of zeroing in on the correct answer.

Solutions: The skills most often used in this lesson are estimating products and quotients. It may prove helpful to quickly review rounding and multiplication of multiples of 10.

Checks: The most commonly used check, and one that students should form a habit of using, is estimation.

Students should also reread the question to ensure that units or other needed explanatory information are included. Students should also look for answers that go

---

PROBLEM SOLVING
Checking for a Reasonable Answer

Some errors in arithmetic can lead to answers that are far from the correct answer. When you solve a problem, think about the reasonableness of the answer. Is it much too great? Is it much too small? You can often spot a wrong answer just by thinking about whether it is reasonable.

> A newly published book on mathematics and architecture sells for $28.95. Library purchases for the first month were reported to be 4,468 copies. What was the total amount paid for those copies?
>
> **a.** $120,000   **b.** $1,200   **c.** $1,200,000

Without computing the exact answer, try to find a reasonable estimate. You can see that choice *b* is much too small and choice *c* is much too large. The most reasonable answer to the problem is choice *a*, or $120,000.

$$
\begin{array}{rcr}
\$28.95 & \rightarrow & \$30.00 \\
\times \quad 4,468 & \rightarrow & \times \quad 4,000 \\
\hline
& & \$120,000.00
\end{array}
$$

Read each problem. Without computing the exact answer, write the letter of the most reasonable answer.

1. Each chapter of the book is illustrated with 83 engravings of buildings. If the book has twenty-five chapters, how many engravings are there in the book?

   a. 200 engravings
   b. 2,000 engravings
   c. 20,000 engravings

2. One bookstore ordered 762 books. If the total cost of the order, including shipping charges, was $23,926.80, what was the total cost per book?

   a. $3.10
   b. $30.00
   c. $310.00

---

against the logic of a situation or against experience; for example, the product or sum of two whole numbers cannot be less than either number.

Read each problem. Without computing the exact
answer, write the letter of the most reasonable answer.

3. An illustration of a square Roman
courtyard showed that there were
6,875 tiles on one edge of the floor.
About how many tiles were there
in the courtyard floor?

a. 49,000
b. 4,900,000
c.) 49,000,000

4. In building a scale model of a
Babylonian building, Janice used
materials worth $2.75. Rachel spent
23 times as much on her model of
the Roman Forum. About how
much did Rachel spend?

a. about $30
b. about $40
c.) about $65

5. Members of the Mideastern High
School archeology club built a
diorama of ancient Babylon. The
original plans called for the total
number of trees, bushes, and plants
to be 14 times the number of
buildings. If 896 buildings were
planned, how many trees, bushes,
and plants would there have been?

a. 8,000
b.) 14,000
c. 100,000

6. The practice of cubing a number
goes back at least as far as the
tenth century. More recently,
Manny was estimating cube roots
in a math contest. The contest's
deciding question was $\sqrt[3]{27,000}$.
What answer should Manny have
given?

a.) 30
b. 130
c. 3,000

7. Louise wanted to determine the
distance from Mercury to Earth. If
Mercury is 36,000,000 miles from
the sun, and Earth is 93,000,000
miles from the sun, which is the
most reasonable estimate of their
distance from each other?

a.) 5×10^7
b. 5×10^8
c. 5×10^6

★8. In around 580 B.C., Pythagoras used
an equation to find the length of
the longest side of a right triangle.
Use the equation $c = \sqrt{a^2 + b^2}$. If a
is 3 m and b is 4 m, how long is c?

a. 0.5 m
b.) 5 m
c. 50 m

Classwork/Homework, page H34

ASSIGNMENT GUIDE

Basic: 1–4
Average: 2–6
Extended: 3–8
Resources
Practice, p. 34   Class/Home, p. H34
Enrich, p. 34

Exercise Analysis
1–5   Check for a reasonable answer
6–8   Check for a reasonable answer with
       exponents

FOLLOW-UP ACTIVITIES

PROBLEM SOLVING
Have the class plan an overnight
trip to a major city anywhere in the country.
Without researching any specific information, have them estimate the cost of the
trip, including transportation, accommoda-
tions, meals, and entertainment. Have
every student contribute, and allow any
suggestion that seems reasonable, as long
as the student can explain it.

CALCULATOR
Materials: 1 calculator that has a
square-root key per group of four

Choose one student from each group and
have that student enter a number that is
greater than 1,000 on the calculator. As it is
entered, the student will tell the number to
the rest of the group. Each group member
will have 30 seconds to write a reasonable
estimate of the square root of the number
on a piece of paper. The student with the
calculator will then press the square-root
key and announce the correct answer. The
student whose estimate was closest to the
actual square root takes the calculator and
repeats the activity.

COMING UP
Some prime real estate!

Warm-Up

Have students write the quotient.

$39 \div 3 =$ (13) $72 \div 8 =$ (9)

$28 \div 4 =$ (7) $60 \div 5 =$ (12)

$81 \div 9 =$ (9) $91 \div 7 =$ (13)

GETTING STARTED

Start with the number 2. Ask students to name the whole numbers that, when multiplied, result in 2. (2 × 1) Make a list. Repeat the procedure for numbers 3 to 15.

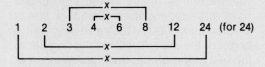

3	4	5	6
3 × 1	2 × 2	5 × 1	3 × 2
	4 × 1		1 × 6

Separate the numbers into two groups: those that have only two factors, and those that have more than two factors. Discuss how the numbers that have only two factors are alike.

TEACHING THE LESSON

A. Point out that when we talk about factors, we mean whole numbers.

B. In listing factors for a composite number, remind students to start with the outermost factors and then work toward the middle.

1   2   3   4   6   8   12   24   (for 24)

C. Point out that 0 is not considered to be prime because it has an infinite number of factors (0 × 1; 0 × 2; and so on). It is not considered composite because it has no *unique* factors.

Checkpoint

The chart lists the common errors students make in identifying factors, prime numbers, and composite numbers.

Correct Answers: 1a, 2a, 3d

Remediation

■ For these errors, have students practice writing both the factors and the multiples of a number until they are clear about the differences between them.

□ For this error, guide students in completing Reteach Master, p. 26.

○ For these errors, guide students through the Manipulative Follow-Up Activity.

Factors, Primes, and Composites

A. In about 300 B.C., the Greek mathematician Euclid used the notion of factors to develop a theorem relating prime numbers to factorization.

A **factor** is any number used in multiplication to produce a product.

A **prime number** is any number greater than 1 whose only factors are itself and 1.

Is 7 a prime number?

Since the only factors of 7 are 7 and 1, 7 is a prime number.

Some other prime numbers are 2, 3, 5, 11, and 13.

B. A number greater than 1 that has more than two factors is called a **composite number.**

Is 12 a prime number or a composite number?

To find the factors of 12, write 12 as the product of different pairs of numbers.

$12 = 1 \times 12$ $12 = 2 \times 6$ $12 = 3 \times 4$

The factors of 12 are 1, 2, 3, 4, 6, and 12.

So, 12 is a composite number because it has factors other than itself and 1.

C. The number 1 is neither prime nor composite, and occasionally is called **unity.** The smallest prime number is 2.

Checkpoint Write the letter of the correct answer.

1. A factor of 24 is ■.   (a.) 6   **b.** 48   **c.** 7   **d.** 96

2. A prime number is ■.   (a.) 2   **b.** 9   **c.** 51   **d.** 25

3. A composite number is ■.   **a.** 5   **b.** 17   **c.** 23   (d.) 57

COMMON ERRORS

Answer Choice	Type of Error
■ 1b, 1d	Writes a multiple instead of a factor
□ 1c	Writes an incorrect factor
○ 2b, 2c, 2d	Writes a composite number instead of a prime number
○ 3a, 3b, 3c	Writes a prime number instead of a composite number

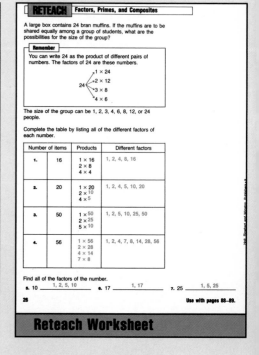

RETEACH Factors, Primes, and Composites

A large box contains 24 bran muffins. If the muffins are to be shared equally among a group of students, what are the possibilities for the size of the group?

Remember
You can write 24 as the product of different pairs of numbers. The factors of 24 are these numbers.

24 ⎰ 1 × 24
    ⎱ 2 × 12
      3 × 8
      4 × 6

The size of the group can be 1, 2, 3, 4, 6, 8, 12, or 24 people.

Complete the table by listing all of the different factors of each number.

Number of items	Products	Different factors
1.	16	1 × 16 2 × 8 4 × 4	1, 2, 4, 8, 16
2.	20	1 × 20 2 × 10 4 × 5	1, 2, 4, 5, 10, 20
3.	50	1 × 50 2 × 25 5 × 10	1, 2, 5, 10, 25, 50
4.	56	1 × 56 2 × 28 4 × 14 7 × 8	1, 2, 4, 7, 8, 14, 28, 56

Find all of the factors of the number.

5. 10 ___ 1, 2, 5, 10   **6.** 17 ___ 1, 17   **7.** 25 ___ 1, 5, 25

26   Use with pages 88–89.

Reteach Worksheet

Find all the factors of each number.

1. 10
1, 2, 5, 10
2. 14
1, 2, 7, 14
3. 15
1, 3, 5, 15
4. 18
1, 2, 3, 6, 9, 18
5. 19
1, 19
6. 24
1, 2, 3, 4, 6, 8, 12, 24
7. 27
1, 3, 9, 27
8. 33
1, 3, 11, 33
9. 38
1, 2, 19, 38
10. 45
1, 3, 5, 9, 15, 45
11. 40
1, 2, 4, 5, 8, 10, 20, 40
12. 55
1, 5, 11, 55
13. 60
1, 2, 3, 4, 5, 6, 10, 12, 15, 20, 30, 60
14. 75
1, 3, 5, 15, 25, 75
15. 85
1, 5, 17, 85

Write *prime* or *composite*.

16. 7
prime
17. 10
composite
18. 14
composite
19. 19
prime
20. 63
composite
21. 29
prime
22. 11
prime
23. 5
prime
24. 4
composite
25. 9
composite
26. 55
composite
27. 60
composite
28. 81
composite
29. 71
prime
30. 15
composite
31. 27
composite
32. 91
composite
33. 87
composite
34. 53
prime
35. 39
composite
36. 58
composite
37. 77
composite
38. 82
composite
39. 90
composite
40. 45
composite

Solve.

41. The **Sieve of Eratosthenes** is a method for finding primes by sifting out composite numbers. To start the sieve, copy the list of numbers and continue to 200. Cross out 1 because it is not prime.

Circle 2 and cross out all numbers that have 2 as a factor.

Circle 3 and cross out all numbers that have 3 as a factor.

Continue in this manner, circling the next prime number and crossing out all numbers that have the circled number as a factor. The remaining numbers should be the prime numbers from 1 to 200.

How many primes are there?
There are 46 primes.

42. Every even number can be written as the sum of two prime numbers. The number 40 is the sum of 37 + 3. What are the other ways to write 40 as the sum of two prime numbers? 29 + 11; 23 + 17

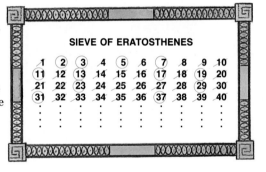

SIEVE OF ERATOSTHENES

ANOTHER LOOK

Divide.

1. $5.95 ÷ 35
$0.17
2. $18.63 ÷ 81
$0.23
3. $229.50 ÷ 450
$0.51
4. $428.17 ÷ 911
$0.47

Classwork/Homework, page H35

89

PRACTICE Factors, Primes, and Composites

Write all the factors of the number.

1. 63 — 1, 3, 7, 9, 21, 63
2. 33 — 1, 3, 11, 33
3. 91 — 1, 7, 13, 91
4. 12 — 1, 2, 3, 4, 6, 12
5. 16 — 1, 2, 4, 8, 16
6. 119 — 1, 7, 17, 119
7. 9 — 1, 3, 9
8. 17 — 1, 17
9. 57 — 1, 3, 19, 57
10. 20 — 1, 2, 4, 5, 10, 20
11. 125 — 1, 5, 25, 125
12. 35 — 1, 5, 7, 35
13. 39 — 1, 3, 13, 39
14. 74 — 1, 2, 37, 74
15. 7 — 1, 7
16. 26 — 1, 2, 13, 26
17. 52 — 1, 2, 4, 13, 26, 52
18. 66 — 1, 2, 3, 6, 11, 22, 33, 66

Write *prime* or *composite*.

19. 109 — prime
20. 17 — prime
21. 18 — composite
22. 29 — prime
23. 79 — prime
24. 52 — composite
25. 72 — composite
26. 19 — prime
27. 39 — composite
28. 96 — composite
29. 91 — composite
30. 59 — prime
31. 47 — prime
32. 144 — composite
33. 2 — prime
34. 71 — prime
35. 57 — composite
36. 36 — composite
37. 13 — prime
38. 189 — composite
39. 300 — composite
40. 3 — prime

Use with pages 88–89.   35

Practice Worksheet

ENRICH Number

The Emirp Corporation of the Alphabeta Star System wants to begin to manufacture prime numbers. The corporation must choose between two recently imported machines. Test the machines for them by completing the tables.

Machine 1:

n	$n^2 - n + 41$	Prime?
0	41	yes
1	41	yes
4	53	yes
12	173	yes
40	1,601	yes
41	1,681	no

This machine does not work for one number. Which number and why? 41; when n = 41, $n^2 - n + 41$ becomes n^2, which is not prime.

Machine 2:

n	$n^2 - 79n + 1,601$	Prime?
0	1,601	yes
1	1,523	yes
2	1,447	yes
20	421	yes
40	41	yes
80	1,681	no

This machine does not work for one number. Which number? 80

Try to invent a prime manufacturing machine for the Emirp Corporation. Use it to manufacture as many primes as you can.

After the students have spent some time working on the solution to this problem, explain that no one has ever discovered a formula for manufacturing primes.

Use with pages 88–89.   35

Enrich Worksheet

Exercise Analysis

1–15   Find factors of composite numbers
16–40   Identify as primes and composites
41–42   Skill applications

You may wish to allow students to use a calculator for some of these exercises.

Another Look

These exercises provide review in division of decimals by whole numbers.

FOLLOW-UP ACTIVITIES

MANIPULATIVES
Materials: blocks or tiles

Blocks or tiles can be used to show whether a number is prime or composite. A prime number of tiles, such as 2, can only form 2 rectangular arrays (1 × 2; 2 × 1).

A composite number of tiles, such as 4, can form more than two rectangular arrays (2 × 2; 1 × 4; 4 × 1).

Have students make all the rectangular arrays for 12, 13, 17, 18, 21, and 24. Have them identify the numbers that could form only 2 arrays (13, 17) and those that could form more than 2 (12, 18, 21, 24).

PROBLEM SOLVING
Twin primes are defined as "a pair of prime numbers whose difference is 2." 3 and 5 are twin primes because 5 − 3 = 2. What are the other twin primes between 1 and 100? (5, 7; 11, 13; 17, 19; 29, 31; 41, 43; 59, 61; 71, 73)

COMING UP
Getting to the root of factor trees

Objective: To find the prime factorization of a number by using a factor tree

Warm-Up
Have students find the following products.

$2^2 \times 3$ (12) $2 \times 3^2 \times 5$ (90)
$2^3 \times 3^2$ (72) 3×5^2 (75)

GETTING STARTED

Exponents can be used to simplify expressions that have several similar factors; for example;

$2 \times 2 \times 2 \times 3 \times 3 = 2^3 \times 3^2 = 72.$

Have students use exponents to simplify these expressions.

$5 \times 3 \times 3 \times 2 \times 5$ ($2 \times 3^2 \times 5^2$)
$2 \times 2 \times 13 \times 13 \times 2 \times 5$
($2^3 \times 5 \times 13^2$)
$7 \times 7 \times 2 \times 3 \times 3$ ($2 \times 3^2 \times 7^2$)

Ask students whether they notice anything about the factors you have written. (They are all prime.)

TEACHING THE LESSON

A. Ask students whether they can think of a reason or a use for prime factorization. Then show them that by multiplying the different prime factors, you can get all the factors of a number. This is especially useful with larger numbers; for example, $36 = 2^2 \times 3^2$. Its factors are 1, 2, 3, 2^2 (4), 2×3 (6), 3^2 (9), $2^2 \times 3$ (12), 2×3^2 (18), and $2^2 \times 3^2$ (36).

B. Remind students that each prime number should be checked to see whether it can be used more than once before going on to the next prime number.

```
2 | 16          2 | 16
2 | 8           2 | 8
2 | 4           (8 is not divisible
2 | 2            by 3, 5, 7, or 11;
    1            so, a student might
(16 = 2⁴)        write 16 = 2 × 8)
```

On the chalkboard, use the division method to factor several other numbers. You may wish to allow students to use calculators while working through this lesson.

Prime Factorization

A. Prime numbers are helpful in factoring because each composite number can be written as the product of prime numbers. This is called the **prime factorization** of the number.

A **factor tree** can be used to find the prime factorization of 120. Begin by choosing any two numbers whose product is 120. Continue until every "branch" ends with a prime factor.

The prime factorization of 120 is $2 \times 3 \times 2 \times 5 \times 2$, or $2 \times 2 \times 3 \times 2 \times 5$. The prime factorization is the same, just the order of the factors is different.

If a factor appears more than once, use exponents to show how many times the factor is used. Write the factors in order. The prime factorization of 120 is $2^3 \times 3 \times 5$.

B. You can also find the prime factorization by using division. Divide by prime numbers in order until the quotient is 1. Use divisibility rules to help you.

```
2 | 30              3 | 231  ← not divisible by 2
3 | 15              7 | 77   ← not divisible by 5
5 | 5              11 | 11
    1                    1
```

The prime   The prime
factorization   factorization
of 30 is   of 231 is
$2 \times 3 \times 5$. $3 \times 7 \times 11$.

COMMON ERRORS

Students often make the mistake of reading only the last row of numbers in a factor tree and taking those for the complete prime factorization.

Remediation
Have students make a habit of circling every prime number in every branch. The prime factorization will then consist of these circled numbers.

Assign Reteach Master, p. 27.

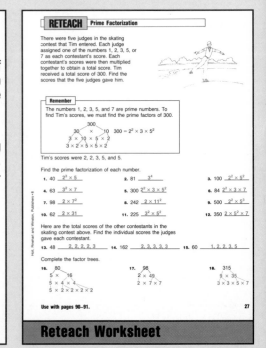

RETEACH | Prime Factorization

There were five judges in the skating contest that Tim entered. Each judge assigned one of the numbers 1, 2, 3, 5, or 7 as each contestant's score. Each contestant's scores were then multiplied together to obtain a total score. Tim received a total score of 300. Find the scores that the five judges gave him.

Remember
The numbers 1, 2, 3, 5, and 7 are prime numbers. To find Tim's scores, we must find the prime factors of 300.

$300 = 2^2 \times 3 \times 5^2$

Tim's scores were 2, 2, 3, 5, and 5.

Find the prime factorization of each number.

1. 40 ___$2^3 \times 5$___   2. 81 ___3^4___   3. 100 ___$2^2 \times 5^2$___
4. 63 ___$3^2 \times 7$___   5. 300 ___$2^2 \times 3 \times 5^2$___   6. 84 ___$2^2 \times 3 \times 7$___
7. 98 ___2×7^2___   8. 242 ___2×11^2___   9. 500 ___$2^2 \times 5^3$___
10. 62 ___2×31___   11. 225 ___$3^2 \times 5^2$___   12. 350 ___$2 \times 5^2 \times 7$___

Here are the total scores of the other contestants in the skating contest above. Find the individual scores the judges gave each contestant.

13. 48 ___2, 2, 2, 2, 3___   14. 162 ___2, 3, 3, 3, 3___   15. 60 ___1, 2, 2, 3, 5___

Complete the factor trees.

16. 80   17. 98   18. 315
   5 × 16   2 × 49   9 × 35
  5 × 4 × 4   2 × 7 × 7   3 × 3 × 5 × 7
5 × 2 × 2 × 2 × 2

Use with pages 90–91.   27

Reteach Worksheet

Find the prime factorization of each number. Use factor trees. Use exponents to write the answer.

1. 12
$2^2 \times 3$
2. 40
$2^3 \times 5$
3. 54
2×3^3
4. 160
$2^5 \times 5$
5. 128
2^7
6. 333
$3^2 \times 37$
7. 108
$2^2 \times 3^3$
8. 300
$2^2 \times 3 \times 5^2$
9. 220
$2^2 \times 5 \times 11$
10. 480
$2^5 \times 3 \times 5$
11. 900
$2^2 \times 3^2 \times 5^2$
12. 750
$2 \times 3 \times 5^3$
13. 960
$2^6 \times 3 \times 5$
14. 620
$2^2 \times 5 \times 31$
15. 824
$2^3 \times 103$
16. 1,260
$2^2 \times 3^2 \times 5 \times 7$
17. 1,402
2×701
18. 1,521
$3^2 \times 13^2$
19. 2,025
$3^4 \times 5^2$
20. 2,431
$11 \times 13 \times 17$

Write the prime factorization of each number. Use exponents.

21. 9
3^2
22. 20
$2^2 \times 5$
23. 27
3^3
24. 64
2^6
25. 35
5×7
26. 80
$2^4 \times 5$
27. 75
3×5^2
28. 94
2×47
29. 135
$3^3 \times 5$
30. 150
$2 \times 3 \times 5^2$
31. 180
$2^2 \times 3^2 \times 5$
32. 48
$2^4 \times 3$
33. 335
5×67
34. 425
$5^2 \times 17$
35. 111
3×37
36. 240
$2^4 \times 3 \times 5$
37. 2,750
$2 \times 5^3 \times 11$
38. 1,960
$2^3 \times 5 \times 7^2$
39. 5,184
$2^6 \times 3^4$
40. 11,475
$3^3 \times 5^2 \times 17$

Write the number for each prime factorization.

41. $2 \times 3 \times 5$ 30

42. $2^2 \times 3 \times 5$ 60

43. $3 \times 5 \times 7^2$
735

44. $5^2 \times 7 \times 11$ 1,925

45. $2^4 \times 3^2 \times 5$ 720

46. $11 \times 13 \times 17$
2,431

Solve.

47. Which prime factors do 24 and 80 share? 2

48. List the shared prime factors of 36 and 144. 2, 3

49. Find the prime factors of 31 and 53. How many factors do they have in common? 1

★50. What is the smallest number that has six different primes in its prime factorization? 30,030

CHALLENGE

Use the Infobank on page 474 to solve. Write the cube roots and break the code.

"What is the most difficult thing to do on a long trip?"

$\sqrt[3]{125}$ $\sqrt[3]{512}$ $\sqrt[3]{343}$ $\sqrt[3]{27}$

$\sqrt[3]{343}$ $\sqrt[3]{64}$ $\sqrt[3]{343}$ $\sqrt[3]{729}$ $\sqrt[3]{216}$

STAY AWAKE

3 = Y
4 = W
5 = S
6 = E
7 = A
8 = T
9 = K

ASSIGNMENT GUIDE

Basic: 1–49 o

Average: 4–46 e, 47–49

Extended: 10–46 e, 47–50, Chlg

Resources
Practice, p. 36   Class/Home, p. H36
Reteach, p. 27
Enrich, p. 36

Exercise Analysis

1–20   Find a number's prime factorization by using factor trees

21–40   Write a number's prime factorization by using exponents

41–46   Write a number from its prime factorization

47–50   Skill applications

You may wish to allow students to use a calculator for some of these exercises.

Challenge

This exercise encourages students to use cube roots in order to decode a puzzle.

FOLLOW-UP ACTIVITIES

COMPUTER

Have students write a program that finds the prime factorization of any number.

```
10 INPUT N
20 FOR F = 2 TO N
30 LET Q = N/F
40 IF Q <>INT(Q) THEN 90
50 IF Q = 1 THEN 100
60 PRINT F; "TIMES";
70 LET N = Q
80 GOTO 30
90 NEXT F
100 PRINT F
110 END
```

PROBLEM SOLVING

Within the set of even natural numbers are numbers that cannot be written as the product of any two members of the set. Such numbers are said to be *E-prime*; for example, 6 is E-prime because $6 = 2 \times 3$, and 3 is not a member of this set. The number 8, though, is *E-composite* because $8 = 4 \times 2$, and both 4 and 2 are members of the set. Have students describe the even natural numbers from 8 to 20 as being either E-prime or E-composite. (E-prime: 10, 14, and 18; E-composite: 8, 12, 16, and 20)

COMING UP

Not so common factors

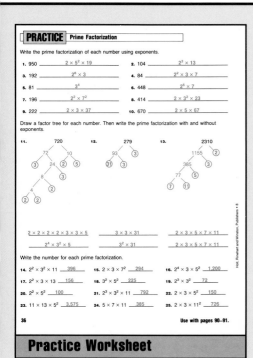

PRACTICE Prime Factorization

Write the prime factorization of each number using exponents.

1. 950 ___$2 \times 5^2 \times 19$___
2. 104 ___$2^3 \times 13$___
3. 192 ___$2^6 \times 3$___
4. 84 ___$2^2 \times 3 \times 7$___
5. 81 ___3^4___
6. 448 ___$2^6 \times 7$___
7. 196 ___$2^2 \times 7^2$___
8. 414 ___$2 \times 3^2 \times 23$___
9. 222 ___$2 \times 3 \times 37$___
10. 670 ___$2 \times 5 \times 67$___

Draw a factor tree for each number. Then write the prime factorization with and without exponents.

11. 720
12. 279
13. 2310

$2 \times 2 \times 2 \times 2 \times 3 \times 3 \times 5$ $3 \times 3 \times 31$ $2 \times 3 \times 5 \times 7 \times 11$
$2^4 \times 3^2 \times 5$ $3^2 \times 31$ $2 \times 3 \times 5 \times 7 \times 11$

Write the number for each prime factorization.

14. $2^2 \times 3^2 \times 11$ ___396___
15. $2 \times 3 \times 7^2$ ___294___
16. $2^4 \times 3 \times 5^2$ ___1,200___
17. $2^2 \times 3 \times 13$ ___156___
18. $3^2 \times 5^2$ ___225___
19. $2^3 \times 3^2$ ___72___
20. $2^2 \times 5^2$ ___100___
21. $2^3 \times 3^2 \times 11$ ___792___
22. $2 \times 3 \times 5^2$ ___150___
23. $11 \times 13 \times 5^2$ ___3,575___
24. $5 \times 7 \times 11$ ___385___
25. $2 \times 3 \times 11^2$ ___726___

36   Use with pages 90–91.

Practice Worksheet

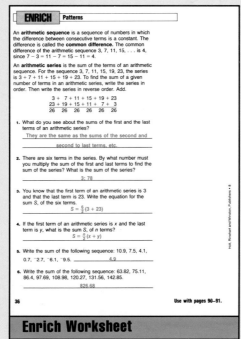

ENRICH Patterns

An **arithmetic sequence** is a sequence of numbers in which the difference between consecutive terms is a constant. The difference is called the **common difference.** The common difference of the arithmetic sequence 3, 7, 11, 15, . . . is 4, since 7 − 3 = 11 − 7 = 15 − 11 = 4.

An **arithmetic series** is the sum of the terms of an arithmetic sequence. For the sequence 3, 7, 11, 15, 19, 23, the series is 3 + 7 + 11 + 15 + 19 + 23. To find the sum of a given number of terms of an arithmetic series, write the series in order. Then write the series in reverse order. Add.

3 + 7 + 11 + 15 + 19 + 23
23 + 19 + 15 + 11 + 7 + 3
26 26 26 26 26 26

1. What do you see about the sums of the first and the last terms of an arithmetic series?
They are the same as the sums of the second and second to last terms, etc.

2. There are six terms in the series. By what number must you multiply the sum of the first and last terms to find the sum of the series? What is the sum of the series?
3; 78

3. You know that the first term of an arithmetic series is 3 and that the last term is 23. Write the equation for the sum S, of the six terms.
$S = \frac{6}{2}(3 + 23)$

4. If the first term of an arithmetic series is x and the last term is y, what is the sum S, of n terms?
$S = \frac{n}{2}(x + y)$

5. Write the sum of the following sequence: 10.9, 7.5, 4.1, 0.7, ⁻2.7, ⁻6.1, ⁻9.5.
4.9

6. Write the sum of the following sequence: 63.82, 75.11, 86.4, 97.69, 108.98, 120.27, 131.56, 142.85.
826.68

36   Use with pages 90–91.

Enrich Worksheet

Objective: To find the greatest common factor by the prime factorization method

Warm-Up

Have students write the prime factorization of each of the following numbers.

114 (2 × 3 × 19)   858 (2 × 3 × 11 × 13)
165 (3 × 5 × 11)   97 (97 × 1)

GETTING STARTED

This is a fun game that makes students think about factors. The strategy is to choose as large a number as possible that has as small and as few factors as possible. Each pair of students makes a list of the numbers from 1 through 36. Player 1 chooses a number, crosses it out, and earns that number of points. Player 2 earns points for all the factors of the number except the number and 1.

For example, Player 1 picks 8, crosses it out, and scores 8 points. Player 2 picks the factors 2 and 4 and scores 6 points. Players alternate until no number is left. The player who has the most points wins.

TEACHING THE LESSON

A. Remind students that to find the GCF by listing factors, they must be careful to list all factors. Students may forget to test some factors, especially larger ones; for example, 286 = 2 × 143. But students may forget to factor 143 (11 × 13). Also, remind students that there is only one GCF, the *largest* common factor.

B. The *common* factors of 60, 42, and 36 can be listed. Although 2 appears twice in 60 and 36 and 3 appears twice in 36, each can be circled only once in all three numbers (as below).

Thus, 3 × 2 is the GCF.

$$60 = 2 \times 2 \times 3 \times 5$$
$$42 = 2 \times 3 \times 7$$
$$36 = 2 \times 2 \times 3 \times 3$$

C. As a sidelight, point out that a fraction is considered to be in simplest form if its numerator and denominator are relatively prime. You may wish to allow students to use calculators while working through this lesson.

Greatest Common Factor (GCF)

A. The rule for finding the **greatest common factor (GCF)** of a set of numbers was probably first used by Boethius, who lived around A.D. 510.

What is the GCF of 12 and 18?

To find the GCF of two numbers, list all the factors of each number.

Then circle the common factors. The GCF is the largest common factor.

Factors of 12: ①, ②, ③, 4 , ⑥, 12

Factors of 18: ①, ②, ③, ⑥, 9 , 18

Common factors: ①, ②, ③, ⑥

GCF: 6

B. Another way to find the GCF is to use prime factorization. To find the GCF of 54, 90, and 126, use exponents to write the prime factorization for each.

Prime factorization of 54: 2×3^3

Prime factorization of 90: $2 \times 3^2 \times 5$

Prime factorization of 126: $2 \times 3^2 \times 7$

Product of common prime factors: 2×3^2

GCF: 18

C. Numbers are called **relatively prime** when their only common factor is 1.

To find the GCF of 8 and 15, factor.

Factors of 8: ①, 2 , 4 , 8

Factors of 15: ①, 3 , 5 , 15

The GCF of 8 and 15 is 1. The numbers are relatively prime.

92

COMMON ERRORS

Students often find the GCF in the prime-factorization method by using the common factors the *greatest* number of times each appears.

Remediation

Have students find the GCF of several numbers by both methods in order to compare answers. In the prime-factorization method, have them circle the common factors the *least* number of times each appears. The GCF will then be their product.

Assign Reteach Master, p. 28.

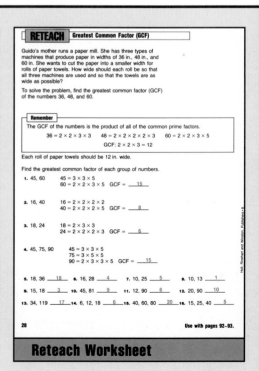

RETEACH Greatest Common Factor (GCF)

Guido's mother runs a paper mill. She has three types of machines that produce paper in widths of 36 in., 48 in., and 60 in. She wants to cut the paper into a smaller width for rolls of paper towels. How wide should each roll be so that all three machines are used and so that the towels are as wide as possible?

To solve the problem, find the greatest common factor (GCF) of the numbers 36, 48, and 60.

Remember

The GCF of the numbers is the product of all the common prime factors.

36 = 2 × 2 × 3 × 3   48 = 2 × 2 × 2 × 2 × 3   60 = 2 × 2 × 3 × 5

GCF: 2 × 2 × 3 = 12

Each roll of paper towels should be 12 in. wide.

Find the greatest common factor of each group of numbers.

1. 45, 60   45 = 3 × 3 × 5
             60 = 2 × 2 × 3 × 5   GCF = __15__

2. 16, 40   16 = 2 × 2 × 2 × 2
             40 = 2 × 2 × 2 × 5   GCF = __8__

3. 18, 24   18 = 2 × 3 × 3
             24 = 2 × 2 × 2 × 3   GCF = __6__

4. 45, 75, 90   45 = 3 × 3 × 5
                 75 = 3 × 5 × 5
                 90 = 2 × 3 × 3 × 5   GCF = __15__

5. 18, 36 __18__ 6. 16, 28 __4__ 7. 10, 25 __5__ 8. 10, 13 __1__

9. 15, 18 __3__ 10. 45, 81 __9__ 11. 12, 90 __6__ 12. 20, 90 __10__

13. 34, 119 __17__ 14. 6, 12, 18 __6__ 15. 40, 60, 80 __20__ 16. 15, 25, 40 __5__

28   Use with pages 92–93.

Reteach Worksheet

List the factors to find the GCF. **Check students' lists.**

1. 27, 81 27
2. 77, 28 7
3. 9, 50 1
4. 10, 48 2

5. 41, 25 1
6. 12, 20 4
7. 20, 35 5
8. 12, 42 6

9. 26, 31, 39 1
10. 15, 33, 54 3
11. 17, 23, 46 1
12. 64, 48, 26 2

Use prime factorization to find the GCF. Use exponents and evaluate.

13. 14, 35 7
14. 12, 60 $2^2 \times 3 = 12$
15. 11, 55 11
16. 15, 40 5

17. 18, 63 $3^2 = 9$
18. 16, 52 $2^2 = 4$
19. 25, 90 5
20. 10, 125 5

21. 27, 63, 45 $3^2 = 9$
22. 32, 40, 58 2
23. 16, 24, 80 $2^3 = 8$
24. 31, 50, 75 1

25. 8, 100 $2^2 = 4$
26. 27, 75, 120 3
27. 24, 42, 54 $2 \times 3 = 6$
28. 360, 756 $2^2 \times 3^2 = 36$

29. 45, 370, 590 5
30. 56, 420 $2^2 \times 7 = 28$
31. 21; 1,087; 3,842 1
32. 204; 3,897 3

Solve.

33. If the GCF of three numbers is 45, what is the smallest that any of the three numbers could be? 45

34. If the GCF of two numbers is 36, what are some of the prime factors of each number? 2, 3

CHALLENGE

The Greek mathematician Euclid discovered an easy way to find the GCF of two numbers.
To find the GCF of 42 and 312

1. Divide the larger number by the smaller.

$$42\overline{)312} \quad \frac{7}{}$$
$$\underline{294}$$

2. Divide the previous divisor by the remainder. Repeat until the remainder is 0.

$$18\overline{)42} \quad \frac{2}{}$$
$$\underline{36}$$

3. The last divisor is the GCF.

Use Euclid's method to find the GCF of these numbers.

$$6\overline{)18} \quad \frac{3}{} \rightarrow 6 \text{ is the GCF.}$$
$$\underline{18}$$
$$0$$

a. 36, 78 6
b. 91, 669 1
c. 146, 722 2

Classwork/Homework, page H37   More practice, page H197   **93**

ASSIGNMENT GUIDE

Basic: 1–12, 13–27 o

Average: 5–12, 13–31 o, 33–34

Extended: 8–12, 14–32 e, 33–34, Chlg

Resources
Practice, p. 37   Class/Home, p. H37
Reteach, p. 28   More Practice, p. H197
Enrich, p. 37

Exercise Analysis

1–12   Find the GCF by the listing method
13–32   Find the GCF by the prime-factorization method
33–34   Skill applications

You may wish to allow students to use a calculator for some of these exercises.

Challenge

This exercise provides an alternate strategy for finding the GCF for a pair of numbers.

FOLLOW-UP ACTIVITIES

PROBLEM SOLVING

The eighth-grade class in a school purchases 38 hamburgers and 57 cans of juice for its annual school picnic. The principal, however, insists that each student who attends must receive exactly the same number of refreshments.

1. What is the largest number of students who can attend under this condition? (19)

2. How many hamburgers can each have? (2)

3. How many cans of juice can each have? (3)

REINFORCEMENT

A number's prime factorization is $2^4 \times 3 \times 5$. The factors of a second number are 1, 2, 4, 5, 8, 10, 16, 20, 40, 80. What is the GCF of the two numbers? (80)

A number's prime factorization is $2^6 \times 3 \times 5^3 \times 7$. A second number's factors are 1, 2, 3, 6, 7, 9, 14, 18, 21, 42, 63, 126. What is the GCF of the numbers? (42)

COMING UP

Last, if not least . . .

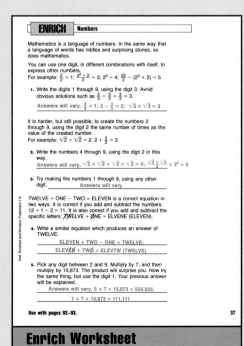

PRACTICE Greatest Common Factor (GCF)

Write the GCF. Find it by listing the factors.

1. 16, 24 8
2. 15, 35 5
3. 24, 72 24
4. 42, 105 21
5. 63, 81 9
6. 24, 49 1
7. 18, 27, 45 9
8. 35, 84 7
9. 12, 20, 28 4
10. 24, 36, 60 12
11. 26, 208 26
12. 88, 121 11

Write the GCF. Find it by using prime factorization.

13. 60, 140 20
14. 96, 128 32
15. 40, 64 8
16. 64, 96, 112 16
17. 81, 108 27
18. 34, 51 17
19. 72, 180 36
20. 15, 80 5
21. 21, 56 7
22. 25, 225 25
23. 60, 84, 114 6
24. 552, 648 24
25. 39, 65, 91 13
26. 115, 138, 184 23
27. 133, 152 19

Use with pages 92–93.   37

Practice Worksheet

ENRICH Numbers

Mathematics is a language of numbers. In the same way that a language of words has riddles and surprising stories, so does mathematics.

You can use one digit, in different combinations with itself, to express other numbers.
For example: $\frac{2}{2} = 1$; $\frac{2^2 + 2}{2} = 3$; $2^2 = 4$; $\frac{22}{2} - (2^2 + 2) = 5$

1. Write the digits 1 through 9, using the digit 3. Avoid obvious solutions such as $\frac{3}{3} + \frac{3}{3} + \frac{3}{3} = 3$.
   Answers will vary. $\frac{3}{3} = 1$; $3 - \frac{3}{3} = 2$; $\sqrt{3} \times \sqrt{3} = 3$

It is harder, but still possible, to create the numbers 2 through 9, using the digit 2 the same number of times as the value of the created number.
For example: $\sqrt{2} \times \sqrt{2} = 2$; $2 + \frac{2}{2} = 3$

2. Write the numbers 4 through 9, using the digit 2 in this way.
   Answers will vary. $\sqrt{2} + \sqrt{2} + \sqrt{2} \times \sqrt{2} = 4$; $\frac{\sqrt{2} \times \sqrt{2}}{2} + 2^2 = 5$

3. Try making the numbers 1 through 9, using any other digit. Answers will vary.

TWELVE + ONE − TWO = ELEVEN is a correct equation in two ways. It is correct if you add and subtract the numbers: 12 + 1 − 2 = 11. It is also correct if you add and subtract the specific letters: TWELVE + ØNE = ELVENE (ELEVEN).

4. Write a similar equation which produces an answer of TWELVE.
   ELEVEN + TWO − ONE = TWELVE;
   ELEVEN + TWØ = ELEVTW (TWELVE)

5. Pick any digit between 2 and 9. Multiply by 7, and then multiply by 15,873. The product will surprise you. Now try the same thing, but use the digit 1. Your previous answer will be explained.
   Answers will vary. $5 \times 7 \times 15,873 = 555,555$;
   $1 \times 7 \times 15,873 = 111,111$

Use with pages 92–93.   37

Enrich Worksheet

Objectives: To find the least common multiple by the listing method and by the prime-factorization method

Warm-Up
Have students find the GCF of the following numbers by the method indicated.

36 and 45: *Listing* (GCF = 9)
210 and 495: *Prime Factorization* (GCF = 3 × 5, or 15)

GETTING STARTED

Have students solve this problem.

Two trains travel between Chicago and New Orleans. One train takes 6 days to complete a round trip, and the other takes 8 days. If they are both in Chicago today, in how many days will they both be in Chicago again? (24 days)

Have students discuss how they found the answer. Show how the trains come to Chicago in multiples of 6 and 8 days.

TEACHING THE LESSON

A. Emphasize the definition of *Least Common Multiple*. Ask the class when finding the LCM is important.

Point out that one of the most important uses of the LCM is to find common denominators for adding and subtracting fractions. Give examples, such as

$\frac{3}{8} + \frac{1}{6}, \frac{2}{3} - \frac{1}{4}$.

B. In this method, 2^2 must be used instead of the 2. When there are like factors, the greatest exponent must be used. It would be wise to spend a few minutes distinguishing between finding the GCF and the LCM by this method.

Checkpoint
The chart lists the common errors students make in finding the multiples of a group of numbers.

Correct Answers: 1d, 2c

Remediation
■ For these errors, have students explain the differences between multiple, common multiple, LCM, and factor.

☐ For this error, guide the students in completing Reteach Master, p. 29.

Least Common Multiple

A. A **multiple** of a number is any product that has the number as a factor.

To find the smallest or the **least common multiple (LCM)** of two numbers, list some of the multiples of each number.

What is the LCM of 6 and 15?

Multiples of 6: 0, 6, 12, 18, 24, 30, 36, 42, 48, 54, 60, . . .

Multiples of 15: 0, 15, 30, 45, 60, 75, . . .

Common multiples: 0, 30, 60, . . .

The smallest nonzero multiple, 30, is the LCM of 6 and 15.

B. Another way to find the LCM of two or more numbers is to use prime factorization.

Find the LCM of 6, 15, and 28.

Prime factorization of 6: 2 × ③

Prime factorization of 15: 3 × ⑤

Prime factorization of 28: ② × ⑦

Different prime factors: 2, 3, 5, 7

Circle the highest power of each prime factor. The LCM is the product of the highest power of each of the different prime factors.

LCM: $2^2 \times 3 \times 5 \times 7$, or 420.

Checkpoint Write the letter of the correct answer.

1. A common multiple of 6 and 12 is ■.
   a. 2   b. 3   c. 6   ⓓ 24

2. The LCM of 9 and 15 is ■.
   a. 3   b. 15   ⓒ 45   d. 135

Math Reasoning, page H21

COMMON ERRORS

Answer Choice	Type of Error
■ 1a, 1b, 1c, 2a	Confuses the multiple with the factor
☐ 2b	Uses the larger number as the LCM
■ 2d	Chooses a common multiple that is not the LCM

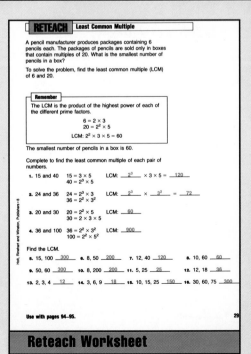

| RETEACH | Least Common Multiple |

A pencil manufacturer produces packages containing 6 pencils each. The packages of pencils are sold only in boxes that contain multiples of 20 pencils in a box. What is the smallest number of pencils in a box?

To solve the problem, find the least common multiple (LCM) of 6 and 20.

Remember
The LCM is the product of the highest power of each of the different prime factors.
6 = 2 × 3
20 = 2² × 5
LCM: 2² × 3 × 5 = 60

The smallest number of pencils in a box is 60.

Complete to find the least common multiple of each pair of numbers.

1. 15 and 40   15 = 3 × 5   LCM: __2³__ × 3 × 5 = __120__
   40 = 2³ × 5

2. 24 and 36   24 = 2³ × 3   LCM: __2³__ × __3²__ = __72__
   36 = 2² × 3²

3. 20 and 30   20 = 2² × 5   LCM: __60__
   30 = 2 × 3 × 5

4. 36 and 100 36 = 2² × 3² LCM: __900__
   100 = 2² × 5²

Find the LCM.

5. 15, 100 __300__   6. 8, 50 __200__   7. 12, 40 __120__   8. 10, 60 __60__

9. 50, 60 __300__   10. 8, 200 __200__   11. 5, 25 __25__   12. 12, 18 __36__

13. 2, 3, 4 __12__   14. 3, 6, 9 __18__   15. 10, 15, 25 __150__   16. 30, 60, 75 __300__

Use with pages 94–95.   29

Reteach Worksheet

List the first five nonzero multiples of each number.

1. 2
2, 4, 6, 8, 10

2. 3
3, 6, 9, 12, 15

3. 5
5, 10, 15, 20, 25

4. 6
6, 12, 18, 24, 30

5. 7
7, 14, 21, 28, 35

6. 9
9, 18, 27, 36, 45

7. 11
11, 22, 33, 44, 55

8. 12
12, 24, 36, 48, 60

9. 20
20, 40, 60, 80, 100

10. 25
25, 50, 75, 100, 125

11. 100
100, 200, 300, 400, 500

12. 500
500, 1,000, 1,500, 2,000, 2,500

List multiples to find the LCM.

13. 24, 30 120

14. 6, 12 12

15. 6, 9 18

16. 3, 5 15

17. 8, 20 40

18. 6, 27 54

19. 10, 12 60

20. 12, 16 48

21. 4, 30 60

22. 17, 3 51

23. 10, 25, 20 100

24. 15, 60, 90 180

Use prime factorizations to find the LCM.

25. 30, 70 210

26. 16, 200 400

27. 36, 54 108

28. 12, 34 204

29. 15, 50 150

30. 42, 84 84

31. 24, 60 120

32. 45, 54 270

33. 14, 27, 35 1,890

34. 25, 42, 45 3,150

35. 6, 15, 150 150

36. 32, 63, 144 2,016

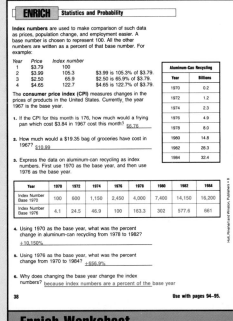

MIDCHAPTER REVIEW

1. Is 42,926 divisible by 3? by 4? by 8?
no; no; no

2. Is 3,970,615 divisible by 2? by 3? by 5?
no; no; yes

3. Indicate whether the number is prime or composite: 127; 91.
prime; composite

Evaluate.

4. 7^2
49

5. 5^3
125

6. 3^4
81

7. 6^4
1,296

8. 8^5
32,768

9. 9^7
4,782,969

Find the square root. Use the table on page 83.

10. $\sqrt{169}$ 13

11. $\sqrt{289}$ 17

12. $\sqrt{1,296}$ 36

13. $\sqrt{26}$ 5.099

14. $\sqrt{38}$ 6.164

Write in scientific notation.

15. 1,800
1.8×10^3

16. 96,320
9.632×10^4

17. 4,001,900
4.0019×10^6

18. 327,000,000
3.27×10^8

Use prime factorization to find the GCF and the LCM.

19. 16, 56
8; 112

20. 112, 220
4; 6,160

21. 786; 1,116
6; 146,196

22. 2,375; 1,775
25; 168,625

Classwork/Homework, page H38

95

ASSIGNMENT GUIDE

Basic: 1–35 o, MCR

Average: 2–36 e, MCR

Extended: 10–12, 14–36 e, MCR

Resources
Practice, p. 38   Class/Home, p. H38
Reteach, p. 29   Reasoning, p. H211
Enrich, p. 38

Exercise Analysis

1–12   List the first five nonzero multiples of a number

13–24   Find the LCM by the listing method

25–36   Find the LCM by the prime-factorization method

You may wish to allow students to use calculators for some of these exercises.

Midchapter Review

This review provides an opportunity for you and students to assess their understanding of concepts and skills developed to this point in the chapter.

FOLLOW-UP ACTIVITIES

MATH COMMUNICATION
Have students research the Euclidean Algorithm for finding the LCM for a pair of numbers if their GCF is known. This rule is based on the fact that the product of the GCF and the LCM of two numbers is equal to the product of the two numbers themselves.

$$GCF(a, b) \times LCM(a, b) = a \times b$$

$$So, LCM = \frac{a \times b}{GCF(a, b)}.$$

Have students find the LCM of 168 and 224 if their GCF is 56.

$$LCM(168, 224) = \frac{168 \times 224}{56} \text{ or } 672$$

Students can verify this LCM by the prime-factorization method.

Use the same method to find the LCM of 388 and 144. (13,968)

COMING UP
Operations have an order.

Objective: To use information from a table to solve problems

Warm-Up

Have students find the following sums.

84 + 71 + 28 + 118 (301)
$2.25 + $7.14 + $0.79 ($10.18)
49 + 209 + 422 + 711 (1,391)
$1.95 + $2.49 + $8.15 ($12.59)

GETTING STARTED

Ask how students know when a bus or train will make a particular stop. (schedule or table) Have students describe the information contained on a train or bus schedule. Point out that a schedule is particularly useful because it can be used each time train or bus information is needed.

Ask volunteers to name other kinds of tables they have seen or used and tell the information that was contained in each. (Examples may include a table of contents in a book, an index, a list of team-sports standings from a newspaper.)

TEACHING THE LESSON

Students often have difficulty interpreting tables because they are unfamiliar with tables and do not read all the information in each classification. The postage-rate table in the lesson should be read in a systematic way. Have students

- scan the table for headings that tell what information the table contains.
- identify the destination.
- identify the letter weight.
- compute the rate by adding the cost for the first ounce and each additional ounce.

Interaction and reinforcement, which are common in small-group work, may benefit some students.

Questions: Students seldom have difficulty understanding what the question is asking. Difficulty may arise, however, because the information needed to answer the question must be found on the table rather than in the problem itself.

Tools: Make sure that students can read the table. Explain that each rate in the table on page 97 is for that weight and under.

Point out that for letters, a fraction of an ounce is treated as an additional ounce; for example, a 2.1-oz letter needs the same postage as a 2.9-oz letter.

Solutions: Students might have difficulty with Problem 5 which requires multiplication of mixed numbers. You may wish to review mixed-number multiplication. This problem also requires very careful reading.

QUESTIONS	TOOLS	SOLUTIONS	CHECKS

PROBLEM SOLVING
Using a Table

Sometimes you can use a *rate* table to find the information you need to solve a problem.

UNITED STATES POSTAGE RATES (1988)

Weight	Rate
Letters—first class, within the United States	
1–11 oz	$0.25 for the first ounce and $0.20 for each additional ounce or fraction of an ounce.
Letters—first class to Mexico	
1–12 oz	$0.25 for the first ounce and $0.20 for each additional ounce or fraction of an ounce.
Letters—surface mail to countries other than Canada and Mexico	
1–8 oz	$0.40 for the first ounce and $0.23 for each additional ounce or fraction of an ounce.

Ben lives in New Hampshire. One day, he went to the post office to mail some letters. He mailed one letter to a friend in Arizona. The letter weighted 2.3 ounces. Ben mailed a second letter to a friend in Mexico. It weighed 5.6 ounces. Finally, he mailed a letter and some photos to a friend in West Germany. That letter weighed 7.4 ounces, and Ben sent it by surface mail. How much postage did Ben buy for each letter?

To find the amount of postage that Ben bought, use the postage-rate table above. A letter that weighs 2.3 ounces, mailed first class within the United States, costs $0.65 ($0.25 + $0.20 + $0.20). A letter that weighs 5.6 ounces, sent first class to Mexico, costs $1.25. A letter that weighs 7.4 ounces, sent by surface mail to West Germany, costs $2.01.

96

You may wish to allow students to use calculators for problem solving.

Checks: Have students check their answers by finding the rate for a package on the table in order to check that the weight is within the range of that rate. Postage for a letter can be checked by

- determining the weight in ounces.
- finding the cost of mailing the first ounce.
- adding the cost of mailing each additional ounce.

Use the table on page 96 and the table at the right to solve.

1. Freddie mailed thank-you notes. He sent 15 one-ounce notes first class to addresses in the United States. How much postage did he pay? **$3.75**

2. Faye wants to send a gift to her aunt in Great Britain, the rate for which is in Rate Group C. How much will it cost her to send a 2-lb 7-oz package air parcel post? **$18.30**

3. Felice has to send a package air parcel post from her company in the United States to Japan. The rate is listed in Rate Group E. The package weighs 5 pounds 14 ounces. How much postage will be required? $45.15

4. Geoffrey paid $15.15 to mail a small package air parcel post to his cousin in Peru, as calculated in Rate Group B. About how much did the package weigh? more than 2 lb and less than 3 lb

5. Cindy mailed letters by surface mail to Greenland, Ethiopia, and Australia. The letter to Ethiopia weighed 1.3 times as much as the letter to Greenland, and the letter to Greenland weighed 1.75 times as much as the letter to Australia. If the letter to Australia weighed 2.6 ounces, how much did Cindy spend on postage in order to mail the three letters? $3.73

6. Henry has a letter that he wants to send to Mexico. The letter weighs 1.1 ounces. Before he seals the envelope, Henry decides to add 4 magazine clippings. Each clipping weighs 0.25 ounces, Henry gives the postal clerk a $1 bill. How much change does he receive? $0.35

UNITED STATES AIR PARCEL POST RATES (1988)

Weight not more than	Rate Group				
	A	B	C	D	E
1 lb	$5.50	$7.15	$8.70	$10.30	$11.95
2	8.30	11.15	13.50	16.10	18.75
3	11.10	15.15	18.30	21.90	25.55
4	13.90	19.15	23.10	27.70	32.35
5	16.70	23.15	27.90	33.50	39.15
6	18.70	26.15	31.90	38.50	45.15
7	20.70	29.15	35.90	43.50	51.15
8	22.70	32.15	39.90	48.50	57.15
9	24.70	35.15	43.90	53.50	63.15
10	26.70	38.15	47.90	58.50	69.15
11	28.70	41.15	51.90	63.50	75.15
12	30.70	44.15	55.90	68.50	81.15
13	32.70	47.15	59.90	73.50	87.15
14	34.70	50.15	63.90	78.50	93.15
15	36.70	53.15	67.90	83.50	99.15
16	38.70	56.15	71.90	88.50	105.15
17	40.70	59.15	75.90	93.50	111.15
18	42.70	62.15	79.90	98.50	117.15
19	44.70	65.15	83.90	103.50	123.15
20	46.70	68.15	87.90	108.50	129.15
21	48.70	71.15	91.90	113.50	135.15
22	50.70	74.15	95.90	118.50	141.15
Each additional 1 lb or fraction of 1 lb	2.00	3.00	4.00	5.00	6.00

Classwork/Homework, pages H39–H40

ASSIGNMENT GUIDE

Basic: 1–4

Average: 2–5

Extended: 2–6

Resources
Practice, pp. 39–40   Class/Home, pp. H39–40

Exercise Analysis
1–6   Use a table to solve a problem

FOLLOW-UP ACTIVITIES

PROBLEM SOLVING
Materials: almanacs

Have students work in groups to locate temperature and precipitation tables in the almanacs for cities in the United States. Have them use information from the tables to answer these questions.
1. Which city or cities had the highest temperature in January? in July?
2. Which city or cities had the lowest temperature in January? in July?
3. Which city or cities had the greatest annual precipitation last year? the least?
4. What was the range between the highest and the lowest temperatures in Kansas City last year?

CALCULATOR
List these letter destinations and weights on the chalkboard.
1. within the United States, 8 oz ($1.41)
2. to Europe, 10 oz ($2.17)
3. to Canada, $9\frac{1}{2}$ oz ($1.84)
4. within the United States, $5\frac{3}{4}$ oz ($1.07)
5. to China, $7\frac{4}{5}$ oz ($1.77)
6. to Mexico, $8\frac{1}{3}$ oz ($1.66)

Have students use the postage-rate table on page 96 and their calculators to find each postage rate for the letters. Point out that many calculators have an automatic repeat function built into the = key. Pressing = consecutively repeats the last function performed; for example, 2 + = = = gives 2 + 2 + 2 + 2 = 8. Encourage students with calculators that have the repeat function to use that function as they solve these problems.

COMING UP
Finding solutions in an orderly way

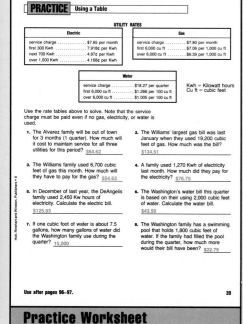

PRACTICE   Using a Table

UTILITY RATES

Electric	
service charge	$7.65 per month
first 300 Kwh	7.918¢ per Kwh
next 700 Kwh	4.87¢ per Kwh
over 1,000 Kwh	4.168¢ per Kwh

Gas	
service charge	$7.80 per month
first 6,000 cu ft	$7.06 per 1,000 cu ft
over 6,000 cu ft	$6.39 per 1,000 cu ft

Water	
service charge	$18.27 per quarter
first 6,000 cu ft	$1.266 per 100 cu ft
over 6,000 cu ft	$1.005 per 100 cu ft

Kwh = Kilowatt hours
Cu ft = cubic feet

Use the rate tables above to solve. Note that the service charge must be paid even if no gas, electricity, or water is used.

1. The Alvarez family will be out of town for 3 months (1 quarter). How much will it cost to maintain service for all three utilities for this period? $64.62

2. The Williams' largest gas bill was last January when they used 19,200 cubic feet of gas. How much was the bill? $134.51

3. The Williams family used 6,700 cubic feet of gas this month. How much will they have to pay for the gas? $54.63

4. A family used 1,270 Kwh of electricity last month. How much did they pay for the electricity? $76.75

5. In December of last year, the DeAngelis family used 2,450 Kwh hours of electricity. Calculate the electric bill. $125.93

6. The Washington's water bill this quarter is based on their using 2,000 cubic feet of water. Calculate the water bill. $43.59

7. If one cubic foot of water is about 7.5 gallons, how many gallons of water did the Washington family use during the quarter? 15,000

8. The Washington family has a swimming pool that holds 1,800 cubic feet of water. If the family had filled the pool during the quarter, how much more would their bill have been? $22.79

Use after pages 96–97.   39

Practice Worksheet

PRACTICE   Using a Table

The table below shows the long-distance rates charged by a phone company for direct-dial calls.

Distance to Called Place (Airline Miles)	Weekday Full Rate 8 AM–5 PM		Evening 35% Discount 5 PM–11 PM		Night 11 PM–8 AM & Weekend 60% Discount	
	initial 1 min	each addl min	initial 1 min	each addl min	initial 1 min	each addl min
1–16 miles	$0.23	$0.15	$0.14	$0.10	$0.09	$0.06
17–30 miles	.33	.21	.21	.14	.13	.09
31–55 miles	.43	.28	.27	.19	.17	.12
56–100 miles	.53	.34	.34	.23	.21	.14
101–172 miles	.62	.40	.40	.26	.24	.16
173–244 miles	.69	.45	.44	.30	.27	.18
245–316 miles	.75	.49	.48	.32	.30	.20

Use the rate table to solve.

1. Linda called Inez at 12 noon on Wednesday. Inez lives 90 miles away. How much did the call cost if Linda and Inez talked for 12 minutes? $4.27

2. How much would Linda have saved if she had made a call of the same length to Inez at 9:30 P.M. on Wednesday? $1.40

3. How much would Linda have saved if she had made a call of the same length to Inez at 11:30 P.M.? $2.52

4. Ben lives in Indianapolis, 294 miles from his aunt. At 8:00 P.M. on Saturday, Ben called his aunt and talked for 17 minutes. How much did the call cost? $3.50

5. The EZ Company does business with a bank 40 miles away. The president of EZ makes a 5-minute call to the bank at 10:00 A.M. on Friday. How much does the call cost? $1.55

6. The EZ Company makes 25 weekly calls to an insurance company, 185 miles away. The calls last an average of 15 minutes each and occur between 9:30 A.M. and 4:30 A.M. on weekdays. How much does the company pay per week for the 25 calls? $174.75

7. If the EZ Company could call the insurance company at 7:30 A.M., how much would it save each week on the 25 phone calls? $105.00

40   Use after pages 96–97.

Practice Worksheet

Warm-Up

Have students perform the following operations mentally, one at a time, in the order
in which they are given.

$15 + 3 \div 3 \times 4 = (18, 6, 24)$
$28 \div 14 \times 10 \div 4 = (2, 20, 5)$
$56 \div 8 + 19 - 11 = (7, 26, 15)$

GETTING STARTED

Write this expression on the board:

$2 + 8 \times 5$

Ask for two volunteers to evaluate it. Have
the second volunteer arrive at a different
value than the first value. The two values
are $(2 + 8) \times 5 = 50$; and $2 + (8 \times 5) = 42$. Tell them that only one of these answers is correct.

Tell students that in this lesson, they will
learn rules for evaluating such expressions. Try to elicit from students why such
rules are essential. (because such expressions must have one meaning, which
everyone can determine)

TEACHING THE LESSON

A. The three examples have been solved
in different orders. You might want to
draw parentheses to show the different
procedures used.

$[(15 + 3) \times 5] - 2 = 88$
$[15 + (3 \times 5)] - 2 = 28$
$(15 + 3) \times (5 - 2) = 54$

Point out when the visual cues of parentheses are not present, a clearly
defined order of operations is needed
before a simple answer (on which
everyone can agree) can be obtained.

B. Within parentheses, the order of operations applies.

Extend the lesson for an example that
has all decimals.

$(2.1 + 3.2 \times 0.5) - 0.2 \times 0.4 + (3.5)^2$
$= (15.87)$

Order of Operations

A. What is $15 + 3 \times 5 - 2$ simplified?

Without rules for simplifying an expression,
$15 + 3 \times 5 - 2$ might yield three different answers.

$15 + 3 \times 5 - 2$	$15 + 3 \times 5 - 2$	$15 + 3 \times 5 - 2$
$18 \times 5 - 2$	$15 + 15 \quad -2$	$18 \times 5 - 2$
$90 - 2$	$30 - 2$	18×3
88?	28?	54?

To avoid this problem, you can use these rules that
specify the order for carrying out the operations.

Rules for the Order of Operations
1. Multiply as indicated by exponents.
2. Multiply and divide from left to right in order.
3. Add and subtract from left to right in order.
4. If parentheses are used, simplify within the
   parentheses first. Use rules 1 through 3.

By following the rules, you can see that
$15 + 3 \times 5 - 2 = 28$.

B. Simplify $3 \cdot 4 + (5^2 + 4 \cdot 2) - 9.82$. · means multiply.

$$3 \cdot 4 + (5^2 + 4 \cdot 2) - 9.82 = 3 \cdot 4 + (25 + 4 \cdot 2) - 9.82$$
$$= 3 \cdot 4 + (25 + 8) - 9.82$$
$$= 3 \cdot 4 + 33 - 9.82$$
$$= 12 + 33 - 9.82$$
$$= 35.18$$

C. Many calculators do not follow the rules for
order of operations. For example, if you use a
calculator to find the value of $6 + 4 \times 3$, you may
get the answer 30, which is not correct.

To get the correct answer, rewrite the expression in
the order that the operations should be performed.

$$6 + 4 \times 3 = 4 \times 3 + 6 = 18$$

COMMON ERRORS

Students often experience great difficulty in remembering the order of the
rules.

Remediation
The order of operations can be ex-
plained by using this equation: $3^3 \times 3 + 3 = 84$. Point out that the operation that has the potential for the
greatest magnitude of change comes
first, exponents; then the next greatest
magnitude of change, multiplication
and division; followed by the smallest
magnitude of change, addition and
subtraction.

Assign Reteach Master, p. 30.

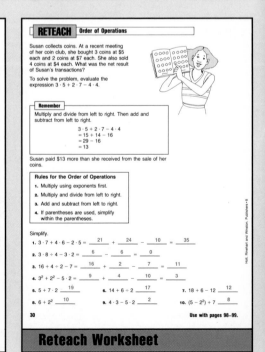

RETEACH   Order of Operations

Susan collects coins. At a recent meeting
of her coin club, she bought 3 coins at $5
each and 2 coins at $7 each. She also sold
4 coins at $4 each. What was the net result
of Susan's transactions?

To solve the problem, evaluate the
expression $3 \cdot 5 + 2 \cdot 7 - 4 \cdot 4$.

Remember

Multiply and divide from left to right. Then add and
subtract from left to right.

$$3 \cdot 5 + 2 \cdot 7 - 4 \cdot 4$$
$$= 15 + 14 - 16$$
$$= 29 - 16$$
$$= 13$$

Susan paid $13 more than she received from the sale of her
coins.

Rules for the Order of Operations
1. Multiply using exponents first.
2. Multiply and divide from left to right.
3. Add and subtract from left to right.
4. If parentheses are used, simplify
   within the parentheses.

Simplify.

1. $3 \cdot 7 + 4 \cdot 6 - 2 \cdot 5$ = __21__ + __24__ − __10__ = __35__

2. $3 \cdot 8 + 4 - 3 \cdot 2$ = __6__ − __6__ = __0__

3. $16 + 4 \div 2 - 7$ = __16__ + __2__ − __7__ = __11__

4. $3^2 + 2^2 - 5 \cdot 2$ = __9__ + __4__ − __10__ = __3__

5. $5 + 7 \cdot 2$ __19__   6. $14 + 6 \div 2$ __17__   7. $18 + 6 - 12$ __12__

8. $6 + 2^2$ __10__   9. $4 \cdot 3 - 5 \cdot 2$ __2__   10. $(5 - 2^2) + 7$ __8__

30   Use with pages 98–99.

Reteach Worksheet

Simplify.

1. $4 + 3 \cdot 2$ 10

2. $9 + 6 \div 3$ 11

3. $14 \div 2 - 2$ 5

4. $11 - 7 + 3$ 7

5. $7 + 5 - 3$ 9

6. $15 \div 3 + 6$ 11

7. $14 + 4 - 18 \div 3$ 12

8. $50 \cdot 4 \div 5 + 6 - 6$ 40

9. $14 + 2 \cdot 5$ 24

10. $8 \cdot 3 - 7$ 17

11. $82 + 2 \cdot 10$ 102

12. $6 \cdot 9 \div 3$ 18

13. $15 \cdot (14 - 2)$ 180

14. $18 - (12 - 3)$ 9

15. $13 - 3^2$ 4

16. $15 + 8^2$ 79

17. $(3 + 6)^2$ 81

18. $(10 - 2)^2$ 64

19. $3 + 6^2$ 39

20. $10 - 2^2$ 6

21. $80 - 8 \cdot (13 - 9)$ 48

22. $19 + (7 + 4)^3$ 1,350

23. $84 - (16 - 8)^2$ 20

24. $18 + 7 \cdot (32 - 6)$ 200

Use parentheses to make each answer true.

25. $9 - (3 + 2) = 4$

26. $(1.8 - 0.8) \cdot 7 = 7$

27. $(4 \cdot 5) - (3 \cdot 5) = 5$

28. $3 + 2 \cdot (6 \div 6) = 5$

29. $(15 \div 5) + 2 = 5$

30. $(10 + 15) \div 5 = 5$

31. $7 \cdot (3 - 3) \div 3 = 0$

32. $(2.9 + 1.1) \cdot 5 = 20$

Write each expression so that a calculator may be used to simplify the expression. Then simplify.

33. $8 + 5 \times 5$
$5 \times 5 + 8 = 33$

34. $18 + 6 \div 2$
$6 \div 2 + 18 = 21$

35. $12 \times (14 - 5)$
$(14 - 5) \times 12 = 108$

36. $7.2 \times (3.4 + 1.2)$
$(3.14 + 1.2) \times 7.2 = 33.12$

37. $18 + 4^2$
$4 \times 4 + 18 = 34$

38. $90 + 2^2 \times 5$
$2 \times 2 \times 5 + 90 = 110$

Write each expression and then simplify it.

39. Add the product of 3 and 2 to 4 squared; then subtract 1.

40. Multiply the difference between 4 squared and 2 squared by 3 squared.

41. What is the value of 2.5 multiplied by 5?

42. Multiply the value of 3 squared minus the product of 2 and 4 by 4.

CHOOSING THE METHOD

Decide which method you would use to compute each exercise: mental math, calculator, or paper and pencil. Explain your answer.

1. $80,000 \div 40$ 12,000

2. $7,452 \div 12$ 621

3. $12\overline{)60,000}$ 5,000

4. $360 \div 0.95$ 378.94736

5. $36\overline{)5,000}$ 138.$\overline{8}$

6. $89.5 \div 0.01$ 8,950

Classwork/Homework, page H41

99

ASSIGNMENT GUIDE

Basic: 1–9, 11–33 o, CTM

Average: 1–6, 8–36 e, CTM

Extended: 2–32 e, 33–36, CTM

Resources
Practice, p. 41   Class/Home, p. H41
Reteach, p. 30   Reasoning, p. H212
Enrich, p. 39

Exercise Analysis
1–24   Use the rules of order of operations to simplify an expression
25–32   Insert parentheses to make the equation true
33–38   Use a calculator to simplify
39–42   Skill applications

Choosing the Method
There is no one way to compute these exercises. Encourage students to find the most efficient methods. Have students explain their decisions.

FOLLOW-UP ACTIVITIES

NUMBER SENSE (Mental Math)
To parallel the exercise in the Warm-Up section, write these exercises on the board, and have students find the answers mentally.

$2 \times 3 + 5 + 7 = (18)$
$40 + 41 \div 9 = (9)$
$3 + 9 \times 7 = (84)$
$18 + 9 \div 3 = (9)$
$18 \times 2 \div 9 = (4)$
$6 + 4 \times 9 \div 3 \times 2 = (60)$

PUZZLES AND GAMES
Have students roll 3 number cubes. Using the 3 numbers and the operations signs $+$ and $\times$, have the students write 10 different expressions such as $3 + 5 \times 2$ and $(5 + 2) \times 3$. Then have the students simplify the expressions that they wrote.

COMING UP
Hunting for x

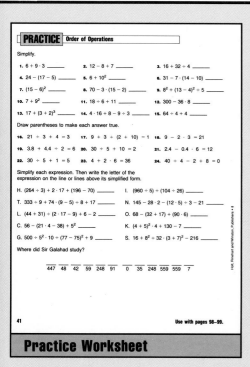

Practice Worksheet

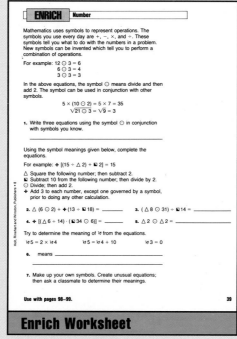

Enrich Worksheet

Warm-Up

Have each student write on a sheet of paper *equal* or *not equal* for each of the following ●'s.
1. $18 + 21$ ● 39 (=)
2. $68 \div 9$ ● 7 (≠)
3. 12×5 ● 60 (=)
4. $99 - 32$ ● 76 (≠)
5. $64 + 8$ ● 72 (=)

GETTING STARTED

Show students the following inequalities.
1. ■ > 7 (8, 9, 10 . . .)
2. ■ < 5 (0, 1, 2, 3, 4)
3. ■ < 2 (0, 1)
4. $5 >$ ■ (0, 1, 2, 3, 4)
5. $7 >$ ■ (0, 1, 2, 3, 4, 5, 6)
6. ■ > 3 (4, 5, 6 . . .)
7. ■ > 11 (12, 13, 14 . . .)
8. $6 >$ ■ (0, 1, 2, 3, 4, 5)

Have them list all the possible whole number answers that can be obtained by using an ellipse where applicable.

TEACHING THE LESSON

A. Describe an equation as a balance that has quantities on both trays. If the trays balance, then the equation is true. If the trays do not balance, the equation is not true. A *variable* is nothing more than a "cloak-and-dagger" number, that is, a number in disguise.

B. In using a replacement set to solve an equation, you *replace* the variable in the equation with the different members of the replacement set in order to determine for which members the equation is true. You may also want to call this *substituting for the variable.*

Equations

A. Solve $x + 3 = 9$.

Equations such as the one above were used by the Egyptians as long ago as 1700 B.C.

$$6 < 9 \qquad 5 + 3 = 8 \qquad 11 + 2 > 7.6 \qquad 13 + 1 \neq 12 \qquad y - 4 = 10$$

All of the above are number sentences because they show the relationship between numbers, but only $5 + 3 = 8$ and $y - 4 = 10$ are **equations.** Equations show **equality.**

The letters in $x + 3 = 9$ and $y - 4 = 10$ are **variables.** They replace numbers. A number sentence that contains a variable is an **algebraic sentence.**

To solve $x + 3 = 9$, substitute members of the replacement set {4,5,6} for the variable. Find the replacement that makes $x + 3 = 9$ a true statement.

Let $x = 4$.

$$x + 3 = 9$$
$$4 + 3 \stackrel{?}{=} 9$$
$$7 \neq 9$$

4 *is not* a solution.

Let $x = 5$.

$$x + 3 = 9$$
$$5 + 3 \stackrel{?}{=} 9$$
$$8 \neq 9$$

5 *is not* a solution.

Let $x = 6$.

$$x + 3 = 9$$
$$6 + 3 \stackrel{?}{=} 9$$
$$9 = 9$$

6 *is* a solution.

Equations of this type have exactly one solution. So, 6 is the solution of $x + 3 = 9$.

B. Use the replacement set {0,1,2,3,4,5,6,7,8,9,10} to solve.

$$n + 3.4 = 8.4$$
$$5 + 3.4 \stackrel{?}{=} 8.4$$
$$8.4 = 8.4$$

5 is the solution.

$$7b = 21$$
7b means 7 · b.
$$7 \cdot 3 \stackrel{?}{=} 21$$
$$21 = 21$$

3 is the solution.

$$\frac{k}{4} = 6$$
$$\frac{24}{4} \stackrel{?}{=} 6$$
$$6 = 6$$

24 *is not* a value in the given replacement set.

So, there is no solution in the replacement set.

100

COMMON ERRORS

When multiplication by a variable is written without the multiplication sign or dot, students may mistakenly add; or they may consider the value of the variable to be trailing digits of a single number whose first digits are those of the numerical factor.

Remediation

Tell students to think of 3x as "3 x's." Tell them that if x is 8, 3x is 3 eights, which is 3 times 8, or 24.

Assign Reteach Master, p. 31.

100

Write *true* if the replacement value is a solution.
Write *false* if it is not.

1. $x + 4 = 9$, if $x = 5$ true

2. $3 + y = 7$, if $y = 3$ false

3. $y - 3 = 5$, if $y = 9$ false

4. $8 - y = 2$, if $y = 6$ true

5. $7x = 21$, if $x = 4$ false

6. $15x = 45$, if $x = 3$ true

7. $y + 7 = 8.5$, if $y = 2.5$ false

8. $\frac{20}{x} = 4$, if $x = 6$ false

9. $\frac{w}{3} = 4$, if $w = 12$ true

10. $3.8 + z = 8$, if $z = 4.2$ true

Use the replacement set $\{0,1,2,3,4,5,6,7,8, \ldots\}$ to find the solution. If there is no solution in the replacement set, write *none*.

11. $x + 5.4 = 9.4$ $x = 4$

12. $x + 1 = 19$ $x = 18$

13. $x + 3.5 = 8.5$ $x = 5$

14. $22 + x = 30$ $x = 8$

15. $x + 0 = 3$ $x = 3$

16. $x - 9 = 12$ $x = 21$

17. $x - 3.5 = 6.5$ $x = 10$

18. $5 - x = 3$ $x = 2$

19. $x - 9 = 9$ $x = 18$

20. $x - 0 = 15$ $x = 15$

21. $4x = 20$ $x = 5$

22. $2x = 16$ $x = 8$

23. $4x = 15$ none

24. $6x = 18$ $x = 3$

25. $3x = 21$ $x = 7$

26. $\frac{x}{6} = 4$ $x = 24$

27. $\frac{x}{2} = 10$ $x = 20$

28. $\frac{12}{x} = 3$ $x = 4$

29. $\frac{x}{5} = 20$ $x = 100$

30. $\frac{x}{4} = 12$ $x = 48$

31. $41 = 9 + x$ $x = 32$

32. $84 + h = 350$ $h = 266$

33. $106 = 125 - z$ $z = 19$

34. $4.8a = 19.2$ $a = 4$

★35. $\frac{118.5}{m} = 39.5$ $m = 3$

★36. $\frac{w}{1.2} = 12$ none

★37. $\frac{1,000}{n} = 100$ $n = 10$

Solve.

38. Does the replacement set $\{2,3,4\}$ include the solution to $3 \cdot 4(x + 2^2) \div 6 = 0$?   no

39. If xx was written instead of x^2, what would the solution to $xx = 64$ be? $x = 8$ (also $^-8$)

ANOTHER LOOK

Subtract.

1. $7 - 2.65$
4.35

2. $12 - 6.312$
5.688

3. $96 - 18.769$
77.231

4. $13.21 - 9$
4.21

5. $46.098 - 7$
39.098

6. $22.36 - 20.84$
1.52

Classwork/Homework, page H42

ASSIGNMENT GUIDE

Basic: 1–10, 11–33 o, AL

Average: 1–10, 12–34 e, 38–39, AL

Extended: 5–10, 12–34 e, 35–39, AL

Resources
Practice, p. 42   Class/Home, p. H42
Reteach, p. 31
Enrich, p. 40

Exercise Analysis
1–10   Decide if the replacement value is a solution to the equation
11–37   Use a replacement set to solve equations
38–39   Skill applications

Another Look
These exercises provide a review of subtracting decimals.

FOLLOW-UP ACTIVITIES

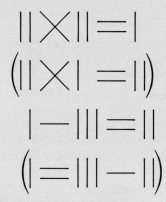

MANIPULATIVES
Materials: match sticks

By changing the position of only one match, how can the following equations be made true?

PROBLEM SOLVING
From the replacement set (8,3,5), find which number in each blank makes a true statement.

$6 - (5) + 7 \times (8) + (3) = 60$

Continue by using similar equations.

COMING UP
Pick and choose.

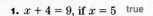

PRACTICE Equations

Write T for true if the replacement value is a solution. Write F for false if it is not.

1. $a + 8 = 9$, if $a = 2$ F

2. $3 \times b = 18$, if $b = 6$ T

3. $\frac{15}{b} = 3.25$, if $b = 4$ F

4. $c - 8 = 3$, if $c = 12$ F

5. $5.6 + c = 7$, if $c = 1.4$ T

6. $\frac{a}{6} = 1$, if $a = 6$ T

7. $3d = 24$, if $d = 9$ F

8. $9 + d = 12$, if $d = 4$ F

9. $7.2 - a = 5.2$, if $a = 2$ T

10. $a - 7 = 3$, if $a = 10$ T

11. $\frac{c}{6} = 2$, if $c = 12$ F

12. $3c = 15$, if $c = 5$ T

Write the solution. Use the replacement set $\{0, 1, 2, \ldots\}$.

13. $x + 3.6 = 7.6$ $x = $ 4

14. $36 = m - 27$ $m = $ 63

15. $g + 49 = 51$ $g = $ 2

16. $105 = z + 47$ $z = $ 58

17. $7 + e = 18$ $e = $ 11

18. $\frac{99}{a} = 3$ $a = $ 33

19. $96 - x = 18$ $x = $ 78

20. $19d = 171$ $d = $ 9

21. $14 - v = 14$ $v = $ 0

22. $\frac{f}{6} = 6$ $f = $ 36

23. $39 = 13a$ $a = $ 3

24. $10.6f = 53$ $f = $ 5

25. $103 = 71 + b$ $b = $ 32

26. $s - 106 = 34$ $s = $ 140

27. $446 = 307 + n$ $n = $ 139

28. $4.4 = \frac{17.6}{x}$ $x = $ 4

29. $\frac{308}{b} = 77$ $b = $ 4

30. $95 + z = 107$ $z = $ 12

31. $27a = 324$ $a = $ 12

32. $136 = r + 27$ $r = $ 109

33. $11 = \frac{121}{r}$ $r = $ 11

34. $c + 26 = 95$ $c = $ 69

35. $147 = 49w$ $w = $ 3

36. $c - 3 = 115$ $c = $ 118

42   Use with pages 100–101.

Practice Worksheet

ENRICH Algebra

1. The time it takes for an object to travel a given distance can be calculated if the speed is known. To find out how long it takes for a car traveling 30 miles per hour to go 60 miles, solve this equation.

$\frac{30 \text{ miles}}{1 \text{ hour}} = \frac{60 \text{ miles}}{x \text{ hours}}$

$x = 2$

2. The speed of light is 186,000 miles per second. Find the speed of light in miles per hour.
$130,000 \times 3,600 = 669,600,000$ miles per hour

3. A rocket ship and its observation satellite travel together at a speed of 130,000 miles per second. The distance between the ship and the satellite is 930,000 miles. A beam of light is reflected from the satellite to a mirror on the ship. Light travels at a speed of 186,000 miles per second. How long does it take for the light to travel from the satellite to the ship and return?   10 seconds

4. From a point on Earth, the satellite appears to be traveling above the ship. An observer watching the ship and the satellite from Earth sees the path of the light beam as shown in the diagram. The total distance of the path that the observer sees is 2,600,000 miles. The speed of the light remains 186,000 miles per second. Calculate how long it takes the light to make its trip between the ship and the satellite, as seen from Earth.   14 seconds

Think about the calculations you made in Problems 2 and 3. How can two different travel times be recorded for the same light beam traveling a fixed distance? The main reason for this phenomenon is that the speed of light does not change, even if the light source itself is moving very fast.

5. What is the speed of the light coming from the lights on a spaceship that moves at 130,000 miles per second?
186,000 miles per second

40   Use with pages 100–101.

Enrich Worksheet

Objective: To choose the correct operation to solve a problem

Warm-Up
Have students compute the answer.

33 × 7 (231)	625 ÷ 25 (25)
71 × 12 (852)	684 ÷ 19 (36)

GETTING STARTED

Materials: 20 books

Display the books and tell students you want to put them in 4 equal stacks. Have students discuss how you might find how many books should be placed in each stack. (Write the division sentence 20 ÷ 4.) Now tell students you want to make 5 stacks of books. Elicit from students that you can divide 20 by 5 to find how many books there will be in each stack. Point out that students can use division to find how many stacks there are or how many books there are in each stack.

TEACHING THE LESSON

Deciding whether to use multiplication or division can often be confusing for students. Have students use a checklist to help them choose the appropriate operation.
● If I know (given numbers)
● And I want to find (number of sets/number in each set)
● Then I can (divide)

Review the two meanings of division: finding the number of sets and finding the number in each set.

Questions: Tell students that the question should give clues for the operation needed to answer it. "How many are there in each?" almost always points to division. A question that asks anything concerning the total rarely involves division.

Tools: Students should make a checklist similar to the one above and in their text. The most telling clue students will have in choosing division over multiplication is that the total number will be given and must be separated into groups of the same size. If the total number is not given but must be found by joining groups of the same size, multiplication should be used.

Solutions: If students have difficulty computing with the chosen operation, have them refer to the appropriate lesson in the text.

Checks: Have students go back to the checklist and substitute the answer for the number they wanted to find to see whether their answer seems reasonable. Checking by using the reverse operation *should not* be encouraged, as students might have used the wrong operation initially.

QUESTIONS	TOOLS	SOLUTIONS	CHECKS

PROBLEM SOLVING
Choosing the Operation

When you are trying to decide how to solve a problem, you can look at the wording and at the question that is asked for hints. You can use these hints to choose the best operation to use to solve the problem.

> Pythagoras was a famous Greek mathematician who taught his classes while walking through the countryside. One year, he had 187 students. He grouped them into 11 classes. Each class had the same number of students in it. How many students were there in each class?

Hints:

If you know	and you want to find	you can
● the number in each set is the same ● the number in each set ● the total number	the number of sets	divide.
● the number in each set is the same ● the total number ● the number of sets	the number in each set	divide.

Once you have chosen the best operation, you can solve the problem.

$$\underset{187}{\text{the total number}} \quad \div \quad \underset{11}{\text{the number of sets}} \quad = \quad \underset{17}{\overset{\text{the number}}{\text{in each set}}}$$

There were 17 students in each class.

Write the letter of the operation you would use to solve each problem.

1. A mechanical device invented in the nineteenth century could draw 3 pictures per hour. It was called the Green Lady. How many pictures could the Green Lady draw in 5 hours?

a. addition   **b.** subtraction
Ⓒ **multiplication** **d.** division

2. A computer called the Imagix can draw 17 pictures per minute. How long would it take the Imagix to draw 289 pictures?

a. addition   **b.** subtraction
c. multiplication Ⓓ **division**

Solve.

3. Jerzy has a colossal abacus that has 52 columns. Each column is 2.5 inches wide. How wide are all the columns together? 130 in.

4. One abacus has 30 columns of 5 beads each. A second abacus has 15 columns of 6 beads each. How many more beads does the first abacus have than the second? 60 beads

5. In 1642, Blaise Pascal built the first mechanical counting machine. The first machine that could do all four mathematical operations was built 178 years later. In which year was the second machine built? 1820

6. Charles Babbage invented an early computer called the Analytical Engine. The machine had 50 counter wheels that could store 1,000 figures each. How many figures could the entire machine store? 50,000 figures

7. The first United States census to be tallied by computer took place in 1890. The idea for the computer was based on the Jacquard fabric loom, which was invented 83 years before the 1890 census. When was the Jacquard loom invented? 1807

★8. Barbara Schwartz is word processing a 196-page report on the history of computers. She is storing the report on disks that hold about 90 pages. How many disks will she need? 3 disks

★9. The Mark I could perform 50 operations per second. ENIAC could perform 50,000 operations in 10 seconds. How many times faster was ENIAC than the Mark I? 100 times faster

★10. When ENIAC was built, it was estimated that it would take 100 engineers 1 year to do a calculation that ENIAC could perform in 2 hours. How many years would it have taken 10 engineers to do a problem that took ENIAC 1 hour? 5 years

Classwork/Homework, page H43

Exercise Analysis
1–2 Choose the correct operation
3–10 Solve

FOLLOW-UP ACTIVITIES

CALCULATOR
Materials: calculator per student or group

Write the following series of numbers on the chalkboard or provide them as a hand-out. Have students work from left to right with their calculators to find the operations needed to complete each number sentence.

- 364 ■ 21 ■ 17 ■ 3,206 ■ 7 = 477 (+, ×, −, ÷)
- 54 ■ 27 ■ 310 ■ 56 ■ 2 ■ 7,000 = 1,736 (÷, +, ×, ÷, −)
- 3,190 ■ 10 ■ 10 ■ 10 ■ 10 = 3,280 (−, ÷, +, ×)
- 62 ■ 15 ■ 30 ■ 90 ■ 476 ■ 20 = 9,720 (×, −, ÷, +, ×)
- 3,690 ■ 421 ■ 6 ■ 25 ■ 28 ■ 71 = 7,313 (−, +, ÷, −, ×)

PROBLEM SOLVING
Divide the class into six groups. Assign each group a given that is listed in the *If You Know* column on page 102. Have the group use the assigned given to write a problem about the number of students in the class. Then have groups exchange problems and solve.

COMING UP
'Tis the occasion for an equation

PRACTICE Choosing the Operation

Choose the operation you would use to solve each problem.

1. The tallest tree in the world is the Howard Libby redwood tree, 366 feet tall. The tallest spruce is a 126-foot blue spruce in Colorado. How many times taller is the redwood than the spruce?
a. add **b.** subtract **c.** multiply Ⓓ divide

2. White pine trees average 100 feet in height. Scotch pine trees average 30 feet less in height. About how tall are most scotch pines?
a. add Ⓑ subtract **c.** multiply **d.** divide

Solve.

3. The diameter of a mature chestnut oak is about 2.5 feet. The diameter of a mature sequoia is about 20 feet. About how many times greater is the diameter of the sequoia than the oak? about 8

4. The General Sherman sequoia tree is 272 feet high. Its lowest branch is 130 feet high. How many feet of the tree contain branches? 142 feet

5. The fastest-growing tree is a type of silk tree which has grown as fast as 2.7 feet in one month. How tall might a tree like this grow in ½ a year? 16.2 feet

6. The wood of a black ironwood tree weighs up to 93 pounds per cubic foot. The wood of the lightest balsa wood tree is 37.2 times lighter. What is the balsa wood's weight per cubic foot? 2.5 pounds

7. The northernmost tree, a Sitka spruce, took 98 years to grow 28 cm. About how many years did it take to grow one cm? 3.5 years

8. The tallest recorded apple tree was 70 feet high. The tallest known shellbark hickory tree was 1.5 times taller. How tall was the hickory? 105 feet

Use after pages 102–103. 43

Practice Worksheet

ENRICH Problem Solving

You are a mathematician who works with historical data. For each problem below, solve by choosing the correct operation or operations.

1. In 490 B.C., Persia invaded Greece with 29,877 soldiers. Athens had 9,959 soldiers. How many Persian soldiers were there to each Greek soldier? 3 soldiers

2. Rome was invaded by Goths in A.D. 410, by Vandals 45 years later and by Ostrogoths 21 years after that. When did the Ostrogoths invade Rome? A.D. 476

3. The area of present-day Austria is 32,374 square miles. The area of present-day Hungary is 35,918 square miles. The two countries were once one country covering 11,909 square miles less than four times the combined area of the two present-day countries. How large was the Austrio-Hungarian Empire? 261,259 square miles

4. Belgium was part of Holland for 15 years after Napolean's defeat. Napolean died in 1821, six years after his defeat. What year did Belgium become independent? 1830

5. Only 23 British prisoners survived from overnight imprisonment in the "Black Hole of Calcutta." Eight more than six times as many soldiers were thrown in the prison. How many died? 123 soldiers

6. The first volume of Shakespeare's plays was published seven years after his death. He was born in 1564 and died at age 52. When was the volume published? 1623

7. In the "Great" London Fire of 1666, 89 churches and 148 times as many houses burned. How many buildings were destroyed? 13,261 buildings

8. Columbus sailed with a crew of 52 on the ship *Santa Maria*. The two other ships, the *Nina* and the *Pinta*, each carried 8 fewer than ½ the crew of the *Santa Maria*. How many people did the 3 ships carry? 89 people

Use with pages 102–103. 41

Enrich Worksheet

Objective: To solve one-step algebraic equations with addition and subtraction

Warm-Up

Have students write *true* or *false* to describe each of the following statements.

$11 - y = 22$, if $y = 8$ (false)

$\frac{20}{z} = 5$, if $z = 4$ (true)

$13 + x = 28$, if $x = 25$ (false)

$4b = 48$, if $b = 12$ (true)

GETTING STARTED

Have students find the missing number in each equation.

$18 - \blacksquare = 2$ (16) $24 + \blacksquare = 35$ (11)

$9.6 - \blacksquare = 8.8$ (0.8) $77 + \blacksquare = 94$ (17)

$19 + \blacksquare = 53$ (34) $51 - \blacksquare = 35$ (16)

Ask students how they went about solving these equations. Show how they can subtract to find a missing term.

TEACHING THE LESSON

A. Give more examples to emphasize the fact that an equation remains true when the same number is added to or subtracted from both sides; for example:

$17.9 + 4 = 21.9$

$17.9 + 4 - 17.9 = 21.9 - 17.9$

$4 = 4$

B. If an equation has several numbers in addition to a variable, the numbers should be combined before performing any operations on both sides of the equation; for example:

$y + 18 - 3.6 - 1.2 + 3 = 44.1$

$y + (18 - 3.6 - 1.2 + 3) = 44.1$

$y + 16.2 = 44.1$

$y + 16.2 - 16.2 = 44.1 - 16.2$

$y = 27.9$

You may wish to allow students to use calculators while working through this lesson.

Checkpoint

The chart lists the common errors students make in solving one-step algebraic equations with addition and subtraction.

Correct Answers: 1c, 2b, 3c

Remediation

■ For these errors, set up a scale balance to show equations. Have students add and subtract weight from only *one* side of the balance and then from both sides. You can use a paper bag to disguise unknown weights.

☐ For these errors, guide the students in completing Reteach Master, p. 32.

Solving Equations (+ and −)

A. It is believed that the earliest methods of solving equations involved testing replacements. Later, however, Arab mathematicians began to use methods that were more convenient than the trial-and-error method.

Because addition and subtraction are inverse operations, one can be used to undo the other.

If you add or subtract the same number on both sides of an equation, the resulting equation has the same solution.

To find the solution of $x + 18 = 54$, subtract 18 from both sides of the equation.

$$x + 18 = 54$$
$$x + 18 - 18 = 54 - 18$$
$$x = 36$$

To check, let $x = 36$.

$$36 + 18 \overset{?}{=} 54$$
$$54 = 54 \; \checkmark$$

So, $x = 36$.

B. To find the solution of $y - 1.5 = 3.5$, add 1.5 to both sides of the equation.

$$y - 1.5 = 3.5$$
$$y - 1.5 + 1.5 = 3.5 + 1.5$$
$$y = 5$$

To check, let $y = 5$.

$$5 - 1.5 \overset{?}{=} 3.5$$
$$3.5 = 3.5 \; \checkmark$$

The solution is 5.

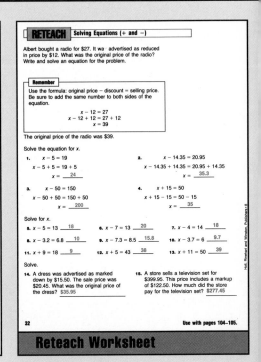

Checkpoint Write the letter of the correct answer.

1. The next step in the solution of $y - 3 = 5$ is ■.

a. $y - 3 + 5 = 5$ **b.** $y - 3 = 5 + 3$ **(c.)** $y - 3 + 3 = 5 + 3$

2. The next step in the solution of $x + 3 = 10$ is ■.

a. $x + 3 - 3 = 10 - 10$ **(b.)** $x + 3 - 3 = 10 - 3$ **c.** $x + 3 - 10 = 10 - 3$

3. The solution of $500 + x = 750$ is ■.

a. $x = 1{,}250$ **b.** $x = 750$ **(c.)** $x = 250$

104

COMMON ERRORS

Answer Choice	Type of Error
☐ 1a	Adds the incorrect number to both sides
☐ 1b	Adds the number only to the right side
■ 2a, 2c	Subtracts a different number from each side
☐ 3a	Adds the number from one side and subtracts it from the other
☐ 3b	Subtracts the number only on the left side

Solve each equation.

1. $x - 12 = 68$
   $x = 80$
2. $b - 27 = 41$
   $b = 68$
3. $c - 2.4 = 6.7$
   $c = 9.1$
4. $y - 15 = 32$
   $y = 47$
5. $w + 805 = 904$
   $w = 99$
6. $r - 9 = 5$
   $r = 14$
7. $x - 6 = 34$
   $x = 40$
8. $t - 14.4 = 16.9$
   $t = 31.3$
9. $9 + y = 84$
   $y = 75$
10. $m + 112 = 146$
    $m = 34$
11. $t - 92 = 109$
    $t = 201$
12. $t + 81.6 = 110.5$
    $t = 28.9$
13. $c - 81 = 53$
    $c = 134$
14. $c + 57.9 = 84.2$
    $c = 26.3$
15. $d - 2.3 = 1.7$
    $d = 4$
16. $x - 5.5 = 7$
    $x = 12.5$
17. $s + 4.6 = 9.7$
    $s = 5.1$
18. $t + 23.4 = 42.3$
    $t = 18.9$
19. $y - 7 = 15$
    $y = 22$
20. $d + 12.8 = 19.7$
    $d = 6.9$
21. $r + 12 = 78$
    $r = 66$
22. $y - 11.2 = 74$
    $y = 85.2$
23. $15 + s = 84$
    $s = 69$
24. $t - 19 = 143$
    $t = 162$
25. $y + 9.5 = 20$
    $y = 10.5$
26. $a + 7.3 = 15.2$
    $a = 7.9$
27. $x + 1.6 = 5.8$
    $x = 4.2$
28. $n + 3.7 = 10.3$
    $n = 6.6$
29. $t - 32.9 = 73.8$
    $t = 106.7$
★30. $c + (6.2 + 3.9) = 25.5$
    $c = 15.4$
★31. $n + 3.7 + 6.9 = 15$
    $n = 4.4$
★32. $m - 2.4 - 3 = 10$
    $m = 15.4$
★33. $(9.5 + 0.8) + m = 15.7$
    $m = 5.4$

FOCUS: REASONING

The geometry that you are familiar with was developed by Euclid 2,000 years ago. In the 1830's, three European mathematicians—the German, Karl Gauss; the Russian, Nikolai Lobachevsky; and the Hungarian, Janos Bolyai—all published works challenging Euclidean geometry.

Many of Europe's top students traveled to study with at least one of these three mathematicians. Of a sample group of 30, 12 studied with Gauss and 9 with Lobachevsky. Of Gauss's students, $\frac{1}{3}$ also studied with Lobachevsky, and another $\frac{1}{3}$ also studied with Bolyai. Of Lobachevsky's students, $\frac{2}{3}$ also studied with Bolyai. 3 students studied with all of them, and 4 students studied with none of them. Use the Venn diagram at the right to find how many studied with Bolyai.
16 students

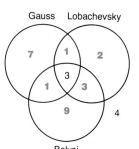

Gauss   Lobachevsky

Bolyai

Classwork/Homework, page H44

More Practice, page H197

105

ASSIGNMENT GUIDE

Basic: 1–21

Average: 1–9, 11–31 o

Extended: 13–33, F

Resources
Practice, p. 44   Class/Home, p. H44
Reteach, p. 32   More Practice, p. H197
Enrich, p. 42

Exercise Analysis

1–29   Solve one-step addition and subtraction equations
30–33   Solve two-step addition and subtraction equations

Focus: REASONING

This problem requires students to use a Venn Diagram to analyze a series of factual statements.

FOLLOW-UP ACTIVITIES

MANIPULATIVES

Materials: balance; 5- and 10-g weights

To illustrate the concept of balancing equations, place an "unknown" mass (10 grams) on the left side of a balance along with a known mass (5 grams). You can use a paper bag for the "unknown" mass. On the right side, place three 5-gram masses. Have a student write the equation for this problem. ($x + 5 = 15$) Then have a student subtract 5 grams from each side of the balance. The unknown mass must then equal the mass on the right side of the scale (10 grams). Continue by using similar examples.

PUZZLES AND GAMES

Have students write and solve equations to complete this magic square.

16	x	y	13
a	11	10	z
9	7	b	c
4	14	15	1

($x = 2$, $y = 3$, $a = 5$, $z = 8$, $b = 6$, $c = 12$)

COMING UP

Multiple madness!

Objective: To solve one-step algebraic equations with multiplication and division

Warm-Up

Have students solve the following equations.

$54 + y = 77$ $(y = 77 - 54 = 23)$
$z - 6.6 = 3.08$ $(z = 3.08 + 6.6 = 9.68)$
$c + 14 + 15 = 29$ $(c = 29 - 14 - 15 = 0)$
$b + 45 = 54.8$ $(b = 54.8 - 45 = 9.8)$

GETTING STARTED

Have students find the missing number in each of the following equations.

$110 ÷ ■ = 10$ (11); $18 ÷ ■ = 10$ (1.8);
$1.5 × ■ = 4.5$ (3); $42 ÷ ■ = 6$ (7);
$2.5 × ■ = 27.5$ (11); $13 × ■ = 44.2$ (3.4)

Discuss how students found their answers.

TEACHING THE LESSON

A. Ask students to explain what each of the following symbols means.

$3s$ (3 times s, or $3 \cdot s$)
$16a$ (16 times a, or $16 \cdot a$)

Reinforce the nature of an equation: Since something *equals* something else, both sides of the equation are equal. When you multiply or divide both sides of an equation by a single number, you are performing the operation on the same number so that the equality will be preserved.

B. Explain that to find the value of a variable, you must *isolate* it, or place it alone, on one side of the equal sign. Extend the lesson by using an equation that has decimals.

$$\frac{m}{1.2} = 3.5$$
$$\frac{m}{1.2} \cdot 1.2 = 3.5 \cdot 1.2$$
$$m = 4.2$$

Remind students to use substitution to check their answers. You may wish to allow students to use calculators while working through this lesson.

Checkpoint

The chart lists the common errors students make in solving one-step algebraic equations with multiplication and division.

Correct Answers: 1b, 2d

Remediation

■ For these errors, have students circle the number next to the variable (or write a 1) as a reminder to divide by the same number.

☐ For these errors, guide students in completing Reteach Master, p. 33.

Solving Equations (× and ÷)

A. Since the multiplication symbol × can become confused with the variable x, either · or no symbol at all is used in equations to mean multiplication.

12 times r can be written $12 \cdot r$ or $12r$.

Since multiplication and division are inverse operations, one can be used to undo the other. If you multiply or divide both sides of an equation by the same number (except 0) the resulting equation has the same solution.

To solve $12r = 132$, divide both sides of the equation by 12.

$$12r = 132 \qquad \text{To check, let } r = 11.$$
$$\frac{12r}{12} = \frac{132}{12} \qquad 12 \cdot 11 \overset{?}{=} 132$$
$$r = 11 \qquad\qquad 132 = 132 ✔$$

So, $r = 11$.

B. To solve $\frac{y}{9} = 43$, multiply both sides by 9.

$$\frac{y}{9} = 43 \qquad \text{To check, let } y = 387.$$
$$9 \cdot \frac{y}{9} = 9 \cdot 43 \qquad \frac{387}{9} \overset{?}{=} 43$$
$$y = 387 \qquad\qquad 43 = 43 ✔$$

The solution is 387.

Checkpoint Write the letter of the correct answer.

1. If $12y = 36$, then $y = ■$.

a. $\frac{1}{3}$ **b.** 3   c. 24   d. 432

2. If $\frac{x}{4} = 32$, then $x = ■$.

a. $\frac{1}{8}$ b. 28   c. 8   **d.** 128

106

Math Reasoning, page H212

COMMON ERRORS

Answer Choice	Type of Error
☐ 1a	Divides incorrectly
☐ 1c	Subtracts instead of divides
■ 1d	Multiplies instead of divides
☐ 2a, 2c	Divides instead of multiplies
☐ 2b	Subtracts instead of multiplies

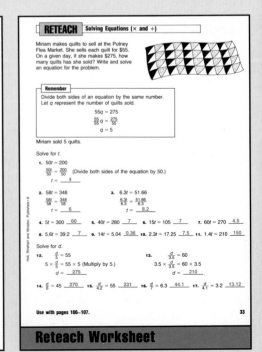

Miriam makes quilts to sell at the Putney Flea Market. She sells each quilt for \$55. On a given day, if she makes \$275, how many quilts has she sold? Write and solve an equation for the problem.

Remember
Divide both sides of an equation by the same number.
Let q represent the number of quilts sold.

$$55q = 275$$
$$\frac{55}{55}q = \frac{275}{55}$$
$$q = 5$$

Miriam sold 5 quilts.

Solve for t.

1. $50t = 200$
$\frac{50t}{50} = \frac{200}{50}$ (Divide both sides of the equation by 50.)
$t = \underline{\ 4\ }$

2. $58t = 348$
$\frac{58t}{58} = \frac{348}{58}$
$t = \underline{\ 6\ }$

3. $6.3t = 51.66$
$\frac{6.3t}{6.3} = \frac{51.66}{6.3}$
$t = \underline{\ 8.2\ }$

4. $5t = 300$ __60__   **5.** $40t = 280$ __7__   **6.** $15t = 105$ __7__   **7.** $60t = 270$ __4.5__

8. $5.6t = 39.2$ __7__   **9.** $14t = 5.04$ __0.36__   **10.** $2.3t = 17.25$ __7.5__   **11.** $1.4t = 210$ __150__

Solve for d.

12. $\frac{d}{5} = 55$
$\frac{d}{5} \times 5 = 55 \times 5$ (Multiply by 5.)
$d = \underline{\ 275\ }$

13. $\frac{d}{3.5} = 60$
$3.5 \times \frac{d}{3.5} = 60 \times 3.5$
$d = \underline{\ 210\ }$

14. $\frac{d}{6} = 45$ __270__   **15.** $\frac{d}{4.2} = 55$ __231__   **16.** $\frac{d}{7} = 6.3$ __44.1__   **17.** $\frac{d}{4.1} = 3.2$ __13.12__

Use with pages 106–107.

33

Reteach Worksheet

Solve.

1. $8k = 64$ $k = 8$

2. $5m = 90$ $m = 18$

3. $2.5c = 10$ $c = 4$

4. $8t = 296$ $t = 37$

5. $1.4z = 4.2$ $z = 3$

6. $0.3k = 42.3$ $k = 141$

7. $12m = 156$ $m = 13$

8. $6m = 774$ $m = 129$

9. $15j = 285$ $j = 19$

10. $4x = 196$ $x = 49$

11. $4.5p = 288$ $p = 64$

12. $4.3t = 8.6$ $t = 2$

13. $0.4c = 0.36$ $c = 0.9$

14. $4m = 232$ $m = 58$

15. $3.6y = 10.8$ $y = 3$

16. $5g = 175$ $g = 35$

17. $\frac{a}{6} = 18$ $a = 108$

18. $\frac{y}{27} = 5$ $y = 135$

19. $\frac{y}{1.5} = 15$ $y = 22.5$

20. $\frac{w}{25} = 7$ $w = 175$

21. $\frac{p}{2} = 13$ $p = 26$

22. $\frac{s}{0.8} = 3.4$ $s = 2.72$

23. $\frac{c}{80} = 7$ $c = 560$

24. $\frac{c}{16} = 20$ $c = 320$

25. $\frac{n}{0.5} = 12$ $n = 6$

26. $\frac{n}{11} = 10$ $n = 110$

27. $\frac{x}{3.3} = 30$ $x = 99$

28. $\frac{b}{0.3} = 30$ $b = 9$

29. $\frac{t}{4} = 2.1$ $t = 8.4$

30. $\frac{c}{20} = 0.5$ $c = 10$

31. $\frac{m}{18} = 7$ $m = 126$

32. $\frac{y}{2} = 256$ $y = 512$

★33. $\frac{y}{7} = 56 - 49$ $y = 49$

CHALLENGE

1. Harvey has a son whose age, raised to the fourth power, is the same as the son's age times 27. How old is Harvey's son? **3 years old**

2. Harvey also has two daughters. Sarah is four times as old as Andrea. Sarah's age raised to the third power is equal to Andrea's age raised to the ninth power. How old are Harvey's daughters?
Sarah is 8, and Andrea is 2.

3. Harvey's mother's birthday is next week. Her present age can be expressed as $a^b \cdot b^a$, where a and b are both single-digit prime factors. How old will Harvey's mother be on her upcoming birthday? **73**

4. Harvey is 5 years older than his wife. The second digit in his wife's age is 2 more than the first digit in her age and 1 more than the first digit in Harvey's age. The sum of the digits in her age is twice the sum of the digits in Harvey's age. How old are Harvey and his wife?
Harvey is 40, and his wife is 35.

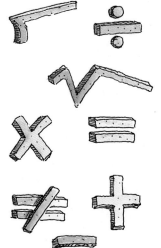

Classwork/Homework, page H45

More Practice, page H197 **107**

Exercise Analysis

1–15   Solve one-step multiplication equations

16–32   Solve one-step division equations

33   Solve two-step equations

Challenge

These problems encourage students to write the correct algebraic expression before solving.

FOLLOW-UP ACTIVITIES

MATH COMMUNICATION

Have students write the algebraic equation for the following statements.

1. Three times a number equals thirty-three. ($3n = 33$)

2. A number divided by five is fifteen. ($\frac{n}{5} = 15$)

3. Forty-eight is equal to six times a number. ($48 = 6n$)

4. Five and five-tenths is equal to a number divided by eight. ($5.5 = \frac{n}{8}$)

*5. Six more than two times a number equals twelve. ($2n + 6 = 12$)

*6. Seven less than four times a number is equal to eight and three-hundredths. ($4n - 7 = 8.03$)

PROBLEM SOLVING

Farmer Brown has 5 times as many sheep as his neighbor, Farmer Ned. Ned, however, has 8 more chickens than his neighbor, Farmer Brown. If Farmer Brown has 25 sheep and 9 chickens, how many chickens and sheep does Farmer Ned own? (Two separate equations must be formed.

$5n = 25$ (sheep) $x - 8 = 9$ (chickens)

$\frac{5n}{5} = \frac{25}{5}$ $x - 8 + 8 = 9 + 8$

$n = 5$ $x = 17$

Farmer Ned has 5 sheep and 17 chickens.)

COMING UP

Learning to do the two-step, without music

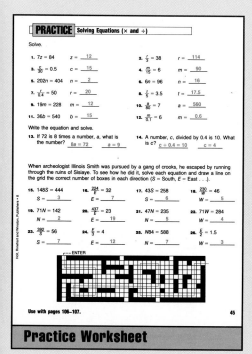

Practice Worksheet

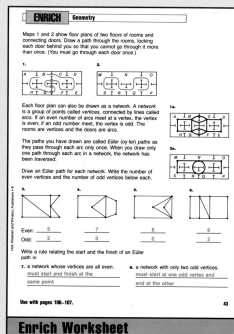

Enrich Worksheet

Objective: To solve two-step algebraic equations

Warm-Up
Have students solve the following equations.

$1.7s = 6.12$ $(s = 3.6)$; $\frac{z}{9} = 81$ $(z = 729)$;

$24x = 1,008$ $(x = 42)$; $\frac{y}{0.8} = 5$ $(y = 4)$

GETTING STARTED

Tell students that you are going to isolate the 3 in this equation by performing several operations on both sides of the equation.

$$(5 \times 3) + 2 = 17$$
$$(5 \times 3) + 2 - 2 = 17 - 2$$
$$5 \times 3 = 15$$
$$5 \times \frac{3}{5} = \frac{15}{5}$$
$$3 = 3$$

Have students work through similar examples.

TEACHING THE LESSON

A. It is usually easier to undo addition and subtraction before performing multiplication and division in two-step equations.

If $3x + 4.6 = 19.6$, then $\frac{3x}{3} + 4.6 \neq \frac{19.6}{3}$.

Point out that this doesn't work because both sides of the equation were not divided by 3: Only part of the left side was divided by 3. If you divide both sides by 3, you get $\frac{(3x + 4.6)}{3} = \frac{19.6}{3}$, but this does not help simplify the expression.

B. Again, point out that if $\frac{r}{5} - 9 = 11$, then $5 \cdot \frac{r}{5} - 9 \neq 11 \cdot 5$ because not all parts of the left side were multiplied by 5.

But $5 \cdot (\frac{r}{5} - 9) = 11 \cdot 5$
$(5 \cdot \frac{r}{5}) - 5 \cdot 9 = 55$
$r - 45 = 55$
$r - 45 + 45 = 55 + 45$
$r = 100$

Checkpoint
The chart lists the common errors students make in solving two-step equations.

Correct Answers: 1a, 2d

Remediation
- ■ For these errors, have students circle the operation they are going to undo in each step as a reminder to perform the correct procedure.
- □ For these errors, guide students in completing Reteach Master, p. 34.

108

Solving Two-Step Equations

A. Solving equations is part of *algebra,* a word that comes from two Arab words that mean "opposition" and "restoration." Opposite operations undo equal terms on one side of an equation and restore them on the other side.

To solve $3x + 4.6 = 19.6$, first subtract 4.6 from both sides of the equation; next divide both sides by 3.

$$3x + 4.6 = 19.6$$
$$3x + 4.6 - 4.6 = 19.6 - 4.6$$
$$3x = 15$$
$$\frac{3x}{3} = \frac{15}{3}$$
$$x = 5.$$

To check, let $x = 5$.
$$3 \cdot 5 + 4.6 \stackrel{?}{=} 19.6$$
$$15 + 4.6 \stackrel{?}{=} 19.6$$
$$19.6 = 19.6 \ ✔$$

B. To solve $\frac{r}{5} - 9 = 11$, first add 9 to both sides of the equation; next multiply both sides by 5.

$$\frac{r}{5} - 9 = 11$$
$$\frac{r}{5} - 9 + 9 = 11 + 9$$
$$\frac{r}{5} = 20$$
$$\frac{r}{5} \cdot 5 = 20 \cdot 5$$
$$r = 100$$

To check, let $r = 100$.
$$\frac{100}{5} - 9 \stackrel{?}{=} 11$$
$$20 - 9 \stackrel{?}{=} 11$$
$$11 = 11 \ ✔$$

Checkpoint Write the letter of the correct answer.

1. The solution of $2x + 8 = 20$ is $x = $ ■.
  (a.) 6 **b.** 2 **c.** 24 **d.** 56

2. The solution of $\frac{t}{2} - 14 = 14$ is $t = $ ■.
  a. 0 **b.** 42 **c.** 14 **(d.)** 56

108

COMMON ERRORS

Answer Choice	Type of Error
□ 1b	Divides before subtracting, divides the left side incorrectly
■ 1c, 1d, 2a, 2c	Chooses the incorrect operation
□ 2b	Multiplies before adding

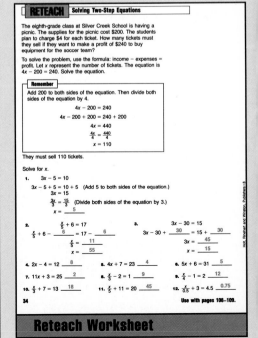

RETEACH Solving Two-Step Equations

The eighth-grade class at Silver Creek School is having a picnic. The supplies for the picnic cost $200. The students plan to charge $4 for each ticket. How many tickets must they sell if they want to make a profit of $240 to buy equipment for the soccer team?

To solve the problem, use the formula: income − expenses = profit. Let x represent the number of tickets. The equation is $4x − 200 = 240$. Solve the equation.

Remember
Add 200 to both sides of the equation. Then divide both sides of the equation by 4.
$$4x − 200 = 240$$
$$4x − 200 + 200 = 240 + 200$$
$$4x = 440$$
$$\frac{4x}{4} = \frac{440}{4}$$
$$x = 110$$

They must sell 110 tickets.

Solve for x.

1. $3x − 5 = 10$
$3x − 5 + 5 = 10 + 5$ (Add 5 to both sides of the equation.)
$3x = 15$
$\frac{3x}{3} = \frac{15}{3}$ (Divide both sides of the equation by 3.)
$x = \underline{5}$

2. $\frac{x}{5} + 6 = 17$
$\frac{x}{5} + 6 - \underline{6} = 17 - \underline{6}$
$\frac{x}{5} = \underline{11}$
$x = \underline{55}$

3. $3x − 30 = 15$
$3x − 30 + \underline{30} = 15 + \underline{30}$
$3x = \underline{45}$
$x = \underline{15}$

4. $2x − 4 = 12$ $\underline{8}$
5. $4x + 7 = 23$ $\underline{4}$
6. $5x + 6 = 31$ $\underline{5}$
7. $11x + 3 = 25$ $\underline{2}$
8. $\frac{x}{3} − 2 = 1$ $\underline{9}$
9. $\frac{x}{4} − 1 = 2$ $\underline{12}$
10. $\frac{x}{3} + 7 = 13$ $\underline{18}$
11. $\frac{x}{5} + 11 = 20$ $\underline{45}$
12. $\frac{x}{0.5} + 3 = 4.5$ $\underline{0.75}$

34   **Use with pages 108–109.**

Reteach Worksheet

Solve. For additional activities, see *Connecting Math Ideas*, page 470.

1. $7n - 12 = 16$
$n = 4$

2. $9d - 27 = 36$
$d = 7$

3. $\frac{m}{4} + 6 = 30$
$m = 96$

4. $\frac{y}{5} - 9 = 11$
$y = 100$

5. $\frac{s}{3} - 15 = 15$
$s = 90$

6. $9x + 5 = 77$
$x = 8$

7. $\frac{x}{4} - 3 = 1$
$x = 16$

8. $\frac{x}{5} + 9 = 14$
$x = 25$

9. $4v + 5 = 37$
$v = 8$

10. $9d - 9 = 9$
$d = 2$

11. $\frac{x}{7} + 4 = 10$
$x = 42$

12. $5m - 4 = 26$
$m = 6$

13. $6z + 3 = 69$
$z = 11$

14. $2a + 9 = 17$
$a = 4$

15. $\frac{h}{5} + 8 = 15$
$h = 35$

16. $\frac{r}{9} - 4 = 7$
$r = 99$

17. $2k - 6 = 8$
$k = 7$

18. $4a + 8 = 32$
$a = 6$

19. $7w - 9 = 12$
$w = 3$

20. $2a - 19 = 31$
$a = 25$

21. $\frac{n}{6} + 8 = 12$
$n = 24$

22. $4j + 7 = 31$
$j = 6$

23. $\frac{h}{8} + 10 = 14$
$h = 32$

24. $\frac{t}{5} - 7 = 13$
$t = 100$

25. $7f - 1 = 27$
$f = 4$

26. $\frac{g}{7} - 3 = 2$
$g = 35$

27. $9c - 4 = 41$
$c = 5$

28. $3n - 3 = 15$
$n = 6$

29. $\frac{s}{9} - 2 = 3$
$s = 45$

30. $\frac{y}{10} + 4 = 16$
$y = 120$

31. $4k - 6 = 34$
$k = 10$

32. $\frac{m}{2} - 5 = 15$
$m = 40$

33. $3y - 11 = 25$
$y = 12$

34. $0.5n + 3 = 8.5$
$n = 11$

35. $24.1 + 6x = 38.5$
$x = 2.4$

36. $3.5 + 2x = 13.5$
$x = 5$

37. $\frac{y}{3.5} + 15 = 17$
$y = 7$

38. $2a - 23 = 40$
$a = 31.5$

39. $3y - 22 = 32$
$y = 18$

CHALLENGE   Patterns, Relations, and Functions

You can use the pattern to find products of numbers that are nearly equal.

$7^2 = 7 \times 7 = 49$
$8 \times 6 = 48$
$9 \times 5 = 45$
$10 \times 4 = 40$

$8^2 = 8 \times 8 = 64$
$9 \times 7 = 63$
$10 \times 6 = 60$
$11 \times 5 = 55$

$9^2 = 9 \times 9 = 81$
$10 \times 8 = 80$
$11 \times 7 = 77$
$12 \times 6 = 72$

Does this pattern hold for all squares? **yes**

Use the pattern to find the following products.

1. 101×99 $100^2 = 10,000$
$101 \times 99 = 9,999$

2. 102×98
$102 \times 98 = 9,996$

3. 103×97
$103 \times 97 = 9,991$

4. 201×199 $200^2 = 40,000;$
$201 \times 199 = 39,999$

5. 202×198
$202 \times 198 = 39,996$

6. 203×197
$203 \times 197 = 39,991$

7. See if you can extend the pattern to find 204×196.
$204 \times 196 = 39,984$

Classwork/Homework, page H46   More Practice, page H198   **109**

ASSIGNMENT GUIDE

Basic: 1–24

Average: 10–39

Extended: 16–39, Chlg

Resources
Practice, p. 46   Class/Home, p. H46
Reteach, p. 34   More Practice, p. H198
Enrich, p. 44

Exercise Analysis
1–39   Solve two-step equations that have whole numbers and decimals

Challenge
These exercises encourage students to use number patterns to simplify products.

FOLLOW-UP ACTIVITIES

PUZZLES AND GAMES
The following procedure will always yield the number 3. Think of a number and add 5 to it. Double the result and subtract 4. Divide the total by 2 and subtract your first number. The number you find is 3.

Have students write the equations for each step to show why this trick works.
1. Think of a number n.
2. Add 5. ($n + 5$)
3. Double the result. ($2[n + 5]$, or $2n + 10$)
4. Subtract 4. ($2n + 10 - 4 = 2n + 6$)
5. Divide by 2. ($[2n + 6]/2 = n + 3$)
6. Subtract the first number. ($n + 3 - n$ or 3) (The answer is always 3.)

MATH COMMUNICATION
On blank cards, write an expression in words on the front and a different one expressed algebraically on the back. Be sure that every expression is shown both ways on different cards. Give each student a card. Have them take turns reading the statements on their cards. As each student reads a card, the other students check to see whether they have the corresponding algebraic expression on their cards; for example:

$2n$	$n - 3$	n^2
3 less than a number	a number squared	twice a number

Play continues until each student has had a turn.

COMING UP
Mathematical composition

109

Objective: To write an equation to solve a problem

Warm-Up

Have students solve for the variable in the following:

$4x - 3 = 13$ ($x = 4$)
$2y + 7 = 21$ ($y = 7$)
$0.5z - 5 = 15$ ($z = 40$)

GETTING STARTED

Write the number 8 on the chalkboard. Divide the class into groups. Challenge students to write as many equations as they can for which 8 is the solution. Have volunteers write their group's equations on the chalkboard. Elicit from students that every number can be the solution to an infinite number of equations. Point out that writing an equation can help students solve problems.

TEACHING THE LESSON

Emphasize that an equation merely shows two expressions that are equal to each other. To help students understand equations, write these equations on the chalkboard and ask students to use phrases to describe them.

● $6n + 7 = 43$ (7 more than 6 times a number is 43.)
● $\frac{n}{6} - 11 = 14$ (11 less than a number divided by 6 is 14.)

Point out that there is more than one way to word these phrases, just as most equations can be written in more than one way. However, students will probably find it easiest to write an equation that follows the wording in the problem as closely as possible.

Questions: Point out that the variable n, or information students need to find, is usually contained in the question. Be sure students realize that the variable in the equation represents the number they are asked to find. In setting up the equation $4n + 3 = 15$, emphasize the fact that 15 is *not* the answer.

Tools: The tools used to find the answer are the given information and how it is related to the answer. This relationship is expressed by the equation itself. Suggest that students who have difficulty writing equations write a list of the information they *know* and what they need to *find* as is outlined in their text.

Solutions: Review solving one- and two-step equations. Emphasize that the same operations must be used on each side of the equation. Students might be confused by the units of measure (*amphora*, *mina*, and *shekel*). You may wish to point out that

110

PROBLEM SOLVING
Writing an Equation

Many word problems can be solved by writing the problem in the form of an equation. When writing an equation, be sure that you state the facts in the problem correctly.

> A basic unit of weight in ancient Babylon was called a *mina*. A Babylonian farmer had two piles of grain to sell. The first pile of grain weighed 15 minas, which was 3 more than 4 times the weight of the second pile of grain. What was the weight of the second pile of grain?

1. List what you know and what you need to find.

Know
● The first pile of grain weighed 15 minas.
● The first pile of grain weighed 3 more than 4 times the second pile of grain.

Find
● the weight of the second pile of grain

2. Think about how you can use the given information to form an equation. Use a variable to represent the number you need to find.
Let n = the weight of the second pile of grain.

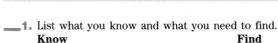

weight of the first pile of grain	was	3	more than	4 times the weight of the second pile of grain
↓	↓	↓	↓	↓
15	=	3	+	4n

Think: You can rewrite the equation as $4n + 3 = 15$.

3. Solve the equation, and write the answer.

$$4n + 3 = 15$$
$$4n + 3 - 3 = 15 - 3$$
$$4n = 12$$
$$\frac{4n}{4} = \frac{12}{4}$$
$$n = 3$$

The second pile of grain weighed 3 minas.

Math Reasoning, page H212

110

---

each is like our pint, pound, or ounce respectively. You may wish to allow students to use calculators for problem solving.

Checks: Substitute the answer in the equation to check. Be sure the correct label is included with the answer so that it makes sense in the problem.

Write the letter of the correct equation.

1. In the 1700's, the United States foot was divided into 1,000 parts. This foot was 33 parts longer than the Roman foot. How many parts long was the Roman foot?

  a. $18 + n = 1,000$
  (b.) $n + 33 = 1,000$
  c. $n - 33 = 1,000$

2. The Venice foot was used in some cities in Italy. This foot was 62 parts longer than 1.1 times the United States foot. How many parts long was the Venice foot?

  a. $\frac{n}{1.1} + 62 = 1,000$
  b. $1.1n + 62 = 1,000$
  (c.) $n - 62 = 1.1 \times 1,000$

Write an equation, and solve.

3. The Antwerp foot was used in Belgium. It was 54 parts shorter than the 1,000-part American foot. How many parts long was the Antwerp foot? *n + 54 = 1,000; 946 parts long*

4. A Babylonian farmer had two bags of dried peas. One bag weighed 35 *shekels*, which was 5 more than twice the weight of the other bag. How much did the other bag weigh? *2n + 5 = 35; 15 shekels*

5. In ancient Rome, an *amphora* was a unit of liquid measure. A container holding 12 amphora of olive oil holds 2 amphora more than $\frac{1}{3}$ as much as a second container. How many amphora of olive oil does the second container hold? *$\frac{n}{3}$ + 2 = 12; 30 amphora*

6. A Roman merchant had 2 containers of honey. The first container held 52 amphora. This amount was 8 less than 3 times the amount of honey in the second container. How many amphora of honey did the second container hold? *3n − 8 = 52; 20 amphora*

7. In a Babylonian market, a farmer sold 2 piles of vegetables. The first pile of vegetables weighed 12 minas, which was 6 minas less than 0.75 times the weight of the second pile of vegetables. What was the weight of the second pile of vegetables? *0.75n − 6 = 12; 24 minas*

★8. In about A.D. 1400, the English foot measured 13.2 inches. The United States *pole* measures 23.76 inches longer than the square of the number of inches in the old English foot. How many inches are there in a United States pole? *n − 23.76 = 13.2²; 198 inches*

Classwork/Homework, page H47

PRACTICE | Writing an Equation

Choose the correct equation.

1. The Mark 2 model of the Trans computer costs $785. This is $45 less than 1.5 times the cost of the Mark 1 model. How much does the Mark 1 model cost?
  (a.) 1.5n − 45 = 785
  b. 1.5n = 785 − 45
  c. n + 45 = 785 − 1.5

2. The Mark 1 model has a memory storage of 32K. The memory of the Mark 2 model is 10K more than 5 times the memory of the Mark 1. How many K's is the Mark 2's memory?
  a. n + 10 = 32 × 5
  b. $\frac{n}{5}$ = 32 + 10
  (c.) n − 10 = 32 × 5

Write an equation, and solve.

3. The Gant printer can print 600 characters per minute. The Nole printer can print 20 characters per minute more than 1.8 times the characters per minute of the Gant printer. How many characters per minute can the Nole printer print?
10n = 4 × 7.80 − 6   1,100 characters

4. The weight of a hard disk unit of a computer is 0.5 times the total weight of the printer and the terminal. The hard disk unit weighs 14.85 kilograms, and the terminal weighs 10.6 kilograms. How many kilograms does the printer weigh?
0.5 (n + 10.6) = 14.85   19.1 kg

5. A pack of 10 soft disks costs $6 less than 4 printer ribbons. Each printer ribbon costs $7.80. What is the cost of each soft disk?
10n + 6 = 4 × 7.80 $2.52

6. Max has $65.00. He buys 5 copies of a computer manual, and his change is $2.75. How much does each copy of the manual cost?
5n = 65 − 2.75 $12.45

7. The total memory of two computers is 192K. The second computer has double the memory of the first computer. How much memory does the second computer have?
3n = 192, n = 64   128K

8. Katrine has programmed a computer so that any number she enters will be squared and then the square will be doubled. If she enters the number 1.2 what will the computer show?
n = 2(1.2²)   2.88

Use after pages 110–111.   47

Practice Worksheet

ENRICH | Problem Solving

Dr. Norton Wood will not write or speak the number 13. His superstition also prevents him from speaking or writing certain other numbers, and he uses equations to avoid these numbers. Write and solve the equations to find some of the numbers he will not use.

1. "132 divided by 6 times my son's age is the square root of 4." How old is Dr. Wood's son?
132 ÷ 6n = √4; 11 years old

2. "If you multiply the number of children I have by 4, the answer is the same as if you divide 16 by the number of my children." How many children does he have?
4n = 16 ÷ 4; 2 children

3. "If you multiply the square of my daughter's age by 4, it is 75 more than the square of my son's age." How old is Dr. Wood's daughter?
4n² = 75 + 11²; 7 years old

4. "In 9 years, my daughter will be half as old as my cousin Jill will be." How old is Jill now?
$\frac{n + 9}{2}$ = 7 + 9; 23 years old

5. "If I live a century, this will be 14 years less than 6 times as long as I have refused to use certain numbers." How long has he refused to use the numbers?
100 = 6n − 14; 19 years

6. "The first digit of my age multiplied by 6 equals 10 more than the first digit of my age multiplied by 4." What is the first digit of Dr. Wood's age?
6n − 10 = 4n; 5

7. "One more than the second digit of my age is the difference between the ages of my children." What is the second digit of Dr. Wood's age?
n + 1 = 11 − 7; 3

8. "When my daughter was born, I was 4.6 times as old as my dog." How old is Dr. Wood's dog?
n − 7 = $\frac{53 − 7}{4.6}$; 17 years old

9. What group of numbers does Dr. Norton Wood refuse to use? The answers to the problems and the number 13 are the first numbers of the group.
prime numbers

10. Write an equation in Dr. Wood's style to avoid writing the next number in the group. Be careful not to use any other numbers in the group.
Answers will vary; the solution is 29.

Use with pages 110–111.   45

Enrich Worksheet

ASSIGNMENT GUIDE

Basic: 1–4

Average: 2–6

Extended: 3–8

Resources
Practice, p. 47   Class/Home, p. H47
Enrich, p. 45   Reasoning, p. H212

Exercise Analysis
1–2 Choose the correct equation
3–8 Write an equation; solve

FOLLOW-UP ACTIVITIES

 PROBLEM SOLVING
Copy the equations on the chalkboard.

$3n - 14 = 49$ $\frac{b}{5} + 7 = 12$

$6.1v + 8 = 69$ $\frac{c}{12.6} - 3 = 19$

Have students write a word problem to correspond to each equation. (Answers will vary.)

 MANIPULATIVES
Materials: balance, 28 pennies or small masses per group

Have students use the balance to demonstrate an equation. When the balance is even, both sides are equal. Write $4n + 6 = 14$ on the chalkboard. Have students place 14 pennies on each pan of the balance. Next have students take 6 pennies from each pan. Divide the remaining pennies in each pan into 4 equal groups. Those groups represent n, which equals 2. Have students work in small groups to challenge one another to write and solve equations, using the balance and pennies to represent their equations.

COMING UP
Wrapping it up

111

Objectives: To determine the least and the greatest products for a given number of digits

Warm-Up

Have students rename the following in words or as numbers: 890,000,841,746; 6,816,777,000,000; 911,030,978,400; 7,000,762; 90,003,051,820; 783,782,000,002; twelve thousand, four hundred, three; two billion, three million, fifty-four hundred; fourteen hundred and eight tenths; fifteen and nine hundredths; and fifty-nine trillion, four million, eight thousand sixty-five.

GETTING STARTED

Have students discuss items that are often counted in thousands, millions, billions, and trillions; for example, populations, budgets, distances.

Form students into three groups. Each group will represent an imaginary country.

Country	Population	Budget
A	3.5 million	24 trillion
B	6.8 million	36 trillion
C	4.7 million	29 trillion

Have each group make up a name and write a description of the country and the demographics of its population. Each group is to make up different categories of expenditures and amounts of money students wish to allocate to each from the budget; for example, education, welfare, public health, defense, transportation, administrative costs.

TEACHING THE LESSON

Explain that most calculators have only an 8-digit display. Have students work the first example on calculators. Explain that there are two ways that a calculator shows numbers too big for the display. Some calculators show E, and the operator is required to move the decimal point eight place values to the right of where it is shown on the display, adding zeros if necessary. This is called the overflow function. Some calculators show the number in ordinary scientific notation. For example,

100,000 × 100,000
    displays: 100.00000 E
or displays: 1   10
12,345,678 × 98,765,432
    displays: 12193262. E
or displays: 1.2193   15

Have each student experiment by calculating with large numbers on his or her calculator to find which method the calculator

CALCULATOR

When you multiply two 1-digit numbers, how many digits can there be in the answer? This answer is obvious: the smallest such product is $0 \times 0 = 0$ and the largest product is $9 \times 9 = 81$. So, there must be 1 or 2 digits in the product of two 1-digit numbers.

Use your calculator (and your problem-solving skills) to complete this chart. See Answer Key.

Number of Digits in the First Factor	Number of Digits in the Second Factor	Smallest Product	Number of Digits in Smallest Product	Largest Product	Number of Digits in Largest Product
1	1	$0 \times 0 = 0$	1	$9 \times 9 = 81$	2
2	2	$10 \times 10 = 100$	3	$99 \times 99 = 9{,}801$	4
3	3	1. ■	2. ■ 5	3. ■	4. ■ 6
4	4	5. ■	6. ■ 7	7. ■	8. ■ 8
5	5	★9. ■	★10. ■ 9	★11. ■	★12. ■ 10
6	6	★13. ■	★14. ■ 11	★15. ■	★16. ■ 12
7	7	★17. ■	★18. ■ 13	★19. ■	★20. ■ 14
2	3	21. $10 \times 100 =$ ■	22. ■ 4	23. $99 \times 999 =$ ■	24. ■ 5
2	4	25. ■	26. ■ 5	27. ■	28. ■ 6
2	5	29. ■	30. ■ 6	31. ■	32. ■ 7
3	4	33. ■	34. ■ 6	35. ■	36. ■ 7
3	5	37. ■	38. ■ 7	39. ■	40. ■ 8
4	7	★41. ■	★42. ■ 10	★43. ■	★44. ■ 11

45. Using an 8-digit calculator, what is the largest whole number that can be multiplied by itself and correctly displayed? 9,999

112

employs. Discuss the accuracy of each of the methods.

Point out that most calculators drop digits when a product is too long for its display. Discuss methods students can use to find these large products. The Distributive Property is sometimes useful. For example:

362 × 536,271,384
= 362 × (536,000,000 + 271,384)
= (362 × 536,000,000) + (362 × 271,384)

362 × 536 equals 194,032 (by the calculator), so 362 × 536,000,000 equals 194,032,000,000, and
362 × 271,384 = 98,241,008.

With pencil and paper, find that the product is:

```
   194,032,000,000
+       98,241,008
   194,130,241,008
```

GROUP PROJECT

Setting Your Own Standards

The problem: How would you measure the weight of objects if you didn't use pounds or ounces? Many ancient measurement systems used a physical object, such as a kernel of corn, as a standard. For example, if 250 corn kernels equaled one pound, a 47-pound dog would weigh 11,750 kernels of corn in an ancient measuring system. What objects would you use as standards for measurement? Consider the key questions, and invent your own system of weights based on one object or several objects. Then find the weight of your object(s) in pounds or ounces. Make a chart like the one below, and calculate the weight of each item by using your new system of weights.

Key Questions
- Will you use one kind of object as a measurement of everything?

- How efficiently will your object(s) measure very heavy items? very light items?

- How easy to handle will large quantities of your object(s) be?

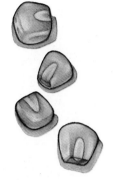

Item	Customary weight	New system
Can of soup	▣	▣
Blue whale	▣	▣
Pizza	▣	▣
Typewriter	▣	▣
Toaster	▣	▣
Toast	▣	▣
Potato	▣	▣

113

ASSIGNMENT GUIDE

Basic:	p. 112, p. 113
Average:	p. 112, p. 113
Extended:	p. 112, p. 113

Objectives: To set a standard of measurement; to calculate weights based upon it

USING THE PAGE

Have students form groups of three or four. Tell them to consider the Key Questions in thinking about objects to use for their standards of measurement. The bulk and weight of these objects should be factors in their decision. They might want to use one object to measure heavy objects and one for light ones.

Each student should suggest a standard to his or her group, and the group should choose one of these as their standard. Each group member should then choose two or three items and estimate or research to find the customary weight of the items. Students should then switch papers and convert each others' items from customary weight to the new measurement standard. Members of each group should also work together to convert the weights in the list on the student page to their new system. When this has been finished, have the group members collaborate to make a chart, such as the one on the pupil page, to organize their data. Display the groups' charts in the classroom, and have students examine each group's system.

To extend this cooperative learning activity, have each group choose another group's measurement standard, and convert the items in their own list to the new measurement standard.

3 CHAPTER TEST

Purpose: The Chapter Test helps to assess students' understanding of the concepts and skills presented in this chapter.

The chart below is designed to help you review the test items by correlating them with the testing objectives that appear in the Chapter Overview.

Item	*Objectives*
1–3	A
4–6	B
7–11	C
12–18	D
19–20	E
21–28	F
32	G
29–31	I
33	H

Bonus
The bonus question may be used for extra credit, or you may want to assign it to students who complete the test before the rest of the class.

Calculator
You may wish to have students use calculators for the problem-solving portions of the test.

Resources
If you prefer to use this Chapter Test as a review exercise, additional testing materials are available in the Teacher's Resource Book.

CHAPTER TEST

Write whether each number is divisible by 2, 3, 4, 5, 6, 8, 9, 10, or none of these numbers. (pages 80–81)

1. 699 by 3

2. 3,168 by 2, 3, 4, 6, 8, 9

3. 4,217 by none of the numbers

Find the square root. (pages 82–83)

4. $\sqrt{16}$ 4

5. $\sqrt{25}$ 5

6. $\sqrt{36}$ 6

Write in scientific notation. (pages 84–85)

7. 480,000 4.8×10^5

8. 3,215,700 3.2157×10^6

9. 619,720 6.1972×10^5

Write in standard form. (pages 84–85)

10. 3.24×10^3 3,240

11. 5.4321×10^6 5,432,100

Write the prime factorization for each number. Use exponents. (pages 90–91)

12. 54 2×3^3

13. 48 $2^4 \times 3$

14. 525 $3 \times 5^2 \times 7$

Find the GCF. (pages 92–93)

15. 14 and 82 2

16. 25, 50, 75 25

Find the LCM. (pages 94–95)

17. 7 and 9 63

18. 4, 9, and 12 36

Simplify. (pages 98–99)

19. $2(7 + 8) \div (9 - 4)$ 6

20. $(36 \div 3^2 + 3) \times (18 - 12)$ 42

Solve. (pages 100–101 and 104–107)

21. $x + 18 = 42$ $x = 24$

22. $a - 9.2 = 4.6$ $a = 13.8$

23. $7y = 56$ $y = 8$

24. $\frac{b}{2} = 8.7$ $b = 17.4$

114

POSTTEST Chapter 3 Page 1

1. Which of the following numbers is divisible by 4?
2,122 2,332 2,582 2,606
______

2. What is $\sqrt{36}$?
______

3. Write 470,000,000 in scientific notation.
______

4. What is the greatest common factor (GCF) of 60 and 42?
______

5. What is the least common multiple (LCM) of 16 and 24?
______

6. John bought a computer for $1,149. Tim bought the same model at another store for $899. How much more did John spend?
Which of the following number sentences could be used to solve this problem?
a. $x = 1{,}149 + 899$ b. $x = 1{,}149 - 899$
c. $x \div 899 = 1{,}149$ d. $899x = 1{,}149$
______

7. Ted ate 4 medium-sized bananas. If each banana contained 0.06 milligrams of vitamin B_1, how much vitamin B_1 did Ted get?
______

8. What is the square root of 64?
______

9. Write 3.7×10^5 in standard form.
______

10. Simplify $9 + 12 \div 3$.
______

Use the information from the chart below for questions 11 and 12.

BUS FARES FROM METROPOLIS TO FOUR TOWNS

To	One way	Round Trip	10-Trip Ticket
Earlimart	$5.70	$11.20	$52.20
Porterville	6.15	12.10	56.60
Tipton	4.40	8.55	40.00
Pixley	5.05	9.90	45.90

11. How much is saved by buying a round-trip ticket rather than buying two one-way tickets to travel by bus from Metropolis to Tipton and back?
______

12. How much is saved per trip by buying a 10-trip ticket from Metropolis to Porterville?
______

Posttest

Name ______ Date ______

POSTTEST Chapter 3 Page 2

13. A factory produced 3,982 calculators in a week at a cost of about $5.00 per calculator. About how much was spent to produce calculators that week? Without computing the exact answer, choose the most reasonable answer.
a. $800 b. $3,987
c. $20,000 d. $2,000,000
______

14. What is the greatest common factor (GCF) of 140, 154, and 196?
______

15. Which of the following numbers is divisible by 9?
32,154 41,283 62,311 73,214
______

16. An apartment building has 10 floors with 4 apartments on each floor. If every apartment is occupied, which of the following numbers is the most reasonable for the number of people who live in the building?
a. 14 b. 114
c. 800 d. 1,800
______

17. If $y + 4.5 = 10.5$, what is y?
______

18. What is the least common multiple (LCM) of the three numbers 18, 60, and 126?
______

19. Simplify $24 + (9 \cdot 2 + 3 \cdot 4)^2$.
______

20. What is $\sqrt{81}$?
______

21. What value of x makes $0.4x = 12.2$ a true statement?
______

22. The average distance from the sun to Mars is about 140 million miles. How would this number be written in scientific notation?
______

23. The number 4,830 is divisible by what single-digit whole numbers greater than 2?
______

Posttest

Solve. (pages 108–109)

25. $4n - 25 = 23$ $n = 12$

26. $\frac{c}{2.1} + 8 = 13$ $c = 10.5$

27. $7m + 6.5 = 41.5$ $m = 5$

28. $\frac{d}{5} - 14 = 2$ $d = 80$

Solve. (pages 86–87 and 110–111)

29. The area a yoke of oxen could plow in one day was called an *acre*. It is 43,560 square feet. There are 9 square feet in 1 square yard. How many square yards are there in 1 acre? **4,840 yd²**

30. It took Margaret 17.5 minutes to walk to school. It took Julie 7.3 minutes less. Find how long it took Julie to get to school. $17.5 - x = 7.3; x = 10.2$

31. A *carat* weighs 200 milligrams, or 3.085 grains troy. How many milligrams does a 24.5-carat stone weigh? How many grains troy does it weigh? $24.5 \times 200 = n, n = 4,900$ mg; $24.5 \times 3.085 = x, x = 75.583$ grains troy

32. Find the prime factors of 312. Then find the prime factors of 520. Use your first answer to see if your second answer is reasonable. $2^3 \times 3 \times 13; 2^3 \times 5 \times 13$

Use the table below to solve. (pages 96–97)

COST OF ELECTRICITY (PER KWH)

	First 250 kwh	Additional kwh
June 1 to September 30	13.28¢	14.26¢
October 1 to May 31	13.28¢	12.41¢

33. The DeFiore household uses 415 kwh of electricity during the month of August. Find the cost of this electricity to the nearest cent. **$56.73**

BONUS

Solve.

The Babylonian *mina* was shaped like a duck and weighed about 640 grams. A swan weighed 30 mina. If you had 70 minas, how many grams would they weigh, and how many swans could you balance on a scale? **44,800 g; 2 swans**

115

For students who have difficulty with written tests, this test can be given orally.

You may wish to test students, orally or in writing, to see if they can explain the steps used in solving selected items. The following table summarizes the procedures for solving key test items.

Ex. 7–9

Writing numbers in scientific notation

To write a number in scientific notation, move the decimal point to the left to form a number between 1 and 10. Then count the number of places the decimal point was moved to determine an exponent of 10. Then write the number times 10 to that power.

Ex. 15–16

Finding the greatest common factor

To find the greatest common factor of two or more numbers, list all the factors of each number. Then circle the common factors. The GCF is the greatest common factor.

Write each number as the product of prime numbers. Begin with 2, because it is the smallest prime number. Continue to write numbers as products until only prime numbers remain. When you have found the prime factorization of each number, find the product of the common prime factors. The product is equal to the GCF.

Ex. 17–19

Finding the least common multiple

To find the least common multiple of two or more numbers, write each number as the product of prime numbers. Multiply the highest power of each of the different prime numbers. The product is equal to the LCM.

Purpose This Reteaching page provides additional instruction for key concepts in the chapter. It is designed for use by students who have had difficulty with these concepts. It can also be used to provide additional practice for students who require it.

USING THE PAGE

The order of operations was taught on pages 98–99.

Review the four statements, explaining *order*. Be sure to give examples of each case on the chalkboard. Explain that unless these rules are used, many different answers can be given for an expression. You may also want to review finding exponents such as 3^2, $(13 - 4)^2$ or 9^2, and $(1 + 2)^2$ because these are often confused by students. Exercises 25 through 30 should be assigned and done on the chalkboard. Emphasize that students can find their mistakes when they give an incorrect answer.

Resources

For other practice and activities related to this chapter, see the Teacher's Resource Book.

RETEACHING

When an expression contains several operations, simplify it in the following order.

1. Simplify powers and roots.

2. If parentheses are used, evaluate the expressions enclosed in parentheses first, and use the order outlined below.

3. Perform multiplications and divisions from left to right.

4. Perform additions and subtractions from left to right.

Simplify $(3^2 \cdot 5) \div (1 + 2^3) + (6 - 3)$.

$$
\begin{aligned}
(3^2 \cdot 5) \div (1 + 2^3) + (6 - 3) &= (9 \cdot 5) \div (1 + 8) + (6 - 3) \\
&= \quad 45 \; \div \quad 9 \; + \quad 3 \\
&= \qquad 5 \qquad + \quad 3 \\
&= \quad 8
\end{aligned}
$$

Simplify each expression.

1. $5 + 6 \cdot 2$ 17   **2.** $9 + 6 - 5$ 10   **3.** $18 \div 6 + 2$ 5

4. $12 \div 2 - 3$ 3   **5.** $3 \cdot (5 + 4)$ 27   **6.** $(3 + 5) \cdot 7$ 56

7. $8 \cdot (30 \div 5)$ 48   **8.** $3 \cdot 4 \cdot (7 + 5)$ 144   **9.** $30 + 20 \div 4$ 35

10. $60 \div (12 + 3)$ 4   **11.** $3 \cdot (4 + 5) \div 9$ 3   **12.** $8 \cdot (4 - 1) \div 6$ 4

13. $7 + 3 \cdot 2 + 16$ 29   **14.** $40 \div (8 - 4) + 5$ 15   **15.** $(5 + 6) \div (12 - 1)$

16. $4^3 \div 4 + 4 - 4$ 16   **17.** $3 + (1 + 2)^2$ 12   **18.** $(9 + 5) \div (2 + 5)$

19. $3^2 \div 1 + (3 + 6)$ 18   **20.** $2 + 2^2 - 2$ 4   **21.** $10 + 6^2$ 46

22. $(19 - 4^2)$ 3   **23.** $(13 - 4)^2$ 81   **24.** $86 - 8 \cdot (4 + 6)$ 6

Use parentheses to make each answer true.

25. $(4 + 6) \div 2 = 5$ **26.** $(9 - 6) \cdot 5 = 15$

27. $14 \div (9 - 2) = 2$ **28.** $36 \div (3 + 6) = 4$

29. $2 \cdot 9 \div (3 + 3) = 3$ **30.** $(12 + 6) \cdot (3 + 3) = 108$

116

ENRICHMENT

Expressions as Rules

Since a **sequence** is a set of numbers written in a particular order, the relationship between a term and its position in the sequence can be expressed as a **rule** for the sequence.

For the sequence 15, 30, 45, 60, 75, . . .

the value of the term is   15, 30, 45, 60, 75, . . .

the number of each term is 1, 2, 3, 3, 4, . . .

The relationship between the number of each term (n) and the value of the term can be expressed as the rule $15n$.

The value of the sixth term would therefore be

$$15 \cdot 6 = 90.$$

Given the rule for a sequence, it is possible to calculate any term of the sequence independently of the others.

Use the rule $3n + 4$ to find the first three terms and the tenth term of the sequence.

$3 \cdot 1 + 4 = 7$
$3 \cdot 2 + 4 = 10$
$3 \cdot 3 + 4 = 13$
$3 \cdot 10 + 4 = 34$

The first three terms of the sequence are 7, 10, and 13. The tenth term is 34.

Write the rule for each sequence.

1. 7, 12, 17, 22, . . . $5n + 2$

2. 4; 16; 64; 256; 1,024; . . . 4^n

3. 1, 4, 9, 16, . . . n^2

4. $4, \frac{5}{2}, 2, \frac{7}{4}, \frac{8}{5}, \ldots$ $\frac{n+3}{n}$

Use each rule to find the first five terms and the thirtieth term.

5. $7n - 4$
3, 10, 17, 24, 31; 206

6. n^3
1; 8; 27; 64; 125; 27,000

7. $\frac{3}{n}$
$3, \frac{3}{2}, 1, \frac{3}{4}, \frac{3}{5}; \frac{1}{10}$

8. $\left(\frac{1}{n+1}\right)^2$
$\frac{1}{4}, \frac{1}{9}, \frac{1}{16}, \frac{1}{25}, \frac{1}{36}; \frac{1}{961}$

117

Purpose This Enrichment page provides an additional challenge for those students whose work throughout the chapter and on the Chapter Test shows a thorough understanding of the material. Alternatively, you may wish to use these exercises as a supplementary lesson for the entire class.

USING THE PAGE

Writing the rules for sequences allows students to compute any term of a sequence without computing the terms that precede it. Emphasize that n is the place of each term in the sequence. In answering Exercises 5 through 8, the numbers 1, 2, 3, 4, 5, and 30 will be substituted into each rule to find those terms of the sequence.

Resources
For additional Enrichment activities, see the Teacher's Resource Book.

This Cumulative Review page provides an opportunity to reinforce students' understanding of the concepts and skills taught in previous chapters.

The chart below is designed to aid you in reviewing the material by specifying the pages on which various concepts and skills were taught.

Item	Page
1	46–47
2	44–45
3	46–47
4	50–51
5	52–53
6	60–61
7	2–3
8	26–27
9	30–31
10	22–23
11	14–15
12	28–29
13	52–53
14	60–61

Each Cumulative Review gives students an opportunity to practice taking tests that are written in a multiple-choice, standardized format. Be sure that students understand that if the correct answer is not among the first three given, then they should select the fourth choice—"not given"—as the correct answer. At least one item per test will require students to give this response.

CUMULATIVE REVIEW

Write the letter of the correct answer.

1. Estimate $324\overline{)9{,}572}$.

a. 3　　　　　b. 30
c. 300　　　　d. 3,000

2. $5{,}000 \div 100$

a. 5　　　　　b. 50
c. 500　　　　d. not given

3. Estimate $9{,}324 \times 5{,}711$.

a. 53,000　　　b. 540,000
c. 54,000,000　d. 5,400,000

4. $40{,}724 \times 296$

a. 11,943,204　b. 12,054,304
c. 12,054,414　d. not given

5. $7{,}008 \div 213$

a. 22 R192　　b. 32
c. 32 R192　　d. not given

6. 0.09872×59

a. 0.482338　　b. 5.71448
c. 5.82448　　d. not given

7. What number is 921 million, 123 thousand?

a. 921,123　　b. 921,100,023
c. 921,123,000　d. not given

8. Estimate $89{,}456 + 98{,}546$.

a. 19,000　　　b. 100,000
c. 190,000　　d. 2,000,000

9. $19.40701 - 1.94072$

a. 17.46629　　b. 18.54773
c. 18.56739　　d. not given

10. Round to thousandths and subtract: $5.80992 - 2.93427$.

a. 2.874　　　b. 2.876
c. 3.744　　　d. not given

11. $6{,}750{,}042 + 7{,}439{,}968 + 318{,}765$

a. 13,497,645　b. 13,871,245
c. 14,190,010　d. not given

12. $721.0409 + 16.939 + 72.104$

a. 729.9452　　b. 810.0839
c. 1,611.6709　d. not given

13. James rented a store for 2 years for $13,380 per year. How much was his monthly rent?

a. $1,115　　　b. $13,380
c. $26,760　　d. not given

14. Irene bought 7 sweaters at $15.50 each and sold them for $5 more each. Find the amount she charged for all the sweaters.

a. $73.50　　　b. $108.50
c. $143.50　　d. not given

CHAPTER  OVERVIEW

FRACTIONS

SUMMARY

Chapter 4 focuses on the computation of fractions and mixed numbers. Comparing, ordering, and estimating the sums, differences, products, and quotients of fractions and mixed numbers, writing fractions as decimals, and solving one- and two-step equations involving fractions and mixed numbers are included.

LESSON SEQUENCE

PROFESSIONAL BACKGROUND

Researchers report that it is common for an adolescent to consider fractions to be two numbers that should be treated separately instead of a rational number with a size of its own.

When they order fractions, students might indicate that $\frac{6}{8}$ is greater than $\frac{3}{4}$ because both its numerator and denominator are greater. In reference to the estimation of fractions, the Second National Assessment of Educational Progress revealed that students often have trouble in the estimation of the sums and the differences of fractions. When asked to estimate the sum of $\frac{12}{13} + \frac{7}{8}$, less than a quarter of the 13-year olds surveyed were able to come up with 2 as an estimate. A shockingly high number estimated 19 or 21.

Though most students learn to multiply and divide fractions by rote memorization of the applicable rules, research indicates that diagrams can help students deepen their understanding and memorization of the rules.

For example, to demonstrate $\frac{1}{3} \div 2$, draw a whole, divide it into thirds, and then divide one of the thirds in half. Or, $\frac{1}{3} \div 2$ can be represented as $\frac{1}{3} \times \frac{1}{2}$, in which case the whole can be shaded $\frac{1}{3}$ vertically and $\frac{1}{2}$ horizontally. The solution is the double-shaded area.

References: See Driscoll (secondary volume, chapter on fractions); Hart; Carpenter et al.;

Behr, Merlyn J., et al. November 1984. "Order and Equivalence of Rational Numbers: A Clinical Teaching Experiment. *Journal for Research in Mathematics Education.*

MATERIALS

calculators
graph paper and rulers

VOCABULARY

equivalent fraction (p. 120)
mixed numbers (p. 122)
least common denominator (p. 124)
common factor (p. 138)
reciprocal (p. 146)
complex fraction (p. 161)

ABOUT THE CHAPTER

Fractions have a prominent role in probability, proportions, and in solving equations. This chapter reviews and extends all that students have learned about fractions. There is one lesson in this chapter in which students are given the opportunity, in a problem-solving setting, to work cooperatively. In this lesson, students are confronted with a real-life situation through which they are encouraged to develop and apply a variety of strategies.

In Chapter 4, students learn about fractions and mixed numbers. Lessons focus on comparing and ordering fractions and mixed numbers as well as on addition, subtraction, multiplication, and division. Students also learn to write fractions as decimals and to solve equations with fractions.

Do not hesitate to show students how to order fractions on a number line. Cross-multiplication is a powerful way to compare and order fractions.

Students often have difficulty subtracting mixed numbers which require that they rename twice. In the second renaming, students must understand that 1 is renamed as a fraction $\frac{n}{n}$, where n is the denominator of the fraction in the mixed number.

In division, students may still have difficulty implementing the rule, "invert the divisor and multiply." Students will benefit from seeing whole-number examples which show that multiplying by the reciprocal of the divisor yields the same result as the division problem.

Estimation can be another way to help students avoid errors when dividing fractions. Have students estimate the answer to a division problem and check the estimate against the answer. The answer should appear reasonable when compared to the estimate, although estimation is not an infallible check.

Calculators can be used with fractions. Every fraction is a division problem. So, students can use calculators to divide the numerator by the denominator in each fraction.

Problem-solving lessons show students how to obtain and use information from a pictograph and how to estimate the answers to problems. Other problem-solving lessons show students how to write and solve a simpler problem and how to interpret a remainder.

The Group Project ends this chapter and actively involves students in planning a handicraft fair.

The Enrichment lesson introduces students to complex fractions. This lesson builds nicely on the content of the chapter. Students will often encounter complex fractions as they solve equations.

USING THE CHAPTER OPENER

Each Chapter Opener presents situational problem-solving activities that can be used to explore the skills taught throughout the chapter. The work sheets can be used by individuals, small groups, or the whole class, depending on the needs of the class. The Chapter Opener focuses on a nonalgorithmic approach to mathematics through real-life situations relevant to students' experiences. Through an interdisciplinary approach, the Chapter Opener helps students explore the relationships between mathematics, other areas of the curriculum, and everyday life while developing different strands of mathematics.

In the Chapter Opener activities, students will use demographics in taking a survey. Students will also explore spatial patterns and relationships.

PROBLEM SOLVING

Obtaining information from an outside source is a necessary skill for solving math problems as well as for addressing real-life problems that confront us every day. In addition to teaching students how to use data not given in a problem, the lesson *Using a Pictograph* in this chapter discusses the organization and labeling of data in pictographs, and instructs students in a step-by-step method of obtaining needed information. This lesson lends itself to small-group work.

The Estimation problem-solving lesson in this chapter focuses on a strategy for determining how accurate an estimate needs to be. *Mathematics Unlimited* suggests that you encourage any student improvisations that increase their estimation skills.

Students are sometimes intimidated by problems that contain numbers with a great many digits or that include fractions or decimals. The lesson Writing a Simpler Problem helps students to find a solution by setting up a parallel problem with much simpler numbers. The problem becomes less intimidating when approached with the simpler numbers, and the steps necessary to solve it become obvious. Once the problem has been solved using simpler numbers, students use the original numbers in the problem and solve.

Unlike problems involving addition, subtraction, or multiplication, division problems do not always produce whole-number solutions. The lesson Interpreting the Quotient and the Remainder instructs students to focus on whether the answer to a problem requires the quotient, the remainder, both the quotient and the remainder, or a rounded quotient. In these situations it is important that the students check the reasonableness of their answers.

Most of the problem-solving lessons in *Mathematics Unlimited* lend themselves to small-group work. In a comfortable group atmosphere, students can brainstorm and discuss various ways to solve problems.

BULLETIN BOARD

"Quilt Sampler"

Materials: paper to cover bulletin board; lettering; push pins; felt-tip pens of assorted colors or crayons; construction paper/poster board; stapler; scissors; note cards; hand-out (blank quilt squares)

Preparation: Cover bulletin board with paper and arrange display lettering. Use paper or poster board to construct a "quilt" frame that has squares measuring 40 in. × 40 in. (This measurement has been calculated for the participation of 25 students and will vary according to the actual number of students. Allow one square, 8 in. × 8 in., per student). Have students draw an 8 in. × 8 in. square on construction paper or poster board and divide it into four parts.

After pp. 152-153: Have students design two of their squares, color them with felt-tip pens or crayons, and leave the alternate squares white. Cut out the squares and attach them in the frame to form a quilt. Give each student a note card on which to write an "of" statement concerning the quilt, for example: $\frac{1}{2}$ of the quilt is white squares; $\frac{1}{2}$ of 100 squares = 50 squares. There are 50 white squares in the quilt. Post the note cards around the quilt.

COMMON ERRORS

Many students experience difficulty when they divide mixed numbers. Students correctly might rename a mixed number, but then forget to find the reciprocal before they multiply. For example, $\frac{1}{4} \div 2\frac{1}{2}$ might be solved as follows:

$$\frac{1}{4} \div 2\frac{1}{2}$$

$$\frac{1}{4} \div \frac{5}{2}$$

$$\frac{1}{4} \times \frac{5}{2} = \frac{5}{8}$$

To remediate this error, be sure that students see that dividing two fractions involves two steps; and that dividing a mixed number involves *three* steps which are:

a. change mixed numbers to fractions
b. find the reciprocal of the divisor
c. multiply the dividend by the reciprocal of the divisor

Have students divide several fractions by other fractions. Then give students mixed numbers to divide, emphasizing that each step needed for dividing 2 fractions must be done.

SPECIAL NEEDS

A review of equivalent fractions is necessary prior to any computation that uses fractions. Remind students of the basic rule: When adding and subtracting, only like objects may be combined or taken from each other.

Although multiplying fractions tends to be easier for students than adding and subtracting them, do not just present the rule. Students might confuse rules, or forget them. Use paper folding to model multiplication, and stress that the × sign means "of"; that is, $\frac{1}{2} \times \frac{1}{2}$ means $\frac{1}{2}$ of $\frac{1}{2}$. Similarly, merely telling students to "invert and multiply" when dividing fractions is not enough to foster understanding. Remind students that their answers should be in simplest form. Have advanced students find the error in the following proof.

$$a = b$$
$$a + b = 2a$$
$$\frac{a + b}{2} = a$$
$$\frac{a + b}{2} - b = a - b$$
$$a + b - 2b = 2(a - b)$$
$$a - b = 2(a - b)$$
$$\frac{a - b}{a - b} = \frac{2(a - b)}{a - b}$$
$$1 = 2$$

(If $a = b$, then $a - b = 0$, and the seventh step is undefined.)

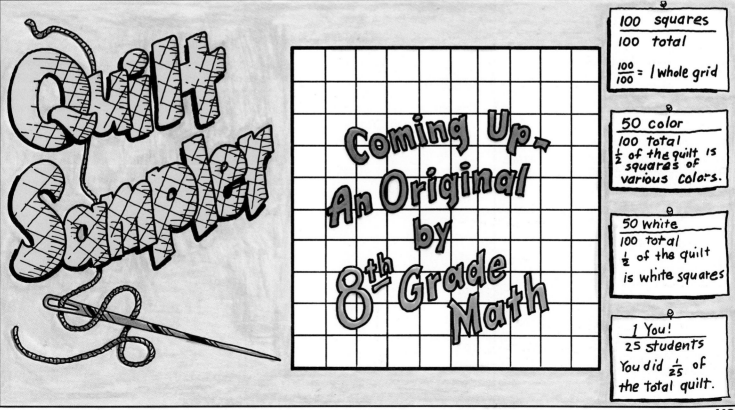

MATH LABS

NUMBER SENSE (Mental Math)

Have each student prepare a set of 20 index cards, 10 with a decimal and 10 with a fraction, and on the other side of the cards have each write his/her name.

Have two students combine their sets of cards, and then take turns turning one card at a time faceup. They should place each card in proper order with the cards that are already faceup on the table to form a number line. When all the cards are on the table, students should be able to write the fractions and decimals in order from greatest to least or from least to greatest. Then they can sort the cards, combine their sets with other students' and repeat the process.

NUMBER SENSE (Estimation)

Have students estimate products of fractions by finding the range of appropriate products. For example, to find the range for $3\frac{3}{4} \cdot 2\frac{1}{3}$, first round both numbers down ($3 \cdot 2 = 6$), then round both numbers up ($4 \cdot 3 = 12$). Therefore, $6 < 3\frac{3}{4} \cdot 2\frac{1}{3} < 12$. The boundaries are 6 and 12.

Have students find the boundaries for each product.

$$3\frac{1}{8} \cdot 6\frac{2}{3} \quad (18, 28)$$

$$5\frac{1}{5} \cdot 7\frac{9}{10} \quad (35, 48)$$

$$6\frac{4}{5} \cdot 8\frac{1}{3} \quad (48, 63)$$

$$4\frac{1}{2} \cdot 2\frac{7}{8} \quad (8, 15)$$

$$9\frac{1}{2} \cdot 3\frac{8}{9} \quad (27, 40)$$

$$7\frac{1}{7} \cdot 4\frac{5}{6} \quad (28, 40)$$

Have students find possible factors for each pair of boundaries listed below (Whole numbers must be as given, fractional numbers will vary.)

$$6 < \left(2\frac{1}{4} \cdot 3\frac{9}{10}\right) < 12$$

$$24 < \left(4\frac{3}{7} \cdot 6\frac{5}{8}\right) < 35$$

$$27 < \left(9\frac{7}{10} \cdot 3\frac{1}{2}\right) < 40$$

$$35 < \left(5\frac{1}{2} \cdot 7\frac{1}{3}\right) < 48$$

CALCULATOR

Because the calculator computes in decimal arithmetic, it will not perform fraction operations. The calculator, however, can be used to perform certain tedious computations within a fraction exercise. For example, $\frac{692}{473} \times \frac{821}{47} = \frac{568132}{22231}$. The calculator can be used to multiply numerators and denominators. Note that you must understand the process of multiplication before you use the calculator. Similarly, for other operations involving fractions, the calculator can be used as an aid in manipulating the computation of fractions.

Calculators should also be available for all problem-solving exercises.

Additional Activities: **Drill and Practice:** Complete this multiplication magic square. The product of each row, column, and diagonal is the same.

$7\frac{1}{2}$		5
	$2\frac{1}{2}$	
$1\frac{1}{4}$		

Exploration: Can you solve this mystery? Begin with 20. Do this code on your calculator.

$$27 \div 1\frac{1}{2} \times 3\frac{3}{8} \div 1\frac{1}{4} \div 1\frac{4}{5} = 27$$

Start with 45, 51. Why does this work?

PLAN AHEAD

This chapter will not require elaborate planning ahead. You will need fractional parts and graph paper.

SUBJECT AREA CONNECTIONS

Here are some activities for reinforcing the concepts presented in this chapter.

- **CONSUMER:** Have students research the number of cents per hour it takes to run a 60-watt light bulb, black and white television, toaster, and VCR. Then have them write these figures (decimals) as fractions of a dollar and multiply to find the cost of running each appliance over various periods of time.

- **SCIENCE:** Have students find the altitude of the highest mountain in North America. Then have them give the altitude of an expedition that has climbed $\frac{1}{4}$, $\frac{1}{3}$, $\frac{1}{2}$, $\frac{2}{3}$, and $\frac{3}{4}$ of the way to the top.

- **CONSUMER:** Have students cut out advertisements from the newspaper for products on sale at $\frac{1}{3}$ and $\frac{1}{2}$ off the regular price. Then have them find either the sale price or the regular price whichever is *not* given.

- **SOCIAL STUDIES:** Students conduct a survey of the number of classmates wearing red, green, brown, and blue clothing. Students write fractions that express the number of classmates wearing each color to the total number of classmates. Students then order the fractions from greatest to least.

PLANNING CALENDAR
ABBREVIATION KEY

Teacher's Resource Book	*Follow-up Activities*
MMW—Making Math Work	CALC—Calculator
P—Practice	CMP—Computer
R—Reteach	CNS—Consumer
E—Enrich	P&G—Puzzles and Games
	MNP—Manipulatives
	MC—Math Connection
	MCM—Math Communication
	NS—Number Sense
	PS—Problem Solving
	RFM—Reinforcement

PLANNING CALENDAR

Pages	Lesson Objectives	Basic	Average	Extended	Class/Home	More Practice	Math Reasoning	Follow-up	Reteach	Practice	Enrich
		ASSIGNMENT GUIDE									
119	Chapter Opener (Use MMW 7,8)	119	119	119							
120,121	To write equivalent fractions	1-20,36-41	1-41o,Chlg	16-41,Chlg	H48		H213	P&G CALC	35	48	46
122,123	To write a mixed number as a fraction and a fraction as a mixed number	1-41o, 43-44,Chlg	2-42e, 43-44,Chlg	1-12,31-44,Chlg	H49			CMP P&G	36	49	47
124,125	To compare and order fractions and mixed numbers	1-29o, 30-32,Calc	2-28e, 30-32,Calc	11-32,Calc	H50			NS RFM	37	50	48
126,127	To use information from a pictograph in solving problems	1-5	2-6	3-8	H51			PS RFM		51	49
128,129	To estimate sums and differences of fractions and mixed numbers	1-8,11-31	1-25,31-32	1-25,31-32	H52			RFM MC	38	52	50
130,131	To add fractions and mixed numbers	1-26,36-37	6-29,36-37	6-17,24-37	H53		H213	RFM PS	39	53	51
132,133	To subtract fractions and mixed numbers	1-16,23-31,36	1-31o, 32-37,Chlg	6-26e, 27-37,Chlg	H54	H198		P&G RFM	40	54	52
134,135	To subtract mixed numbers with renaming	1-20,37-38,MCR	5-24,37-38,MCR	21-38,MCR	H55			NS NS	41	55	53
136,137	To estimate in problem solving	1-4	2-5	3-6	H56			PS RFM		56	54
138,139	To multiply fractions	1-23,32-35,AL	1-23o, 24-35,AL	2-22e, 24-35,AL	H57			PS RFM	42	57	55
140,141	To estimate products and quotients using rational numbers	1-37o	1-39o, 40	2-38e, 39-40	H58			NS	43	58	56
142,143	To multiply mixed numbers	1-20e, 32-33,AL	1-19o, 21-34,AL	13-35,AL	H59		H213	RFM PS	44	59	57
144,145	To answer a question by writing a simpler problem	1-4	2-6	3-9	H60			PS		60	58
146,147	To divide fractions	1-25,31-32	6-32,Chlg	11-33,Chlg	H61			PS P&G	45	61	59
148,149	To divide mixed numbers	1-8,9-23o,33-36,F	1-23o, 25-26,F	2-24e, 25-36,F	H62	H199	H214	P&G PS	46	62	60
150,151	To explore writing decimals as fractions and fractions as decimals	150,151	150,151	150,151	H63	H199	H214	RFM CMP	47	63	61
152,153	To solve equations involving fractions	1-12,16-17,NS	1-15o, 17-19,NS	2-16e, 17-19,NS	H64		H214	MCM CMP	48	64	62
154,155	To interpret quotients and remainders in solving problems	1-5	2-6	5-10	H65					65	63
156	Logical Reasoning: To identify subsets and disjoint sets; to use a Venn diagram	156	156	156							
157	Group Project: To compare costs	157	157	157							

158,159 Chapter Test   160 Reteaching   161 Enrichment   162,163 Technology   164 Cumulative Review

TESTS

A. To find a fraction equivalent to a given fraction
B. To compare and order fractions and mixed numbers
C. To write a fraction as a whole or mixed number, and vice versa
D. To add or subtract fractions and mixed numbers
E. To multiply or divide fractions and mixed numbers
F. To write a fraction as a decimal, and vice versa
G. To solve one-step and two-step equations that involve fractions
H. To estimate sums, differences, products, and quotients of fractions and mixed numbers
I. To use information from a pictograph to solve problems
J. To write a simpler problem as a strategy for solving problems
K. To interpret the quotient and the remainder

FAMILY INVOLVEMENT

Family Involvement for Chapter 4 encourages family members to make a time schedule that shows the number of hours per week they spend on ordinary daily activities (breakfast, lunch, hobbies, physical exercise, work, school, watching television, and performing household chores.) After recording how many hours they spend each week on each activity, they must determine the fraction of each week they spend performing each activity. They are to compare the fractions to find out who spent the most, the least, or equal time on each activity. Students and their families are then to write the ideal amount of time that they would like to spend on each activity in a week and convert the figures into fractions of a week. Then they are to compare the ideal times to the real times. Family members are then to discuss ways in which they can spend their time doing what they would most like to do.

STUDENT RESOURCES

Bibliography

American Heritage Illustrated History of the United States, Vol. 2: Colonial America. Great Neck, NY: Choice Publishing, Inc., 1988.

Comins, Jeremy. *Totems, Decoys, and Covered Wagons.* New York: Lothrop, Lee, and Shepard Company, 1976.

Duncan, Jim. *Practical Math Skills—Junior High Level.* Carthage, IL: Good Apple, Inc., 1989.

Fisher, Timothy. *Hammocks, Hassocks, and Hideaways: Furniture Kids Can Build for Themselves.* Reading, Massachusetts: Addison-Wesley, 1980.

Loeper, John J. *The Shop on High Street: The Toys and Games of Early America.* New York: Atheneum, 1978.

Films

Between Rational Numbers. 7 minutes. Color. 1970. Distributed by Silver Burdett, Summit, N.J.

Dividing with Fractions—Reciprocals. Color. 1970. Distributed by Silver Burdett, Summit, N.J.

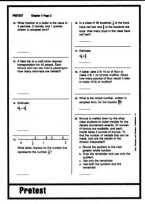

Which American handicrafts are you familiar with? Do you know anyone who enjoys whittling, making pottery, basket weaving, leather tooling, or quilting? Most craftspeople use mathematics when they design their crafts. Choose a craft. Which math skills might you need?

4 FRACTIONS

Objective: To explore problems related to hobbies

Direct students to look at the picture of the potter's wheel. Talk with students about their crafts or hobbies. If any student's craft is pottery, have him or her explain how a potter's wheel is used. Ask students which math skills they might need for making pottery; for wood-working; for quilting; for carving. (Answers will vary.)

SMALL GROUP
Statistics and Probability
Materials: Making Math Work page 7 per student

Instruct students to poll their families and friends about their favorite crafts. Have them organize this information into demographic categories as suggested and record it on the chart. When this information has been gathered and organized, have students record the information on a double-bar graph. Tell them to use a different color bar for each category. Remind students to title their graphs and label each axis. Have groups compare their graphs to find which craft is the most popular.

INDIVIDUAL
Geometry
Materials: Making Math Work page 8

Have each student complete Making Math Work page 8. Encourage students to be creative in designing the quilts. Have volunteers sketch several designs on the chalkboard. Then have students complete the rest of the work sheet. Ask students how they would alter their designs to fit all the different quilt sizes.

WHOLE CLASS
Patterns
Materials: completed Making Math Work page 8

Using the quilt squares shown on Making Math Work page 8, sketch several patterns of squares on the chalkboard, and have students predict the next 4 squares in each pattern. Two possible patterns are listed below, but you may want to develop your own if students have difficulty with these or find them too easy.
- a b b c c c d d d a a b b b (cccc)
- a b a c a d b a b c b d c a c b (cdda)

Discovering the patterns in these series of squares will give students valuable experience in defining *visual/spatial relationships*. Challenge students to come to the chalkboard, sketch quilt patterns of their own, and ask other students to continue the patterns.

MAKING MATH WORK

How would you go about polling different people in your community to find out which craft is their favorite craft? How many people would you poll? One way to record your information is to use demographic categories. You can group people into different classifications (male or female, younger than age 21 or older than age 21, and so on). Use the chart below to record your information. Check students' charts.

Craft	Category:_____	Category:_____

Now use a double-bar graph to show results. What is the favorite craft of the community? Check students' graphs.

How are the results different for different groups?
Answers will vary.

Use with pupil page 119.　　　　Making Math Work **7**

Making Math Work

MAKING MATH WORK

Plan a patchwork quilt. You will use four different kinds of material cut into 5½-inch squares. Look at the part of the quilt shown. Then complete the quilt plan.

Sketch your quilt here. Check students' sketches.

How much of each kind of material will you need to make each of the following quilts? How many squares will you need to make? Check students' tables.

Type of quilt	Squares of each material	Total squares
King quilt (102 in. x 102 in.)		
Queen quilt (90 in. x 102 in.)		
Full quilt (81 in. x 96 in.)		
Twin quilt (72 in. x 96 in.)		
Baby quilt (34 in. x 44 in.)		

If each square takes 2½ hours to make, how long will it take to complete each quilt? If each square is ¼ square foot, how many square feet of material will you need for each quilt? Check students' tables.

Type of quilt	Time	Square feet
King quilt (102 in. x 102 in.)		
Queen quilt (90 in. x 102 in.)		
Full quilt (81 in. x 96 in.)		
Twin quilt (72 in. x 96 in.)		
Baby quilt (34 in. x 44 in.)		

8 Making Math Work　　　　**Use with pupil page 119.**

Making Math Work

Objective: To find equivalent fractions

Warm-Up
Have students find the LCM of each set.

12 and 18 (36)   20 and 15 (60)
2, 6, and 8 (24)   3, 5, and 10 (30)

Have them find the GCF of each set.

18 and 20 (2)   12 and 16 (4)
9, 12, and 15 (3)   20, 300, and 80 (20)

GETTING STARTED

Materials: paper, crayons

Have each student fold a piece of paper into thirds and shade $\frac{2}{3}$. Then have them fold the paper in half and name the new fraction for the shaded part. ($\frac{4}{6}$)

Have them refold to find $\frac{8}{12}$ and $\frac{16}{24}$.

Write: $\frac{2}{3} = \frac{4}{6} = \frac{8}{12} = \frac{16}{24}$.

Have students explain why these fractions are equivalent. Ask whether they can think of a more efficient method of finding equivalent fractions.

TEACHING THE LESSON

A. Review the concepts of *numerator* and *denominator* as needed. Give examples of fractions as part of a whole and part of a group. Pay particular attention to fractions that equal 1.

B. Point out that when we multiply or divide the numerator and the denominator by the same number, the result is the same as multiplying by 1. Review the Identity Property of Multiplication.

C. Some students may prefer to use cross products to find the missing term.

$$\frac{2}{3} = \frac{n}{12}$$
$$3n = 24$$
$$n = 8$$

D. Ask students to think of other ways to prove that two or more fractions are equivalent. Two possibilities are
- simplifying one or both fractions;

$$\frac{3}{5} = \frac{3}{5} \qquad \frac{12}{20} = \frac{12 \div 4}{20 \div 4} = \frac{3}{5}$$

- renaming, using a common denominator.

$$\frac{3}{5} = \frac{3 \times 4}{5 \times 4} = \frac{12}{20} \qquad \frac{12}{20} = \frac{12}{20}$$

Equivalent Fractions

A. A fraction can be used to represent part of a whole or part of a set.

Equivalent fractions name the same number but use different terms. The fractions $\frac{1}{2}$, $\frac{2}{4}$, and $\frac{4}{8}$ are equivalent fractions.

B. To find an equivalent fraction, you can multiply or divide the numerator and the denominator of a fraction by the same number.

$$\text{numerator} \longrightarrow \frac{2}{3} = \frac{2 \times 2}{3 \times 2} = \frac{4}{6} \qquad \frac{6}{12} = \frac{6 \div 6}{12 \div 6} = \frac{1}{2}$$
$$\text{denominator} \longrightarrow \frac{2}{3} = \frac{2 \times 3}{3 \times 3} = \frac{6}{9} \qquad \frac{6}{12} = \frac{6 \div 2}{12 \div 2} = \frac{3}{6}$$

A fraction is in simplest form if the **greatest common factor (GCF)** of the numerator and the denominator is 1.

To write a fraction in simplest form, divide the numerator and the denominator by the GCF.

Write $\frac{15}{21}$ in simplest form.

$$\frac{15}{21} = \frac{15 \div 3}{21 \div 3} = \frac{5}{7}$$

Think:
The GCF of 15 and 21 is 3.

C. To find the missing term in $\frac{2}{3} = \frac{n}{12}$

Think: $3 \times \blacksquare = 12$. $3 \times 4 = 12$

Multiply 2 by 4. $\frac{2}{3} = \frac{2 \times 4}{3 \times 4} = \frac{8}{12}$ So, $n = 8$.

D. Use cross products to find whether two fractions are equivalent.

Are $\frac{3}{5}$ and $\frac{12}{20}$ equivalent?   Are $\frac{2}{9}$ and $\frac{1}{3}$ equivalent?

$$3 \times 20 = 60 \qquad\qquad 2 \times 3 = 6$$
$$5 \times 12 = 60 \qquad\qquad 9 \times 1 = 9$$

Yes, since $60 = 60$, $\frac{3}{5} = \frac{12}{20}$.   No, since $9 \neq 6$, $\frac{2}{9} \neq \frac{1}{3}$.

120   Math Reasoning, page H213

COMMON ERRORS

Some students might not understand the need to use the GCF in writing a fraction in simplest form; for example, they will simplify $\frac{4}{9}$ to $\frac{2}{3}$ because 2 is a factor of 4 and 3 is a factor of 9.

Remediation
For this error, have students list the factors of the numerator and the denominator in order to identify the greatest common factor.

$$\frac{18\ (1, 2, 3, \textbf{6}, 9, 18)}{24\ (1, 2, 3, 4, \textbf{6}, 8, 12, 24)} \qquad \frac{18 \div 6}{24 \div 6} = \frac{3}{4}$$

Assign Reteach Master, p. 35.

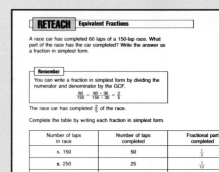

RETEACH Equivalent Fractions

A race car has completed 60 laps of a 150-lap race. What part of the race has the car completed? Write the answer as a fraction in simplest form.

Remember
You can write a fraction in simplest form by dividing the numerator and denominator by the GCF.
$\frac{60}{150} = \frac{60 \div 30}{150 \div 30} = \frac{2}{5}$

The race car has completed $\frac{2}{5}$ of the race.

Complete the table by writing each fraction in simplest form.

Number of laps in race	Number of laps completed	Fractional part completed
1. 150	50	$\frac{1}{3}$
2. 250	25	$\frac{1}{10}$
3. 100	8	$\frac{2}{25}$
4. 80	60	$\frac{3}{4}$

Write in simplest form.

5. $\frac{10}{16}$ $\frac{5}{8}$ 6. $\frac{40}{100}$ $\frac{2}{5}$ 7. $\frac{16}{48}$ $\frac{1}{3}$ 8. $\frac{10}{25}$ $\frac{2}{5}$

9. $\frac{12}{18}$ $\frac{2}{3}$ 10. $\frac{18}{24}$ $\frac{3}{4}$ 11. $\frac{12}{30}$ $\frac{2}{5}$ 12. $\frac{16}{24}$ $\frac{2}{3}$

13. $\frac{90}{110}$ $\frac{9}{11}$ 14. $\frac{18}{34}$ $\frac{9}{17}$ 15. $\frac{20}{32}$ $\frac{5}{8}$ 16. $\frac{48}{64}$ $\frac{3}{4}$

Use with pages 120–121.   35

Reteach Worksheet

Write two equivalent fractions for each. Answers will vary.

1. $\frac{3}{4}$ $\frac{6}{8}, \frac{9}{12}$ **2.** $\frac{1}{5}$ $\frac{2}{10}, \frac{3}{15}$ **3.** $\frac{2}{7}$ $\frac{6}{21}, \frac{8}{28}$ **4.** $\frac{3}{8}$ $\frac{6}{16}, \frac{12}{32}$ **5.** $\frac{4}{9}$ $\frac{8}{18}, \frac{12}{27}$

Write the fraction in simplest form.

6. $\frac{8}{12}$ $\frac{2}{3}$ **7.** $\frac{14}{21}$ $\frac{2}{3}$ **8.** $\frac{15}{20}$ $\frac{3}{4}$ **9.** $\frac{9}{10}$ $\frac{9}{10}$ **10.** $\frac{55}{80}$ $\frac{11}{16}$

Find the missing term.

11. $\frac{1}{4} = \frac{n}{12}$ 3 **12.** $\frac{2}{3} = \frac{n}{15}$ 10 **13.** $\frac{5}{9} = \frac{n}{27}$ 15 **14.** $\frac{1}{3} = \frac{n}{18}$ 6 **15.** $\frac{5}{6} = \frac{n}{30}$ 25

16. $\frac{2}{7} = \frac{n}{21}$ 6 **17.** $\frac{1}{10} = \frac{n}{100}$ 10 **18.** $\frac{3}{8} = \frac{n}{32}$ 12 **19.** $\frac{3}{2} = \frac{n}{24}$ 36 **20.** $\frac{5}{1} = \frac{n}{4}$ 20

21. $\frac{6}{7} = \frac{18}{n}$ 21 **22.** $\frac{1}{5} = \frac{25}{n}$ 125 **23.** $\frac{2}{3} = \frac{16}{n}$ 24 **24.** $\frac{5}{9} = \frac{30}{n}$ 54 **25.** $\frac{2}{7} = \frac{18}{n}$ 63

26. $\frac{5}{4} = \frac{35}{n}$ 28 **27.** $\frac{3}{4} = \frac{18}{n}$ 24 **28.** $\frac{1}{2} = \frac{49}{n}$ 98 **29.** $\frac{6}{8} = \frac{36}{n}$ 48 **30.** $\frac{5}{6} = \frac{20}{n}$ 24

31. $\frac{4}{5} = \frac{n}{15}$ 12 **32.** $\frac{8}{1} = \frac{48}{n}$ 6 **33.** $\frac{2}{3} = \frac{6}{n}$ 9 **34.** $\frac{3}{5} = \frac{n}{15}$ 9 **35.** $\frac{5}{9} = \frac{n}{36}$ 20

Use cross products to write = or ≠ for the ●.

36. $\frac{3}{4}$ ● $\frac{12}{16}$ = **37.** $\frac{5}{6}$ ● $\frac{7}{9}$ ≠ **38.** $\frac{5}{8}$ ● $\frac{12}{16}$ ≠ **39.** $\frac{9}{15}$ ● $\frac{3}{5}$ = **40.** $\frac{1}{6}$ ● $\frac{1}{3}$ ≠

Solve.

41. A class made wax candles for a history project. That day, 4 of the 28 students in the class were absent. What fraction of the class made candles? Write your answer in simplest form. $\frac{6}{7}$ of the class

CHALLENGE **Patterns, Relations, and Functions**

What fraction of each figure is shaded?

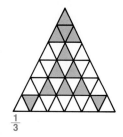
$\frac{1}{3}$

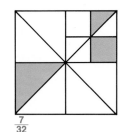
$\frac{7}{32}$

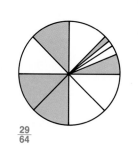
$\frac{29}{64}$

ASSIGNMENT GUIDE

Basic:	1–20, 36–41
Average:	1–41 o, Chlg
Extended:	16–41, Chlg

Resources
Practice, p. 48   Class/Home, p. H48
Reteach, p. 35   Reasoning, p. H213
Enrich, p. 46

Exercise Analysis

1–5	Write two equivalent fractions
6–10	Write a fraction in simplest form
11–35	Find the missing term of an equivalent fraction
36–40	Use cross products to determine whether fractions are equivalent
41	Skill application

Challenge

The key is to use the denominator of the smallest shaded section to rename each shaded section. In the square, the smallest shaded section represents $\frac{1}{32}$; in the circle, $\frac{1}{64}$.

FOLLOW-UP ACTIVITIES

PUZZLES AND GAMES
Have students use the clues to solve each riddle.

● What has no wings but can fly?

  Clues: first $\frac{3}{7}$ of *helpful*, middle $\frac{1}{7}$ of *minimum*, first $\frac{3}{4}$ of *cope*, last $\frac{1}{2}$ of *winter*

● It's 100 years old!

  Clues: first $\frac{3}{4}$ of *cent*, middle $\frac{3}{7}$ of *natural*, middle $\frac{1}{3}$ of *rye*

Have students make up similar riddles.

CALCULATOR
Have each student write a calculator sentence for finding each missing term, and then have each student key it in.

● $\frac{5}{6} = \frac{x}{30}$ (5 ⊠ 30 ÷ 6 ⊟ 25)

● $\frac{3}{x} = \frac{198}{462}$ (3 ⊠ 462 ÷ 198 ⊟ 7)

● $\frac{x}{12} = \frac{176}{192}$ (176 ⊠ 12 ÷ 192 ⊟ 11)

● $\frac{17}{20} = \frac{1,071}{x}$ (1,071 ⊠ 20 ÷ 17 ⊟ 1,260)

COMING UP

Fractions get mixed up.

Warm-Up

Have students compute each example mentally.

$3 \times 7 + 4$ (25)	$8 \times 6 + 4$ (52)
$7 \times 8 + 7$ (63)	$4 \times 10 + 7$ (47)
$6 \times 12 + 11$ (83)	$9 \times 16 + 9$ (153)

GETTING STARTED

Explain that a recipe for Colonial Tea calls for $\frac{1}{3}$ teaspoon honey per cup of tea.

Point out the inconvenience of measuring $\frac{1}{3}$ teaspoon 16 times. Ask students to think of an easier way.

TEACHING THE LESSON

A. Reinforce the concepts of mixed numbers and fractions greater than 1 by having students draw models to show the following.

$$2\frac{1}{2} \qquad 5\frac{3}{4} \qquad \frac{8}{3} \qquad \frac{15}{8}$$

B. Have students calculate mentally.
- How many thirds are in 3? (9)
- Add two more thirds. How many thirds are there now? (11) Write: $3\frac{2}{3} = \frac{11}{3}$

Repeat with similar examples.

C. Use models as needed to show the concept that underlies the computation.
- How many groups of 6 are there in 34? (5)
- What part of a group is left? ($\frac{4}{6}$)
- Write the whole number and fraction. ($5\frac{4}{6}$)
- Simplify, if necessary. ($5\frac{2}{3}$)

Checkpoint

The chart lists the common errors students make when renaming mixed numbers as fractions.

Correct Answers: 1b, 2b

Remediation

■ For these errors, have students rewrite each mixed number as the sum of a whole number and a fraction. After they have renamed the mixed number, have them compare the fraction to this sum to check whether the answer is reasonable.

□ For these errors, assign Reteach Master, p. 36.

Mixed Numbers

A. A **mixed number** is the sum of a whole number and a fraction.

$5\frac{1}{3}$ means $5 + \frac{1}{3}$.

Every mixed number is equivalent to a fraction.

$$5\frac{1}{3} = 5 + \frac{1}{3} = \frac{15}{3} + \frac{1}{3} = \frac{16}{3}$$

B. You can use a shortcut to write a mixed number as a fraction. Write $5\frac{1}{2}$ as a fraction.

Multiply the whole number by the denominator.	Add the numerator to the product.	Write the sum over the denominator.
$5\frac{1}{2} \longrightarrow 2 \times 5 = 10$	$10 + 1 = 11$	$\frac{11}{2}$

So, $5\frac{1}{2} = \frac{11}{2}$.

C. Fractions greater than 1 can be written as mixed numbers. Write $\frac{34}{6}$ as a mixed number.

$$\frac{34}{6} \longrightarrow \begin{array}{r} 5 \\ 6\overline{)34} \\ 30 \\ \hline 4 \end{array} \begin{array}{l} \leftarrow \text{whole-} \\ \text{number} \\ \text{part} \end{array} \qquad \frac{4}{6} \leftarrow \text{fraction} \qquad 5\frac{4}{6} = 5\frac{2}{3}$$

So, the fraction $\frac{34}{6}$ can be written as the mixed number $5\frac{2}{3}$.

Checkpoint Write the letter of the correct answer.

Choose the equivalent fraction.

1. $3\frac{2}{3} = \blacksquare$

  a. $\frac{9}{3}$ **(b.)** $\frac{11}{3}$ **c.** $\frac{12}{3}$ **d.** $\frac{15}{3}$

2. $2\frac{5}{7} = \blacksquare$

  a. $\frac{12}{7}$ **(b.)** $\frac{19}{7}$ **c.** $\frac{49}{7}$ **d.** $\frac{70}{7}$

122

COMMON ERRORS

Answer Choice	Type of Error
■ 1a	Fails to add the numerator to the renamed whole number
□ 1c	Adds the whole number and the denominator and then multiplies by the numerator
□ 1d, 2c	Adds the whole number and the numerator and then multiplies by the denominator
■ 2a	Adds the numerator and the denominator
□ 2d	Multiplies the whole number by the numerator and then multiplies by the denominator

---

Write the mixed number as a fraction.

1. $5\frac{1}{3}$ $\frac{16}{3}$ 2. $2\frac{1}{2}$ $\frac{5}{2}$ 3. $6\frac{2}{3}$ $\frac{20}{3}$ 4. $9\frac{4}{5}$ $\frac{49}{5}$ 5. $5\frac{3}{4}$ $\frac{23}{4}$ 6. $7\frac{1}{9}$ $\frac{64}{9}$

7. $2\frac{6}{7}$ $\frac{20}{7}$ 8. $9\frac{7}{8}$ $\frac{79}{8}$ 9. $3\frac{4}{5}$ $\frac{19}{5}$ 10. $1\frac{12}{13}$ $\frac{25}{13}$ 11. $10\frac{10}{11}$ $\frac{120}{11}$ 12. $6\frac{1}{9}$ $\frac{55}{9}$

13. $7\frac{1}{3}$ $\frac{22}{3}$ 14. $1\frac{1}{9}$ $\frac{10}{9}$ 15. $2\frac{5}{6}$ $\frac{17}{6}$ 16. $7\frac{8}{9}$ $\frac{71}{9}$ 17. $5\frac{9}{10}$ $\frac{59}{10}$ 18. $7\frac{8}{10}$ $\frac{78}{10}$

Write the fraction as a whole number or a mixed
number in simplest form.

19. $\frac{22}{5}$ $4\frac{2}{5}$ 20. $\frac{10}{6}$ $1\frac{2}{3}$ 21. $\frac{32}{9}$ $3\frac{5}{9}$ 22. $\frac{45}{7}$ $6\frac{3}{7}$ 23. $\frac{23}{2}$ $11\frac{1}{2}$ 24. $\frac{86}{40}$ $2\frac{3}{20}$

25. $\frac{71}{20}$ $3\frac{11}{20}$ 26. $\frac{12}{3}$ 4 27. $\frac{15}{9}$ $1\frac{2}{3}$ 28. $\frac{17}{16}$ $1\frac{1}{16}$ 29. $\frac{21}{8}$ $2\frac{5}{8}$ 30. $\frac{23}{5}$ $4\frac{3}{5}$

31. $\frac{39}{10}$ $3\frac{9}{10}$ 32. $\frac{5}{4}$ $1\frac{1}{4}$ 33. $\frac{18}{5}$ $3\frac{3}{5}$ 34. $\frac{23}{9}$ $2\frac{5}{9}$ 35. $\frac{17}{10}$ $1\frac{7}{10}$ 36. $\frac{18}{17}$ $1\frac{1}{17}$

37. $\frac{36}{7}$ $5\frac{1}{7}$ 38. $\frac{42}{9}$ $4\frac{2}{3}$ 39. $\frac{43}{9}$ $4\frac{7}{9}$ 40. $\frac{25}{7}$ $3\frac{4}{7}$ 41. $\frac{8}{1}$ 8 42. $\frac{24}{5}$ $4\frac{4}{5}$

Solve. For Problem 44, use the Infobank.

43. Pete is making wooden legs for
stools. He needs 4 legs for each
stool. If Pete has made 34 legs,
how many stools can he make?
How many legs will be left?
8 stools; 2 legs

44. Use the information on page 474 to
solve. Find the materials that can
be used to make a basket. List the
materials which come in $\frac{3}{8}$-in.
widths.
flat reed, flat oval reed, round reed

CHALLENGE

What fraction of a dollar is each coin?

$\frac{1}{100}$ $\frac{1}{20}$ $\frac{1}{10}$ $\frac{1}{4}$ $\frac{1}{2}$

What fraction are they of $100?

$\frac{1}{10,000}$ $\frac{1}{2,000}$ $\frac{1}{1,000}$ $\frac{1}{400}$ $\frac{1}{200}$

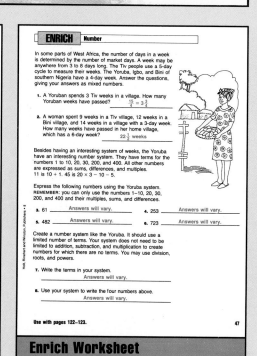

Practice Worksheet

Enrich Worksheet

ASSIGNMENT GUIDE

Basic: 1–41 o, 43–44, Chlg

Average: 2–42 e, 43–44, Chlg

Extended: 1–12, 31–44, Chlg

Resources
Practice, p. 49   Class/Home, p. H49
Reteach, p. 36
Enrich, p. 47

Exercise Analysis

1–18   Write a mixed number as a fraction

19–42   Write a fraction as a whole number or a mixed number

43   Skill application

44   Data collection and computation

Challenge

To find what fraction each coin is of $1,000,
guide students to realize that since 1¢ =
$\frac{1}{100}$ of $1 and $1 = $\frac{1}{1,000}$ of $1,000, 1¢ of
$1,000 = $\frac{1}{100} \times \frac{1}{1,000} = \frac{1}{100,000}$.

FOLLOW-UP ACTIVITIES

COMPUTER
Have students write a program that
will rename a fraction greater than 1 as a
mixed number and a mixed number as a
fraction.

```
10 INPUT "WHAT IS TO BE RENAMED";
   A$
20 IF A$ = "MIXED NUMBER" THEN 50
30 IF A$ = "FRACTION" THEN 100
40 GOTO 10
50 REM RENAMING A MIXED NUMBER
60 INPUT "WHOLE NUMBER, NUMERA-
   TOR, DENOMINATOR"; W,N,D
70 LET G = W*D + N
80 PRINT G; "/"; D
90 GOTO 150
100 REM RENAMING A FRACTION
110 INPUT "NUMERATOR, DENOMINA-
    TOR"; N,D
120 LET Y = INT (N/D)
130 LET Z = N – Y*D
140 PRINT Y; " "; Z; "/"D
150 END
```

PUZZLES AND GAMES
Have students write four 9's so that
they will equal 100. (99$\frac{9}{9}$)

COMING UP
Line up the fractions.

4 | FRACTIONS

Objectives: To compare and order fractions and mixed numbers

Warm-Up

Have students find the LCM of each.

5 and 8 (40)	4 and 10 (20)
2, 3, and 5 (30)	4, 7, and 8 (56)

GETTING STARTED

Materials: graph paper, ruler

Have students draw a 4-inch line segment on graph paper, mark off 1-inch segments, and label them $\frac{1}{4}$, $\frac{2}{4}$, $\frac{3}{4}$, and $\frac{4}{4}$. Tell students to draw a perpendicular line at $\frac{4}{4}$. Then have them draw a 5-inch line segment from the left endpoint of the original line segment to the perpendicular line (they will have a right triangle). Students should mark off 1-inch segments on this line and from each of these points should draw lines perpendicular to and intersecting the first line. Tell them to mark these points of intersection $\frac{1}{5}$, $\frac{2}{5}$, $\frac{3}{5}$, $\frac{4}{5}$, and $\frac{5}{5}$. Then have students use this line as a number line, and ask them which is greater—$\frac{3}{4}$ or $\frac{4}{5}$. $\left(\frac{4}{5}\right)$

TEACHING THE LESSON

A. As you discuss the text example, point out that $\frac{15}{12} = 1\frac{3}{12}$ and that $\frac{20}{12} = 1\frac{8}{12}$.

Point out that fractions that have like numerators can also be compared easily: the greater the denominator, the lesser the fraction. For example, $\frac{7}{12} < \frac{7}{10}$.

Have students compare each pair of fractions.

- $\frac{8}{27}$ ● $\frac{8}{23}$ (<)
- $\frac{6}{210}$ ● $\frac{6}{232}$ (>)

B. Point out that the LCM need not be used and that any common multiple will work.

C. You may want to have students apply the procedure for comparing mixed numbers to examples such as:

- $3\frac{5}{80}$ ● $3\frac{5}{8}$ (<)
- $7\frac{4}{50}$ ● $7\frac{4}{7}$ (<)

D. Use the following example to demonstrate that the procedure is the same for ordering fractions less than 1, fractions greater than 1, and mixed numbers.

Write $\frac{2}{3}$, $\frac{7}{6}$, $1\frac{5}{12}$, and $\frac{3}{4}$ in order from the greatest to the least. $\left(1\frac{5}{12}, \frac{7}{6}, \frac{3}{4}, \frac{2}{3}\right)$

Comparing and Ordering Fractions and Mixed Numbers

A. A number line can be used to compare fractions.

Number line showing $\frac{1}{4}$, $\frac{1}{3}$, $\frac{1}{2}$, $\frac{2}{3}$, $\frac{3}{4}$, 1, $1\frac{1}{4}$, $1\frac{1}{2}$, $1\frac{2}{3}$, $1\frac{3}{4}$, 2 and below: $\frac{1}{12}$, $\frac{2}{12}$, $\frac{3}{12}$, $\frac{4}{12}$, $\frac{5}{12}$, $\frac{6}{12}$, $\frac{7}{12}$, $\frac{8}{12}$, $\frac{9}{12}$, $\frac{10}{12}$, $\frac{11}{12}$, $\frac{12}{12}$, $\frac{13}{12}$, $\frac{14}{12}$, $\frac{15}{12}$, $\frac{16}{12}$, $\frac{17}{12}$, $\frac{18}{12}$, $\frac{19}{12}$, $\frac{20}{12}$, $\frac{21}{12}$, $\frac{22}{12}$, $\frac{23}{12}$, $\frac{24}{12}$

To compare fractions that have like denominators, compare their numerators. From the number line, you can see that $\frac{7}{12} > \frac{5}{12}$, $\frac{15}{12} < \frac{20}{12}$, and $1\frac{1}{4} < 1\frac{2}{3}$.

B. Compare fractions that have unlike denominators by writing equivalent fractions and comparing numerators.

Compare $\frac{3}{5}$ and $\frac{5}{8}$.

Find the **least common multiple (LCM)** of 5 and 8. The **least common denominator (LCD)** is 40.

$$\frac{3}{5} = \frac{24}{40} \qquad\qquad \frac{5}{8} = \frac{25}{40}$$

Since $24 < 25$, $\frac{24}{40} < \frac{25}{40}$ and $\frac{3}{5} < \frac{5}{8}$.

C. You can also compare mixed numbers. First compare the whole numbers; then compare the fractions.

Compare $3\frac{2}{3}$ and $3\frac{1}{2}$.

$3 = 3 \qquad \frac{2}{3} = \frac{4}{6} \qquad \frac{1}{2} = \frac{3}{6} \qquad \frac{4}{6} > \frac{3}{6} \qquad$ So, $3\frac{2}{3} > 3\frac{1}{2}$.

D. To order fractions and mixed numbers, compare.

Order $\frac{3}{4}$, $\frac{2}{5}$, and $\frac{5}{6}$.

$$\frac{3}{4} = \frac{45}{60} \qquad \frac{2}{5} = \frac{24}{60} \qquad \frac{5}{6} = \frac{50}{60}$$

So, $\frac{2}{5} < \frac{3}{4} < \frac{5}{6}$.

Order $4\frac{1}{5}$, $4\frac{3}{10}$, and $4\frac{2}{7}$.

$$4 = 4 = 4$$

$$\frac{1}{5} = \frac{14}{70} \qquad \frac{3}{10} = \frac{21}{70} \qquad \frac{2}{7} = \frac{20}{70}$$

So, $4\frac{1}{5} < 4\frac{2}{7} < 4\frac{3}{10}$.

From least to greatest: $\frac{2}{5}$, $\frac{3}{4}$, $\frac{5}{6}$

From greatest to least: $\frac{5}{6}$, $\frac{3}{4}$, $\frac{2}{5}$

From least to greatest: $4\frac{1}{5}$, $4\frac{2}{7}$, $4\frac{3}{10}$

From greatest to least: $4\frac{3}{10}$, $4\frac{2}{7}$, $4\frac{1}{5}$

124

COMMON ERRORS

Some students might conclude that $3\frac{8}{15} > 3\frac{3}{4}$ because they think the greater number of parts indicates a greater fraction.

Remediation

For this error, use diagrams to review the fundamental concept that for wholes of equal size, the greater the number of parts, the smaller each part becomes. Explain that $\frac{3}{4} > \frac{3}{6}$ because fourths are greater than sixths and a number of fourths is therefore greater than the same number of sixths.

Assign Reteach Master, p. 37.

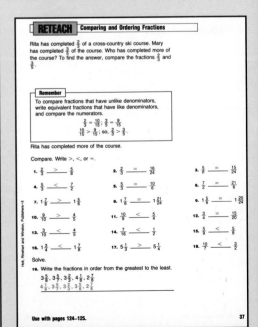

Compare. Write $>$, $<$, or $=$ for ●.

1. $\frac{3}{5}$ ● $\frac{4}{5}$ $<$ 2. $\frac{2}{3}$ ● $\frac{1}{3}$ $>$ 3. $\frac{4}{9}$ ● $\frac{8}{9}$ $<$ 4. $\frac{7}{8}$ ● $\frac{1}{8}$ $>$ 5. $\frac{3}{4}$ ● $\frac{1}{4}$ $>$

6. $\frac{6}{7}$ ● $\frac{7}{8}$ $<$ 7. $\frac{5}{9}$ ● $\frac{4}{5}$ $<$ 8. $\frac{2}{3}$ ● $\frac{1}{2}$ $>$ 9. $\frac{3}{8}$ ● $\frac{3}{4}$ $<$ 10. $\frac{9}{10}$ ● $\frac{2}{3}$ $>$

11. $\frac{8}{4}$ ● $\frac{7}{8}$ $>$ 12. $\frac{10}{11}$ ● $\frac{5}{6}$ $>$ 13. $\frac{4}{7}$ ● $\frac{8}{9}$ $<$ 14. $\frac{1}{6}$ ● $\frac{9}{10}$ $<$ 15. $\frac{7}{9}$ ● $\frac{3}{5}$ $>$

16. $3\frac{1}{6}$ ● $4\frac{5}{6}$ $<$ 17. $2\frac{3}{7}$ ● $2\frac{1}{7}$ $>$ 18. $5\frac{1}{3}$ ● $6\frac{2}{3}$ $<$ 19. $8\frac{1}{4}$ ● $8\frac{3}{4}$ $<$

20. $6\frac{1}{5}$ ● $3\frac{1}{8}$ $>$ 21. $4\frac{1}{9}$ ● $4\frac{1}{8}$ $<$ 22. $5\frac{5}{9}$ ● $4\frac{7}{10}$ $>$ 23. $6\frac{2}{3}$ ● $7\frac{8}{9}$ $<$

Order from the least to the greatest.

24. $\frac{5}{6}, \frac{2}{9}, \frac{1}{3}$ $\frac{2}{9}, \frac{1}{3}, \frac{5}{6}$ 25. $\frac{3}{4}, \frac{1}{4}, \frac{5}{8}$ $\frac{1}{4}, \frac{5}{8}, \frac{3}{4}$ 26. $\frac{3}{5}, \frac{3}{10}, \frac{13}{15}, 2\frac{1}{15}$
$\frac{3}{10}, \frac{3}{5}, \frac{13}{15}, 2\frac{1}{15}$

Order from the greatest to the least.

27. $\frac{1}{6}, \frac{1}{2}, \frac{3}{4}$ $\frac{3}{4}, \frac{1}{2}, \frac{1}{6}$ 28. $\frac{2}{3}, \frac{2}{15}, \frac{3}{5}$ $\frac{2}{3}, \frac{3}{5}, \frac{2}{15}$ 29. $\frac{4}{7}, \frac{1}{2}, \frac{3}{4}, 1\frac{1}{8}$
$1\frac{1}{8}, \frac{3}{4}, \frac{4}{7}, \frac{1}{2}$

Solve.

30. A standard double-bed quilt is 16 patches across and 27 patches long. How many patches are in the quilt?
432 patches

31. Design your own quilt square. Write problems to compare fractions or whole numbers. **Answers will vary.**

32. A quilt uses 8 triangles and 1 square of red fabric, 12 triangles of black fabric, 4 triangles and 2 squares of checked fabric, and 4 squares of floral fabric. If each triangle is $\frac{1}{4}$ the size of a square, which fabric is used the most? **floral fabric**

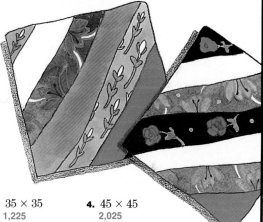

CALCULATOR

Use a calculator to find each product.

1. 15×15 225   2. 25×25 625   3. 35×35 1,225   4. 45×45 2,025

Find a pattern to help you predict:

5. 65×65 4,225   6. 75×75 5,625   7. 85×85 7,225   8. 95×95 9,025

Classwork/Homework, page H50

125

ASSIGNMENT GUIDE

Basic: 1–29 o, 30–32, Calc

Average: 2–28 e, 30–32, Calc

Extended: 11–32, Calc

Resources
Practice, p. 50   Class/Home, p. H50
Reteach, p. 37
Enrich, p. 48

Exercise Analysis

1–15   Compare fractions
16–23   Compare mixed numbers
24–26   Order fractions from the least to the greatest
27–29   Order fractions from the greatest to the least
30, 32   Skill applications
31   Problem formulation

Calculator

Students use their calculators to find a pattern of products. Then they use this pattern to predict other products.

FOLLOW-UP ACTIVITIES

NUMBER SENSE (Mental Math)

Have students use $=$ or $\neq$ to make each statement true.

$3\frac{1}{8}$ ● $2\frac{9}{8}$ $(=)$ $3\frac{3}{2}$ ● $4\frac{2}{7}$ $(\neq)$ $5\frac{6}{4}$ ● $3\frac{3}{1}$ $(\neq)$

$4\frac{8}{3}$ ● $6\frac{1}{3}$ $(\neq)$ $1\frac{9}{2}$ ● $7\frac{1}{8}$ $(\neq)$ $6\frac{12}{4}$ ● $1\frac{48}{6}$ $(=)$

$7\frac{1}{3}$ ● $5\frac{14}{16}$ $(\neq)$ $6\frac{5}{3}$ ● $7\frac{1}{3}$ $(\neq)$ $1\frac{19}{6}$ ● $4\frac{1}{6}$ $(=)$

$1\frac{15}{12}$ ● $2\frac{1}{4}$ $(=)$ $3\frac{20}{3}$ ● $9\frac{2}{3}$ $(=)$ $5\frac{1}{8}$ ● $1\frac{25}{6}$ $(\neq)$

REINFORCEMENT

Have students write the missing numerators or denominators that will make the sentence true. (Answers will vary. Possible answers are given.)

$\frac{1}{■} > \frac{■}{2} > \frac{3}{■} > \frac{■}{4} > \frac{5}{■} > \frac{■}{6}$
(1)   (1)   (1)   (1)   (1)   (1)
(1)   (7)   (21)

$\frac{1}{■} < \frac{1}{■} < \frac{1}{■} < \frac{1}{■} < \frac{1}{■} < \frac{1}{■}$
(6)   (5)   (4)   (3)   (2)   (1)

$\frac{1}{■} > \frac{2}{■} > \frac{3}{■} > \frac{4}{■} > \frac{5}{■} > \frac{6}{■}$
(1)   (3)   (5)   (7)   (9)   (11)

COMING UP

Can you picture that?

PRACTICE · Comparing Fractions and Mixed Numbers

Compare. Write $>$, $<$, or $=$ in the circle. Use the LCD.

Write the numbers in order from the least to the greatest.

Solve.

29. Marie drank $1\frac{3}{5}$ cups of juice. Roger drank $1\frac{2}{3}$ cups of juice. Who drank more juice? Marie

30. Lila has two different recipes for banana bread. Recipe A uses $3\frac{1}{4}$ cups of bananas. Recipe B uses $3\frac{7}{8}$ cups of bananas. Which recipe uses less? Recipe A

50   Use with pages 124–125.

Practice Worksheet

ENRICH · Number

It was a very rainy autumn. Many of the fall sports events were rained out. Ranking of the teams in the AA South division was difficult, because all the teams played different numbers of games. The chart gives each school's record in each sport, expressed as a fraction of events won over events played.

School	Soccer	Lacrosse	Football	Field Hockey	Track & Field
Sunnyside	$\frac{8}{19}$	$\frac{6}{12}$	$\frac{6}{11}$	$\frac{5}{8}$	$\frac{6}{10}$
Franklin	$\frac{7}{18}$	$\frac{7}{11}$	$\frac{8}{11}$	$\frac{5}{9}$	$\frac{6}{10}$
Central	$\frac{5}{18}$	$\frac{5}{9}$	$\frac{7}{12}$	$\frac{7}{9}$	$\frac{4}{11}$
Lincoln	$\frac{6}{17}$	$\frac{7}{13}$	$\frac{6}{10}$	$\frac{6}{9}$	$\frac{5}{11}$
Cleveland	$\frac{10}{19}$	$\frac{8}{14}$	$\frac{4}{9}$	$\frac{7}{12}$	$\frac{7}{12}$
Northwoods	$\frac{9}{19}$	$\frac{7}{12}$	$\frac{5}{11}$	$\frac{6}{10}$	$\frac{5}{9}$

For each sport, list the teams in order from the school with the best record to the school with the worst record.

1. Soccer:
Cleveland, Northwoods, Central, Sunnyside, Franklin, Lincoln

2. Lacrosse:
Franklin, Northwoods, Cleveland, Central, Lincoln, Sunnyside

3. Football:
Lincoln, Central, Sunnyside, Franklin, Northwoods, Cleveland

4. Field Hockey:
Central, Franklin, Lincoln, Sunnyside, Northwoods, Cleveland

5. Track & Field:
Sunnyside, Cleveland, Northwoods, Franklin, Lincoln, Central

48   Use with pages 124–125.

Enrich Worksheet

Objective: To use information from a pictograph

Warm-Up
Have students compute the following.

5 · 20 (100)   6 · 18 (108)
13^2 (169) 15^2 (225)

GETTING STARTED

Discuss with students the use of international traveler's aid symbols. Elicit from them descriptions of some of the familiar ones; for example, the symbols for rest rooms, fuel stations, highway-side restaurants, do-not-enter signs, and no-smoking signs.

TEACHING THE LESSON

Pictographs are one information source that appear with increasing frequency in newspapers, magazines, and television news shows. They are also one of the easiest sources to read. Tell students that in reading a pictograph, the first step is to read the title and labels. The titles and labels will tell students the information that is contained in the pictograph. Students should next read the legend to identify what each symbol stands for. They can then read the graph by multiplying the number of symbols next to each heading by the number of items each symbol represents. Explain to students that a half symbol represents one half the number of items a whole symbol represents.

Questions: As with reading any outside information source, one problem some students will encounter with the question is that the information needed to answer the question is not in the exercise itself. Have students familiarize themselves with the pictograph before they approach the problems.

Tools: Explain to students that pictographs are used for comparing data and are similar in that respect to bar graphs. They provide a quick visual comparison for finding such information as greatest, least, range, and so on. One common problem students face is reading information from the graph incorrectly. By familiarizing themselves with the key to the symbols used in the graph before they look at the questions, students can often avoid this problem.

Solutions: Many errors result from mistakes in reading the graphs. Have students review the key to the symbols used in the graphs.

PROBLEM SOLVING
Using a Pictograph

A pictograph is a kind of graph that uses pictures or symbols to represent quantities of items. Use the pictograph below to answer this question. How many shirts were hand-painted?

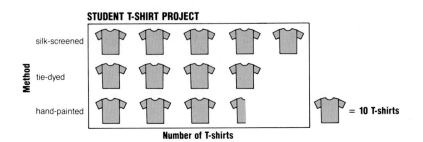

STUDENT T-SHIRT PROJECT

Method: silk-screened / tie-dyed / hand-painted

Number of T-shirts

= 10 T-shirts

- The title tells you that this pictograph shows the number of T-shirts decorated for a student project.
- The key tells you that each symbol stands for 10 T-shirts. This means that half of a T-shirt symbol stands for half of 10, or 5.
- You can find the number of shirts that were hand-painted by counting the symbols in that row. There are $3\frac{1}{2}$ symbols. The 3 symbols stand for 30 shirts; the $\frac{1}{2}$ symbol stands for 5 shirts; so, there is a total of 35 shirts.

Use the T-shirt pictograph to answer each question. Write the letter of the correct answer.

1. How many T-shirts were tie-dyed?

a. 4
b. 40
c. 45

2. Which method of decoration was the most popular?

a. silk-screening
b. tie-dyeing
c. hand-painting

126

Checks: Have students check the accuracy of the information read from the graph. Be sure that students understand what each symbol represents and that they have correctly counted the number of symbols.

The pictograph below displays the average weekly basket sales in Jane's shop. Use the pictograph to help you solve each question.

JANE'S BASKET SHOP: AVERAGE WEEKLY SALES

Kind of basket:
reed, cane, ash-splint, oak splint, sea-grass, raffia, sisal

Number sold

 = 16 baskets

3. How many more reed baskets than raffia baskets were sold weekly? **16 more baskets**

4. On the average, how many ash-splint baskets are sold in a week? **72 baskets**

5. About how many sea-grass baskets are sold in a week?
56 baskets

6. Which kind of basket is the most popular?
cane basket

7. Which kind of basket is the least popular?
sisal basket

8. Which three kinds of baskets are the best-sellers?
cane, oak splint, and reed

Classwork/Homework, page H51

ASSIGNMENT GUIDE

Basic: 1–5

Average: 2–6

Extended: 3–8

Resources
Practice, p. 51   Class/Home, p. H51
Enrich, p. 49

Exercise Analysis
1–2 Use a pictograph to choose the correct answer
3–8 Use information from a pictograph to solve a problem

FOLLOW-UP ACTIVITIES

PROBLEM SOLVING
Materials: business or science magazines with pictographs

Separate students into groups of four. Have each group find a pictograph in a magazine. Each group should define exactly the information that is contained in the pictograph and then write five or six questions based on that information. Groups will then exchange pictographs and questions and answer them.

REINFORCEMENT
Tell students that information in a pictograph has often been rounded; for example, if each symbol represents 100, the information might be rounded to the nearest 50.

List the information below on the chalkboard. Tell students that it is to be displayed in a pictograph and that the symbol used will represent 100 items. Half symbols will also be used. Have them round each number accordingly and determine the number of symbols needed.

The Pottery Shed: Monthly Sales

Mugs	282	(300; 3 symbols)
Bowls	541	(550; 5½ symbols)
Plates	309	(300; 3 symbols)
Jugs	128	(150; 1½ symbols)
Ashtrays	672	(650; 6½ symbols)

COMING UP
Sums and differences, more or less

PRACTICE Using a Pictograph

PIZZA PALACE SALES

Monday	⊗⊗⊗⊗⊗
Tuesday	⊗⊗⊗⊗⊗◖
Wednesday	⊗⊗⊗⊗⊗
Thursday	⊗⊗⊗⊗⊗
Friday	⊗⊗⊗⊗⊗⊗⊗◖
Saturday	⊗⊗⊗⊗⊗⊗
Sunday	⊗⊗⊗⊗⊗◖

⊗ = 50 pizzas

The pictograph above shows the average sales of pizzas for various days of the week. Use the pictograph to solve.

1. On which day are the most pizzas sold? Friday

2. On which days are the least pizzas sold?
Monday and Wednesday

3. How many more pizzas are normally sold on Thursday than on Sunday? 75

4. What is the average number of pizzas sold per week?
2,450

5. How many more pizzas does the Palace normally sell during the week (Monday through Friday) than on weekends? 1,050

6. When there is a Friday night football game, the Pizza Palace sales are usually 1.6 times the normal Friday sales. About how many are sold on a football Friday? 680

7. During a holiday weekend the sales on Friday, Saturday, and Sunday are usually 1.5 times the usual sales. Calculate the sales for each of these three days during the holiday weekend. (Round to the nearest whole number.) Friday 638; Saturday 563; Sunday 488

8. If the average profit on a pizza is $2.63, how much profit does the Pizza Palace earn on the sales of pizzas during an average week? $6,443.50

Use after pages 126–127.   51

Practice Worksheet

ENRICH Problem Solving

🌳 = 1,000 trees 🌳 = 750 trees 🌳 = 500 trees 🌳 = 250 trees

	Walnut	Oak	Poplar	Cottonwood
Number of trees reaching maturity this year	🌳🌳🌳🌳	🌳🌳🌳🌳🌳	🌳🌳🌳🌳🌳🌳	🌳🌳🌳🌳🌳
Time required to reach maturity	80 years	80 years	50 years	40 years
Number of board feet per tree	150	300	400	400

You are the manager of a large tree farm. The table above provides you with some of the information you need to plan your operations. Use the data to answer the questions.

1. You have received an order for 800,000 board feet of walnut. Can you fill the order? no

2. How many board feet of oak will you be able to sell this year?
1,950,000 board feet

3. A company has offered to purchase all of your available poplar for $0.22 per board foot. How much income will your crop produce this year? $946,000

4. Cottonwood trees cost about $1.25 per tree every year in farming costs. How much does your farm have invested in this year's cottonwood crop? $512,500

5. A lumber company agrees to harvest and haul all of your mature walnut trees. The company will pay you $0.15 per board foot. How much profit will you make? $102,500

6. A competing tree farm has produced 1,215,000 board feet of walnut this year. How many times as large was its crop as your crop?
1.8 times as large

7. If oak and walnut trees cost the same amount per year to grow, and a board foot of walnut sells for 1.75 times as much as a board foot of oak, which tree would provide the more profitable crop? oak

8. If all of your trees are harvested when they reach maturity, and the same type of tree is immediately planted in place of the harvested tree, how many years will there be between identical crops of trees? 200 years

Use with pages 126–127.   49

Enrich Worksheet

127

Warm-Up

Have students use < or > to compare the fractions.

$\frac{3}{8}$ ● $\frac{1}{2}$ (<)

$\frac{7}{8}$ ● $\frac{3}{4}$ (>)

$\frac{2}{3}$ ● $\frac{1}{2}$ (>)

$\frac{1}{4}$ ● $\frac{2}{5}$ (<)

GETTING STARTED

Discuss a shopping trip in which four items are to be purchased: a record for $12.47; a book for $8.49; a notebook for $7.44; and a pen for $2.49. Estimate whether everything can be bought for $30.00. Disregard sales tax. (By rounding to dollars, yes: 8.49 ≈ 8.00; 12.47 ≈ 12.00; 7.44 ≈ 7.00; and 2.49 ≈ 2.00. Total $29.00.) Discuss with students that although $29 is a reasonable estimate, it is not useful for making sure there is enough money. It would be better to round up the costs to get an overestimate. (12.47≈13.00, 8.47≈9.00, 7.44≈ 8.00, 2.49≈3.00, total $33.00).

Discuss the possibility of rounding to half-dollars. Rework the estimate. (8.49 ≈ 8.50; 12.47 ≈ 12.50, 7.44 ≈ 7.50, and 2.49 ≈ 2.50. Total $31.00. Therefore, the individual could not purchase all four items.)

TEACHING THE LESSON

Materials: fraction discs of various denominators

A. Use fraction discs to allow students to observe visually the approximation of fractions.

$\frac{7}{8} \approx 1$ $\frac{3}{5} \approx \frac{1}{2}$ $\frac{1}{8} \approx 0$

$\frac{2}{5} \approx \frac{1}{2}$ $\frac{1}{6} \approx 0$ $\frac{5}{6} \approx 1$

Stress that speed is a primary objective of estimation: If it takes as long to estimate as it does to find exact answers, you might as well add.

B. Emphasize that estimating does not give an exact answer, but a good approximation.

For subtraction, the whole numbers are subtracted first and then adjusted higher (+) or lower (−), depending on the comparison of the fractional numbers.

Estimating Sums and Differences

A. Marcy needs at least 9 oz of wool to knit a scarf. Her grandmother gives Marcy $1\frac{3}{4}$ oz of red wool, $2\frac{3}{8}$ oz of green wool, and $3\frac{1}{5}$ oz of yellow wool. Will that be enough?

You do not need to know the exact weight of the wool, only that it weighs at least 9 oz. So, estimate $1\frac{3}{4} + 2\frac{3}{8} + 3\frac{1}{5}$.

Add the whole numbers. Adjust by approximating the fractions with 0, $\frac{1}{2}$, or 1.

$1 + 2 + 3 = 6$ $\frac{3}{4} \approx 1$; $\frac{3}{8} \approx \frac{1}{2}$; $\frac{1}{5} \approx 0$

Estimate: $6 + 1 + \frac{1}{2} + 0 = 7\frac{1}{2}$.

≈ means "is approximately equal to."

So, $1\frac{3}{4} + 2\frac{3}{8} + 3\frac{1}{5} < 9$.

Marcy doesn't have enough wool to knit a scarf.

Another example:

$4\frac{7}{8} + \frac{1}{9} + \frac{5}{12} + 3\frac{4}{5}$

Think: $4 + 3 = 7$; $\frac{7}{8} \approx 1$; $\frac{1}{9} \approx 0$; $\frac{5}{12} \approx \frac{1}{2}$; $\frac{4}{5} \approx 1$.

Estimate: $7 + 1 + 0 + \frac{1}{2} + 1 = 9\frac{1}{2}$.

B. You can estimate differences in a similar way.

Estimate $6\frac{7}{9} - 2\frac{3}{5}$.

Subtract the whole numbers. Adjust by comparing the fractional parts.

$6 - 2 = 4$ $\frac{7}{9} > \frac{3}{5}$; so, adjust up.

So, $6\frac{7}{9} - 2\frac{3}{5} > 4$

Estimate 4^+, or slightly more than 4.

Another example:

$12\frac{1}{8} - 9\frac{2}{3}$

Think: $12 - 9 = 3$; $\frac{1}{8} < \frac{2}{3}$; so, adjust down.

Estimate 3^-, or slightly less than 3.

128

COMMON ERRORS

Some students question the possibility of several "right" answers to an estimation problem because they do not thoroughly understand estimation.

Remediation

For this error, have students work through several word problems that require a "yes-no" answer rather than an exact number. For example:

Andy has three pieces of wire, $3\frac{2}{3}$ ft, $5\frac{1}{7}$ ft, and $2\frac{5}{6}$ ft long. Does he have enough to reach 10 ft across a room? (yes)

Assign Reteach Master, p. 38.

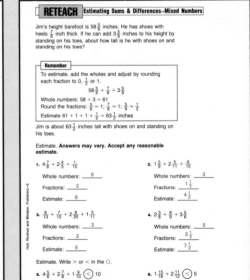

RETEACH Estimating Sums & Differences–Mixed Numbers

Jim's height barefoot is $58\frac{5}{8}$ inches. He has shoes with heels $\frac{7}{8}$ inch thick. If he can add $3\frac{5}{9}$ inches to his height by standing on his toes, about how tall is he with shoes on and standing on his toes?

Remember

To estimate, add the wholes and adjust by rounding each fraction to 0, $\frac{1}{2}$ or 1.

$58\frac{5}{8} + \frac{7}{8} + 3\frac{5}{9}$

Whole numbers: $58 + 3 = 61$
Round the fractions: $\frac{5}{8} \approx 1$; $\frac{7}{8} \approx 1$; $\frac{5}{9} \approx \frac{1}{2}$

Estimate $61 + 1 + 1 + \frac{1}{2} = 63\frac{1}{2}$ inches

Jim is about $63\frac{1}{2}$ inches tall with shoes on and standing on his toes.

Estimate. **Answers may vary. Accept any reasonable estimate.**

1. $4\frac{7}{8} + 2\frac{4}{9} + \frac{1}{15}$

Whole numbers: __6__

Fractions: __2__

Estimate: __8__

2. $1\frac{5}{9} + 2\frac{5}{11} + \frac{8}{15}$

Whole numbers: __3__

Fractions: $1\frac{1}{2}$

Estimate: $4\frac{1}{2}$

3. $\frac{6}{13} + \frac{7}{15} + 2\frac{9}{20} + 1\frac{5}{11}$

Whole numbers: __3__

Fractions: __2__

Estimate: __5__

4. $2\frac{3}{8} + \frac{8}{9} + 3\frac{5}{6}$

Whole numbers: __5__

Fractions: $2\frac{1}{2}$

Estimate: $7\frac{1}{2}$

Estimate. Write > or < in the ○.

5. $4\frac{5}{8} + 2\frac{7}{8} + 1\frac{9}{10}$ (<) 10

6. $1\frac{15}{16} + 2\frac{11}{12}$ (<) 5

7. $2\frac{1}{9} + 1\frac{1}{16} + \frac{3}{25}$ (>) 3

8. $9\frac{9}{10} + 1\frac{5}{20} + 2\frac{7}{15}$ (<) 14

38   Use with pages 128–129.

Reteach Worksheet

Estimate. **Answers may vary. Accept any reasonable estimate.**

1. $2\frac{6}{7} + 3\frac{7}{9}$ 7⁻ **2.** $4\frac{8}{9} + 2\frac{6}{7}$ 8⁻ **3.** $5\frac{3}{5} + 1\frac{2}{7}$ 6–8 **4.** $3\frac{1}{9} + 5\frac{9}{10}$ 8–10

5. $4\frac{7}{8} - 1\frac{3}{7}$ 3⁺ **6.** $3\frac{2}{5} - 1\frac{1}{8}$ 2⁺ **7.** $9\frac{7}{8} - 4\frac{3}{5}$ 5⁺ **8.** $8\frac{3}{7} - 4\frac{4}{5}$ 4⁻

9. $\left(34\frac{1}{8} - 28\frac{3}{7}\right) + \left(11\frac{5}{9} - 4\frac{2}{7}\right)$ 12–14 **10.** $\left(16\frac{7}{11} + 4\frac{1}{9}\right) - \left(3\frac{4}{9} + 12\frac{3}{10}\right)$ 4–6

Estimate. Write > or < for ●.

11. $2\frac{6}{7} + 3\frac{8}{9}$ ● 7 < **12.** $4\frac{3}{4} + 3\frac{9}{10}$ ● 8 > **13.** $2\frac{1}{8} + 1\frac{5}{9}$ ● 4 <

14. $3\frac{4}{5} + 4\frac{2}{9}$ ● 9 < **15.** $5\frac{3}{10} + 3\frac{1}{9}$ ● 8 > **16.** $4\frac{1}{5} + 1\frac{3}{4}$ ● 6 <

17. $3\frac{7}{8} + 2\frac{6}{7} + 4\frac{1}{9}$ ● 12 < **18.** $\frac{6}{7} + 3\frac{1}{6} + 4\frac{3}{5}$ ● 8 >

19. $5\frac{1}{5} - 2\frac{4}{7}$ ● 3 < **20.** $6\frac{1}{2} - 2\frac{7}{8}$ ● 3 > **21.** $7\frac{3}{5} - 2\frac{1}{9}$ ● 5 >

22. $6\frac{1}{7} - 1\frac{4}{5}$ ● 5 < **23.** $9\frac{3}{4} - 5\frac{2}{5}$ ● 4 > **24.** $7\frac{1}{5} - 3\frac{2}{9}$ ● 5 <

25. $\left(9\frac{6}{7} - 4\frac{3}{4}\right) + \left(6\frac{1}{8} - 2\frac{2}{3}\right)$ ● 10 < **26.** $\left(4\frac{7}{8} + 2\frac{6}{7}\right) - \left(1\frac{1}{8} + 2\frac{4}{5}\right)$ ● 6 <

Write the letter of the correct answer. Choose the best estimate.

27. $2\frac{7}{8} + 3\frac{8}{11}$ **a.** about 5 **b.** about 6 **ⓒ** about 7

28. $4\frac{3}{4} + 2\frac{4}{5}$ **a.** about 6 **ⓑ** about 8 **c.** about 9

29. $6\frac{7}{8} - 2\frac{4}{9}$ **a.** about 2 **ⓑ** about 4 **c.** about 8

30. $8\frac{4}{5} - 3\frac{3}{7}$ **a.** about 3 **b.** about 4 **ⓒ** about 5

Solve.

31. During Barclay's yearly leftover-handspun-wool sale, a pound of lamb's wool costs $25.00. Becky buys $3\frac{3}{4}$ oz of grey wool, $4\frac{2}{5}$ oz of white wool, and $2\frac{7}{16}$ oz of brown wool. Does she spend more or less than $25.00? **less than $25.00**

32. Joan goes on a shopping spree and buys $24\frac{3}{4}$ oz of different-colored wools. She really only needs about 18 oz. Becky offers to buy some of the wool from Joan. She picks three balls weighing $2\frac{4}{5}$ oz, $3\frac{2}{9}$ oz, and $1\frac{7}{8}$ oz. Can Joan let her buy them? **no**

Classwork/Homework, page H52

129

ASSIGNMENT GUIDE

Basic: 1–8, 11–31

Average: 1–25, 31–32

Extended: 1–25, 31–32

Resources
Practice, p. 52   Class/Home, p. H52
Reteach, p. 38
Enrich, p. 50

Exercise Analysis
1–10 Estimate the sum or difference of mixed numbers
11–18 Estimate a sum compared to a given answer
19–24 Estimate a difference and compare to a given answer
25–30 Mixed practice
31–32 Skill applications

REINFORCEMENT
Have students decide whether the following differences should be adjusted up or down.
1. $7\frac{5}{6} - 4\frac{9}{10}$ (down)
2. $5\frac{3}{5} - 1\frac{1}{4}$ (up)
3. $7\frac{2}{9} - 6\frac{2}{7}$ (down)
4. $3\frac{1}{3} - 2\frac{2}{9}$ (up)
5. $8\frac{6}{8} - 4\frac{3}{5}$ (up)
6. $12\frac{9}{11} - 8\frac{3}{4}$ (up)

MATH CONNECTION (Consumer)
Have students bring in recipes and estimate the size of the bowl needed to hold all the listed ingredients for each recipe. Use a 1-quart, 2-quart, or 4-quart bowl.

Hint: 4 cups equals 1 quart.

Example:

$3\frac{1}{2}$ cups flour ≈ $3\frac{1}{2}$ cups

$3\frac{1}{3}$ cups sugar ≈ 3 or $3\frac{1}{2}$ cups

$\frac{3}{4}$ cup of milk ≈ 1 cup

$1\frac{7}{8}$ cups water ≈ + 2 cups
_____
$9\frac{1}{2}$ or 10 cups
need a 4-quart bowl

COMING UP
Fractions are taking shape. Tomorrow's Follow-Up shows how.

PRACTICE Estimating Sums and Differences

Write > or < for ○.

1. $1\frac{1}{9} + 2\frac{3}{8}$ (>) 3 **2.** $2\frac{4}{5} + 1\frac{7}{8}$ (<) 5

3. $4\frac{8}{9} + 3\frac{5}{7}$ (<) 9 **4.** $7\frac{8}{11} + 6\frac{7}{9}$ (>) 13

5. $6\frac{1}{7} + 5\frac{3}{19}$ (>) 11 **6.** $8\frac{1}{7} + 13\frac{2}{21}$ (<) 22

7. $4\frac{7}{8} + 2\frac{6}{11}$ (>) 7 **8.** $4\frac{5}{8} + 1\frac{9}{11}$ (<) 7

9. $14\frac{5}{8} + 9\frac{3}{9}$ (<) 23 **10.** $\frac{4}{7} + \frac{5}{9}$ (>) 1

11. $2\frac{5}{7} + 3\frac{5}{8}$ (<) 6 **12.** $6\frac{3}{11} + 2\frac{5}{19}$ (<) 9

13. $14\frac{8}{11} + 1\frac{3}{4}$ (>) 16 **14.** $3\frac{9}{10} + 1\frac{5}{7}$ (>) 5

15. $7\frac{2}{3} + 6\frac{5}{9}$ (>) 14 **16.** $4 - 2\frac{1}{8}$ (<) 2

17. $3\frac{1}{5} - 1\frac{7}{8}$ (>) 1 **18.** $8\frac{7}{8} - 5\frac{1}{5}$ (>) 3

19. $9\frac{7}{8} - 2\frac{1}{15}$ (>) 7 **20.** $5\frac{4}{9} - 1\frac{3}{11}$ (>) 4

21. $12\frac{2}{3} - 5\frac{9}{10}$ (>) 6 **22.** $6\frac{1}{11} - 1\frac{5}{9}$ (>) 3

23. $15\frac{7}{11} - 3\frac{5}{12}$ (>) 12 **24.** $20\frac{7}{8} - 10\frac{3}{7}$ (>) 10

Solve.

25. Do the apples and oranges weigh more than 8 pounds altogether? no

26. Do the bananas and berries weigh more than 4 pounds altogether? yes

27. Which two bags of fruit weigh about 5 pounds? berries and oranges or apples and pears

50

Holt, Rinehart and Winston, Publishers • 8

Practice Worksheet

ENRICH Patterns

A **geometric sequence** is a sequence of numbers in which each term is equal to the previous term multiplied by a constant factor. The constant factor is called the **common ratio**. To find the common ratio, divide each term by the term that comes directly before it.

5, 20, 80, 320, . . .

The above is a geometric sequence because there is a common ratio between consecutive terms:

$\frac{20}{5} = \frac{80}{20} = \frac{320}{80} = 4$ (the common ratio)

Find the common ratio, *r*, and the next term of each sequence.

1. 3, 1.5, 0.75, 0.375, . . . *r* = 0.5 next term = 0.1875

2. ⁻2, 4, ⁻8, 16, . . . *r* = ⁻2 next term = ⁻32

3. 1.3, 1.3, 1.3, 1.3, . . . *r* = 1 next term = 1.3

4. $5x, 5\frac{x}{2}, 5\frac{x}{4}, 5\frac{x}{8}, \ldots$ *r* = $\frac{x}{2}$ next term = $5\frac{x}{16}$

5. Write a geometric sequence in which the common ratio is ⁻1.
any sequence in the form 5, ⁻5, 5, ⁻5, 5, ⁻5

6. Write a geometric sequence in which the common ratio is √2.
any sequence in the form 1, √2, 2, 2√2, 4, 4√2, 8

If 3 is the first term of a geometric sequence with a common ratio 4, then the terms will be

3, 3 × 4, 3 × 4 × 4, 3 × 4 × 4 × 4, . . .

7. Use exponents to express the sequence, and give the fifth term.

$3, 3 \times 4, 3 \times 4^2, 3 \times 4^3, 3 \times 4^4$

8. If 48 is the third term of the above sequence, try to find the formula for the sixth term.

sixth term = $3 \times 4^{6-1}$, or 3×4^5

50 Use with pages 128–129.

Holt, Rinehart and Winston, Publishers • 8

Enrich Worksheet

Warm-Up

Have students estimate the sum.

$5\frac{7}{8} + 6\frac{13}{14}$ (13) $\qquad$ $5\frac{1}{9} + 6\frac{3}{40}$ (11)

$5\frac{5}{6} + 6\frac{1}{8}$ (12) $\qquad$ $5\frac{7}{9} + 6\frac{6}{7}$ (13)

$5\frac{2}{9} + 6\frac{5}{23}$ (11) $\qquad$ $5\frac{1}{7} + 6\frac{8}{9}$ (12)

GETTING STARTED

Discuss situations in everyday life that involve the addition of fractions and of mixed numbers. Challenge the class to come up with ten examples. List them in categories such as sports, hobbies, shopping, cooking, and so on.

TEACHING THE LESSON

A. Concentrate on renaming the sum as a mixed number. Have students add and simplify the sum of:
- $\frac{11}{12} + \frac{11}{12}$ ($1\frac{5}{6}$)
- $\frac{13}{16} + \frac{15}{16}$ ($1\frac{3}{4}$)

B. When adding mixed numbers and fractions, some students may find it helpful to draw a line to separate the whole-number parts from the fraction parts.

$$
\begin{array}{c|c}
5 & \frac{1}{2} \\
 & \\
 & \frac{3}{4} \\
 & \\
+1 & \frac{1}{3} \\
\hline
 & \\
\end{array}
\qquad
\begin{array}{c|c}
5 & \frac{1}{2} = \frac{6}{12} \\
 & \\
 & \frac{3}{4} = \frac{9}{12} \\
 & \\
+1 & \frac{1}{3} = \frac{4}{12} \\
\hline
6 & \frac{19}{12} \\
6 & +1\frac{7}{12} = 7\frac{7}{12}
\end{array}
$$

Checkpoint

The chart lists the common errors students make when adding fractions and mixed numbers.

Correct Answers: 1b, 2d, 3d, 4a

Remediation

■ For these errors, draw models to show the addition of fractions. Emphasize the fact that when adding the numerators, the denominator does not change.

□ For these errors, assign Reteach Master, p. 39.

△ For this error, refer students to the examples on p. 120.

Adding Fractions and Mixed Numbers

A. A toy banjo was constructed in two pieces. The circular body was $\frac{1}{4}$ yd in diameter and the neck was $\frac{3}{4}$ yd long. How long was the banjo?

To add fractions with like denominators, add the numerators. Use the same denominator. Write in simplest form.

$$\frac{1}{4} + \frac{3}{4} = \frac{1+3}{4} = \frac{4}{4}, \text{ or } 1.$$

The banjo was 1 yd long.

B. Add $5\frac{1}{2} + \frac{3}{4} + 1\frac{1}{3}$.

To add fractions and mixed numbers with unlike denominators, find equivalent fractions.

Write each fraction with a common denominator.

Think: The LCD is 12.

$$
\begin{aligned}
5\frac{1}{2} &= 5\frac{6}{12} \\
\frac{3}{4} &= \frac{9}{12} \\
+ 1\frac{1}{3} &= 1\frac{4}{12}
\end{aligned}
$$

Add.

$$
\begin{aligned}
5\frac{1}{2} &= 5\frac{6}{12} \\
\frac{3}{4} &= \frac{9}{12} \\
+ 1\frac{1}{3} &= 1\frac{4}{12} \\
\hline
&6\frac{19}{12}
\end{aligned}
$$

Simplify the sum.

$$6\frac{19}{12} = 6 + 1\frac{7}{12} = 7\frac{7}{12}$$

Checkpoint   Write the letter of the correct answer.

Add.

1. $\frac{3}{7} + \frac{5}{14}$ $\qquad$ **a.** $\frac{8}{21}$ $\qquad$ ⓑ $\frac{11}{14}$ $\qquad$ **c.** 8 $\qquad$ **d.** $\frac{1}{21}$

2. $\frac{3}{5} + \frac{3}{4}$ $\qquad$ **a.** $\frac{6}{9}$ $\qquad$ **b.** $\frac{6}{5}$ $\qquad$ **c.** $\frac{27}{20}$ $\qquad$ ⓓ $1\frac{7}{20}$

3. $3\frac{5}{6} + 1\frac{2}{3}$ $\qquad$ **a.** $1\frac{2}{3}$ $\qquad$ **b.** $4\frac{7}{9}$ $\qquad$ **c.** $4\frac{2}{3}$ $\qquad$ ⓓ $5\frac{1}{2}$

4. $2\frac{1}{2} + 4\frac{4}{5} + \frac{3}{4}$ $\qquad$ ⓐ $8\frac{1}{20}$ $\qquad$ **b.** $6\frac{41}{20}$ $\qquad$ **c.** 8 $\qquad$ **d.** 9

130 $\qquad\qquad\qquad\qquad$ Math Reasoning, page H213

COMMON ERRORS

Answer Choice	Type of Error
■ 1a, 2a, 3b	Adds the numerators and the denominators
□ 1c	Adds the numerators; omits the denominators
□ 1d	Adds the denominators; omits the numerators
□ 2b, 4c	Fails to use the common denominator
△ 2c, 4b	Fails to simplify the answer
□ 3a	Omits an addend
■ 3c	Omits the fractional part of an addend
□ 4d	Estimates the answer

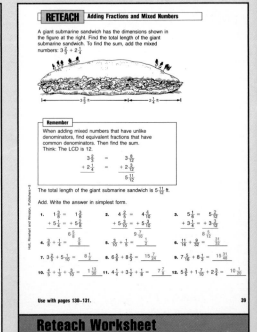

RETEACH Adding Fractions and Mixed Numbers

A giant submarine sandwich has the dimensions shown in the figure at the right. Find the total length of the giant submarine sandwich. To find the sum, add the mixed numbers: $3\frac{2}{5} + 2\frac{1}{4}$

Remember

When adding mixed numbers that have unlike denominators, find equivalent fractions that have common denominators. Then find the sum.
Think: The LCD is 12.

$$
\begin{aligned}
3\frac{2}{5} &= \quad 3\frac{8}{20} \\
+ 2\frac{1}{4} &= \quad + 2\frac{5}{20} \\
\hline
&\quad 5\frac{11}{20}
\end{aligned}
$$

The total length of the giant submarine sandwich is $5\frac{11}{20}$ ft.

Add. Write the answer in simplest form.

1. $1\frac{3}{8} = 1\frac{3}{8}$
   $+ 5\frac{1}{4} = + 5\frac{2}{8}$
   _____
   $6\frac{5}{8}$

2. $4\frac{2}{5} = 4\frac{4}{10}$
   $+ 5\frac{3}{10} = + 5\frac{3}{10}$
   _____
   $9\frac{7}{10}$

3. $5\frac{1}{4} = 5\frac{3}{12}$
   $+ 3\frac{1}{4} = + 3\frac{9}{12}$
   _____
   $8\frac{5}{12}$

4. $\frac{3}{8} + \frac{1}{4} = \frac{5}{8}$

5. $\frac{3}{10} + \frac{1}{5} = \frac{1}{2}$

6. $\frac{11}{16} + \frac{9}{32} = \frac{31}{32}$

7. $3\frac{2}{5} + 5\frac{1}{10} = 8\frac{1}{2}$

8. $6\frac{3}{8} + 8\frac{2}{3} = 15\frac{1}{24}$

9. $7\frac{5}{16} + 8\frac{1}{3} = 15\frac{31}{48}$

10. $\frac{4}{5} + \frac{1}{3} + \frac{3}{10} = 1\frac{13}{30}$

11. $4\frac{1}{4} + 3\frac{1}{2} + \frac{1}{8} = 7\frac{7}{8}$

12. $5\frac{3}{8} + 1\frac{7}{10} + 2\frac{3}{4} = 10\frac{1}{20}$

Use with pages 130–131. $\qquad\qquad$ 39

Reteach Worksheet

Add. Write the answer in simplest form.

1. $\frac{1}{6} + \frac{5}{6}$ 1   **2.** $\frac{4}{5} + \frac{2}{5}$ $1\frac{1}{5}$ **3.** $\frac{7}{12} + \frac{1}{12}$ $\frac{2}{3}$ **4.** $\frac{1}{2} + \frac{1}{2}$ 1   **5.** $\frac{5}{9} + \frac{5}{9}$ $1\frac{1}{9}$

6. $\begin{array}{r}\frac{3}{4}\\+\frac{1}{2}\\\hline\end{array}$ $1\frac{1}{4}$ **7.** $\begin{array}{r}\frac{7}{8}\\+\frac{3}{4}\\\hline\end{array}$ $1\frac{5}{8}$ **8.** $\begin{array}{r}\frac{11}{12}\\+\frac{3}{4}\\\hline\end{array}$ $1\frac{2}{3}$ **9.** $\begin{array}{r}\frac{4}{5}\\+\frac{7}{10}\\\hline\end{array}$ $1\frac{1}{2}$ **10.** $\begin{array}{r}\frac{3}{4}\\+\frac{2}{7}\\\hline\end{array}$ $1\frac{1}{28}$ **11.** $\begin{array}{r}\frac{2}{15}\\+\frac{1}{5}\\\hline\end{array}$ $\frac{1}{3}$

12. $\begin{array}{r}6\frac{1}{2}\\+\frac{2}{3}\\\hline\end{array}$ $7\frac{1}{6}$ **13.** $\begin{array}{r}2\frac{1}{6}\\+\frac{1}{5}\\\hline\end{array}$ $2\frac{11}{30}$ **14.** $\begin{array}{r}\frac{4}{5}\\+1\frac{1}{2}\\\hline\end{array}$ $2\frac{3}{10}$ **15.** $\begin{array}{r}\frac{2}{3}\\+7\frac{1}{5}\\\hline\end{array}$ $7\frac{13}{15}$ **16.** $\begin{array}{r}3\frac{1}{5}\\+\frac{2}{3}\\\hline\end{array}$ $3\frac{13}{15}$ **17.** $\begin{array}{r}6\frac{1}{4}\\+\frac{3}{8}\\\hline\end{array}$ $6\frac{5}{8}$

18. $\begin{array}{r}7\frac{1}{3}\\+3\frac{1}{2}\\\hline\end{array}$ $10\frac{5}{6}$ **19.** $\begin{array}{r}2\frac{7}{8}\\+5\frac{3}{9}\\\hline\end{array}$ $8\frac{5}{24}$ **20.** $\begin{array}{r}1\frac{4}{5}\\+3\frac{1}{3}\\\hline\end{array}$ $5\frac{2}{15}$ **21.** $\begin{array}{r}2\frac{1}{6}\\+3\frac{2}{3}\\\hline\end{array}$ $5\frac{5}{6}$ **22.** $\begin{array}{r}5\frac{5}{6}\\+1\frac{1}{3}\\\hline\end{array}$ $6\frac{23}{24}$ **23.** $\begin{array}{r}4\frac{5}{9}\\+2\frac{2}{3}\\\hline\end{array}$ $7\frac{2}{9}$

24. $6\frac{1}{3} + \frac{1}{2} + \frac{4}{5}$ $7\frac{19}{30}$ **25.** $3\frac{1}{2} + \frac{2}{3} + \frac{7}{9}$ $4\frac{17}{18}$ **26.** $\frac{1}{6} + 8\frac{1}{3} + 1\frac{1}{4}$ $9\frac{3}{4}$

27. $\frac{4}{5} + \frac{1}{8} + 3\frac{2}{5}$ $4\frac{13}{40}$ **28.** $1\frac{3}{4} + \frac{1}{2} + \frac{5}{6}$ $3\frac{1}{12}$ **29.** $\frac{8}{9} + \frac{5}{6} + 2\frac{1}{3}$ $4\frac{1}{18}$

30. $\begin{array}{r}3\frac{1}{6}\\2\frac{1}{5}\\+\frac{4}{5}\\\hline 6\frac{1}{6}\end{array}$ **31.** $\begin{array}{r}1\frac{1}{8}\\3\frac{1}{6}\\+\frac{1}{2}\\\hline 4\frac{19}{24}\end{array}$ **32.** $\begin{array}{r}\frac{2}{3}\\1\frac{1}{6}\\+4\frac{1}{2}\\\hline 6\frac{1}{3}\end{array}$ **33.** $\begin{array}{r}3\frac{1}{8}\\\frac{3}{4}\\+1\frac{1}{8}\\\hline 5\end{array}$ **34.** $\begin{array}{r}5\frac{1}{6}\\\frac{2}{5}\\+3\frac{3}{10}\\\hline 8\frac{13}{15}\end{array}$ **35.** $\begin{array}{r}\frac{4}{5}\\1\frac{1}{10}\\+4\frac{1}{2}\\\hline 6\frac{2}{5}\end{array}$

Solve.

36. A craftsworker worked for $5\frac{1}{2}$ hours Monday, $6\frac{1}{4}$ hours Tuesday, and $7\frac{1}{2}$ hours Wednesday to construct a stringed instrument. How many hours did it take? $19\frac{1}{4}$ hours

37. A wood-carver had two pieces of wood. One piece was $1\frac{3}{8}$ ft long and the other $1\frac{1}{4}$ ft long. Which was the longer piece? $1\frac{3}{8}$ feet

ASSIGNMENT GUIDE

Basic: 1–26, 36–37

Average: 6–29, 36–37

Extended: 6–17, 24–37

Resources
Practice, p. 53   Class/Home, p. H53
Reteach, p. 39   Reasoning, p. H213
Enrich, p. 51

Exercise Analysis
1–5   Add fractions that have like denominators
6–11   Add fractions that have unlike denominators
12–23   Add fractions and mixed numbers that have unlike denominators
24–35   Add three fraction and mixed-number addends
36–37   Skill applications

FOLLOW-UP ACTIVITIES

 REINFORCEMENT
Have students write the following mixed numbers in opposite circles so that the sum of each pair equals $6\frac{3}{4}$: $1\frac{1}{4}$, $2\frac{1}{8}$, $3\frac{1}{3}$, $3\frac{5}{12}$, $4\frac{5}{8}$, $5\frac{1}{2}$.

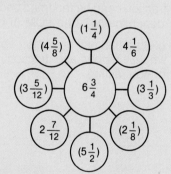

PROBLEM SOLVING
Have students find each missing number. Suggest that they first use estimation to determine a reasonable answer and then substitute that answer and add to check.

● $5\frac{6}{7} + \blacksquare \frac{4}{5} = 8\frac{23}{35}$ (2)

● $3\frac{7}{8} + 4\frac{1}{\blacksquare} = 8\frac{3}{8}$ (2)

● $1\frac{3}{\blacksquare} + 7\frac{6}{15} = 9$ (5)

★ $\blacksquare \frac{3}{\blacksquare} + 12\frac{2}{3} = 15\frac{2}{21}$ (2,7)

COMING UP
Less is more.

Objective: To subtract fractions and mixed numbers

Warm-Up

Have students write each sum in simplest form.

$\frac{1}{3} + \frac{2}{5}$ $\left(\frac{11}{15}\right)$, $\frac{1}{6} + \frac{3}{8}$ $\left(\frac{13}{24}\right)$, $5\frac{2}{3} + 4\frac{1}{8}$ $\left(9\frac{19}{24}\right)$, $7\frac{5}{12} + 8\frac{3}{10}$ $\left(15\frac{43}{60}\right)$

GETTING STARTED

Have students solve this problem.

• The Explorers Club went on a hike. Group A hiked $10\frac{3}{4}$ miles. Group B hiked $5\frac{1}{4}$ miles. How much farther did Group A hike? ($5\frac{1}{2}$ miles)

Ask volunteers to tell how they found their answers. Encourage those who subtracted to describe the steps they followed.

TEACHING THE LESSON

A. Point out that students can apply to subtracting fractions much of what they have learned about adding fractions, such as renaming with common denominators.

B. Use another example such as $\frac{5}{8} - \frac{1}{4}$ to remind students that sometimes only one fraction need be renamed because one denominator is the LCM of both.

C. Some students may prefer to separate the whole number and fraction parts before subtracting.

$$\begin{array}{r|l} 3 & \frac{3}{4} \\ \hline -2 & \frac{1}{2} \\ \end{array} \qquad \begin{array}{r|l} 3 & \frac{3}{4} = \frac{3}{4} \\ \hline -2 & \frac{1}{2} = \frac{2}{4} \\ \hline 1 & \frac{1}{4} \\ \end{array}$$

Checkpoint

The chart lists the common errors students make when subtracting fractions and mixed numbers.

Correct Answers: 1a, 2b, 3d, 4b

Remediation

■ For this error, have students practice renaming fractions as equivalent fractions.

☐ For these errors, assign Reteach Master, p. 40.

△ For this error, refer students to the examples on p. 120.

Subtracting Fractions and Mixed Numbers

A. To subtract fractions that have like denominators, subtract the numerators. Use the same denominator.

$$\frac{7}{8} - \frac{3}{8} = \frac{7-3}{8} = \frac{4}{8}, \text{ or } \frac{1}{2}.$$

B. To subtract fractions with unlike denominators, find the LCD.

Subtract $\frac{6}{7} - \frac{2}{3}$.

Write each fraction with a common denominator. Subtract.

$$\begin{array}{r} \frac{6}{7} = \frac{18}{21} \\ -\frac{2}{3} = \frac{14}{21} \\ \hline \frac{4}{21} \end{array}$$

Think: 21 is the LCD.

C. To subtract mixed numbers, subtract the fractions. Then subtract the whole numbers.

Subtract $3\frac{3}{4} - 2\frac{1}{2}$.

Find fractions that have a common denominator.	Subtract the fractions.	Subtract the whole numbers.
$3\frac{3}{4} = 3\frac{3}{4}$ $-2\frac{1}{2} = 2\frac{2}{4}$	$3\frac{3}{4}$ $-2\frac{2}{4}$ $\frac{1}{4}$	$3\frac{3}{4}$ $-2\frac{2}{4}$ $1\frac{1}{4}$

Checkpoint Write the letter of the correct answer.

Subtract.

1. $\frac{8}{11} - \frac{3}{11}$ ⓐ $\frac{5}{11}$ **b.** $\frac{11}{22}$ **c.** $\frac{11}{11}$ **d.** 5

2. $\frac{5}{6} - \frac{1}{3}$ **a.** $\frac{2}{6}$ ⓑ $\frac{1}{2}$ **c.** $\frac{4}{6}$ **d.** $\frac{4}{3}$

3. $4\frac{3}{4} - 1\frac{1}{4}$ **a.** 6   **b.** 1   **c.** $\frac{1}{2}$ ⓓ $3\frac{1}{2}$

4. $2\frac{19}{24} - 1\frac{3}{8}$ **a.** $1\frac{5}{24}$ ⓑ $1\frac{5}{12}$ **c.** $1\frac{10}{12}$ **d.** $4\frac{1}{6}$

132

COMMON ERRORS

Answer Choice	Type of Error
☐ 1b, 1c, 3a, 3b, 4d	Adds instead of subtracts
☐ 1d	Omits the denominator
■ 2a	Fails to rename correctly
■ 2c, 2d	Fails to rename
☐ 3c	Omits whole-number part
△ 4a, 4c	Fails to simplify correctly

Subtract. Write the answer in simplest form.

1. $\dfrac{6}{7} - \dfrac{3}{7}$ $\dfrac{3}{7}$ 2. $\dfrac{9}{11} - \dfrac{2}{11}$ $\dfrac{7}{11}$ 3. $\dfrac{3}{4} - \dfrac{1}{4}$ $\dfrac{1}{2}$ 4. $\dfrac{4}{5} - \dfrac{2}{5}$ $\dfrac{2}{5}$ 5. $\dfrac{7}{9} - \dfrac{4}{9}$ $\dfrac{1}{3}$

6. $\dfrac{12}{21} - \dfrac{3}{7}$ $\dfrac{1}{7}$ 7. $\dfrac{13}{24} - \dfrac{1}{6}$ $\dfrac{3}{8}$ 8. $\dfrac{1}{2} - \dfrac{1}{6}$ $\dfrac{1}{3}$ 9. $\dfrac{2}{3} - \dfrac{2}{9}$ $\dfrac{4}{9}$ 10. $\dfrac{3}{4} - \dfrac{5}{8}$ $\dfrac{1}{8}$

11. $\begin{array}{r} \frac{19}{21} \\ -\ \frac{6}{7} \\ \hline \frac{1}{21} \end{array}$ 12. $\begin{array}{r} \frac{5}{9} \\ -\ \frac{1}{3} \\ \hline \frac{2}{9} \end{array}$ 13. $\begin{array}{r} \frac{5}{8} \\ -\ \frac{1}{2} \\ \hline \frac{1}{8} \end{array}$ 14. $\begin{array}{r} \frac{3}{7} \\ -\ \frac{1}{14} \\ \hline \frac{5}{14} \end{array}$ 15. $\begin{array}{r} \frac{2}{3} \\ -\ \frac{1}{6} \\ \hline \frac{1}{2} \end{array}$ 16. $\begin{array}{r} \frac{3}{4} \\ -\ \frac{5}{12} \\ \hline \frac{1}{3} \end{array}$

17. $\begin{array}{r} \frac{7}{8} \\ -\ \frac{2}{3} \\ \hline \frac{5}{24} \end{array}$ 18. $\begin{array}{r} \frac{1}{2} \\ -\ \frac{5}{11} \\ \hline \frac{1}{22} \end{array}$ 19. $\begin{array}{r} \frac{7}{8} \\ -\ \frac{2}{5} \\ \hline \frac{19}{40} \end{array}$ 20. $\begin{array}{r} \frac{5}{6} \\ -\ \frac{1}{9} \\ \hline \frac{13}{18} \end{array}$ 21. $\begin{array}{r} \frac{3}{4} \\ -\ \frac{2}{5} \\ \hline \frac{7}{20} \end{array}$ 22. $\begin{array}{r} \frac{4}{5} \\ -\ \frac{5}{7} \\ \hline \frac{3}{35} \end{array}$

23. $6\dfrac{2}{3} - 5\dfrac{1}{3}$ $1\dfrac{1}{3}$ 24. $7\dfrac{3}{4} - 4\dfrac{3}{4}$ 3 25. $10\dfrac{4}{5} - 2\dfrac{2}{5}$ $8\dfrac{2}{5}$ 26. $12\dfrac{5}{6} - 4\dfrac{1}{6}$ $8\dfrac{2}{3}$

27. $\begin{array}{r} 4\frac{3}{4} \\ -\ 1\frac{1}{2} \\ \hline 3\frac{1}{4} \end{array}$ 28. $\begin{array}{r} 5\frac{6}{7} \\ -\ 3\frac{2}{3} \\ \hline 2\frac{4}{21} \end{array}$ 29. $\begin{array}{r} 2\frac{8}{9} \\ -\ 1\frac{3}{4} \\ \hline 1\frac{5}{36} \end{array}$ 30. $\begin{array}{r} 3\frac{3}{8} \\ -\ 2\frac{1}{4} \\ \hline 1\frac{1}{8} \end{array}$ 31. $\begin{array}{r} 4\frac{5}{8} \\ -\ 2\frac{2}{5} \\ \hline 2\frac{9}{40} \end{array}$

32. $\dfrac{7}{8} - \dfrac{2}{3}$ $\dfrac{5}{24}$ 33. $3\dfrac{9}{10} - 1\dfrac{5}{6}$ $2\dfrac{1}{15}$ 34. $\dfrac{33}{41} - \dfrac{1}{2}$ $\dfrac{25}{82}$ 35. $7\dfrac{22}{29} - 5\dfrac{2}{3}$ $2\dfrac{8}{87}$

Solve.

36. Karen bought $\dfrac{1}{2}$ of a hide. She needed $\dfrac{3}{8}$ of a hide to make a leather shoulder bag. Did she have enough? How much leather was left? Yes; $\dfrac{1}{8}$ of a hide was left.

37. Tanning hides makes them soft. Jerry spends $\dfrac{1}{2}$ hour on the tanning process. Ron spends $3\dfrac{1}{4}$ hours tanning. Write a subtraction problem that uses this information. Answers will vary.

CHALLENGE   Patterns, Relations, and Functions

Study the fractions below.

$\dfrac{1}{2} - \dfrac{1}{4} - \dfrac{1}{8} - \dfrac{1}{16} - \dfrac{1}{32} - \dfrac{1}{64} \cdots$

As you subtract each fraction, what pattern do you notice?
The difference is the last fraction you subtracted.
The fraction gets closer to zero.
Will you ever reach zero?   no

ASSIGNMENT GUIDE

Basic: 1–16, 23–31, 36

Average: 1–31 o, 32–37, Chlg

Extended: 6–26 e, 27–37, Chlg

Resources
Practice, p. 54   Class/Home, p. H54
Reteach, p. 40   More Practice, p. H198
Enrich, p. 52

Exercise Analysis

1–22	Subtract fractions
23–31	Subtract mixed numbers
32–35	Mixed practice
36	Skill application
37	Problem formulation

Challenge

Point out that what is being subtracted each time is $\frac{1}{2}$ of the previous number. The pattern will never result in a difference of zero because any number, no matter how small, can always be halved.

FOLLOW-UP ACTIVITIES

PUZZLES AND GAMES
In the square below, a vertical move represents addition, whereas a horizontal move represents subtraction. Have students find the results of each indicated move.

$2\frac{5}{6}$	$6\frac{11}{12}$	$5\frac{1}{3}$
$8\frac{1}{12}$	$1\frac{1}{12}$	$\frac{3}{4}$
$3\frac{1}{4}$	$7\frac{1}{6}$	$4\frac{2}{3}$

- $2\frac{5}{6}$ ↓↓ $(14\frac{1}{6})$
- $6\frac{11}{12}$ ←↓ $(12\frac{1}{6})$
- $4\frac{2}{3}$ ↑←↓ $(11\frac{1}{2})$
- $*3\frac{1}{4}$ ↑↑→ $(7\frac{1}{4})$

REINFORCEMENT

The ancient Egyptians used unit fractions exclusively. They did not have a symbol for $\frac{2}{3}$ but wrote it as $\frac{1}{2} + \frac{1}{6}$ or as $\frac{1}{3} + \frac{1}{3}$. Rename each fraction first as the sum of two unit fractions and then as the sum of three unit fractions.

- $\dfrac{3}{4}$ $\left(\dfrac{1}{2} + \dfrac{1}{4}, \dfrac{1}{4} + \dfrac{1}{4} + \dfrac{1}{4} \text{ or } \dfrac{1}{3} + \dfrac{1}{3} + \dfrac{1}{12}\right)$
- $\dfrac{7}{12}$ $\left(\dfrac{1}{2} + \dfrac{1}{12} \text{ or } \dfrac{1}{3} + \dfrac{1}{4}, \dfrac{1}{12} + \dfrac{1}{6} + \dfrac{1}{3}\right)$
- $\dfrac{5}{6}$ $\left(\dfrac{1}{3} + \dfrac{1}{2}, \dfrac{1}{3} + \dfrac{1}{3} + \dfrac{1}{6}\right)$
- $\dfrac{5}{8}$ $\left(\dfrac{1}{2} + \dfrac{1}{8}, \dfrac{1}{4} + \dfrac{1}{4} + \dfrac{1}{8}\right)$

COMING UP
The borrowers

Objective: To subtract mixed numbers with renaming

Warm-Up

Have students estimate each difference.

$7\frac{5}{6} - 3\frac{1}{4}$ (5) $8\frac{1}{3} - 2\frac{5}{6}$ (5)

$9\frac{1}{4} - 6\frac{7}{9}$ (2) $7\frac{2}{3} - 4\frac{5}{6}$ (3)

$5\frac{1}{3} - 2\frac{1}{2}$ $(2\frac{1}{2})$ $10\frac{2}{5} - 8\frac{1}{3}$ $(2\frac{1}{2})$

$6\frac{1}{4} - 1\frac{7}{8}$ (4) $3\frac{1}{2} - 1\frac{2}{3}$ $(1\frac{1}{2})$

GETTING STARTED

Point out that just as we sometimes need to rename when subtracting from a whole number, we sometimes need to rename a mixed number as well. Draw a diagram to illustrate renaming $3\frac{1}{4}$ as $2\frac{5}{4}$.

$3\frac{1}{4}$ = $2\frac{5}{4}$

Use similar models as needed to help students rename these fractions.

$4\frac{1}{2} = 3\frac{3}{2}$; $6\frac{1}{3} = 5\frac{4}{3}$; $2\frac{3}{8} = 1\frac{11}{8}$

TEACHING THE LESSON

A. You may wish to use a model to illustrate the subtraction in the example. Point out that 1 can easily be renamed as a fraction that has any denominator; for example, $1 = \frac{7}{7} = \frac{11}{11} = \frac{3}{3}$, and so on. Therefore, $1\frac{3}{7} = \frac{7}{7} + \frac{3}{7} = \frac{10}{7}$.

B. Other examples:

$6\frac{1}{3} - 2\frac{3}{4}$ $\left(3\frac{7}{12}\right)$; $10 - 5\frac{5}{6}$ $\left(4\frac{1}{6}\right)$

Checkpoint

The chart lists the common errors students make when subtracting mixed numbers.

Correct Answers: 1c, 2a, 3b

Remediation

■ For this error, have students draw a model for each problem and then cross out corresponding parts to ensure that the subtraction is completed.

□ For these errors, assign Reteach Master, p. 41.

△ For this error, refer students to the examples on p. 132.

Subtracting Mixed Numbers with Renaming

A. Greg has $7\frac{1}{8}$ yd of round reed. He uses $3\frac{3}{8}$ yd for a basket. How much round reed does he have left?

Find $7\frac{1}{8} - 3\frac{3}{8}$.

Write in vertical form.	Compare fractions. Rename if necessary.	Subtract. Simplify if necessary.
$7\frac{1}{8}$ $- 3\frac{3}{8}$	$\frac{1}{8} < \frac{3}{8}$ $7\frac{1}{8} = 6 + 1\frac{1}{8} = 6\frac{9}{8}$	$7\frac{1}{8} = 6\frac{9}{8}$ $- 3\frac{3}{8} = 3\frac{3}{8}$ $\overline{\quad 3\frac{6}{8} = 3\frac{3}{4}}$

He has $3\frac{3}{4}$ yd of round reed left.

B. Subtract $6\frac{1}{5} - 2\frac{3}{4}$.

Find fractions that have a common denominator.	Compare fractions. Rename if necessary.	Subtract.
$6\frac{1}{5} = 6\frac{4}{20}$ $- 2\frac{3}{4} = 2\frac{15}{20}$	$\frac{4}{20} < \frac{15}{20}$ $6\frac{4}{20} = 5 + 1\frac{4}{20} = 5\frac{24}{20}$	$6\frac{1}{5} = 5\frac{24}{20}$ $- 2\frac{3}{4} = 2\frac{15}{20}$ $\overline{\quad 3\frac{9}{20}}$

Other examples:

$8 = 7\frac{6}{6}$
$- 2\frac{1}{6} = 2\frac{1}{6}$
$\overline{\quad 5\frac{5}{6}}$

$3\frac{1}{4} = 2\frac{5}{4}$
$- 1\frac{3}{4} = 1\frac{3}{4}$
$\overline{\quad 1\frac{2}{4} = 1\frac{1}{2}}$

Checkpoint Write the letter of the correct answer.

Subtract.

1. $7\frac{7}{9} - 3\frac{4}{9} = \blacksquare$ **a.** $3\frac{3}{9}$ **b.** $4\frac{3}{9}$ **ⓒ** $4\frac{1}{3}$ **d.** $7\frac{1}{3}$

2. $9 - 4\frac{5}{6} = \blacksquare$ **ⓐ** $4\frac{1}{6}$ **b.** 5 **c.** $6\frac{5}{6}$ **d.** $13\frac{5}{6}$

3. $5\frac{1}{4} - 4\frac{1}{3} = \blacksquare$ **a.** $\frac{1}{3}$ **ⓑ** $\frac{11}{12}$ **c.** $1\frac{1}{12}$ **d.** $1\frac{11}{12}$

134

COMMON ERRORS

Answer Choice	Type of Error
△ 1a, 3c	Makes an error in computation
□ 1b	Fails to simplify the answer
■ 1d, 2b	Fails to subtract completely
□ 2c, 3a, 3d	Renames incorrectly
□ 2d	Adds instead of subtracts

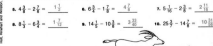

Subtract. Write the answer in simplest form.

1. $4\frac{1}{4} - 2\frac{3}{4}$ $1\frac{1}{2}$
2. $5\frac{1}{3} - 3\frac{2}{3}$ $1\frac{2}{3}$
3. $6\frac{3}{5} - 1\frac{4}{5}$ $4\frac{4}{5}$
4. $2\frac{3}{8} - 1\frac{7}{8}$ $\frac{1}{2}$

5. $6\frac{5}{8}$
$-3\frac{3}{4}$
$2\frac{7}{8}$

6. $3\frac{1}{6}$
$-1\frac{1}{2}$
$1\frac{2}{3}$

7. $2\frac{2}{5}$
$-1\frac{7}{10}$
$\frac{7}{10}$

8. $3\frac{3}{8}$
$-1\frac{1}{2}$
$1\frac{7}{8}$

9. $9\frac{2}{3}$
$-3\frac{5}{6}$
$5\frac{5}{6}$

10. $5\frac{3}{5}$
$-2\frac{9}{10}$
$2\frac{7}{10}$

11. 5
$-3\frac{1}{3}$
$1\frac{2}{3}$

12. 3
$-1\frac{1}{9}$
$1\frac{8}{9}$

13. 6
$-5\frac{7}{9}$
$\frac{2}{9}$

14. 12
$-6\frac{4}{5}$
$5\frac{1}{5}$

15. 13
$-7\frac{6}{11}$
$5\frac{5}{11}$

16. 9
$-2\frac{2}{3}$
$6\frac{1}{3}$

17. $8 - 7\frac{1}{4}$ $\frac{3}{4}$
18. $19 - 3\frac{2}{3}$ $15\frac{1}{3}$
19. $7 - 3\frac{5}{6}$ $3\frac{1}{6}$
20. $5 - 4\frac{4}{7}$ $\frac{3}{7}$

21. $6\frac{2}{3} - 5\frac{6}{7}$ $\frac{17}{21}$
22. $3\frac{3}{10} - 1\frac{2}{3}$ $1\frac{19}{30}$
23. $18\frac{1}{2} - 7\frac{7}{9}$ $10\frac{13}{18}$
24. $6\frac{1}{4} - 5\frac{3}{5}$ $\frac{13}{20}$

25. $5\frac{1}{5}$
$-2\frac{2}{3}$
$2\frac{8}{15}$

26. $2\frac{1}{6}$
$-1\frac{2}{5}$
$\frac{23}{30}$

27. $3\frac{1}{8}$
$-1\frac{2}{3}$
$1\frac{11}{24}$

28. $15\frac{3}{10}$
$-6\frac{2}{3}$
$8\frac{19}{30}$

29. $17\frac{3}{8}$
$-8\frac{3}{5}$
$8\frac{31}{40}$

30. $4\frac{1}{12}$
$-3\frac{2}{9}$
$\frac{31}{36}$

31. 9
$-\frac{13}{15}$
$8\frac{2}{15}$

32. $6\frac{1}{4}$
$-3\frac{5}{8}$
$2\frac{5}{8}$

33. $4\frac{1}{4}$
$-1\frac{3}{4}$
$2\frac{1}{2}$

34. 2
$-1\frac{8}{17}$
$\frac{9}{17}$

35. $5\frac{1}{6}$
$-2\frac{7}{8}$
$2\frac{7}{24}$

36. 3
$-1\frac{11}{12}$
$1\frac{1}{12}$

Solve.

37. At the end of the day, Jocelyn had $68\frac{3}{4}$ ft of round reed. If she started the day with $92\frac{1}{2}$ ft, how much round reed did Jocelyn use during the day? $23\frac{3}{4}$ ft

38. Greg started with 50 feet of flat reed. He used $24\frac{1}{2}$ feet on one basket, $12\frac{2}{3}$ feet on another, and $11\frac{1}{4}$ feet on a third. How much did he have left? $1\frac{7}{12}$ ft

MIDCHAPTER REVIEW

Add. Write the answer in simplest form.

1. $\frac{3}{7} + \frac{2}{7}$ $\frac{5}{7}$
2. $\frac{5}{8} + \frac{3}{5}$ $1\frac{9}{40}$
3. $2\frac{4}{9} + \frac{7}{9}$ $3\frac{2}{9}$
4. $3\frac{3}{4} + 7\frac{11}{16}$ $11\frac{7}{16}$
5. $2\frac{1}{5} + \frac{9}{11} + 3\frac{7}{10}$ $6\frac{79}{110}$

Subtract. Write the answer in simplest form.

6. $\frac{7}{8} - \frac{3}{8}$ $\frac{1}{2}$
7. $\frac{5}{9} - \frac{7}{18}$ $\frac{1}{6}$
8. $\frac{9}{11} - \frac{3}{4}$ $\frac{3}{44}$
9. $4\frac{3}{5} - 2\frac{2}{5}$ $2\frac{1}{5}$
10. $7\frac{1}{2} - 3\frac{5}{16}$ $4\frac{3}{16}$

11. $5\frac{3}{10} - 1\frac{1}{15}$ $4\frac{7}{30}$
12. $9\frac{5}{8} - 2\frac{7}{8}$ $6\frac{3}{4}$
13. $12 - 3\frac{5}{6}$ $8\frac{1}{6}$
14. $2\frac{5}{9} - 1\frac{9}{11}$ $\frac{73}{99}$
15. $18\frac{1}{4} - 12\frac{9}{17}$ $5\frac{49}{68}$

Classwork/Homework, page H55

135

ASSIGNMENT GUIDE

Basic: 1–20, 37–38, MCR

Average: 5–24, 37–38, MCR

Extended: 21–38, MCR

Resources
Practice, p. 55   Class/Home, p. H55
Reteach, p. 41
Enrich, p. 53

Exercise Analysis

1–4   Subtract mixed numbers that have like denominators
5–10 Subtract mixed numbers that have unlike denominators
11–20 Subtract a mixed number from a whole number
21–36 Mixed practice
37–38 Skill applications

Midchapter Review

This review provides an opportunity for you and students to assess their understanding of concepts and skills developed to this point in the chapter.

FOLLOW-UP ACTIVITIES

NUMBER SENSE (Estimation)

Have students use estimation to compare each sum or difference.

- $4\frac{1}{4} - 2\frac{2}{3}$ ● $3\frac{5}{6} - 1\frac{7}{8}$ (<)
- $5\frac{1}{2} + 4\frac{5}{8}$ ● $10\frac{1}{3} - 1\frac{5}{6}$ (>)
- $5\frac{5}{6} - 1\frac{1}{2}$ ● $3\frac{2}{7} + 1\frac{5}{7}$ (<)
- $9\frac{1}{3} - 3\frac{1}{2}$ ● $4\frac{4}{5} + 1\frac{1}{2}$ (<)

NUMBER SENSE (Mental Math)

Have students perform each series of computations mentally.

$\frac{1}{2} + \frac{1}{4} + 3\frac{1}{8} - 1\frac{3}{8} + 3\frac{5}{6} - 4\frac{3}{4} + 9\frac{5}{12} - 7\frac{5}{8} - 3\frac{1}{8}$

$(\frac{1}{4})$

COMING UP

On or about

PRACTICE | Subtracting Mixed Numbers with Renaming

Subtract. Write the answer in simplest form.

1. $16\frac{1}{5}$ $-15\frac{1}{2}$ $\frac{7}{10}$
2. $19\frac{1}{2}$ $-14\frac{1}{3}$ $5\frac{1}{6}$
3. $17\frac{4}{5}$ $-10\frac{7}{10}$ $7\frac{1}{10}$
4. 16 $-7\frac{3}{5}$ $8\frac{2}{5}$
5. $8\frac{4}{5}$ $-2\frac{1}{4}$ $6\frac{11}{20}$

6. $16\frac{2}{5}$ $-5\frac{4}{5}$ $10\frac{3}{5}$
7. 9 $-2\frac{1}{5}$ $6\frac{4}{5}$
8. $16\frac{2}{5}$ $-5\frac{4}{5}$ $10\frac{19}{20}$
9. $12\frac{5}{8}$ $-9\frac{1}{4}$ $3\frac{3}{8}$
10. $9\frac{1}{2}$ $-3\frac{3}{8}$ $6\frac{1}{8}$

11. $12\frac{1}{2}$ $-10\frac{3}{8}$ $1\frac{11}{18}$
12. 19 $-2\frac{1}{2}$ $16\frac{1}{2}$
13. $15\frac{1}{3}$ $-14\frac{1}{6}$ $1\frac{1}{6}$
14. 5 $-2\frac{7}{8}$ $2\frac{5}{8}$
15. $19\frac{7}{8}$ $-10\frac{3}{8}$ $7\frac{3}{8}$

16. $13\frac{1}{2}$ $-4\frac{1}{3}$ $9\frac{9}{10}$
17. $4\frac{2}{9}$ $-1\frac{1}{3}$ $3\frac{7}{9}$
18. $10\frac{1}{4}$ $-3\frac{5}{8}$ $6\frac{7}{12}$
19. $18\frac{4}{7}$ $-5\frac{1}{2}$ $13\frac{1}{14}$
20. $10\frac{1}{3}$ $-5\frac{1}{3}$ $\frac{2}{9}$

21. 5 $-3\frac{2}{3}$ $1\frac{1}{3}$
22. $3\frac{1}{2}$ $-2\frac{2}{5}$ 1
23. 14 $-1\frac{5}{6}$ $12\frac{1}{6}$
24. $9\frac{3}{4}$ $-5\frac{1}{3}$ $4\frac{5}{12}$
25. $19\frac{7}{8}$ $-11\frac{1}{2}$ $8\frac{3}{8}$

26. $12\frac{1}{2} - 11\frac{7}{12}$ $\frac{11}{18}$
27. $10\frac{1}{2} - 4\frac{3}{7}$ $6\frac{1}{14}$
28. $11\frac{3}{4} - 2\frac{9}{10}$ $8\frac{17}{20}$
29. $20 - 2\frac{7}{10}$ $17\frac{3}{10}$
30. $11\frac{1}{4} - 1\frac{2}{3}$ $10\frac{1}{3}$
31. $10\frac{2}{3} - 9\frac{1}{6}$ $1\frac{1}{2}$
32. $18\frac{1}{4} - 13\frac{1}{6}$ $5\frac{1}{12}$
33. $13 - 6\frac{5}{8}$ $6\frac{3}{8}$
34. $10\frac{2}{3} - 7\frac{3}{8}$ $2\frac{8}{...}$
35. $10\frac{3}{4} - 2\frac{1}{3}$ $8\frac{5}{12}$

ENRICH | Measurement

You can find the day of the week of any date in history even if you don't have a calendar for that year.

Leap years occur in every year divisible by 4 and in every century year divisible by 400. (The year 2000 will be a leap year; the years 1700, 1800, and 1900 were not).

1. How many complete weeks and how many extra days are there in a nonleap year? in a leap year?
   52 complete weeks, one day; 52 complete weeks, two days

2. If January 1 is a Monday, on what day will December 31 fall in a nonleap year?
   Monday; Tuesday

3. The year 1984 was a leap year. Which years have been leap years between 1963 and 1984?
   1964, 1968, 1972, 1976, 1980

4. January 1, 1970, was on a Thursday. What day was January 1 in the year you were born?
   Answers will vary.

By using the chart below, you can tell the dates and days of the week for any year in history or in the future.

S	M	T	W	Th	F	S
				1	2	3
4	5	6	7	8	9	10
11	12	13	14	15	16	17
18	19	20	21	22	23	24
25	26	27	28	29	30	31

Imagine sliding the box back and forth across the chart to see all the possible monthly patterns.

5. What information do you need in order to use the chart for any given year?
   the day of the week for any date that year; whether or not the year is a leap year

6. What was the first day of the week for each month in your birth year? Use the chart, and remember the number of days in each month.
   Answers will vary.

Practice Worksheet | **Enrich Worksheet**

Objective: To solve problems by estimation

Warm-Up

Have students estimate the following sums and differences.

$1\frac{1}{4} + 3\frac{5}{8}$ (5) $16\frac{3}{8} + 9\frac{13}{16}$ (26)

$7\frac{3}{4} - 2\frac{5}{8}$ (5) $22\frac{7}{10} - 6\frac{4}{5}$ (16)

GETTING STARTED

Tell students that you are going to make 4 shelves from a piece of board 48 in. long. Each shelf will be $11\frac{7}{8}$ in. long. You want to know if the board is long enough. Have students discuss how to solve the problem. Students may suggest dividing 48 by $11\frac{7}{8}$ or estimating $48 \div 12$. Point out that they should *overestimate* or round up to make sure there will be enough board.

TEACHING THE LESSON

Students must learn to decide how accurate an estimate needs to be. Explain to students that if an estimate will provide an adequate answer to a problem, they must still decide

- whether to *overestimate* or *underestimate*.
- how accurate the estimate needs to be.

In the lesson problem, the first estimate of 12 inches is not exact enough because the underestimate gives a length very close to $13\frac{5}{16}$. An overestimate is more desirable in this instance because it is better to have more wood than not enough. By rounding each length to the nearest half inch, a more accurate estimate can be found.

Questions: The most essential choice in answering the question is deciding the necessary level or exactness. In the lesson problem, the width of the saw cut must also be considered. Since this width cannot be predicted with any certainty, the best approach is to overestimate the length of the board needed. Stress the importance of first deciding whether an overestimate, an underestimate, or an exact answer is needed in each problem.

Tools: Explain that the front-end method is good for underestimating an answer. If students' estimates are too small but very close to what is needed, students should round to a smaller unit and estimate again. Discuss alternate methods of estimating. Do not discourage these methods if they are effective. Point out that there is no "best" method of estimating.

Solutions: You may wish to review addition of fractions.

136

PROBLEM SOLVING
Estimation

Once you have decided to estimate, you have to decide how accurate your estimate needs to be.

> Julia is building a bird feeder. The wooden sides of the feeder are to measure $6\frac{3}{8}$ in. long and $5\frac{3}{4}$ in. wide. Can she cut the 2 sides from a piece of wood $13\frac{5}{16}$ in. long and 6 in. wide?

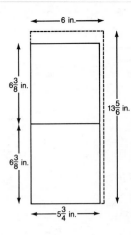

To solve this problem, you can first draw a sketch. Since $5\frac{3}{4} < 6$, you can see that the piece of wood is wide enough. To discover whether it is long enough, you can round the length of each side to the nearest inch and multiply by 2.

$$6\frac{3}{8} \longrightarrow 6$$
$$2 \times 6 = 12$$

The length of the 2 sides put end to end is about 12 inches.

Of course $13\frac{5}{16}$ is greater than 12, but the lengths are fairly close. You may want to estimate more closely. You can do this by rounding $6\frac{3}{8}$ in. to the nearest $\frac{1}{2}$ in., and then multiplying by 2.

$$6\frac{3}{8} \longrightarrow 6\frac{1}{2}$$
$$2 \times 6\frac{1}{2} = 13$$

Since $13\frac{5}{16} > 13$, the actual length of the piece of wood is greater than the two bird-feeder sides placed end to end. Julia can cut the sides from the piece of wood.

136

Checks: Have students consider the reasonableness of their estimates rather than checking the estimates by computation. Encourage students to rely on their estimates without computing.

Use estimation to solve each problem. Write an exact answer when needed.

1. George is making a quilt. He wants to use 5 colors. He will need $1\frac{3}{8}$ yards of each color. He finds two matching pieces of red fabric. One is $1\frac{1}{8}$ yards long, the other is $\frac{1}{2}$ yard long. Can he use these pieces as one of his colors? **yes**

2. George has five scraps of green fabric. Their lengths are $\frac{5}{8}$ yard, $\frac{1}{5}$ yard, $\frac{1}{4}$ yard, $\frac{3}{8}$ yard, and $\frac{1}{2}$ yard. He needs $1\frac{3}{8}$ yards. Does he have enough green fabric for the quilt? **yes**

3. George's quilt will contain 36 squares. For each square, he needs 2 red triangles and 4 blue triangles. How many triangles of each color should he cut for the quilt? **72 red triangles; 144 blue triangles**

4. George decides to add a white border. The border will measure 10 in. wide and 320 in. long. He has several scraps of white material, that measure 10 in. wide. Their lengths are $8\frac{1}{2}$ in., $19\frac{3}{8}$ in., $33\frac{1}{4}$ in., $41\frac{5}{8}$ in., $48\frac{1}{4}$ in., $61\frac{1}{4}$ in., and $68\frac{1}{4}$ in. Will he have enough fabric to make the border? **no**

5. Elisa is helping George by making the back portion of the quilt. It will measure 80 in. wide and 80 in. long. She is using three pieces of fabric. Each piece measures 80 in. in length. Their widths are $27\frac{1}{2}$ in., $21\frac{3}{4}$ in., and $11\frac{1}{8}$ in. Does she have enough material to make the back? **no**

6. Elisa is also helping to sew the front of the quilt to the back. If George had done this job alone, it would have taken him about $6\frac{3}{4}$ hours to finish it. Elisa works at the same rate as George. How much time should they allow for sewing the back to the front? **about $3\frac{1}{2}$ hours**

ASSIGNMENT GUIDE

Basic:	1–4
Average:	2–5
Extended:	3–6

Resources
Practice, p. 56   Class/Home p. H56
Enrich, p. 54

Exercise Analysis
1–6 Solve by estimating or finding the exact answer

FOLLOW-UP ACTIVITIES

PROBLEM SOLVING
Copy the chart and problems on the chalkboard or provide it as a handout.

Size	Lengths available				
	4 ft	6 ft	8 ft	10 ft	12 ft
2 × 4	yes	yes	yes	yes	yes
2 × 6	yes	no	yes	no	yes
2 × 8	no	yes	yes	yes	no
2 × 10	no	no	yes	no	yes

1. You need eight $3\frac{1}{2}$-foot lengths of 2 × 4.
2. You need fourteen $2\frac{1}{4}$-foot lengths of 2 × 10.
3. You need four $5\frac{3}{8}$-foot lengths and two $3\frac{3}{4}$-foot lengths of 2 × 6.
4. You need one $2\frac{1}{2}$-foot length, one $3\frac{1}{4}$-foot length, and four $6\frac{1}{8}$-foot lengths of 2 × 8.
5. You need twenty-two $7\frac{1}{2}$-foot lengths and eighteen $2\frac{1}{4}$-foot lengths of 2 × 4.

Have students estimate what piece of lumber they would buy in order to leave the least amount of waste. (Answers will vary.)

REINFORCEMENT
Materials: yardsticks per group

Have students work in small groups to plan how they would construct bookshelves to hold the math books for the class. Have students decide and measure
● where in the classroom the shelves could be built.
● the length of each shelf.
● the width of each shelf.
● which pieces of wood on the chart above would be most practical to buy.

COMING UP
"Times" when fractions are "productive"

Practice Worksheet

Enrich Worksheet

137

Objective: To multiply fractions

Warm-Up
Have students find the GCF of each pair.

24 and 30 (6)   21 and 28 (7)
24 and 40 (8)   36 and 54 (18)

GETTING STARTED

Pose the following problem.
- The Gold family bought $\frac{2}{3}$ acre of land. They turned $\frac{1}{4}$ of their land into a vegetable garden. What fraction of an acre is the size of their garden?

Discuss possible solutions. Draw a diagram to show the answer.

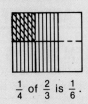

$\frac{1}{4}$ of $\frac{2}{3}$ is $\frac{1}{6}$.

TEACHING THE LESSON

A. Point out that whenever we multiply by a fraction less than 1, the product is always less than the other factor. This is because multiplying by a fraction less than 1 means finding that part of the other factor.

B. Demonstrate the value of the shortcut by having students multiply the following fractions first without simplifying and then with simplifying.

$$\frac{7}{12} \times \frac{48}{56} = \frac{336}{672} = \frac{336 \div 336}{672 \div 336} = \frac{1}{2}$$

$$\frac{7}{12} \times \frac{48}{56} = \frac{7}{12} \times \frac{48}{56} = \frac{4}{8} = \frac{1}{2}$$

In the Other Examples section, use the example with three factors to emphasize the fact that simplifying can occur between any numerator and any denominator. For students who want to know why the shortcut works, point out that they are actually dividing by $\frac{n}{n}$, or 1. The digits change, but the value stays the same.

Multiplying Fractions

A. When Martha makes patchwork quilts, she sews patches into blocks of 8 first, before sewing the blocks together to form a quilt. Of the part of the quilt shown, $\frac{5}{8}$ is flannel. Of that part, $\frac{4}{5}$ is plaid flannel. What fraction of the block shown is plaid flannel?

Find $\frac{4}{5}$ of $\frac{5}{8}$. $\boxed{\textit{Of} \text{ means multiply.}}$

To multiply fractions, multiply the numerators and multiply the denominators. Write the product in simplest form.

$$\frac{4}{5} \times \frac{5}{8} = \frac{4 \times 5}{5 \times 8} = \frac{20}{40} = \frac{1}{2}$$

Of the part of the quilt shown, $\frac{1}{2}$ is plaid flannel.

B. When you multiply fractions, you may want to take a shortcut and simplify first. To simplify, divide the numerators and denominators by a common factor.

Find $\frac{5}{9} \times \frac{21}{25}$.

3 is a common factor of 9 and 21. Divide each by 3. $\frac{5}{\underset{3}{9}} \times \frac{\overset{7}{21}}{25}$

5 is a common factor of 5 and 25. Divide by 5. $\frac{\overset{1}{5}}{\underset{3}{9}} \times \frac{\overset{7}{21}}{\underset{5}{25}}$

Multiply. $\frac{\overset{1}{5}}{\underset{3}{9}} \times \frac{\overset{7}{21}}{\underset{5}{25}} = \frac{1 \times 7}{3 \times 5} = \frac{7}{15}$

Other examples:

$\frac{5}{8} \times \frac{4}{7}$

$\frac{\overset{}{5}}{\underset{2}{8}} \times \frac{\overset{1}{4}}{7} = \frac{5 \times 1}{2 \times 7} = \frac{5}{14}$

$\frac{3}{7} \times \frac{5}{6} \times \frac{7}{10}$

$\frac{\overset{1}{3}}{\underset{1}{7}} \times \frac{\overset{1}{5}}{\underset{2}{6}} \times \frac{\overset{1}{7}}{\underset{2}{10}} = \frac{1 \times 1 \times 1}{1 \times 2 \times 2} = \frac{1}{4}$

COMMON ERRORS

Some students might apply the shortcut incorrectly by reducing pairs of denominators.

$$\frac{7}{15} \times \frac{1}{5} = \frac{7}{\underset{3}{15}} \times \frac{1}{\underset{1}{5}} = \frac{7}{3}$$

Remediation
For this error, emphasize the fact that reducing can only take place across the fraction bar. Have students check that their answer is reasonable by comparing the product to the factors. If it is larger than either factor, it must be incorrect as long as one of the factors is less than one.

Assign Reteach Master, p. 42.

RETEACH Multiplying Fractions

A recipe calls for $\frac{3}{8}$ cup raisins. Mike wants to make $\frac{2}{3}$ of the recipe. How many cups of raisins should he use? To find the answer, multiply the fractions.

Remember
When multiplying fractions, you may simplify first. Then multiply the numerators and multiply the denominators.

$$\frac{3}{8} \times \frac{2}{3} = \frac{3 \times 2}{8 \times 3} = \frac{1 \times 1}{4 \times 1} = \frac{1}{4}$$

He should use $\frac{1}{4}$ cup raisins.

Multiply. Write the answer in simplest form.

1. $\frac{3}{5} \times \frac{5}{7} = \frac{3 \times 5}{5 \times 7} = \frac{3}{7}$

2. $\frac{2}{3} \times \frac{3}{14} = \frac{2 \times 3}{3 \times 14} = \frac{1}{7}$

3. $\frac{5}{7} \times \frac{5}{8} = \frac{5 \times 5}{7 \times 8} = \frac{15}{28}$

4. $\frac{5}{12} \times \frac{8}{15} = \frac{5 \times 8}{12 \times 15} = \frac{2}{9}$

5. $\frac{9}{14} \times \frac{2}{9} = \frac{1}{7}$ 6. $\frac{11}{12} \times \frac{5}{7} = \frac{11}{21}$ 7. $\frac{2}{3} \times \frac{6}{5} = \frac{1}{10}$ 8. $\frac{1}{16} \times \frac{4}{5} = \frac{1}{4}$

9. $\frac{4}{7} \times \frac{21}{32} = \frac{3}{8}$ 10. $\frac{7}{8} \times \frac{1}{7} = \frac{1}{8}$ 11. $\frac{21}{40} \times \frac{5}{7} = \frac{3}{8}$ 12. $\frac{21}{40} \times \frac{11}{14} \times \frac{10}{11} = \frac{3}{8}$

Solve.

13. A recipe calls for $\frac{7}{8}$ cup wheat germ. How much wheat germ should be used for $\frac{2}{5}$ of the recipe? $\frac{7}{20}$ cup

14. A chili recipe requires $\frac{3}{4}$ lb chopped beef. How much chopped beef would be used in $\frac{4}{5}$ of the recipe? $\frac{3}{5}$ lb

15. A recipe for 25 people requires $\frac{7}{8}$ tablespoon mixed herbs. Sam is cooking for 20 people. How much mixed herbs should he use? $\frac{7}{10}$ tablespoon

42   Use with pages 138–139.

Reteach Worksheet

Multiply. Write the answer in simplest form.

1. $\frac{2}{9} \times \frac{1}{3}$ $\frac{2}{27}$ 2. $\frac{4}{7} \times \frac{8}{9}$ $\frac{32}{63}$ 3. $\frac{2}{4} \times \frac{1}{11}$ $\frac{3}{44}$ 4. $\frac{2}{3} \times \frac{4}{5}$ $\frac{8}{15}$ 5. $\frac{5}{9} \times \frac{1}{9}$ $\frac{5}{81}$

6. $\frac{1}{3} \times \frac{3}{4}$ $\frac{1}{4}$ 7. $\frac{3}{8} \times \frac{4}{9}$ $\frac{1}{6}$ 8. $\frac{5}{7} \times \frac{14}{15}$ $\frac{2}{3}$ 9. $\frac{12}{17} \times \frac{5}{12}$ $\frac{5}{17}$ 10. $\frac{4}{5} \times \frac{1}{8}$ $\frac{1}{10}$

11. $\frac{9}{10} \times \frac{35}{36}$ $\frac{7}{8}$ 12. $\frac{7}{8} \times \frac{12}{21}$ $\frac{1}{2}$ 13. $\frac{2}{5} \times \frac{8}{9}$ $\frac{16}{45}$ 14. $\frac{42}{55} \times \frac{25}{28}$ $\frac{15}{22}$ 15. $\frac{8}{9} \times \frac{18}{24}$ $\frac{2}{3}$

16. $\frac{2}{3} \times \frac{1}{4} \times \frac{5}{7}$ $\frac{5}{42}$ 17. $\frac{2}{5} \times \frac{1}{4} \times \frac{5}{6}$ $\frac{1}{12}$ 18. $\frac{1}{6} \times \frac{1}{2} \times \frac{3}{5}$ $\frac{1}{20}$ 19. $\frac{5}{9} \times \frac{2}{3} \times \frac{1}{6}$ $\frac{5}{81}$

20. $\frac{7}{8} \times \frac{8}{9} \times \frac{9}{21}$ $\frac{1}{3}$ 21. $\frac{3}{8} \times \frac{2}{7} \times \frac{1}{6}$ $\frac{1}{56}$ 22. $\frac{6}{14} \times \frac{1}{3} \times \frac{7}{8}$ $\frac{1}{8}$ 23. $\frac{5}{6} \times \frac{12}{25} \times \frac{25}{26}$ $\frac{5}{13}$

24. $\frac{5}{6} \times \frac{1}{2}$ $\frac{5}{12}$ 25. $\frac{3}{4} \times \frac{2}{3}$ $\frac{1}{2}$ 26. $\frac{1}{2} \times \frac{3}{7}$ $\frac{3}{14}$ 27. $\frac{5}{6} \times \frac{1}{10} \times \frac{3}{4}$ $\frac{1}{16}$

28. $\frac{3}{16} \times \frac{5}{9} \times \frac{1}{2}$ $\frac{5}{96}$ 29. $\frac{2}{3} \times \frac{9}{10} \times \frac{20}{21}$ $\frac{4}{7}$ 30. $\frac{4}{7} \times \frac{3}{5}$ $\frac{12}{35}$ 31. $\frac{3}{16} \times \frac{4}{5}$ $\frac{3}{20}$

Solve.

32. Sara had $\frac{3}{4}$ yd of embroidery floss with which to stitch her name. She used $\frac{1}{2}$ of the floss. How much floss did she use? $\frac{3}{8}$ yd

33. In an embroidery group, $\frac{2}{3}$ of the members use a cross-stitch on their samplers. Of these, $\frac{1}{2}$ also use stem stitch. What part of the embroidery group uses stem stitch?
$\frac{1}{3}$ of the group

34. Of Mr. Brooks's class, $\frac{5}{6}$ know how to do the satin stitch. Of these, $\frac{1}{4}$ know how to do the chain stitch. What part of Mr. Brooks's students know how to do the chain stitch?
$\frac{5}{24}$ of the students

35. Bob was practicing the French knot on $\frac{3}{4}$ yd of embroidery floss. After 1 hour, he had used up $\frac{3}{4}$ of the embroidery floss he started with. How much embroidery floss did he have left? $\frac{3}{16}$ yd

ANOTHER LOOK

Write in standard form.

1. $6 \cdot 10^2$
600

2. $32 \cdot 10^5$
3,200,000

3. $711 \cdot 10^4$
7,110,000

4. $16.8 \cdot 10^3$
16,800

5. $72.4 \cdot 10^5$
7,240,000

6. $4.06 \cdot 10^1$
40.6

7. $33.92 \cdot 10^6$
33,920,000

8. $12.089 \cdot 10^8$
1,208,900,000

9. $947.628 \cdot 10^{10}$
9,476,280,000,000

Classwork/Homework, page H57

139

ASSIGNMENT GUIDE

Basic: 1–23, 32–35, AL

Average: 1–23 o, 24–35, AL

Extended: 2–22 e, 24–35, AL

Resources
Practice, p. 57   Class/Home, p. H57
Reteach, p. 42
Enrich, p. 55

Exercise Analysis

1–5	Multiply two fractions
6–15	Use the shortcut to multiply two fractions
16–23	Use the shortcut to multiply three fractions
24–31	Mixed practice
32–35	Skill applications

Another Look

This review provides maintenance for writing the standard form for products given in exponential form.

FOLLOW-UP ACTIVITIES

PROBLEM SOLVING
Have students solve these problems.

● Stewart buys $\frac{2}{3}$ yard of electrical wire so that he can fix his clock. After his repairs, he finds that he has $\frac{1}{3}$ yard left. What part of his purchase did he use? ($\frac{1}{2}$)

● Laura's stew recipe calls for $\frac{2}{3}$ cup of chili powder. Its yield, however, is 2 gallons, and Laura wants to make only $\frac{1}{2}$ gallon. How much chili powder should she use? ($\frac{1}{6}$ cup)

REINFORCEMENT
Have students draw diagrams to find each answer.

$\frac{2}{3}$ of 15 $\frac{5}{6}$ of 24

$\frac{2}{3}$ of $\frac{1}{2}$ $\frac{1}{4}$ of $\frac{2}{3}$

COMING UP
More or less

Objectives: To estimate products and quotients using rational numbers

Warm-Up

Have students round these fractions and mixed numbers to the nearest whole number.

$2\frac{3}{4}$ (3); $8\frac{1}{2}$ (9); $4\frac{1}{5}$ (4); $6\frac{7}{8}$ (7)

Have students compare the following by using >, <, or =.

$3\frac{7}{8} \bullet 3\frac{5}{6}$ (>)

$2\frac{1}{2} \bullet 2\frac{3}{6}$ (=)

$1\frac{7}{9} \bullet 2\frac{1}{3}$ (<)

$3\frac{4}{5} \bullet 2\frac{2}{3}$ (>)

TEACHING THE LESSON

A. Emphasize that when rounding mixed numbers, students should round both numbers to the nearer whole number. Fractions of $\frac{1}{2}$ or larger round to the next higher whole number.

Give students these guidelines for rounding mixed numbers to estimate products.

- If both are rounded up, adjust product down.

  $1\frac{5}{8} \times 3\frac{4}{5} \approx 2 \times 4 \approx 8^-$

- If both are rounded down, adjust product up.

  $3\frac{1}{3} \times 4\frac{1}{5} \approx 3 \times 4 \approx 12^+$

- If one rounds up and one rounds down, do not adjust product.

  $2\frac{1}{3} \times 3\frac{7}{8} \approx 2 \times 4 \approx 8$

When multiplying a fraction times a whole number, students can round the fraction to $\frac{1}{2}$, 0, or 1.

B. Give students these guidelines for rounding mixed numbers to find quotients.

- If dividend > divisor, the quotient > 1.

  $\frac{4}{5} \div \frac{1}{2} > 1 \left(\frac{4}{5} > \frac{1}{2}\right)$

- If dividend < divisor, the quotient < 1.

  $\frac{1}{2} \div \frac{4}{5} < 1 \left(\frac{1}{2} < \frac{4}{5}\right)$

140

Estimating Products and Quotients

A. Handmade quilts are insulated with a material called *batting*. A full-size quilt measures about $8\frac{1}{3}$ feet by $9\frac{1}{2}$ feet. About how many square feet of batting are needed for the quilt?

Estimate $8\frac{1}{3} \times 9\frac{1}{2}$.

Round each factor to the nearest whole number. Then, multiply the rounded factors.

$$8\frac{1}{3} \times 9\frac{1}{2}$$
$$\downarrow \qquad \downarrow$$
$$8 \times 10 = 80$$

About 80 square feet of batting are needed for a double quilt.

$\boxed{\frac{3}{8} \text{ is close to } \frac{1}{2}}$

Other examples:

$6\frac{1}{4} \times 9\frac{1}{3}$ $9\frac{5}{8} \times 3\frac{3}{4}$ $\frac{3}{8} \times 15\frac{1}{2}$

$\downarrow \quad \downarrow$ $\downarrow \quad \downarrow$ $\downarrow \qquad \downarrow$

$6 \times 9 = 54^+$ $10 \times 4 = 40^-$ $\frac{1}{2} \times 16 = 8^-$, or $\frac{3}{8} \times 16 = 6^-$

Estimate: 54^+ Estimate: 40^- Estimate: 8^- or 6^-

B. $4\frac{7}{8} \div 3\frac{3}{4}$.

Compare the quotient to 1.	Round the factors to numbers that divide easily.	Divide the rounded numbers.

$4\frac{7}{8} > 3\frac{3}{4}$. So, the quotient is greater than 1.

Estimate: 1^+

$$4\frac{7}{8} \div 3\frac{3}{4}$$
$$\downarrow \qquad \downarrow$$
$$4 \div 4$$

$$4 \div 4 = 1$$

Other examples:

$11\frac{2}{3} \div 6\frac{1}{5}$ $\frac{4}{5} \div 2\frac{1}{3}$

$\downarrow \qquad \downarrow$ $\downarrow \qquad \downarrow$

$12 \div 6 = 2 \leftarrow$ $\boxed{11\frac{2}{3} > 6\frac{1}{5}}$ So, the quotient is greater than 1. $1 \div 2 = \frac{1}{2}$ $\boxed{\frac{4}{5} < 2\frac{1}{3}}$. So, the quotient is less than 1.

Estimate: 2   Estimate: $\frac{1}{2}$

140

COMMON ERRORS

$4\frac{7}{8} \times 1\frac{2}{3} \approx 4$

Students might "drop" the fractional part of a mixed number when estimating.

Remediation

For this error, illustrate the difference when just "dropping" the fraction, rounding the fraction, and the exact number.

Rounded: $5 \times 2 = 10$

Exact: $4\frac{7}{8} \times 1\frac{2}{3} = 8\frac{1}{8}$

Have student verbally work through several problems.

Assign Reteach Master, p. 43

RETEACH   Estimating Products and Quotients

A box of soap weighs $3\frac{6}{8}$ pounds. There are $2\frac{3}{4}$ boxes of soap in the laundry room. If 15 pounds of soap are needed each month, is there a month's supply of soap?

Remember

When multiplying fractions
- If both factors are rounded up, an **overestimate** is produced
- If both factors are rounded down, an **underestimate** is produced

An exact answer is not needed to answer this question; so, estimate. When estimating with fractions, think about the numbers involved.

$2\frac{3}{4} \times 3\frac{6}{8}$ about 4   Both numbers were rounded up, so $3 \times 4 = 12$ is an overestimate.

  about 3

There is not a month's supply of soap.

Estimate. Choose the best answer.

1. $3\frac{1}{3} \times 4\frac{1}{7}$ a. under 12   b. over 12
2. $5\frac{7}{8} \times 3\frac{8}{11}$ a. under 15   b. over 15
3. $2\frac{8}{9} \times 3\frac{7}{8}$ c. under 12   b. over 12
4. $5\frac{1}{2} \times 3\frac{5}{13}$ a. under 15   b. over 15
5. $7\frac{1}{2} \times 3\frac{5}{13}$ a. under 21   b. over 21
6. $4\frac{2}{7} \times 2\frac{8}{9}$ c. under 15   b. over 15
7. $5\frac{1}{8} \times 2\frac{1}{9}$ a. under 10   b. over 10
8. $7\frac{1}{9} \times 8\frac{1}{8}$ a. under 56   b. over 56
9. $5\frac{1}{10} \times 6\frac{7}{8}$ a. under 30   b. over 30
10. $6\frac{3}{4} \times 1\frac{7}{8}$ c. under 14   b. over 14

Use with pages 140–141.

43

Reteach Worksheet

Estimate. **Answers may vary. Accept any reasonable estimate.**

1. $6\frac{1}{3} \times 4\frac{7}{8}$ 30
2. $3\frac{3}{4} \times 2\frac{5}{6}$ 12⁻
3. $1\frac{1}{6} \times 3\frac{1}{4}$ 3⁺
4. $8\frac{1}{5} \times 3\frac{2}{3}$ 32

5. $5 \times 4\frac{5}{7}$ 25⁻
6. $3\frac{2}{3} \times 6$ 24⁻
7. $5\frac{1}{2} \times 2\frac{1}{3}$ 12
8. $7\frac{2}{5} \times 5$ 35⁺

9. $\frac{7}{16} \times 3\frac{2}{3}$ 2
10. $\frac{9}{10} \times 7\frac{5}{8}$ $7\frac{5}{8}$⁻
11. $\frac{1}{3} \times 8\frac{5}{8}$ 3⁻
12. $\frac{3}{4} \times 12\frac{1}{6}$ 9⁺

Estimate. Write > or < for ●.

13. $6\frac{1}{4} \div 3\frac{1}{2} ● 1$ >
14. $\frac{3}{8} \div 2\frac{1}{2} ● 1$ <
15. $3\frac{1}{5} \div 3\frac{1}{2} ● 1$ <

16. $5\frac{1}{8} \div \frac{9}{10} ● 1$ >
17. $1\frac{2}{3} \div 5\frac{1}{2} ● 1$ <
18. $\frac{15}{16} \div \frac{3}{5} ● 1$ >

Estimate. **Answers may vary. Accept any reasonable estimate.**

19. $3\frac{3}{4} \div 2$ 2
20. $6\frac{1}{3} \div 3\frac{1}{8}$ 2
21. $3\frac{1}{2} \div 5\frac{7}{8}$ $\frac{2}{3}$
22. $1\frac{1}{16} \div 4\frac{1}{4}$ $\frac{1}{4}$

23. $5\frac{1}{6} \div 3$ $\frac{5}{3}$
24. $2\frac{3}{8} \div \frac{7}{8}$ 2
25. $1\frac{3}{4} \div 5\frac{1}{4}$ $\frac{2}{5}$
26. $6\frac{1}{4} \div 3\frac{1}{4}$ 2

Estimate. Write > or < for ●.

27. $5\frac{1}{3} \times 6\frac{1}{4} ● 30$ >
28. $8\frac{3}{4} \times 2\frac{1}{2} ● 27$ <
29. $8\frac{1}{2} \times 1\frac{3}{4} ● 10$ >

30. $\frac{7}{9} \times 3\frac{5}{6} ● 4$ <
31. $1\frac{1}{3} \times 8\frac{5}{6} ● 8$ >
32. $6\frac{3}{4} \times 2\frac{4}{5} ● 13$ >

33. $6\frac{1}{2} \div 1\frac{7}{8} ● 3$ >
34. $3\frac{4}{5} \div 2 ● 2$ <
35. $8\frac{1}{3} \div 2\frac{7}{8} ● 4$ <

36. $\frac{9}{10} \div 2\frac{7}{8} ● \frac{1}{2}$ <
37. $1\frac{1}{3} \div 5\frac{3}{8} ● 3$ <
38. $8\frac{5}{8} \div 2\frac{7}{8} ● 2$ >

Solve.

39. A baby quilt measures about $2\frac{2}{3}$ feet by $3\frac{1}{2}$ feet. About how many square feet of batting are needed to insulate the quilt?
9–12 square feet

40. Sue is making a quilt for her mother as a birthday gift. She has about $9\frac{1}{2}$ sections left to quilt. Her mother's birthday is about $4\frac{1}{2}$ weeks away. About how many sections per week must she quilt to finish the gift on time? about 2 sections

Classwork/Homework, page H58

141

ASSIGNMENT GUIDE

Basic: 1–37 o
Average: 1–39 o, 40
Extended: 2–38 e, 39–40

Resources
Practice, p. 58   Class/Home, p. H58
Reteach, p. 43
Enrich, p. 56

Exercise Analysis
1–12 Estimate the product of mixed numbers, whole numbers, and fractions
13–18 Compare quotients to 1
19–26 Estimate quotients
27–38 Estimate to compare products and quotients
39–40 Skill applications

FOLLOW-UP ACTIVITIES

NUMBER SENSE (Estimation)
Sometimes when estimating products, you want to know the lowest and the highest possible number. To do so is to find the "boundaries" of the problem.

$$3\frac{3}{4} \times 2\frac{1}{3}$$

First round both numbers down: $3 \times 2 = 6$.

Then, round both numbers up: $4 \times 3 = 12$.

Therefore, $6 < (3\frac{3}{4} \times 2\frac{1}{3}) < 12$.

The boundaries are 6 and 12.

Find the boundaries for the following problems.

1. $3\frac{1}{8} \times 6\frac{2}{3}$ (18, 28)

2. $5\frac{1}{5} \times 7\frac{9}{10}$ (35, 48)

3. $6\frac{4}{5} \times 8\frac{1}{3}$ (48, 63)

4. $4\frac{1}{2} \times 2\frac{7}{8}$ (8, 15)

5. $9\frac{1}{2} \times 3\frac{8}{9}$ (27, 40)

COMING UP
Give more power to fractions in tomorrow's Follow-Up.

PRACTICE · Estimating Products and Quotients

Write > or < for ○.

1. $2\frac{1}{8} \times 1\frac{1}{9} \bigcirc 2$ >
2. $3\frac{2}{7} \times 2\frac{1}{8} \bigcirc 12$ <
3. $4\frac{1}{7} \times 2 \bigcirc 8$ >
4. $5\frac{5}{8} \times 4\frac{3}{4} \bigcirc 30$ <
5. $3\frac{4}{5} \times 5 \bigcirc 20$ <
6. $2\frac{3}{4} \times 2\frac{7}{8} \bigcirc 9$ <
7. $6 \times 5\frac{7}{11} \bigcirc 30$ >
8. $\frac{7}{8} \times 5 \bigcirc 5$ <
9. $8\frac{1}{3} \times 2\frac{1}{8} \bigcirc 16$ >
10. $3\frac{1}{7} \times 12\frac{7}{8} \bigcirc 36$ >
11. $4\frac{4}{5} \times 2 \bigcirc 8$ >
12. $14\frac{7}{8} \times 2\frac{9}{10} \bigcirc 45$ <
13. $\frac{4}{5} \div \frac{1}{9} \bigcirc 1$ >
14. $\frac{1}{9} \div \frac{4}{5} \bigcirc 1$ <
15. $1\frac{1}{2} \div 2 \bigcirc 1$ <
16. $2\frac{1}{4} \div 1\frac{7}{8} \bigcirc 1$ >
17. $7\frac{3}{4} \div 8\frac{1}{8} \bigcirc 1$ <
18. $5\frac{1}{3} \div 2\frac{7}{8} \bigcirc 1$ >

Estimate. Answers will vary. Accept any reasonable estimates.

19. $15\frac{1}{7} \div 4\frac{11}{14}$ 3–4
20. $6\frac{1}{7} \div 1\frac{8}{9}$ 3–4
21. $5\frac{1}{8} \div \frac{9}{10}$ 5–6
22. $28\frac{7}{9} \div 8\frac{1}{4}$ 3–4
23. $10\frac{2}{3} \div 4\frac{1}{7}$ 2–3
24. $6\frac{1}{7} \div 1\frac{3}{4}$ 3–4
25. $5\frac{7}{8} \div 2\frac{9}{11}$ 2–3
26. $8\frac{1}{11} \times 7\frac{5}{9}$ 56–60
27. $3\frac{8}{9} \times 7\frac{10}{11}$ 28–32
28. $14\frac{1}{8} \times 2\frac{1}{15}$ 28–30
29. $1\frac{1}{9} \times 5\frac{1}{8}$ 5–6
30. $\frac{9}{10} \times 5\frac{4}{5}$ 5–6

58   Use with pages 140–141.

Practice Worksheet

ENRICH · Number

The Galaxy's Greatest Hits is a laser disc being produced by the Galactic Recording Studio. Disc jockeys at radio stations on the planet Octum, which uses a base-eight number system, and the planet Binaria, which uses a base-two number system, will need to know the length of each song on the disc. The base-eight system uses the digits 0 to 7, and each place is 8 times the value of the place to the right of it. The base-two system uses the digits 0 and 1, and each place is 2 times the value of the place to the right of it.

1. Fill in the chart for the base-eight numbers 0 to 7 and the corresponding base-two numbers.

Base 8	0_8	1_8	2_8	3_8	4_8	5_8	6_8	7_8
Base 2	0_2	1_2	10_2	11_2	100_2	101_2	110_2	111_2

To convert $10{,}011_2$ to a base number, separate it into groups of three digits from *right* to *left*. Your last group has less than three digits. Use the chart to write the corresponding base-eight number for each group of digits. If a group begins with a zero, ignore the zero.

$$10{,}011_2 = 23_8$$

To convert 41_8 to a base-two counterpart, write each base-eight number in its base-two counterpart. If a group of base-two numbers is less than three digits, add zeros in front of the number to make it three digits long.

$$41_8 = 100{,}001_2$$

2. Fill in the laser disc jacket chart for the length of each song in seconds.

Side 1	Binaria	Octum
Song 1	$11{,}111{,}001_2$	371_8
Song 2	$100{,}110{,}011_2$	463_8
Song 3	$11{,}001{,}011_2$	313_8

Side 2	Binaria	Octum
Song 4	$110{,}010{,}101_2$	625_8
Song 5	$100{,}010{,}011_2$	423_8
Song 6	$101{,}110{,}001_2$	561_8

It is possible to convert from one base to any other base. We have this simple system to convert between base two and base eight because 8 is a power of 2.

3. Would a similar system work for converting between base five and base eight? Why or why not? No; 8 is not a power of 5.

56   Use with pages 140–141.

Enrich Worksheet

Objective: To multiply mixed numbers

Warm-Up

Have students estimate each product.

$5\frac{1}{3} \times 6\frac{7}{8}$ (35); $2\frac{5}{6} \times 3\frac{1}{4}$ (9)

$1\frac{1}{9} \times 8\frac{4}{5}$ (9); $4\frac{3}{4} \times 6\frac{4}{5}$ (35⁻)

$2\frac{1}{5} \times 9\frac{1}{6}$ (18⁺); $3\frac{1}{4} \times 6\frac{1}{7}$ (18⁺)

GETTING STARTED

Write the following on the chalkboard.

$2\frac{1}{3} \times 4\frac{1}{2}$

Encourage students to devise their own method of finding the product. If a hint is needed, tell them that the procedure for multiplying fractions can also work for multiplying mixed numbers.

TEACHING THE LESSON

Students do not need to learn any new skills to multiply mixed numbers; instead, they merely have to apply several skills that they have already acquired. Emphasize the advantage of estimating the product before multiplying. Have students first estimate and then multiply each product.

$4\frac{3}{4} \times 6\frac{2}{5}$ $\left(30\frac{2}{5}\right)$; $9\frac{5}{6} \times 3$ $\left(29\frac{1}{2}\right)$; $6 \times \frac{7}{8} \times 4\frac{2}{3}$ $\left(24\frac{1}{2}\right)$

Checkpoint

The chart lists the common errors students make when multiplying mixed numbers.

Correct Answers: 1b, 2d, 3c, 4d

Remediation

■ For these errors, have students rewrite each mixed number as the sum of a whole number and a fraction. Then have them rewrite the product by using the Distributive Property to illustrate the multiplication.

$2\frac{2}{3} \times 1\frac{4}{5} = (2 + \frac{2}{3}) \times (1 + \frac{4}{5})$

$\quad = 2(1 + \frac{4}{5}) + \frac{2}{3}(1 + \frac{4}{5})$

$\quad = 2(1) + 2(\frac{4}{5}) + \frac{2}{3}(1) + \frac{2}{3}(\frac{4}{5})$

□ For these errors, assign Reteach Master, p. 44.

△ For this error, refer students to the examples on p. 138.

Multiplying Mixed Numbers

A. To multiply $1\frac{3}{5} \times 3\frac{1}{8}$, write both mixed numbers as fractions.

Multiply $1\frac{3}{5} \times 3\frac{1}{8}$.

Write fractions for both numbers.

$1\frac{3}{5} \times 3\frac{1}{8} = \frac{8}{5} \times \frac{\overset{1}{\cancel{25}}}{\cancel{8}} = \frac{1 \times 5}{1 \times 1} = 5$

Multiply $5 \times 2\frac{6}{7}$.

Write whole numbers as fractions.

$5 \times 2\frac{6}{7} = \frac{5 \times 20}{1 \times 7} = \frac{100}{7} = 14\frac{2}{7}$

Other examples:

Multiply $3\frac{3}{4} \times \frac{4}{15}$.

$3\frac{3}{4} \times \frac{4}{15}$

$\frac{15}{4} \times \frac{4}{15}$

$\frac{\overset{1}{\cancel{15}} \times \overset{1}{\cancel{4}}}{\underset{1}{\cancel{4}} \times \underset{1}{\cancel{15}}} = \frac{1}{1} = 1$

Multiply $\frac{5}{9} \times 3\frac{6}{7} \times \frac{1}{5}$.

$\frac{5}{9} \times 3\frac{6}{7} \times \frac{1}{5}$

$\frac{5}{9} \times \frac{27}{7} \times \frac{1}{5}$

$\frac{\overset{1}{\cancel{5}} \times \overset{3}{\cancel{27}} \times 1}{\underset{1}{\cancel{9}} \times 7 \times \underset{1}{\cancel{5}}} = \frac{3}{7}$

Checkpoint Write the letter of the correct answer.

Multiply.

1. $3\frac{3}{5} \times 2\frac{2}{9}$ 　　　 **a.** $6\frac{1}{9}$　 **ⓑ** 8　　 **c.** 10　　 **d.** 72

2. $8\frac{1}{3} \times 5$ 　　　 **a.** 15　 **b.** 40　 **c.** $40\frac{1}{3}$ **ⓓ** $41\frac{2}{3}$

3. $1\frac{2}{7} \times 4\frac{2}{3}$ 　　 **a.** 4　 **b.** $4\frac{4}{21}$ **ⓒ** 6　 **d.** $\frac{126}{7}$

4. $1\frac{3}{4} \times 3\frac{2}{3} \times 3\frac{3}{11}$ 　 **a.** $\frac{21}{4}$ **b.** 9　 **c.** $9\frac{3}{22}$ **ⓓ** 21

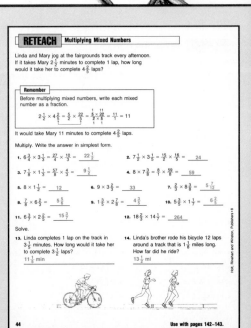

Math Reasoning, page H213

COMMON ERRORS

Answer Choice	Type of Error
□ 1a	Fails to rename before multiplying
△ 1c, 1d, 3d, 4a	Makes errors in computation
□ 2a	Renames incorrectly
■ 2b, 3a, 4b	Fails to multiply the fractional part of a mixed number
■ 2c, 3b, 4c	Multiplies whole-number parts, multiplies fraction parts, and then adds

---

RETEACH Multiplying Mixed Numbers

Linda and Mary jog at the fairgrounds track every afternoon. If it takes Mary $2\frac{1}{5}$ minutes to complete 1 lap, how long would it take her to complete $4\frac{2}{5}$ laps?

Remember
Before multiplying mixed numbers, write each mixed number as a fraction.

$2\frac{1}{5} \times 4\frac{2}{5} = \frac{5}{5} \times \frac{22}{5} = \frac{5 \times 22}{5 \times 5} = \frac{11}{1} = 11$

It would take Mary 11 minutes to complete $4\frac{2}{5}$ laps.

Multiply. Write the answer in simplest form.

1. $6\frac{3}{4} \times 3\frac{1}{3} = \frac{27}{4} \times \frac{10}{3} = $ ___ $22\frac{1}{2}$　　 2. $7\frac{1}{2} \times 3\frac{1}{5} = \frac{15}{2} \times \frac{16}{5} = $ ___ 24

3. $7\frac{1}{8} \times 1\frac{1}{3} = \frac{57}{8} \times \frac{4}{3} = $ ___ $9\frac{1}{2}$　　 4. $8 \times 7\frac{3}{8} = \frac{8}{1} \times \frac{59}{8} = $ ___ 59

5. $8 \times 1\frac{1}{2} = $ ___ 12　 6. $9 \times 3\frac{6}{3} = $ ___ 33　 7. $\frac{7}{8} \times 8\frac{2}{6} = $ ___ $5\frac{7}{12}$

8. $\frac{7}{8} \times 6\frac{2}{3} = $ ___ $5\frac{5}{6}$　 9. $1\frac{3}{5} \times 2\frac{7}{8} = $ ___ $4\frac{3}{5}$　 10. $5\frac{3}{8} \times 1\frac{1}{7} = $ ___ $6\frac{1}{7}$

11. $6\frac{3}{7} \times 2\frac{4}{9} = $ ___ $15\frac{5}{7}$　 12. $18\frac{2}{3} \times 14\frac{1}{7} = $ ___ 264

Solve.

13. Linda completes 1 lap on the track in $3\frac{1}{7}$ minutes. How long would it take her to complete $3\frac{1}{2}$ laps? ___ $11\frac{1}{2}$ min

14. Linda's brother rode his bicycle 12 laps around a track that is $1\frac{1}{8}$ miles long. How far did he ride? ___ $13\frac{1}{2}$ mi

44　　　　　　　Use with pages 142–143.

Reteach Worksheet

Multiply. Write the answer in simplest form.

1. $2\frac{4}{5} \times 2\frac{1}{2}$ 7

2. $5\frac{1}{3} \times 1\frac{3}{4}$ $9\frac{1}{3}$

3. $7\frac{5}{7} \times 4\frac{5}{9}$ $35\frac{1}{7}$

4. $3\frac{7}{11} \times 3\frac{2}{3}$ $13\frac{1}{3}$

5. $5\frac{3}{8} \times 3\frac{15}{15}$ $21\frac{1}{2}$

6. $10\frac{2}{3} \times 7\frac{3}{4}$ $82\frac{2}{3}$

7. $5\frac{7}{9} \times 13\frac{1}{2}$ 78

8. $8\frac{5}{8} \times 2\frac{4}{5}$ $24\frac{3}{20}$

9. $13\frac{3}{4} \times 12$ 165

10. $6\frac{4}{5} \times 20$ 136

11. $35 \times 3\frac{1}{7}$ 110

12. $50 \times 7\frac{9}{20}$ $372\frac{1}{2}$

13. $3\frac{2}{3} \times \frac{15}{22}$ $2\frac{1}{2}$

14. $\frac{5}{8} \times 4\frac{4}{5}$ 3

15. $\frac{3}{5} \times 4\frac{1}{2}$ $2\frac{7}{10}$

16. $25\frac{1}{5} \times \frac{4}{5}$ $20\frac{4}{25}$

17. $6 \times \frac{7}{12}$ $3\frac{1}{2}$

18. $\frac{8}{15} \times 10$ $5\frac{1}{3}$

19. $24 \times \frac{5}{2}$ 60

20. $\frac{11}{9} \times 99$ 121

21. $4\frac{1}{4} \times 3\frac{2}{3}$ $15\frac{7}{12}$

22. $6\frac{3}{8} \times 2\frac{4}{9}$ $15\frac{7}{12}$

23. $9 \times 5\frac{2}{3}$ 51

24. $8\frac{5}{6} \times 12$ 106

25. $5\frac{3}{8} \times 20$ $107\frac{1}{2}$

26. $36 \times 2\frac{1}{3}$ 84

27. $10 \times \frac{13}{15}$ $8\frac{2}{3}$

28. $\frac{20}{7} \times 84$ 240

29. $4\frac{2}{3} \times 2\frac{1}{2} \times 3\frac{4}{5}$ $44\frac{1}{3}$

30. $3\frac{5}{7} \times \frac{24}{8} \times 3\frac{10}{13}$ 42

31. $\frac{2}{3} \times 2\frac{1}{8} \times \frac{3}{2}$ $2\frac{1}{8}$

Solve.

32. It takes Susan 6 min to complete 1 row of her knitting. About how long will it take her to complete $7\frac{1}{2}$ rows? 45 min

33. Bill is making a Mexican hat that will have a $6\frac{1}{2}$-in.-wide brim. The brim is $1\frac{7}{8}$ in. short of that width now. How wide is the brim? $4\frac{5}{8}$ inches

★34. Nancy uses $6\frac{1}{4}$ skeins of wool to make one sweater. How many skeins has Nancy used if she has half-finished her fourth sweater? $21\frac{7}{8}$ skeins

★35. Chris needs to knit 120 rows to complete one sweater. It takes him 4 min to knit 1 row. He completed $3\frac{1}{2}$ sweaters this month. How much time did he spend on them? 28 hours

ANOTHER LOOK

Solve.

1. Cassius makes cameo scenes carved on small pieces of onyx. During the past 18 years, he carved an average of 38 pieces per year. What is the total number of pieces he carved? 684 pieces

2. Eileen constructs lobster traps and sells them for $12.85 each. During her year in Cape Cod, she sold 412 traps. How much money did she earn from these sales? $5,294.20

ASSIGNMENT GUIDE

Basic: 2–20 e, 32–33, AL

Average: 1–19 o, 21–34, AL

Extended: 13–35, AL

Resources

Practice, p. 59   Class/Home, p. H59
Reteach, p. 44   More Practice, p. H198
Enrich, p. 57   Reasoning, p. H213

Exercise Analysis

1–8   Multiply two mixed numbers
9–12   Multiply a mixed number by a whole number
13–20 Multiply a mixed number or whole number by a fraction
21–31 Mixed practice
32–35 Skill applications

Another Look

This review provides maintenance for word problems involving the multiplication of whole numbers and money.

FOLLOW-UP ACTIVITIES

REINFORCEMENT
Have students find each product. If students encounter difficulty, suggest that they first evaluate each power.

- $\frac{2^3}{3^2} \times \frac{5^2}{2^2} \times \frac{3^3}{8^2}$ $\left(2\frac{11}{32}\right)$

- $\frac{8^2}{9^2} \times \frac{3^2}{2^2} \times \frac{5^2}{4^2} \times \frac{6^2}{7^2}$ $\left(2\frac{2}{49}\right)$

- $\frac{2^3}{3^3} \times \frac{5^3}{4^3} \times \frac{6^3}{10^3} \times \frac{8^3}{9^3}$ $\left(\frac{64}{729}\right)$

PROBLEM SOLVING
Have students identify each pattern and write the next three numbers.

$2\frac{1}{2}, 3\frac{1}{4}, 4$ $\left(\text{Add } \frac{3}{4}; 4\frac{3}{4}, 5\frac{1}{2}, 6\frac{1}{4}\right)$

$20\frac{3}{4}, 18\frac{1}{12}, 15\frac{5}{12}$ $\left(\text{Subtract } 2\frac{2}{3}; 12\frac{3}{4}, 10\frac{1}{12}, 7\frac{5}{12}\right)$

$\frac{1}{100}, \frac{1}{40}, \frac{1}{16}$ $\left(\text{Multiply by } 2\frac{1}{2}; \frac{5}{32}, \frac{25}{64}, \frac{125}{128}\right)$

COMING UP
Taking it easy

Objective:

Objective: To answer a question by writing a simpler problem

Warm-Up
Have students compute the answers.

$40,000 \times 80$ (3,200,000)
$7,500 \times 600$ (4,500,000)
$\frac{4}{5} \times 90$ (72) $\frac{7}{8} \times 46 \left(40\frac{1}{4}\right)$

GETTING STARTED

Write these problems on the chalkboard.
- A crafts shop sells an average of $5,183.26 worth of merchandise per week. How much merchandise does it sell over a 47-week period?
- Lana sells $8 worth of paper flowers in an hour. How much does she sell in 8 hours?

Ask students which problem is easier to solve and why. (The second problem has simpler numbers.)

Point out that the only difference between the problems is the size of the numbers. Have students choose simpler numbers to estimate the answer to the first problem.

TEACHING THE LESSON

If students substitute simpler numbers for those that are difficult, they can focus on the operation needed to solve the problem. When they have determined *how* to solve the problem, they can substitute the actual numbers for simpler numbers to find the answer. Simpler numbers might include
- estimated whole numbers.
- any simple whole number (not necessarily related to the actual number).

Questions: Tell students that the key to figuring out how to set up a problem is to work backward from what the question asks (what is needed) to what is known.

Tools: The tools are the simpler numbers that are chosen. Emphasize that if rounding the original numbers does not help students to see the operation needed, they should rewrite the problem using much smaller numbers so that the math involved is only basic facts.

Solutions: Once the problem is set up correctly, students should not encounter much difficulty with the computation. You may wish to allow students to use calculators for problem solving.

Emphasize the parallels between solving the simpler problem and solving the original problem. Problem 6 may be confusing to students because it asks about how many blankets there are. Students could legitimately answer about 1.

| QUESTIONS | TOOLS | SOLUTIONS | CHECKS |

PROBLEM SOLVING
Writing a Simpler Problem

Some problems look harder than they are. It may help you to solve problems that contain decimals, fractions, or large numbers if you substitute simpler numbers for these numbers. Once you have solved the problem with simpler numbers, solve it with the actual numbers.

> Last year, a button factory produced 1,283 plastic buttons per week for 46 weeks and 1,720 wood buttons per week for the next 6 weeks. How many buttons did the factory produce during the 52 weeks?

Substitute simpler numbers, and break the problem down into small steps.

Use the actual numbers.

___ 1. $1,000 \times 50 = 50,000$ (number of plastic buttons for 46 weeks)

$1,283 \times 46 = 59,018$

___ 2. $2,000 \times 10 = 20,000$ (number of wood buttons for 6 weeks)

$1,720 \times 6 = 10,320$

___ 3. $50,000 + 20,000 = 70,000$ (buttons produced in 52 weeks)

$59,018 + 10,320 = 69,338$ (buttons produced in 52 weeks)

Write the letter of the better plan for simplifying the problem.

1. Members of the sewing club spend $2.43 for materials to make each pot holder. If the members want to make a $1.69 profit per pot holder, how much should they charge for 15 pot holders?

(a.) **Step 1:** $2 + $2 = $4
   Step 2: $4 \times 15 = $60

b. **Step 1:** $2 \times 15 = $30
   Step 2: $30 + $2 = $32

144 ▬▬▬▬▬▬▬▬▬▬▬

Checks: Students who solve *only* the simpler problem should be aware immediately that their answers are unreasonable. Remind students to substitute their answers back into the original problem.

Write the letter of the better plan for simplifying the problem.

2. The knitters at the Software Yarn Shop knit 16,800 stitches to make 10 place mats. They produce 386 place mats in 5 days. How many stitches do they knit each day?

a. Step 1: $390 \div 10 = 39$
Step 2: $39 \times 5 = 195$
Step 3: $195 \times 17,000 = 3,315,000$

b. Step 1: $390 \div 5 = 78$
Step 2: $17,000 \div 10 = 1,700$
Step 3: $1,700 \times 78 = 132,600$

Solve. Simplify the problem if you need to.

3. Mr. Clark's recipe calls for $87\frac{1}{2}$ apples to make 25 bowls of applesauce. If he wants to make 95 bowls of applesauce, how many apples does he need? $332\frac{1}{2}$ apples

4. From 1978 through 1986, the Stoneware Shop dyed 1,570 skeins of wool per year. From 1987 through 1990, the shop dyed 1,610 skeins per year. What is the shop's total production from 1978 to 1990? 20,570 skeins

5. Sheila makes cotton batik dress fabric. She uses $6\frac{4}{5}$ packages of dye for every 34 dresses. If she wants to make 85 dresses, how many packages of dye does she need? 17 packages

6. A group of 12 weavers produces $10\frac{1}{2}$ blankets per day. About how many blankets per day should Don expect to weave when he joins the group? $\frac{7}{8}$ of a blanket

7. The Country Shop produces $20\frac{1}{2}$ dozen candles per day. During the holidays, the shop increases production by $\frac{1}{3}$. How many more candles than normal does the shop produce during a 7-day holiday period? 574 candles

8. Brad will use 3 bags of tiles for a mosaic floor. The bags contain 4,878 tiles, 6,585 tiles, and 9,681 tiles. Brad uses $\frac{2}{3}$ of the tiles from each bag for the floor. How many tiles does he use? 14,096 tiles

9. The Antique Artisans make a colonial table set. Each set contains 2 oak chairs and 1 oak table. They use $11\frac{1}{2}$ ft^2 of oak for each chair and $17\frac{3}{4}$ ft^2 of oak for each table. They make 9 sets per week. How much wood do they use per week? $366\frac{3}{4}$ ft^2

Classwork/Homework, page H60

ASSIGNMENT GUIDE

Basic: 1–4
Average: 2–6
Extended: 3–9

Resources
Practice, p. 60 Class/Home, p. H60
Enrich, p. 58

Exercise Analysis

1–2 Choose the best plan for a simpler problem
3–9 Use simpler numbers to write a number sentence; solve

FOLLOW-UP ACTIVITIES

PROBLEM SOLVING
Materials: calculator per student (optional)

Prepare a handout with the following problems and equations. Have students match each problem with the appropriate simpler number equation. Then have students use their calculators to solve the original problems.

a. $(100 - 30) \times 50 = 3,500$
b. $1 \times \frac{1}{2} \times 250 = 125$
c. $(150 \times 50) + (20 \times 30) = 8,100$
d. $[(500 \times 300) + (150 \times 40)] \div (300 + 40) = 459$

1. A bookbinder packages 147 crates of books with 65 books in each and 16 crates with 30 books in each. What is the total number of books packaged? (**c**; 10,035)

2. A history book contains 36 four-color illustrations and 114 black-and-white illustrations. In a crate of 45 books, how many more black-and-white illustrations than four-color illustrations are there? (**a**; 3,510)

3. Of the 252 pages in a book, $\frac{7}{9}$ have illustrations. Of those pages, $\frac{3}{4}$ have four-color illustrations. How many pages of four-color illustrations are there? (**b**; 147)

4. There is an average of 482 words on each page that is all text. There is an average of 142 words on each page with illustrations. There are 312 all-text pages and 38 illustration pages. To the nearest whole number, what is the average number of words on each page? (**d**; 445)

COMING UP
Fractions of the first division

Objective: To divide fractions

Warm-Up

Have students find each missing factor.

$\frac{2}{5} \times \blacksquare = 1$ $\left(2\frac{1}{2}\right)$ $\frac{5}{8} \times \blacksquare = 1$ $\left(1\frac{3}{5}\right)$

$\blacksquare \times \frac{7}{6} = 1$ $\left(\frac{6}{7}\right)$ $\blacksquare \times \frac{1}{3} = 1$ (3)

$1\frac{1}{2} \times \blacksquare = 1$ $\left(\frac{2}{3}\right)$ $\frac{1}{4} \times \blacksquare = 1$ (4)

GETTING STARTED

Pose the following problem.

● The distance around the running track near Joan's house is $\frac{1}{4}$ mile. If she wants to run $\frac{3}{4}$ mile, how many laps should she run? (3)

Ask volunteers to demonstrate how they found the answer. Then ask: Suppose Joan wanted to run only $\frac{2}{3}$ mile. How many laps should she run? $\left(2\frac{2}{3}\right)$ Discuss possible solutions.

TEACHING THE LESSON

If needed, review the position of the dividend, divisor, and quotient in a division example written in horizontal form. Demonstrate the following algebraic proof for the division algorithm.

$$\frac{a}{b} \div \frac{c}{d} = \frac{\frac{a}{b}}{\frac{c}{d}} = \frac{\frac{a}{b} \times \frac{d}{c}}{\frac{c}{d} \times \frac{d}{c}}$$

$$= \frac{a}{b} \times \frac{d}{c}$$

reciprocals

Checkpoint

The chart lists the common errors students make when dividing fractions.

Correct Answers: 1d, 2b, 3c, 4a

Remediation

■ For this error, have students check that their answer is reasonable by comparing the quotient to the dividend and the divisor. When dividing by a fraction less than 1, the quotient will always be greater than the dividend.

☐ For this error, assign Reteach Master, p. 45.

△ For this error, refer students to the examples on p. 138.

Dividing Fractions

Rhoda has $\frac{3}{4}$ yard of silver beads to be used as spacers in necklaces. If each necklace needs $\frac{3}{8}$ yard of beads, how many necklaces can be made?

Divide $\frac{3}{4} \div \frac{3}{8}$.

Find the **reciprocal** of the divisor.

Two numbers are reciprocals if their product is 1.

$\frac{8}{3} \times \frac{3}{8} = \frac{24}{24} = 1$

So, the reciprocal of $\frac{3}{8}$ is $\frac{8}{3}$.

Multiply by the reciprocal of the divisor.

$\frac{3}{4} \div \frac{3}{8} = \frac{3}{4} \times \frac{8}{3}$

Two necklaces can be made.

Simplify and multiply.

$\frac{3}{4} \div \frac{3}{8} = \frac{3}{\underset{1}{4}} \times \frac{\overset{2}{8}}{\underset{1}{3}} = \frac{2}{1} = 2$

Other examples:

Divide $\frac{3}{5} \div \frac{9}{10}$.

$\frac{3}{5} \div \frac{9}{10} = \frac{3}{5} \times \frac{10}{9} = \frac{\overset{1}{3}}{5} \times \frac{\overset{2}{10}}{\underset{3}{9}} = \frac{2}{3}$

Divide $\frac{2}{3} \div \frac{1}{8}$.

$\frac{2}{3} \div \frac{1}{8} = \frac{2}{3} \times \frac{8}{1} = \frac{16}{3} = 5\frac{1}{3}$

Checkpoint Write the letter of the correct answer.

Divide.

1. $\frac{2}{7} \div \frac{1}{9}$ a. $\frac{2}{63}$ b. $\frac{7}{18}$ c. $1\frac{3}{8}$ ⓓ $2\frac{4}{7}$

2. $\frac{1}{4} \div \frac{3}{8}$ a. $\frac{3}{32}$ ⓑ $\frac{2}{3}$ c. $\frac{3}{4}$ d. $1\frac{1}{2}$

3. $\frac{3}{4} \div \frac{15}{12}$ a. $\frac{45}{48}$ b. $1\frac{2}{3}$ ⓒ $\frac{3}{5}$ d. $\frac{2}{3}$

4. $\frac{7}{8} \div \frac{21}{24}$ ⓐ 1 b. $\frac{147}{192}$ c. $\frac{10}{11}$ d. $\frac{7}{8}$

146

COMMON ERRORS

Answer Choice	Type of Error
■ 1a, 2a, 3a, 4b	Multiplies without finding a reciprocal
☐ 1b, 2d, 3b	Reciprocates the dividend
△ 1c, 2c, 3d, 4c	Makes an error in computation
☐ 4d	Adds the numerators and the denominators

Write the reciprocal.

1. $\frac{3}{4}$ $\frac{4}{3}$ **2.** $\frac{1}{5}$ $\frac{5}{1}$ **3.** $\frac{1}{4}$ $\frac{4}{1}$ **4.** $\frac{4}{5}$ $\frac{5}{4}$ **5.** $\frac{9}{10}$ $\frac{10}{9}$

6. $\frac{6}{7}$ $\frac{7}{6}$ **7.** $\frac{7}{9}$ $\frac{9}{7}$ **8.** $\frac{3}{8}$ $\frac{8}{3}$ **9.** $\frac{5}{9}$ $\frac{9}{5}$ **10.** $\frac{7}{8}$ $\frac{8}{7}$

Divide. Write the answer in simplest form.

11. $\frac{1}{3} \div \frac{1}{6}$ 2   **12.** $\frac{2}{3} \div \frac{2}{9}$ 3   **13.** $\frac{5}{7} \div \frac{1}{7}$ 5   **14.** $\frac{3}{4} \div \frac{3}{16}$ 4   **15.** $\frac{5}{9} \div \frac{5}{18}$ 2

16. $\frac{3}{8} \div \frac{2}{5}$ $\frac{15}{16}$ **17.** $\frac{1}{3} \div \frac{5}{6}$ $\frac{2}{5}$ **18.** $\frac{1}{2} \div \frac{6}{7}$ $\frac{7}{12}$ **19.** $\frac{1}{4} \div \frac{3}{5}$ $\frac{5}{12}$ **20.** $\frac{1}{6} \div \frac{2}{5}$ $\frac{5}{12}$

21. $\frac{6}{7} \div \frac{4}{5}$ $1\frac{1}{14}$ **22.** $\frac{9}{8} \div \frac{1}{7}$ $7\frac{7}{8}$ **23.** $\frac{4}{5} \div \frac{7}{9}$ $1\frac{1}{35}$ **24.** $\frac{6}{11} \div \frac{5}{33}$ $3\frac{3}{5}$ **25.** $\frac{7}{8} \div \frac{4}{5}$ $1\frac{3}{32}$

26. $\frac{4}{9} \div \frac{3}{7}$ $1\frac{1}{27}$ **27.** $\frac{2}{7} \div \frac{4}{11}$ $\frac{11}{14}$ **28.** $\frac{3}{7} \div \frac{1}{7}$ 3   **29.** $\frac{1}{5} \div \frac{4}{15}$ $\frac{3}{4}$ **30.** $\frac{8}{9} \div \frac{18}{25}$ $1\frac{19}{81}$

Solve.

31. Beads that are $\frac{1}{16}$ inch in diameter are strung into a necklace. How many beads are needed for $\frac{3}{4}$ inch?
12 beads

★33. Frank has oblong onyx beads and coral beads. Each onyx bead is $\frac{3}{8}$ in. long, and each coral bead is $\frac{1}{2}$ in. long. How many times a coral bead's length is an onyx bead's length? $\frac{3}{4}$ **times**

32. Suzanne has $\frac{3}{4}$ yard of cord on which to string beads. How long is $\frac{1}{2}$ this length? $\frac{3}{8}$ **yard**

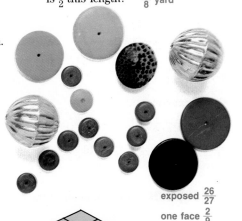

CHALLENGE

The large cube on the right is made of twenty-seven smaller cubes. What fraction of the smaller cubes are exposed? What fraction of the smaller cubes have exactly one exposed face? two exposed faces? three? four? five? six? no exposed faces?

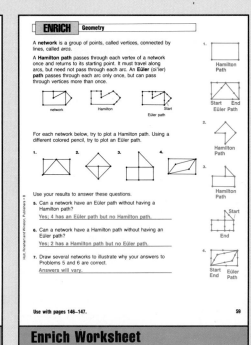

exposed $\frac{26}{27}$
one face $\frac{2}{9}$
two faces $\frac{4}{9}$
three faces $\frac{8}{27}$
four faces 0
five faces 0
six faces 0
no faces $\frac{1}{27}$

For additional activities, see *Connecting Math Ideas*, page 470.

ASSIGNMENT GUIDE

Basic:	1–25, 31–32
Average:	6–32, Chlg
Extended:	11–33, Chlg

Resources
Practice, p. 61   Class/Home, p. H61
Reteach, p. 45
Enrich, p. 59

Exercise Analysis
1–10   Write a reciprocal
11–30   Divide a fraction by a fraction
31–33   Skill applications

Challenge
Some students may find it helpful to construct the cube from blocks, mark the exposed surfaces, and then dismantle the cube to find the answers.

FOLLOW-UP ACTIVITIES

PROBLEM SOLVING
Listed below are inputs and outputs from a computer. Have students suggest some possible operations that the computer could have performed in each case. (Answers will vary.)

Input	$\frac{2}{5}$	$\frac{7}{8}$	$\frac{3}{4}$	$\frac{1}{2}$	1
Output	$\frac{4}{5}$	$\frac{7}{2}$	1	$\frac{5}{14}$	$\frac{1}{4}$

PUZZLES AND GAMES
Provide the following as a handout.

Start $\frac{1}{2}$	$\frac{8}{10}$ ←	$\frac{7}{8}$	$\frac{3}{7}$ ←	$\frac{2}{9}$
$\frac{1}{4}$	$\frac{10}{12}$	$\frac{7}{9}$	$\frac{7}{2}$ ←	$\frac{3}{5}$
$\frac{4}{5}$	$\frac{6}{5}$	Finish	$\frac{6}{9}$	$\frac{1}{6}$
$\frac{5}{6}$	$\frac{3}{5}$	$\frac{4}{7}$ →	$\frac{7}{8}$	$\frac{2}{5}$
$\frac{3}{4}$ →	$\frac{1}{8}$ →	$\frac{1}{3}$ →	$\frac{8}{9}$ →	$\frac{9}{10}$

Instruct students to start at the square indicated and follow the arrows, multiplying if moving vertically and dividing if moving horizontally. Have them find the value of the open square. ($\frac{1}{5}$)

COMING UP
Mix and match

147

Objective: To divide mixed numbers

Warm-Up

Have students rename each as a fraction mentally.

$1\frac{3}{4}$ $(\frac{7}{4})$ $2\frac{2}{5}$ $(\frac{12}{5})$ $4\frac{1}{5}$ $(\frac{21}{5})$ $3\frac{2}{3}$ $(\frac{11}{3})$

$6\frac{3}{7}$ $(\frac{45}{7})$ $5\frac{4}{9}$ $(\frac{49}{9})$ $9\frac{3}{4}$ $(\frac{39}{4})$ $7\frac{5}{6}$ $(\frac{47}{6})$

GETTING STARTED

Write the following on the chalkboard.

- Greg has a board $7\frac{1}{2}$ feet long. How many $1\frac{1}{4}$ foot-long sections can he cut from the board?

Ask which operation is needed to find the answer. (division) Guide students to discovering the algorithm for dividing mixed numbers. If a hint is needed, suggest that they rename the mixed numbers as fractions.

TEACHING THE LESSON

A. Have students practice finding the reciprocal of a mixed number using examples such as those below. $3\frac{4}{5}$ $(\frac{5}{19})$; $9\frac{1}{3}$ $(\frac{3}{28})$; $8\frac{3}{4}$ $(\frac{4}{35})$

B. Emphasize the fact that writing a whole number as a fraction that has a denominator of 1 makes it easier to follow the procedure for dividing fractions.

You may wish to extend the example in the Other Examples section to include those shown below.

$3\frac{1}{4} \div 2\left(1\frac{5}{8}\right); 7 \div 15\left(\frac{7}{15}\right); 2 \div 3\frac{1}{5}\left(\frac{5}{8}\right)$

Checkpoint

The chart lists the common errors students make when dividing mixed numbers.

Correct Answers: 1b, 2c, 3b, 4a

Remediation

■ For these errors, have students identify the parts of a division example. Remind them that the number by which we divide is the divisor. As the first step in completing the following examples, have students circle the divisor and find its reciprocal.

$3\frac{1}{4} \div 1\frac{1}{2}$ $\left(2\frac{1}{6}\right)$; $\frac{5}{8} \div 4$ $\left(\frac{5}{32}\right)$; $6 \div \frac{4}{9}$ $\left(13\frac{1}{2}\right)$

□ For this error, assign Reteach Master, p. 46.

△ For this error, refer students to the examples on p. 120.

Dividing Mixed Numbers

A. A dowel is used to make axles for wooden trains. From a dowel $10\frac{2}{3}$ inches long, how many axles can be made if each axle is $2\frac{2}{3}$ inches long?

Divide $10\frac{2}{3} \div 2\frac{2}{3}$.

Since you will divide by $2\frac{2}{3}$, you must find its reciprocal.

$2\frac{2}{3} = \frac{8}{3}$ $\frac{8}{3} \times \frac{3}{8} = 1$

Write fractions for both numbers.

$10\frac{2}{3} \div 2\frac{2}{3} = \frac{32}{3} \div \frac{8}{3}$

Multiply by the reciprocal. Simplify.

$\overset{4}{\underset{1}{\frac{32}{3}}} \times \overset{1}{\underset{1}{\frac{3}{8}}} = \frac{4}{1} = 4$

Four axles can be made.

B. Divide $3 \div 7\frac{4}{5}$.

Write whole numbers and mixed numbers as fractions.

$3 \div 7\frac{4}{5} = \frac{3}{1} \div \frac{39}{5}$

Multiply.

$\frac{3}{1} \times \underset{13}{\overset{1}{\frac{5}{39}}} = \frac{5}{13}$

Other examples:

Divide $6\frac{3}{4} \div \frac{5}{8}$.

$\frac{27}{4} \div \frac{5}{8} = \frac{27}{4} \times \underset{1}{\overset{2}{\frac{8}{5}}} = \frac{54}{5} = 10\frac{4}{5}$

Divide $8 \div \frac{2}{9}$.

$\frac{8}{1} \div \frac{2}{9} = \underset{1}{\overset{4}{\frac{8}{1}}} \times \frac{9}{2} = \frac{36}{1} = 36$

Checkpoint   Write the letter of the correct answer.

Divide.

1. $3\frac{1}{3} \div 1\frac{1}{5}$ **a.** $\frac{9}{25}$ **b.** $2\frac{7}{9}$ **c.** $2\frac{14}{18}$ **d.** 4

2. $5 \div 1\frac{1}{4}$ **a.** $\frac{1}{4}$ **b.** $\frac{4}{25}$ **c.** 4 **d.** $6\frac{1}{4}$

3. $1\frac{3}{7} \div 1\frac{2}{3}$ **a.** $1\frac{1}{6}$ **b.** $\frac{6}{7}$ **c.** $2\frac{8}{21}$ **d.** $3\frac{3}{7}$

4. $6\frac{3}{5} \div 9$ **a.** $\frac{11}{15}$ **b.** $\frac{3}{5}$ **c.** $1\frac{4}{11}$ **d.** $15\frac{3}{5}$

148   Math Reasoning, page H214

COMMON ERRORS

Answer Choice	Type of Error
■ 1a, 2a, 3a, 4c	Finds a reciprocal of the dividend
△ 1c	Fails to simplify the answer
□ 1d, 2d, 3c, 3d, 4d	Uses the incorrect operation
■ 2b	Finds a reciprocal of both terms
△ 4b	Makes an error in computation

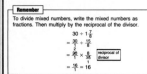

RETEACH Dividing Mixed Numbers

Luis is building a table in his wood shop. To build the tabletop, he is using boards that are $1\frac{7}{8}$ in. wide. If the table is supposed to be 30 in. wide, how many boards does he need? To find the answer, divide: $30 \div 1\frac{7}{8}$.

Remember

To divide mixed numbers, write the mixed numbers as fractions. Then multiply by the reciprocal of the divisor.

$30 \div 1\frac{7}{8}$
$= \frac{30}{1} \div \frac{15}{8}$
$= \frac{30}{1} \times \frac{8}{15}$ reciprocal of divisor
$= \frac{16}{1} = 16$

Luis needs 16 boards for the tabletop.

Divide. Write the answer in simplest form.

1. $30 \div 2\frac{1}{2} = \frac{30}{1} \div \frac{5}{2} = \frac{30}{1} \times \frac{2}{5} = \underline{12}$ 2. $18 \div 3\frac{1}{3} = \frac{18}{1} \div \frac{10}{3} = \frac{18}{1} \times \frac{3}{10} = \underline{5\frac{2}{5}}$

3. $3\frac{5}{8} \div 2\frac{1}{4} = \frac{29}{8} \div \frac{9}{4} = \underline{3\frac{5}{8}}$ 4. $3\frac{1}{4} \div 1\frac{7}{8} = \frac{13}{4} \div \frac{15}{8} = \underline{1\frac{11}{15}}$

5. $28 \div 1\frac{7}{8} = \underline{14\frac{14}{15}}$ 6. $20 \div 1\frac{4}{5} = \underline{11\frac{1}{9}}$ 7. $16 \div 1\frac{1}{4} = \underline{12\frac{4}{5}}$

8. $1\frac{1}{5} \div \frac{4}{5} = \underline{1\frac{1}{2}}$ 9. $2\frac{3}{8} \div \frac{1}{2} = \underline{4\frac{3}{4}}$ 10. $14\frac{3}{4} \div 1\frac{7}{8} = \underline{7\frac{13}{15}}$

11. $6\frac{3}{10} \div 2\frac{1}{4} = \underline{2\frac{13}{15}}$ 12. $8\frac{1}{2} \div 2\frac{3}{8} = \underline{3\frac{7}{24}}$ 13. $7\frac{2}{3} \div \frac{2}{7} = \underline{25\frac{8}{12}}$

Solve.

14. A piece of plywood 96 inches long was cut into strips that were each $3\frac{1}{4}$ inches wide. How many strips were there? 29 strips

15. A piece of plywood was cut into strips that each measured $5\frac{7}{8}$ in. If the piece of plywood was 48 in. long, how many strips were there? 8 strips

46   Use with pages 148–149.

Reteach Worksheet

Divide. Write the answer in simplest form.

1. $3\frac{1}{4} \div 1\frac{3}{4}$ $1\frac{6}{7}$ **2.** $4\frac{1}{3} \div 1\frac{2}{3}$ $2\frac{3}{5}$ **3.** $4\frac{5}{8} \div 2\frac{1}{8}$ $2\frac{3}{17}$ **4.** $2\frac{1}{5} \div 1\frac{3}{5}$ $1\frac{3}{8}$

5. $5 \div 2\frac{1}{2}$ 2 **6.** $10 \div 3\frac{1}{3}$ 3 **7.** $16 \div 1\frac{7}{9}$ 9 **8.** $2 \div 1\frac{7}{8}$ $1\frac{1}{15}$

9. $2 \div 1\frac{1}{4}$ $1\frac{3}{5}$ **10.** $6 \div 3\frac{2}{5}$ $1\frac{13}{17}$ **11.** $7 \div 4\frac{1}{9}$ $1\frac{26}{37}$ **12.** $12 \div 3\frac{4}{5}$ $3\frac{3}{19}$

13. $2 \div \frac{7}{8}$ $2\frac{2}{7}$ **14.** $4 \div \frac{3}{4}$ $5\frac{1}{3}$ **15.** $12 \div \frac{3}{5}$ 20 **16.** $7 \div \frac{2}{3}$ $10\frac{1}{2}$

17. $9\frac{9}{10} \div \frac{4}{5}$ $12\frac{3}{8}$ **18.** $6\frac{2}{3} \div \frac{5}{6}$ 8 **19.** $12\frac{1}{3} \div \frac{1}{9}$ 111 **20.** $11\frac{5}{9} \div \frac{1}{4}$ $46\frac{2}{9}$

21. $6\frac{6}{7} \div \frac{6}{7}$ 8 **22.** $4\frac{1}{2} \div \frac{1}{3}$ $13\frac{1}{2}$ **23.** $9\frac{9}{10} \div \frac{9}{10}$ 11 **24.** $13\frac{1}{10} \div \frac{6}{7}$ $15\frac{17}{60}$

25. $9\frac{1}{3} \div 3\frac{2}{3}$ $2\frac{6}{11}$ **26.** $14\frac{1}{4} \div \frac{5}{9}$ $25\frac{13}{20}$ **27.** $6 \div 3\frac{2}{3}$ $1\frac{7}{11}$ **28.** $10\frac{1}{5} \div 5\frac{4}{5}$ $1\frac{22}{29}$

29. $7 \div \frac{7}{9}$ 9 **30.** $4 \div 4\frac{5}{9}$ $\frac{36}{41}$ **31.** $5\frac{1}{6} \div 2\frac{1}{4}$ $2\frac{8}{27}$ **32.** $6\frac{1}{3} \div \frac{2}{9}$ $28\frac{1}{2}$

Solve.

33. Larry bought a piece of wood $34\frac{1}{2}$ inches long to build crossing gates. He cut the wood into 6 pieces of equal length. How long was each piece? $5\frac{3}{4}$ in.

34. George laid down a length of track that was $5\frac{3}{4}$ feet long. He used 5 sections of equal length. How long was each section? $1\frac{3}{20}$ ft

35. Paula wanted to have rugs of equal length for each of her 4 miniature houses. She used up a strip of blue felt $6\frac{3}{4}$ inches long. How long was each rug? $1\frac{11}{16}$ in.

36. In 10 minutes, Lisa's train goes around the track $7\frac{1}{2}$ times. How long does it take the train to go around the track once? $1\frac{1}{3}$ min, or 80 s

NUMBER SENSE

Two of these answers are unreasonable. Estimate to find them. Tell why they are unreasonable.

2, 3 are unreasonable. Answers will vary.

1. $2\frac{1}{3} \times \frac{9}{10} = 2\frac{1}{10}$ **2.** $3\frac{3}{8} \times \frac{4}{5} = 5\frac{2}{5}$

3. $5\frac{2}{3} \div 1\frac{1}{6} = 6\frac{5}{6}$ **4.** $3\frac{1}{2} \div \frac{7}{8} = 4$

ASSIGNMENT GUIDE

Basic: 1–8, 9–23 o, 33–36, NS

Average: 1–23 o, 25–36, NS

Extended: 2–24 e, 25–36, NS

Resources
Practice, p. 62   Class/Home, p. H62
Reteach, p. 46   More Practice, p. H199
Enrich, p. 60   Reasoning, p. H214

Exercise Analysis
1–12   Divide by a mixed number
13–24   Divide by a fraction
25–32   Mixed practice
33–36   Skill applications

Number Sense
This activity provides students with practice in determining whether or not an answer is reasonable.

FOLLOW-UP ACTIVITIES

PUZZLES AND GAMES
Have students fill in each circle with $\frac{1}{2}$, $\frac{3}{4}$, or $\frac{7}{8}$ so that each row and each column form true statements. Each fraction can be used more than once in a given column. Operations should be performed sequentially.

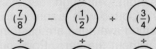
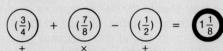
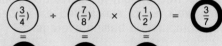

PROBLEM SOLVING
Have students solve this problem.
- If a snail climbs a 30-foot flagpole at the rate of $1\frac{1}{2}$ feet per day but slips back $\frac{3}{4}$ foot each night, when will it reach the top? (the evening of the thirty-ninth day)

COMING UP
News about decimals bears repeating.

Objective: To explore writing decimals as fractions and fractions as decimals

Warm-Up

Have students find each quotient mentally.

$\frac{36}{9}$ (4) $\frac{42}{7}$ (6) $\frac{39}{3}$ (13)

$\frac{125}{25}$ (5) $\frac{720}{24}$ (30) $\frac{1750}{50}$ (35)

GETTING STARTED

Write the following on the chalkboard, and have each student write at least one other way of representing each problem.

$$\frac{3}{4} \qquad 4\overline{)5} \qquad 10 \div 3$$

Foster a class discussion about the fact that any of the three methods used above can be used to write each of these problems (for example, $4\overline{)3} = 3 \div 4 = \frac{3}{4}$). Be sure that students realize that all fractions are division problems and that any division problem can be written as a fraction.

TEACHING THE LESSON

Materials: calculators

You may wish to have students work on this lesson either in groups of four or as a class. Have students read through the problem and each of the clues. Be sure they understand that to find a batting average they should divide the number of hits by the number of times at bat and that it is customary to round this decimal to the nearest thousandth. Although decimals are commonly reported with a zero in the ones place, batting averages are customarily reported without the zero. Point out that a *walk* is not considered an *at bat* when computing a batting average.

For question 1, have students divide each number of hits by the number of times at bat and make a list of decimal equivalents. They can then work through the clues, matching each player with a batting average, and make a table listing the decimal equivalents for question 2. The seven clues identify the batting averages of seven players. Students can find the other two players' batting averages through trial and error by trying to match up old and new statistics to the one remaining new batting average (.450—Barbara). Guide students to realize that this batting average can be converted to a fraction by writing .450 as $\frac{450}{1000}$ and simplifying it to $\frac{9}{20}$. Students can then check to see which batting statistics can also be simplified to this fraction.

When they find decimal equivalents, students will discover that those for Monica

---

Decimals and Fractions

Help! The scorekeeper has lost the scorebook and does not know what the batting averages are. The coach has a list of the batting statistics for the starting players through the end of last week, but he does not know which statistic is for which player. The scorekeeper has a piece of scrap paper on which she had computed the current batting averages of 4 starting players, but she does not know which average belongs to which player. She has come to your math class for help.

Here is what she knows:

- Batting statistics up to the end of last week.

  | Hits | 24 | 39 | 37 | 23 | 18 | 21 | 21 | 19 | 35 |
  | At Bats | 64 | 96 | 80 | 50 | 80 | 70 | 60 | 50 | 63 |

  0.375; 0.40625; 0.4625; 0.46; 0.225; 0.3; 0.35; 0.38; 0.555 . . .

- To find a batting average, divide the number of hits by the number of at bats and show the quotient rounded to the nearest thousandth. Also, drop the zero before the decimal point. Four of the batting averages until today are

  .375   .200   .450   .333

- Statistics from this week for each player:

	At Bats	Hits
Barbara	10	4
Gene	10	0
Fred	11	3
Monica	12	3
Lisa	14	5
Bob	14	5
Daniela	12	4
Juan	10	4
Kelly	10	6

- Other clues:

  Fred insists that his batting average at the end of last week was .375.

  Daniela does not remember her batting average from last week, but she knows she's been at bat a total of 75 times.

New Statistics		
27/60	0.45	.450
18/90	0.2	.200
27/75	0.36	.360
24/72	0.3	.333
24/64	0.375	.375
44/110	0.4	.400
39/75	0.52	.520
25/80	0.3125	.313
43/90	0.47	.478

His statistics then must have been $\frac{24}{64}$.

She has 12 at bats this week; last weeks statistics for her were $\frac{35}{63}$.

Math Reasoning, page H214

---

and Kelly repeat and that the rest of them terminate. Make sure they understand that the bar goes over only those digits within the decimal that repeat (e.g., $0.4777 \ldots = 0.4\overline{7}$).

Point out that if the denominator of a simplified fraction contains a prime factor other than 2 or 5, the fraction will be a repeating decimal. Lead students to discover that this is so because 2 and 5 are factors of powers of 10, whereas 3, 7, and so forth are not.

In $\frac{1}{12}$, for example, the prime factors of 12 are $2 \times 2 \times 3$. Therefore, the decimal equivalent is a repeating decimal. $(0.08\overline{3})$

Have students determine whether the decimal equivalent of each fraction is terminating or repeating: $\frac{3}{4}$ (T), $\frac{2}{3}$ (R), $\frac{5}{9}$ (R), $\frac{7}{15}$ (R), $\frac{9}{20}$ (T).

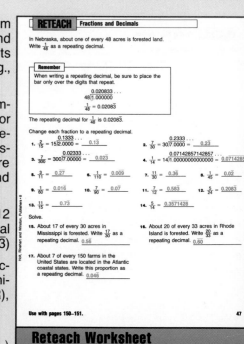

RETEACH | Fractions and Decimals

In Nebraska, about one of every 48 acres is forested land. Write $\frac{1}{48}$ as a repeating decimal.

Remember
When writing a repeating decimal, be sure to place the bar only over the digits that repeat.

$$\begin{array}{r} 0.020833\ldots \\ 48\overline{)1.000000} \end{array}$$

$\frac{1}{48} = 0.020\overline{83}$

The repeating decimal for $\frac{1}{48}$ is $0.020\overline{83}$.

Change each fraction to a repeating decimal.

1. $\frac{2}{15} = 15\overline{)2.0000}$ ___0.1333...___ ___0.13___

2. $\frac{7}{30} = 30\overline{)7.0000}$ ___0.2333...___ ___0.2$\overline{3}$___

3. $\frac{7}{300} = 300\overline{)7.00000}$ ___0.02333...___ ___0.02$\overline{3}$___

4. $\frac{1}{14} = 14\overline{)1.00000000000000}$ ___0.07142857142857...___ ___0.0$\overline{714285}$___

5. $\frac{3}{11} =$ ___0.$\overline{27}$___

6. $\frac{1}{110} =$ ___0.0$\overline{09}$___

7. $\frac{11}{30} =$ ___0.3$\overline{6}$___

8. $\frac{1}{45} =$ ___0.0$\overline{2}$___

9. $\frac{1}{60} =$ ___0.01$\overline{6}$___

10. $\frac{7}{90} =$ ___0.0$\overline{7}$___

11. $\frac{7}{12} =$ ___0.58$\overline{3}$___

12. $\frac{5}{24} =$ ___0.208$\overline{3}$___

13. $\frac{11}{15} =$ ___0.7$\overline{3}$___

14. $\frac{5}{14} =$ ___0.3$\overline{571428}$___

Solve.

15. About 17 of every 30 acres in Mississippi is forested. Write $\frac{17}{30}$ as a repeating decimal. ___0.5$\overline{6}$___

16. About 20 of every 33 acres in Rhode Island is forested. Write $\frac{20}{33}$ as a repeating decimal. ___0.$\overline{60}$___

17. About 7 of every 150 farms in the United States are located in the Atlantic coastal states. Write this proportion as a repeating decimal. ___0.04$\overline{6}$___

Use with pages 150–151. ___47___

Reteach Worksheet

(Continued on p. 151.)

Juan's batting average at the end of last week included only one nonzero digit.

Kelly's mother knows that Kelly has a total of 43 hits this year.

The girl who has been at bat a total of 72 times knows that all the digits in her current batting average are the same.

The boy whose latest batting average is .200 has a total of 18 hits.

Bob has more hits than anyone else on the team.

It must have been .300 or $\frac{21}{70}$.

She has 6 hits this week, and so she was $\frac{37}{80}$ last week.

Her latest average is .333, and so her new statistics must be $\frac{24}{72}$—Monica.

His statistics last week must have been $\frac{18}{80}$, and so he has no hits this week—Gene. He has 5 hits this week—he must have had 39 hits through the end of last week for a total of 44 hits (Kelly has 43).

Thinking as a Team

1. Use a calculator to convert the batting statistics through the end of last week into decimal form. How can you use this information and the clues to compute the batting statistics for each player? See page 150 and above.

2. Make a table showing the latest batting statistics in fractional form. Compute the decimal equivalents for each. See page 150.

3. How would you find the decimal equivalent of $\frac{2}{3}$ on a calculator? Decimals such as 0.666 ... are called **repeating decimals**. The pattern of the digits is unending. You can write a repeating decimal by putting a bar over the digits that repeat (0.$\bar{6}$). What decimal equivalents in your table are repeating decimals? 0.$\bar{3}$; 0.4$\bar{7}$

4. How would you find the decimal equivalent of $\frac{9}{20}$ on a calculator? Decimals such as 0.45 are called **terminating decimals** because they end instead of repeat. What decimal equivalents in your table are terminating decimals? 0.45; 0.2; 0.36; 0.375; 0.4; 0.52; 0.3125

5. Find everyone's batting average. Who has the best batting average? See page 150. Daniela.

Congratulations! You have analyzed the scorekeeper's data and helped her use logical reasoning to argue to a correct conclusion.

Classwork/Homework, page H63   More Practice, page H199   **151**

ASSIGNMENT GUIDE

Basic:	p. 150, p. 151
Average:	p. 150, p. 151
Extended:	p. 150, p. 151

Resources
Practice, p. 63   Class/Home, p. H63
Reteach, p. 47   More Practice, p. H199
Enrich, p. 61   Reasoning, p. H214

Have students investigate to find out how they can write a mixed number as a decimal. (Write as a fraction greater than one and then divide and rewrite the fractional part as a decimal.) Give them the following numbers to write as decimals or fractions.

$1\frac{3}{5}$ (1.6) 3.75 ($3\frac{3}{4}$) $7\frac{1}{8}$ (7.125) $4\frac{2}{9}$(4.$\bar{2}$)

11.35 ($11\frac{7}{20}$)

Refer students who need additional practice to More Practice page 483 in the back of the pupil's book.

FOLLOW-UP ACTIVITIES

REINFORCEMENT
Ask students to find the decimal equivalents for $\frac{1}{9}$ (0.$\bar{1}$), $\frac{2}{9}$ (0.$\bar{2}$), and $\frac{3}{9}$ (0.$\bar{3}$). Ask them to continue this pattern through $\frac{8}{9}$, and then ask whether students think this pattern holds for $\frac{9}{9}$. Students may be surprised to learn that $\frac{9}{9}$ equals 0.$\bar{9}$. This repeating decimal (0.9999 . . .) represents a sequence that converges to (equals) 1. Students may find this easier to understand after they find the difference in the problem 1 − 0.9. If they say 1 − 0.999 = 0.001, extend the decimal to 0.9999 and show them that the difference is even smaller.

COMPUTER
Have students write a program to find the decimal equivalents of sevenths.

```
10 FOR N = 1 TO 7
20 LET D = N / 7
30 PRINT N;"/7",D
40 NEXT N
50 END
```

COMING UP
Teatime

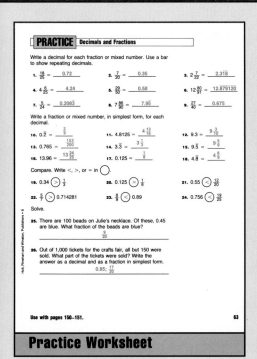

Practice Worksheet

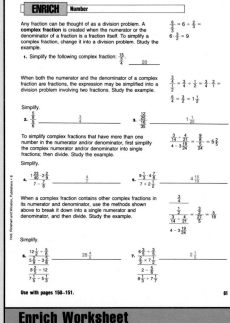

Enrich Worksheet

Objective: To solve equations involving fractions

Warm-Up
Have students solve each equation mentally.

$3s = 15$ $(s = 5)$ $\quad$ $14 + q = 26$ $(q = 12)$

$x - 8 = 23$ $\quad$ $\frac{x}{3} = 7$ $(x = 21)$

$(x = 31)$

GETTING STARTED

Have students perform each operation. Have them start with $8\frac{1}{2}$.
- Multiply by $\frac{3}{8}$.
- Add $2\frac{1}{2}$.
- Subtract $2\frac{1}{2}$.
- Divide by $\frac{3}{8}$.

The result should be $8\frac{1}{2}$. Discuss what happened. Guide students to recall that because addition and subtraction are inverse operations, as are multiplication and division, one operation undoes the other.

TEACHING THE LESSON

A. Some students may find it easier to solve equations involving addition and subtraction if they are rewritten as shown below.

$$\begin{array}{r} x + 3\frac{3}{4} = 8\frac{1}{2} \\ -3\frac{3}{4} \quad -3\frac{3}{4} \\ \hline x \qquad = 4\frac{3}{4} \end{array}$$

$$\begin{array}{r} x - 1\frac{1}{2} = 7 \\ +1\frac{1}{2} \quad +1\frac{1}{2} \\ \hline x \qquad = 8\frac{1}{2} \end{array}$$

B. Extend the instruction by showing how to solve an equation involving division.

$$x \div \frac{3}{4} = 4 \ (x = 3)$$

C. Emphasize the fact that when solving two-step equations, students should add or subtract first and then multiply or divide. Some students may find it helpful to know that by doing so, they are reversing the order of operations.

Before assigning exercises as independent work, guide students through the examples below.

$$1\frac{1}{4}r + 3\frac{2}{3} = 12 \qquad \left(r = 6\frac{2}{3}\right)$$
$$6\frac{1}{2}d - 2\frac{3}{4} = 10 \qquad \left(d = 1\frac{25}{26}\right)$$

Solving Equations with Fractions

A. A potter needed to make a teapot and teacups. He used $3\frac{3}{4}$ packages of clay for the teapot. If he started with $8\frac{1}{2}$ packages of clay, how much clay did he have left for the teacups?

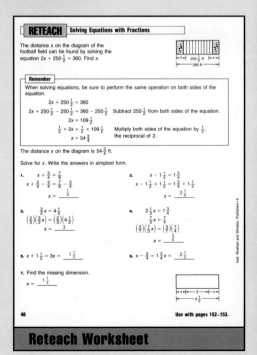

Clay for the teacups		Clay used for the teapot		Clay started with
x	$+$	$3\frac{3}{4}$	$=$	$8\frac{1}{2}$
x	$+ 3\frac{3}{4} - 3\frac{3}{4}$		$=$	$8\frac{1}{2} - 3\frac{3}{4}$
	x		$=$	$4\frac{3}{4}$

He had $4\frac{3}{4}$ packages of clay left for the teacups.

B. Solve.

$$\frac{3}{4}s = 5$$

$$\frac{3}{4}s = 5$$

$$\frac{4}{3} \cdot \frac{3}{4}s = \frac{4}{3} \cdot \frac{5}{1}$$ Multiply both sides by the reciprocal of $\frac{3}{4}$.

$$s = \frac{20}{3}$$

$$s = 6\frac{2}{3}$$

Check.

$$\frac{3}{4}s = 5$$

$$\frac{3}{4} \cdot 6\frac{2}{3} \stackrel{?}{=} 5$$

$$\frac{3}{\cancel{4}} \cdot \frac{\cancel{20}}{\cancel{3}} \stackrel{?}{=} 5$$

$$5 = 5 ✓$$

C. Solve. $\frac{5}{8}d + 4\frac{1}{4} = 16\frac{3}{4}$

$$\frac{5}{8}d + 4\frac{1}{4} = 16\frac{3}{4}$$

$$\frac{5}{8}d + 4\frac{1}{4} - 4\frac{1}{4} = 16\frac{3}{4} - 4\frac{1}{4}$$

$$\frac{8}{5} \cdot \frac{5}{8}d = \frac{8}{5} \cdot 12\frac{1}{2}$$

$$d = \frac{\cancel{8}}{\cancel{5}} \cdot \frac{\cancel{25}}{\cancel{2}}$$

$$d = 20$$

152

Math Reasoning, page H214

COMMON ERRORS

Some students might incorrectly compensate for an operation performed on one side of the equation by undoing the operation on the other side.

$$\begin{array}{r} x + 2 = 5 \\ -2 + 2 \\ \hline x = 7 \end{array}$$

Remediation
For this error, emphasize the fact that the same operation must be performed on both sides of the equation. Have students check their answers either by substituting their answers into the original equation or by performing the same operations on a known equality such as $1 = 1$.

Assign Reteach Master, p. 48.

Solve. Write the answer in simplest form.

1. $x + 1\frac{1}{6} = 5\frac{1}{8}$ **2.** $z + 2\frac{3}{8} = 8\frac{7}{12}$ **3.** $y - 4\frac{1}{4} = 3\frac{1}{5}$ **4.** $b - 12\frac{7}{8} = 9\frac{5}{9}$

$x = 3\frac{23}{24}$ $z = 6\frac{5}{24}$ $y = 7\frac{9}{20}$ $b = 22\frac{31}{72}$

5. $\frac{1}{6}r = 3$ **6.** $1\frac{3}{4}c = 9\frac{1}{4}$ **7.** $f \div \frac{2}{5} = 4$ **8.** $k \div 2\frac{5}{4} = 8\frac{5}{4}$

$r = 18$ $c = 5\frac{2}{7}$ $f = 1\frac{3}{5}$ $k = 30\frac{1}{16}$

9. $12\frac{1}{3}h + 3 = 21\frac{1}{3}$ **10.** $3\frac{7}{9}t - 2\frac{8}{9} = 5$ **11.** $5\frac{2}{9}f - 7\frac{2}{3} = 23$ **12.** $3\frac{3}{16}u + \frac{3}{8} = 4\frac{3}{8}$

$h = 1\frac{18}{37}$ $t = 2\frac{3}{34}$ $f = 5\frac{41}{47}$ $u = 1\frac{13}{51}$

13. $a + 2\frac{1}{2} = 9$ **14.** $\frac{1}{8}n = 6\frac{1}{4}$ **15.** $\frac{1}{2}d + 1\frac{1}{2} = 5$ **★16.** $12\frac{1}{4} + 3\frac{1}{6} = 21\frac{3}{6}w$

$a = 6\frac{1}{2}$ $n = 50$ $d = 7$ $w = \frac{185}{258}$

Solve.

17. It takes a potter $\frac{3}{4}$ hour to make 1 bowl. How many bowls will the potter make in 33 hours? (Write an equation, and let b = number of bowls.) $\frac{3}{4}b = 33$; $b = 44$ bowls

18. A potter used 10 packages of clay to make bowls. If 1 bowl took $1\frac{1}{4}$ packages, how many bowls did he make? (Let b = the number of bowls.) $1\frac{1}{4}b = 10$; $b = 8$; 8 bowls

19. Suppose that you want to buy a set of soup bowls. You consider a set of 8 soup bowls that sells for $20 at a discount store. Then you visit a local potter who sells handcrafted bowls for $5.00 each. The less expensive bowls are mass produced and of lower quality than the pottery bowls. Both types of bowls will serve the same purpose. Would you rather buy more of the less expensive bowls, or fewer bowls of better quality for the same price? Why? Answers will vary.

NUMBER SENSE

Mentally match the equations that have the same solution.

1. $a + 2 = 11$ b   **a.** $4 = \frac{v}{2} + 1$

2. $\frac{b}{4} + 6 = 6$ c   **b.** $7 = w - 2$

3. $5c + 5 = 30$ e   **c.** $5 = x + 5$

4. $12 - 2d = 0$ a   **d.** $8 = 4 + \frac{y}{2}$

5. $e + 2 = 10$ d   **e.** $0 = \frac{z}{5} - 1$

Classwork/Homework, page H64

153

ASSIGNMENT GUIDE

Basic: 1–12, 16–17, NS

Average: 1–15 o, 17–19, NS

Extended: 2–16 e, 17–19, NS

Resources
Practice, p. 64   Class/Home, p. H64
Reteach, p. 48   Reasoning, p. H214
Enrich, p. 62

Exercise Analysis

1–8   Solve a one-step equation
9–16   Solve a two-step equation
17–18 Skill applications
19   Problem formulation

Number Sense
The activity provides students with practice in solving equations mentally.

FOLLOW-UP ACTIVITIES

MATH COMMUNICATION
Have students write equations to solve each problem.
- One third less than two is how much less than one half less than three? ($\frac{5}{6}$)
- What part of three is one third of two? ($\frac{2}{9}$)
- One fourth of five is what part of three? ($\frac{5}{12}$)
- Two less than one half of twelve is what part of five? ($\frac{4}{5}$)
- One third less than two is how much less than one half more than three? ($1\frac{5}{6}$)

COMPUTER
Have students write a program that will give the Celsius equivalents for the following Fahrenheit temperatures: zero, the freezing point of water (32°), the temperature of the human body (98.6°), and the boiling point of water (212°).

```
10 PRINT  "FAHRENHEIT",  "CELSIUS"
20 READ F
30 LET C = (F − 32) * 5/9
40 PRINT F,,C
50 IF F<>212 GOTO 20
60 DATA 0, 32, 98.6, 212
70 END
```

COMING UP
All that remains

PRACTICE Solving Equations with Fractions

Solve. Write the answer in simplest form.

1. $x + 2\frac{1}{3} = 7$ $x =$ ___ $4\frac{2}{3}$ **2.** $n - 4\frac{3}{5} = 12\frac{1}{3}$ $n =$ ___ $16\frac{14}{15}$

3. $\frac{1}{9}a + 3\frac{2}{3} = 4\frac{1}{2}$ $a =$ ___ $7\frac{1}{2}$ **4.** $1\frac{3}{4}b - 13 = 2\frac{1}{4}$ $b =$ ___ $8\frac{5}{7}$

5. $3\frac{1}{3}w + \frac{2}{3} = 20\frac{1}{2}$ $w =$ ___ $5\frac{19}{20}$ **6.** $3\frac{3}{10}r + 2\frac{1}{3} = 1\frac{5}{9}$ $r =$ ___ $1\frac{8}{27}$

7. $\frac{1}{2}g + \frac{4}{3} = 7$ $g =$ ___ $11\frac{1}{3}$ **8.** $\frac{4}{9}s - 2 = 14$ $s =$ ___ 36

Solve each equation. To unscramble the limerick, write the words from each box in the correct space below.

$3X + 5 = 9$	$\frac{5}{3}X = 15$	$2X \div 3 = 14$
$X =$ ___ 15	$X =$ ___ 9	$X =$ ___ 21
WHEN HE ROSE	EXCEEDINGLY NEAT	WHO WAS SO
$5\frac{1}{4}X = 42$	$3\frac{2}{3}X = 44$	$1\frac{3}{5}X = 32$
$X =$ ___ 8	$X =$ ___ 12	$X =$ ___ 20
ON HIS HEAD	THERE WAS A	HIS FEET
$\frac{5}{12}X + 1 = 21$	$7X - 3 = 39$	$\frac{8}{5}X = 2\frac{2}{3}$
$X =$ ___ 48	$X =$ ___ 6	$X =$ ___ 3
OUT OF BED	DID DIRTY	HE STOOD
$3\frac{3}{7}X - 5 = 19$	$\frac{X}{23} + 13 = 14$	$5X - 2\frac{2}{7} = 7\frac{4}{7}$
$X =$ ___ 7	$X =$ ___ 23	$X =$ ___ 2
FROM CRETE	YOUNG FELLOW	AND NEVER

12	THERE WAS A	23	YOUNG FELLOW	7	FROM CRETE
21	WHO WAS SO	9	EXCEEDINGLY NEAT	15	WHEN HE ROSE
48	OUT OF BED	3	HE STOOD	8	ON HIS HEAD
2	AND NEVER	6	DID DIRTY	20	HIS FEET

64   Use with pages 152–153.

Practice Worksheet

ENRICH Algebra

1. At a baseball game between the Pittsfield All Stars and the Rock City Bombers, $\frac{2}{3}$ of the fans in Section C cheered for the All Stars. Of the remainder, $\frac{1}{2}$ cheered for the Bombers. In all, 250 people in Section C were cheering either for the All Stars or the Bombers. How many people were sitting in Section C?

To solve this problem, you must use an equation.
Let x = total number of fans in Section C.
$\frac{2}{3}x$ = number of All Stars fans
$\frac{1}{3}x$ = remainder; therefore,
$\frac{1}{2}(\frac{1}{3}x)$ = number of Bombers fans
250 = total fans cheering for either team
Set up the equation and solve.
All Star fans + Bomber fans = total cheering for either team
$\frac{2}{3}x + \frac{1}{2}(\frac{1}{3}x) = 250$ **Answer:** $x = 300$

2. In Section D, $\frac{1}{4}$ of the fans cheered for the Bombers. Of the remainder, $\frac{1}{3}$ were for the All Stars. A surprising 185 people in Section D didn't care who won the game. How many people were sitting in Section D?
$\frac{1}{4}x + \frac{1}{3}(\frac{3}{4}x) + 185 = x$ **Answer:** $x = 370$

3. In Section E, $\frac{3}{5}$ of the audience was from Pittsfield. Of the remainder, $\frac{3}{5}$ lived in Rock City; $\frac{1}{4}$ lived in Rock Falls, which is near Rock City; and the rest came from out of state. In all, 136 people in Section E were from Pittsfield, Rock City, or Rock Falls. How many people were sitting in Section E?
$\frac{3}{5}x + \frac{3}{5}(\frac{2}{5}x) + \frac{1}{4}(\frac{2}{5}x) = 136$ **Answer:** $x = 160$

4. The peanut vendor sold $\frac{1}{3}$ of her supply to fans in Section C, $\frac{2}{5}$ of the remainder to Section D, and another $\frac{1}{3}$ of the remainder to Section E. She has 50 bags of peanuts left. How many bags did she start with?
$\frac{1}{3}x + \frac{2}{5}(\frac{2}{3}x) + \frac{1}{3}(\frac{2}{5}x) + 50 = x$ **Answer:** $x = 270$

62   Use with pages 152–153.

Enrich Worksheet

Objectives: To interpret quotients and remainders in solving problems

Warm-Up

To prepare students for this lesson, have them compute the following: $48 \div 6$ (8); $48 \div 7 \left(6\frac{6}{7}\right)$; $49 \div 7$ (7); $49 \div 6.$ $\left(8\frac{1}{6}\right)$

GETTING STARTED

Separate the class into groups according to the following specifications.
- students wearing glasses
- students whose last names contain an S
- students whose first names contain two vowels
- students wearing blue jeans

Some students may fit in more than one category. Challenge the class to develop a category that describes the students that fit in *none* of the categories.

TEACHING THE LESSON

This lesson deals with interpreting the remainder and the quotient when solving division problems. Guide students through each of the four introductory problems, highlighting the differences in the way the remainder is or isn't applied in the solution. In the first problem, be sure students understand that the quotient is the number of full classes and that the remainder is the number of students left. Obviously, Jim cannot hold $\frac{6}{8}$ of a class; so, the quotient is rounded up to the next whole number. In reading the second problem, emphasize the fact that the key to interpreting the quotient and the remainder is the realization that each student receives an *equal* amount. Therefore, the sheets of glass are divided into 8 equal parts, and no rounding should take place. Problem 3 asks how many glass cutters will be *left* after 8 boxes are full. This should immediately alert students to look for a remainder. In the fourth question, the fact that they want to know how many *whole* frames can be made should indicate to students that they are dealing *only* with the quotient.

Questions: Correct identification of the question is essential in deciding how to interpret the quotient and remainder. Suggest that students look for the key words in a question; such as *equal amount, left*, and so on. Challenge students to develop different questions for each problem that would require a different interpretation of the quotient and remainder.

Tools: It may be helpful to have students find the form of the answer (whole number, fraction, and so on) and the label attached to it before actually solving the problem. This will make easier the decision of how to interpret the remainder once the division

---

QUESTIONS	TOOLS	SOLUTIONS	CHECKS

PROBLEM SOLVING
Interpreting the Quotient and the Remainder

Sometimes, when you divide, the answer is not a whole number. If the answer is a quotient with a remainder, be sure your answer really answers the question.

1. Jim gives classes in creating stained-glass windows. He allows a maximum of 8 students per class, and 30 people have applied. How many classes should Jim schedule?

$$\begin{array}{r} 3\,\text{R}6 \\ 8)\overline{30} \\ \underline{24} \\ 6 \end{array}$$

Look at the quotient.
Look at the remainder.
Round the quotient up to the next-greater whole number.

Jim should schedule 4 classes.

2. There are $10\frac{2}{3}$ dozen sheets of colored glass given to each class. Each of the 8 students receives an equal amount. How much glass does each student receive?

$10\frac{2}{3} \div 8 \qquad \frac{32}{3} \div 8$ Look at the quotient.
Look at the remainder.

$\overset{4}{\cancel{\frac{32}{3}}} \times \frac{1}{\cancel{8}_1} \qquad \frac{4}{3} = 1\frac{1}{3}$ Use both the quotient and the remainder.

Each student will receive $1\frac{1}{3}$ dozen, or 16, pieces of glass.

3. Jim is storing glass cutters. He has only 8 boxes. The cutters fit 4 to a box, and there are 34 glass cutters. How many cutters will not be boxed?

$$\begin{array}{r} 8\,\text{R}2 \\ 4)\overline{34} \\ \underline{32} \\ 2 \end{array}$$

Look at the quotient.
Look at the remainder.
Use only the remainder.

There will be 2 cutters that will not be boxed.

4. Seven feet of framing are needed to frame each project. If framing is purchased in 8-ft lengths, how many frames can be made from 16 ft of framing?

$$\begin{array}{r} 2\,\text{R}2 \\ 7)\overline{16} \\ \underline{14} \\ 2 \end{array}$$

Look at the quotient.
Look at the remainder.
Use only the quotient.

Two frames can be made from 16 ft of framing.

154

---

has been worked out. Also suggest that after students have worked the division problem, they might identify exactly what each number represents before listing a solution; for example, in the first introductory problem, 8 = the students in one class; 30 = the total number of students; 3 = the number of full classes; 6 = the number of students left.

Solutions: The computational part of the problem should not be a major source of trouble, but you may want to review with students the ways in which a remainder can be expressed. (whole number, fraction, decimal, and so on.)

Checks: The most-helpful check will be the check for the reasonableness and logic of an answer when it is substituted into the problem. Students should also use multiplication and addition to check the accuracy of their division.

Write the letter of the correct answer.

1. Jackie made a mold for ceramic tiles. The mold produces 8 tiles at a time. If Jackie wants to make 78 tiles, how many times must she fill the mold?

$$78 \div 8 = 9\frac{3}{4}$$

a. 9 times
b. $9\frac{3}{4}$ times
c. 10 times

Solve.

3. Samantha buys a piece of canvas that measures 90 square feet. How many paintings that measure 7 square feet can she paint on the canvas? **12 paintings**

5. Joanna has 2,000 strands of natural cane. How many baskets can she weave if the pattern for each basket calls for 94 strands of cane? **21 baskets**

7. Barbara is selling handmade pot holders at 3 for $5.50. What is the lowest price that Barbara should charge for 1 pot holder? **$1.84**

9. Fiona works in brass. It costs her $12.80 to craft 6 brass nameplates. She sells one to a friend at cost. How much does the friend pay for the nameplate? **$2.14**

2. Margo's candle shop produces 700 candles per day. If the shop packs 6 candles to a box, how many boxes are needed per day?

$$700 \div 6 = 116 \text{ R}4$$

a. 116 boxes
b. $116\frac{1}{2}$ boxes
c. 117 boxes

4. A design for a bowl 10 in. in diameter and 5 in. high calls for $1\frac{3}{4}$ lb of clay. There are 6 lb of clay. How much clay remains if 3 bowls are made? $\frac{3}{4}$ **pound of clay**

6. To string a necklace, Jesse needs 236 small beads. The crafts store sells small beads in bags of 75 beads each. How many bags must Jesse buy? **4 bags**

8. Eduardo uses $\frac{3}{4}$ sheet of red glass for each stained-glass window he is working on. If he plans to make 5 windows, how many sheets of red glass does he need to buy? **4 sheets**

★10. Lattia is molding pewter figurines. For every 10.5-ounce figurine, she must pour 12 ounces of molten pewter. What percent of the pewter is waste? **12.5%**

Classwork/Homework, page H65

ASSIGNMENT GUIDE

Basic: 1–5
Average: 2–6
Extended: 5–10

Resources
Practice, p. 65 Class/Home, p. H65
Enrich, p. 63

Exercise Analysis
1–2 Choose the correct answer
3–10 Skill applications

FOLLOW-UP ACTIVITIES

PROBLEM SOLVING
Separate students into groups of four. Give each group a division exercise that has a remainder, such as 98 ÷ 12. Have a member of each group use this exercise to write a problem for each of the four strategies shown on page 154 (1 strategy per student). Then have groups challenge one another with problems they have written.

CALCULATOR

Materials: calculators

Discuss with students the use of calculators for division and the form of the remainder (decimal). Write 684 ÷ 25 = 27 R9 on the chalkboard. Then write out the following sequence and have students perform it on their calculators. Explain that in this way, they can quickly convert decimal remainders back to whole numbers by simply multiplying.

$$684 \div 25 = 27.36 - 27 = 0.36 \times 25 = 9$$

For some calculators, the multiplication will not always result in a whole number but will be very close and should be rounded, as in the problem below. Ask students to explain why this is true.

$$1{,}117 \div 14 \approx 79.785714 - 79 \approx$$
$$0.785714 \times 14 \approx 10.999996 \rightarrow 11$$

COMING UP
Be reasonable!

Objectives: To identify subsets and disjoint sets; to use a Venn diagram

Warm-Up

Have students write *true* or *false* for each of the following statements.

1. All dogs are animals. (true)
2. All cats are animals. (true)
3. All dogs are cats. (false)
4. Some dogs are cats. (false)
5. No dogs are cats. (true)

GETTING STARTED

Tell students that a set represents the group of all things with a certain characteristic or set of characteristics. Have them think of a few examples of sets. Then draw the Venn diagram below on the chalkboard to illustrate the relationships between the set of all dogs, all cats, and all animals.

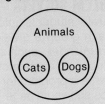

Point out that a Venn diagram makes it easier to visualize the relationship between sets and to determine which statements about a set are true and which are not.

TEACHING THE LESSON

Point out to students that the phrase *each of the 33 campers* tells them how large the entire set of campers is. Call their attention to the use of the word *the*, and ask how the meaning would be different if the sentence read *Each of 33 campers took exactly one crafts course.* (The entire set of campers would not necessarily be limited to 33.) Remind students that the word *exactly* means *no more and no less*.

Elicit from students the difference between the use of the definite article *the* in the sentence *9 campers took the Indian-jewelry course,* and the indefinite article *a* in the sentence *14 campers took a jewelry course.* (The word *the* implies that there is exactly one Indian-jewelry course; the word *a* implies that there is at least one jewelry course, but that there may be more than one.)

Review the meaning of *disjoint sets* ("sets which are not joined or do not overlap at all") and the ⊂ notation for subset.

Point out that students can easily remember which way the symbol ⊂ faces by remembering that a subset is *contained* in the larger set, because the symbol ⊂ looks almost exactly like the letter **C,** the first letter of the word *contained.* They can remember that A ⊂ B means A is a subset of B, or A is contained in B.

LOGICAL REASONING

At summer camp, each of the 33 campers took exactly one crafts course. A total of 9 campers took the Indian-jewelry course. Of the campers, 8 took the leather class and 14 took a jewelry course. The remaining campers took the stained-glass course. How many campers took the stained-glass course?

Every Indian-jewelry student is a jewelry student. So, {Indian-jewelry students} is a **subset** of {jewelry students}.
Write: {Indian-jewelry students} ⊂ {jewelry students}.

No students are taking both a jewelry class and the leather class. So, {leather students} and {jewelry students} are **disjoint** sets.

There are 33 − 14 − 8 = 11 campers taking the stained-glass course.

VENN DIAGRAM

14 − 9

Jewelry

Indian jewelry

9

8

Leather

Stained glass — 33 − 14 − 8

Write A ⊂ B, B ⊂ A, or A and B are disjoint.

1. A = {leather belts}
   B = {belts}   *A ⊂ B*

2. A = {gold jewelry}
   B = {silver jewelry}
   A and B are disjoint.

3. A = {windows}   *B ⊂ A*
   B = {stained-glass windows}

4. A = {necklaces}
   B = {bracelets}
   A and B are disjoint.

5. A = {metallic jewelry}
   B = {silver necklaces}
   B ⊂ A

6. A = {leather crafts}
   B = {leather belts}   *B ⊂ A*

Use a Venn diagram to solve.

The jewelry class made 24 necklaces from either gemstones or beads. They made 35 bracelets from either silver, beads, or gemstones. They made 23 pieces of jewelry from gems and 19 pieces of jewelry from beads. They made 9 beaded necklaces.

7. How many necklaces were made from gems? 15
8. How many beaded bracelets did they make? 10
9. How many bracelets were made from gems? 8
10. How many bracelets were made from silver? 17

156

Finally, point out the importance of reading through all the information in a problem before setting up a Venn diagram and the importance of starting with the largest set or sets first and then filling in the subsets.

GROUP PROJECT

A Crafty Way to Raise Money

The problem: Your school has been invited to participate in an American Handicrafts Fair to raise money for charity. Your school has been offered a choice of the following three crafts: basket weaving, rug hooking, or beaded jewelry making.

Using the chart and the questions below, decide which handicraft would probably be the wisest choice.

Materials		Cost	Tools	Time to make each	Projected selling price	Estimated number that would be sold
Baskets	wicker	$4.00 per basket	scissors	3 hours	$5.75	200
Rugs	yarn	$44.25 per rug	metal hook	60 hours	$65.00	50
	cotton backing	$7.50 per rug				
Jewelry	beads	$4.50 per necklace	pliers	1 hour	$8.50	125
	string and clasp	$.50 each				

Key Questions
- Which craft item is the least expensive to make?
- Which item is the least time-consuming to make?
- Which item will sell for the highest price?
- Which item will probably sell most successfully?

157

ASSIGNMENT GUIDE

Basic:	p. 156, p. 157
Average:	p. 156, p. 157
Extended:	p. 156, p. 157

Objective: To compare costs to find the most cost-efficient item

USING THE PAGE

Have students work in groups of three or four. Have each group discuss the proper sequence of steps needed to determine which craft would be best. Remind students to carefully consider the Key Questions when determining how to approach this problem. Have one student in each group write down the specific steps agreed upon for evaluating the different crafts. When this is done, have groups do the actual calculations to determine the most profitable craft (beads). Remind students to also consider factors, such as the labor involved in each craft. They should realize that it may be difficult to find enough volunteers for the job if making the craft is very time-consuming.

To extend this cooperative learning activity, have each group devise their own chart with the following information: reasonable cost of materials, time expenditures, selling prices, and estimated sales for any of three different crafts, such as pottery, sewing, leathercraft, and wood carving, making one craft the most profitable. Then have groups exchange charts and calculate which of the three crafts they are given is the most cost-effective. Groups can then check their answers with the group that devised the chart.

Purpose: The Chapter Test helps to assess students' understanding of the concepts and skills presented in this chapter.

The chart below is designed to help you review the test items by correlating them with the testing objectives that appear in the Chapter Overview.

Item	Objectives
1–3	A
4–9	C
10–15	B
16–21	D
22–24	H
25–30	E
31–36	F
37–40	G
41	I
42	J
43	K

Bonus
The bonus questions may be used for extra credit, or you may want to assign them to students who complete the test before the rest of the class.

Calculator
You may wish to have students use calculators for the problem-solving portions of the test.

Resources
If you prefer to use this Chapter Test as a review exercise, additional testing materials are available in the Teacher's Resource Book.

CHAPTER TEST

Write in simplest form. Then write two fractions that are equivalent to each fraction. (pages 120–121)

1. $\frac{10}{12}$ $\frac{5}{6}$ Answers will vary.   2. $\frac{35}{56}$ $\frac{5}{8}$ Answers will vary.   3. $\frac{21}{87}$ $\frac{7}{29}$ Answers will va

Write a fraction for each whole number or mixed number. (pages 122–123)

4. $4\frac{3}{8}$ $\frac{35}{8}$ 5. 5 $\frac{5}{1}$ 6. $9\frac{2}{5}$ $\frac{47}{5}$

Write a whole number or mixed number for each fraction. (pages 122–123)

7. $\frac{48}{9}$ $5\frac{1}{3}$ 8. $\frac{85}{5}$ 17 9. $\frac{98}{3}$ $32\frac{2}{3}$

Compare. Use >, <, or = for ●. (pages 124–125)

10. $\frac{2}{3}$ ● $\frac{12}{18}$ $=$ 11. $1\frac{3}{8}$ ● $\frac{15}{8}$ $<$ 12. $\frac{3}{4}$ ● $\frac{6}{12}$ $>$

Order from the greatest to the least. (pages 124–125)

13. $\frac{5}{8}, \frac{2}{3}, \frac{3}{4}, \frac{4}{9}$ 14. $2\frac{5}{6}, 2\frac{2}{9}, 2\frac{1}{4}, 2\frac{9}{12}$ 15. $1\frac{2}{3}, 1\frac{3}{4}, 2\frac{1}{5}, 1\frac{1}{2}$
$\frac{3}{4}, \frac{2}{3}, \frac{5}{8}, \frac{4}{9}$ $2\frac{5}{6}, 2\frac{9}{12}, 2\frac{1}{4}, 2\frac{2}{9}$ $2\frac{1}{5}, 1\frac{3}{4}, 1\frac{2}{3}, 1\frac{1}{2}$

Add or subtract. Write the answer in simplest form. (pages 130–135)

16. $\frac{5}{7} + \frac{3}{7} + \frac{4}{7}$ $1\frac{5}{7}$ 17. $\frac{2}{3} + \frac{7}{9} + \frac{1}{9}$ $1\frac{5}{9}$ 18. $5\frac{1}{4} + 3\frac{5}{6} + 1\frac{1}{3}$ $10\frac{5}{12}$

19. $\frac{5}{8} - \frac{3}{8}$ $\frac{1}{4}$ 20. $\frac{1}{2} - \frac{1}{5}$ $\frac{3}{10}$ 21. $4\frac{2}{7} - 1\frac{1}{3}$ $2\frac{20}{21}$

Estimate. (pages 128–129 and 140–141)
Answers may vary. Accept any reasonable estimate.

22. $5\frac{3}{4} + 2\frac{4}{5} - 1\frac{3}{5}$ $7–8$ 23. $7\frac{1}{6} \times 6\frac{1}{8}$ 42^+ 24. $8\frac{1}{4} \div 2\frac{1}{5}$ $3–4$

Multiply or divide. Write the answer in simplest form.
(pages 138–139, 142–143, and 146–149)

25. $\frac{3}{4} \times \frac{4}{5}$ $\frac{3}{5}$ 26. $4 \times \frac{8}{9}$ $3\frac{5}{9}$ 27. $2\frac{1}{2} \times \frac{3}{7}$ $1\frac{1}{14}$

28. $\frac{2}{9} \div \frac{4}{5}$ $\frac{5}{18}$ 29. $\frac{5}{7} \div 6$ $\frac{5}{42}$ 30. $1\frac{3}{4} \div \frac{2}{3}$ $2\frac{5}{8}$

158

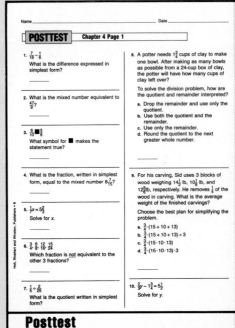

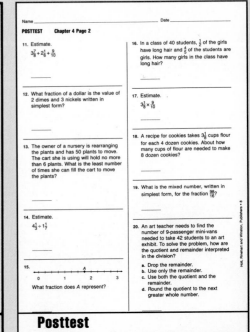

For students who have difficulty with written tests, this test can be given orally.

You may wish to test students, orally or in writing, to see if they can explain the steps used in solving selected items. The following table summarizes the procedures for solving key test items.

Ex. 16–21

Adding or subtracting fractions and mixed numbers

To add or subtract fractions that have like denominators, add or subtract the numerators and keep the denominator. To add or subtract fractions that have unlike denominators, first write them as equivalent fractions with the least common denominator by finding the LCM of the denominators. Then add or subtract the numerators. For mixed numbers, first write them as fractions; then follow the steps above. For both fractions and mixed numbers, write answers in simplest form.

Ex. 31–36

Writing decimals as fractions and fractions as decimals

To write a decimal as a fraction, use the digits to the right of the decimal point as the numerator. To find the denominator, count the number of digits to the right of the decimal point (tenths, hundredths, thousandths, and so on). Rewrite fractions in simplest form, if necessary. To write a fraction as a decimal, divide the numerator by the denominator. To show a repeating decimal, place a bar over the digit(s) that repeat(s).

Write each decimal as a fraction, and write each fraction as a decimal. (pages 150–151)

31. 0.4 $\frac{2}{5}$ **32.** 0.85 $\frac{17}{20}$ **33.** 0.065 $\frac{13}{200}$ **34.** $\frac{2}{9}$ $0.\bar{2}$ **35.** $\frac{7}{20}$ 0.35 **36.** $\frac{4}{15}$ $0.2\bar{6}$

Solve. (pages 152–153)

37. $\frac{3}{5}x = \frac{2}{3}$ **38.** $y \div \frac{3}{5} = 7$ **39.** $\frac{1}{2}d - 1\frac{1}{2} = 7$ **40.** $3\frac{1}{4}x + 2\frac{3}{8} = 5\frac{7}{8}$

$x = 1\frac{1}{9}$ $y = 4\frac{1}{5}$ $d = 17$ $x = 1\frac{1}{13}$

Solve. Solve a simpler problem where necessary.
(pages 126–127, 136–137, 144–145, and 154–155)

41. The County Fair of Oakley recorded the number of quilts entered in the Best Quilt Contest each year. The results are listed in the pictograph at the right. If the trend of quilt entries continues during the next five years, will the number of entries in 1994 exceed 80 quilts? **yes**

QUILTS ENTERED IN CONTEST

Year	
1989	⊠ ⊠ ⊠ ⊠ ⊠ ⊠ ⊠ ⊠
1988	⊠ ⊠ ⊠ ⊠ ⊠ ⊠ ⊠ ⊠
1987	⊠ ⊠ ⊠ ⊠ ⊠ ⊠ ⊠
1986	⊠ ⊠ ⊠ ⊠ ⊠ ⊠
1985	⊠ ⊠ ⊠ ⊠ ⊠ ⊠

⊠ **8 quilts**

42. Bert sells necklaces at the fair. If each necklace is made of 3 large ceramic beads and 4 small ceramic beads that have 12 brass spacers on either side of each bead, how many of each item must he buy for 18 necklaces? **54 large beads, 72 small beads, and 1,728 spacers**

43. Use the pictograph to find the average number of quilts entered in the Best Quilt Contest during the last five years. In which year(s) was the number of entries greater than the average? If quilts are shown with no more than 6 per display area, how many display areas were needed in 1989? **55.2 quilts; 1988 and 1989; 11 display areas**

BONUS

Use the table to find what fraction of the total cost the small beads are.
$\frac{1}{36}$

Cost of Necklaces	
Large beads	$1.25 each
Small beads	$0.25 each
Spacers	$0.50 bag
Cord and findings	$7.00

159

159

Purpose This Reteaching page provides additional instruction for key concepts in the chapter. It is designed for use by students who have had difficulty with these concepts. It can also be used to provide additional practice for students who require it.

USING THE PAGE

Mixed-number addition and subtraction was taught on pages 130–135.

Work through the addition example. Point out that the fractions given do not have the same denominator. Review finding equivalent fractions using the LCD of 20. Also point out that the fraction in the sum $\frac{29}{20}$ must be renamed as $1\frac{9}{20}$. Work through the subtraction problem. Again, stress the fact that 3 and 4 are unlike denominators so that an LCD must be used to find equivalent fractions. Explain why it is necessary to rename before students can subtract. Stress that answers should always be in simplest form.

Resources

For other practice and activities related to this chapter, see the Teacher's Resource Book.

RETEACHING

A. Add $1\frac{1}{5} + 4\frac{3}{4} + 1\frac{1}{2}$.

To add mixed numbers that have unlike denominators, find equivalent fractions.

Find the LCM of the denominators 5, 4, and 2. The LCD is 20.

Write each fraction, using like denominators.

$$1\frac{1}{5} = 1\frac{4}{20}$$
$$4\frac{3}{4} = 4\frac{15}{20}$$
$$+ 1\frac{1}{2} = 1\frac{10}{20}$$

Add.

$$1\frac{1}{5} = 1\frac{4}{20}$$
$$4\frac{3}{4} = 4\frac{15}{20}$$
$$+ 1\frac{1}{2} = 1\frac{10}{20}$$
$$6\frac{29}{20}$$

Simplify the sum.

$$6\frac{29}{20} = 6 + 1\frac{9}{20} = 7\frac{9}{20}$$

B. Subtract $4\frac{1}{3} - 1\frac{3}{4}$.

To subtract mixed numbers that have unlike denominators, find fractions that have like denominators.

Rename fractions.

$$4\frac{1}{3} = 4\frac{4}{12}$$
$$- 1\frac{3}{4} = 1\frac{9}{12}$$

Compare fractions.

$$\frac{4}{12} < \frac{9}{12} \quad \text{So, rename.}$$
$$4\frac{4}{12} = 3 + 1\frac{4}{12} = 3\frac{16}{12}$$

Subtract.

$$4\frac{1}{3} = 3\frac{16}{12}$$
$$- 1\frac{3}{4} = 1\frac{9}{12}$$
$$2\frac{7}{12}$$

> Subtract the fractions and then the whole numbers.

Add. Write the answer in simplest form.

1. $4\frac{3}{8} + 2\frac{2}{3}$ $7\frac{1}{24}$
2. $2\frac{3}{5} + 7\frac{2}{3}$ $10\frac{4}{15}$
3. $4\frac{5}{6} + 2\frac{3}{5}$ $7\frac{13}{30}$
4. $3\frac{1}{4} + 5\frac{1}{6} + 1\frac{2}{3}$ $10\frac{1}{12}$
5. $2\frac{1}{2} + 1\frac{1}{6} + 10\frac{4}{5}$ $14\frac{7}{15}$
6. $11\frac{3}{10} + 1\frac{1}{6} + 8\frac{3}{4}$ $21\frac{13}{60}$

Subtract. Write the answer in simplest form.

7. $3\frac{2}{5} - 1\frac{9}{10}$ $1\frac{1}{2}$
8. $9\frac{1}{8} - 6\frac{1}{2}$ $2\frac{5}{8}$
9. $6\frac{1}{3} - 4\frac{5}{6}$ $1\frac{1}{2}$
10. $5\frac{1}{4} - 3\frac{5}{6}$ $1\frac{5}{12}$
11. $7\frac{1}{7} - 5\frac{1}{3}$ $1\frac{17}{21}$
12. $9\frac{2}{3} - 6\frac{7}{8}$ $2\frac{19}{24}$

160

ENRICHMENT

Complex Fractions

A **complex fraction** is a fraction in which the numerator or the denominator or both have a fraction as a term.

You can simplify complex fractions by dividing.

$$\frac{\frac{19}{9}}{\frac{2}{3}} = \frac{19}{9} \div \frac{2}{3}$$

Divide. $\quad \frac{19}{9} \div \frac{2}{3} = \frac{19}{\cancel{9}} \times \frac{\cancel{3}}{2} = \frac{19}{6} = 3\frac{1}{6}$

Sometimes you have to simplify the numerator or the denominator or both first.

$$\frac{2\frac{2}{3} + \frac{1}{6}}{\frac{1}{2} + \frac{1}{3}} = \frac{\frac{8}{3} + \frac{1}{6}}{\frac{1}{2} + \frac{1}{3}} = \frac{\frac{16}{6} + \frac{1}{6}}{\frac{3}{6} + \frac{2}{6}} = \frac{\frac{17}{6}}{\frac{5}{6}} =$$

$$\frac{17}{6} \div \frac{5}{6} = \frac{17}{\cancel{6}} \times \frac{\cancel{6}}{5} = \frac{17}{5} = 3\frac{2}{5}$$

Simplify.

1. $\dfrac{\frac{1}{4}}{\frac{1}{6}}$ $1\frac{1}{2}$

2. $\dfrac{\frac{2}{3}}{\frac{1}{3}}$ 2

3. $\dfrac{\frac{8}{9}}{\frac{1}{3}}$ $2\frac{2}{3}$

4. $\dfrac{\frac{4}{5}}{\frac{1}{2}}$ $1\frac{3}{5}$

5. $\dfrac{\frac{1}{5}}{\frac{6}{7}}$ $\frac{7}{30}$

6. $\dfrac{\frac{4}{7}}{\frac{3}{8}}$ $1\frac{11}{21}$

7. $\dfrac{\frac{1}{9}}{\frac{7}{8}}$ $\frac{8}{63}$

8. $\dfrac{\frac{2}{5}}{\frac{9}{10}}$ $\frac{4}{9}$

9. $\dfrac{\frac{1}{3}}{3}$ $\frac{1}{9}$

10. $\dfrac{\frac{1}{3}}{9}$ $\frac{1}{27}$

11. $\dfrac{\frac{1}{4}}{2}$ $\frac{1}{8}$

12. $\dfrac{\frac{1}{3}}{2}$ $\frac{1}{6}$

13. $\dfrac{\frac{1}{4}}{6}$ $\frac{1}{24}$

14. $\dfrac{\frac{6}{7}}{3}$ $\frac{2}{7}$

15. $\dfrac{\frac{5}{6}}{2}$ $\frac{5}{12}$

16. $\dfrac{\frac{1}{9}}{3}$ $\frac{1}{27}$

17. $\dfrac{\frac{2}{5} + 1\frac{1}{10}}{\frac{1}{2} + \frac{3}{5}}$ $1\frac{4}{11}$

18. $\dfrac{1\frac{2}{3} - \frac{1}{6}}{\frac{1}{3} + \frac{1}{2}}$ $1\frac{4}{5}$

19. $\dfrac{\frac{1}{2} + 3\frac{3}{5}}{1\frac{3}{20} + \frac{7}{10}}$ $2\frac{8}{37}$

20. $\dfrac{1\frac{1}{3} - \frac{3}{5}}{1\frac{1}{2} + \frac{7}{9}}$ $\frac{66}{205}$

21. $\dfrac{\frac{1}{3} + 3\frac{9}{10}}{\frac{1}{6} - \frac{1}{8}}$ $101\frac{3}{5}$

22. $\dfrac{4\frac{1}{3} + 9\frac{1}{3}}{\frac{1}{2} + 1\frac{1}{4}}$ $7\frac{17}{21}$

23. $\dfrac{1\frac{6}{7} - \frac{1}{4}}{\frac{1}{9} + \frac{3}{4}}$ $1\frac{188}{217}$

24. $\dfrac{3\frac{2}{3} + \frac{4}{9}}{1\frac{4}{5} - \frac{2}{3}}$ $3\frac{32}{51}$

161

Purpose This Enrichment page provides an additional challenge for those students whose work throughout the chapter and on the Chapter Test shows a thorough understanding of the material. Alternatively, you may wish to use these exercises as a supplementary lesson for the entire class.

USING THE PAGE

In introducing this lesson, remind students that every fraction is a division problem. Every complex fraction, therefore, is merely a complex division problem and can be rewritten in simpler form. Tell students to simplify what is above and below the line before dividing the numerator by the denominator. Most student errors occur in the use of reciprocals in division.

Resources
For additional Enrichment activities, see the Teacher's Resource Book.

Objectives: To use BASIC PRINT, LET, and IF...THEN statements in programs that rename fractions as decimals

Warm-Up

Copy the following exercises onto the chalkboard, and have students multiply to find the answers.

$$\frac{2}{3} \times \frac{3}{4} \left(\frac{1}{2}\right) \qquad \frac{1}{10} \times \frac{6}{31} \left(\frac{3}{155}\right)$$

$$\frac{7}{23} \times \frac{2}{3} \left(\frac{14}{69}\right) \qquad \frac{7}{9} \times \frac{4}{5} \left(\frac{28}{45}\right)$$

GETTING STARTED

Begin with students a discussion that centers around the concept of a fraction. Elicit from students when fractions are used to describe amounts in everyday living. (Half a gallon of milk, $\frac{3}{4}$ of a tank of gasoline in the car, recipes that call for fractions of a cup or a tablespoon of ingredients are examples.)

Using the idea of fractions in everyday life, point out that all the examples given are easy to use because they represent amounts that are easy to recognize. One can readily see when something is divided in half, or into eighths, or into quarters. Very often, however, fractions are not easily recognized. It would be difficult to recognize $\frac{17}{209}$ of an amount. Explain to students that, when finding an amount, a fraction often must be renamed as a decimal. Point out that this may be the case when a nonfractional answer is required or when a decimal makes finding the answer easier. An example of this occurs when students are performing computations on a calculator. Multiplying fractional amounts can be a tedious process, although it is less tedious than using pencil and paper. Have students explain the algorithm necessary for multiplying two fractions on a calculator. Elicit from them that when they divide the numerator by the denominator of each fraction, they are renaming the fractions as decimals.

TEACHING THE LESSON

If students have had no previous BASIC experience, it is recommended that this lesson be taught in three class sessions. Students begin this lesson by running a simple program to rename fractions as decimals.

This program illustrates some essential computer concepts. The first is the use of the PRINT statement to echo the programmer's voice when the program is run. By using this statement immediately following the line number, students can have the computer print information statements. Point out to students that the non-

---

TECHNOLOGY

This BASIC program renames fractions as decimals.

```
10 PRINT "TYPE THE NUMERATOR": INPUT N
20 PRINT "TYPE THE DENOMINATOR": INPUT D
30 PRINT N "/" D "=" N/D
```

When you RUN this program, your screen might look like this.
TYPE THE NUMERATOR
? 2
TYPE THE DENOMINATOR
? 5
2/5 = 0.4

1. Add a line to this program to be sure that the denominator is not zero.   25 IF D = 0 THEN GOTO 20

For any two fractions $\frac{a}{b}$ and $\frac{c}{d}$ (where $b \neq 0$ and $d \neq 0$), the product of the fractions is $\frac{a}{b} \cdot \frac{c}{d}$, or $\frac{ac}{bd}$. You can use this program to multiply two fractions.

```
10 PRINT "FIRST NUMERATOR": INPUT A
20 PRINT "FIRST DENOMINATOR": INPUT B
30 PRINT "SECOND NUMERATOR": INPUT C
40 PRINT "SECOND DENOMINATOR": INPUT D
50 LET AC = A * C
60 LET BD = B * D
70 PRINT A "/" B "TIMES" C "/" D "EQUALS" AC "/" BD
```

2. Add two lines to this program to check that the denominators are not zero.

25 IF B = 0 THEN GOTO 20
45 IF D = 0 THEN GOTO 40

3. Show what your screen will look like when you RUN this program and multiply $\frac{5}{6}$ times $\frac{1}{9}$.

```
FIRST NUMERATOR
? 5
FIRST DENOMINATOR
? 6
SECOND NUMERATOR
? 1
SECOND DENOMINATOR
? 9
5/6 TIMES 1/9 EQUALS 5/54
```

---

numerical information in a PRINT statement must be enclosed in quotation marks, as in the instruction "TYPE THE NUMERATOR" on program line 10. Following this PRINT statement, a colon is followed by the opportunity to input a variable for the numerator. Line 20 of the program repeats these concepts, but asks in this case for a denominator. The final line of the program instructs the computer to PRINT the numerator, the fraction bar (appearing in quotation marks because it is nonnumeric), the denominator, the equal sign (in quotation marks), and the quotient of the division of the fraction, a decimal equivalent.

The next section introduces a new program in which two fractions are multiplied. The first four lines call for inputting two fractions, $\frac{A}{B}$ and $\frac{C}{D}$. Lines 50 and 60 instruct the computer to perform the multiplication

first of the numerators and then of the denominators. Line 70 has the compute print the original fractions and their prod uct. The exercise then requires student to add a pair of IF...THEN and GOTC statements to check that the denomina tors are not equal to 0 (a number canno be divided by zero).

You can use a semicolon to help you print two statements directly following each other. Here is a program that uses semicolons.

```
10 LET A = 7
20 PRINT A; " IS EQUAL";
30 PRINT " TO " ; A
```

When you RUN this program, your screen will look like this.

7 IS EQUAL TO 7

In line 20, the semicolon after the A made the value of A and the words IS EQUAL print next to each other on the same line. Semicolons do not affect anything that is inside quotation marks. The semicolon at the end of line 20 causes the material from line 30 to print next to the material from line 20.

Here is the fraction-multiplication program rewritten to contain semicolons.

```
10 PRINT "FIRST NUMERATOR"; : INPUT A
20 PRINT "FIRST DENOMINATOR"; : INPUT B
30 PRINT "SECOND NUMERATOR"; : INPUT C
40 PRINT "SECOND DENOMINATOR"; : INPUT D
50 LET AC = A * C
60 LET BD = B * D
70 PRINT A; "/";B; "TIMES"; C; "/";D; "EQUALS"; AC; "/"; BD
```

Notice the semicolon in line 10. It made the question mark from the INPUT statement print right after FIRST NUMERATOR.

4. Write a program to find the sum of two fractions. The expression for the sum of two fractions $\frac{a}{b}$ and $\frac{c}{d}$ is $\frac{ad + bc}{bd}$. Remember to check the denominators to be sure that neither one is zero.

```
10  PRINT "FIRST NUMERATOR"; : INPUT A       60  IF D = 0 THEN GOTO 50
20  PRINT "FIRST DENOMINATOR"; : INPUT B     70  LET AD = A * D
30  IF B = 0 THEN GOTO 20                     80  LET BC = B * C
40  PRINT "SECOND NUMERATOR"; : INPUT C       90  LET BD = B * D
50  PRINT "SECOND DENOMINATOR"; : INPUT D    100  LET N = AD + BC
                                             110  PRINT A; "/"; B; "PLUS"; C; "/";
                                                  D; "EQUALS"; N; "/"; BD
```

163

FOLLOW-UP ACTIVITIES

COMPUTER

Materials: computers with disk drives, formatted floppy disks

Have students identify the parts of the computer. (monitor, keyboard, computer, disk drive) Point out that not all computers are in this configuration. Some have all the components as one unit or the monitor and the disk drive together. Explain that once a BASIC program has been entered into the computer, it is in the computer's memory. When the computer is turned off, or you type NEW, the program is cleared from memory. Show the class a floppy disk. Explain that a disk allows you to save a program or data for future use.

Information is stored magnetically on a disk in much the same way that sound is stored on a cassette tape. Before you can use a new disk, it must be formatted or initialized. (Check your computer manual to find out how this is done.) Programs may be saved on a disk by typing the system command SAVE and a name for the program. (This is the procedure for the Apple computer. Please refer to your computer manual to find out how to save a program on a disk.) Have students perform the following exercise at the computer.

1. Insert an initialized disk into the disk drive, and close the door.
2. Type a simple BASIC program into the computer.
3. Type SAVE (space) and a name for the program.
4. Type CATALOG. (This command may differ on other computers.) Check to find out whether your program name appears on the list.
5. Type NEW.
6. Type LIST.
7. Type LOAD and the name of your program.
8. Type LIST.
9. Type RUN.

Elicit from students where the program is after each stage of the exercise. (2. computer; 3. computer and disk; 4. computer and disk; 5. disk; 6. disk; 7. computer and disk; 8. computer and disk)

On page 163, students are shown that by including a semicolon, statements can be made to print immediately following each other on the same line. Be sure students understand that a semicolon does not affect anything that is enclosed by quotation marks. Following the modified fraction-multiplication program, students are asked to write their own fraction-addition program that includes semicolons. While students may not actually run these programs, be sure they have checked each program carefully to correct any bugs that may prevent a program from running.

Purpose This Cumulative Review page provides an opportunity to reinforce students' understanding of the concepts and skills taught in previous chapters.

The chart below is designed to aid you in reviewing the material by specifying the pages on which various concepts and skills were taught.

Item	Page
1	80–81
2	82–83
3	82–83
4	90–91
5	84–85
6	94–95
7	56–57
8	58–59
9	64–65
10	60–61
11	66–67
12	22–23
13	110–111
14	110–111

Each Cumulative Review gives students an opportunity to practice taking tests that are written in a multiple-choice, standardized format. Be sure that students understand that if the correct answer is not among the first three given, then they should select the fourth choice—"not given"—as the correct answer. At least one item per test will require students to give this response.

CUMULATIVE REVIEW

Write the letter of the correct answer.

1. Which number is divisible by 9?

a. 291   b. 837
c. 982   d. not given

2. What is the square root of 81?

a. 9   b. 17
c. 27   d. not given

3. Evaluate 7^4.

a. 53   b. 343
c. 2,401   d. not given

4. What is the prime factorization of 54?

a. $3^3 \times 2$ b. $3^2 \times 2^3$
c. 34   d. not given

5. What is the standard number for 6.75×10^5?

a. 0.00675   b. 675,000
c. 6,750,000   d. not given

6. What is the LCM of 3, 16, and 24?

a. 24   b. 64
c. 48   d. not given

7. $106.02 \times 1,000$

a. 0.10602   b. 10,602
c. 106,020   d. not given

8. Estimate 24.72×0.49.

a. 8   b. 10
c. 12^+ d. 20^+

9. $712.38 \div 62$

a. 1,149   b. 11.49
c. 114.8   d. not given

10. 0.703×0.04

a. 0.002802   b. 0.02812
c. 0.2812   d. not given

11. $0.718116 \div 0.042$

a. 17.098   b. 17.98
c. 170.98   d. not given

12. Round to the nearest hundredth and subtract: $62.84572 - 3.99398$.

a. 58.8   b. 58.84
c. 58.86   d. not given

13. By walking 9 km, Max walked 3 km less than four times as far as Joe. Write an equation and solve to find how far Joe walked.

a. $1\frac{1}{2}$ km   b. 3 km
c. 24 km   d. not given

14. Selina collected 240 cans and bottles to return to the collection center. She had 10 more cans than bottles. Write an equation and solve to find how many cans she had.

a. 110   b. 115
c. 230   d. not given

164

CHAPTER  OVERVIEW

MEASUREMENT

SUMMARY

Chapter 5 deals with metric and customary units of measure, with time, and with temperature in the Celsius and Fahrenheit scales. Included are lessons about estimating by choosing the best unit, choosing the best measure, and about changing between units and denominate numbers.

LESSON SEQUENCE

PROFESSIONAL BACKGROUND

Studies indicate that real measurement is abandoned too early to suit the need of many students. It is not surprising, then, that researchers who interpreted the results of the Second National Assessment of Educational Progress concluded that students' performance on more advanced topics such as perimeter, area, and volume were among the least understood of the content areas in the assessment.

Although students are familiar with measurement, their knowledge tends to be superficial. From the beginning, they should be measuring actual objects for their length, volume, mass, capacity, or temperature. Have students continue to use a variety of units and different measurement systems to measure each object. Measurements should be rewritten in other units within the same system. Also ask students to use various scales and to find scale measurements, and thus give them experience in the multiplication or division of whole numbers, fractions, and decimals.

Finally, provide students with ample and regular practice in the estimation of measurement. Research analysis shows that the most effective activities involve either giving students an object and asking them to estimate its measurement, or giving them a measurement and asking them to suggest an object for which that measurement would be a reasonable estimate.

References: See Bright; Carpenter et al.; and Hart.

MATERIALS

cardboard strips
drinking straws
string
tape measures
metric rulers
centimeter-square graph paper
index cards
1-liter containers
sand and beans
gram cubes
red Cuisinaire rods
pebbles
small plastic bags
pan balances
10 cm × 10 cm × 10 cm clear plastic cubes
1 cm^3 wood cubes
measuring beakers
water
centimeter cubes
newspapers, magazines
health education books
boxes
plastic foam
spring scale
micrometer
laboratory balance
thermometer
Sartorius balance
graduated cylinder
pH meter
clock face with hour hand
airline schedules

VOCABULARY

meter, kilometer, hectometer, dekameter, decimeter, centimeter, millimeter (p. 166)
liter (p. 168)
mass (p. 170)
capacity (p. 170)
cubic centimeter (p. 170)
volume (p. 170)
customary units (p. 174)
precision (p. 180)
greatest possible error (p. 180)
elapsed time (p. 182)
time zones (p. 186)
Fahrenheit/Celsius (p. 188)

ABOUT THE CHAPTER

The use of metric units of measure is becoming more popular in this country. They are the most common units of measure in the rest of the world. It is important that students learn both the customary and metric units of measurement taught in this chapter. There is a lesson in this chapter in which students are given the opportunity, in a real-life problem-solving situation, to work cooperatively.

In Chapter Five, students learn about metric and customary units of length, mass (weight), capacity, and volume. Students also learn about precision and greatest possible error. Other lessons focus on time and on Celsius and Fahrenheit temperature.

To help students understand the metric system, build on the similarity between the structure of this system and the structure of our place-value number system. Students should be familiar with the metric prefixes and their numerical meanings. Students should be aware of how easy it is to rename metric units.

This chapter offers many opportunities for active student involvement. Do not hesitate to give students actual measuring tasks, particularly involving length, capacity, and mass.

Estimation may be more useful in measurement than in any other area of mathematics. After all, many of our everyday measurement activities involve estimates rather than precise measurements. Students should be able to present reasonable estimates of length, area, capacity, mass, and temperature. We recommend this general strategy for teaching measurement lessons. First ask students to write an estimate of the measurement. Then ask students to determine the actual measurement. Finally, have students compare their estimates with the actual measures. This procedure should result in more accurate estimates and more precise measurements.

Calculators can be used effectively to rename metric measurements and customary measurements.

Problem-solving lessons show students how to determine which question the problem is asking, and how to use the distance formula $d = rt$ to solve problems. Other lessons show students how to find information from a road map, and give students an opportunity to choose the strategy or method needed to solve a problem.

The Group Project actively involves students, and asks them to design a futuristic car while remaining within a price limit. Students have many opportunities to use their calculators and their imaginations as they design the car.

The Enrichment lesson introduces the concept of significant digits and accuracy. The lesson builds on the content of this chapter to develop this important distinction between precision and accuracy.

USING THE CHAPTER OPENER

Each Chapter Opener presents situational problem-solving activities that can be used to motivate the skills taught throughout the chapter. The work sheets can be used by individuals, small groups, or the whole class, depending on the needs of the class. Some students might be ready to use the Chapter Opener at the beginning of the chapter; others might first need to develop the skills taught in the chapter.

Students should be encouraged to use the calculator when appropriate. The Chapter Opener focuses on a nonalgorithmic approach to real-life situations relevant to students' experiences. Through an interdisciplinary approach, the Chapter Opener helps students to explore the relationship between mathematics, other areas of the curriculum, and everyday life while developing different strands of mathematics.

In the Chapter Opener activities, students make tables. They will also become familiar with the factors involved in choosing and buying an automobile and the methods for researching those factors.

PROBLEM SOLVING

Learning to ask the right questions in real-life situations is the goal of the lesson Choosing/Writing a Sensible Question. The approach in *Mathematics Unlimited* is to set up a situation or event and to then have students formulate questions that must be asked to plan the event and make it a success. In order to augment the comprehensiveness of the questions asked, have students speculate about the possible results if certain questions are not asked. Encourage students to think not only about the general situation as presented but also about specific problems that must be handled.

Although the Choosing the Strategy or Method lessons in *Mathematics Unlimited* exercise the problem-solving skills learned to that point, they do more than provide practice. To solve the problems in the lesson, students must first determine which problem-solving strategy to apply, and then apply it correctly. Because more than one strategy can often be applied to each problem, the lesson is ideal for small-group work. Working in groups, students can share ideas and brainstorm—two useful techniques that keep students from getting stuck.

The Using a Formula lesson introduces the formula $d = rt$, or distance = rate × time. Although most problems involving formulas can be solved with a close reading, suggest that students memorize this formula because they are likely to encounter it at some later point. Have students identify what number in each problem will be substituted for each letter in the formula. The ability to solve for each term in a formula can ease computations that could otherwise prove difficult for the students.

Obtaining information from an outside source is a skill necessary for solving math problems as well as for addressing real-life problems. In addition to its general aim of teaching students how to use data not included in the text of the problem, the lesson To Use Information from a Road Map in this chapter discusses the organization and labeling of data on road maps and instructs students in methods of obtaining needed information from such maps. This lesson lends itself to small-group work. By encouraging the noncritical, idea-gathering technique of brainstorming, you can help students recognize that there is usually more than one way to solve any problem.

BULLETIN BOARD

"Time Travel"

Materials: poster-board strip for lettering; map of the United States, including time zones; 2 envelopes; index cards; felt-tip pen

Preparation: Display map of the United States on the board and attach title above it as shown. Label and attach two envelopes at bottom of board, one to contain elapsed time problems and the other to hold time zone problems. Write problems on index cards about elapsed time, such as "A college student drove from San Diego to Seattle. If he started at 9:00 A.M. and arrived the next day at 1:30 A.M., how long did the trip take?" ($16\frac{1}{2}$ hours). Write answers on back of cards. Place problems in appropriate envelope. Write time zone problems, such as "A couple drove from Chicago to Boston. They left at 3:30 P.M. on Thursday. If the trip took 23 hours, what day and time did they arrive?" (3:30 P.M., Friday). Write answers on back of cards and place in appropriate envelope.

After pp. 182-183: Have students select problems from the Elapsed Time envelope and solve them, checking their answers on the back of cards.

After pp. 186-187: Have students select problems from the Time Zones envelope, solve them, and check their answers.

COMMON ERRORS

Students sometimes have difficulty understanding precision and accuracy. The terms seem nearly synonymous to many students, and they easily confuse the mathematical meaning of each. It seems natural to students that it means the same thing to say that a measurement is *accurate* to the nearest meter, or *precise* to the nearest meter.

To remediate this error, explain that precision and accuracy have distinct mathematical meanings. Accuracy tells the number of significant digits. For example, if 260 m is accurate to the nearest 10 m, there are 2 significant digits; if 260 m is accurate to the nearest meter, there are 3 significant digits, and the measurement is more accurate.

Precision gives the amount of possible error in a measurement. Be sure students understand that a measure is precise to $\frac{1}{2}$ the unit in which it is stated. For example, if 260 meters is accurate to the nearest 10 meters, then the precision is 5 meters. Explain that this means the exact measurement is within 5 meters of the stated measurement, either more or less.

SPECIAL NEEDS

A major area of difficulty in this chapter is understanding the differences between volume, capacity, and mass. To help students overcome this difficulty, provide hands-on experiences. Provide rectangular prisms, rounded containers, centimeter cubes, unifix cubes, sand, and water for student use. Before measuring, have students make a chart with the headings *Volume, Capacity,* and *Mass* listed across the top and the names of the measuring containers listed down one side. Guide students to find the number of basic units (cubes) it would take to fill each container, and have them list these findings in the *Volume* column. Make sure that they include the appropriate units. Have students continue to use manipulatives, and complete the chart. The concept of time (as opposed to telling time) may also cause problems for some students. Provide numerous realistic situations ("School dismisses at 2:45 P.M. today, and you need to be back for practice in 1 hour 15 minutes. At what time should you return?") to practice this concept. Help students learn to budget their time.

Have interested students research the evolution of weights and measures. They may be surprised to find that many common units are derived from earlier practices and implementations. Have them write a very short play to present their findings.

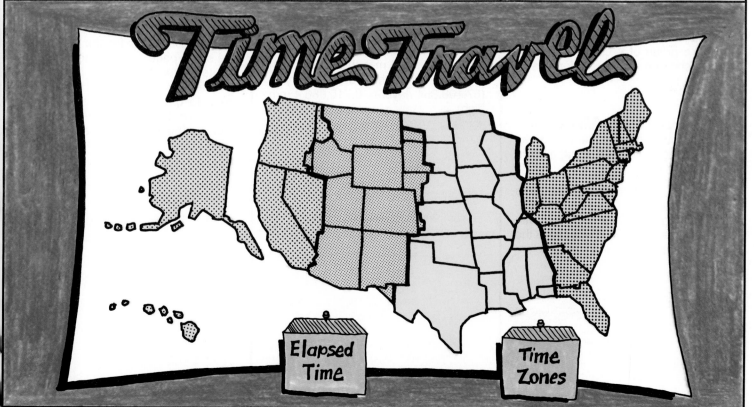

MATH LABS

 NUMBER SENSE (Estimation)
Materials: rulers

Have students work in pairs to prepare a list of 10 objects that are available in the classroom, then have them take turns estimating the length of each object in yards, feet, or inches. They can measure the objects to check their estimates and then record the differences between the estimates and the measured lengths.

PUZZLES AND GAMES
Materials: student-made set of 40 index cards, 10 with lengths in meters, 10 with equivalent lengths in centimeters, 10 with equivalent lengths in kilometers, 10 with equivalent lengths in millimeters.

Students work in groups of 3–4, place the cards facedown on a table in a 4 × 10 array and take turns turning 2 cards faceup to see if the lengths are equivalent. When the two lengths are equivalent, the cards are removed from the array and kept by the student. When they are not equivalent, the cards are turned facedown in their original places.

Students continue until all the cards are matched. The winner is the student with the most cards.

Students also can be given seven cards each. The remaining cards are put in a pile facedown in the center of the table. Students try to get a group of 3 and a group of 4 cards, with each group showing equivalent lengths in different units.

PUZZLES AND GAMES
Materials: 24 student-prepared index cards, each with a capacity in cm^3, kL, or m^3

Working in pairs, students take turns picking a card and then giving the possible dimensions of a container with the given capacity. Students check the reasonableness of each other's answers.

CALCULATOR

Effective use of measurement requires a thorough understanding of the terms and principles involved. The calculator cannot manipulate the ideas and concepts. However, measurement applications usually involve computations. These computations can be performed on a calculator; for example, the computing of units of measurement—length, capacity, and mass—in metrical terms; or length, capacity, and weight in customary measures. Because many of these computations are tedious or time consuming, the use of a calculator is helpful.

Students should have calculators available for all problem-solving activities.

Additional Activities: **Drill and Practice:** Suppose 4.3 and 9.2 have been rounded to the nearest tenth. Before rounding, 4.3 could have been as small as 4.25 or as large as 4.34; 9.2 could have been as small as 9.15 or as large as 9.24. What is the error range for 4.3 × 9.2? (4.25 × 9.15, 4.34 × 9.24) If 3.8 and 7.5 have been rounded to the nearest tenth, what is the error range for 3.8 × 7.5?

Exploration: Suppose you fold a piece of paper in half, making two layers. Fold it again, making four layers. Continue the process. How many layers will there be after 26 folds? If the paper is 0.1 mm thick, how high is the stack? Is this possible? Try it. (67,108,864 layers; 6,710,886.4 mm high)

SUBJECT AREA CONNECTIONS

These Subject Area Connections are useful for reinforcing the concepts presented in this chapter.

p. 171-Science: Students find the densities of various substances on a list, given the mass and volume of each, and the formula for density. ($D = MV$)

p. 175-Library Skills: Students research the origins and measures of a digit, a span, a cubit, and a fathom.

p. 177-Health: Students adapt recipes taken from magazines and newspapers to plan lunch menus large enough for their class. Adapted recipes include the lowest price per unit and total cost.

p. 181-Science: Students find relative precision of equipment that is used in the school science department.

p. 187-Science: Students use the scientific concept of *local noon* to find the exact longitude of their town.

PLAN AHEAD

You will need to supply 1,000 cm^3 clear plastic cubes, 1 cm^3 wood cubes, pan balances, measuring beakers, and water for the activity on T.E. p. 170. You will need to prepare for Remediation on T.E. p. 176 and supply calculators for the activity on the same page. You will need to supply items from the science department for the activity on T.E. p. 181. You will need to prepare index cards for the activity on T.E. p. 183. The activity on T.E. p. 189 will require a computer.

PLANNING CALENDAR

Pages	Lesson Objectives	ASSIGNMENT GUIDE			Class/ Home	More Practice	Math Reasoning	Follow-up	Reteach	Practice	Enrich
		Basic	Average	Extended							
165	Chapter Opener (Use MMW 9,10)	165	165	165							
166,167	To express length in metric units	1-6,7-25o,28,NS	2-6,8-26e,28-29, NS	4-6,8-26e,27-30, NS	H66		H215	NS MNP	49	66	64
168,169	To express capacity and mass using metric units	1-4,5-21o,23-35o, 38	1-39o,40	6-36e,37-41,Chlg	H67		H215	MNP NS	50	67	65
170,171	To explore relationships among metric units of volume, capacity, and mass	170,171	170,171	170,171	H68	H199		MC	51	68	66
172,173	To choose/write a sensible question	1-4	2-6	3-8	H69			PS CALC		69	67
174,175	To express length in customary units	1-4,5-27o,32-36, NS	2-30e,32-37,NS	5-27o,29-37,NS	H70	H200	H215	MC RFM	52	70	68
176,177	To express capacity and weight using customary units	1-19o,24-30,MCR	2-22e,24-30, MCR	8-20e,21-31,MCR	H71	H200		MC MNP	53	71	69
178,179	To practice choosing and using methods and strategies for solving problems	1-9	2-16e	1-15o,16	H72 H73			CALC CALC		72-73	
180,181	To explore precision and determine greatest possible error	180,181	180,181	180,181	H74	H200		MC MNP	54	74	70
182,183	To understand the relationship between units of time and to calculate elapsed time	1-6,8-28e,Chlg	1-6,9-27o,28, Chlg	2-20e,22-28,Chlg	H75		H216	MNP RFM	55	75	71
184,185	To use a formula ($d = rt$) in problem solving	1-5	3-8	5-10	H76			PS CALC		76	72
186,187	To determine time across time zones	1-12,13-27o	1-12,14-26e,27	4-16e,17-29,Chlg	H77		H216	MC MC	56	77	73
188,189	To measure temperature using both the Fahrenheit and Celsius scales	1-15,18,AL	4-19,AL	4-19,AL	H78		H216	MNP CMP	57	78	74
190,191	To use information from a road map to solve problems	1-6,10	1-4,8-10	4-10	H79			PS CALC		79	75
192	Calculator: To compare, add, and subtract distances	192	192	192							
193	Group Project: To choose among options; to stay within a budget	193	193	193							

194,195	Chapter Test
196	Reteaching
197	Enrichment
198	Cumulative Review

ABBREVIATION KEY

Teacher's Resource Book	Follow-up Activities	MC—Math Connection
MMW—Making Math Work	CALC—Calculator	MCM—Math Communication
P—Practice	CMP—Computer	NS—Number Sense
R—Reteach	P&G—Puzzles and Games	PS—Problem Solving
E—Enrich	MNP—Manipulatives	RFM—Reinforcement

SOFTWARE
Mathematics Unlimited Problem-Solving Software
Strategies: Problem-Solving

TESTS

A. To choose the appropriate metric or customary unit of length, mass, or capacity

B. To change between measures of length, mass, volume, or capacity in the metric and customary systems

C. To add and subtract with regrouping in the customary system

D. To find temperature changes (Fahrenheit and Celsius)

E. To add, subtract, or change between units of time

F. To find elapsed time across time zones

G. To formulate sensible questions

H. To use the formula $d = rt$ to solve problems

I. To use information from a road map to solve problems

FAMILY INVOLVEMENT

Family Involvement for Chapter 5 encourages family members to plan and prepare an evening meal. They are to choose an appetizer or soup, a main course, and dessert from a cookbook. Students and their families are to decide how many servings and how much of each ingredient will be needed. A chart has been provided for family members to use in recording the various amounts needed in the recipe. Family members then calculate the increase in the amount of each ingredient needed in order to make enough dinner for the family and two friends.

Additional activities might include an examination of the contents of the refrigerator. Have family members record the total quantity of all the liquid items and the total weight of all the solid items in the refrigerator. Family members should be encouraged to create a chart on which to record the measurements taken in customary units as well as in metric units. To complete the chart, they will have to convert customary units to metric units and vice versa depending on the original unit of measurement.

STUDENT RESOURCES

Bibliography

Griesbach, Ellen and Taylor, Jerry. *The Prentice-Hall Encyclopedia of Mathematics.* Englewood Cliffs, New Jersey: Prentice-Hall, Inc., 1982.

Knudson, Richard L. *Restoring Yesterday's Cars.* Minneapolis: Lerner Publications Co., 1983.

Waitley, Douglas. *The Roads We Traveled: An Amusing History of the Automobile.* New York: Julian Messner, a division of Simon & Schuster, Inc., 1979.

Films

Meters, Liters, and Kilograms. 23 minutes. Color. 1974. Distributed by Perennial Education, Inc., Highland Park, Ill.

Pretest

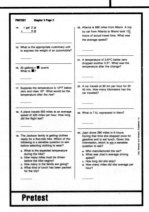

Pretest

Suppose you had a driver's license, and you wanted to buy a car. Which factors would you consider in choosing a car? Which car would you choose, and why would you choose it?

5 MEASUREMENT

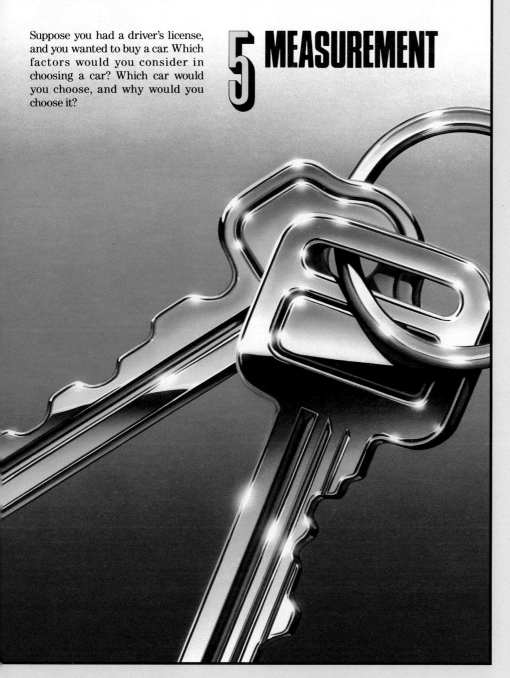

Objective: To explore problems related to automobiles

Direct students to look at the picture of car keys. Ask them whether any of their families have recently purchased new cars. If so, discuss the cars they bought and the reasons they had for buying them.

SMALL GROUP
Statistics and Probability
Materials: Making Math Work page 9 per student, automotive magazines

Have each student in the group choose a car he or she likes and research information such as its fuel consumption, its repair record, and details about its appearance. Have students rate the information obtained for each car by comparing it to information available about other cars on the market. Suggest that they use automotive magazines to research this information. Then have students use this information to calculate the cost of maintaining these cars for one year. Suggest that students call or visit a local service station to find the approximate cost of each of the services listed on page 9. After they have done so, have groups compare cars they selected to those selected by other groups in the class. Which car received the best overall rating? Which cars required the lowest maintenance costs?

INDIVIDUAL
Number
Materials: Making Math Work page 10 per student, automotive magazines

Have each student complete Making Math Work page 10. Tell students to assume that the price information given is for the cars they choose and ask them to choose which options they would like to have and can afford. Discuss the second part of the page with students. Ask them why the value of most cars depreciates and why the value of a few cars does not. Suggest that after a given period (say, 20 years), the value of a well-maintained car begins to appreciate. Discuss the reasons for this, and ask what a 50-year-old restored car might be worth compared to its original value.

WHOLE CLASS
Logic
Discuss with students the purchase of a car and all the factors that must be taken into consideration. Write a list on the chalkboard of the things most people want a car to contain. Do they want small cars or large cars? Do they want sports cars or family cars? How much can they spend?

Warm-Up

Have students do the following computations mentally.

$2.3 \times 100 \ (230)$ $0.805 \times 1,000 \ (805)$

$\dfrac{4.54}{10} \ (0.454)$ $\dfrac{75.9}{1,000} \ (0.0759)$

GETTING STARTED

Materials: 2 or more of each of the following, precut in various lengths: cardboard strips, drinking straws, string, chalk, erasers, pencils, and rubber bands

Have students measure the length of their desks with one of the materials. Discuss the relative merits of measuring with the different materials.

Point out that all units of measure should be both accurate and easy to duplicate. Those that change their shape (rubber bands) or size (chalk) with use are of little value.

TEACHING THE LESSON

A. A meter is slightly longer than a yard. Each prefix added to the word meter changes its meaning.

milli- means "thousandth" ($\frac{1}{1,000}$).
centi- means "hundredth" ($\frac{1}{100}$).
deci- means "tenth" ($\frac{1}{10}$).
deka- means "ten" (10).
hecto- means "hundred" (100).
kilo- means "thousand" (1,000).

B. Point out that when renaming a larger unit with a smaller unit, you move from left to right on the chart and move the decimal point from left to right the number of places moved on the chart; when renaming a smaller unit with a larger unit, move from right to left.

Checkpoint

The chart lists the common errors students make in estimating and renaming linear measures.

Correct Answers: 1b, 2b

Remediation

■ Help students become familiar with metric units of length by relating units to the lengths of their arms and legs.

○ For this error, assign the Manipulative Follow-Up Activity.

□ For these errors, assign Reteach Master, p. 49.

Metric Units of Length

A. The **meter (m)** is the basic metric unit of length. All other units are related to the meter.

kilometer	hectometer	dekameter	meter	decimeter	centimeter	millimeter
km	hm	dam	m	dm	cm	mm
1,000 m	100 m	10 m	1 m	0.1 m	0.01 m	0.001 m

The width of a car door is about 1 m.

The thickness of a seat belt is about 1 mm.

To the nearest centimeter, the car key is 6 cm long.

To the nearest millimeter, the car key is 59 mm long.

B. The metric system is based on powers of 10.

To rename a larger unit with a smaller unit, multiply.

$5 \text{ km} = \blacksquare \text{ m}$ $0.06 \text{ m} = \blacksquare \text{ cm}$
$5 \times 1,000 = 5,000$ $0.06 \times 100 = 6$
$5 \text{ km} = 5,000 \text{ m}$ $0.06 \text{ m} = 6 \text{ cm}$

To rename a smaller unit with a larger unit, divide.

$300 \text{ cm} = \blacksquare \text{ m}$ $37 \text{ m} = \blacksquare \text{ km}$
$300 \div 100 = 3$ $37 \div 1,000 = 0.037$
$300 \text{ cm} = 3 \text{ m}$ $37 \text{ m} = 0.037 \text{ km}$

Checkpoint Write the letter of the correct answer.

1. Choose the best measure for the length of a gas pedal.

a. 20 mm **(b.)** 20 cm
c. 200 cm **d.** 20 m

2. Choose the missing number.
$9 \text{ cm} = \blacksquare \text{ mm}$

a. 0.9 **(b.)** 90
c. 900 **d.** 9,000

166 Math Reasoning, page H215

COMMON ERRORS

Answer Choice	Type of Error
■ 1a, 1c, 1d	Confuses units of length
○ 2a	Moves decimal point in wrong direction
□ 2c, 2d	Moves decimal point too far in correct direction

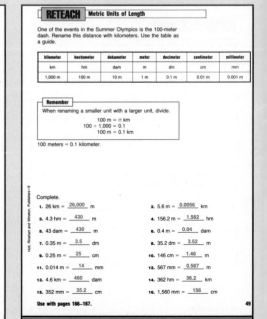

RETEACH Metric Units of Length

One of the events in the Summer Olympics is the 100-meter dash. Rename this distance with kilometers. Use the table as a guide.

kilometer	hectometer	dekameter	meter	decimeter	centimeter	millimeter
km	hm	dam	m	dm	cm	mm
1,000 m	100 m	10 m	1 m	0.1 m	0.01 m	0.001 m

Remember

When renaming a smaller unit with a larger unit, divide.

$100 \text{ m} = \blacksquare \text{ km}$
$100 \div 1,000 = 0.1$
$100 \text{ m} = 0.1 \text{ km}$

100 meters = 0.1 kilometer.

Complete.

1. $26 \text{ km} = \underline{26,000} \text{ m}$ 2. $5.6 \text{ m} = \underline{0.0056} \text{ km}$
3. $4.3 \text{ hm} = \underline{430} \text{ m}$ 4. $156.2 \text{ m} = \underline{1.562} \text{ hm}$
5. $43 \text{ dam} = \underline{430} \text{ m}$ 6. $0.4 \text{ m} = \underline{0.04} \text{ dam}$
7. $0.35 \text{ m} = \underline{3.5} \text{ dm}$ 8. $35.2 \text{ dm} = \underline{3.52} \text{ m}$
9. $0.25 \text{ m} = \underline{25} \text{ cm}$ 10. $146 \text{ cm} = \underline{1.46} \text{ m}$
11. $0.014 \text{ m} = \underline{14} \text{ mm}$ 12. $567 \text{ mm} = \underline{0.567} \text{ m}$
13. $4.6 \text{ m} = \underline{460} \text{ dam}$ 14. $362 \text{ hm} = \underline{36.2} \text{ km}$
15. $352 \text{ mm} = \underline{35.2} \text{ cm}$ 16. $1,560 \text{ mm} = \underline{156} \text{ cm}$

Use with pages 166–167. 49

Reteach Worksheet

Write the unit used to measure

1. distance on a map   cm or km

2. the distance between cities.   km

3. the length of a car.   m

4. the width of a tire.   cm

Choose the best estimate. Write the letter of the correct answer.

5. the length of a windshield wiper

a. 35 mm   **b.** 35 cm   **c.** 35 m

6. the diameter of a headlight

a. 0.15 km   **b.** 1.5 m   **c.** 15 cm

Complete.

7. 26 km = ▆ m   26,000

8. 60 cm = ▆ mm   600

9. 7 m = ▆ cm
700

10. 13 m = ▆ cm   1,300

11. 2 m = ▆ mm   2,000

12. 5 km = ▆ m
5,000

13. 8,000 cm = ▆ mm   80,000

14. 72 cm = ▆ mm   720

15. 9 m = ▆ cm
900

16. 4,000 m = ▆ km   4

17. 2,000 cm = ▆ m   20

18. 5,000 mm = ▆ cm
500

19. 7,600 m = ▆ km   7.6

20. 200 m = ▆ km   0.2

21. 1,500 mm = ▆ m
1.5

22. 1.9 m = ▆ cm   190

23. 0.6 m = ▆ cm   60

24. 3.5 km = ▆ m
3,500

25. 7 mm = ▆ m   0.007

★**26.** 0.2 dm = ▆ m   0.02

★**27.** 19 dam = ▆ dm
1,900

Solve. For Problem 30, use the Infobank.

28. Car upholstery is sold at the Auto Supply Shop. The clerk has two lengths in blue. One length is 3.04 m long. The other is 189 cm long. Which piece is longer?
the 3.04-m piece

29. The distance between two cities is 743.8 km. If Joyce has driven 408.9 km, how much farther does she need to drive to reach the other city?   334.9 km

30. Use the information on page 475 to solve. The Quiet Achiever, a solar-powered car, arrived in Sydney, Australia, on January 7, 1983, after having crossed the entire continent. How many kilometers is it from Port Augusta to Orange?   1,049 km

NUMBER SENSE

Calculate mentally.

1. 100 cm = ▆ m   1

2. 1 m = ▆ mm
1,000

3. 2,000 m = ▆ km   2

4. 5 m = ▆ cm
500

5. 40 cm = ▆ mm   400

6. 10 km = ▆ m
10,000

7. 4,000 mm = ▆ m   4

8. 1 mm = ▆ m
0.001

ASSIGNMENT GUIDE

Basic: 1–6, 7–25 *o*, 28, NS

Average: 2–6, 8–26 *e*, 28–29, NS

Extended: 4–6, 8–26 *e*, 27–30, NS

Resources
Practice, p. 66   Class/Home, p. H66
Reteach, p. 49   Reasoning, p. H215
Enrich, p. 64

Exercise Analysis

1–4	Select appropriate unit of length
5–6	Estimate metric lengths
7–27	Rename units
28–29	Skill applications
30	Data collection and computation

Number Sense

These exercises provide additional practice in understanding the relationship between metric units.

FOLLOW-UP ACTIVITIES

NUMBER SENSE (Estimation)

Materials: books, pencils, clips, shoes, coins, desks, chair seats, and metric rulers

Have students record their estimation of the metric length of two objects in millimeters, two objects in centimeters, and two objects in decimeters. Then have students use all three metric units to measure and record the length of each object. Discuss the differences between the estimations. Ask if some units were easier than others for estimating and measuring.

MANIPULATIVES

Materials: metric rulers, tape measures, or centimeter-square graph-paper strips, 6 index cards per student with lengths for easily measured classroom objects in millimeters, centimeters, or decimeters

Have students work in groups of two to four, with each student in turn picking a length card and then using a metric measure to find an object in the room that matches the same length. Continue until all cards have been used.

COMING UP

Follow the liter.

Practice Worksheet

Enrich Worksheet

Objectives: To express capacity and mass using metric units

Warm-Up
Have students complete the following.

2.7 m = _____ cm (270)
5.62 km = _____ m (5,620)
35 mm = _____ cm (3.5)
770 mm = _____ hm (0.0077)

GETTING STARTED

Materials: different-shaped 1-liter containers, 1 container labeled *Liter*, sand, water, or beans for pouring

Ask which container has the greatest capacity. Ask who can suggest a way to find the capacity of each container. Volunteers can pour sand, water, or beans to find the capacity of containers. The container labeled *Liter* can be used to identify the common capacity.

TEACHING THE LESSON

A. Remind students that the prefixes learned in the previous lesson may be used here.

30 mL means $\frac{30}{1,000}$ L, or 0.030 L;
6 kL means 6 × 1,000 L, or 6,000 L.

B. The mass of a paper clip is about 1 g. The mass of a nickel is about 5 g. 1 L of water has a mass of 1 kg.

C. Remind students to move the decimal point one place value for each change in unit size, from left to right for a smaller unit and from right to left for a larger unit.

Checkpoint
The chart lists the common errors students make in metric conversions that involve capacity and mass.

Correct Answers: 1c, 2a

Remediation
■ For this error, use the following activity.

■ Materials: pan balance, gram and kilogram masses (or cube-a-grams), classroom objects

Have students use the balance and masses to find the mass of classroom objects. Students should record the mass of each object in one metric unit and rename with the other unit.

○ For this error, assign the Manipulative Follow-Up Activity.

□ For these errors, assign Reteach Master, p. 50.

Metric Units of Capacity and Mass

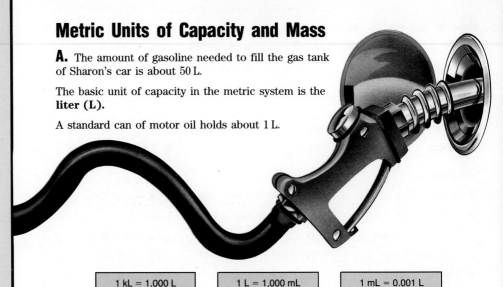

A. The amount of gasoline needed to fill the gas tank of Sharon's car is about 50 L.

The basic unit of capacity in the metric system is the **liter (L).**

A standard can of motor oil holds about 1 L.

1 kL = 1,000 L	1 L = 1,000 mL	1 mL = 0.001 L

B. The **gram (g)** is the basic unit of mass in the metric system.

The mass of a gasoline credit card is about 12 g.

1 kg = 1,000 g	1 g = 1,000 mg	1 mg = 0.001 g

C. To rename one unit of mass or capacity with another unit, multiply or divide by a power of 10.

To rename a larger unit with a smaller unit, multiply.

$$3.8 \text{ kL} = \blacksquare \text{ L}$$
$$3.8 \times 1,000 = 3,800$$
$$3.8 \text{ kL} = 3,800 \text{ L}$$

To rename a smaller unit with a larger unit, divide.

$$500 \text{ g} = \blacksquare \text{ kg}$$
$$500 \div 1,000 = 0.5$$
$$500 \text{ g} = 0.5 \text{ kg}$$

Checkpoint   Write the letter of the correct answer.

1. Choose the best estimate for the mass of an automobile.

a. 175 g   b. 750 kg
c. 1,750 kg   d. 1,750 L

2. Choose the missing number. 80 L = ■ kL

a. 0.08   b. 0.8
c. 8   d. 80

168   Math Reasoning, page H215

COMMON ERRORS

Answer Choice	Type of Error
○ 1a	Confuses units of mass
□ 1b	Chooses correct unit, incorrect number
■ 1d	Chooses wrong unit of measure
■ 2b, 2c	Places decimal point incorrectly
■ 2d	Chooses wrong operation

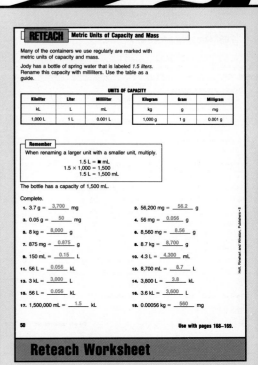

RETEACH Metric Units of Capacity and Mass

Many of the containers we use regularly are marked with metric units of capacity and mass.

Jody has a bottle of spring water that is labeled *1.5 liters*. Rename this capacity with milliliters. Use the table as a guide.

UNITS OF CAPACITY

Kiloliter	Liter	Milliliter		Kilogram	Gram	Milligram
kL	L	mL		kg	g	mg
1,000 L	1 L	0.001 L		1,000 g	1 g	0.001 g

Remember
When renaming a larger unit with a smaller unit, multiply.
1.5 L = ■ mL
1.5 × 1,000 = 1,500
1.5 L = 1,500 mL

The bottle has a capacity of 1,500 mL.

Complete.

1. 3.7 g = _3,700_ mg
2. 56,200 mg = _56.2_ g
3. 0.05 g = _50_ mg
4. 56 mg = _0.056_ g
5. 8 kg = _8,000_ g
6. 8,560 mg = _8.56_ g
7. 875 mg = _0.875_ g
8. 8.7 kg = _8,700_ g
9. 150 mL = _0.15_ L
10. 4.3 L = _4,300_ mL
11. 56 L = _0.056_ kL
12. 8,700 mL = _8.7_ L
13. 3 kL = _3,000_ L
14. 3,800 L = _3.8_ kL
15. 56 L = _0.056_ kL
16. 3.6 kL = _3,600_ L
17. 1,500,000 mL = _1.5_ kL
18. 0.00056 kg = _560_ mg

50   Use with pages 168–169.

Holt, Rinehart and Winston, Publishers • 5

Reteach Worksheet

Write the unit used to measure

1. the mass of a car engine. kg

2. the capacity of a car's gas tank. L

3. the length of the fuel line. cm

4. a drop of motor oil. mL

Complete.

5. 1 kg = ■ g 1,000

6. 2 g = ■ mg 2,000

7. 2 L = ■ mL
2,000

8. 90 mg = ■ g 0.09

9. 350 mL = ■ L 0.35

10. 702 L = ■ kL
0.702

11. 7 mL = ■ L 0.007

12. 7,000 L = ■ kL 7

13. 1,005 g = ■ kg
1.005

14. 16,000 g = ■ kg 16

15. 8,400 mg = ■ g 8.4

16. 5,500 g = ■ kg
5.5

17. 8.2 kg = ■ g 8,200

18. 0.4 L = ■ mL 400

19. 6.5 g = ■ mg
6,500

20. 0.025 kL = ■ mL 25,000

21. 0.0525 kg = ■ g 52.5

★22. 4.5 g = ■ cg
450

Compare. Write >, <, or = for ●.

23. 1 kg ● 100 g >

24. 1 L ● 0.1 kL <

25. 1 mg ● 0.001 g
=

26. 5 kL ● 5,000 L =

27. 800 mL ● 8 L <

28. 9 g ● 900 mg
>

29. 3.2 L ● 3,200 mL =

30. 0.7 kg ● 70 g >

31. 25 mg ● 0.0025 g
>

32. 19 g ● 0.19 kg <

33. 10 L ● 10,000 mL =

34. 89 mL ● 0.89 L
<

35. 0.46 g ● 460 mg =

★36. 0.01 kg ● 100,000 mg <

★37. 0.56 L ● 5.6 cL
>

Solve.

38. When the gas tank of Paul's car is empty, it costs $22.80 to fill it. If gasoline costs $0.38 per liter, how many liters does the tank hold?
60 L

39. The gas tank of Sarah's car holds 50 liters of gasoline. If gasoline costs $0.30 per liter, how much does it cost Sarah to fill the tank?
$15.00

40. Select five foreign cars and compare the mass of each. Which car has the largest mass?
Answers will vary.

★41. Al's car gets 12 km/L of gas. If gas costs $0.35/L, how much will Al spend on gas to drive 60 km?
$1.75

CHALLENGE

Mr. Stanton is cooking dinner. He must sauté vegetables for exactly 7 min, but he has no clock and his watch is broken. He does, however, have two egg timers—one 3-min timer and one 5-min timer. How can he time 7 min? See Answer Key.

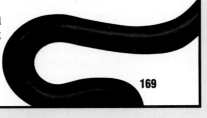

Classwork/Homework, page H67

169

ASSIGNMENT GUIDE

Basic: 1–4, 5–21 o, 23–35 o, 38

Average: 1–39 o, 40

Extended: 6–36 e, 37–41, Chlg

Resources
Practice, p. 67   Class/Home, p. H67
Reteach, p. 50   Reasoning, p. H215
Enrich, p. 65

Exercise Analysis

1–4	Write the appropriate units of measure
5–22	Rename units
23–37	Compare metric units
38–39, 41	Skill applications
40	Data collection

Challenge
This puzzle requires students to use logical reasoning to solve the problem.

FOLLOW-UP ACTIVITIES

MANIPULATIVE
Materials: gram cubes, red cuisin-aire rods, or other 1-g masses, different-sized pebbles, small plastic bags, pan balances (Balances can be made from hanger, string, and two plastic containers or paper plates.)

Have students determine and record the mass of five different-sized pebbles and calculate the number of each type of pebble they would need for a set of mass that measures 1 g, 5 g, 10 g, 100 g, 500 g, or 1 kg. They can put pebbles into plastic bags to make one set of masses with which to measure objects in the classroom. (Pebbles per gram will vary.)

NUMBER SENSE (Mental Math)
Have students complete the following equations without pencil or paper.

500 mL + 0.2 L + 500 mL = _____ L
(1.2)
250 mg + 600 mg + 150 mg = _____ g
(1.0)
1.9 kL + 300 L + 2.1 kL + 700 L = _____ kL (5.0)
80 g + 40 g + 20 g + 60 g = _____ g
(200)
3.3 kg + 5.9 kg − 0.3 kg + 0.1 kg = _____ kg (9.0)

COMING UP
Mass-ive volumes

Warm-Up

Read each metric pair. Have students write <, >, or = for the ●.

25 mm ● 2.5 cm (=)
0.1 kg ● 0.090 g (>)
20 g ● 3,000 mg (>)
788 mL ● 7.88 L (<)
0.65 kL ● 6,500 L (<)
15 dm ● 0.15 dam (=)

GETTING STARTED

Ask students why they think that ice cubes in an ice-cube tray often extend above the edge of the individual cube holder. (because water expands when it freezes) Ask whether any students have ever held the lid of a jar under warm water to make it easier to unscrew. Challenge them to explain why this works. (because heat causes the lid to expand, separating it from the jar)

TEACHING THE LESSON

Materials: 1 cm³ wood cube, 1,000 cm³ plastic cube (open at the top), balance with masses, measuring beaker, water bottle per group of students

Because of the depth of the conceptual development involved, this lesson may be addressed in several class periods. You may want to have students work through the developmental parts of this lesson in groups of four and have a class discussion for Thinking as a Team. Students' balances should have a capacity of at least 1 kg (per pan). If you do not have access to balances of this capacity, have students fill the plastic cube only to the first mark so that they will have 100 cm³ of water with which to find the capacity and the mass.

Make sure that students understand that the volume of the small wooden cube is the amount of space that it occupies. (1 cm³) Using the larger plastic cube, however, students are to find the volume of the *inside* of the container, or the volume of matter that it can hold.

Ask them whether this volume is the same as the volume of the container itself. (no) Point out that students are to find the volume only to the top line, not to the very edge, of the cube. Ask them what methods they used to find the volume of the cube.

Remind students to be careful not to spill any water when they are trying to find the capacity of the plastic cube, for this might affect the reliability of their measurements. Lead students to realize that they can

---

Relating Metric Measures

Within the metric system there are simple relationships among the measures of volume, capacity, and mass. This lesson will help you explore these relationships.

The **volume** of an object is the amount of space it occupies. Volume is measured in cubic units. At the right is a picture of a cube with a volume of 1 cubic centimeter (1 cm³). Each edge of this cube is 1 centimeter (cm) long.

Step 1: Copy the table below. You will complete the table as you work through the rest of this lesson.

CUBES

Edge Length	Volume	Capacity	Mass of Water
1 cm	a. ■ 1 cm³	b. ■ 1 mL	c. ■ 1 g
10 cm	d. ■ 1,000 cm³	e. ■ 1,000 mL	f. ■ 1,000 g
100 cm	g. ■ 1 m³	h. ■ 1,000 L (1 kL)	i. ■ 1,000 kg (1t)

Step 2: Take a large hollow cube that has a 10 cm edge.

- Find the volume of the inside of the cube in cubic centimeters. You might use little cubes of volume 1 cm³ to help you.

- Discuss the method you used with your teammates.

- Record your answer next to letter *d* in the table. Be sure to include the unit of measurement (cm³).

170

---

compensate for the mass of the cube itself by placing an empty cube (or an equal mass) on the other pan or by adjusting the riders that many balances have (they might want to do this before Step 3).

For the Thinking as a Team section, students will complete their tables. Discuss the precision of students' measurements, and ask whether any students got different answers. For question 2, make sure that students realize that because the volume of the small wooden cube is $\frac{1}{1000}$ the volume of the large plastic cube, the capacity of the wooden cube and the mass of water that it could contain are also $\frac{1}{1000}$ that of the plastic cube. For question 3, students should fill out blanks *a, b,* and *c* in the table in order to see the basic unifying relationship of metric measures:
1 cm³→1 mL→1 g of water. For question 4, make sure that students see that the

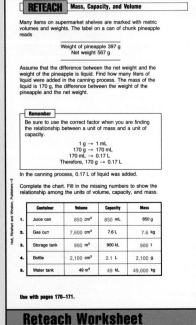

(Continued on p. 171.)

Step 3: Fill a bottle with water, and then use the water to fill your large cube.

- Use a measuring beaker to measure the amount of water in your cube in millimeters.

- Record the capacity of the cube in milliliters (mL) next to the letter *e* in your table.

Step 4: Find the mass of the water in your large cube. Use a scale or balance.

- How did you adjust for the mass of the cube itself?

- Record your answer in grams (g) next to the letter *f* in your table.

> Answers may vary—students could compensate by placing extra weight on the other pan or by adjusting the rider on the balance arm.

Thinking as a Team

Look again at the picture of the cube that has a volume of 1 cm³.

1. How does the volume of this cube compare to the volume of the large cube? Its volume is $\frac{1}{1,000}$th the volume of the large cube.
2. What would be the volume and the mass of the water that would fill the small cube? What is the capacity of the small cube? See table on page 170.
3. Record your answers next to the letters *a*, *b*, and *c* in the table. Be sure to include the units of measurement.
4. Imagine a cube that has edges that are 100 cm long. Fill out the last row of the table. A mass of 1,000 kg is 1 metric ton. See table on page 170.
5. Discuss the relationships among the volume, the capacity, and the mass of water.

> The volume–capacity relationships always hold, but the mass relationship depends on the density of the substance.

6. Do you think that the same relationships hold for other substances such as sand? Experiment.

For additional activities, see ***Connecting Math Ideas***, page 470.

ASSIGNMENT GUIDE

Basic: p. 170, p. 171

Average: p. 170, p. 171

Extended: p. 170, p. 171

Resources
Practice, p. 68   Class/Home, p. H68
Reteach, p. 51   More Practice, p. H199
Enrich, p. 66

volume of the largest cube would be 1,000 times that of the plastic cube. Students should discover the relationship that this reveals: 1 m³→1,000 L (1kL)→1,000 kg (1 t). For question 6, foster a discussion concerning the fact that the relationships for volume and capacity always hold but that the mass of a particular amount of a substance depends on that substance's density (defined as mass per unit volume).

FOLLOW-UP ACTIVITIES

MATH CONNECTION
(Science)

The *density* of a substance is the ratio of its mass to its volume. The standard used is water, with a density of $\frac{1g}{cm^3}$ at 4°C.

Given the formula $D = \frac{M}{V}$, have students find the density of the following.

Mass = 50 g; Volume = 100 cm³
$\left(D = \dfrac{0.5g}{cm^3} \right)$

Mass = 25 g; Volume = 10 cm³
$\left(D = \dfrac{2.5g}{cm^3} \right)$

Mass = 6.6 g; Volume = 30 cm³
$\left(D = \dfrac{0.22g}{cm^3} \right)$

Mass = 100 mg; Volume = 0.1cm³
$\left(D = \dfrac{1.0g}{cm^3} \right)$

COMING UP
It's inching up!

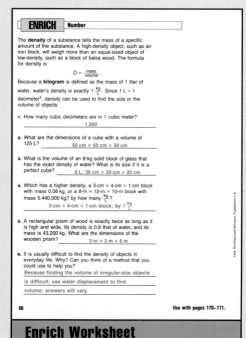

ectives. To choose/write a sensible
question

Warm-Up

To prepare students for this lesson, have
them compute the following.

27 × 6 (162)   38 × 9 (342)
556 ÷ 4 (139)   1,120 ÷ 32 (35)

GETTING STARTED

To incite students to think about how decisions are made, instruct them to draw up a
list of the different things they would like to
do over the coming weekend. Have them
estimate how long each activity or project
will take and draw up a plan listing when
they will do each activity in order to fit all the
activities into the weekend. Then have students discuss the questions they asked
themselves and the information they
needed to formulate their plans.

TEACHING THE LESSON

This lesson deals with formulating appropriate questions for different situations.
There is no actual computation involved.
Guide students through the introductory
page. Students are given a situation and a
general question: How much should they
charge for each copy of their magazine?
They must gather the information necessary to answer this. Choosing the correct
questions to ask is the first step. Note that
on page 172, there are several questions.
Students must decide which of these are
pertinent and which have no bearing on the
situation. In order to do this, students
should ask themselves "Will the answer to
this question bring me any closer to a decision?" If it will, it is a pertinent question.

Questions: This is a good situation for
class discussion. Students will respond
positively to such a situation because there
are no definite answers. Encourage students to look beyond their questions and
answers to the consequences of their actions. Ask them what situations might or
might not develop if certain questions are
not raised. Do not discourage creativity but
focus instead on thoroughness and on
formulating questions to answer specific
problems.

Tools: A good suggestion here is to have
students write lists of information that
might be needed for a certain situation and
to formulate appropriate questions based
on that list. Discuss the brainstorming approach with students.

Solutions: No computation is done in this
lesson.

PROBLEM SOLVING
Choosing/Writing a Sensible Question

Asking the right questions can help you organize
information and make appropriate decisions.

Jake and Becky decided to publish a newsletter that
would feature events and news about cars, trucks, and
tractors. Jake named the newsletter *Motor Mouth*.
They realized that there would be expenses involved in
putting *Motor Mouth* together and in reproducing it.
They had enough money for the first issue. After that,
they hoped the price of each newsletter would cover
its cost of production.

Becky and Jake have to decide on a price per copy for
Motor Mouth. Answering which of these questions will
help them make a decision?

- How much will it cost to reproduce each copy?
  Computing how much it will cost to reproduce each
  copy is important. The price per copy will have to
  be at least as great as that amount.

- How long will it take to write one issue? Because
  the writers, Becky and Jake, do not plan to receive
  salaries, this information will not affect the price.

- What supplies, if any, will they have to buy? It is
  important to determine what supplies they will have
  to buy. Their cost will be part of the cost of
  production.

172

Checks: Have students check for completeness. Ask students, if all the questions
they have listed are answered, whether
their plans for the magazine will be complete.

Read each statement. Then formulate questions that Becky and Jake should answer before making a decision. Answers may vary. Sample questions are given.

1. The owner of Taco Stop asked Becky to publish his advertisements in *Motor Mouth*.

How much money should they charge for advertising space?

2. Ezra offered to write movie reviews for *Motor Mouth* in return for the price of the movie tickets.

Would the added subscription revenue from the movie reviews justify the cost of the tickets?

3. After the first 2 issues, *Motor Mouth* began to receive from 18 to 30 letters per week. Some offered suggestions. Others contained news and other interesting information. Mary suggested that they publish the letters.

Would the added subscription revenue from the letters justify the loss of space for advertising and articles?

4. People began to ask how much it would cost to subscribe to *Motor Mouth* and have issues mailed to their homes.

How much would postage cost?

5. Sara told them about a county fair that features tractor-pulling and mud-bogging events and suggested that they sell *Motor Mouth* there.

Would there be many people at the fair who would want to buy *Motor Mouth*?

6. Becky took some great photographs of the mud-bogging contest for the newsletter. She shot and developed 2 rolls of film.

How much space should they devote to a mud-bogging contest?

7. Both Becky's and Jake's families were planning to go away on vacation for the month of August.

Should they hire someone to put out *Motor Mouth* that month?

★8. After one year, *Motor Mouth* is selling well and has a large list of subscribers. Several people want to join the staff.

How much money would they be able to pay staff members?

Classwork/Homework, page H69

ASSIGNMENT GUIDE

Basic: 1–4

Average: 2–6

Extended: 3–8

Resources
Practice, p. 69   Class/Home, p. H69
Enrich, p. 67

Exercise Analysis
1–8 Formulate questions

FOLLOW-UP ACTIVITIES

PROBLEM SOLVING
Have students plan a class talent show. Discuss what will need to be done to prepare for the project and separate the class into several groups, one group to deal with each aspect of the project. Have each group draft a list of questions that will have to be answered. When all groups have finished, write out their questions on the chalkboard and discuss them with the entire class. Be sure all aspects of the talent show have been planned.

CALCULATOR
Write the following number series on the chalkboard: 816449362516941.

Tell students that there is a pattern to the series. Then separate the class into small groups and have them formulate questions about the series that they could answer to discover the pattern. Encourage them to use a calculator to help them formulate and answer questions about the series. (Answers will vary; possible questions include: Does the series build from left to right or from right to left? If it builds from the right, is there a constant number that is added to each digit to get to the next one? subtracted? The series is descending squares: $9^2, 8^2, \ldots 1^2$.

COMING UP
A lesson that goes the whole nine yards

Practice Worksheet

Enrich Worksheet

Objective: To express length in customary units

Warm-Up

Have students perform these operations and write the answers as whole numbers or mixed numbers in simplest form.

$4\frac{2}{3} \cdot 12$ (56) $36 \div 15 \left(2\frac{2}{5}\right)$

$5,280 \div 7 \left(754\frac{2}{7}\right)$ $1,760 \cdot 1.5$ (2,640)

GETTING STARTED

Ask students questions, the answers to which will most likely be in customary units of length, such as:
- What size belts would you look for in a clothing store? (usually 20 in. to 36 in.)
- What inseam length would you look for in pants? (usually 33 in. to 37 in.)

Discuss the fact that the United States is one of a few countries in which customary units of length are still the most commonly used.

Ask them to estimate
- the length of an unsharpened pencil. (about 7 in.)
- the length of an audio cassette. (about 4 in.)
- the height of the classroom doorway. (about 7 ft)

TEACHING THE LESSON

A. Introduce the origins of customary units of measure. An *inch* was the width of a man's thumb. A *foot* was adapted from the length of a king's own foot and varied from 10 to 13 inches. A *yard* was the girth of an Anglo-Saxon king. The *mile* comes from the Latin phrase *milia passuum*, "a thousand paces," and was based on the Roman pace of 5 feet.

Remind students that when they rename a smaller unit with a larger unit, the number of units in their answer will be less. Conversely, when they rename a larger unit with a smaller unit, the number of units will be greater.

B. Provide additional examples for adding and subtracting mixed units of linear measure, such as:

2 ft + 2 ft (1 yd 1 ft)
1 ft + 2 ft + 2ft (1 yd 2 ft)
2 yd 1 ft − 2 ft (1 yd 2 ft)
3 ft 8 in. + 4 in. (4 ft)

174

Customary Units of Length

A. The graph at the right shows the total stopping distance (reaction distance + breaking distance) of a car. How many yards will it take for a car to stop if it is going 50 mph?

From the graph, it takes 165 ft to stop. To answer in yards, you need to know the customary units of length.

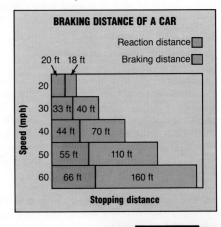

BRAKING DISTANCE OF A CAR

Reaction distance ☐
Braking distance ☐

Speed (mph)	Stopping distance
20	20 ft, 18 ft
30	33 ft, 40 ft
40	44 ft, 70 ft
50	55 ft, 110 ft
60	66 ft, 160 ft

> 12 inches (in.) = 1 foot (ft)
> 36 in. =   3 ft   = 1 yard (yd)
> 5,280 ft = 1,760 yd = 1 mile (mi)

To rename a smaller unit with a larger unit, divide.

165 ft = ■ yd
165 ÷ 3 ⟵ [3 ft = 1 yd]
165 ft = 55 yd

The total stopping distance is 55 yd.

To rename a larger unit with a smaller unit, multiply.

$\frac{3}{4}$ ft = ■ in.
$\frac{3}{4}$ × 12 ⟵ [12 in. = 1 ft]
$\frac{3}{4}$ ft = 9 in.

B. Sometimes when you compute with measures, you have to rename the units.

Add.

  5 yd 2 ft
+ 8 yd 2 ft
13 yd 4 ft, ⟵ 1 yd 1 ft
or 14 yd 1 ft

Subtract.

4 yd 10 in. ⟶ 3 yd 46 in.
− 2 yd 16 in. ⟶ − 2 yd 16 in.
             1 yd 30 in.

174   Math Reasoning, page H215

COMMON ERRORS

When adding or subtracting customary units of length, some students will rename as they do in base ten.

Remediation

Have students use a yardstick to measure and record the length of a desk, a chair, a windowsill, a chalkboard, a table, and a door frame in inches. Then have them rename each length with feet and inches, with yards and inches, with yards and feet, and with yards, feet, and inches.

Assign Reteach Master, p. 52.

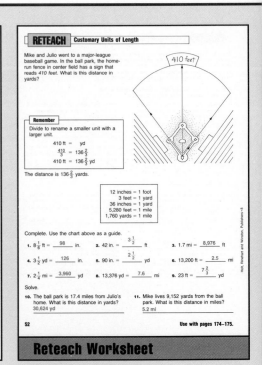

RETEACH Customary Units of Length

Mike and Julio went to a major-league baseball game. In the ball park, the home-run fence in center field has a sign that reads *410 feet*. What is this distance in yards?

410 feet

Remember
Divide to rename a smaller unit with a larger unit.

410 ft =   yd
$\frac{410}{3}$ = 136$\frac{2}{3}$
410 ft = 136$\frac{2}{3}$ yd

The distance is 136$\frac{2}{3}$ yards.

> 12 inches = 1 foot
> 3 feet = 1 yard
> 36 inches = 1 yard
> 5,280 feet = 1 mile
> 1,760 yards = 1 mile

Complete. Use the chart above as a guide.

1. 8$\frac{1}{8}$ ft = __98__ in.
2. 42 in. = __3$\frac{1}{2}$__ ft
3. 1.7 mi = __8,976__ ft
4. 3$\frac{1}{2}$ yd = __126__ in.
5. 90 in. = __2$\frac{1}{2}$__ yd
6. 13,200 ft = __2.5__ mi
7. 2$\frac{1}{4}$ mi = __3,960__ yd
8. 13,376 yd = __7.6__ mi
9. 23 ft = __7$\frac{2}{3}$__ yd

Solve.

10. The ball park is 17.4 miles from Julio's home. What is this distance in yards?
30,624 yd

11. Mike lives 9,152 yards from the ball park. What is this distance in miles?
5.2 mi

52   Use with pages 174–175.

Reteach Worksheet

Choose the best measure. Write the letter of the correct answer.

1. the width of a tire tread

(a.) $\frac{1}{2}$ in. **b.** $\frac{1}{2}$ ft **c.** $\frac{1}{2}$ yd

2. the height of a car bumper

a. 10 ft (b.) 21 in. **c.** 3 yd

3. the length of a car

a. 14 in. (b.) 15 ft **c.** 12 yd

4. the width of a car headlight

(a.) 7 in. **b.** 12 ft **c.** 7 yd

Complete.

5. 15 ft = ▮ in. 180

6. 3 mi = ▮ yd 5,280

7. 16 yd = ▮ ft 48

8. 3 yd = ▮ in. 108

9. 2 mi = ▮ yd 3,520

10. 11 ft = ▮ in. 132

11. 84 in. = ▮ ft 7

12. 51 ft = ▮ yd 17

13. 10,560 ft = ▮ mi 2

14. 96 in. = ▮ ft 8

15. 144 in. = ▮ yd 4

16. 180 in. = ▮ yd 5

17. $6\frac{1}{2}$ ft = ▮ in. 78

18. $7\frac{1}{3}$ yd = ▮ ft 22

19. $1\frac{1}{5}$ mi = ▮ ft 6,336

20. $7\frac{1}{4}$ ft = ▮ in. 87

21. $2\frac{1}{2}$ yd = ▮ in. 90

22. $3\frac{1}{2}$ mi = ▮ ft 18,480

23. 30 in. = ▮ ft $2\frac{1}{2}$

24. 60 in. = ▮ yd $1\frac{2}{3}$

25. 10 ft = ▮ yd $3\frac{1}{3}$

26. 51 in. = ▮ ft $4\frac{1}{4}$

27. 2,640 yd = ▮ mi $1\frac{1}{2}$

28. 29,040 ft = ▮ mi $5\frac{1}{2}$

★**29.** 2 ft 7 in. = ▮ in. 31

★**30.** 4 yd 5 in. = ▮ in. 149

★**31.** 9 yd 2 ft = ▮ in. 348

Add or subtract.

32.   2 ft 4 in.
       + 3 ft 5 in.
       ————————
        5 ft 9 in.

33.   8 yd 2 ft
       − 3 yd 1 ft
       ————————
        5 yd 1 ft

34. 14 yd 2 ft
       + 6 yd 2 ft
       ————————
       21 yd 1 ft

35. 17 ft 4 in.
       − 8 ft 7 in.
       ————————
        8 ft 9 in.

Solve.

36. A mechanic installed an exhaust pipe that is $1\frac{2}{3}$ ft long. How many inches long is the pipe? 20 in.

37. The mechanic joined a pipe that is $1\frac{2}{3}$ ft long to a pipe that is $2\frac{1}{2}$ ft long. Find the total length of the pipe. $4\frac{1}{6}$ ft, or 4 ft 2 in.

NUMBER SENSE

Calculate mentally. Answer in the largest possible unit.

1. 1 ft + 8 in. + 4 in. 2 ft

2. 9 in. + 7 in. + 8 in. 2 ft

3. 1 yd + 2 ft + 8 in. + 4 in. 2 yd

4. 2 ft + 4 ft + 3 ft 3 yd

5. 2 yd + 30 in. + 6 in. 3 yd

6. 3 in. + 2 in. + 7 in. 1 ft

7. 1 ft + 11 in. + 1 in. 2 ft

8. 2 ft + 8 in. + 4 in. 1 yd

9. 1 yd + 2 ft + 10 in. + 2 in. 2 yd

ASSIGNMENT GUIDE

Basic: 1–4, 5–27 o, 32–36, NS

Average: 2–30 e, 32–37, NS

Extended: 5–27 o, 29–37, NS

Resources
Practice, p. 70   Class/Home, p. H70
Reteach, p. 52   More Practice, p. H200
Enrich, p. 68   Reasoning, p. H215

Exercise Analysis

1–4   Estimate with customary units
5–31   Rename units
32–35   Add and subtract units
36–37   Skill applications

Number Sense

These exercises require students to rename and add customary units mentally.

FOLLOW-UP ACTIVITIES

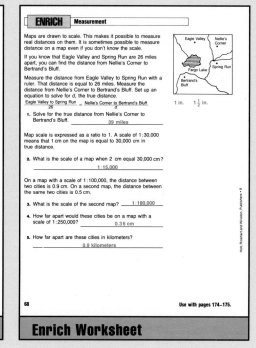

MATH CONNECTION
(Library skills)

There are many other units of length seldom used today. Have students find the origins and the measures of the following units.

- digit (from L. *digitus*, meaning "finger"; the length equal to the width of a finger—$\frac{3}{4}$ inches)
- span (from the Anglo-Saxon *span*; the distance from the tip of the little finger to the tip of the thumb when the hand is outstretched—9 inches)
- cubit (from L. *cubitum*, meaning "elbow"; the length from the elbow to the tip of the middle finger—18 inches)
- fathom (from the Anglo Saxon *faethom*, meaning "embrace"; the length of outstretched arms from fingertip to fingertip—6 feet)

REINFORCEMENT

Have students use a yardstick to measure the length and the width in inches of the classroom, a hallway, a desk, or a table and to record the measurements. They can rename the dimensions with feet and inches and with yards, feet, and inches.

Variation: Students can rename their measurements with spans (1 span = 9 inches) or with cubits (1 cubit = 18 inches)

COMING UP
Fill 'er up!

PRACTICE Customary Units of Length

| 12 inches (in.) = 1 foot (ft) |
| 36 in. = 3 ft = 1 yard (yd) |
| 5,280 ft = 1,760 yd = 1 mile (mi) |

Write the unit used to measure

1. the height of a refrigerator. foot

2. a tennis court. yard or foot

3. the distance to the moon. mile

4. the width of a shelf. inch

What is the middle of India? To find out, match the measurement on the left with its equivalent on the right. Then copy the letters into the numbered blanks below.

5. $\frac{1}{4}$ ft   **H.** 92 ft
6. 1,104 in.   **L.** $2\frac{1}{3}$ ft
7. 84 ft   **T.** 61 ft
8. 32 in.   **D.** $\frac{1}{4}$ mi
9. 92 yd   **T.** 3 in.
10. $\frac{3}{4}$ mi   **E.** 276 ft
11. $20\frac{1}{3}$ yd   **E.** 28 yd
12. 63 ft   **T.** 3,960 ft
13. 129 in.   **R.** $10\frac{3}{4}$ ft
14. 440 yd   **E.** 21 yd

T H E L E T T E R D
5 6 7   8 9 10 11 12 13   14

70   Use with pages 174–175.

Practice Worksheet

ENRICH Measurement

Maps are drawn to scale. This makes it possible to measure real distances on them. It is sometimes possible to measure distance on a map even if you don't know the scale.

If you know that Eagle Valley and Spring Run are 26 miles apart, you can find the distance from Nellie's Corner to Bertrand's Bluff.

Measure the distance from Eagle Valley to Spring Run with a ruler. That distance is equal to 26 miles. Measure the distance from Nellie's Corner to Bertrand's Bluff. Set up an equation to solve for *d*, the true distance.

$$\frac{\text{Eagle Valley to Spring Run}}{26} = \frac{\text{Nellie's Corner to Bertrand's Bluff}}{d}$$

1 in. $1\frac{1}{2}$ in.

1. Solve for the true distance from Nellie's Corner to Bertrand's Bluff. 39 miles

Map scale is expressed as a ratio to 1. A scale of 1:30,000 means that 1 cm on the map is equal to 30,000 cm in true distance.

2. What is the scale of a map when 2 cm equal 30,000 cm? 1:15,000

On a map with a scale of 1:100,000, the distance between two cities is 0.9 cm. On a second map, the distance between the same two cities is 0.5 cm.

3. What is the scale of the second map? 1:180,000

4. How far apart would these cities be on a map with a scale of 1:250,000? 0.36 cm

5. How far apart are these cities in kilometers? 0.9 kilometers

68   Use with pages 174–175.

Enrich Worksheet

Objectives: To express capacity and weight using customary units

Warm-Up

Have students perform these operations mentally and give answers as fractions, whole numbers, or mixed numbers in simplest form.

$$\frac{1}{8} \cdot 12 \left(1\frac{1}{2}\right) \qquad\qquad \frac{2}{3} \cdot 1.4 \left(\frac{14}{15}\right)$$

$$4 \div \frac{1}{2} \ (8) \qquad\qquad \frac{1}{2} \div \frac{1}{4} \ (2)$$

GETTING STARTED

Ask students to name everyday situations in which they measure liquids. (Possible answers include: when cooking, when taking liquid medicines, when preparing plant-nutrient solutions, when making solutions in the science lab.) Make a list of the units of liquid measure with which students are familiar.

TEACHING THE LESSON

A. Have students make the following table of equivalents.

How many	Ounces	Cups	Pints	Quarts	Gallons
Ounces	x	8	16	32	128
Cups	$\frac{1}{8}$	x	2	4	16
Pints	$\frac{1}{16}$	$\frac{1}{2}$	x	2	8
Quarts	$\frac{1}{32}$	$\frac{1}{4}$	$\frac{1}{2}$	x	4
Gallons	$\frac{1}{128}$	$\frac{1}{16}$	$\frac{1}{8}$	$\frac{1}{4}$	x

B. Have students make a chart of equivalents for units of weight.

How many	Ounces	Pounds	Tons
Ounces	x	16	32,000
Pounds	$\frac{1}{16}$	x	2,000
Tons	$\frac{1}{32,000}$	$\frac{1}{2,000}$	x

Checkpoint

The chart lists the common errors students make in using customary units of capacity and mass.

Correct Answers: 1c, 2b

Remediation

■ For this error, give students various objects to hold. Have them estimate the weight of each object. Change the objects daily until they can distinguish between ounces and pounds.

☐ For these errors, assign Reteach Master, p. 53.

○ For this error, assign the Manipulative Follow-Up Activity.

Customary Units of Capacity and Weight

A. In the United States, gasoline and oil are measured in **customary units.** The customary units of capacity are shown below.

> 8 fluid ounces (fl oz) = 1 cup (c)
> 2 c = 1 pint (pt)
> 2 pt = 1 quart (qt)
> 4 qt = 1 gallon (gal)

To rename a larger unit with a smaller unit, multiply.

$$\frac{1}{2} \text{ gal} = \blacksquare \text{ qt}$$
$$\frac{1}{2} \times 4 = 2 \quad\longleftarrow\quad \boxed{4 \text{ qt} = 1 \text{ gal}}$$
$$\frac{1}{2} \text{ gal} = 2 \text{ qt}$$

To rename a smaller unit with a larger unit, divide.

$$144 \text{ fl oz} = \blacksquare \text{ c}$$
$$144 \div 8 = 18$$
$$144 \text{ fl oz} = 18 \text{ c}$$

B. The customary units of weight are shown in this table.

> 16 ounces (oz) = 1 pound (lb)
> 2,000 lb = 1 ton (T)

$$3\frac{1}{4} \text{ T} = \blacksquare \text{ lb}$$
$$3\frac{1}{4} \times 2{,}000 = 6{,}500$$
$$3\frac{1}{4} \text{ T} = 6{,}500 \text{ lb}$$

$$40 \text{ oz} = \blacksquare \text{ lb}$$
$$40 \div 16 = 2\frac{1}{2}$$
$$40 \text{ oz} = 2\frac{1}{2} \text{ lb}$$

Checkpoint Write the letter of the correct answer.

1. 11 pt = ■

a. $5\frac{1}{2}$ pt   b. 5 qt

(c.) $5\frac{1}{2}$ qt   d. 22 qt

2. Choose the best estimate for the weight of an automobile tire.

a. 15 oz   (b.) 15 lb
c. 150 lb   d. 1.5 T

176

COMMON ERRORS

Answer Choice	Type of Error
☐ 1a	Uses correct operation, incorrect units
☐ 1b	Forgets to include fraction
☐ 1d	Uses wrong operation
■ 2a, 2d	Confuses customary units of weight
○ 2c	Chooses correct unit but wrong number

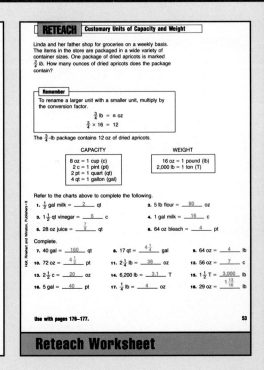

RETEACH Customary Units of Capacity and Weight

Linda and her father shop for groceries on a weekly basis. The items in the store are packaged in a wide variety of container sizes. One package of dried apricots is marked $\frac{3}{4}$ lb. How many ounces of dried apricots does the package contain?

Remember
To rename a larger unit with a smaller unit, multiply by the conversion factor.
$$\frac{3}{4} \text{ lb} = \blacksquare \text{ oz}$$
$$\frac{3}{4} \times 16 = 12$$

The $\frac{3}{4}$-lb package contains 12 oz of dried apricots.

CAPACITY	WEIGHT
8 oz = 1 cup (c)	16 oz = 1 pound (lb)
2 c = 1 pint (pt)	2,000 lb = 1 ton (T)
2 pt = 1 quart (qt)	
4 qt = 1 gallon (gal)	

Refer to the charts above to complete the following.

1. $\frac{1}{2}$ gal milk = __2__ qt
2. 5 lb flour = __80__ oz
3. $1\frac{1}{2}$ qt vinegar = __6__ c
4. 1 gal milk = __16__ c
5. 28 oz juice = __$\frac{7}{8}$__ qt
6. 64 oz bleach = __4__ pt

Complete.

7. 40 gal = __160__ qt
8. 17 qt = __$4\frac{1}{4}$__ gal
9. 64 oz = __4__ lb
10. 72 oz = __$4\frac{1}{2}$__ pt
11. $2\frac{1}{4}$ lb = __36__ oz
12. 56 oz = __7__ c
13. $2\frac{1}{2}$ c = __20__ oz
14. 6,200 lb = __3.1__ T
15. $1\frac{1}{2}$ T = __3,000__ lb
16. 5 gal = __40__ pt
17. $\frac{1}{4}$ lb = __4__ oz
18. 29 oz = __$1\frac{13}{16}$__ lb

Use with pages 176–177.

53

Reteach Worksheet

Choose the best measure. Write the letter of the correct answer.

1. the capacity of a car's gas tank
a. 20 c   **b.** 20 pt
c. 20 qt   **(d.)** 20 gal

2. the weight of a car
a. 4,000 oz   **b.** 100 lb
(c.) 2 T   **d.** 200 T

Complete.

3. 3 qt = ■ pt   6
4. 12 gal = ■ qt   48
5. 5 lb = ■ oz   80

6. 9 qt = ■ c   36
7. 3 T = ■ lb   6,000
8. 2 c = ■ fl oz   16

9. 32 fl oz = ■ c   4
10. 64 oz = ■ lb   4
11. 12 qt = ■ gal   3

12. 4,000 lb = ■ T   2
13. 16 pt = ■ gal   2
14. 16 c = ■ gal   1

15. $3\frac{1}{2}$ gal = ■ qt   14
16. $2\frac{1}{4}$ c = ■ fl oz   18
17. $5\frac{1}{2}$ lb = ■ oz   88

18. 24 oz = ■ lb $1\frac{1}{2}$
19. 5,000 lb = ■ T $2\frac{1}{2}$
20. 17 qt = ■ gal $4\frac{1}{4}$

★21. 3 lb 7 oz = ■ oz   55
★22. 7 gal 3 qt = ■ qt   31
★23. 47 oz = ■ lb ■ oz   2, 15

Add or subtract.

24. 3 lb 9 oz + 6 lb 7 oz   10 lb
25. 4 gal 3 qt 1 pt + 6 gal 2 qt 1 pt   11 gal 2 qt
26. 7 lb 4 oz − 2 lb 9 oz   4 lb 11 oz
27. 6 gal 1 qt − 2 gal 3 qt   3 gal 2 qt

Solve.

28. Carol had two 2-gallon containers of gasoline. One container was full and the other half full. How many quarts did she have?   12 qt

29. Bill pays $11.95 per quart for Shine Perfect car wax. He bought 3 quarts. How much money did he spend? $35.85

30. Find out how many gallons of gasoline your local filling station pumps per week. How much is this per month?   Answers will vary.

31. Auto Tar Remover is sold for $2.79 per quart. If Dennis buys 90 gallons, how much does he pay? $1,004.40

MIDCHAPTER REVIEW

Complete.

1. 17 km = ■ m   17,000
2. 4,100 mg = ■ g   4.1
3. 22,000 mL = ■ L   22

4. 288 in. = ■ yd   8
5. 14 lb = ■ oz   224
6. 7 gal = ■ qt   28

Classwork/Homework, page H71   More Practice, page H200   **177**

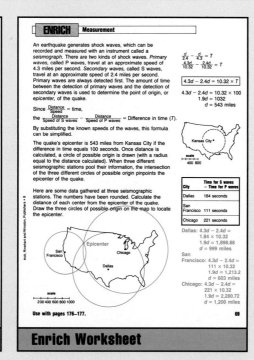

177

Objective: To practice choosing and using methods and strategies for solving problems

Warm-Up

To prepare students for this lesson, have them compute the following.

$z + 17 = 25$ (8) $9 - r = 4$ (5)

$12x = 54$ (4.5) $\frac{t}{20} = 6$ (120)

GETTING STARTED

Review with students the problem-solving strategies that have already been presented by asking students to name as many strategies as they can. As each strategy is named, ask students to quickly make up a problem that could be solved using that strategy. Encourage creativity.

TEACHING THE LESSON

These pages are designed to provide students with a chance to use their problem-solving skills. Students have to come up with an appropriate strategy for each problem and make use of that strategy. If students are having trouble, they should try something else or move on to the next problem and return later to the difficult one. You may want to have students work in groups to complete these pages. You may wish to allow students to use calculators for problem solving.

Students may benefit from a review of the problem-solving strategies taught to this point in the text.

Estimation, pp. 54–55, 136–137

4-Step Plan, pp. 16–17

Using Data from Outside Sources, Including Infobank, pp. 24–25

Using a Graph, pp. 32–33

Identifying Extra/Needed Information, pp. 48–49

Choosing the Operation, pp. 62–63, 102–103

Solving Multistep Problems/Making a Plan, pp. 68–69

Checking for a Reasonable Answer, pp. 86–87

Using a Table, pp. 96–97

Writing an Equation, pp. 110–111

Using a Pictograph, pp. 126–127

Writing a Simpler Problem, pp. 144–145

Interpreting the Quotient and Remainder, pp. 154–155

Choosing/Writing a Sensible Question, pp. 172–173

178

QUESTIONS	TOOLS	SOLUTIONS	CHECKS

PROBLEM SOLVING
Choosing a Strategy or Method

Write the strategy or method you choose. Then solve.   Strategies and methods will vary.

> Estimation
> Using a Graph
> Identifying Extra/Needed Information
> Choosing the Operation
> Solving Multi-step Problems
> Checking for a Reasonable Answer
> Using a Table
> Writing an Equation
> Interpreting the Quotient and the Remainder

1. A flower shop sells long-stemmed roses for $1.50 each. If the store pays $6.00 per dozen for the roses, how much profit does it make if it sells 5 dozen? Choosing the operation; $60.00

2. A customer in a flower shop bought 3 roses at $1.50 each, 4 gladioli at $0.85 each, and a plant for $12.50. How much did the customer spend? Choosing the operation; $20.40

3. The Grimm Forest has an average of 150 trees per acre. If the forest covers 210 acres, about how many trees are there? Estimation; about 30,000 trees

4. On one map, 1 inch equals 24.5 miles. The map shows the distance from Montreal, Quebec, to Burlington, Vermont, to be about 5 inches. What is the approximate distance between those places? Estimation; about 125 miles

5. In a music poll, 55 people said they preferred folk music. This was 12 fewer than those who said they preferred jazz. How many people preferred jazz? Writing an equation;

6. Penny caught 10 fish on a camping trip. This number was 2 more than $\frac{2}{3}$ of the number of fish Jan caught. How many fish did Jan catch? Writing an equation; 12 fish

7. The supermarket uses plastic sacks that can hold up to 4 kilograms of groceries. Mr. Jackson's groceries weigh about 22 kilograms. How many sacks should the clerk use? Interpreting the quotient; 6 sacks

8. Susan has $30.00 to spend on herself and her brother at the amusement park. Admission tickets cost $9.50 each, and she plans on paying $5.00 each for lunch. Does Susan have enough money? Estimation; yes

9. Mrs. McGhee needs 33 feet of wood to complete a fence. The wood is sold in 8-foot sections. How many sections of wood must she buy? Interpreting the quotient; 5 sections

178

Choose a strategy or method and solve.

10. At a fashion show, each of 50 buyers placed an order for $10,000 worth of fashion items. If $3,000 of each order was spent for jewelry, what was the total spent for other items? $350,000

11. A van carries racks of coats from a warehouse to a store. The van carries 320 coats per trip. If the store will sell half the number of coats for $235 and the rest for $350, what is the value of the coats carried in 8 trips? $748,800

12. Robbie's mother can spend $9,500 for a new car. She sees a model she likes for $8,754.50, but she wants some options that cost $257.30, $315.75, and $214.47. Does she have enough money to buy the car and the options? no

13. Hal wants to buy a car that will cost him a total of $8,568. He can pay for it in 36 monthly payments. His other monthly expenses amount to $76.15, $37.58, $146.25, $322.74, and $176.42. His monthly income is $1,080. Can he afford to buy the car? yes

Use the double bar graph at the right to solve.

14. On what day did the 1990 attendance first surpass the 1989 attendance? Saturday

15. To the nearest thousand, how many more people attended the fair on the Friday of 1989 than on the Friday of 1990? 40,000 more people

16. Was the combined attendance on the Fridays of 1989 and 1990 more than or less than the attendance on the Saturday of 1990? less than

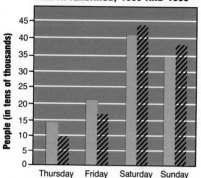

FAIR ATTENDANCE, 1989 AND 1990

1989
1990

Classwork/Homework, pages H72–H73

ASSIGNMENT GUIDE

Basic: 1–6
Average: 2–12 e
Extended: 1–13 o

Resources
Practice, pp. 72–3   Class/Home, pp. H72–3

Exercise Analysis
1–9   Choose an appropriate strategy or method
10–16   Mixed Practice

FOLLOW-UP ACTIVITIES

 CALCULATOR
Materials: calculator per student

Choose a number at random and write it on the chalkboard. Have students use calculators to come up with a number sentence that results in your number. Tell students that they are allowed to use only the four calculator functions ($+$, $-$, $\times$, $\div$) and a single digit, but that they can also use each as many times as necessary. The object of the game is to arrive at the goal number by using the fewest possible keystrokes within a time limit of three minutes. After three minutes have elapsed, ask for students' number sentences. The shortest sentence wins. After students have the knack of the game, choose not only the goal number for them but also the digit they must use to find it; for example: goal = 23; digit = 4.

$4 + 4 + 4 \div 4 + 4 + 4 + 4 + 4 + 4 = 23$
(18 keystrokes)

 CALCULATOR
Materials: calculator per student

Tell students that it is possible to multiply numbers whose product is too large for a calculator display if they use the following method. Have them first split the large number into two smaller numbers between the ones period and the thousands period and then multiply each group of periods separately. When they have found the two products, have them attach three zeros for the three digits they took off, and add to arrive at the final product.

654,718   Multiply 718 × 594 = 426,492
×   594   Multiply 654 × 594 = 388,476

Add.   426,492
+ 388,476,000   (Add these three 388,902,492 zeros.)
654,718 × 594 = 388,902,492

COMING UP
Precision counts!

179

Objectives: To explore precision and determine greatest possible error

Warm-Up

Have students rename the following with millimeters and order them from the least to the greatest.

2 dm (200 mm); 5 cm (50 mm); 370 m (370,000 mm); 0.21 m (210 mm); 0.003 km, (3,000 mm); 0.06 m (60 mm); 5,380 mm (50 mm; 60 mm; 200 mm; 210 mm; 3,000 mm; 5,380 mm; 370,000 mm)

GETTING STARTED

List the following items on the chalkboard.
● the length of the classroom
● the width of a pencil
● the distance from home to school
● the diameter of a clock face

Foster discussion among students about what unit of measure might be appropriate to use when measuring each of these items. Point out that it would not make sense to use a very small unit to try to measure a large item. For example, ask students why it probably would not be appropriate to measure the length of the classroom in millimeters.

TEACHING THE LESSON

Materials: centimeter rulers

There are two approaches that you can use in teaching this lesson: (1) have students work individually through the developmental questions and convene in groups of four to work on Thinking/Working as a Team or (2) have students work through the developmental parts in groups of four and have a class discussion for Thinking/Working as a Team.

A. Have students discuss the question at the top of the page. Challenge them to name several items, each of which could be reported as a meter in length. Have them measure each of the lines on the page to the nearest centimeter. They should see that although all 3 lines are obviously *not* exactly equal in length, all of them measure 7 centimeters.

For question 1, elicit from students that the measurements to the nearest millimeter are more *precise* because the unit of measure is smaller. This may become clearer to students if you ask whether the top and bottom lines have to be equal when measured to the nearest *tenth* of a millimeter. (not necessarily) Lead them to realize that any item that has a length between 6.5 cm and 7.5 cm can be reported as 7 cm in

---

Precision and Greatest Possible Error

A. Do you think that all items reported as a meter in length are exactly 1 meter long? You can use a centimeter ruler to help you explore how measurements are reported.

_____

_____

_____

Step 1: Measure each of the line segments above to the nearest centimeter.

● Which line segments have the same measurement to the nearest centimeter?
all 3 line segments
● Which line segments appear to be exactly equal in length? the top and bottom line segments

Step 2: Measure each of the line segments above to the nearest millimeter.

● Which line segments have the same measurement to the nearest millimeter?
the top and bottom line segments

Thinking as a Team

The **precision** of a measurement is related to the unit of measure used. The smaller the unit of measure, the more precise the measurement.

1. Which measurements are more precise, those reported in Step 1 or those reported in Step 2?
those reported in Step 2
2. What is the length of the shortest line segment that could be reported as 7 cm? 6.5 cm

3. What is the length of the longest line segment that could be reported as 7 cm? 7.5 cm

4. How much more or less than the reported measurement could the actual length of the line segment be? 0.5 cm

180

---

length and any object reported as 7 cm can be up to 0.5 cm greater or less than 7 cm.

B. Students should be led to understand that any reported measurement has a *greatest possible error* of plus or minus 0.5 units of measure used. In other words, an object whose reported measurement was 14 in. could have an actual measure of anywhere between 13.5 in. and 14.5 in.

Guide students to discover that no measurement is ever exact because an object could, theoretically, always be measured more precisely (i.e., to a smaller unit of measure).

Have students discuss the greatest error that would be allowable in each of several situations. Make sure that they

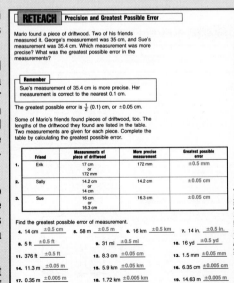

(*Continued on p. 181.*)

B. Because the actual measurement could be at most 0.5 units greater or less than the reported measurement, the **greatest possible error** can be written as ±0.5 units. This is read as "plus or minus 0.5 units."

- Do you think any measurement is ever exact? Discuss your reasoning with the group.

No, because any measurement could be made more precisely (i.e., to a smaller unit).

- Discuss with your group situations in which different degrees of precision would be necessary. What is the greatest possible error allowable in each situation? *Answers will vary.*

- When the course for a 10-km road race is measured, do you think the greatest possible error is +0.5 km? How precise do you think the measurement should be? *No; measurement to the nearest meter might be appropriate.*

Working as a Team

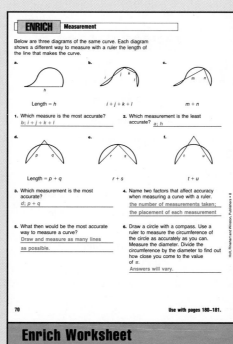

When serving, a tennis player must hit the ball into the opponent's service court, which is in the shape of a rectangle $13\frac{1}{2}$ feet by 21 feet.

Phyllis and Jorge are painting lines on a tennis court. Phyllis marks off the lines for the service court at 13 feet and 20 feet 6 inches. Jorge insists the measurements should be precise to the nearest inch. Phyllis says that because the measurements are given to the nearest foot, the greatest error allowable is $\frac{1}{2}$ foot either way and the error will make only a very small difference. She tells Jorge that the greatest possible error in area will be only 6 inches × 6 inches, or 36 square inches. Jorge says the error will be much greater. Carefully draw a picture of the court showing how the error in measurement actually affects the area. Then tell who is right. *Jorge*

1. What is the greatest possible error in area? *2,448 in.²*

2. What percent of the total area is this? *about 6%*

3. Do you think that the error in area might be significant in a tennis tournament? Discuss your reasons with the members of your team. *It very likely would be.*

Classwork/Homework, page H74   More Practice, page H200   **181**

---

understand that an error of ±0.5 km would *not* be acceptable for the measurement of the course of a 10-km race. The concept of greatest possible error is further developed in the Working as a Team section. Make sure that students realize after working through this section that the measurement of an object can be *more* precise than the way in which it is reported (for example, a measurement of 48 in., although precise to the nearest *inch,* is commonly reported as 4 *ft*).

ASSIGNMENT GUIDE

Basic: p. 180, p. 181

Average: p. 180, p. 181

Extended: p. 180, p. 181

Resources
Practice, p. 74   Class/Home, p. H74
Reteach, p. 54   More Practice, p. H200
Enrich, p. 70

FOLLOW-UP ACTIVITIES

MATH CONNECTION (Science)

The results of many science experiments often depend on the precision of the equipment used. Have students find the precision of the equipment used in the science department in your school. Equipment that might be checked includes a spring scale, micrometers, a laboratory balance, thermometers, a Sartorius balance, an oscilloscope, a graduated cylinder, and a pH meter.

MANIPULATIVES

Materials: a 100-ft tape, a 50-ft tape, a standard yardstick, a meter stick, a metric tape with millimeter markings per class

Have students measure the length of the classroom floor (or, if possible, the gym floor) using the different measurement tools. Which measurement is more precise? Why? (The metric tape will be more precise because it uses the smallest units of measurement.)

COMING UP
Travel time!

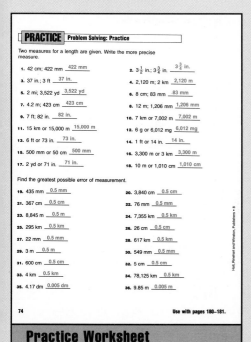

PRACTICE Problem Solving: Practice

Two measures for a length are given. Write the more precise measure.

1. 42 cm; 422 mm *422 mm*
2. $3\frac{1}{2}$ in.; $3\frac{3}{4}$ in. *$3\frac{3}{4}$ in.*
3. 37 in.; 3 ft *37 in.*
4. 2,120 m; 2 km *2,120 m*
5. 2 mi; 3,522 yd *3,522 yd*
6. 8 cm; 83 mm *83 mm*
7. 4.2 m; 423 cm *423 cm*
8. 12 m; 1,206 mm *1,206 mm*
9. 7 ft; 82 in. *82 in.*
10. 7 km or 7,002 m *7,002 m*
11. 15 km or 15,000 m *15,000 m*
12. 6 g or 6,012 mg *6,012 mg*
13. 6 ft or 73 in. *73 in.*
14. 1 ft or 14 in. *14 in.*
15. 500 mm or 50 cm *500 mm*
16. 3,300 m or 3 km *3,300 m*
17. 2 yd or 71 in. *71 in.*
18. 10 m or 1,010 cm *1,010 cm*

Find the greatest possible error of measurement.

19. 435 mm *0.5 mm*
20. 3,840 cm *0.5 cm*
21. 367 cm *0.5 cm*
22. 76 mm *0.5 mm*
23. 8,845 m *0.5 m*
24. 7,355 km *0.5 km*
25. 295 km *0.5 km*
26. 26 cm *0.5 cm*
27. 22 mm *0.5 mm*
28. 617 km *0.5 km*
29. 3 m *0.5 m*
30. 549 mm *0.5 mm*
31. 600 cm *0.5 cm*
32. 5 cm *0.5 cm*
33. 4 km *0.5 km*
34. 78,125 km *0.5 km*
35. 4.17 dm *0.005 dm*
36. 9.85 m *0.005 m*

74   Use with pages 180–181.

Holt, Rinehart and Winston, Publishers • 8

Practice Worksheet

ENRICH Measurement

Below are three diagrams of the same curve. Each diagram shows a different way to measure with a ruler the length of the line that makes the curve.

Length = h   i + j + k + l   m + n

1. Which measure is the most accurate? *b; i + j + k + l*
2. Which measurement is the least accurate? *a; h*

Length = p + q   r + s   t + u

3. Which measurement is the most accurate? *d; p + q*
4. Name two factors that affect accuracy when measuring a curve with a ruler. *the number of measurements taken; the placement of each measurement*

5. What then would be the most accurate way to measure a curve? *Draw and measure as many lines as possible.*
6. Draw a circle with a compass. Use a ruler to measure the circumference of the circle as accurately as you can. Measure the diameter. Divide the circumference by the diameter to find out how close you come to the value of π. *Answers will vary.*

70   Use with pages 180–181.

Holt, Rinehart and Winston, Publishers • 8

Enrich Worksheet

181

OB....tives. To understand the relationship between units of time and to calculate
elapsed time

Warm-Up

6 ft 5 in.	3 m 20 cm	4 lb
+ 2 ft 8 in.	− 80 cm	− 5 oz
(9 ft 1 in.)	(2 m 40 cm)	(3 lb 11 oz)

GETTING STARTED

Write the time on the chalkboard (for example, 9:45 A.M., 2:15 P.M.). Discuss different
ways of reading time (for example, 9:45
A.M. is 9 h 45 min, 45 min past 9, 15 min to
10, a quarter to 10, etc.) and the meaning
of A.M.. Repeat for 10:30 P.M. Ask why we
say *half past, a quarter to, o'clock.* Discuss
the relationship of these terms to the shape
of an analog clock and to the screen of a
digital clock.

TEACHING THE LESSON

A. In discussing units of time, point out
that the length of a day is the only unit
dictated by the rotation of Earth and
that the year is the only unit dictated by
its revolution. Early Sumerians, who
believed there were 360 days in a year,
divided the day into cycles of 6, 60, and
6 times 60. (360) We still use 24 h/d,
60 min/h, and 60 s/min.

Checkpoint

The chart lists the common errors students
make in dealing with time.

Correct Answers: 1b, 2c, 3b

Remediation

■ For this error, guide students in writing
fractions in simplest form. Before dividing, have them list the factors of the
numerator and the denominator and
determine the GCF.

○ For this error, assign the Manipulative
Follow-Up Activity.

□ For these errors, assign Reteach Master, p. 55.

Time and Elapsed Time

Ty left Scranton, Pennsylvania, at 9:30 A.M., and arrived
in Wheeling, West Virginia, at 5:15 P.M. How long did
the trip take?

The amount of time between events is called the
elapsed time.

60 seconds (s) = 1 minute (min)	1 week (wk) = 7 d
60 min = 1 hour (h)	1 year (y) = 365 d or 12 months (mo)
24 h = 1 day (d)	100 y = 1 century

$$5 \text{ h } 15 \text{ min (P.M.)} \longrightarrow \quad 17 \text{ h } 15 \text{ min} = \quad 16 \text{ h } 75 \text{ min}$$
$$- 9 \text{ h } 30 \text{ min (A.M.)} \longrightarrow \quad - 9 \text{ h } 30 \text{ min} = \quad - 9 \text{ h } 30 \text{ min}$$
$$\overline{\quad\quad\quad\quad\quad\quad\quad\quad\quad\quad 7 \text{ h } 45 \text{ min}}$$

Both times now
mean "starting
from midnight."

The trip took 7 h 45 min.

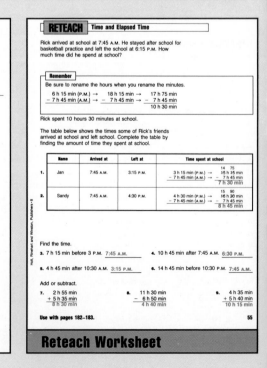

Checkpoint Write the letter of the correct answer.

1. Choose the correct time for 5 h 45 min after 8:30 A.M.

a. 2:15 A.M.   **b.** 2:15 P.M.   **c.** 1:75 P.M.   **d.** 1:15 P.M.

2. Choose the elapsed time between 10:45 A.M. and 1:15 P.M.

a. 3 h   **b.** 3 h 30 min   **c.** 2 h 30 min   **d.** 2 h 20 min

3. Choose the missing number. 48 min = ■ h

a. $1\frac{1}{4}$ **b.** $\frac{4}{5}$ **c.** 0   **d.** $\frac{24}{30}$

182   Math Reasoning, page H216

COMMON ERRORS

Answer Choice	Type of Error
○ 1a	Uses A.M. instead of P.M.
□ 1c	Fails to rename
□ 1d, 3c, 3d	Renames incorrectly
□ 2a	Uses only hours
□ 2b	Fails to name hours correctly
□ 2d	Renames only 50 min in subtraction
■ 3a	Transposes numerator and denominator

RETEACH Time and Elapsed Time

Rick arrived at school at 7:45 A.M. He stayed after school for
basketball practice and left the school at 6:15 P.M. How
much time did he spend at school?

Remember
Be sure to rename the hours when you rename the minutes.

$$6 \text{ h } 15 \text{ min (P.M.)} \rightarrow 18 \text{ h } 15 \text{ min} \rightarrow 17 \text{ h } 75 \text{ min}$$
$$- 7 \text{ h } 45 \text{ min (A.M.)} \rightarrow - 7 \text{ h } 45 \text{ min} \rightarrow - 7 \text{ h } 45 \text{ min}$$
$$\overline{\quad\quad\quad\quad\quad\quad\quad 10 \text{ h } 30 \text{ min}}$$

Rick spent 10 hours 30 minutes at school.

The table below shows the times some of Rick's friends
arrived at school and left school. Complete the table by
finding the amount of time they spent at school.

	Name	Arrived at	Left at	Time spent at school
1.	Jan	7:45 A.M.	3:15 P.M.	3 h 15 min (P.M.) → 15 h 15 min − 7 h 45 min (A.M.) → − 7 h 45 min **7 h 30 min**
2.	Sandy	7:45 A.M.	4:30 P.M.	4 h 30 min (P.M.) → 16 h 30 min − 7 h 45 min (A.M.) → − 7 h 45 min **8 h 45 min**

Find the time.

3. 7 h 15 min before 3 P.M. 7:45 A.M.   **4.** 10 h 45 min after 7:45 A.M. 6:30 P.M.

5. 4 h 45 min after 10:30 A.M. 3:15 P.M.   **6.** 14 h 45 min before 10:30 P.M. 7:45 A.M.

Add or subtract.

7. 2 h 55 min + 5 h 35 min 8 h 30 min	**8.** 11 h 30 min − 6 h 50 min 4 h 40 min	**9.** 4 h 35 min + 5 h 40 min 10 h 15 min

Use with pages 182–183.   55

Reteach Worksheet

Find the time.

1. 2 h 35 min before 12:15 P.M.
   9:40 A.M.
3. 5 h 55 min after 10:30 P.M.   4:25 A.M.

2. 8 h 12 min after 9:00 A.M.
   5:12 P.M.
4. 3 h 18 min before 1:10 P.M.
   9:52 A.M.

5. 6 h 47 min before 12:50 A.M.
   6:03 P.M.

6. 9 h 25 min after 6:00 A.M.
   3:25 P.M.

Find the elapsed time between

7. 5:00 A.M. and 3:15 P.M.   10 h 15 min

8. 8:05 P.M. and 11:00 P.M.
   2 h 55 min

9. 7:21 A.M. and 12 noon.   4 h 39 min

10. 6:52 A.M. and 2:45 P.M.
    7 h 53 min

11. 4:10 P.M. and 1:20 A.M.   9 h 10 min

12. 11:20 P.M. and 11:50 A.M.
    12 h 30 min

Write the missing number.

13. 3 min = ■ s   180

14. $2\frac{1}{2}$ h = ■ min   150

15. $\frac{3}{4}$ d = ■ h   18

16. 48 h = ■ d   2

17. 75 s = ■ min $1\frac{1}{4}$

18. 100 min = ■ h $1\frac{2}{3}$

19. 30 s = ■ min $\frac{1}{2}$

20. 60 h = ■ d $2\frac{1}{2}$

21. $5\frac{1}{2}$ h = ■ min
    330

Add or subtract.

22.   3 h 20 min
     + 5 h 30 min
      8 h 50 min

23.   5 min 36 s
     + 10 min 42 s
      16 min 18 s

24.   15 h 20 min
     − 7 h 17 min
      8 h 3 min

25.   12 min 15 s
     − 10 min 45 s
      1 min 30 s

Solve.

26. Mr. Thomas drove nonstop from New York City to Washington, D.C. He left New York at 5:00 A.M. If the trip took 5 h 43 min, at what time did he arrive in Washington?
    10:43 A.M.

27. Ms. Van Mirt has to be in Denver at 10:30 A.M. She lives 3 h 45 min away. If it takes her 45 min to dress and eat, at what time should she get up in the morning?   6:00 A.M.

28. Plan a four-day car trip to three cities in your area. Outline a time schedule that includes the total driving time.   Answers will vary.

CHALLENGE

A **hectare** is a measure of land area.

1 hectare (ha) = 10,000 square meters (m²)

A square field 100 meters on a side would be an example of a hectare. Give the dimensions of another rectangle that would cover 1 hectare. Estimate how many hectares your school yard is.   Answers will vary.

ASSIGNMENT GUIDE

Basic: 1–6, 8–28 e, Chlg

Average: 1–6, 9–27 o, 28, Chlg

Extended: 2–20 e, 22–28, Chlg

Resources
Practice, p. 75   Class/Home, p. H75
Reteach, p. 55   Reasoning, p. H216
Enrich, p. 71

Exercise Analysis

1–6	Compute the time before or after a given time
7–12	Compute elapsed time
13–21	Rename units of time
22–25	Add or subtract units of time
26–27	Skill applications
28	Data collection and computation

Challenge

This activity applies metric concepts to area. An example of about 1 hectare is the area covered by the Empire State Building.

FOLLOW-UP ACTIVITIES

MANIPULATIVES
Materials: 52 index cards

Have groups of two to four students prepare 52 "time" cards. Each card shows one of the following: an analog clock face with time showing, a time in words (omit A.M. or P.M.), a digital clock time including A.M. or P.M.

Deal five cards to each student in the group. Use the rules for rummy. Cards with no A.M. or P.M. markings are wild. The object is to acquire sets of three cards; the elapsed time between the times on two of the cards is shown on the third. The game ends when a player discards all cards.

REINFORCEMENT
Materials: clock face, hour hand

Use materials to demonstrate addition, subtraction, multiplication, and division in base 12.

3 + 5 = 8   7 + 6 = 1   2 − 4 = 10

Have students solve these equations in base 12.

4 + 6 = (10)   5 + 11 = (4)
3 − 10 = (5)   7 − 8 = (11)

COMING UP
Watch it lag!

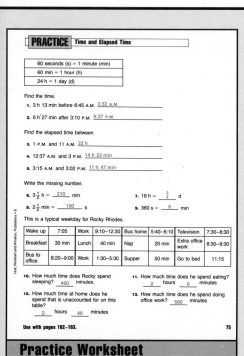

PRACTICE   Time and Elapsed Time

60 seconds (s) = 1 minute (min)
60 min = 1 hour (h)
24 h = 1 day (d)

Find the time.

1. 3 h 13 min before 6:45 A.M.   3:32 A.M.

2. 6 h 27 min after 3:10 P.M.   9:37 P.M.

Find the elapsed time between

3. 1 P.M. and 11 A.M.   22 h

4. 12:37 A.M. and 3 P.M.   14 h 23 min

5. 3:15 A.M. and 3:02 P.M.   11 h 47 min

Write the missing number.

6. $3\frac{1}{2}$ h = ___ 210 ___ min

7. 18 h = $\frac{3}{4}$ d

8. $2\frac{1}{2}$ min = ___ 150 ___ s

9. 360 s = ___ 6 ___ min

This is a typical weekday for Rocky Rhodes.

Wake up	7:05	Work	9:10–12:30	Bus home	5:40–6:10	Television	7:30–8:30
Breakfast	30 min	Lunch	40 min	Nap	20 min	Extra office work	8:30–9:30
Bus to office	8:20–9:00	Work	1:30–5:30	Supper	50 min	Go to bed	11:15

10. How much time does Rocky spend sleeping?   490   minutes.

11. How much time does he spend eating?   2   hours   0   minutes

12. How much time at home does he spend that is unaccounted for on this table?   2   hours   40   minutes

13. How much time does he spend doing office work?   500   minutes

Use with pages 182–183.   75

Practice Worksheet

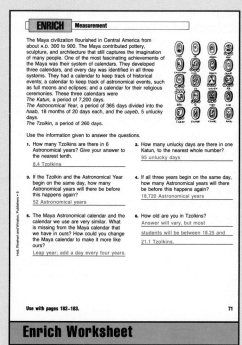

ENRICH   Measurement

The Maya civilization flourished in Central America from about A.D. 300 to 900. The Maya contributed pottery, sculpture, and architecture that still captures the imagination of many people. One of the most fascinating achievements of the Maya was their system of calendars. They developed three calendars, and every day was identified in all three systems. They had a calendar to keep track of historical events; a calendar to keep track of astronomical events, such as full moons and eclipses; and a calendar for their religious ceremonies. These three calendars were
The Katun, a period of 7,200 days.
The Astronomical Year, a period of 365 days divided into the *haab*, 18 months of 20 days each, and the *uayeb*, 5 unlucky days.
The Tzolkin, a period of 260 days.

Use the information given to answer the questions.

1. How many Tzolkins are there in 6 Astronomical years? Give your answer to the nearest tenth.
   8.4 Tzolkins

2. How many unlucky days are there in one Katun, to the nearest whole number?
   95 unlucky days

3. If the Tzolkin and the Astronomical Year begin on the same day, how many Astronomical years will there be before this happens again?
   52 Astronomical years

4. If all three years begin on the same day, how many Astronomical years will there be before this happens again?
   18,720 Astronomical years

5. The Maya Astronomical calendar and the calendar we use are very similar. What is missing from the Maya calendar that we have in ours? How could you change the Maya calendar to make it more like ours?
   Leap year; add a day every four years.

6. How old are you in Tzolkins?
   Answer will vary, but most students will be between 18.25 and 21.1 Tzolkins.

Use with pages 182–183.   71

Enrich Worksheet

Objective: To use an appropriate formula to find needed information

Warm-Up

Have students solve the following exercises.

18 ÷ 3 (6)   12 × 4 (48)
3.9 × 16 (62.4)   108.75 ÷ 15 (7.25)
4.7 × 5.2 (24.44)   102 × 0.5 (51)

GETTING STARTED

Tell the class that you left on a trip at 12:00 and drove 45 miles per hour until 3:20. Have the class determine

- how many miles you traveled from 12:00 to 1:00. (45 miles)
- the miles you traveled from 1:00 to 2:00. (45 miles)
- the miles you traveled from 2:00 to 3:00. (45 miles)
- the miles you traveled from 3:00 to 3:20. (Remind the class that this is $\frac{1}{3}$ hour.) (15 miles)

Ask the class how to find the distance you traveled from these numbers. (Add them: 45 + 45 + 45 + 15 = 150.) Ask the class for an easier way to determine the distance covered. (Multiply the speed by the amount of time traveled: 45 × $3\frac{1}{3}$ = 150.)

TEACHING THE LESSON

Students will often encounter formulas in mathematics, science, and in everyday life. Have students memorize this formula. Tell them that they will often have to use formulas from memory.

Another example:

A train goes 70 mi/h for 3 h 45 min. How far does it go?

$d = rt$

$d = (70) \times \left(3\frac{3}{4}\right)$

$d = 262\frac{1}{2}$

$r = 262\frac{1}{2} \div 3\frac{3}{4}$

$t = 262\frac{1}{2} \div 70$

Questions: Questions in this lesson will be easily understood if students are careful when determining whether the missing variable is the distance traveled, the time it took to travel, or the rate.

Tools: Some students may incorrectly assign the d variable for r or t. Remind students to substitute carefully, using a rearrangement of the formula if necessary.

Remind students that care must be taken when using formulas in order to ensure that the same units are used consistently. Em-

---

| QUESTIONS | TOOLS | SOLUTIONS | CHECKS |

PROBLEM SOLVING
Using a Formula ($d = rt$)

The distance a vehicle has moved can be calculated when you know the vehicle's average speed and the amount of time for which it has been moving.

To calculate the distance, use the formula $d = rt$, where
 d = distance
 r = rate of travel (speed)
 t = time.

> Rachel is driving from Springfield, Missouri, to Fort Wayne, Indiana. If she drives for 2 hours 15 minutes at 50 miles per hour, how far has she traveled?

To solve a problem by using a formula, follow these general rules.

1. Use the correct formula.

2. Substitute values in the formula.

3. Solve the equation.

4. Write the answer, using the correct unit.

Use the formula $d = rt$, and evaluate.

$t = 2\frac{1}{4}$ hours $d = rt$

$r = 50$ miles per hour $d = (50)\left(2\frac{1}{4}\right)$

$d = 112\frac{1}{2}$

She traveled $112\frac{1}{2}$ mi.

You can use other forms of the distance formula to find the time or the rate.

To solve for t: $t = d \div r$ $t = 112\frac{1}{2} \div 50$

To solve for r: $r = d \div t$ $r = 112\frac{1}{2} \div 2\frac{1}{4}$

184

---

phasize that minutes must be renamed with fractions of hours when r is expressed as distance per hour.

Some students may also have difficulty understanding the derivation of the formulas for t and r. If so, use $d = rt$, and give an example such as $d = 100$ km and $r = 50$ km/h to show that 100 km = 50 km/h × t. The need to divide d by r to solve for t should then be apparent.

Solutions: One common error is to incorrectly express t as hours and minutes instead of hours and fractions of hours; for example, a student may write $4\frac{1}{2}$ h as 4.30 instead of $4\frac{1}{2}$. This often occurs when solving for t: 4.25 h is often confused for 4 h 25 min instead of 4 h 15 min. To find the number of minutes in 0.25 h, multiply 60 by 0.25.

Checks: Have students look at the first equation in which numbers were substituted in the formula: Was each number substituted for the correct variable? Students may also estimate to check the reasonableness of their answers.

Write the letter of the formula that will help you solve the problem.

1. A race-car driver drove her car 3.3 kilometers in 1.1 minutes. What was her average speed?

a. $r = \frac{d}{t}$

b. $t = \frac{d}{r}$

c. $d = rt$

2. Mr. Shane drove his car 340 miles. His average speed was 20 mph. How long did his trip take?

a. $r = \frac{d}{t}$

b. $t = \frac{d}{r}$

c. $d = rt$

Solve.

3. Tim drove from Chicago, Illinois, to Evansville, Indiana, in 5 hours 45 minutes. His average speed was 52 mph. About how far is Evansville from Chicago? 299 mi

4. Durango, Mexico, lies between Mazatlán and Fresnillo. Durango is 325 kilometers from Mazatlán and 291 kilometers from Fresnillo. How far is Mazatlán from Fresnillo by way of Durango? 616 km

5. Duncan drove from Davenport, Iowa, to Des Moines, Iowa, a distance of 176 miles. At what rate of speed did he travel if he reached Des Moines in 4 hours? 44 mi/h

6. Leaving home, Carol drove at 45 mph for 30 minutes. Then she drove at 30 mph for 15 minutes to reach her office. How far did she drive to reach her office? 30 mi

7. Jeff and Ann rode on a train from Rome, Italy, to Florence, Italy. The trip took 4.5 hours, and the train's average speed was 96 kilometers per hour. About how far is it from Rome to Florence? 432 km

8. Jack drove from his home in Eugene, Oregon, to Portland, Oregon. The distance between the two cities is approximately 173 kilometers. The trip took Jack about $2\frac{1}{2}$ hours. What was his average speed? 69.2 km/h

9. In 1928, Mr. DeQuincy drove his Model-J Duesenberg 1,845 miles from Los Angeles, California, to St. Louis, Missouri. The trip took 26 hours. To the nearest mile per hour, what was Mr. DeQuincy's average rate of speed? 71 mi/h

★10. At 9:00 A.M., Sandi and Kim each begin to drive from Richmond, Virginia, to Harrisburg, Pennsylvania, a distance of 228 miles. Sandi drove at 50 mph, and Kim drove at 55 mph. How much sooner did Kim reach Harrisburg than Sandi? 25 minutes

Classwork/Homework, page H76

Exercise Analysis
1–2   Identify the proper formula
3–10   Skill applications

FOLLOW-UP ACTIVITIES

PROBLEM SOLVING
Tim wants to know how far it is from his house to his parents' house, but the odometer in his car is broken. Tim realized that if he drove at a steady speed, he could time his trip to find the distance. Since he had to drive at several different speeds, he broke his trip up into segments:

- 4 min at 25 mi/h
- 1 min at stop light
- 80 min at 45 mi/h
- 1 min at stop light
- 12 min at 40 mi/h
- 8 min at 25 mi/h

How far is it from Tim's house to his parents' house? (73 miles)

CALCULATOR
A calculator's memory can be used to store a single number that will be used repeatedly in related calculations. This often occurs when one variable in a formula is a constant; for example, let $r = 50$ mi/h. Place it in the memory by pressing 50 M or M +. Then to find d when $t = 4$ h, just press 4 × MR = to find the answer: 200. To then find d when $t = 12$ h, just press 12 × MR = to find 600.

Have students place the designated numbers into a calculator's memory and then use the calculator to solve the series of questions. At 55 mi/h, how far will you go in 3 h? (165 m) $2\frac{3}{4}$ h? $\left(151\frac{1}{4}\text{ m}\right)$ 6 h? (330 m)

How long will it take to go 210 miles at 35 mi/h? (6 h) 50 mi/h? $\left(4\frac{1}{5}\text{ h}\right)$ 500 mi/h? (0.42 h)

How fast are you going if in $2\frac{1}{2}$ h you drive 90 m? (36 mi/h) 120 m? (48 mi/h) 65 m? (26 mi/h)

Remind students to convert fractions such as $\frac{3}{4}$ to 0.75, and so on.

COMING UP
Time is on my side.

Objective: To determine time across time zones

Warm-Up

Divide the class into rows of four for a relay race. Have the first student in each row do the first exercise. When the first student is finished, the second student does the second exercise, and so on. The first row of students that finishes all examples correctly wins the race.

$3\frac{1}{7}$ wk = (22) d $2\frac{1}{2}$ min = (150) s

36 min = $\left(\frac{3}{5}\right)$ h   96 h = (4) d

GETTING STARTED

Ask students to explain the following puzzle.

Three airplanes leave New York at 1:00 P.M. and travel 600 mi/h. One plane travels approximately 2,100 mi, arriving in Denver, Colorado, at about 2:30 P.M. A second plane travels approximately 2,700 mi, arriving in Caracas, Venezuela, at about 6:00 P.M. The third plane travels approximately 1,700 mi, arriving in St. Johns, Canada, at about 5:00 P.M. Why are there differences in arrival time?

(Denver and St. Johns are in different time zones from New York; Caracas is in the same time zone as New York, but the travel distances are different.)

TEACHING THE LESSON

A. Help students to see the relationship between time zones and *longitude*. Earth is divided into 360 degrees of *longitude*. Greenwich is located on 0° longitude, the prime meridian. The international date line is located at 180° longitude. There is a 12-hour difference between them. This is why a day is taken away when crossing the date line going east, and added when crossing the date line going west. Time zones were introduced in 1918 to simplify traveling problems.

Time Zones

Mr. McCarthy plans to drive from Washington, D.C., to Seattle, Washington. He will drive 10 h per day. The trip takes 56 h. He leaves on Monday and each day begins driving at 9:00 A.M. by his watch, which remains on D.C. time. When will he arrive in Seattle?

Earth is divided into twenty-four time zones. Universal Coordinated Time is the first time zone. The time changes to one hour earlier for each time zone going west. The time changes to one hour later for each time zone going east. The Continental United States has four time zones.

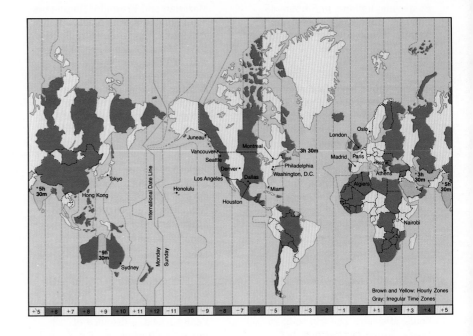

Because Mr McCarthy will pass through four time zones going west, he will arrive in Seattle at 12:00 P.M. Saturday.

186   Math Reasoning, page H216

COMMON ERRORS

Students often lose track of when to add or subtract hours in elapsed times across time zones.

Remediation

Have students mark west (*W*) or east (*E*) next to the locations whose times are being compared. Remind them that *W* means to subtract 1 hour for each zone, and that *E* means to add 1 hour for each zone.

Assign Reteach Master, p. 56.

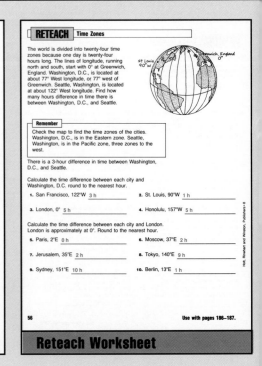

RETEACH Time Zones

The world is divided into twenty-four time zones because one day is twenty-four hours long. The lines of longitude, running north and south, start with 0° at Greenwich, England. Washington, D.C., is located at about 77° West longitude, or 77° west of Greenwich. Seattle, Washington, is located at about 122° West longitude. Find how many hours difference in time there is between Washington, D.C., and Seattle.

Remember

Check the map to find the time zones of the cities. Washington, D.C., is in the Eastern zone. Seattle, Washington, is in the Pacific zone, three zones to the west.

There is a 3-hour difference in time between Washington, D.C., and Seattle.

Calculate the time difference between each city and Washington, D.C. round to the nearest hour.

1. San Francisco, 122°W 3 h   2. St. Louis, 90°W 1 h

3. London, 0° 5 h   4. Honolulu, 157°W 5 h

Calculate the time difference between each city and London. London is approximately at 0°. Round to the nearest hour.

5. Paris, 2°E 0 h   6. Moscow, 37°E 2 h

7. Jerusalem, 35°E 2 h   8. Tokyo, 140°E 9 h

9. Sydney, 151°E 10 h   10. Berlin, 13°E 1 h

56   Use with pages 186–187.

Reteach Worksheet

It is 9:00 A.M. Friday in Denver. Write the time in each city.

1. Los Angeles
8:00 A.M.
2. Houston
10:00 A.M.
3. Miami
11:00 A.M.
4. Juneau
7:00 A.M.
5. Montreal
11:00 A.M.
6. Honolulu
6:00 A.M.
7. Seattle
8:00 A.M.
8. Philadelphia
11:00 A.M.

It is 4:00 P.M. Tuesday in Paris. Write the time in each city.

9. London
3:00 P.M.
10. Oslo 4:00 P.M.
11. Athens
5:00 P.M.
12. Washington, D.C.
10:00 A.M.
13. Hong Kong
11:00 P.M.
14. Nairobi
6:00 P.M.
15. Vancouver
7:00 A.M.
16. Dallas
9:00 A.M.

It is 5:30 A.M. Thursday in Tokyo. Write the time in each city.

17. Hong Kong
4:30 A.M.
18. Sydney
6:30 A.M.
19. Paris
9:30 P.M. Wed.
20. Seattle
12:30 A.M. Wed.
21. London
8:30 P.M. Wed.
22. Athens
10:30 P.M. Wed.
23. Algiers
8:30 P.M. Wed.
24. Madrid
9:30 P.M. Wed.

Solve. For problem 29, use the Infobank.

25. Ms. Howland drove from Houston to Los Angeles. She left at 8 A.M. and arrived 3 days 2 hours later. What time was it in Los Angeles when she arrived? 8 A.M.

26. Mr. Su drove from Seattle to Montreal. When he arrived, it was 7:00 A.M. on Friday. What time and what day was it in Seattle?

4:00 A.M., Friday

27. Plan a two-week trip to the Orient. Determine departure and arrival dates and times for each city on your tour. Answers will vary.

28. Ms. Traetta flew from Miami to Sydney, Australia. It was 9:00 P.M. on March 18 when she arrived. What time and date was it in Miami? 6 A.M., March 18

29. Use the information on page 475 to solve. The Quiet Achiever is a solar-powered car. Its average velocity is 25 km/h. At this rate, how long would it take the Achiever to travel from Broken Hill to Dubbo? 30 h

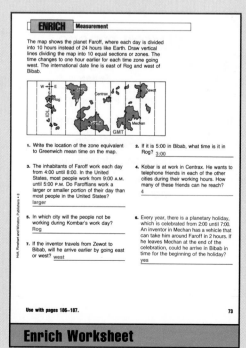

CHALLENGE

A pilot of a supersonic plane told his young son that when he leaves New York at 10:00 A.M. Eastern time, he arrives in Los Angeles at 9:30 A.M. Pacific time. The young boy looked puzzled and then asked, "If you keep going at the same speed and fly all the way around the world, will you arrive back in New York before you left?" What is wrong with this thinking?

Classwork/Homework, page H77
See Answer Key.
187

ASSIGNMENT GUIDE

Basic: 1–12, 13–27 o

Average: 1–12, 14–26 e, 27

Extended: 4–16 e, 17–29, Chlg

Resources
Practice, p. 77   Class/Home, p. H77
Reteach, p. 56   Reasoning, p. H216
Enrich, p. 73

Exercise Analysis

1–24	Write the time in different time zones
25–26, 28–29	Skill applications
27	Data collection and computation

Challenge

This problem asks students to incorporate knowledge of the international date line and the concept of time zones to solve a logical-reasoning problem.

FOLLOW-UP ACTIVITIES

MATH CONNECTION (Consumer)
Materials: schedules of various airlines

Have students make lists of airlines that travel to the same destination and calculate the travel time for each flight. Which airline has the best time to a given destination? (Answers will vary.)

Variation: Have students compute the cost of telephone calls of various lengths made at various times of day. A local phone book contains the rates.

MATH CONNECTION (Science)
Although official times are standard throughout time zones, *local times* can vary as much as 4 minutes from one town to another. To find the exact local time for any city, scientists use the concept of *local noon.* (Local noon occurs when the sun is most directly overhead.)

*The time for local noon can be used to calculate the exact longitude of your town. Through observation, find the difference in minutes between local noon and noon on the clock. Then divide by 4 to find the degrees east or west of the center of your standard time zone.

Consult a detailed atlas of your region for pertinent longitudinal and mileage data.

COMING UP
Cool it!

Warm-Up

Have students perform the following operations mentally.

72 + 13 (85)   71 − 12 (59)
26.5 + 21 (47.5)   26.5 − 21 (5.5)
12 + 11.5 (23.5)   12 − 11.5 (0.5)

GETTING STARTED

Materials: newspaper reports of daily temperatures in different cities, picture or chalk drawing of a Fahrenheit thermometer showing 100°, 0°, ⁻10° with lines marking 10° intervals

Have volunteers read the temperatures for cities such as Miami, Dallas, San Diego, Anchorage, and Fairbanks. Point out that some of the listed temperatures may be above zero degrees on the thermometer and some may be below zero degrees. Ask volunteers to write each city's temperature in the appropriate place on the thermometer.

TEACHING THE LESSON

A. The two points of reference on the Fahrenheit scale are 32° and 212°—the freezing point and boiling point of water. The corresponding points on the Celsius scale are 0° and 100°.

Have students read the classroom thermometer. Discuss where the mercury will be when the temperature is 5° warmer and when it is 15° cooler. Have students refer to scales to find each of the following temperatures.

75°F + 8°F = (83°F)
20°C + 2°C − 10°C = (12°C)

14°C − 6°C + 1°C − 3°C = (6°C)
⁻20°C − 1°C + 11°C + 6°C + 5°C = (1°C)

Checkpoint

The chart lists the common errors students make in exercises involving temperature.

Correct Answers: 1b, 2a

Remediation

■ For these errors, guide students in drawing a number line to help them model changes in temperature on both the Celsius and the Fahrenheit scales.

☐ For these errors, assign Reteach Master, p. 57.

Temperature

The temperature of the burning gases in the cylinder of a car can reach as high as 4,500°F. The cooling system keeps the temperature of the engine between 160°F and 180°F.

Temperature can be measured in degrees Fahrenheit (°F) or degrees Celsius (°C).

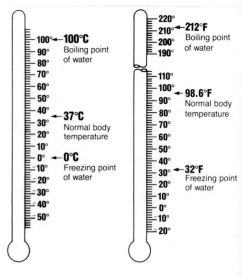

Suppose the temperature is ⁻14°C and rises 16°. What is the temperature now?

Look at the Celsius thermometer. Start at ⁻14°C and move 16 units up. The temperature now is 2°C.

Checkpoint Write the letter of the correct answer.

1. Choose the best estimate for the temperature of a refrigerated apple.

a. 0°C   (b.) 10°C
c. 20°C   d. 40°C

2. The temperature is 4°F; it drops 7°. What is the temperature now?

(a.) ⁻3°F   b. 3°F
c. ⁻7°F   d. ⁻11°F

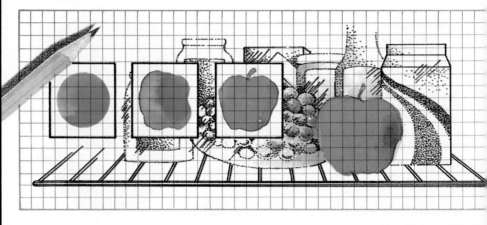

188   Math Reasoning, page H216

COMMON ERRORS

Answer Choice	Type of Error
☐ 1a, 1c	Estimates incorrectly
■ 1d	Estimates for Fahrenheit
☐ 2b	Uses incorrect sign
■ 2c	Disregards starting point
☐ 2d	Uses wrong operation and wrong sign

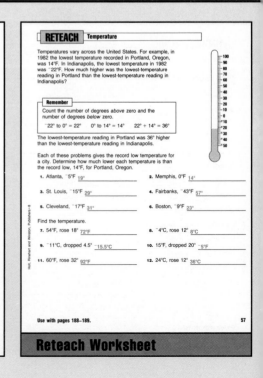

RETEACH Temperature

Temperatures vary across the United States. For example, in 1982 the lowest temperature recorded in Portland, Oregon, was 14°F. In Indianapolis, the lowest temperature in 1982 was ⁻22°F. How much higher was the lowest-temperature reading in Portland than the lowest-temperature reading in Indianapolis?

Remember
Count the number of degrees *above* zero and the number of degrees *below* zero.
⁻22° to 0° = 22°   0° to 14° = 14°   22° + 14° = 36°

The lowest-temperature reading in Portland was 36° higher than the lowest-temperature reading in Indianapolis.

Each of these problems gives the record low temperature for a city. Determine how much lower each temperature is than the record low, 14°F, for Portland, Oregon.

1. Atlanta, ⁻5°F 19°   2. Memphis, 0°F 14°
3. St. Louis, ⁻15°F 29°   4. Fairbanks, ⁻43°F 57°
5. Cleveland, ⁻17°F 31°   6. Boston, ⁻9°F 23°

Find the temperature.
7. 54°F, rose 18° 72°F   8. ⁻4°C, rose 12° 8°C
9. ⁻11°C, dropped 4.5° ⁻15.5°C   10. 15°F, dropped 20° ⁻5°F
11. 60°F, rose 32° 92°F   12. 24°C, rose 12° 36°C

Use with pages 188–189.   57

Reteach Worksheet

Choose the best estimate. Write the letter of the correct answer.

1. room temperature   **a.** 55°F   **(b.)** 68°F   **c.** 78°F

2. a medium oven   **a.** 32°F   **b.** 100°F   **(c.)** 350°F

3. a freezer   **a.** ⁻100°F   **(b.)** ⁻5°F   **c.** 22°F

Find the temperature.

4. 12°F, rose 15°   27°F   **5.** ⁻10°F, dropped 5°   ⁻15°F   **6.** ⁻7°F, rose 18°
                                                                            11°F

Find the change in temperature.

7. 18°F to 35°F   17°   **8.** ⁻12°F to ⁻17°F   ⁻5°   **9.** ⁻18°F to 7°F
                                                                           25°

Choose the best estimate. Write the letter of the correct answer.

10. a cold day   **(a.)** 5°C   **b.** 20°C   **c.** 32°C

11. a warm day   **a.** 75°C   **b.** 50°C   **(c.)** 25°C

Find the temperature.

12. 35.7°C, rose 7°   42.7°C   **13.** ⁻18.2°C, dropped 0.5°   **14.** ⁻12.7°C, rose 18.5°
                                                  ⁻18.7°C   5.8°C

Find the change in temperature.

15. 38.2°C to 47.9°C   9.7°   **16.** ⁻12°C to ⁻20.4°C   ⁻8.4°   **17.** ⁻4.6°C to 14.2°C
                                                                              18.8°

Solve.

18. An antifreeze composed of ethylene glycol mixed with water has a boiling point of 223°F. How does this compare with the boiling point of water?   11° higher

19. Research in your school library to find the average temperature inside a carburetor during combustion.
Answers will vary.

ANOTHER LOOK

Find the product.

1. $4 \cdot 5^2$ 100   **2.** $3^2 \cdot 3^2$ 81   **3.** $2 \cdot 3^2 \cdot 4^2$ 288   **4.** $2^2 \cdot 4^3$ 256   **5.** $2^3 \cdot 7 \cdot 11$
                                                                                            616

Give the prime factorization of each number.

6. 45 $3^2 \cdot 5$ **7.** 36 $2^2 \cdot 3^2$ **8.** 175 $5^2 \cdot 7$ **9.** 169 13^2 **10.** 572
                                                                                                   $2^2 \cdot 11 \cdot 13$

Classwork/Homework, page H78   **189**

ASSIGNMENT GUIDE

Basic: 1–15, 18, AL

Average: 4–19, AL

Extended: 4–19, AL

Resources
Practice, p. 78   Class/Home, p. H78
Reteach, p. 57   Reasoning, p. H216
Enrich, p. 74

Exercise Analysis

1–3	Select the best estimate, Fahrenheit
4–9	Compute temperature or change in temperature (Fahrenheit)
10–11	Select the best estimate, Celsius.
12–17	Compute temperature or change in temperature (Celsius)
18	Skill application
19	Data collection

Another Look

These exercises provide reviews of computing with exponents and of finding the prime factorization of a number.

FOLLOW-UP ACTIVITIES

MANIPULATIVES

Materials: construction paper, magazine pictures of events associated with certain temperatures; for example, a beach scene, a yard sale, people skiing

Have students paste one picture on each sheet of construction paper. Below each picture, write three different temperatures.

Using these as flash cards, have students pick the most reasonable temperature for the event pictured.

COMPUTER

Have students enter and run the following program:

```
10      REM C TO F
30      PRINT TAB (10); "CELSIUS";
        TAB (20); "FAHRENHEIT"
40      PRINT:PRINT
50      FOR C = 100 TO -50 STEP -10
60      LET F = 9*C/5 + 32
70      FOR I = 1 TO 740: NEXT I
80      PRINT TAB (12); C;
        TAB (22); F
90      NEXT C
100     END
```

This program prints a table showing Celsius measures being renamed with Fahrenheit measures.

COMING UP
On the road again

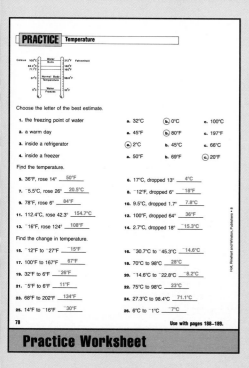

PRACTICE Temperature

Choose the letter of the best estimate.

1. the freezing point of water   **a.** 32°C   **(b.)** 0°C   **c.** 100°C

2. a warm day   **a.** 45°F   **(b.)** 80°F   **c.** 197°F

3. inside a refrigerator   **(a.)** 2°C   **b.** 45°C   **c.** 66°C

4. inside a freezer   **a.** 50°F   **b.** 69°F   **(c.)** 20°F

Find the temperature.

5. 36°F, rose 14°   50°F   **6.** 17°C, dropped 13°   4°C

7. ⁻5.5°C, rose 26°   20.5°C   **8.** ⁻12°F, dropped 6°   ⁻18°F

9. 78°F, rose 6°   84°F   **10.** 9.5°C, dropped 1.7°   7.8°C

11. 112.4°F, rose 42.3°   154.7°F   **12.** 100°F, dropped 64°   36°F

13. ⁻16°F, rose 124°   108°F   **14.** 2.7°C, dropped 18°   ⁻15.3°C

Find the change in temperature.

15. ⁻12°F to ⁻27°F   ⁻15°F   **16.** ⁻30.7°C to ⁻45.3°C   ⁻14.6°C

17. 100°F to 167°F   67°F   **18.** 70°C to 98°C   28°C

19. 32°F to 6°F   ⁻26°F   **20.** ⁻14.6°C to ⁻22.8°C   ⁻8.2°C

21. ⁻5°F to 6°F   11°F   **22.** 75°C to 98°C   23°C

23. 68°F to 202°F   134°F   **24.** 27.3°C to 98.4°C   71.1°C

25. 14°F to ⁻16°F   ⁻30°F   **26.** 6°C to ⁻1°C   ⁻7°C

78   **Use with pages 188–189.**

Practice Worksheet

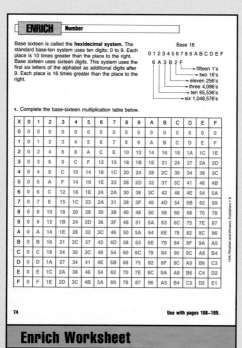

ENRICH Number

Base sixteen is called the **hexidecimal system.** The standard base-ten system uses ten digits: 0 to 9. Each place is 10 times greater than the place to the right. Base sixteen uses sixteen digits. This system uses the first six letters of the alphabet as additional digits after 9. Each place is 16 times greater than the place to the right.

Base 16
0 1 2 3 4 5 6 7 8 9 A B C D E F
6 A 3 B 2 F
— fifteen 1's
— two 16's
— eleven 256's
— three 4,096's
— ten 65,536's
— six 1,048,576's

1. Complete the base-sixteen multiplication table below.

X	0	1	2	3	4	5	6	7	8	9	A	B	C	D	E	F
0	0	0	0	0	0	0	0	0	0	0	0	0	0	0	0	0
1	0	1	2	3	4	5	6	7	8	9	A	B	C	D	E	F
2	0	2	4	6	8	A	C	E	10	12	14	16	18	1A	1C	1E
3	0	3	6	9	C	F	12	15	18	1B	1E	21	24	27	2A	2D
4	0	4	8	C	10	14	18	1C	20	24	28	2C	30	34	38	3C
5	0	5	A	F	14	19	1E	23	28	2D	32	37	3C	41	46	4B
6	0	6	C	12	18	1E	24	2A	30	36	3C	42	48	4E	54	5A
7	0	7	E	15	1C	23	2A	31	38	3F	46	4D	54	5B	62	69
8	0	8	10	18	20	28	30	38	40	48	50	58	60	68	70	78
9	0	9	12	1B	24	2D	36	3F	48	51	5A	63	6C	75	7E	87
A	0	A	14	1E	28	32	3C	46	50	5A	64	6E	78	82	8C	96
B	0	B	16	21	2C	37	42	4D	58	63	6E	79	84	8F	9A	A5
C	0	C	18	24	30	3C	48	54	60	6C	78	84	90	9C	A8	B4
D	0	D	1A	27	34	41	4E	5B	68	75	82	8F	9C	A9	B6	C3
E	0	E	1C	2A	38	46	54	62	70	7E	8C	9A	A8	B6	C4	D2
F	0	F	1E	2D	3C	4B	5A	69	78	87	96	A5	B4	C3	D2	E1

74   **Use with pages 188–189.**

Enrich Worksheet

Objectives: To use information from a road map

Warm-Up

Have students find the following distances.

84.2 km + 17 km − 12.5 km (88.7 km)

29,000 mi ÷ 120 $\left(241\frac{2}{3} \text{ mi}\right)$

7.82 mi × 365 (2,854.3 mi)

(500 km ÷ 4) + 325 km (450 km)

(62 mi × 5) + (18.4 mi × 7) (438.8 mi)

GETTING STARTED

Have a volunteer come to the front of the class and attempt to describe the route from the school to his or her home. Tell the volunteer to describe the route as accurately as possible. Encourage the use of visual aids. The student will probably draw a map on the chalkboard. Discuss the utility of maps.

TEACHING THE LESSON

Most people will have occasion to use a road map fairly often during their lives. Familiarity with the information contained on maps will be of use to students in numerous situations.

Questions: Encourage students to ask interpretive questions when reading a map. For instance, if the shortest distance between two points is via a local road students may ask such questions as "Might it be quicker to travel via a main highway, since the speed limit is higher and there will be no traffic lights?" Conversely, if speed is not a vital consideration students may wish to ask such questions as "Which route will be the most pleasant to travel?"

Tools: Review the mileage legend with students, particularly the use of red ticks to show the ends of each mileage segment. Some students may also need to review the differences among the types of roads on the map.

Students may benefit from working these problems in groups. Some students may be familiar with road maps and may be able to share their knowledge with other students.

Solutions: Students may have to be reminded of the formula $d = rt$, relating distance, speed, and time traveled.

Checks: Students should check the map to verify distances they have used to solve the problems. Computations can be checked for mathematical accuracy.

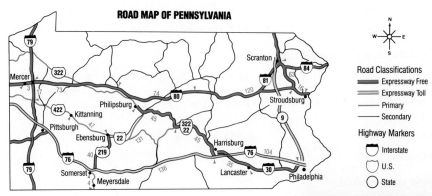

| QUESTIONS | TOOLS | SOLUTIONS | CHECKS |

PROBLEM SOLVING
Using a Road Map

A road map is a good source of information about routes and distances between places.

This is how data are shown on a road map.

- The map title tells you the area or region that the map shows.
- The map key at the right identifies road classifications and highway markers.
- Mileage is indicated by red numbers between red tick marks.

Karen uses this road map of Pennsylvania to plan her trip from Philipsburg to Harrisburg. She wants to know how many miles she will travel.

- Locate Philipsburg and Harrisburg.
- Find the shortest route that connects them.
- Find the mileage symbols and the numerals along the route between Harrisburg and Philipsburg.

The trip will be 90 miles.

190

Solve. Use the road map on page 190 to answer each question.

1. Kirby drives from Philadelphia to Lancaster. What road is the most direct route? Interstate 30

2. Monica lives in Meyersdale and is planning to drive to Ebensburg and back. About how many miles will she travel? about 88 miles

3. Millie drove from Kittanning to Ebensburg and from Ebensburg to Somerset. Approximately how many miles did she drive on the expressway, and how many miles did she drive on a primary road?
approximately 40 miles of expressway; about 47 miles of primary road

4. Aaron drove from the junction of routes 79 and 80 to the junction of routes 79 and 422. If he drove at 50 miles per hour, about how long did that trip take him? about 20 minutes

5. Mr. Lee is planning to drive from Stroudsburg to Mercer. What is the shortest route? About how long will the trip take him if he drives at 45 mph? Interstate 80; about 6 hours 20 minutes.

6. Ronnie drove on Route 76 from Philadelphia to Somerset and back. Her company paid her expenses, including gas and a travel allowance of $0.17 per mile. How much was she reimbursed if she spent $17.50 for gas? $99.10

7. Mrs. Davis plans to drive from Philadelphia to Harrisburg and then back to Lancaster. Her car gets 21 miles per gallon. About how many gallons of gas will Mrs. Davis use? about 6.6 gallons

8. Anthony wants to drive from Meyersdale to Somerset and then on to Ebensburg. If he averages 49 miles per hour and stops for a half hour to eat lunch, how long will the trip take? about 1 hour 24 minutes

9. Lenny has to drive from Harrisburg to Somerset, but he doesn't want to take a toll road. How much longer will the trip be if he travels on routes 22 and 219? 80 miles

10. Interstate highways that have even numbers run east and west. Odd numbered interstate highways run north and south. If you left Pittsburgh and traveled an odd-numbered interstate highway, then an even-numbered one, then another odd-numbered one, in what directions would you have gone? north or south; east or west; north or south

Classwork/Homework, page H79

ASSIGNMENT GUIDE

Basic:	1–6, 10
Average:	1–4, 8–10
Extended:	4–10

Resources
Practice, p. 79   Class/Home, p. H79
Enrich, p. 75

Exercise Analysis
1–10   Data collection and computation

FOLLOW-UP ACTIVITIES

PROBLEM SOLVING
Have students find a road map of your state or region. Have each student use the map to plan a trip of approximately 500 miles. Students should list the roads they would take, the places they would visit, and the distances between those places.

Tell students that actual road maps are often less clearly labeled than the map in the text. Mileage symbols often represent distance between intersections of highways.

If students have difficulty finding a map, your library probably has a United States road atlas.

CALCULATOR
Have students use a calculator to solve the following problems.
1. Mrs. Stevenson lives in Lancaster and drives to work in Harrisburg every day. She works 50 five-day weeks per year. If it costs her an average of $0.28 per mile for all the expenses associated with driving (price of car, gas, insurance, and so on), how much does she spend every year to commute to Harrisburg? ($4,900)
2. Mr. Gonzales drives from Somerset to Harrisburg and back every week for a business meeting. Mr. Gonzales's company pays him $0.35 per mile plus $10 per trip for parking. If Mr. Gonzales were paid this money only once per year, how much would he receive? ($5,470.40)

Coming Up
Math and machines

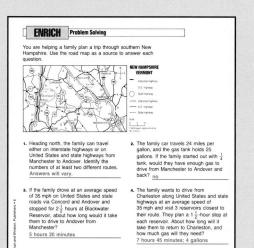

PRACTICE Using a Road Map

Solve. Use the road map to answer each question.

CALIFORNIA

— Freeways
— Principal through Highways
— Other divided highways
— Other roads
○ National Interstate
○ U.S. ○ State
Scale

1. Martin drives from Las Vegas, Nevada, to Ludlow, California, via Barstow, California. What are the numbers of the highways he will drive on? 15, 40

2. About how far along the freeways is it from Las Vegas, Nevada, to Needles, California (on Route 40 near Arizona)? 287 miles

3. Samuel drives on Route 58 from Bakersfield to Barstow. His car travels 20 miles per gallon. If he has 6 gallons of gas in his tank, can he complete his trip without buying more gas? no

4. Muriel's mother begins her trip from San Fernando to Paso Robles on Route 5. Muriel's father drives from Ventura to Paso Robles. Does one of them drive farther? Who and by how much?
Yes; Muriel's mother drives about 25 more miles.

5. Naomi's car travels 25 miles per gallon. If gas costs her $1.05 per gallon, about how much will she have to spend on gas to make the longer trip described in Problem 4? $7.77

6. Lebec is halfway between Bakersfield and San Fernando. Mojave is directly east of Lebec. Armand wants to drive on the freeway from Mojave to Lebec. Would it be quicker for him to go through Bakersfield or through San Fernando? through Bakersfield

Use after pages 190–191.   79

Practice Worksheet

ENRICH Problem Solving

You are helping a family plan a trip through southern New Hampshire. Use the road map as a source to answer each question.

NEW HAMPSHIRE VERMONT
— Interstate highway
— U.S. highway
○ State highway
— Interstate highway
— U.S. highway
Scale

1. Heading north, the family can travel either on interstate highways or on United States and state highways from Manchester to Andover. Identify the numbers of at least two different routes.
Answers will vary.

2. The family car travels 24 miles per gallon, and the gas tank holds 25 gallons. If the family started out with $\frac{1}{4}$ tank, would they have enough gas to drive from Manchester to Andover and back? no

3. If the family drove at an average speed of 35 mph on United States and state roads via Concord and Andover and stopped for $2\frac{1}{2}$ hours at Blackwater Reservoir, about how long would it take them to drive to Andover from Manchester? 5 hours 20 minutes

4. The family wants to drive from Charleston along United States and state highways at an average speed of 35 mph and visit 3 reservoirs closest to their route. They plan a $1\frac{1}{2}$-hour stop at each reservoir. About how long will it take them to return to Charleston, and how much gas will they need? 7 hours 45 minutes; 4 gallons

Use after pages 190–191.   75

Enrich Worksheet

Objectives: To compare, add, and subtract distances

Warm-Up
Estimate the following.

1. 4,896
    − 1,248
    (3,000–4,000)

2. 2,374
    6,889
    + 7,921
    (15,000–18,000)

3. 9,789
    − 1,423
    (8,000–9,000)

4. 10,984
    7,720
    2,041
    + 993
    (19,000–23,000)

(Answers may vary. Accept any reasonable estimate.)

GETTING STARTED

Have students plan a trip to a nearby city. They should estimate the cost and the time required for the trip based on using various kinds of transportation.

TEACHING THE LESSON

Point out that although students will not have to use calculators to solve some of these problems, calculators would be useful because they allow students to find the total distances of given routes quickly. Students should be encouraged to estimate before they use their calculators.

CALCULATOR

Use your calculator and the table to solve.

Distances are given in kilometers.

	Chicago	Denver	Houston	Los Angeles	Miami	New York	St. Louis	Seattle
Denver, CO	1,463							
Houston, TX	1,503	1,408						
Los Angeles, CA	2,806	1,350	2,208					
Miami, FL	1,916	2,762	1,543	3,750				
New York, NY	1,163	2,618	2,279	3,948	1,757			
St. Louis, MO	413	1,257	1,090	2,544	1,719	1,419		
Seattle, WA	2,790	1,642	3,034	1,543	4,385	3,875	2,752	
Washington, DC	953	2,375	1,938	3,682	1,481	346	1,138	3,721

1. Compare the two routes.
   (a) Los Angeles to St. Louis to New York 3,963 km
   (b) Los Angeles to New York 3,948 km
   Which route from Los Angeles to New York is shorter? b.   how much shorter? 15 km

2. Compare these two routes.
   (a) Houston to St. Louis to Washington, D.C. 2,228 km
   (b) Houston to Washington, D.C. 1,938 km
   Which route from Houston to Washington, D.C., is longer? a   how much longer? 290 km

3. Determine the shortest route from Miami to Seattle, stopping at one of the cities on the chart. Which city would you stop at? Denver

4. You are planning a route from Denver to Chicago, that is as close to 2,000 km as possible, making as many stops as you wish. Which route would you use? Answers will vary.

5. You have won an airline contest. Your prize is 10,000 km of free flying. You must start from the city nearest you and return to the same city. Which route would you take to use as much of the 10,000 km without going over? Answers will vary.

192

GROUP PROJECT

A Wild and Crazy Car

The problem: Lucky you! In a promotional super-raffle, you alone won the new car, the fabulous Funmobile of the Future! Along with the car, you were given $10,000 to spend on any group of options you want. Choose your options from the list below. Put together a package, and make sure you don't exceed your budget.

Funmobile Options

- Power steering $810.00
- Power brakes $645.00
- Power windows $860.00
- Rear-window wipers $692.00
- Laser defroster $1,350.00
- Deluxe covered roof seats $1,675.00
- OmniScopic see-all windshield $1,815.00
- Telekinetic TV telephone $2,160.00
- Backseat hot tub $2,662.50
- Pseudoconvertible Night Sky Simulator $2,545.00
- Moto-Mini golf course $4,750.00
- Continental climate control $1,235.00
- Solid-gold designer hubcaps (each) $1,672.50
- Accu-Sound SuperStereo system $1,685.00
- Automated ComputoKitchen $4,653.50

193

ASSIGNMENT GUIDE

Basic:	p. 192, p. 193
Average:	p. 192, p. 193
Extended:	p. 192, p. 193

Objectives: To choose among options; to stay within a budget

USING THE PAGE

Students are given the opportunity to exercise their individual preferences, while staying within a budget. Working this project in groups is a good exercise in accommodating varied tastes.

Separate the class into groups of three or four. Students should first consider individually their own preferred options, and then express them to the group. After each student has stated his or her preferences, the group as a whole should determine which combination of options is most attractive. Point out that some options, such as power steering or rear-window wipers, are practical and could make the car more pleasant to drive at all times; other options, such as the golf course, are fun but useful only occasionally.

Have each group determine which of their favorite options they can afford with the given budget. Point out that some expensive items can be sacrificed to allow the purchase of several smaller items. If desired, each group can read the list of their combination of options to the class, noting the total cost. A tally could be kept to see which three options were the most popular.

To extend this activity, have groups determine which options they would choose if the budget were only $6,000; or if it were $15,000. Then survey the groups to see which were the three most popular options in each circumstance.

Purpose: The Chapter Test helps to assess students' understanding of the concepts and skills presented in this chapter.

The chart below is designed to help you review the test items by correlating them with the testing objectives that appear in the Chapter Overview.

Item	Objectives
1–8	A
9–17	B
18–21	C
22–23	E
24–25	D
26–27	E
28	F
29	H
30	I
31	G
32–33	B

Bonus
The bonus questions may be used for extra credit, or you may want to assign them to students who complete the test before the rest of the class.

Calculator
You may wish to have students use calculators for the problem-solving portions of the test.

Resources
If you prefer to use this Chapter Test as a review exercise, additional testing materials are available in the Teacher's Resource Book.

CHAPTER TEST

Give the appropriate metric unit to measure each. (pages 166–169)

1. sack of oranges kg

2. bottle of vanilla extract mL

3. a hike km

4. slice of melon g

Give the appropriate customary unit to measure each. (pages 174–177)

5. bottle of honey oz

6. gasoline gal

7. sack of potatoes lb

8. length of a shoe in.

Complete. (pages 166–171 and 174–177)

9. $5{,}000 \text{ cm} = \blacksquare \text{ m}$ 50

10. $0.07 \text{ L} = \blacksquare \text{ mL}$ 70

11. $250 \text{ L} = \blacksquare \text{ kL}$ 0.

12. $8 \text{ mL} = \blacksquare \text{ g of water}$ 8

13. $0.005 \text{ g} = \blacksquare \text{ mg}$ 5

14. $6 \text{ gal} = \blacksquare \text{ qt}$ 24

15. $18 \text{ lb} = \blacksquare \text{ oz}$ 288

16. $144 \text{ oz} = \blacksquare \text{ lb}$ 9

17. $5 \text{ yd} = \blacksquare \text{ ft}$ 15

Add or subtract. (pages 174–177, 182–183)

18.
$$\begin{array}{r} 8 \text{ lb } 11 \text{ oz} \\ + 2 \text{ lb } 9 \text{ oz} \\ \hline 11 \text{ lb } 4 \text{ oz} \end{array}$$

19.
$$\begin{array}{r} 3 \text{ yd } 2 \text{ ft} \\ + 2 \text{ yd } 2 \text{ ft} \\ \hline 6 \text{ yd } 1 \text{ ft} \end{array}$$

20.
$$\begin{array}{r} 5 \text{ qt } 1 \text{ c} \\ - 3 \text{ qt } 3 \text{ c} \\ \hline 1 \text{ qt } 2 \text{ c} \end{array}$$

21.
$$\begin{array}{r} 6 \text{ gal } 5 \text{ pt} \\ - 2 \text{ gal } 5 \text{ pt} \\ \hline 4 \text{ gal} \end{array}$$

22.
$$\begin{array}{r} 2 \text{ h } 45 \text{ min} \\ + 6 \text{ h } 20 \text{ min} \\ \hline 9 \text{ h } 5 \text{ min} \end{array}$$

23.
$$\begin{array}{r} 5 \text{ h } 12 \text{ min} \\ - 2 \text{ h } 35 \text{ min} \\ \hline 2 \text{ h } 37 \text{ min} \end{array}$$

Write the degree change. (pages 188–189)

24. $^-4°F$ to $^-50°F$ 46°F

25. $^-8°C$ to $31°C$ 39°C

194

POSTTEST   Chapter 5 Page 1

1. What is the appropriate metric unit of length for measuring the distance around the trunk of a small tree?

2. What is the change in temperature from 15°C to ⁻6°C?

3. How many ounces are in 15 pounds of bananas?

4. How much water does it take to fill a one cubic centimeter box?

5.
$$\begin{array}{r} 4 \text{ h } 40 \text{ min} \\ - 1 \text{ h } 45 \text{ min} \end{array}$$

6. A mixture of salt and water has a freezing point of 27°F. How much higher or lower is this than 32°, the freezing point of pure water?

7.
$$\begin{array}{r} 2 \text{ h } 15 \text{ min} \\ + 5 \text{ h } 50 \text{ min} \end{array}$$

8. What is the appropriate customary unit used to measure the height of a car?

9.
$$\begin{array}{r} 6 \text{ gal } 2 \text{ qt} \\ - 4 \text{ gal } 3 \text{ qt} \end{array}$$

10. A race car drove 3.4 kilometers in 1.2 minutes. Given this information which would be a sensible question to ask?
 a. What was the color of the car?
 b. What is the distance around the track?
 c. How long did it take to finish the race?
 d. At what speed was the car traveling?

11.
$$\begin{array}{r} 4 \text{ ft } 3 \text{ in.} \\ - 2 \text{ ft } 7 \text{ in.} \end{array}$$

12. What is the appropriate metric unit for expressing the mass of a person?
 a. kilogram   b. gram
 c. liter   d. millimeter

13. What is 8 cm expressed in mm?

Posttest

POSTTEST   Chapter 5 Page 2

14.
$$\begin{array}{r} 3 \text{ lb } 8 \text{ oz} \\ + 4 \text{ lb } 10 \text{ oz} \end{array}$$

15. What is the appropriate customary unit used to measure the weight of a sack of apples?

16. 64 quarts = ■ gallons
 What is ■?

17. The temperature late one January afternoon was 45°F. Early the next morning the temperature had fallen to 5° below freezing. How much had the temperature changed on the Fahrenheit scale?

18. A plane travels at an average speed of 400 miles per hour from Metropolis to Tropicana. How long does the flight take if the cities are 1,300 miles apart?

19. At Roosevelt High School, a committee from the senior class is planning to work on the yearbook. Which of the following is not a sensible question to ask?
 a. What will the cost be to each senior member?
 b. What activities should be highlighted?
 c. How much advertising should be included?
 d. How many pages are in the school's newspaper?

20. Eric rode his bike from 9:30 AM to 1:00 PM. If he traveled a total distance of 28 miles, what was his average speed in miles per hour?

21. The morning temperature was 13°C. The temperature rose 9° by noon. What was the temperature at noon?

22. A train travels from Hometown to Picksley at an average speed of 70 km per hour. If the trip takes 2 h 30 min, how far apart are the two cities?

Posttest

Find the elapsed time between each. (pages 182–183)

26. 3:00 A.M. and 2:20 P.M.
11 h 20 min

27. 11:15 P.M. and 2:14 A.M.
2 h 59 min

28. Denver is 7 time zones west of London, England. If you left London at 1:30 P.M. and flew for 11 hours, what time would it be in Denver when your plane arrived? (pages 186–187)
5:30 P.M.

Solve. (pages 168–169, 172–173, 176–177, 184–185, and 190–191)

29. The longest scheduled bus route is Across Australia Coach Lines, which travels 3,389 mi and takes about 76 h. To the nearest tenth, what is the average speed of the bus? 44.6 mph

30. Wendell's newspaper route required him to drive 85 mi/d. His map scale was 1.5 cm equals 5 mi. How many centimeters would represent his route?
25.5 cm

31. Wendell earns $1,000 per month delivering newspapers. He is considering buying a new car that will cost him $350 per month. Formulate a question that he should answer before making a decision. Answers may vary.
What are his other monthly expenses?

32. Lynn has used 7,000 mL of car wax this year. Change this amount to the most appropriate metric unit. 7 L

33. If Dennis wants to fill eight 2-quart containers with oil, how many gallons of oil must he purchase?
4 gal

BONUS

Solve.

A bolt has 40 yards of cloth. If a bolt is enough fabric to upholster $2\frac{1}{2}$ automobiles, how many yards are necessary for each car? If you can only purchase the cloth in bolts, how many bolts must you buy for 18 cars? 16 yd; 8 bolts

195

For students who have difficulty with written tests, this test can be given orally.

You may wish to test students, orally or in writing, to see if they can explain the steps used in solving selected items. The following summarizes the procedures for solving key test items.

Ex. 18–23

Adding or subtracting customary measures

To add or subtract customary measures, rename smaller units with larger units by multiplying, or rename larger units with smaller units by dividing as necessary. Then add or subtract.

POSTTEST   Chapter 5 Page 3

23. An average eighth-grade student has a mass of 40 kilograms. What is this mass expressed in grams?

24. Jill can mow a lawn with a riding mower in 2 hours. Which of the following is not a sensible question to ask?
a. What color is the mower?
b. What time does she start mowing?
c. What type of mower is to be used?
d. What is the size of the lawn?

25. What is the appropriate metric unit used to measure the capacity of a car's gas tank?

26. 10 yd 2 ft
+ 2 yd 1 ft

27. A car traveled at 50 mph for 2 h 45 min. How many miles did the car travel?

28. At Roosevelt Junior High, an 80% average for four tests is required to get on the "B" honor roll. John received grades of 72%, 78%, 81% and 85% on his first four tests. Which of the following is not a sensible question to ask?
a. Will John make the "B" honor roll?
b. What is the average of 72%, 78%, 81% and 85%?
c. What is the number of scores above 80%?
d. What day was he absent from school?

29. Andrew's 9-hour work shift has two 20-minute rest breaks and a 20-minute lunch break. How many hours does he spend working?

30. How many minutes are there in $2\frac{3}{4}$ hours?

31. John's height is 5 ft 8 in. What is his height expressed in inches?

32. What is the appropriate customary unit used to measure a can of motor oil?

Posttest

POSTTEST   Chapter 5 Page 4

Use the following map for questions 33 to 36.

33. What is the distance between Oklahoma City and Tulsa?

34. What route would you follow to go from Stratford to Calvin?

35. Chris drives from Henryetta to Oklahoma City. What road is the most direct route?

36. Michael drove from Tulsa to Lawton. The trip took 4 hours. What was his average speed?

Use the following map for questions 37 to 40.

37. Mrs. Gonzales and her family drove across the United States from New York to Los Angeles. The trip took 5 days 5 hours. They left New York at 8 AM. At what time did they arrive in Los Angeles?

38. Mario places a call at 11:05 PM from Johnson City to his Aunt Lisa who lives in Pittsburgh. At what time will Aunt Lisa's telephone ring?

39. When it is 1:00 PM in Salt Lake City, what is the time in Cincinnati?

40. A traveler gained 3 hours on a non-stop flight. The plane left the East Coast at 1:00 PM and arrived on the West Coast at 3:15 PM. How many hours did the flight take?

Posttest

USING THE PAGE

This skill was originally taught on pages 166–167.

Remind students that powers of 10 and metric prefixes are used to name metric units of capacity, mass, and length. The relationship between units in the metric system is the same whether the measurement involves length, capacity, or mass. Review the lengths given until students are sure of the relationship among them, based on the prefixes. Work through the examples and point out how to move the decimal point in the proper direction. Point out that, in some cases, zeros must be added to the given number.

Resources

For other practice and activities related to this chapter, see the Teacher's Resource Book.

196

RETEACHING

The **meter** is the standard metric unit of length. Powers of 10 and metric prefixes are used to name metric units of length.

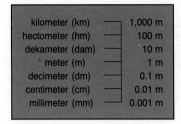

kilometer (km)	1,000 m
hectometer (hm)	100 m
dekameter (dam)	10 m
meter (m)	1 m
decimeter (dm)	0.1 m
centimeter (cm)	0.01 m
millimeter (mm)	0.001 m

Use the chart to rename metric units. Count the steps on the chart from the given unit to the desired unit.

To rename 20 km in meters, move the decimal point to the **right** one place for each step you counted **down**. The meter is three steps down. So, move the decimal point three places to the right.

$$20 \text{ km} = 20.000 = 20{,}000 \text{ m}$$

To rename 500 mm in centimeters, move the decimal point to the **left** one place for each step you counted **up**. The centimeter is one step up. So, move the decimal point one place to the left.

$$500 \text{ mm} = 50.0 = 50 \text{ cm}$$

Complete.

1. 300 cm = ▓ m   3.0
2. 250 mm = ▓ m   0.25
3. 0.7 m = ▓ mm   700
4. 0.9 km = ▓ cm   90,000
5. 40 cm = ▓ km   0.00040
6. 0.92 m = ▓ cm   92
7. 25 cm = ▓ m   0.25
8. 0.2 m = ▓ mm   200
9. 3,500 mm = ▓ m   3.5
10. 9 km = ▓ m   9,000
11. 1.5 cm = ▓ m   0.015
12. 1,400,000 mm = ▓ km   1
13. 0.32 m = ▓ mm   320
14. 0.005 m = ▓ cm   0.5
15. 520 m = ▓ km   0.52
16. 26 mm = ▓ dam   0.0026
17. 0.027 km = ▓ cm   2,700
18. 22,000 m = ▓ km   22
19. 934,000 cm = ▓ km   9.34
20. 340 dm = ▓ hm   0.34
21. 0.46 km = ▓ mm   460,00

Calculate mentally.

1. 30 cm = ▓ m   0.3
2. 500 m = ▓ hm   5
3. 20 dam = ▓ m   200
4. 2 hm = ▓ dm   2

ENRICHMENT

Significant Digits and Accuracy

Significant digits indicate the number of times a unit of measurement is contained in that measurement.

Measurement	120 m	12 m	120.4 m	0.048 cm	3.06 cm
Unit of measure	1 m	1 m	0.1 m	0.001 cm	0.01 cm
Number of units	120	12	1,204	48	306
Significant digits	1, 2, 0	1, 2	1, 2, 0, 4	4, 8	3, 0, 6
Number of significant digits	3	2	4	2	3

When comparing two measurements, the one with the greater number of significant digits is more **accurate.** The one with the smaller unit of measure is more **precise.**

0.048 cm ⟵ more *precise* (unit = 0.001 cm)

3.06 cm ⟵ more *accurate* (three significant digits)

When you compute by using measurement, how you round your answer depends on what operations you are using.

To find the accuracy of a sum or difference, round the answer to the place of the least precise measurement.

$$
\begin{array}{rl}
1.6 & \text{ft} \longleftarrow \text{least precise} \\
3.542 & \text{ft} \qquad \text{measurement} \\
+\ 2.32 & \text{ft} \\
\hline
7.462 & = 7.5\ \text{ft} \\
& \text{(rounded to tenths)}
\end{array}
$$

To find the accuracy of a product or quotient, round the answer to the same number of significant digits as the measurement that has the fewest significant digits.

6.09 m × 0.025 m = 0.15225 = 0.15 m

↑ three significant digits   ↑ two significant digits   ↑ rounded to two significant digits

Compute. Round your answer to the correct number of significant digits.

1. 8.15 m + 7.275 m + 3.7 m   19.1 m
2. 47 in. × 0.902 in.   42 in.²
3. 27.6 ft − 0.048 ft   27.6 ft
4. 0.033 cm² ÷ 8 cm   0.004 cm

197

Purpose This Enrichment page provides an additional challenge for those students whose work throughout the chapter and on the Chapter Test shows a thorough understanding of the material. Alternatively, you may wish to use these exercises as a supplementary lesson for the entire class.

USING THE PAGE

Explain to students that significant digits are the only digits in a number, which is attached to a measurement, that tell how many times the unit of measurement is used. As such, they indicate the accuracy of a measurement—the more significant digits, the greater the accuracy. Contrast *accuracy* with *precision* for the benefit of students who have trouble understanding the difference.

Discuss with students why the accuracy of an answer cannot be greater than that of the measurements used in the problem. Relate it to situations where such accuracy is essential.

Resources

For additional Enrichment activities, see the Teacher's Resource Book.

Purpose This Cumulative Review page provides an opportunity to reinforce students' understanding of the concepts and skills taught in previous chapters.

The chart below is designed to aid you in reviewing the material by specifying the pages on which various concepts and skills were taught.

Item	Page
1	120–121
2	130–131
3	132–133
4	142–143
5	148–149
6	92–93
7	98–99
8	104–105
9	106–107
10	66–67
11	66–67
12	144–145
13	110–111

Each Cumulative Review gives students an opportunity to practice taking tests that are written in a multiple-choice, standardized format. Be sure that students understand that if the correct answer is not among the first three given, then they should select the fourth choice—"not given"—as the correct answer. At least one item per test will require students to give this response.

CUMULATIVE REVIEW

Write the letter of the correct answer.

1. What is an equivalent fraction for $\frac{12}{14}$?

   a. $\frac{6}{7}$ b. $1\frac{1}{6}$

   c. $\frac{8}{10}$ d. not given

2. $8\frac{1}{3} + 4\frac{3}{4}$

   a. $3\frac{7}{12}$ b. 11

   c. $13\frac{1}{12}$ d. not given

3. $5\frac{1}{8} - 3\frac{5}{6}$

   a. $1\frac{7}{24}$ b. $1\frac{1}{2}$

   c. $2\frac{1}{14}$ d. not given

4. $5\frac{2}{7} \times 3\frac{2}{3}$

   a. $15\frac{4}{21}$ b. $17\frac{1}{3}$

   c. $19\frac{8}{21}$ d. not given

5. $4\frac{3}{8} \div 2\frac{3}{4}$

   a. $1\frac{12}{19}$ b. $2\frac{1}{2}$

   c. 4 d. not given

6. Choose the GCF of 14, 56, and 91.

   a. 3 b. 7

   c. 14 d. not given

7. Simplify
   $2.4(16.5 - 5) \div 2(0.951 + 0.549)$.

   a. 3 b. 9.2

   c. 15.159 d. not given

8. Solve for d: $d - 73 = 126$.

   a. 53
   b. 126
   c. 199
   d. not given

9. Solve for x: $\frac{x}{2.4} = 17.03$.

   a. 7.1
   b. 14.64
   c. 40.896
   d. not given

10. $402.5\overline{)4{,}037.075}$

    a. 1.003
    b. 10.03
    c. 10.3
    d. not given

11. Estimate: $76.59\overline{)759.67}$.

    a. 8 b. 100
    c. 10 d. 800

12. Ahmed had $\frac{2}{3}$ of his assets invested. Of his investments, $\frac{3}{4}$ were in mutual funds. What fraction of his money was invested in other ways? Use a simpler problem to write an equation to solve.

    a. $\frac{1}{6}$ b. $\frac{3}{16}$
    c. $\frac{1}{2}$ d. not given

13. 5 more than 6 times a number is 23. Write an equation and solve for the number.

    a. 3 b. 4.67
    c. 128 d. not given

198

RATIO, PROPORTION, PERCENT

SUMMARY

Chapter 6 covers ratios, rates, proportions, and scale drawings, followed by a survey of the three cases of percent. Also included are changing among percents, fractions, and decimals; and the percent of increase and decrease.

LESSON SEQUENCE

PROFESSIONAL BACKGROUND

Research shows that many students have a tendency to add in proportion problems, even when the resulting ratio is not equivalent to the original ratio. For example, given $\frac{6}{8} = \frac{?}{12}$, some students might think that since 12 is 4 more than 8, that you may add 4 to 6 and the answer will be 10.

One difficulty is that many students see fractions as two numbers with little relation to each other. The results of a recent National Assessment of Educational Progress emphasize the point. They indicate that a large percentage of adolescents see little or no connection among the four aspects of fractions or rational numbers:
• measure—three-fourths of a unit
• quotient—three divided by four
• ratio—three to four
• operator—three for every four.
To remediate this difficulty, guide students to solve proportion problems based on:
• concrete models such as balance scales in which distance and weight on one side is proportional to distance and weight on the other side
• situations in everyday life such as making scale drawings.

Researchers have also found that frequent discussion of terms such as "proportion," "ratio," "graph," and "approximation" in which students are challenged to find examples in everyday life help considerably.

Resources: See Hart; Carpenter et al.;

Jackson, Michael B., and E. Ray Phillips. November, 1983. "Vocabulary Instruction in Ratio and Proportion for Seventh Graders." *Journal for Research in Mathematics Education.*

MATERIALS

yardsticks
red and blue paper
map
blueprint
scale model
toothpicks
graph paper
centimeter-grid paper
counters
health textbooks
6 large cards
tacks
facsimile coins
newspaper advertisements
sales catalog

VOCABULARY

ratio (p. 200)
equal ratios (p. 200)
simplest form (p. 200)
rate (p. 200)
unit rate (p. 200)
proportion (p. 202)
cross products (p. 202)
scale drawings (p. 206)
percent (p. 208)
percent increase (p. 226)
percent decrease (p. 226)
inverse proportions, (p. 235)

ABOUT THE CHAPTER

The concepts and skills introduced in this chapter are among the most difficult for eighth-grade students to master. These concepts and skills build directly on fraction and decimal concepts and skills which were covered earlier in the text.

In Chapter Six, students learn about ratios, rates, proportions, and scale drawings. Lessons about percents, decimals, and fractions lead to the three cases of percent:
• finding the percent of a number
• finding the percent
• finding the total number

The chapter closes with lessons about using proportions to solve percent problems and about percent of increase and decrease.

Students need a clear understanding of the relationship of decimals to fractions to work with percent. You will want to be alert to students who are having difficulty with these concepts as you teach the first few lessons in this chapter. Do not hesitate to review concepts that students do not understand.

The Reteaching lesson for this chapter focuses on fractions, decimals, and percents. You may want to turn to it for additional review.

The chapter is focused on the three important cases of percent. Those students who fully understand the relationships among the three will find it much easier to complete the computations.

Students should have practical experience with percents. Newspaper sale announcements and information about percent increases in sales or prices are useful sources of information.

Calculators can certainly be used effectively to carry out computations related to percents. Calculators that have fully functional percent keys can be used to directly find the percent of increase or decrease.

Problem-solving lessons show students how to use proportions to solve problems, and how to make an organized list to solve nonroutine problems. Other problem-solving lessons show students how to use the interest formula ($I = prt$), and how to find and use information from a circle graph.

The Group Project actively involves students in planning a day when students in the class will take over as teachers. The project gives students

an opportunity to apply problem solving and other mathematical concepts and skills.

The Enrichment lesson introduces students to inverse proportions. In particular, the lesson shows students how rate is inversely proportional to time. Students are also introduced to formulas that involve constants.

USING THE CHAPTER OPENER

Each Chapter Opener presents situational problem-solving activities that can be used to motivate the skills taught throughout the chapter. The work sheets can be used by individuals, small groups, or the whole class, depending on the needs of the class. Some students might be ready to use the Chapter Opener at the beginning of the chapter; others might first need to develop the skills taught in the chapter.

Students should be encouraged to use the calculator when appropriate. The Chapter Opener focuses on a nonalgorithmic approach to real-life situations relevant to students' experiences. Through an interdisciplinary approach, the Chapter Opener helps students to explore the relationship between mathematics, other areas of the curriculum, and everyday life while developing different strands of mathematics.

In the Chapter Opener activities, students will learn about pet care and make a budget related to pet care. Students will also learn the considerations that must be made before choosing a pet.

PROBLEM SOLVING

The lesson Writing a Proportion addresses a skill that is useful in many real-life situations, such as in making a scale drawing or in changing a recipe. This lesson focuses on solving word problems by rewriting them as proportions. Emphasize to students that a proportion is a comparison of two equal ratios. Review the use of cross products to find a missing term in equal ratios. In setting up the proportion, explain that because the ratios are equal the terms must be parallel. This process is made easier if the terms to be used are first given labels.

The lesson Making an Organized List/Acting It Out instructs students to solve combination problems by acting out the problem situation and constructing ordered sample spaces, or organized lists. Such a list allows students to be sure that all combinations have been explored. Emphasize that a list should be developed logically, using one element at a time. This will ensure that all possible options have been examined. Students may benefit from small-group work on these problems.

The lesson Using a Formula introduces the formula $I = prt$, or Interest = principal × rate × time. Although most problems involving formulas can be solved with a close reading, suggest that students memorize this formula because they are likely to encounter it at some later point. Have students identify what number in each problem will be substituted for each letter in the formula. The ability to solve for each term in a formula can ease computations that could otherwise prove difficult for students.

Obtaining information from an outside source is a skill necessary for solving math problems as well as for addressing real-life problems. In addition to its general aim of teaching students how to use data not included in the text of the problems, the lesson Using a Circle Graph in this chapter discusses the organization and labeling of data in circle graphs and instructs students in methods of obtaining needed information from such graphs. This lesson lends itself to small-group work.

BULLETIN BOARD

"The Work Force"

Materials: paper to cover bulletin board (can use help-wanted section of newspaper); lettering; large cut-out or outline of United States; 4 paper circles; 8 paper strips; pens or markers

Preparation: Cover bulletin board with paper and arrange display lettering. Construct four circle graphs with the following angles darkened: 158°, 61°, 10°, and 3°. Write titles of four graphs and four numbers on paper strips as shown. (Data for graphs taken from "Employment and Earnings," a Department of Labor publication, United States Government, July, 1985. Population information taken from "United States Statistical Abstracts," July 1, 1984.) Attach the outline of the United States; circle graphs and titles as shown. Write population count in outline of United States and numbers under each title as shown.

After pp. 200-201: Have class express the four numbers shown as ratios and in fractional form. Write on board after they have finished.

After pp. 210-211: Have students calculate the decimal equivalents of fractions previously found (0.026, 0.0073, 0.174, 0.436). Write on board.

After pp. 212-213: Have students express the four numbers as percentages (2.6%, 0.70%, 17.4%, 43.6%). Write on board.

COMMON ERRORS

Some students have difficulty finding the percent of increase or decrease in a number or measurement.

For example: An $8.00 record is on sale for $7.00. What is the percent of decrease in the price?

In solving this problem, students might become confused about whether the percent should be found using the original price or the lower price.

To remediate this error, have students determine what has been decreased or increased. Be sure they see that the *original* price (or other quantity) has been decreased or increased.

To find the percent increase or decrease, then, they find the amount of the increase or decrease. Then they form a fraction with that number as the numerator, and with the original quantity as the denominator. Then this fraction is used in a proportion:

$$\frac{\$1.00}{\$8.00} = \frac{n}{100}$$
$$8.00n = 100.0$$
$$n = 0.125 \text{ or } 12.5\%$$

SPECIAL NEEDS

Fractions, decimals, and percents are closely related and, therefore, should be taught together. Review equivalent fractions, first using concrete materials (fraction strips, pattern blocks) and the identity property for students having difficulty with these concepts. Any ratio that has a denominator of 100 can be expressed as a percent. (per hundred) To help students perceive the relevance of this concept, have them cut items from newspapers or magazines which show percents. (sale ads or bank interests, weather predictions) Have students determine fractional and decimal equivalents so that they understand the relationship among the three concepts. Have them picture the representations whenever possible.

Word problems involving percent can also be an area of difficulty for some students. Remind students that, in these problems, *of* is usually translated as *times,* and *is* generally represents *equals* in the equation. Problems might require much drill and practice. Have students find ads in the paper that indicate "30% off original price" or "$100 is a 20% savings," and let them figure the costs.

Provide students with an answer; for example, 135%, 40, or $\frac{17}{20}$. Have them make up as many different kinds of questions that have that answer as they can.

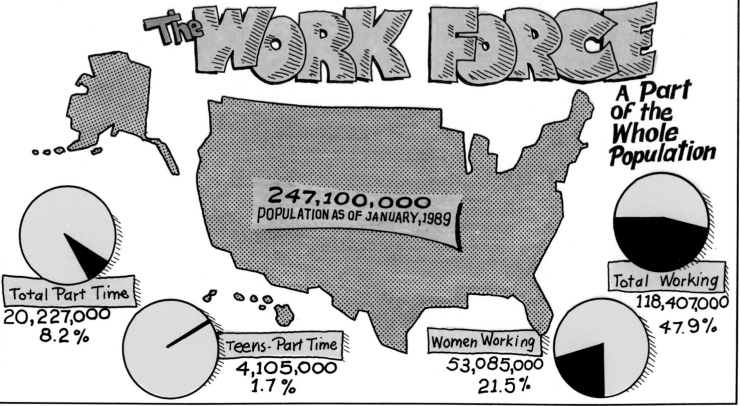

MATH LABS

PUZZLES AND GAMES
Materials: one cube with a fraction on each face and one cube with a numeral from 1–6 on each face

Two or three students take turns tossing the cubes. The single numeral will be the numerator of another fraction. After the toss, the student gives the appropriate term to complete the proportion. For example, a student tosses $\frac{1}{2}$ and 4. $\frac{1}{2} = \frac{4}{?}$; the missing term is 8.

PUZZLES AND GAMES
Materials: student-made set of 36 index cards: 12 with percents; 12 with equivalent decimals; and 12 with equivalent fractions

Working in groups of 3–4, students place the cards facedown on a table in a 6 × 6 array. They take turns turning three cards faceup in place to see if they are equivalent decimals, percents, and fractions. When the three values are equivalent, the cards are removed from the array and kept by the student. When they are not equivalent, the cards are turned facedown in their original place. Students continue until all the cards are matched. The winner is the student with the most cards.

REINFORCEMENT
Materials: 15 cards, each with a scale in mm, cm, dm, m

Have students list 6 objects in the room that can be easily measured. Each student should measure one object in mm, cm, dm, or m and randomly select a card with a scale on it. If the scale is the same as the unit used for the actual measurement, they select another scale. Students should then find the scale measurement for the object.

CALCULATOR

Ratio, Proportion, and Percent
Many computations of ratio, proportion, and percent are tedious and time consuming. A calculator can assist with these computations; for example, the solving of proportions usually involves division and multiplication. The calculator can perform the arithmetic, but students must understand the process in order to obtain the correct result. Percent exercises also cause difficulty for many students. Pressing only the %̄ key on the calculator seldom produces the correct result. Therefore, students need to learn the underlying principles of percent, and how the %̄ key functions on a calculator.

Students should have calculators available for all problem-solving activities.

Additional Activities: **Drill and Practice:** Make a list of the number of hours in a day that you eat, sleep, work, study, watch TV, and attend school. Determine the percent of the day that you spend doing each activity.

Exploration: Find the number n that makes each pair of ratios equal.

$$\frac{n}{5} = \frac{20}{n}\,(10)$$
$$\frac{n}{3} = \frac{27}{n}\,(9)$$
$$\frac{n}{4} = \frac{9}{n}\,(6)$$
$$\frac{n}{2} = \frac{8}{n}\,(4)$$

SUBJECT AREA CONNECTIONS

Here are some activities for reinforcing the concepts presented in this chapter.
- **Social Studies:** Have students find the ratio of teachers to students in their school.
- **Social Studies:** Have students find the approximate percent of increase or decrease in their town's population from 1960 to the present.
- **Art:** Have students measure the classroom to the nearest meter or foot. Then have them make a scale drawing.
- **Language Arts:** Have students choose a current-events topic. Have each of them look through a magazine or a newspaper, and find what percent of the total number of articles is about their topic.
- **Physical Education:** Have students do as many sit-ups as possible in five minutes. Have each of them divide to find their rate of sit-ups per minute.

PLAN AHEAD

You will not need to prepare anything elaborate for this chapter.

PLANNING CALENDAR
ABBREVIATION KEY

Teacher's Resource Book	Follow-up Activities
MMW—Making Math Work	CALC—Calculator
P—Practice	CMP—Computer
R—Reteach	CNS—Consumer
E—Enrich	P&G—Puzzles and Games
	MNP—Manipulatives
	MC—Math Connection
	MCM—Math Communication
	NS—Number Sense
	PS—Problem Solving
	RFM—Reinforcement

PLANNING CALENDAR

Pages	Lesson Objectives	Basic	Average	Extended	Class/Home	More Practice	Math Reasoning	Follow-up	Reteach	Practice	Enrich
		ASSIGNMENT GUIDE									
199	Chapter Opener (Use MMW 11,12)	199	199	199							
200,201	To write ratios, equal ratios, and rates	1-20,28-29,36-37, AL	2-30e, 32-37,AL	1-31o, 32-37,AL	H80		H217	MNP RFM	58	80	76
202,203	To identify a proportion and solve for a missing term	1-16,29,31-33	1-29o, 31-33	6-28e, 29-33,Chlg	H81			PS MNP	59	81	77
204,205	To solve problems using proportions	1-4	2-6	3-8	H82			PS CALC		82	78
206,207	To calculate actual and scale measurements from scale drawings	1-9	1-9	1-9,Chlg	H83			NS PS	60	83	79
208,209	To identify and write a percent for a fraction or ratio	1-19,23-27	5-27,NS1-5	9-27,NS	H84			MNP	61	84	80
210,211	To write a decimal as a percent and a percent as a decimal	1-20,33-36,F	1-19o, 21-36,F	2-20e, 25-36,F	H85		H217	PS PS	62	85	81
212,213	To write a fraction as a percent and a percent as a fraction	1-22,31-34,AL	1-23o, 25-34,AL	6-24e, 25-34,AL	H86	H201	H217	PS NS	63	86	82
214,215	To make an organized list in problem solving	1-5	1-6	2-8	H87 H88			PS CMP		87-88	
216,217	To find the percent of a number	1-20,29-32,MCR	1-19o, 21-32, MCR	9-32,MCR	H89			MC NS	64	89	83
218,219	To find what percent one number is of another	1-16,22-25,NS1-4	1-19o, 22-25, NS1-4	19-25,NS	H90			P&G MC	65	90	84
220,221	To find a number when a percent of it is known	1-18,21-23,NS	1-23,NS	1-23,NS	H91		H218	PS MC	66	91	85
222,223	To use a formula to compute simple interest ($i = prt$)	1-4	2-6	4-8	H92			PS CALC		92	86
224,225	To use a proportion to solve a percent problem	1-19o, 21-23	1-13o, 15-23	2-14e, 15-23,Chlg	H87	H201		RFM MC	67	93	87
226,227	To find the percent of increase or decrease	1-12,16-17	1-12,16-19,F	1-11o, 13-19,F	H94		H218	CMP	68	94	88
228,229	To use information from a circle graph to solve problems	1-7	3-9	4-14	H95			PS CMP		95	89
230	Math Communication: To recognize math abbreviations	230	230	230							
231	Group Project: To plan a curriculum; to budget time; to make a schedule	231	231	231							

232,233	Chapter Test
234	Reteaching
235	Enrichment
236,237	Technology
238	Cumulative Review

TESTS

A. To solve proportions
B. To find actual measure, given scale and scale measurement, and vice versa
C. To write a decimal or a fraction as a percent, and vice versa
D. To find the percent of a number
E. To find what percent a number is of a given number
F. To find the number, given a percent of the number
G. To find the percent of increase or decrease
H. To write a proportion to solve problems
I. To make an organized list to solve problems
J. To use the formula $I = prt$ to solve problems
K. To use information from a circle graph to solve problems

FAMILY INVOLVEMENT

Family Involvement for Chapter 6 encourages family members to design a dream house. They must choose an appropriate scale and sketch a general design on graph paper. After all the rooms have been drawn, each family member is to choose one or two rooms and draw them to scale based on a floor plan showing the placement of furniture. The completed rooms are to be cut out and pasted together on a piece of plain paper, which will then show the completed design for the house.

Additional activities might include encouraging family members to use some basic proportions (1:2, 1:3, or 2:3, etc.) to make a simple scale drawing of one or two rooms in their home. The drawings should show floor and wall dimensions as well as the placement of furniture and other large objects in the room.

STUDENT RESOURCES

Bibliography

Greene, Linda. *Careers in the Computer Industry.* New York: Franklin Watts, Inc., 1983.

Males, Carolyn, and Roberta Feigen. *Life After High School: A Career Planning Guide.* Englewood Cliffs, NJ: Messner, 1986.

Studio D Staff and Irit Adler. *Picture Puzzles for the Super-Smart.* New York: Sterling Publishing Co., Inc., 1985.

Films

The Golden Section. 18 minutes. Color. 1968. Distributed by Macmillan Films, Inc., Mt. Vernon, N.Y.

Ratio. 8 minutes. Color. 1970. Distributed by Silver Burdett, Summit, N.J.

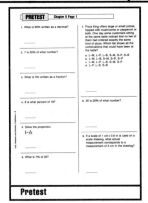

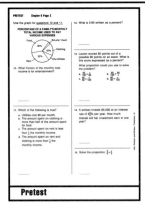

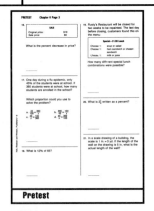

Suppose you wanted to buy a dog. If you were solely responsible for the purchase and the care of your pet, which kind of dog would you buy? What kind of part-time job would you need in order to purchase and pay for the care of the dog?

6 RATIO, PROPORTION, PERCENT

Objective: To explore problems involving pet care

Direct students to look at the picture of the puppy. Ask how many students have pets. Ask any who have unusual pets to discuss them with the class. Have students share stories about their pets.

WHOLE CLASS
Logic
Encourage a class discussion on the care of a pet. Concentrate on the responsibilities involved and the cost of pet care. Write on the chalkboard a list of questions students think should be answered before deciding whether to buy a pet and what kind of pet to buy. If some students are considering getting pets for the entire family, suggest that they decide beforehand who will perform each of the chores involved in caring for the pets.

SMALL GROUP
Statistics and Probability
Materials: Making Math Work page 12 per student, resource materials

Have each student complete a copy of Making Math Work page 12. Have students determine what kinds of expenses are involved in caring for a pet and list them in the first column of the chart. Then have them research the cost and the frequency of each of these items. Suggest that they get this information from books or by consulting with a veterinarian or owner of a pet store. Because some costs are peculiar to caring for a particular kind of dog, have students write equations that reflect the costs of various dogs.

INDIVIDUAL
Number
Materials: Making Math Work page 11 per student

Have each student complete a copy of Making Math Work page 11. Have students use the totals from Making Math Work page 12 to fill in the first part of page 11. (If they have not completed page 12, have them estimate the costs of caring for a dog.) Suggest that they research different jobs that may be available to them in the area and choose one that they would enjoy doing. Have them use this information to complete the remainder of page 11. Discuss what they might do with any extra money they earned from their jobs.

▎MAKING MATH WORK

Suppose you wanted to buy a dog. Calculate the costs involved. Answers will vary.

Type of dog _____

Cost: Vaccinations:

Leash/collar: License:

Total:

How would you earn money to buy your dog? Could you find a part-time job? What would it be? Answers will vary.

Type of job: Rate of pay:

Number of hours for which you will work before you can buy the dog:

How would you afford to feed your dog? Answers will vary.

Cost of dog food (1 month):

Type of job: Rate of pay:

Number of hours of work each month:

Use the information above to complete the budget sheet. Check students' tables.

	Hours worked	Income	Expense	Cost	Balance
September					
October					
November					
December					
January					
February					
March					
April					
May					
June					
July					
August					

Making Math Work

▎MAKING MATH WORK

How would you make a budget and compute the costs of caring for your dog? First, find out what your expenses will be for the year. Which accessories would you buy? Which kind or kinds of food would you feed it? What are some costs of vaccines? How often would you have to buy some of the items? Add to the list below; then find your estimated budget figure. Answers will vary. Check students' tables.

Expense	Cost	How often?	Total price
Food			
Vaccines			

Making Math Work

Objectives: To write ratios, equal ratios, and rates

Warm-Up
Have the students write each fraction in simplest form.

$\frac{20}{30}$ $\left(\frac{2}{3}\right)$ $\frac{3}{15}$ $\left(\frac{1}{5}\right)$ $\frac{14}{21}$ $\left(\frac{2}{3}\right)$ $\frac{6}{8}$ $\left(\frac{3}{4}\right)$

$\frac{21}{42}$ $\left(\frac{1}{2}\right)$ $\frac{8}{15}$ $\left(\frac{8}{15}\right)$ $\frac{9}{12}$ $\left(\frac{3}{4}\right)$ $\frac{15}{40}$ $\left(\frac{3}{8}\right)$

GETTING STARTED

Draw a domino on the chalkboard with 6 dots on the left and 1 dot on the right. Ask: How many dots are there on the left compared to the dots on the right? (6 to 1) Draw a second domino under the first with the same number of dots on each side. Ask: The total number of dots has changed, but has the relationship changed between the number of dots on the left and the number of dots on the right? (no) Have students explain that though there are now more dots, there are still 6 dots on the left for each 1 dot on the right.

TEACHING THE LESSON

A. Extend the lesson by asking students to find the ratio of: CPR hours to total hours (8:24); total hours to basic first-aid hours (24:16); total hours to CPR hours (24:8); basic first-aid hours to total hours. (16:24)

Stress that the first quantity mentioned is the first term of the ratio and that the second quantity mentioned is the second term.

B. Explain to students that they can find equal ratios by using what they know about equivalent fractions.

C. Explain that when two rates are equal, one could write the same units on the top and the same units on the bottom; for example, $\frac{\$30}{8\,h} = \frac{\$3.75}{1\,h}$. Point out that the rate is the relationship between the amount of money ($30) and hours (8), while the ratio is the relationship between $30 per 8 h worked and $3.75 per 1 h worked. Emphasize the fact that the terms in a ratio are generally the same units. The terms in a rate, however, are *always* different units because a rate expresses something *per* something.

Ratios and Rates

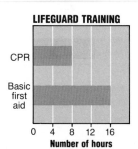

A. Oceanville has a special lifeguard-training program. The program includes 16 hours of instruction in basic first aid and 8 hours of instruction in cardiopulmonary resuscitation (CPR). What is the ratio of the number of hours of CPR instruction to the number of hours of basic first-aid instruction?

A **ratio** is a comparison of two numbers. The ratio of CPR hours to basic first-aid hours is 8 to 16, or 8:16, or $\frac{8}{16}$. Each ratio is read "8 to 16."

The numbers 8 and 16 are called the **terms** of the ratio. The order of terms in a ratio is important. The ratio 16:8 is *not* the same as the ratio 8:16.

$$\frac{8}{16} \quad \begin{array}{l}\leftarrow \text{ first term} \\ \leftarrow \text{ second term}\end{array}$$

B. For every 1 hour of CPR instruction, there are 2 hours of basic first-aid instruction. So, you can also use the ratio 1:2 to compare the CPR instruction and the basic first-aid instruction.

These are **equal ratios.** $\qquad \frac{8}{16} = \frac{1}{2} \leftarrow$ This ratio is in **simplest form.**

Equal ratios can be found by multiplying or dividing both terms of a ratio by the same number (not zero).

$$\frac{2}{3} = \frac{2 \times 6}{3 \times 6} = \frac{12}{18} \qquad\qquad \frac{80}{100} = \frac{80 \div 20}{100 \div 20} = \frac{4}{5}$$

C. A **rate** is a ratio that compares two different kinds of units. For example, if John earned $30 in 8 hours, the rate of earnings to hours is

$$\begin{array}{l}\text{dollars} \longrightarrow \\ \text{hours} \longrightarrow\end{array} \frac{30}{8} = \frac{30 \div 8}{8 \div 8} = \frac{3.75}{1}.$$

When the second term is one unit, the rate is called a **unit rate.** The unit rate $\frac{3.75}{1}$ indicates that John earns $3.75 per hour.

Math Reasoning, page H217

LIFEGUARD TRAINING

COMMON ERRORS

Students might interchange the terms of a ratio; for example, Joe earned $15 and Betty earned $18. The ratio of Betty's earnings to Joe's is 18:15, not 15:18.

Remediation
Have students
- identify the question: Betty's to Joe's.
- write the terms: $18 to $15.
- write the ratio and then simplify: 18:15, or 6:5.

Assign Reteach Master, p 58.

RETEACH Ratios and Rates

John received 350 votes in the class election. His opponent received 250 votes. What is the ratio of the number of votes John received to the number of votes his opponent received? Write the ratio as a fraction in its simplest form.

Remember
Be sure to select the correct values for the terms in the ratio.

$$350:250$$
$$\frac{350}{250} = \frac{7 \cdot 50}{5 \cdot 50} = \frac{7}{5}$$

The ratio of John's votes to his opponent's votes is $\frac{7}{5}$.

As new class president, John polled the students on several issues about the school. The results are shown in the table. Complete the table by writing the ratio of the "for" votes to the number of "against" votes. Write all fractions in their simplest form.

Issue	"For" votes	"Against" votes	Ratio	Fraction
1.	300	60	300:60	$\frac{5}{1}$
2.	240	120	240:120	$\frac{2}{1}$
3.	180	180	180:180	$\frac{1}{1}$
4.	60	300	60:300	$\frac{1}{5}$
5.	350	10	350:10	$\frac{35}{1}$
6.	124	216	124:216	$\frac{31}{54}$
7.	20	340	20:340	$\frac{1}{17}$
8.	270	95	270:95	$\frac{54}{19}$
9.	185	175	185:175	$\frac{37}{35}$
10.	310	50	310:50	$\frac{31}{5}$

58   Use with pages 200–201.

Reteach Worksheet

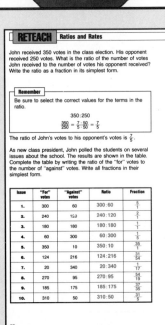

Write each ratio in fraction form.

1. 3 to 2 $\frac{3}{2}$　　**2.** 6:7 $\frac{6}{7}$　　**3.** 9 to 1 $\frac{9}{1}$　　**4.** 7 to 10 $\frac{7}{10}$

5. 6 to 17 $\frac{6}{17}$　　**6.** 5:4 $\frac{5}{4}$　　**7.** 7:5 $\frac{7}{5}$　　**8.** 1 to 3 $\frac{1}{3}$

Write each ratio as a fraction in simplest form.

9. $\frac{10}{20}$ $\frac{1}{2}$　　**10.** $\frac{9}{6}$ $\frac{3}{2}$　　**11.** $\frac{4}{2}$ $\frac{2}{1}$　　**12.** 16:6 $\frac{8}{3}$　　**13.** $\frac{18}{12}$ $\frac{3}{2}$　　**14.** 5 to 45 $\frac{1}{9}$

15. 90:40 $\frac{9}{4}$　　**16.** $\frac{15}{10}$ $\frac{3}{2}$　　**17.** $\frac{60}{100}$ $\frac{3}{5}$　　**18.** 17 to 35 $\frac{17}{35}$　　**19.** $\frac{22}{6}$ $\frac{11}{3}$　　**20.** 64:24 $\frac{8}{3}$

21. 9:12 $\frac{3}{4}$　　**22.** 28 to 7 $\frac{4}{1}$　　**23.** 1.2 to 4.8 $\frac{1}{4}$　　**24.** 8:80 $\frac{1}{10}$　　**25.** 2.6 to 5.2 $\frac{1}{2}$

26. 4 wins to 12 losses $\frac{1}{3}$　　　　**27.** 8 present to 15 absent $\frac{8}{15}$

Write three equal ratios.　　*Answers will vary. Sample answers are given.*

28. $\frac{1}{3}$ $\frac{2}{6}, \frac{3}{9}, \frac{4}{12}$　　**29.** $\frac{9}{2}$ $\frac{18}{4}, \frac{27}{6}, \frac{36}{8}$　　**30.** $\frac{6}{1}$ $\frac{12}{2}, \frac{18}{3}, \frac{24}{4}$　　**31.** $\frac{7}{5}$ $\frac{14}{10}, \frac{21}{15}, \frac{28}{20}$

Write the unit rate.

32. 125 yards in 25 seconds
5 yards per second

33. 180 pages in 3 hours
60 pages per hour

34. $24 for 3 books $8 per book

35. 28 pounds in 4 weeks
7 pounds per week

Solve. For Problem 37, use the Infobank.

36. A group of 9 students entered the lifeguard course. All but 2 finished the course. What is the ratio of those finishing the course to those entering? 7:9

37. Use the information on page 475 to solve. Wendell's doctor has advised him not to eat any foods that have added salt. Should Wendell have a bowl of Heidi's soup?
No, because it contains added salt.

ANOTHER LOOK

Find the greatest common factor for each pair of numbers.

1. 4, 12 4　　**2.** 6, 21 3　　**3.** 10, 35 5　　**4.** 14, 63 7　　**5.** 48, 231 3

Find the least common multiple for each pair of numbers.

6. 3, 7 21　　**7.** 5, 9 45　　**8.** 12, 32 96　　**9.** 16, 44 176　　**10.** 45, 99 495

Find the least common denominator for each pair of fractions.

11. $\frac{1}{2}, \frac{3}{4}$ 4　　**12.** $\frac{2}{3}, \frac{3}{5}$ 15　　**13.** $\frac{2}{7}, \frac{3}{4}$ 28　　**14.** $\frac{2}{9}, \frac{1}{3}$ 9　　**15.** $\frac{3}{4}, \frac{7}{12}$ 12

Classwork/Homework, page H80

201

ASSIGNMENT GUIDE

Basic:　1–20, 28–29, 36–37, AL

Average:　2–30 e, 32–37, AL

Extended:　1–31 o, 32–37, AL

Resources
Practice, p. 80　　Class/Home, p. H80
Reteach, p. 58　　Reasoning, p. H217
Enrich, p. 76

Exercise Analysis
1–8　　Write a ratio in fraction form
9–27　　Write a ratio in simplest form
28–31　　Write equal ratios
32–35　　Find a unit rate
36　　Skill application
37　　Data collection and computation

You may wish to allow students to use calculators to complete some of the exercises.

Another Look
This review provides maintenance for finding greatest common factors and least common multiples.

FOLLOW-UP ACTIVITIES

MANIPULATIVES
Materials: yardsticks

Have students measure the classroom to the nearest foot to find the following ratios of
- length of room to width of room.
- length of room to height of room.
- width of room to height of room.
- height of room to length of room.
- height of room to width of room.

REINFORCEMENT
Have students give examples of ratios from other subjects and from outside of school; for example, 3 TV sets to 1 stereo recorder.

COMING UP
It will take "extreme means" to solve tomorrow's problems.

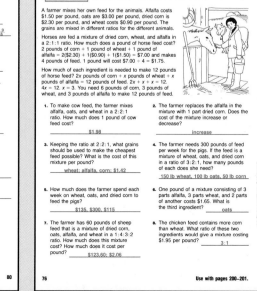

PRACTICE　Ratios and Rates

Write each ratio in fraction form. Simplify where necessary.

1. 5 to 3 $\frac{5}{3}$　　**2.** 1:14 $\frac{1}{14}$　　**3.** 1.5 to 4.5 $\frac{1}{3}$

4. 6:6 $\frac{1}{1}$　　**5.** 24.8:13.4 $\frac{12.4}{6.7}$　　**6.** 101.9 to 98.6 $\frac{101.9}{98.6}$

7. 3:5 $\frac{3}{5}$　　**8.** 1,295 to 1,187 $\frac{1,295}{1,187}$　　**9.** 12:19 $\frac{12}{19}$

10. 10 to 100 $\frac{1}{10}$　　**11.** 25 to 63 $\frac{25}{63}$　　**12.** 3:20 $\frac{3}{20}$

13. 15 to 10 $\frac{3}{2}$　　**14.** 13:80 $\frac{13}{80}$　　**15.** 65 to 200 $\frac{13}{40}$

16. 2:1 $\frac{2}{1}$　　**17.** 136 to 358 $\frac{68}{179}$　　**18.** 746:746 $\frac{1}{1}$

19. 5:450 $\frac{1}{90}$　　**20.** 28 to 29 $\frac{28}{29}$　　**21.** 8 to 64 $\frac{1}{8}$

22. 100 to 200 $\frac{1}{2}$　　**23.** 4.1:1.6 $\frac{4.1}{1.6}$　　**24.** 10:15 $\frac{2}{3}$

25. 61:33 $\frac{61}{33}$　　**26.** 4.2 to 1.4 $\frac{3}{1}$　　**27.** 3:11 $\frac{3}{11}$

28. 5 motorcycles to 4 bicycles $\frac{5}{4}$　　**29.** 28 cars to 8 motorcycles $\frac{7}{2}$

30. 2 bikers to 30 motorists $\frac{1}{15}$　　**31.** 400 miles in 5 hours $\frac{80}{1}$

Write the unit rate.

32. $3,600 for 3 motorcycles
$1,200 per motorcycle

33. 16 riders for 16 motorcycles
1 rider per motorcycle

34. 175 miles in 3.5 hours
50 miles per hour

35. 212.5 miles on 2.5 gallons of gas
85 miles per gallon

Use with pages 200–201.　　80

Practice Worksheet

ENRICH　Algebra

A farmer mixes her own feed for the animals. Alfalfa costs $1.50 per pound, oats are $3.00 per pound, dried corn is $2.30 per pound, and wheat costs $0.90 per pound. The grains are mixed in different ratios for the different animals.

Horses are fed a mixture of dried corn, wheat, and alfalfa in a 2:1:1 ratio. How much does a pound of horse feed cost? 2 pounds of corn + 1 pound of wheat + 1 pound of alfalfa = 2($2.30) + 1($0.90) + 1($1.50) = $7.00 and makes 4 pounds of feed. 1 pound will cost $7.00 ÷ 4 = $1.75.

How much of each ingredient is needed to make 12 pounds of horse feed? 2x pounds of corn + x pounds of wheat + x pounds of alfalfa = 12 pounds of feed. 2x + x + x = 12. 4x = 12. x = 3. You need 6 pounds of corn, 3 pounds of wheat, and 3 pounds of alfalfa to make 12 pounds of feed.

1. To make cow feed, the farmer mixes alfalfa, oats, and wheat in a 2:2:1 ratio. How much does 1 pound of cow feed cost?
$1.98

2. The farmer replaces the alfalfa in the mixture with 1 part dried corn. Does the cost of the mixture increase or decrease?
increase

3. Keeping the ratio at 2:2:1, what grains should be used to make the cheapest feed possible? What is the cost of this mixture per pound?
wheat, alfalfa, corn; $1.42

4. The farmer needs 300 pounds of feed per week for the pigs. If the feed is a mixture of wheat, oats, and dried corn in a ratio of 3:2:1, how many pounds of each does she need?
150 lb wheat, 100 lb oats, 50 lb corn

5. How much does the farmer spend each week on wheat, oats, and dried corn to feed the pigs?
$135, $300, $115

6. One pound of a mixture consisting of 3 parts alfalfa, 3 parts wheat, and 2 parts of another costs $1.65. What is the third ingredient?
oats

7. The farmer has 60 pounds of sheep feed that is a mixture of dried corn, oats, alfalfa, and wheat in a 1:4:3:2 ratio. How much does this mixture cost? How much does it cost per pound?
$123.60; $2.06

8. The chicken feed contains more corn than wheat. What ratio of these two ingredients would give a mixture costing $1.95 per pound?
3:1

Use with pages 200–201.　　76

Enrich Worksheet

Objectives: To identify a proportion and solve for a missing term

Warm-Up
Have students solve each of the following equations mentally.

$4x = 2 \cdot 2$ ($x = 1$)
$9y = 6 \cdot 6$ ($y = 4$)
$15c = 20 \cdot 24$ ($c = 32$)
$18z = 9 \cdot 8$ ($z = 4$)

GETTING STARTED

Materials: 20 counters (5 of one color and 15 of another) per student

Have students count their counters. Have them write a ratio expressing the numerical relationship between the two colors (e.g., 5 white: 15 red, or $\frac{5}{15}$). Now ask students to arrange all of the counters into five identical sets, each containing both colors. Have them express the contents of one set as a ratio (1 white: 3 red, or $\frac{1}{3}$). Ask: Are the two ratios equal? (yes) Have students tell how they know this. Then have them combine the contents of 2 sets and write the resulting ratio. ($\frac{2}{6}$) Repeat, using 3 sets and 4 sets. ($\frac{3}{9}$) Ask which ratios are equal. (all) Have volunteers show why.

TEACHING THE LESSON

A. Call attention to the terms *extremes* and *means*. Have a volunteer use this vocabulary to explain cross products.

In setting up proportions, students often interchange the terms of the second ratio; for example, they might write $\frac{2 \text{ (teachers)}}{20 \text{ (students)}} = \frac{x \text{ (students)}}{3 \text{ (teachers)}}$ and find the wrong number of students.

B. Write $24:40 = 15:x$ on the chalkboard. Point out that when the proportion is written in this form, you don't have to rewrite it to cross multiply. Multiply the end terms and then multiply the middle terms of the proportion and proceed to solve for x.

$$24:40 = 15:x$$
$$24x = 15 \cdot 40$$
$$24x = 600$$
$$x = 25$$

In the Other Examples section, note that the second example introduces a ratio in which one term is not a whole number.

Proportions

A. Lori is comparing catalogs of two computer schools. One catalog states that 27 out of 30 of our graduates find jobs. The other catalog states that 90 out of 100 of our graduates find jobs. So, Lori compares the ratios 27:30 and 90:100.

An equation that shows that two ratios are equal is called a **proportion**. You can use **cross products** to determine whether two ratios are equal.

extremes → $\frac{27}{30} \overset{?}{=} \frac{90}{100}$ ← means
means → ← extremes

$$27 \cdot 100 \overset{?}{=} 30 \cdot 90$$
$$2,700 = 2,700$$

The cross products are equal. So, the ratios are equal.
$\frac{27}{30} = \frac{90}{100}$ is a proportion.

Two ratios such as $\frac{27}{30}$ and $\frac{64}{70}$ are not equal, because their cross products are not equal.

$$27 \cdot 70 \overset{?}{=} 30 \cdot 64$$
$$1,890 \neq 1,920$$

B. Sometimes you are given a proportion that has a variable in one of its ratios. You *solve* the proportion when you find the correct value for x. You can use cross products.

Cross multiply.	Solve.	Check: $\frac{24}{40} \overset{?}{=} \frac{15}{25}$
$\frac{24}{40} = \frac{15}{x}$	$\frac{24x}{24} = \frac{600}{24}$	$\frac{3}{5} = \frac{3}{5}$ ✔
$24 \cdot x = 40 \cdot 15$	$x = 25$	
$24x = 600$		

Other examples:

$$\frac{14}{10} = \frac{x}{15}$$
$$14 \cdot 15 = 10 \cdot x$$
$$210 = 10x$$
$$\frac{210}{10} = \frac{10x}{10}$$
$$21 = x$$

Check: $\frac{14}{10} \overset{?}{=} \frac{21}{15}$.

$$\frac{7}{5} = \frac{7}{5} ✔$$

$$\frac{1.25}{x} = \frac{5}{9}$$
$$1.25 \cdot 9 = x \cdot 5$$
$$11.25 = 5x$$
$$\frac{11.25}{5} = \frac{5x}{5}$$
$$2.25 = x$$

Check: $\frac{1.25}{2.25} \overset{?}{=} \frac{5}{9}$.

$$\frac{1.25 \times 4}{2.25 \times 4} = \frac{5}{9}$$
$$\frac{5}{9} = \frac{5}{9} ✔$$

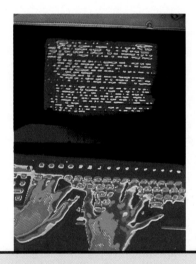

COMMON ERRORS

When given a proportion, some students multiply the numerators, multiply the denominators, and set the products as equal. For example, given $\frac{3}{4} = \frac{x}{8}$, they would find $3x = 32$.

Remediation
Encourage these students to draw arrows before multiplying to help them remember to cross multiply.

$$\frac{3}{4} \qquad \frac{x}{8}$$

Assign Reteach Master, p. 59.

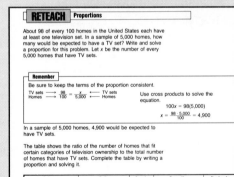

Are the ratios equal? Write *yes* or *no*.

1. $\frac{3}{6}, \frac{5}{4}$ no
2. $\frac{18}{6}, \frac{6}{2}$ yes
3. $\frac{6}{9}, \frac{10}{15}$ yes
4. $\frac{20}{4}, \frac{106}{21}$ no

5. $\frac{4}{16}, \frac{12}{48}$ yes
6. $\frac{30}{40}, \frac{80}{100}$ no
7. $\frac{4}{8}, \frac{105}{210}$ yes
8. $\frac{50}{60}, \frac{60}{50}$ no

Solve each proportion.

9. $\frac{6}{9} = \frac{8}{x}$ x = 12
10. $\frac{6}{5} = \frac{30}{x}$ x = 25
11. $\frac{21}{28} = \frac{6}{x}$ x = 8
12. $\frac{12}{4} = \frac{15}{x}$
    x = 5

13. $\frac{4}{12} = \frac{x}{15}$ x = 5
14. $\frac{8}{20} = \frac{x}{25}$ x = 10
15. $\frac{15}{21} = \frac{x}{35}$ x = 25
16. $\frac{20}{12} = \frac{x}{33}$
    x = 55

17. $\frac{12}{x} = \frac{8}{10}$ x = 15
18. $\frac{16}{x} = \frac{8}{4}$ x = 8
19. $\frac{9}{x} = \frac{60}{80}$ x = 12
20. $\frac{36}{x} = \frac{45}{50}$
    x = 40

21. $\frac{x}{10} = \frac{36}{20}$ x = 18
22. $\frac{x}{18} = \frac{6}{9}$ x = 12
23. $\frac{x}{4} = \frac{180}{30}$ x = 24
24. $\frac{x}{50} = \frac{21}{75}$
    x = 14

25. $\frac{1.2}{x} = \frac{6}{9}$ x = 1.8
26. $\frac{10}{14} = \frac{x}{10.5}$ x = 7.5
27. $\frac{9}{3.5} = \frac{18}{x}$ x = 7
28. $\frac{x}{3.6} = \frac{60}{80}$
    x = 2.7

Write a proportion and solve for x.

29. The ratio of 18 to 15 is equal to the ratio of x to 40.
    18 : 15 = x : 40; x = 48

★30. The ratio of $13\frac{1}{2}$ to $3\frac{3}{8}$ is equal to the ratio of 48 to x.
    $13\frac{1}{2} : 3\frac{3}{8} = 48 : x$; x = 12

Solve.

31. One school states that 3 of every 5 students have part-time jobs. Another school says that 60 of every 100 students have part-time jobs. Are these equal ratios? yes

32. A school admits 3 of every 4 people who apply. If 120 people apply, how many will probably be admitted? 90 people

33. A school states that 80 of its 96 graduates in computer science found jobs in their field. What is this ratio in simplest form? $\frac{5}{6}$

CHALLENGE

Use the digits 1, 2, 3, 6, 7, 9, and 0 to find the value each letter represents in the problem below.
Other solutions are possible.

$$\begin{array}{r} \text{SUN} \\ + \text{FUN} \\ \hline \text{SWIM} \end{array}$$

$S = 1, U = 3, N = 6$
$F = 9, W = 0, I = 7, M = 2$

Classwork/Homework, page H81   **203**

ASSIGNMENT GUIDE

Basic: 1–16, 29, 31–33

Average: 1–29 o, 31–33

Extended: 6–28 e, 29–33, Chlg

Resources
Practice, p. 81   Class/Home, p. H81
Reteach, p. 59
Enrich, p. 77

Exercise Analysis

1–8   Identify equal ratios
9–28   Find the missing term
29, 30 Write a proportion and solve
31–33 Skill applications

You may wish to allow students to use calculators to complete some of the exercises.

Challenge

For students not adept at reasoning, several hints might be necessary. Give only one hint at a time.

● When adding two 1-digit numbers, the only number that can be regrouped is a 1. Therefore, $S = 1$.
When adding a number to itself, the sum must be even. Therefore, M must be 0, 2, or 6. Ask students why M cannot be 0.

FOLLOW-UP ACTIVITIES

PROBLEM SOLVING

Using 4 and 6 as the extremes and 3 and 8 as the means, find how many true proportions can be written.

$\left(\frac{4}{3} = \frac{8}{6}, \frac{4}{8} = \frac{3}{6}, \frac{6}{3} = \frac{8}{4}, \frac{6}{8} = \frac{3}{4}\right)$

MANIPULATIVES

Materials: yardsticks

Have students use yardsticks to solve such proportions as:

$\frac{3}{4} = \frac{x}{12} (x = 9); \frac{7}{8} = \frac{x}{16} (x = 14)$

Have students write the known proportion; for example, 4 : 12. Then they should count sets of 4 on the yardstick (beginning at 0) until they reach 12. (3 sets) Next have them mark off an equal number of sets of 3 on the yardstick to find the missing term.

COMING UP

To scale it up or to scale it down: that is the task!

Objective: To solve problems using proportions

Warm-Up
Have students solve the following proportions.

$\frac{3}{8} = \frac{n}{48}$ (18); $\frac{15}{n} = \frac{5}{11}$ (33); $\frac{n}{17} = \frac{12}{68}$ (3);

$\frac{24}{18} = \frac{10}{n}$ (7.5)

GETTING STARTED

Tell the class that examples of proportions used in everyday life are numerous. Ask students to think of situations in which proportions are used. (unit pricing, in recipes, and in reading map and model scales)

TEACHING THE LESSON

As an example of using a proportion, poll the students for their favorite vegetable. Write a ratio on the chalkboard for each choice; for example, the number of students choosing carrots to the number of students in class. Then write proportions comparing each ratio to the total number of students in the school. Solve to find how many students with each preference you would expect to find in the school, if your class is typical.

Questions: Students are not likely to encounter difficulties in understanding the question. Be sure students realize that problems such as the introductory one call for a specific amount of a particular ingredient, not merely a factor by which the recipe is increased.

Tools: The most frequent problem students will encounter in this area is sorting the given information in a problem and recognizing it as a situation that calls for a proportion. Remind students that a *proportion* is a comparision of two equal ratios. When presented with a problem in which they must increase or decrease the amount of something, have them look for an equal ratio. The easiest way to spot the numbers needed for this ratio is by looking for numbers that have the same label, such as *16 servings* and *6 servings*.

Solutions: Students will probably run into the most difficulty setting up the proportion. Assist them by labeling the numbers in the introductory problem, for example, *given number of servings, reduced number of servings,* and so on. Be sure they realize that the ratios will always be set up in a parallel manner with the same item on either the top or the bottom in *both* ratios. It may also be necessary to note that in converting an entire recipe, it would be easier to simplify the given ratio in order to com-

pute a factor first and then to multiply each item by this factor. Point out, however, that this factor is not all that is asked for in most problems.

Check: To check their solutions, students should rewrite the problem, set up the proportion again, and substitute their answer. Students should check to see not only that their numbers are correct, but also that the answer itself makes sense.

| QUESTIONS | TOOLS | SOLUTIONS | CHECKS |

PROBLEM SOLVING
Writing a Proportion

Sometimes you can use a proportion to solve a problem.

Patrick is studying to become a chef. For one of his assignments, he has to convert a recipe that yields 16 servings to one that will yield 6 servings. The recipe, for an eggplant casserole, calls for $\frac{2}{3}$ cup of grated cheese. How much will he need for the recipe that will yield only 6 servings?

To find out how much cheese he needs, write a proportion.

Let n = the amount of cheese required in the 6-serving recipe.

$$\underset{\substack{\text{cheese in the} \\ \text{original recipe} \\ \text{servings in the} \\ \text{original recipe}}}{} \frac{\frac{2}{3}}{16} = \frac{n}{6} \underset{\substack{\text{cheese in the} \\ \text{new recipe} \\ \text{servings in the} \\ \text{new recipe}}}{}$$

You cannot rename either fraction, and so, the next step is to cross multiply.

$$16 \cdot n = \frac{2}{3} \cdot 6$$

Solve for n.
$$16n = 4$$
$$n = \frac{4}{16} \text{ or } \frac{1}{4}$$

Patrick will need $\frac{1}{4}$ cup of cheese.

- Why is it usually important to keep a specific ratio between ingredients when changing the amount of servings for a recipe?
  So your new recipe will taste and look the same as your original recipe.

Write the letter of the correct proportion.

1. Anthony's assignment is to make chili for 80 people. He has a recipe that serves 35 people. It calls for 8 pounds of ground beef. How many pounds of ground beef will he need in order to serve 80 people?

a. $\frac{80}{8} = \frac{8}{n}$ **b.** $\frac{1}{10} = \frac{35}{n}$ **(c.)** $\frac{8}{35} = \frac{n}{80}$

2. Jack needs 2 quarts of salad dressing for 80 people. The recipe for 3 cups of salad dressing calls for $\frac{1}{4}$ cup of vinegar. How much vinegar will Jack need for 2 quarts of dressing?

a. $\frac{\frac{1}{4}}{8} = \frac{8}{n}$ **b.** $\frac{2}{3} = \frac{n}{\frac{1}{4}}$ **(c.)** $\frac{\frac{1}{4}}{3} = \frac{n}{8}$

Solve. Use a proportion when appropriate.

3. For the final exam, the students at the Culinary Institute are making dinner for all the teachers. Mark is supposed to make 17 loaves of bread. If he uses $5\frac{3}{4}$ cups of whole-wheat flour for 2 loaves, how many cups will he need to use for 17 loaves?

$\frac{5\frac{3}{4}}{2} = \frac{n}{17}$; $n = 48\frac{7}{8}$ cups

4. Angela has been assigned to make her famous sauce. Her recipe calls for boiling the sauce until it is reduced by $\frac{1}{3}$. If she wants $3\frac{1}{3}$ cups of reduced sauce, how many cups will she need to begin with?
5 cups

5. Carol conducted a survey to find out how many people preferred fried chicken to roasted chicken. She found that the ratio of fried-chicken lovers to roasted-chicken lovers was 7 to 4. If 224 people preferred fried chicken, how many people were polled in the survey?

$\frac{7}{4} = \frac{224}{n}$; $n = 128$; 352 people

6. Raul made a fruit drink by using 1 part orange concentrate to 1 part lemon concentrate to 6 parts water. If he used 24 ounces of orange concentrate, how much water did he use? If there were 130 calories in each 8-ounce cup, how many calories were there in 24 ounces of fruit drink?   144 oz water; 390 calories

7. Sue usually buys avocados for guacamole at $0.89 each. Avocados are on sale at $0.79 each or 2 for $1.50. If she decides to spend $7.00 on avocados, how many can she buy, and how much money will she have left?   9 avocados and $0.21 left

8. The Griffin Restaurant offers a dinner for $27.50. The owner's cost for each dinner is $25.00, giving him a 10% profit. To increase the profit to 13%, how much more will he need to charge for this dinner? $0.75

Classwork/Homework, page H82

ASSIGNMENT GUIDE

Basic:	1–4
Average:	2–6
Extended:	3–8

Resources
Practice, p. 82   Class/Home, p. H82
Enrich, p. 78

Exercise Analysis
1–2   Choose the correct proportion
3–6   Solve using a proportion
7   Interpret the remainder
8   Multistep problem

FOLLOW-UP ACTIVITIES

PROBLEM SOLVING
Materials: grocery-store newspaper advertisements with unit prices per group

Draw up a shopping list of six or so common grocery items. Have each group "shop" the newspaper advertisements for the items listed, computing unit prices for each item and identifying which price is the lowest. Each group will then choose the most economical store, the one with the lowest total for all the items combined.

CALCULATOR
Materials: 1 calculator per student

Have students solve the following proportions on a calculator.

$\frac{27}{216} = \frac{n}{456}$ $(n = 57)$; $\frac{3,210}{n} = \frac{57,535}{11,507}$

$(n = 642)$; $\frac{n}{12.4185} = \frac{12.92}{1.09832}$

$(n = 146.08403)$; $\frac{4.58}{0.421} = \frac{7.963}{n}$

$(n = 0.73197)$

COMING UP
Scaled-down problems

Warm-Up

Write the following proportions on the board, and have students complete them.

- 1 is to 5 as 4 is to _____ (20)
- 8 is to 10 as 4 is to _____ (5)
- 7 is to 9 as 21 is to _____ (27)
- 33 is to 36 as 11 is to _____ (12)

GETTING STARTED

Materials: map and blueprint

Display a map and a blueprint or a scale model of something very small. Ask students to suggest ways in which these are similar. Elicit the notion that they are both representations of things either too large or too small to display in their actual sizes. Have students discuss the advantages of using a map or a blueprint.

TEACHING THE LESSON

A. Some students may invert the problem to read $\frac{1 m}{2 cm} = \frac{x m}{11 cm}$, or $\frac{2 cm}{11 cm} = \frac{1 m}{x m}$. These are also acceptable proportions. The important thing is that the same units are in the same position; for example, in $\frac{2 cm}{11 cm} = \frac{1 m}{x m}$, the same units are on the left.

B. Encourage students to write sentences such as the following to describe the proportion.

The scale is 4 m are equal to 1 cm. Therefore, 10 m are equal to x cm.

You may wish to allow students to use calculators while working through this lesson.

Checkpoint

The chart lists the common errors students make in using scale drawings.

Correct Answers: 1d, 2b

Remediation

■ Review the cross-products method of solving proportions. Continue until students can successfully solve several examples. Also you might have students write the units beside each term in the proportion to identify what unit x should be. Then have students review the word problem to check whether their answers are reasonable.

☐ Assign Reteach Master, p. 60.

Scale Drawings

A. Enrique is studying to be a landscape architect. He prepares a scale drawing that has a scale of 2 cm = 1 m. In his drawing, a spruce tree is located 11 cm from the building. What is the actual distance from the tree to the building?

Let x = the actual distance from the tree to the building. Use the scale to write a proportion.

distance in drawing (cm) $\longrightarrow$ $\frac{2}{1} = \frac{11}{x}$ $\longleftarrow$ distance in drawing (cm)
actual distance (m) $\longrightarrow$ $\qquad$ $\longleftarrow$ actual distance (m)

$$2x = 11$$
$$\frac{2x}{2} = \frac{11}{2}$$
$$x = 5.5$$

Cross multiply and find x.

The actual distance is 5.5 m.

B. Suppose you plan to use the scale 1 cm = 4 m to prepare a scale drawing. If the actual length of an object is 10 m, what will be its length in the scale drawing?

Let x = the length in the drawing. Write a proportion.

length in drawing (cm) $\longrightarrow$ $\frac{1}{4} = \frac{x}{10}$ $\longleftarrow$ length in drawing (cm)
actual length (m) $\longrightarrow$ $\qquad$ $\longleftarrow$ actual length (m)

$$10 = 4x$$
$$\frac{10}{4} = \frac{4x}{4}$$
$$2.5 = x$$

Cross multiply and find x.

The length in the drawing will be 2.5 cm.

Checkpoint — Write the letter of the correct answer.

Find the missing measurement.

1. Scale: 1 cm = 2 m
Drawing measurement: 6 cm
Actual measurement: ▨

- **a.** 3 cm
- **b.** 12 cm
- **c.** 3 m
- **d.** 12 m

2. Scale: 3 in. = 5 ft
Actual measurement: 10 ft
Drawing measurement: ▨

- **a.** $1\frac{1}{2}$ in.
- **b.** 6 in.
- **c.** 6 ft
- **d.** 150 ft

206

COMMON ERRORS

Answer Choice	Type of Error
☐ 1a, 2d	Uses incorrect proportion; uses incorrect unit of measure
■ 1b, 2c	Uses incorrect unit of measure
☐ 1c, 2a	Uses incorrect proportion

RETEACH | Scale Drawing

The Smiths like the floor plan that they found in a magazine. The scale of the drawing is 1 cm = 2 m. Write a proportion to find x, the length of the home. The drawing is 7.2 cm long.

Remember
Make sure the terms in the equation are consistent.

Length in drawing (cm) $\longrightarrow$ $\frac{1}{2} = \frac{7.2}{x}$ $\longleftarrow$ Length in drawing (cm)
Actual length (m) $\qquad$ Actual length (m)

$$x = 2 \cdot 7.2 = 14.4$$

The length of the home is about 14.4 m.

For each drawing dimension, write a proportion that represents the actual length. Solve the proportions and round each answer to the nearest tenth.

Dimension	Drawing length	Scale ratio	Proportion	Actual length
1. Width	4.8 cm	1 cm = 2 m	$\frac{1}{2} = \frac{4.8}{x}$	9.6 m
2. Length, Room D	2.7 cm	1 cm = 2 m	$\frac{1}{2} = \frac{2.7}{x}$	5.4 m
3. Width, Room D	2.6 cm	1 cm = 2 m	$\frac{1}{2} = \frac{2.6}{x}$	5.2 m

Use the scale 1 cm = 2 m to write a proportion for the actual length. Solve the proportion.

- **4.** Length of room C (2.5 cm) 5 m
- **5.** Width of room C (1.8 cm) 3.6 m
- **6.** Length of room E (4.3 cm) 8.6 m
- **7.** Width of room E (2.1 cm) 4.2 m
- **8.** Length of room B (1.9 cm) 3.8 m
- **9.** Width of room B (0.4 cm) 0.8 m
- **10.** Length of room A (2.4 cm) 4.8 m
- **11.** Width of room A (2.2 cm) 4.4 m

Solve.

12. A drawing has a line that is 14.5 cm long. The scale of the drawing is 1 cm = 10.5 m. Find the actual length represented by the line. 152.25 m

60

Use with pages 206–207.

Reteach Worksheet

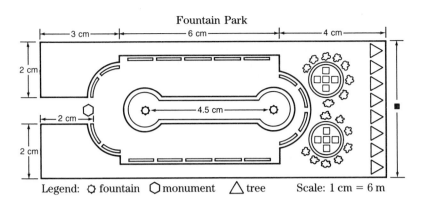

Fountain Park

| 3 cm | 6 cm | 4 cm |

2 cm

2 cm

2 cm

4.5 cm

Legend: ⬡ fountain ⬡ monument △ tree   Scale: 1 cm = 6 m

1. Use a centimeter ruler to find the width of the park in the drawing.   5 cm

Use the scale drawing to find the actual

2. length of the park.   78 m

3. width of the park.   30 m

4. width of the park entrance.   6 m

5. distance between the fountains.   27 m

Solve.

6. The lawn area in front of a post office is 3 meters wide. How wide should it be in a scale drawing if a scale of 1 cm = 0.5 m is used?   **6 cm wide**

7. A landscape architect is preparing a scale drawing of a shrub border that has a scale of $\frac{1}{2}$ in. = 1 ft. If the border is $35\frac{1}{2}$ ft long, how long should it be in the drawing? $17\frac{3}{4}$ in. long

8. A scale drawing of the town park is prepared that has a scale of 1 cm = 8 m. If the distance from the drinking fountain to the bandstand is 8.5 cm, what is the actual distance?   **68 m**

9. Choose a rectangular area, such as a classroom or school yard, and find its length and width. Select an appropriate scale, and prepare a scale drawing based on your measurements.   **Check students' drawings.**

CHALLENGE

You have 6 toothpicks. How can you arrange them so you have four equilateral triangles, all having sides 1 toothpick long?

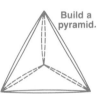

Build a pyramid.

Classwork/Homework, page H83

ASSIGNMENT GUIDE

Basic: 1–9

Average: 1–9

Extended: 1–9, Chlg

Resources
Practice, p. 83   Class/Home, p. H83
Reteach, p. 60
Enrich, p. 79

Exercise Analysis

1   Measure a distance in a scale drawing with a centimeter ruler
2–5   Find an actual measurement
6–8   Skill applications
9   Data collection and computation

You may wish to allow students to use calculators to complete some of the exercises.

Challenge

The manipulation of toothpicks may help students to discover that three dimensions are necessary to solve this problem.

FOLLOW-UP ACTIVITIES

NUMBER SENSE (Estimation)

Have students decide on a scale that would be necessary to put the following on a sheet of 8-in. by 11-in. paper.
- the classroom
- the whole school
- the city
- the state
- the continental United States (1 in. = 275 mi)
- Earth (1 in. = 2,300 mi)

Have students consult an atlas to find how accurate their estimates were.

PROBLEM SOLVING

Point out that a 1 in. : 12 ft ratio can also be expressed in simplest form as 1 : 144. Next remind students that the models they buy in hobby stores are scale models. Then have them solve such problems as the following.
- Kevin buys a 1 : 9 model of a motorcycle. When built, the model is 8 in. long. How long is the actual motorcycle? (6 ft)
- Sarah is building a 1 : 48 model airplane. The actual plane is 66 ft long. How long, in inches, will the model be? ($16\frac{1}{2}$ in.)

COMING UP

The sweet smell of per "cent"!

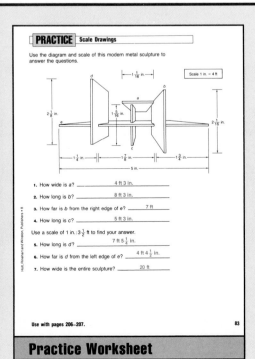

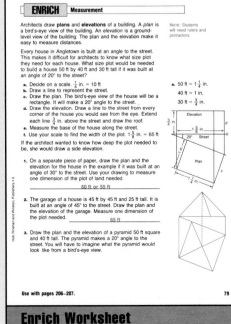

Objectives: To identify and write a percent for a fraction or a ratio

Warm-Up
Have students write an equivalent ratio that has a denominator of 100 for each.

$\frac{2}{5}\left(\frac{40}{100}\right)$; $\frac{4}{1}\left(\frac{400}{100}\right)$; $\frac{12}{25}\left(\frac{48}{100}\right)$; $\frac{6}{15}\left(\frac{40}{100}\right)$;

$\frac{7}{10}\left(\frac{70}{100}\right)$; $\frac{15}{20}\left(\frac{75}{100}\right)$; $\frac{45}{50}\left(\frac{90}{100}\right)$;

$\frac{27}{30}\left(\frac{90}{100}\right)$; $\frac{5}{8}\left(\frac{62.5}{100}\right)$; $\frac{3}{2}\left(\frac{150}{100}\right)$

GETTING STARTED

Have students discuss where they have seen numbers used as percents; for example, a sale tag that is marked 50% off. Have students identify how percents are used and what they mean.

TEACHING THE LESSON

A. To aid students in remembering that percent is a ratio that has a second term of 100, point out that the percent symbol is actually made up of the digits in 100. At first, it was written as *00*, but then it became *0/0*, or %. Explain that *percent* means "per hundred."

B. Students may question the possibility of percents greater than 100, as in the case of $\frac{7}{5}$. One possible example of this might be: There were 5 members in the club last year. Then 2 new members joined. The club's attendance is now $\frac{7}{5}$, or 140% of what it was last year.

C. Emphasize that 0.375% means $\frac{0.375}{100}$ and is not equal to the decimal 0.375. It is actually 0.00375.

You may also want to extend the instruction to include percents that involve mixed numbers, such as expressing the ratio 2:3 as $66\frac{2}{3}\%$.

The Meaning of Percent

A. This year's graduating class at Lakeland High School has 100 students, and 17 of them plan to attend the community college. You can express this information

as a ratio.   as a fraction.   as a decimal.

17 to 100, $\frac{17}{100}$ 0.17
or 17:100

You can also use a percent. **Percent (%)** means "per hundred."

So, 17% of Lakeland's graduates plan to attend the community college.

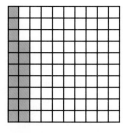

The 10-by-10 figure represents the 100 graduates. Of the squares, 17 are shaded.

B. To write a percent for a fraction, you can find an equivalent fraction that has 100 as the denominator.

Write $\frac{1}{2}$ as a percent.   Write $\frac{7}{5}$ as a percent.

$\frac{1}{2} = \frac{x}{100}$ $\frac{7}{5} = \frac{x}{100}$

$\frac{1}{2} = \frac{1 \cdot 50}{2 \cdot 50} = \frac{50}{100}$ $\frac{7}{5} = \frac{7 \cdot 20}{5 \cdot 20} = \frac{140}{100}$

The fraction $\frac{1}{2} = \frac{50}{100}$, or 50%.   The fraction $\frac{7}{5} = \frac{140}{100}$, or 140%.

C. To write a percent for the ratio of a part to the whole, find an equal ratio that has 100 as the second term.

Express the ratio 9:20   Express the ratio 3 to 800
as a percent.   as a percent.

9:20 is $\frac{9}{20}$ ← part ← whole   3 to 800 is $\frac{3}{800}$ ← part ← whole

$\frac{9}{20} = \frac{x}{100}$ $\frac{3}{800} = \frac{x}{100}$

$900 = 20x$ $300 = 800x$

$\frac{900}{20} = \frac{20x}{20}$ $\frac{300}{800} = \frac{800x}{800}$

$45 = x$ $0.375 = x$

The ratio 9:20 is equal to   The ratio 3 to 800 is equal to
45:100, or 45%.   0.375:100, or 0.375%.

208

COMMON ERRORS

Some students might encounter difficulty recognizing when denominators can be multiplied by a factor to find 100.

Remediation
List the pairs of factors that can be multiplied to find 100. (2, 50; 4, 25; 5, 20; 10, 10)

Using such examples as $\frac{7}{50}$ (14%) and $\frac{3}{5}$ (60%), have students multiply the numerator and denominator by the appropriate factor.

Point out that when the denominator is 100, the numerator will be the percent.

Assign Reteach Master, p. 61.

Reteach Worksheet

Write as a percent.

1. $\frac{12}{100}$ 12% **2.** $\frac{3}{100}$ 3%   **3.** 99 of 100 99% **4.** 7:100 7%

5. $\frac{77}{100}$ 77% **6.** 13 per hundred 13% **7.** 11:100 11% **8.** 1 of 100 1%

9. $\frac{3}{10}$ 30% **10.** $\frac{10}{10,000}$ 0.1% **11.** $\frac{7}{10}$ 70% **12.** $\frac{426}{200}$ 213%

13. $\frac{3}{2}$ 150% **14.** $\frac{3}{5}$ 60% **15.** $\frac{9}{1,200}$ 0.75% **16.** $\frac{12}{25}$ 48%

Write each ratio as a percent.

17. 7:50 14% **18.** 13:20 65% **19.** 5:8 62.5% **★20.** 1 to 3 $33\frac{1}{3}$%

21. 5 students of 100 students 5% **22.** 2 scholarships per 25 students 8%

Solve. For Problem 24, use the Infobank.

23. Of the 100 graduates at Lakeland High School, 31 plan to attend an out-of-state college. What percent plan to attend an out-of-state college? 31%

24. Use the information on page 475 to solve. In grams, what is the United States Recommended Daily Allowance of protein? 48

25. This year, Fairview High School has a graduating class of 80 students. Of the 80 students, 6 plan to enter the military. What percent plan to enter the military? 7.5%

26. Of this year's 80 graduates at Fairview High School, 57 have found summer jobs. What percent have found summer jobs? 71.25%

27. Survey 10 of your classmates to determine the career that each is preparing for. Write each result as a fraction and then as a percent.
Answers will vary.

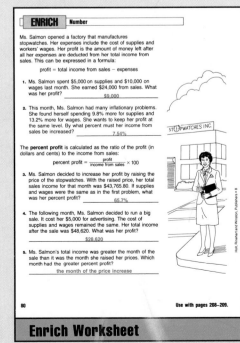

NUMBER SENSE

Change each fraction to a percent.

1. $\frac{3}{4}$ 75% **2.** $\frac{2}{5}$ 40% **3.** $\frac{9}{10}$ 90% **4.** $\frac{4}{5}$ 80% **5.** $\frac{6}{5}$ 120%

6. $\frac{1}{4}$ 25% **7.** $\frac{5}{4}$ 125% **8.** $\frac{3}{20}$ 15% **9.** $\frac{3}{25}$ 12% **10.** $\frac{41}{50}$ 82%

Classwork/Homework, page H84

209

ASSIGNMENT GUIDE

Basic: 1–19, 23–27

Average: 5–27, NS 1–5

Extended: 9–27, NS

Resources
Practice, p. 84 Class/Home, p. H84
Reteach, p. 61
Enrich, p. 80

Exercise Analysis
1–22 Write a ratio as a percent
23, 25–26 Skill applications
24, 27 Data collection and computation

You may wish to allow students to use calculators for some of these exercises.

Number Sense
The "Backward Z" method may help students to solve these exercises.

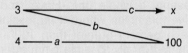

Step A: 4 × ■ equals 100. (25)
Step B: 25 times 3 is what number? (75)
Step C: $\frac{3}{4} = \frac{75}{100}$, or 75%.

FOLLOW-UP ACTIVITIES

MANIPULATIVES
On graph paper, draw these figures.

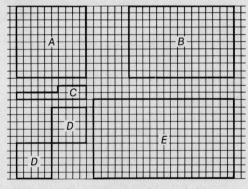

Ask:
• If A = 100%, what percent of A is each of the other shapes? (B: 150%, C: 14%, D: 50%, E: 220%)
• If D = 100%, how do all the other percentages change? (They double.)
• If E = 100%, what is A? ($45.\overline{45}$%)

COMING UP
Write on with percents and decimals!

209

Objectives:
To write a decimal as a percent and a percent as a decimal

Warm-Up
Have students write decimal equivalents for such fractions as:

$\frac{12.5}{100}$ (0.125); $\frac{33}{100}$ (0.33); $\frac{9}{10}$ (0.9); $\frac{5}{8}$ (0.625).

GETTING STARTED

Materials: centimeter grid paper

Give each student two sheets of centimeter grid paper. Have them count off and then draw a border around 5 squares each 10 cm × 10 cm. Tell students to shade enough centimeter squares to show the following percents: 8%, 41%, 28%, 245%, 150%.

TEACHING THE LESSON

A. Explain that 100% = 1 because it represents a whole unit. Have students give examples where it is possible to have percent greater than 100% and where it is only possible to have percent less than 100%.

B. Tell students that they will always know how many places to move the decimal point if they remember that *percent* means "per hundred" and that there are two decimal places in hundredths.

C. Extend the lesson by having students write each of the following as a percent.

0.72 (72%), 0.07 (7%), 0.015 (1.5%), 3.2 (320%), 4.005 (400.5%), 32 (3,200%), 17.2 (1,720%)

Checkpoint
The chart lists the common errors students make in renaming decimals and percents.

Correct Answers: 1a, 2b, 3d, 4b

Remediation
■ For these errors, emphasize that *percent* means "per hundred." Point out that to write a percent as a decimal, divide by 100; to rewrite a decimal as a percent, multiply by 100. For either, move the decimal point two places. Have students rewrite each of the multiple choices in Checkpoint Questions 1 and 2 as percents and in Questions 3 and 4 as decimals.

☐ For these errors, assign Reteach Master, p. 62.

210

Percents and Decimals

A. Ben plans to become a reporter. This summer he is working part-time in a newsroom and spends 35% of his salary for school expenses.

You can write a decimal to describe the part of Ben's salary spent for school expenses.

35% means 35 per 100, or $\frac{35}{100}$.

35% = 0.35

B. You can use a shortcut to write a percent as a decimal. Move the decimal point two places to the left and omit the percent sign.

18% = 0.18 = 0.18
225% = 2.25 = 2.25

3.5% = 0.035 = 0.035
0.6% = 0.006 = 0.006

> Add zeros as necessary.

C. You can also write a decimal as a percent. Move the decimal point two places to the right and write the percent sign.

0.32 = 0.32% = 32%
0.07 = 0.07% = 7%

4 = 4.00% = 400%
0.015 = 0.015 % = 1.5%

> Add zeros as necessary.

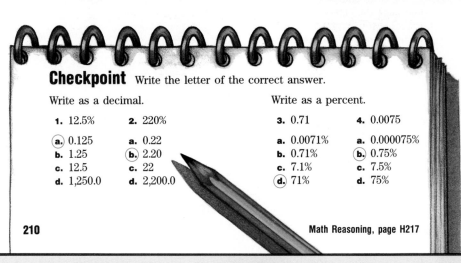

Checkpoint
Write the letter of the correct answer.

Write as a decimal.

1. 12.5%
   - **(a.)** 0.125
   - b. 1.25
   - c. 12.5
   - d. 1,250.0

2. 220%
   - a. 0.22
   - **(b.)** 2.20
   - c. 22
   - d. 2,200.0

Write as a percent.

3. 0.71
   - a. 0.0071%
   - b. 0.71%
   - c. 7.1%
   - **(d.)** 71%

4. 0.0075
   - a. 0.000075%
   - **(b.)** 0.75%
   - c. 7.5%
   - d. 75%

210

Math Reasoning, page H217

COMMON ERRORS

Answer Choice	Type of Error
■ 1b, 2c, 3c	Moves decimal point only one place
☐ 1c	Drops percent sign without moving decimal point
☐ 1d, 2d, 3a, 4a	Moves decimal point in incorrect direction
■ 2a, 4c	Moves decimal point three places
☐ 3b	Adds percent sign without moving decimal point
☐ 4d	Ignores place value

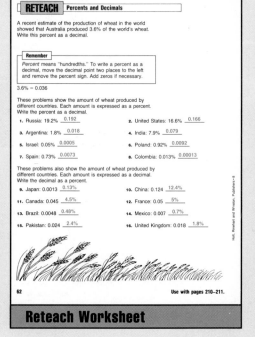

RETEACH Percents and Decimals

A recent estimate of the production of wheat in the world showed that Australia produced 3.6% of the world's wheat. Write this percent as a decimal.

> **Remember**
> *Percent* means "hundredths." To write a percent as a decimal, move the decimal point two places to the left and remove the percent sign. Add zeros if necessary.

3.6% = 0.036

These problems show the amount of wheat produced by different countries. Each amount is expressed as a percent. Write the percent as a decimal.

1. Russia: 19.2% _0.192_
2. United States: 16.6% _0.166_
3. Argentina: 1.8% _0.018_
4. India: 7.9% _0.079_
5. Israel: 0.05% _0.0005_
6. Poland: 0.92% _0.0092_
7. Spain: 0.73% _0.0073_
8. Colombia: 0.013% _0.00013_

These problems also show the amount of wheat produced by different countries. Each amount is expressed as a decimal. Write the decimal as a percent.

9. Japan: 0.0013 _0.13%_
10. China: 0.124 _12.4%_
11. Canada: 0.045 _4.5%_
12. France: 0.05 _5%_
13. Brazil: 0.0048 _0.48%_
14. Mexico: 0.007 _0.7%_
15. Pakistan: 0.024 _2.4%_
16. United Kingdom: 0.018 _1.8%_

62

Use with pages 210–211.

Reteach Worksheet

Write as a decimal.

1. 13% 0.13   **2.** 99% 0.99   **3.** 8% 0.08   **4.** 62% 0.62

5. 150% 1.50   **6.** 500% 5.0   **7.** 354% 3.54   **8.** 247% 2.47

9. 1.8% 0.018   **10.** 0.9% 0.009   **11.** 12.5% 0.125   **12.** 6.25% 0.0625

Write as a percent.

13. 0.83 83%   **14.** 0.32 32%   **15.** 0.60 60%   **16.** 0.07 7%

17. 3.68 368%   **18.** 5.00 500%   **19.** 1.04 104%   **20.** 7.50 750%

21. 0.4 40%   **22.** 6 600%   **23.** 1.2 120%   **24.** 9 900%

25. 0.005 0.5%   **26.** 1.005 100.5%   **27.** 0.0057 0.57%   **28.** 0.0125 1.25%

Copy and complete the table.

Percent	8.25%	925%	0.38% **31.** ■	1.25% **32.** ■
Decimal	0.0825 **29.** ■	9.25 **30.** ■	0.0038	0.0125

Solve.

33. The staff issued a special edition of the paper for the opening of the baseball season. The number of copies printed of the special edition was 2.1 times the usual number. What percent was this? 210%

34. Gwen questioned the reporters about their education. Of 10 reporters, 4 had gone to journalism school. What percent went to journalism school? Write this percent as a decimal. 40%; 0.40

35. When Gwen works overtime, she earns 1.5 times her regular wage. What is this number written as a percent? 150%

36. In a newspaper or a magazine, find a graph that has percents. Redraw the graph. Use decimals for the percents. Check students' graphs.

FOCUS: REASONING

"My name is William McShane. I have as many brothers as sisters, but each of my sisters has twice as many brothers as sisters."

QUESTION: How many boys and how many girls are there in the McShane family? 4 boys; 3 girls

ASSIGNMENT GUIDE

Basic: 1–20, 33–36, F

Average: 1–19 o, 21–36, F

Extended: 2–20 e, 25–36, F

Resources
Practice, p. 85   Class/Home, p. H85
Reteach, p. 62   Reasoning, p. H217
Enrich, p. 81

Exercise Analysis

1–12   Write a percent as a decimal
13–28   Write a decimal as a percent
29–32   Mixed practice
33–35   Skill applications
36   Data collection and computation

You may wish to allow students to use calculators for some of these exercises.

Focus: Reasoning

The use of trial and error is acceptable, but encourage students to solve the problem algebraically. Using the variables G (girls), B (boys), and R (William's brothers), we can see that:

$$G = R; B = R + 1$$
$$B = 2 (G - 1)$$

Therefore: $R + 1 = 2 (R - 1)$
$$R + 1 = 2R - 2$$
$$3 = R$$
$$4 = B$$

FOLLOW-UP ACTIVITIES

PROBLEM SOLVING
Have students identify what is wrong with the following statements.

- The price of the car was cut 150%. (No price can be cut more than 100% because a 100% cut would result in a car that costs nothing.)
- The store doubled its inventory of shirts; in other words, it increased the number of shirts 200%. (If something doubles, it increases 100%.)
- The swim shop became a self-service shop after the summer when it reduced its staff by 130%. (No more than 100% of its staff could be let go because a 100% reduction means that there would be no one left.)

PROBLEM SOLVING
Have students record the class attendance for a week. Then have them calculate the increase or decrease in attendance from one day to the next.

COMING UP
We present a fraction and a percent.

Objectives: To write a fraction as a percent and a percent as a fraction

Warm-Up
Have students find the missing term in each proportion.

$\frac{9}{20} = \frac{x}{100}$ (45); $\frac{3}{4} = \frac{x}{100}$ (75);

$\frac{2}{3} = \frac{x}{100}$ $\left(66\frac{2}{3}\right)$; $\frac{3}{250} = \frac{x}{1,000}$ (12);

$\frac{3}{50} = \frac{x}{100}$ (6); $\frac{17}{50} = \frac{x}{10,000}$ (3,400)

GETTING STARTED

Remind students that any fraction $\frac{a}{b}$ always means $a \div b$. Next demonstrate that if $b > a$, the quotient is always a decimal less than 1. Point out that they already know how to rewrite a fraction as a decimal as well as how to rewrite a decimal as a fraction. Ask: How would you rewrite a fraction as a percent? (Divide the denominator by the numerator and multiply by 100.)

TEACHING THE LESSON

A. Have students name the fractions, in simplest form, that correspond to each percent.

0.5% $\left(\frac{1}{200}\right)$ $12\frac{1}{2}\%$ $\left(\frac{1}{8}\right)$

3% $\left(\frac{3}{100}\right)$ $14\frac{2}{7}\%$ $\left(\frac{1}{7}\right)$

37.5% $\left(\frac{3}{8}\right)$

B. Have students name all the possible factors of 100. Ask: Why are fractions that have denominators that are factors of 100 simple to change to percents?

In the Other Examples section, an alternate strategy for writing a percent for a mixed number is to rename the mixed number with a fraction greater than 1. Then divide.

Percents and Fractions

A. Before entering the state veterinary school, 75% of the students completed four years of college. What fraction of the students is this?

To write a percent as a fraction, use 100 as the denominator and write the answer in simplest form.

$$75\% = \frac{75}{100} = \frac{75 \div 25}{100 \div 25} = \frac{3}{4}$$

$\frac{3}{4}$ of the students completed four years of college.

B. There are two ways to write a fraction as a percent. One way is to find an equivalent fraction that has a denominator of 100.

$$\frac{1}{4} = \frac{25}{100} = 25\%$$

The other way is to use division to find a decimal.

Division is convenient for a fraction such as $\frac{7}{8}$ because the denominator 8 is not a factor of 100.

$$\frac{1}{4} \longrightarrow 4\overline{)1.00} \quad 0.25 = 25\%$$

Sometimes you must divide beyond the hundredths place.

$$\frac{7}{8} \longrightarrow 8\overline{)7.000} \quad 0.875 = 87.5\%, \text{ or } 87\frac{1}{2}\%$$

Other examples:

percents to fractions

$$28\% = \frac{28}{100} = \frac{7}{25}$$

$$83\frac{1}{3}\% = \frac{83\frac{1}{3}}{100} = 83\frac{1}{3} \div 100$$
$$= \frac{\overset{5}{\cancel{250}}}{3} \times \frac{1}{\underset{2}{\cancel{100}}} = \frac{5}{6}$$

$$165\% = \frac{165}{100} = \frac{33}{20} = 1\frac{13}{20}$$

fractions to percents

$$\frac{2}{5} = \frac{40}{100} = 40\%$$

$$\frac{2}{3} = 3\overline{)2.00} \quad 0.66\frac{2}{3} = 66\frac{2}{3}\%$$

$$1\frac{3}{5} = \underbrace{1}_{100\%} + \underbrace{\frac{3}{5}}_{60\%} = 160\%$$

Math Reasoning, page H217

COMMON ERRORS

Some students might have difficulty with the concept of a percent being a decimal, such as 87.5%.

Remediation
Have students use graph paper to show the difference between 87.5% and 87% and between $25\frac{1}{2}\%$ and 25%.

Assign Reteach Master, p. 63.

RETEACH Percents and Fractions

The statistics of the basketball team show that Amy made 5 of 8 free throws in last week's game. What percent of her free throws did she make?

Remember
Write the fraction as a decimal. Then move the decimal point two places to the right and write the percent sign.
$$8\overline{)5.000} \quad 0.625 \quad \frac{5}{8} = 0.625 = 62.5\%$$

Amy made 62.5% of her free throws.

Write each fraction as a percent.

1. $\frac{4}{8}$ _50%_   2. $\frac{14}{25}$ _56%_   3. $\frac{3}{8}$ _37$\frac{1}{2}$%_   4. $\frac{1}{6}$ _16$\frac{2}{3}$%_   5. $\frac{1}{8}$ _12$\frac{1}{2}$%_

6. $\frac{3}{4}$ _75%_   7. $\frac{17}{50}$ _34%_   8. $\frac{2}{9}$ _22$\frac{2}{9}$%_   9. $\frac{9}{25}$ _36%_   10. $\frac{0}{21}$ _0%_

Write each percent as a fraction in simplest form.

11. 60% $\frac{3}{5}$ 12. 40% $\frac{2}{5}$ 13. 45% $\frac{9}{20}$ 14. $31\frac{1}{4}$% $\frac{5}{16}$ 15. $66\frac{2}{3}$% $\frac{2}{3}$

16. 87% $\frac{87}{100}$ 17. 48% $\frac{12}{25}$ 18. $62\frac{1}{2}$% $\frac{5}{8}$ 19. $9\frac{1}{2}$% $\frac{19}{200}$ 20. $\frac{0}{25}$% _0_

Use with pages 212–213.   63

Reteach Worksheet

Write as a fraction, a whole number, or a mixed number. Express all fractions in simplest form.

1. 10% $\frac{1}{10}$

2. 25% $\frac{1}{4}$

3. 95% $\frac{19}{20}$

4. 56% $\frac{14}{25}$

5. $12\frac{1}{2}\%$ $\frac{1}{8}$

6. $14\frac{2}{7}\%$ $\frac{1}{7}$

7. $2\frac{1}{2}\%$ $\frac{1}{40}$

8. $66\frac{2}{3}\%$ $\frac{2}{3}$

9. 175% $1\frac{3}{4}$

10. 280% $2\frac{4}{5}$

11. 200% 2

12. 550% $5\frac{1}{2}$

Write as a percent.

13. $\frac{1}{2}$ 50%

14. $\frac{7}{10}$ 70%

15. $\frac{22}{25}$ 88%

16. $\frac{49}{50}$ 98%

17. $\frac{1}{11}$ $9\frac{1}{11}\%$

18. $\frac{5}{12}$ $41\frac{2}{3}\%$

19. $\frac{11}{40}$ $27\frac{1}{2}\%$

20. $\frac{4}{7}$ $57\frac{1}{7}\%$

21. $1\frac{4}{5}$ 180%

22. $3\frac{1}{2}$ 350%

23. $2\frac{2}{3}$ $266\frac{2}{3}\%$

★24. $5\frac{1}{9}$ $511\frac{1}{9}\%$

Copy and write the missing fraction, mixed number, or percent.

25. $91\frac{2}{3}\% = $ ■ $\frac{11}{12}$

26. ■% $= \frac{1}{6}$ $16\frac{2}{3}$

27. $62\frac{1}{2}\% = $ ■ $\frac{5}{8}$

28. ■% = 32.5 3,250

29. $112\frac{1}{2}\% = $ ■ $1\frac{1}{8}$

★30. ■% $= \frac{80}{30}$ $266\frac{2}{3}$

Solve.

31. Of all veterinarians, $\frac{1}{3}$ are specialists in treating small animals. What percent of veterinarians specialize in this area? $33\frac{1}{3}\%$

32. Of the 36,000 veterinarians in the United States, 7.5% work for the federal government. What is this percent written as a fraction? $\frac{3}{40}$

33. A student in veterinary school estimates that she spends $\frac{1}{8}$ of her time working with animals. What is this fraction written as a percent? $12\frac{1}{2}\%$

34. A young veterinarian who borrowed money to attend school spends $16\frac{2}{3}\%$ of his income to repay the loan. What fraction of his income is this? $\frac{1}{6}$

ANOTHER LOOK

Divide. Write the quotient in simplest form.

1. $\frac{3}{4} \div \frac{3}{8}$ 2

2. $\frac{6}{9} \div \frac{1}{3}$ 2

3. $\frac{4}{5} \div \frac{6}{10}$ $1\frac{1}{3}$

4. $\frac{9}{15} \div \frac{2}{6}$ $1\frac{4}{5}$

5. $\frac{8}{3} \div \frac{3}{4}$ $3\frac{5}{9}$

6. $\frac{7}{6} \div \frac{3}{5}$ $1\frac{17}{18}$

7. $\frac{4}{9} \div \frac{11}{6}$ $\frac{8}{33}$

8. $\frac{18}{13} \div \frac{6}{5}$ $1\frac{2}{13}$

Classwork/Homework, page H86   More Practice, page H201   **213**

ASSIGNMENT GUIDE

Basic: 1–22, 31–34, AL

Average: 1–23 o, 25–34, AL

Extended: 6–24 e, 25–34, AL

Resources

Practice, p. 86   Class/Home, p. H86
Reteach, p. 63   More Practice, p. H201
Enrich, p. 82   Reasoning, p. H217

Exercise Analysis

1–12   Write a percent as a fraction or as a mixed number

13–20   Write a fraction as a whole-number percent or as a mixed-number percent

21–24   Write a mixed number as a percent

25–30   Mixed practice

31–34   Skill applications

You may wish to allow students to use a calculator for some of these exercises.

Another Look

This review provides maintenance for the division of fractions.

FOLLOW-UP ACTIVITIES

PROBLEM SOLVING

Have students solve this problem.

• Mrs. Young's homeroom class met prior to first period. After homeroom class, 35% of the group went to English class, $\frac{1}{10}$ went to band practice, $\frac{1}{5}$ went to history class, 15% went to science class, and the rest of them stayed for math class. Write the number that stayed for math class as a fraction and as a percent of the whole group. (20%, $\frac{1}{5}$)

To vary the problem, use your own math class and the classes your students will attend after math class.

NUMBER SENSE (Estimation)

Have students estimate whether the fraction is greater than or less than the percent. Then have them find the correct answer.

$\frac{2}{3}$ ■ 50% (>) $\frac{5}{7}$ ■ 50% (>)

$\frac{5}{6}$ ■ 75% (>) $\frac{2}{9}$ ■ 25% (<)

$\frac{1}{8}$ ■ 25% (<) $\frac{2}{11}$ ■ 25% (<)

COMING UP

Find it! Find the part of the whole!

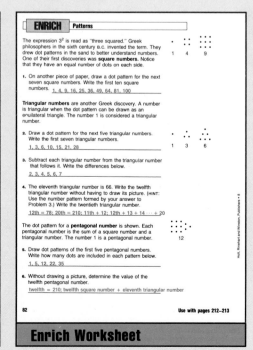

213

Objective: To solve a problem by making an organized list

Warm-Up

To prepare students for this lesson, have them compute the following sums mentally.

- 10 plus 9 plus 8 plus 7 plus 6 plus 5 plus 4 plus 3 plus 2 plus 1 (55)
- 14 plus 13 plus 12 plus 11 plus 10 plus 9 plus 8 plus 7 (84)

GETTING STARTED

Ask students to think of the different purposes for which lists are made. Three such purposes are

- as a checklist or reminder; for example, grocery lists, lists of chores, and so on.
- to arrange the various components of a task into an order or sequence; for example, a list of directions for assembly of a model, a list of directions for travel, and so on.
- to rank things in an order or to otherwise arrange information; for example, a list of election results, a list of the tallest buildings in the world, and so on.

Have students think of examples of each type of list. Then ask if students can think of any more uses for lists. Tell them that today's lesson is about one type of list used to organize information.

TEACHING THE LESSON

The major reason for making an organized list is to avoid omissions when finding a set of combinations; for example, to find all the possible committees of 3 people that can be formed from a group of 5 people (*A,B,C,D,E*), construct an organized list using a strategy similar to the following.

- Start with 2 people (A-B), and match them with each possible third person. (*A,B,C; A,B,D; A,B,E*)
- Then change the original pair to include one different person (*A-C*), and repeat the above process. (*A,C,D: A,C,E*)

Repeat until all possible values have been substituted. Remember not to repeat combinations. The list should look like this: *A,B,C,; A,B,D; A,B,E; A,C,D; A,C,E; A,D,E; B,C,D; B,C,E; B,D,E; C,D,E.*

Questions: Students often find it difficult to decide whether or not order is important. Make sure students understand that a meeting between Phil and Annette is the same as a meeting between Annette and Phil.

Tools: Make sure students set up a list of abbreviations to use. Remind students to look for the same combinations in different orders, for example, *A-B-C, A-C-B.*

214

| QUESTIONS | TOOLS | SOLUTIONS | CHECKS |

PROBLEM SOLVING
Making an Organized List/Acting it Out

Making an organized list can help you solve certain word problems. Here is an example.

Students
Phil
Annette
Rodrigo
Twyla
Griffin
Miko
Sal
Lee

> Bernard is teaching a course in job hunting to eight college students. He wants to set up interviews in which every student will meet with every other student. How many meetings will take place?

Use slips of paper with the names of the students to *act out* the different combinations of students.

Make an organized list of each pair. Use each student's first initial.

P–A, P–R, P–T, P–G, P–M, P–S, P–L
A–R, A–T, A–G, A–M, A–S, A–L
R–T, R–G, R–M, R–S, R–L
T–G, T–M, T–S, T–L
G–M, G–S, G–L
M–S, M–L
S–L   A total of 28 meetings will take place.

Remember that each pair of students needs to meet only once. For example, A–P is the same pair as P–A.

Solve.

1. Bill is registering for night classes at a local college. He can take two classes on Wednesday night, but there are four offered that interest him: English literature, BASIC, sociology, and journalism. Complete the list of the course combinations Bill could take. Use the first initial of each course.

    E–B, ▪–▪, ▪–▪   E–S, E–J
    B–S, ▪–▪,   B–J
    ▪–▪   S–J

2. The writing-workshop instructor puts students together in groups of three to criticize one another's work. The students in the workshop are Verna, Maurice, Ophelia, Seth, Carla, and Andrea. Complete the list of combinations of six students in groups of three.

    V–M–O, V–M–S, ▪–▪–▪, ▪–▪–▪,   V-M-C, V-M-A
    V–O–S, V–O–C, ▪–▪–▪,   V–O–A,
    ▪–▪–▪, V–S–A, V–C–A   V–S–C,
    M–O–S, ▪–▪–▪, ▪–▪–▪,   M–O–C, M–O–
    ▪–▪–▪, M–S–A, M–C–A   M–S–C,
    ▪–▪–▪, O–S–A, O–C–A   O–S–C
    ▪–▪–▪   S–C–A

214

Solutions: This lesson involves organization rather than computation. Mathematical computation is not used.

Checks: As a check, have students try to put together combinations of items that are listed in an order opposite to that which students have been using. Have them check to see that these combinations appear on their lists.

Solve. Check students' lists. The number of combinations is given.

3. Deborah is a textbook designer. For a two-color geometric figure, she must choose from four color overlays: black, red, blue, and yellow. List all the possible color combinations for the geometric figure. 6 combinations

4. Liza's chamber-music class is giving a benefit concert of works by Haydn, Mozart, Dvořák, and Brahms. Liza will play two pieces with the class. Make a list of all the combinations of works she could play. 6 combinations

5. Lori is a floral designer. She wants to use five colors in a particular arrangement of flowers. She has white carnations, yellow daisies, blue iris, orange lilies, red chrysanthemums, lavender chrysanthemums, pink tulips, and green ferns. Make a list of all the color combinations Lori could use in her arrangement. 56 combinations

6. Frederico is an apprentice tiler. He is installing a floor based on a design that uses tiles of four colors. Frederico can use eight colors: earth, copper, gray, turquoise, white, olive, lemon, and black. Make a list that shows each combination of colors Frederico could use. 70 combinations

7. Kevrok has a reading list of twelve novels for his American literature course—one each by Twain, James, Irving, Dreiser, Crane, Fitzgerald, Hemingway, Faulkner, Warren, Mailer, Roth, and Barth. His professor told him to read any ten from the list. How many combinations of novels could Kevrok read? 66 combinations

8. Drew is a carpentry teacher. His students work with pine, oak, cherry, walnut and maple wood finishes. Drew can only supervise two types of wood finishes each class. Make a list of all the wood finish combinations that Drew could supervise. 10 combinations

Classwork/Homework, pages H87–H88

Exercise Analysis
1–8   Make an organized list

FOLLOW-UP ACTIVITIES

🔑 PROBLEM SOLVING
Give this imaginary scenario to students.

Your school is having a career day. 6 different people will come and give workshops in different career areas. Each student can attend 4 workshops. The areas are medicine, engineering, computers, the arts, teaching, and government. Have students make a list of the different combinations of workshops that they could attend. *(M,E,C,A; M,E,C,T; M,E,C,G; M,E,A,T; M,E,A,G; M,E,G,T; M,C,A,T; M,C,A,G; M,C,G,T; M,A,T,G; E,C,A,T; E,C,A,G; E,C,T,G; E,A,T,G; C,A,T,G)*

💻 COMPUTER
Have students write a program that asks three math questions and has a different response for each right and wrong answer. (six responses altogether) After each of these responses, include a time-delay loop that keeps the next question from being printed for several seconds. Here is one possible program with the first set of responses.

```
10 INPUT "10*20 "; A1
20 IF A1 = 10*20 THEN PRINT "THAT'S
   RIGHT!" GOTO 50
30 PRINT "THE CORRECT ANSWER
   IS", 10*20
40 FOR X = 1 TO 1500:NEXT X
```

Line 50 should be the next input statement.

COMING UP
Ending the search

Objective: To find the percent of a number

Warm-Up
Have students find the following products mentally.

0.30 · 40 (12); 0.75 · 28 (21);
0.125 · 50 (6.25); 0.25 · 84 (21);
1.4 · 50 (70); 3.375 · 200 (675)

GETTING STARTED

Place 10 counters on the table. Ask: How many counters are 40% of those on the table? (4) Have some volunteers explain how they found their answers. (Two possible methods are to write the percent as a fraction that has a denominator equal to the number of counters or to use a proportion.)

Tell students that in this lesson, they will learn a one-step method for solving such problems.

TEACHING THE LESSON

A. After teaching the model example, pose this problem.

Janine's boss, Sally, earns 315% of what Janine earns. If Janine earns $6/h, what is Sally's hourly wage?

$x = 3.15 · 6 = 18.90$

Sally earns $18.90 per hour.

B. Use the following example to demonstrate that if a mixed-number percent that has a denominator of 3 or 9 is written as a decimal, computation is impossible because the decimal repeats.

$33\frac{1}{3}\%$ of $48 = 0.\overline{33} \times 48$

The only solution is to rewrite the percent as a fraction.

Note that the Other Examples section includes percents less than 1% and greater than 100%.

You many wish to allow students to use calculators while working through this lesson.

Finding the Percent of a Number

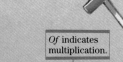

A. Janine is an apprentice electrician. Her four-year apprenticeship combines classroom instruction with practical experience. In her first year, she is paid 40% of the hourly wage for union electricians. If that wage is $15 per hour, what is her hourly wage in the first year?

Of indicates multiplication.

Let x = the number.

Write an equation and solve.

Janine earns $6 per hour in the first year.

You can also use a fraction to solve the problem.

$40\% = \frac{40}{100} = \frac{2}{5}$

Think: What number is 40% of 15?

$$x = 0.40 · 15$$
$$x = 6$$

Write an equation and solve. The answer is the same.

$$x = \frac{2}{5} · 15$$
$$x = 6$$

B. To find a percent of a number, sometimes it is easier to use a fraction. At other times, it is easier to use a decimal.

Find $66\frac{2}{3}\%$ of 510.

Use a fraction. $66\frac{2}{3}\% = \frac{2}{3}$

Write an equation and solve.

What is 7.5% of 68?
Use a decimal. $7.5\% = 0.075$
Write an equation and solve.

Think: What number is $66\frac{2}{3}\%$ of 510?

$$x = \frac{2}{3} · 510$$
$$x = 340$$

$$x = 0.075 · 68$$
$$x = 5.1$$

Other examples:

Find 0.2% of 800.
$x = 0.002 · 800$
$x = 1.6$

Find 175% of 60.
$x = 1.75 · 60$
$x = 105$

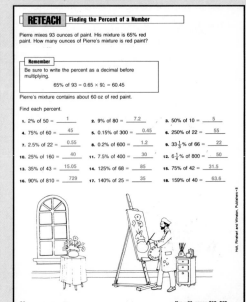

216

Math Reasoning, page H218

COMMON ERRORS
Some students might have difficulty writing the correct equation.

Remediation
You can correct this error by having these students practice setting up equations. Stress the process of moving from words to equations.

What number is 35% of 200?

$$n = 0.35 • 200$$

$$n = 70$$

Assign Reteach Master, p. 64.

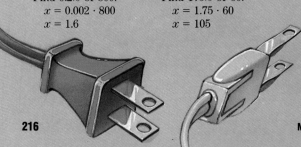

Find the percent of the number.

1. 10% of 20
   2
2. 70% of 200
   140
3. 50% of 80
   40
4. 75% of $40
   $30
5. 8% of 48
   3.84
6. 30% of 50
   15
7. 15% of $30
   $4.50
8. 2% of 250
   5
9. $66\frac{2}{3}$% of 33
   22
10. $12\frac{1}{2}$% of 72
    9
11. $16\frac{2}{3}$% of $96
    $16.00
12. $6\frac{1}{4}$% of 64
    4
13. 1.5% of 400
    6
14. 0.5% of 444
    2.22
15. 7.5% of $160
    $12.00
16. 2.75% of 200
    5.5
17. 260% of 20
    52
18. $37\frac{1}{2}$% of 80
    30
19. 0.9% of $300
    $2.70
20. $14\frac{2}{7}$% of 84
    12

Solve.

21. Find 63% of 500. 315

22. 110% of 96 is what number? 105.6

23. What is $84\frac{2}{3}$% of $150? $127

24. Find 7.5% of $2,100. $157.50

25. 0.5% of 65 is what number? 0.325

26. Find 0.08% of 500. 0.4

27. What number is 85.5% of 70? 59.85

28. What number is 99.5% of 200? 199

29. During one 40-hour week, Janine spent 25% of her time in class. How many hours did she spend in class? 10 hours

30. On Jason's current electrical job, there are 3 experienced electricians for every apprentice. What is the ratio of experienced electricians to apprentices?
    3:1 experienced to apprentice

31. A second-year apprentice earns 55% of the union wage, and a third-year apprentice earns 75% of it. If the union wage is $15 per hour, what is the difference in hourly earnings between a second- and a third-year apprentice? $3.00 difference

32. There are 560,000 licensed electricians in the United States. Of these, 52% are construction electricians. How many construction electricians are there?
    291,200 construction electricians

MIDCHAPTER REVIEW

Write as a percent.

1. $\frac{4}{5}$
   80%
2. $\frac{7}{7}$
   100%
3. $3\frac{7}{10}$
   370%
4. 0.54
   54%
5. 3.08
   308%

Write as a decimal and as a fraction or mixed number.

6. 20%
   0.2; $\frac{1}{5}$
7. 42%
   0.42; $\frac{21}{50}$
8. 360%
   3.6; $3\frac{3}{5}$
9. 37.5%
   0.375; $\frac{3}{8}$
10. $62\frac{1}{2}$%
    0.625; $\frac{5}{8}$ **217**

Classwork/Homework, page H89

ASSIGNMENT GUIDE

Basic: 1–20, 29–32, MCR

Average: 1–19 o, 21–32, MCR

Extended: 9–32, MCR

Resources

Practice, p. 89   Class/Home, p. H89
Reteach, p. 64   Reasoning, p. H218
Enrich, p. 83

Exercise Analysis

1–8	Find a whole-number percent
9–12	Find a mixed-number percent
13–16	Find a decimal percent
17–28	Mixed practice
29–32	Skill applications

You may wish to allow students to use a calculator for some of these exercises.

Midchapter Review

This review provides an opportunity for you and students to assess their understanding of concepts and skills developed to this point in the chapter.

FOLLOW-UP ACTIVITIES

MATH CONNECTION (Consumer)

Listed below are the regular prices and the sale discounts being offered by each of three record stores. Have students calculate the sale price at each store in order to determine which is offering the best buy.

Store	Regular Price	Sale Discount
Spin	$10.90	40% off ($6.54)
Discworld	$7.50	16% off ($6.30)
Trax	$8.00	$\frac{1}{5}$ off ($6.40)

(Discworld offers the best buy.)

NUMBER SENSE (Mental Math)

Have students find 10% of each of the following.

3 (0.3)   95 (9.5)   129 (12.9)
390 (39)   875 (87.5) $174 ($17.40)

Then have them find 1% of the same numbers.

3 (0.03)   95 (0.95)   129 (1.29)
390 (3.9)   875 (8.75) $174 ($1.74)

COMING UP

The percents in the great divide!

Objective: To find what percent one number is of another

Warm-Up

Have students solve the following equations.

$4n = 3$ (0.75) $5n = 2$ (0.4)
$9n = 3$ (0.333) $8n = 5$ (0.625)
$22.5n = 9$ (0.4) $4.04n = 22.422$ (5.55)

GETTING STARTED

Use this example or substitute exact details from your class.

An eighth-grade math class has 30 students enrolled. On Monday, 6 students were absent. What percent of the students were absent?

Have students express this as a ratio (6:30), as a fraction ($\frac{6}{30}$), as a decimal (0.20), and as a percent. (20%)

Repeat with such similar examples as the percent of the school orchestra that are string players. Point out that in today's lesson, students will learn a simpler method of finding the percent.

TEACHING THE LESSON

A. Students who encounter difficulty with the correct equation may be helped by emphasizing the alignment shown on the lesson page. Guide students through similar examples.

B. Explain that to find the percent of a number, multiply; to find the percent one number is of another, divide. Also use examples similar to $750 = n \cdot 3$ to show that when the part is greater than the whole, the percent is greater than 100%. You may wish to allow students to use calculators while working through this lesson.

Checkpoint

The chart lists the common errors students make in finding what percent one number is of another.

Correct Answers: 1b, 2c, 3c, 4a

Remediation

■ For these errors, have students complete the equation *unknown* % × *whole* = *part*, using such questions as: What percent of 9 is 35? What percent of 32 is 7? What percent of 15 is 86?

☐ For this error, assign Reteach Master, p. 65.

Finding What Percent

A. Gifford Hospital has a 35-hour training course for volunteer workers. Students in the course spend 21 hours on patient care. What percent of the course is spent on patient care?

Let n = the percent.   Think: What percent of 35 is 21?

Write an equation. $n \cdot 35 = 21$

$$35n = 21$$

Solve. $$\frac{35n}{35} = \frac{21}{35}$$

$$n = \frac{3}{5} = 0.60, \text{ or } 60\%$$

So, 60% of the course is spent on patient care.

B. What percent of 6 is 15?

$$n \cdot 6 = 15$$
$$6n = 15$$
$$\frac{6n}{6} = \frac{15}{6}$$
$$n = 2.5, \text{ or } 250\%$$

3 is what percent of 750?

$$3 = n \cdot 750$$
$$3 = 750n$$
$$\frac{3}{750} = \frac{750n}{750}$$
$$0.004 = n \qquad 0.004 \longrightarrow 0.4\%$$
$$0.4\% = n$$

Another example:

What percent of \$19.50 is \$6.50?

$$n \cdot 19.5 = 6.5$$
$$19.5n = 6.5$$
$$\frac{19.5n}{19.5} = \frac{6.5}{19.5}$$
$$n = \frac{1}{3}, \text{ or } 33\frac{1}{3}\%$$

Checkpoint Write the letter of the correct answer.

1. What percent of 20 is 5?

a. 100%   **b.** 25%   **c.** 40%   **d.** 400%

2. What percent of 72 is 90?

a. 1.25%   **b.** 80%   **c.** 125%   **d.** 2.8%

3. What percent of 16 is 6?

a. 96%   **b.** $266\frac{2}{3}\%$ **c.** $37\frac{1}{2}\%$ **d.** 10%

4. What percent of 50 is 0.5?

a. 1%   **b.** 25%   **c.** 100%   **d.** 49.5%

218

COMMON ERRORS

Answer Choice	Type of Error
■ 1a, 1c, 1d, 2b, 2d, 3a, 3b, 3d, 4b, 4c, 4d	Writes equation incorrectly
☐ 2a	Adds percent sign to quotient

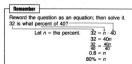

RETEACH Finding the Percent

A box of Fruit Bran lists the ingredients for an average 40-g serving. The serving contains 32 g of carbohydrates. What percent of the Fruit Bran is carbohydrates?

Remember
Reword the question as an equation; then solve it.
32 is what percent of 40?

Let n = the percent. $32 = n \cdot 40$
$$32 = 40n$$
$$\frac{32}{40} = \frac{40n}{40}$$
$$0.8 = n$$
$$80\% = n$$

The serving contains 80% carbohydrates.

A 50-g serving of a cereal contains various ingredients in the amounts shown in the table. Compose a problem statement that asks what percent of the serving each ingredient represents. Use each problem statement to write and solve an equation to find the percent.

Ingredient	Amount	Problem statement	Equation	Percent
1. Protein	4 g	4 is what percent of 50	$4 = n \cdot 50$	8%
2. Fat	1.25 g	1.25 is what percent of 50	$1.25 = n \cdot 50$	2.5%
3. Sodium	0.25 g	0.25 is what percent of 50	$0.25 = n \cdot 50$	0.5%
4. Potassium	0.275 g	0.275 is what percent of 50	$0.275 = n \cdot 50$	0.55%
5. Starch	18 g	18 is what percent of 50	$18 = n \cdot 50$	36%
6. Sugar	14 g	14 is what percent of 50	$14 = n \cdot 50$	28%
7. Dietary fiber	4.8 g	4.8 is what percent of 50	$4.8 = n \cdot 50$	9.6%
8. Vitamin B₆	0.0006 g	0.0006 is what percent of 50	$0.0006 = n \cdot 50$	0.0012%
9. Niacin	0.005 g	0.005 is what percent of 50	$0.005 = n \cdot 50$	0.01%
10. Calcium	0.22 g	0.22 is what percent of 50	$0.22 = n \cdot 50$	0.44%

Use with pages 218–219.   65

Reteach Worksheet

Find the percent.

1. What percent of 50 is 10? 20%

2. 1.6 is what percent of 6.4? 25%

3. 4.5 is what percent of 90? 5%

4. What percent of 485 is 97? 20%

5. What percent of 110 is 60.5? 55%

6. 1,250 is what percent of 5,000? 25%

7. 9 is what percent of 6? 150%

8. 34 is what percent of 17? 200%

9. 81.25 is what percent of 65? 125%

10. What percent of 10 is 12? 120%

11. 1.5 is what percent of 300? 0.5%

12. What percent of 400 is 2? 0.5%

13. 0.15 is what percent of 300? 0.05%

14. What percent of 200 is 0.125? 0.0625%

15. 30 is what percent of 36? $83\frac{1}{3}$%

16. What percent of 24 is 4? $16\frac{2}{3}$%

17. 98 is what percent of 1,000? 9.8%

18. 12.5 is what percent of 40? 31.25%

19. 6 is what percent of 600? 1%

20. What percent of 180 is 4.5? 2.5%

★**21.** Suppose x and y are whole numbers, and x is 15% of y. List three pairs of possible values for x and y. 3 and 20; 6 and 40; 9 and 60; Answers will vary.

Solve.

22. A volunteer course was started that had 25 people. Of those enrolled, 4 volunteers transferred to another course. What percent completed the original course? 84%

23. The hospital has 180 volunteers. Teenagers comprise $\frac{1}{3}$ of the volunteers. What percent of the volunteers are teenagers? $33\frac{1}{3}$% teenagers

24. In one group, all 18 volunteers plan careers in medicine. Of this number, 3 plan to become surgeons. What percent of the volunteer group plans to become surgeons? $16\frac{2}{3}$%

25. Hospital officials would like volunteers to contribute a total of 900 hours per week. Last week, volunteers contributed a total of 840 hours. What percent of the desired total is this? $93\frac{1}{3}$%

NUMBER SENSE

Compute mentally by changing percents to fractions.

1. 60% of 15
9

2. 75% of 240
180

3. $33\frac{1}{3}$% of 420
140

4. 40% of 35
14

5. 45% of 80
36

6. $12\frac{1}{2}$% of 80
10

7. 140% of 250
350

8. $87\frac{1}{2}$% of 160
140

Classwork/Homework, page H90

219

ASSIGNMENT GUIDE

Basic: 1–16, 22–25, NS 1–4

Average: 1–19 o, 22–25, NS 1–4

Extended: 9–25, NS

Resources
Practice, p. 90   Class/Home, p. H90
Reteach, p. 65
Enrich, p. 84

Exercise Analysis
1–10   Find the whole-number percent
11–14   Find the decimal percent
15–16   Find the mixed-number percent
17–21   Mixed practice
22–25   Skill applications

You may wish to allow students to use calculators to complete some of the exercises.

Number Sense
Point out that these problems can be further simplified by writing the percents as fractions in simplest form.

FOLLOW-UP ACTIVITIES

PUZZLES AND GAMES
Using the following fractions, decimals, and percents, solve the magic square so that the sum in every direction, horizontal, vertical, and diagonal, is 150%. Use $\frac{1}{20}$, 0.6, $\frac{1}{4}$, $\frac{1}{2}$, 0.4, 0.75, 15%, $\frac{19}{20}$, and 85%.

(85%)	($\frac{1}{20}$)	(0.6)
($\frac{1}{4}$)	($\frac{1}{2}$)	(0.75)
(0.4)	($\frac{19}{20}$)	(15%)

- Change all values to percents.
- Put $\frac{1}{2}$ in the center.

MATH CONNECTION
(Health)
Materials: health textbooks

Have students find the percent of their diets that each of the basic food families should represent. Then have them calculate the percent of their diet that should consist of carbohydrates, of whole grains, of vegetables, and so on.

COMING UP
Tomorrow, percents will be "totaled."

Objective: To find a number when a percent of it is known

Warm-Up
Have students solve the equations.

$0.15x = 30$ ($x = 200$)
$0.75x = 60$ ($x = 80$)
$0.3x = 20$ $\left(x = 66\frac{2}{3}\right)$
$0.55x = 49.5$ ($x = 90$)

GETTING STARTED

Materials: 6 large cards with legends *Whole*, *Part*, *Percent*, *Times*, *Equals*, and *Unknown*; tacks

Tack the cards on a bulletin board as shown.

Percent Times Whole Equals Part

Have students tack the *Unknown* card over the other appropriate card in order to represent these problems.
• Find the percent of a number. (Percent Times Whole Equals Unknown)
• Find the percent one number is of another. (Unknown Times Whole Equals Part)
• Find a number when a percent of it is known. (Percent Times Unknown Equals Part)

TEACHING THE LESSON

A. Point out that if the percent is less than 100%, the whole will always be greater than the known part. If the percent is greater than 100%, the whole will be smaller than the part.

B. Review the most-common repeating decimals and their fractional equivalents.

$0.\overline{33} = \frac{1}{3}$ $0.1\overline{6} = \frac{1}{6}$
$0.\overline{66} = \frac{2}{3}$ $0.8\overline{3} = \frac{5}{6}$

You may wish to allow students to use calculators while working through this lesson.

Checkpoint
The chart lists the common errors students make in solving for the total number.

Correct Answers: 1c, 2d

Remediation
■ For this error, work individually with students, reviewing the placement of the decimal point in division.

☐ For these errors, assign Reteach Master, p. 66.

220

Finding the Total Number

A. Andrew earns $480 per week as a computer programmer trainee. This amount is 75% of the salary for an experienced programmer. What is the salary of an experienced programmer?

Let x = the number.

Think: 75% of what number is 480?

Write an equation. $0.75 \cdot x = 480$

Solve.
$$0.75x = 480$$
$$\frac{0.75x}{0.75} = \frac{480}{0.75}$$
$$x = 640$$

An experienced programmer earns $640 per week.

B. In some problems, it is easier to use a fraction for the percent.

54 is $66\frac{2}{3}$% of what number?

$54 = \frac{2}{3} \cdot x$ $\boxed{66\frac{2}{3}\% = \frac{2}{3}}$

$54 = \frac{2}{3}x$

$\frac{3}{2} \cdot 54 = \frac{3}{2} \cdot \frac{2}{3}x$

$81 = x$

So, 54 is $66\frac{2}{3}$% of 81.

Other examples:

0.3% of what number is 12?

$0.003 \cdot x = 12$
$0.003x = 12$
$\frac{0.003x}{0.003} = \frac{12}{0.003}$
$x = 4{,}000$

91 is 130% of what number?

$91 = 1.3 \cdot x$
$91 = 1.3x$
$\frac{91}{1.3} = \frac{1.3x}{1.3}$
$70 = x$

Checkpoint Write the letter of the correct answer.

1. 10 is 50% of what number?

a. 0.2   **b.** 5   **c.** 20   **d.** 25

2. $12\frac{1}{2}$% of what number is 8?

a. 1   **b.** 16   **c.** 0.64   **d.** 64

220   Math Reasoning, page H218

COMMON ERRORS

Answer Choice	Type of Error
☐ 1b, 2a	Multiplies instead of dividing
☐ 1d, 2b	Makes error in computation
■ 1a	Incorrect placement of decimal point

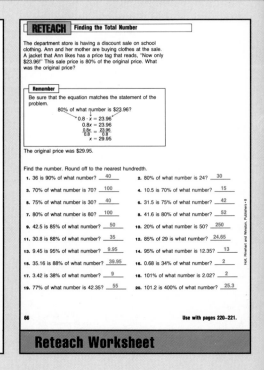

Find the number.

1. 10% of what number is 30? **300**

2. 40 is 80% of what number? **50**

3. 16 is 25% of what number? **64**

4. 81 is 90% of what number? **90**

5. 65% of what number is 260? **400**

6. 92% of what number is 50.6? **55**

7. $12\frac{1}{2}$% of what number is 4? **32**

8. $87\frac{1}{2}$% of what number is 70? **80**

9. $6\frac{1}{4}$% of what number is 2? **32**

10. $23\frac{1}{3}$ is $16\frac{2}{3}$% of what number? **140**

11. 0.5% of what number is 2.5? **500**

12. 0.04% of what number is 1? **2,500**

13. 147 is 350% of what number? **42**

14. 42 is 100% of what number? **42**

15. 12.75 is 15% of what number? **85**

16. 68.75 is 55% of what number? **125**

17. 0.325 is 20% of what number? **1.625**

18. 75% of what number is 14.25? **19**

★19. If x is 125% of y, then y is what percent of x? **80%**

★20. If x is 45% of y, then y is what percent of x? **$222\frac{2}{9}$%**

Solve.

21. A company employs 180 computer programmers. This is 45% of the employees in the company. How many employees are there in the company? **400 employees**

22. Susan earns 60% of the salary of a systems analyst. If a systems analyst earns $900 per week, how much does Susan earn? **$540 per week**

23. Computer Graphics Inc. spent $1,400 advertising for new programmers. If this amount was 125% of the budgeted amount, how much had been budgeted? **$1,120 budgeted**

NUMBER SENSE

Choose the correct answer.

1. 10% of 130   a. 1.3   **b. 13**   c. 130   d. 1,300
2. 1% of 200   a. 0.2   **b. 2**   c. 20   d. 200
3. 100% of 40   a. 0.4   b. 4   **c. 40**   d. 4,000
4. 10% of 70   a. 0.7   **b. 7**   c. 70   d. 700
5. 100% of 350   a. 3.5   b. 35   **c. 350**   d. 35,000
6. 1% of 500   a. 0.5   **b. 5**   c. 50   d. 500

Classwork/Homework, page H91

221

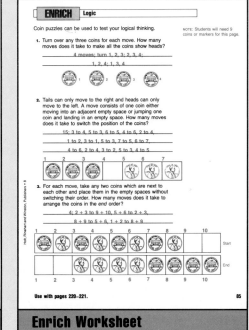

ASSIGNMENT GUIDE

Basic: 1–18, 21–23, NS

Average: 1–23, NS

Extended: 1–23, NS

Resources
Practice, p. 91   Class/Home, p. H91
Reteach, p. 66   Reasoning, p. H218
Enrich, p. 85

Exercise Analysis

1–6   Find the total number using a whole-number percent

7–10   Find the total number using a mixed-number percent

11–12   Find the total number using a decimal percent

13–14   Find the total number using a percent greater than or equal to 100%

15–20   Mixed practice

21–23   Skill applications

You may wish to allow students to use calculators to complete some of the exercises.

Number Sense
This activity provides practice in finding the percent of a number.

FOLLOW-UP ACTIVITIES

PROBLEM SOLVING
Have students solve each of these problems.
- Bob is 75% as old as Ted, who is 50% as old as Jim. If Bob is 9, how old is Jim? (24)
- Sandi has 80% as much money as June, who has 80% as much as Jill. If Sandi has $12.80, how much does Jill have? ($20.00)

MATH COMMUNICATION
Have students write a question to describe each equation.
- $n \cdot 25 = 8$
  (What percent of 25 is 8?)
- $0.32 \cdot n = 8$
  (8 is 32% of what number?)
- $\frac{1}{6} n = 3$
  (3 is $16\frac{2}{3}$% of what number?)

COMING UP
The "pro's" have it!

221

Objective: To use a formula to compute simple interest

Warm-Up
To prepare students for this lesson, have them compute the following percents.

25% of 120 (30)
14% of 210 (29.4)
32 is ■% of 200 (16)
156 is 30% of ■ (520)

GETTING STARTED

Discuss the differences between current interest rates on loans and interest rates on savings. Bring a newspaper to class and compare some of the interest rates listed in bank advertisements.

TEACHING THE LESSON

Be sure students are using the correct formula. Students should try to learn the $I = prt$ formula by heart. Explain to students that the symbols in the formula are variables and can be replaced by numbers. When the correct values are substituted for the variables, the resulting equation can be solved to give the answer to the problem.

Questions: Be sure that students understand down payment. Explain that this is the part of the total cost that is *not* borrowed. The principal is found by subtracting the down payment from the cost.

Tools: Be sure students identify the information in the problem that should be used as p, as r, and as t. Check to see that students understand what *principal*, *rate*, and *time* mean. One problem students frequently encounter is using the correct units of measurement (*interest in dollars, principal in dollars, rate as a percent, time in years*). Explain to students that an interest rate is usually a yearly rate.

Explain that in loans covered by $I = prt$, interest is calculated on the basis of the original principal, even though some of that principal may already have been paid.

Solutions: Computational problems may arise in problems with percents. Review with students the three cases of percent and relate them to the $I = prt$ formula (solving for I or t, solving for r, and solving for p). The most common difficulty students will have is using the formula to solve for a variable other than I.

In Problems 4 and 8, students must subtract the down payment to find the principal.

Checks: To check their answers, have students substitute them into the original formula and solve for another figure that is given in the problem. Also, have students check to see that their answers are expressed in correct units.

| QUESTIONS | TOOLS | SOLUTIONS | CHECKS |

PROBLEM SOLVING
Using a Formula ($I = prt$)

Interest is a fee someone pays for borrowing money from a bank or a lending agency. Interest is also the set fee that a bank pays to customers for the use of their money. The amount of money borrowed or saved is called the *principal*, and the interest rate is a percent of the principal. Time is expressed in years.

> Maureen is planning a career as a forest ranger. The books for the second semester of her sophomore year in college will cost $350. She can pay only $50 of her book bill and will have to borrow the rest. If the bank agrees to lend her the money for 6 months at an interest rate of 8%, how much interest will she pay?

To solve a problem by using a formula, follow these general rules.

1. Use the correct formula.
2. Substitute values in the formula.
3. Solve the equation.
4. Write the answer.

To calculate the interest, use the formula $I = prt$, where

I = interest

p = principal ($350 − $50 = $300)

r = rate (8%)

t = time $\left(6 \text{ months or } \frac{1}{2} \text{ year} = 0.5\right)$.

Therefore, $I = \$300 \times 0.08 \times 0.5 = \$12$.

Maureen will pay $12 in interest.

You can use other forms of the interest formula to find the principal, the rate, or the time.

To calculate the principal, use $p = I \div rt$.
To calculate the rate, use $r = I \div pt$.
To calculate the time in years, use $t = I \div pr$.

Write the letter of the correct form of the interest formula.

1. Mark paid $1,500 in interest on money he borrowed for 3 years in order to attend a computer-training program. If the interest rate was 10%, how much did he borrow?

a. $t = I \div pr$
b. $r = I \div pt$
c. $I = prt$
d. $p = I \div rt$ (circled)

2. Christine wants to borrow $2,000 in order to take a foreign-language course. If she borrows the money for 2 years at an interest rate of 12%, how much will she pay in interest?

a. $t = I \div pr$
b. $r = I \div pt$
c. $I = prt$ (circled)
d. $p = I \div rt$

Solve. Use the correct form of the interest formula.

3. Joan borrowed $3,000 from her father to use as a down payment on a new car. She agreed to pay him back at a yearly rate of $12\frac{1}{2}\%$ over a period of 3 years. How much interest will she pay him?
$1,125

4. Ralph's college tuition for one year is $5,500. He pays 20% down and takes out a loan for the balance at a rate of 6% a year for 6 years. What is the total amount he will repay? **$5,984**

5. On a loan of $804, Arthur paid interest that amounted to $192.96 over 2 years. He made monthly payments of $41.54. What was the rate of interest at which he borrowed the money? **12%**

6. Mr. and Mrs. Whitkin drove 478 miles from Houston, Texas, to Tulsa, Oklahoma, to take their son back to college. If their average driving speed was 52 miles per hour, how long—to the nearest hour—did it take them to reach Tulsa? **9 hours**

7. At the end of 45 months, Cindy paid $1,881 in interest on money she borrowed to go to a business school. If she paid interest at an annual rate of $15\frac{1}{5}\%$ on the loan, how much did she borrow? **$3,300**

★8. The Carsons bought their son a personal computer that cost $1,850. They paid 10% down and agreed to pay the balance plus interest in equal monthly payments for 24 months. If the annual interest rate is 16%, how much are their monthly payments, rounded to the nearest dollar? **$92**

Classwork/Homework, page H92

ASSIGNMENT GUIDE

Basic:	1–4
Average:	2–6
Extended:	4–8

Resources
Practice, p. 92   Class/Home, p. H92
Enrich, p. 86

Exercise Analysis

1–2 Choose the correct form of the formula
3 Find the interest
4 Find the total payment
5 Find the interest rate
6 Find the amount of time
7 Find the principal
8 Find the loan payments

FOLLOW-UP ACTIVITIES

 PROBLEM SOLVING
Materials: 1 newspaper per group

Have each group check through the newspaper for interest rates on both savings accounts and on loans. Using one specific interest rate that they have found for savings accounts and one for a loan, have them compute how much money a bank makes in 1 year when it takes $5,000 that a customer has invested in a savings account and loans it out to someone else.

 CALCULATOR
Materials: 1 calculator per student

Write this word problem on the chalkboard. Henry has deposited $500 into a savings account that pays 7.5% interest per year. It pays the interest every 3 months. The interest paid is added to the original total, all of which earns interest in the next 3 months. Have students find the total amount Henry will have in 1 year. ($538.57)

COMING UP
Percents for utilitarians

Objective: To use a proportion to solve a percent problem

Warm-Up
Have students find the missing term in each of the proportions below.

$\frac{45}{100} = \frac{x}{84}$ ($x = 37.8$)

$\frac{x}{100} = \frac{39}{273}$ ($x = 14\frac{2}{7}$)

GETTING STARTED

Write the following on the chalkboard.

Bill installs cable for television. He charges $32 for a one-set hook up, but he charges only 80% of that price for each set if more than one set is hooked up. How much does Bill charge per set to hook up two? ($25.60)

Tell students to solve the problem without using the equation

$x = 0.80 \cdot 32$.

Then have some volunteers explain how they found the answer.

TEACHING THE LESSON

A. Remind students that the percent is the part of 100, which is the whole.

B. Several hints may be useful in determining which numbers correspond to the terms of the proportion.
- *Of a given number* means that number is the "part."
- *A given number is* or *is a given number* means that number is the "whole."

C. Guide students through the following examples to emphasize the importance of working carefully when computing with fractions and decimals.

2.5% of 300 is what number?

$\frac{2.5}{100} = \frac{n}{300}$

$100n = 750$

$n = 7.5$

What number is $33\frac{1}{3}$% of 150?

$\frac{33\frac{1}{3}}{100} = \frac{n}{150}$

$100n = 33\frac{1}{3} \times 150$

$100n = \frac{100}{3} \times 150$

$100n = 5{,}000$

$n = 50$

You many wish to allow students to use calculators while working through this lesson.

Percent Using Proportions

A. Of the 120 students in one barber school, 85% are less than 25 years old. How many students are less than 25 years old?

You can use a proportion to find a percent of a number. In this problem, you want to find 85% of 120.

REMEMBER: 85% means $\frac{85}{100}$. Set up another ratio that equals $\frac{85}{100}$. Let $x =$ the number of students less than age 25.

Write a proportion.

part $\longrightarrow$ $\frac{85}{100} = \frac{x}{120}$ $\longleftarrow$ part
whole $\longrightarrow$ $\phantom{\frac{85}{100} = {}}$ $\longleftarrow$ whole

Cross multiply and solve.

$85 \cdot 120 = 100 \cdot x$
$10{,}200 = 100x$
$102 = x$

So, 102 students are less than 25 years old.

B. You can use a proportion to find what percent one number is of another.

What percent of 24 is 3?

Write a proportion.

part $\longrightarrow$ $\frac{x}{100} = \frac{3}{24}$
whole $\longrightarrow$

Cross multiply and solve.

$x \cdot 24 = 100 \cdot 3$
$24x = 300$
$x = 12\frac{1}{2}$

So, 3 is $12\frac{1}{2}$% of 24.

C. You can use a proportion to find a number when you know a percent of the number.

20% of what number is 1.7?

Write a proportion.

part $\longrightarrow$ $\frac{20}{100} = \frac{1.7}{x}$
whole $\longrightarrow$

Cross multiply and solve.

$20 \cdot x = 100 \cdot 1.7$
$20x = 170$
$x = 8.5$

So, 20% of 8.5 is 1.7.

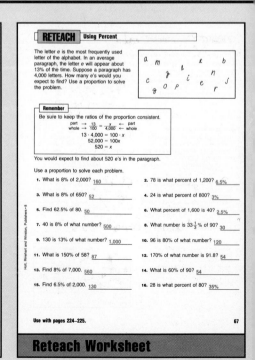

224

COMMON ERRORS

Students might change the percent to a decimal and then include the decimal in the proportion; for example, 20% of 15 is what number?

$20\% = 0.20$

$\frac{0.20}{100} = \frac{x}{15}$

$x = 0.03$

Remediation
To correct this error, review the meaning of *percent* and have students write percents as fractions that have denominators of 100.

Assign Reteach Master, p. 67.

Use a proportion to solve each problem.

1. What is 40% of 160? *64*
2. Find 25% of 48. *12*
3. What number is 15% of 400? *60*
4. What is 150% of 30? *45*
5. What percent of 50 is 35? *70%*
6. 16 is what percent of 48? *33⅓%*
7. 2.2 is what percent of 8.8? *25%*
8. What percent of 600 is 3? *.5%*
9. 60% of what number is 63? *105*
10. 1.9 is 10% of what number? *19*
11. 18 is 200% of what number? *9*
12. 175 is 25% of what number? *43.75*
13. What number is 7% of 300? *21*
14. 22 is 55% of what number? *40*
15. What percent of 140 is 7? *5%*
16. Find 75% of 150. *112.5*
17. 65 is what percent of 120? *54%*
18. What is $33\frac{1}{3}$% of 99? *33*
19. 1.1 is what percent of 55? *2%*
20. What is 87.5% of 56? *49*

Solve.

21. An apprentice barber earns about $260 a week. This is about 65% of what an experienced barber earns. How much does an experienced barber earn? *$400*

22. Of the 112,000 barbers in this country, 5% are women. Use a proportion to find the number of women barbers. *5,600*

23. The training program at one barber school lasts 10 months. Tuition costs $1,900. In addition, the student must buy a personal set of tools for $600. Tools make up what percent of the combined cost of tuition and tools?

CHALLENGE

Rita owns a boutique. When an item arrives, Rita marks it up 60% from the buying price. If it does not sell after 9 weeks, she takes 25% off its price. Four weeks later, if it is still in the shop, she takes 30% off that price. If it sells at this price, does she earn or lose money on it? What percent of the original buying price is her earnings or her loss?

Classwork/Homework, page H93
More Practice, page H201

225

ASSIGNMENT GUIDE

Basic: 1–19 *o*, 21–23

Average: 1–13 *o*, 15–23

Extended: 2–14 *e*, 15–23, Chlg

Resources
Practice, p. 93   Class/Home, p. H93
Reteach, p. 67   More Practice, p. H201
Enrich, p. 87

Exercise Analysis

1–4   Use a proportion to find the percent of a number

5–8   Use a proportion to find the percent one number is of another

9–12   Use a proportion to find the total number

13–20 Mixed practice

21–23 Skill applications

You may wish to allow students to use calculators to complete some of the exercises.

Challenge

Students must recognize that *marking up 60%* means "multiplying by 60% or by .60."

FOLLOW-UP ACTIVITIES

REINFORCEMENT
Materials: facsimile coins

Give each student two facsimile coins. Ask: The first coin is what percent of the second? For example; a nickel is what percent of a quarter? (20%)

Variation: Have students list all comparisons equal to a given percent. (20%— nickel: quarter; dime: half dollar, etc.)

MATH CONNECTION (Consumer)
Materials: newspaper advertisements

Have students calculate the prices for various items listed in the ads if food items are 72% of the advertised prices, an item of clothing is 63% of the advertised price, a piece of furniture is 91% of the advertised price, and a piece of electronic equipment is 96% of the advertised price. (Answers will vary.)

COMING UP
The ups and downs of percents

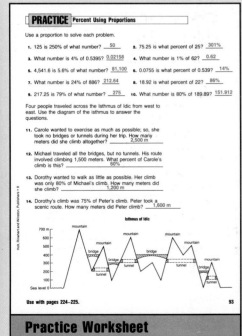

Objectives: To find the percent of increase or decrease

Warm-Up

Have students identify whether the following numbers increased or decreased and by how much.

- Shirt prices go from $20 to $15. (decrease of $5)
- The class size goes from 30 to 21. (decrease of 9)
- The fare goes from $6 to $12. (increase of $6)
- The number of fish in the tank goes from 10 to 3 to 8. (decrease of 7, increase of 5)

GETTING STARTED

Ask students: What percent of $20 is $5? (25%) What percent of $6 is $12? (200%) What percent of 10 is 8? (80%)

TEACHING THE LESSON

A. Some students may find the following model helpful in writing the appropriate equation to find the percent of increase or decrease.

Percent of original = change

unknown × 60 = 15

B. Emphasize the fact that to find the percent of increase or decrease, one must find the percent that the *amount* of increase or decrease is of the original amount.

Also remind students that percent of decrease can never exceed 100 because a 100% decrease results in 0.

You may wish to allow students to use calculators while working through this lesson.

Percent of Increase and Decrease

A. A technical college is expanding its program in civil engineering. There are now 60 students in the program. If there will be 15 more students next year, what is the percent of increase?

Let n = the percent.   Think: What percent of 60 is 15?

$$n \cdot 60 = 15$$

Write an equation. $60n = 15$

Solve. $n = \dfrac{15}{60}$ ← amount of change ← original amount

The percent of increase is 25%. $n = \dfrac{1}{4}$, or 25%

Suppose that the enrollment was originally 80 students, and it decreased by 16. What is the percent of decrease?

Let n = the percent.   Think: What percent of 80 is 16?

$$n \cdot 80 = 16$$

Write an equation. $80n = 16$

Solve. $n = \dfrac{16}{80}$

$$n = \dfrac{1}{5}, \text{ or } 20\%$$

The percent of decrease is 20%.

B. Sometimes you need to compute the amount of change before you can find the percent of increase or decrease.

At the start of a term, there were 20 students in one surveying class. At the end, there were only 18. What is the percent of decrease?

Compute the amount of change.

$$20 - 18 = 2$$

Write an equation and solve it.

$$n \cdot 20 = 2$$
$$20n = 2$$
$$n = \dfrac{2}{20} = \dfrac{1}{10}, \text{ or } 10\%$$

The percent of decrease is 10%.

226   Math Reasoning, page H218

COMMON ERRORS

Some students might not use the starting amount as the whole and the final amount as the part.

Remediation

Have these students label the starting amount and the final amount before writing the equation.

Assign Reteach Master, p. 68.

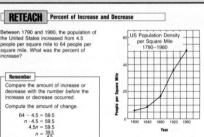

RETEACH | Percent of Increase and Decrease

Between 1790 and 1980, the population of the United States increased from 4.5 people per square mile to 64 people per square mile. What was the percent of increase?

US Population Density per Square Mile 1790–1980

Remember

Compare the amount of increase or decrease with the number before the increase or decrease occurred.

Compute the amount of change.

$$64 - 4.5 = 59.5$$
$$n \cdot 4.5 = 59.5$$
$$4.5n = 59.5$$
$$n = \dfrac{59.5}{4.5}$$
$$n = 13.22 = 1,322\%$$

The population per square mile increased by 1,322%.

The table shows the population per square mile in various years. Write an expression for the percent of increase or decrease.

Year and population density	Year and population density	Amount of increase or decrease	Expression for rate of increase or decrease
1. 1790 4.5	1800 6.1	6.1 − 4.5	$\frac{6.1-4.5}{4.5}$
2. 1800 6.1	1810 4.3	6.1 − 4.3	$\frac{6.1-4.3}{6.1}$
3. 1810 4.3	1820 5.5	5.5 − 4.3	$\frac{5.5-4.3}{4.3}$

For each problem, the population density is given for two years. Find the percent of increase or decrease in population density. Round to the nearest 0.1%.

4. 1820—5.5, 1830—7.4 __34.5%__   5. 1840—9.8, 1850—7.9 __19.4%__

6. 1880—14.2, 1890—17.8 __25.4%__   7. 1900—21.5, 1910—26 __20.9%__

68   Use with pages 226–227.

Reteach Worksheet

Find the percent of increase or decrease.

1. Original value: 50
Increase: 18 **36%**

2. Original price: $21
Decrease: $7 **$33\frac{1}{3}%$**

3. Original value: 90
Increase: 15 **$16\frac{2}{3}%$**

4. Original price: $100
New price: $140 **40%**

5. Original value: 500
New value: 625 **25%**

6. Original value: 22
New value: 33 **50%**

7. Original value: 50
New value: 35 **30%**

8. Original value: 240
New value: 96 **60%**

9. Original price: $72
New price: $60 **$16\frac{2}{3}%$**

10. Original Price: $12
New price: $15 **25%**

11. Original price: $15
New price: $12 **20%**

12. Change: 10
Original value: 200 **5%**

Find the missing number.

★13. Original value: ■
New value: $18.90
Percent of
increase: 12.5%
$16.80

★14. Original value: ■
New value: $44.50
Percent of
decrease: $28\frac{4}{7}%$
$62.30

★15. Original value: ■
Increase: 72,000
Percent of
increase: 56.25%
128,000

Solve.

16. Last year, Les earned $8.50 per hour working on a surveying job. This year he has been offered $9.35 per hour for the same job. What is the percent of increase?
10% increase

17. Carolyn needs a total of 72 credits for an associate degree in civil-engineering technology. If 6 of those are credits in surveying, what percent are credits in surveying?
$8\frac{1}{3}%$

18. Paul spent $28.80 on a school jacket. If the same jacket sold for $21.60 last semester, what is the percent of increase? **$33\frac{1}{3}%$ increase**

19. Compare the number of students in your class now with the number at the beginning of the school year. Find the percent of increase or decrease. **Answers will vary.**

FOCUS: REASONING

Write the conclusion.

If this item did not cost less, you did not buy it on sale.

If you bought this item at Relangers, it did not cost less.

You bought this item on sale. **You did not buy this item at Relangers.**

Classwork/Homework, page H94

227

ASSIGNMENT GUIDE

Basic: 1–12, 16–17

Average: 1–12, 16–19, F

Extended: 1–11 o, 13–19, F

Resources
Practice, p. 94   Class/Home, p. H94
Reteach, p. 68   Reasoning, p. H218
Enrich, p. 88

Exercise Analysis
1–12   Find the percent of increase or decrease
13–15   Find the original value
16–18   Skill applications
19   Data collection and computation

You may wish to allow students to use a calculator to complete some of the exercises.

Focus: Reasoning
A more concrete example might be helpful as a foundation for students before assigning the problem in the text.

If this pet is not a cat, it is not a dog. If it was purchased at a pet store, it is not a cat. You bought it at a pet store. Conclusion? (It is not a cat or a dog.)

FOLLOW-UP ACTIVITIES

COMPUTER
Have students write computer programs that will find the percent of increase or decrease.

```
10  INPUT "ORIGINAL, NEW VALUE";
    O, N
20  IF O = N THEN 90
30  IF O > N THEN LET A$ =
    "DECREASE"
40  IF O < N THEN LET A$ =
    "INCREASE"
50  LET C = ABS (O-N)
60  LET P = (C/O) * 100
70  PRINT "THE PERCENT OF"; A$;
    "IS"; P; "%"
80  STOP
90  PRINT "THERE HAS BEEN NO
    CHANGE"
100 END
```

COMING UP
Properly apportioned parts problems

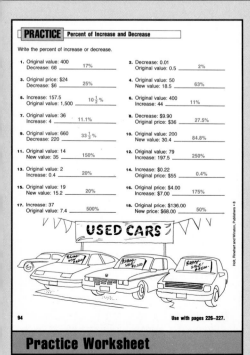

PRACTICE Percent of Increase and Decrease

Write the percent of increase or decrease.

1. Original value: 400
Decrease: 68 **17%**

2. Decrease: 0.01
Original value: 0.5 **2%**

3. Original price: $24
Decrease: $6 **25%**

4. Original value: 50
New value: 18.5 **63%**

5. Increase: 157.5
Original value: 1,500 **$10\frac{1}{2}%$**

6. Original value: 400
Increase: 44 **11%**

7. Original value: 36
Increase: 4 **11.1%**

8. Decrease: $9.90
Original price: $36 **27.5%**

9. Original value: 660
Decrease: 220 **$33\frac{1}{3}%$**

10. Original value: 200
New value: 30.4 **84.8%**

11. Original value: 14
New value: 35 **150%**

12. Original value: 79
Increase: 197.5 **250%**

13. Original value: 2
Increase: 0.4 **20%**

14. Increase: $0.22
Original price: $55 **0.4%**

15. Original value: 19
New value: 15.2 **20%**

16. Original price: $4.00
Increase: $7.00 **175%**

17. Increase: 37
Original value: 7.4 **500%**

18. Original price: $136.00
New price: $68.00 **50%**

USED CARS

94   Use with pages 226–227.

Practice Worksheet

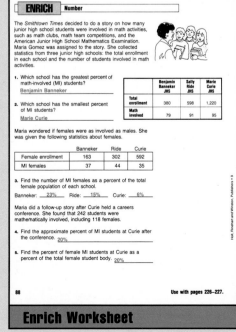

ENRICH Number

The *Smithtown Times* decided to do a story on how many junior high school students were involved in math activities, such as math clubs, math team competitions, and the American Junior High School Mathematics Examination. Maria Gomez was assigned to the story. She collected statistics from three junior high schools: the total enrollment in each school and the number of students involved in math activities.

1. Which school has the greatest percent of math-involved (MI) students?
Benjamin Banneker

2. Which school has the smallest percent of MI students?
Marie Curie

	Benjamin Banneker JHS	Sally Ride JHS	Marie Curie JHS
Total enrollment	380	598	1,220
Math involved	79	91	95

Maria wondered if females were as involved as males. She was given the following statistics about females.

	Banneker	Ride	Curie
Female enrollment	163	302	592
MI females	37	44	35

3. Find the number of MI females as a percent of the total female population of each school.
Banneker: **23%** Ride: **15%** Curie: **6%**

Maria did a follow-up story after Curie held a careers conference. She found that 242 students were mathematically involved, including 118 females.

4. Find the approximate percent of MI students at Curie after the conference. **20%**

5. Find the percent of female MI students at Curie as a percent of the total female student body. **20%**

88   Use with pages 226–227.

Enrich Worksheet

227

Objectives: To use information from a circle graph

Warm-Up
Have students compute the following.

20% of 140 (28)	35% of 480 (168)
0.64 · 125 (80)	5.2 · 485 (2,522)

GETTING STARTED

Discuss with students the careers they plan to pursue. Make a list on the chalkboard of each field that students name and of the number of students who plan to enter it. For each category, find the percent of the total number of students. Relate this list to a circle graph, and explain that such a list must be made before a circle graph can be drawn.

TEACHING THE LESSON

Tell students that *circle graphs* are used to show the parts of a whole. Emphasize that circle graphs are different from other graphs in that they show how a whole is divided into parts. Circle graphs are often used to show how budgets are planned or how revenue is to be spent. Be sure students recognize that the entire circle graph on page 228 represents 160 students and that each part of the graph shows a percent of this total. Note that in using whole-number percents for a circle graph, it is sometimes necessary to round the numbers being used. This may result in a total percentage that is slightly less than or slightly greater than 100%.

Questions: One of the major problems students face when using graphs is that the necessary information is not within the exercise itself. Have students examine the graph and the information it contains before they attempt to answer the questions.

Tools: Make sure students correctly transfer information from the graph. Students will sometimes confuse the percentages listed for the actual number of students in each category. Be sure students reread all explanatory material in and around the graph.

Solutions: One of the most frequent errors students make with circle graphs is in using percents. Review all three cases of percent and place special emphasis on finding a percent of a number.

Checks: Students should check to see that they correctly copied information from the graph. Point out that it might be a good idea to estimate an answer before solving so they will have something to check their final answer against.

QUESTIONS	TOOLS	SOLUTIONS	CHECKS

PROBLEM SOLVING
Using a Circle Graph

A circle graph shows how a total amount is divided into parts. For example, the circle graph below was divided into parts based on the percent each part is of the whole. The larger the percent, the larger the part.

Use the circle graph to answer this question. How many students plan to enter the field of medicine?

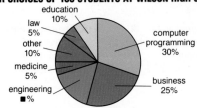

CAREER CHOICES OF 160 STUDENTS AT WILSON HIGH SCHOOL

- education 10%
- law 5%
- other 10%
- medicine 5%
- engineering ■%
- computer programming 30%
- business 25%

- • The title tells you that this graph shows the career choices made by 160 students at one school.

- • Each part of the graph shows what percent of the students have chosen a particular career. These percents must add up to 100%.

- • The size of each part shows the size of its percent. Find the part labeled *medicine*. What percent is this part?

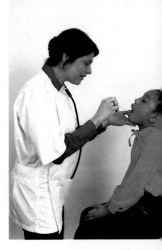

The graph tells you that 5% of the students have chosen medicine.

Find 5% of 160.

Use a fraction. $5\% = \frac{5}{100} = \frac{1}{20}$

Write an equation, and solve. $x = \frac{1}{20} \cdot 160$

$$x = 8$$

A total of 8 students plan to enter the field of medicine.

Can you use the circle graph on page 228 to answer each question? Write *yes* or *no*.

1. Did more students choose computer programming as a career than any other category? **yes**

2. How many career choices are there in the category labeled *other*? **no**

3. Is the number of students who chose computer programming as a career double the number of students who chose engineering as a career? **yes**

Use the circle graph on page 228 to solve each problem. If you cannot use the circle graph to answer a question, write *not enough information*.

4. What percent of the students plan to have careers in engineering? **15%**

5. How many students plan to have careers in engineering? **24 students**

6. How many students plan to follow a career in business? **40 students**

7. How many students plan to have a career in law? **8 students**

8. Which other field was chosen by the same number of students as law? **medicine**

9. How many more students plan to enter computer programming than the field of education? **32 students**

10. Which two fields combined represent the career choices of more than half the students? **computer programming and business**

11. How many students plan to have careers in farming and agriculture? **not enough information**

12. If half the students who chose business as a career intend to become accountants, how many students plan to become accountants? **20 students**

13. One fourth of the students who chose engineering as a career intend to become electrical engineers. How many students are planning to become electrical engineers? **6 students**

14. Notice that 10% of the students chose a career in the category labeled *other*. If three fourths of the students in this category chose a military career, how many students plan to enter the military? **12 students**

Classwork/Homework, page H95

ASSIGNMENT GUIDE

Basic:	1–7
Average:	3–9
Extended:	4–14

Resources
Practice, p. 95   Class/Home, p. H95
Enrich, p. 89

Exercise Analysis
1–3 Decide whether a question can be answered from a circle graph
4–14 Use a circle graph to solve

FOLLOW-UP ACTIVITIES

PROBLEM SOLVING
Materials: newspapers and magazines per group

Have each group look through newspapers and magazines for examples of circle graphs. Have each group write a set of ten problems that can be answered with information from a circle graph. Have groups exchange graphs and questions and solve problems.

CALCULATOR
Materials: 1 calculator per student

Copy the circle graph below onto the chalkboard. Explain to students that circle graphs can also use fractions of a whole instead of percents. Have them copy the graph and find the number of scouts who are each age.

10 (120); 11 (64); 12 (56); 13 (30); 14 (25); 15 (16); 16 (8); 17 (1)

Age in years of
320 Sea Scouts

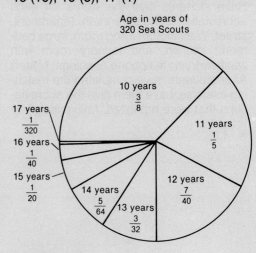

COMING UP
Two out of three R's

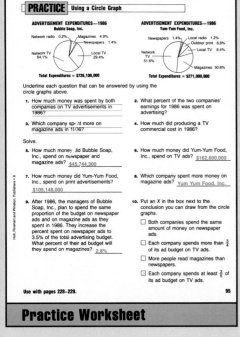

Practice Worksheet

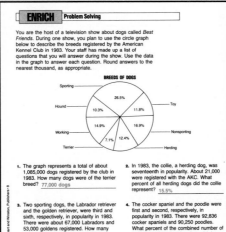

Enrich Worksheet

Objective: To recognize math abbreviations

Warm-Up
Write the following on the chalkboard, and have students solve.
1. 20% of 5■ = ■0 (0, 1)
2. 50% of ■5■ = 7■ (1, 0, 5)
3. 60% of ■0 = 2■ (4, 4)
4. 10% of ■6■ = 4■ (4, 0, 6)

GETTING STARTED

Write the following on the chalkboard.

HEAD
HEELS

Explain to students that this is a puzzle that stands for an abbreviation of a familiar phrase. Elicit from students, or tell them, that it stands for the expression "head over heels."

Write the following on the chalkboard, and have students work in pairs to solve each puzzle.

meal²   BAN ANA
(square meal)   (banana split)

THERE   W A T E R
 A   feet feet
 N   feet feet
 G   feet feet
(hang in there)   (6 feet under water)

linklinklink   PERFECT BDOY
linklinklink   PERFECT BOYD
link   link   PERFECT BYOD
(the missing link)   (nobody's perfect)

Encourage students to create abbreviation puzzles of their own.

TEACHING THE LESSON

Have students give the words for each abbreviation in the paragraph. (apartment, street, Washington; living room; large bedroom; kitchen, and laundry room with washer/dryer; telephone evenings; Mister) After students have completed the matching exercise, have them give the abbreviations that were not listed. (min/minute)

MATH COMMUNICATION

Read this want ad.

FOR RENT: Sunny apt on Green St Seattle Wash. Liv rm, lg bdrm, kit & laun rm w/ w/d. Tel eves (206) 687–2478, ask for Mr Toms.

The ad contains some familiar abbreviations. An abbreviation is a quick way of writing a word that is used frequently.

When you read mathematics, you will find many abbreviations for commonly used terms.

Match the abbreviation with its meaning.

1. A.M.   g   **a.** ante morem   **b.** second

2. s   b   **c.** commutative   **d.** minute

3. cm   h   **e.** mile   **f.** subtract

4. mi   e   **g.** ante meridiem   **h.** centimeter

Write an appropriate abbreviation for each missing word in each sentence below.

5. A pint of liquid will fill two 1-■ measures.   c

6. One ■ equals a thousandth of a meter.   mm

7. Eighteen inches is $1\frac{1}{2}$■.   ft

8. Nine feet equals 108 ■.   in.

9. A fence that measures 3,520 yd is about 2 ■ long.   mi

10. A hundredth of a meter is 1 ■.   cm

11. Ten o'clock, between midnight and noon, is 10:00 ■.   A.M.

12. Twelve ■ is about 3 months.   wk

13. Four quarts equals one ■.   gal

14. A cup of liquid is 8 ■.   fl oz

15. Ten hours past 10:30 in the morning is 8:30 ■.   P.M.

16. Jack drove his car 4,312 meters, or 4.312 ■.   km

17. Lenna's lasagna called for $\frac{1}{2}$ cup tomato sauce or 4 ■.   oz

18. When he applied for a library card, Carl had to fill in the ■, ■, and ■ he was born.   mo, d, y

19. In 1984, Gabriella Dorio ran the 1,500-m run in 4 ■ 03.26 ■.   min, s

20. In July, the average temperature in Egypt is about 34°■.   C

230

GROUP PROJECT

Teachers for a Day

The problem: You and your classmates are going to become teachers for one week. You will have 6 hours per day to teach the subjects you are learning about now. You must decide who will teach each subject, how it will be taught, and how teaching time will be budgeted for each day of the week. Consider the questions below. Discuss them with your classmates, and make a schedule for the week.

Key Questions

- How will you decide who will teach which subject? Will you have a different teacher for each subject?

- Which of the listed subjects will you teach?

Science	Art
Social Studies	Music
Math	Home economics
English	Industrial arts
Foreign Language	Physical education

- What other subjects should be included?

- Do some subjects require more time than others to teach?

- What activities should you include (for example: lunch, assembly, study hall)?

TEACHING SCHEDULE

	Monday	Tuesday	Wednesday	Thursday	Friday
9:00					
9:45					
10:30					
11:15					
12:00					
12:45					
1:30					
2:15					
3:00					

231

Objectives: To plan a curriculum; to budget time; to make a schedule

USING THE PAGE

Separate the class into groups of five to seven. Have each group discuss and list the variables to consider in this project. In the schedule, they should list the subjects to be taught, when they should be taught, and who should teach them. Have each group divide responsibility for teaching all classes among themselves. Students should volunteer to teach classes they enjoy or in which they excel. Each teacher should have approximately the same class load, though some teachers will teach more than one class.

Remind groups that a different schedule is needed for each day of the week, because classes such as music or industrial arts are usually not offered each day. Also, such courses might be offered as optional classes in the same time period.

Groups should discuss and vote on the different choices for classes, teachers, and other matters. Remind students to use the Key Questions to guide their decisions.

To extend this cooperative learning activity, have each group plan schedules for a summer camp. Students should volunteer to teach subjects they would like to know or enjoy, such as bicycle maintenance, bread baking, flute playing, swimming, or fishing. Each group should plan a daily schedule, combining their subjects with other typical camp activities.

Purpose: The Chapter Test helps to assess students' understanding of the concepts and skills presented in this chapter.

The chart below is designed to help you review the test items by correlating them with the testing objectives that appear in the Chapter Overview.

Item	Objectives
1–3	A
4–7	B
8–15	C
16–18	D
19–21	E
22–25	F
26–29	G
30	H
31	I
32	J
33–34	K

Bonus

The bonus questions may be used for extra credit, or you may want to assign them to students who complete the test before the rest of the class.

Calculator

You may wish to have students use calculators for the problem-solving portions of the test.

Resources

If you prefer to use this Chapter Test as a review exercise, additional testing materials are available in the Teacher's Resource Book.

CHAPTER TEST

Solve the proportions. (pages 202–203)

1. $\frac{7}{a} = \frac{28}{44}$ $a = 11$

2. $\frac{3}{5} = \frac{y}{30}$ $y = 18$

3. $\frac{b}{9} = \frac{2}{3}$ b

The scale of a drawing is 1.5 cm = 10 m. (pages 206–207)

4. What length does 6 cm represent? 40 m

5. How many centimeters represent 25 m? 3.75 cm

On a drawing, $7\frac{1}{2}$ cm represents 135 m. (pages 206–207)

6. The scale is 1 cm = ■ m? 18 m

7. What distance does 3 cm represent? 54 m

Write each fraction or decimal as a percent. (pages 208–213)

8. $\frac{4}{5}$ 80%

9. $2\frac{19}{50}$ 238%

10. 0.83 83%

11. 3.097 309.7%

Write each percent as a fraction and as a decimal. (pages 208–213)

12. 32% $\frac{8}{25}$; 0.32

13. 21.6% $\frac{27}{125}$; 0.216

14. 620% $6\frac{1}{5}$; 6.2

15. 0.3% $\frac{3}{1,000}$; 0.0

Solve. (pages 216–221)

16. 26% of 480 124.8

17. 2.8% of 325 9.1

18. 130% of 67 87.10

19. 338 is what percent of 845? 40%

20. 987 is what percent of 282? 350%

21. 0.5 is what percent of 200? 0.25%

22. 160 is 25% of what number? 640

23. 1,050 is 140% of what number? 750

24. 75.85 is $9\frac{1}{4}$% of what number? 820

25. 180.9 is 22.5% of what number? 804

Give the percent of the increase or the decrease. (pages 226–227)

26. $260 is marked up to $338. 30% increase

27. $400 is marked down to $340. 15% decrease

28. 180 is changed to 259.2. 44% increase

29. 46 is changed to 43.47. $5\frac{1}{2}$% decrease

232

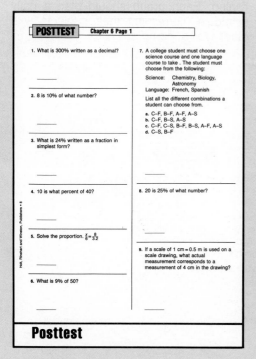

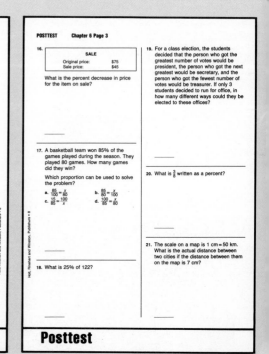

Solve. (pages 204–205, 214–215, 222–223, and 228–229)

30. A magazine conducted a survey to find how many high school graduates preferred the sales profession to one in advertising. The published report stated that the ratio of potential salespersons to advertisers was 3 to 2. If 621 graduates preferred sales, how many graduates were polled in this survey? $\frac{3}{2} = \frac{621}{n}$; $n = 414$; **1,035 graduates**

31. Sue tutors new secretaries in dictation. She tutors only two students at a time. There are four secretaries who have applied: Dorinda, Lois, Ella, and Christopher. Use the initial of each name to find the possible combinations she could teach. **D–L, D–E, D–C, L–E, L–C, E–C**

32. John earned $350 at his job. If he invests this money at 8.75% simple interest yearly, how much will he earn in 1 year? **$30.63**

Use the circle graph at the right for Exercises 33–34.

33. Angadish College offers 4 different programs. If the total student body is 13,145 students, how many students are there in the business program? **2,629 students**

34. Suppose the total of business and engineering students is 6,525. Find the number of students in the student **body.** **14,500 students**

ANGADISH COLLEGE STUDENT BODY

18% Science students
37% Liberal arts students
20% Business students
25% Engineering students

BONUS

Solve.

After last year's graduation, 95 students of a class of 475 went into business. This year, 130 students of a class of 520 went into business after graduation. In terms of percent, how many more students went into business this year? **5% more**

233

For students who have difficulty with written tests, this test can be given orally.

You may wish to test students, orally or in writing, to see if they can explain the steps used in solving selected items. The following table summarizes the procedures for solving key test items.

Ex. 1–3

Solving proportions

To solve a proportion that has a variable in one of its ratios, use cross products to find the correct value for the variable. Cross-multiply and solve.

Ex. 8–11

Writing fractions or decimals as percents

To write a decimal as a percent, move the decimal point two places to the right, and write the percent sign. To write a fraction as a percent, first check to see if the denominator is a factor of 100. If so, write an equivalent fraction that has a denominator of 100. The numerator will be the percent. If the denominator is not a factor of 100, divide the numerator by the denominator to obtain a decimal; then rewrite as a percent, using the method above.

Ex. 16–25

Finding a percent of a number, finding what percent a number is of another, and finding the total number

To find a percent of a number, solve for *x* by multiplying the number by the percent that is expressed as a decimal or a fraction. To find what percent a number is of another, divide the first number by the second number, and multiply by 100%. To find the total number, given a number that is a stated percent of the number, let *x* equal the total number and write an equation. Solve for *x* by dividing the number that represents part of the total number by the stated percent.

POSTTEST Chapter 6 Page 4

22. The price of a suit was reduced from $250 to $175. What was the percent decrease in price?

23. The price of an article was raised from $10 to $11. What was the percent increase?

24. A man bought a stereo that cost $500 and paid for it over a period of one year. If the total amount that he paid was $575, what was the rate of interest?

25. What percent of 90 is 9?

26. A model airplane has a wingspan of 20 cm. The wingspan of the real airplane was 60 m. What does a scale of 1 cm represent?

27. Carla has $1,050 in her savings account. If the bank pays interest every three months and the interest rate is $5\frac{1}{4}$% per year, how much interest should Carla get at the end of three months?

28. Solve the proportion. $\frac{8}{x} = \frac{4}{6}$

29. On a scale drawing of a monument, the scale is 1 cm = 8 m. What is the distance between two statues on the drawing if the actual distance between them is 72 meters?

30. At Washington Junior High School, 45% of the students are girls. If there are 135 girls, how many students are enrolled?

31. A student answered 27 test questions correctly. If this was 60% of the questions, how many questions were on the test?

Posttest

POSTTEST Chapter 6 Page 5

32. 36 is 12% of what number?

33. Solve the proportion. $\frac{13}{11} = \frac{4}{x}$

34. From a bicycle shop, one can rent 3-speed or 10-speed bikes. The bikes come in three colors: red, blue, and green. On a particular day, the owner noticed that each bike rented was a different combination of color and speed from all the others. List all the different combinations of bikes that could have been rented that day.

   a. 3–R, 3–B, 10–R, 10–B
   b. 3–R, 10–R, 10–B
   c. 3–R, 3–B, 3–G, 10–R, 10–B, 10–G
   d. 3–B, 3–G, 10–R, 10–B, 10–G

Use the circle graph for questions 35 and 36.

Out-of-doors
Help People 30% 20% Lab or Office
Small Business 20% 25% Large Business Firm

The graph shows the results of a survey of 120 students. Each student was asked to select from five types of occupations the one that he or she would prefer.

35. How many of the students surveyed preferred a large business?

36. How many of the students surveyed preferred to work out-of-doors?

Posttest

POSTTEST Chapter 6 Page 6

37. A woman was buying a new car. She could choose between a two-door or a four-door model, with either a hard top or a vinyl top, and in either blue or green. How many possible combinations are there to choose from?

38. What percent of 40 is 8?

39. A 30 oz jar of oil-and-vinegar salad dressing contains 60% oil. How many ounces of oil does the jar contain?

40. Juan made one deposit in his savings account at the beginning of last year. His savings account earned $42 in interest. If the interest rate was $5\frac{1}{4}$% per year and interest is paid yearly, what was the amount of his original deposit?

41. What is 200% of $60?

42. What is 0.6% of 280?

43. 48 is what percent of 16?

44. The original price of a coat was $60. Over a period of a year the price increased to $72. What was the percent increase in price?

Posttest

Purpose This Reteaching page provides additional instruction for key concepts in the chapter. It is designed for use by students who have had difficulty with these concepts. It can also be used to provide additional practice for students who require it.

USING THE PAGE

These skills were taught on pages 210–213.

Remind students that given fractions as well as given percents can be written as decimals. Review how to write a given percent as a decimal and also how to write a given decimal as a percent. Also remind students how to use division to write a given fraction as a percent, as shown in the example. Review the method of writing a given percent as a fraction, as shown in the second example. Be sure students are aware of these relationships before you assign the exercises.

Resources

For other practice and activities related to this chapter, see the Teacher's Resource Book.

RETEACHING

$\frac{1}{2}$, 0.5, and 50% all have the same value.

A. To change a fraction to a decimal, divide its numerator by its denominator.

Express $\frac{5}{8}$ as a decimal and as a percent.

$$\frac{5}{8} \rightarrow 8\overline{)5.000} \quad \begin{array}{r} 0.625 \\ \underline{4\,8} \\ 20 \\ \underline{16} \\ 40 \\ \underline{40} \end{array}$$

To change a decimal to a percent, multiply the decimal by 100 and write the percent sign.

$\frac{5}{8} = 0.625$

$0.625 \cdot 100 = 62.5\%$

So, $\frac{5}{8} = 0.625 = 62.5\%$

B. To write a percent as a decimal, move the decimal point two places to the left and remove the percent sign.

Express 45% as a decimal and as a fraction.

$45\% = 0.45$

To rewrite the decimal as a fraction, write the decimal (without the decimal point) in the numerator. The denominator is the power of 10 indicated by the number of places in the decimal. Express the fraction in simplest form.

$0.45 = \frac{45}{100} = \frac{9}{20}$

So, $45\% = 0.45 = \frac{9}{20}$

Copy and complete the chart at right.

Fraction		Decimal	Percent
$\frac{3}{4}$		**1.** ▦ 0.75	**2.** ▦ 75%
3. ▦	$\frac{13}{25}$	0.52	**4.** ▦ 52%
$\frac{7}{8}$		**5.** ▦ 0.875	**6.** ▦ 87.5%
7. ▦	$\frac{3}{5}$	**8.** ▦ 0.6	60%
9. ▦	$\frac{1}{4}$	**10.** ▦ 0.25	25%
11. ▦	$\frac{3}{8}$	0.375	**12.** ▦ 37.5%
$\frac{17}{20}$		**13.** ▦ 0.85	**14.** ▦ 85%
15. ▦	$\frac{2}{5}$	0.4	**16.** ▦ 40%

234

ENRICHMENT

Inverse Proportions

The formula used to compute distance is

rate × time = distance.

With this formula, different pairs of rate and time factors can produce a distance of 200 mi.

r	×	t	=	d
100	×	2	=	200
50	×	4	=	200
40	×	5	=	200
20	×	10	=	200

Notice that if distance, d, remains constant, the time, t, increases as the rate, r, decreases. Rate is said to be **inversely proportional** to time. Since the rate multiplied by the time is constant, we can express this relation as $rt = k$, where k is the constant.

Write the following relation as a formula. Use k as the constant.

If a fixed sum of money is to be spent, the number of articles, n, that can be bought is inversely proportional to the cost, c, of an article.

Since the product of n and c must be constant, the formula is

$$nc = k.$$

Write each relation as a formula. Use k as the constant.

1. If the area of a rectangle is constant, the length varies inversely with the width. $lw = k$

2. If annual income is fixed, the principal that must be invested varies inversely with the rate of interest. $pr = k$

3. If a weekly salary is fixed, the amount of money earned per hour varies inversely with the number of hours worked. $mh = k$

★4. If a force remains constant, the amount of mass used varies inversely with its acceleration. $ma = k$

235

Purpose
This Enrichment page provides an additional challenge for those students whose work throughout the chapter and on the Chapter Test shows a thorough understanding of the material. Alternatively, you may wish to use these exercises as a supplementary lesson for the entire class.

USING THE PAGE

In any formula (or equation) of the form $d = rt$, if the d side remains constant, the terms of the other side must be inversely proportional; that is, as one increases, the other decreases. A constant in such a formula is usually represented by the letter k. The other two variables can be any factors whose product is the constant; for example, $rt = 200$, $r = 400$, $t = 0.5$. After students have finished the problems on this page, present them with the formula $E = mc^2$. Tell them E is the amount of energy released when mass m is changed to energy, and c is the speed of light (300,000 km/s), a constant. If they solve for c^2, the equation reads $c^2 = \frac{E}{m}$, and E and m are *directly proportional*—both increase or decrease together. Discuss how large E must be to have $\frac{E}{m}$ equal c^2, and relate it to the enormous amount of energy released from a minute amount of mass.

Resources
For additional Enrichment activities, see the Teacher's Resource Book.

Objective: To use the INT function in BASIC to round numbers

Warm-Up
Have students estimate the following sums and products in two ways: first by rounding each number *down* to the nearest integer and then by rounding each number *up* to the nearest integer. Discuss the answers.

4.6 + 2.1 + 7.4 (13;16)
6.9 + 3.4 + 8.4 (17;20)
4.3 × 8.1 (32;45)
9.2 × 1.7 (9;20)

GETTING STARTED

Materials: several long cash-register tapes

Ask students to describe situations in which they would use rounded numbers. Possible answers include making sure you have enough money in a supermarket, estimating the amount of carpet you would need for a room, or estimating the amount of time it will take to do your homework.

Ask students whether they have ever seen an item marked *3 for $1.00.* If they were to purchase just one of the items, how much would that item cost? ($0.34; supermarkets always round the price up to the nearest whole cent.) Ask students whether they can think of other situations in which numbers are always rounded in one direction only. (tax on an item; the length of a nonleap year)

TEACHING THE LESSON

[*Note:* Italics denote activities that require use of a computer.]

Although students are very familiar with the concept of rounding numbers, they need to recognize that the INT function does not actually round off numbers. The INT function rounds numbers down to the next integer. So, INT (2.5) = 2 and INT (−2.5) = −3. In order to round numbers to the *nearest* integer, 0.5 must be added to a number before the INT function is applied. The process used to round a number to the nearest ten (see Exercise 10) is to move the tens place temporarily to the ones place, round to the nearest whole number, and then restore the original place value. So, 10 * INT (38.6 / 10 + .5) rounds 38 to the nearest ten in 3 steps.
1. 38.6 / 10 places the tens digit in the ones place.
2. INT (3.86 + .5) rounds 3.86 to 4.
3. 10 * 4 restores the 4 to the tens place. The rounded result is 40.

Remind students that a REM statement can help them to remember what a program or a part of a program does. Write the EVEN OR ODD program on the chalk-

---

TECHNOLOGY

You can use the INTEGER FUNCTION with BASIC to round a number down to the nearest integer. If you enter PRINT INT(2.7), your computer will print this. 2

For negative numbers, INT also rounds numbers downward. INT does not simply cut off the decimal part of a number. If you enter PRINT INT(−12 − 0.5), the computer will print this. −13.

Write what the instruction will print.

1. PRINT INT (9.6) 9   **2.** PRINT INT (−1.5) −2

3. PRINT INT (3.55) 3   **4.** PRINT INT (−5 * 0.5) −3

5. PRINT INT (13/3) 4   **6.** PRINT INT (−9/4) −3

Here is a program that tells whether a number is even or odd. If you divide an even number by 2, the result will always be an integer. If you divide an odd number by 2, the result is never an integer.

```
10 PRINT "TYPE A NUMBER"; : INPUT N
20 IF N/2 = INT (N/2) THEN PRINT N; "IS EVEN"
30 IF N/2 < > INT (N/2) THEN PRINT N; "IS ODD"
```

7. Write two runs of this program, one showing an odd number and the other showing an even number.

```
TYPE A NUMBER ? 2
2 IS EVEN
TYPE A NUMBER ? 3
3 IS ODD
```

8. Write a program to test whether a number is evenly divisible by 3.
```
10 PRINT "TYPE A NUMBER"; : INPUT N
20 IF N/3 = INT (N/3) THEN PRINT N; "IS DIVISIBLE BY 3"
30 IF N/3 < > INT (N/3) THEN PRINT N; "IS NOT DIVISIBLE BY 3"
```

---

board. Identify it with a REM statement.

```
5 REM EVEN OR ODD
```

Sometimes you want to round a number to the nearest integer, instead of rounding down. This means that any number that has a decimal of 0.5 or greater, will be rounded up, and any number that has a decimal of less than 0.5 will be rounded down.

Here's how to use the INT function to round a number.

```
10 PRINT "TYPE A DECIMAL"; : INPUT D
20 LET N = INT (D + .5)
30 PRINT D; "ROUNDS TO"; N
```

If you type the number 4.7 into this program, the computer will add .5 to it and produce 5.2. The integer value of 5.2 is 5. The rounded value of 4.7 is 5.

If you type the number 4.3 into this program, the computer will add .5 to it and produce 4.8. The integer value of 4.8 is 4, so the rounded value of 4.3 is 4.

9. Edit (replace lines or write new lines) the program to tell you whether the number is rounded up or down. Here are some sample RUNs of your program.

TYPE A DECIMAL ? 8.5   30 IF N > D THEN PRINT D; "ROUNDS UP TO"; N
8.5 ROUNDS UP TO 9   40 IF N < D THEN PRINT D; "ROUNDS DOWN TO"; N

TYPE A DECIMAL ? 5.2
5.2 ROUNDS DOWN TO 5

10. Write a program that will round numbers to the nearest ten.

```
10 PRINT "TYPE A DECIMAL"; : INPUT D
20 LET N = 10 * INT (D/10 + .5)
30 PRINT D; "ROUNDS TO"; N
```

237

ASSIGNMENT GUIDE

Basic: 1–10

Average: 1–10

Extended: 1–10

FOLLOW-UP ACTIVITIES

 COMPUTER
Materials: computer

Remind students that a computer has the capacity to generate random numbers. In BASIC, you must use the command RND. Have students enter and run the following program.

```
5 REM RANDOM NUMBERS
10 PRINT RND (1)
20 GOTO 5
```

This program will generate random decimal fractions between 0 and 1. You can edit this program to generate random whole numbers between 0 and 9.

```
10 REM LET X BE A RANDOM NUMBER
15 X = RND (1)
20 REM MULTIPLY X BY 10 TO GET
   NUMBERS > 1
25 X = X * 10
30 REM ROUND THE FRACTION
35 X = INT (X)
40 PRINT X
50 GOTO 10
```

Have students change the numbers in lines 15 and 25. For example, they might try 15 X = RND(6) and 25 X = X * 100. What is the outcome?

Here is a statement that will generate random numbers from 1 to 6.

PRINT INT (6 * RND(1)) + 1

This statement can be used twice with an identifying PRINT statement to simulate a pair of number cubes. The computer can then be used instead of number cubes for playing a game.

```
10 REM NUMBER CUBES
15 PRINT "FIRST NUMBER CUBE"
20 PRINT INT(6 * RND(1)) + 1
25 PRINT "SECOND NUMBER CUBE"
30 PRINT INT(6 * RND(1)) + 1
```

Ask students the following questions.
1. *Why do you multiply the random number by 6? (to find a number between 0 and 5)*
2. *Why do you add 1? (to eliminate the 0 and to raise the range of numbers to between 1 and 6)*

Purpose This Cumulative Review page provides an opportunity to reinforce students' understanding of the concepts and skills taught in previous chapters.

The chart below is designed to aid you in reviewing the material by specifying the pages on which various concepts and skills were taught.

Item	Page
1	166–167
2	168–169
3	60–61
4	168–169
5	176–177
6	174–175
7	150–151
8	124–125
9	152–153
10	106–107
11	108–109
12	56–57
13	184–185
14	48–49

Each Cumulative Review gives students an opportunity to practice taking tests that are written in a multiple-choice, standardized format. Be sure that students understand that if the correct answer is not among the first three given, then they should select the fourth choice—"not given"—as the correct answer. At least one item per test will require students to give this response.

CUMULATIVE REVIEW

Write the letter of the correct answer.

1. Complete: $284.7 \text{ m} = \blacksquare \text{ km}$.

a. 0.2847   b. 2.847
c. 28.47   d. not given

2. Choose the appropriate unit to measure cranberry juice.

a. meters   b. liters
c. grams   d. not given

3. $7 \times 42.95 \text{ L}$

a. 30.035 L   b. 300.65 L
c. 3006.5 L   d. not given

4. Complete: $0.038 \text{ g} = \blacksquare \text{ mg}$.

a. 0.0038   b. 0.38
c. 3.8   d. not given

5. Complete: $7 \text{ gal } 8 \text{ pt} = \blacksquare \text{ qt}$.

a. 29   b. 30
c. 32   d. not given

6. $18 \text{ ft } 9 \text{ in.} - 11 \text{ ft } 11 \text{ in.}$

a. 6 ft 10 in.   b. 7 ft 2 in.
c. 7 ft 11 in.   d. not given

7. Write 0.64 as a fraction.

a. $\frac{2}{3}$ b. $\frac{3}{5}$
c. $\frac{16}{25}$ d. not given

8. Order $\frac{2}{3}, \frac{3}{7}, \frac{7}{19}$ from the least to the greatest.

a. $\frac{7}{19}, \frac{3}{7}, \frac{2}{3}$ b. $\frac{3}{7}, \frac{2}{3}, \frac{7}{19}$
c. $\frac{3}{7}, \frac{7}{19}, \frac{2}{3}$ d. not given

9. Solve for r: $\frac{2}{3}r = \frac{4}{5}$.

a. $\frac{5}{6}$ b. 1
c. $1\frac{1}{5}$ d. not given

10. Solve for c: $24c = 168$.

a. 7   b. 144
c. 3,032   d. not given

11. Solve for m: $\frac{m}{8} - 41 = 23$.

a. 8   b. 64
c. 512   d. not given

12. $28.34 \div 1,000$

a. 0.02834
b. 2.834
c. 2,834
d. not given

13. Andrea drove 297 mi in 5 h 24 min. At what rate did she drive?

a. 50 mph
b. 55 mph
c. 60 mph
d. not given

14. At Lily's yarn sale, Lilycot costs $1.75 per 35-g ball. Lilycot used to cost $3.25 per ball. How much would it cost to knit a sweater requiring 900 g of Lilycot?

a. $43.75
b. $45.50
c. $81.25
d. not given

238

CHAPTER 7 OVERVIEW

INTEGERS, RATIONALS, REALS

SUMMARY

Chapter 7 deals with integers, rationals, and reals. Included are lessons on the addition, subtraction, multiplication, and division of integers and rational numbers, the use of integers as exponents, the defining of real and irrational numbers, and the graphing of real numbers.

LESSON SEQUENCE

PROFESSIONAL BACKGROUND

Eighth grade is the last chance for students to make key connections among various concepts and skills before high school mathematics. As mentioned in earlier chapters, many students perceive a fraction only as two numbers together, having little or no relationship to each other. These students might think that $\frac{4}{8}$ is greater than $\frac{2}{4}$ because the constituent numbers are larger. This impairs their ability to compare and order rational numbers.

Many students find it difficult to conceptualize the connection between fractions and rational numbers as well as the meaning of place value in decimals. One study of misconceptions quotes 14-year olds who say, "0.8— that's about equal to $\frac{1}{8}$," and "0.45 hours is 45 minutes." In another study, about a third of the 12-year olds surveyed could not determine, given 4.06 and 4.5, which number was the greater.

Thus, it is important to stress basic concepts in rational number work, such as units in fractions and place value in decimals, and to help students see critical connections between rational numbers and such applications as proportional reasoning.

References: See Behr et al.; Carpenter et al.; Hart et al.

Bell, Alan, et al. 1981. "Choice of Operation in Verbal Problems with Decimal Numbers." *Educational Studies in Mathematics,* 12: 399–420.

MATERIALS

container
index cards
pan balances
paper clips
calculators
graph paper
rulers

VOCABULARY

integers (p. 240)
absolute value (p. 240)
negative (p. 240)
positive (p. 240)
negative exponent (p. 254)
rational numbers (p. 258)
terminating decimals (p. 266)
repeating decimals (p. 266)
irrational numbers (p. 266)
real numbers (p. 266)
coordinate plane (p. 268)
real-number plane (p. 268)
origin (p. 268)
ordered pair (p. 268)
quadrants (p. 268)
radicals (p. 277)

ABOUT THE CHAPTER

Until now, students have been learning about positive whole numbers and fractions. In this chapter, students' knowledge is extended to negative numbers. This is the second of four chapters in this text which directly prepare students for algebra. There is one lesson in this chapter in which students are given the opportunity, in a problem-solving setting, to work cooperatively. In this lesson, students are confronted with a real-life situation through which they are encouraged to develop and apply a variety of strategies.

In Chapter 7, students learn about integers and rational numbers. They learn how to add, subtract, multiply, and divide integers and rational numbers. Students also learn how integers can be used as exponents and about real numbers and graphing integers, rational numbers, and real numbers.

The number line is the most explicit way of presenting integers and rational numbers. Do not hesitate to use it to help students locate, order, add, and subtract integers and rational numbers.

There is no easy way of explaining how the sign of the product or quotient is reached—same signs, positive answer; different signs, negative answer. It is probably best not to develop an involved explanation for students. Rather, rely on the patterns developed in the text.

Students must coordinate two rules—for inverting the divisor and determining the sign of the quotient—when they divide rational numbers. You may want to devote additional time to this.

Graphing numbers in the coordinate plane is a particularly important skill. You may want students to draw designs on the coordinate plane and then represent these designs with a list of ordered pairs. Other students can try to reproduce the patterns from the list of ordered pairs.

Estimation is a particularly effective way to check that an answer is reasonable. Calculators should be used to do cumbersome or difficult calculations. Students should know how to add, subtract, multiply, and divide integers on a calculator. You should be aware that not all calculators are the same.

Problem-solving lessons in this chapter show students how to get and use information from a graph and how to check that the solution to a problem answers the question. Other problem-solving lessons show students how to identify subgoals to be reached when solving a problem and give students an opportunity to choose strategies or methods for solving problems.

The Group Project actively involves students and asks them to plan a trip that Magellan took in the 1500s. Magellan's trip lasted about three years, but students are to plan the trip using modern means of transportation.

The Enrichment lesson introduces students to addition and subtraction of radicals.

USING THE CHAPTER OPENER

Each Chapter Opener presents situational problem-solving activities that can be used to explore the skills taught throughout the chapter. The work sheets can be used by individuals, small groups, or the whole class, depending on the needs of the class. The Chapter Opener focuses on a nonalgorithmic approach to mathematics through real-life situations relevant to the children's experiences. Through an interdisciplinary approach, the Chapter Opener helps children explore the relationships between mathematics, other areas of the curriculum, and everyday life while developing different strands of mathematics.

The Chapter Opener activities deal with making maps and coordinate grids. Students will navigate through caves using only coordinates to guide them.

PROBLEM SOLVING

The lesson *Using Graphs* requires students to draw on data from an outside source to solve problems. A major stumbling block for many students stems from the fact that the information they need is physically separate from the problem they must solve. Some students may also be unfamiliar with the data source they must read and interpret. The lesson discusses the organization and labeling of broken-line and bar graphs, how they are read, and when they are used. This chapter includes a lesson on choosing and using strategies and methods for solving problems. Once students choose a plan of action they must apply it correctly to solve the problem. Because more than one strategy can often be employed for each problem, the Choosing a Strategy or Method lesson is ideal for work in small groups in which students can brainstorm and share ideas to keep each other from getting stuck.

The lesson Checking That the Solution Answers the Question focuses on multiple-choice problems that may include correct answers to two or more very different but related questions.

Students are taught a strategy which will help them choose the pertinent question and check that their answers address the information specifically sought in the question. The Solving Multi-step Problems/Making a Plan lesson addresses those math problems that cannot be solved unless one or more intermediate operations are performed first.

The *Mathematics Unlimited* approach to solving these problems is to have students identify the information they need to find in order to solve the problem and make a plan listing the intermediate calculations in the order in which they must be performed to solve the problem. Be aware that some students may mistakenly believe that multistep problems contain extra information. Most of the problem-solving lessons in *Mathematics Unlimited* lend themselves to small-group work. In a comfortable group atmosphere, students can brainstorm and discuss various ways to solve problems.

BULLETIN BOARD

"Climb Every Mountain"

Materials: paper to cover board; lettering; felt-tip pens; poster board for game pieces; push pins; stapler; 3 envelopes; index cards

Preparation: Draw the outline of a mountain as shown. Cut out game pieces on which students can write their initials, and attach them to the board with push pins. In intervals of 150 feet, mark off from 0 to 1,000 feet on the mountain. Attach three envelopes to the bottom of the board. On index cards, write examples of addition and subtraction of integers, with like and unlike signs, write the answers on the back of the cards, and place them in the first envelope, marked *Snowshoes.* On separate index cards, write examples of addition and subtraction of rational numbers, with like and unlike signs, note the answers on the back of the cards, and place them in the second envelope, marked *Ice Pick.* On the remaining index cards, write examples of division and multiplication of real numbers, note the answers on the back of the cards, and place them in the third envelope, marked *Rope.*

After pp. 242-243: Have students solve examples from the envelopes. For each correct answer, they advance their game pieces up the mountain by the appropriate number of feet.

COMMON ERRORS

Students sometimes have difficulty using the correct sign when they divide integers. Two common errors of this variety are made by students. One error made is to give a negative quotient even when both dividend and divisor are negative. The other error made is to ignore negative signs in the dividend and in the divisor and then to give a positive quotient.

A helpful remediation for these errors is to have students check division problems that involve integers by using the related multiplication sentence. Students are more likely to remember to apply the rules when multiplying. Also many students find it easier to master the rules of multiplication of integers.

SPECIAL NEEDS

The idea of anything being less than zero is difficult for some students to grasp, and it warrants review. Relate negative numbers to previous encounters that the students might have had. For example, ask whether they would rather be outside in ⁻18° weather or in ⁻1° weather. Have students use a number line to see that numbers become larger from left to right on the line. Review basic facts before proceeding to addition and subtraction of integers.

Although adding and subtracting integers with like signs should not present problems, use two-color counters, assigning one color to represent positive numbers and the second color to represent negative numbers. Have students model addition of integers with unlike signs by using these counters. Review multiplication as repeated addition with the two-color counters. Tell students the rule for multiplying a negative by a negative and the rule for dividing a negative by a negative. You may wish to have students write these rules on note cards and keep them handy for reference.

Challenge students to use their math vocabulary to make math "jokes." For example:

I might be radical, but you're unreal!

$\sqrt{14}$ $\sqrt{-6.2}$

239C

MATH LABS

COMPUTER

Have students write a program that will evaluate exponential expressions such as $a^b + a^c$; $a^b - a^c$; $a^b \times a^c$; or $a^b \div a^c$.

```
10 INPUT "FIRST TERM: BASE,
   EXPONENT"; B, E
20 LET S = B^E
30 INPUT "OPERATION, BASE,
   EXPONENT (0,0,0 IF NO
   MORE)"; O$, B, E
40 IF O$ = "0" THEN 100
50 IF O$ = " + " THEN LET S =
   S + B^E
60 IF O$ = " − " THEN LET S =
   S − B^E
70 IF O$ = "*" THEN LET S =
   S*B^E
80 IF O$ = "/" THEN LET S =
   S/B^E
90 GOTO 30
100 PRINT S
110 END
```

MATH CONNECTION

Have students evaluate each expression.
• Sixteen plus negative four. (12)
• Fourteen minus negative sixteen. (30)
• One third to the negative third power. (27)
• The difference six minus negative two divided by negative four times eight. (−16)
• Two fifths divided by negative one half then raised to the negative fourth power. ($\frac{625}{256}$)

MATH CONNECTION

Have students use positive and negative integers and rational numbers to represent each of the following.

At midnight, the temperature was 34°F. Over the next 6 hours, it fell 4°, and then rose 13° during the 2 hours after that. ($^+34 + {}^-4 + {}^+13$)

Cynthia had $1,230 in her bank account on Monday. On Tuesday, she paid her $378 rent. On Thursday, she wrote a check for her credit-card bill of $178. On Friday, she deposited her $324 paycheck. ($^+1,230 + {}^-378 + {}^-178 + {}^+324$)

At the beginning of his party, Terry filled a bowl with 5 pounds of raw vegetables. Halfway through, he took out the 2.3 pounds that were left so that he could wash the bowl. When he put the vegetables back, he put in $3\frac{1}{4}$ pounds. ($^+5 + {}^-2.3 + {}^+3\frac{1}{4}$)

CALCULATOR

Many students have difficulty understanding integers, rationals and reals. Many of these topics can be explored by using a calculator. For example, the properties of the operations on integers can be illustrated (for example, the product of negative integers). Also, properties of the rationals can be explored, for example, between any two rationals there exists another rational. See the exploration activity below.

Students should have calculators available for all problem-solving activities.

Additional Activities: **Drill and Practice:** Verify these unusual power patterns:

$$2^2 + 3^2 + 6^2 = 7^2$$
$$3^2 + 4^2 + 12^2 = 13^2$$
$$5^2 + 6^2 + 30^2 = 31^2$$
$$19^2 + 20^2 + 380^2 = 381^2$$

Exploration: "The Big Squeeze": Begin with $\frac{1}{2}$ and $\frac{3}{4}$. Find the number halfway between $\frac{1}{2}$ and $\frac{3}{4}$ and then halfway between $\frac{1}{2}$ and the result of the first step. Continue for 10 steps. ($\frac{5}{8}$, $\frac{9}{16}$, $\frac{17}{32}$, $\frac{33}{64}$, $\frac{65}{128}$, $\frac{129}{256}$, $\frac{257}{512}$, $\frac{513}{1,024}$, $\frac{1,025}{2,048}$, $\frac{2,049}{4,096}$)

SUBJECT AREA CONNECTIONS

The Subject Area Connections are useful for reinforcing the concepts presented in this chapter.

p. 251-Science: Students use the formula for uniform velocity (velocity = distance ÷ time) to determine the velocity of an object that has fallen.

p. 255-Science: Students write percents in scientific notation.

p. 269-Social Studies: Students research cartography.

Here are some other ideas for reinforcing these concepts.
• **SOCIAL STUDIES:** Students choose several companies listed on the stock market page of the newspaper and record the daily price fluctuations for a week. Students compare the beginning stock prices and daily changes in terms of positive or negative numbers and determine the price of each stock at the end of the week.
• **LIBRARY SKILLS:** Have students research the official language and population of each country in South America. Have them calculate approximately how many people speak each language.

PLAN AHEAD

You will need to write the properties of integers on slips of paper for the activity on T.E. p. 242. You will need to prepare index cards for the activity on T.E. p. 243. You will need calculators for the activity on T.E. p. 261.

PLANNING CALENDAR
ABBREVIATION KEY

Teacher's Resource Book	*Follow-up Activities*
MMW—Making Math Work	CALC—Calculator
P—Practice	CMP—Computer
R—Reteach	CNS—Consumer
E—Enrich	P&G—Puzzles and Games
	MNP—Manipulatives
	MC—Math Connection
	MCM—Math Communication
	NS—Number Sense
	PS—Problem Solving
	RFM—Reinforcement

PLANNING CALENDAR

Pages	Lesson Objectives	ASSIGNMENT GUIDE			Class/Home	More Practice	Math Reasoning	Follow-up	Reteach	Practice	Enrich
		Basic	Average	Extended							
239	Chapter Opener (Use MMW 13,14)	239	239	239							
240,241	To identify, compare and order integers	1-10,11-39o	1-10,12-40e, Chlg	15-44, Chlg	H96		H219	CMP PS	69	96	90
242,243	To define the properties of integers	1-31o,33-35,Calc	2-32e,33-36,Calc	10-32e,33-38,Calc	H97			P&G	70	97	91
244,245	To add integers	1-8, 9-41o,NS	1-7o,10-42e,NS	10-42e,NS	H98		H219	MC NS	71	98	92
246,247	To subtract integers	1-8, 9-45o,46-48	1-8, 10-44e,46-49	10-44e,46-49	H99			NS PS	72	99	93
248,249	To use information from a graph to solve problems	1-6, 9-10	3-12	5-16	H100			PS MC		100	94
250,251	To explore the multiplication of integers	250,251	250,251	250,251	H101			P&G MC	73	101	95
252,253	To explore the division of integers	252,253	252,253	252,253	H102	H201	H219	PS NS	74	102	96
254,255	To define the meaning of negative exponents and to express numbers in scientific notation	1-39o,MCR	2-40e,MCR	2-40e,MCR	H103			MC CMP	75	103	97
256,257	To practice choosing and using methods and strategies for solving problems	1-12	2-18e	1-19o	H104 H105			CALC CALC		104-105	
258,259	To define and graph rational numbers	1-10,11-29o, 31,Chlg1	1-10,12-34e, Chlg1-2	1-26e,27-34,Chlg	H106		H220	P&G CMP	76	106	98
260,261	To add and subtract rational numbers	1-12,13-37o,NS	6-44e,NS	9-32e,34-44,NS	H107	H202		PS CALC	77	107	99
262,263	To check that the solution answers the question in problem solving	1-6	2-8	3-10	H108			PS		108	100
264,265	To multiply and divide rational numbers	1-43o,NS	2-4,5-43o,NS	9-45o,NS	H109		H220	RFM PS	78	109	101
266,267	To explore rational and irrational numbers and terminating and repeating decimals and their relation to real numbers	266,267	266,267	266,267	H110	H202		PS	79	110	102
268,269	To graph ordered pairs on a real number plane	1-32	1-33	9-35	H111		H220	P&G MC	80	111	103
270,271	To solve multi-step problems/making a plan in problem solving	1-5	2-6	2,4-8	H112					112	104
272	Calculator: To use the compound-interest formula	272	272	272							
273	Group Project: To plan a trip; to draw its route on a map	273	273	273							

274,275	Chapter Test
276	Reteaching
277	Enrichment
278	Cumulative Review

SOFTWARE
Mathematics Unlimited Problem-Solving Software
Strategies: Problem Solving

TESTS

A. To compare and order integers

B. To add or subtract integers

C. To multiply or divide integers

D. To write a decimal in scientific notation, using negative exponents

E. To compare and order rational numbers

F. To add or subtract rational numbers

G. To multiply or divide rational numbers

H. To name or locate an ordered pair in a coordinate plane

I. To use information from a graph that has a scale above and below zero to solve problems

J. To check that the solution answers the question

K. To identify subgoals and solve multistep problems

FAMILY INVOLVEMENT

Family Involvement for Chapter 7 encourages family members to use a map to plot the coordinates of several important places in their neighborhood. They are first asked to find or sketch a map of their neighborhood and to list on it all the important places near their home such as the school, the grocery store, and the homes of friends. Then they are to copy a grid onto a sheet of tracing paper and place it over the map. The coordinates of all the places they have marked are to be found and routes from their home to each location are to be plotted along the streets shown on the map. Family members are to list the coordinates as a set of directions and challenge one another to trace the route and name the location.

Additional activities might include the creation of a line map on which family members can locate some of the most prominent landmarks on the route from their home to the school. Family members should note the distances between each landmark and illustrate the nature of each landmark.

STUDENT RESOURCES

Bibliography

Asimov, Isaac. *Asimov on Numbers.* Garden City, New York: Doubleday and Company, Inc., 1977.

Collins, Michael. *Flying to the Moon and Other Strange Places.* New York: Farrar, Strauss and Giroux.

Settle, Mary Lee. *Waterworld.* New York: E. P. Dutton, Inc., 1984.

Films

Infinity. 17 minutes. Color. 1972. Distributed by AIMS Instructional Media, Glendale, Calif.

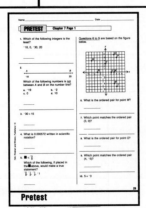

Pretest

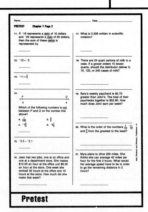

Pretest

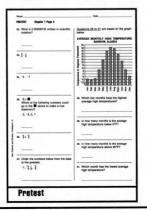

Pretest

Pretest

You are only 50 feet below a cave entrance. The temperature is 10°C. The tunnel to your right is 6 feet wide. All the other tunnels are 2 feet wide. What is your next move? Finish writing the text for the new computer game, Spelunking Adventure. The player's goal is to find the cave exit without becoming stuck or frozen. Remember too, that cave temperatures often fall well below zero and that players may move in any direction.

7 INTEGERS, RATIONALS, REALS

Objective: To explore problems related to coordinate graphing

Direct students to look at the picture of the miner's hat. Tell them that miners have to deal with harsh, dangerous conditions because they work in tunnels all day. They must determine the precise location of each job site so that they will be able to get out of the tunnel quickly in an emergency. Tell students to think of a tunnel as a series of coordinates that will help them determine where miners are in a tunnel and which direction will lead them out of it.

WHOLE CLASS
Geometry
Materials: Making Math Work page 13

Instruct students how to play Spelunking Adventure. Draw a sample model of the coordinate grid on the chalkboard. Remind students that there must be a way out of the tunnel. Discuss how coordinates can aid in determining one's position in a tunnel. Emphasize the difficulty involved in determining where one is in relation to the opening when only dark tunnels surround one.

INDIVIDUAL
Logic
Materials: Making Math Work pages 13 and 14

Have students construct their own mazes by using the grid on Making Math Work page 14. Suggest that each student plan and sketch the maze before drawing it on the work sheet.

SMALL GROUP
Algebra
Materials: completed Making Math Work page 14

Have students trade their completed Making Math Work page 14. While one student tries to work his or her way out of the tunnel, the creator of the maze should let that student know how he or she is doing. Each student should be given two chances to try to complete the mazes created by the other members of the group. Remind students to use the coordinates to determine where they have been, where they are now, and where they should move next. Whoever makes it through all the tunnels created by his or her group has earned the right to be called a Spelunking Expert!

MAKING MATH WORK

Play Spelunking Adventure. The object of the game is to have a friend try to reach the cave opening by finding the correct pathway through a maze that you create. Your friend can move 1 square (in any direction) per turn. The only rule is that your friend cannot stay at a negative temperature or at a negative elevation for more than three consecutive turns.

Use the grid on page 14, and draw a maze of tunnels so that there is at least one correct pathway from the starting point to the cave opening. Then number each open square. Here is an example of what a part of the cave could look like.

10		9
8	7	6
5		4
3	2	1 Start

Square	Temperature	Elevation
1	10°C	-50 ft
2	15°C	0 ft
3	16°C	10 ft
4	9°C	-40 ft
5	14°C	-5 ft
6	-10°C	100 ft
7	0°C	-70 ft
8	15°C	0 ft
9	-11°C	-109 ft
10	14°C	-10 ft

Next, use a positive or a negative integer to assign a temperature and an elevation to each numbered square. Make a table on a separate piece of paper to keep track of the ordered pairs of temperature and elevation.

Use with pupil page 239.   Making Math Work **13**

Making Math Work

MAKING MATH WORK

Use this sheet to plan your pathways for the spelunking adventure. Remember that you cannot spend more than three consecutive turns at negative altitudes or at negative temperatures. Good luck. Check students' mazes.

	A	B	C	D	E	F	G	H	I	J
1										
2										
3			Cave opening							
4										
5										
6										
7										
8										
9								Start		

Spelunking notes:

14   Making Math Work   Use with pupil page 239.

Making Math Work

Objectives: To identify, compare, and order integers.

Warm-Up

Have students arrange the following numbers in order from the least to the greatest.

$1.2, \frac{1}{2}, 0.8, 2\frac{1}{4}, 2.1, 1.7, \frac{8}{4}$

$\left(\frac{1}{2}, 0.8, 1.2, 1.7, \frac{8}{4}, 2.1, 2\frac{1}{4}\right)$

GETTING STARTED

Write on the chalkboard $18 - 6 = (12)$. Call on a volunteer to give the difference. Repeat for $12 - 6 = (6)$; $6 - 6 = (0)$.

Discuss the pattern that has been formed, and ask what the next subtraction example will be. $(0 - 6 = \blacksquare)$

Ask whether the subtraction is possible and if so, how students would write the answer. Point out that today's lesson will introduce numbers less than 0.

TEACHING THE LESSON

A. Point out that when indicating the number of whole-number intervals from zero, you express integers in magnitude or distance; when demonstrating negative and positive integers to the left or to the right of zero, you express direction.

B. Mention that opposite integers always represent the same magnitude of distance but that with the exception of zero, they lie in opposite directions and express different signs.

C. Absolute value can also be defined in this way. When x is positive,
$$|x| = x.$$
When x is negative,
$$|x| = {}^-x.$$
The integer's distance from 0 is the key to determining its absolute value.

D. Extend the instruction by having students order the following integers from the least to the greatest. $3, {}^-2, 1, {}^-4, {}^-5$
$({}^-5, {}^-4, {}^-2, 1, 3)$

Checkpoint

The chart lists the common errors students make when dealing with integers.

Correct Answers: 1b, 2d

Remediation

■ Have students use a number line to find the opposites of the following integers.

$2 ({}^-2); 6 ({}^-6); 9 ({}^-9); 0 (0)$

□ For these errors, assign Reteach Master, p. 69.

The Meaning of Integers

A. Integers are located at whole-number distances from zero (0) on a number line. Integers to the left of zero are **negative,** and integers to the right of zero are **positive.** Although zero is an integer, it is neither positive nor negative.

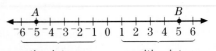

negative integers   positive integers

Point A is at negative 5 $({}^-5)$.
Point B is at positive 5 $({}^+5)$, or (5).
Positive integers are customarily written without the positive sign.

B. Each integer has an opposite that is an equal distance from zero in the opposite direction.

${}^-6$ is the opposite of 6.
4 is the opposite of ${}^-4$.
0 is the opposite of 0.

C. An integer's **absolute value** is its distance from zero. The distance is never negative.

The absolute value of ${}^-5$ is 5.
Write $|{}^-5| = 5$.

The absolute value of 5 is 5.
Write: $|5| = 5$.

D. Integers increase in value from left to right on the number line, and decrease in value from right to left.

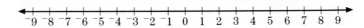

${}^-8$ is to the left of ${}^-5$.   So, ${}^-8 < {}^-5$.   2 is to the right of ${}^-4$.   So, $2 > {}^-4$.

To order the integers 7, ${}^-6$, 4, 0, and ${}^-3$ from the least to the greatest, think of them on a number line. Write them in order from left to right.

${}^-6, {}^-3, 0, 4, 7$

To order the same integers from the greatest to the least, think of the numbers from right to left.

$7, 4, 0, {}^-3, {}^-6$

Checkpoint   Write the letter of the correct answer.

1. Which of the following is *not* true?

a. $|{}^-3| = 3$ (**b.**) $|6| = {}^-6$
c. $|0| = 0$ **d.** ${}^-3 < 7$

2. Order ${}^-3$, 0, 4, and ${}^-7$ from the least to the greatest.

a. $0, {}^-3, 4, {}^-7$ **b.** $0, 4, {}^-3, {}^-7$
c. ${}^-3, {}^-7, 0, 4$ (**d.**) ${}^-7, {}^-3, 0, 4$

COMMON ERRORS

Answer Choice	Type of Error
□ 1a, 1c	Misunderstands the absolute value symbol
■ 1d, 2b	Misunderstands the concept of negative numbers
□ 2a	Uses the absolute value to order the integers
□ 2c	Orders negative numbers as if they were positive integers

---

RETEACH   The Meaning of Integers

Numbers to the left of zero are called **negative numbers** or **negative integers.** Numbers to the right of zero are called **positive numbers** or **positive integers.**

Zero is neither positive nor negative. The positive integers, the negative integers, and zero can be shown on a number line.

Negative integers   Zero   Positive integers

Integers to the right are larger and integers to the left are smaller.
Each integer has an opposite.

The opposite of ${}^+2$ is ${}^-2$.
The opposite of ${}^-3$ is ${}^+3$.
The opposite of 0 is 0.

Hence, a number plus its opposite is zero.

${}^+2 + ({}^-2) = 0$
${}^-3 + ({}^+3) = 0$
$0 + 0 = 0$

Write the integer for each point on the number line.

1. point A ${}^+8$ 2. point B ${}^+5$ 3. point C ${}^+1$
4. point D ${}^-2$ 5. point E ${}^-6$ 6. point F ${}^+4$
7. point G ${}^-8$ 8. point H ${}^-4$ 9. point I ${}^-10$

Write each phrase as an integer.

11. 30°F below zero ${}^-30°$ 12. A gain of 50 pounds ${}^+50$
13. 1,500 feet below sea level ${}^-1,500$ 14. Nine feet above flood stage ${}^+9$

Use with pages 240–241.   69

Reteach Worksheet

Write an integer for each point on the number line.

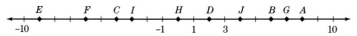

E   F   C   I   H   D   J   B   G   A
-10   -1   1   3   10

1. Point A 8   **2.** Point B 6   **3.** Point C $^-4$ **4.** Point D 2   **5.** Point E $^-9$

6. Point F $^-6$ **7.** Point G 7   **8.** Point H 0   **9.** Point I $^-3$ **10.** Point J 4

Write each phrase as an integer.

11. 80°F below zero $^-80$°F

12. a gain of 23 yards   23 yd

13. 7 ft below flood stage $^-7$ ft

14. 200 miles above sea level   200 mi

Write the opposite of each integer.

15. 13 $^-13$ **16.** $^-8$ 8   **17.** 25 $^-25$ **18.** $^-110$ 110   **19.** $^-76$ 76

Find the absolute value.

20. $|24|$ 24   **21.** $|^-7|$ 7   **22.** $|^-91|$ 91   **23.** $|28|$ 28   **24.** $|^-96|$ 96

Compare. Write >, <, or = for ●.

25. $^-9$ ● 4   <   **26.** $^-7$ ● $^-5$ <   **27.** 0 ● $^-3$ >   **28.** $^-1$ ● $^-1$ =

29. 6 ● $^-5$ >   **30.** 8 ● $^-8$ >   **31.** $^-62$ ● $^-47$ <   **32.** 26 ● $^-27$ >

Order each set of integers from the least to the greatest.

33. 4, $^-4$, $^-7$, $^-9$
$^-9$, $^-7$, $^-4$, 4

34. 42, 0, $^-41$, $^-1$
$^-41$, $^-1$, 0, 42

35. 6, 7, 9, $^-7$, $^-6$
$^-7$, $^-6$, 6, 7, 9

36. 1, $^-2$, $^-4$, $^-6$, 0
$^-6$, $^-4$, $^-2$, 0, 1

37. 20, $^-21$, 10, $^-19$
$^-21$, $^-19$, 10, 20

38. 0, $^-5$, 6, 9, $^-10$
$^-10$, $^-5$, 0, 6, 9

Order each set of integers from the greatest to the least.

39. 21, 3, $^-8$, 0, 8
21, 8, 3, 0, $^-8$

40. 1, 0, $^-1$, 3, 4
4, 3, 1, 0, $^-1$

41. $^-14$, $^-17$, $^-8$, $^-10$, $^-6$
$^-6$, $^-8$, $^-10$, $^-14$, $^-17$

42. 11, $^-10$, 14, 7, $^-6$
14, 11, 7, $^-6$, $^-10$

43. 8, 14, $^-15$, 17, $^-3$
17, 14, 8, $^-3$, $^-15$

44. $^-21$, 16, 7, $^-5$, $^-4$
16, 7, $^-4$, $^-5$, $^-21$

CHALLENGE

To compare the absolute value of two integers, compare their distances from zero.

$|^-8| > |^-5|$ $|^-4| < |^-5|$ $|^-3| > |2|$

Compare. Write >, <, or = for ●.

1. $|^-35|$ ● $|^-9|$ >   **2.** $|42|$ ● $|^-42|$ =   **3.** $|^-61|$ ● $|28|$ >   **4.** $|72|$ ● $|^-3|$ >

ASSIGNMENT GUIDE

Basic: 1–10, 11–39 o

Average: 1–10, 12–40 e, Chlg

Extended: 15–44, Chlg

Resources
Practice, p. 96   Class/Home, p. H96
Reteach, p. 69   Reasoning, p. H219
Enrich, p. 90

Exercise Analysis

1–10	Identify an integer on a number line
11–14	Write an integer for a word phrase
15–19	Write the opposite integer
20–24	Find the absolute value
25–32	Compare two integers
33–44	Order integers

Challenge

These exercises reinforce students' understanding that the sign of the integers is of no importance when comparing the absolute value.

FOLLOW-UP ACTIVITIES

COMPUTER

Have students write a program that lists all the integers between an integer and its opposite.

```
(10 REM NUMBER LINE
 20 INPUT N
 30 FOR X = 0 TO ABS(2*N)
 40 PRINT −ABS(N) + X,
 50 NEXT X
 60 END)
```

PROBLEM SOLVING

Have each student draw a number line to aid in finding the mystery integers described below.

● A negative integer has an absolute value three times as great as that of a positive integer. They are 12 units apart on the number line. Name the integers. ($^-9$, 3)

● When you move along the number line from this negative integer to its opposite and then continue an additional 3 units from 0, you wind up at 7. Name the original integer. ($^-4$)

● When dividing the absolute value of a negative integer into the absolute value of a positive integer, the quotient is 4. They are 10 units apart on the number line. Name the integers. ($^-2$, 8)

COMING UP
Caving in to integers . . .

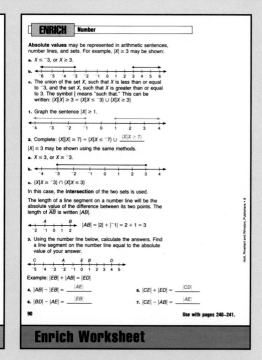

Practice Worksheet

Enrich Worksheet

Objectives: To define the properties of integers

Warm-Up
Have students mentally compute the following examples.

$6 \cdot (13 - 8) + 4$ (34)
$13 - (144 \div 12)$ (1)
$5^2 \times (12 - 8)$ (100)
$18 + (401 - 331)$ (88)

GETTING STARTED

Materials: a container

Write each of the following properties on a slip of paper, and put the slips into a container. Then call each volunteer to select a slip and write on the chalkboard an equation containing whole numbers, which illustrates each of these properties.
1. Identity Property of Addition
2. Distributive Property of Multiplication
3. Commutative Property of Addition
4. Associative Property of Multiplication
5. Identity Property of Multiplication
6. Commutative Property of Multiplication
7. Property of Zero for Multiplication
8. Associative Property of Addition

TEACHING THE LESSON

After discussing the properties of integers, extend the instruction by having students find the missing integers or variables in equations such as the following.

$^{-}21 + 13 = \blacksquare + {}^{-}21$ (13)
$(^{-}8 \cdot 6) \cdot {}^{-}4 = {}^{-}8 \cdot (\blacksquare \cdot {}^{-}4)$ (6)
$d \cdot 1 = 1 \cdot \blacksquare$ (d)
$p(q + r) = (\blacksquare \cdot q) + (\blacksquare \cdot r)$ (p, p)

Properties of Integers

The properties for the addition and multiplication of whole numbers also apply to integers. The letters a, b, and c represent integers.

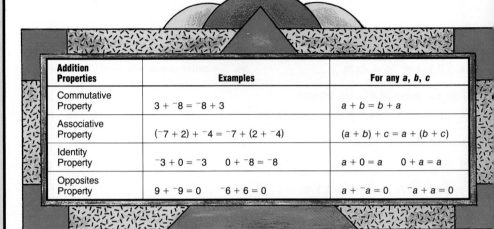

Addition Properties	Examples	For any a, b, c
Commutative Property	$3 + {}^{-}8 = {}^{-}8 + 3$	$a + b = b + a$
Associative Property	$({}^{-}7 + 2) + {}^{-}4 = {}^{-}7 + (2 + {}^{-}4)$	$(a + b) + c = a + (b + c)$
Identity Property	$^{-}3 + 0 = {}^{-}3 \qquad 0 + {}^{-}8 = {}^{-}8$	$a + 0 = a \qquad 0 + a = a$
Opposites Property	$9 + {}^{-}9 = 0 \qquad {}^{-}6 + 6 = 0$	$a + {}^{-}a = 0 \qquad {}^{-}a + a = 0$

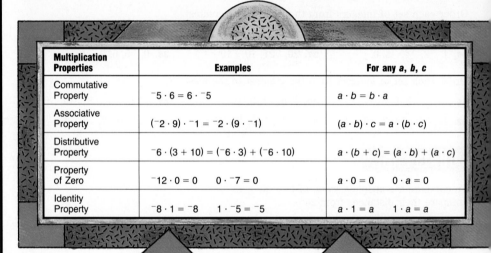

Multiplication Properties	Examples	For any a, b, c
Commutative Property	$^{-}5 \cdot 6 = 6 \cdot {}^{-}5$	$a \cdot b = b \cdot a$
Associative Property	$(^{-}2 \cdot 9) \cdot {}^{-}1 = {}^{-}2 \cdot (9 \cdot {}^{-}1)$	$(a \cdot b) \cdot c = a \cdot (b \cdot c)$
Distributive Property	$^{-}6 \cdot (3 + 10) = ({}^{-}6 \cdot 3) + ({}^{-}6 \cdot 10)$	$a \cdot (b + c) = (a \cdot b) + (a \cdot c)$
Property of Zero	$^{-}12 \cdot 0 = 0 \qquad 0 \cdot {}^{-}7 = 0$	$a \cdot 0 = 0 \qquad 0 \cdot a = 0$
Identity Property	$^{-}8 \cdot 1 = {}^{-}8 \qquad 1 \cdot {}^{-}5 = {}^{-}5$	$a \cdot 1 = a \qquad 1 \cdot a = a$

242

COMMON ERRORS

Students often misplace signs when completing equations demonstrating properties.

Remediation
Have students circle each sign at the left side of the example before completing it. After completing the example, students can review the problem to determine whether the signs have been handled correctly. They need not concentrate on the numbers.

Assign Reteach Master, p. 70.

RETEACH | **Properties of Integers**

Cindy and Donald were vacationing at the beach. The first day, Cindy found 15 seashells and Donald found 18. The second day, Cindy found 18 shells and Donald found 15. Without adding, which property can you use to show that they each found the same number of shells?

Remember
The Commutative Property of Addition
$15 + 18 = 18 + 15$

The 15 and 18 have **commuted**, or changed places.

Use the properties of integers to find the missing integers.

1. $2 + ({}^{-}5) = ({}^{-}5) + \underline{2}$
2. $(3 + 8) + \underline{5} = 3 + (8 + 5)$
3. $6(3 + 5) = 6 \cdot \underline{3} + 6 \cdot 5$
4. $^{-}10({}^{-}5 + 7) = {}^{-}10 \cdot {}^{-}5 + {}^{-}10 \cdot \underline{7}$
5. $9 + \underline{0} = 9$
6. $\underline{15} + 0 = 15$
7. $24 \cdot \underline{1} = 24$
8. $\underline{^{-}37} \cdot 1 = {}^{-}37$
9. $12 + \underline{^{-}12} = 0$
10. $\underline{13} + {}^{-}13 = 0$

Write the property.

11. $5(6 + 8) = 5 \cdot 6 + 5 \cdot 8$ — Distributive
12. $({}^{-}3 + 5) + 7 = {}^{-}3 + (5 + 7)$ — Associative
13. $9 + 0 = 9$ — Identity Property of Addition
14. $25 \cdot 1 = 25$ — Identity Property of Multiplication
15. $^{-}7 + 7 = 0$ — Opposite
16. $^{-}13 \cdot 0 = 0$ — Multiplication of zero
17. $^{-}12 + {}^{-}25 = {}^{-}25 + {}^{-}12$ — Commutative Property of Addition
18. $9 \cdot {}^{-}2 = {}^{-}2 \cdot 9$ — Commutative Property of Multiplication

70 | Use with pages 242–243

Reteach Worksheet

Use the properties to find the missing integer.

1. $7 + {}^-11 = \blacksquare + 7$ ${}^-11$

2. ${}^-12 + 0 = \blacksquare$ ${}^-12$

3. ${}^-5 + (3 + {}^-10) = ({}^-5 + \blacksquare) + {}^-10$ 3

4. ${}^-8 \cdot 0 = \blacksquare$ 0

5. ${}^-9 \cdot (6 \cdot 5) = ({}^-9 \cdot 6) \cdot \blacksquare$ 5

6. $13 \cdot {}^-18 = {}^-18 \cdot \blacksquare$ 13

7. $5 + {}^-5 = \blacksquare$ 0

8. $7 \cdot ({}^-10 + 6) = (7 \cdot \blacksquare) + (7 \cdot 6)$ ${}^-10$

9. ${}^-4 \cdot \blacksquare = {}^-20 \cdot {}^-4$ ${}^-20$

10. $(17 + \blacksquare) + {}^-1 = 17 + (8 + {}^-1)$ 8

11. $16 \cdot ({}^-8 \cdot \blacksquare) = (16 \cdot {}^-8) \cdot 14$ 14

12. ${}^-22 \cdot (6 + \blacksquare) = ({}^-22 \cdot 6) + ({}^-22 \cdot 5)$ 5

13. ${}^-3 \cdot 0 = n$ 0

14. $n \cdot 1 = {}^-12$ ${}^-12$

15. $n + 0 = {}^-32$ ${}^-32$

16. ${}^-19 + n = 10 + {}^-19$ 10

17. $(n + 0) + 6 = {}^-4 + (0 + 6)$ ${}^-4$

18. ${}^-4 + n = 0$ 4

Use the Commutative Property to write an equivalent expression.

19. ${}^-8 + 7$ $7 + {}^-8$

20. $13 \cdot {}^-9$ ${}^-9 \cdot 13$

21. ${}^-22 \cdot {}^-20$ ${}^-20 \cdot {}^-22$

22. $43 + {}^-81$ ${}^-81 + 43$

23. $n + 2$ $2 + n$

24. $3 \cdot r$ $r \cdot 3$

25. $x + {}^-9$ ${}^-9 + x$

26. $y \cdot {}^-8$ ${}^-8 \cdot y$

Use the Associative Property to write an equivalent expression.

27. $10 + ({}^-9 + {}^-15)$ $(10 + {}^-9) + {}^-15$

28. $(38 \cdot {}^-2) \cdot {}^-3$ $38 \cdot ({}^-2 \cdot {}^-3)$

29. $7 \cdot (56 \cdot {}^-31)$ $(7 \cdot 56) \cdot {}^-31$

30. ${}^-9 + ({}^-6 + x)$ $({}^-9 + {}^-6) + x$

31. ${}^-8 \cdot (y \cdot {}^-4)$ $({}^-8 \cdot y) \cdot {}^-4$

32. $(16 \cdot {}^-16) \cdot {}^-r$ $16 \cdot ({}^-16 \cdot {}^-r)$

Use the Distributive Property to write an equivalent expression.

33. $5 \cdot ({}^-8 + 10)$ $(5 \cdot {}^-8) + (5 \cdot 10)$

34. $(6 \cdot y) + (6 \cdot x)$ $6 \cdot (y + x)$

35. $({}^-8 \cdot 21) + ({}^-8 \cdot 5)$ ${}^-8 \cdot (21 + 5)$

36. $x \cdot (6 + 4)$ $(x \cdot 6) + (x \cdot 4)$

★37. $({}^-37 + 3) \cdot {}^-16$ $({}^-16 \cdot {}^-37) + ({}^-16 \cdot 3)$

★38. $({}^-8 + 8) \cdot y$ $(y \cdot {}^-8) + (y \cdot 8)$

CALCULATOR

To find the prime factorization of a number on a calculator, divide by the lowest prime number (2, 3, 5, 7, 11, …) until you get a whole number. Continue to divide each resulting quotient by the least prime number that gives a whole number as an answer. $40 \div 2 \to 20 \div 2 \to 10 \div 2 \to 5$ So $40 = 2^3 \cdot 5$. Use a calculator to find the prime factorization.

1. 24 $2^3 \cdot 3$ **2.** 100 $2^2 \cdot 5^2$ **3.** 525 $3 \cdot 5^2 \cdot 7$ **4.** 1,617 $3 \cdot 7^2 \cdot 11$

Classwork/Homework, page H97

243

ASSIGNMENT GUIDE

Basic: 1–31 *o*, 33–35, Calc

Average: 2–32 *e*, 33–36, Calc

Extended: 10–32 *e*, 33–38, Calc

Resources
Practice, p. 97   Class/Home, p. H97
Reteach, p. 70
Enrich, p. 91

Exercise Analysis
1–18 Find the missing integer
19–26 Apply the Commutative Property
27–32 Apply the Associative Property
33–38 Apply the Distributive Property

Calculator
For these exercises, students should keep a tally of the number of times they have divided by the lowest prime number.

FOLLOW-UP ACTIVITIES

PUZZLES AND GAMES
Materials: 30 index cards

On each of the first 15 cards, write the name of one of the addition or multiplication properties of integers. On the next 15 cards, write a numerical example for each property (${}^-8 + 6 = 6 + {}^-8$).

Keep the cards separate, shuffle each pile and then place them face down. A volunteer chooses 2 cards in an attempt to match the cards, that is, to match the property with the example. Other students should verify each match. When a match has been made, the cards should be removed. Play continues until all cards have been matched.

COMING UP
Learning to be divisive with integers

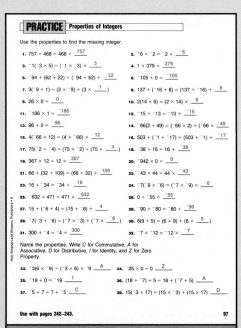

Practice Worksheet

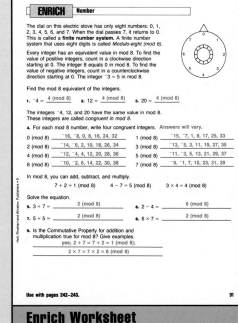

Enrich Worksheet

Warm-Up

Have students copy and complete the following table.

Integer	Opposite	Absolute value
$^+7$		
$^-9$		
0		
$^-45$		
$^-392$		

GETTING STARTED

Materials: balance, paper clips, strip of paper, pencil per group

Have students work in small groups to make number scales for their balances. They should position the strip of paper behind the pointer of the balance. Then they should place one paper clip at a time in the right pan and write positive integers 1, 2, 3, and so on to indicate the pointer position after each paper clip has been added. Have them remove the paper clips from the right pan and repeat the procedure for the left pan. Tell them to mark $^-1$, $^-2$, $^-3$, . . . for the pointer position after each paper clip has been added. Tell them also that they will use the scale to add integers and that positive integers will go on the right and negative integers will go on the left. Give them the following example: $4 + ^-2$. Have students put four paper clips on the right pan and two on the left. Ask them to read the scale (2). Repeat by using these examples: $3 + ^-2$ (1); $^-2 + 1$ (3).

TEACHING THE LESSON

A. Extend the instruction by using a number line to add the following.

$$3 + 5; \quad ^-2 + ^-4$$

B. Emphasize the fact that the sum of two positive integers will always be positive; the sum of two negative integers will always be negative.

C. Explain that integers that have opposite signs represent distances from 0 in opposite directions. When such integers are added, the shorter distance "cancels" part of the longer. The sum is what remains of the longer (the difference between the two absolute values) and carries its sign. Encourage each student who encounters difficulty to draw a number line.

Adding Integers

A. The entrance to a cave is 20 m below the surface. The main chamber's floor is 30 m below the entrance. Write an integer for the location of the main chamber's floor. To find the location of the main chamber's floor, use a number line and start at 0. Add $^-20 + ^-30$.

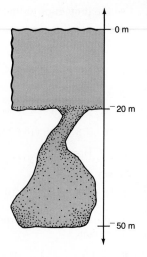

Begin at 0, and move left to 20. From there, move left 30 more.

The main chamber's floor is 50 m below the surface. This is written as $^-50$.

B. If two integers have the same sign, add their absolute values, and use the sign of the addends.

$$20 + 30 \rightarrow |20| + |30| \rightarrow 50 \qquad ^-20 + ^-30 \rightarrow |20| + |30| \rightarrow ^-50$$

C. You can also add integers with unlike signs.

Add $6 + ^-5$.

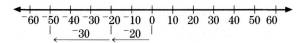

Begin at 0, and move right to 6. From there, move 5 to the left.

$$6 + ^-5 = 1$$

Add $^-6 + 5$.

Begin at 0, and move left to $^-6$. From there, move 5 to the right.

$$^-6 + 5 = ^-1$$

To find the sum of two integers that have different signs, subtract their absolute values. Then use the sign of the addend that has the greater absolute value.

$$6 + ^-5 \rightarrow |6| - |^-5| \rightarrow 1$$
$$^-6 + 5 \rightarrow |^-6| - |5| \rightarrow ^-1$$

COMMON ERRORS

Students are sometimes confused about why $^-6$ is less than $^-5$ but has a greater absolute value.

Remediation

Absolute value refers to the distance of an integer from 0 irrespective of its sign. Use a number line to show that any integer to the left of 0 is less than any integer to its right and greater than any integer to its left, as was the case for whole numbers.

Assign Reteach Master, p. 71.

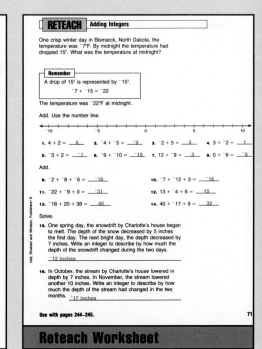

RETEACH Adding Integers

One crisp winter day in Bismarck, North Dakota, the temperature was $^-7$°F. By midnight the temperature had dropped 15°. What was the temperature at midnight?

Remember
A drop of 15° is represented by $^-15$°.
$$^-7 + ^-15 = ^-22$$

The temperature was $^-22$°F at midnight.

Add. Use the number line.

1. $4 + 2 =$ ___6___   2. $^-4 + ^-5 =$ ___$^-9$___   3. $^-2 + 5 =$ ___3___   4. $3 + ^-2 +$ ___1___

5. $^-3 + 2 =$ ___$^-1$___   6. $^-9 + ^-10 =$ ___$^-19$___   7. $12 + ^-9 =$ ___3___   8. $0 + ^-6 =$ ___$^-6$___

Add.

9. $^-2 + ^-8 + ^-6 =$ ___$^-16$___   10. $^-7 + ^-12 + 3 =$ ___$^-16$___

11. $^-22 + ^-9 + 0 =$ ___$^-31$___   12. $13 + ^-4 + 6 =$ ___15___

13. $^-18 + 20 + 38 =$ ___40___   14. $40 + ^-17 + 9 =$ ___32___

Solve.

15. One spring day, the snowdrift by Charlotte's house began to melt. The depth of the snow decreased by 5 inches the first day. The next bright day, the depth decreased by 7 inches. Write an integer to describe by how much the depth of the snowdrift changed during the two days.
___$^-12$ inches___

16. In October, the stream by Charlotte's house lowered in depth by 7 inches. In November, the stream lowered another 10 inches. Write an integer to describe by how much the depth of the stream had changed in the two months. ___$^-17$ inches___

Use with pages 244–245.   71

Reteach Worksheet

Add. Use the number line.

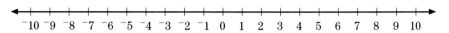

1. 3 + 2 5
2. ⁻4 + ⁻3 ⁻7
3. ⁻5 + 2 ⁻3
4. 3 + ⁻1 2
5. (⁻4 + 2) + ⁻1 ⁻3
6. (⁻2 + ⁻3) + ⁻4 ⁻9
7. (6 + ⁻1) + ⁻2 3
8. (⁻3 + ⁻2) + 0 ⁻5

Add.

9. 7 + 4 11
10. ⁻3 + ⁻6 ⁻9
11. ⁻10 + ⁻21 ⁻31
12. 18 + 32 50
13. 12 + ⁻8 4
14. 6 + ⁻2 4
15. ⁻7 + 18 11
16. 18 + ⁻7 11
17. ⁻10 + 8 ⁻2
18. 25 + ⁻30 ⁻5
19. 81 + ⁻72 9
20. ⁻72 + 81 9
21. ⁻7 + 9 2
22. ⁻46 + ⁻1 ⁻47
23. 12 + ⁻12 0
24. 62 + ⁻80 ⁻18
25. 3 + ⁻114 ⁻111
26. ⁻7 + 8 1
27. ⁻356 + ⁻85 ⁻441
28. ⁻211 + 437 226
29. ⁻2 + (⁻6 + ⁻8) ⁻16
30. (⁻2 + ⁻6) + ⁻8 ⁻16
31. (⁻9 + ⁻22) + 0 ⁻31
32. 14 + (⁻3 + 6) 17
33. (28 + 30) + ⁻18 40
34. 28 + (30 + ⁻18) 40
35. (⁻10 + ⁻10) + 25 5
36. 47 + (⁻130 + ⁻2) ⁻85
37. (⁻45 + 8) + ⁻23 ⁻60
38. ⁻611 + (89 + 12) ⁻510
39. (⁻611 + 89) + 12 ⁻510
40. (338 + 109) + ⁻447 0

Solve. For Problem 42, use the Infobank.

41. The depth of the deepest point in the Atlantic Ocean is 30,246 ft below sea level. The deepest point in the Pacific Ocean is 5,052 ft lower. What is the depth of the deepest point in the Pacific Ocean? 35,298 ft

42. Use the information on page 476 to solve. Find the span of years between the founding of Geneva and the founding of Madrid. 950 years

NUMBER SENSE

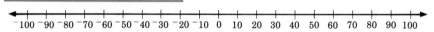

Solve.

1. Start at 0. Add 30. Subtract 40. Add 10. Subtract 50. ⁻50
2. Start at 0. Subtract 50. Add 20. Subtract 40. Add 70. Add 20. 20
3. Start at ⁻20. Subtract 30. Add 60. Add 20. Subtract 80. Add 100. 50

Classwork/Homework, page H98   245

pages 244-245

ASSIGNMENT GUIDE

Basic: 1–8, 9–41 o, NS
Average: 1–7 o, 10–42 e, NS
Extended: 10–42 e, NS

Resources
Practice, p. 98   Class/Home, p. H98
Reteach, p. 71   Reasoning, p. H219
Enrich, p. 92

Exercise Analysis

1–8   Add integers by using a number line
9–28   Add integers
29–40   Add three integers
41–42   Skill applications

Number Sense

This activity provides practice in adding and subtracting integers that are multiples of 10, using a number line.

FOLLOW-UP ACTIVITIES

MATH CONNECTION (Consumer) A clothing store keeps a log of its sales and its daily cost of doing business. Its profit-and-loss statement for a typical week is shown below. Have students calculate the store's net profit for each day of the week and the total week.

DAY	INCOME ($)	EXPENSES ($)	PROFIT ($)
Monday	⁺135	⁻65	(⁺70)
Tuesday	⁺88	⁻101	(⁻13)
Wednesday	⁺215	⁻142	(⁺73)
Thursday	⁺177	⁻125	(⁺52)
Friday	⁺150	⁻172	(⁻22)

(The weekly net profit is $160.)

NUMBER SENSE (Mental Math) Have students find compatible integers that will facilitate addition.

⁻25 + ⁻35 + 25 = (⁻35)
64 + ⁻25 + ⁻14 = (25)
⁻13 + 18 + ⁻7 + 12 = (10)
87 + ⁻15 + ⁻17 + 15 = (70)

COMING UP

Watch out for falling temperatures!

PRACTICE Adding Integers

Add.
1. 11 + 5 = 16
2. 2,931 + ⁻685 = 2,246
3. 458 + ⁻393 = 65
4. ⁻62 + ⁻71 = ⁻133
5. 674 + ⁻39 + 102 = 737
6. ⁻603 + 906 = 303
7. 815 + 281 = 1,096
8. 9 + ⁻12 = ⁻3
9. ⁻763 + 54 = ⁻709
10. (36 + ⁻27) + 446 = 455
11. ⁻698 + (⁻32 + 250) = ⁻480
12. ⁻8,815 + ⁻9,776 = ⁻18,591
13. ⁻310 + ⁻908 = ⁻1,218
14. (358 + 1,024) + ⁻761 = 621
15. 562 + ⁻593 = ⁻31
16. ⁻176 + ⁻229 = ⁻405
17. 103 + ⁻702 = ⁻599
18. ⁻894 + ⁻979 = ⁻1,873
19. ⁻84 + ⁻22 = ⁻106
20. 94 + ⁻87 = 7
21. (⁻95 + 521) + ⁻299 = 127
22. ⁻838 + ⁻719 = ⁻1,557
23. ⁻1,432 + 1,098 = ⁻334
24. 239 + ⁻184 + ⁻313 = ⁻258
25. ⁻51 + ⁻98 = ⁻149
26. 952 + ⁻398 = 554

Can you drive through Integer City? Find the sum of the first two integers and write your answer in the first circle. Find the sum of your answer and the next integer, and write it in the circle that follows. Continue in this way to drive through Integer City.

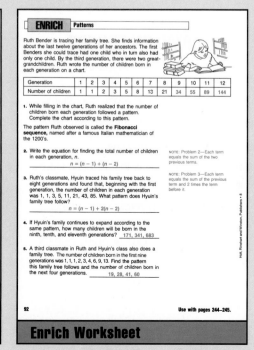

98   Use with pages 244–245.

Practice Worksheet

ENRICH Patterns

Ruth Bender is tracing her family tree. She finds information about the last twelve generations of her ancestors. The first Benders she could trace had one child who in turn also had only one child. By the third generation, there were two great-grandchildren. Ruth wrote the number of children born in each generation on a chart.

Generation	1	2	3	4	5	6	7	8	9	10	11	12
Number of children	1	1	2	3	5	8	13	21	34	55	89	144

1. While filling in the chart, Ruth realized that the number of children born each generation followed a pattern. Complete the chart according to this pattern.

The pattern Ruth observed is called the **Fibonacci sequence**, named after a famous Italian mathematician of the 1200's.

2. Write the equation for finding the total number of children in each generation, n.

NOTE: Problem 2—Each term equals the sum of the two previous terms.

$$n = (n - 1) + (n - 2)$$

3. Ruth's classmate, Hyuin traced his family tree back to eight generations and found that, beginning with the first generation, the number of children in each generation was 1, 1, 3, 5, 11, 21, 43, 85. What pattern does Hyuin's family tree follow?

NOTE: Problem 3—Each term equals the sum of the previous term and 2 times the term before it.

$$n = (n - 1) + 2(n - 2)$$

4. If Hyuin's family continues to expand according to the same pattern, how many children will be born in the ninth, tenth, and eleventh generations? 171, 341, 683

5. A third classmate in Ruth and Hyuin's class also does a family tree. The number of children born in the first nine generations was 1, 1, 2, 3, 4, 6, 9, 13. Find the pattern this family tree follows and the number of children born in the next four generations. 19, 28, 41, 60

92   Use with pages 244–245.

Enrich Worksheet

245

Objective: To subtract integers

Warm-Up

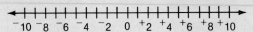

Have students use the number line to find
- the integer that is 4 units to the right of 1 (5); ⁻2 (2); 0 (4); ⁻4. (0);
- the integer that is 5 units to the left of ⁻1 (⁻6); 3 (⁻2); 4 (⁻1); ⁻3. (⁻8)

GETTING STARTED

Write the following expressions, and ask which two are equivalent.

$5 - 1$ $5 + 1$ $5 + {}^-1$

After students have identified the first and third as equivalent, have them try these.

$6 + {}^-3$ $6 + 3$ $6 - 3$

Summarize the results.

$5 - 1 = 4$ $6 + {}^-3 = 3$
$5 + {}^-1 = 4$ $6 - 3 = 3$
$5 - 1 = 5 + {}^-1$ $6 - 3 = 6 + {}^-3$

Discuss why the expressions are equal.

TEACHING THE LESSON

Use a number line to help students understand the subtraction of integers.

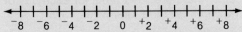

Remind students that they can use inverse operations to find a missing number; for example $8 - 3 = n$. Think: $3 + n = 8$.

Have students apply the same strategy to subtract the following.

$6 - 2$ $^-9 - {}^-3$
$1 - 4$ $^-3 - {}^-5$
$10 - {}^-3$ $^-8 - 2$

Checkpoint
The chart lists the common errors students make when subtracting integers.

Correct Answers: 1b, 2d, 3b, 4b

Remediation
■ Have students practice writing opposites to simplify subtraction examples.

$^-3 - 4 \ ({}^-3 + {}^-4)$
$12 - 8 \ (12 + {}^-8)$
$5 - 9 \ (5 + {}^-9)$
$^-8 - {}^-6 \ ({}^-8 + 6)$

△ For this error, refer students to examples on p. 7.

☐ For these errors, assign Reteach Master, p. 72.

Subtracting Integers

A scientist stationed at the McMurdo research station in Antarctica recorded a temperature drop of 4°F between morning and evening. The temperature in the morning was ⁻28°F. What was the temperature after the drop?

To find the temperature at McMurdo, subtract.

Refer to the picture of the thermometer. $^-28 - 4 = {}^-32$

Another way to subtract an integer is to add its opposite.

$^-28 - 4$
$^-28 + {}^-4 = {}^-32$

The temperature after the drop was ⁻32°F.

Other examples:

Subtract.

$^-7 - {}^-6$	$10 - 12$	$25 - {}^-14$
↓ ↓	↓ ↓	↓ ↓
$^-7 + 6 = {}^-1$	$10 + {}^-12 = {}^-2$	$25 + 14 = 39$
$^-7 - {}^-6 = {}^-1$	$10 - 12 = {}^-2$	$25 - {}^-14 = 39$

Checkpoint Write the letter of the correct answer.

Subtract.

1. $^-5 - 2$ a. $^-10$ ⓑ $^-7$ c. $^-3$ d. 3

2. $9 - {}^-4$ a. $^-13$ b. $^-5$ c. 5 ⓓ 13

3. $^-11 - {}^-2$ a. $^-14$ ⓑ $^-9$ c. 9 d. 13

4. $4 - 14$ a. $^-18$ ⓑ $^-10$ c. $^-4$ d. 18

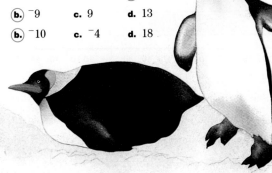

246

COMMON ERRORS

Answer Choice	Type of Error
☐ 1a, 4d	Uses the wrong operation
☐ 1c, 2b	Subtracts the absolute values and applies the sign of greater or lesser value
■ 1d, 2c	Subtracts the absolute values
■ 2a, 3c	Uses the wrong sign
△ 3a, 4c	Makes error in basic facts
☐ 3d, 4a	Subtracts incorrectly after assuming the wrong sign for one integer

---

Rewrite each using addition.

1. $^-5 - 6$
   $^-5 + ^-6$
2. $9 - ^-4$
   $9 + 4$
3. $7 - 9$
   $7 + ^-9$
4. $^-4 - ^-6$
   $^-4 + 6$
5. $14 - 20$
   $14 + ^-20$
6. $^-10 - 30$
   $^-10 + ^-30$
7. $^-11 - ^-2$
   $^-11 + 2$
8. $8 - ^-9$
   $8 + 9$

Subtract.

9. $^-9 - 7$ $^-16$
10. $^-6 - 2$ $^-8$
11. $^-12 - 18$ $^-30$
12. $18 - ^-12$ 30

13. $14 - ^-3$ 17
14. $7 - ^-8$ 15
15. $21 - ^-1$ 22
16. $4 - ^-10$ 14

17. $^-5 - ^-4$ $^-1$
18. $^-11 - ^-6$ $^-5$
19. $^-8 - ^-5$ $^-3$
20. $8 - 5$ 3

21. $^-17 - ^-19$ 2
22. $^-6 - ^-3$ $^-3$
23. $^-56 - ^-61$ 5
24. $^-18 - ^-18$ 0

25. $7 - 41$ $^-34$
26. $15 - 20$ $^-5$
27. $38 - 167$ $^-129$
28. $49 - 50$ $^-1$

29. $12 - ^-8$ 20
30. $^-37 - 40$ $^-77$
31. $37 - ^-40$ 77
32. $8 - ^-111$ 119

33. $63 - 78$ $^-15$
34. $^-301 - ^-28$ $^-273$
35. $538 - 746$ $^-208$
36. $^-80 - ^-80$ 0

Compute. Perform operations within parentheses first.

37. $^-7 + (6 + 8)$ 7
38. $3 - (^-4 + 2)$ 5
39. $^-12 - (^-6 + ^-9)$ 3

40. $(^-18 - 4) + ^-7$ $^-29$
41. $^-36 - (4 + ^-8)$ $^-32$
42. $101 + (^-7 - ^-7)$ 101

43. $(^-36 - 31) + 18$ $^-49$
44. $(^-146 - 52) + ^-27$ $^-225$
45. $^-87 + (^-87 - 0)$ $^-174$

Solve.

46. The average temperature in Antarctica is $^-60°F$. In the winter, the temperature can drop another 60°. What would this temperature be? $^-120°F$

47. If the temperature is $^-46°C$ in the morning at an Antarctic research center, how many degrees must the temperature rise to reach 0°C? $46°C$

48. In Chicago the high for a day was 7°F and the low was $^-4°F$. What was the difference between the two temperatures? $11°F$

49. In Fargo, North Dakota, the high for a day was $^-5°F$ and the low was $^-17°F$. What was the difference between the two temperatures? $12°F$

Classwork/Homework, page H99

247

Exercise Analysis

1–8   Rewrite a subtraction example as addition
9–36   Subtract integers
37–45   Evaluate an expression that involves adding and subtracting integers
46–49   Skill applications

FOLLOW-UP ACTIVITIES

NUMBER SENSE (Mental Math)
Have students mentally compute the following.

$^-2 + ^-6 + 5$ ($^-3$)
$4 - 8 - ^-7$ (3)
$^-3 - 7 - ^-2$ ($^-8$)
$9 + ^-4 + ^-5$ (0)
$^-6 - ^-2 + 8$ (4)
$4 - ^-7 - 9 + ^-6$ ($^-4$)

PROBLEM SOLVING
A frog sits at the bottom of a 20-foot well. Every hour, it hops up 5 feet and then slides back 3 feet. At this rate, how long will it take for the frog to get out of the well? (The net gain every hour is 2 feet. But after eight hours, the frog will hop from a height of 16 feet to 21 feet, and will not slide back into the well.)

COMING UP
Get the picture?

Objectives: To use information from broken-line and bar graphs

Warm-Up

Have students compute averages for the following groups of numbers.
- 26, 42, 38, 29, 40, 53 (38)
- 7.4, 8.2, 5.0, 13.1, 9.6, 10.5, 11.3 (9.3)
- 0.21, 0.96, 0.42, 0.81, 10 (2.48)

GETTING STARTED

Discuss with students the uses of each of the following: broken-line graphs (for showing changes), bar graphs (for comparing data), double-bar graphs (for comparing two related sets of data), and circle graphs (for dividing a whole into parts). Have students give examples of specific types of information which might be shown on each type of graph. (Accept all reasonable answers.)

TEACHING THE LESSON

Broken-line and bar graphs are two of the most commonly used information sources. They are especially common in the business world where data on profits, sales, or production are frequently presented in graph form. Emphasize that broken-line graphs are usually used to show how a set of data changes over time and to spot trends. Profits and sales over a period of time are often charted this way. Bar graphs are used to compare data, such as the production rates of several manufacturing plants for a given month or year.

In using the graphs on page 248, be sure students know that they are dealing with monthly averages and that information for specific days or measurements cannot be found on the graphs. Also point out that the first interval on the vertical axis on each graph is condensed and that this is indicated by the jagged line.

Questions: Have students who encounter difficulty with the question define exactly what type of information the graph provides and develop a general idea of what that information is. By noticing the shape of the broken line or the heights of the bars, students should be able to formulate an idea about the data and trends.

Tools: Help students to see that the slope of a section of line indicates temperature increase or decrease and how drastic that change was, relative to other months. The answer to Problem 12 can be found by simply finding the longest bar.

A common error students might make in solving Problems 13–16 is that they may fail to realize that the vertical scales for the two graphs are different. Tell students that

PROBLEM SOLVING
Using Graphs

The broken-line graph below shows variations in the average monthly temperature in Fairbanks, Alaska.

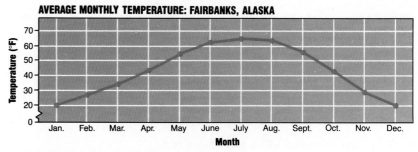

AVERAGE MONTHLY TEMPERATURE: FAIRBANKS, ALASKA

- The title describes the purpose of the graph.
- The scale along the vertical axis shows the temperature in degrees Fahrenheit. The temperature did not go below 20°F, and so, the graph shows a break in the scale between 20°F and 0°F.
- The labels along the horizontal axis show the months.
- Each point on the graph shows the average temperature for the month. Lines between the points make the graph easy to read.

The bar graph below shows the average monthly temperature in Juneau, Alaska.

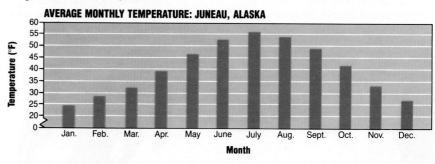

AVERAGE MONTHLY TEMPERATURE: JUNEAU, ALASKA

248

when comparing two graphs, it is always necessary to check the scales before making visual judgments. Students may also mistakenly infer intermediate temperatures on a broken-line graph. Point out that the lines simply connect the monthly averages to help show trends and do not indicate known information.

Solutions: Some subtraction is required. Be sure students realize that comparing two numbers requires subtraction.

Checks: Have students check to see that they have read the scale correctly (correct intervals, correct units), especially in comparing graphs. It is also fairly easy to estimate a reasonable range of answers for these problems.

ASSIGNMENT GUIDE

Basic: 1–6, 9–10

Average: 3–12

Extended: 5–16

Resources
Practice, p. 100   Class/Home, p. H100
Enrich, p. 94

Can you use the broken-line graph or the bar graph to answer each question? Write either *yes* or *no*.

1. What is the lowest average temperature in Fairbanks? **yes**

2. What was the temperature in Fairbanks on August 5? **no**

3. What is the hottest month in Juneau? **yes**

4. What was the temperature on the coldest day on record in Barrow? **no**

Use the broken-line graph to answer each question.

5. Between which months does the average temperature in Fairbanks increase?
January–July

6. Between which months does the average temperature in Fairbanks decrease?
July–December

7. Between which months does the average temperature not vary by more than 5 degrees?
June–July; July–August; December–January

8. Which average temperature change was greater, September to October or October to November?
September to October

Use the bar graph to answer each question.

9. Between which months does the average temperature in Juneau increase?
January–July

10. Between which months does the average temperature in Juneau decrease?
July–January

11. What is the difference in degrees between the highest and the lowest average temperatures in Juneau? **32°F**

12. Which is the hottest month in Juneau? **July**

Use the broken-line graph and the bar graph to answer each question.

13. Which city has the highest average temperature? During which month?
Fairbanks; July

14. Which city has the lowest average temperature? During which months?
Fairbanks; December, January

15. Which city has the greatest temperature increase between two months; between which months and how many degrees of difference? **Fairbanks; April–May; 11°F**

16. Which city has the least temperature difference between two months; which months and how many degrees of difference?
Fairbanks; December—January; 0°F

Classwork/Homework, page H100

Exercise Analysis

1–4 Decide whether the question can be answered from the graph
5–8 Use information from a broken-line graph to solve a problem
9–12 Use information from a bar graph to solve a problem
13–16 Compare information on two graphs to solve a problem

FOLLOW-UP ACTIVITIES

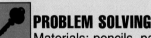
PROBLEM SOLVING
Materials: pencils, paper

Use the scores from an old math test to make a broken-line graph. Make a list on the chalkboard of the scores. Use an interval width of 5 points, and record the number of students whose score fell in each interval. Have students decide on a title for the graph and on labels for each of the scales. Then graph the points and connect them with lines. Explain to the students that a normal distribution of test scores would graph as a *bell curve*, the peak of the curve being the most common score. Discuss with students why a graph of scores might not show such a curve and how to make such a curve more likely.

MATH CONNECTION (Consumer)
Materials: newspapers from past several weeks

One set of data that often appears on a broken-line graph is a record of stock prices. Have students compile a chart of the Dow Jones Industrial average for the past several weeks. Explain that the average is that of a number of leading stocks and is used as a general indicator of stock-market trends and as one indicator of the strength of the economy. Have students graph the Dow Jones closing average for each day and connect these points with lines. They must decide on the numbers on the scales and then label and title the graph. Remind students that the first interval on the vertical scale should be condensed. Discuss the trends that can be seen from the graph.

COMING UP
Less is more, when multiplied by less.

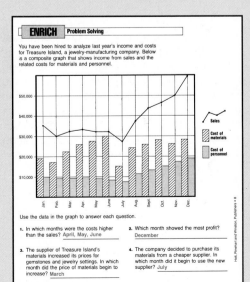

Practice Worksheet

Enrich Worksheet

Warm-Up

Have students multiply the following.

12 · 12 (144)   13 · 9 · 2 (234)
5 · 11 · 8 (440)   17 · 22 (374)

GETTING STARTED

Pose the following problem.

An oil company is exploring for oil. It uses negative integers to report the elevation of the drilling bit below the surface (e.g., it reports 8 m below the surface as ⁻8 m). Each day the company drills 8 m deeper into the group. At the end of 7 days, what is the elevation of the drill bit? (⁻56 m) At ⁻82 m the company hits oil and starts to withdraw the drill bit at 4 meters per hour. After 6 hours, what is the elevation of the drill bit? (⁻58 m)

Ask students to explain how they found the answers. Discuss whether there is a method that would be more efficient than repeated addition.

TEACHING THE LESSON

You may wish to have students work through the developmental parts of this lesson in groups of four and have a class discussion for Thinking as a Team.

Students should realize after reading the first two paragraphs that when the turtle moves backward and Dominick plays the tape in reverse, it appears as though the turtle is moving forward. This concept that the opposite of an opposite duplicates the original may serve as a model that will help students understand how the product of two negative integers is a positive number. In the first pattern of multiplication examples, students should see that the product decreases by a constant amount as the second factor decreases. Seeing this pattern will enable them to predict that when the second factor is less than zero, the product will also be less than zero. Students should also see that the products in the second pattern increase and should be able to predict that the product of two negative integers will be positive.

Have students work together to complete the table on page 251. Write the following exercises on the chalkboard, and ask for volunteers to give the products.

4 · ⁻3 (⁻12) ⁻7 · 6 (⁻42)   13 · ⁻5 (⁻65)
⁻8 · ⁻9 (72) 16 · ⁻8 (⁻128) ⁻15 · ⁻10 (150)

From the exercises given in question 1, students should conclude for question 2

Multiplying Integers

Dominick uses his video camera to record the actions of his remarkable pet turtle.

When the turtle moves forward and Dominick plays the video tape in reverse, what action appears on the screen? When the turtle moves backward, how does it appear on the screen if the tape is played normally? What would happen if the turtle were backing up and Dominick played the tape in reverse? the turtle moves in reverse; in reverse; forward

How does the remarkable turtle provide a model for finding the sign when you multiply integers? The rules work in parallel ways.

The following patterns suggest the rules that you might have discovered above.

Do you see a pattern developing in the right-hand column? Copy and complete the table.

$3 \times 3 = 9$
$3 \times 2 = 6$
$3 \times 1 = 3$
$3 \times 0 = 0$

How does the pattern suggest a general rule for multiplying a positive number by a negative number? It suggests their product is negative.

$3 \times {}^-1 = \blacksquare$ ⁻3
$3 \times {}^-2 = \blacksquare$ ⁻6
$3 \times {}^-3 = \blacksquare$ ⁻9

Do you recall why it is true that $3 \times {}^-3$ equals ${}^-3 \times 3$? because of the commutative property of multiplication

Copy and complete this table. Do you see a pattern in the right-hand column? yes

${}^-3 \times 3 = {}^-9$
${}^-3 \times 2 = {}^-6$
${}^-3 \times 1 = {}^-3$
${}^-3 \times 0 = 0$

How does this pattern suggest a general rule for finding the product of two negative numbers? It suggests their product is positive.

${}^-3 \times {}^-1 = \blacksquare$ 3
${}^-3 \times {}^-2 = \blacksquare$ 6
${}^-3 \times {}^-3 = \blacksquare$ 9

250

---

that when the number of negative factors is odd, the product is negative and that when the number of negative factors is even, the product is positive. For question 4, make sure that students realize that the double negative in Mr. Cyan's warning is equivalent to a positive statement. Ask them what parallels they can draw between this situation and the multiplication of integers.

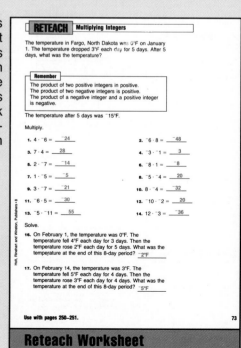

Thinking as a Team

Copy and complete the table shown below, using what you have learned about determining the sign of the product of two integers.

Discuss with your group how you determine the sign. Discuss ways to remember the rules for the sign of a product.

Sign of first number	Sign of second number	Sign of product	
positive	positive	■	positive
positive	negative	■	negative
negative	positive	■	negative
negative	negative	■	positive

1. What happens when more than two integers are multiplied?

Is $^-2 \times {}^-3 \times 4$ positive or negative? positive

What about $^-2 \times {}^-3 \times {}^-4$? negative

What about $^-2 \times {}^-3 \times {}^-4 \times {}^-5$? positive

Discuss with your group the methods you used to find these products?

2. Describe the patterns for the products when more than two negative integers are multiplied.

An odd number of negative factors gives a negative product; an even number gives a positive product.

3. On a local quiz show a player gets 10 points (+10) for each correct answer and loses 5 points ($^-5$) for each incorrect answer. After eight answers, the player has earned the following number of points:

$$10 + 10 + {}^-5 + 10 + {}^-5 + {}^-5 + {}^-5 + 10$$

Describe several different ways to find the player's score. Answers will vary—students could add or multiply.

4. Mr. Cyan told his children, "Be careful, that chemical is not nonpoisonous!" How could Mr. Cyan have warned his children by using a simpler phrase?

"Be careful, that chemical is poisonous!"

ASSIGNMENT GUIDE

Basic:	p. 250, p. 251
Average:	p. 250, p. 251
Extended:	p. 250, p. 251

Resources
Practice, p. 101   Class/Home, p. H101
Reteach, p. 73
Enrich, p. 95

FOLLOW-UP ACTIVITIES

PUZZLES AND GAMES
Have students complete the magic square below. The combined product of all the integers in any row, diagonal, or column is always the same. (216)

$(^+12)$	$^-1$	$(^-18)$
$(^-9)$	$^+6$	$^-4$
$^-2$	$(^-36)$	$^+3$

MATH CONNECTION (Science)
The velocity of a falling object is found by multiplying its acceleration by the time of its fall. (Velocity = acceleration × time.) Use the data below to find the velocity of an object that has fallen from an airplane.

Velocity (m/s)	Acceleration	Time
$(^-19.6)$	$^-9.8$ m/s^2	2 sec
$(^-49)$	$^-9.8$ m/s^2	5 sec
$(^-98)$	$^-9.8$ m/s^2	10 sec
$(^-147)$	$^-9.8$ m/s^2	15 sec

COMING UP
Multiplication's mate

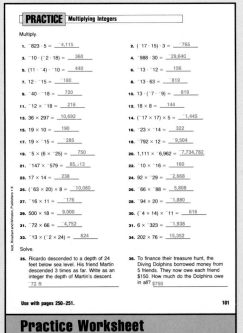

Practice Worksheet

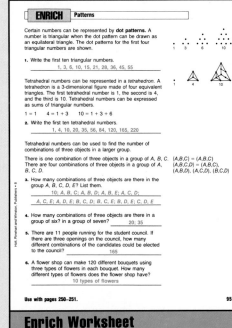

Enrich Worksheet

Objective: To explore the division of integers

Warm-Up

Have students find the product of the following factors.

$^-8 \cdot 9$ ($^-72$)

$^-12 \cdot {}^-34$ (408)

$28 \cdot {}^-17$ ($^-476$)

$^-6 \cdot (3 \cdot {}^-11)$ (198)

GETTING STARTED

Review multiplication as the inverse operation of division. Write $8 \times 7 = n$ on the chalkboard. Have students write the two related division problems ($n \div 7 = 8$, $n \div 8 = 7$). Tell the class that multiplication and division are inverse operations in problems involving integers as well. Write $^-18 \times {}^-5 = n$ on the chalkboard. Have students write the two related division problems ($n \div {}^-18 = {}^-5$, $n \div {}^-5 = {}^-18$).

TEACHING THE LESSON

There are two approaches that you can use in teaching this lesson: (1) have students work individually through the developmental parts and convene in groups of four to work on Thinking as a Team or (2) have students work through the developmental parts in groups of four and have a class discussion for Thinking as a Team.

Have students complete the multiplication sentences and the related division sentences. Students should be able to answer question 1 by looking at the patterns in these division sentences. Make sure that they are aware of the relationship between the rules for the multiplication of integers and those for the division of integers. For question 2, some discussion should be focused on calculators that do not operate on the basis of the method indicated. Point out that certain calculators cannot perform operations with negative integers such as $35 \div {}^-7$. Ask students how they could apply the rules they have formulated to perform the following exercises on such calculators.

$78 \div {}^-13$ ($^-6$) $^-152 \div 8$ ($^-19$)

$^-1,457 \div {}^-31$ (47)

For question 3, you may wish to review the order of operations with whole numbers.

Have students work through the problem on page 253 by first subtracting costs from sales to find the profit or loss for each time period. Elicit from them that they should use a positive integer in the case of a profit and a negative integer in the case of a loss to record their answers. Then have students divide to find each company's aver-

---

Dividing Integers

Just as multiplication and division of whole numbers are related, so are multiplication and division of integers. With that in mind, try these multiplication and division exercises mentally. Use multiplication to check the division results.

$7 \times 5 = \blacksquare$ 35 $35 \div 7 = \blacksquare$ 5

$^-7 \times 5 = \blacksquare$ $^-35$ $^-35 \div {}^-7 = \blacksquare$ 5

$7 \times {}^-5 = \blacksquare$ $^-35$ $^-35 \div 7 = \blacksquare$ $^-5$

$^-7 \times {}^-5 = \blacksquare$ 35 $35 \div {}^-7 = \blacksquare$ $^-5$

Did you get the correct sign in each case? Which answers are negative? Which are positive?

Thinking as a Team

1. What is the relationship between multiplication of integers and division of integers? Use what you have learned about multiplication of integers to write a set of rules for the division of integers. When is the quotient positive? When is the quotient negative?

   > If two integers have like signs, their quotient is positive; if two integers have unlike signs, their quotient is negative.

2. Can you use a calculator to divide integers? Not all calculators accept data in the same way. To divide 35 by $^-7$ on many calculators, you could do this:

   $\boxed{3}\ \boxed{5}\ \boxed{\div}\ \boxed{7}\ \boxed{+/-}\ \boxed{=}$

   Does your calculator work this way? What display results? Do any calculators in your group work differently?

   > $^-5$; some calculators require one to press the $\boxed{-}$ key before pressing $\boxed{7}$.

3. You use the same order of operations to simplify expressions that contain integers as you use to simplify expressions that contain whole numbers. Simplify the following expressions.

   $^-75 \div (^-5 - 10)$ 5

   $200 \div (^-25 \div 10)$ $^-80$

   $[18 \div (^-2)] \div [3 \times (^-3)]$ 1

252   Math Reasoning, page H219

---

age monthly profit or loss and multiply to predict each company's expected yearly profit or loss. Guide students to realize that the monthly and yearly figures are, at best, estimates and that the longer the period of time on which they are based, the most likely they are to be accurate.

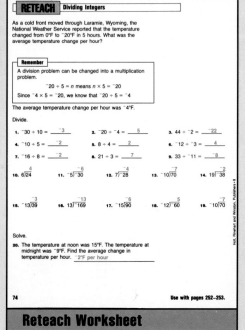

You are writing a social studies report on the companies that have opened in your city during the last year. In the newspaper you read the total sales and the total costs of each company for different periods of time. To find the company's profit or loss, you can subtract total costs from total sales. If the number is positive, then it is a profit. If the number is negative, then it is a loss.

Copy the table. Use positive and negative integers to represent the missing figures.

Company	Time Period	Total Sales	Total Costs	Profit or Loss	Yearly Profit or Loss	Monthly Profit or Loss
Perelli Plastics	3 mos.	80,000	89,000	⁻9,000	⁻36,000	⁻3,000
Smith Foundry	6 mos.	158,000	140,000	18,000	36,000	3,000
Dirks Tires	4 mos.	56,000	64,000	⁻8,000	⁻24,000	⁻2,000
Kraus Metal Co.	2 mos.	24,000	20,000	4,000	24,000	2,000
A-1 Advertising	3 mos.	19,000	17,600	1,400	5,600	466.67
Diamax Inc.	8 mos.	132,000	136,000	⁻4,000	⁻6,000	⁻500

Thinking as a Team

Review how you found the yearly and monthly figures for each company.

- Are the yearly and monthly figures exact? What does the yearly figure for each company mean? Do you think that the yearly and monthly figures are more accurate for some companies than for others? Discuss your answers and reasoning with the other teams in your class.

No; the expected profit or loss for the year; the greater the number of months reported, the more accurate the yearly and the average monthly figures are.

Classwork/Homework, page H102   **More Practice, page H201**   **253**

ASSIGNMENT GUIDE

Basic: p. 252, p. 253
Average: p. 252, p. 253
Extended: p. 252, p. 253

Resources
Practice, p. 102   Class/Home, p. H102
Reteach, p. 74   More Practice, p. H201
Enrich, p. 96   Reasoning, p. H219

FOLLOW-UP ACTIVITIES

PROBLEM SOLVING
Solve for *n* in the following.

$n + ^-22 = 41$ (63)
$4n - ^-10 = ^-62$ ($^-18$)
$n - 16 = ^-3$ (13)
$21n + ^-42 = 63$ (5)
$(^-48 - ^-96) \div (^-3 \cdot 4) = n$ ($^-4$)

NUMBER SENSE (Estimation)
Have students use rounding to estimate the following quotients.

$\frac{^-509}{21}$ ($^-25$) $\frac{^-396}{^-42}$ (10)

$\frac{1,211}{^-58}$ ($^-20$) $^-742 \div 47$ ($^-15$)

COMING UP
Expounding on exponents

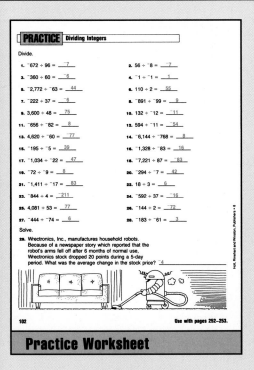

Practice Worksheet

Enrich Worksheet

253

Warm-Up

Have students evaluate

5^3 (125); 3^6 (729);
11^4 (14,641)

GETTING STARTED

Have students write the following numbers in scientific notation.

32,159 ($3.2159 \cdot 10^4$)
22,000,000 ($2.2 \cdot 10^7$)
987,000 ($9.87 \cdot 10^5$)

Have students write the standard form of the following.

$1.128 \cdot 10^2$ (112.8)
$4.85 \cdot 10^6$ (4,850,000)
$7.03 \cdot 10^0$ (7.03)

Point out that in each case, the value of the exponent indicates the number of places to the right the decimal point is moved.

TEACHING THE LESSON

A. Use the following examples to show how integers with exponents can be written as fractions. Positive exponents indicate the number of times the base number is a factor in the numerator. Negative exponents indicate the number of times the base number is a factor in the denominator.

$$10^3 = \frac{10 \cdot 10 \cdot 10}{1} \qquad 10^{-3} = \frac{1}{10 \cdot 10 \cdot 10}$$

$$8^{-2} = \frac{1}{8 \cdot 8} \qquad 7^5 = \frac{7 \cdot 7 \cdot 7 \cdot 7 \cdot 7}{1}$$

B. Ask students to explain why numbers such as $0.44 \cdot 10^8$ and $25.26 \cdot 10^8$ are not considered to be expressed in scientific notation.

C. Extend the instruction by having students write $1.823 \cdot 10^{-5}$ in standard form. (0.00001823)

D. Other examples:

$9^5 \cdot 9^3$ (9^8)
$2^7 \cdot 2^2$ (2^9)
$6^2 \cdot 6^3$ (6^5)

E. Extend the lesson by using the following example.

$$\frac{3^8 \cdot 3^{-2}}{3^1 \cdot 3^{-3}} \quad (3^8)$$

Integers as Exponents

A. You can use integers as exponents. Study the pattern.

$$10^1 = 10$$
$$10^0 = 1$$
$$10^{-1} = \frac{1}{10}$$
$$10^{-2} = \frac{1}{10^2} = \frac{1}{10 \cdot 10} = \frac{1}{100}$$

Other examples:

$$5^{-1} = \frac{1}{5}$$
$$3^{-2} = \frac{1}{3^2} = \frac{1}{3 \cdot 3} = \frac{1}{9}$$
$$10^{-3} = \frac{1}{10^3} = \frac{1}{10 \cdot 10 \cdot 10} = \frac{1}{1,000}$$

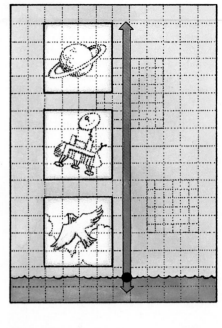

B. A very large number can be written in **scientific notation** by writing the number as a product of two factors. One factor is between 1 and 10. The other factor is a power of 10.

$42,500 = 4.25 \cdot 10,000$

So, $42,500 = 4.25 \cdot 10^4$.

C. Numbers less than 1 can be written in scientific notation by using a negative power of 10. To write $3.76 \cdot 10^{-4}$ in standard form, move the decimal point four places to the left.

$3.76 \cdot 10^{-4} = 0\ 0\ 0\ 0\ 3.7\ 6$

So, $3.76 \cdot 10^{-4} = 0.000376$.

D. Simplify $4^2 \cdot 4^3$.

$4^2 \cdot 4^3 = (4 \cdot 4) \cdot (4 \cdot 4 \cdot 4) = 4^5 = 1,024$

You can also multiply powers with the same base by adding the exponents.

$4^2 \cdot 4^3 = 4^{(2 + 3)} = 4^5$

Another example:

$3^4 \cdot 3^{-5} = 3^{(4 + {}^{-}5)} = 3^{-1}$

E. Simplify $6^4 \div 6^2$.

$6^4 \div 6^2 = \frac{6 \cdot 6 \cdot 6 \cdot 6}{6 \cdot 6} = 6 \cdot 6 = 6^2 = 36$

You can also divide powers with the same base by subtracting the exponents.

$6^4 \div 6^2 = 6^{(4 - 2)} = 6^2$

Another example:

$8^{-2} \div 8^{-5} = 8^{({}^{-}2 - {}^{-}5)} = 8^3$

254

COMMON ERRORS

Students might be confused about whether to add or subtract exponents with unlike signs when they multiply or divide.

Remediation
Have students write exercises in standard form to see which operation is appropriate.

$7^2 \cdot 7^{-6} =$

$$(7 \cdot 7) \cdot (\frac{1}{7 \cdot 7 \cdot 7 \cdot 7 \cdot 7 \cdot 7}) = \frac{7 \cdot 7}{7 \cdot 7 \cdot 7 \cdot 7 \cdot 7 \cdot 7}$$

$$\frac{1}{7 \cdot 7 \cdot 7 \cdot 7} = 7^{-4}$$

Assign Reteach Master, p. 75.

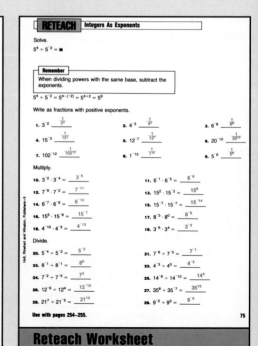

Write as fractions with positive exponents.

1. 2^{-2} $\frac{1}{2^2}$ **2.** 4^{-3} $\frac{1}{4^3}$ **3.** 8^{-6} $\frac{1}{8^6}$ **4.** 14^{-5} $\frac{1}{14^5}$

5. 21^{-8} $\frac{1}{21^8}$ **6.** 30^{-10} $\frac{1}{30^{10}}$ **7.** 142^{-14} $\frac{1}{142^{14}}$ **8.** 1^{-20} $\frac{1}{1^{20}}$

Write in scientific notation.

9. 0.143 $1.43 \cdot 10^{-1}$ **10.** 0.089 $8.9 \cdot 10^{-2}$ **11.** 0.0406 $4.06 \cdot 10^{-2}$ **12.** 0.000461 $4.61 \cdot 10^{-4}$

13. 0.000092 $9.2 \cdot 10^{-5}$ **14.** 0.000723 $7.23 \cdot 10^{-4}$ **15.** 0.00846 $8.46 \cdot 10^{-3}$ **16.** 0.000452 $4.52 \cdot 10^{-4}$

Write in standard form.

17. $2.5 \cdot 10^{-2}$ 0.025 **18.** $3.78 \cdot 10^{-4}$ 0.000378 **19.** $1.6 \cdot 10^{-6}$ 0.0000016 **20.** $7.219 \cdot 10^{-5}$ 0.00007219

21. $3.84 \cdot 10^{-8}$ 0.0000000384 **22.** $9.92 \cdot 10^{-9}$ 0.00000000992 **23.** $4.32 \cdot 10^{-3}$ 0.00432 **24.** $5.702 \cdot 10^{-7}$ 0.0000005702

Simplify.

25. $2^{-2} \cdot 2^{-4}$ 2^{-6} **26.** $5^{-1} \cdot 5^{-5}$ 5^{-6}

27. $8^{-9} \cdot 8^{-2}$ 8^{-11} **28.** $12^2 \cdot 12^{-2}$ 12^0, or 1

29. $7^{-6} \cdot 7^4$ 7^{-2} **30.** $16^{-8} \cdot 16^{-8}$ 16^{-16}

31. $10^{-6} \cdot 10^5$ 10^{-1} **32.** $22^{-10} \cdot 22^{-3}$ 22^{-13}

33. $6^{-4} \div 6^{-2}$ 6^{-2} **34.** $9^{-6} \div 9^{-5}$ 9^{-1}

35. $7^{-1} \div 7^{-1}$ 7^0, or 1 **36.** $5^{-4} \div 5^0$ 5^{-4}

37. $\frac{8^{-2}}{8^{-5}}$ 8^3 **38.** $\frac{13^{-6}}{13^{-10}}$ 13^4

39. $\frac{21^{-6}}{21^4}$ 21^{-10} **40.** $\frac{36^8}{36^{-7}}$ 36^{15}

For additional activities, see
Connecting Math Ideas on page 471.

MIDCHAPTER REVIEW

Compute.

1. $^-6 + 3 + ^-9$ $^-12$ **2.** $^-63 + 19 + ^-7$ $^-51$ **3.** $^-6 + ^-3 + ^-4$ $^-13$ **4.** $6 + ^-13 + ^-7$ $^-14$

5. $49 - 63$ $^-14$ **6.** $^-4 - ^-4$ 0 **7.** $8 - ^-11$ 19 **8.** $^-7 - 8$ $^-15$

9. $2 \cdot ^-3$ $^-6$ **10.** $^-12 \cdot ^-2$ 24 **11.** $1 \cdot ^-1$ $^-1$ **12.** $^-13 \cdot 7$ $^-91$

13. $\frac{32}{8}$ 4 **14.** $^-40 \div ^-2$ 20 **15.** $\frac{^-25}{^-5}$ 5 **16.** $^-144 \div 12$ $^-12$

Simplify.

17. $6^{-2} \cdot 6^{-3}$ 6^{-5} **18.** $10^{-3} \cdot 10^{13}$ 10^{10} **19.** $23^{-4} \div 23^0$ 23^{-4} **20.** $7^{-4} \div 7^{-2}$ 7^{-2}

Classwork/Homework, page H103

255

ASSIGNMENT GUIDE

Basic: 1–39 o, MCR

Average: 2–40 e, MCR

Extended: 2–40 e, MCR

Resources
Practice, p. 103   Class/Home, p. H103
Reteach, p. 75
Enrich, p. 97

Exercise Analysis

1–8 Write a negative exponent as a fraction with a positive exponent
9–16 Write a decimal in scientific notation
17–24 Write a number in scientific notation in standard form
25–32 Multiply numbers with negative exponents
33–40 Divide negative exponents

Midchapter Review

These exercises provide an opportunity for you and your students to assess their understanding of concepts and skills developed to this point in the chapter.

FOLLOW-UP ACTIVITIES

MATH CONNECTION
(Science)

Have students write each percent using scientific notation.

COMPOSITION OF DRY AIR

Substance	Percent	Scientific Notation
Nitrogen	78.1	$(7.81 \cdot 10^1)$
Oxygen	20.9	$(2.09 \cdot 10^1)$
Argon	0.934	$(9.34 \cdot 10^{-1})$
Helium	0.00053	$(5.3 \cdot 10^{-4})$
Neon	0.0018	$(1.8 \cdot 10^{-3})$

COMPUTER
Have students write a program that will print any decimal number less than 0 in scientific notation. The program below is a good start.

```
(10 LET E=1
20 INPUT N
30 LET S=N*10^E
40 IF S > =1 THEN 70
50 LET E=E+1
60 GOTO 30
70 PRINT S; "TIMES 10 TO THE NEGA-
   TIVE"; E
80 END)
```

COMING UP
Making perfect

Objective: To practice choosing and using methods and strategies for solving problems

Warm-Up

To prepare students for this lesson, have them compute the following.

64% of 3,910 (2,502.4)
117.64 is what percent of 692? (17%)
3,071.2 is 55% of what number? (5,584)

GETTING STARTED

Ask several student volunteers to come forward and write a word problem of their own on the chalkboard. Have other students in the class solve these problems.

TEACHING THE LESSON

These problem-solving pages allow students to choose strategies from those strategies already taught in the textbook. Students also choose the appropriate method for solving each problem. This means students must find an effective approach for each problem and must correctly implement the strategy and method they have chosen. Remind students that they should not stay stuck on a problem; they should try another approach or move on and return later. It might be helpful to have students work these problems in small groups. Encourage students to choose the most efficient method.

You may wish to review the problem-solving skills presented to this point in the text.

Estimation, pp. 9–11, 54–55, 136–137

4-Step Plan, pp. 16–17

Using Data from Outside Sources, Including Infobank, pp. 24–25

Using a Graph, pp. 32–33, 248–249

Identifying Extra/Needed Information, pp. 48–49

Choosing the Operation, pp. 62–63, 102–103

Solving Multistep Problems/Making a Plan, pp. 68–69

Checking for a Reasonable Answer, pp. 86–87

Using a Table, pp. 96–97

Writing an Equation, pp. 110–111

Using a Pictograph, pp. 126–127

Writing a Simpler Problem, pp. 144–145

Interpreting the Quotient and Remainder, pp. 154–155

Choosing/Writing a Sensible Question, pp. 172–173

Using a Formula, pp. 184–185, 222–223

Using a Road Map, pp. 190–191

Writing a Proportion, pp. 204–205

Making an Organized List, pp. 214–215

Using a Circle Graph, pp. 228–229

| QUESTIONS | TOOLS | SOLUTIONS | CHECKS |

PROBLEM SOLVING
Choosing a Strategy or Method

Write the strategy or method you choose. Then solve. Strategies and methods will vary.

1. For 9 years, an automobile maker produced an average of 3,425,600 cars per year. In the tenth year, the company made 2,747,500 cars. What was the average production rate for 10 years? Solving multi-step problems; 3,357,790 cars

2. From 1984 through 1989, Artie grew an average of $173\frac{1}{2}$ bushels of tomatoes per year. In 1990, he grew $185\frac{3}{4}$ bushels. What was the average number of bushels grown through 1990? Solving multi-step problems; $175\frac{1}{4}$ bushels

3. A hardware store sells solder in 25-foot rolls. Jerry needs 137 feet of solder. How many rolls does he need to buy? Interpreting the quotient; 6 rolls

4. A magazine distributor packs magazines in bundles of 50. How many bundles can be made from 35,700 magazines? Interpreting the quotient; 714 bundles

5. In 1987, the most money spent by a single advertiser was $1,557,800,000. Of this, 21% was spent on network TV. How much money did this advertiser spend on network TV? Choosing the operation; $327,138,000

6. How much of the total amount spent on advertising in Exercise 5 was not spent on network TV? Choosing the operation; $1,230,662,000

7. Last month, Robbie used the rowing machine $7\frac{1}{2}$ hours more than his father did. Robbie used the rowing machine for $35\frac{3}{4}$ hours. For how many hours did his father use the machine? Writing an equation; $28\frac{1}{4}$ hours

8. Carl made 6 equal payments on a new pair of ice skates. Each payment was $18.42. What was the total cost of the skates? Choosing the operation; $110.52

9. Susan has saved $150.00 to have 2 new tires put on her car. The tires cost $52.50 each, and the labor costs $18.50. Balancing costs $11.75. Does Susan have enough money to pay for everything? Estimation; yes

10. On Wednesday, 22 students visited a museum and paid a total of $116.60 for admission. They all paid the same amount. About how much was the admission per student? Estimation; about $5.00

Estimation
Using a Graph
Choosing the Operation
Solving Multi-step Problems
Checking for a Reasonable Answer
Writing an Equation
Interpreting the Quotient and the Remainder
Using a Formula
Using a Road Map
Making an Organized List

256

Solve if possible. Identify any needed information.

11. On their vacation, Marie and her family went from Portland, Maine, to Cleveland, Ohio. They spent $535.00. What were their average daily expenses?
need to know length of trip

12. Chris and Anita began to hike at 7:35 one morning. They hiked for $2\frac{1}{2}$ hours, stopped for 20 minutes, and hiked again for $1\frac{3}{4}$ hours. What time was it then? **12:10 P.M.**

Choose a strategy or method and solve.

13. A man on a unicycle set a record by traveling 100 miles in about $7\frac{3}{4}$ hours. What was his average rate of speed for the distance, rounded to the nearest mile per hour? **13 mph**

14. A team of cyclists rode at an average speed of 21 miles per hour for 2 hours 36 minutes. How far did they ride? **54.6 miles**

15. Dave's father bought a stereo for $857.50. He paid $90 down and arranged to finance the rest for one year at 19%. How much did he pay for the stereo? **$1,003.33**

16. Antonia paid $420.75 in interest on a loan of $1,700 for a period of 18 months. What was the rate of interest on the loan?
1.375% per month

17. Use the map at the right. What major route would you take from Macon to Atlanta, and how far would you travel?
Route 75; 80 miles

18. Use the map at the right. Driving at an average speed of 48 miles per hour, how long would it take to go from Chattanooga, Tennessee, to Atlanta, Georgia?
about 2 hours

19. Look back at the problems you have solved. Which of these problems seemed difficult? What strategy or method did you use? Is there more than one way to solve these problems? Share ideas with your classmates. **Answers will vary.**

Classwork/Homework, pages H104–H105

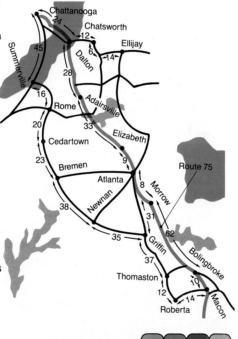

ASSIGNMENT GUIDE

Basic: 1–12

Average: 2–18 e

Extended: 1–19 o

Resources
Practice, pp. 104–5   Class/Home, pp. H104–5

Exercise Analysis
1–18   Choose an appropriate strategy or method

FOLLOW-UP ACTIVITIES

CALCULATOR
Materials: calculator per student

Have students take the number of the month of their birth and enter it into their calculators. Then have them multiply by 100 and add to that the date of their birth. They should then multiply by 2, add 9, multiply by 5, add 8, multiply by 10, and subtract 422. Students should then add the last two digits of the year of their birth and subtract 108. Ask what the result is. (The display should read their birth month, date, and year.)

CALCULATOR
Materials: calculator per student

Tell students it is possible to divide a dividend that has too many digits if they break apart the problem into two problems.

$$26\overline{)4{,}589{,}042{,}848}$$

- First divide the billions and millions with your calculator.

$$26\overline{)4{,}589\text{ million}} = 176\text{ R13 million}$$

- Add the remainder to the remainder of the dividend.

$$13{,}000{,}000 + 42{,}848 = 13{,}042{,}848$$

- Divide this sum by the divisor.

$$26\overline{)13{,}042{,}848} = 501{,}648$$

- Add the quotients. If there is a remainder from the last step, attach it to the quotient.

$$176{,}000{,}000$$
$$+\quad 501{,}648$$
$$\overline{176{,}501{,}648}$$

$$26\overline{)4{,}589{,}042{,}848} = 176{,}501{,}648$$

COMING UP
Numbers can be reasonable.

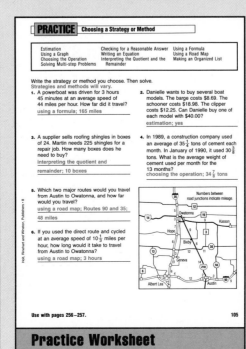

Objectives: To define and graph rational numbers

Warm-Up
Have students order the following fractions from the least to the greatest.

$\frac{2}{3}, \frac{5}{4}, \frac{4}{5}, 1\frac{3}{5}, 0, \frac{3}{2}$

$\left(0, \frac{2}{3}, \frac{4}{5}, \frac{5}{4}, \frac{3}{2}, 1\frac{3}{5}\right)$

GETTING STARTED

Draw the following.

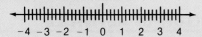

$-4 \quad -3 \quad -2 \quad -1 \quad 0 \quad 1 \quad 2 \quad 3 \quad 4$

Have volunteers come forward and locate the following points.

3	⁻4	$-1\frac{1}{5}$
3.2	⁻2.4	$\frac{-7}{5}$

Point out that in addition to showing positive and negative integers, a number line can also be used to show positive and negative fractions and mixed numbers.

TEACHING THE LESSON

A. Explain that a number is considered to be a rational number if it can be written as a fraction when both the numerator and the denominator are integers. All whole numbers are considered rational because they can be written as the ratio of themselves and 1 (for example, $5 = \frac{5}{1}$). Point out that 0 is also considered to be a rational number when it is written as the fraction $\frac{0}{9}$.

Note that any two rational numbers, a and ^-a, are *opposites* if their sum is 0.

B. Extend the instruction by having students order the following rational numbers from the least to the greatest.

$^-6.1, 0, \frac{-1}{2}, 0.45, \frac{-3}{9}, \frac{1}{3}$

$\left(^-6.1, \frac{-1}{2}, \frac{-3}{9}, 0, \frac{1}{3}, 0.45\right)$

Point out that when a rational number in decimal form is compared to one in fraction form, it is sometimes necessary to convert one to the other; for example, $0.75 = \frac{3}{4}$.

Rational Numbers

A. A **rational number** is a number that can be written as a ratio of two integers, where the denominator is not zero. Integers, fractions, and mixed numbers are rational numbers.

$^-3 = \frac{^-3}{1}$ So, $^-3$ is rational.

$^-1\frac{3}{5} = \frac{^-8}{5}$ So, $^-1\frac{3}{5}$ is rational.

$0.75 = \frac{3}{4}$ So, 0.75 is rational.

$0.\overline{3} = \frac{1}{3}$ So, $0.\overline{3}$ is rational.

Every rational number can be named by a terminating or a repeating decimal. A number such as 0.010010001 . . . is nonterminating and nonrepeating. 0.010010001 . . . represents a number that is not rational.

Point A is the rational number $^-2\frac{1}{2}$, or $^-2.5$.
Point B is the rational number $\frac{2}{3}$.
$\frac{^-2}{3}$ and $\frac{2}{3}$ are opposites. $^-2.5$ and 2.5 are opposites.

B. To compare two rational numbers, compare as you would compare integers. The number to the right on a number line is greater. The number to the left on the number line is less.

$^-3 < ^-1.\overline{3} \qquad 2\frac{1}{4} > \frac{^-2}{3}$

To order the rational numbers $0.75, 0, ^-1\frac{3}{5}, \frac{^-2}{3},$ and $\frac{2}{3}$ from the least to the greatest, think of the number line from the left to the right.

$^-1\frac{3}{5}, \frac{^-2}{3}, 0, \frac{2}{3}, 0.75$

To order the same rational numbers from the greatest to the least, think of the number line from the right to the left.

$0.75, \frac{2}{3}, 0, \frac{^-2}{3}, ^-1\frac{3}{5}$

Math Reasoning, page H220

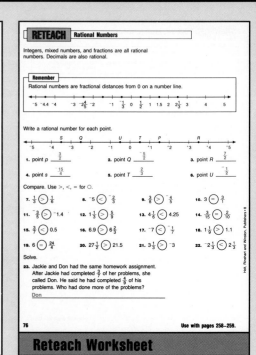

COMMON ERRORS

Students sometimes order rational numbers without regard to their signs as if all of them were positive.

Remediation
Have students group by sign the numbers to be ordered. If needed, have them plot each number on a number line. Then have students compare all the negative rational numbers before they compare the positive rational numbers.

Assign Reteach Master, p. 76.

RETEACH Rational Numbers

Integers, mixed numbers, and fractions are all rational numbers. Decimals are also rational.

Remember
Rational numbers are fractional distances from 0 on a number line.

$^-5 \quad ^-4.4 \quad ^-4 \qquad ^-3 \quad ^-2\frac{4}{5} \quad ^-2 \qquad ^-1 \quad \frac{^-1}{3} \quad 0 \quad \frac{1}{2} \quad 1 \quad 1.5 \quad 2 \quad 2\frac{2}{3} \quad 3 \qquad 4 \qquad 5$

Write a rational number for each point.

1. point p ___
2. point Q ___
3. point R ___
4. point s ___
5. point T ___
6. point U ___

Compare. Use >, <, = for ○.

7. $\frac{1}{3} ○ \frac{1}{6}$
8. $^-5 ○ \frac{^-2}{3}$
9. $\frac{3}{8} ○ \frac{4}{5}$
10. $3 ○ \frac{3}{4}$
11. $\frac{^-3}{5} ○ ^-1.4$
12. $1\frac{1}{3} ○ \frac{5}{3}$
13. $4\frac{1}{8} ○ 4.25$
14. $\frac{3}{5} ○ \frac{2}{10}$
15. $\frac{3}{4} ○ 0.5$
16. $6.9 ○ 6\frac{2}{3}$
17. $^-7 ○ \frac{^-1}{7}$
18. $1\frac{1}{3} ○ 1.1$
19. $6 ○ \frac{24}{4}$
20. $27\frac{1}{2} ○ 21.5$
21. $3\frac{1}{3} ○ ^-3$
22. $^-2\frac{1}{3} ○ 2\frac{1}{3}$

Solve.

23. Jackie and Don had the same homework assignment. After Jackie had completed $\frac{3}{4}$ of her problems, she called Don. He said he had completed $\frac{4}{5}$ of his problems. Who had done more of the problems?
Don

76   Use with pages 258–259.

Reteach Worksheet

Write the rational number for each point.

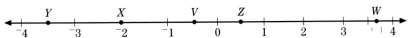

1. Point V **2.** Point W **3.** Point X **4.** Point Y **5.** Point Z
$-\frac{1}{2}$, or -0.5 $3\frac{2}{3}$, or $3.\overline{6}$ -2 -3.5, or $-3\frac{1}{2}$ $\frac{1}{2}$, or 0.5

Write the opposite of the rational number.

6. $-4\frac{1}{2}$ $4\frac{1}{2}$ **7.** 28 -28 **8.** -0.95 0.95 **9.** $\frac{8}{15}$ $-\frac{8}{15}$ **10.** $2\frac{4}{5}$ $-2\frac{4}{5}$

Compare. Use $>$, $<$, or $=$ for ●.

11. $\frac{1}{2}$ ● $\frac{1}{4}$ $>$ **12.** -6 ● $-\frac{2}{3}$ $<$ **13.** $\frac{4}{5}$ ● $-\frac{3}{8}$ $>$ **14.** 2 ● $\frac{2}{1}$ $=$

15. -1.4 ● $-\frac{3}{5}$ $<$ **16.** $1\frac{1}{2}$ ● $\frac{4}{9}$ $>$ **17.** $6\frac{1}{4}$ ● 6.25 $=$ **18.** $-\frac{3}{2}$ ● $-\frac{15}{10}$ $=$

19. $\frac{4}{7}$ ● $0.\overline{5}$ $>$ **20.** 9.6 ● $8\frac{3}{8}$ $>$ **21.** -5 ● $-\frac{1}{5}$ $<$ **22.** $1\frac{1}{8}$ ● $1.\overline{1}$ $>$

23. 4 ● $\frac{24}{6}$ $=$ **24.** 37.5 ● $37\frac{1}{2}$ $=$ **25.** $8\frac{1}{8}$ ● -8 $>$ **26.** $-6.\overline{3}$ ● $-6\frac{1}{3}$ $=$

Order from the greatest to the least.

27. $-\frac{3}{2}$, 2, 0.2 2, 0.2, $-\frac{3}{2}$ **28.** $1\frac{1}{8}$, $1.\overline{3}$, -0.6 $1.\overline{3}$, $1\frac{1}{8}$, -0.6

29. -4, $-\frac{4}{2}$, $-1\frac{3}{8}$, 4.7 4.7, $-1\frac{3}{8}$, $-\frac{4}{2}$, -4 **30.** $\frac{3}{7}$, $2\frac{1}{7}$, $-6.\overline{3}$, $-2\frac{1}{7}$ $2\frac{1}{7}$, $\frac{3}{7}$, $-2\frac{1}{7}$, $-6.\overline{3}$

Order from the least to the greatest.

31. -2.4, $-\frac{9}{2}$, -3 $-\frac{9}{2}$, -3, -2.4 **32.** $1\frac{5}{7}$, $\frac{13}{7}$, $1.\overline{5}$ $1.\overline{5}$, $1\frac{5}{7}$, $\frac{13}{7}$

33. $-3\frac{1}{2}$, $-3.\overline{5}$, $\frac{7}{8}$, 4 $-3.\overline{5}$, $-3\frac{1}{2}$, $\frac{7}{8}$, 4 **34.** $-1\frac{1}{5}$, $\frac{7}{9}$, $1.\overline{4}$, 2.0 $-1\frac{1}{5}$, $\frac{7}{9}$, $1.\overline{4}$, 2.0

CHALLENGE

Between any two different rational numbers there is an infinite number of rational numbers. For example, between 2.7 and 2.8 there are 2.75, 2.76, 2.763, 2.764, and so on.

Name four rational numbers between each pair of rational numbers.   **Answers will vary.**

1. -1.35, -1.34 **2.** $\frac{2}{3}$, $\frac{3}{4}$ **3.** $1\frac{1}{3}$, 1.4

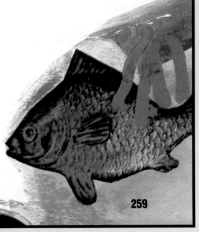

Classwork/Homework, page H106

259

ASSIGNMENT GUIDE

Basic: 1–10, 11–29 o, 31, Chlg 1

Average: 1–10, 12–34 e, Chlg 1–2

Extended: 1–26 e, 27–34, Chlg

Resources
Practice, p. 106   Class/Home, p. H106
Reteach, p. 76   Reasoning, p. H220
Enrich, p. 98

Exercise Analysis
1–5   Identify a rational number on a number line
6–10   Write the opposite of a rational number
11–26   Compare rational numbers
27–34   Order rational numbers

Challenge
These exercises encourage students to extend the concept of rational numbers and to become aware of the property of density of numbers on a number line.

FOLLOW-UP ACTIVITIES

PUZZLES AND GAMES
Have students use each of the ten digits exactly once to write the number 41. Tell them that they can use any of the four operations and can include exponents.

$(41 = 78 - 39 + 1^4 + \frac{2}{5} + 0.6)$

COMPUTER
Have students write a program that will find n rational numbers between any two values A and B that are entered into the computer. The value n must be a whole number 1 or greater.

```
(10 INPUT "BETWEEN WHICH VALUES";A,B
 20 INPUT "HOW MANY NUMBERS";N
 30 FOR X = 1 TO N
 40 LET M = (A + B)/2
 50 PRINT M
 60 LET A = M
 70 NEXT X
 80 END)
```

Encourage students to "stump" the computer by entering numbers like 1.11111111 and 1.11111112. The computer is a finite machine and rational numbers are infinite.

COMING UP
Adding and subtracting the rational way

259

Objectives: To add and subtract rational numbers

Warm-Up
Have students add and subtract the following integers.

$^-5 + {}^-2$ ($^-7$); $^-3 - {}^-2 + 4$ (3);
$11 - {}^-5 + {}^-2$ (14); $^-4 - {}^-4$ (0)

GETTING STARTED

Draw the following.

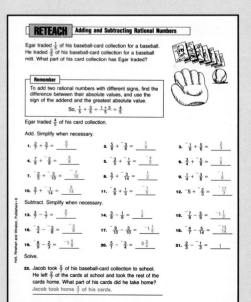

-4 -3 -2 -1 0 1 2 3 4

Have a volunteer locate $1\frac{1}{5}$ on the line. Ask what would have to be done to add $1\frac{3}{5}$ to $1\frac{1}{5}$. (Move to the right $1\frac{3}{5}$ units.) Have the volunteer locate this sum.

Have the volunteer locate $^-2.5$, and then ask what needs to be done to add $^-0.8$ to $^-2.5$. (Move 0.8 units to the left.) Locate this sum on the line. Repeat the exercise for the following.

$^-3.4 - {}^-2.8$ $3\frac{1}{2} + {}^-4.65$

$1.95 + {}^-4$ $2.6 - {}^-3\frac{1}{4}$

TEACHING THE LESSON

A. Point out that the rules for adding rational numbers parallel those for adding integers.

In the Other Examples section, review adding fractions with unlike denominators if necessary. Emphasize the fact that the negative sign must appear outside the parentheses once the fractions have been written as absolute values.

Emphasize also that the addition of two rational numbers with different signs involves comparing addends. The goal is to find the sign of the addend with the greater absolute value.

B. Extend the lesson by using a more complicated example.

$^-4.3 - {}^-0.7 + {}^-2.1 - 4$ ($^-9.7$)

Tell the class that the Commutative Property of Addition holds for the addition of rational numbers.

Again, note that the rules for subtracting rational numbers parallel those for subtracting integers.

Adding and Subtracting Rational Numbers

A. The deepest part of the Pacific Ocean was measured to be 6.77 mi below sea level in 1951. Eight years later, the deepest part was measured to be 0.08 mi lower. What was the new lowest depth?

To add and subtract rational numbers, combine the rules for adding and subtracting integers and fractions.

To add two rational numbers that have the same signs, add their absolute values and use the sign of the addends.

Add $^-6.77 + {}^-0.08$.

$^-6.77 + {}^-0.08 = |^-6.77| + |^-0.08| = {}^-6.85$

The new lowest depth is 6.85 mi.

Other examples:

Add $\frac{3}{4} + \frac{1}{2}$.

$\frac{3}{4} + \frac{1}{2} = \left|\frac{3}{4}\right| + \left|\frac{2}{4}\right| = \frac{3+2}{4} = 1\frac{1}{4}$

Add $^-\frac{3}{4} + {}^-\frac{1}{2}$.

$^-\frac{3}{4} + {}^-\frac{1}{2} = {}^-\left(\frac{3}{4} + \frac{2}{4}\right) = {}^-\left(\frac{3+2}{4}\right) = {}^-1\frac{1}{4}$

To add two rational numbers that have different signs, find the difference between their absolute values, and use the sign of the addend that has the greater absolute value.

Add $^-\frac{3}{7} + \frac{1}{3}$.

$^-\frac{3}{7} + \frac{1}{3} = {}^-\left(\frac{9}{21} - \frac{7}{21}\right) = {}^-\left(\frac{9-7}{21}\right) = {}^-\frac{2}{21}$

Add $0.32 + {}^-0.4$.

$0.32 + {}^-0.4 = {}^-(0.40 - 0.32)$
$= {}^-0.08$

B. To subtract a rational number, add its opposite.

Subtract $^-\frac{4}{5} - \frac{2}{5}$.

$^-\frac{4}{5} - \frac{2}{5} = {}^-\frac{4}{5} + {}^-\frac{2}{5} = \frac{^-4 + {}^-2}{5}$
$= {}^-\frac{6}{5} = {}^-1\frac{1}{5}$

Subtract $\frac{7}{8} - {}^-\frac{5}{8}$.

$\frac{7}{8} - {}^-\frac{5}{8} = \frac{7}{8} + \frac{5}{8} = \frac{12}{8} = 1\frac{4}{8} = 1\frac{1}{2}$

Subtract $^-12.5 - 10.4$.

$^-12.5 - 10.4 = {}^-12.5 + {}^-10.4$
$= {}^-22.9$

Subtract $^-2.26 - {}^-4.31$.

$^-2.26 - {}^-4.31 = {}^-2.26 + 4.31 = 2.05$

260

COMMON ERRORS

Students often confuse signs when they add rational numbers.

Remediation
Give students examples such as the following. Have them write the sign of the answer before adding or subtracting. In order to do this, have them first identify the rational number with the greater absolute value.

$^-4.25 + 8.63 = |8.63| - |4.25| = {}^+4.38$

Assign Reteach Master, p. 77.

Add. Simplify when necessary.

1. $\frac{2}{3} + \frac{^-1}{3}$ $\frac{1}{3}$
2. $\frac{^-3}{4} + \frac{3}{4}$ 0
3. $\frac{^-1}{6} + \frac{^-5}{6}$ $^-1$
4. $\frac{^-4}{5} + \frac{^-3}{5}$ $^-1\frac{2}{5}$

5. $\frac{7}{8} + \frac{^-5}{8}$ $\frac{1}{4}$
6. $\frac{3}{4} + \frac{^-7}{8}$ $^-\frac{1}{8}$
7. $\frac{^-2}{5} + \frac{^-3}{10}$ $^-\frac{7}{10}$
8. $\frac{^-5}{7} + \frac{3}{14}$ $^-\frac{13}{14}$

9. $\frac{4}{27} + \frac{^-1}{9}$ $\frac{1}{27}$
10. $\frac{^-1}{5} + \frac{2}{7}$ $\frac{3}{35}$
11. $\frac{^-3}{8} + 2$ $1\frac{5}{8}$
12. $^-4 + \frac{^-4}{15}$ $^-4\frac{4}{15}$

13. $0.4 + ^-0.7$ $^-0.3$
14. $^-2.1 + ^-3.5$ $^-5.6$
15. $^-6.21 + ^-4.13$ $^-10.34$

16. $^-7.24 + 2.18$ $^-5.06$
17. $^-2.4 + 3.12$ 0.72
18. $0.3 + ^-3.12$ $^-2.82$

19. $^-2.86 + ^-2$ $^-4.86$
20. $1.76 + ^-0.06$ 1.70
21. $^-4 + ^-0.04$ $^-4.04$

Subtract. Simplify when necessary.

22. $\frac{^-3}{8} - \frac{1}{8}$ $^-\frac{1}{2}$
23. $\frac{^-7}{16} - \frac{^-5}{16}$ $^-\frac{1}{8}$
24. $\frac{2}{5} - \frac{^-3}{5}$ 1
25. $\frac{4}{7} - \frac{^-6}{7}$ $1\frac{3}{7}$

26. $\frac{^-9}{10} - \frac{^-3}{10}$ $^-\frac{3}{5}$
27. $\frac{^-4}{7} - \frac{^-3}{14}$ $^-\frac{5}{14}$
28. $\frac{^-8}{15} - \frac{3}{5}$ $^-1\frac{2}{15}$
29. $\frac{^-3}{4} - \frac{^-7}{8}$ $\frac{1}{8}$

30. $\frac{^-5}{9} - \frac{5}{18}$ $^-\frac{5}{6}$
31. $\frac{2}{3} - \frac{^-1}{2}$ $1\frac{1}{6}$
32. $3 - \frac{^-4}{5}$ $3\frac{4}{5}$
33. $\frac{^-1}{9} - ^-2$ $1\frac{8}{9}$

34. $1.2 - ^-0.7$ 1.9
35. $^-3.6 - ^-2.1$ $^-1.5$
36. $^-4.52 - 0.76$ $^-5.28$

37. $^-5.35 - ^-5.35$ 0
38. $0.67 - ^-1.2$ 1.87
39. $3.82 - ^-2.34$ 6.16

40. $^-7.6 - 0.05$ $^-7.65$
41. $^-12.4 - ^-14.57$ 2.17
42. $^-0.22 - 1.02$ $^-1.24$

Solve.

43. The brightness of stars is called their *visual magnitude*. Sirius has a magnitude of $^-1.58$. Alpha Centauri has a magnitude 1.64 greater than Sirius. What is the magnitude of Alpha Centauri?   0.06

44. The brightest star in the Leo constellation has a visual magnitude of 1.36. The star Canopus has a visual magnitude of $^-0.86$. What is the difference between their visual magnitudes?   2.22

NUMBER SENSE

Write the reciprocal.

1. $^-\frac{1}{2}$ $^-2$
2. $\frac{4}{5}$ $\frac{5}{4}$
3. $^-\frac{7}{8}$ $^-\frac{8}{7}$
4. $^-2$ $^-\frac{1}{2}$
5. $1\frac{3}{4}$ $\frac{4}{7}$

6. $^-2\frac{5}{7}$ $^-\frac{7}{19}$
7. $4\frac{3}{4}$ $\frac{4}{19}$
8. $^-2\frac{1}{3}$ $^-\frac{3}{7}$
9. $^-1\frac{5}{6}$ $^-\frac{6}{11}$
10. $1\frac{7}{8}$ $\frac{8}{15}$

Exercise Analysis
1–21   Add rational numbers
22–42   Subtract rational numbers
43–44   Skill applications

Number Sense
These exercises provide practice in finding the reciprocal of a rational number, a skill that will be useful in the upcoming lesson.

FOLLOW-UP ACTIVITIES

PROBLEM SOLVING
Have students solve the following problems.
1. The boiling point of chlorine is $^-34.1$°C. Its melting point is $^-101$°C. What is the difference between its boiling and melting points? (66.9°C)
2. The melting point of fluorine is 32°C below its boiling point. If the boiling point of fluorine is $^-188$°C, what is its melting point? ($^-220$°C)
3. The boiling point of bromine is 65.88°C above its melting point. If its melting point is $^-7.08$°C, what is its boiling point? (58.8°C)

CALCULATOR
Have students use calculators to evaluate the following expressions. Point out that they may need to apply the rules for adding and subtracting rational numbers *before* entering the numbers.

$^-2.3 + 1.7 - 0.9$
$(0 - 2.3 + 1.7 - 0.9 = ^-1.5)$
$\frac{5}{4} + ^-1.1 - 2.6$
$(5 \div 4 - 1.1 - 2.6 = ^-2.45)$
$^-4.76 - ^-0.76 + 1.8 - 3.9$
$(0 - 4.76 + 0.76 + 1.8 - 3.9 = ^-6.1)$
$5.4 - 1.046 + ^-2.23 + 3.6$
$(5.4 + 3.6 - 1.046 - 2.23 = 5.724)$

COMING UP
An answer is nice, but the answer is much nicer.

Warm-Up

To prepare students for this lesson, have them compute the following.

$^-20 \times 12$ ($^-240$) $36 \times ^-15$ ($^-540$)
$^-40 \times ^-50$ (2,000) $^-8 \times 108$ ($^-864$)

GETTING STARTED

As an introduction to this lesson, ask students to pay close attention while you read the following aloud, and then have them give answers. (Read it only once.)

Railroad crossing, look out for cars—can you spell it, without any *r*'s?

The answer is, of course, *i-t*. The exercise emphasizes the need for finding what the question actually asks before trying to answer it. See how many students correctly answer this one.

I have 57 apples. I give all but 18 of them away. How many apples do I have left? (18)

TEACHING THE LESSON

It is important for students to realize that not all problems ask for numbers, even though computation may be involved in finding the solution. When faced with a problem involving math, students often tend to perform the computation involved and stop when they arrive at a numerical answer. Frequently, even when students realize the problem calls for other information, by the time they have set up and completed the computation involved they have forgotten what the problem originally asked. This is especially true in testing situations where there is anxiety about finishing on time. The emphasis in teaching this lesson should be on reading and comprehension. Explain to students that math deals not only with numbers, but also with logic and with the relationships among anything that can be ordered. It may be helpful to spend some time reading the problems on pages 262 and 263 aloud to students (books closed) and asking them to identify the question in each and in what form the answer will be.

Questions: The key to understanding the question is taking the time to read it carefully. Too often, students skim over a problem, pick out the numbers, perform the necessary computation, and present the numerical answer as the solution to the problem without ever knowing what the problem asks. Tell students that reading skills are just as important in the study of math and science as they are in the study of literature. Have them decide what form

the solution will take before actually performing the computation.

Tools: Be sure students realize that there are several ways to go about answering most of these problems. In the first introductory problem, it would be just as correct to add 2,200 and 650, to add 100 to that sum, and to check if the answer is greater than 4,000.

Solutions: You may wish to review the use of negative exponents, emphasizing the fact that the smaller the absolute value of a negative exponent, on a number the greater the value of the number.

Checks: The most important check here is for the reasonableness of the answer—does the solution fit the problem? If so, students should then work backward through their computation, checking it for accuracy.

| QUESTIONS | TOOLS | SOLUTIONS | CHECKS |

PROBLEM SOLVING
Checking That the Solution Answers the Question

Some problems call for answers that are not just numbers with labels. Pay special attention to the question that is asked in a problem. Be sure that your answer actually answers the question.

Deepstar-4000, a minisub used for undersea exploration, can reach a maximum depth of 4,000 ft. During one trip, it descended to a depth of 2,200 ft; then it descended another 650 ft. Did it descend to within 100 ft of its maximum depth?

Which is the correct answer?

a. 2,850 ft
b. 1,150 ft
c. No, it did not descend to within 100 ft of its maximum depth.

$$\begin{array}{r} 2,200 \\ +\ \ 650 \\ \hline 2,850 \end{array} \qquad \begin{array}{r} 4,000 \\ -\ \ 100 \\ \hline 3,900 \end{array}$$

$$2,850 < 3,900$$

The number of feet to which the minisub must descend if it is to be within 100 feet of its maximum depth

The correct answer is *c*. The problem does not ask for a numerical solution; it asks a question that can only be answered with a yes or no.

On another trip, Deepstar-4000 descended to a depth of 3,200 ft; then it descended another 250 ft. How far did it descend in all?

Which is the correct answer?
a. 3,450 ft
b. No, it did not descend to within 100 ft of its maximum depth.
c. 2,950 ft

The correct answer is *a*. This time, the problem requires a numerical solution. It is a matter of simple addition.

Which statement answers the question? Write the letter of the correct answer.

1. A chart used by a scientist has a scale from 0 to ⁻325 ft. Every ⁻25 ft, there is a special mark on the scale. Are there more than 15 special marks on the scale?

   a. Yes, there are more than 15 special marks.
   b. No, there are fewer than 15 special marks.
   c. 13 special marks

2. The maximum depth of a minisub is 3,945 ft. A trip calls for the minisub to descend first to a depth of 1,945 ft and then to descend another 1,890 ft. Will the sub descend to within 200 ft of its maximum depth?

   a. 3,835 ft   **b.** 110 ft
   c. Yes, it will descend to within 200 ft of its maximum depth.

Solve.

3. The minisub's marine biologist arranged 3 microscopic sea creatures by size, from the largest to the smallest. The creatures were labeled as follows:
   a. 1.75×10^{-5} meters
   b. 0.95×10^{-6}
   c. 1.21×10^{-4}.
   Was the order **c, b, a**? no

4. A minisub touched the ocean bottom in one spot at 3,450 ft. Its mechanical arm reached out and dug $\frac{1}{8}$ ft into the ocean floor. Then the arm probed 4 times deeper. Was the depth of the last probe greater or less than 3,460 ft from sea level? less than

5. An explorer minisub descends in stages of 400 ft at a time. The descent takes 8 min per stage. After 32 min, is the sub above or below 1,800 ft? above

6. A minisub was transported on a truck that drove 8.4 kilometers in 24 minutes. What was the rate of speed of the truck in kilometers per hour? 21 km/h

7. The ocean depth at one place is $\frac{3}{5}$ mi. A minisub descended to $\frac{2}{3}$ of the depth. Did the sub descend more than 2,000 ft? yes

8. A sea creature measures 4.75×10^{-2} meters long. It has tiny stripes every 0.25×10^{-3} meters. Does the creature have more than 180 stripes? yes

9. A robot minisub descends at a rate of 5 meters per minute. It reaches the end of its cable in 15 minutes. Can the robot minisub descend below 100 meters? no

10. A minisub descended to a depth of $2\frac{1}{8}$ mi. It then ascended $\frac{3}{8}$ mi before descending $2\frac{3}{8}$ mi. What depth is the minisub at now?
    $4\frac{1}{8}$ mi

Claswork/Homework, page H108

ASSIGNMENT GUIDE

Basic: 1–6

Average: 2–8

Extended: 3–10

Resources
Practice, p. 108   Class/Home, p. H108
Enrich, p. 100

Exercise Analysis
1–2   Choose the correct answer
3–10 Skill applications

FOLLOW-UP ACTIVITIES

PROBLEM SOLVING
Read aloud each of the following situations and ask each student to write at least two problems that could be answered from the information given. Do not limit students' questions. Accept *any* problems that could be answered using the given information. Encourage creativity.

1. An explorer uncovers a huge system of 27 caves that stretches through an entire mountain. He estimates the total walking distance through the caves to be 8 miles. The straight-line distance through the mountain is 5 miles.

2. In one cave is a row of stalactites and stalagmites that form an almost solid wall. The tallest part of this wall is 15 yards high and the shortest part is 8 inches high.

3. In analyzing the mineral content of a stalactite, a scientist finds that it is 78% limestone and 3% iron.

4. Of the 27 caves, animal life is found in all but 3 and plant life is found in all.

5. The explorer estimates that there are 200 bats in one cave and 1,000 bats in the entire system of caves.

6. The total walking distance through the caves is 8 miles. Of this distance, $\frac{5}{7}$ of it stretches through just 4 caves. The longest of these caves is $2\frac{1}{2}$ miles.

COMING UP
A rational approach to multiplication and division

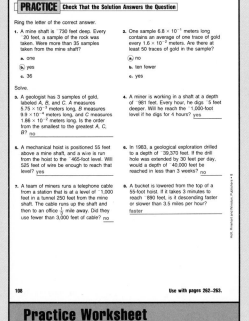

Practice Worksheet

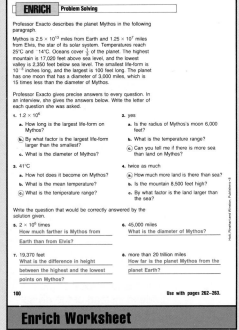

Enrich Worksheet

Objectives: To multiply and divide rational numbers

Warm-Up
Multiply and divide the following.

$2\frac{1}{8} \cdot \frac{8}{9}$ $\left(1\frac{8}{9}\right)$ $3.84 \div 1.6$ (2.4)

$\frac{3}{5} \div 3\frac{1}{5}$ $\left(\frac{3}{16}\right)$ $7.9 \cdot 1.1$ (8.69)

GETTING STARTED

Write the following equations on the board.

$^-2 \cdot 3 = ^-6$ $^-2 = ^-6 \div 3$

Then write them in fractional form.

$\frac{^-2}{1} \cdot \frac{3}{1} = \frac{^-6}{1}$ $\frac{^-2}{1} = \frac{^-6}{3}$

Ask students whether the equality is still true. Elicit from them that because each factor has been replaced by its equivalent, the equality still holds.

TEACHING THE LESSON

A. Point out that the negative sign in front of a fraction applies to either the numerator or the denominator. Give the following examples to demonstrate that altering its position does not alter the sign of the answer.

$$\frac{^-1}{3} \cdot \frac{^-1}{2} = \left(\frac{^-1}{3}\right) \cdot \left(\frac{^-1}{2}\right) = \frac{1}{6}$$

$$\frac{^-1}{3} \cdot \frac{^-1}{2} = \frac{^-1 \cdot ^-1}{3 \cdot 2} = \frac{1}{6}$$

B. Extend the lesson by combining multiplication and division in the following example.

$$\frac{^-3.5}{0.5} \cdot \frac{0.75}{^-0.375} = (14)$$

Checkpoint
The chart lists the common errors students make in multiplying or dividing rational numbers.

Correct Answers: 1c, 2b, 3d

Remediation
■ For these errors, have students solve a simpler example by ignoring the sign at first. After they have arrived at the solution, have them apply the rules for multiplication or division in order to choose the correct sign.

☐ For these errors, assign Reteach Master, p. 78.

△ For this error, refer students to the examples on p. 121.

Multiplying and Dividing Rational Numbers

A. To multiply rational numbers, use the rules for multiplying integers, decimals, and fractions.

If two rational numbers have like signs, their product is positive.

Multiply $\frac{^-1}{3} \cdot \frac{^-1}{2}$.

$\frac{^-1}{3} \cdot \frac{^-1}{2} = \frac{^-1 \cdot ^-1}{3 \cdot 2} = \frac{1}{6}$

Multiply $^-0.4 \cdot ^-1.2$.

$^-0.4 \cdot ^-1.2 = 0.48$

If two rational numbers have unlike signs, their product is negative.

Multiply $\frac{^-1}{2} \cdot \frac{3}{4}$.

$\frac{^-1}{2} \cdot \frac{3}{4} = \frac{^-1 \cdot 3}{2 \cdot 4} = \frac{^-3}{8}$

Multiply $4.2 \cdot ^-3.1$.

$4.2 \cdot ^-3.1 = ^-13.02$

B. Divide rational numbers by combining the rules for dividing integers, decimals, and fractions.

If two rational numbers have like signs, their quotient is positive.

Divide $^-1\frac{1}{2} \div ^-\frac{3}{8}$.

$^-1\frac{1}{2} \div ^-\frac{3}{8} = \frac{^-3}{2} \div \frac{^-3}{8}$
$= \frac{^-3}{2} \cdot \frac{^-8}{3}$
$= \frac{^-3 \cdot ^-8}{2 \cdot 3} = \frac{24}{6} = 4$

Divide $^-4.5 \div ^-18.0$.

$^-4.5 \div ^-18.0 = 0.25$

If two rational numbers have unlike signs, their quotient is negative.

Divide $\frac{3}{4} \div ^-\frac{3}{8}$.

$\frac{3}{4} \div ^-\frac{3}{8} = \frac{3}{4} \cdot \frac{^-8}{3} =$
$\frac{3 \cdot ^-8}{4 \cdot 3} =$
$\frac{^-24}{12} = ^-2$

Divide $1.2 \div ^-0.4$.

$1.2 \div ^-0.4 = ^-3$

Checkpoint   Write the letter of the correct answer.

Multiply or divide.

1. $\frac{^-2}{3} \cdot \frac{^-4}{5}$ a. $\frac{^-8}{15}$ b. $\frac{^-10}{12}$ c. $\frac{8}{15}$ d. $\frac{6}{15}$

2. $\frac{1}{8} \cdot \frac{^-4}{5}$ a. $\frac{5}{20}$ b. $\frac{^-1}{10}$ c. $\frac{^-5}{32}$ d. $\frac{4}{10}$

3. $^-1\frac{1}{4} \div \frac{^-5}{8}$ a. $\frac{25}{32}$ b. $\frac{^-2}{1}$ c. $\frac{1}{2}$ d. 2

Math Reasoning, page H220

COMMON ERRORS

Answer Choice	Type of Error
■ 1a	Uses the wrong sign
■ 1b	Uses the wrong operation and the wrong sign
☐ 1d	Adds the numerators, multiplies the denominators
☐ 2a, 2c, 3a	Uses the wrong operation
△ 2d	Uses the wrong sign; reduces the denominator but not the numerator
■ 3b	Uses the wrong sign; does not simplify
☐ 3c	Uses the reciprocal of the dividend instead of the divisor

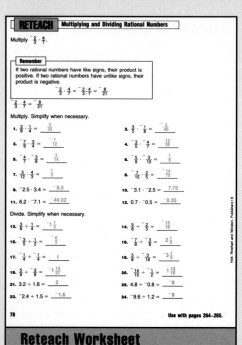

Reteach Worksheet

Multiply. Simplify when necessary.

1. $^-\frac{3}{8} \cdot \frac{1}{4}$ $^-\frac{3}{32}$ 2. $\frac{1}{2} \cdot ^-\frac{5}{16}$ $^-\frac{5}{32}$ 3. $^-\frac{7}{9} \cdot ^-\frac{3}{4}$ $\frac{7}{12}$ 4. $^-\frac{2}{5} \cdot ^-\frac{5}{8}$ $\frac{1}{4}$

5. $^-\frac{4}{7} \cdot ^-\frac{7}{8}$ $\frac{1}{2}$ 6. $^-\frac{5}{9} \cdot ^-\frac{2}{3}$ $\frac{10}{27}$ 7. $\frac{7}{12} \cdot \frac{3}{4}$ $\frac{7}{16}$ 8. $^-\frac{2}{15} \cdot \frac{7}{11}$ $^-\frac{14}{165}$

9. $1\frac{1}{4} \cdot ^-\frac{3}{8}$ $^-\frac{15}{32}$ 10. $^-\frac{5}{6} \cdot ^-2\frac{5}{8}$ $2\frac{3}{16}$ 11. $^-2\frac{3}{5} \cdot 4$ $^-10\frac{2}{5}$ 12. $^-1\frac{1}{9} \cdot ^-2\frac{3}{7}$ $2\frac{44}{63}$

13. $\frac{1}{4} \cdot ^-\frac{2}{5}$ $^-\frac{1}{10}$ 14. $\frac{2}{3} \cdot ^-1\frac{1}{4}$ $^-\frac{5}{6}$ 15. $^-1\frac{2}{5} \cdot ^-4$ $5\frac{3}{5}$ 16. $^-\frac{1}{4} \cdot ^-3$ $\frac{3}{4}$

17. $0.7 \cdot ^-3.5$ $^-2.45$ 18. $^-1.2 \cdot ^-4.4$ 5.28 19. $^-3.7 \cdot 3.71$ $^-13.727$

20. $^-2.63 \cdot ^-1.45$ 3.8135 21. $^-4.3 \cdot 0.08$ $^-0.344$ 22. $^-14.67 \cdot ^-6.2$ 90.954

23. $^-9.5 \cdot 3.703$ $^-35.1785$ 24. $^-1.14 \cdot ^-0.07$ 0.0798 25. $^-6.2 \cdot ^-1.45$ 8.99

Divide. Simplify when necessary.

26. $^-\frac{3}{4} \div \frac{1}{8}$ $^-6$ 27. $^-\frac{5}{8} \div ^-\frac{2}{3}$ $\frac{15}{16}$ 28. $\frac{1}{2} \div ^-\frac{3}{5}$ $^-\frac{5}{6}$ 29. $^-\frac{7}{8} \div ^-\frac{3}{8}$ $2\frac{1}{3}$

30. $^-\frac{1}{4} \div \frac{1}{4}$ $^-1$ 31. $\frac{3}{8} \div ^-\frac{5}{16}$ $^-1\frac{1}{5}$ 32. $\frac{5}{9} \div ^-\frac{3}{8}$ $^-1\frac{13}{27}$ 33. $^-\frac{1}{2} \div ^-\frac{14}{15}$ $\frac{15}{28}$

34. $\frac{3}{8} \div ^-2$ $^-\frac{3}{16}$ 35. $^-2\frac{2}{3} \div ^-\frac{7}{16}$ $6\frac{2}{21}$ 36. $^-\frac{3}{4} \div 4$ $^-\frac{3}{16}$ 37. $^-5 \div \frac{7}{7}$ $^-5$

38. $^-4.8 \div ^-0.6$ 8 39. $^-2.5 \div 1.5$ $^-1.\overline{6}$ 40. $7.28 \div ^-0.08$ $^-91$

41. $^-6.66 \div ^-1.11$ 6 42. $^-9.39 \div 0.3$ $^-31.3$ 43. $^-1.2 \div ^-1.44$ $0.8\overline{3}$

44. $^-18.3 \div 0.183$ $^-100$ 45. $^-3.185 \div ^-2.45$ 1.3 46. $^-0.8 \div ^-3.2$ 0.25

NUMBER SENSE

Copy and complete the table.

	1%	10%	100%
98	0.98	9.8	98
540	5.40	54.0	540
1,900	19.00	190.0	1,900
3,000	30.00	300.0	3,000

Classwork/Homework, page H109

265

ASSIGNMENT GUIDE

Basic: 1–43 o, NS

Average: 2–4, 5–43 o, NS

Extended: 9–45 o, NS

Resources
Practice, p. 109   Class/Home, p. H109
Reteach, p. 78   Reasoning, p. H220
Enrich, p. 101

Exercise Analysis
1–25   Multiply rational numbers
26–46 Divide rational numbers

You may wish to allow students to use calculators for some of these exercises.

Number Sense
This activity provides practice in finding the percent of a number.

FOLLOW-UP ACTIVITIES

REINFORCEMENT
Have students use the order of operations to evaluate the following expressions.

$^-\frac{1}{2} + \frac{2}{3} \cdot ^-\frac{3}{4}$ $(^-1)$

$1.2 \cdot ^-0.6 - ^-4.2$ (3.48)

$^-\frac{3.5}{0.7} - \frac{2}{7} \cdot ^-2\frac{1}{3}$ $(^-5\frac{2}{3})$

$0.56 \div ^-0.8 - ^-1.2 \cdot 12$ (13.7)

Repeat the exercise by using similar examples.

PROBLEM SOLVING
The Ringle Supply Company keeps a running inventory of all parts shipped (−) as well as all parts received (+). Have students solve the following problems.
- On Monday, 1,089 feet of cable were shipped during a 7.5-hour period. On the average, what was the net change in the inventory of cable each hour? ($^-145.2$ feet)
- On Wednesday, $\frac{1}{8}$ of the 3,816 jars received were damaged and then immediately returned. That day the company also shipped $\frac{1}{6}$ of an order for 22,800. What was the net change in the jar inventory? ($^-461$ jars)
- On Friday, $\frac{5}{9}$ of the inventory of electrical fuses was shipped out. If there were 2,124 fuses in stock, what was the net change in the fuse inventory? ($^-1,180$ fuses)

COMING UP
Really big real numbers . . .

PRACTICE Multiplying and Dividing Rational Numbers

Multiply or divide. Simplify when necessary.

1. $^-0.2 \cdot 0.81$ = $^-0.162$ 2. $^-6.16 \div 0.7$ = $^-8.8$
3. $^-\frac{2}{9} \cdot ^-\frac{3}{4}$ = $\frac{1}{6}$ 4. $1\frac{1}{3} \div 1\frac{1}{4}$ = $1\frac{1}{15}$
5. $^-0.8 \cdot ^-0.6$ = 0.48 6. $2.37 \div 0.1$ = 23.7
7. $9\frac{1}{10} \cdot 8\frac{3}{7}$ = $76\frac{7}{10}$ 8. $^-\frac{1}{3} \div \frac{3}{7}$ = $^-\frac{7}{9}$
9. $9.1 \cdot ^-0.45$ = $^-4.095$ 10. $0.99 \div 0.05$ = 19.8
11. $\frac{2}{3} \cdot ^-10\frac{1}{2}$ = $^-7$ 12. $\frac{2}{7} \div ^-1$ = $^-\frac{2}{7}$
13. $1.34 \cdot 0.07$ = 0.0938 14. $5.52 \div ^-6$ = $^-0.92$
15. $^-\frac{2}{3} \cdot ^-3$ = 2 16. $^-16 \div \frac{5}{7}$ = $^-22\frac{2}{5}$
17. $^-0.13 \cdot ^-3.9$ = 0.507 18. $0.06 \div 0.3$ = 0.2
19. $\frac{3}{4} \cdot \frac{2}{9}$ = $\frac{1}{6}$ 20. $6\frac{1}{2} \div 1\frac{4}{9}$ = $4\frac{1}{2}$
21. $^-9.5 \cdot 12.7$ = $^-120.65$ 22. $^-8.4 \div ^-4.2$ = 2
23. $^-9 \div \frac{7}{2}$ = $^-2\frac{4}{7}$ 24. $9\frac{3}{7} \div 1\frac{1}{3}$ = $7\frac{1}{14}$
25. $^-0.05 \cdot ^-16$ = 0.8 26. $1.4 \div ^-7$ = $^-0.2$
27. $^-\frac{3}{4} \cdot 10\frac{2}{3}$ = $^-8$ 28. $^-\frac{1}{4} \div ^-1$ = $\frac{1}{4}$
29. $^-0.05 \cdot 1.7$ = $^-0.085$ 30. $2.79 \div 3.1$ = 0.9
31. $9\frac{3}{5} \cdot 2\frac{7}{12}$ = 26 32. $9\frac{1}{10} \div \frac{7}{9}$ = $11\frac{7}{10}$

33. Ahmed has a summer job finishing tables for a furniture maker. He can finish $2\frac{1}{3}$ tables per week (7 days). The furniture maker received an order for 13 tables that must be done in five weeks and one day. Will Ahmed be able to finish them all on time? If not, how many will the furniture maker have to finish himself?
no; 1 table

Use with pages 264–265.   109

Practice Worksheet

ENRICH Number

Look at the equation 1 + 5 + 6 = 2 + 3 + 7. If each number is squared, the equation is still true: $1^2 + 5^2 + 6^2 = 2^2 + 3^2 + 7^2$. This is called a **multigrade**. A *multigrade* is an equation in which each side is an equal sum, and the sides are still equal after each term has been raised to a power. If the same number is added to each term of a multigrade, a new multigrade is created: (1 + 2) + (5 + 2) + (6 + 2) = (2 + 2) + (3 + 2) + (7 + 2) = 3 + 7 + 8 = 4 + 5 + 9. This is a second-order multigrade.

1. Square each term of the new multigrade.
9 + 49 + 64 = 16 + 25 + 81

To create a second-order multigrade:
a. begin with a simple equality: 2 + 5 = 3 + 4.
b. add the same number to each term: 6 + 9 = 7 + 8.
c. reverse the sides of the second equation: 7 + 8 = 6 + 9.
d. combine the two equations: 2 + 5 + 7 + 8 = 3 + 4 + 6 + 9.

Create four second-order multigrades of your own.
2. Answers will vary.   3. Answers will vary.
4. Answers will vary.   5. Answers will vary.

A third-order multigrade is one in which you can either square or cube the terms of the equation and the equation is still true. To create a third-order multigrade, add the same number to each term in a second-order multigrade. Reverse the sides of one of the equations and combine them. If 6 is added to each term in the multigrade 2 + 5 + 7 + 8 = 3 + 4 + 6 + 9, the multigrade becomes 8 + 11 + 13 + 14 = 9 + 10 + 12 + 15. Reversing the sides of the second equation and combining the equations creates a third-order multigrade:
2 + 5 + 7 + 8 + 9 + 10 + 12 + 15 = 3 + 4 + 6 + 9 + 8 + 11 + 13 + 14. Terms which appear on both sides of the equation cancel.

Create a third-order multigrade from each of the second-order multigrades you created.
6. Answers will vary.   7. Answers will vary.
8. Answers will vary.   9. Answers will vary.

Use with pages 264–265.   101

Enrich Worksheet

Holt, Rinehart and Winston, Publishers • 8

Objective: To explore rational and irrational numbers, terminating and repeating decimals, and their relation to real numbers.

Warm-Up

Write the following examples on the chalkboard for students to complete.

$\left(\frac{-1}{2}\right)^2 \left(\frac{1}{4}\right)$ $(0.25)^2 \ (0.0625)$

$\left(\frac{-2}{3}\right)^2 \left(\frac{4}{9}\right)$ $(^-1.8)^2 \ (3.24)$

GETTING STARTED

Discuss with students the kinds of numbers they have learned about to this point in the text. List the following on the chalkboard.

whole numbers
decimals
fractions
integers
rational numbers

Elicit from students why the category of rational numbers includes all the other categories. Emphasize the fact that rational numbers include only terminating and repeating decimals. Ask whether students can imagine other kinds of numbers that might not terminate or repeat as decimals. Explain that they will learn about such numbers in this lesson.

TEACHING THE LESSON

There are two approaches that you can use in teaching this lesson: (1) have students work individually through the developmental questions and convene in groups of four to work on Thinking as a Team, or (2) have students work through the developmental parts in groups of four and have a class discussion for Thinking as a Team.

Review with students the definition of rational numbers. Remind them that they can order the given rational numbers by finding the decimal equivalent of each fraction. Make sure that students realize that nonrepeating, nonterminating decimals are *irrational numbers* and that rational and irrational numbers together compose the set of real numbers.

In the Thinking as a Team section, students can estimate the value of irrational square roots by trial and error. Because $\sqrt{5}$ is between $\sqrt{4}$ and $\sqrt{9}$, students can conclude that $\sqrt{5}$ is between 2 and 3.

Students can then try to find the squares of 2.1, 2.2, and so on until they find which is closest to 5. (2.2) For question 3, ask students which two perfect squares 20 is between. (16 and 25) After they have esti-

---

Real Numbers

Every point on the number line corresponds to a real number. For example, point A corresponds to the real number 2. The point midway between A and B must correspond to 2.5. What number corresponds to the point one unit to the left of 2.5? **1.5**

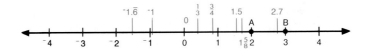

A real number in decimal form may repeat or terminate, or it may neither repeat nor terminate. Real numbers that repeat or terminate are called **rational** numbers.

2.5 terminates. The decimal equivalent of $2\frac{1}{3}$ is 2.333.... This decimal repeats and can be written $2.\bar{3}$.

Thinking as a Team _____

1. Copy the number line shown above. Then show the approximate location of each of the following real numbers. Which numbers, as decimals, are repeating? Which terminate? You may use your calculator. **$\frac{1}{3}$ and $^-1.\bar{6}$ repeat—the rest terminate.**

   $1.5 \qquad ^-1 \qquad \frac{1}{3} \qquad ^-1.\bar{6} \qquad \frac{3}{4} \qquad 0 \qquad 2.7 \qquad 1\frac{5}{8}$

2. Do you or any of your friends have a calculator that has a ☑ key? If so, press ② ☑ on this calculator. Does the decimal form of $\sqrt{2}$ appear to repeat? How about $\sqrt{3}$? $\sqrt{4}$? $\sqrt{5}$?

   None of them appear to repeat.

Real numbers that cannot be written as terminating or repeating decimals are called **irrational** numbers. The square root of a whole number is either another whole number or an irrational number. Thus $\sqrt{4}$ is rational, but $\sqrt{6}$ is irrational. Numbers such as 0.10110111011110... are also irrational because, although their digits follow a pattern, they do not repeat.

266

---

mated $\sqrt{20}$ to the nearest tenth (4.5), have them estimate each of the following to the nearest tenth.

$\sqrt{7}$ (2.6) $\qquad \sqrt{13}$ (3.6) $\qquad \sqrt{57}$ (7.5)
$\sqrt{238}$ (15.4)

Guide students to realize that a calculator cannot actually display an irrational number because such a number never can have a repeating pattern in its digits but has an infinite number of digits. For question 5, students should be able to see that $\frac{1}{11}$, $\frac{1}{7}$, and $\frac{1}{13}$ are rational numbers because they are expressed as ratios of integers. Lead them to discover that rationality is *not* always obvious to one who looks at the decimal equivalent displayed on a calculator because the calculator displays only 8 digits. The pattern for $\frac{1}{11}$ can easily be seen, and the pattern for $\frac{1}{7}$ $(\frac{1}{7} = 0.142857)$ can almost be seen on a calculator, but the

(Continued on p. 267.)

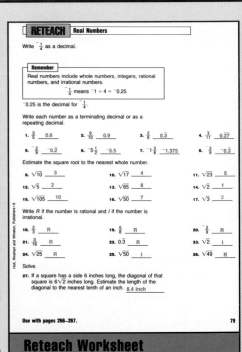

Reteach Worksheet

Thinking as a Team

You can estimate the square root of a number by using perfect squares that are near the number.

1. $\sqrt{5}$ is between $\sqrt{4}$ and $\sqrt{9}$, and so $\sqrt{5}$ is between what two numbers? **2 and 3**

2. How can you estimate $\sqrt{5}$ to the nearest tenth?
   Try 2.3^2, 2.4^2 and so on.

3. What is $\sqrt{20}$ to the nearest tenth? **4.5**

4. Enter any number on your calculator. Is the number shown on your display rational or irrational? Can your calculator actually display an irrational number? **rational; no**

5. Are the numbers $\frac{1}{11}$, $\frac{1}{7}$, and $\frac{1}{13}$ rational or irrational?
   rational
   How do you know? **They are ratios of integers.**
   Using your calculator, look at the decimal form of $\frac{1}{11}$, $\frac{1}{7}$, and $\frac{1}{13}$. Can you tell whether each of these decimals is rational from looking at your calculator? Why or why not?

   No, students cannot tell this from an 8-digit calculator because there may be a larger number of repeating digits.

Classify the following real numbers as rational or irrational. Your calculator will help.

$\sqrt{9}$ R $\frac{1}{6}$ R $\sqrt{8}$ I 1.2 R $^-4$ R $0.\overline{7}$ R $\sqrt{7}$ I $\frac{3}{5}$ R $\frac{1}{11}$ R 0 R

Which of these numbers are integers? Which are whole numbers? Can a number be both rational and irrational?
$\sqrt{9}$, $^-4$, 0; $\sqrt{9}$, 0; no

Thinking as a Team

1. In this Venn Diagram, each circle represents one of the following number sets: real numbers, rational numbers, irrational numbers, integers, and whole numbers. Identify each of these sets with the letters A, B, C, D, and E. **A—whole numbers; B—integers; C—rational numbers; D—irrational numbers; E—real numbers**

2. Decide which of the following statements are true:

   All rational numbers are real numbers. **true**
   If a number is an integer, then it is rational. **true**
   If a number is negative, then it is not a whole number. **true**
   Some rational numbers are irrational. **false**
   Every rational number is an integer. **false**

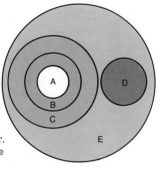

ASSIGNMENT GUIDE

Basic: p. 266, p. 267
Average: p. 266, p. 267
Extended: p. 266, p. 267

Resources
Practice, p. 110   Class/Home, p. H110
Reteach, p. 79   More Practice, p. H202
Enrich, p. 102

pattern for $\frac{1}{13}$ ($\frac{1}{13} = 0.\overline{076923}$) is not so obvious. In fact, students may think that the decimal terminates because most calculators drop the eighth digit, which is a zero.

The Venn diagram at the bottom of the page should be a useful tool in helping students keep track of the relationship among different sets of numbers. Have students support or disprove each statement in question 2 by giving an example. Refer students who need additional practice to More Practice page 486 in the back of the textbook.

FOLLOW-UP ACTIVITIES

PROBLEM SOLVING

Copy the following problem and its solution onto the chalkboard, and tell students they can use a similar method to find the fractional equivalent of any repeating decimal.

$$n = 0.8\overline{3}$$
$$100n = 83.\overline{33}$$
$$10n = 8.\overline{33}$$
$$90n = 75$$
$$n = \frac{75}{90} = \frac{5}{6}$$

Have students use this method to find the fractional equivalents of these repeating decimals.

$0.1\overline{6}$ $\left(\frac{1}{6}\right)$ $0.\overline{7}$ $\left(\frac{7}{9}\right)$ $0.\overline{45}$ $\left(\frac{5}{11}\right)$

$0.4\overline{6}$ $\left(\frac{7}{15}\right)$

COMING UP
Quite plainly, plotting points for pairs

Warm-Up

Have students identify the following numbers as either rational (R) or irrational (I).

$\dfrac{-11}{\sqrt{64}}$ (R)   3.14 (R)   0.050050005 . . . (I)

$\sqrt{100}$ (R) $\dfrac{-\sqrt{3}}{-2}$ (I) $\dfrac{527}{85}$ (R)

GETTING STARTED

Draw the following graph and table on the chalkboard.

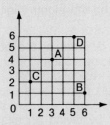

Point	Location	
	Across	Up
A	(3)	(4)
D	(5)	(6)
(C)	1	2
(B)	6	1

Have students review the procedure for locating and naming points on a coordinate grid by referring to the graph to complete the table.

TEACHING THE LESSON

Explain that each coordinate in an ordered pair is a point of reference to some known standard, that is, it indicates distance from either the x- or y-axis. Show that the exact location of the ordered pair can be found by drawing two lines of reference—one from the x-axis and the other from the y-axis—and observing the point of intersection.

Extend the instruction by having students identify the quadrant in which each of the following ordered pairs is located.

($^-$3.2, 5.8) (II)   ($\dfrac{-5}{9}$, $\dfrac{-1}{9}$) (III)

($2\frac{1}{4}$, $^-$0.3) (IV)   (3, 12.1) (I)

Graphing Real Numbers

You have used real numbers to locate points on a number line. You can also use real numbers to locate points in a plane, called a **coordinate plane,** or a **real-number plane.**

The x-axis and y-axis are real-number lines. Their intersection is the **origin,** and is described by the **ordered pair** (0,0).

Every point in the real-number plane can be described by an ordered pair of real numbers.

The x-axis and the y-axis divide the real-number plane into four **quadrants.**

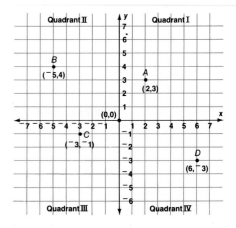

Ordered pairs in Quadrant I have the form (+,+). (2,3) are the coordinates of point A in Quadrant I.

Ordered pairs in Quadrant II have the form ($-$,+). ($^-$5,4) are the coordinates of point B in Quadrant II.

Ordered pairs in Quadrant III have the form ($-$,$-$). ($^-$3,$^-$1) are the coordinates of point C in Quadrant III.

Ordered pairs in Quadrant IV have the form (+,$-$). (6,$^-$3) are the coordinates of point D in Quadrant IV.

Graph the ordered pair ($^-$4,2).

To graph ($^-$4,2), move 4 to the left of the origin (0,0) along the x-axis. Then move 2 up from the x-axis.

Graph the ordered pair $\left(1\frac{1}{2}, ^-2\right)$.

To graph $1\frac{1}{2}$, move right $1\frac{1}{2}$, or $\frac{1}{2}$ of the way between 1 and 2 along the x-axis. Then move 2 down from the x-axis.

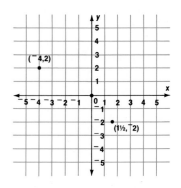

COMMON ERRORS

Students often confuse positive and negative coordinates when graphing on a real-number plane.

Remediation

Games such as Battleship often help make concrete the concept of plotting points. Have students think of the sign of the x-coordinate as meaning either left ($-$) or right (+) and of the y-coordinate as being either up (+) or down ($-$).

Assign Reteach Master, p. 80.

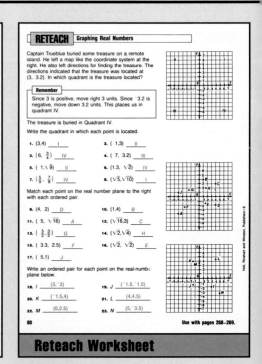

Write the quadrant in which each point is located.

1. $(4,3)$ I
2. $(2,^-1)$ IV
3. $\left(\dfrac{^-3}{4},6\right)$ II
4. $(^-7,^-2.\overline{3})$ III

5. $(3,^-1)$ IV
6. $(3.1,2)$ I
7. $\left(\dfrac{7}{8},\dfrac{^-5}{9}\right)$ IV
8. $(^-2,4)$ II

Match each ordered pair with a point in the real-number plane at the right.

9. $(^-2,1)$ F
10. $(4,6)$ C

11. $\left(\dfrac{3}{4},^-3\right)$ L
12. $(5,1.3)$ K

13. $(^-1.\overline{6},^-3)$ R
14. $(2,3)$ B

15. $\left(\dfrac{^-7}{9},2\dfrac{2}{3}\right)$ D
16. $(^-2,5)$ A

17. $(^-4,^-0.5)$ N
18. $(3,^-3.3)$ P

19. $\left(5\dfrac{1}{8},^-3\dfrac{7}{11}\right)$ G
20. $(5.5,3.5)$ E

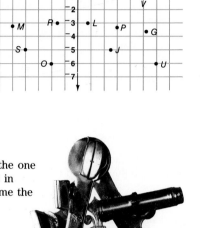

Write an ordered pair for each point in the real-number plane at the right.

21. H $(^-5,3)$
22. I $(2,5)$
23. J $(2.5,^-5)$
24. M $(^-5,^-3.2)$
25. O $(^-2,^-6)$
26. Q $(0,0)$
27. S $(^-4,^-5)$
28. T $(^-4,5.3)$
29. U $(6,^-6)$
30. V $(5,^-1)$

On graph paper, draw a real-number plane like the one above. Graph each point and connect the points in order. Connect the last point to the first and name the figure.

31. $(^-2,2), (4,2), (2,^-2), (^-4,^-2)$ parallelogram

32. $(^-6,3), (^-6,^-3), (6,^-3), (6,3)$ rectangle

33. $(1,^-3), (1,3), (^-5,^-3)$ triangle

34. $(^-4,4), (^-4,^-4), (4,^-4), (4,4)$ square

35. $(^-2,2), (^-1,2), (2,^-2), (2,2), (3,2), (3,^-3), (1,^-3),$
$(^-1,^-1), (^-1,^-3), (^-2,^-3)$ the letter N

Classwork/Homework, page H111

269

ASSIGNMENT GUIDE

Basic: 1–32

Average: 1–33

Extended: 9–35

Resources
Practice, p. 111   Class/Home, p. H111
Reteach, p. 80   Reasoning, p. H220
Enrich, p. 103

Exercise Analysis

1–8   Identify the quadrant in which a point is located
9–20   Locate an ordered pair
21–30   Write ordered pairs for given points
31–35   Plot a figure in a real-number plane

FOLLOW-UP ACTIVITIES

PUZZLES AND GAMES
Materials: graph paper and rulers

Have each student draw a coordinate plane. Then have the class form groups of four. Have one student in each group secretly plot a line that should extend across 3 specific points on the plane horizontally, vertically, or diagonally. The remaining students are then to guess the location of the line by asking about specific locations. The first player to guess its location wins.

MATH CONNECTION
(Social studies)
Have students research the science of mapmaking (cartography). They should focus on the following areas.
1. When did mapmaking become a science? (during the Age of Exploration)
2. What is a map projection? (a way of showing a curved surface on a flat piece of paper)
3. What are the three basic kinds of map projections? (Mercator; conic; polar)

COMING UP
Does anyone have plans?

PRACTICE Graphing Real Numbers

Use graph I to answer Problems 1 through 6.
1. What are the coordinates of point D? $(^-1, 0.25)$
2. What are the coordinates of point S? $(0.75, ^-0.75)$
3. What are the coordinates of point L? $(0.5, 0.75)$
4. Graph point H at (1.25,0.75).
5. Graph point T at $(^-0.75, ^-0.25)$.
6. Graph point J at $(^-0.5,1.25)$.
Use graph II to answer Problems 7 through 12.
7. Graph point M at (0.75, ^-0.5).
8. Graph point N at $(^-0.25,1)$.
9. Graph point P at $(^-0.75, ^-0.5)$.
10. Graph point Q at (1.25,1).
11. In which quadrant would $(^-4.5, 6.2)$ be? II
12. In which quadrant would $(3.1415, ^-4.6)$ be? IV

Use with pages 268–269.   111

Practice Worksheet

ENRICH Measurement

Two forms of carbon exist in the natural world—C_{12} and C_{14}. C_{14} undergoes radioactive decay at a steady rate. Its decay is said to have a half-life of 5,700 years. This means that a sample of C_{14} will deteriorate to half its original weight every 5,700 years. A sample of 100 g of C_{14} will deteriorate to 50 g after 5,700 years. In 11,400 years, it will deteriorate to 25 g. The process continues until the sample has completely disintegrated.

1. A sample of C_{14} weighs 512 g. How much will it weigh after 11,400 years?
128 g

2. How much will the sample weigh after 39,900 years?
4 g

3. How many years will it take for a 512-g sample to weigh only 1 g?
51,300 years

Radioactive decay in a living organism cannot be detected because the organism is constantly replacing its decayed C_{14} atoms with "new" C_{14} atoms from the environment. This replacement no longer occurs after death. In "dead" tissue, the amount of C_{12} stays the same. The amount of C_{14} diminishes by half after each successive half-life of 5,700 years. Shown below are C_{12}:C_{14} ratios for a specimen during its first two half-lives:

1×10^{12}:1	when living
1×10^{12}:0.5	after 5,700 years (1 half-life)
1×10^{12}:0.25	after 11,400 years (2 half-lives)

4. Scientists use C_{12}:C_{14} ratios to determine the approximate age of specimens. Complete the table.

Specimen	Amount of C_{12}	Amount of C_{14}	Approximate age
A	4×10^2 g	4×10^{-10} g	alive
B	5×10^3 g	1.25×10^{-9} g	11,400 years
C	30 g	9.375×10^{-13} g	28,500 years
D	32,000 g	6.25×10^{-11} g	51,300 years

Use with pages 268–269.   103

Enrich Worksheet

269

Objective: To make a plan to solve a multistep problem

Warm-Up

Have students rename each of the following measurements with meters.

418 cm (4.18 m)   180 mm (0.18 m)
19 mm (0.019 m)   34 km (34,000 m)
36,214 cm (362.14 m)   0.289 km (289 m)

GETTING STARTED

Draw these figures on the board.

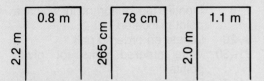

Tell the class that these are the measurements of three door frames. Ask the class the following questions: "If you were buying wood to make these door frames, how would you find how much wood you need?" (Answers will vary and will probably involve simple addition.) "Would you want to express the total in meters or in centimeters?" (meters; Only one set of measurements would need to be renamed.) "Would you rename centimeters with meters separately and add, or would you add the centimeters and rename the answer with meters?" (Rename the answer since that would require only one renaming.) Tell the class that you often have to rename units before solving a problem.

TEACHING THE LESSON

Students will often look at the data in a problem and simply think, "What must I do to these numbers to get what I need?" This is an inefficient problem-solving strategy because it is indirect. By making a plan first, students learn to focus directly on what is asked and how to solve for it before beginning manipulation of supplied data.

Questions: The questions require a careful reading. Point out that each multistep problem contains *two* questions—the one identifying unstated data and the one asking the problem's question.

Tools: There are three critical steps to the approach taught in the lesson.
● Determine what the questions ask for.
● Identify unstated data.
● Use stated and unstated data to solve the problem.

The final step is critical. Students must realize that they may have to derive the data needed to solve the problem from data that is not included in the problem itself.

PROBLEM SOLVING
Solving Multistep Problems/Making a Plan

You may need to make more than one calculation to solve some problems. Before you can answer the question that is asked, you may have to find some data that are not stated. You can often compute with the numbers that are stated to find the numbers you need. Making a plan can help you solve such problems.

> Ms. Cronin, a geologist, discovered some plant fossils in a cave 30 meters below sea level. The next day, she dug 25 centimeters deeper and found more plant fossils. On the third day, she dug twice as far as on the second day and found several insect fossils. How many meters below sea level were the insect fossils Ms. Cronin discovered on the third day?

Unstated data: number of meters dug the second day
number of meters dug the third day

Plan
___ **1.** Rename 25 centimeters with meters.

___ **2.** Multiply Step 1's answer by 2.

___ **3.** Add the total number of meters found in steps 1 and 2 to the depth of the cave.

Rename 25 centimeters with meters; divide 25 by 100.

$25 \div 100 = 0.25$ $25 \text{ cm} = 0.25 \text{ m}$

Multiply 0.25 m by 2 to find the number of meters dug the third day.

$0.25 \times 2 = 0.50$ She dug 0.50 m.

Add the answers found in steps 1 and 2 to the depth of the cave.

$30 + 0.25 + 0.50 = 30.75$

The insect fossils Ms. Cronin discovered on the third day were 30.75 meters below sea level.

Explain the above outline to students. This method will help students focus on needed data.

Some students may also benefit from writing a word equation or several word equations; for example: cave depth + day 2 dig + day 3 dig = total depth.

Solutions: Renaming among metric units of length is used extensively. Students may benefit from reviewing these measurement equalities. You may wish to allow students to use calculators when solving these problems.

Checks: Students can review the computations for each step of the plan. The problem should also be reread after solving to check the reasonableness of the answer.

Complete the plan for solving each problem by writing the missing steps.

1. After digging for 3 days, a geologist discovered plant fossils at a distance of 24.5 m below sea level. On Thursday, he dug 185 cm deeper and found more plant fossils. On Friday, he dug three times as far as on Thursday and found several animal fossils. How many meters below sea level were the animal fossils?

— **1.** Rename 185 cm with meters.

— **2.** Multiply Step 1's answers by 3.

— **3.** Add 24.5 to the sum of Step 1 and Step 2.

2. Ms. Cronin recorded the depths at which fossils were found on a recent search. She recorded findings at depths of 0.66 meters, 0.62 meters, 64.5 centimeters, and 65.4 centimeters. At what depth was the deepest fossil found?

— **1.** Rename 64.5 centimeters with meters.

— **2.** Convert 65.4 centimeters to meters.

— **3.** Choose the largest number.

Make a plan for each problem. Solve. Check students' plan.

3. From a floating platform, a drill is lowered to a depth of 6.2 kilometers. The drill goes 9.5 meters into the sea floor and then is withdrawn 750 centimeters. How many meters below sea level did the tip of the drill reach? 6,209.5 meters

5. From a cavern 1.75 kilometers below sea level, a diver releases a flare that travels to the surface of the sea at the rate of 15 meters per second. How many meters from the surface was the flare 12 seconds after firing? 1,570 meters

7. The maximum depth of the Atlantic Ocean is 8.65 kilometers. A geologist took a water sample from a level that was $\frac{2}{5}$ this depth. At how many meters from the surface was the sample taken? 3,460 meters

4. A section of a petrified tree measures 1,296 cm long. A geologist cuts it into 4 sections, and each section is cut in half to form a research sample. How many meters are in a research sample? 1.62 meters

6. Ms. Cronin took out a loan to build a laboratory for examining and displaying fossils. She repaid a total of $18,562.50 on a loan of $16,500. What was the rate of interest on the 1-year loan? 12.5% interest

8. Ms. Cronin supervised 2 research sites. At the first site her assistants dug 1.6 m the first day and 2.4 m the next day. At the second site they dug 1.7 m the first day and 2.2 m the second day. At which site was the deeper hole dug? first site

Classwork/Homework, page H112

ASSIGNMENT GUIDE

Basic: 1–5

Average: 2–6

Extended: 2, 4–8

Resources
Practice, p. 112   Class/Home, p. H112
Enrich, p. 104

Exercise Analysis
1–2 Complete a problem-solving plan
3–8 Skill applications

FOLLOW-UP ACTIVITIES

PROBLEM SOLVING
Have students write a plan and solve the following problem. Tell them that light travels 3.0×10^8 m/s.

Zena's new spacecraft travels exactly one half the speed of light. The first part of her trip, to the planet Planetron, took exactly 164 days. The next part of her journey, to the Fill'er Up space station, took exactly 120 days. Since then, she has traveled for another 24 days. How far has she traveled?

(Sample plan:
a. Find the number of days traveled.
b. Find the number of seconds per day.
c. Multiply **a** times **b**.
d. Multiply $\frac{1}{2} \times 3.0 \times 10^8$ m/s by **c**. (Answer: 4×10^{15} m)

CALCULATOR
The four function keys of most calculators are often designed to function as an = key also. This permits the user to solve a string of operations without pressing = each time; for example, 2 + 9 + 4 − 8 can be solved by pressing 2 + 9 + 4 − 8 = instead of 2 + 9 = +4 = − 8 = . Have each student find out how each method affects the order of operations on his or her calculator. (Calculators vary.) Then have students use calculators to solve these problems.

● 28 × 64 ÷ 19 × 12 (1,131.7894)
● 2,850 ÷ 15 × 7 (1,330)
● 28,426 − 3,450 − 7,981 (16,995)
● (4,921 + 7,855) × 0.25 (3,194)
● 284 + 9,985 + 7 (1,467)

COMING UP
Buttoning up

Objective: To use the compound-interest formula

Warm-Up

Have students solve the following simple interest problems by finding how much interest would be charged.

1. $I = 10\%$
   $P = \$1,000$ ($100)
   $T = 1$ year
2. $I = 5\%$
   $P = \$2,000$ ($100)
   $T = 1$ year
3. $I = 7\frac{1}{2}\%$
   $P = \$4,000$ ($300)
   $T = 1$ year

GETTING STARTED

Discuss with students the various kinds of bank accounts available today. Point out that there is a great variety of interest rates available and the way that such rates are paid. Also, point out that these accounts rarely pay simple interest. Discuss the formula with students. Have them explain what each term means.

TEACHING THE LESSON

Discuss the formula with students. Have them explain what each term means.

Point out that in order to use this formula on a calculator, they must change the order in which they perform the operations. They should find the exponent first and save it. Then they should find $r \div n$ and add the quotient to 1. Next, they are to use the sum as a factor to be multiplied by the number of times indicated by the exponent. This product is then to be multiplied by the principal. Students should round the answer to the nearest cent. Some calculators may require students to enter the number and then the command for each step. This process can be made easier by entering the results of each operation into the memory and then recalling it each time it is needed.

Note that in the third step of the example, some calculators will require the following keystrokes rather than those shown.
1 . 0 2 5 × × = = =

CALCULATOR

Most savings accounts pay compound interest. This means that the bank pays interest on both the money in the account and the interest earned. The formula for computing compound interest is:

$$a = p \cdot \left(1 + \frac{r}{n}\right)^{(n \cdot y)}$$

a = amount of money after all of the interest is paid
p = the principal, or the money deposited
r = the annual rate of interest written as a decimal
n = the number of times a year interest is compounded
y = the number of years the principal is left in the account

Harry deposits $1,000 into his savings account. This account earns 10% interest, compounded quarterly (4 times a year). How much money will be in the account if he leaves it in for a year?

Press: [4] [×] [1] [=] — The display should show 4. This tells you what the exponent will be.

Press: [.] [1] [÷] [4] [+] [1] [=] — The display should show 1.025. Raise this number to the exponent found in the first step.

Press: [1] [.] [0] [2] [5] [×] [1] [.] [0] [2] [5] [=] [=] [=] — The display should show 1.1038128. Multiply this by the principal.

Press: [1] [0] [0] [0] [×] [1] [.] [1] [0] [3] [8] [1] [2] [8] [=] — The display should show 1103.8128. Round this amount to the nearest hundredth.

There will be $1,103.81 in the account at the end of a year.

Use a calculator to solve.

1. Ronnie deposits $2,000 into an account that earns 8% interest, compounded twice a year. How much money will be in the account if she leaves it in for 2 years? **$2,339.72**

2. Pablo deposits $4,000 into an account that earns 12% interest, compounded yearly. How much money will be in the account if he leaves it in for 3 years? **$5,619.71**

3. In the example, suppose that Harry had rounded 1.025 to 1.03 before calculating the interest. Would the error have been very great? Explain. Yes; interest would have been $125.51. The digits in 1.025 are all significant and should not be rounded.

272

GROUP PROJECT

Circling the World

The problem: The first circumnavigation of the world occurred in the 1500's. The sea voyage, undertaken by Ferdinand Magellan, took three years. Today, you can travel around the world in a fraction of that time. You can travel by ship, by jet, and, to a great extent, by car, train, or bus. Using the questions below, plan a trip around the world. Draw your route on a map.

Key Questions

- How many weeks, months, or years will you allow for your trip?

- How many stops will you make?

- At which places will you stop?

- How long will you stay in each place?

- How will you travel from each place to the next? What forms of transportation will you use?

- What preparations will you make before leaving on your trip?

- Can you estimate how much your trip will cost?

- Suppose you want to spend the least time traveling and the most time visiting places. What would be the minimum amount of time you'd have to allow for traveling?

- How many miles do you plan to travel each day?

273

ASSIGNMENT GUIDE

Basic:	p. 272, p. 273
Average:	p. 272, p. 273
Extended:	p. 272, p. 273

Objectives: To plan a trip; to draw its route on a map

USING THE PAGE

Materials: world atlas, books on geography, blank outline map of the world, color pencils per group

Organize students into groups of four to six. Have students consider individually places where they would like to go on the group's trip. When each student has presented to the group his or her preferred stops, the group then should plan a relatively direct route, including as many of the desired stops as is practical. Remind groups to consider the Key Questions in planning their trips.

Have each group use color pencils to chart their route around the world on an outline map. Group members should each have the opportunity to find and mark various places on the outline map. Groups should also estimate the length and cost of the trip and the total mileage they will log. Members of each group should also take turns naming things to do before departure, and one group member should write down a list of all these considerations.

To extend this cooperative learning activity, have each group write a diary for one day or one week of their trip. Have them record each location, their method of transport to that place, the highlights of the place as they imagine it or have read about it, the number of miles logged that day traveling or just sightseeing, and daily expenses.

Purpose: The Chapter Test helps to assess students' understanding of the concepts and skills presented in this chapter.

The chart below is designed to help you review the test items by correlating them with the testing objectives that appear in the Chapter Overview.

Item	Objectives
1–5	A
6–7	B
8–11	C
12–14	D
15–17	E
18	F
19–20	G
21	F
22–23	G
24–26	C
27–31	H
32–35	I,J,K

Bonus
The bonus question may be used for extra credit, or you may want to assign it to students who complete the test before the rest of the class.

Calculator
You may wish to have students use calculators for the problem-solving portions of the test.

Resources
If you prefer to use this Chapter Test as a review exercise, additional testing materials are available in the Teacher's Resource Book.

CHAPTER TEST

Compare. Write $>$, $<$, or $=$ for ●. (pages 240–241)

1. $^-3$ ● $^-3$ $=$

2. $^-6$ ● $^-2$ $<$

3. 4 ● $^-5$ $>$

Order from the greatest to the least. (pages 240–241 and 258–259)

4. $16, ^-3, 37, ^-49, 2, ^-24$
$37, 16, 2, ^-3, ^-24, ^-49$

5. $^-1\frac{1}{2}, ^-2, 0.5, \frac{4}{7}$
$\frac{4}{7}, 0.5, ^-1\frac{1}{2}, ^-2$

Add, subtract, multiply, or divide. (pages 244–247 and 250–253)

6. $^-10 + ^-4 + 3$ $^-11$

7. $^-21 - 4 - ^-3$ $^-22$

8. $^-2 \cdot 21$ $^-42$

9. $^-4 \cdot ^-5$ 20

10. $32 \div ^-8$ $^-4$

11. $^-81 \div ^-9$ 9

Write in scientific notation. (pages 254–255)

12. 0.187 $1.87 \cdot 10^{-1}$

13. 0.00586 $5.86 \cdot 10^{-3}$

14. 0.00604 $6.04 \cdot 10$

Compare. Write $>$, $<$, or $=$ for ●. (pages 258–259)

15. $^-1.2$ ● $^-\frac{4}{9}$ $<$

16. $\frac{6}{11}$ ● $^-1\frac{1}{3}$ $>$

17. 9.6 ● $9\frac{3}{5}$ $=$

Add, subtract, multiply, or divide. (pages 260–261 and 264–265)

18. $^-\frac{1}{5} + \frac{2}{5} - \frac{4}{5}$ $^-\frac{3}{5}$

19. $^-\frac{3}{5} \cdot ^-\frac{4}{11}$ $\frac{12}{55}$

20. $^-\frac{2}{3} \cdot \frac{3}{8}$ $^-\frac{1}{4}$

21. $^-3.7 + ^-2.8 - ^-3.5$ $^-3$

22. $^-\frac{4}{5} \div \frac{1}{6}$ $^-4\frac{4}{5}$

23. $^-7.68 \div ^-3.2$ 2.4

Write as a terminating or a repeating decimal. (pages 266–267)

24. $^-\frac{5}{11}$ $^-0.\overline{45}$

25. $\frac{5}{8}$ 0.625

26. $\frac{7}{18}$ $0.38\overline{}$

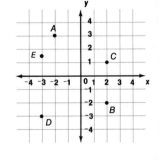

Use the graph for Exercises 27–31. (pages 268–269)
Write the ordered pair for each point.

27. A $(^-2,3)$

28. C $(2,1)$

Write the point for the ordered pair.

29. $(2,^-2)$ B

30. $\left(^-3, 1\frac{1}{2}\right)$ E

31. $(^-3,^-3)$ D

274

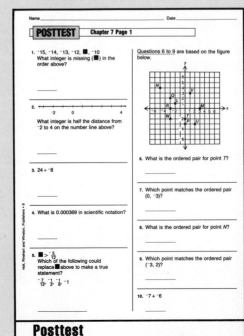

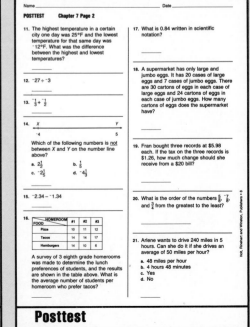

Solve. Use the graph to answer Exercises 32–35. Make sure that your solution answers the question. (pages 248–249, 256–257, 262–263, and 270–271)

32. During Expedition TLO, Marcel recorded the temperature at 12 noon and at 12 midnight for a week. Find the average temperature at midnight for the week. ⁻12°C

33. Was the difference in temperature for Day 4 greater than or less than the difference in temperature for Day 7? less than

34. What was the difference in temperature between noon on Day 2 and noon on Day 6? 3°C

35. What was the average temperature at 12 noon for the week? Round your answer to the nearest tenth of a degree. 6.7°C

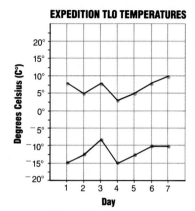

EXPEDITION TLO TEMPERATURES

Blue = 12 noon
Red = 12 midnight

BONUS

Solve.

If one day the temperature was ⁻15°C at midnight, ⁻10°C at 3 A.M., ⁻3°C at 6 A.M., 0°C at 9 A.M., and 5°C at noon, which interval showed the greatest degree of change in temperature? What was the change in degrees? 3 A.M. to 6 A.M.; 7°C

275

For students who have difficulty with written tests, this test can be given orally.

You may wish to test students, orally or in writing, to see if they can explain the steps used in solving selected items. The following summarizes the procedures for solving key test items.

Ex. 12–14

Writing numbers less than 1 in scientific notation using a negative power of 10

To write a number that is less than 1 in scientific notation, write the first factor by moving the decimal point to the right to form a number between 1 and 10. Write the second factor as a negative power of 10, counting the number of places the decimal point was moved to determine the exponent. Then write the first factor times the negative exponent of 10.

Ex. 18–23

Adding, subtracting, multiplying, and dividing rational numbers

To add two rational numbers that have the same signs, add their absolute values and use the sign of the addends. To add two rational numbers that have different signs, find the difference between their absolute values and use the sign of the addend that has the greater absolute value.

To subtract a rational number, add its opposite. To multiply or divide two rational numbers, remember that if two rational numbers have like signs, their product or quotient is positive. If two rational numbers have unlike signs, their product or quotient is negative.

POSTTEST   Chapter 7 Page 3

22. What is 0.000045 written in scientific notation?

23. ⁸⁄₉ ÷ ¹⁄₄

24. ⁻15 · ⁻5

25. ■ < ⁻4
Which of the following integers, if placed in the ■ above, would make a true statement?
⁻10, ⁻3, 0, 2

26. ⁻⁵⁄₁₂ + ⁻²⁄₁₂

27. Order the numbers below from the greatest to the least.
³⁄₄, ⁻¹⁄₂, 0, ²⁄₃

Questions 28 to 31 are based on the graph below.

ESTIMATED HOTTEST TEMPERATURES ON SURFACES OF THE PLANETS

28. Which planet has the highest estimated hottest temperature?

29. Which three planets have the lowest estimated hottest temperatures?

30. How many planets have estimated hottest temperatures that are below 0°F?

31. Which planets have estimated hottest temperatures that are greater than the Earth's?

Posttest

POSTTEST   Chapter 7 Page 4

32. ⁻10 − ⁻8

33. 7⅘ ÷ ⁻3

34. Order the integers below from the greatest to the least.
1, ⁻3, ⁻9, 5

35. ⁻3⅕ − ⁻2³⁄₁₀

36. Sandra has $14.75. She wants to buy a book for $13.95. If the tax is $0.98, does she have enough money?
a. $0.18   b. $14.93
c. yes   d. no

37. ⁻1 · ⁻1 · ⁻1

38. ⁻1.44 ÷ ⁻1.2

39. Which is the greater mass, 500 grams or 4 kilograms?

40. ⁻4.4 · 1.2

41. 10 − (⁻8 + 5)

42. What is 0.0223 written in scientific notation?

43. A drilling rig drills an oil well at the rate of 5 feet per minute. How far does it drill in 3 hours?

44. The record low temperature in January for Kansas is ⁻35°F. During one week in January, the high temperature in Kansas on Monday was 20°F and it dropped 30° that night. The high on Tuesday was 10°F and it dropped 16° that night. Did the temperature set a new record low for January on Monday or Tuesday?
a. 46°
b. ⁻10°
c. No
d. Yes, it dropped both nights.

Posttest

Purpose This Reteaching page provides additional instruction for key concepts in the chapter. It is designed for use by students who have had difficulty with these concepts. It can also be used to provide additional practice for students who require it.

USING THE PAGE

Integers as exponents were taught on pages 254–255.

Review powers of 10 as an introduction to this page. Emphasize to students that a power of 10 can be converted to exponential form by counting the number of zeros to find the exponent. Extend this to moving the decimal point with negative exponents. Be sure students realize that when they write a number in scientific notation, the first number should be between 1 and 10. Tell students that a negative exponent is the same as the inverse of a positive exponent with the same absolute value $(4^{-3} = \left(\frac{1}{4^3}\right) = \frac{1}{64})$.

Exponents with the same base can be multiplied or divided simply by adding or subtracting the exponents. Emphasize the fact that this can be done only if the bases are the same.

Resources

For other practice and activities related to this chapter, see the Teacher's Resource Book.

RETEACHING

A. Recall that a number in scientific notation is the product of a number between 1 and 10 and a power of 10. When a number smaller than 1 is expressed in scientific notation, the power of 10 has a negative exponent.

Express 659,000 in scientific notation.

$$659,000 = 6.59 \cdot 10,000$$
$$= 6.59 \cdot 10^5 \longleftarrow \text{scientific notation}$$

Express 0.00286 in scientific notation.

$$0.00286 = 2.86 \cdot 0.001$$
$$= 2.86 \cdot 10^{-3} \longleftarrow \text{scientific notation}$$

The exponent shows how many places the decimal point must be moved to write the number in standard form. Move the decimal point to the right with a positive exponent. Move the decimal point to the left with a negative exponent.

B. To multiply (or divide) numbers that are powers of the same base, use the following rules.

1. To multiply powers of the same base, add exponents.
2. To divide powers of the same base, subtract exponents.

Multiply $5^4 \cdot 5^3$.
$$5^4 \cdot 5^3 = 5^{4+3} = 5^7 \quad \text{Add exponents.}$$
$$\text{Base remains the same.}$$

Divide $7^5 \div 7^2$.
$$7^5 \div 7^2 = 7^{5-2} = 7^3 \quad \text{Subtract exponents.}$$
$$\text{Base remains the same.}$$

Express each number in scientific notation.

1. 2,300
$2.3 \cdot 10^3$

2. 60,350
$6.035 \cdot 10^4$

3. 84,000
$8.4 \cdot 10^4$

4. 750,000
$7.5 \cdot 10^5$

5. 0.000426
$4.26 \cdot 10^{-4}$

6. 0.0583
$5.83 \cdot 10^{-2}$

7. 0.000063
$6.3 \cdot 10^{-5}$

8. 0.00000312
$3.12 \cdot 10^{-6}$

Multiply or divide.

9. $8^2 \cdot 8^3$
8^5

10. $6^{-2} \cdot 6^3$
6

11. $5 \cdot 5^4$
5^5

12. $2^{-4} \cdot 2^{-2}$
2^{-6}

13. $5^4 \div 5$
5^3

14. $3^6 \div 3^{-2}$
3^8

15. $4^7 \div 4^5$
4^2

16. $9^{-2} \div 9^3$
9^{-5}

276

ENRICHMENT

Adding and Subtracting with Radicals

In a **radical expression** such as $3\sqrt{2}$, the number under the radical sign is called the **radicand**. The number in front of the radical sign is called the **coefficient**. If two radical expressions have the same radicand, they are called **like radicals**.

$5\sqrt{2}$ and $7\sqrt{2}$ are like radicals because they both contain the same radicand (2).

Like radical expressions can be combined by adding (or subtracting) their coefficients.

Add. $5\sqrt{2} + 7\sqrt{2} = (5 + 7)\sqrt{2}$
$\qquad\qquad\quad = 12\sqrt{2}$

Subtract. $3\sqrt{6} - 5\sqrt{6} = (3 - 5)\sqrt{6}$
$\qquad\qquad\qquad\quad = {}^{-}2\sqrt{6}$

Only expressions containing like radicals can be combined. However, some expressions that appear to have no like radicals can be combined after each radical is simplified.

Simplify and combine $\sqrt{75} - \sqrt{27} + \sqrt{12}$.

$\sqrt{75} = \sqrt{25 \cdot 3} = \sqrt{25} \cdot \sqrt{3} = 5\sqrt{3}$
$\sqrt{27} = \sqrt{9 \cdot 3} = \sqrt{9} \cdot \sqrt{3} = 3\sqrt{3}$
$\sqrt{12} = \sqrt{4 \cdot 3} = \sqrt{4} \cdot \sqrt{3} = 2\sqrt{3}$
$5\sqrt{3} - 3\sqrt{3} + 2\sqrt{3} = (5 - 3 + 2)\sqrt{3}$
$\qquad\qquad\qquad\qquad\quad = 4\sqrt{3}$

Think:
$\sqrt{a \cdot b} = \sqrt{a} \cdot \sqrt{b}$

Check with a calculator: $\boxed{3}\ \boxed{\sqrt{\ }}\ \boxed{\times}\ \boxed{4}\ \boxed{=}$ ← Both displays should show 6.928203.

$\boxed{7}\ \boxed{5}\ \boxed{\sqrt{\ }}\ \boxed{-}\ \boxed{2}\ \boxed{7}\ \boxed{\sqrt{\ }}\ \boxed{+}\ \boxed{1}\ \boxed{2}\ \boxed{\sqrt{\ }}\ \boxed{=}$

Simplify and combine where possible.

1. $4\sqrt{10} + 2\sqrt{10} - 5\sqrt{10}$
$\sqrt{10}$

2. $7\sqrt{7} - 2\sqrt{7} + 3\sqrt{7} + 3\sqrt{7}$
$11\sqrt{7}$

3. $\sqrt{5} + 7\sqrt{2} - 4\sqrt{2} + 7\sqrt{5}$
$8\sqrt{5} + 3\sqrt{2}$

4. $4\sqrt{3} + 6\sqrt{2} + 4\sqrt{11} - \sqrt{3}$
$3\sqrt{3} + 6\sqrt{2} + 4\sqrt{11}$

5. $3\sqrt{44} + \sqrt{99} - 7\sqrt{11}$
$2\sqrt{11}$

6. $12\sqrt{7} - \sqrt{63} + 5\sqrt{112}$
$29\sqrt{7}$

7. $2\sqrt{13} - 4\sqrt{13} + \sqrt{13}$
$^{-}\sqrt{13}$

8. $^{-}6\sqrt{3} + {}^{-}2\sqrt{3} + 14\sqrt{3}$
$6\sqrt{3}$

9. $^{-}3\sqrt{2} + 4\sqrt{17} + {}^{-}2\sqrt{2} - {}^{-}\sqrt{17}$
$^{-}5\sqrt{2} + 5\sqrt{17}$

10. $\sqrt{5} - \sqrt{5} + \sqrt{23} + {}^{-}6\sqrt{3}$
$\sqrt{23} + {}^{-}6\sqrt{3}$

277

Purpose This Enrichment page provides an additional challenge for those students whose work throughout the chapter and on the Chapter Test shows a thorough understanding of the material. Alternatively, you may wish to use these exercises as a supplementary lesson for the entire class.

USING THE PAGE

Write $3\sqrt{2}$ on the chalkboard. Tell students that a mathematical expression with a square-root sign in it is called a *radical expression*, $\sqrt{2}$ is the *radical*, 2 is the *radicand*, and 3 is the *coefficient*. Emphasize that only *like radicals*—those that have the same radicand—can be combined. This becomes obvious if students estimate the value of a radical and substitute that value back into the expression or equation. Be sure students understand that the value of radicals can only be estimated to a certain number of places and that they are nonterminating, nonrepeating decimals. Sometimes, however, a radical can be simplified to some extent. In order to do this, students should look for a perfect square factor in the radicand. This factor can then be evaluated and attached to the new radical.

Resources
For additional Enrichment activities, see the Teacher's Resource Book.

Purpose This Cumulative Review page provides an opportunity to reinforce students' understanding of the concepts and skills taught in previous chapters.

The chart below is designed to aid you in reviewing the material by specifying the pages on which various concepts and skills were taught.

Item	Page
1	200–201
2	202–203
3	212–213
4	210–211
5	216–217
6	212–213
7	188–189
8	166–167
9	176–177
10	142–143
11	150–151
12	88–89
13	152–153
14	206–207

Each Cumulative Review gives students an opportunity to practice taking tests that are written in a multiple-choice, standardized format. Be sure that students understand that if the correct answer is not among the first three given, then they should select the fourth choice—"not given"—as the correct answer. At least one item per test will require students to give this response.

CUMULATIVE REVIEW

Write the letter of the correct answer.

1. What is $3:7$ written as a fraction?

a. $\frac{7}{21}$　　**b.** $\frac{3}{7}$

c. $2\frac{1}{3}$　　d. not given

2. Solve for c: $\frac{3}{5} = \frac{c}{15}$.

a. 3　　**b.** 9

c. 25　　d. not given

3. What is 723% written as a fraction?

a. $\frac{723}{1,000}$　　**b.** $\frac{723}{100}$

c. 723　　d. not given

4. What is 4.03 written as a percent?

a. $4\frac{3}{100}$　　b. 40.3%

c. $40\frac{3}{10}$　　**d.** not given

5. What is 24.6% of 242?

a. 59.532　　b. 584.32

c. 4,953.2　　d. not given

6. What is $4\frac{3}{5}$ written as a percent?

a. 4.6%　　b. 60%

c. 460%　　d. not given

7. What is the temperature change from 33°C to ⁻5°C?

a. 28°C　　**b.** 38°C

c. 39°C　　d. not given

8. $3.25 \text{ m} + 7.10 \text{ cm} = \blacksquare \text{ cm}$

a. 10.35　　**b.** 332.10

c. 396　　d. not given

9. Choose the appropriate unit to measure flour.

a. inches　　b. quarts

c. pounds　　d. not given

10. $4\frac{2}{5} \times 7\frac{1}{8}$

a. $\frac{176}{285}$　　b. $28\frac{1}{20}$

c. $32\frac{7}{20}$　　**d.** not given

11. What is $\frac{3}{7}$ written as a decimal rounded to the nearest hundredth?

a. 0.42　　b. 0.429

c. 0.43　　d. not given

12. Of 11, 43, and 57, which is not prime?

a. 11　　b. 43

c. 57　　d. not given

13. Janice wanted to bake a dozen muffins, but the recipe she had would yield 36. How much milk should she use if the recipe called for $2\frac{1}{4}$ c?

a. $\frac{1}{3}$ c　　**b.** $\frac{3}{4}$ c

c. $\frac{5}{5}$ c　　d. not given

14. Ed's map has a scale of 1 in. = 20 mi. The distance between two cities on this map is 8.45 in. How far apart are the cities?

a. 4.9 mi　　b. 52.25 mi

c. 169 mi　　d. not given

278

CHAPTER  OVERVIEW

EQUATIONS AND INEQUALITIES ONE VARIABLE

SUMMARY

Chapter 8 focuses on equations and inequalities. Included are lessons on solving one- and two-step equations and inequalities in one variable by using integers, rationals, and reals, writing one- and two-step equations for word problems, and solving and graphing equations and inequalities on the number line.

LESSON SEQUENCE

PROFESSIONAL BACKGROUND

As might be expected, studies have shown that many adolescents encounter difficulty in understanding the meaning and the use of variables. For instance, some students believe that the equations

$$6a + 5 = 35$$
$$6x + 5 = 35$$

have different solutions because the variable has changed. To help these students, use a variety of letters and stress their meaning when equations are constructed. Take care to use the correct language when topics in algebra are discussed. For instance, emphasize the distinction between "Let c equal the number of cars," and "Let c equal cars."

Keep in mind that in earlier grades, equations were based on action statements such as "$7 + 8$ equals (or yields) 15." In algebra, equations are suddenly equivalence statements as in $6x + 4 = x$. To help students internalize this new role, research suggests that teachers work through a sequence of activities that proceeds from the concrete to the abstract. For example, write an equation and cover the unknown with your hand, a box, or a piece of paper. After some practice, draw a rectangle or triangle to represent the variable. Finally, as students grasp the notion of algebraic equivalence, use letters for the unknowns.

Resources: See Herscovics and Kieran; and Driscoll (secondary volume, chapter on algebra).

MATERIALS

pan balances and paper clips
index cards

VOCABULARY

algebraic expression (p. 280)
inequality (p. 292)

ABOUT THE CHAPTER

This is the third of four chapters in this text that are specially designed to prepare students for algebra. It is this chapter which is the crucial one that can make the difference for students. It brings together all that students have learned about integers and rational numbers with all they have learned about solving equations and extends it to solving inequalities.

In Chapter 8, students learn to evaluate and solve 1- and 2-step equations using integers and rational numbers. Students learn to write equations to solve word problems. Students also learn to solve 1- and 2-step inequalities and to graph equations and inequalities.

You have already taught students how to solve equations. The challenge in this chapter is for them to extend solving equations to include integers and rational numbers. It may be appropriate to review some of the concepts covered in Chapter 3. We don't want students to move beyond this chapter without understanding it thoroughly.

Inequalities are solved in much the same way as equations. Indeed, the similarity between the two methods should be emphasized. Using the method of a test point to solve an inequality avoids formal instruction on the properties of inequalities.

The problem-solving lessons in the chapter show students how to choose and write an equation and how to use the guess-and-check method of solving nonroutine problems. Other problem-solving lessons show students how to look for another way to solve a problem and how to get and use information from a schedule.

The Group Project actively involves students as the prime-time scheduler for a television network. Students must take into account factors such as competition, potential sponsors, and the size of the audience as they plan the schedule. This problem-solving project gives students an opportunity to apply problem-solving and other mathematical concepts and skills.

The Enrichment lesson shows students how to solve equations in one variable with exponents. This lesson, which is a natural extension of the chapter, actually shows students how to solve simple quadratic equations.

USING THE CHAPTER OPENER

Each Chapter Opener presents situational problem-solving activities that can be used to explore the skills taught throughout the chapter. The work sheets can be used by individuals, small groups, or the whole class, depending on the needs of the class. The Chapter Opener focuses on a nonalgorithmic approach to mathematics through real-life situations relevant to the children's experiences. Through an interdisciplinary approach, the Chapter Opener helps children explore the relationships between mathematics, other areas of the curriculum, and everyday life while developing different strands of mathematics.

In the Chapter Opener activities, students will use demographics to plan an advertising campaign. Students will also choose a product and develop an advertising budget and a commercial for their product.

PROBLEM SOLVING

The lesson Writing an Equation builds upon the lesson Choosing the Operation. Before they can write an equation, students will need to determine what operations to use. *Mathematics Unlimited* emphasizes a conceptual reasoning approach, in which students sort through the given information, rather than rely on key terms to signal specific operations. Keep in mind that more than one equation may achieve the correct solution and that some equations can be written two ways. For example, $n + 6 = 17$ can also be written as $17 - 6 = n$. The lesson Guessing and Checking focuses on problems characterized by a set of conditions, all of which must be satisfied in the correct answer. The guess-and-check strategy, can help students to explore a problem more deeply, and to avoid random guesses. The method is often useful for discovering whether a pattern exists. An effective test-taking tool, it can also be used when solving multiple-choice problems.

The lesson Making a Table to Find a Pattern teaches students how to analyze and define the relationship between a given set of numbers. Students learn that a pattern recurs as the numbers are compared in increasing intervals: the relationship between the first and second number is the same as that between the second and the third, the third and fourth, and so on. The lesson teaches students to draw tables which make the pattern easier to find. Once the pattern is deciphered, students can extend the tables to find the solution to the problem.

In the lesson Using a Schedule students practice using data not included in the text of a problem. The lesson focuses on how departure and arrival times are organized in a train schedule and on how to use this information, in combination with information obtained from the time-zone map on P.E. page 186, to solve the given problem. Using a Schedule offers an excellent opportunity for small-group work.

Most of the problem-solving lessons in *Mathematics Unlimited* lend themselves to small-group work. Small groups furnish the opportunity for students to develop cooperative attitudes and group decision-making skills.

BULLETIN BOARD

"At The Movies"

Materials: paper to cover bulletin board; lettering; felt-tip pens; movie posters or magazine and newspaper ads for movies, brought in by students and by teacher; string or yarn; push pins; poster-board strips

Preparation: Cover bulletin board with paper and arrange movie ads or posters to the left of the board as shown. Below each picture, on poster-board strip, write a sentence related to movies, such as, *There were 3 more lighting technicians than sound technicians on the set.* Write an algebraic expression for each sentence on the back of each strip, for example: *x + 3.* Attach the strips to the board. Use a push pin to fasten a length of string to the right of each picture. On the right-hand side of the board, on poster-board strips, write the algebraic expressions which correspond to the sentences on the left-hand side of the board. Attach a push pin to the left of each expression. Be sure that the corresponding algebraic expressions are not written in the same order as the sentences.

After pp. 280-281: Have students use the string and push pins to connect the sentences on the left with the correct algebraic expressions on the right. Ask them to check the answers on the back of each sentence.

COMMON ERRORS

Students sometimes have difficulty solving equations that involve integers. In concentrating on the operations needed to solve for a variable, they overlook the rules of operations. A student might proceed as follows:

$$a/-2 = -3$$
$$(a/-2) \cdot 2 = -3 \cdot 2$$
$$a = -6$$

To remediate this type of error, review the rules governing integers with like and unlike signs for all operations. Then work several examples on the board carefully, step by step. Use the above example and emphasize which operation must be used on both sides of the equation to solve for *a*. Have students determine what operation needs to be performed on *a/−2* to get *a* by itself? (Multiply it by −2.) Then have students find what they need to do to the equation *a/−2 = −3* to solve for *a*? (Multiply both sides by −2.) Finally ask: How do we simplify *(a/−2) · −2 = −3 · −2?* (*a = 6*)

They should write down each step carefully and to make sure that all operations are performed on both sides of the equation.

SPECIAL NEEDS

Guide students who are having difficulty with equations to an understanding of inverse properties. Thoroughly review the concepts $^+n + {}^-n = 0$ and $\frac{1}{n} \times \frac{n}{1} = 1$, prior to solving equations. Remind students that equations must always remain "balanced." Therefore, in order not to disturb this "balance," whatever operation is performed on one side of the equation must also be performed on the other side. Introduce the terms *(variable, coefficient, equation),* and always use correct terminology. Make sure that students know that the variable represents a number or numbers which make the equation true. Equations can be checked easily by having each student substitute their numerical solution for the variable. Initially, they may use a "guess and check" method that is based on logical reasoning. To solve the equation algebraically, have them set up the equation so that the variable stands alone on one side. Continue to stress the concepts of "balance" and inverse properties. Proceed to two-step equations only after the process for solving one-step equations is mastered.

Challenge students to find out about women mathematicians and to report about one of them to the class.

MATH LABS

COMPUTER

Provide the program below as a handout, and have students analyze it and explain the function of each program line.

To aid students in their analysis, ask
- What does it do? (It tests the user's ability to solve the two-step equation $3x + 8 = 22$.)
- When does the computer give a hint? (After the second incorrect response.)

```
10  DATA "3X + 8 = 22",
    "SUBTRACT", "8", "DIVIDE
    BY", "3"
20  READ A$
30  PRINT A$
40  INPUT "FIRST STEP TO
    SOLVE";X$
50  GOSUB 100
60  INPUT "CORRECT. SECOND
    STEP TO SOLVE":X$
70  GOSUB 100
80  PRINT "CORRECT."
90  END
100 REM SUBROUTINE FOR
    TESTING RESPONSES
110 READ A$
120 READ B$
130 LET C$ = A$ + B$
140 IF C$ = X$ THEN RETURN
150 INPUT "INCORRECT. TRY
    AGAIN";X$
160 IF C$ = X$ THEN RETURN
170 PRINT "INCORRECT. HINT:
    ";A$;
180 INPUT X$
190 IF X$ = B$ THEN RETURN
200 GOTO 170
```

PUZZLES AND GAMES

Have students color in those line segments indicated by each inequality or pair of inequalities to find the answer to the following question: In which year was "Rowan and Martin's Laugh-In" the top rated network TV show? (1969)

a) $9 < 7x + 2 < 23$
b) $\frac{11}{2} < \frac{x}{4} + 5 < \frac{23}{4}$
c) $\frac{-5}{3} < \frac{x}{3} - 2 < \frac{4}{3}$
d) $-3 < 4x - 7 < 5$
e) $\frac{-16}{3} < \frac{4x}{3} < -4$ or $-\frac{8}{3} < \frac{4x}{3} < -\frac{4}{3}$
f) $\frac{-4}{7} < \frac{2x}{7} + \frac{4}{7} < -\frac{2}{7}$ or
   $0 < \frac{2x}{7} + \frac{4}{7} < \frac{2}{7}$
g) $\frac{-14}{5} < \frac{3x}{5} - \frac{2}{5} < \frac{-11}{5}$ or
   $\frac{-8}{5} < \frac{3x}{5} - \frac{2}{5} < -1$

CALCULATOR

Equations and inequalities, two of the fundamental topics in the introductory study of algebra, are very important. Students need to have a thorough understanding of the concepts of variable, equation, inequality, and solution set. Although the calculator will not solve equations, calculator codes can be written to solve some equations. In this way, a student should acquire a strong foundation and preparation for the study of more complex algebraic concepts.

Students should use calculators for all problem-solving activities.

Additional Activities: **Drill and Practice:** The following calculator code solves $AX = B$ where A and B are constants. In the code $A = 8.6$, $B = 7.4$. CODE: $7.4 \div 8.6 = $.
Find X for each of the following pairs of A and B: (9.3, 6.4), (17.41, 93.2)

Exploration: Develop a calculator code to solve the equation $AX + B = C$ where A, B, and C are constants.

SUBJECT AREA CONNECTIONS

These activities are useful for reinforcing the concepts presented in this chapter.

p. 283-Science: Students are given the Ohm formula and variables to solve for current, voltage, or resistance. This involves solving a two-step equation.

Here are some other activities for presenting these concepts.
- **ART:** Have students measure 1 teaspoon of blue paint and enough yellow paint to create a vivid green color. Have students write a one-variable equation to express the mixture.
- **SOCIAL STUDIES:** Have students survey the entire class regarding each person's favorite radio station. Have students graph the results.

PLAN AHEAD

You will need to prepare index cards for the activity on T.E. p. 287.

PLANNING CALENDAR

Pages	Lesson Objectives	Basic	Average	Extended	Class/Home	More Practice	Math Reasoning	Follow-up	Reteach	Practice	Enrich
		ASSIGNMENT GUIDE									
279	Chapter Opener (Use MMW 15,16)	279	279	279							
280,281	To write and evaluate an algebraic equation	1-6,11-16,29-31	1-13,20-25,29-31	1-10,11-27o,29-31	H113		H221	NS CALC	81	113	105
282,283	To solve a one-step equation	1-12,13-33o,34-35, NS	1-22,34-35,NS	13-35,NS	H114			NS MC	82	114	106
284,285	To solve a two-step equation	1-17,34-37,NS1-8	2-32e,34-37,NS	1-33o,34-37,NS	H115	H203	H221	CALC PS	83	115	107
286,287	To write a word problem from an equation	1-8,MCR	1-10,MCR	1-12,MCR	H116			MCM RFM	84	116	108
288,289	To write an equation to solve a problem	1-4	2-6	3-8	H117			PS CALC		117	109
290,291	To use the guess-and-check strategy to solve problems	1-4	2-5	3-6	H118 H119			PS CALC		118-119	
292,293	To define an inequality and solve given a replacement set	1-13,18-28e, Calc1-11o	1-5,6-22e,24-28, Calc	1-5,14-29,Calc	H120		H222	NS CMP	85	120	110
294,295	To solve a one-step inequality	1-8,9-31o	1-4,6-32e,33-34	6-32e,33-34,Chlg	H121	H203	H222	MCM MC	86	121	111
296,297	To organize information in a table and look for a pattern to solve problems	1-4	3-4,6-7	3-7	H122 H123			PS CALC		122-123	
298,299	To solve a two-step inequality	1-16,33-34,NS	1-31o,33-34,NS	2-32e,33-34,NS	H124	H203		PS RFM	87	124	112
300,301	To solve and graph equations and inequalities on a number line	1-12,17-28,33	5-15,17-28,33-34	9-16,25-34,Chlg	H125		H222	PS RFM	88	125	113
302,303	To use information from a schedule in problem solving	1-4	2-6	3-8	H126			PS RFM		126	114
304	Logical Reasoning: To define *logical equivalence* and the *if/then conditional* by using a truth table; to determine the truth value of conditional	304	304	304							
305	Group Project: To plan TV programming; to make a schedule	305	305	305							

306,307	Chapter Test
308	Reteaching
309	Enrichment
310,311	Technology
312	Cumulative Review

SOFTWARE

Mathematics Unlimited Problem-Solving Software
  Strategies: Problem Solving

ABBREVIATION KEY

Teacher's Resource Book
MMW—Making Math Work
P—Practice
R—Reteach
E—Enrich

Follow-up Activities
CALC—Calculator
CMP—Computer
P&G—Puzzles and Games
MNP—Manipulatives

MC—Math Connection
MCM—Math Communication
NS—Number Sense
PS—Problem Solving
RFM—Reinforcement

TESTS

A. To evaluate algebraic expressions
B. To solve one-step and two-step equations that involve rational numbers
C. To solve one-step inequalities
D. To solve two-step inequalities
E. To graph an equation or inequality
F. To write an equation for a problem, and solve
G. To use a guess-and-check strategy to solve problems
H. To organize information in a table to find a pattern to solve problems
I. To use information from a schedule to solve problems

FAMILY INVOLVEMENT

Family Involvement for Chapter 8 encourages family members to set up a family-run business in which furniture kits can be bought, assembled, and sold. Family members are asked to consider decisions such as who will assemble the kits, who will finish them, who will keep records, and during which hours the business should be open. It should be pointed out that calculating the retail price of the items to be sold is an important aspect of running a family business. Family members are asked to add the cost of wages and benefits as part of their calculations. They are then to calculate 15% of the cost as profit. The retail cost is to be added to the wholesale price to get the retail price. Family members should then estimate the profits that they expect their family-run business to earn.

Additional activities might include finding the current prices of several items in the home such as electric appliances, furniture, electronic equipment, and lawnmowers. Then family members should calculate the sales tax. If the state has no sales tax, have family members calculate a tax rate of 6%.

STUDENT RESOURCES

Bibliography

Jenkins, Gerald, and Anne Wild. *Mathematical Curiosities.* New York: Parkwest Publications, Inc., 1986.

Mintern, Helen. *Television and Video.* New York: Franklin Watts, 1984.

O'Connor, Jane, and Katy Hall. *Magic in the Movies: The Story of Special Effects.* Garden City, New York: Doubleday and Company, Inc., 1980.

Smart, Margaret A. *Focus on Pre-Algebra.* Hayward, CA: Activity Resources Co., Inc., 1983.

Films

Two Laws of Algebra. 4 minutes. Color. 1973. Distributed by Pyramid Films, Santa Monica, Calif.

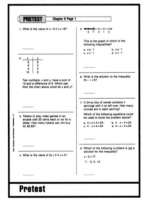

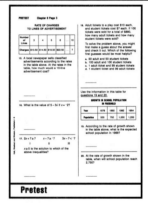

Which factors do you think affect the cost of advertising on national television programs? Think of a product you would like to sell. Plan when and how you would advertise it. Can you come up with equations that you could use to show the costs of making the commercial and of showing it once, twice, or ten times?

8 EQUATIONS AND INEQUALITIES
One Variable

Objectives: To explore problems related to advertising

Direct students to look at the picture of the test products. Ask them what they know about the advertising industry. Discuss the various ways in which advertising pervades their lives—through television, radio, newspapers, billboards, and so on.

SMALL GROUP
Statistics and Probability
Materials: Making Math Work page 15 per student

Have each student complete a copy of Making Math Work page 15. Ask each group to come up with a product, either imaginary or real, that they would like to sell. Then have each group develop a profile of who they think would be the typical consumer of the product. Explain that products are marketed in this way in the real world, but that the actual research is much more thorough. Finally, have each group choose four television shows on which they could air advertisements to expose their product to viewers who fit the profile of the ideal consumer.

INDIVIDUAL
Algebra
Materials: Making Math Work page 16 per student

Have each student complete a copy of Making Math Work page 16. Suggest that students come up with equations representing total advertising costs based on such variables as number and length of commercials. As a challenge, have students get together and plan the commercial time for all their products for an entire day. Tell them that the average half-hour television show includes about 10 minutes of commercials.

WHOLE CLASS
Patterns and Functions
Materials: completed Making Math Work page 15 per student

Ask volunteers to take the last instruction on Making Math Work page 15 one step further and write a television commercial. Then have those students briefly present their commercials to the class. Tell them to use other students as actors if necessary and any props that are available. Encourage students to be as creative as possible.

Discuss with the class why the commercial does or does not work, keeping in mind that the point of a commercial is to induce people to buy the product.

Objectives: To write and evaluate an algebraic expression

Warm-Up
Have students write a numerical statement for each sentence.
- One more than five is six. (5 + 1 = 6)
- Two less than three is one. (3 − 2 = 1)
- Five more than two is seven. (2 + 5 = 7)

GETTING STARTED

Tell students that *x* can stand for any number. Then have each student write a numerical expression to represent each statement.
- six less than a number (*x* − 6)
- triple a number (3*x*)

TEACHING THE LESSON

A. Explain that an algebraic expression compares an unknown quantity to a known quantity.

B. Guide students through writing each word expression in numerical form.
- twice the sum of 9 and 12 (2[9 + 12])
- 78 less than the quotient of *y* divided by 12 ([$\frac{y}{12}$] − 78)

Use the following example to demonstrate that word phrases can be ambiguous: *three times a number plus two* could be 3*n* + 2 or 3(*n* + 2).

C. Point out that although expressions can have an infinite number of possible values, most equations in one variable produce only one solution.

Ask students whether they can think of an equation in one variable that has more than one solution. (*y*² = 9; *y* = [⁺3, ⁻3])

Checkpoint
The chart lists the common errors students make when writing and evaluating algebraic expressions.

Correct Answers: 1b, 2a

Remediation
■ For this error, have students contrast statements such as: "seven is less than thirteen" with "seven less than thirteen."

☐ For these errors, assign Reteach Master, p. 81.

△ For this error, refer students to the examples on p. 250.

Algebraic Expressions

A. TV station WYZX programs 2 more hours of news during the afternoon than it programs during the morning. An **algebraic expression** can represent this relationship.

Let *m* equal the amount of news programming during the morning. Then *m* + 2 will equal the amount of news programming during the afternoon.

The variable *m* represents a number.

B. Algebraic expressions can be written from word phrases.

Word Phrase	*Algebraic Expression*
four more than a number	$n + 4$
twice as much as a number	$2n$
negative seven plus three fourths of a number	$^-7 + \frac{3}{4}n$

C. Evaluate the expression $2 + y$, if $y = {}^-1, 0,$ and 3.

$$\begin{array}{cc} 2 + y & \quad 2 + y \\ \downarrow \quad \downarrow & \quad \downarrow \quad \downarrow \\ 2 + {}^-1 & \quad 2 + 0 \\ 1 & \quad 2 \end{array}$$

$$\begin{array}{c} 2 + y \\ \downarrow \quad \downarrow \\ 2 + 3 \\ 5 \end{array}$$

Checkpoint Write the letter of the correct answer.

1. An algebraic expression for seven less than *m* would be ■.

   a. $7 < m$ **b.** $m - 7$ **c.** $m + 7$ **d.** $7 - m$

2. Evaluate ^-4c, when $c = 5$.

   a. $^-20$ **b.** $^-1\frac{1}{4}$ **c.** $^-\frac{4}{5}$ **d.** 20

280   Math Reasoning, page H221

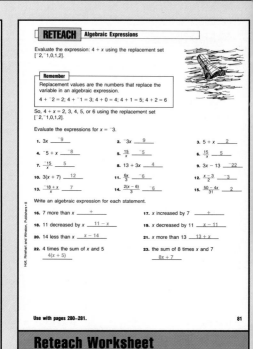

COMMON ERRORS

Answer Choice	Type of Error
■ 1a	Mistakes *is less than* for *less than*
☐ 1c, 2b, 2c	Uses the incorrect operation
☐ 1d	Transposes terms
△ 2d	Omits the negative sign in the product

Write each as an algebraic expression.

1. eight less than y $y - 8$

2. four multiplied by x $4x$

3. the total of a and 6 $a + 6$

4. five more than d $d + 5$

5. c decreased by 6 $c - 6$

6. r times 3 $3r$

7. 7 divided by a $\frac{7}{a}$

8. c divided by 4 $\frac{c}{4}$

9. twice the sum of t and 5 $2(t + 5)$

10. a increased by 11 $a + 11$

Evaluate each expression, if the variable equals 0, 1, 2, 3, and 4.

11. $3 + t$
3, 4, 5, 6, 7

12. $t - 4$
$^-4, ^-3, ^-2, ^-1, 0$

13. $4t$
0, 4, 8, 12, 16

14. $\frac{m}{3}$
$0, \frac{1}{3}, \frac{2}{3}, 1, 1\frac{1}{3}$

15. $b + 11$
11, 12, 13, 14, 15

16. $20 - y$
20, 19, 18, 17, 16

17. $3(x + 2)$
6, 9, 12, 15, 18

18. $2x - 3$
$^-3, ^-1, 1, 3, 5$

19. $16 + 3w$
16, 19, 22, 25, 28

Evaluate each expression, if the variable equals $^-3, ^-2, ^-1, 0,$ and 1.

20. $m + 1$
$^-2, ^-1, 0, 1, 2$

21. $m - 5$ $^-8, ^-7, ^-6, ^-5, ^-4$

22. $5x$ $^-15, ^-10, ^-5, 0, 5$

23. $4(x - 3)$
$^-24, ^-20, ^-16, ^-12, ^-8$

24. $\frac{(y + 2)}{3}$ $^-\frac{1}{3}, 0, \frac{1}{3}, \frac{2}{3}, 1$

25. $\frac{4}{(6 + y)}$ $1\frac{1}{3}, 1, \frac{4}{5}, \frac{2}{3}, \frac{4}{7}$

26. $3m + 5$
$^-4, ^-1, 2, 5, 8$

27. $10 - 2y$
16, 14, 12, 10, 8

28. $(m + 2) \cdot 2$
$^-2, 0, 2, 4, 6$

Solve.

29. WYZX broadcasts a dance program each day of the week. Write an expression that represents the number of times the program is broadcast in a given number (w) of weeks. $7w$

30. The total number of soap operas that were aired last year was p. If the same number of soap operas were aired daily, write an expression to show how many shows were aired each day. $\frac{p}{365}$

31. In 1984, people in 63.8 million households in the United States watched public television at least once per month. If the number is projected to be 95.7 million households in 1994, how many more households can be expected to watch public television in 1994?
31.9 million more households

Classwork/Homework, page H113

281

ASSIGNMENT GUIDE

Basic: 1–6, 11–16, 29–31

Average: 1–13, 20–25, 29–31

Extended: 1–10, 11–27 o, 29–31

Resources
Practice, p. 113   Class/Home, p. H113
Reteach, p. 81   Reasoning, p. H221
Enrich, p. 105

Exercise Analysis
1–10   Write a word phrase as an algebraic expression
11–28   Evaluate an algebraic expression given a replacement set
29–31   Skill applications

FOLLOW-UP ACTIVITIES

NUMBER SENSE (Mental Math)
Have students simplify each word phrase mentally.
- three times the sum of four and six (30)
- 36 divided by the sum of 8 and 4 (3)
- twice the difference between 100 and 75 (50)
- six times the square root of 49 (42)
- the difference between 6^2 and 3^2 (27)

CALCULATOR
For each expression, have each student write a sentence based on the use of a calculator and then use it to evaluate the expression.
- $3.6 + [1.5 \cdot (n - 6)]$, if $n = 8$
  (8 $-$ 6 $\times$ 1.5 $+$ 3.6 $=$ 6.6)
- $[8 \cdot (\frac{a}{4} + \frac{b}{4})] - 12$, if $a = 5, b = 7$
  (5 $+$ 7 $+$ 4 $\times$ 8 $-$ 12 $=$ 12)
- $(^-6 + \frac{c}{3}) \cdot (\frac{5}{d} \cdot 4)$, if $c = 36, d = ^-10$
  (36 $\div$ 3 $-$ 6 $\times$ 5 $+$ 10 $+/-$ $\times$ 4 $=$ $^-12$)

On some calculators, the = key must be pressed after each operation. Thus, in the first example the keystrokes must be 8 $-$ 6 $=$ $\times$ (etc.).

COMING UP
The real thing!

Objective: To solve a one-step equation

Warm-Up

Have students simplify each of the following expressions.

$^-3 + 4$ (1) $^-8 \div 2$ ($^-4$)

$5 - ^-3$ (8) $72 + ^-51$ (21)

$^-6 \times 7$ ($^-42$) $^-35 - ^-18$ ($^-17$)

$28 \div ^-4$ ($^-7$) $4 \cdot ^-5$ ($^-20$)

GETTING STARTED

Materials: balance, paper clips, 2 identical pieces of paper, pencil per pair of students

Have students work in pairs. Have one student wrap from 1 to 5 paper clips in a piece of paper, mark it *x*, and place this packet and several loose paper clips on the left pan of the balance. He or she should then place on the right pan the other piece of paper and enough paper clips to balance the mass on the left pan. The second student should write an equation to describe the situation and then remove from both pans the same number of paper clips until all that remains on the left pan is *x*. Finally, the student should unwrap the packet to verify that *x* is equal to the number of paper clips remaining on the right pan.

TEACHING THE LESSON

A. You may wish to review the rules for operations with real numbers.

B. Ask students to tell the general rule for subtracting integers. (To subtract an integer, add its opposite.)

Remind students that in order to check an answer, the value for the variable should be substituted into the original equation and then the equation should be simplified and its equality checked.

Checkpoint

The chart lists the common errors students make when solving one-step equations.

Correct Answers: 1a, 2a, 3c, 4a

Remediation

■ For these errors, have students review the rules for operations with integers; then before they solve each problem, have them write which operation must be performed on both sides of the equation.

□ For this error, assign Reteach Master, p. 82.

△ For these errors, refer students to the examples on p. 66.

Solving One-Step Equations

To solve equations that have real numbers, remember the rules for operations that involve real numbers.

A. Solve and check.

$$x + 3 = ^-12$$
$$x + 3 - 3 = ^-12 - 3$$
$$x = ^-15$$

$$x + ^-3 = ^-12$$
$$x + ^-3 - (^-3) = ^-12 - (^-3)$$
$$x = ^-9$$

Check.
$$^-15 + 3 \overset{?}{=} ^-12$$
$$^-12 = ^-12 ✔$$

Check.
$$^-9 + ^-3 \overset{?}{=} ^-12$$
$$^-12 = ^-12 ✔$$

B. Solve and check one-step equations that involve real numbers. Remember that operations must be performed on both sides of an equation.

$$d - \frac{1}{8} = \frac{^-3}{4}$$
$$d - \frac{1}{8} + \frac{1}{8} = \frac{^-3}{4} + \frac{1}{8}$$
$$d = \frac{^-6}{8} + \frac{1}{8}$$
$$d = \frac{^-5}{8}$$

$$d - \frac{^-1}{8} = \frac{^-3}{4}$$
$$d - \frac{^-1}{8} + \frac{^-1}{8} = \frac{^-3}{4} + \frac{^-1}{8}$$
$$d = \frac{^-6}{8} - \frac{1}{8}$$
$$d = \frac{^-7}{8}$$

Other examples:

$$^-4c = 12$$
$$\frac{^-4c}{^-4} = \frac{12}{^-4}$$
$$c = ^-3$$

Check.
$$^-4 \cdot ^-3 \overset{?}{=} 12$$
$$12 = 12 ✔$$

$$\frac{^-y}{2.5} = ^-5$$
$$\frac{^-y}{2.5} \cdot ^-2.5 = ^-5 \cdot ^-2.5$$
$$y = 12.5$$

Check.
$$\frac{^-12.5}{2.5} \overset{?}{=} ^-5$$
$$^-5 = ^-5 ✔$$

Checkpoint Write the letter of the correct answer.

Solve.

1. $y - 3 = ^-15$; $y = ■$

(a.) $^-12$ b. $^-5$ c. 12   d. 18

2. $0.2c = ^-20$; $c = ■$

(a.) $^-100$ b. $^-10$ c. 10   d. 100

3. $y - ^-12 = 15$; $y = ■$

a. $^-3$ b. $-\frac{4}{5}$ (c.) 3   d. 27

4. $\frac{1}{2}x = ^-4$; $x = ■$

(a.) $^-8$ b. $^-2$ c. 2   d. 8

COMMON ERRORS

Answer Choice	Type of Error
■ 1b, 3b, 4b	Uses the incorrect operation
□ 1c, 2d, 3a, 4d	Uses the incorrect sign
■ 1d, 3d	Fails to understand the rules for operating with real numbers
△ 2b	Makes an error in computation
△ 2c	Makes an error in computation; uses the incorrect sign
■ 4c	Uses the incorrect operation; uses the incorrect sign

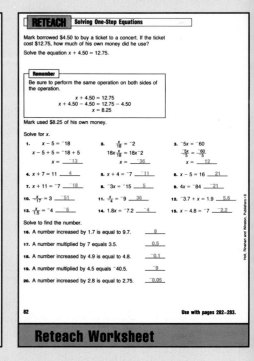

RETEACH Solving One-Step Equations

Mark borrowed $4.50 to buy a ticket to a concert. If the ticket cost $12.75, how much of his own money did he use?

Solve the equation x + 4.50 = 12.75.

Remember
Be sure to perform the same operation on both sides of the operation.

$$x + 4.50 = 12.75$$
$$x + 4.50 - 4.50 = 12.75 - 4.50$$
$$x = 8.25$$

Mark used $8.25 of his own money.

Solve for x.

1. $x - 5 = ^-18$
$x - 5 + 5 = ^-18 + 5$
$x = \underline{^-13}$

2. $\frac{x}{18} = ^-2$
$18x\frac{x}{18} = 18x^-2$
$x = \underline{^-36}$

3. $^-5x = ^-60$
$\frac{^-5x}{^-5} = \frac{^-60}{^-5}$
$x = \underline{12}$

4. $x + 7 = 11$ $\underline{4}$

5. $x + 4 = ^-7$ $\underline{^-11}$

6. $x - 5 = 16$ $\underline{21}$

7. $x + 11 = ^-7$ $\underline{^-18}$

8. $^-3x = ^-15$ $\underline{5}$

9. $4x = ^-84$ $\underline{^-21}$

10. $\frac{x}{^-17} = 3$ $\underline{^-51}$

11. $\frac{x}{4} = ^-9$ $\underline{^-36}$

12. $^-3.7 + x = 1.9$ $\underline{5.6}$

13. $\frac{x}{1.5} = ^-4$ $\underline{^-6}$

14. $1.8x = ^-7.2$ $\underline{^-4}$

15. $x - 4.8 = ^-7$ $\underline{^-2.2}$

Solve to find the number.

16. A number increased by 1.7 is equal to 9.7. $\underline{8}$

17. A number multiplied by 7 equals 3.5. $\underline{0.5}$

18. A number increased by 4.9 is equal to 4.8. $\underline{^-0.1}$

19. A number multiplied by 4.5 equals $^-40.5$. $\underline{^-9}$

20. A number increased by 2.8 is equal to 2.75. $\underline{^-0.05}$

82   Use with pages 282–283.

Reteach Worksheet

Solve and check.

1. $a + 3 = {}^-19$ $a = {}^-22$

2. $c + \frac{3}{4} = \frac{5}{8}$ $c = \frac{{}^-1}{8}$

3. ${}^-2.8 + x = 3.2$
   $x = 6$

4. $e - 6 = {}^-12$ $e = {}^-6$

5. $g - 16 = {}^-4$ $g = 12$

6. $y - 4.3 = {}^-2.1$
   $y = 2.2$

7. $7x = {}^-21$ $x = {}^-3$

8. $9y = {}^-36$ $y = {}^-4$

9. $5.3x = {}^-21.2$
   $x = {}^-4$

10. $\frac{{}^-x}{4} = {}^-13$ $x = 52$

11. $\frac{y}{2} = {}^-26$ $y = {}^-52$

12. $\frac{m}{2.5} = {}^-10$ $m = {}^-25$

13. ${}^-5 + t = 17$ $t = 22$

14. $a + {}^-2 = {}^-9$
    $a = {}^-7$

15. $r - {}^-3 = 6$
    $r = 3$

16. ${}^-7 - p = {}^-9$
    $p = 2$

17. ${}^-6d = 42$
    $d = {}^-7$

18. $8c = {}^-64$
    $c = {}^-8$

19. $\frac{{}^-m}{3} = {}^-8$ $m = 24$

20. $\frac{r}{5} = {}^-3$ $r = {}^-15$

21. $a + \frac{1}{2} = {}^-1\frac{1}{2}$
    $a = {}^-2$

22. $c - \left(\frac{{}^-2}{3}\right) = \frac{1}{9}$
    $c = \frac{{}^-5}{9}$

23. $4x = \frac{{}^-3}{5}$
    $x = \frac{{}^-3}{20}$

24. $\frac{\frac{y}{2}}{3} = {}^-6$
    $y = {}^-4$

25. $c + {}^-0.5 = {}^-2.8$
    $c = {}^-2.3$

26. ${}^-1.7 + y = 3.2$
    $y = 4.9$

27. $d + 0.8 = {}^-3.2$
    $d = {}^-4$

28. $y - 0.7 = 0.4$
    $y = 1.1$

29. ${}^-0.6\,m = 0.72$
    $m = {}^-1.2$

30. $2.3y = {}^-9.2$
    $y = {}^-4$

31. $\frac{r}{0.7} = {}^-0.6$
    $r = 0.42$

32. $\frac{{}^-t}{0.3} = 5$
    $t = {}^-1.5$

33. $\frac{0.4}{x} = {}^-0.2$
    $x = {}^-2$

Solve. For Problem 35, use the Infobank.

34. The audience for a new movie's first night was 320. This was twice the number of people who attended the movie the second night. If x represents the second night's audience, how many people attended the movie the second night? (HINT: Use an equation to solve.) **160 people**

35. Use the information on page 476 to solve. A TV set projects 60 frames per second. In which region or country would you find this TV set? Write an equation and solve. (HINT: Let x = the number of pictures per second.) **North America; South America; Japan; 2x = 60, or x = 30**

NUMBER SENSE

Compute mentally.

1. $7z = 14$
   $z = 2$

2. $y + 8 = 20$
   $y = 12$

3. $\frac{a}{6} = 4$
   $a = 24$

4. $f - 15 = 15$
   $f = 30$

5. $\frac{h}{4} = 5$
   $h = 20$

6. $m + 9 = {}^-1$
   $m = {}^-10$

7. $3r = {}^-18$
   $r = {}^-6$

8. $18 + k = 12$
   $k = {}^-6$

9. $t + {}^-6 = 4$
   $t = 10$

10. ${}^-12v = 0$
    $v = 0$

11. $\frac{u}{2} = 4$
    $u = {}^-8$

12. $b - {}^-5 = 10$
    $b = 5$

283

PRACTICE | Solving One-Step Equations

Solve.

1. $n + 9\frac{1}{4} = 13\frac{3}{8}$ _____ $4\frac{1}{8}$

2. $r + 759 = 529$ _____ $r = {}^-230$

3. $\frac{1}{7}c = 6$ _____ $c = 42$

4. $\frac{1}{23}w = 15$ _____ $w = 345$

5. $0.5w = 1.415$ _____ $w = 2.83$

6. ${}^-71.3n = 63.457$ _____ $n = {}^-0.89$

7. $d + 0.069 = 0.139$ _____ $d = 0.07$

8. $0.004 - n = {}^-0.636$ _____ $n = 0.64$

9. $4t = {}^-28$ _____ $t = {}^-7$

10. $n - \frac{5}{12} = \frac{7}{12}$ _____ $n = 1$

11. $z - \frac{1}{3} = \frac{4}{15}$ _____ $z = \frac{3}{5}$

12. $4\frac{1}{2} + b = {}^-1\frac{2}{5}$ _____ $b = {}^-5\frac{9}{10}$

13. $10\frac{1}{2}n = 6\frac{9}{16}$ _____ $n = \frac{5}{8}$

14. $n - \frac{2}{7} = \frac{3}{14}$ _____ $n = \frac{1}{2}$

15. $a - 733 = 129$ _____ $a = 862$

16. ${}^-0.55h = 4.40$ _____ $h = {}^-8$

17. ${}^-0.41 = 0.09$ _____ $n = 0.5$

18. $25 - p = 7$ _____ $p = 18$

19. $c + \frac{3}{10} = \frac{31}{70}$ _____ $c = \frac{1}{7}$

20. $w + 6\frac{1}{2} = 10\frac{1}{4}$ _____ $w = 3\frac{3}{4}$

21. $12.4d = 111.6$ _____ $d = 9$

22. $94.2 - w = 19.65$ _____ $w = 74.55$

23. $b - 93 = {}^-12$ _____ $b = 81$

24. $\frac{3}{8}m = {}^-\frac{27}{80}$ _____ $m = {}^-\frac{9}{10}$

25. $211 + z = 657$ _____ $z = 446$

26. ${}^-203 - z = 420$ _____ $z = {}^-623$

27. ${}^-16 - t = 40$ _____ $t = {}^-56$

28. $6.174 + n = 5.324$ _____ $n = {}^-0.85$

29. ${}^-\frac{1}{9}r = 9$ _____ $r = {}^-81$

30. $6.4n = 352.64$ _____ $n = 55.1$

31. The state in which Melissa and Edward live requires a nickel deposit on all soft-drink containers. Edward and Melissa collect containers to cash in for the deposit. After one week, Melissa had 75 containers, which was $1\frac{1}{2}$ times as many as Edward had collected. The number of containers Melissa collected is given by the equation $1\frac{1}{2}n = 75$. How many bottles and cans did Edward collect? _____ 50

114   Use with pages 282–283.

Practice Worksheet

ENRICH | Geometry

The area of a region made up of unit squares can be computed by **Pick's Formula**. A point is drawn at each corner of each square. The first step in finding the formula is to look at figures that have points of unit measure on their perimeters only.

1. Complete the chart.

Perimeter points (P)	4	6	8	10	12
Area measured in unit squares (A)	1	2	3	4	5

2. When the area increases by one, how many perimeter points are added? _____ 2

3. Write the formula for the area (A) of a figure with perimeter points only. The points are defined as P. (HINT: The number of perimeter points must be divided by 2.) $A = \frac{P}{2} - 1$

The figures below show regions that have interior points as well as perimeter points.

4. Complete the chart.

Perimeter points (P)	8	10	10	14	14
Interior points (I)	1	2	1	2	4
Area (A)	4	6	5	8	10

5. Write Pick's Formula for finding the area of an enclosed region that has P perimeter points and I interior points. (Use the formula for the area of a region with perimeter points only to help you.) $A = \left(\frac{P}{2} - 1\right) + I$

106   Use with pages 282–283.

Enrich Worksheet

ASSIGNMENT GUIDE

Basic: 1–12, 13–33 o, 34–35, NS

Average: 1–22, 34–35, NS

Extended: 13–35, NS

Resources
Practice, p. 114   Class/Home, p. H114
Reteach, p. 82   Reasoning, p. H221
Enrich, p. 106

Exercise Analysis

1–33   Solve a one-step equation
34   Skill applications
35   Data collection and computation

Number Sense

These exercises provide practice in solving one-step equations mentally.

FOLLOW-UP ACTIVITIES

MATH CONNECTION (Science)

Explain that for every electrical circuit, the relationship among the current, the voltage, and the resistance is shown below.

$$\text{Current } (I) = \frac{\text{Voltage } (V)}{\text{Resistance } (R)}$$

Have students complete the chart.

I (amps)	V (volts)	R (ohms)
(0.5)	25	50
(0.75)	30	40
15	(6.0)	0.4
6	(15.0)	2.5
12	24	(2.0)
0.4	5	(12.5)

MATH CONNECTION (Consumer)

Have each student write an equation and use it to solve each problem.

- Six oranges cost $1.00 at the market. Lily has $8.50 to spend on oranges. How many can she buy? (51)
- Halloween pumpkins cost $5.75. Mrs. Mullen wants to buy pumpkins to decorate her restaurant and is willing to spend up to $23.00. How many can she buy? (4)

COMING UP

Double plays

283

Objective: To solve a two-step equation

Warm-Up

Have students solve each equation.

$-7 + c = -21$ $(c = -14)$ $\frac{r}{5.8} = 3$ $(r = 17.4)$

$b - \frac{-7}{8} = \frac{3}{4}$ $(b = \frac{-1}{8})$ $\frac{3}{5}p = 15$ $(p = 25)$

GETTING STARTED

Write the equation $3x = 9$ on the chalk-board, and have students copy it. Then read aloud the following instructions.

- Divide both sides by 14.
- Add 71 to both sides.
- Add $^-71$ to both sides.
- Simplify (to $\frac{3x}{14} = \frac{9}{14}$).
- Multiply both sides by $\frac{14}{3}$.

Discuss the answer, pointing out that the same result would have been obtained by dividing both sides by 3. Emphasize the fact that any number of operations can be performed on both sides of an equation without changing its solution.

TEACHING THE LESSON

A. Explain that the general equation for this problem would consist of two variables: the number of adults' tickets sold and the number of children's tickets sold. ($5a + 2c = 374$) Not until the value of the second variable is supplied can the equation be solved. Without a value for c, there would be no single answer.

B. Point out that in order to solve a two-step equation, the order of operations is usually reversed: addition and subtraction are reversed first and then multiplication and division are reversed. This would not be the case, however, for an equation such as $5(x + 3) = 22$.

In the Another Example section, the second step requires division by a fraction. A quick review of reciprocals may be helpful.

Solving Two-Step Equations

A. At the Bijou, movie tickets for adults cost $5 each, and tickets for children under 12 years of age cost $2 each. One evening, the total ticket sales were $374. If 12 child tickets were sold, how many adult tickets were sold?

A two-step equation can be used to answer the question.

If you let x represent the number of adults, then $5x$ represents the cost of the adult tickets. The cost of the child tickets was $12 \cdot \$2$, or $24.

$$5x + 24 = 374$$
$$5x + 24 - 24 = 374 - 24$$
$$5x = 350$$
$$\frac{5x}{5} = \frac{350}{5}$$
$$x = 70$$

To check, let $x = 70$.
$$5 \cdot 70 + 24 \stackrel{?}{=} 374$$
$$350 + 24 \stackrel{?}{=} 374$$
$$374 = 374 \ ✔$$

That evening, 70 adult tickets were sold.

B. To solve a two-step equation, you must "undo" both operations.

Solve $\frac{x}{0.03} - 0.5 = 3.5$.
$$\frac{x}{0.03} - 0.5 = 3.5$$
$$\frac{x}{0.03} - 0.5 + 0.5 = 3.5 + 0.5$$
$$\frac{x}{0.03} = 4$$
$$\frac{x}{0.03} \cdot 0.03 = 4 \cdot 0.03$$
$$x = 0.12$$

Check.
$$\frac{0.12}{0.03} - 0.5 \stackrel{?}{=} 3.5$$
$$4 - 0.5 \stackrel{?}{=} 3.5$$
$$3.5 = 3.5 \ ✔$$

Another example: Solve $\frac{2}{3}x - {}^-4 = 26$.
$$\frac{2}{3}x - {}^-4 - {}^+4 = 26 - {}^+4$$
$$\frac{2x}{3} \cdot \frac{3}{2} = 22 \cdot \frac{3}{2}$$
$$x = 33$$

Check.
$$\frac{2}{3} \cdot 33 - {}^-4 \stackrel{?}{=} 26$$
$$22 - {}^-4 \stackrel{?}{=} 26$$
$$26 = 26 \ ✔$$

Math Reasoning, page H221

COMMON ERRORS

Students often lose track of the steps they are performing and consequently reverse only one operation or reverse the operation on only one side of the equation.

Remediation

For these errors, have students make a simple checklist of steps to be followed in solving an equation. Then have them check off each step after it is completed.

Assign Reteach Master, p. 83.

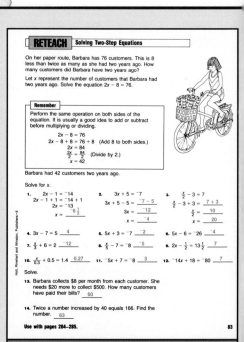

RETEACH | Solving Two-Step Equations

On her paper route, Barbara has 76 customers. This is 8 less than twice as many as she had two years ago. How many customers did Barbara have two years ago?

Let x represent the number of customers that Barbara had two years ago. Solve the equation $2x - 8 = 76$.

Remember

Perform the same operation on both sides of the equation. It is usually a good idea to add or subtract before multiplying or dividing.

$2x - 8 = 76$
$2x - 8 + 8 = 76 + 8$ (Add 8 to both sides.)
$2x = 84$
$\frac{2x}{2} = \frac{84}{2}$ (Divide by 2.)
$x = 42$

Barbara had 42 customers two years ago.

Solve for x.

1. $2x - 1 = {}^-14$
$2x - 1 + 1 = {}^-14 + 1$
$2x = {}^-13$
$x = \underline{{}^-6\frac{1}{2}}$

2. $3x + 5 = {}^-7$
$3x + 5 - 5 = \underline{{}^-7 - 5}$
$3x = \underline{{}^-12}$
$x = \underline{{}^-4}$

3. $\frac{x}{2} - 3 = 7$
$\frac{x}{2} - 3 + 3 = \underline{7 + 3}$
$\frac{x}{2} = \underline{10}$
$x = \underline{20}$

4. $3x - 7 = 5$ $\underline{4}$

5. $5x + 3 = {}^-7$ $\underline{{}^-2}$

6. $5x - 6 = {}^-26$ $\underline{{}^-4}$

7. $\frac{x}{3} + 6 = 2$ $\underline{{}^-12}$

8. $\frac{x}{5} - 7 = {}^-8$ $\underline{{}^-5}$

9. $2x - \frac{1}{2} = 13\frac{1}{2}$ $\underline{7}$

10. $\frac{x}{0.3} + 0.5 = 1.4$ $\underline{0.27}$

11. $^-5x + 7 = {}^-8$ $\underline{3}$

12. $^-14x + 18 = {}^-80$ $\underline{7}$

Solve.

13. Barbara collects $8 per month from each customer. She needs $20 more to collect $500. How many customers have paid their bills? $\underline{60}$

14. Twice a number increased by 40 equals 166. Find the number. $\underline{63}$

Use with pages 284–285. 83

Reteach Worksheet

Solve and check.

1. $5x + 7 = 32$
  $x = 5$

2. $8y + 9 = 49$
  $y = 5$

3. $2g - 18 = 42$
  $g = 30$

4. $9m - 9 = 72$
  $m = 9$

5. $\frac{b}{2} + 7 = 10$
  $b = 6$

6. $\frac{p}{9} + 1 = 8$
  $p = 63$

7. $\frac{x}{5} - 3 = 2$
  $x = 25$

8. $\frac{c}{5} - 1 = 9$
  $c = 50$

9. $0.5r - 7 = 13$
  $r = 40$

10. $8d - 0.9 = 4.7$
  $d = 0.7$

11. $3.6y + 3.2 = 15.8$
  $y = 3.5$

12. $0.06x + 3.6 = 3.6042$
  $x = 0.07$

13. $0.08t - 4 = 16$
  $t = 250$

14. $\frac{s}{0.5} + 4 = 8$
  $s = 2$

15. $\frac{e}{6} + 2.7 = 6$
  $e = 19.8$

16. $\frac{w}{3.2} - 14 = 27$
  $w = 131.2$

17. $\frac{t}{3} - 4.25 = 7.25$
  $t = 34.5$

18. $\frac{2}{5}t + 7 = 21$
  $t = 35$

19. $3g + \frac{4}{5} = 9\frac{4}{5}$
  $g = 3$

20. $\frac{3}{4}z - 2 = 4$
  $z = 8$

21. $7n - \frac{3}{7} = 20\frac{4}{7}$
  $n = 3$

22. $\frac{5}{6}r + 20 = 40$
  $r = 24$

23. $\frac{2}{3}p - 6 = 2$
  $p = 12$

24. $6c - \frac{1}{3} = 11\frac{2}{3}$
  $c = 2$

25. $9a + \frac{7}{10} = 3\frac{2}{5}$
  $a = \frac{3}{10}$

26. $^-7x + 8 = ^-20$
  $x = 4$

27. $^-5c + 5 = ^-15$
  $c = 4$

28. $4y - ^-3 = ^-25$
  $y = ^-7$

29. $^-7f + ^-3 = ^-45$
  $f = 6$

30. $^-\frac{s}{3} - 4 = ^-10$
  $s = 18$

31. $^-\frac{b}{5} + 8 = 14$
  $b = ^-30$

32. $^-\frac{x}{1} - 9 = ^-15$
  $x = 6$

33. $^-\frac{z}{7} + 4 = 8$
  $z = ^-28$

Write an equation for each and solve.

34. Six more than eight times a number is thirty. What is the number? (HINT: Let n = the number.) $6 + 8n = 30; n = 3$

35. Five less than a number divided by four is two. What is the number? (HINT: Let n = the number.)
  $\frac{n}{4} - 5 = 2; n = 28$

36. In one year, the Orpheum presents 21 movies, which is 5 more than the number of movies presented by the Bijou. How many movies does the Bijou present? (HINT: Let m = the number of movies at the Bijou.) $m + 5 = 21; m = 16$ movies

37. If film is projected at the rate of 24 frames per second, how many frames will be projected in 3 minutes? (HINT: Let f = the number of frames.)
  $f = 24 \cdot 60 \cdot 3; f = 4{,}320$ frames

NUMBER SENSE

Compute mentally.

1. $21 \div 3 = \blacksquare$
  7

2. $75 \div 25 = \blacksquare$
  3

3. $220 \div 11 = \blacksquare$
  20

4. $240 \div 3 = \blacksquare$
  80

5. $150 \div 5 = \blacksquare$
  30

6. $144 \div 6 = \blacksquare$
  24

7. $81 \div 3 = \blacksquare$
  27

8. $120 \div 40 = \blacksquare$
  3

9. $720 \div 8 = \blacksquare$
  90

10. $360 \div 12 = \blacksquare$
  30

11. $164 \div 4 = \blacksquare$
  41

12. $275 \div 11 = \blacksquare$
  25

ASSIGNMENT GUIDE

Basic: 1–17, 34–37, NS 1–8

Average: 2–32 e, 34–37, NS

Extended: 1–33 o, 34–37, NS

Resources
Practice, p. 115   Class/Home, p. H115
Reteach, p. 83   More Practice, p. H203
Enrich, p. 107   Reasoning, p. H221

Exercise Analysis
1–33   Solve a two-step equation
34–37   Skill applications

Number Sense
This exercise provides practice in dividing mentally.

FOLLOW-UP ACTIVITIES

CALCULATOR
Explain that students can use calculators to solve two-step equations. First, enter the number at the right side of the equation and then perform the correct sequence of operations that should be performed on both sides of the equation to solve for the variable. For example, to solve $3x + 5 = 110$, enter 110, subtract 5, and then divide by 3 to display 35.

Have students use calculators to solve each equation.

$6x + 81 = 327$ ($x = 41$)
$9y - 21 = 267$ ($y = 32$)
$\frac{x}{5} + 68 = 144$ ($x = 380$)
$27y - 116 = 532$ ($y = 24$)

PROBLEM SOLVING
Have students solve this problem.
- One movie theater sells a box of buttered popcorn for $0.75, and another theater sells the same box for only $0.50. If both theaters sell $75 worth of popcorn in one afternoon and each sells the same number of boxes, how much money does each theater receive?

(Let x = the number of boxes of popcorn each theater sells. From the equation $\$0.75x + \$0.50x = \$75$, we find that $x = 60$ boxes. Therefore, the first theater receives $0.75 \cdot 60$, or $45, and the second theater receives $0.50 \cdot 60$, or $30. Check: $45 + $30 = $75.)

COMING UP
Loquacious equations

Objective: To write a word problem from an equation

Warm-Up

Have students solve each equation.

$4b - 10 = ^-6$ $(b = 1)$

$1.7 + \frac{c}{3} = ^-2.2$ $(c = ^-11.7)$

$\frac{2}{3}d - \frac{1}{3} = 1\frac{1}{3}$ $(d = \frac{5}{2}, \text{ or } 2\frac{1}{2})$

$^-0.8e + ^-1.4 = 7$ $(e = ^-10.5)$

GETTING STARTED

Have students think of an object such as a horse. Tell them that x will stand for this object. Have them evaluate $x + 4$. Ask: Does this make sense? If not, why not? (No, you cannot add a number to an object.) Ask: How can you change the meaning of x to make $x + 4$ make sense? (Show that if you let $x =$ the number of horses, $x + 4$ can mean 4 horses more than x horses.) Explain that in word problems, variables stand for numbers of things, not the things themselves.

TEACHING THE LESSON

A. Have students suggest other possible word problems for the same equation. The following offers one suggestion.

- Some students went out on a Friday night. They spent $3 each for movie tickets and $9 for sandwiches and juice. If they spent a total of $15, how many students were there?

Remind students that the answers must be realistic; for example, ask: If $4p = 18$, why would it be unrealistic for p to represent the number of people who go to a movie theater that charges $4 for a ticket? (because it would mean that $4\frac{1}{2}$ of the people went to the theater, which is nonsensical.)

B. Ask students how the problem would have changed if the numbers had been doubled.

$8c + 12 = ^-4$

(More prizes would have been given away, more profit would have been earned from sandwiches, and the net loss would have been greater, but the cost per prize would have remained $2.)

How would the problem have changed if the equation had been $4c + 6 = ^+2$? (The booth owners would have had a net profit of $2 from the day's receipts, and the cost per prize would have been $1.)

Word Problems from Equations

A. You can write word problems from equations.

What word problem could be represented by $3m + 9 = 15$?

Let $9 be the cost of a blank cassette tape.
Let $3 be the cost of a movie rental at Video Corner.
Let $15 be the total that Neville Adams spent at Video Corner for tapes and movies.

Here is a possible word problem: Neville Adams rented movies at $3 each at Video Corner and bought one blank cassette tape for $9. His total bill was $15. How many movies did he rent?

Solve. $3m + 9 = 15.$ Check. $3(2) + 9 \stackrel{?}{=} 15$
            $3m = 6$ $6 + 9 \stackrel{?}{=} 15$
             $m = 2$ $15 = 15$ ✔

He rented 2 movies.

B. What word problem could be represented by $4c + 6 = ^-2$?

Let 4 be the number of free prizes.
Let $6 be the profit from the sale of sandwiches.
Let $^-$$2 be the net loss from the day's receipts at the street fair.

Here is a possible word problem: The owners of one booth at the street fair gave away 4 free prizes and earned $6 profit on the sandwiches they sold. If $^-$$2 is the net loss from the day's receipts, how much did it cost the owners for each prize they gave away?

Solve. $4c + 6 = ^-2$ Check. $4(^-2) + 6 \stackrel{?}{=} ^-2$
            $4c = ^-8$ $^-8 + 6 \stackrel{?}{=} ^-2$
             $c = ^-2$ $^-2 = ^-2$ ✔

It cost the owners $2 for each prize they gave away, or $^-$$2.

COMMON ERRORS

Some students may have difficulty imagining situations for word problems.

Remediation

For this error, provide students with an equation and a situation but apply the situation to only one of the terms in the equation. Then have students suggest what the other numbers in the equation might represent. This practice should ease students into making connections between equations and real-life situations.

Assign Reteach Master, p. 84.

Match the equation to the word problem.

1. $2v = 8$ a
2. $2k + 8 = 40$ d
3. $8r + 40 = 640$ b
4. $\frac{g}{2} = 8$ c

a. Edna watched television twice as much as she watched her VCR. If she watched television for 8 hours, how much time did she spend watching her VCR?

b. Tommy paid $40 as a down payment on a new television/VCR package. He paid the balance in 8 equal installments. If the total cost was $640, how much was each payment?

c. Marvin's television set was half as old as his radio. If his television set was 8 years old, how old was his radio?

d. Because Rudy had cable TV, he could watch 8 more stations than Pam. Counting twice the stations that they both could watch, they could watch 40 stations in all. How many stations could Pam watch?

Write a word problem for each equation.
Answers will vary.

5. $v - 3 = 27$

Let 3 be the number of videotapes returned to the manufacturer.

6. $\frac{u}{21} = 5$

Let $21 be the cost of one radio.

Write a word problem for each equation. Then solve and check.   For word problems, answers will vary.

7. $x - 10 = 31$
$x = 41$

8. $a + 7 = 9$
$a = 2$

9. $6p = 204$
$p = 34$

10. $\frac{b}{3} = 1$
$b = 3$

11. $z - 4 = 3$
$z = 7$

12. $\frac{m}{10} = 9$
$m = 90$

MIDCHAPTER REVIEW

Evaluate each algebraic expression if the variable equals $^-2$, $^-1$, 0, 3, and 4.

1. $x + 7$
5, 6, 7, 10, 11

2. $4a - 12$
$^-20$, $^-16$, $^-12$, 0, 4

3. $\frac{6}{(f + 8)}$
1, $\frac{6}{7}$, $\frac{3}{4}$, $\frac{6}{11}$, $\frac{1}{2}$

Solve and check.

4. $y + 19 = 8$ $y = ^-11$

5. $v - 36 = 40$ $v = 76$

6. $\frac{1}{4}p = ^-8$ $p = ^-32$

7. $9z - 2 = ^-20$ $z = ^-2$

8. $^-\frac{r}{1.6} + 4 = 12$ $r = ^-12.8$

9. $^-7m - \frac{7}{8} = 48\frac{1}{8}$
$m = ^-7$

Practice Worksheet

Enrich Worksheet

ASSIGNMENT GUIDE

Basic: 1–8, MCR
Average: 1–10, MCR
Extended: 1–12, MCR

Resources
Practice, p. 116   Class/Home, p. H116
Reteach, p. 84
Enrich, p. 108

Exercise Analysis
1–4   Match an equation to a word problem
5–12 Write a word problem for an equation

Midchapter Review
This review provides an opportunity for you and students to assess their understanding of concepts and skills developed to this point in the chapter.

FOLLOW-UP ACTIVITIES

MATH COMMUNICATION
Have students solve each equation, and then present the answer in a statement.

1. $y + 82 = 110$; there are y people on the bus and 82 people in the restaurant. (After the 28 people from the bus joined the 82 people in the restaurant, there were 110 people in the restaurant.)

2. $5x - 35 = 50$; there are x feet per board, 5 boards, and 35 feet of board have already been used. (If you start with 5 boards of 17 feet each and use 35 feet of board, you will have 50 feet of board left.)

3. $2s + 3{,}500 = 4{,}246$; there are s shoppers, 3,500 shoes for sale, and a total of 4,246 shoes in the store. (If you add the shoes of the 373 shoppers, 2 per shopper, to the 3,500 shoes for sale, then there are 4,246 shoes in the store altogether.)

REINFORCEMENT
Materials: index cards

On each card, write three similar equations. On the back of each card, print a word problem for one of the equations. While displaying the equations, read the word problem and have students pick the equation that correctly represents the problem.

COMING UP
It's equal, right?

Objective: To write an equation to solve a problem

Warm-Up

To prepare students for this lesson, have them solve the following equations.

$12z + 56 = 272$ (18)

$\frac{f}{9.8} + 16 = 12$ ($^-39.2$)

$\frac{2}{5}p + {-8} = {^-2}$ (15)

$\frac{^-7}{8}g - 14 = {^-9.1}$ ($^-5.6$)

GETTING STARTED

Have students work in pairs. The first student thinks of a sentence and then lists its words and punctuation out of order. The second student must then try to put the sentence in order. Students then reverse roles.

TEACHING THE LESSON

Tell students that the model presented on this page can be used in all the problems in this lesson. By listing the given data and assigning variables to the unknown data, students can more clearly see the question they are being asked. The equation needed to find the variable will answer the question.

Questions: The question posed in the problem will be easier to understand if students set up the information beforehand.

Tools: Students may have difficulty setting up the equation so that it states the data given in the problem. Emphasize the idea that students should first break apart the problem into individual pieces of information; for example, 38 people in *Thunderbolt*; *Thunderbolt's* cast is 20 more than $\frac{3}{5}$ of *Skytrail's*. Students should then write mathematical terms or expressions for each piece of information and arrange these terms or expressions in the order in which the problem presents them.

Solutions: Review solving equations and computing with fractions.

Checks: Be sure that the right terms have been used in the equation and that it repeats what the problem says. Substitute the solution into the equation to check that the equation was solved correctly. Then change the equation back into word form to be sure the solution answers the question that was asked. Check that the proper labels or units are used with the answer.

QUESTIONS	TOOLS	SOLUTIONS	CHECKS

PROBLEM SOLVING
Writing an Equation

Writing a problem in equation form will often help you find the solution to a word problem.

> Jerry Davis recently directed a cast of 38 people in the movie *Thunderbolt*. The cast consisted of 20 more than $\frac{3}{5}$ of the number of people in the cast of another movie called *Skytrail*. How many people were there in the cast of *Skytrail*?

1. List what you know and what you need to find.

Know

- There were 38 people in the cast of *Thunderbolt*.
- *Thunderbolt's* cast contained 20 more than $\frac{3}{5}$ of the number of people in the cast of *Skytrail*.

Find

- the number of people in the cast of the movie *Skytrail*

2. Think about how you can use the given information to form an equation. Use a variable to represent the number you need to find. Let $n =$ number of people in the cast of *Skytrail*.

number of people in the cast of *Thunderbolt*	was	20	more than	$\frac{3}{5}$ of the number of people in the cast of *Skytrail*
↓	↓	↓		↓
38	=	20	+	$\frac{3}{5}n$

Think: You can rewrite this equation as $\frac{3}{5}n + 20 = 38$.

3. Solve the equation and write the answer.

$\frac{3}{5}n + 20 = 38 \qquad \frac{3}{5}n + 20 - 20 = 38 - 20$

$\frac{3}{5}n = 18 \qquad \frac{5}{3} \cdot \frac{3}{5}n = 18 \cdot \frac{5}{3}$

$n = 30$; There were 30 people in the cast of *Skytrail*.

288

Write the letter of the correct equation.

1. The Majestic Theater will show 17 cartoons during a festival. This is $\frac{1}{3}$ the number of cartoons it plans to show during the year. How many cartoons will the theater show during the year?

a. $n + \frac{1}{3} = 17$

b. $\frac{1}{3}n = 17$

c. $n - 17 = \frac{1}{3}$

2. Last week 274 people attended the premiere of a movie. This number was 14 fewer than twice the number of people who attended the last premiere at this theater. How many people attended the last premiere?

a. $274 = 2n - 14$

b. $\frac{274}{2} = n - 14$

c. $274 + 14 = \frac{n}{2}$

Solve. Use an equation where appropriate.

3. One Hollywood studio owns enough science fiction movies to show 2 movies a day for 52 days. This number is 20 more than a rival studio owns. How many science fiction movies does the rival studio own?

$52 \times 2 = 20 + n$; 84 movies

4. Mr. Von Meck directed a cast of 19 people in a new movie. This cast had 3 fewer people than $\frac{2}{3}$ of the cast in his previous movie. How many actors and actresses were cast in his previous movie?

$19 = \frac{2}{3}x - 3$; 33 people

5. In April 5,530 people saw films at the Fox Theater. This number was 122 fewer than $\frac{4}{5}$ of the attendance at that theater in March. How many people saw films at the Fox Theater in March?

$5{,}530 = \frac{4}{5}n - 122$; 7,065 people

6. The special effects for *Skytrail*, a new adventure movie, cost $2,370,000. This was $\frac{1}{5}$ of the total cost of making the movie. How much did it cost to make *Skytrail*?

$\$2{,}370{,}000 = \frac{1}{5}n$; $11,850,000

7. Anna manages a movie theater that features classic movies. Anna has scheduled 23 musical comedies for an upcoming movie festival. The number of musical comedies scheduled is 5 more than 3 times the number of mysteries scheduled for the festival. How many mysteries has Anna scheduled for the festival?

$23 = 3n + 5$; 6 mysteries

8. Tom's costume for his new role cost $2,560. In his previous role his costume cost $30 more than $\frac{1}{8}$ of the cost of the costume for his new role. How much did his costume for his previous role cost?

$\frac{1}{8}(\$2{,}560) + 30 = n$; $350

Classwork/Homework, page H117

ASSIGNMENT GUIDE

Basic: 1–4

Average: 2–6

Extended: 3–8

Resources
Practice, p. 117 Class/Home, p. H117
Enrich, p. 109

Exercise Analysis
1–2 Choose the correct equation
3–8 Write an equation and solve the problem

FOLLOW-UP ACTIVITIES

PROBLEM SOLVING
Read the following problems aloud, and have students write and solve equations for them as quickly as possible.

- A certain number when multiplied by 6 and added to 4 is 40. What is that number? (6)
- The product of a certain number and 14 is 16 less than 142. What is that number? (9)
- When the quotient of a certain number and 5 is added to 28, the sum is 56. What is the number? (140)
- $\frac{3}{4}$ of a certain number is 17 less than the number itself. What is that number? (68)
- $\frac{7}{12}$ of a certain number is 42 more than ⁻35. What is that number? (12)
- The quotient of a certain number divided by ⁻11 is 21 less than 62. What is that number? (⁻451)
- The product of the opposite of a certain number and 13 is 24 more than 80. What is that number? (⁻8)

CALCULATOR
Materials: calculator per group of students

Have students enter the following numbers and signs into the calculators in an order that will yield the greatest possible answer and also in an order that will yield the smallest possible answer. (Answers depend on type of calculator. Sample answers are shown.)

5 5 5 9 6 × = (greatest: 655 × 95 = 62,255; least: 559 × 56 = 31,304)

1 5 8 8 9 × = (greatest: 881 × 95 = 83,695; least: 5,889 × 1 = 5,889)

3 3 4 5 5 6 + × = (greatest: 6 + 5 × 5433 = 59,763; least: 345 + 56 × 3 = 1,203)

COMING UP
Guess what?

Objective: To use the guess-and-check strategy to solve problems

Warm-Up
Have students estimate the following.

148 ÷ 21 (7)   785 ÷ 120 (8)
28 × 14 (300)   2,320 × 17 (40,000)
69 × 125 (8,400)   68,925 ÷ 87 (700)
9,000,281 ÷ 855 (10,000)

Answers may vary. Accept any reasonable estimate.

GETTING STARTED

Have the class find the number which, raised to the fourth power, is 83,521. Have students make a series of estimates. First, is 83,521 greater or less than 10^4? (greater) Have students multiply to find 20^4. (160,000) Point out that the number must be between 10 and 20. Have students continue until they find the answer. (17)

TEACHING THE LESSON

Sometimes the solution to a problem will have to satisfy several different requirements. When these requirements are unrelated, finding the answer deductively is difficult since students will not know where to begin their line of reasoning. Instead, students should guess and then check their guess against each of the requirements. Subsequent guesses should come closer to the answer until, through the process of elimination, an answer is found.

Questions: The questions require only a close reading for comprehension.

Tools: The guess-and-check strategy is useful for refining successive guesses. The main tool is to use the check to understand why the guess was not a solution. Once students understand why a guess did not work, they can propose an alternate that is more likely to work. Have students write down each guess and then write down why it is not a solution (sum of digits too large, square of number less than sum of cubes of digits, and so on). This will help students use the check to improve subsequent guesses. Discuss with students why, in the instructional problem, Sally first tried to meet requirements 1 and 3, using requirements 2 and 4 as checks. (Requirements 1 and 3, taken together, have a much smaller group of possible answers than do the others.)

Solutions: Squares and cubes of numbers are used extensively. Review these skills if necessary.

Checks: Since checks are an integral part of the strategy, answers will be checked

---

PROBLEM SOLVING
Guessing and Checking

Sometimes you can solve a problem by using the conditions given, first to guess at and then to check the answer.

Number Explorers is a TV math show that presents everything from games to plays. Sally, a game contestant, has to guess two 2-digit numbers that meet the following requirements.

1. Each of the two numbers has two different digits.
2. Both numbers must have the same digits, but the digits are reversed.
3. The sum of the 2 digits must be 12.
4. The product of the 2 digits must be a number cubed.

For the first guess, Sally picks two numbers that meet requirements 1 and 3—they are 2-digits, and the sum of the 2 digits is 12. The first guess is 57 and 84.

Then, she checks them against the other requirements and finds that the numbers 57 and 84 do not meet requirement 2—they must have the same digits but those digits must be reversed. Her second guess is 48 and 84.

When she checks this guess against requirement 4, she finds that the product of the two digits—32—is not a number cubed.

Sally continues to guess and check until she finds the pair of numbers that meets all four requirements.

Of all the possible pairs of numbers, only 39 and 93 meet the fourth requirement. The product of their digits—27—equals a number cubed—3. The 2-digit numbers are therefore 39 and 93.

290

---

continually. Encourage students to make a list of the separate requirements that must be met for each problem.

Solve. If you use the guess-and-check strategy, show your guesses and how you checked them.

1. For a party, the people who work on *Number Explorers* baked giant loaves of bread in geometric shapes. They bought 28 bags of flour, rye flour in 2-pound bags and wheat flour in 5-pound bags. They bought the same number of pounds of each kind of flour. How many bags of each kind of flour did they buy? twenty 2-lb bags of rye flour; eight 5-lb bags of wheat flour

2. One contestant must find a 2-digit number that is less than 20. When each of its digits is squared and the two squared numbers are added together, their sum is 3 less than the original number. What is the number? 13

3. To find the number of production workers on the show, find this number. It is a 2-digit number between 75 and 90. When its digits are added together and the sum is squared, the answer is the original number. What is the number of workers? 81 workers

4. One contestant wins a prize by correctly guessing a 3-digit number between 140 and 160. When each digit is cubed and the three cubed numbers are added together, the sum equals the number. What is the number? 153

5. One week, the show features automorphic numbers. An *automorphic number* is one whose square ends with the number. An example is 25, whose square is 625. There are 2 automorphic numbers between 2 and 10. What are they? 5 and 6

6. Contestants on the show are given prizes based on the number of points they score. For every 3 points, a contestant is given $25 worth of prizes. Linda Randizi scored 969 points. How much money were her prizes worth? $8,075

k/Homework, pages H118–H119

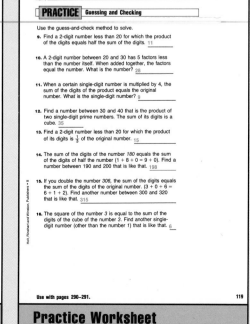

ASSIGNMENT GUIDE

Basic: 1–4

Average: 2–5

Extended: 3–6

Resources
Practice, pp. 118–9   Class/Home, pp. H118–9

Exercise Analysis
1–6 Skill applications

FOLLOW-UP ACTIVITIES

PROBLEM SOLVING
Have students find the missing numbers.

1. A number has fewer than 8 digits and more than 5. Its prime factors are 2, 3, 5, and 7. It is a perfect square. Its second and fourth digits are the same. What is the number? (*Hint*: If a number is a perfect square, all its prime factors must be present in multiples of 2.) (396,900)

2. A 4-digit number is a perfect cube. It is also a palindrome. What is the number and its cube root? (*Hint*: A *numerical palindrome* is a number that reads the same from right to left as from left to right.) (1331; 11)

CALCULATOR
Have students use a calculator to check their guesses to the solution for the following problems.

1. Both digits of a 2-digit number are the same. When the number is squared and the result is divided by 11, the answer is 704. What is the number? (88)

2. A 5-digit number is a perfect cube whose cube root is between 20 and 30. The sum of the digits of the number is the cube root. What is the number? (19,683)

3. A certain percent of a 3-digit number is 819. Either the percent or the number is the product of 91 and 4. The percent is less than the number. What is the number, and what is the percent? (364; 225%)

COMING UP
More or less

Objectives: To define an inequality and solve given a replacement set

Warm-Up
Have students use $=$ or $\neq$ to indicate whether each equation is true for $x = {}^-3$.

$x + 3 \bullet 0 \ (=)$

$\dfrac{x}{^-3} \bullet {}^-1 \ (\neq)$

$7 - x \bullet 4 \ (\neq)$

$4x \bullet {}^-12 \ (=)$

GETTING STARTED

Review briefly the $>$ and $<$ symbols. Then have students write inequalities for the following sentences.
- The square of 2 is less than 7. ($2^2 < 7$)
- Ninety-five divided by 17 is greater than 5. ($95 \div 17 > 5$)
- The sum of x and y and z is greater than 50. ($x + y + z > 50$)

TEACHING THE LESSON

A. Emphasize the fact that an inequality in a variable yields a solution set that consists of a range of numbers. Explain that $t < {}^-10$ means that t can be any number less than $^-10$.

B. Tell students that they can solve an inequality simply by inserting each element of the replacement set into the inequality and determining whether the inequality is true for that element.

Note that inequalities in the Other Examples section are solved given the replacement set of real numbers. Point out that care must be taken not to leave out possible solutions; for example, if only 3 and 5 were tested for $t + 3 > 7$, a student might write $t > 5$ for the solution, whereas $t > 4$ is the correct solution.

Inequalities

A. An inequality is a number sentence that has any of the following symbols: $>$, $<$, $\geq$, $\leq$, or $\neq$.

$\geq$ means "is greater than or equal to."
$\leq$ means "is less than or equal to."

Word Sentence	Inequality
The temperature is less than $^-10°$F.	$t < {}^-10$
The cost is greater than or equal to $5.	$c \geq 5$
The weight of the fish plus 5 oz is less than or equal to 32 oz.	$f + 5 \leq 32$
A drop of 3°C in the temperature results in a temperature greater than $^-12$°C.	$t - 3 > {}^-12$

B. You can solve an inequality by finding all the values in the **replacement set** that make the inequality a true statement.

Solve $x < {}^-3$. Use the replacement set $\{{}^-5, {}^-4, {}^-3\}$.

Try $^-5$.	Try $^-4$.	Try $^-3$.
$x < {}^-3$	$x < {}^-3$	$x < {}^-3$
$^-5 \bullet {}^-3$	$^-4 \bullet {}^-3$	$^-3 \bullet {}^-3$
$^-5 < {}^-3$ ✔	$^-4 < {}^-3$ ✔	$^-3 = {}^-3$
$^-5$ is a solution.	$^-4$ is a solution.	$^-3$ is not a solution.

So, the values $^-5$ and $^-4$ in the replacement set are solutions to the inequality.

Other examples:

Solve. Use all real numbers as the replacement set.

$p + 7 \geq 0$

Try 7.	$7 + 7 \bullet 0$	$14 \geq 0$ ✔
Try 0.	$0 + 7 \bullet 0$	$7 \geq 0$ ✔
Try $^-7$.	$^-7 + 7 \bullet 0$	$0 \geq 0$ ✔
Try $^-8$.	$^-8 + 7 \bullet 0$	$^-1 < 0$

So, all real numbers $\geq {}^-7$ are solutions of the inequality.

$\dfrac{x}{2} < {}^-2$

Try 0.	$\dfrac{0}{2} \bullet {}^-2$	$0 > {}^-2$
Try $^-4$.	$\dfrac{^-4}{2} \bullet {}^-2$	$^-2 = {}^-2$
Try $^-5$.	$\dfrac{^-5}{2} \bullet {}^-2$	$^-2\frac{1}{2} < {}^-2$ ✔

So, all real numbers $< {}^-4$ are solutions of the inequality.

Math Reasoning, page H222

COMMON ERRORS

For inequalities such as $m - 7 \leq 0$, some students may have difficulty in deciding whether $m \geq 7$ or $m \leq 7$.

Remediation
For this error, have students locate replacement values on a number line drawn on the chalkboard. By testing one replacement value after another in numerical order, they should develop a sense of the direction in which solutions to inequalities lie.

Assign Reteach Master, p. 85.

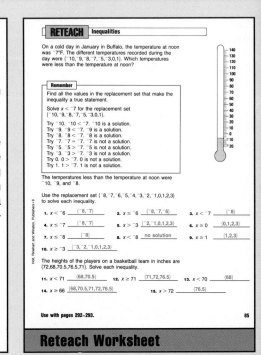

RETEACH | Inequalities

On a cold day in January in Buffalo, the temperature at noon was $^-7$°F. The different temperatures recorded during the day were ($^-10$,$^-9$,$^-8$,$^-7$,$^-5$,$^-3$,0,1). Which temperatures were less than the temperature at noon?

Remember
Find all the values in the replacement set that make the inequality a true statement.

Solve $x < {}^-7$ for the replacement set ($^-10$,$^-9$,$^-8$,$^-7$,$^-5$,$^-3$,0,1).

Try $^-10$. $^-10 < {}^-7$. $^-10$ is a solution.
Try $^-9$. $^-9 < {}^-7$. $^-9$ is a solution.
Try $^-8$. $^-8 < {}^-7$. $^-8$ is a solution.
Try $^-7$. $^-7 = {}^-7$. $^-7$ is not a solution.
Try $^-5$. $^-5 > {}^-7$. $^-5$ is not a solution.
Try $^-3$. $^-3 > {}^-7$. $^-3$ is not a solution.
Try 0. $0 > {}^-7$. 0 is not a solution.
Try 1. $1 > {}^-7$. 1 is not a solution.

The temperatures less than the temperature at noon were $^-10$, $^-9$, and $^-8$.

Use the replacement set ($^-8$,$^-7$,$^-6$,$^-5$,$^-4$,$^-3$,$^-2$,$^-1$,0,1,2,3) to solve each inequality.

1. $x < {}^-6$ ___$(^-8,^-7)$___ **2.** $x \leq {}^-6$ ___$(^-8,^-7,^-6)$___ **3.** $x < {}^-7$ ___$(^-8)$___

4. $x \leq {}^-7$ ___$(^-8,^-7)$___ **5.** $x > {}^-3$ ___$(^-2,^-1,0,1,2,3)$___ **6.** $x \geq 0$ ___$(0,1,2,3)$___

7. $x \leq {}^-8$ ___$(^-8)$___ **8.** $x < {}^-8$ ___no solution___ **9.** $x \geq 1$ ___$(1,2,3)$___

10. $x \geq {}^-3$ ___$(^-3,^-2,^-1,0,1,2,3)$___

The heights of the players on a basketball team in inches are (72,68,70.5,76.5,71). Solve each inequality.

11. $x < 71$ ___$(68,70.5)$___ **12.** $x \geq 71$ ___$(71,72,76.5)$___ **13.** $x < 70$ ___(68)___

14. $x \geq 66$ ___$(68,70.5,71,72,76.5)$___ **15.** $x > 72$ ___(76.5)___

Use with pages 292–293.

85

Reteach Worksheet

Match each statement with an inequality.

1. The weight is greater than 6 pounds. b
2. The watermelons weigh less than 6 kg. c
3. The length of the rope is greater than 20 feet. d
4. The cost of 6 peaches is greater than or equal to $1. a
5. One quarter of the number of lemons in the basket is less than 20. e

a. $6p \geq 1$
b. $w > 6$
c. $w < 6$
d. $l > 20$
e. $\frac{1}{4}f < 20$

Use the replacement set {0,1,2,3,4,5,6,7}.
Solve.

6. $x < 4$
$x = 0, 1, 2, 3$
7. $a \geq 3$
$a = 3, 4, 5, 6, 7$
8. $y < 2$
$y = 0, 1$
9. $b \geq 5$
$b = 5, 6, 7$
10. $r \leq 7$
$r = 0, 1, 2, 3, 4, 5, 6, 7$
11. $c \leq 4$
$c = 0, 1, 2, 3, 4$
12. $b \leq 1$
$b = 0, 1$
13. $g < 3$
$g = 0, 1, 2$
14. $m \geq 3 + 4$
$m = 7$
15. $r > 7 - 3$
$r = 5, 6, 7$
16. $d < 1 \cdot 4$
$d = 0, 1, 2, 3$
17. $h > \frac{10}{2}$
$h = 6, 7$

Use the replacement set {⁻5,⁻4,⁻3,⁻2,⁻1,0,1,2,3,4,5}.
Solve.

$t = ⁻5, ⁻4, ⁻3, ⁻2, ⁻1, 0, 1, 2, 3, 4$

18. $x + 2 > 5$
$x = 4, 5$
19. $y + ⁻1 \leq ⁻3$
$y = ⁻2, ⁻3, ⁻4, ⁻5$
20. $t - 5 < 0$
21. $3r \geq ⁻3$
$r = ⁻1, 0, 1, 2, 3, 4, 5$
22. $\frac{s}{4} \leq ⁻1$
$s = ⁻4, ⁻5$
★23. $⁻2n > 6$
$n = ⁻4, ⁻5$

Use the replacement set of all real numbers.
Solve.

24. $q + 10 > 2$
all real numbers > ⁻8
25. $x - 21 > ⁻5$
all real numbers > 16
26. $\frac{y}{3} \leq ⁻19$
all real numbers ≤ ⁻57
27. $12m < 252$
all real numbers < 21
28. $\frac{p}{7} \leq ⁻52$
all real numbers ≤ ⁻364
★29. $33x \neq 2{,}508$
all real numbers except 76

CALCULATOR

Compare. Use >, <, or = for ●.

1. $\sqrt{3} + \sqrt{7} ● \sqrt{10}$
>
2. $\sqrt{13} ● \sqrt{2} + \sqrt{11}$
<
3. $\sqrt{3} + \sqrt{5} ● \sqrt{7} + \sqrt{1}$
>
4. $\sqrt{13} - \sqrt{5} ● \sqrt{8}$
<
5. $\sqrt{15} - \sqrt{12} ● \sqrt{3}$
<
6. $\sqrt{11} - \sqrt{3} ● \sqrt{13} - \sqrt{5}$
>
7. $\sqrt{3} \cdot \sqrt{4} ● \sqrt{12}$
=
8. $\sqrt{2} \cdot \sqrt{8} ● \sqrt{16}$
=
9. $\sqrt{2} \cdot \sqrt{3} \cdot \sqrt{5} ● \sqrt{30}$
=
10. $\frac{\sqrt{20}}{\sqrt{5}} ● \sqrt{4}$
=
11. $\frac{\sqrt{9}}{\sqrt{3}} \cdot \sqrt{2} ● \sqrt{6}$
=
12. $\frac{\sqrt{8}}{\sqrt{4}} \cdot \sqrt{2} ● \sqrt{4}$
=

Classwork/Homework, page H120

ASSIGNMENT GUIDE

Basic: 1–13, 18–28 e, Calc 1–11 o

Average: 1–5, 6–22 e, 24–28, Calc

Extended: 1–5, 14–29, Calc

Resources
Practice, p. 120   Class/Home, p. H120
Reteach, p. 85   Reasoning, p. H222
Enrich, p. 110

Exercise Analysis

1–5   Match a word sentence to an inequality

6–17   Solve an inequality for a replacement set of whole numbers

18–23 Solve an inequality given a replacement set of integers

24–29 Solve an inequality given a replacement set of real numbers

Calculator

These exercises extend the concept of square root to more complicated calculations.

FOLLOW-UP ACTIVITIES

NUMBER SENSE (Estimation)

Tell students that solutions to inequalities can be estimated; for example, if $4y < 401$, $y <$ about 100. Have students estimate solutions to these inequalities.

$26x < 100$	($x <$ about 4)
$8x > 58$	($x >$ about 7)
$x \div 11 < 14$	($x <$ about 140)
$50x > 201$	($x >$ about 4)
$x \div 49 > 8$	($x >$ about 400)

COMPUTER

Have students write a program that will print only the values from the replacement set (⁻3,0,3,6,9) that satisfy $n - 6 \leq ⁻3$.

```
10 DATA ⁻3, 0, 3, 6, 9
20 FOR X = 1 TO 5
30 READ N
40 IF N − 6 <= ⁻3 THEN PRINT N
50 NEXT X
60 END
```

COMING UP

A motion picture "extra"-vaganza!

PRACTICE Inequalities

Use the real numbers as the replacement set. Write the letter of the solution set of the inequality.

1. $4y < 4$ — f
2. $3 + y \geq 1$ — m
3. $\frac{5}{y} = 5$ — e
4. $y - 1 > 8$ — r
5. $\frac{1}{2}y \leq ⁻3$ — o
6. $2y > 8$ — k
7. $y - 2 \geq 2$ — c
8. $\frac{1}{8}y \geq 2$ — g
9. $⁻1 + y > 1$ — l
10. $\frac{1}{3}y > 15$ — j
11. $3y = 0$ — h
12. $y + 2 > ⁻8$ — b
13. $y - 4 \leq 5$ — i
14. $y + 1 = ⁻4$ — d
15. $y - 2 > ⁻96$ — n
16. $\frac{1}{4}y \geq ⁻4$ — q
17. $5y \geq 95$ — a
18. $3y < ⁻9$ — p

a. $y = \{19,20,21,\ldots\}$
b. $y = \{⁻9,⁻8,⁻7,\ldots\}$
c. $y = \{4,5,6,7 \ldots\}$
d. $y = \{⁻5\}$
e. $y = \{1\}$
f. $y = \{\ldots ⁻2,⁻1,0\}$
g. $y = \{16,17,18,\ldots\}$
h. $y = \{0\}$
i. $y = \{\ldots 7,8,9\}$
j. $y = \{46,47,48,\ldots\}$
k. $y = \{5,6,7,\ldots\}$
l. $y = \{3,4,5,\ldots\}$
m. $y = \{⁻2,⁻1,0,\ldots\}$
n. $y = \{⁻93,⁻92,⁻91,\ldots\}$
o. $y = \{\ldots ⁻8,⁻7,⁻6\}$
p. $y = \{\ldots ⁻6,⁻5,⁻4\}$
q. $y = \{⁻16,⁻15,⁻14,\ldots\}$
r. $y = \{10, 11, 12,\ldots\}$

120   Use with pages 292–293.

Practice Worksheet

ENRICH Number

Ned and the Noise Buffoons are going on a concert tour. Ned is trying to decide if he should buy and insure an electric guitar for the tour. Ned's guitar will cost $865. Ned has plenty of money in the bank. He estimates that there is a 2% chance that it will be lost on the tour and a 20% chance that it will be damaged. He thinks that any damage done could be repaired for $100. He calculates that the probable cost for the guitar on tour will be ($865 × 2%) + ($100 × 20%) = $37.30.

For $40.00, Ned can purchase insurance for his guitar. The insurance policy is a $50.00 deductible, which means that Ned would have to pay the first $50.00 of any claim he made. If Ned does buy insurance, there is a 100% chance that he will pay the $40.00 premium, a 2% chance that he will pay the $50.00 deductible if his guitar is lost, and a 20% chance that he will pay the $50.00 deductible for any damage. He calculates his probable cost on the tour as ($40 × 100%) + ($50 × 2%) + ($50 × 20%) = $51.00

1. Based on cost, should Ned buy insurance for his guitar?
no

The other members of the Buffoons want to know if they should buy and insure their instruments. The chance of any of their equipment being lost is the same as Ned's, 2%.

Big Bub: His drums will cost $1,430 and he estimates that there is a 10% chance that they will receive $300 worth of damage.

Billy the Risk: His electric piano will cost $972, and he estimates a 25% chance of damage, with repairs costing $200.

Billy can purchase the same policy as Ned, at the same price, but Bub would have to pay a $60.00 premium for a $75.00 deductible policy.

What is the probable cost for

2. Billy, if he does not buy insurance? $69.44
3. Billy, if he does buy insurance? $53.50
4. Bub, if he does not buy insurance? $58.60
5. Bub, if he does buy insurance? $69.00

110   Use with pages 292–293.

Enrich Worksheet

Objective: To solve a one-step inequality

Warm-Up

Have students determine which elements of the replacement set ($^-4, ^-3, ^-2, ^-1, 0$) are solutions for each inequality.

$n < 0$ ($^-4, ^-3, ^-2, ^-1$)
$2a > ^-4$ ($^-1, 0$)
$m - 3 > ^-3$ (none)
$\frac{d}{4} \leq ^-1$ ($^-4$)

GETTING STARTED

Tell the class that there are certain key phrases that signal an inequality. Write $>$, $<$, $\geq$, and $\leq$ on the chalkboard. Ask students to think of as many word phrases as they can for each situation; (for example, $>$: *greater than, more than, faster than,* and so on; $\leq$: *or less, at most, up to,* and so on.)

TEACHING THE LESSON

Discourage them from bypassing the conversion steps to and from an inequality because this may lead to difficulties later on. Also note that no negative coefficients appear in any of these inequalities. If students ask about this kind of inequality, tell them that a special set of rules governs such inequalities and that they are used for more advanced work in algebra.

Solving One-Step Inequalities

A movie needs extras for a crowd scene. Each extra is paid $50. If the budget allows no more than $4,500 for extras, how many can be hired?

Let x represent the number of extras. Then, $50x \leq 4,500$.

To solve an inequality, solve the related equation. Then write the correct inequality for the solution.

$50x \leq 4,500$
$50x = 4,500$ Use the related equation.
$\frac{50x}{50} = \frac{4,500}{50}$ Divide by 50.
$x = 90$ Think: Is $x \leq 90$ the solution?

Test any value less than 90 to find out.
If you try 0 for x, $50 \cdot 0 \leq 4,500$. So, $x \leq 90$.

No more than 90 extras can be hired.

Other examples:

Solve $a + 7.5 \geq 9.4$.
Use the related equation.

$a + 7.5 = 9.4$
$a + 7.5 - 7.5 = 9.4 - 7.5$
$a = 1.9$ Is $a \geq 1.9$ the solution?
Try 10 for a. $\frac{10}{2.5} > 2$. So, $a \geq 1.9$.

Solve $\frac{4}{5}s \geq 20$.
Use the related equation.
$\frac{4}{5}s = 20$

$\frac{4}{5}s \cdot \frac{5}{4} = \overset{5}{\cancel{20}} \cdot \frac{5}{\cancel{4}\,1}$

$s = 25$ Is $s \geq 25$ the solution?
Try 30 for s. $\frac{4}{5} \cdot 30 \geq 20$.
So, $s \geq 25$.

Solve $\frac{p}{7} \neq 49$.
Use the related equation.

$\frac{p}{7} = 49$
$\frac{p}{7} \cdot 7 = 49 \cdot 7$
$p = 343$
So, $p \neq 343$.

Solve $t - 4 \leq 6$.
Use the related equation.

$t - 4 = 6$
$t - 4 + 4 = 6 + 4$
$t = 10$ Is $t \leq 10$ the solution?
Try 8 for t. $8 - 4 \leq 6$.
So, $t \leq 10$.

COMMON ERRORS

Students will sometimes forget to convert the related equation back to an inequality.

Remediation

For this error, have each student draw a circle around the equal sign in each step of the solution; for example:

$7x \geq 616$
$7x \bullet 616 \; (=)$
$\frac{7x}{7} \bullet \frac{616}{7} \; (=)$
$x \bullet 88 \; (=)$
$x \geq 88$

Assign Reteach Master, p. 86.

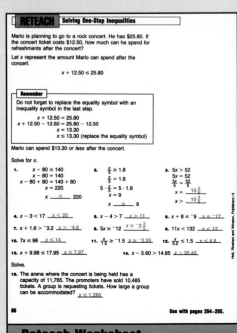

RETEACH   Solving One-Step Inequalities

Mario is planning to go to a rock concert. He has $25.80. If the concert ticket costs $12.50, how much can he spend for refreshments after the concert?

Let x represent the amount Mario can spend after the concert.

$$x + 12.50 \leq 25.80$$

Remember
Do not forget to replace the equality symbol with an inequality symbol in the last step.

$x + 12.50 = 25.80$
$x + 12.50 - 12.50 = 25.80 - 12.50$
$x = 13.30$
$x \leq 13.30$ (replace the equality symbol)

Mario can spend $13.30 *or less* after the concert.

Solve for x.

1. $x - 80 \leq 140$
$x - 80 = 140$
$x - 80 + 80 = 140 + 80$
$x = 220$
$x \;\underline{\leq}\; 220$

2. $\frac{x}{5} \geq 1.8$
$\frac{x}{5} = 1.8$
$5 \cdot \frac{x}{5} = 5 \cdot 1.8$
$x = 9$
$x \;\underline{\geq}\; 9$

3. $5x > 52$
$5x = 52$
$\frac{5x}{5} = \frac{52}{5}$
$x = 10\frac{2}{5}$
$x > \underline{10\frac{2}{5}}$

4. $x - 3 < 17$ $\underline{x < 20}$
5. $x - 4 > 7$ $\underline{x > 11}$
6. $x + 8 \leq ^-9$ $\underline{x \leq ^-17}$

7. $x + 1.6 > ^-3.2$ $\underline{x > ^-4.8}$
8. $5x \geq ^-12$ $\underline{x \geq ^-2\frac{2}{5}}$
9. $11x < 132$ $\underline{x < 12}$

10. $7x \leq 98$ $\underline{x \leq 14}$
11. $\frac{x}{15} \geq ^-1.5$ $\underline{x \geq ^-22.5}$
12. $\frac{x}{32} \leq 1.5$ $\underline{x \leq 48}$

13. $x + 9.98 \leq 17.95$ $\underline{x \leq 7.97}$
14. $x - 5.60 > 14.85$ $\underline{x > 20.45}$

Solve.

15. The arena where the concert is being held has a capacity of 11,765. The promoters have sold 10,485 tickets. A group is requesting tickets. How large a group can be accommodated? $\underline{x \leq 1,280}$

86   Use with pages 294–295.

Reteach Worksheet

Solve.

1. $x + 2 < 8$
$x < 6$

2. $a + 4 \geq 9$
$a \geq 5$

3. $r - 1 > 7$
$r > 8$

4. $x - 5 \leq 3$
$x \leq 8$

5. $3g > 24$
$g > 8$

6. $7b < 21$
$b < 3$

7. $\frac{d}{6} \leq 10$
$d \leq 60$

8. $\frac{m}{4} > 6$
$m > 24$

9. $x - 0.3 \neq 0.7$
$x \neq 1$

10. $y + 1.3 \geq 2.4$
$y \geq 1.1$

11. $c + 2.4 > 4.2$
$c > 1.8$

12. $k - 4.8 \leq 6.3$
$k \leq 11.1$

13. $0.6m \leq 3.6$
$m \leq 6$

14. $1.2t > 4.8$
$t > 4$

15. $\frac{q}{2.7} \geq 0.3$
$q \geq 0.81$

16. $\frac{m}{1.6} < 0.6$
$m < 0.96$

17. $a - \frac{1}{4} \geq \frac{3}{4}$ $a \geq 1$

18. $c - \frac{3}{8} > \frac{4}{8}$ $c > \frac{7}{8}$

19. $s + \frac{1}{2} \geq \frac{2}{5}$
$s \geq \frac{1}{15}$

20. $y + \frac{1}{8} \leq \frac{4}{5}$ $y \leq \frac{27}{40}$

21. $\frac{1}{2}c \geq \frac{3}{5}$ $c \geq 1\frac{1}{5}$

22. $\frac{2}{3}t \leq \frac{4}{5}$ $t \leq 1\frac{1}{5}$

23. $\frac{r}{\frac{1}{3}} \neq \frac{2}{3}$ $r \neq \frac{2}{9}$

24. $\frac{y}{\frac{1}{5}} \leq \frac{2}{5}$ $y \leq \frac{2}{25}$

25. $e - 7 \neq {}^-3$
$e \neq 4$

26. $x - 3 > {}^-8$
$x > {}^-5$

27. $x + 5 > {}^-3$
$x > {}^-8$

28. $g + 9 \leq {}^-18$
$g \leq {}^-27$

29. $\frac{y}{3} \leq 2$ $y \leq 6$

30. $\frac{d}{5} > 5$ $d > 25$

31. $6m < {}^-3.6$
$m < {}^-0.6$

32. $3r < 12$ $r < 4$

Solve.

33. Last week, 7 people were selected for a scene in the school play. The director wants no more than 29 people in the scene. Write an inequality, and solve to find how many more people can be selected for the scene. $x + 7 \leq 29$; no more than 22 more people

34. The leading player, Angela Greene, receives a salary of $175 per day. How many days will it take her to earn $2,275? **13 days**

CHALLENGE

To simplify expressions such as $2x + 4 + 3x + 7$, first, group the like terms, variables with identical variables, and whole numbers with whole numbers.

Add the like terms.

$2x + 3x + 4 + 7$
$5x \quad + \quad 11$

Simplify each expression.

1. $4x + 3x + 7 + 10$
$7x + 17$

2. $6y + 8 + 3y + 4$
$9y + 12$

3. $7 + 12 + 19z + 1 + 2z$
$21z + 20$

4. $5a + 3 + 176 + 18a + a$
$24a + 179$

Use with pages 294–295.   121
Practice Worksheet

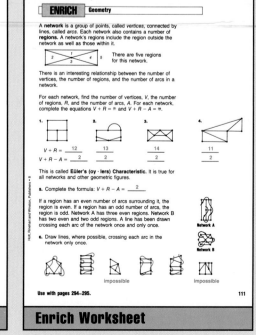

Use with pages 294–295.   111
Enrich Worksheet

ASSIGNMENT GUIDE

Basic:	1–8, 9–31 o
Average:	1–4, 6–32 e, 33–34
Extended:	6–32 e, 33–34, Chlg

Resources
Practice, p. 121	Class/Home, p. H121
Reteach, p. 86	More Practice, p. H203
Enrich, p. 111	Reasoning, p. H222

Exercise Analysis
1–32   Solve an inequality
33–34   Skill applications

Challenge
This activity introduces a skill that is fundamental to solving algebraic equations and word problems and to proving theorems in geometry and so on.

FOLLOW-UP ACTIVITIES

MATH COMMUNICATION
Explain that two or more inequalities can be combined into one simpler statement if the same variable is involved; for example, if $y < 3$ and $y \geq 0$, then both statements can be written as $0 \leq y < 3$.

Have students combine each pair of inequalities into a simpler statement.

1. $x < 5$ and $x > 1$ $(1 < x < 5)$
2. $z \leq {}^-2$ and $z \geq {}^-4$ $({}^-4 \leq z \leq {}^-2)$
3. $b > 1$ and $b \leq 10$ $(1 < b \leq 10)$
4. $f \leq \frac{4}{5}$ and $f > \frac{{}^-1}{5}$ $(\frac{{}^-1}{5} < f \leq \frac{4}{5})$
5. $t < 2.45$ and $t > {}^-0.1$
   $({}^-0.1 < t < 2.45)$
*6. $2m \leq {}^-4$ and $m > {}^-5$
   $({}^-5 < m \leq {}^-2)$
*7. $p < 3$ and $3p > {}^-9$ $({}^-3 < p < 3)$

MATH CONNECTION (Consumer)
Have students write and solve an inequality for each of the following problems.

- Tickets to a baseball game cost $6.50. Tim wants to buy as many as he can, but he has only $26. How many tickets can he buy? ($6.50x \leq 26; $x \leq 4$. He can buy a maximum of 4 tickets.)
- Paint costs $3.75 per tube. Jenny has $18. How many tubes can she buy? ($3.75x \leq 18; $x \leq 4.8$. Jenny can buy a maximum of 4 tubes.)

COMING UP
Pat Tern is the new Jon Seagull.

Objective: To organize information to find a pattern

Warm-Up
Have students write the next three numbers in each pattern.
- 13, 26, 39 . . . (52, 65, 78)
- 201, 185, 169 . . . (153, 137, 121)
- 6, 18, 54 . . . (162, 486, 1,458)
- 256, 128, 64 . . . (32, 16, 8)

GETTING STARTED

Have students recall how postage rates are charged (base rate for first ounce, additional charge for additional ounce or fraction thereof). Ask students how they would find the postage for a 9.25-oz letter if the first $1\frac{3}{4}$ oz costs 20¢ and each additional $1\frac{3}{4}$ oz costs 17¢. Draw this table on the board.

20¢	37¢	54¢	71¢	88¢	105¢
$1\frac{3}{4}$	$3\frac{1}{2}$	$5\frac{1}{4}$	7	$8\frac{3}{4}$	$10\frac{1}{2}$

Tell students that another way this information might be shown is by giving examples of letter weights and postage; for example, $1\frac{3}{4}$ oz = 20¢, $5\frac{1}{4}$ oz = 54¢, and $8\frac{3}{4}$ oz = 88¢. Tell them that this lesson will help them find patterns for such examples.

TEACHING THE LESSON

Students often will encounter information in the form of a pattern which must be extended to find additional information. Patterns are often formed with two sets of numbers, the relationship between which may be unclear. This lesson teaches students to organize the information into a table to find the pattern in both sets of numbers and the relationship between these patterns.

Questions: If students have trouble with a question, have them begin a table first. This may help them understand the supplied information. Point out that these are really multistep problems. The unstated information is the relationship between the patterns.

Tools: The most important tool is the table. In the table, the pattern in each set of numbers is more easily observed and extended. Remind students to carefully align the related numbers so that all numbers correspond accurately.

Remind students that patterns can have any starting point; for example, 7.284, 10.284, 13.284 is a pattern that begins at 7.284 and in which 3 is added to find the next number in the pattern.

Solutions: Only basic operations are used in the lesson.

QUESTIONS	TOOLS	SOLUTIONS	CHECKS

PROBLEM SOLVING
Making a Table To Find a Pattern

You can use a table to help you find a pattern that will enable you to solve a problem.

> To help promote its new movie, *Galaxy Dragonfighter*, Fallotte Enterprises created a video game about the movie's hero. For the next week, Fallotte is offering cash prizes to players who score high in the game. A score of 75,000 points in a single game wins a $2 prize. Scoring 77,250 points wins $2.50, scoring 79,500 wins $3.00, and so on. Shawn won $5.00. How many points did he score?

Make a table.

Points Scored	Prize
75,000	$2.00
77,250	$2.50
79,500	$3.00

The table makes it easier to see the pattern. For every 2,250 points scored, the player wins another $0.50. To find out how many points Shawn scored, continue the table until you reach the prize that he won—$5.00.

Points Scored	Prize
75,000	$2.00
77,250	$2.50
79,500	$3.00
81,750	$3.50
84,000	$4.00
86,250	$4.50
88,500	$5.00

Shawn scored at least 88,500 points.

296

Checks: Students should reread the question after solving to ensure completion. Each separate pattern should be checked for accuracy.

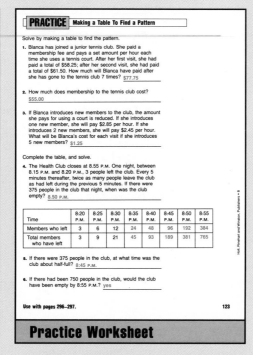

Solve. Make a table if needed.

1. Julie scored 95,250 points playing the *Galaxy Dragonfighter* game. What was the cash prize that she won? **$6.50**

2. How many points would a player have to score to win the top prize—$8.00? **102,000 points**

3. *The Danville Times* charges $31.75 for a 3-line classified advertisement. A 4-line ad costs $41.10, a 5-line ad costs $50.45, a 6-line ad costs $59.80, and so on. How much will Mr. Simmons pay if he wants to take out a help-wanted ad that runs 9 lines? **$87.85**

4. How much would it cost to place a 7-line ad in *The Danville Times*? **$69.15**

5. To rent 4 video tapes at the Tape City Video Shop, you need $63.80. To rent 5 tapes, you need $67.60; to rent 6 tapes, you need $71.40; and so on. If you need a membership in order to rent even 1 tape and if you get 3 tapes rent free when you buy a membership, how much does a membership cost? How much does it cost to rent 9 tapes? **Membership costs $60.00; 9 tapes cost $82.80.**

6. A throng of Hollywood stars arrived at the gala opening of a new movie. The first person through the door of the theater was the star of the movie. Each time the theater doors opened thereafter, 4 more stars entered than had entered previously. If the theater doors opened and closed 15 times, how many stars attended the opening of the movie? Copy and complete the table.

Door openings	1	2	3	4	5	6	7	8	9	10	11	12	13	14	15
Stars entered	1	5	9	13	17	21	25	29	33	37	41	45	49	53	57
Total stars	1	6	15	28	45	66	91	120	153	190	231	276	325	378	435

435

7. After the doors had opened 9 times, how many stars were there in the theater? **153**

Classwork/Homework, pages H122–H123

ASSIGNMENT GUIDE

Basic: 1–4

Average: 3–4, 6–7

Extended: 3–7

Resources
Practice, pp. 122–3   Class/Home, pp. H122–3

Exercise Analysis
1–2 Extend the table in the lesson
3–7 Draw a table to find a pattern

FOLLOW-UP ACTIVITIES

PROBLEM SOLVING
Have students make a table to solve these problems.

1. The E-Z-Read Encyclopedia Company began an incentive program for its sales force. Ted sold three 12-volume sets last week and received a bonus of $9.00. Mackenzie sold five 10-volume sets and received a bonus of $12.50. Marie sold 8 of the company's 5-volume junior sets and received $10.00. James sold 3 copies of the 20-volume jumbo encyclopedia. What was his bonus? ($15.00)

2. What was Jessica's bonus if she sold 5 junior sets and 4 jumbo sets? ($26.25)

CALCULATOR
Have students use a calculator to solve the following problems.

1. A video game called Intergalactic Milk Deliverer gives an extra tankful of gas to the space deliverer when 500,000 bottles of milk have been delivered. The next tankful of gas comes when 855,000 bottles of milk have been delivered, and the next tankful after 1,210,000. How many bottles of milk must be delivered in order to win 5 extra tankfuls of gas? (1,920,000)

2. Daisy scored 3,340,000 points. How many extra tankfuls of gas did she win? (9)

COMING UP
Step, step, solve!

297

Warm-Up
Have students solve each inequality.

$4r \geq {}^-16 \ (r \geq {}^-4)$

$\frac{2p}{3} < 8 \ (p < 12)$

$s - 6 \leq {}^-5 \ (s \leq 1)$

$1.7q > 8.5 \ (q > 5)$

GETTING STARTED

Have students write an equation for the following word problem.

- Melissa spent $3.40 at the grocery store. She spent $1.20 on milk and the rest on 11 apples. How much did each apple cost? ($1.20 + 11x = $3.40)

Ask students how they would change the equation if the word problem changed to include the following information.

- Melissa had $3.40. She bought milk for $1.20 and 11 apples. What is the most each apple might have cost? ($1.20 + 11x \leq $3.40)

Tell students that this is a two-step inequality that, like one-step inequalities, can be solved by using the related equation.

TEACHING THE LESSON

Point out that the key phrase that signals an inequality in the first example consists of the words "84 days or *less*." Ask the class why an inequality is needed. Guide them to realize that 84 days is a maximum, a number that cannot be exceeded. Any number of days 84 or fewer would be acceptable. So, $\leq$ is used. In the case of a minimum such as "seventy-five customers per night were needed for the play to break even," an inequality can also be used.

Checkpoint
The chart lists the common errors students make when solving two-step inequalities.

Correct Answers: 1a, 2b

Remediation
- For this error, have students check their answers by replacing the variable with values not in the solution set to determine whether they do indeed make the inequality false.

☐ For these errors, assign Reteach Master, p. 87.

298

Solving Two-Step Inequalities

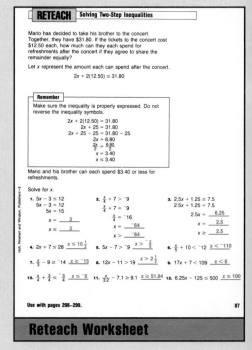

Shigeko has 7 scenes left to tape for her television drama. She has already spent 56 days on the project, which must be finished in a total of 84 days or less. How many days can she spend on the average on each remaining scene?

The problem can be represented as a two-step inequality. Let x represent the number of days she can spend on each scene; then $7x$ represents the total time that remains.

$$7x + 56 \leq 84$$

$$7x + 56 - 56 = 84 - 56 \quad \text{Use the related equation.}$$

$$7x = 28$$

$$\frac{7x}{7} = \frac{28}{7}$$

$$x = 4 \qquad \text{Is } x \leq 4 \text{ the solution?}$$

Try 0 for x. $7 \cdot 0 + 56 \leq 84$ So, $x \leq 4$.

She can spend on the average 4 days or less on each remaining scene.

Another example:

Solve. Use the replacement set of real numbers.

$$\frac{x}{2} + 4 < 7$$

$$\frac{x}{2} + 4 - 4 = 7 - 4 \quad \text{Use the related equation.}$$

$$\frac{x}{2} = 3$$

$$\frac{x}{2} \cdot 2 = 3 \cdot 2$$

$$x = 6 \qquad \text{Is } x < 6 \text{ the solution?}$$

Try 2 for x. $\frac{2}{2} + 4 < 7$. So, $x < 6$.

Any number less than 6 will be in the solution set.

Checkpoint Write the letter of the correct answer.

Solve.

1. $2x + 3 < 9$ **ⓐ** $x < 3$ **b.** $x = 3$ **c.** $x < 6$ **d.** $x < 12$

2. $4x + 4 \leq 16$ **a.** $x \geq 3$ **ⓑ** $x \leq 3$ **c.** $x \leq 5$ **d.** $x > 3$

298

COMMON ERRORS

Answer Choice	Type of Error
☐ 1b	Fails to return the related equation to an inequality
☐ 1c	Fails to perform the same operation on both sides of the related equation
☐ 1d, 2c	Uses the incorrect operation
■ 2a, 2d	Uses the incorrect inequality symbol

RETEACH Solving Two-Step Inequalities

Mario has decided to take his brother to the concert. Together, they have $31.80. If the tickets to the concert cost $12.50 each, how much can they each spend for refreshments after the concert if they agree to share the remainder equally?

Let x represent the amount each can spend after the concert.

$$2x + 2(12.50) \leq 31.80$$

Remember
Make sure the inequality is properly expressed. Do not reverse the inequality symbols.

$$2x + 2(12.50) = 31.80$$
$$2x + 25 = 31.80$$
$$2x + 25 - 25 = 31.80 - 25$$
$$2x = 6.80$$
$$\frac{2x}{2} = \frac{6.80}{2}$$
$$x = 3.40$$
$$x \leq 3.40$$

Mario and his brother can each spend $3.40 or less for refreshments.

Solve for x.

1. $5x - 3 \leq 12$
$5x - 3 = 12$
$5x = 15$
$x = \underline{3}$
$x \leq \underline{3}$

2. $\frac{x}{4} + 7 > {}^-9$
$\frac{x}{4} + 7 = {}^-9$
$\frac{x}{4} = {}^-16$
$x = \underline{{}^-64}$
$x > \underline{{}^-64}$

3. $2.5x + 1.25 \geq 7.5$
$2.5x + 1.25 = 7.5$
$2.5x = \underline{6.25}$
$x = \underline{2.5}$
$x \geq \underline{2.5}$

4. $2x + 7 \leq 28$ $\underline{x \leq 10\frac{1}{2}}$ **5.** $5x - 7 > {}^-9$ $\underline{x > {}^-\frac{2}{5}}$ **6.** $\frac{x}{5} + 10 < {}^-12$ $\underline{x < {}^-110}$

7. $\frac{x}{3} - 9 \geq {}^-14$ $\underline{x \geq {}^-15}$ **8.** $12x - 11 > 19$ $\underline{x > 2\frac{1}{2}}$ **9.** $17x + 7 < 109$ $\underline{x < 6}$

10. $\frac{x}{4} + \frac{3}{4} \leq {}^-\frac{3}{4}$ $\underline{x \leq {}^-6}$ **11.** $\frac{x}{3.2} - 7.1 \geq 9.1$ $\underline{x \geq 51.84}$ **12.** $6.25x - 125 \leq 500$ $\underline{x \leq 100}$

Use with pages 298–299.   87

Reteach Worksheet

Solve.

1. $2x + 3 < 5$
$x < 1$

2. $4a - 2 > 6$
$a > 2$

3. $3y - 1 < 5$
$y < 2$

4. $6z + 3 > 15$
$z > 2$

5. $\frac{b}{2} + 4 > 2$
$b > {}^-4$

6. $\frac{k}{3} - 1 > 1$
$k > 6$

7. $\frac{d}{12} + 4 \geq 7$
$d \geq 36$

8. $\frac{t}{8} - 7 \geq 7$
$t \geq 112$

9. $7c - 5.7 > 51$
$c > 8.1$

10. $8.2g + 8 < 24.4$
$g < 2$

11. $1.2t + 4 > 100$
$t > 80$

12. $1.2m - 4 \leq 2$
$m \leq 5$

13. $\frac{t}{3} - 0.2 \geq 0.6$
$t \geq 2.4$

14. $\frac{c}{12} + 1.6 > 1.7$
$c > 1.2$

15. $\frac{m}{0.5} - 3.1 \leq 59$
$m \leq 31.05$

16. $\frac{y}{0.6} + 4 > 8$
$y > 2.4$

17. $7y - \frac{2}{5} < 48\frac{3}{5}$
$y < 7$

18. $6c - 2\frac{1}{4} < 39\frac{3}{4}$
$c < 7$

19. $\frac{2}{3}y + 9 \geq 21$
$y \geq 18$

20. $\frac{3}{5}n + 8 > 17$
$n > 15$

21. $\frac{m}{3} + \frac{1}{8} \neq \frac{4}{8}$
$m \neq 1\frac{1}{8}$

22. $\frac{x}{2} - \frac{3}{4} \leq \frac{3}{4}$
$x \leq 3$

23. $\frac{l}{2} - \frac{1}{5} > \frac{3}{5}$
$l > 1\frac{3}{5}$

24. $\frac{d}{4} + \frac{1}{12} < \frac{4}{12}$
$d < 1$

25. $8e + 4 < 36$
$e < 4$

26. $9s - {}^-7 \geq 25$
$s \geq 2$

27. $4b + {}^-2 \neq {}^-6$
$b \neq {}^-1$

28. $2m - 9 > 19$
$m > 14$

29. $\frac{a}{2} + {}^-9 \geq 6$
$a \geq 30$

30. $\frac{z}{6} - 14 \leq 2$
$z \leq 96$

31. $\frac{r}{7} - {}^-3 > 4$
$r > 7$

32. $\frac{n}{4} + 2 < 7$
$n < 20$

Solve. For Problem 34, use the Infobank.

33. Write an inequality; then solve. Toby and Sam are saving to buy a TV that costs $147. If Toby has saved $25 more than Sam, but they do not have enough as yet, how much have they each saved?
$2x + 25 < 147$; Sam has saved less than $61; Toby has saved less than $86.

34. Use the information on page 476 to solve. What is the number of frames projected by a TV set in Europe if it has projected 2,500 lines. Write an equation; then solve. (HINT: Let x = the number of frames projected.)
$625x = 2,500$
$x = 4$
4 frames

NUMBER SENSE

How can we estimate $\frac{348 \times 17}{9}$?

Think about numbers that are easier to compute mentally.

$350 \times \frac{18}{9}$		$\frac{360}{9} \times 20$		$\frac{350 \times 20}{10}$
350×2	or	40×20	or	350×2
700		800		700

Both 700 and 800 are good estimates.

Think of easier numbers, and estimate. Other estimates are possible.

1. $\frac{478 \times 36}{7}$ 2,500

2. $\frac{713 \times 65}{8}$ 5,600

3. $\frac{94 \times 198 \times 14}{7 \times 46}$ 800

Classwork/Homework, page H124

More Practice, page H203   **299**

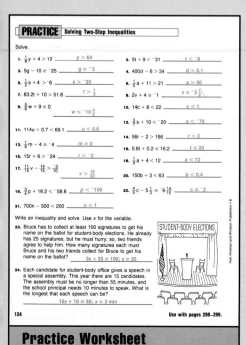

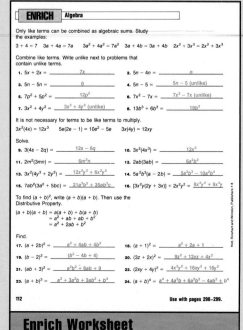

ASSIGNMENT GUIDE

Basic: 1–16, 33–34, NS

Average: 1–31 o, 33–34, NS

Extended: 2–32 e, 33–34, NS

Resources
Practice, p. 124   Class/Home, p. H124
Reteach, p. 87   More Practice, p. H203
Enrich, p. 112

Exercise Analysis
1–32   Solve a two-step inequality
33   Skill application
34   Data collection and computation

Number Sense
These exercises encourage students to simplify products by searching for compatible numbers.

FOLLOW-UP ACTIVITIES

PROBLEM SOLVING
Have students solve each two-sided inequality.
- $4 < 4x - 8 < 12$ $(3 < x < 5)$
- ${}^-0.9 < 0.3x < 4.5$ $({}^-3 < x < 15)$
- $\frac{3}{4} > \frac{y}{2} - \frac{1}{4} > \frac{1}{4}$ $(2 > y > 1)$
- ${}^-6 > 2b + {}^-5 > {}^-10$ $(\frac{-1}{2} > b > \frac{-5}{2})$

For students who encounter difficulty, show that they can break the two-sided inequality apart. For example,

$4 < 4x - 8 < 12$ can be written as
$4 < 4x - 8$ and $4x - 8 < 12$.

REINFORCEMENT
Have students solve this problem. A television director contracted to pay a camera technician $450 for one week. The director must also pay the technician an extra $125 per day for each day more than a week that the shoot runs. If the most the director can afford to pay the technician is $825.00, for how many days can the shoot run? (10 days)

COMING UP
Graphic scenes

299

Objectives: To solve and graph equations and inequalities on a number line

Warm-Up

Have students solve each inequality.
- $0.4s - 5.1 > 10.3$ ($s > 38.5$)
- $\frac{2d}{7} + \frac{4}{7} \leq \frac{5}{7}$ ($d \leq \frac{1}{2}$)
- $3c + {}^-8 < {}^-11$ ($c < {}^-1$)
- $9v - 18 > 27$ ($v > 5$)

GETTING STARTED

Draw a number line numbered from $^-10$ to 10 on the chalkboard. Above it write this inequality: $x > {}^-1$. Plot each of the following numbers on the number line, asking students whether each satisfies the inequality.

3 (yes)	$^-5$ (no)	8 (yes)
0 (yes)	$-\frac{1}{2}$ (yes)	5 (yes)

Have several volunteers plot other values of x that satisfy the inequality. Then ask the class whether the numbers below, which are not on the number line, satisfy the inequality.

15	50	100	285	500

(All satisfy the inequality.) Ask where these numbers would be if the number line were extended. (All would be to the right.)

TEACHING THE LESSON

Ask students how they would graph $x \neq 3$.

Have a volunteer come to the board and draw the number line.

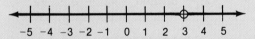

Checkpoint

The chart lists the common errors students make when graphing inequalities.

Correct Answers: 1c, 2b

Remediation

■ For these errors, review the meaning of open and filled circles on a number line. Have students first consider the specified value. If the inequality symbol is $\geq$ or $\leq$, have them draw a solid circle at the point on the number line. If the inequality symbol is $>$ or $<$, have them draw an open circle.

□ For these errors, assign Reteach Master, p. 88.

Graphing Equations and Inequalities

The solution to an equation or an inequality can be shown as a point or a set of points on a number line.

$x = 3$

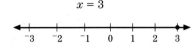

$x > 3$

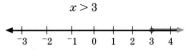

The open circle indicates the solution does not include 3.

Graph $\frac{y}{2.5} > 2$.
Use the related equation to solve.

$$\frac{y}{2.5} = 2$$
$$\frac{y}{2.5} \cdot 2.5 = 2 \cdot 2.5$$
$$y = 5 \quad \text{Is } y > 5 \text{ the solution?}$$

Try 10. $\frac{10}{2.5} > 2$. So, $y > 5$.

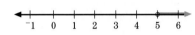

The ray indicates that all real numbers greater than 5 are solutions; 5 is not a solution.

Graph $45x \leq 270$.
Use the related equation to solve.

$$45x = 270$$
$$\frac{45x}{45} = \frac{270}{45}$$
$$x = 6 \quad \text{Is } x \leq 6 \text{ the solution?}$$

Try 0. $45 \cdot 0 \leq 270$. So, $x \leq 6$.

The ray indicates that all real numbers less than or equal to 6 are solutions.

Checkpoint Write the letter of the correct answer.

Choose the equation or inequality that matches each graph.

1.

2.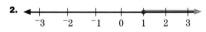

a. $x = {}^-1$	**b.** $x > {}^-1$	
(c.) $x < {}^-1$	**d.** $x \geq {}^-1$	

a. $a \leq 1$	**(b.)** $a \geq 1$	
c. $a > 1$	**d.** $a < 1$	

300

Math Reasoning, page H222

COMMON ERRORS

Answer Choice	Type of Error
■ 1a	Mistakes the open circle for the designation of a point
□ 1b, 2a	Mistakes the direction of inequality
■ 1d	Includes an open circle in a solution set
■ 2c	Fails to include the end point of the ray in the solution set
□ 2d	Mistakes the direction of inequality; fails to include the end point of the ray in the solution set

---

RETEACH | Graphing Equations and Inequalities

Solve and graph the inequality $2x + 5 \leq 1$.

$$2x + 5 = 1$$
$$2x + 5 - 5 = 1 - 5$$
$$2x = {}^-4$$
$$x = {}^-2$$
$$x \leq {}^-2$$

Remember

$x \leq {}^-2$ translates as $x = {}^-2$ or x is to the left of $^-2$ on a graph.

Write an inequality that matches the graph.

1. $x < 1$
2. $x > 3$
3. $x \geq {}^-2$
4. $x \leq {}^-1$
5. $x < 2$
6. $x > 0$
7. $x \leq 5$
8. $x \geq 100$

Solve each equation and graph the inequality on a separate sheet of paper. 9–15: Check students' graphs.

9. $2x \geq 4$	$x \geq 2$	10. $3x \leq {}^-3$	$x \leq {}^-1$	11. $x + 3 > {}^-5$	$x > {}^-8$
12. $\frac{x}{5} + 3 < {}^-4$	$x < {}^-35$	13. $3x - 6 \leq 15$	$x \leq 7$	14. $3.2x - 5.1 \geq 1.3$	$x \geq 2$

88

Use with pages 300–301.

Reteach Worksheet

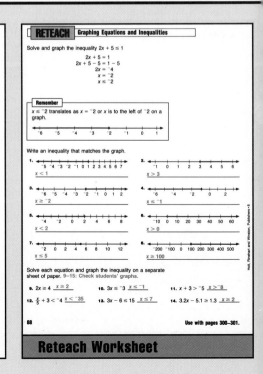

Solve and graph the inequality.   Check students' graphs.

1. $x - 8 > 7$
   $x > 15$
2. $z + 5.5 > 8$
   $z > 2.5$
3. $\frac{y}{2} \le 3$
   $y \le 6$
4. $4c > 12$
   $c > 3$
5. $\frac{1}{4}a \ge 4$
   $a \ge 16$
6. $w - {}^-7 \le 15$
   $w \le 8$
7. $\frac{3}{4}r < 3$
   $r < 4$
8. $7c \ne 2.8$
   $c \ne 0.4$
9. $2x - 5 < 1$
   $x < 3$
10. $\frac{y}{2} + 5 > 6$
    $y > 2$
11. $0.3p + 0.3 \le 1.2$
    $p \le 3$
12. $\frac{m}{2} + {}^-2 < 10$
    $m < 24$
13. $3b + \frac{2}{3} \ge 3\frac{10}{15}$
    $b \ge 1$
14. $\frac{c}{2.5} - 7 \le 3.4$
    $c \le 26$
15. $\frac{3}{5}n + 2 > 5$
    $n > 5$
★16. $\frac{5}{9}g + 2.7 \ne 4.75$
    $g \ne 3.69$

Solve and graph the equation.   Check students' graphs.

17. $c - 9 = 3$
    $c = 12$
18. $b - 1.28 = 8.72$
    $b = 10$
19. $9t = 7$
    $t = \frac{7}{9}$
20. $a - 8 = {}^-4$
    $a = 4$
21. $\frac{x}{4} = \frac{3}{4}$
    $x = {}^-3$
22. $p + 0.78 = 18$
    $p = 17.22$
23. ${}^-4c = {}^-16$
    $c = 4$
24. $\frac{e}{6} = \frac{2}{3}$
    $e = 4$
25. $2x + 10 = 18$
    $x = 4$
26. ${}^-12 + p = 4$
    $p = 16$
27. $x + 5.7 = 18.3$
    $x = 12.6$
28. ${}^-2b - 5 = {}^-7$
    $b = 1$
29. $\frac{r}{2} - 2 = 2$
    $r = 8$
★30. $\frac{s}{2} + 2 = 2$
    $s = 0$
★31. ${}^-4c - 8 = {}^-8$
    $c = 0$
★32. ${}^-k + 3 = {}^-4$
    $k = 7$

Solve.

33. Time the lengths of commercials in minutes during an hour of TV programming. Write equations to represent the relation between the total commercial time and the remaining time. Solve to find the program time. Graph the solution.
    Answers will vary.

★34. Maria sells station time for commercials. Yesterday she sold 2 minutes more than she sold the day before. These two days are still less than her record total sale of 8 minutes in two days. Write and graph an inequality to represent the number of minutes sold yesterday and the day before.
    $2x + 2 < 8$
    Check students' graphs.

CHALLENGE   Patterns, Relations, and Functions

To solve these inequalities, test values for the variable, and graph the solution set.

Check students' graphs.
1. ${}^-x > 2$
2. ${}^-y < {}^-6$
3. $\frac{x}{2} + 4 \ge 7$
4. ${}^-5a + 4 \le 24$

Classwork/Homework, page H125

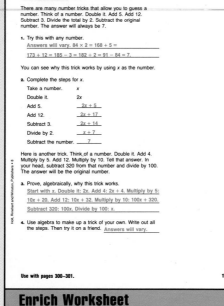

301

Holt, Rinehart and Winston, Publishers • 8

PRACTICE   Graphing Equations and Inequalities

Solve and graph the equation or inequality.

1. $x + 4 < {}^-2$ _____ $x < {}^-6$
2. $2a + 3 = {}^-3$ _____ $a = {}^-3$
3. $\frac{1}{2}h \le {}^-7$ _____ $h \le {}^-14$
4. $7m > {}^-14$ _____ $m > {}^-2$
5. $\frac{1}{5}y - 3 = {}^-2$ _____ $y = 5$
6. $8b - 4 = {}^-4$ _____ $b = 0$
7. $\frac{1}{6}v - 1 \le 0$ _____ $v \le 6$
8. $n + 6 > 8$ _____ $n > 2$
9. $14r - 20 < 22$ _____ $r < 3$
10. $z - 6 \ge 6$ _____ $z \ge 12$

Use with pages 300–301.   125

Practice Worksheet

ENRICH   Patterns

There are many number tricks that allow you to guess a number. Think of a number. Double it. Add 5. Add 12. Subtract 3. Divide the total by 2. Subtract the original number. The answer will always be 7.

1. Try this with any number.
   Answers will vary. 84 × 2 = 168 + 5 =
   173 + 12 = 185 − 3 = 182 ÷ 2 = 91 − 84 = 7.

You can see why this trick works by using x as the number.

2. Complete the steps for x.
   Take a number. x
   Double it. $2x$
   Add 5. $2x + 5$
   Add 12. $2x + 17$
   Subtract 3. $2x + 14$
   Divide by 2. $x + 7$
   Subtract the number. 7

Here is another trick. Think of a number. Double it. Add 4. Multiply by 5. Add 12. Multiply by 10. Tell that answer. In your head, subtract 320 from that number and divide by 100. The answer will be the original number.

3. Prove, algebraically, why this trick works.
   Start with x. Double it: 2x. Add 4: 2x + 4. Multiply by 5:
   10x + 20. Add 12: 10x + 32. Multiply by 10: 100x + 320.
   Subtract 320: 100x. Divide by 100: x.

4. Use algebra to make up a trick of your own. Write out all the steps. Then try it on a friend. Answers will vary.

Use with pages 300–301.   113

Enrich Worksheet

ASSIGNMENT GUIDE

Basic:	1–12, 17–28, 33
Average:	5–15, 17–28, 33–34
Extended:	9–16, 25–34, Chlg

Resources
Practice, p. 125   Class/Home, p. H125
Reteach, p. 88   Reasoning, p. H222
Enrich, p. 113

Exercise Analysis
1–16   Solve and graph an inequality
17–32 Solve and graph an equation
33   Problem formulation
34   Skill application

Challenge
Because students have not been taught that negative coefficients require a reversal of the symbol, they will have to use trial and error to solve these problems.

When students have finished (or encountered difficulty), help them formulate the rule.

FOLLOW-UP ACTIVITIES

PROBLEM SOLVING
Have students graph each set of inequalities. Explain that *and* means that both inequalities must be satisfied, whereas *or* means that only one must be satisfied.
- $x \ge 5$ or $x < 3$
- $x > {}^-2$ and $x > 1$
- $x \le 0$ or $x > 2$
- $x < {}^-1$ and $x > 1$

REINFORCEMENT
Have students write the inequality graphed on each number line.

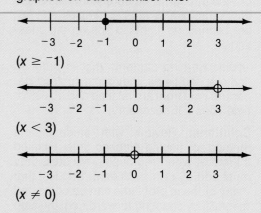

($x \ge {}^-1$)

($x < 3$)

($x \ne 0$)

COMING UP
I can't help but wonder where I'm bound.

Objective. To use information from a schedule

Warm-Up

Have students mentally compute the following elapsed times.

6:00 A.M. to 11:00 A.M. (5 h)
7:30 A.M. to 1:30 P.M. (6 h)
12:45 P.M. to 7:00 P.M. (6 h, 15 min)
9:45 A.M. to 3:15 P.M. (5 h, 30 min)

GETTING STARTED

Discuss with students their past travel experiences. Ask them about the amount of time they spent on an airplane, a train, or a bus. Ask them to relate any experiences in which their flight or train was late and they missed connections. Ask if they used a schedule for any transportation that they used.

TEACHING THE LESSON

Explain to students that reading a bus, train, or airline schedule is an essential skill today. Discuss the meaning of each heading on the schedule. Emphasize that it is important to know which time zones are referred to on the schedule. The departure and arrival times listed always refer to the time zones followed in their respective cities. Chicago follows Central Standard Time (CST) and New York follows Eastern Standard Time (EST). Note that there is a 1-hour difference between these time zones. Flight 914 arrives in New York at 4:54 P.M. EST, but at 3:54 P.M. CST. Mention should also be made of Mountain Standard Time (1 h earlier than CST) and Pacific Standard Time (1 h earlier than MST).

Questions: The questions asked in this lesson involve either finding elapsed time or finding departure/arrival times. For Exercises 5 through 8, be sure students realize they must use several schedules and figure connecting flights to answer the questions.

Tools: Remind students that in order to find elapsed times, they must subtract departure time from arrival time and adjust for time zones, if necessary.

Solutions: Review with students the method for finding elapsed time. Remind them that when regrouping minutes, they must add 60 (1 h = 60 min). Suggest that many of these problems can be computed mentally by counting forward from the time of departure. Also be sure students realize that there may be more than one correct solution to problems that ask what flight a person could take to arrive at a destination by a certain time.

302

PROBLEM SOLVING
Using a Schedule

A plane schedule shows you where and when each plane stops along its route. You can use a time-zone map to find the difference in time between two places that are in different time zones.

> The International Film and Video Convention is being held in New York City. Travis will travel from Chicago, Illinois, to New York, New York. Here is the plane schedule he will use.

Here is the information you should study on this kind of schedule:

- The main heading tells you where the plane leaves from.

- The subheading tells you where the plane is flying to.

- The columns show you the plane's departure time, its arrival time, and the flight number.

- The *a* or the *p* after the times shows you whether the time is A.M. or P.M.

- The capital letters *(CST)* show the time zone of the city of departure *(Central Standard Time)*.

Use the schedule and the time-zone map on page 186 to answer this question.

Travis decides to take the 2:00 P.M. flight to New York. At what time will he arrive, and how long will the flight take?

Look at the schedule. Locate the entry under New York that shows the 2:00 P.M. departure time. Now look at the time-zone map on page 186. Chicago is in the Central time zone, and New York is in the Eastern time zone. When it is 4:54 P.M. in New York, it is 3:54 P.M. in Chicago. The flight will take 1 hour 54 minutes.

302

Chicago, Illinois (CST)		
To New York, New York		
Leave	Arrive	Flight
6:15a	9:09a	928
6:44a	9:42a	256
7:00a	9:55a	900
8:00a	10:53a	902
8:35a	11:27a	258
9:00a	11:55a	904
10:00a	12:52p	906
11:00a	1:49p	908
11:15a	2:20p	304
1 1:30a	2:22p	518
11:46a	3:22p	390
11:48a	2:47p	760
12:00p	2:50p	910
1:00p	3:50p	912
2:00p	4:54p	914
2:15p	5:11p	122
2:15p	5:30p	790
3:00p	5:53p	916
4:00p	7:00p	918
4:43p	7:59p	152
4:43p	7:43p	584
4:44p	8:39p	782
5:00p	7:59p	920
5:10p	8:18p	104
6:00p	8:57p	922
7:00p	10:00p	924
8:00p	10:50p	926
8:15p	11:14p	220
8:15p	11:14p	308

Checks: Have students check to see that they have read the information correctly and accounted for A.M. and P.M. in setting up the problem so that the correct label is used in the answer. Also, have students be sure they have correctly compensated for different time zones. Suggest that they check the reasonableness of their answers.

Use the plane schedule on page 302 to solve each problem. Write either *true* or *false*.

1. Flight 518 leaves Chicago at 11:30 A.M. and arrives in New York at 2:22 P.M. true

2. If Travis takes Flight 920, he will arrive in New York at 8:39 P.M. false

3. Flight 760 takes 5 minutes longer than Flight 914. true

4. If Travis takes Flight 928, the trip will take him 1 hour and 54 minutes. true

Use the plane schedules on pages 302 and 303 to answer each question.

5. Elaine, an independent filmmaker from Seattle, Washington, has to change planes in Denver, Colorado, before flying to New York. Which flights could she take from Seattle if she wants to arrive in New York by 6:00 P.M.?
210 (leaves at 6:35 A.M.) or 288 (leaves at 8:00 A.M.)

6. Elaine, flying from Seattle, takes the earliest possible connecting flight in Denver and arrives in New York on time. How much time did she spend on the entire trip?
8 hours 19 minutes

★7. Donald, a film critic, wants to leave Denver, Colorado, before 8:00 in the morning. He can fly directly to New York or fly to Chicago, change planes, and save some money on plane fare. Which flight takes more time? How much more time does it take?
The New York flight takes 1 hour 33 minutes longer.

★8. Donald decides to save money and change planes in Chicago, but his plane is late and he doesn't arrive in Chicago until 11:35 A.M. Which flights could he take from Chicago and still arrive in New York before 5:00 P.M.? How long would each flight take?
Flight 390 (2 h 36 min); Flight 760 (1 h 59 min); Flight 910 (1 h 50 min); Flight 912 (1 h 50 min); Flight 914 (1 h 54 min)

Classwork/Homework, page H126

Seattle, Washington (PST)		
To Denver, Colorado		
Leave	Arrive	Flight
6:35a	10:04a	210
8:00a	11:27a	288
12:05p	3:27p	18
2:15p	6:37p	748
2:55p	6:17p	434
3:30p	10:15p	1257

Denver, Colorado (MST)		
To Chicago, Illinois		
Leave	Arrive	Flight
7:35a	10:40a	518
10:12a	1:28p	26
10:54a	3:08p	576
11:01a	2:15p	916
11:03a	3:50p	482
11:04a	3:55p	670
12:55p	4:05p	376
4:00p	7:18p	296
4:09p	8:52p	328
5:35p	8:47p	276
6:57p	11:01p	636
7:15p	10:19p	254
8:35p	11:39p	278
3:00a	6:01a	888

To New York, New York		
Leave	Arrive	Flight
7:35a	3:22p	518
8:15a	1:40p	164
10:12a	4:54p	26
10:51a	5:50p	642
11:00a	4:35p	210
11:01a	5:53p	916
11:09a	4:51p	160
12:25p	6:00p	162
12:55p	8:39p	376
4:20p	9:55p	174
4:21p	10:00p	178
3:00a	9:42a	888

ASSIGNMENT GUIDE

Basic:	1–4
Average:	2–6
Extended:	3–8

Resources
Practice, p. 126   Class/Home, p. H126
Enrich, p. 114

Exercise Analysis
1–8 Use information from airline schedules to solve a problem

FOLLOW-UP ACTIVITIES

PROBLEM SOLVING
Materials: airline, train, or bus schedules

Have each student plan a round-trip to a distant city. Have students draw up travel plans listing flight, train, or bus numbers; times of departure and arrival; any connections that must be made; and elapsed time for each portion of the trip.

REINFORCEMENT
Discuss with students the advantages of 24-hour clocks and the situations in which they are used, such as military life. Have students write up daily schedules for themselves and then convert them to 24-hour time.

COMING UP
A reasonable lesson

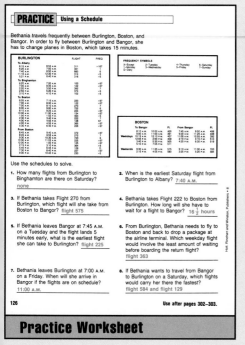

Practice Worksheet

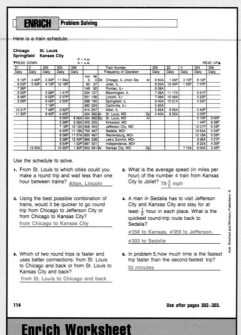

Enrich Worksheet

Objectives: To define *logical equivalence* and the *if/then conditional* by using a truth table; to determine the truth value of conditional

Warm-Up
Write the sentence *x* > *y* on the chalkboard and have students say whether the statement is *true* or *false* for each set of values for *x* and *y*.

x = 6, *y* = 6 (*f*)   *x* = 6, *y* = 5 (*t*)
x = 5, *y* = 6 (*f*)   *x* ≥ *y* + 1 (*t*)

GETTING STARTED

Ask students how many possibilities they think there are for the statement *x* > 9. Elicit from the class that there are two possibilities, *true* or *false*, and elicit the conditions for each. (true if *x* > 9, and false if *x* ≤ 9)

Point out that all logical statements are either true or false. Then ask students if they think the sentence *Please shut the door* is a logical statement and why it is or why it is not. (It is not logical because the sentence asserts nothing and, therefore, there are no conditions under which it is either true or false.) Then have students make up three sentences each and have classmates determine whether the sentences are logical statements.

TEACHING THE LESSON

Point out that all logical statements are either true or false, but logic tells you nothing about whether a statement is actually true or false. The logician's job is simply to determine what conditions would have to be met in order for a statement to be true.

A. Emphasize the fact that to say that two statements are logically equivalent is not to say that they mean the same thing but only that the conditions which make one true make the other true as well. Two statements are logically equivalent if whenever one is true the other is true and if whenever one is false the other is false. Have students try to think of other pairs of logical equivalent statements; for example, *Today is Sunday* and *Tomorrow is Monday*.

B. Point out that the statement *If P then Q* is logically equivalent to the statement *Not P, or Q*. In other words, *If P then Q* is true whenever not *P* obtains and it is true whenever *Q* obtains. Emphasize that it is only false when *P* obtains and *Q* does not; the statement makes no claims about *Q* when *P* does not obtain.

C. Ask students if they think *If P then Q* is logically equivalent to *If Q then P* (it is

304

LOGICAL REASONING

A. Logical statements are always either true or false. Two statements are equivalent if each is true when the other is true. The table below shows that statements *p* and *q* are equivalent.

p: *x* is greater than or equal to 8.
q: *x* is not less than 8.

	p	*q*
if *x* < 8	false	false
if *x* = 8	true	true
if *x* > 8	true	true

B. A statement such as "*If* tomorrow is Thursday, *then* the weather will be clear" is a **conditional statement.** The statement only promises clear weather if tomorrow is a Thursday. So, it is only false on a Thursday that is not clear. This relationship is shown in the **truth table.**

p: Tomorrow is Thursday.
q: The weather will be clear.

Notice that the conditional statement **if p, then q** is true unless *p* is true and *q* is false.

p	*q*	if *p*, then *q*
true	true	**true**
true	false	**false**
false	true	**true**
false	false	**true**

C. The statement **if q, then p** is the **converse** of the statement **if p, then q.** If a conditional statement is true, its converse may or may not be true.

Statement: If *x* > 5, then *x* > 2. ⟵ true for any *x*
Converse: If *x* > 2, then *x* > 5. ⟵ false for *x* = 3 or *x* = 4

Solve by using *p*: Mr. Watson's car is green.
                          q: Mr. Watson's car is a two-door.

1. Is the statement **if p, then q** *true* or *false* if Mr. Watson's car is

   a. a brown two-door?   true   **c.** a green four-door?   false
   b. a green two-door?   true   **d.** a blue four-door?   true

2. Write the converse of **if p, then q.** Is the converse true or false if Mr. Watson's car is

   a. a red five-door?   true   **c.** a blue two-door?   false
   b. a green two-door?   true   **d.** a green four-door?   true

304

---

not). Have a student volunteer come to the chalkboard and complete the truth table for *If Q then P* and compare it to the truth table for *If P then Q* on the lesson page. Then have student compare the truth conditions for *If P then Q* and its converse *If Q then P*. (Both conditionals are true when both *P* and *Q* are true or when both *P* and *Q* are false.)

Remind students to use a truth table when trying to determine whether a conditional statement is true of false.

GROUP PROJECT

Choose Your Channel

The problem: Your class is in charge of the prime-time schedule for a new TV network. Divide the class into 7 teams. Each team will be responsible for the schedule for one night. Look in TV guides to find out what the competition is doing. Then decide what kinds of shows to do, and make out a schedule like the one below to create balanced programming for the week.

Key Facts
- You must compete with the other networks to attract a share of the viewing audience.

- You need sponsors and advertisers, and so, your shows cannot be too controversial; but you also cannot let your advertisers determine the content of your programming.

- Each team must convince the rest of the class to approve its schedule.

Key Questions
- How do you decide whether a show should be 1 hour or $\frac{1}{2}$ hour long?

- What kinds of shows will you schedule?

- At what time would you schedule news? movies? variety shows? family shows? series?

- What kinds of specials would you schedule?

P.M. VIEWING							
	Mon.	Tue.	Wed.	Thurs.	Fri.	Sat.	Sun.
8:00	?	?	?	?	?	?	?
8:30	?	?	?	?	?	?	?
9:00	?	?	?	?	?	?	?
9:30	?	?	?	?	?	?	?
10:00	?	?	?	?	?	?	?
10:30	?	?	?	?	?	?	?

305

ASSIGNMENT GUIDE

Basic:	p. 304, p. 305
Average:	p. 304, p. 305
Extended:	p. 304, p. 305

Objectives: To plan TV programming; to make a schedule

USING THE PAGE

Materials: TV listings

Separate the class into groups representing seven competing TV networks that will run programs opposite each other for one week in prime time, from 7:00 P.M. to 11:00 P.M. Encourage groups to be creative in thinking of programs that would appeal to a wide audience. To begin, groups should discuss the Key Questions. Remind groups to plan a variety of shows, to balance them within an evening and throughout the week, and to be aware of the times at which their target audiences are likely to be watching. For instance, shows appealing to young children should be scheduled early in the evening.

Each group member should suggest shows, and the group should vote on which shows to place in each spot in the schedule. Have group members collaborate in writing a schedule in a form such as the one on the pupil page.

After the schedules are complete, groups can take turns presenting their programming in each time slot to the class. Have each member of the class write which program he or she would watch at each time slot and tabulate the results. Have each network revise its schedule based on the reaction of the class to the programs presented.

To extend this cooperative learning activity, tell students that they are going to plan programming for a new cable network that will be shown only to subscribers. Have them plan more attractive and controversial shows that they think will interest their target audience without worrying about advertisers' disapproval. Have students make lists of shows they might like to see if they and not the advertisers dictated the content of the schedule.

8 CHAPTER TEST

Purpose: The Chapter Test helps to assess students' understanding of the concepts and skills presented in this chapter.

The chart below is designed to help you review the test items by correlating them with the testing objectives that appear in the Chapter Overview.

Item	*Objectives*
1–3	A
4–12	B
13–18	B
19–21	C
22–24	D
25–30	E
31	I
32	F
33	G
34	F
35	H

Bonus

The bonus question may be used for extra credit, or you may want to assign it to students who complete the test before the rest of the class.

Calculator

You may wish to have students use calculators for the problem-solving portions of the test.

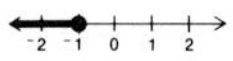

Resources

If you prefer to use this Chapter Test as a review exercise, additional testing materials are available in the Teacher's Resource Book.

CHAPTER TEST

Evaluate each expression if the variable equals 0, $^{-}3$, and 2. (pages 280–281)

1. $a + 4$ 4; 1; 6 **2.** $3b$ 0; $^{-}9$; 6 **3.** $\frac{x}{5}$ 0; $\frac{^{-}3}{5}$; $\frac{2}{5}$

Solve. (pages 282–285)

4. $^{-}3x = {}^{-}24$ $x = 8$ **5.** $\frac{a}{^{-}2.7} = 4.1$ $a = {}^{-}11.07$ **6.** $b - {}^{-}\frac{1}{4} = \frac{3}{8}$ $b =$

7. $^{-}4d + 2 = 18$ $d = {}^{-}4$ **8.** $\frac{s}{3.2} - {}^{-}6 = 2$ $s = {}^{-}12.8$ **9.** $^{-}\frac{5}{6}m - 3 = 7$ $m = {}^{-}$

10. $\frac{g}{^{-}3} + 17 = 32$ $g = {}^{-}45$ **11.** $0.6k - {}^{-}8 = 11.6$ $k = 6$ **12.** $\frac{z}{\frac{^{-}1}{5}} + {}^{-}2 = 13$ $z = {}^{-}$

Write a word problem for each equation then solve and check. (pages 286–287) For word problems, answers will vary.

13. $n - 18 = 40$ $n = 58$ **14.** $\frac{p}{7} = 5$ $p = 35$ **15.** $2x = 174$ $x = 87$

16. $r + 25 = 180$ $r = 155$ **17.** $6t = 48$ $t = 8$ **18.** $\frac{15}{z} = 5$ $z = 3$

Solve. (pages 294–295 and 298–299)

19. $x + 5 > {}^{-}3$ $x > {}^{-}8$ **20.** $a - {}^{-}\frac{4}{7} < 1\frac{1}{2}$ $a < \frac{13}{14}$ **21.** $\frac{y}{6.2} \geq 3.4$ $y \geq 21$

22. $\frac{t}{0.4} + 2 > 3$ $t > 0.4$ **23.** $\frac{d}{4} + \frac{2}{9} < 1\frac{1}{18}$ $d < 3\frac{1}{3}$ **24.** $2x - {}^{-}3 \neq 6$ $x \neq$

Solve and graph each equation. (pages 300–301) Check students' graphs.

25. $3e - 4 = 11$ $e = 5$ **26.** $\frac{f}{^{-}5} - 5 = {}^{-}7$ $f = 10$ **27.** $\frac{t}{^{-}2} - 4 = 9$ $t = {}^{-}26$

Solve and graph each inequality. (pages 300–301) Check students' graphs.

28. $3a - 7 > 8$ $a > 5$ **29.** $\frac{c}{2.5} - 4 \leq 6$ $c \leq 25$ **30.** $5c + {}^{-}3 > 12$ $c > 3$

Name ______________________ Date __________

POSTTEST Chapter 8 Page 1

1. What is the value of $x + 5$ if $x = 8$?

2.

x	y
5	2
3	4
6	2
7	12

Two numbers, x and y, have a product of 12 and a sum of 7. Which pair from the chart above could be x and y?

3. A video club rents video tapes at \$3.00 each to non-members and \$2.00 each to members. If membership in the club costs \$10.00, how much will a person who will rent 25 video tapes save by joining the club first?

4. What is the value of $4 + 3x$ if $x = 2$?

5.

This is the graph of which of the following inequalities?

a. $x < {}^{-}1$ b. $x > {}^{-}1$
c. $x \leq {}^{-}1$ d. $x \geq {}^{-}1$

6. What is the solution to the inequality $4x - 2 \leq 10$?

7. In one day a cable company made a profit of \$165 from new subscriptions. The total cost to the company for hooking up the new customers was \$75. If there were 8 new customers, what is the cost to each customer for a new subscription?

Which of the following equations can be used to solve the problem above?

a. $8x - 75 = 165$ b. $8x + 165 = 75$
c. $8x + 75 = 165$ d. $8 \cdot (x + 75) = 165$

8. Which of the following numbers is not a solution to the inequality $\frac{x}{5} \geq {}^{-}3$?

$^{-}20$, $^{-}15$, $^{-}10$, 0

Posttest

Name ______________________ Date __________

POSTTEST Chapter 8 Page 2

9. To solve $x - 7 = 13$, what would need to be done to both sides of the equation?

Use the schedule below for questions 10 and 11.

FLIGHT SCHEDULE FROM TWIN FALLS

To:	Leave	Arrive
Danville	9:05 AM	11:20 AM
Brunswick	10:30 AM	1:57 PM
Manchester	11:30 AM	3:30 PM
Lewistown	11:35 PM	2:25 AM

Note: All cities are in the same time zone.

10. How long is the flight from Twin Falls to Lewistown?

11. Which flight shown takes the least amount of time?

12. Puzzle: There are 20 animals in a barnyard. Some are rabbits and the rest are chickens. If there are 64 animal feet in the barnyard, how many rabbits are there?

A class decided to use guess-and-check to solve the puzzle above. They guessed that there were 16 rabbits. Which of the following is true?

a. 16 is right because it is less than 20.
b. 16 is right because $16 \times 4 = 64$.
c. 16 is too big.
d. 16 is too small.

13. What is the solution to the inequality $2y - 6 < {}^{-}8$?

14. The admission price for an adult is twice the price for a child. If the admission of one adult and one child was \$6.75, how much did the child's admission cost?

Posttest

Name ______________________ Date __________

POSTTEST Chapter 8 Page 3

Day	2	3	4	5	6
Number of Calls	150	200	250	300	350

15. A local TV station started a contest in which viewers phoned in their answers to a question. The table above shows the number of phone calls per day. If the rate of increase remains the same, how many phone calls should the TV station expect on the 10th day of the contest?

16. What is the value of $7 - 2x$ if $x = 5$?

17. $4x + 7 < 15$ (I) $6x - 2 < {}^{-}2$ (II) $\frac{x}{2} + 1 < 2$ (III)

$x < 0$ is the solution to which of the above inequalities?

18. At a school carnival 200 tacos were sold. At first they were selling for \$2 each, but the price was reduced to \$1 each. Altogether, \$240 was collected. How many tacos were sold at each price?

To solve the problem above, you might first make a guess about the answer and check it out. Which of the following first guesses would be the most helpful?

a. 4 tacos at \$2 and 196 tacos at \$1
b. 196 tacos at \$2 and 4 tacos at \$1
c. 200 tacos at \$2 and 200 tacos at \$1
d. 100 tacos at \$2 and 100 tacos at \$1

Use the following information in this table for questions 19 and 20.

POPULATION GROWTH IN ELMWOOD (to the nearest thousand)

Year	1950	1960	1970	1980
Population	20,000	21,000	23,000	26,000

19. If the pattern continues, what will the population of Elmwood be in 1990?

20. If the pattern continues, in what year will the population of Elmwood be nearest to 40,000?

Posttest

Solve. (pages 288–289, 290–291, 296–297, and 302–303)

31. José read the schedule to plan his TV viewing. Would it be possible for him to watch the entire drama on Channel 16 at 9 P.M. and also to watch the comedy on Channel 15 at 9:30 P.M.? **no**

TV Programs This Evening		
9:00	(15)	Sports
	(16)	Drama
9:30	(15)	Comedy
10:00	(14)	Film
	(16)	Sports

32. The cost of special effects for a new movie was $3,472,800. This amount was $\frac{1}{5}$ of the total cost of making the movie. Write an equation and solve to find the cost of making the movie. $\frac{1}{5}x = 3{,}472{,}800$; $x = \$17{,}364{,}000$

33. A game show contestant must find a 3-digit number that is divisible by 3 and by 5. The first two digits (but not the third) are the same and the sum of the 3 digits is less than 20. What is the number? **225**

34. In May 2,345 people attended a comedy film at the Century Theater. This was 106 fewer than $\frac{3}{4}$ of the attendance at that theater in December. Write an equation and solve to find how many people attended the Century Theater in December. $\frac{3}{4}x - 106 = 2{,}345$; $x = 3{,}268$ people

35. *The Village Gazette* charges $29.75 for a 4-line advertisement. A 5-line ad costs $38.20, a 6-line ad costs $46.65, a 7-line ad costs $55.10, and so on. How much will Mrs. Webb pay for a 10-line ad? **$80.45**

BONUS

Solve.

For $126.94, Lynne purchased 3 movies and rented 4 films. If the rental fee was $2.86 per film, write an equation and solve to find the cost of purchasing a movie. $3x + 4(\$2.86) = \$126.94$; $x = \$38.50$

For students who have difficulty with written tests, this test can be given orally.

You may wish to test students, orally or in writing, to see if they can explain the steps used in solving selected items. The following summarizes the procedures for solving key test items.

Ex. 1–3

Evaluating algebraic expressions

To evaluate algebraic expressions, given values for the variable, substitute each given value for the variable and evaluate.

Ex. 4–12

Solving one- and two-step equations

To solve one-step equations that have real numbers, use the same procedures for whole numbers, fractions, and decimals, but remember the rules for operations that involve real numbers. To solve two-step equations, remember to undo both operations.

Ex. 19–24

Solving inequalities

To solve an inequality, use the related equation. Then replace the inequality symbol in the last step. Remember that usually more than one number will make the inequality true.

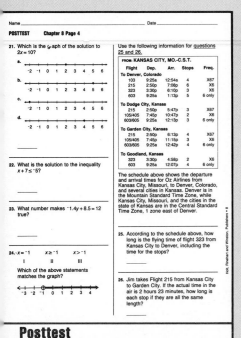

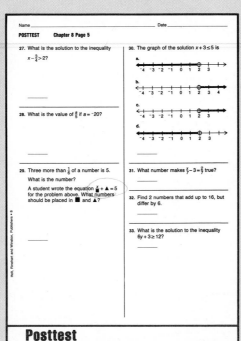

Purpose

Purpose This Reteaching page provides additional instruction for key concepts in the chapter. It is designed for use by students who have had difficulty with these concepts. It can also be used to provide additional practice for students who require it.

USING THE PAGE

Solving algebraic equations is taught on pages 282–285.

When reteaching this skill, emphasize to students that an equation shows equality—two quantities that are equal. It follows that, if both sides are equal, an operation performed on one side must also be performed on the other. Once students understand this concept, move on to "undoing" operations by performing inverse operations. Tell students that addition or subtraction is done first, and then multiplication or division is performed to solve for the variable. Solutions to equations are written in the form $x = 3.5$. Have students check their solutions by substituting them back into equations in place of the variable and then solving the number sentences to see if they are true.

Resources

For other practice and activities related to this chapter, see the Teacher's Resource Book.

RETEACHING

To solve an algebraic equation means to find the values of the variable that make the equation true. If there is one operation in the variable expression, use the inverse operation on both sides of the equation. If there are two operations in the variable expression, add or subtract first, and then solve for the variable.

Solve.
$$1.8x + 1.6 = 7.9$$
$$1.8x + 1.6 - 1.6 = 7.9 - 1.6$$
$$1.8x = 6.3$$
$$\frac{1.8x}{1.8} = \frac{6.3}{1.8}$$
$$x = 3.5$$

To check, let $x = 3.5$.
$$1.8 \cdot 3.5 + 1.6 \stackrel{?}{=} 7.9$$
$$6.3 + 1.6 \stackrel{?}{=} 7.9$$
$$7.9 = 7.9 ✔$$

Solve.
$$\frac{3}{4}x - 3 = {}^-9$$
$$\frac{3}{4}x - 3 + 3 = {}^-9 + 3$$
$$\frac{3}{4}x = {}^-6$$
$$\frac{4}{3} \cdot \frac{3}{4}x = \frac{4}{3} \cdot {}^-6$$
$$x = {}^-8$$

To check, let $x = {}^-8$.
$$\frac{3}{4} \cdot {}^-8 - 3 \stackrel{?}{=} {}^-9$$
$${}^-6 - 3 \stackrel{?}{=} {}^-9$$
$${}^-9 \stackrel{?}{=} {}^-9 ✔$$

Solve and check.

1. $9x - 18 = 72$
   $x = 10$

2. $\frac{1}{2}x + 3 = 12$
   $x = 18$

3. $\frac{x}{5} - 3 = 6.5$
   $x = 47.5$

4. $8x - 0.9 = 4.7$
   $x = 0.7$

5. $\frac{3}{4}x + 6 = 21$
   $x = 20$

6. $\frac{2}{3}x - 6 = 2$
   $x = 12$

7. $6x - \frac{1}{3} = 12\frac{2}{3}$
   $x = 2\frac{1}{6}$

8. $^-5x + 10 = 25$
   $x = {}^-3$

9. $^-7x + 3 = {}^-39$
   $x = 6$

10. $\frac{x}{^-2} + 4 = 8$
    $x = {}^-8$

11. $\frac{3}{4}x - 4 = 2$
    $x = 8$

12. $\frac{x}{1.6} - 3.2 = 3.2$
    $x = 10.24$

13. $\frac{x}{0.5} + 4 = 8$
    $x = 2$

14. $0.2x + 3.2 = 6$
    $x = 14$

15. $\frac{x}{3} - 4.25 = 7.25$
    $x = 34.5$

16. $\frac{x}{7} + 4 = 8$
    $x = 28$

17. $4x + 1.2 = {}^-5.6$
    $x = {}^-1.7$

18. $^-6x - {}^-3 = {}^-7.8$
    $x = 1.8$

19. $\frac{x}{9} + 17 = 46$
    $x = 261$

20. $^-3x + 21 = 63$
    $x = {}^-14$

21. $\frac{^-x}{8} - 10\frac{1}{2} = {}^-30$
    $x = 156$

22. $\frac{x}{13} + {}^-4 = {}^-4$
    $x = 0$

23. $16x - {}^-7.5 = 76.3$
    $x = 4.3$

24. $^-9x + {}^-1\frac{3}{8} = 64\frac{5}{8}$
    $x = {}^-7\frac{1}{3}$

25. $\frac{5}{x} - 1.7 = 0.3$
    $x = 2.5$

26. $\frac{^-3}{5}x + 6 = 5\frac{1}{4}$
    $x = 1\frac{1}{4}$

27. $\frac{14}{x} - 7.2 = 17.2$
    $x = 1.4$

308

ENRICHMENT

Solving Algebraic Equations in One Variable With Exponents

An algebraic equation is called a **quadratic or second-degree equation** when 2 is the largest exponent used. Every quadratic equation has two roots or solutions.

When the quadratic equation has only one variable term, its two roots are found by

1. isolating the variable term.
2. taking the square root of each side.
3. checking the resulting roots.

Solve. $x^2 = 64$

$x = \pm \sqrt{64}$

$\boxed{\pm \text{ means one root is positive and the other is negative.}}$

$x = {}^{\pm}8$

Check. $8^2 \overset{?}{=} 64 \qquad ({}^-8)^2 \overset{?}{=} 64$

$\qquad 64 = 64 \; \vee \qquad 64 = 64 \; \vee$

So, the two roots of $x^2 = 64$ are 8 and $^-8$.

Solve. $\qquad 4x^2 = x^2 + 48$

$4x^2 - x^2 = 48$

$3x^2 = 48$

$x^2 = 16$

$x = \pm \sqrt{16}$

$x = {}^{\pm}4$

Check. $4(4)^2 \overset{?}{=} 4^2 + 48 \qquad 4({}^-4)^2 \overset{?}{=} ({}^-4)^2 + 48$

$\quad 4 \cdot 16 \overset{?}{=} 16 + 48 \qquad 4 \cdot 16 \overset{?}{=} 16 + 48$

$\qquad 64 = 64 \; \vee \qquad\qquad 64 = 64 \; \vee$

The roots are 4 and $^-4$.

Solve and check.

1. $x^2 = 49$
$x = {}^{\pm}7$

2. $x^2 = 121$
$x = {}^{\pm}11$

3. $x^2 = 625$
$x = {}^{\pm}25$

4. $x^2 = 20$
$x = {}^{\pm}2\sqrt{5}$

5. $x^2 = 72$
$x = {}^{\pm}6\sqrt{2}$

6. $x^2 = 125$
$x = {}^{\pm}5\sqrt{5}$

7. $3x^2 = 12$
$x = {}^{\pm}2$

8. $4x^2 = 36$
$x = {}^{\pm}3$

9. $6x^2 = 96$
$x = {}^{\pm}4$

10. $5x^2 = 90$
$x = {}^{\pm}3\sqrt{2}$

11. $7x^2 = 686$
$x = {}^{\pm}7\sqrt{2}$

12. $10x^2 = 360$
$x = {}^{\pm}6$

309

Purpose This Enrichment page provides an additional challenge for those students whose work throughout the chapter and on the Chapter Test shows a thorough understanding of the material. Alternatively, you may wish to use these exercises as a supplementary lesson for the entire class.

USING THE PAGE

Define the term *quadratic equation* (or *second-degree equation*) on the chalkboard. Explain that every quadratic equation of this type has two roots—one negative, one positive—because every positive number has two square roots—one negative, one positive $(8 \cdot 8 = 64,\; {}^-8 \cdot {}^-8 = 64, \; \sqrt{64} = 8$ and ${}^-\sqrt{64} = {}^-8$. Have students solve a quadratic equation in one variable the way they would solve any equation in one variable—by isolating the variable on one side of the equation and performing the same operations to both sides. In solving quadratic equations, the final operation performed on both sides is the finding of the two square roots. Remind students that negative numbers do not have square roots.

Resources
For additional Enrichment activities, see the Teacher's Resource Book.

Objectives: To use BASIC to solve computations that involve exponents and scientific notation

Warm-Up

Elicit from students the process by which exponents are computed. Have students compute the following exponents.

3^2 (9)	5^4 (625)	8^3 (512)
3^5 (243)	4^5 (1,024)	

Then, using their answers to the above exercises, have students write each number by using scientific notation.

9 (9×10^0) 625 (6.25×10^2)
512 (5.12×10^2) 243 (2.43×10^2)
1,024 (1.024×10^3)

GETTING STARTED

Begin with students a discussion about the computer as a counting machine. Elicit from students that the function of the computer is to keep track of and to modify long, organized chains of numbers. By keeping track of these numbers in their memories, computers can perform complex calculations. Have students suggest some examples from science and industry that show how computers are used for such operations. (Examples might include computing space-shuttle orbits and landings, predicting the path of comets, or designing a new automobile or a building.) Point out to students that in all these situations, specific programs are used for a number of different needs. Explain to students that two very common computer applications involve finding the values of exponents and scientific notation.

TEACHING THE LESSON

The focus of this lesson is on the concept of exponents rather than on any specific computer-programming skill. As the lesson explains, different computers use variations on the exponent symbol (^). The manual for your school's computer should be consulted for the specific symbol. At this point, students should have a firm grasp of both the concept of exponents and the rudimentary BASIC commands. The lesson itself focuses on recognizing the concepts and practicing them. The preliminary exercise of the lesson is simply to find the number values for a series of exponents.

The second part of the lesson involves what students know mathematically as order of operations. Explain to students that when a computer is faced with a series of different operations, it will do operations in parentheses first, then exponents, then multiplication and division from left to right, and then addition and subtraction from left

TECHNOLOGY

You can use BASIC to solve computational problems that contain exponents. For example, to find the value of 2^3, you can type this. PRINT 2^3
The computer will print this. 8

On some computers, you use the ↑ symbol instead of the ^ symbol. Other computers may use other symbols.

Write what the instruction will print.

1. PRINT 8^2 64 **2.** PRINT 5^3 125 **3.** PRINT 2^4 16 **4.** PRINT 10^5 100,000

If you give the computer an instruction with several operations, it will use the same rules for computing that you have learned. The computer does operations in the following order:

1. Operations within parentheses
2. Exponents
3. Multiplication and division (left to right)
4. Addition and subtraction (left to right)

If a multiplication operation and a division operation occur in the same exercise, the computer will first do the computation that is on the left.

Write what the computer will print when you give this instruction:

5. PRINT 5 * 2^2 20   **6.** PRINT (5 * 2)^2 100
7. PRINT 16 − 4^2 0   **8.** PRINT (2 * 5)^3/(2^2) 250

310

to right. Students practice this order by writing the response to a PRINT command followed by a number sentence.

Once students have an understanding of exponents and computer order of operations, students are introduced to scientific notation as a means of writing very long numbers in a short form. It is also explained that the computer will use scientific notation to write the number if the number exceeds nine digits.

In this way, students are exposed to the notions of computer representation of numbers and of exponents as they are used for showing powers of 10. Students practice recognizing and interpreting this notation in a series of PRINT statement exercises.

Scientific Notation is a shorthand way to write very large or very small numbers. Your computer uses scientific notation to represent any number that has more than 9 digits. For instance, 670,000,000,000 is represented as 6.7 E 11.

This means 6.7 times 10^{11}. Another way to think of this is to move the decimal point 11 places to the right.

The number 0.000000000067 is represented as 6.7 E −11.

This means 6.7 times 10^{-11}, or move the decimal point 11 places to the left.

The computer always moves the decimal point far enough so that the number to the left of the E is a number between 1 and 10, followed by a decimal point and the number of decimal places needed up to 8.

Write what the instruction will print.

9. PRINT .00000000000038   3.8 E−13

10. PRINT 73000000000000000   7.3 E 15

11. PRINT 11ˆ9   2.3579477 E 09

12. PRINT 10ˆ10   1.0 E 10   Different computers may print with a slightly different format.

13. PRINT 10ˆ−17   1.0 E −17

311

FOLLOW-UP ACTIVITIES

 COMPUTER

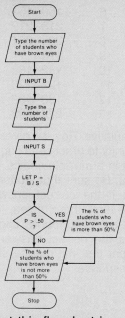

Explain that this flowchart is a plan for a program to find out whether more than 50% of the students in the class have brown eyes. Use data from the class to follow the flowchart. Elicit from students a BASIC program for this flowchart. Write it on the chalkboard.

```
(10 PRINT "TYPE THE NUMBER OF
    STUDENTS WHO HAVE BROWN
    EYES"
20 INPUT B
30 PRINT "TYPE THE NUMBER OF
    STUDENTS"
40 INPUT S
50 LET P = B/S
60 IF P > .50 THEN PRINT "THE % OF
    STUDENTS WHO HAVE BROWN
    EYES IS MORE THAN 50%"
70 IF P <= .50 THEN PRINT "THE % OF
    STUDENTS WHO HAVE BROWN
    EYES IS NOT MORE THAN 50%"
80 END)
```

Discuss why line 70 uses <= instead of just <. (The decision diamond determined only that P was *not greater than 0.50*.) Elicit from students how to find out whether P is equal to 0.50. (Add another decision box to the flowchart: "IS P = 0.50?") Explain that using more than one decision diamond or IF...THEN statement is made easier with a GOTO statement.

311

Purpose This Cumulative Review page provides an opportunity to reinforce students' understanding of the concepts and skills taught in previous chapters.

The chart below is designed to aid you in reviewing the material by specifying the pages on which various concepts and skills were taught.

Item	*Page*
1	244–245
2	246–247
3	250–251
4	240–241
5	84–85
6	150–151
7	218–219
8	220–221
9	176–177
10	182–183
11	122–123
12	188–189
13	222–223

Each Cumulative Review gives students an opportunity to practice taking tests that are written in a multiple-choice, standardized format. Be sure that students understand that if the correct answer is not among the first three given, then they should select the fourth choice—"not given"—as the correct answer. At least one item per test will require students to give this response.

CUMULATIVE REVIEW

Write the letter of the correct answer.

1. $7 + {}^-14$
   a. $^-21$ (b.) $^-7$ c. 7 d. not given

2. $^-72 - {}^-31$
   a. $^-103$ (b.) $^-41$ c. 41 d. not given

3. $^-23 \times {}^-14$
   a. $^-9$ b. 37 c. $^-122$ (d.) not given

4. Order from the greatest to the least: $^-7$, 4, $^-82$, $^-14$.
   (a.) 4, $^-7$, $^-14$, $^-82$
   b. $^-82$, $^-14$, $^-7$, 4
   c. $^-82$, 4, $^-7$, $^-14$
   d. not given

5. What is 0.07824 written in scientific notation?
   a. 7.824×10^{-3} (b.) 7.824×10^{-2} c. $7{,}824 \times 10^{-2}$ d. not given

6. Order $^-5\frac{4}{5}$, 7.25, $^-43.3$, $2\frac{1}{8}$ from the least to the greatest.
   (a.) $^-43.3$, $^-5\frac{4}{5}$, $2\frac{1}{8}$, 7.25
   b. $2\frac{1}{8}$, $^-5\frac{4}{5}$, 7.25, $^-43.3$
   c. 7.25, $2\frac{1}{8}$, $^-5\frac{4}{5}$, $^-43.3$
   d. not given

7. 3.54 is what percent of 472?
   a. 13% b. 25% c. 76% (d.) not given

8. 299.04 is 84% of what number?
   a. 234 (b.) 356 c. 451 d. not given

9. Complete: 272 oz = ■ lb.
   (a.) 17 b. 23 c. 27.2 d. not given

10. 7 h 42 min + 16 h 39 min
    a. 9 h 3 min
    b. 23 h 3 min
    (c.) 24 h 21 min
    d. not given

11. What is $\frac{52}{9}$ as a mixed number?
    a. $5\frac{2}{9}$ (b.) $5\frac{7}{9}$ c. $7\frac{2}{9}$ d. not given

12. Frieda left New York when the temperature was 42°F. When she arrived in Nome, Alaska, the temperature was 9°F below zero. What was the change in the number of degrees?
    a. 33°F (b.) 51°F c. 52°F d. not given

13. Floyd's savings account pays an annual yield of 6.03% interest. To the nearest dollar, how much interest did he gain on $2,000 over a 3-year period if the interest was reinvested each year?
    a. $361 b. $371 (c.) $384 d. not given

312

CHAPTER  OVERVIEW

STATISTICS AND PROBABILITY

SUMMARY

Chapter 9 deals with statistics and probability. Lessons on the measures of central tendency, possible outcomes, permutations and combinations, independent and dependent events, and prediction, as well as histograms and various graphs, are included.

LESSON SEQUENCE

PROFESSIONAL BACKGROUND

Along with the growing body of educational research on statistics and probability, related topics such as fractions, graphing, and conditional reasoning, still provide useful insights for teaching mathematics.

A recent National Assessment of Educational Progress indicated that students have difficulty with permutations and combinations. The vast majority of 17-year olds could do only the most basic combinations. This implies the need for more emphasis on the use of graphic devices such as tree diagrams.

Adolescents benefit from models of conditional reasoning ("if-then" and "whether-then" constructions). When hypotheses, possibilities, and logical reasoning are regularly discussed and used, many students can be aided in the development of their probability concepts and skills.

Research also demonstrates the importance of the teacher's use of vocabulary. In the National Assessment, changing the word "mean" to "average" improved performance considerably among both 13- and 17-year olds. Having students discuss and use terms in statistics can help their work in this area. Research further indicates a considerable distinction between a student's ability to interpret statistical graphs, tables, and charts, and to construct them in order to represent statistical problems, as well as a considerable distinction between a student's ability to plot discrete quantities on a graph and make graphs that represent continuous relationships.

References: See NCTM Yearbook on Statistics and Probability; Carpenter et al.; and Hart.

MATERIALS

geoboards and rubber bands
newspapers and magazines
construction paper and scissors
counters of 3 different colors
number cubes
pennies
calculators
pencils and pens
paper bag
chalk
crayon
52-card deck

VOCABULARY

data (p. 314)
frequency table (p. 314)
relative frequency (p. 314)
range (p. 314)
mode (p. 316)
mean/average (p. 316)
median (p. 316)
measures of central tendency (p. 316)
bimodal (p. 316)
bar graph (p. 318)
histogram (p. 318)
scattergram (p. 320)
positive correlation (p. 320)
negative correlation (p. 320)
broken-line graph (p. 322)
double broken-line graph (p. 322)
circle graph (p. 324)
possible outcomes (p. 328)
tree diagram (p. 328)
sample space (p. 328)
factorial (p. 330)
permutations (p. 330)
combinations (p. 332)
equally likely (p. 334)
impossible/certain (p. 334)
probability (p. 334)
independent events (p. 336)
dependent events (p. 340)
prediction (p. 342)
normal curve (p. 351)

ABOUT THE CHAPTER

Statistics gives us a way to organize and examine information and then to draw reasonable conclusions from this information. Probability is a way of determining the likelihood that some event will, or will not, happen. These topics have increased importance in a contemporary curriculum and give students an opportunity to apply what they have learned about fractions and graphs. There are 3 lessons in this chapter in which students are given the opportunity, in problem-solving settings, to work cooperatively. In these lessons, students are confronted with real-life situations through which they are encouraged to develop and apply a variety of strategies.

In Chapter 9, students learn how to arrange data, how to find the mean, median, and mode, and how to graph data on bar graphs, circle graphs, and broken-line graphs. Other lessons show students how to find permutations and combinations of outcomes. Students also learn to find the probability of an event, including the different methods used to find the probability of independent and dependent events.

It is most important that students understand that both statistics and probability are inexact sciences. The measures of central tendency—mean, median, and mode—and the range give us a certain kind of information about data only.

The probability of an event gives us some idea about the likelihood that it will happen. The probability of flipping a penny and getting heads is $\frac{1}{2}$. However, we could flip a penny 50 times and get only a few heads, or none at all. Probability tells us that, over the long run, there will be about as many heads as tails.

Probability is about experimentation, and students should have many opportunities to conduct their own probability experiments. Students should flip coins, spin spinners, and conduct other probability experiments. This is how they will learn what probability is all about.

Estimation plays an important role in probability. Students should be encouraged to estimate the likelihood of an event and then compare the outcome to their estimate.

Problem-solving lessons in the chapter show students how to get and use information from a scattergram and how to select notation to solve nonroutine problems. Other problem-solving lessons show students how to get and use information from a sample and how to avoid misinterpreting information from a graph or from statistics.

The Group Project actively involves students in deciding on combinations of events for a sports day. The Enrichment lesson introduces students to the normal curve, an important frequency distribution in statistics.

USING THE CHAPTER OPENER

Each Chapter Opener presents situational problem-solving activities that can be used to explore the skills taught throughout the chapter. The work sheets can be used by individuals, small groups, or the whole class, depending on the needs of the class. The Chapter Opener focuses on a nonalgorithmic approach to mathematics through real-life situations relevant to the children's experiences. Through an interdisciplinary approach, the Chapter Opener helps children explore the relationships between mathematics, other areas of the curriculum, and everyday life while developing different strands of mathematics.

In the Chapter Opener activities, students will learn to conduct a survey. They will also learn how to use a survey to predict characteristics for a population. Students will learn to find measures of central tendency in real-life situations and to use these measures to make judgments about a whole.

PROBLEM SOLVING

The lesson Using a Scattergram focuses on how a scattergram is organized, labeled, and read. Students can use this skill to solve problems that require them to interpret whether a correlation exists between two sets of data.

The lesson Using Samples requires students to draw on data from an outside source to solve problems. As with other lessons in which information integral to the problem solving is separate from the text, students learn how to use the sample data for their own purposes. The problems of how to read a sample, how to draw conclusions from its data, and how to use the sample data to make projections, are all addressed. This lesson lends itself to the non-critical, idea-gathering technique of brainstorming in a small-group setting.

The lesson Selecting Notation teaches students mathematical shorthand that will help them to solve certain types of problems.

Students may become confused when faced with selecting the appropriate notation for a given problem-solving situation. The lesson examines several forms of notation useful to solving a variety of problems, including some with probability. It offers another excellent chance to involve students in small-group work.

The lesson Interpreting a Graph goes one step farther than those lessons in which students were required to draw on data from an outside source. To solve these problems, students must compare two different sets of data expressed as broken-line graphs. The twist to this type of comparison is that the two graphs are drawn to different scales. The lesson focuses on how to evaluate two outside sources—their axes and data—so that they can be accurately compared in the process of solving a problem.

Most of the problem-solving lessons in *Mathematics Unlimited* lend themselves to small group work. In a comfortable group atmosphere, students can brainstorm and discuss various ways to solve problems.

BULLETIN BOARD

"What A Game!"

Materials: paper to cover the bulletin board; lettering; poster board; pictures and newspaper clippings of a special sports event; push pins or tacks; felt-tip pens

Preparation: Cover the board with paper and arrange display lettering. Cut four large rectangles from poster board, label them, and post as shown. Gather pictures, newspaper articles, and statistics from a recent sports event and mount them across the board as shown. On the chart shown, football statistics have been chosen as topics for the frequency tables, but choices may vary.

After pp. 314-315: Have students help construct and post frequency tables for these topics as shown: **A:** Yards Gained Per Quarter For Home Team; **B:** Penalty Yards Per Quarter, Per Team; **C:** Accumulated Points Scored Per Quarter; **D:** How Points Were Scored (Touchdown, field goal, etc.)

After pp. 318-319: Have students help construct a bar graph for Topic **A** and a double-bar graph for Topic **B.** Post it in the appropriate box beside the table.

After pp. 322-323: Have students help construct a broken-line graph for Topic **C.** Post in appropriate box.

COMMON ERRORS

Students often have difficulty identifying permutations and combinations, and often confuse the two. To remediate this error, focus on review of the meaning of the permutations and combinations. Emphasize that permutations involve order, while combinations do not. In other words, A-B is a different permutation than B-A, but the two are the same combination.

Combinations are found by using multiplication and division only. An important hint for students to remember is that combinations involve two quantities: the number of items in the larger group, and the number of items in the combination group. For example, a combination question could take a form such as: How many combinations of three can one make from a group of five? If the two quantities are the same, for example, "how many combinations of five can be made from a group of five?", then the answer would be 1.

SPECIAL NEEDS

Probability terms and ideas are used by students daily: "I'll probably pull a B on that test"; "The odds are the Cubs will win the pennant"; "I'll bet two to one it will be sunny tomorrow." Use concrete materials to determine that the probability of an event occurring is the ratio of the number of ways the event can occur to the total number of possible events. Allow students to work out probability problems with manipulatives before having them perform the computations. Allow them to perform "experiments" to find whether or not their data is true. The more trials they perform, the more accurate their data will be. For example, have them flip a coin 100 times to find the number of times heads turns up. Perhaps after doing this they will better understand a fifty–fifty chance of an event occurring.

Have interested students select two financial stocks from those listed in your local paper. Have them record the performance of those stocks each day for a month. Have them graph the results, and make predictions based on their graphs.

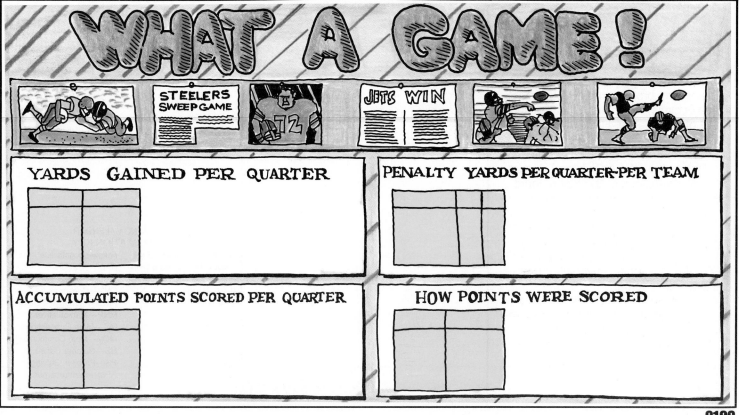

MATH LABS

COMPUTER

Have students write a program that will use the data for a circle graph to compute the appropriate central angles for each section of the graph.

```
 10 LET X = 1
 20 INPUT "TOTAL AMOUNT"; T
 30 INPUT "SECTION: LABEL,
    AMOUNT (0,0 IF NO
    MORE)";L$(X),A(X)
 40 IF L$(X) = "0" THEN 90
 50 LET C(X) = INT(A(X)/T*360)
 60 LET S = S + C(X)
 70 LET X = X + 1
 80 GOTO 30
 90 PRINT
100 PRINT
110 PRINT "SECTION",
    "DEGREES"
120 FOR Z = 1 TO X - 1
130 PRINT L$(Z), C(Z)
140 NEXT Z
150 END
```

MATH COMMUNICATION

Have students make a graph to illustrate the information below.

Of the 48 teams that competed in the 1984 NCAA Division II Basketball Championship, two had 17 regular-season wins, five had 18, two had 19, five had 20, four had 21, six had 22, three had 23, six had 24, five had 25, three had 26, four had 27, one had 28, and two had 29.

PROBLEM SOLVING

Have students determine which type of graph (bar, double bar, histogram, broken line, double broken line or circle) would best illustrate each set of data below. Have them explain their answers.

• The number of games won and lost by the NCAA Division I Basketball champions of the last 5 years.
• The points-per-game average of the NCAA Division I scoring leader of each of the last ten years.
• The breakdown of playing time in minutes per game of the members of the Columbia University men's basketball team.
• The NCAA Division II percentage leaders in both field goals and free throws over the last 8 years.

CALCULATOR

Computations involved in the study of statistics and probability are usually tedious and time-consuming. Without a calculator (or computing device), many students would refuse to do them. The calculator permits students to investigate the ideas of probability and statistics without being totally frustrated by the calculations. For example, combinations and permutations involve factorials, which are tiresome to compute.

Students should be encouraged to use calculators for all problem-solving activities.

Additional Activities: **Drill and Practice:** Make a table of factorials. What is the largest factorial that you can compute on an 8-digit calculator?

Exploration: Make a chart of Pascal's triangle that shows 30 rows.

SUBJECT AREA CONNECTIONS

These Subject Area Connections are useful for reinforcing the concepts presented in this chapter.

p. 319-Social Studies: Students research state populations. Then make a frequency table and bar graph.

p. 321-Science: Students investigate the negative and positive correlations in a scientific formula.

p. 325-Science: Students represent the chemical make up of the human body on a bar graph.

Here are some other ideas for reinforcing these concepts.

Social Studies: Have students measure and record the height of each class member. Have them design a graph to show the various heights. Find the median, mode, and mean height.

Language Arts: Have students choose a paragraph from a newspaper and count the number of times each letter of the alphabet is used. Design a graph to show the relative frequency of each letter's occurrence.

PLAN AHEAD

You will need geoboards and rubber bands for the activity on T.E. p. 323. You will need newspapers and magazines for the activity on T.E. p. 323. You will need to prepare cut-out figures for the Getting Started on T.E. p. 328. You will need calculators for the activities on T.E. pp. 331 and 333. You will need a 52-card deck for the activity on T.E. p. 341 and a large number of pennies for the activity on T.E. p. 342.

PLANNING CALENDAR
ABBREVIATION KEY

Teacher's Resource Book	Follow-up Activities
MMW—Making Math Work	CALC—Calculator
P—Practice	CMP—Computer
R—Reteach	CNS—Consumer
E—Enrich	P&G—Puzzles and Games
	MNP—Manipulatives
	MC—Math Connection
	MCM—Math Communication
	NS—Number Sense
	PS—Problem Solving
	RFM—Reinforcement

PLANNING CALENDAR

| Pages | Lesson Objectives | ASSIGNMENT GUIDE | | | Class/Home | More Practice | Math Reasoning | Follow-up | Reteach | Practice | Enrich |
		Basic	Average	Extended							
313	Chapter Opener (Use MMW 17,18)	313	313	313							
314,315	To organize raw data into a frequency table	1-11	1-12	1-13	H127			MC RFM	89	127	115
316,317	To define and calculate median, mode, and mean	1-24	7-30	10-33	H128	H204	H223	CMP PS	90	128	116
318,319	To make and read a bar graph and a histogram	1-3,5-7	2-7	1-7	H129			PS MC	91	129	117
320,321	To use information from a scattergram in problem solving	1-5	2-6	4-10	H130			PS MC		130	118
322,323	To make and read a broken line graph	1-3,MCR	1-4,MCR	2-4,MCR	H131		H223	MNP RFM	92	131	119
324,325	To make and read a circle graph	1-4,7-10	2-5,7-12	3-12	H132			MC NS	93	132	120
326,327	To use information from samples to solve problems	1-3,5	1-6	1-7	H133 H134			PS CALC		133-134	
328,329	To calculate the number of possible outcomes	1-10	5-11	5-12	H135		H223	RFM P&G	94	135	121
330,331	To explore permutations and combinations	330,331	330,331	330,331				PS			122
332,333	To explore the numerical relationship between permutations and combinations	332,333	332,333	332,333	H136 H137	H204	H224	CALC P&G	95-96	136-137	123
334,335	To define and calculate probability	1-16,33-34	10-24,33-34	17-34	H138			CMP PS	97	138	124
336,337	To calculate the probability of independent events	1-14,23-24,CTM	7-19,23-24,CTM	7-24,CTM	H139			PS RFM	98	139	125
338,339	To select and use a proper notation in problem solving	1-3	2-4	2-3,5	H140			PS CALC		140	126
340,341	To calculate the probability of dependent events	1-14,Chlg1-2	9-20,Chlg1-4	9-22,Chlg	H141			PS PS	99	141	127
342,343	To explore mathematical prediction	342,343	342,343	342,343	H142			PS	100	142	128
344,345	To correctly interpret information from graphs	1-3	2-5	3-7	H143 H144					143-144	
346	Calculator: To find the mean of a set of numbers	346	346	346							
347	Group Project: To plan a sports competition; to write rules	347	347	347							

348,349	Chapter Test	351	Enrichment
350	Reteaching	352	Cumulative Review

TESTS

A. To collect and record data by making a table, bar graph, histogram, broken-line graph, circle graph, or pictograph

B. To find the mean, median, mode, and range

C. To find all possible permutations of a set of objects

D. To find all possible combinations of a set of objects

E. To list the elements of a sample space for an experiment

F. To find the probability of a simple event

G. To find the probability of independent events

H. To find the probability of dependent events

I. To compute the expectation of an event for a given number of trials

J. To select appropriate notation to aid in solving problems

K. To interpret information from graphs and statistics

FAMILY INVOLVEMENT

Family Involvement for Chapter 9 encourages family members to keep a daily record of the local temperature for a week. The high and low temperatures reached each day are to be listed in appropriate columns of a chart. At the end of the week, family members are to find the mean and the median of the daily highs and the daily lows. These statistics are to be written on a table showing temperature data. Then the mean and the median of all the highs and lows recorded for the week are to be calculated. Finally, the statistics are to be analyzed in order to predict the high and low temperatures of the next day.

Additional activities might involve finding the temperature inside the home at two different times during the day (i.e., in the morning and in the evening). Family members should keep a record of the measurements taken during the course of two or three days and make a bar graph showing temperature variations inside their home. To extend this activity, family members should record temperatures twice a day for two weeks and then make a double-bar graph comparing the average daily temperature for each week.

STUDENT RESOURCES

Bibliography

Allen, Anne. *Sports for the Handicapped.* New York: Walker and Company, 1981.

Frontier Press Company Staff. *Lincoln Library of Sports Champions.* Columbus: Frontier Press Co., 1989.

Gardner, Robert. *Science & Sports.* New York: Franklin Watts, 1988.

Izenberg, Jerry. *Great Latin Sports Figures: The Proud People.* Garden City, New York: Doubleday and Company, Inc., 1976.

Films

Estimation: Am I Close? 21 minutes. Color videotape. 1985. *Challenger of the Unknown* series. Distributed by the American Association for the Advancement of Science, Washington D.C.

Inferential Statistics I. 21 minutes. Color. 1975. Distributed by Media Guild, Solana Beach, Calif.

Statistics at a Glance. 28 minutes. Color. 1972. Distributed by Media Guild, Solana Beach, Calif.

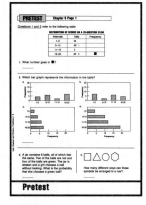

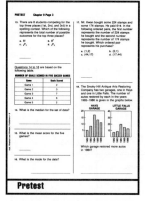

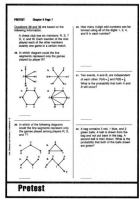

What is the most popular spectator sport in your school? Do boys and girls have the same favorites or different ones? Does the answer differ according to the age of the people you question? How would you take a sample that would give you reliable information about the preferences of the students in your school?

9 STATISTICS AND PROBABILITY

Objective: To explore problems related to taking a survey

Direct students to look at the picture of the stadium seats. Ask how many students have attended professional sporting events. Which events do most students prefer? Do they think that their favorite is the favorite of the whole school? These last two questions can be answered by taking a survey.

INDIVIDUAL
Statistics and Probability
Materials: Making Math Work page 18 per student

Have students complete Making Math Work page 18. Then have them find the statistics for another player on the same team. Ask them whether these statistics are sufficient to enable them to compare performances and then determine which player has had a greater impact on the whole league. Also, ask students whether they can tell which player has been more beneficial to the team.

SMALL GROUP
Statistics and Probability
Materials: Making Math Work page 17 per student

Have each student complete the survey. Students should tally the responses as a group, which will give them a greater number of responses. Tell them that the reliability of a survey is based on obtaining as many responses as possible. Have students compare individual surveys to see whether they obtained similar results. Ask whether individual results are similar to the results obtained by the group as a whole. Have students come up with other problems or questions that can be answered by taking a survey.

MAKING MATH WORK

Are the sports that adults watch different from the sports that younger people watch? How would you find out? Make a list of ten sports below. Then survey the people in your community to find out which sports they like. Remember to keep track of the age groups of the people you survey. Check students' charts.

Sports list	Age group
1.	
2.	
3.	
4.	
5.	
6.	
7.	
8.	
9.	
10.	

Number of people surveyed:

Average age group:

In the space below, write a statement that describes the relationship between the people's age groups and the sports people prefer to watch.

_____
_____
_____
_____

Use with pupil page 313.   Making Math Work 17

Making Math Work

MAKING MATH WORK

Choose a favorite player from any baseball team. Analyze the statistics and the records of this team to find the averages asked for below. Then compare your favorite player's statistics with the team's statistics. How does your favorite player compare? Check students' charts.

	Team's statistics	Player's statistics
Name of team: _____		Name of player: _____ Position: _____
Average height:		
Average weight:		
Average age:		
Average weight:		
Average runs:		
Average runs batted in:		
Average stolen bases:		
Average strikeouts:		
Average outs:		
Average errors:		
Average years in the league:		
Average years on the team:		

18 Making Math Work   Use with pupil page 313.

Making Math Work

WHOLE CLASS
Statistics and Probability
Conduct a survey. Ask students which kind of music they prefer. Then ask who their favorite recording artist is. Before you obtain their answers, have students write their predictions about the preferences of the whole class on a piece of paper. Remind students that their responses can be different from their predictions. Ask them to guess what percentage of the class will make the correct predictions. Ask them to speculate about whether a survey of all eight grades would yield the same results as a survey of the whole class. Discuss survey results in the context of generalizations.

Objective: To organize raw data into a frequency table

Warm-Up

Have students find the percent each is of 15.

$3 (20\%); 8 \left(53\frac{1}{3}\%\right); 15 (100\%); 5 \left(33\frac{1}{3}\%\right)$

Then have them find the percent each is of 24.

$6 (25\%); 18 (75\%); 16 \left(66\frac{2}{3}\%\right); 48 (200\%)$

GETTING STARTED

Conduct a survey of students' favorite colors, holidays, rock groups, and so on. Have them write their choices on slips of paper. Then discuss ways of organizing and presenting these data.

TEACHING THE LESSON

A. Point out that the lowest interval must include the lowest datum but need not begin with it. This applies to the highest interval and the highest datum as well. Nevertheless, the range of the intervals must include both the highest and the lowest datum.

Explain that relative frequencies are customarily rounded to the nearest percent.

Ask students on what day of the month they were born. List each response on the chalkboard. Make a table after students have chosen its title and its intervals. Then have them make a tally of the data, count the frequencies, and calculate the relative frequencies. Ask:
- During which interval do the most birthdays occur? the least?
- Do the total frequencies equal the number of students in class? (yes)
- Do the relative frequencies add up to 100%? (If not, this reflects the percent lost or gained in the rounding. In this case, point out that the total frequencies always reflect 100% of the tallies.)

B. Emphasize the fact that the range indicates the spread, or dispersion, of the data. Have students think of situations in which knowing the range would be useful. For example, if someone wanted to wade across a stream, he or she would rather know that the depth ranges from 2 feet to 10 feet than know that the average depth is 6 feet.

Arranging Data

A. Between 1954 and 1976, Hank Aaron hit 755 home runs. The number of home runs he hit each year is listed below.

13, 39, 24, 44, 20, 27, 40, 32, 38, 12, 26, 31, 44, 47, 10, 44, 45, 39, 34, 30, 44, 29, 40

In how many of the years did Hank Aaron hit 40 or more home runs?

It is easier to find the answer if the numerical information, or **data,** is organized into intervals. In the **frequency table** at the right, the data (number of home runs per year) is organized into **intervals.** The size of each interval, called its **width,** is 10 home runs ($20 - 10 = 10$, $30 - 20 = 10$, and so on). For each year's number, a **tally mark** is made next to the appropriate interval. The **relative frequency** is the ratio of the frequency for the interval to the total frequency.

Hank Aaron hit 40 or more home runs in 8 of the 23 years, or about 35% of the time.

$\frac{8}{23} \approx 0.35$, or 35%

B. Find the range for the set of data given above.

The **range** is the difference between the greatest and the least number in a set of data. You can tell from the frequency table that the greatest number is between 40 and 49, and that the least number is between 10 and 19.

  Greatest number = 47
  Least number = 10
  Range = 47 − 10 = 37

So, the range for the given set of data is 37.

314

NUMBER OF HOME RUNS

Intervals	Tally	Frequency	Relative frequency
10–19	III	3	13%
20–29	IH1	5	22%
30–39	IH1 II	7	30%
40–49	IH1 III	8	35%
Total		23	100%

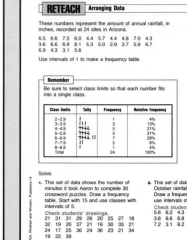

COMMON ERRORS

Some students might try to calculate the range from the intervals of the frequency table rather than from the data.

Remediation
For this error, have students change the intervals of the table made in Part A. Then have them recalculate the range. Emphasize the fact that changing the intervals has no effect on the data and therefore no effect on the range.

Assign Reteach Master, p. 89.

Reteach Worksheet

Use the data to solve Exercises 1–6.

The most home runs hit per year in each of the major leagues for 1980–1989 was 48, 41, 31, 22, 37, 39, 40, 39, 36, 43, 37, 40, 37, 40, 49, 49, 39, 42, 47, and 36.

1. Make a frequency table. Start with 20 and use intervals that have a width of 5. (The first interval is 20–24.) See Answer Key.

2. For how many years did the major leaguers hit 45 or more home runs? **4 years**

3. For what percent of the years were 30–34 home runs hit? **5%**

4. For what percent of the years were 35–39 home runs hit? **40%**

5. Which interval of home runs has the greatest frequency? **35–39**

6. What is the range of the home runs hit? **27**

Use the data to solve Exercises 7–11.

The average number of points per game of the NBA scoring leaders for 1965–1989 was 34.7, 33.5, 35.6, 27.1, 28.4, 31.2, 31.7, 34.8, 34.0, 30.8, 34.5, 31.1, 31.1, 27.2, 29.6, 33.1, 30.7, 32.3, 28.4, 30.6, 32.9, 30.3, 37.1, 35.0, and 32.5.

7. Make a frequency table. Start with 25 and use intervals that have a width of 5. (The first interval is 25–29.9.) See Answer Key.

8. What is the range for this set of data? **10.0**

9. Which interval has the greatest frequency? **30–34.9**

10. In how many years was the average 35 or above? **3 years**

11. What percent of the scoring leaders had an average between 25 and 29.9? **20%**

Solve. For Problem 13, use the Infobank.

12. Make a frequency table to organize this data of the years of football played by the all-time leading scorers. See Answer Key.

13. Use the information on page 477 to solve. Which scoring champion had the highest scoring average for one season? During which year did he accomplish this?
Wilt Chamberlain; 1962

ALL-TIME LEADING SCORERS

Player	Years played	Player	Years played
Bahr	13	Bakken	17
Blanda	26	Cappelletti	11
Cox	15	Groza	17
Leahy	15	Moseley	16
Stenerud	19	Turner	16

Classwork/Homework, page H127

315

315

ASSIGNMENT GUIDE

Basic: 1–11

Average: 1–12

Extended: 1–13

Resources
Practice, p. 127   Class/Home, p. H127
Reteach, p. 89
Enrich, p. 115

Exercise Analysis
1–12   Make and read a frequency table
13   Data collection and computation

You may wish to allow students to use calculators for some of these exercises.

FOLLOW-UP ACTIVITIES

MATH CONNECTION (Consumer)
Have students work in small groups to collect 10 to 20 ads for a particular item such as a car or a television. Then have them organize the prices into a frequency table. Have each group present its table to the class. Discuss the factors that account for differences in price.

REINFORCEMENT
Survey the class and collect data on one of the topics below. Have students organize the data into a frequency table.
● birth month (January 1–January 31 and so forth as intervals)
● distance of students' homes from school in miles
● number of brothers and sisters
● height

COMING UP
A not-so-nasty average

PRACTICE — Arranging Data

The average scores for Masters Bowling Tournament champions from 1973 to 1984 were 218, 234, 213, 220, 218, 200, 202, 206, 218, 205, 212, 212.

1. Make a frequency table. Start with 200, and use intervals that have a width of 5. Complete the average score, tally, frequency, and relative frequency for each interval.

Average score	Tally	Frequency	Relative frequency
200–204	//	2	16.7%
205–209	//	2	16.7%
210–214	///	3	25%
215–219	///	3	25%
220–224	/	1	8.3%
225–229		0	0%
230–234	/	1	8.3%

2. What is the range for the set of data? 34

3. In how many years was the average 205–209? 2

4. For what percent of the years was the average 215–219? 25%

From 1969 to 1983, the amounts for the Professional Golf Association's leading money winners were as follows: $175,223; $157,037; $244,490; $320,542; $308,362; $353,201; $323,149; $266,438; $310,653; $362,429; $462,636; $530,808; $375,699; $446,462; $426,668.

5. Make a frequency table. Start with $100,000 and use intervals that have a width of $50,000. (The first is $100,000–$149,999.) Complete the average score, tally, frequency, and relative frequency for each interval.

Winnings	Tally	Frequency	Relative frequency
$100,000–$149,999		0	0%
$150,000–$199,999	//	2	13.3%
$200,000–$249,999	/	1	6.7%
$250,000–$299,999	/	1	6.7%
$300,000–$349,999	////	4	26.7%
$350,000–$399,999	///	3	20%
$400,000–$449,999	//	2	13.3%
$450,000–$499,999	/	1	6.7%
$500,000–$549,999	/	1	6.7%

6. What is the range for this set of data? $373,771

7. For what percent of the years were the winnings $100,000–$249,999? 20%

8. For what percent of the years were the winnings $350,000 or more? Round to the nearest tens place value. 46.7%

Use with pages 314–315.   127

Practice Worksheet

ENRICH — Statistics and Probability

The letter that is used most frequently in the English language is the letter E. The next most frequent letters are T, A, O, I, R, and N. The letters used least often are Q, Z, K, X, and J.

Knowing the frequency with which letters occur can often help you decipher a code. It is also useful to think about short words: a single-letter word is usually either a or I, and a double-letter word is commonly to, in, an, as, and so on. If you have already found the code for a, the double-letter word with a could only be an, am, as, or at. Similarly, if you know that a word is tw_, the blank can be only an o.

The paragraph below is a **cryptogram** and has been written in a code where each letter is substituted for another letter of the alphabet.

1. Decipher the cryptogram. Fill in the blanks. Whenever you can deduce a letter, fill in all the other blanks that use the same coded letter. Some of the blanks have already been filled in. Think about the two letters that can appear next to each other in different places in a word, and about the single-letter word that would be capitalized in the middle of a sentence.

Qeshh pho vhsh rkqqkof anvo cq c qcdih. Noh rcka, "K ikjh ecp", coa noh rcka, "K ikjh behhrh." Qeh qesa noh innjha cq qeh qkph coa ahbkaha qn ihcwh qehp qn qehks dskiikcoq bnowhsrcqkno. "Kg K an onq ihcwh onv, K vkii ecwh qn ehcs c inq pnsh dcinohl."

Three men were sitting down at a table. One said, "I like ham," and one said "I like cheese." The third one looked at the time and decided to leave them to their brilliant conversation. "If I do not leave now, I will have to hear a lot more baloney."

2. Write your own cryptogram. See if a friend can decode it. Answers will vary.

Use with pages 314–315.   115

Enrich Worksheet

Objectives: To define and calculate median, mode, and mean

Warm-Up
Have students find each quotient.

$(22 + 31 + 28 + 34 + 30) \div 5$ (29)
$(12 + 18 + 13 + 16 + 13) \div 5$ (14.4)
$(102 + 113 + 97 + 110) \div 4$ (105.5)
$(7 + 9 + 8 + 4 + 8 + 9 + 11 + 8) \div 8$ (8)

GETTING STARTED

Use the following situation to launch a general discussion of the uses of statistics.

The Lakewood Movie Theater kept a record of how many tickets were sold each day for a week.

Mon. Tues. Wed. Thurs. Fri. Sat. Sun.
176　204　367　385　　427　436　372

Ask, "If you had to use one number to describe the number of tickets sold on any one day, what would it be?" Encourage students to explain their methods of finding the answers.

Discuss why it is useful to describe an entire set of data by using one number.

TEACHING THE LESSON

A. Explain that when data are listed sequentially, the median is the midpoint. Half the data are above and half are below this point. The median need not itself belong to the original set. Have students suggest applications of median and mode. (Median track times are useful in differentiating faster runners from slower runners. Given a set of test scores, the mode would be the number that was scored most often.)

B. Use the following set of data to explain the difference between median and mean.

20, 20, 22, 28, 80

For this set, the median is 22 but the mean is 34. Ask: Which is the better indicator of the trend?

Point out that because median and mean are computed differently, they should be interpreted differently. If these data represented test scores, then the median would be a more appropriate measure because an average score that only one person scored higher than would not be very informative. If, however, these data represented the number of cans collected on a recycling drive, then the "per person" measure of the mean would be quite useful.

Median, Mode, and Mean

A. The first women's Olympic long-jump competition occurred in 1948, and the record jump was 18 ft $8\frac{1}{4}$ in. The distances for a high school women's long-jump competition are listed in the table.

Find the median and mode for this set of data.

High School Women's Long Jump	
12 ft 6 in.	11 ft 4 in.
15 ft 8 in.	9 ft 9 in.
12 ft 2 in.	10 ft 1 in.
14 ft 7 in.	16 ft 2 in.
14 ft 6 in.	16 ft 9 in.

The **median** is the middle number in a set of data when the numbers are listed in order. When there are two middle numbers, add the two middle numbers and divide by 2 to find the median.

$$\frac{12 \text{ ft } 6 \text{ in.} + 14 \text{ ft } 6 \text{ in.}}{2} = 13 \text{ ft } 6 \text{ in.}$$

The median is 13 ft 6 in.

The **mode** is the number that appears most often in the set. In the given set of data, there is no mode because all of the long jumps are of different distances. A set of data can have more than one mode. For example, the following set of data has two modes.

38, 21, 29, 38, 5, 21

Both 38 and 21 are modes.

B. The Olympic Pentathlon is a contest of five events. What is the mean score for the five scores shown at the right?

The **mean,** or **average,** is the sum of the numbers divided by the number of addends. To find the mean score, add the scores and divide by the number of events.

$$\frac{1,100 + 956 + 1,300 + 978 + 1,135}{5} = \frac{5,469}{5} = 1,093.8$$

The mean score for the Pentathlon is 1,093.8 points.

The mean, median, and mode are called **measures of central tendency.**

PENTATHLON

Event	Score
Riding	1,100
Fencing	956
Swimming	1,300
Shooting	978
Running	1,135

316

Math Reasoning, page H223

COMMON ERRORS

Some students might fail to include repeated data in calculating the median or the mean.

Remediation
For this error, have students order the data and then count the number of items in the group. After calculating the median, they should check that there are as many data above the median as there are below that point. After calculating the mean, students should check to see that the number of data matches the number of addends and the divisor.

Assign Reteach Master, p. 90.

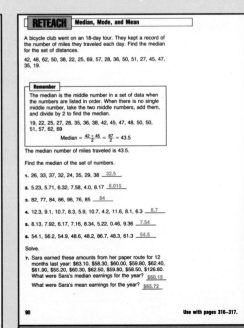

RETEACH | Median, Mode, and Mean

A bicycle club went on an 18-day tour. They kept a record of the number of miles they traveled each day. Find the median for the set of distances.

42, 48, 62, 50, 38, 22, 25, 69, 57, 28, 36, 50, 51, 27, 45, 47, 35, 19.

Remember

The median is the middle number in a set of data when the numbers are listed in order. When there is no single middle number, take the two middle numbers, add them, and divide by 2 to find the median.

19, 22, 25, 27, 28, 35, 36, 38, 42, 45, 47, 48, 50, 50, 51, 57, 62, 69

Median = $\frac{42 + 45}{2} = \frac{87}{2} = 43.5$

The median number of miles traveled is 43.5.

Find the median of the set of numbers.

1. 26, 33, 37, 32, 24, 35, 29, 38 _32.5_
2. 5.23, 5.71, 6.32, 7.58, 4.0, 8.17 _6.015_
3. 82, 77, 84, 86, 98, 76, 85 _84_
4. 12.3, 9.1, 10.7, 8.3, 5.9, 10.7, 4.2, 11.6, 8.1, 6.3 _8.7_
5. 8.13, 7.92, 6.17, 7.16, 8.34, 5.22, 0.46, 9.36 _7.54_
6. 54.1, 56.2, 54.9, 48.6, 48.2, 86.7, 48.3, 61.3 _54.5_

Solve.

7. Sara earned these amounts from her paper route for 12 months last year: $63.10, $58.30, $60.00, $59.80, $62.40, $61.90, $55.20, $60.30, $62.50, $59.80, $58.50, $126.80. What were Sara's median earnings for the year? _$60.15_
What were Sara's mean earnings for the year? _$65.72_

90　Use with pages 316–317.

Reteach Worksheet

For each set of data find the median, mode, and mean.
Round to the nearest thousandth.

Set of data	Median	Mode	Mean
78, 96, 83, 78, 94	**1.** 83	**2.** 78	**3.** 85.8
132, 249, 365, 418, 253, 372	**4.** 309	**5.** no mode	**6.** 298.167
5,697; 5,432; 5,574; 5,459; 5,357; 5,495; 5,697; 5,459	5,477 **7.**	5,459 and 5,697 **8.**	5,521.25 **9.**
0.5, 0.8, 0.6, 1.1, 0.9, 0.1, 0.5	**10.** 0.6	**11.** 0.5	**12.** 0.643
1.12, 2.37, 3.46, 1.29, 2.87, 3.46	**13.** 2.62	**14.** 3.46	**15.** 2.428
4.002, 4.215, 3.84, 4.215, 3.906, 3.84, 3.002, 4.215	3.954 **16.**	**17.** 4.215	3.904 **18.**
6, $3\frac{1}{2}$, $4\frac{3}{4}$, $5\frac{1}{4}$, 5, $4\frac{1}{2}$, $4\frac{3}{4}$, $4\frac{3}{4}$	**19.** $4\frac{3}{4}$	**20.** $4\frac{3}{4}$	**21.** $4\frac{13}{16}$, or 4.813
$7\frac{2}{3}$, $6\frac{1}{2}$, 4, $5\frac{1}{3}$, 8, $7\frac{1}{2}$	**22.** 7	**23.** no mode	**24.** $6\frac{1}{2}$, or 6.5
7 ft 5 in., 12 ft 3 in., 7 ft 9 in., 6 ft 5 in., 10 ft 6 in., 7 ft 9 in.	7 ft 9 in. **25.**	7 ft 9 in. **26.**	8 ft $8\frac{1}{6}$ in. ★**27.**
3 lb 8 oz, 2 lb 15 oz, 4 lb 3 oz, 3 lb, 4 lb 5 oz, 2 lb 8 oz, 3 lb 10 oz	3 lb 8 oz **28.**	no mode **29.**	3 lb 7 oz ★**30.**

Solve. For Problem 33, use the Infobank.

The table lists the salary distribution for twelve professional basketball players.

31. Find the median, mode, and mean.
$325,000; $250,000; $400,000

★**32.** Imagine that the highest-paid player retires and is replaced by another player. If the mean of the team members' salaries is now $325,000, what is the salary of the new player? $100,000

33. Use the information on page 477 to solve. To the nearest whole number, find the mean number of points that Bob McAdoo scored over the years that he was NBA scoring leader.   2,506 points

Salary	Frequency
$70,000	1
$100,000	1
$130,000	1
$250,000	3
$400,000	2
$600,000	2
$750,000	1
$1,000,000	1

ASSIGNMENT GUIDE

Basic: 1–24

Average: 7–30

Extended: 10–33

Resources
Practice, p. 128   Class/Home, p. H128
Reteach, p. 90   More Practice, p. H204
Enrich, p. 116   Reasoning, p. H223

Exercise Analysis

1–9   Find the median, mode, and mean of a given set of whole numbers
10–18   Find the median, mode, and mean of a given set of decimals
19–24   Find the median, mode, and mean of a given set of fractions
25–30   Find the median, mode, and mean of a given set of linear or weight measurements
31–32   Skill applications
33   Data collection and computation

You may wish to allow students to use calculators for some of these exercises.

FOLLOW-UP ACTIVITIES

COMPUTER
Have students write a program to find the median of an ordered set of data.

```
(10 LET N = 0
20 LET N = N + 1
30 INPUT "DATUM"; D(N)
40 INPUT "ANOTHER (YES OR NO)";A$
50 IF A$ = "YES" THEN 20
60 LET W = N/2
70 IF W = INT(W) THEN 100
80 LET M = D(INT(W) + 1)
90 GOTO 110
100 LET M = (D(W) + D(W + 1))/2
110 PRINT "THE MEDIAN IS"; M
120 END)
```

PROBLEM SOLVING
Have students solve this problem.
• The Lubinsky Jukebox Company decided to analyze data about records selected by jukebox customers. Median, mode, and mean were calculated. Two of these measures were discarded but the third was reported to a radio station. Which measure did the station obtain? Why? (The mode; because it indicates the most popular record.)

COMING UP
A picture is worth a thousand words.

317

Objectives: To make and read a bar graph and a histogram

Warm-Up
Have students organize the following data about favorite softball positions into a frequency table.

1B, 3B, 2B, OF, OF, 1B, 1B, P, SS, SS, C, OF, OF, 3B, P, OF, 3B, 1B, P, C

GETTING STARTED
Conduct a survey of the number of record albums each student owns. Have students organize these data into a frequency table. Then ask them to suggest ways these data could be represented graphically.

TEACHING THE LESSON
A. Pose the following problems.
- The four eighth-grade English classes at Ochs Junior High took the same grammar test. What is the most efficient method of organizing the data to compare the scores of each class? (Find the mean score of each class.)

Discuss the steps involved in making the corresponding bar graph. Use the example to point out the necessity of using *breaks* in a scale if information is not continual or applicable from zero to the first given set of data.

B. Ask students how they would make the histogram that would best display the distribution of all eighth-grade scores. (Make a frequency table for all the scores and then show the score intervals along one axis and the frequency of each score along the other axis. Draw the bars with no space between them.)

Bar Graphs and Histograms

A. The average age of athletes in different sports varies. This chart lists the mean (average) age of Olympic athletes in four sports.

Graphs are used to make it easy to see relationships among data. To make several comparisons between two sets of data, draw a **double-bar graph.**

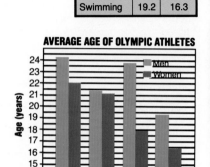

MEAN AGE		
Sport	Men	Women
Canoeing	24.2	22.0
Diving	21.3	21.1
Gymnastics	23.6	17.8
Swimming	19.2	16.3

1. Choose a scale. Be sure that the largest number on the scale is greater than the largest number that will be plotted. The break in the vertical scale shows that the portion of the graph between 0 and 15 is not being shown.

2. Label the axes of the graph.

3. Draw a bar for each item. You can use vertical bars or horizontal bars.

4. Make a key and choose a title for your graph.

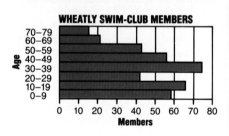

B. The Wheatly Municipal Swim Club conducted a survey of the ages of its members. Draw a histogram to show the distribution of the data.

A **histogram** is a bar graph that shows the frequencies of intervals of data. The histogram below is made from the table at the right.

To make a histogram, follow these steps.

1. Make a frequency table.
2. Choose a scale.
3. Label the axes of the histogram.
4. Draw a bar to show the frequency of each interval of data.
5. Choose a title for your histogram.

Age	Frequency	Age	Frequency
0–9	58	40–49	56
10–19	66	50–59	43
20–29	42	60–69	21
30–39	74	70–79	15

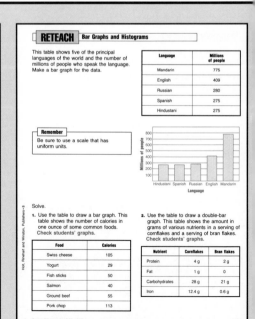

318

COMMON ERRORS
Some students might incorrectly devise a scale that is not inclusive of all the data.

Remediation
For this error, have students first find the range of the data and then make sure that the labeling of the axes is inclusive of the range.

Assign Reteach Master, p. 91.

RETEACH Bar Graphs and Histograms

This table shows five of the principal languages of the world and the number of millions of people who speak the language. Make a bar graph for the data.

Language	Millions of people
Mandarin	775
English	409
Russian	280
Spanish	275
Hindustani	275

Remember
Be sure to use a scale that has uniform units.

Solve.

1. Use the table to draw a bar graph. This table shows the number of calories in one ounce of some common foods. Check students' graphs.

Food	Calories
Swiss cheese	105
Yogurt	29
Fish sticks	50
Salmon	40
Ground beef	55
Pork chop	113

2. Use the table to draw a double-bar graph. This table shows the amount in grams of various nutrients in a serving of cornflakes and a serving of bran flakes. Check students' graphs.

Nutrient	Cornflakes	Bran flakes
Protein	4 g	2 g
Fat	1 g	0
Carbohydrates	28 g	21 g
Iron	12.4 g	0.6 g

Use with pages 318–319.

91

Reteach Worksheet

Use the tables in Exercises 1 and 2 to make bar graphs. **Check students' graphs.**

1. COLLEGE FOOTBALL STADIUMS

School	Capacity
Alabama	59,000
Florida	72,000
Iowa State	50,000
Michigan U.	102,000
Utah U.	35,000
Virginia U.	42,000

2. LEADING LIFETIME PASSERS

Player	Yards
Joe Montana	27,533
Otto Graham	23,584
Danny White	21,959
Roger Staubach	22,700
Sonny Jurgensen	32,224
Boomer Esiason	14,825

Use the tables in Exercises 3 and 4 to make double-bar graphs. **Check students' graphs.**

3. NATIONAL HOCKEY LEAGUE

Team	87–88 Wins	88–89 Wins
N.Y. Islanders	39	28
Washington	38	41
Philadelphia	38	36
N.Y. Rangers	36	37
New Jersey	38	27
Pittsburgh	36	40

4. RECORD AUTO SPEEDS

Year	Indianapolis	Daytona
1983	162.117	155.979
1984	163.621	150.994
1985	152.982	172.265
1986	170.722	148.124
1987	162.175	176.263
1988	149.809	137.531
1989	167.581	148.466

For Exercises 5–7, refer to the table on the years of football played by the leading rushers. Choose intervals that have widths of 2 years, beginning with 6–7.

ALL-TIME LEADING RUSHERS

Player	Years played	Player	Years played
Payton	13	Simpson	11
Dorsett	12	Dickerson	6
Brown	9	Perry	16
Harris	13	Campbell	8
Riggins	14	Taylor	10

5. How many intervals are needed?
5 intervals

6. Make a frequency table.
See Answer Key.

7. Graph the information in a histogram. See Answer Key.

319

Exercise Analysis
1–2 Make a bar graph
3–4 Make a double-bar graph
5–7 Make a histogram

FOLLOW-UP ACTIVITIES

PROBLEM SOLVING
Tell students that sometimes it is convenient to show values above and below a particular value, such as 0°C or 0 feet above sea level, on a bar graph. This is called a *floating-axis bar graph* because the horizontal axis "floats" in the middle of the graph and the bars stretch up and down from it.

Guide students in using a floating-axis bar graph to plot the following data.
● This year's junior golf tournament was held at Sandy Rock. The scores against par of the first six players to finish were Sam, ⁺4; Joanna, ⁺1; Betty, ⁻1; Jon, even; Rudy, ⁻4; Amber, ⁺5.

MATH CONNECTION
(Social studies)
Have students research the population of each state. Encourage them to
● organize the data into a frequency table. (Intervals of 3 million people would be appropriate.)
● make the corresponding bar graph.

COMING UP
Data is dispersed.

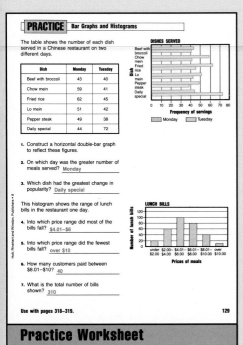

Practice Worksheet

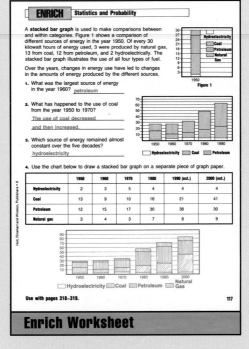

Enrich Worksheet

Objective: To use information from a scattergram

Warm-Up

To prepare students for this lesson, have them compute the following.

$$\frac{k}{80} = 4 \; (320) \qquad\qquad 6k = 180 \; (30)$$

$$4.8k = 96 \; (20) \qquad\qquad 5 = \frac{k}{3.2} \; (16)$$

GETTING STARTED

Ask the class: What is the relationship between a basketball player's height and the likelihood that he or she can dunk the basketball? (In general, the taller the player, the greater the likelihood that he or she can dunk the ball.) Ask if there are exceptions to this tendency. Point out that some shorter people can jump very high, and some taller people do not jump very well. Nonetheless, the relationship between height and the ability to dunk the ball is true *in general.* Tell the class that in this lesson, they will learn a method for observing the relationship between two different factors.

TEACHING THE LESSON

A *scattergram* is a graph of two sets of data that shows whether or not a correlation exists between the data. Note that in the scattergrams on pages 320 and 321 there are, in many cases, more than one value for any specific reading on an axis. In the scattergram at the top of page 321, there are 3 players aged 36 and 2 players aged 40. Point out to students how this differs from a broken-line or bar graph. Be sure all students understand the terms *positive correlation, negative correlation,* and *no correlation.*

Questions: Tell students that the location of an individual point is of less importance than the way in which most of the points cluster. Students may have difficulty understanding what a positive or negative correlation means.

Suggest that they imagine a positive effect or increase on one set of data. If this causes a positive effect on the other set of data, there is a positive correlation. If it causes a negative effect on the other set of data, there is a negative correlation. If it causes no apparent effect, there is no correlation between the two sets of data.

Tools: Make sure that students read and understand the labels on the axes of the scattergram. The most obvious difficulty students face is one of deciding whether or not a set of points shows a correlation. The visual effect of a correlation may be enhanced if students hold the scattergram at

---

| QUESTIONS | TOOLS | SOLUTIONS | CHECKS |

PROBLEM SOLVING
Using a Scattergram

A **scattergram** is a useful tool for showing whether a correlation exists between two sets of data.

The graph below is a scattergram. It shows the batting average and the age of each member of the Hodge's Hardware Little League team. A dashed line drawn through the points, as shown, makes it easy to see a correlation between the two sets of data.

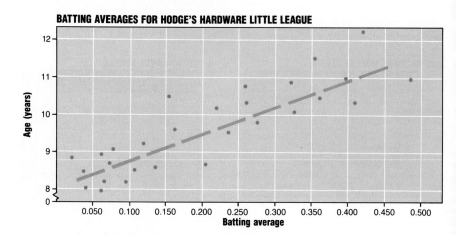

BATTING AVERAGES FOR HODGE'S HARDWARE LITTLE LEAGUE

From the scattergram, you can see that as a player's age increases, that player's batting average also increases. This is known as a **positive correlation** because both sets of data increase or decrease together, and the dashed line slants upward to show a positive correlation.

In a **negative correlation,** one set of data increases as the other decreases. The dashed line slants downward to show a negative correlation.

If no dashed line can be drawn close to the points, there is said to be **no correlation** between the two sets of data.

320

---

arm's length. It should then become apparent whether or not there is a pattern in the data. The pattern can be verified by drawing a line. Again, be sure students understand that the only information that should be gathered from a scattergram is the presence or absence of a correlation.

Solutions: There is no computation involved in this lesson.

Checks: Suggest that students read the graph scales and predict what type of correlation, if any, would be expected. Check that they correctly interpret the upward or downward slope of a line as a positive or negative correlation.

Use the scattergram below to solve.

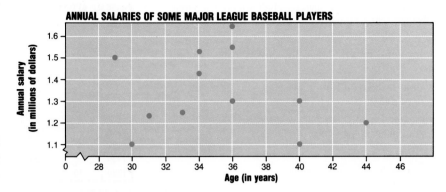

ANNUAL SALARIES OF SOME MAJOR LEAGUE BASEBALL PLAYERS

1. What correlation, if any, do you see between the two sets of data?
no correlation

2. What does the answer to Question 1 tell you about the relationship between the two sets of data?
There is no relationship between age and salary.

3. What correlation would you expect to see if you graphed a similar scattergram for accountants? As age increases, salary should also increase.

For each scattergram below, write *positive correlation*, *negative correlation* or *no correlation*.

4.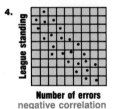
Number of errors
negative correlation

5.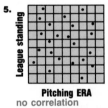
Pitching ERA
no correlation

6.
Team batting average
positive correlation

Tell which kind of correlation you would probably see in each scattergram.

7. A scattergram that shows the distance from an archery target and shooting accuracy. negative correlation

8. A scattergram that shows the speed at which a discus is tossed and the time it stays aloft. positive correlation

9. A scattergram that shows the weight of goalies and the number of saves they made. no correlation

10. A scattergram that shows the speed of ski jumpers and the length of their jumps. positive correlation

Classwork/Homework, page H130

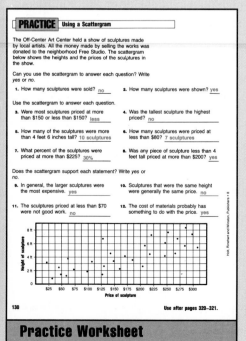
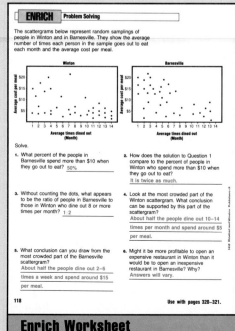
ASSIGNMENT GUIDE

Basic: 1–5

Average: 2–6

Extended: 4–10

Resources
Practice, p. 130   Class/Home, p. H130
Enrich, p. 118

Exercise Analysis
1–6   Identify correlation in a scattergram
7–10   Identify correlation between two sets of data

FOLLOW-UP ACTIVITIES

PROBLEM SOLVING
Materials: drawing paper, felt-tip pens, per group

Have each group make a list of their ages and the ages of their brothers and sisters. Then have students estimate the height of each person on the list. Have each group use this information to make a scattergram. Decide on intervals for the axes, on labels, and on a title for the graph. Have the groups plot the ages and the estimated heights, decide whether there is a correlation, and draw a dashed line through the points. Most graphs should show a positive correlation between age and height. Some graphs may show no correlation. Discuss why this is possible. Ask students if they would expect to see a correlation between the ages and heights of adults. (no)

MATH CONNECTION
(Science)
To investigate positive and negative correlation in scientific formulas, write the formula $d = rt$ on the board. Have students recall that d = distance, r = rate (or speed), and t = time. Have students use a scattergram, if needed, to determine whether each two factors listed are positively or negatively correlated when the third factor is constant.

- At a constant rate, is there a negative or a positive correlation between distance and time spent traveling? (positive)
- For a constant time of travel, is there a negative or positive correlation between distance and rate? (positive)
- For a constant distance, is there a positive or a negative correlation between time traveled and rate? (negative)

COMING UP
Lines in pieces

Objectives: To make and read a broken-line graph

Warm-Up
Have students find the median, mode, mean, and range of the following data.

49, 34, 37, 39, 49, 52, 36, 37, 41, 35, 40, 36, 47, 51, 37, 32, 37, 41, 51, 35
(median: 38; mode: 37; mean: 40.8; range: 20)

GETTING STARTED

Write the following sets of data on the chalkboard.

ANNUAL PRECIPITATION

City	Amount
Cairo	0.4 in.
Hong Kong	85 in.
Seattle	34 in.
Stockholm	24 in.
Sydney	44.8 in.

ANNUAL PRECIPITATION IN SEATTLE

Month	Inches
Jan.	5.8
Feb.	4.2
Mar.	3.6
Apr.	2.5
May	1.7
Jun.	1.5
Jul.	0.7
Aug.	1.1
Sep.	2.0
Oct.	3.9
Nov.	5.9
Dec.	5.9

Discuss how the two sets of data are similar and how they are different. Students should realize that one set involves *comparing* amounts of precipitation, whereas the other charts the *change* over time in precipitation for one city.

TEACHING THE LESSON

Relate the example on the lesson page to the discussion in Getting Started by pointing out that bar graphs are frequently used to show comparisons, whereas broken-line graphs are better suited to show changes in an event over time.

Point out that when making a double-broken-line graph, each line must be distinguishable from the other. Suggest that students make one line dotted and the other solid or that they use a different color for each line. Also, point out that a double-broken-line graph requires a key to tell which line is which.

Broken-Line Graphs

The table at the right lists baseball attendance from 1982 to 1989. Compare the attendance at baseball games during these years.

A **broken-line graph** usually shows change over a period of time.

A **double broken-line** graph is used to compare two sets of data.

To make a double broken-line graph, follow these steps.

1. Round the data to an appropriate scale unit. In this case, the numbers are already rounded to the nearest million.

2. Draw a graph, and use the chosen scale unit to label the vertical axis. Then label the horizontal axis. Note that the periods of time are generally represented on the horizontal axis.

3. To plot on the graph the data points from one league, start at 1982 on the horizontal axis. For the American League, place the dot halfway between 22 million and 24 million, directly above 1982. Continue in this manner to plot the remaining points for the American League.

4. Use line segments to connect all the points for the American League in order. Then plot the points for for the National League, and connect them in the same way. Make a key and choose a title for your graph.

Between which years was there the greatest increase in the National League?

The greatest increase occurred between 1986 and 1987.

BASEBALL ATTENDANCE (IN MILLIONS)

Year	League	
	American	National
1982	23	22
1983	24	22
1984	24	22
1985	24	22
1986	25	22
1987	27	25
1988	28	24
1989	30	25

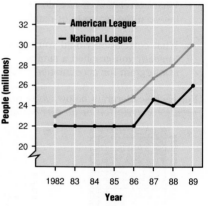

BASEBALL ATTENDANCE

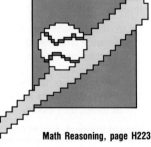

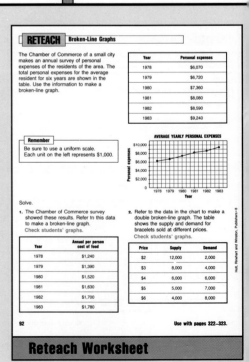

Math Reasoning, page H223

COMMON ERRORS

Some students will choose intervals that are inappropriate for the data. The result will be a graph that is either too large (interval too small) or too dense (interval too large).

Remediation
Have students practice writing intervals by having them round the following data to the nearest thousand and then sketch three graphs based on intervals of 2,000; 10,000; and 5,000. Discuss which scale works best.

Visitors to Seaside Park

M	T	W
3,845	5,614	10,314
Th	F	Sa
12,469	23,965	28,416

Assign Reteach Master, p. 92.

RETEACH Broken-Line Graphs

The Chamber of Commerce of a small city makes an annual survey of personal expenses of the residents of the area. The total personal expenses for the average resident for six years are shown in the table. Use the information to make a broken-line graph.

Year	Personal expenses
1978	$6,070
1979	$6,720
1980	$7,360
1981	$8,080
1982	$8,590
1983	$9,240

Remember
Be sure to use a uniform scale. Each unit on the left represents $1,000.

AVERAGE YEARLY PERSONAL EXPENSES

Solve.

1. The Chamber of Commerce survey showed these results. Refer to this data to make a broken-line graph.
Check students' graphs.

Year	Annual per person cost of food
1978	$1,240
1979	$1,390
1980	$1,520
1981	$1,630
1982	$1,700
1983	$1,780

2. Refer to the data in the chart to make a double broken-line graph. The table shows the supply and demand for bracelets sold at different prices.
Check students' graphs.

Price	Supply	Demand
$2	12,000	2,000
$3	8,000	4,000
$4	6,000	6,000
$5	5,000	7,000
$6	4,000	8,000

92

Use with pages 322–323.

Reteach Worksheet

322

1. Use the data to make a broken-line graph. Check students' graphs.

LEAGUE BOWLING AVERAGES

Year	Averages
1985	219.834
1986	221.662
1987	218.535
1988	223.699
1989	212.844
1990	216.645

2. Use the data to make a double broken-line graph. Check students' graphs.

BOATS (MILLIONS)

Year	Inboard	Sail
1985	1.1	0.9
1986	1.3	0.9
1987	1.2	1.0
1988	1.2	1.0
1989	1.3	1.1
1990	1.4	1.1

Solve.

THE OLYMPIC GAMES

— Summer
— Winter

Nations represented (number) / Year

3. Are more nations represented in the summer or in the winter games?
summer games

4. Why are there two breaks in the graph? The games were not played during these years.

MIDCHAPTER REVIEW

Use the data to solve Exercises 1–4.

The best player on the local women's basketball team scored 318 points during the season. The number of points she scored in each game are 16, 18, 10, 20, 21, 6, 17, 15, 20, 12, 15, 18, 10, 18, 20, 21, 9, 14, 18, and 20.

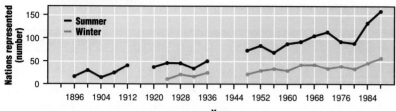

1. What is the range of points she scored during the season? 15

2. Find the mean, median, and mode or modes for this set of data. 15.9; 17.5; 18 and 20

3. Make a frequency table for her scores. Use an interval width of 5, starting with 5–9. See Answer Key.

4. Draw a broken-line graph with the data. Check students' graphs.

Classwork/Homework, page H131

323

323

Objectives: To make and read a circle graph

Warm-Up
Have students give the degree of the angle equivalent to each of the following fractions of a circle.

$\frac{1}{4}$ (90°) $\qquad$ $\frac{2}{3}$ (240°) $\qquad$ $\frac{1}{2}$ (180°)

$\frac{1}{10}$ (36°) $\qquad$ $\frac{1}{6}$ (60°) $\qquad$ $\frac{3}{4}$ (270°)

$\frac{1}{8}$ (45°) $\qquad$ $\frac{1}{12}$ (30°) $\qquad$ $\frac{5}{6}$ (300°)

GETTING STARTED

Explain that a central angle is an angle whose vertex is the center of a circle. Demonstrate the construction of a central angle of 90° by using a protractor and a straight-edge.

Have students construct the following central angles: 30°, 40°, 144°, 315°. Then have them identify the fraction of the circle that each angle cuts out or intercepts. ($\frac{1}{12}$, $\frac{1}{9}$, $\frac{2}{5}$, $\frac{7}{8}$)

TEACHING THE LESSON

A. Tell students that they can round both the intermediary percents and the degree measures. If they round, however, the degree measures must add up to 360°, though the percents need not add up to exactly 100%.

Point out that it is often useful to rename repeating decimal percents as fractions when finding the degree measures of central angles. For example, if an item is $33\frac{1}{3}$% of the whole, it is easier to find the appropriate central angle by multiplying $\frac{1}{3} \cdot 360°$.

B. Explain that though circle graphs provide clear representations of the distribution of a whole, those representations are only approximate because of the amount of rounding that is often necessary before they can be constructed.

You may wish to allow students to use calculators while working through the lesson.

324

Circle Graphs

A. The chart at the right lists the favorite sports of 872 students.

A **circle graph** is often used to show how a whole quantity is divided into parts. Circle graphs are used to display data in fraction, decimal, or percent form.

To make a circle graph, follow these steps.

1. Find the percent of the total for each item.
2. Calculate the measure of each central angle.
3. Use a protractor to draw each central angle.
4. Label the graph and choose a title.

FAVORITE SPORTS

Sport	Number of students
Soccer	123
Softball	67
Tennis	297
Volleyball	318
Other	67

Sport	Number of students	Percent of total	Central angles of graph
Soccer	123	$\frac{123}{872} \approx 14\%$	14% of 360° ≈ 50°
Softball	67	$\frac{67}{872} \approx 8\%$	8% of 360° ≈ 29°
Tennis	297	$\frac{297}{872} \approx 34\%$	34% of 360° ≈ 122°
Volleyball	318	$\frac{318}{872} \approx 36\%$	36% of 360° ≈ 130°
Other	67	$\frac{67}{872} \approx 8\%$	8% of 360° ≈ 29°
Total	872	100%	360°

B. Which two sports together were preferred by about $\frac{2}{3}$ of the students?

Look at the graph.

You can see that together volleyball and tennis were preferred by about $\frac{2}{3}$ of the students.

324

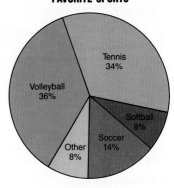

FAVORITE SPORTS

Tennis 34% · Volleyball 36% · Softball 8% · Soccer 14% · Other 8%

COMMON ERRORS

Some students might have difficulty calculating the appropriate degree measures for central angles.

Remediation
Have students practice finding a percent of 360 by using fractions, terminating decimals, and repeating decimal percents. Emphasize the appropriate renaming of percents as fractions or decimals.

$12\frac{1}{2}$% (45) 17.5% (63) 28.3% (102)

Assign Reteach Master, p. 93.

Use each set of data to make a circle graph. Check students' graphs.

1. groups of people watching the Super Bowl on television

Men	Women	Teens	Children
48%	35%	7%	10%
173°	126°	25°	36°

2. groups of people watching the World Series on television

Men	Women	Teens	Children
52%	38%	5%	5%
187°	137°	18°	18°

3. COLLEGE FOOTBALL GAMES ALABAMA

Won	Lost	Tied
641	226	43
252°	90°	18°

4. COLLEGE FOOTBALL GAMES TULSA

Won	Lost	Tied
421	261	26
248°	90°	22°

5. AFTER-SCHOOL FALL SPORTS CLUBS

Sport	Number of participants	
Football	73	68°
Gymnastics	42	39°
Ice hockey	24	22°
Soccer	85	79°
Volleyball	164	152°

6. AFTER-SCHOOL SPRING SPORTS CLUBS

Sport	Number of participants	
Basketball	98	86°
Soccer	128	112°
Softball	66	58°
Tennis	90	79°
Track	28	25°

Selecting an Appropriate Format • Tell which type of graph would best display the data. Answers may vary.

7. the percent of earnings spent for food, rent, clothing, utilities, and entertainment circle graph

8. the monthly profit earned by a company for a year broken-line graph

9. the frequency of scores between 50 and 60, 60 and 70, 70 and 80, and 80 and 90 on a math test histogram

10. the heights of the six tallest buildings in the United States bar graph

11. the daily high and low temperatures for a city for a month double broken-line graph

12. the weights of 26 members of a football team bar graph

Classwork/Homework, page H132

325

ASSIGNMENT GUIDE

Basic: 1–4, 7–10

Average: 2–5, 7–12

Extended: 3–12

Resources
Practice, p. 132   Class/Home, p. H132
Reteach, p. 93
Enrich, p. 120

Exercise Analysis
1–2 Make a circle graph given the percents of a whole
3–4 Make a circle graph given the fractional parts of a whole
5–6 Make a circle graph
7–12 Select appropriate format

You may wish to allow students to use calculators for some of these exercises.

FOLLOW-UP ACTIVITIES

MATH CONNECTION (Science)
Point out that six elements make up 99% of the human body. They are calcium (1.5%), carbon (18%), hydrogen (10%), nitrogen (3%), oxygen (65%), and phosphorus (1.5%). All other elements make up 1%.

Have students represent this information in a circle graph. Then have them use their body weights to calculate the amount of each element in their bodies.

NUMBER SENSE (Estimation)
Have each student conduct research if necessary before making a circle graph to represent one of the following.
● the spending of allowance
● the five largest expenses listed in the federal budget (Have students group all other expenses as a sixth part labeled *Other*.)

Then have them exchange graphs, giving the total number represented by the graph. Students can then estimate the values of each item shown on the graphs, and return the papers to be checked.

COMING UP
For eggs' sample, use 2 chicken yolks.

PRACTICE Circle Graphs

1. Use a compass and a protractor to construct a circle graph that shows the number of pages each person contributed to the Chess Club's newsletter. Use the first letter of each person's name to represent his or her contribution. Mark each part of the graph with the percent that it represents.

Andre	4	Eva	2
Beth	4	Franco	8
Carlos	4	Gordon	6
Dionne	2	Helga	2

2. What is the measure of the central angle of the part that represents Carlos's contribution? 45

3. What fraction of the total did Gordon contribute? $\frac{3}{16}$

4. What fraction of the total did Andre contribute? $\frac{1}{8}$

5. What fraction of the total did Andre, Dionne, and Beth contribute together? $\frac{5}{16}$

6. What is the ratio of Gordon's contribution compared to Eva's? 3:1

Selecting an Appropriate Format • Tell which type of graph would best display the data. Answers may vary.

7. the monthly temperatures of a city for a year broken-line graph

8. the lengths of the eight longest rivers in the world bar graph

9. the percent of space used for clothing, sporting goods, kitchen appliances, and furniture circle graph

10. the frequency of weights between 100–110 lbs, 110–120 lbs, 120–130 lbs, and 130–140 lbs histogram

11. the percent of a garden used for azaleas, petunias, roses, and geraniums circle graph

12. the monthly precipitation in 2 different cities for 12 months double broken-line graph

132   Use with pages 324–325.

Practice Worksheet

ENRICH Statistics and Probability

The symbol σ represents the standard deviation. Standard deviation is used to help evaluate data in relationship to the mean. A large standard deviation tells you that measurements are spread out around the mean. A small standard deviation tells you that measurements are grouped more closely around the mean.

To find the standard deviation for the group of measurements 16, 17, 18, 19, 20, 21, 24, and 25:

1. Find the mean of the group.
$(16 + 17 + 18 + 19 + 20 + 21 + 24 + 25) \div 8 = 20$

The difference between each measurement and the mean is called the *deviation (d)*.

2. Complete the line on the chart for the deviation of each measurement. Then square the deviation.

Measurement	16	17	18	19	20	21	24	25
Deviation (d)	⁻4	⁻3	⁻2	⁻1	0	⁺1	⁺4	⁺5
d^2	16	9	4	1	0	1	16	25

3. Add the squares of the deviations. 72

4. Divide by the number of measurements. $72 \div 8 = 9$

5. Find the square root. This is the standard deviation. $\sqrt{9} = 3$

The formula for standard deviation is $\sigma = \sqrt{\frac{\Sigma d^2}{n}}$

Solve.

6. A gem dealer has 6 bags of diamonds. The number of stones in each packet are 29, 31, 31, 34, 35, and 38. Calculate the standard deviation for the number of diamonds in the group of packages. $\sigma = 3$

7. The dealer has 8 amethysts which are about the same size. He weighs them and finds that the carat weights are 13, 15, 15, 16, 17, 17, 17, and 18. Calculate the standard deviation for the weight of amethysts in the group. $\sigma = 1.5$

120   Use with pages 324–325.

Enrich Worksheet

325

Objective: To use information from a sample to solve a problem

Warm-Up
To prepare students for this lesson, have them compute the following percents.

32% of 300 (96)
17% of 150 (25.5)
110% of 2,660 (2,926)
400% of 7.6 (30.4)

GETTING STARTED

Take a poll to identify the number of left-handed students in the class. Write this number on the chalkboard as a percent of the total number of students in the class. Then write the number of students in the entire school on the chalkboard. Ask students to determine from the data the total number of left-handed students in the school.

TEACHING THE LESSON

In teaching this lesson, emphasize that when using information from a sample, one assumes that the ratio of the data found in the sample is equal to the ratio of the data found in the entire population. In this way, it is possible to predict characteristics for a whole population. In order for the predictions to have any degree of accuracy, however, the sample must be as representative as possible of the whole population. Explain that a random sample is not necessarily a representative one. All of the characteristics that may affect the needed information must be accounted for. On page 327, because age may have a bearing on whether or not people approve of a politician's performance, the sample must take into account the ages of those interviewed. In order to answer Question 2, students must determine how much of the population is age 18–30 (36%, or 10,800), what percentage of people polled in that age bracket disapproved (41%), and how many people in the total population age 18–30 disapproved (41% of 10,800, or about 4,400).

Questions: Some students may find a percentage of the total population when they are asked for a percentage of the sample, and vice versa.

Tools: Be sure students realize that they must find a percentage of the sample before they can find the percentage of the entire population. Suggest that one alternate method of solving these problems is to set up and solve a proportion; for example: How many people in the total population are opposed to the referendum? $\frac{50}{125} = \frac{n}{7,250}$; $n = 2,900$

| QUESTIONS | TOOLS | SOLUTIONS | CHECKS |

PROBLEM SOLVING
Using a Sample

Sampling is a method of obtaining information. It can be used to draw conclusions about the opinions of a particular population by questioning a representative group.

Castle Rock is going to have a referendum on the ballot in the upcoming election. It asks if the town should raise money for the library by increasing taxes. *The Castle Rock Newsletter* conducted a poll before the election to find out if the referendum would pass. They used a sample of 125 people of a population of 7,250.

ARE YOU IN FAVOR OF THE REFERENDUM?	
Yes	60
No	50
Undecided	15

What percent of the sample favored the referendum?

60 of 125
60 ÷ 125 = 0.48
0.48 = 48%
48% of the sample favored the referendum.

You can use this poll to make predictions about the whole population if you assume that the views of the people in the sample are representative of those of the whole population.

According to the poll, how many in the total population favor the referendum?

48% = 0.48
0.48 × 7,250 = 3,480

About 3,500 people in Castle Rock favor the referendum.

326

Solutions: Review the algorithms for solving the three cases of percent. You may wish to allow students to use calculators when solving these problems.

Checks: Have students check their answers by working the problems backward using inverse operations. Once students have broken a population into percents, have them verify that the total of separate percents equals 100.

Use the table below to answer the exercises.

The Metropolis, a daily newspaper, conducted a poll on the performance of the mayor after two years in office. They questioned three groups of 400 people each, of the city's 30,000 population. They carefully chose the people they questioned so that the views of the people in the sample would be representative of the whole population. (The numbers in parentheses show the percent of the total population that each age group represents.)

AGE GROUP	18–30 (36%)	31–60 (30%)	OVER AGE 60 (12%)
Approve	192	168	144
Disapprove	164	156	176
Undecided	44	76	80
Total	400	400	400

1. Which age group(s) approved of the mayor's performance by more than 40%?
   18–30 age group; 31–60 age group
2. According to the poll, how many people in the total population aged 18–30 (to the nearest 100) disapproved of the mayor's performance? 4,400 people
3. In which age group were 20% of the people undecided? over 60 age group
4. From the results of the survey, *The Metropolis* predicts that the mayor will be reelected during the next election. Do you agree or disagree with the prediction? Explain. Answers will vary.
5. What is meant by the statement "they carefully chose the people they questioned"? People were chosen who were not biased for or against the mayor.
6. Suppose the mayor is in the 18–30 age group. Do you think this fact would bias the results of those people in the 18–30 age group? Explain. Answers will vary.

Classwork/Homework, pages H133–H134

ASSIGNMENT GUIDE

Basic:	1–3, 5
Average:	1–6
Extended:	1–7

Resources
Practice, pp. 133–4   Class/Home, pp. H133–4

Exercise Analysis
1–6 Data collection and computation

FOLLOW-UP ACTIVITIES

PROBLEM SOLVING
Materials: newspapers and magazines that present polls and surveys

Have students look through newspapers and magazines to find the results of surveys and polls. Then have them each write several questions relating to these. Have them challenge one another with these questions.

CALCULATOR
Materials: calculators, pencils, paper

Read the following problems aloud and have students use calculators to solve.

Emphasize that they can use either percents or proportions to solve. Have them round their answers to the nearest whole number.
- In a sample of 430 people, 112 have blond hair. If the total population is 14,240 people, about how many blond-haired people would you expect to find? (3,709)
- In a sample of 703 people, 362 are found to be over the age of 40. About how many people over the age of 40 would you expect to find in a population of 35,000? (18,023)
- In a sample of 5,245 people, 1,713 jog. Out of a total population of 118,927, about how many joggers could you expect to find? (38,841)

COMING UP
There is some possibility here!

Tweed Polls, Inc., conducted a poll to ask residents of Ringford (population 16,000) their opinions about the choice of a raccoon as the new town mascot. Three groups of 250 people each were questioned. The table below shows their responses.

Age group	15–25	26–45	Older than 45
Percent of the town population	25%	40%	20%
Approve	115	90	120
Disapprove	100	105	80
Undecided	35	55	50

Assume that the poll is representative of the opinions of all Ringford residents in the age groups sampled. Use the table to solve.

1. Which age group voiced the greatest difference of opinion between approval and disapproval? Older than 45
2. What percent of the 26–45 age group was undecided? 22%
3. In which age group did 40% of the people disapprove? 15–25
4. How many Ringford residents are more than 45 years old? 3,200 residents
5. How many Ringford residents in the 15–25 age group disapproved? 1,600 residents
6. How many Ringford residents in the 26–45 age group approved? 2,304 residents
7. What percent of all Ringford residents 15 years of age and older disapproved? 39%
8. How many residents of Ringford are less than 15 years of age? 2,400 residents
9. If 80% of the undecideds in the older-than-45 age group had disapproved and 20% had approved, would the majority of the age group have disapproved? no
10. Do the majority of residents of Ringford who are 15 years of age and older approve or disapprove? approve

Use with pages 326–327. 133

Practice Worksheet

To find out whether passengers would use a new service, Airways North conducted a poll. The results are shown below.

Age	20–40	20–40	Older than 40	Older than 40
Career	Self-employed	Executives	Self-employed	Executives
Percent of total first-class passengers	20%	28%	12%	24%
Will use the service	150	210	175	270
Will not use the service	200	240	215	170
Undecided	150	50	110	60

A total of 8,260 passengers fly first class between New York and Rome each month. Based on the assumption that the passengers in the poll represent all of Airways North's first-class passengers, solve.

1. What percent of self-employed passengers questioned said they would use the new service? 32.5%
2. Suppose that Airways North had questioned only executives older than 40, and the results showed that 60% of those polled would use the new service. Would this poll be a good indicator of the total population of passengers? Explain your answer. No; the sample would be biased.
3. To the nearest person, how many passengers are likely to use the service? 3,325 passengers
4. If Airways North reduced the fare paid by executives by 10%, they expect that 75% of the undecided executives would use the new service. The airline, however, would have to book at least 3,100 passengers per month to make a profit. Can they obtain that number of passengers if they reduce the fare for executives? yes
5. To make a profit, Airways North needs at least 2,750 passengers to use its new service each month. Using only the categories represented in the poll, should the new service be started? yes
6. How many passengers will the airline have if it reduces the fare? not enough information

134

Practice Worksheet

Use after pages 326–327.

Objective: To calculate the number of possible outcomes

Warm-Up
Have students find each product mentally.

4 · 4 · 4 (64)	5 · 3 · 4 (60)
3 · 8 · 12 (288)	5 · 7 · 2 (70)
3 · 9 · 4 (108)	6 · 6 · 6 (216)

GETTING STARTED

Materials: white, orange, and blue construction paper, scissors

Pose the following problem to students: Mr. Howard, the athletic director of the junior high school, wants to purchase new gym uniforms. The school's colors are orange and blue. Mr. Howard is willing to consider white also but only for the shirts. From how many different color pairings for the shirt and for the shorts can Mr. Howard choose? Have students cut out figures from construction paper to represent shorts and shirts. Tell them to put together each possible pairing of colors for the uniforms and then list the pairings (for example, orange–orange). Ask how many pairings are possible. (6)

TEACHING THE LESSON

A. Guide the students through this additional example.

On Sports Day, Southpoint Junior High schedules only three periods. During each period, students can choose from among a varying number of sports. Softball, volleyball, and football are offered during Period 1; water polo and jogging during Period 2; and archery, bicycling, and gymnastics during Period 3. Have each student draw a tree diagram to illustrate the possible choices. Then have students use letter codes to list the sample space.

B. Point out that when many choices are involved, tree diagrams become unwieldy. At a convention, for instance, the daily schedule might be divided into eight periods and eight workshops might be held per period. Emphasize the usefulness of a formula in such cases.

Have students apply the formula to find the number of possible choices a Southpoint Junior High student could make on Sports Day. Have them check their answers against their answers from Part A.

Possible Outcomes

A. For gym class, Bob may be assigned to football or soccer in the fall. He may be assigned to baseball, jogging, or tennis in the spring. What are the **possible outcomes?**

You can use a **tree diagram** to find the number of possible outcomes.

Each branch of the tree lists a possible outcome.

Count the possible outcomes.

The tree diagram lists 6 possible outcomes.

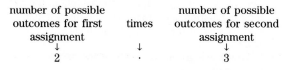

TREE DIAGRAM

Fall assignment	Spring assignment	Possible outcomes
football	baseball	football–baseball
	jogging	football–jogging
	tennis	football–tennis
soccer	baseball	soccer–baseball
	jogging	soccer–jogging
	tennis	soccer–tennis

The **sample space** consists of the 6 possible outcomes. You can use these letters to list the outcomes: *FB, FJ, FT, SB, SJ,* and *ST.*

F stands for football, *B* stands for baseball, and so on.

B. Both the fall sports can be paired with all the spring sports. You can multiply to find the total number of possible outcomes.

number of possible outcomes for first assignment	times	number of possible outcomes for second assignment	=	number of possible outcomes for both assignments
↓	↓	↓	↓	↓
2	·	3	=	6

If you are making two or more choices, the total number of possible outcomes is the product of the number of possible outcomes for each choice.

Math Reasoning, page H223

COMMON ERRORS

Some students might add instead of multiply the number of possible outcomes for each event when finding the number of possible outcomes of a series of events.

Remediation
For this error, have students check their answers by drawing tree diagrams or sample spaces.

Assign Reteach Master, p. 94.

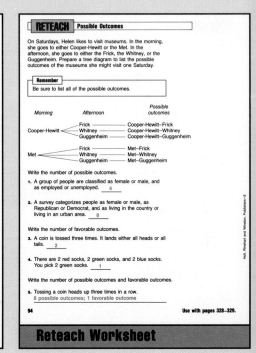

You are going to spin these two spinners.

First spinner   Second spinner

1. Copy and complete the tree diagram to show the possible outcomes.

2. Copy and complete the sample space.
1*A*, 1*B*, 2*A*, ■, ■, ■ 2*B*, 3*A*, 3*B*

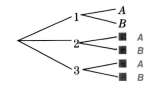

3. How many possible outcomes are there? 6

4. Is the number of possible outcomes equal to 3 · 2? yes

You are going to choose one card from each row.

5. Draw a tree diagram to show the possible outcomes.
See diagram to right.

6. List the outcomes in space.
★ +,★ √,★ ✳,□ +,□ √,□ ✳,
△ +,△ √,△ ✳,○ +,○ √,○ ✳

7. How many possible outcomes are there? 12

8. Is the number of possible outcomes equal to 4 · 3? yes

Solve.

9. Bob has 5 shirts in his closet and 3 pairs of pants. He is going to choose one shirt and one pair of pants. How many different outfits can he choose? 15 outfits

10. Maria has 4 skirts and 6 blouses in her closet. She is going to choose one skirt and one blouse. How many different outfits can she choose? 24 outfits

11. There are 3 routes from Ashton to Centerville and 3 routes from Centerville to Sterling. How many routes are there from Ashton to Sterling through Centerville?
9 routes

12. There are 2 routes from Plainedge to Bellmore and 4 routes from Bellmore to Talmont. How many routes are there from Plainedge to Talmont through Bellmore?
8 routes

Classwork/Homework, page H135

329

Exercise Analysis
1–8   Construct a tree diagram to find the possible outcomes
9–12   Skill applications

FOLLOW-UP ACTIVITIES

REINFORCEMENT
Explain that when many choices are possible, tree diagrams can become unmanageable. In such cases, a matrix such as the one shown below can be helpful.

	A	B	C	D	E
1	A1	B1	C1	D1	E1
2	A2	B2	C2	D2	E2

- Elaine's travel agent knows of 4 routes from Atlanta to Norfolk and 5 from Norfolk to Philadelphia.

Have each student write a matrix for all the possible routes from Atlanta to Philadelphia via Norfolk. Suggest that each student assign codes to each subroute.

PUZZLES AND GAMES
Draw the figure at the left on the chalkboard.

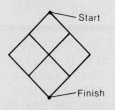
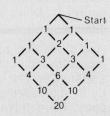

Have students find the number of different ways to get from Start to Finish, moving down only along the lines. If desired, students can complete a similar 3 × 3 array. (The problem can be explained by using the figure at the right, which is a 3 × 3 array that shows the number of possible routes to each point.)

COMING UP
Forever changes

Objective: To explore permutations and combinations

Warm-Up
Have students find each product mentally.

$4 \cdot 3 \cdot 2 \cdot 1$ (24)
$5 \cdot 4 \cdot 3 \cdot 2$ (120)
$6 \cdot 5 \cdot 4 \cdot 3$ (360)
$7 \cdot 6 \cdot 5 \cdot 4$ (840)

GETTING STARTED

Materials: group of 3 different colored counters per student

Ask students to arrange the counters in as many different groups of 2 different colored counters as possible. They should have 3 groups of 2 counters each. Then ask students how many ways each of these groups can be arranged in a different order. They should see that each group of 2 can be arranged in 2 different orders. Finally, ask students to arrange the counters in as many different *ordered* groups of 2 different colored counters as possible. Students should have 6 groups of 2 ordered counters.

TEACHING THE LESSON

Because of the depth of the conceptual development involved, this lesson and the following lesson may be addressed in several class periods. The Reteach and Practice worksheets should not be assigned until the following lesson has been completed. You may wish to have students work through the developmental parts of this lesson in groups of four and have a class discussion for Thinking as a Team.

Have students read through the introductory problem and discuss the questions in the Thinking as a Team section. Make sure that students realize that order is important in John's proposal but not in Ms. Baker's.

Help students to see that they can solve a group of simpler problems by making lists and that they can look at these solutions to try to find patterns and make generalizations. Have them complete the lists of combinations and permutations for 4 students taken 2 at a time. Then ask them to make similar lists for a group of 5 students taken 2 at a time and a group of 6 students taken 2 at a time. Ask them whether they can see a pattern developing in the way the number of permutations and combinations increases. If so, ask them to extend this pattern to predict the number of combinations and permutations for a group of 7 students taken 2 at a time. (21 combinations, 42 permutations)

Permutations and Combinations

Ms. Baker rushed into her eighth grade class one day and exclaimed, "The mayor has decided that our class will send a team to represent the city in the state Mathematics Challenge! We have to pick three representatives from the ten students in the class, and I think they should go to the competition as equal partners."

"I disagree," said John, the resident mathematics whiz. "Let's send a captain, assistant captain, and a secretary. I think that the team will be better organized that way."

Ms. Baker thought for a moment and responded, "Very well, John, if you can tell me in three tries how many teams are possible if we go along with my idea or with your idea, then I'll agree to your proposal."

"That's easy, ten times three equals thirty teams," John said quickly.

"Haste makes waste," Ms. Baker replied. "Try again."

John started to hedge. "Well, both proposals involve the same number of possible teams, right?"

"Wrong!" said Ms. Baker. The class got more excited as John grew nervous.

Thinking as a Team

What is John to do? How is it possible that one proposal would result in more teams than the other proposal? Discuss with your teammates. Try to determine which proposal would result in more teams and, if possible, the number of teams involved in each proposal.

John's proposal has more possible teams because order is important, while in Ms. Baker's proposal order is not important.

John did not understand the difference between ordered arrangements, or permutations, and unordered arrangements, or combinations. Ms. Baker's proposal involved combinations. John's proposal involved permutations.

330

Have students investigate the relationship between the number of permutations and the number of combinations in each of the cases that they have seen. Then have them make lists to find the numbers of combinations and permutations that would be possible if 3 students were chosen from groups of 4, 5, and 6. (4, 24; 10, 60; 20, 120) Ask in how many ways a group of 3 students can be ordered. (6)

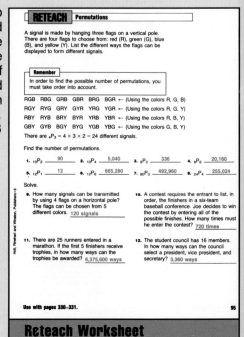

John decided to try a simple experiment to help him see the difference between permutations and combinations. He would make organized lists to see how many permutations and combinations could be made if 2 team members were being chosen from a group of 4 students: Allen, Biff, Carla, and Dione. Complete each of the lists on your own.

Combinations	Permutations
Allen–Biff	Allen–Biff, Biff–Allen
Allen–Carla	Allen–Carla, Carla–Allen
Allen–Dione....	Allen–Dione....

Thinking as a Team

1. How many combinations are there? 6

2. How many ways can each combination be ordered?
2 ways

3. How many permutations are there? 12

4. Can you generalize about whether there will be more combinations or more permutations for any arrangement of things? **more permutations (assuming the number being selected is more than 1)**

5. How can you relate the number of combinations, the number of ways in which each combination can be ordered, and the number of permutations?

No. of combinations × no. of ways of ordering each = no. of permutations.

When is order important? When is order unimportant? Determine whether order is important in finding the number of arrangements in each problem. **Accept all reasonable answers that students can defend logically.**

- You are inviting four of your friends for a dinner.

- You are placing three of your records on a turntable to be played.

- You are mixing five different components for fertilizer for your garden.

- You are planning a party, and you plan to ask six guests to park their six cars in your driveway.

Thinking as a Team

1. Different members of your team may interpret each of the four problems differently. Discuss your answers and the various interpretations involved.

2. Explain how Ms. Baker's proposal involved combinations, whereas John's proposal involved permutations.

331

ASSIGNMENT GUIDE

Basic: p. 330, p. 331

Average: p. 330, p. 331

Extended: p. 330, p. 331

Resources
Enrich, p. 122

FOLLOW-UP ACTIVITIES

PROBLEM SOLVING
Give students the following problems. Have them make organized lists to solve them.

- Louise is arranging 3 books on a shelf. In how many ways can she arrange them? (6)
- In how many ways can she arrange 4 books? (24)
- Giuseppe has a group of 4 books, but only 3 of them will fit on a shelf. How many different groups of 3 can he put on the shelf if the order of the books does not matter? (4)
- How many groups of 3 books can he put on the shelf if the order *does* matter? (24)
- Claudette has to pick 4 dancers from a group of 5 for a chorus line. If the order does not matter, how many groups of 4 can she pick? (5)
- How many groups can she pick if the order *does* matter? (120)

COMING UP
The combination platter

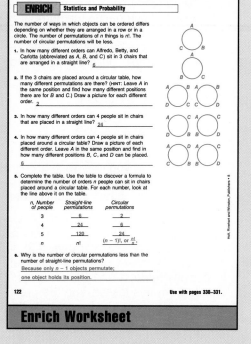

PRACTICE Permutations and Combinations

Write the number of permutations.

1. $_7P_2$ __42__
2. $_5P_4$ __120__
3. $_9P_6$ __60,480__
4. $_8P_3$ __336__
5. $_{10}P_2$ __90__
6. $_6P_3$ __120__
7. $_{12}P_5$ __95,040__
8. $_{20}P_4$ __116,280__
9. $_{15}P_6$ __3,603,600__
10. $_{17}P_3$ __4,080__
11. $_{100}P_2$ __9,900__
12. $_{40}P_5$ __78,960,960__

13. Evaluate 10! __3,628,800__

Find the factorial.

14. 3! + 3! __12__
15. 8! ÷ 5! __336__
16. 4 × 4! __96__
17. 2! × 7! __10,080__
18. 9! + 6! __363,600__
19. 21! ÷ 18! __7,980__
20. 3 × 5! __360__
21. 7! ÷ 4 __1,260__
22. 10! ÷ 5! __30,240__

Write *true* or *false*.

23. 9 × 8! = 9! __true__
24. 64! ÷ 63! = 64 __true__
25. 3! + 5! = 8! __false__
26. 47! ÷ 47 = 46! __true__
27. 5! × 4! = 20! __false__
28. 10! ÷ 7! = 720 __true__

Solve.

29. Peter Possible has 25 different books on his shelf. In how many ways can he pick 3 books? __13,800 ways__

30. Mary Maybe has 16 different bottles of perfume. In how many ways can she arrange them 5 at a time? __524,160 ways__

31. In how many different ways can 8 people line up in front of a movie box office? __40,320 ways__

32. In how many ways can 7 photographs be hung in a horizontal line? __5,040 ways__

136   Use with pages 330–331.

Practice Worksheet

ENRICH Statistics and Probability

The number of ways in which objects can be ordered differs depending on whether they are arranged in a row or in a circle. The number of permutations of *n* things is *n*!. The number of circular permutations will be less.

1. How many different orders can Alfredo, Betty, and Carlotta (abbreviated as *A*, *B*, and *C*) sit in 3 chairs that are arranged in a straight line? __6__

2. If the 3 chairs are placed around a circular table, how many different permutations are there? (HINT: Leave *A* in the same position and find how many different positions there are for *B* and *C*.) Draw a picture for each different order. __2__

3. In how many different orders can 4 people sit in chairs that are placed in a straight line? __24__

4. In how many different orders can 4 people sit in chairs placed around a circular table? Draw a picture of each different order. Leave *A* in the same position and find in how many different positions *B*, *C*, and *D* can be placed. __6__

5. Complete the table. Use the table to discover a formula to determine the number of orders *n* people can sit in chairs placed around a circular table. For each number, look at the line above it on the table.

n, Number of people	Straight-line permutations	Circular permutations
3	6	2
4	24	6
5	120	24
n	n!	(n − 1)!, or $\frac{n!}{n}$

6. Why is the number of circular permutations less than the number of straight-line permutations?
__Because only n − 1 objects permutate;__
__one object holds its position.__

122   Use with pages 330–331.

Enrich Worksheet

331

Objectives: To explore the numerical relationship between permutations and combinations and determine the number of permutations and combinations

Warm-Up

Have students evaluate each.

$\frac{4 \cdot 3 \cdot 2}{3 \cdot 2 \cdot 1}$ (4) $\frac{5 \cdot 4 \cdot 3 \cdot 2}{4 \cdot 3 \cdot 2 \cdot 1}$ (5) $\frac{6 \cdot 5 \cdot 4 \cdot 3}{4 \cdot 3 \cdot 2 \cdot 1}$ (15)

GETTING STARTED

Pose the following problem to students.
• The eighth grade class is putting on a play. 6 people try out for 3 parts.

Have students make an organized list to find the number of possible combinations of people for the three parts. (20) Ask students in how many ways each of these combinations can be ordered. (6)

TEACHING THE LESSON

Materials: calculators

Because of the depth of conceptual development involved, this lesson may take several class periods. You may wish to have students work through this lesson in groups of four or have a class discussion. You may wish to allow students to use calculators for some of the computations in this lesson.

A. Have students discuss why it is a good strategy to solve the problem by examining how many permutations there are of one combination. (You can find the relationship between the number of positions in a combination and the number of permutations of that combination without listing all of the combinations or permutations.) Students should realize that making a list is impractical because of the large number of combinations and permutations. Discuss with students how they can determine the number of permutations by multiplying the number of choices for each position. They should discover that the number of choices decreases for each position. Lead students to understand that they can find the total number of combinations by dividing the total number of permutations by the number of permutations for one combination.

B. Read through this section with the class. Point out the various notations used when computing the number of combinations and permutations. Have students write the correct notation for the problem they just solved. Elicit that to find how many ways a given number of objects can be ordered, they should

---

Numbers of Permutations and Combinations

A. To satisfy Ms. Baker's request from the last lesson, John had to find the number of possible combinations and the number of possible permutations when 3 students are selected from a class of 10 students.

Thinking as a Team

John chose one combination of 3 students to examine. He started to make a list to determine all of the permutations that can be formed using those 3 students. Copy and complete the list.

Combination	Permutations		
	Captain	*Asst. Capt.*	*Secretary*
John, Kim, Alice	John	Alice	Kim
	John	Kim	Alice

How many permutations are there?   6 permutations

Choose another combination of 3 students and find how many permutations there are. What numerical relationship is there between the combinations and the permutations for each combination?   6 permutations; for every combination of 3 students there are 6 permutations

To solve John's problem you need to find the number of combinations of 3 students there are in a group of 10 students. Would you make a list? Why not?   no; list would become tedious and unmanagable

It is easier to find the number of permutations; then you divide to find the number of combinations. You can find the total number of permutations or teams by multiplying.

• In a class of 10 students, how many possible choices are there for captain?   10 choices
• After a captain is selected, how many students are left to choose an assistant from?   9 choices
• How many choices are there left for secretary?   8 choices

```
        ┌ choices for captain
        │ ┌ choices for assistant captain
        │ │ ┌ choices for secretary
        ↓ ↓ ↓
     10 · 9 · 8 = ■   720
```

332   Math Reasoning, page H224

---

find the factorial of that number. Further elicit that computing the number of combinations can be made easier by simplifying before multiplying. Write the following example on the chalkboard.

$$_7C_5 = \frac{_7P_5}{5!} = \frac{7 \cdot 6 \cdot 5 \cdot 4 \cdot 3}{5 \cdot 4 \cdot 3 \cdot 2 \cdot 1}$$

$$= \frac{7 \cdot 6 \cdot \cancel{5} \cdot \cancel{4} \cdot \cancel{3}}{\cancel{5} \cdot \cancel{4} \cdot \cancel{3} \cdot 2 \cdot 1} = \frac{42}{2} = 21$$

After they complete the Thinking as a Team problems, you may wish to have students write problems on their own, share them with other students, then solve them.

Refer students who need additional practice to More Practice page 488 in the back of the textbook. You may wish to assign Reteach and Practice worksheets from this lesson and the previous lesson after students complete this lesson.

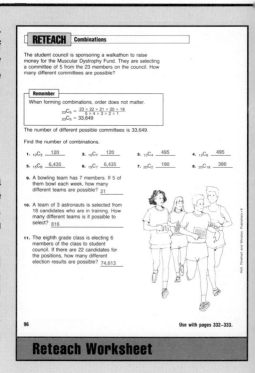

RETEACH Combinations

The student council is sponsoring a walkathon to raise money for the Muscular Dystrophy Fund. They are selecting a committee of 5 from the 23 members on the council. How many different committees are possible?

Remember
When forming combinations, order does not matter.
$_{23}C_5 = \frac{23 \times 22 \times 21 \times 20 \times 19}{5 \times 4 \times 3 \times 2 \times 1}$
$_{23}C_5 = 33,649$

The number of different possible committees is 33,649.

Find the number of combinations.

1. $_{10}C_3$ ___120___
2. $_{10}C_7$ ___120___
3. $_{12}C_4$ ___495___
4. $_{12}C_8$ ___495___
5. $_{15}C_8$ ___6,435___
6. $_{15}C_7$ ___6,435___
7. $_{20}C_2$ ___190___
8. $_{20}C_{18}$ ___380___

9. A bowling team has 7 members. If 5 of them bowl each week, how many different teams are possible? ___21___

10. A team of 3 astronauts is selected from 18 candidates who are in training. How many different teams is it possible to select? ___816___

11. The eighth grade class is electing 6 members of the class to student council. If there are 22 candidates for the positions, how many different election results are possible? ___74,613___

96   Use with pages 332–333.

Reteach Worksheet

- What is the total number of permutations? 720 permutations
- How many combinations are there? 120 combinations
- How many teams are possible using John's idea? 720 teams
- How many teams are possible using Ms. Baker's idea? 120 teams

B. Some special notation is used in discussing permutations and combinations.

In the case you just solved, you found the numbers of permutations possible when 3 objects are chosen from a group of 10 objects. This is written as $_{10}P_3$.

$$_{10}P_3 = 10 \cdot 9 \cdot 8 = 720$$

number of choices ↗   number of positions ↗

The notation 3! is used to show the product of 3 and all counting numbers less than 3, and is read "three factorial."

$$3! = 3 \cdot 2 \cdot 1 = 6$$

In the case you just solved you found that the number of ways in which 3 objects can be ordered is 3! or 6. You then found the number of combinations possible for 3 objects chosen from a group of 10 objects by dividing $_{10}P_3$ by 6. This can be written:

$$_{10}C_3 = \frac{_{10}P_3}{3!} = \frac{10 \cdot 9 \cdot 8}{3 \cdot 2 \cdot 1} = 120$$

Thinking as a Team

Discuss the solutions to each of the following with other teams.

1. In how many ways can a president and vice president be chosen in a class of 15 students? $_{15}P_2 = 210$
2. How many basketball teams of 5 members each can be made from a group of 12 students? $_{12}C_5 = 792$
3. How many committees of 3 can be formed from a class of 18 students? $_{18}C_3 = 816$

ASSIGNMENT GUIDE

Basic:	p. 332, p. 333
Average:	p. 332, p. 333
Extended:	p. 332, p. 333

Resources

Practice, pp. 136–7	Class/Home, pp. H136–7
Reteach, pp. 95–6	More Practice, p. H204
Enrich, p. 123	Reasoning, p. H224

FOLLOW-UP ACTIVITIES

CALCULATOR
Have students use calculators to find the number of possible combinations of 50 people in a drama class in each play.

2-person play (1,225)
3-person play (19,600)
4-person play (230,300)
5-person play (2,118,760)

PUZZLES AND GAMES
Using any operational signs, including exponents and roots, make each equation true. (Possible solutions are displayed at the right.)

$$1 \; 1 \; 1 = 6 \quad ((1 + 1 + 1)!)$$
$$2 \; 2 \; 2 = 6 \quad (2 + 2 + 2)$$
$$3 \; 3 \; 3 = 6 \quad (3 \times 3 - 3)$$
$$4 \; 4 \; 4 = 6 \quad (\sqrt{4} + \sqrt{4} + \sqrt{4})$$
$$5 \; 5 \; 5 = 6 \quad (5 \div 5 + 5)$$
$$6 \; 6 \; 6 = 6 \quad (6 + 6 - 6)$$
$$7 \; 7 \; 7 = 6 \quad ((7^2 - 7) \div 7)$$
$$8 \; 8 \; 8 = 6 \quad (\sqrt[3]{8} + \sqrt[3]{8} + \sqrt[3]{8})$$
$$9 \; 9 \; 9 = 6 \quad ((9 + 9) \div \sqrt{9})$$

COMING UP
Is that possible? Probably!

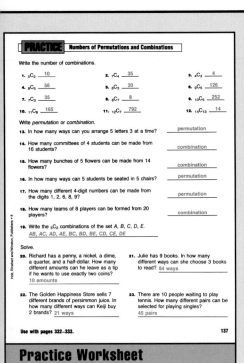

PRACTICE — Numbers of Permutations and Combinations

Write the number of combinations.

1. $_5C_2$ __10__   2. $_7C_4$ __35__   3. $_4C_3$ __4__
4. $_8C_5$ __56__   5. $_6C_3$ __20__   6. $_9C_5$ __126__
7. $_7C_3$ __35__   8. $_8C_7$ __8__   9. $_{10}C_5$ __252__
10. $_{11}C_8$ __165__   11. $_{12}C_7$ __792__   12. $_{14}C_{13}$ __14__

Write *permutation* or *combination*.

13. In how many ways can you arrange 5 letters 3 at a time? __permutation__
14. How many committees of 4 students can be made from 16 students? __combination__
15. How many bunches of 5 flowers can be made from 14 flowers? __combination__
16. In how many ways can 5 students be seated in 5 chairs? __permutation__
17. How many different 4-digit numbers can be made from the digits 1, 2, 6, 8, 9? __permutation__
18. How many teams of 8 players can be formed from 20 players? __combination__
19. Write the $_5C_2$ combinations of the set A, B, C, D, E. __AB, AC, AD, AE, BC, BD, BE, CD, CE, DE__

Solve.

20. Richard has a penny, a nickel, a dime, a quarter, and a half-dollar. How many different amounts can he leave as a tip if he wants to use exactly two coins? __10 amounts__
21. Julie has 9 books. In how many different ways can she choose 3 books to read? __84 ways__
22. The Golden Happiness Store sells 7 different brands of persimmon juice. In how many different ways can Keiji buy 2 brands? __21 ways__
23. There are 10 people waiting to play tennis. How many different pairs can be selected for playing singles? __45 pairs__

Use with pages 332–333.   137

Practice Worksheet

ENRICH — Statistics and Probability

The number of permutations of a string of digits or letters is the factorial of the number of items in the string. If a number or object is repeated in the string, there will be fewer permutations—abc will have 3!, or 6, permutations: abc, acb, cab, cba, bac, and bca; aba will have only 3 permutations: aba, aab, and baa.

Although the word *MISSISSIPPI* has 11 letters in it, it will have less than 11! permutations. To find the number of permutations, count the number of repeating letters and the number of times each repeats. *I* repeats 4 times; S, 4 times; P, 2 times. Divide 11! by 4! × 4! × 2!, the factorials of the letters that repeat.

The number of permutations of the word *MISSISSIPPI* will be:

$$\frac{11!}{4! \times 4! \times 2!} = \frac{11 \times 10 \times 9 \times 8 \times 7 \times 6 \times 5 \times 4 \times 3 \times 2 \times 1}{4 \times 3 \times 2 \times 1 \times 4 \times 3 \times 2 \times 1 \times 2 \times 1} = \frac{11 \times 10 \times 9 \times 7 \times 5}{1} = 34,650$$

1. How many permutations are there of the number 77,667? __10__
2. How many 5-letter permutations are there in MADAM? __30__
3. How many 8-digit permutations are there in the number 12,341,235? __5,040__
4. How many 7-letter permutations are there in the word BALLOON? __1,260__
5. Write three 4-letter words that will each have 12 permutations. __Answers will vary; one repeating letter.__
6. Write three 6-digit numbers that will each have 60 permutations. __Answers will vary; 333,221.__
7. How many different ways can a cowhand stack 3 straw hats and 4 felt hats? __35__
8. How many different ways can you distribute 5 pintos and 4 stallions to 9 cowhands? __126__
9. How many different ways can you distribute 3 wagons, 4 buggies, and 4 carts to 11 families if each family is to get one vehicle? __11,550__
10. Draw a line between the words with the same number of possible permutations.

COWBOY ─ INDIAN
TONTO ─ LASSOS
ROPES ─ HORSES
KANSAS ─ TEEPEE

Use with pages 332–333.   123

Enrich Worksheet

333

Objectives: To define and calculate probability

Warm-Up
Have students rewrite each ratio as a percent.

3:4 (75%) 1:2 (50%) 4:5 (80%)

$\frac{1}{8}$ (12.5%) $\frac{2}{3}$ $\left(66\frac{2}{3}\%\right)$ $\frac{9}{10}$ (90%)

5:5 (100%) 0:7 (0%) 3:1 (300%)

GETTING STARTED

Materials: 4 black pencils, 1 red pencil, paper bag

Place the 5 pencils in the bag. Draw a tally chart labeled *Black* and *Red* on the chalkboard.

Have a volunteer pick a pencil out of the bag without looking. Mark the pick on the tally chart, and then return the pencil to the bag. Repeat until every student has selected a pencil.

Count the number of times a black pencil was selected. Have students write a ratio to represent black selections to the total number of selections. Repeat for red. Ask: What do the ratios indicate? (The ratios will more closely approach 4:5 and 1:5 as the number of repetitions of the experiment increases.)

TEACHING THE LESSON

A. Emphasize the fact that probabilities are found by dividing favorable outcomes by possible outcomes. Then extend the lesson by pointing out that what students already know about possible outcomes, permutations, and combinations can be useful in finding the denominator of a probability.

B. Guide students through the intermediate steps in the solution.

$P(R) = \frac{0}{6} = 0$

$P(W, Y, \text{ or } G) = \frac{(2 + 1 + 3)}{6} = 1$

C. Point out that the probability of not picking a white tennis ball is the complement of the probability of picking a white tennis ball. Since $P(\text{white}) = \frac{2}{6}$, $P(\text{not white}) = 1 - P(\text{white}) = \frac{4}{6}$, or $\frac{2}{3}$.

Probability

A. Mr. Thomas has a bag of tennis balls. Of them, 3 are green, 2 are white, and 1 is yellow. He is going to pick a tennis ball without looking. This is called picking a tennis ball **at random.** He is **equally likely** to pick any one of the tennis balls.

What is the **probability** of picking a green tennis ball?

The probability of picking a green tennis ball can be written as P(*G*).

$P(G) = \frac{\text{number of favorable outcomes}}{\text{number of possible outcomes}}$

There are 6 possible outcomes; 3 of the outcomes are favorable because there are 3 green tennis balls.

So, $P(G) = \frac{3}{6} = \frac{1}{2}$.

The probability of picking a green tennis ball is $\frac{1}{2}$, or 50%.

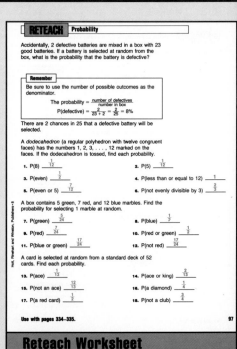

B. An event consists of 0, 1, or more possible outcomes.

What is the probability of picking a red tennis ball?

Since there is no red tennis ball in the bag, the event is **impossible.** If an event will never occur, the probability is 0.

$P(\text{red}) = 0$

What is the probability of picking a white, yellow, or green tennis ball?

Since any one of the tennis balls will be either white, yellow, or green, the event is **certain.** If an event will always occur, the probability is 1.

$P(\text{white, yellow, or green}) = 1$

C. What is the probability of not picking a white tennis ball?

Since 4 tennis balls are not white, there are 4 possible favorable outcomes.

$P(\text{not white}) = \frac{4}{6} = \frac{2}{3}$

D. There are 5 cards in a hat. They are 1, 2, 3, 4, and 5. If a card is picked at random, what is the probability that it is greater than 3? Since there are 2 cards greater than 3, P(greater than 3) $= \frac{2}{5}$.

334 Math Reasoning, page H224

COMMON ERRORS

Some students might have difficulty seeing more than one favorable outcome. For instance, if picking a green ball is the favorable outcome and there are 3 green balls, students may find only one favorable outcome because only one green ball is to be picked.

Remediation
For this error, demonstrate the multiplicity of outcomes by having students number each set of like outcomes. For example, the green balls could be numbered *G1*, *G2*, and *G3*. By numbering them in that way, students can see that P(*G*) is equivalent to P(*G1*, *G2*, or *G3*).

Assign Reteach Master, p. 97.

Find each probability in Exercises 1–32.

Toss a number cube once. The numbers on the 6 faces are 1, 2, 3, 4, 5, and 6.

1. P(5) $\frac{1}{6}$

2. P(odd) $\frac{1}{2}$

3. P(3 or 6) $\frac{1}{3}$

4. P(less than 5) $\frac{2}{3}$

5. P(not 1) $\frac{5}{6}$

6. P(9) 0

7. P(greater than 3) $\frac{1}{2}$

8. P(even or odd) 1

9. P(2, 3, or 4) $\frac{1}{2}$

Choose 1 marble without looking.

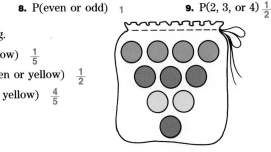

10. P(blue) $\frac{2}{5}$

11. P(yellow) $\frac{1}{5}$

12. P(not green) $\frac{7}{10}$

13. P(green or yellow) $\frac{1}{2}$

14. P(white) 0

15. P(not yellow) $\frac{4}{5}$

16. P(not red and not blue) $\frac{1}{2}$

Pick 1 card at random.

17. P(blue) $\frac{3}{10}$

18. P(A) $\frac{1}{5}$

19. P(green or red) $\frac{7}{10}$

20. P(F) $\frac{1}{10}$

21. P(vowel) $\frac{3}{10}$

22. P(A or B) $\frac{2}{5}$

23. P(not D) $\frac{4}{5}$

24. P(blue or C) $\frac{1}{2}$

Pick 1 card at random.

25. P(even) $\frac{1}{2}$

26. P(less than 4) $\frac{1}{4}$

27. P(a multiple of 4) $\frac{1}{4}$

28. P(a multiple of 2) $\frac{1}{2}$

29. P(a prime) $\frac{1}{2}$

30. P(a factor of 25) $\frac{1}{8}$

31. P(greater than 4) $\frac{5}{8}$

32. P(a factor of 24) $\frac{5}{8}$

Solve.

33. In a raffle for a 10-speed bike, 250 tickets are sold. What is the probability of winning if you buy 10 tickets? $\frac{1}{25}$

34. Sue collects old dimes. She has 6 dimes from 1941, 5 dimes from 1932, and 1 dime from 1930 in her pocket. If she picks 1 dime, what is the probability she will pick a dime older than 1932? $\frac{1}{12}$

Classwork/Homework, page H138

335

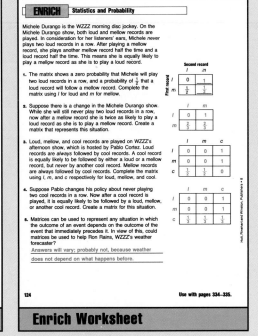
Exercise Analysis
1–32 Find the probability of an event
33–34 Skill applications

FOLLOW-UP ACTIVITIES

COMPUTER
Have the students write a program that will simulate the tossing of a coin and keep a tally of the way it lands.

```
(10 INPUT "HOW MANY TOSSES"; N
 20 FOR A = 1 TO N
 30 LET X = INT(RND(A)*2)
 40 IF X = 0 THEN LET T = T + 1
 50 IF X = 1 THEN LET H = H + 1
 60 NEXT A
 70 PRINT H; "HEADS AND";T;"TAILS"
 80 END)
```

PROBLEM SOLVING
Have students solve this problem.
- Quentin was the last person to buy tickets in a raffle. Before he bought a ticket, 375 tickets had been sold. Based on the purchase of 1 ticket, what are Quentin's chances of winning? ($\frac{1}{376}$) on 5 tickets? ($\frac{5}{380}$, or $\frac{1}{76}$) on 25 tickets? ($\frac{25}{400}$, or $\frac{1}{16}$) Would Quentin's chances be 100 times better if he bought 100 tickets instead of 1? If not, why not? (Not quite, because although Quentin would greatly increase his chances by buying so many tickets, he would also slightly decrease them by raising the number of possible outcomes by increasing the number of tickets.)

COMING UP
A declaration of independence

Objectives. To calculate the probability of independent events

Warm-Up

Have students calculate the probability of picking each colored pencil from a bag containing 2 blue, 4 red, 1 green, and 1 purple.

P(blue) $\left(\frac{2}{8}, \text{ or } \frac{1}{4}\right)$ P(green) $\left(\frac{1}{8}\right)$

P(red) $\left(\frac{4}{8}, \text{ or } \frac{1}{2}\right)$ P(yellow) $\left(\frac{0}{8}, \text{ or } 0\right)$

P(blue or red) $\left(\frac{6}{8}, \text{ or } \frac{3}{4}\right)$

P(blue, red, green, or purple) $\left(\frac{8}{8}, \text{ or } 1\right)$

GETTING STARTED

Pose the following situation.

- Fred plays on a 10-member softball team. On any given day, Fred may play any of the 10 positions.

Have students suggest ways to find the probability of Fred's playing catcher one day and pitcher the next. (One method is to calculate the number of possible outcomes. (100) Because there is only one favorable outcome, the probability is $\frac{1}{100}$.)

TEACHING THE LESSON

A. Emphasize the necesssity of returning the cap to the box. If the cap is not returned, there will be fewer possible outcomes, for the second pick would be dependent on the first pick.

B. Have students formulate a rule for finding the probability of three independent events. (P(A,B,C,) = P(A) · P(B) · P(C)) Then have them apply the rule to find the probability of a coin landing heads up 8 times in a row. ($\frac{1}{256}$, or $\left[\frac{1}{2}\right]^8$)

Checkpoint

The chart lists the common errors students make when finding the probability of independent events.

Correct Answers: 1a, 2b

Remediation

☐ For these errors, assign Reteach Master, p. 98.

Independent Events

A. Mr. Ramos has 2 caps that have a fish on them, 3 caps that have a boat on them, and 1 cap that has waves on it. Without looking, he picks a cap from the box. He puts it back. He picks another cap. What is the probability that he picks a cap that has a fish followed by a cap that has a boat?

Find the probability of each event. Since Mr. Ramos replaces the first hat, the outcome of the second event does not depend on the outcome of the first event. These are **independent events.**

P(fish) = $\frac{2}{6}$ or $\frac{1}{3}$

P(boat) = $\frac{3}{6}$ or $\frac{1}{2}$

If A and B are independent events, you can multiply to find the probability of event A and event B both occurring.

$P(A,B) = P(A) \cdot P(B)$

$P(\text{fish, boat}) = P(\text{fish}) \cdot P(\text{boat}) = \frac{1}{3} \cdot \frac{1}{2} = \frac{1}{6}$

So, the probability of picking a hat that has a fish followed by a hat that has a boat is $\frac{1}{6}$.

B. Toss a coin and then spin the spinner. What is the probability of tossing heads and spinning red?

P(heads) = $\frac{1}{2}$ P(red) = $\frac{2}{5}$

$P(\text{heads, red}) = P(\text{heads}) \cdot P(\text{red}) = \frac{1}{\underset{1}{2}} \cdot \frac{\overset{1}{2}}{5} = \frac{1}{5}$

The probability of tossing heads and spinning red is $\frac{1}{5}$.

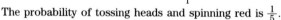
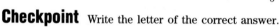

Checkpoint Write the letter of the correct answer.

Use the coin and spinner above to find the probability.

1. P(heads, green) = ■

   a. $\frac{1}{10}$ **b.** $\frac{7}{10}$ **c.** $\frac{1}{5}$ **d.** $\frac{1}{2}$

2. P(red or blue, tails) = ■

   a. $\frac{5}{8}$ **b.** $\frac{2}{5}$ **c.** $\frac{1}{2}$ **d.** $\frac{4}{5}$

336

Math Reasoning, page H224

COMMON ERRORS

Answer Choice	Type of Error
☐ 1b	Adds the probabilities instead of multipying them
☐ 1c, 1d, 2c, 2d	Writes the probability of only one event
☐ 2a	Inverts the probability of the second event

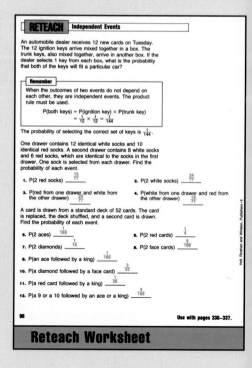

Reteach Worksheet

336

Find each probability in Exercises 1–27.

Toss a number cube 2 times. The numbers on the 6 faces are 1, 2, 3, 4, 5, and 6.

1. P(1,6) $\frac{1}{36}$ **2.** P(2,7) 0   **3.** P(even, odd) $\frac{1}{4}$

4. P(1 or 2, 3) $\frac{1}{18}$ **5.** P(not 6, 3) $\frac{5}{36}$ **6.** P(greater than 3, 1) $\frac{1}{12}$

Spin both spinners.

7. P(red, 2) $\frac{1}{8}$ **8.** P(green, 6) $\frac{3}{32}$

9. P(yellow, 2 or 4) $\frac{1}{16}$ **10.** P(red, 4 or 8) $\frac{1}{4}$

11. P(not red, even) $\frac{1}{2}$ **12.** P(not green, not 8) $\frac{15}{32}$

13. P(red, odd) 0   **14.** P(green or blue, 4 or 8) $\frac{3}{16}$

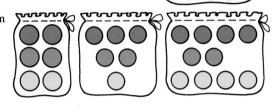

Pick 1 marble at random, replace it, and pick another marble at random.

15. P(blue, red) $\frac{1}{12}$ **16.** P(red, yellow) $\frac{1}{16}$

17. P(green, green) $\frac{1}{36}$ **18.** P(blue, not blue) $\frac{2}{9}$

19. P(red or green, blue) $\frac{5}{36}$

Pick 1 marble at random from each bag.

★**20.** P(red, blue, yellow) $\frac{2}{45}$

★**21.** P(blue, red, yellow) $\frac{1}{15}$

★**22.** P(three reds) $\frac{1}{15}$

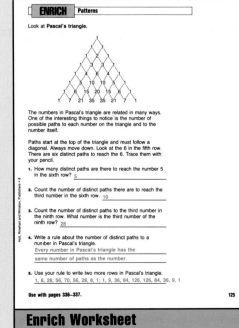

Solve.

23. Alim and Lina each choose at random a number from 1 to 4. What is the probability that they choose the same number? $\frac{1}{4}$

24. Kara tosses a coin 2 times. The first time she tosses heads. What is the probability that she tosses tails the second time? $\frac{1}{2}$

CHOOSING THE METHOD

Decide which method you would use to compute each exercise: mental math, calculator, or paper and pencil. Explain your answer.

1. 500×30 **2.** 49×51 **3.** 0.23×41.2 **4.** 6.10×20.5
   15,000   2,499   9.476   125.05

ASSIGNMENT GUIDE

Basic: 1–14, 23–24, CTM

Average: 7–19, 23–24, CTM

Extended: 7–24, CTM

Resources
Practice, p. 139   Class/Home, p. H139
Reteach, p. 98   Reasoning, p. H224
Enrich, p. 125

Exercise Analysis
1–19   Find the probability of two independent events
20–22   Find the probability of three independent events
23–24   Skill applications

Choosing the Method
Students must choose the most efficient method for computing the answers to these exercises. Have students explain their choices.

FOLLOW-UP ACTIVITIES

PROBLEM SOLVING
Have students use a spinner divided into quarters (1 blue, 1 red, 2 green) to help them solve the following problem.
● Thalia finds P(green) to be $\frac{2}{3}$. She says that she divided 2 favorable outcomes (the 2 green quarters) by 3 possible outcomes (blue, red, or green). Is Thalia correct? If not, what is P(green), and how did Thalia err? (No; $\frac{1}{2}$; Thalia erred by not realizing that just as the 2 green quarters count as 2 favorable outcomes, they also count as 2 possible outcomes.)

REINFORCEMENT
Have each student find the probability or write a formula for finding the probability.
● A six-sided number cube is tossed 3 times. What is the probability of side x being rolled every time? ($\frac{1}{216}$)
● The same cube is rolled n times. What is the probability of side x being rolled every time? ($[\frac{1}{6}]^n$) of side x or side y being rolled each time? ($[\frac{1}{3}]^n$)

COMING UP
Some notation that is not musical

337

Objectives: To select and use a proper notation

Warm-Up

Have students solve the following inequalities.

- $x + 5 > 14$ $(x > 9)$
- $3x - 12 \leq 45$ $(x \leq 19)$
- $(y \div 6) + 8 \geq 12$ $(y \geq 24)$
- $7y + 65 \leq 352$ $(y \leq 41)$

GETTING STARTED

Have students write the following information in the simplest form possible.

Game 1: Perez, 12 points; Smith, 10 points
Game 2: Perez, 18 points; Smith, 9 points
Game 3: Perez, 11 points; Smith, 16 points
Game 4: Perez, 8 points; Smith, 14 points
Game 5: Perez, 13 points; Smith, 15 points

Have students list the facts that can be found from these numbers; for example, who scored the most points in the five games; who scored the most points in a game more often; who had the highest average per game; and so on.

Ask students how they organized their chart. Have students come to the board to show their format. Tell the class that it is helpful to organize such information as simply as possible. Tell the class that in this lesson, they will learn a shorthand way of writing this type of information.

TEACHING THE LESSON

Students will encounter many situations in which effective formatting of information will be a crucial element in developing a problem-solving strategy. Different ways of organizing data can themselves suggest problem-solving strategies. Ordered pairs offer an important shorthand method of expressing two related qualities and emphasizing their relationship.

These problems require logical reasoning as well as notating skills. Tell the class that ordered pairs are used in the example to keep track of the amount of water in each container at each step.

Questions: Point out to students that the solution to the water problem consists of the ten combinations needed to result in the desired combination (5, 0).

Tools: The problem that students are most likely to experience will be confusion over the ordering of pairs. Students should be encouraged to write down what each element in the ordered pair represents (the key to their pairs). Students experiencing difficulties should be reminded to look at their key to the ordered pairs before writing each new pair.

| QUESTIONS | TOOLS | SOLUTIONS | CHECKS |

PROBLEM SOLVING
Selecting Notation

In the past, you have used symbols for variables to help solve a word problem. In mathematics, it is possible to use different kinds of notation or symbols to represent the facts of a problem and to assist you in finding the solution.

> The water boy for the football team needed exactly 5 liters of water to fill the water dispenser. If he had only a 7-liter container and a 3-liter container, how could he fill and empty these two containers so that he could return from the locker room with exactly 5 liters of water?

- You can order pairs to represent the water in each container at any given time.

For example, the ordered pair (5,2) means

$$\left(\begin{matrix} 5 \text{ liters of water} \\ \text{in 7-liter container} \end{matrix} \right) \text{ and } \left(\begin{matrix} 2 \text{ liters of water} \\ \text{in 3-liter container} \end{matrix} \right)$$

The sequence $(0,0) \rightarrow (0,3) \rightarrow (3,0)$ means that 3 liters of water were first poured into the 3-liter container. These 3 liters were then poured into the 7-liter container.

- Use the ordered pairs to represent the sequence of pourings needed to obtain exactly 5 liters.

$$(0,3) \rightarrow (3,0) \rightarrow (3,3) \rightarrow (6,0)$$
$$(6,3) \rightarrow (7,2) \rightarrow (0,2) \rightarrow (2,0)$$
$$(2,3) \rightarrow (5,0)$$

An ordered pair is one of many different kinds of notation that is helpful in solving problems.

Another type of notation which you have used earlier in this chapter is $P(G)$. On page 334, the notation $P(G)$ represents the probability of picking a green tennis ball.

Solutions: Students will have to compute quantities of coins and stamps of different denominations. The rules for order of operations may need review.

Checks: Students can check their ordered pairs against their key. For the coin and stamp problems, they can also total the value of coins or stamps represented by each pair.

Select the appropriate notation, and solve. Write the letter of the correct answer.

1. There are 5 members of a handball club. They decided that every member of the club should play every other member once. Use geometric notation to find out how many games had to be played? (HINT: use a dot to represent a member of the club and a line segment to represent a game played.)

a.   b.   c.   d.

2. How many combinations of 10¢ stamps and 2¢ stamps equal 46¢ worth of postage? Choose the notation that represents the correct combinations. The first number of each ordered pair represents 10¢ stamps, and the second number represents 2¢ stamps.

a. (5,1), (1,7), (3,4), (4,10), (2,13)
b. (4,3), (2,13), (2,8), (2,18)
c. (1,20), (2,10), (1,18)
d. (4,3), (3,8), (2,13), (1,18)

Solve. Use notation where appropriate.

3. While hiking, 2 friends decide to separate. They have a water jug that contains 6 pints of water. They also have a 4-pint canteen and a 1-pint canteen. How can 2 friends divide the water evenly between themselves? Use ordered pairs.
(6,0,0) → (2,4,0) → (2,3,1) → (3,3,0)

4. Janine sells perfume at a department store. She earns $3 per hour plus $0.50 commission on every bottle she sells. One day, she works from 10:00 A.M. to 3:00 P.M. and sells 14 bottles of perfume. How much did she earn that day? $22

5. Jack Griffin pays for $3.75 worth of bandages with a $5 bill. How many combinations of dimes and nickels might Jack receive in change?
12 combinations
(1,23); (2,21); (3,19); (4,17); (5,15); (6,13); (7,11); (8,9); (9,7); (10,5); (11,3); (12,1)

Classwork/Homework, page H140

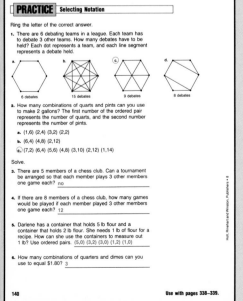
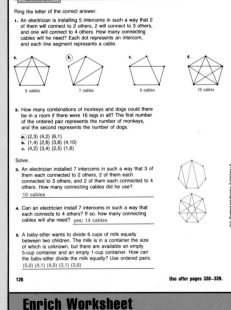
ASSIGNMENT GUIDE

Basic: 1–3
Average: 2–4
Extended: 2–3, 5

Resources
Practice, p. 140   Class/Home, p. H140
Enrich, p. 126

Exercise Analysis
1–2 Choose the letter of the correct notation
3–5 Skill applications

FOLLOW-UP ACTIVITIES

PROBLEM SOLVING
Have students solve the following problems involving ordered triples.

- Edward left the house with $8.00. He went to the store, spent some money, and came home with one or more $1.00 bills. Use ordered triples to show how much money Edward might have had (or spent) at each step in his trip. [(8-1-7), (8-2-6), (8-3-5), (8-5-3), (8-6-2), and so on.]

- Tina, Lily, and Sally were buying a present for their mother's birthday. The present cost $13.00. Tina and Sally agreed that they would spend the same amount. Use ordered triples to show the different possible whole-dollar amounts that the girls might pay. [(1-11-1), (2-9-2), (3-7-3), (4-5-4), (5-3-5), (6-1-6)]

CALCULATOR
Many calculators have a memory in which you can store, add, and subtract numbers. This memory function is especially useful in solving equations with many steps; for example, to solve (3 × 23) + (944 × 0.35), press 3 × 23 = M+ or M+= (whichever your calculator has), 944 × 0.35 = M+ or M+=. Then press MR or RM to recall the total in the memory.

The following are ordered quadruples, giving the number of pennies, nickels, dimes, and quarters that several people have. Have students use the calculator to find the amount of money each person has.
- Eva (7,4,8,3) ($1.82)
- Rick (12,3,6,7) ($2.62)
- Pat (3,13,5,5) ($2.43)
- Louise (1,9,4,13) ($4.11)
- Anthony (7,14,11,15) ($5.62)
- Martha (17,11,19,14) ($6.12)

COMING UP
That depends!

Objective. To calculate the probability of dependent events

Warm-Up
Have students find each product.

$\frac{7}{9} \cdot \frac{3}{8} \left(\frac{7}{24}\right)$ $\qquad$ $\frac{2}{7} \cdot \frac{5}{6} \left(\frac{5}{21}\right)$

$\frac{8}{11} \cdot \frac{1}{10} \left(\frac{4}{55}\right)$ $\qquad$ $\frac{5}{6} \cdot \frac{2}{5} \left(\frac{1}{3}\right)$

$\frac{5}{8} \cdot \frac{4}{7} \left(\frac{5}{14}\right)$ $\qquad$ $\frac{1}{9} \cdot \frac{7}{8} \left(\frac{7}{72}\right)$

GETTING STARTED

Materials: 5 clear and 5 opaque marbles

Have a volunteer pick a marble out of a bag, replace it, and then pick out another. Ask: What is the probability that both marbles will be clear? ($\frac{1}{4}$)

Repeat the experiment to illustrate the difference between replacing and not replacing items. Do not replace the first marble. Ask: Has P(clear, then clear) changed? (yes) How could you find the new probability? (Consider the second pick a separate event. Because P(A,B) = P(A) · P(B), P(clear, then clear) = $\frac{1}{2}$ · P(second clear). If a clear marble had been removed, then P(second clear) would have dropped to $\frac{4}{9}$. So, P(clear, then clear) = $\frac{2}{9}$.)

TEACHING THE LESSON

A. Emphasize the fact that when calculating the probability of a second event that is dependent on the first, it is necessary to assume that the outcome of the first event is favorable.

B. Extend the lesson to 3 events.
- P(green, then yellow, then red) ($\frac{1}{60}$)
- P(yellow, then green, then red) ($\frac{1}{60}$)
- P(green, then green, then red) ($\frac{1}{20}$)

Checkpoint
The chart lists the common errors students make when finding the probability of dependent events.

Correct Answers: 1b, 2d

Remediation
■ For this error, have students rewrite each P(A,B) as the product of P(A) and P(B) before solving.

□ For this error, assign Reteach Master, p. 99.

△ For this error, refer students to the examples on p. 138.

Dependent Events

A. Mrs. Waltham went to watch sailboat races with friends. She brought 2 tuna sandwiches and 5 cheese sandwiches in a picnic basket. Mrs. Waltham picked a sandwich at random and took it from the basket. Her friend Kim picked a sandwich at random from the basket. What is the probability they both picked tuna sandwiches?

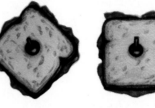

These two events are **dependent events.** The outcome of the first choice affects the probabilities of the outcomes of the second choice because the first sandwich was not replaced.

Find the probability of each event.

P(tuna) = $\frac{2}{7}$ $\qquad$ P(tuna after tuna) = $\frac{1}{6}$ ← There is 1 tuna sandwich left.
$\qquad$ ← There are 6 sandwiches left.

P(tuna, then tuna) = P(tuna) · P(tuna after tuna) = $\frac{\overset{1}{\cancel{2}}}{7} \cdot \frac{1}{\underset{3}{\cancel{6}}} = \frac{1}{21}$

The probability that they both picked tuna sandwiches is $\frac{1}{21}$.

B. Pick a marble from the bag without looking. Do not replace it. Pick another marble. What is the probability of picking a red and then a green marble?

P(red) = $\frac{3}{10}$ $\qquad$ P(green after red) = $\frac{4}{9}$

P(red, then green) = P(red) · P(green after red) = $\frac{\overset{1}{\cancel{3}}}{\underset{5}{\cancel{10}}} \cdot \frac{\overset{2}{\cancel{4}}}{\underset{3}{\cancel{9}}} = \frac{2}{15}$

Checkpoint Write the letter of the correct answer.

Refer to the bag of marbles above.

1. P(red, then blue) = ▦

a. $\frac{3}{10}$ ⓑ. $\frac{1}{15}$ c. $\frac{2}{9}$ d. $\frac{2}{45}$

2. P(blue, then blue) = ▦

a. $\frac{1}{9}$ b. $\frac{1}{15}$ c. $\frac{1}{5}$ ⓓ. $\frac{1}{45}$

340

COMMON ERRORS

Answer Choice	Type of Error
■ 1a, 1c, 2a, 2c	Writes the probability of only one event
△ 1d	Makes an error in computation
□ 2b	Fails to reduce the numerator of the probability of the second event

---

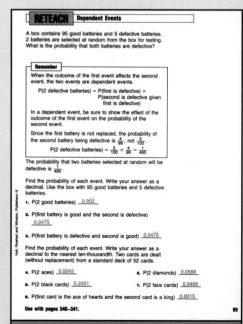

A box contains 95 good batteries and 5 defective batteries. 2 batteries are selected at random from the box for testing. What is the probability that both batteries are defective?

Remember
When the outcome of the first event affects the second event, the two events are dependent events.

P(2 defective batteries) = P(first is defective) × P(second is defective given first is defective)

In a dependent event, be sure to show the effect of the outcome of the first event on the probability of the second event.

Since the first battery is not replaced, the probability of the second battery being defective is $\frac{4}{99}$, not $\frac{5}{100}$.

P(2 defective batteries) = $\frac{5}{100} \times \frac{4}{99} = \frac{1}{495}$

The probability that two batteries selected at random will be defective is $\frac{1}{495}$.

Find the probability of each event. Write your answer as a decimal. Use the box with 95 good batteries and 5 defective batteries.

1. P(2 good batteries) _0.902_

2. P(first battery is good and the second is defective) _0.0479_

3. P(first battery is defective and second is good) _0.0479_

Find the probability of each event. Write your answer as a decimal to the nearest ten-thousandth. Two cards are dealt (without replacement) from a standard deck of 52 cards.

4. P(2 aces) _0.0045_ **5.** P(2 diamonds) _0.0588_

6. P(2 black cards) _0.2451_ **7.** P(2 face cards) _0.0498_

8. P(first card is the ace of hearts and the second card is a king) _0.0015_

Use with pages 340–341.

99

Reteach Worksheet

Find each probability in Exercises 1–22. Assume that the marbles and cards are picked at random.

Pick a marble. Do not replace it. Pick a second marble.

1. P(green, then red) $\frac{1}{5}$ 2. P(red, then blue) $\frac{1}{15}$

3. P(green, then blue) $\frac{1}{10}$ 4. P(blue, then green) $\frac{1}{10}$

5. P(not green, then green) $\frac{3}{10}$ 6. P(yellow, then red) 0

7. P(red, then red) $\frac{1}{15}$ 8. P(not blue, then blue) $\frac{1}{6}$

Pick a marble. Do not replace it. Pick a second marble.

9. P(blue, then red) $\frac{2}{9}$ 10. P(red, then green) $\frac{2}{45}$

11. P(blue, then green) $\frac{1}{18}$ 12. P(not blue, then blue) $\frac{5}{18}$

13. P(red, then red) $\frac{2}{15}$ 14. P(blue, then blue) $\frac{2}{9}$

Pick a card. Do not replace it. Pick a second card.

15. P(red 1, then blue 1) $\frac{1}{56}$ 16. P(2, then 4) $\frac{1}{14}$

17. P(red, then blue) $\frac{2}{7}$ 18. P(3, then red 4) $\frac{1}{28}$

19. P(red or blue, then 3) $\frac{2}{7}$ 20. P(not 2, then not 3) $\frac{15}{28}$

★21. P(1 or 3, then 2 or 4) ★22. P(not odd, then 3) $\frac{2}{7}$
$\frac{2}{7}$

CHALLENGE

There were 9 boxes in a grab bag, 5 red and 4 green. All the boxes felt the same. There were calculators in 4 of the red boxes and in 2 of the green boxes. Sarah reached in and chose a box without looking.

What is each probability?

1. Sarah chose a red box. $\frac{5}{9}$

2. Sarah chose a green box. $\frac{4}{9}$

3. Sarah chose a box containing a calculator. $\frac{2}{3}$

4. Sarah chose a box containing a calculator if she chose a green box. $\frac{1}{2}$

5. Sarah chose a box containing a calculator if she chose a red box. $\frac{4}{5}$

6. Sarah chose a red box if the box she chose contained a calculator. $\frac{2}{3}$

Classwork/Homework, page H141

341

ASSIGNMENT GUIDE

Basic: 1–14, Chlg 1–2

Average: 9–20, Chlg 1–4

Extended: 9–22, Chlg

Resources
Practice, p. 141   Class/Home, p. H141
Reteach, p. 99
Enrich, p. 127

Exercise Analysis
1–22   Find the probability of dependent events

Challenge
If students encounter difficulty, suggest that they sketch each grab bag and its contents.

FOLLOW-UP ACTIVITIES

PROBLEM SOLVING
When Tina went to New York City, she went to the Museum of Modern Art, the Solomon R. Guggenheim Museum, the Whitney Museum of American Art, and the Metropolitan Museum of Art, in that order. Miles plans on visiting the same museums when he goes to New York. What is the probability that he will go to them in the exact same order? ($\frac{1}{24}$)

PROBLEM SOLVING
Pose the following situation.
- Scott plays on an 8-member basketball team. His coach's system works in this way: The 5-player lineup is divided into 4 positions: point guard (PG), shooting guard (SG), center (C), and forward (F). There are 2 forwards.

Have students write probability word problems about Scott's team. Then have them exchange papers, solve one another's problems, and return the papers to be checked.

COMING UP
What will be?

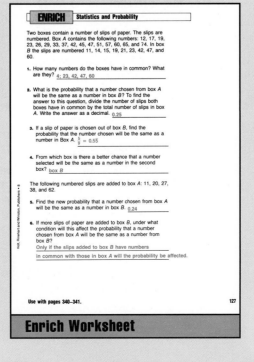

Objective: To explore mathematical prediction

Warm-Up

Have students find each product mentally.

$\frac{2}{5} \cdot 25$ (10) $\frac{1}{12} \cdot 144$ (12)

$\frac{8}{9} \cdot 729$ (648) $\frac{7}{8} \cdot 64$ (56)

$\frac{3}{8} \cdot 440$ (165) $\frac{5}{7} \cdot 196$ (140)

GETTING STARTED

Materials: number cube per pair of students

Have students work in pairs. Each student will choose a digit between 1 and 6, will roll the number cube 24 times, and will record the number of times the chosen digit turned up in 24 rolls. Ask students which member of the pair obtained his or her digit more often and whether this means that the digit is more likely to turn up in subsequent rolls. (no) Ask what the probability is of turning up any one digit in 1 roll. ($\frac{1}{6}$) Then ask students to predict the number of times a 3 would turn up in 24 rolls based on this probability. (4)

TEACHING THE LESSON

Materials: 50–100 pennies per group of 4 students

Because of the depth of the conceptual development involved, this lesson may be addressed in several periods. Have students work through the developmental parts of this lesson in groups of four and have a class discussion for Thinking as a Team.

A. Lead students to realize that the pennies in their samples can be placed in categories according to their minting dates. Review with them the making of bar graphs and histograms, reminding them to choose an appropriate interval and to label each axis. Question 4 under Working as a Team may warrant class discussion. The mode (or possibly the median) might be the most appropriate measure of central tendency for these data. Question 2 in the Thinking as a Team section can be answered in the form of a percent or a fraction.

For question 7, guide students to realize that the possibility that they might not have in their sample even one penny that was minted more than 20 years ago does *not* make the probability zero.

Point out that because the class predictions are based on a larger sample

---

Prediction

A. In this lesson your team will conduct an experiment by gathering sample data and making a prediction.

Working as a Team

1. Gather a sample of between 50 and 100 pennies.

2. Describe your sample to the class. How can pennies be categorized? By date of minting, by mass, and so on.

3. Use a bar graph or a histogram to display the minting dates of the coins in your sample.
Check students' graphs.

4. Before you choose a penny at random, about how old would you expect it to be? Would you use the mean, the median, or the mode of your sample to help you make this prediction? Answers will vary.

Thinking as a Team

Use your sample of pennies to make the predictions:
Check students' answers.

1. What percent of pennies now in circulation were minted before 1975?

2. What is the probability that a penny now in circulation was minted more than 20 years ago?

3. Of those pennies now in circulation, in what year were more minted than in any other?

4. About 50% of the pennies now in circulation were minted prior to what year?

Now share your team's sample data with the class. Using the class data, find or predict:

5. The total number of pennies sampled

6. The class distribution of minting dates

7. The probability that a penny now in circulation was minted more than 20 years ago.

8. The percent of pennies in circulation that were minted before 1975. Is this different from your team's prediction? Why? A different sample is used.

---

space they are likely to be more accurate than those based on the team samples. For question 10, point out that a double-bar graph (or a pair of circle graphs) that shows percents of pennies minted each year would be an appropriate device for comparing class-based and team-based data. Students can answer question 11 by checking an almanac or contacting the Mint or the Treasury Department.

B. For section B, students should figure out that there are 17,576 possible 3-letter sequences. This is *not* a permutation problem because each of the 26 letters can be used more than once ($26 \times 26 \times 26 = 17,576$). The time required to list these sequences would prove to be prohibitive. (As a challenge

(*Continued on p. 343.*)

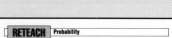

RETEACH | Probability

A poll of voters for class president showed that out of 120 respondents, 40 voted for James. If a student who did not participate in the poll is selected at random, what is the probability that the student will have voted for James?

Remember
A prediction based on empirical probability does not require you to know the total number of possible outcomes.

$P(\text{vote for James}) = \frac{40}{120} = 0.33 = 33\%.$

The probability that a student selected at random will have voted for James is 33%.

Maria conducted polls that asked students their opinions on several issues about the school. What is the probability that a student, chosen at random, will favor the issue? Write your answer as a percent.

Issue	Votes	Favor Issue	Probability
1.	100	50	50%
2.	105	21	20%
3.	100	60	60%
4.	150	15	10%
5.	108	27	25%
6.	110	33	30%
7.	150	6	4%
8.	160	160	100%

The poll for class vice-president shows that 32 voters favor Linda, 68 favor Mary, and 60 favor Wanda. The poll has a total of 160 respondents. If a student is chosen at random, find these probabilities. Write your answer as a percent.

9. P(student favors Linda) 20%   10. P(student favors Mary) 42.5%

11. P(student favors Wanda) 37.5%

100   Use with pages 342–343.

Reteach Worksheet

9. Do you think that your team's predictions are likely to be more or less accurate than the class-based predictions? Why?

Team predictions are likely to be less accurate because they are based on a smaller sample space.

10. Place the class data on minting dates on a double-bar graph to compare it to your team's sample data. How can you use a graph to show clearly the similarities of or the differences between these two groups of data? Compare percents or fractions.

11. How can you find out how many coins are actually minted each year?

Check an almanac or contact the Treasury Department.

B. The license plate on Ceanne's new car reads 586 BUG. If every license plate contains 3 letters and 3 digits, what do you think is the probability that any license plate chosen at random will spell a 3-letter word in the English language?

Thinking as a Team

1. Could you list all possible 3-letter sequences that could appear on license plates? How would you do it? The 17,576 possible sequences would make this difficult, but perhaps a computer could do it quickly.

2. Should your list include sequences in which the same letter appears twice? yes

3. How could you gather data from an experiment to make a prediction? Pick at random sequences of 3 letters and tally the number of words created.

4. What are the advantages of making a list? What are the advantages of doing an experiment?

5. How would you decide what method to use? Check students' answers.

6. Can you think of another way to solve the problem?

Classwork/Homework, page H142

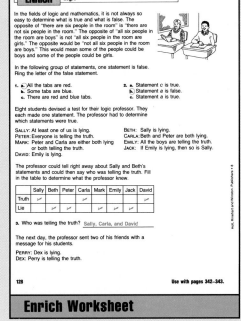

343

ASSIGNMENT GUIDE

Basic: p. 342, p. 343

Average: p. 342, p. 343

Extended: p. 342, p. 343

Resources
Practice, p. 142 Class/Home, p. H142
Reteach, p. 100
Enrich, p. 128

you might ask students to write a computer program that could create such a list.) You may want to discuss whether such a list could be made smaller by ruling out certain letter combinations (e.g., no word can contain 3 consonants) and whether those rules might make it practical to create a list. Discuss whether a partial list would give a reliable answer concerning the probability of a word appearing. An experiment involving a smaller collection of 3-letter sequences picked at random is another approach. Discuss how reliable the results would be. Ask students how they could improve the reliabilities of their empirical probabilities (probabilities found through observation). (Increase the size of the sample space.) Discuss whether finding the solution to a simpler problem might help (e.g., finding the probability that a 2-letter sequence forms a word).

FOLLOW-UP ACTIVITIES

PROBLEM SOLVING
Materials: red and black marbles, bags

Form the class into groups, and give each group a bag containing 3 black and 2 red marbles. Have a member of each group pick out a marble, replace it, and then pick out two more and not replace them.

Have students calculate the probability that all three marbles will be black. ($\frac{9}{50}$) Ask: If this experiment were repeated 50 times, how many times could that result be expected? (9) Have students repeat the experiment 50 times and compare the results with the expectation.

COMING UP
Is there an interpreter in the house?

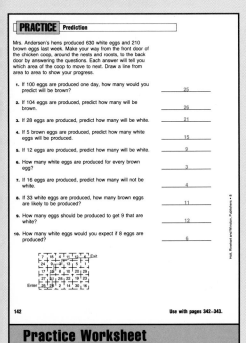

Practice Worksheet

Enrich Worksheet

343

Objective: To correctly interpret information from graphs

Warm-Up

Have students write >, < or = for each ●.
- ● 12 mm ● 6 cm (<)
- ● 0.78 km ● 103 m (>)
- ● 0.7 L ● 700 mL (=)
- ● 1,500 cm ● 1.5 km (<)
- ● 6.3 g ● 63 kg (<)
- ● 11,000 m ● 1.1 km (>)

GETTING STARTED

Present students with the following puzzle. There are 2 rows of 3 students in a class. The first row consists of Reggie, Janet, and Robert. Janet is 5 ft 0 in. tall. There is a 6-in. difference between her height and Reggie's. Robert, at 5 ft 3 in., is midway between Janet and Reggie in height. The second row consists of Zoe, Pat, and Michael. There is a 9-in. difference between the tallest and shortest student in this row. Pat, at 5 ft 0 in., is between Zoe and Michael in height. Zoe is 2 in. shorter. Who is the tallest student in the two rows? (Michael)

TEACHING THE LESSON

The emphasis in this lesson is on correctly reading the scales on a graph. This is especially important when comparing two graphs. Students must learn that the lines (or bars, and so on) found on a graph merely show the data listed on the scale. When one compares graphs, one is actually comparing the numbers indicated on each graph's scale.

Guide students through this introductory problem, pointing out that the scale on one graph is shown in increments of 20 yards, while the scale of the other is shown in increments of 50 yards. This lesson lends itself to small group work.

Questions: Point out to students that most of the questions in the lesson have two-part answers; for example, the name of the school that scored the most runs, and the number of runs it scored. This forces students to do more than just a quick visual comparison and helps eliminate the errors they are likely to make.

Tools: Suggest that before students start to answer the questions relating to a pair of graphs, they first find the range of information on each graph. By seeing both the highest and the lowest values for each graph beforehand, students should have a better idea of just how the two graphs relate to each other. Students should also be cautioned to check the horizontal scales when comparing graphs in order to correctly interpret them.

| QUESTIONS | TOOLS | SOLUTIONS | CHECKS |

PROBLEM SOLVING
Interpreting a Graph

Graphs are helpful tools for showing and comparing information. Sometimes, however, the comparison can be misleading; so, you must be careful to correctly interpret the given information.

These graphs show the total yardage gained by the football teams of 2 colleges in each of the first 6 games of the season.

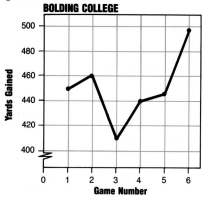

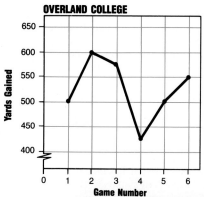

Use the information shown on the graphs to answer the question.

Which school gained the greater number of yards in one game?

At first glance, it may seem that Bolding gained more, during the sixth game. But the vertical axis of the left graph is shown in steps of 20 yards, whereas that of the right graph is shown in steps of 50 yards. The greatest number of yards gained by Bolding, in the sixth game, is 490 yards. In the second game, Overland gained 600 yards.

The greater number of yards gained in one game was achieved by Overland College, in the second game.

Solutions: There is no computation involved in this lesson.

Checks: As a check, students might sketch a double-line graph of their own with information from both graphs on it. This should make comparisons between the information fairly easy.

Use the graphs on page 344 to answer these questions.

1. How many yards did Bolding College gain in the second game? 460 yards

2. How many yards did Overland College gain in the first game? 500 yards

3. Which college gained the least number of yards in a single game, how many yards were gained, and in which game?
Bolding College; 410 yards; the third game

The graphs below represent the number of runs scored in each game of a six-game series by two high schools.

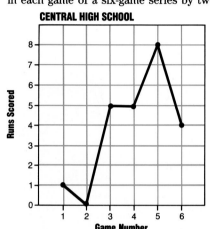

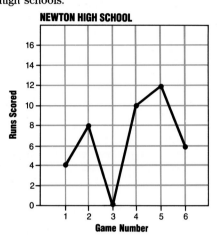

4. Which school had the greater number of runs in one game, and how many runs was it? Newton High; 12 runs

5. Which school scored the fewer number of runs in the 6-game series, and how many runs did it score?
Central High; 23 runs

6. How many runs did each school score in the fourth game? Central High: 5 runs; Newton High: 10 runs

7. Which school scored the same number of runs in two consecutive games, how many runs were scored, and in which games? Central High; 5 runs; third and fourth games

Classwork/Homework, pages H143–H144

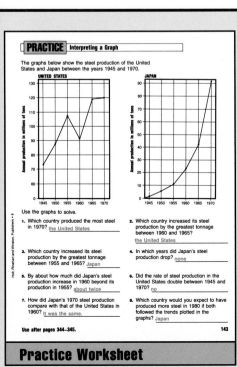

PRACTICE Interpreting a Graph

The graphs below show the steel production of the United States and Japan between the years 1945 and 1970.

UNITED STATES JAPAN

Use the graphs to solve.

1. Which country produced the most steel in 1970? the United States

2. Which country increased its steel production by the greatest tonnage between 1960 and 1965? the United States

3. Which country increased its steel production by the greatest tonnage between 1955 and 1965? Japan

4. In which years did Japan's steel production drop? none

5. By about how much did Japan's steel production increase by 1960 beyond its production in 1955? about twice

6. Did the rate of steel production in the United States double between 1945 and 1970? no

7. How did Japan's 1970 steel production compare with that of the United States in 1960? it was the same.

Use after pages 344–345. 143

Practice Worksheet

PRACTICE Interpreting a Graph

Dobbs Industries started two new companies, Waveform, Inc., and Micromonitor, Inc. Dobbs invested the same amount of money in each company, but did not invest any further amounts after the two companies started operations in January 1979. The graphs below show the performance of each company from 1979 to 1984.

WAVEFORM, INC. MICROMONITOR, INC.

- - - - Total Income
——— Total Expenses

1. Which company made the most profit in 1983? Waveform

2. In which year did both companies make the same amount of profit? 1981

3. Which company performed better between the years 1979 and 1981? Micromonitor

4. If Dobbs Industries had invested $50,000 in each company, in which year would the accumulated profits of Waveform, Inc., have been enough to repay Dobbs' investment in Waveform? 1983

5. In which year could Micromonitor, Inc., repay Dobbs' investment in Micromonitor? 1981

6. If Dobbs Industries expected yearly interest of 5% on its investment, in which year could Micromonitor repay Dobbs Industries? 1983

144 Use after pages 344–345.

Practice Worksheet

Holt, Rinehart and Winston, Publishers • 8

ASSIGNMENT GUIDE

Basic:	1–3
Average:	2–5
Extended:	3–7

Resources
Practice, pp. 143–4   Class/Home, pp. H143–4

Exercise Analysis
1–7   Interpret correctly information from a pair of graphs

FOLLOW-UP ACTIVITIES

 **PROBLEM SOLVING**
Tell students that the six baseball games listed on the graphs on page 345 were all the games played in one season between Central High School and its crosstown rival, Newton High School. Ask students to make a table that lists the team that won each game. Then tell them that the six football games listed in the graphs on page 344 were all between Bolding and Overland Colleges. Tell them that in each game, the team that gained more yards won the game. Ask them to make a table that lists the winner of each game.

PROBLEM SOLVING
Copy the information below onto the chalkboard. Ask students to graph on a separate graph the number of goals each team scored. Have them use a different interval for the vertical scale of each graph so that the graphs look the same when they are placed side by side (except for the vertical scales).

Number of Goals Scored By the Hodges High School and Dant High School Hockey Teams During the 1985–86 Season

Game	Goals	
	Hodges	*Dant*
1	1	2
2	0	0
3	3	6
4	2	4
5	4	8
6	0	0
7	1	2
8	0	0
9	4	8
10	6	12

COMING UP
Making an impression

Objective: To find the mean of a set of numbers

Warm-Up

Form the class into two teams. Have them solve these exercises mentally. The student who answers first wins a point for his or her team. An incorrect answer gives a point to the other team.

2 + 3 + 5 + 4 = (14)
4 + 2 + 7 + 1 = (14)
7 + 5 + 1 + 4 = (17)
4 + 5 + 7 + 9 = (25)
6 + 6 + 3 + 6 = (21)
5 + 2 + 4 + 4 = (15)
7 + 4 + 8 + 3 = (22)
6 + 1 + 5 + 2 = (14)

GETTING STARTED

Have students imagine a baseball pitcher in the major league who wins 18 games in his first season and 20 games in his second season. What is his average number of wins per season? (19)

Have students imagine a baseball player who hits 26 home runs in his first season and 30 in his second season. What is his average number of home runs per season? (28)

Have students imagine a baseball player who steals 30 bases in his first season and 40 in his second season. What is his average number of stolen bases per season? (35)

TEACHING THE LESSON

Have students work the example problem. Point out that the questions on baseball statistics involved the same kind of calculation on a simpler level.

Before doing these problems, have students use the benchmarks to calculate answers to the questions on baseball statistics.

Students should estimate the answer before using their calculators. They should also note the partial sum to be sure they are adding correctly.

Point out to students that it is easy to make an error when finding an average on a calculator because of the large number of computations involved. Using a benchmark is advantageous because it keeps the sum small, and thus errors in entering digits can more easily be detected.

CALCULATOR

To find the mean of these test scores, you could add them on a calculator and divide by the total number of scores.

Scores: 20, 25, 26, 29, 26, 24

Press: [2][0][+][2][5][+][2][6][+][2][9][+][2][6][+][2][4][÷][6][=]

The mean is 25. Another way to find the mean is to pick a number less than or equal to the least number as a "benchmark." Suppose 20 is chosen as the benchmark. Add the differences between each number and the benchmark. Then find the mean of the differences.

Scores: 20, 25, 26, 29, 26, 24

difference from 20: 0, 5, 6, 9, 6, 4

Press: [0][+][5][+][6][+][9][+][6][+][4][÷][6][=]

The mean of the differences is 5. Add it to the benchmark, 20. You get 25. The advantage of this method is that you have smaller numbers to enter and can check the total on the screen more easily as you go.

Find the mean of these numbers, using benchmarks. Find the differences mentally.

1. Test scores of 52, 54, 56, 50, 58; use 50 as the benchmark.   54

2. Prices of $100, $120, $110, $115, $130; use $100 as the benchmark. $115

3. Scores of 38, 35, 32, 33, 31, 39, 40, 41   36.125

4. Heights of 55 in., 56 in., 57 in., 58 in.   56.5 in.

5. Weights of 150 lb, 160 lb, 152 lb, 161 lb, 155 lb, 158 lb   156 lb

346

GROUP PROJECT

Rules of the Game

The problem: Your class is in charge of setting up a sports competition. All of you are tired of the same old sports. You decide to come up with a new kind of competition. How will you agree on which events to include and what the rules will be? Referring to the facts and the questions below, plan the competition, and write a book of rules.

Key Facts

- Many sports consist of a combination of events. The decathlon, for instance, features ten events, including races, jumping, and javelin throwing. The modern pentathlon consists of horseback riding, swimming, running, fencing, and marksmanship.

- Recently developed sports include the triathlon, which consists of swimming, cycling, and running.

- Games in which goals are scored include field hockey, ice hockey, soccer, and polo, which is played on horseback.

- Scoring differs from sport to sport, and winners may be decided on the basis of points, fastest times, highest and farthest marks, or a combination of these methods.

Key Questions

- Will players compete individually or in teams?

- How many events will there be?

- Will you need a field or other special area? If so, what will be its dimensions? How will you indicate boundary lines or goal lines?

- How will the events be scored?

347

Objectives: To plan a sports competition; to write rules

USING THE PAGE

Discuss the Key Facts and Key Questions with the class. Then separate students into groups of four or five. Tell them to come up with a new kind of sports competition by inventing new sports or modifying the rules of existing sports to make them different. Each group should plan one new event and write the rules for playing that event, including methods of scoring and the criteria for winning—how many games win an event, or, if it is a multiple event such as the triathlon, how the winner of the entire competition is decided from the results of the individual events. Then each group should present its new event to the class. The class should critique each event, and each group should then modify the rules or criteria for winning as a result of the class discussion.

To extend this cooperative learning activity, have students write a program of events to be distributed at the competition. Include dates, locations, times of events, and names of players or teams on the program.

Purpose: The Chapter Test helps to assess students' understanding of the concepts and skills presented in this chapter.

The chart below is designed to help you review the test items by correlating them with the testing objectives that appear in the Chapter Overview.

Item	Objectives
1	A
2–5	B
6	E
7	C
8	D
9–12	F
13–15	G
16–19	H
20–22	I
23	J
24–25	K

Calculator

You may wish to have students use calculators for the problem-solving portions of the test.

Resources

If you prefer to use this Chapter Test as a review exercise, additional testing materials are available in the Teacher's Resource Book.

CHAPTER TEST

TY COBB'S SEASON
BATTING AVERAGES

1921	0.389
1922	0.401
1923	0.340
1924	0.338
1925	0.378

FREQUENCY TABLE

Interval	Frequency	Relative Frequency
0.330–0.349	2	40%
0.350–0.369	—	——
0.370–0.389	2	40%
0.390–0.409	1	20%

Use Ty Cobb's season batting averages to solve Exercises 1–5. (pages 314–317)

1. Make a frequency table. Start with 0.330 and use intervals of 0.020. See table above.

2. What is the range of these batting averages? 0.063

3. What is the median? 0.378

4. What is the mean? 0.369

5. Is there a mode? no

6. A baseball player is practicing hitting. Each time at bat there are two possible outcomes: to get a hit (H), or to miss the ball (M). Draw a tree diagram to show the possible outcomes for four times at bat. How many possible outcomes are there? (pages 328–329) 16 possible outcomes

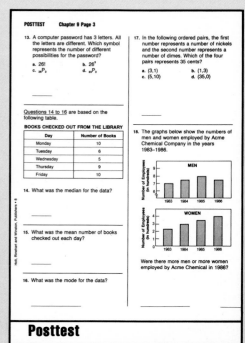

7. A team is holding elections. There are 5 members running for three positions: manager, captain, and treasurer. In how many ways can the three positions be filled? (pages 330–333) $5 \cdot 4 \cdot 3 = 60$

8. There are 9 members on the school basketball team. How many different combinations of 5 can be formed from the 9 members? (pages 330–333) 126

If a number cube is tossed, what is the probability that the number on the cube will be (pages 334–335)

9. even? $\frac{1}{2}$

10. odd? $\frac{1}{2}$

11. less than 3? $\frac{1}{3}$

12. 5? $\frac{1}{6}$

348

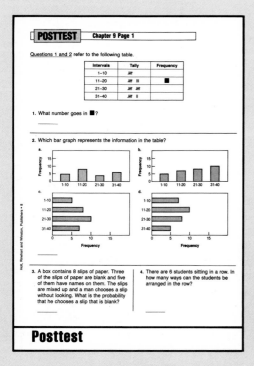

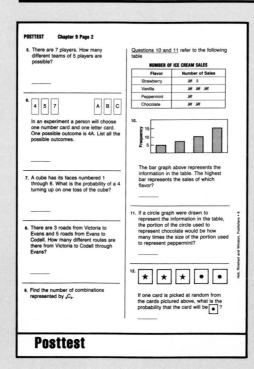

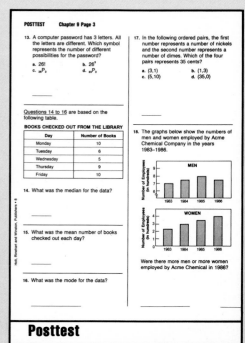

A number cube is tossed twice. Find the probability. (pages 336–337)

13. P(two 3's) $\frac{1}{36}$ **14.** P(even, odd) $\frac{1}{4}$ **15.** P(less than 3, 6) $\frac{1}{18}$

Pick a card. Do not replace it. Pick a second card. Find each probability. (pages 340–341)

16. P(blue, then green) $\frac{1}{3}$

17. P(2, then 4) $\frac{1}{12}$

18. P(1 or 4, then 2 or 3) $\frac{1}{3}$

19. P(4, then blue) $\frac{1}{6}$

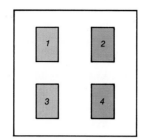

You are going to toss a number cube 300 times. Predict the number of times the outcome will be (pages 342–343)

20. 6. 50 **21.** even. 150 **22.** less than 3. 100

23. There are 4 members on the chess team. They decide that every member should play every other member once. Use geometric notation to find out how many games have to be played. (pages 338–339) 6 games

Woodville has a referendum on the ballot for the upcoming election. A newspaper conducted a poll on the referendum. The poll used a sample of 450 voters of a voting population of 2,500 people. The results of the poll are listed below. (pages 326–327)

Yes	279
No	117
Undecided	54

24. What percent of Woodville's voting population was included in the newspaper poll? 18%

25. What percent of voters in the sample favored the referendum? 62%

349

For students who have difficulty with written tests, this test can be given orally.

You may wish to test students, orally or in writing, to see if they can explain the steps used in solving selected items. The following table summarizes the procedures for solving key test items.

Ex. 2–5

Finding the range, median, mean, and mode for a set of data

The *range* is the difference between the greatest and the least number in a set of data.

The *median* is the middle number in a set of data when the numbers are listed in order. When there are two middle numbers, add the two middle numbers and divide by 2 to find the median.

The *mean* is the sum of the numbers in a set of data divided by the number of addends. The mean is also called the *average*.

The *mode* is the number that appears most often in a set of data. There may be no mode or more than one mode in a set of data.

Ex. 9–22

Predicting probability

To predict probability, divide the number of favorable outcomes by the number of possible outcomes. In predicting the probability of independent events, the outcome of the second event does not depend on the outcome of the first event. With dependent events, the outcome of the first event affects the probabilities of the outcomes of the second event.

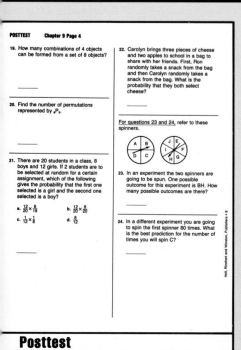

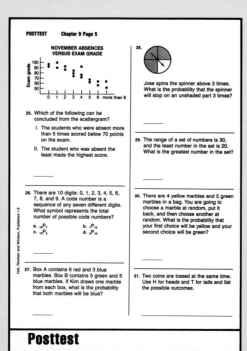

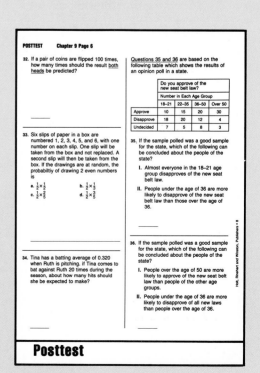

Purpose This Reteaching page provides additional instruction for key concepts in the chapter. It is designed for use by students who have had difficulty with these concepts. It can also be used to provide additional practice for students who require it.

USING THE PAGE

Range, mode, median, and mean are taught on pages 314–317.

These are called the *measures of central tendency* for a set of data. Have students define each of these terms. If the set of data is arranged from the least to the greatest, it will be easier to find the range (which is the difference between the least and the greatest) and the median (which is the middle term in a set of ordered data). If there is an even number of terms in a set of data, the median is found by averaging the middle two terms. The mode is the term that appears most frequently. Not all sets of data have modes. The mean is the average of all the terms.

Resources

For other practice and activities related to this chapter, see the Teacher's Resource Book.

RETEACHING

Statisticians frequently use data in order to make comparisons. To help make meaningful comparisons, they use the range, mode, median, and mean.

Paul received the following scores on his mathematics tests during the second marking period: 99, 75, 86, 66, 80, 100, 75, and 76.

Arrange the scores from the greatest to the least.	100, 99, 86, 80, 76, 75, 75, 66

The **range** is the difference between the highest and the lowest scores.

$$100 - 66 = 34$$

range = 34

The **mode** is the score that occurs most frequently.

mode = 75

The **median** is the middle number of the scores. If there are an even number of scores, add the two middle numbers and divide by 2.

median = 78

The **mean** is the sum of the scores divided by the number of scores.

$$\frac{657}{8} = 82.125$$

mean = 82.125

Find the range, mode, median, and mean for each set of numbers. Round to the nearest hundredth.

1. 23, 21, 31, 29, 31
   10; 31; 29; 27
2. 10, 4, 12, 8, 14, 4, 4
   10; 4; 8; 8
3. 62, 68, 64, 60, 65, 68
   8; 68; 64.5; 64.5
4. 95, 79, 86, 80, 95, 75
   20; 95; 83; 85
5. 86, 92, 92, 85, 75
   17; 92; 86; 86
6. 170, 100, 200, 150, 170, 85
   115; 170; 160; 145.83
7. 8, 3, 6, 5, 9, 5
   6; 5; 5.5; 6
8. 6, 10, 12, 17, 24, 35, 1
   34; none; 12; 15
9. 50, 75, 75, 40, 90, 65, 35
   55; 75; 65; 61.43
10. 75, 70, 80, 95, 135, 135, 135
    65; 135; 95; 103.57
11. 35, 40, 50, 60, 70
    35; none; 50; 51
12. 85, 75, 90, 70, 70, 100, 80
    30; 70; 80; 81.43
13. 110, 130, 122, 138, 114, 125, 136
    28; none; 125; 125
14. 15, 17, 20, 20, 20, 22, 23, 24, 26
    11; 20; 20; 20.78
15. 24, 36, 48, 24, 30, 49, 40, 25, 26, 30
    25; 24 and 30; 30; 33.2
16. 24, 30, 22, 17, 36, 51, 81, 24, 31, 49, 13, 18, 25
    68; 24; 25; 32.38
17. 134, 137, 134, 136, 133, 135, 135, 134, 130, 135, 134
    7; 134; 134; 134.27

350

ENRICHMENT

The Normal Curve

Try this experiment. Toss 10 pennies all at once, and count the number of pennies that turn up heads. Record the number. Repeat this procedure 99 more times. Use the data to make a frequency-distribution table. The table probably will look something like the one at the right.

Notice that the values closest to the center have the highest frequency, and the values closest to the ends have the lowest frequency. This pattern of scores is called a **normal distribution**. When a normal distribution is graphed, a bell-shaped curve results that is called a **normal curve.**

Number of heads per toss	Tally	Frequency
0	I	1
1	II	2
2	III	3
3	IHI IHI I	11
4	IHI IHI IHI IIII	19
5	IHI IHI IHI IHI IHI	25
6	IHI IHI IHI IHI	20
7	IHI IHI II	12
8	IHI	5
9	I	1
10	I	1

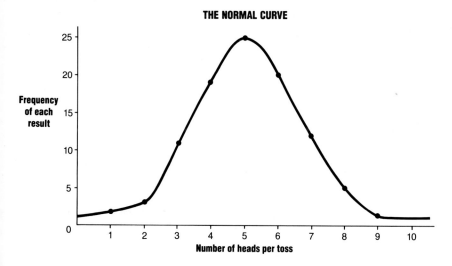

THE NORMAL CURVE

Draw a frequency-distribution table of the heights of all the boys in the eighth grade. Graph the distribution. Is the graph a normal curve? Tables and graphs will vary.

351

Purpose This Cumulative Review page provides an opportunity to reinforce students' understanding of the concepts and skills taught in previous chapters.

The chart below is designed to aid you in reviewing the material by specifying the pages on which various concepts and skills were taught.

Each Cumulative Review gives students an opportunity to practice taking tests that are written in a multiple-choice, standardized format. Be sure that students understand that if the correct answer is not among the first three given, then they should select the fourth choice—"not given"—as the correct answer. At least one item per test will require students to give this response.

CUMULATIVE REVIEW

Write the letter of the correct answer.

1. Evaluate ^-7g when $g = 6$.

   a. $^-42$ **b.** $\frac{^-6}{7}$

   c. $1\frac{1}{4}$ **d.** not given

2. Solve for t: $^-6t = 84$.

   a. $^-24$ **b.** $^-14$

   c. 90 **d.** not given

3. Solve for y: $\frac{y}{^-4} - 16 = 4$.

   a. $^-80$ **b.** $^-16$

   c. $^-5$ **d.** not given

4. 70 is 7 more than 3 times a number. Use an equation to solve.

   a. 21 **b.** $25\frac{2}{3}$

   c. 189 **d.** not given

5. Solve for n: $\frac{n}{7} < 21$.

   a. $n < 3$ **b.** $n < 28$

   c. $n < 147$ **d.** not given

6. $\frac{4}{7} + \frac{^-2}{7}$

   a. $\frac{^-2}{7}$ **b.** $\frac{2}{7}$

   c. $\frac{6}{7}$ **d.** not given

7. $\frac{^-3}{4} \times \frac{^-2}{11}$

   a. $\frac{^-3}{22}$ **b.** $\frac{8}{23}$

   c. $\frac{1}{3}$ **d.** not given

8. A \$68.00 item now sells for \$80.24. Calculate the percent of increase.

   a. 15%   **b.** 17%

   c. 18%   **d.** not given

9. Jack's flight left New York at 7:35 A.M. Eastern time and landed in San Diego at 11:10 A.M. Pacific time. For how long did he fly?

   a. 3 h 35 min   **b.** 4 h 25 min

   c. 6 h 35 min   **d.** not given

10. Jenny bought 17 pages of sheet music and 3 guitar picks. She paid a total of \$42.15. The picks were 3 for \$0.50. Use an equation to find the cost of a page of sheet music.

   a. \$2.13   **b.** \$2.45

   c. \$3.45   **d.** not given

11. The circle graph shows how the budget for the town of Millindale is spent. What is the ratio of the amount spent on education to the amount spent on public works?

   a. $1:2$ **b.** $2:1$

   c. $2.1:1$ **d.** not given

352

CHAPTER  OVERVIEW

GEOMETRY

SUMMARY

Chapter 10 deals with geometric concepts and skills. Included are a variety of constructions and lessons measuring, drawing, and classifying angles and polygons. Identifying lines, parts of a circle, similar and congruent polygons, lines of symmetry, and reflections, translations, and rotations is also discussed.

LESSON SEQUENCE

PROFESSIONAL BACKGROUND

A recent National Assessment of Educational Progress confirmed that students generally could recognize geometric figures, but they were much less successful in their ability to analyze properties of figures. Research has shown that recognition precedes analysis as a distinct level of geometric understanding necessary for understanding deductive geometry.

Although work with properties has been avoided prior to high school, research clearly shows that middle-school students are indeed capable of doing more analysis of geometric properties than the schools have been providing, as long as attention is given to vocabulary and visualization. The National Assessment says that when the words "same size and shape" were used, students were considerably more successful than when the word "congruent" was used. Words such as "similar," "symmetric," "parallel," and "perpendicular" present similar problems. One study shows that the concept of similarity can be especially confusing, and that the substitution of the words "same shape" is not sufficient for clarity. Careful discussion with many examples, including student-generated ones, should accompany any work on geometric properties.

"Right triangle" and "altitude" also present difficulties. About half of junior-high students in one study did not judge tilted or inverted examples to be true right angles, and only about 10 percent were able to draw the altitude of an obtuse triangle.

Resources: See Driscoll (secondary volume, chapter on geometry); and Carpenter et al.

MATERIALS

acetate sheets
compasses
contour maps
toothpicks
tangram
construction paper

VOCABULARY

ABOUT THE CHAPTER

This chapter develops the concepts that prepare students for high school geometry.

In Chapter 10, students learn about the fundamental ideas of geometry (point, line, plane, ray, line segment, etc.), as well as the various types of angles, triangles, and polygons. Students learn to construct and bisect line segments and angles. One lesson focuses on the circle while other lessons show students how to identify congruent and similar polygons and construct congruent triangles. The chapter ends with lessons on symmetry, reflections, translations, and rotations.

Students must master the vocabulary of geometry, and much of what is presented in this chapter is vocabulary and definition. Use the techniques here that you would employ to help students master reading vocabulary words.

Students may have difficulty grasping the idea of similar polygons. A brief review of ratio and proportion may be in order when teaching this lesson. Do not hesitate to have students prepare cutout models of similar polygons to help them grasp the concept.

The lessons on symmetry, reflections, translations, and rotations represent an approach to geometry that is gaining favor in more and more schools. Encourage students to explore patterns and to actually move, rotate, and reflect (with mirrors) the various geometric shapes.

Students should have opportunities to estimate whether two figures are congruent or similar. Then have students determine the relationship between the polygons and compare it with their estimate.

Problem-solving lessons in the chapter show students how to work backward to solve nonroutine problems and give students an opportunity to choose the strategies and methods needed to solve problems. Other problem-solving lessons show students how to draw a picture to solve a problem and how to get information from a data source.

The Group Project actively involves students in planning a teen recreation center. Students have an opportunity to combine concepts and skills from geometry and measurement with arithmetic skills as they work on this project.

The Enrichment lesson shows students how to construct regular polygons. This lesson builds directly and gives students additional work with the compass and straightedge.

USING THE CHAPTER OPENER

Each Chapter Opener presents situational problem-solving activities that can be used to explore the skills taught throughout the chapter. The work sheets can be used by individuals, small groups, or the whole class, depending on the needs of the class. The Chapter Opener focuses on a nonalgorithmic approach to mathematics through real-life situations relevant to the children's experiences. Through an interdisciplinary approach, the Chapter Opener helps children explore the relationships between mathematics, other areas of the curriculum, and everyday life while developing different strands of mathematics.

In the Chapter Opener activities, students will make scale drawings and explore the ways in which geometry is used in designing and constructing buildings. Students will also make use of ratios and proportions to measure objects indirectly.

PROBLEM SOLVING

As well as providing a review of problem-solving skills learned thus far, the Choosing a Strategy or Method lessons in *Mathematics Unlimited* challenge students to select the best problem-solving strategy. Once students choose a plan of action, they must apply it correctly to solve the problems. Because more than one strategy can often be employed for each problem, these lessons are ideal for work in small groups in which students can brainstorm and share ideas to keep each other from getting stuck.

The lesson Drawing a Picture focuses on the use of drawings to make the problem-solving process easier. Problems that include measurement are often appropriate for drawing pictures. Students may encounter difficulty when trying to transform the words in a problem into a diagram. Small-group work which encourages brainstorming—a non-critical, idea-gathering technique—may produce useful drawings.

The lesson Using Outside Sources Including the Infobank teaches students how to look elsewhere for information needed to solve a problem. When faced with a problem that calls for more information, students commonly do not know how to determine what information they need in order to solve the problem. The lesson introduces a strategy for determining the kind of information needed to solve the problem. The lesson also reviews how to read and interpret data from a table, as well as how to compare two separate pieces of data to solve a given problem. Using Outside Sources Including the Infobank lends itself nicely to group work in which students can brainstorm different methods for finding pertinent information.

The Working Backward lesson draws from the skills developed in Choosing the Operation and Writing an Equation. The problems, which give the final result of a series of operations, require students to devise an equation to determine the original number. The equation is then computed in reverse. Students who fail to read questions carefully may have difficulty with this type of problem.

BULLETIN BOARD

"The World Of Polygons"

Materials: paper to cover bulletin board; lettering; felt-tip pens; push pins, tacks or stapler; poster board; construction paper, assorted colors; pictures from magazines

Preparation: Cover bulletin board with paper and arrange the display lettering. Use blue construction paper to cut out an octagonal "globe" and a stand. Position on the board. Label one of two construction-paper titles *Key* and the other *In Our World.* Place them on the board as shown. Post pictures from magazines under *In Our World.* Make construction-paper "continents" as shown below.

After pp. 366-367: Place the triangular continent on the globe. Identify the types of triangles in the key. Have students find pictures which illustrate the use of triangles in our world. Mount them on the board.

After pp. 368-369: Place quadrilateral, pentagonal, and hexagonal continents on the globe. Identify the parts of each continent in the key. Have students find pictures which illustrate the use of these polygons in everyday life. Mount them on the board.

COMMON ERRORS

Some students will have difficulty understanding and identifying translations, reflections, and rotations. For example, students will become confused when they must identify whether the second figure is a translation, reflection, or rotation of the first figure:

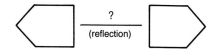

To remediate this problem, equate the newer terms learned for these operations (translation, reflection, rotation) with the more graphic terms students learned in earlier grades (slide, flip, turn).

Use the board to show how a translated figure has been slid, a reflected figure has been flipped, and a rotated figure has been turned.

It may help to explain reflections by using the idea of a mirror. Rotation can also be explained by defining the word rotate. (To turn around a point)

SPECIAL NEEDS

Take advantage of the tangible, activity-oriented nature of geometry to allow learners to build perceptual-motor skills. Use concrete examples to illustrate each definition, property, and classification that is discussed. With your prompting, students will notice geometry shapes all around them.

Students may have difficulty memorizing rules, characteristics, and properties of triangles and other polygons. After reviewing angle classification, provide students with a variety of cut-out triangles, and have them place each under the proper heading on a chart. Continue this method with other polygons, providing the students with specific names for each after they have placed them on their charts. Encourage students to keep a scrapbook with pictures that represent each shape. A mirror can be used to effectively show symmetry, reflections, translations, and rotations. Definitions need not be given until after the tasks are performed.

Have advanced students make a Möbius strip by cutting a rectangle of paper about 3 cm × 30 cm, giving the paper a half-twist, and pasting together the two short sides. How many surfaces does it have? (1) Have each of them cut the strip lengthwise, and describe what happens.

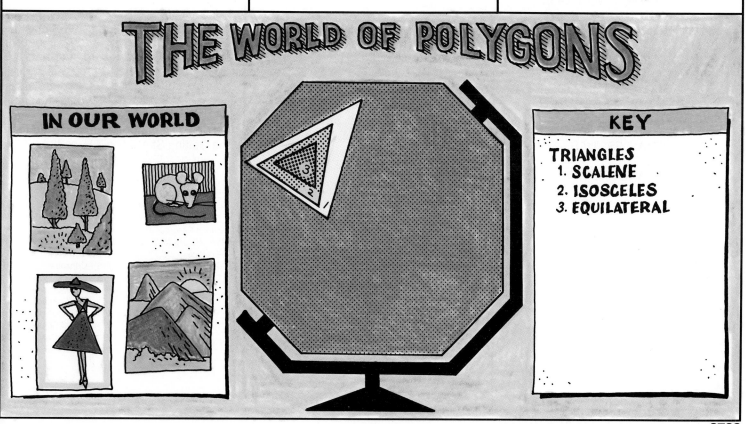

MATH LABS

PUZZLES AND GAMES

Have students use the figure below to make a Venn diagram that illustrates the relationship of a quadrilateral to its subsets (squares, rectangles, and parallelograms).

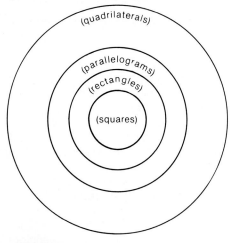

COMPUTER

Have students write a program that will input the name of a figure with between 3 and 10 sides and then output the number of sides which that figure has.

```
10  DATA "TRIANGLE",
    "QUADRILATERAL",
    "PENTAGON", "HEXAGON"
20  DATA "HEPTAGON",
    "OCTAGON", "NONAGON",
    "DECAGON"
30  INPUT "NAME OF FIGURE ";
    F$
40  FOR X = 3 TO 10
50  READ A$(X)
60  IF A$(X) = F$ THEN 80
70  NEXT X
80  RESTORE
85  IF X = 11 GOTO 30
90  PRINT "A" ; F$; "HAS"; X;
    "SIDES"
100 INPUT "ANOTHER? YES OR
    NO"; Y$
110 IF Y$ = "YES" THEN 30
120 END
```

CALCULATOR

Most topics in geometry are not solvable by using a calculator. These concepts, ideas, and principles are not computation topics. Hence, they must be learned and understood before using a calculator. Very few topics in geometry involve numbers that generate computations that can be performed on a calculator. Some of these include the measurement of angles and segments of length and number patterns, for example, the number of diagonals in polygons.

Although there are few calculations in geometry, students should have calculators available for problem-solving activities.

Additional Activities: **Drill and Practice:** Two triangles are similar, *a* and *b* are the lengths of sides in one triangle; *A* and *B* are the corresponding lengths in the second triangle. Complete the chart.

Exploration: Construct a chart showing the number of diagonals in regular polygons of *n* sides (begin with a square and then a pentagon, a hexagon, and so on).

SUBJECT AREA CONNECTIONS

These activities are useful for reinforcing the concepts presented in this chapter.

p. 365-Science: Students look at a contour map and suggest a reason why contours never meet.

p. 367-Home Economics: Students design kitchens.

Here are some other ideas for reinforcing these concepts.

- **SOCIAL STUDIES:** Show students an overhead picture or diagram of a baseball field. Have them identify the geometric forms. (square, line segment, right angle, arc) Ask them to locate the center point of the circle, one of whose arcs is the infield boundary. (the center of the pitcher's mound)
- **LIBRARY SKILLS:** Have students research a famous building of their choice and identify the geometric forms in its structure.

PLAN AHEAD

You will need acetate sheets and felt-tip pens for the Getting Started on T.E. p. 356. You will need to prepare handouts for the activities on T.E. pp. 357 and 377. You will need compasses and straightedges for the Getting Started and the activities on T.E. pp. 358, 361, and 373. You will need a contour map for the activities on T.E. p. 365. You will need pictures of structures made of congruent polygons for the Getting Started on T.E. p. 374. You will need toothpicks and index cards for the activities on T.E. p. 375. You will need construction paper of different colors, scissors, tangrams, and rulers for the activities on. T.E. p. 381. You will need a spinner, a paper figure, and tape for the Getting Started on T.E. p. 384.

PLANNING CALENDAR
ABBREVIATION KEY

Teacher's Resource Book	*Follow-up Activities*
MMW—Making Math Work	CALC—Calculator
P—Practice	CMP—Computer
R—Reteach	CNS—Consumer
E—Enrich	P&G—Puzzles and Games
	MNP—Manipulatives
	MC—Math Connection
	MCM—Math Communication
	NS—Number Sense
	PS—Problem Solving
	RFM—Reinforcement

PLANNING CALENDAR

Pages	Lesson Objectives	ASSIGNMENT GUIDE			Class/Home	More Practice	Math Reasoning	Follow-up	Reteach	Practice	Enrich
		Basic	Average	Extended							
353	Chapter Opener (Use MMW 19,20)	353	353	353							
354,355	To define and identify basic geometric terms and concepts	1-20,22-32e	8-24,25-31o	12-32	H145			P&G MC	101	145	129
356,357	To identify and measure an angle	1-21,22-36e	1-12,14-36e	1-12,13-37o	H146		H225	RFM P&G	102	146	130
358,359	To construct congruent line segments and angles	1-4,7-10	1-10	1-10,Chlg	H147			RFM	103	147	131
360,361	To bisect a line segment and an angle	1-8,AL	1-9,AL	1-10,AL	H148		H225	RFM MNP	104	148	132
362,363	To solve problems by working backward	1-4	2-5	3-6	H149 H150			PS CALC		149-150	
364,365	To define and construct parallel and perpendicular lines	1-23,27-35o,36-37	4-22e,24-37	5-23o,24-37	H151			PS MC	105	151	133
366,367	To classify a triangle	1-13,19-29o	1-10,12-30e	5-10,11-25o,27-30	H152		H225	MC MNP RFM	106	152	134
368,369	To identify a polygon	1-7,9-16,MCR	4-18,MCR	4-20,MCR	H153		H226	MCM CMP	107	153	135
370,371	To practice choosing and using methods and strategies for solving problems	1-15o,16	2-16e	7-16	H154 H155			CALC CALC		154-155	
372,373	To identify parts of a circle	1-13,19-29o	1-14,19-29	12-29	H156			MC RFM	108	156	136
374,375	To identify the corresponding parts of congruent polygons	1-13	1-4,6-20e	1-9o,11-21	H157			P&G P&G	109	157	137
376,377	To identify and construct congruent triangles	1-9	1-12	1-13	H158			PS RFM	110	158	138
378,379	To draw a picture to solve a problem	1-3	3-6	2-6e	H159			PS CMP		159	139
380,381	To identify corresponding parts of similar polygons and use proportions to find their measures	1-9,10-20e,22-33	5-13,18-23	5-23	H160		H226	MNP MNP	111	160	140
382,383	To identify and draw lines of symmetry and reflection	1-4,7-14	1-14,Chlg	1-14,Chlg	H161		H226	RFM MCM	112	161	141
384,385	To define and draw translations and rotations	1-8	1-8	1-8,Chlg	H162			PS PS	113	162	142
386,387	To use information from the Infobank in problem solving	1-4	3-8	3-10	H163			PS RFM		163	143
388	Math Communication: To recognize directional patterns in math	388	388	388							
389	Group Project: To design a recreation center; to make a scale drawing	389	389	389							

390,391   Chapter Test   393   Enrichment   396   Cumulative Review
392   Reteaching   394,395   Technology

TESTS

A. To name points, lines, line segments, and rays and to identify parallel and perpendicular lines

B. To name, measure, and classify angles and to find the complement or supplement of an angle

C. To construct an angle or segment congruent to a given angle or segment and to construct the bisector of a line segment or an angle

D. To find the measures of vertical, alternate interior, and corresponding angles

E. To construct perpendicular or parallel lines

F. To classify triangles according to the measures of their angles or sides and to find the measure of an angle, given the measures of the other two angles

G. To identify and name polygons and to find the measure of an angle given the measures of the other interior angles

H. To identify the parts of a circle

I. To identify congruent figures and lines of symmetry

J. To solve problems that involve corresponding parts of similar polygons

K. To identify translations, rotations, or reflections

L. To use working backward as a strategy to solve problems

M. To draw a picture to solve a problem

FAMILY INVOLVEMENT

Family Involvement for Chapter 10 encourages family members to design a family crest or coat of arms. A list of the distinctive attributes of the family is to be written on a piece of paper. The list should include the things the family does together, the family business or trade, a nickname or a pun of the family surname, a prominent ancestor, and a distinguished or famous member of the family. After completing the list, family members are to draw pictures, emblems, or symbols for each item. A compass and a ruler are to be used to draw the family crest. Favorite pictures, emblems, or symbols are to be drawn onto the sketch of the crest. The completed designs are to be sketched on a sheet of mat board and colored with felt-tip pens or paintbrushes. To extend the activity, family members may choose to embroider the family crest as a tapestry.

Additional activities might include drawing a simple design of the interior of the main room of the home by using only basic geometric lines and shapes. Every figure in the design should be simplified in order to emphasize the basic geometric shape.

STUDENT RESOURCES

Bibliography

Giblin, James Cross. *The Skyscraper Book.* New York: Thomas Y. Crowell, 1981.

Laycock, Mary and Manuel Dominques. *Discover It!* Hayward, CA: Activity Resources Co., 1986.

Laycock, Mary, et al. *Geoblocks & Geojackets: Metric Version.* Hayward, CA: Activity Resources Co., Inc., 1988.

Films

Curves of Constant Width. 16 minutes. Color. 1974. Distributed by International Film Bureau, Chicago, Ill.

Journey to the Center of a Triangle. 8 minutes. Color. 1976. Distributed by International Film Bureau, Chicago, Ill.

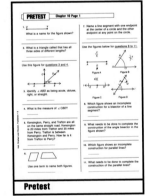

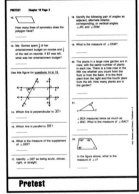

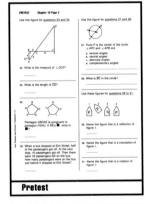

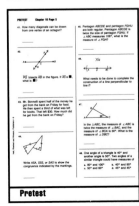

The design of every house includes geometric shapes. Which geometric shapes can you find in the design of the house in which you live? Use at least five different geometric shapes to make a design for a new house.

10 GEOMETRY

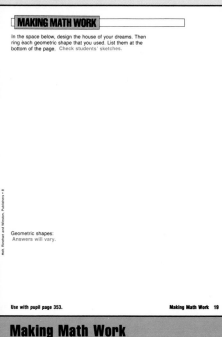

MAKING MATH WORK

In the space below, design the house of your dreams. Then ring each geometric shape that you used. List them at the bottom of the page. Check students' sketches.

Geometric shapes:
Answers will vary.

Use with pupil page 353.

Making Math Work **19**

Making Math Work

MAKING MATH WORK Making Math Work

How tall is the building in which you live? You can find out by using only a yardstick. You can use indirect measurement to help you find the height of the building.

Your house's height: _____ = Your height: _____

Your house's shadow's height: _____ Your shadow's height: _____

20 Making Math Work

Use with pupil page 353.

Making Math Work

Objectives: To explore problems involving geometry and houses

Direct students to look at the pictures of houses. Ask them to name the various geometric shapes they can see in the pictures shown on this page. Discuss geometric forms used in architecture to make a structure that is pleasing to the eye. Emphasize the balance between these forms and the repetition of certain forms. Discuss the relationship between architecture and art.

SMALL GROUP
Measurement
Materials: Making Math Work page 20 per student, yardstick per group

Have each student in the group complete Making Math Work page 20. Explain that the ratio of the length of an individual's shadow to his or her height is equal to the ratio of the length of any object's shadow to its height. Ask why it is important that both shadows be measured at the same time of day. After students have completed page 20, form the class into groups and ask them to calculate the heights of objects around the school (and the school itself) in the same manner.

INDIVIDUAL
Geometry
Materials: Making Math Work page 19, ruler, pencils, compass per student

Have each student complete Making Math Work page 19. Tell students that they can use any perspective they wish in designing their house—floor plan, front view, cutaway, and so on. Have them use as many geometric shapes as possible. Remind them of the importance of balance and repetition in making a structure that is pleasing to the eye. Encourage them to be as creative as possible and to use whatever designs their imaginations dream up.

WHOLE CLASS
Patterns and Functions
Materials: ruler, compass, chalk

Work with the class to design the floor plan for a new school building. Discuss the features a new school building should have. Emphasize improvements that could be made in the existing building. Encourage imaginative ideas. List the features on the chalkboard, and have volunteers sketch an orderly and logical floor plan.

Objectives: To identify and define basic geometric terms and concepts

Warm-Up
Provide students with everyday objects that have easily identifiable shapes such as flying discs (circles), telephone push buttons (squares), calculators (rectangles), and triangular musical instruments (triangles). Have them name the shapes and describe the characteristics of each.

GETTING STARTED

Have students make a list of all the geometric terms they know. Discuss these terms, paying particular attention to the need for a consistent vocabulary of geometry in order to describe shapes such as those in the Warm-Up. Then have the students suggest real-life situations, or occupations such as carpentry, surveying, architecture, design, and navigation, for which a vocabulary of geometry would be necessary.

TEACHING THE LESSON

Explain that in geometry, some basic ideas are not proved but are accepted. These ideas are often best described by illustration.

Display two sheets of paper at different angles. Use them to define a *plane*. Point out that if extended, the two planes would intersect.

Then on one of the sheets, at random mark points *A* and *G*. Fold the paper so that *A* and *G* are on the fold. Ask: Can other points be placed on the fold? (yes) Then ask: How many more points can be placed on the fold? (an infinite number) Unfold the paper. Draw line *AG*, and use it to define a *line*. Then use $\overline{AG}$ to define a *line segment* and $\overrightarrow{AG}$ to define a *ray*. Draw $\overleftrightarrow{XQ}$ intersecting $\overleftrightarrow{AG}$ at *M*, and use it to define *intersecting lines*. Then draw $\overleftrightarrow{JC}$ parallel to $\overleftrightarrow{XQ}$, and use it to define *parallel lines*. Draw a line on the second sheet of paper, and define *skew lines* by holding the sheets at different angles.

Basic Ideas

Terms and ideas in geometry	Picture
point *A*: is an exact location in space.	• *A*
line *CD*, or *DC*: $\overleftrightarrow{CD}$ or $\overleftrightarrow{DC}$ names a straight path of points that continues infinitely in two directions. Another name for $\overleftrightarrow{CD}$ is line *l*.	
ray *EC*, or *EF*: $\overrightarrow{EC}$ or $\overrightarrow{EF}$ names part of a line that has one endpoint and continues infinitely in one direction.	
angle *XYZ*, or *ZYX*: $\angle XYZ$ or $\angle ZYX$ names two rays with a common endpoint. Another name for $\angle XYZ$ is $\angle Y$, or $\angle 1$.	
line segment *GH*, or *HG*: $\overline{GH}$ or $\overline{HG}$ names part of a line with two endpoints.	
plane *T*: is a flat surface that continues infinitely in all directions.	
intersecting lines: $\overleftrightarrow{AB}$ and $\overleftrightarrow{CD}$ are lines that meet at a point *P*.	
parallel lines: $\overleftrightarrow{RS}$ and $\overleftrightarrow{TU}$ are lines in a plane that do not intersect.	
skew lines: $\overleftrightarrow{AB}$ and $\overleftrightarrow{CD}$ are lines that do not intersect and are not parallel. Skew lines lie in different planes.	
congruent segments: $\overline{LM}$ and $\overline{QR}$ are two line segments that have the same length. $\overline{LM} \cong \overline{QR}$. The symbol $\cong$ means "is congruent to."	
midpoint: *M* marks a point that separates a line segment into two congruent segments.	

354

COMMON ERRORS

Some students might label angles incorrectly, using lowercase letters ($\angle abc$) or neglecting to place the vertex in the middle ($\angle ACB$).

Remediation
For these errors, have students write the vertex, or common endpoint, first and then the points on either side.

$\angle \_ B \_ \angle ABC$

Assign Reteach Master, p. 101.

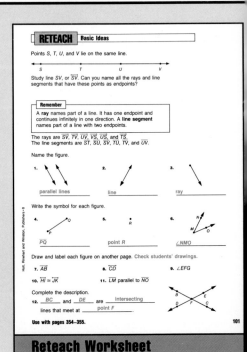

Reteach Worksheet

Name the figure.

1. ——•——————→ **ray**

2. **intersecting lines**

3. • **point**

4. 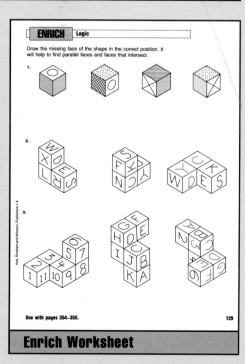 **parallel lines**

5. 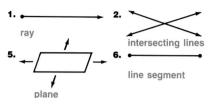 **plane**

6. ←————————→ **line segment**

7. ←——•————•——→ **line**

Write the symbol for each figure.

8. N • **point N**

9. ←——•——•——→ R S **RS**

10. •——————• P ——→ M **PM**

11. •————————• K   L **KL**

Draw and label each figure. **Check students' drawings.**

12. point F   13. $\overline{BC}$ 14. plane J   15. $\overleftrightarrow{EF}$

16. $\overrightarrow{GH}$ 17. $\overleftrightarrow{EF}$ is parallel to $\overleftrightarrow{GH}$.   18. $\overleftrightarrow{KL}$ intersects $\overleftrightarrow{MN}$.

Points A, B, C, and D lie on the same line.

←——•————•————•————•——→
  A   B   C   D

19. Name all the line segments that have these points as endpoints.
$\overline{AB}$; $\overline{AC}$; $\overline{AD}$; $\overline{BC}$; $\overline{BD}$; $\overline{CD}$

20. Name all the rays that have these points as endpoints.
$\overrightarrow{AD}$; $\overrightarrow{BD}$; $\overrightarrow{CD}$; $\overrightarrow{DA}$; $\overrightarrow{CA}$; $\overrightarrow{BA}$

Write *true* if the statement is true. Write *false* if it is false.

21.
$\overline{AB} \cong \overline{CD}$
false

22.
$\overline{EF} \cong \overline{GH}$
true

23.
$\overline{JK} \cong \overline{LM}$
true

24.
$\overline{NP} \cong \overline{RS}$
false

Use the number line to complete each statement.

  A F B   C G D   E
←—+——+——+——+——+——+——+——+——+——+——+——+——+——→
 ⁻6 ⁻5 ⁻4 ⁻3 ⁻2 ⁻1 0 1 2 3 4 5 6 7

25. $\overline{AB} \cong$ ■
CD

26. $\overline{CB} \cong$ ■
CE

27. $\overline{AC} \cong$ ■
BD or FG

28. The midpoint of $\overline{AB}$ is ■.   F

29. The midpoint of $\overline{CD}$ is ■.   G

Find the length of each segment whose midpoint is M.

30.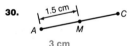
3 cm

31.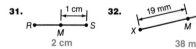
2 cm

32.
38 mm

ASSIGNMENT GUIDE

Basic: 1–20, 22–32 e

Average: 8–24, 25–31 o

Extended: 12–32

Resources
Practice, p. 145   Class/Home, p. H145
Reteach, p. 101
Enrich, p. 129

Exercise Analysis

1–7   Identify a figure
8–11   Write the symbol for a figure
12–18 Draw a figure
19–20 Name line segments and rays
21–27 Identify congruent segments
28–29 Identify a midpoint
30–32 Use a midpoint to find the length of a line segment

FOLLOW-UP ACTIVITIES

PUZZLES AND GAMES
Pose the following puzzle.
• A coach tells his team to form 6 equal rows and assemble 5 players in each row so that the coach can place himself at a point equidistant from each row. "But," the team captain says, "there are only 24 of us."

Can the team do what the coach has asked? (yes, by using the formation shown below)

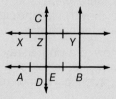

MATH COMMUNICATION
Write the following on the chalkboard. $\overleftrightarrow{CD}$ intersects $\overleftrightarrow{AB}$ at E, which is the midpoint of $\overline{AB}$. $\overleftrightarrow{XY}$ is parallel to $\overleftrightarrow{AB}$ and intersects $\overleftrightarrow{CD}$ at Z, which is the midpoint of $\overline{XY}$. $\overline{XZ}$ is congruent to $\overline{YZ}$ and to $\overline{AE}$. $\overleftrightarrow{BY}$ is parallel to $\overleftrightarrow{CD}$.

Have students draw the figure described above. (A diagram of the figure is given below.)

            C
            |
  ←—•——•——+——•——→
    X   Z | Y
  ←————————+————————→
    A   D | E   B
            |

COMING UP
What's your angle?

355

Warm-Up

Draw the following on the chalkboard.

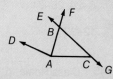

Have students list all the possible ways to name the angles of the triangle.

(∠ABC, ∠CBA, ∠ABG, ∠GBA, ∠BCA, ∠ACB, ∠ECA, ∠ACE, ∠CAB, ∠BAC, ∠CAF, ∠FAC)

GETTING STARTED

Materials: acetate sheets, felt-tip pens, pictures of modern architecture

Cover each picture with an acetate sheet. Have students use the pens to highlight the angles in each building. Ask: Can you think of any categories that might help you classify the angles? Elicit the notion of classification by the size of the opening of an angle rather than by the length of its sides.

TEACHING THE LESSON

A. Explain that the measure of an angle is not linear but radial: It does not matter how long the sides of the angle are but rather what part of a circle the sides would cut out, or intercept.

B. Draw $\overleftrightarrow{AB}$ and place a straightedge marked ($\overrightarrow{AC}$) over it. Rotate the straightedge completely around A, pausing at about 45°, 90°, 135°, and 180°. Have students name each ∠BAC. (acute, right, obtuse, straight)

Ask: How many degrees has $\overrightarrow{AC}$ rotated? (360°) Have a volunteer draw the circular path of C. Point out that the Babylonians, who invented the degree, thought there were 360 days in the year. So, they divided the circle into 360 parts, one for each day.

C. Show how drawing a ray inside the angle from the vertex of a right angle always produces complementary angles.

D. Show how drawing a ray from the vertex of a straight angle always produces supplementary angles.

Angles and Angle Measure

A. For any **angle,** the common endpoint is called the **vertex,** and the rays are called the **sides** of the angle.

Find the measure of the angle formed at the peak of the roof shown in the drawing.

To find the measure of an angle, use an instrument called a **protractor.** Place the center of the protractor at A (the peak of the roof). Place the 0° mark of one scale on one side of the angle. Read that same scale where the other side of the angle intersects it. The angle formed at the peak of the roof is 101°. You can write m∠BAC = 101. m means "measure of."

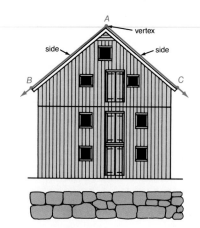

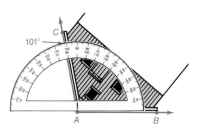

B. An angle can be classified according to its measure (m).

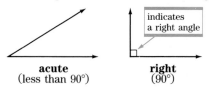

acute (less than 90°)	**right** (90°)
obtuse (greater than 90° but less than 180°)	**straight** (180°)

indicates a right angle

C. Two angles whose measures have a sum of 90° are **complementary** angles.

∠A and ∠B are *complements* of each other.

D. Two angles whose measures have a sum of 180° are **supplementary** angles.

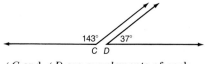

∠C and ∠D are *supplements* of each other.

COMMON ERRORS

Some students might have difficulty reading the protractor.

Remediation

Draw a 60° angle for students. For students who find the measure of an angle such as the one shown above to be within 10° of 60° (but not 60°), check to see whether they are placing the vertex and the baseline correctly.

Students who answer 120° are reading the incorrect scale on the protractor.

Assign Reteach Master, p. 102.

RETEACH Angles and Angle Measure

If angles A and B are supplementary angles and m∠A = 95° find the measure of angle B.

Remember

A pair of angles is made up of **supplementary angles** if the sum of the measures of the angles equals 180°.

Let x represent the number of degrees in the measure of angle B.

$$m\angle A + m\angle B = 180$$
$$95 + x = 180$$

Subtract 95 from both sides of the equation.

$$95 - 95 + x = 180 - 95$$
$$x = 75$$

The measure of angle B is 75°.

Complete the table by finding the measure of x. Angles A and B are complementary.

	Degrees in m∠A	Degrees in m∠B	Equation	x
1.	40	x	40 + x = 90	50
2.	45	x	45 + x = 90	45
3.	x	85	x + 85 = 90	5
4.	x	67	x + 67 = 90	23

Complete the table by finding the measure of x. Angles C and D are supplementary.

	Degrees in m∠C	Degrees in m∠D	Equation	x
5.	40	x	40 + x = 180	140
6.	67	x	67 + x = 180	113
7.	x	53	x + 53 = 180	127
8.	x	46	x + 46 = 180	134

Use with pages 356–357.

Reteach Worksheet

Use a protractor to measure each angle.

1. 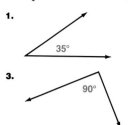 35°

2. 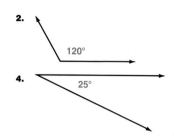 120°

3. 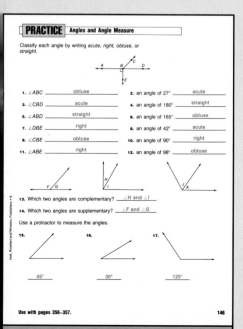 90°

4. 25°

Draw an angle that has the given measure. **Check students' drawings.**

5. 27° **6.** 124° **7.** 90° **8.** 61° **9.** 180°

Use the angle shown to complete.

10. Its vertex is ■. *N*

11. Its sides are ■. $\overrightarrow{NT}$; $\overrightarrow{ND}$

12. Three ways to identify the angle are ■.
∠DNT; ∠TND; ∠N

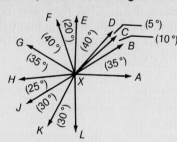

Classify each angle as *acute, right, obtuse,* or *straight.*

13.  right
14. obtuse
15. straight
16. acute

17. 148° obtuse **18.** 180° straight **19.** 17° acute **20.** 83° acute **21.** 90° right

Classify each pair of angles as *complementary, supplementary,* or *neither.*

22. 67°, 13° neither **23.** 141°, 39° supplementary **24.** 2°, 88° complementary **25.** 45°, 45° complementary

Find the complement of an angle that has the given measure.

26. 31° 59° **27.** 74° 16° **28.** 11° 79° **29.** 48° 42° **30.** 86° 4°

Find the supplement of an angle that has the given measure.

31. 64° 116° **32.** 112° 68° **33.** 13° 167° **34.** 128° 52° **35.** 160° 20°

Solve.

36. Draw and label the complementary angles that have equal degree measures.
45°, 45° Check students' drawings.

★37. What is the degree measure of an angle that is 4 times the measure of its supplement? 144°

Classwork/Homework, page H146

357

ASSIGNMENT GUIDE

Basic: 1–21, 22–36 *e*

Average: 1–12, 14–36 *e*

Extended: 1–12, 13–37 *o*

Resources
Practice, p. 146   Class/Home, p. H146
Reteach, p. 102   Reasoning, p. H225
Enrich, p. 130

Exercise Analysis
1–4   Measure an angle
5–9   Draw an angle
10–25 Classify the angle or pair of angles
26–30 Find the complement
31–35 Find the supplement
36–37 Skill applications

FOLLOW-UP ACTIVITIES

REINFORCEMENT
Have students draw the complement and then the supplement of each angle.
● 77° (13°, 103°)
● 34° (56°, 146°)
● 109°—supplement only (71°)
● 90° (0°, 90°)

PUZZLES AND GAMES
Prepare the following as a handout.

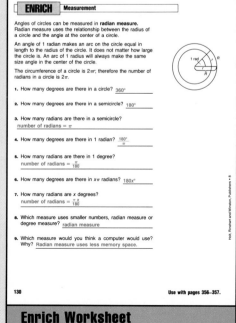

Have students complete the magic square below by measuring the named angles with a protractor. All rows, columns, and diagonals should add up to 180°.

∠EXF (20°)	∠BXC (10°)	∠AXE (90°)	∠LXJ (60°)
∠HXK (55°)	∠EXA (90°)	∠DXC (5°)	∠JXK (30°)
∠DXA (50°)	∠GXJ (60°)	∠HXJ (25°)	∠CXA (45°)
∠BXE (55°)	∠FXE (20°)	∠DXF (60°)	∠CXE (45°)

COMING UP
A construction crew is needed!

PRACTICE Angles and Angle Measure

Classify each angle by writing acute, right, obtuse, or straight.

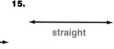

1. ∠ABC ___ obtuse
2. an angle of 27° ___ acute
3. ∠CBD ___ acute
4. an angle of 180° ___ straight
5. ∠ABD ___ straight
6. an angle of 165° ___ obtuse
7. ∠DBE ___ right
8. an angle of 42° ___ acute
9. ∠CBE ___ obtuse
10. an angle of 90° ___ right
11. ∠ABE ___ right
12. an angle of 98° ___ obtuse

13. Which two angles are complementary? ___ ∠H and ∠I
14. Which two angles are supplementary? ___ ∠F and ∠G

Use a protractor to measure the angles.

15. ___ 45° 16. ___ 30° 17. ___ 125°

Use with pages 356–357.   146

Practice Worksheet

ENRICH Measurement

Angles of circles can be measured in **radian measure.**
Radian measure uses the relationship between the radius of a circle and the angle at the center of a circle.

An angle of 1 radian makes an arc on the circle equal in length to the radius of the circle. It does not matter how large the circle is. An arc of 1 radius will always make the same size angle in the center of the circle.
The circumference of a circle is 2π; therefore the number of radians in a circle is 2π.

1. How many degrees are there in a circle? ___ 360°

2. How many degrees are there in a semicircle? ___ 180°

3. How many radians are there in a semicircle?
number of radians = π

4. How many degrees are there in 1 radian? ___ $\frac{180°}{\pi}$

5. How many radians are there in 1 degree?
number of radians = $\frac{\pi}{180}$

6. How many degrees are there in xπ radians? ___ 180x°

7. How many radians are there in x degrees?
number of radians = $\frac{\pi x}{180}$

8. Which measure uses smaller numbers, radian measure or degree measure? ___ radian measure

9. Which measure would you think a computer would use? Why? ___ Radian measure uses less memory space.

Use with pages 356–357.

130

Enrich Worksheet

357

Objectives: To construct congruent line segments and angles

Warm-Up
Have each student use a straightedge to draw an acute angle and an obtuse angle. Then have the student estimate to try to draw angles congruent to those already constructed. Have students exchange papers and use protractors to determine how close they came.

GETTING STARTED

Materials: compasses

Demonstrate how to use the compass. *Emphasize*: Hold only the knob without putting pressure on the points; tilt at a 60° angle from the paper; and guide, do not push, the pencil point. Have students improve their technique by making circles.

TEACHING THE LESSON

A. Have students practice this construction by drawing line segments and then copying them. Have them check their work by measuring the line segments with a ruler.
Stress that constructions require the use of an *unmarked* straightedge. Thus, the marks on a regular ruler are to be ignored.

B. Have students practice this construction by drawing acute angles and then copying them. Use right and obtuse angles and repeat the procedure. Have students use protractors to check and measure their work.

Constructing Congruent Line Segments and Angles

In geometry, a **construction** is a drawing for which only a compass and a straightedge are used.

A. Construct a line segment congruent to $\overline{AB}$.

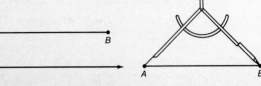

Draw a ray, and label its endpoint P.

Open the compass to the length of $\overline{AB}$.

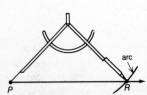

Using the same compass opening, place the compass point on P, and draw an arc. $\overline{PR} \cong \overline{AB}$

B. Construct an angle congruent to $\angle S$.

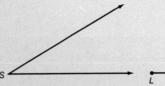

Draw a ray $\overrightarrow{LM}$.

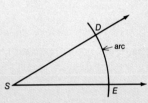

Place the compass point at S, and draw an arc that intersects both sides of $\angle S$. Label the points D and E.

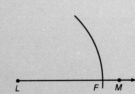

Using the same compass opening, place the compass point at L, and draw an arc. Label the point F on $\overrightarrow{LM}$.

Place the compass points on D and E.

Use the same compass opening to draw an arc from F that intersects the first arc at G. Draw $\overrightarrow{LG}$. $\angle L \cong \angle S$

358

COMMON ERRORS

Some students might have difficulty constructing angles because they are not careful when using the compass.

Remediation
For this error, have students construct several circles and arcs. Work with them to develop a light, smooth touch.

Assign Reteach Master, p. 103.

Copy the figures, and use them to construct the following.

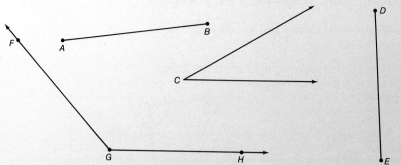

1. Construct a line segment congruent to $\overline{AB}$.
2. Construct an angle congruent to $\angle C$.
3. Construct a line segment congruent to $\overline{DE}$.
4. Construct an angle congruent to $\angle FGH$.
★ 5. Construct a line segment whose length is equal to the length of $\overline{AB}$ + the length of $\overline{DE}$.
★ 6. Construct an angle whose measure is equal to m$\angle FGH$ − m$\angle C$.
   Check students' constructions.

Draw the figure, and construct a figure congruent to it.

7. Draw a line segment. Construct a line segment congruent to it.
8. Draw a right angle. Construct an angle congruent to it.
9. Draw complementary angles. Construct angles congruent to them.
10. Draw supplementary angles. Construct angles congruent to them. Check students' constructions.

CHALLENGE

Find the diameter of this circle.
10 in.

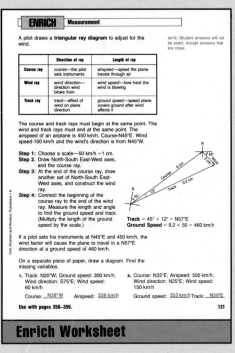

Classwork/Homework, page H147

359

ASSIGNMENT GUIDE

Basic: 1–4, 7–10

Average: 1–10

Extended: 1–10, Chlg

Resources
Practice, p. 147   Class/Home, p. H147
Reteach, p. 103
Enrich, p. 131

Exercise Analysis
1–10   Construct a line segment or angle congruent to a given line segment or angle

Challenge
Offer the following hints for those students who encounter difficulty.
1. All the angles of the figure are right angles. So, the figure must be a rectangle.
2. The diagonals of a rectangle are always congruent line segments.

Therefore, if one diagonal is 5 in., the other must be 5 in. The other diagonal, of course, is the radius of the circle, and the diameter is therefore 10 in.

FOLLOW-UP ACTIVITIES

REINFORCEMENT
Have each student use a straight-edge to draw two line segments and two angles. Have pairs of students exchange papers and copy the figures drawn by the other. Then have students return the papers to be checked by measuring with a ruler and a protractor.

COMING UP
Cut your work in half!

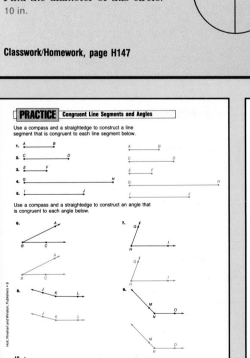

Practice Worksheet

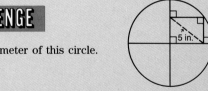

Enrich Worksheet

Objectives: To bisect a line segment and an angle

Warm-Up
Have students answer *True* or *False* to statements such as the following.
- All lines contain line segments. (T)
- All rays are made up of points. (T)
- All lines are made up of rays. (T)
- All line segments are lines. (F)
- All nonintersecting lines are parallel. (F)
- All nonparallel lines are intersecting. (F)

GETTING STARTED

Materials: paper, ruler, per student

Have students draw a 6-inch line segment on a piece of paper and fold the paper so that the ends of the segment meet exactly. Ask them to measure each of the two segments. Then have students draw another line segment along the fold line. Ask them whether they think that this new segment is perpendicular to the original one. (yes) Next, have students draw an angle and fold the piece of paper so that both of the angle's rays fit exactly on top of each other. Tell them to draw another ray along the fold line and to note that the endpoint of this ray is located at the vertex of the angle. Ask students whether they think the two new adjacent angles that have been formed are congruent. (yes)

TEACHING THE LESSON

A. Copy the example on the chalkboard. Set the compass to an opening greater than the length of $\overline{AB}$ to show that any opening greater than $\frac{1}{2}$ the length of $\overline{AB}$ will work. Then set the compass to an opening less than $\frac{1}{2}$ the length of $\overline{AB}$. Point out that this opening will not work because the arcs will not intersect.

B. Tell students that this method will always work regardless of the size of the compass opening. Use the diagram below to prove this.

Open the compass to any radius. Mark the arcs on $\angle A$, and label the intersections B and C. Draw $\overline{BC}$ and label its midpoint D. Open the compass wider, draw the arcs on $\angle A$, and label the intersections X and Y. Then draw $\overleftrightarrow{XY}$ and label its midpoint Z. Show that $\overleftrightarrow{AD}$ and $\overleftrightarrow{AZ}$ are the same line.

Bisecting Line Segments and Angles

Architects use a straightedge and a compass to bisect line segments and angles on blueprints.

A. To **bisect a line segment** means to divide it into two congruent segments. Bisect $\overline{AB}$.

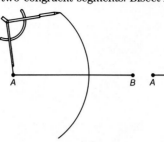
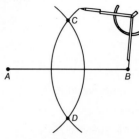
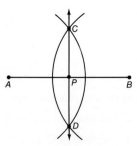

Open the compass to more than $\frac{1}{2}$ the length of $\overline{AB}$. Place the compass point at A, and draw an arc.

Without changing the compass opening, place the compass point at B, and draw another arc. Label the intersections C and D.

Use a straightedge to connect points C and D. $\overleftrightarrow{CD}$ bisects $\overline{AB}$ at P. $\overline{AP} \cong \overline{PB}$. $\overleftrightarrow{CD}$ is the bisector of AB.

B. To **bisect an angle** means to divide it into two congruent angles. Bisect $\angle Y$.

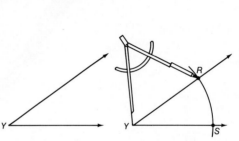

Place the compass point at Y, and draw an arc that intersects both sides of $\angle Y$. Label the points R and S.

Use the same compass opening to draw intersecting arcs from R and S. Label the point Z. Draw $\overrightarrow{YZ}$. $\overrightarrow{YZ}$ bisects $\angle Y$. $\angle RYZ \cong \angle ZYS$. $\overrightarrow{YZ}$ is the bisector of $\angle RYS$.

COMMON ERRORS

While bisecting, students might make large holes in their papers around the point of the compass. This may impair the accuracy of their constructions.

Remediation
For this error, have students demonstrate the construction process. Watch how each student holds the compass, whether the student turns the paper rather than the compass, and so on. Demonstrate the proper way to hold and use the compass.

Assign Reteach Master, p. 104.

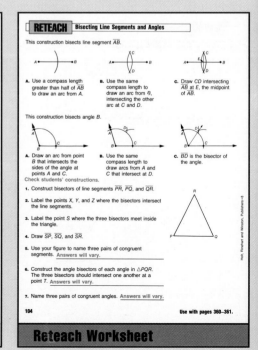

Use the figures to complete.

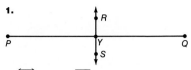

1.

$\overrightarrow{RS}$ bisects $\overline{PQ}$.

$\overline{PY} \cong \blacksquare \ \overline{YQ}$

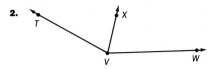

2.

$\overrightarrow{VX}$ bisects $\angle TVW$.

$\angle WVX \cong \blacksquare \ \angle XVT$

Complete.

3. $\overleftrightarrow{EF}$ bisects $\overline{GH}$ at N.

$\overline{GN} \cong \blacksquare \ \overline{NH}$

4. $\overrightarrow{MK}$ bisects $\angle LMN$.

$\angle LMK \cong \blacksquare \ \angle KMN$

Copy each figure. Use each to construct the following: **Check students' constructions.**

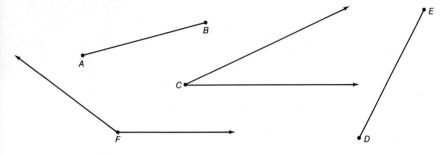

5. the bisector of $\overline{AB}$

6. the bisector of $\angle C$

7. the bisector of $\overline{DE}$

8. the bisector of $\angle F$

Draw any triangle. **Check students' constructions.**

9. Construct the bisector of each side of the triangle. Do these bisectors intersect at one point? **yes**

10. Construct the bisector of each angle in the triangle. Do the angle bisectors intersect at one point? **yes**

ANOTHER LOOK

Evaluate. Use the replacement set $\{^-2, ^-1, 0, 1, 2\}$.

8. $^-2\frac{4}{9}, \ ^-1\frac{2}{9}, \ 0, \ 1\frac{2}{9}, \ 2\frac{4}{9}$

1. $7 + n$
5, 6, 7, 8, 9

2. $n - 11$
$^-13, \ ^-12, \ ^-11, \ ^-10, \ ^-9$

3. $21n$
$^-42, \ ^-21, \ 0, \ 21, \ 42$

4. $\frac{n}{4}$
$^-\frac{1}{2}, \ ^-\frac{1}{4}, \ 0, \ \frac{1}{4}, \ \frac{1}{2}$

5. $\frac{2}{3} + n$
$^-1\frac{1}{3}, \ ^-\frac{1}{3}, \ \frac{2}{3}, \ 1\frac{2}{3}, \ 2\frac{2}{3}$

6. $n - 17.8$
$^-19.8, \ ^-18.8, \ ^-17.8,$
$^-16.8, \ ^-15.8$

7. $0.052n$
$^-0.104, \ ^-0.052, \ 0,$
$0.052, \ 0.104$

8. $\frac{n}{9} \ 11$

361

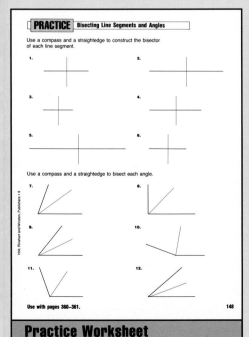

ASSIGNMENT GUIDE

Basic: 1–8, AL

Average: 1–9, AL

Extended: 1–10, AL

Resources
Practice, p. 148   Class/Home, p. H148
Reteach, p. 104   Reasoning, p. H225
Enrich, p. 132

Exercise Analysis

1–4   Use the bisector to name a congruent line segment or angle
5–10   Construct a bisector

Another Look

This review provides maintenance for the use of replacement sets in evaluating an expression.

FOLLOW-UP ACTIVITIES

REINFORCEMENT

Using only compasses and straightedges, have each student construct straight angle ABC with B as the midpoint of $\overline{AC}$. Next, have them draw at random a ray $\overrightarrow{BD}$. Then have pairs of students exchange papers and construct angles congruent to $\frac{1}{2}$ of $\angle DBC$ and $\frac{3}{4}$ of $\angle ABD$. The papers should be returned and checked by measuring with protractors.

MANIPULATIVES

Give each student a sheet of paper to be folded as shown below.

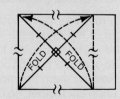

Point out that each fold bisects its corner angle, that the area defined is a square, and that the folds bisect each other at a 90° angle.

Ask students to devise a test whereby one would use only a straightedge and a right angle to tell whether any rectangle was also a square. (Use the straightedge to draw the diagonals of the rectangle and then line up the right angle at the intersection. If the diagonals form a right angle, then the figure is a square.)

COMING UP

Want to get somewhere? Go backward!

Objective: To solve problems by working backward

Warm-Up

Write the following examples on the chalkboard. Have students find the answers.

$\frac{1}{4} \cdot 36$ (9); $\frac{3}{8} \cdot 48$ (18); $0.52 \cdot 4$ (2.08); $\frac{1}{2}x + 3 = 11$ ($x = 16$); $y \cdot \left(\frac{3}{4}\right) = 15$ ($y = 20$)

GETTING STARTED

Draw a 6-square by 6-square grid on the chalkboard. Put a mark in one of the squares. Have a student give four directions to move the mark to a new square; for example: Move up 2, move to the left 1, and so on. Then ask another student to reverse the directions to undo the sequence and move the mark back to where it started. Relate this activity to the strategy of working backward to solve a problem.

TEACHING THE LESSON

In working backward, it is important that students first organize the forward sequence of directions. Once this sequence is established, they can more easily reverse the order and operation.

Questions: Make sure students read the question carefully. Students often encounter problems because they answer the question as would be expected if one worked forward. Careful attention must be paid to exactly what is asked for. Students will be able to identify the correct question by writing the sequence of events or operations and then reversing that sequence.

Tools: Students may have some trouble with the order of the reversals. Writing out the sequence will help. Explain to students that individual operations must be reversed or undone. Remind them that addition and subtraction undo each other; so do multiplication and division.

Solutions: Because much of the work on these pages deals with fractions, it may help to quickly review multiplication and division of fractions. Also review the steps in solving equations.

Checks: The solutions to these problems can be easily checked by substituting them into the beginning of the equation and working the problem forward.

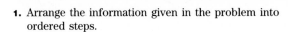

| QUESTIONS | TOOLS | SOLUTIONS | CHECKS |

PROBLEM SOLVING
Working Backward

Some problems give the final result of a series of operations and ask for the original number. You work backward to solve such problems.

> James led a tour through the historic nineteenth-century storefronts in Kansas City. Then, $\frac{2}{5}$ of the group left for lunch. The tour went on to the nation's first major shopping center, which was built in 1922. Half of the remaining group stayed there. James took the last 6 people on a special bus tour. How many people were there on the tour originally?

1. Arrange the information given in the problem into ordered steps.

2. Write an equation for each step.

the number of people in the tour	the number after $\frac{2}{5}$ left	half in the center	other half with James
x	$x - \frac{2}{5}x = \frac{3}{5}x$ $\frac{3}{5}x = y$	$\frac{1}{2}y = z$	$z = 6$

3. Work backward, and solve each equation.

How many people were with the tour in the shopping center?

Since $z = 6$ and $\frac{1}{2}y = z$, then $\frac{1}{2}y = 6$.

$$2 \cdot \frac{1}{2}y = 2 \cdot 6$$
$$y = 12$$

How many people were with the tour originally?

Since $y = 12$ and $\frac{3}{5}x = y$, then $\frac{3}{5}x = 12$.

$$\frac{5}{3} \cdot \frac{3}{5}x = \frac{5}{3} \cdot 12$$
$$x = 20$$

There were originally 20 people on the tour.

Check your answer.	number in tour	that number minus $\frac{2}{5}$ of it	$\frac{1}{2}$ the difference
	20	$20 - \left(\frac{2}{5} \cdot 20\right)$ $20 - 8 = 12$	$\frac{1}{2} \cdot 12 = 6$ The answer is correct.

Work backward. Then write the letter of the correct answer.

1. Of her weekly allowance, Sara spent $\frac{1}{6}$ to buy 12 postcards of historic houses and $\frac{1}{3}$ to buy a book about architecture. Sara had $7.50 of her weekly allowance left after these purchases. What is Sara's weekly allowance?

   a. $12.50   **b.** $15.00   c. $22.50

2. Thelma had some baseball cards. She gave 11 to her brother and divided the remainder equally among herself and 3 friends. Her share consisted of 19 cards. How many cards did she have originally?

   a. 90   b. 48   **c.** 87

Solve.

3. Mrs. Cole's class visited the Mount Pleasant Estate. Half the class toured the grounds. Of those who did not tour the grounds, $\frac{1}{3}$ began the tour in the drawing room and 5 began in the kitchen. This left 3, who began the tour in the basement. How many students were there in the class?
   24 students

4. A team of three painters painted one tower of a suspension bridge. The first painter painted $\frac{1}{4}$ of the tower. The second painter painted $\frac{1}{2}$ the remaining part. The third painter painted a 24-foot section. That left a 16-foot section to be painted by all three painters. How tall is the bridge tower?   **106 $\frac{2}{3}$ feet**

5. The idea for a national monument in St. Louis was conceived 14 years before construction began. It took 20 years to build the Great Archway, but 2 of those years were spent finishing the interior. St. Louis planned a twenty-fifth birthday party to commemorate the building of the exterior of the arch. The party was held in 1990. In which year was the idea for the monument conceived?   **1933**

6. It took 4 months to pour all the concrete required to build the Hoover Dam. In March, 0.62 million cubic meters of concrete were poured. In April, 0.21 million cubic meters less than the March amount were poured. In May, twice the April amount was poured. That left 0.63 million cubic meters to be poured in June. How many cubic meters of concrete are there in the dam?   **2.48 million cubic meters**

Classwork/Homework, pages H149–H150

ASSIGNMENT GUIDE

Basic: 1–4
Average: 2–5
Extended: 3–6

Resources
Practice, pp. 149-50   Class/Home, pp. H149–50

Exercise Analysis
1–2   Choose the correct answer
3–6   Solve by working backward

FOLLOW-UP ACTIVITIES

PROBLEM SOLVING
Have students solve this problem.

Allison read $\frac{1}{8}$ of the books in her bookcase last summer. She read the same number of fiction books as nonfiction books. One fourth of the fiction books were books of poetry. If Allison read 2 books of poetry last summer, how many books are there in her bookcase? (128)

CALCULATOR
Materials: 1 calculator per student

Enter a number into your calculator. Perform a series of six operations on the calculator, announcing each operation to the class as it is entered and having students write them on paper. Announce the final number on your calculator and have students find the original number on their own calculators. The one who computes the number first becomes the announcer.

COMING UP
The construction industry

PRACTICE   Working Backward

Work backward. Ring the letter of the correct answer.

1. Alex is painting a house. He uses $\frac{1}{3}$ of the paint he bought on the dining room. He uses twice as much on the living room as on the kitchen, where he uses $1\frac{1}{2}$ gallons. He has $1\frac{1}{2}$ gallons of paint left. How much paint did Alex buy?
   a. 12 gallons
   b. 16 gallons
   c. 9 gallons

2. Naomi is cleaning out a storeroom at the paint shop. She puts $\frac{1}{2}$ the paint on display in the shop and takes $\frac{1}{3}$ of what is left to the basement. Although she takes $\frac{3}{4}$ of the remaining paint home, there are still 7 gallons left in the storeroom. How much paint was in the storeroom before she cleaned it?
   a. 168 gallons
   b. 112 gallons
   c. 56 gallons

Solve.

3. It took Nancy and Ramon 3 weeks to paint a house in their spare time. During the second week, they used $3\frac{1}{2}$ fewer gallons of paint than they used in the first week. In the third week, they used 13 gallons, which was twice as many as the number of gallons used in the second week. How much paint did they use?
   $29\frac{1}{2}$ gallons

4. Toku follows a budget to buy supplies to paint his room. He spends $\frac{1}{2}$ of his budget on a roller, a tray, and tape. He spends $12.27 on paint, and of the remaining money, he spends $\frac{2}{3}$ on a trim brush, which costs $3.82. How much money has he budgeted? $36.00

5. Susan wants to use blue, yellow, green, and pink paint to decorate her house. She needs 3 times as much blue paint as yellow paint and $\frac{1}{2}$ as much yellow paint as green paint. She needs $3\frac{1}{4}$ gallons of pink paint, which is $\frac{3}{4}$ of a gallon more than the green paint she needs. How much paint does Susan need in all?
   $10\frac{3}{4}$ gallons

6. Colleen's family plans to paint the windows of their house. Her father will paint twice as many windows as her mother, and Colleen and her 2 brothers will paint an equal number of the rest of the windows. Colleen decides to do her own share and her mother's share and paints 7 windows, which is one less than her father's share. How many windows are there?   21 windows

Use with pages 362–363.   149

Practice Worksheet

PRACTICE   Working Backward

Work backward. Ring the letter of the correct answer.

1. In the first act of a play, all the actors were onstage. The second act opened with $\frac{1}{3}$ the actors onstage, and then 5 actors left. After that, $\frac{1}{2}$ the remaining actors left, and 4 actors remained onstage. How many actors were onstage in the first act?
   a. 36   **b.** 26   c. 28

2. Sam bought 8 of his friends tickets for a play. Each ticket cost $8.70. He also bought 2 books of plays, each costing $4.45. He spent exactly $\frac{1}{2}$ the money he had left for a record that cost $6.20. How much money did Sam originally have?
   a. $90.90   b. $84.70   c. $67.10

Solve.

3. In one scene of a play, 23 lines were spoken by the lead actor. The rest of the lines were spoken by Roger and Francis. Francis spoke twice as many lines as Roger, who had 9 lines. How many lines were spoken in the scene?   50 lines

4. Rufus is in charge of lighting a play. Half the lights he uses are white. Of the remaining lights, $\frac{1}{3}$ have red filters, and 4 have blue filters. The 10 lights left have yellow filters. How many lights does Rufus use for the play?   42 lights

5. Sally took money from her bank account to go out of town for an audition. She spent $54.00 for a round-trip bus ticket and $\frac{1}{3}$ of the remaining money for her hotel bill. She spent $7.90 for food and arrived home with $15.10. How much money did Sally take from her bank account? $100.00

6. Act I of a play lasts $\frac{2}{3}$ the time of the whole play. There is a 15-minute intermission. In Act II, Jack's speech takes up $\frac{1}{2}$ the time, and the rest is divided equally between speeches made by Rosa and Zoe. Zoe talks for 6 minutes, and the play ends at 8:17 P.M. When did the play begin?   6:50 P.M.

7. At intermission, Xavier sold refreshments. Of the items he had, $\frac{1}{5}$ were granola bars and $\frac{1}{2}$ the remaining items were containers of popcorn. The rest were divided equally among apples, rice cakes, and containers of yogurt. Xavier sold the 8 apples he had. How many items did he originally have?   60 items

8. Information about a play took up $\frac{1}{3}$ of the pages in the program. Information about the actors took up $\frac{1}{4}$ of the remaining pages. Information about the director, the producer, and the designer took up 2 pages, the same number of pages devoted to the actors. How many pages were there in the program?   12 pages

150   Use with pages 362–363.

Practice Worksheet

Objectives: To define and construct parallel and perpendicular lines

Warm-Up
Have students use straightedges to draw a pair of parallel lines. Have students check one another's work. (Have each student draw a transversal. Show students a pair of angles that should be congruent, and let them measure with protractors.)

GETTING STARTED

Draw the following on the chalkboard.

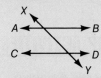

Tell students that $\overleftrightarrow{AB} \parallel \overleftrightarrow{CD}$. Then have them identify pairs of supplementary angles. Ask: Which angles may be congruent?

TEACHING THE LESSON

A. Use the following steps to prove that vertical angles are congruent.
1. $\angle 1 + \angle 2 = 180°$
2. $\angle 2 + \angle 3 = 180°$
3. Therefore, $\angle 1 + \angle 2 = \angle 2 + \angle 3$
4. $\angle 1 = \angle 3$

B. Point out that this method works because the constructed angle and $\angle 1$ are corresponding angles that are congruent if the lines are parallel. Conversely, if corresponding (or alternate interior) angles are drawn congruent, then the lines must be parallel.

C. Emphasize the fact that although the methods for constructing a bisector and a perpendicular may seem similar, they are not necessarily the same. A bisector intersects a line segment at its midpoint, whereas a perpendicular may intersect at any point as long as it intersects at a 90° angle.

364

Perpendicular and Parallel Lines

A. In the drawing shown on the right, line l is parallel to line m, or $l \parallel m$. Line n is perpendicular to line p, or $n \perp p$. **Perpendicular** lines intersect to form right angles.

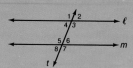

Line t is a **transversal** that intersects lines l and m forming eight angles. Since $l \parallel m$, the following angle relationships are true. For example, $\angle 1$ and $\angle 3$, and $\angle 6$ and $\angle 8$ are **vertical angles** and are congruent. $\angle 1$ and $\angle 2$, and $\angle 6$ and $\angle 7$ are **adjacent angles** and are supplementary. $\angle 4$ and $\angle 6$, and $\angle 3$ and $\angle 5$ are **alternate interior angles** and are congruent. Finally, $\angle 2$ and $\angle 6$, and $\angle 4$ and $\angle 8$ are **corresponding angles** and are congruent.

B. Construct a line parallel to line l.

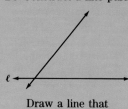 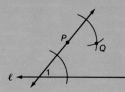 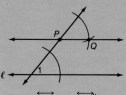

| Draw a line that intersects line l at any point. | At any point P on this line, construct an angle congruent to $\angle 1$. Label the point Q. | Draw $\overrightarrow{PQ}$. $\overrightarrow{PQ} \parallel l$ |

C. Construct a line perpendicular to line l.

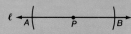 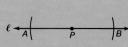 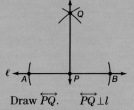

| With the compass opening the same, draw two arcs from P that intersect l. Label the points A and B. | Open the compass farther and place its point at A and then at B, draw intersecting arcs. Label the point Q. | Draw $\overrightarrow{PQ}$. $\overrightarrow{PQ} \perp l$ |

364

COMMON ERRORS

Some students might draw nonintersecting arcs when constructing a perpendicular.

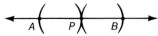

In this figure, the compass opening used to mark A and B is also used to draw the arcs.

Remediation
For this error, tell students that in order for the arcs to intersect, the compass opening that generates them must be greater than the original opening.

Assign Reteach Master, p. 105.

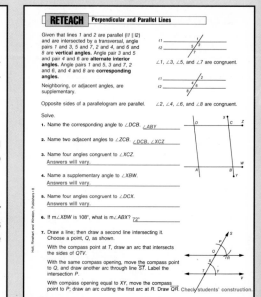

Identify each pair of lines as *parallel* or as *perpendicular*.

1. a pair of lines that intersect to form right angles
   perpendicular

2.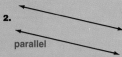
   parallel

3.
   perpendicular

In the given figure, $l \| m$. Identify each pair of angles as *vertical, adjacent, alternate interior,* or *corresponding* angles.

4. ∠1 and ∠8
   vertical

5. ∠3 and ∠8
   alternate interior

6. ∠6 and ∠7
   corresponding

7. ∠3 and ∠5
   adjacent

8. ∠4 and ∠5
   corresponding

9. ∠5 and ∠7
   vertical

10. ∠1 and ∠6
   adjacent

11. ∠5 and ∠6
   alternate interior

12. ∠2 and ∠5
   adjacent

13. ∠4 and ∠6
   vertical

14. ∠2 and ∠3
   vertical

In the same figure, name each pair of angles as *congruent* or *supplementary*.

15. ∠7 and ∠8
   supplementary

16. ∠4 and ∠2
   supplementary

17. ∠7 and ∠1
   supplementary

18. ∠6 and ∠4
   congruent

19. ∠5 and ∠6
   congruent

20. ∠2 and ∠3
   congruent

21. ∠4 and ∠1
   supplementary

22. ∠1 and ∠3
   congruent

23. ∠7 and ∠2
   supplementary

Complete. Use the same figure as above.

24. If m∠6 = 57°, m∠4 = ▓ 57°

25. If m∠6 = 57°, m∠1 = ▓ 123°

In the given figure, $\overleftrightarrow{AB} \| \overleftrightarrow{CD}$. Write *true* if the angles are congruent. Write *false* if the angles are not congruent.

26. ∠AEG ≅ ∠BEF
   true

27. ∠DFH ≅ ∠DFG
   false

28. ∠AEH ≅ ∠CFH
   true

29. ∠BEH ≅ ∠GFC
   true

30. ∠DFH ≅ ∠HFC
   false

31. ∠EFD ≅ ∠CFH
   true

Use this figure to find the measure of each angle. $l \| m$ and m∠6 = 145°.

32. m∠7 145°

33. m∠5 145°

34. m∠2 145°

35. m∠8 35°

Solve. Check students' constructions.

36. Draw a line. Construct a line parallel to it.

37. Draw a line. Construct a line perpendicular to it.

Classwork/Homework, page H151

365

ASSIGNMENT GUIDE

Basic: 1–23, 27–35 o, 36–37

Average: 4–22 e, 24–37

Extended: 5–23 o, 24–37

Resources
Practice, p. 151 Class/Home, p. H151
Reteach, p. 105
Enrich, p. 133

Exercise Analysis
1–3   Identify parallel and perpendicular lines
4–31   Identify a pair of angles
32–35   Find the measure of an angle
36–37   Construct a line perpendicular or parallel to a given line

FOLLOW-UP ACTIVITIES

PROBLEM SOLVING
Have each student use only a compass and a straightedge to construct a square. (Draw $\overline{AB}$. Construct perpendiculars at A and B. Set the compass opening to $\overline{AB}$. Place the point at A, and where the arc intersects the perpendicular, mark D. Repeat to find C on the perpendicular at B. Draw $\overline{CD}$ to complete square ABCD.) Repeat the procedure by drawing only one perpendicular. (Draw perpendicular lines AB and CD. Draw a circle whose center is the intersection of those lines. Complete the square by drawing line segments to connect the points where the circle intersects $\overleftrightarrow{AB}$ and $\overleftrightarrow{CD}$.)

MATH CONNECTION
(Science)
Materials: a map with contour lines

Display the map, and point out the contour lines. Have volunteers suggest explanations for them and amend them as necessary. Point out that like parallel lines, contour lines never meet. Ask why. (because no location can have two different elevations)

COMING UP
You're acute, kid; so, don't be obtuse.

Objective: To classify a triangle

Warm-Up

Have students identify the type of each angle and compute its supplement mentally.

40° (acute, 140°); 75° (acute, 105°); 180° (straight, 0°); 135° (obtuse, 45°); 2° (acute, 178°); 100° (obtuse, 80°); 90° (right, 90°); 116° (obtuse, 64°)

GETTING STARTED

Materials: 4 strips of poster board containing a fastener at one end

Connect three of the poster-board strips to form a triangle. Ask whether the shape of the triangle can be changed. (no, not without unfastening the strips because a triangle is a rigid figure) Allow students to check their answers by trying to move the sides of the triangle.

Then add the fourth strip to form a parallelogram. Ask whether its shape can be changed. (yes) Point out that because squares are not rigid figures, engineers have had to use triangles in constructing bridges, the Eiffel Tower, and so on.

TEACHING THE LESSON

A. Explain that *scalene* comes from the Greek. It means "uneven" or "odd." *Isosceles* also comes from the Greek. It means "equal leg." *Equilateral* comes from the Latin. It means "equal side."

B. Emphasize the fact that for a triangle to be an acute triangle, all three of its interior angles must be acute. If merely one angle of a triangle is right or obtuse, then the triangle would be a right or an obtuse triangle, respectively.

C. Have students cut triangles out of construction paper and label their vertices *A*, *B*, and *C*. Then have them rip off the vertices to demonstrate that by fitting all three into a straight angle, the sum of the angles of a triangle is 180°.

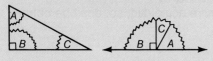

Classifying Triangles

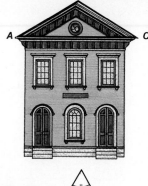

The Southport Savings Bank in Southport, Connecticut, was built in 1854. Notice the triangle-shaped roof. What kind of a triangle is it?

A **triangle** is a closed figure that has three line segments that form its **sides.** You can use the **vertices** of a triangle to name it. Triangle *ABC* is written △*ABC*.

A. A triangle can be named according to the lengths of its sides.

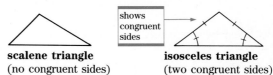

scalene triangle
(no congruent sides)

isosceles triangle
(two congruent sides)

equilateral triangle
(three congruent sides)

The roof of the bank forms an isosceles triangle.

B. A triangle also can be named according to the measures of its angles.

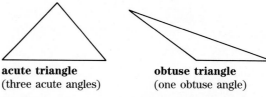

acute triangle
(three acute angles)

obtuse triangle
(one obtuse angle)

right triangle
(one right angle)

The roof of the bank also forms an obtuse triangle.

C. In any triangle, the sum of the measures of the angles is 180°.
33° + 132° + 15° = 180°

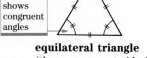

An **exterior angle** of a triangle is formed by extending a side of the triangle. The measure of an exterior angle of a triangle is equal to the sum of the measures of the two opposite interior angles of the triangle. In the figure, m∠4 = m∠1 + m∠2.

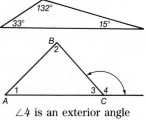

∠4 is an exterior angle of △*ABC*.

Math Reasoning, page H225

COMMON ERRORS

In forming an exterior angle, some students might become confused because they do not know which side of the triangle to extend.

Remediation

For this error, use the diagram to show that any one side can be extended. If $\overline{AC}$ is extended, ∠*Y* results. If $\overline{BC}$ is extended, ∠*X* results. But make sure students understand that ∠*X* and ∠*Y* are congruent vertical angles.

Assign Reteach Master, p. 106.

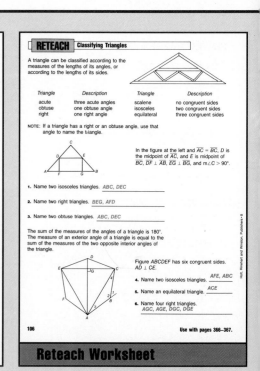

Reteach Worksheet

Complete.

1. A triangle that has at least two congruent sides is called ▪. **isosceles**

2. A triangle that has a 97° angle is called ▪. **obtuse**

3. If the sum of the measures of two angles of a triangle is 124°, the measure of the third angle is ▪. **56°**

4. In the accompanying figure, the measure of the exterior angle is ▪. **145°**

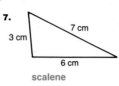

Name each triangle according to the lengths of its sides.

5.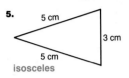

isosceles

6.

equilateral

7.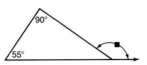

scalene

Name each triangle according to the measures of its angles.

8.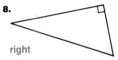

right

9.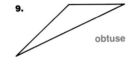

obtuse

10.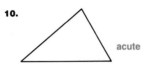

acute

Given the measure of two angles of a triangle, find the measure of the third angle.

11. 48° and 71° 61°   **12.** 90° and 15° 75°   **13.** 117° and 27° 36°   **14.** 13° and 141° 26°

15. 90° and 45° 45°   **16.** 30° and 60° 90°   **17.** 60° and 60° 60°   **18.** 30° and 90° 60°

Draw each figure. **Check students' drawings.**

19. an acute scalene triangle

20. an equilateral triangle

21. an isosceles right triangle

22. an obtuse scalene triangle

23. an equiangular triangle

24. a right scalene triangle

25. an obtuse isosceles triangle

26. an acute isosceles triangle

Determine the measure of each angle in the figure.

27. m∠*1* 32°   **28.** m∠*2* 148°

29. m∠*3* 58°   **30.** m∠*4* 154°

Write *acute, obtuse,* or *right;* and *equilateral, scalene,* or *isosceles* to classify each triangle.

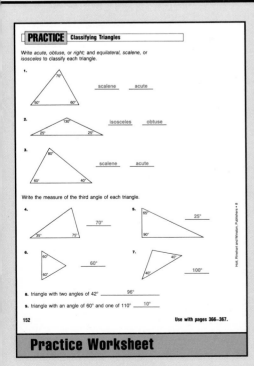

1. scalene   acute

2. isosceles   obtuse

3. scalene   acute

Write the measure of the third angle of each triangle.

4. 70°   **5.** 25°

6. 60°   **7.** 100°

8. triangle with two angles of 42° 96°

9. triangle with an angle of 60° and one of 110° 10°

A tangent to a circle touches the circumference of a circle at only one point. $\overline{AB}$ and $\overline{CD}$ are tangents to circle O.

For any triangle, a circle can be drawn that fits exactly inside the triangle; the sides of the triangle will be tangents of the circle. This is called the *in-circle* of the triangle.

To construct the in-circle, you must construct a perpendicular line from a point to a line.

To construct the perpendicular from *S* to line *TU*:

1. Place the compass point on *S* and draw two arcs on $\overline{TU}$. Mark these points *Q* and *R*.

2. Construct the perpendicular bisector of $\overline{QR}$.

3. Is point *S* on this line? why?
Yes. The point *S* is midway between points *Q* and *R*.

4. Draw a triangle *FGH*.

5. Bisect two angles of the triangle. Label the point where the bisectors meet *X*.

6. Bisect the third angle. Does *X* lie on this bisector? yes

7. Construct a perpendicular line from *X* to each side of the triangle. Measure the lines with a compass. What do you find? They are all the same length.

8. Use *X* as the center to construct the in-circle.

9. What is the angle of intersection of the radius of a circle and a tangent to a circle? 90°

10. Construct the in-circle of triangle *JKL*.

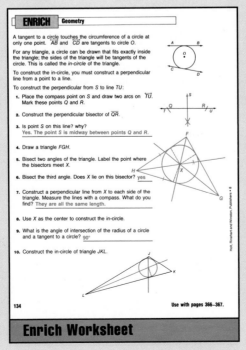

Practice Worksheet   **Enrich Worksheet**

Exercise Analysis
1–2   Name a triangle
3–4   Find the measure of a third angle or an exterior angle
5–10   Name a triangle
11–18   Find the measure of a third angle
19–26   Draw a triangle
27–30   Find the measure of a third angle or an exterior angle

FOLLOW-UP ACTIVITIES

MATH CONNECTION
(Home Economics)
When designing a kitchen, architects pay particular attention to what they call the *triangle of efficiency*. This triangle is defined as that which connects the sink, the stove, and the refrigerator. Give students uniform sheets of paper and have them outline the triangle of efficiency as they design kitchens. Then have them discuss how the design of their triangles affects the functioning of the kitchen. Have each student classify the triangle.

MANIPULATIVES
Materials: assorted triangles cut out of construction paper

Hold up the triangles one at a time, and have volunteers name them according to sides and angles. Repeat this procedure by holding the triangles by different vertices at different angles.

REINFORCEMENT
Have students determine whether the following triangles are possible.
- a triangle with three acute angles (yes)
- a triangle with three obtuse angles (no)
- a triangle with one obtuse angle and one right angle (no)
- an isosceles triangle with a right angle (yes)
- an equilateral triangle with a right angle (no)

COMING UP
Polly gone? We'll find her tomorrow.

Objective: To identify a polygon

Warm-Up
Give students two angles of a triangle such as those listed below and have them find the measure of the third angle.

16°, 90° (74°)   57°, 105° (18°)
167°, 8° (5°)   20°, 69° (91°)

GETTING STARTED

Materials: congruent right isosceles triangles made from cardboard or heavy paper

Put two triangles together to form a square. Ask: What is the sum of the measures of the angles of a square? (Because a square has four right angles, the sum is 360°.) Separate the triangles, and point out that the sum of 360° is confirmed because the sum of the angles of each triangle is 180° and there are two triangles.

Repeat the procedure by using the triangles to form a pentagon or a hexagon. Show that only the angles that are part of a vertex of the polygon contribute to the sum of its angles.

TEACHING THE LESSON

A. Distinguish between concave ("the kind that go in") and convex ("the kind that go out") polygons. Demonstrate a common test: For a polygon to be convex, no line joining two vertices may pass outside the polygon. Consequently, a concave polygon is one in which at least one line joining two vertices passes outside the polygon.

convex   concave

B. Point out that each segment joining opposite vertices of both the rhombus and the square is a perpendicular bisector of the other.

You might also note that it is most common to name a quadrilateral according to the narrowest class to which it belongs.

C. Explain that students can use this method as a quick way to find the measure of each interior angle of a regular polygon. Because all the angles of a regular polygon are congruent, all students have to do is calculate the sum of the measures of the angles and then divide by the number of angles, which is equal to the number of sides.

368

Polygons

A. The figures shown below are examples of **polygons**. A polygon is named according to the number of its sides.

A **regular polygon** has congruent sides and congruent angles.

Sides	Polygon
three	triangle
four	quadrilateral
five	pentagon
six	hexagon
seven	heptagon
eight	octagon
nine	nonagon
ten	decagon

pentagon   regular pentagon   quadrilateral   hexagon

B. Here are some kinds of **quadrilaterals**.

parallelogram
opposite sides parallel and congruent

rectangle
parallelogram has four right angles

square
rectangle has four congruent sides

rhombus
parallelogram has four congruent sides

trapezoid
quadrilateral has only two parallel sides

C. A **diagonal** is a line segment other than a side that joins two vertices of a polygon.

The diagonals in this 5-sided polygon (pentagon) divide it into $5 - 2$, or 3 triangles. So, the sum of the measures of the pentagon's interior angles is $3 \cdot 180$. For a polygon of n sides, the interior angle sum is $(n - 2) \cdot 180$.

For a pentagon $ABCDE$,
$$\text{sum for } ABCDE = (n - 2) \cdot 180$$
$$(5 - 2) \cdot 180$$
$$3 \quad \cdot 180 = 540$$

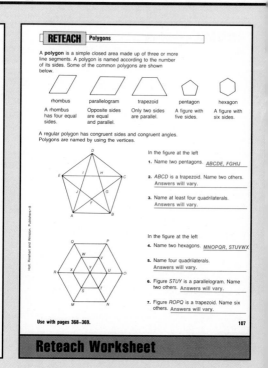

368

Math Reasoning, page H226

COMMON ERRORS

Some students might have difficulty in substituting the proper value for the sum of the measure of the interior angles of a polygon.

Remediation
For this error, have students review the prefixes that denote the number of sides of a polygon. This is the number to be substituted for n. Making a chart may be helpful.

Assign Reteach Master, p. 107.

RETEACH Polygons

A **polygon** is a simple closed area made up of three or more line segments. A polygon is named according to the number of its sides. Some of the common polygons are shown below.

rhombus
A rhombus has four equal sides.

parallelogram
Opposite sides are equal and parallel.

trapezoid
Only two sides are parallel.

pentagon
A figure with five sides.

hexagon
A figure with six sides.

A regular polygon has congruent sides and congruent angles. Polygons are named by using the vertices.

In the figure at the left
1. Name two pentagons. *ABCDE, FGHIJ*

2. ABCD is a trapezoid. Name two others. Answers will vary.

3. Name at least four quadrilaterals. Answers will vary.

In the figure at the left
4. Name two hexagons. *MNOPQR, STUVWX*

5. Name four quadrilaterals. Answers will vary.

6. Figure STUY is a parallelogram. Name two others. Answers will vary.

7. Figure ROPQ is a trapezoid. Name six others. Answers will vary.

Use with pages 368–369.   107

Reteach Worksheet

Name each polygon. Indicate if it is regular.

1.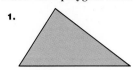
triangle

2.
regular pentagon

3.
decagon

4.
regular hexagon

5.
regular octagon

6.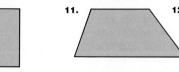
quadrilateral

7. Trace the hexagon. How many diagonals can be drawn from any one vertex? **three diagonals**

8. Trace the octagon. How many diagonals can be drawn from any one vertex? **five diagonals**

Name each quadrilateral.

9.
rhombus

10.
rectangle

11.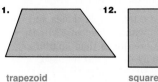
trapezoid

12.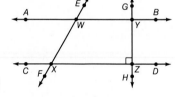
square

For each polygon, find the sum of the measures of the interior angles.

13. triangle
180°

14. octagon
1,080°

15. pentagon
540°

16. nonagon
1,260°

17. hexagon
720°

18. quadrilateral
360°

19. decagon
1,440°

20. heptagon
900°

MIDCHAPTER REVIEW

In the figure at right, $\overline{AB} \| \overline{CD}$. Identify each of the following. **Other answers are possible.**

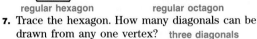

1. a point A
2. four lines $\overline{AB}$; $\overline{CD}$; $\overline{EF}$; $\overline{GH}$
3. two rays $\overrightarrow{WA}$; $\overrightarrow{YB}$
4. two line segments $\overline{WX}$; $\overline{YZ}$

5. two acute angles
∠AWX; ∠WXZ
6. two obtuse angles
∠CXW; ∠XWY
7. two straight angles
∠AWY; ∠CXZ
8. two right angles
∠WYZ; ∠XZY
9. two congruent angles
∠AWX; ∠EWY
10. two supplementary angles
∠AWX; ∠XWY
11. two vertical angles
∠CXF; ∠WXZ
12. two adjacent angles
∠AWX; ∠XWY
13. two corresponding angles
∠EWY; ∠WXZ

Classwork/Homework, page H153

369

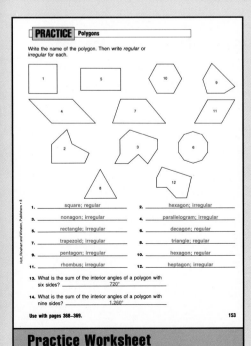
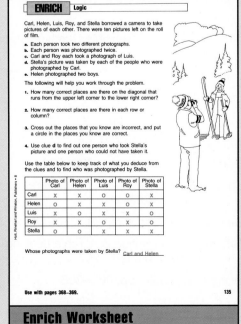
Exercise Analysis
1–6   Name a polygon
7–8   Draw diagonals
9–12   Name a quadrilateral
13–20   Find the sum of the measures of the interior angles of a polygon

You may wish to allow students to use calculators for some of these exercises.

Midchapter Review
This review provides an opportunity for you and students to assess their understanding of concepts and skills developed to this point in the chapter.

FOLLOW-UP ACTIVITIES

MATH COMMUNICATION
Have students match each prefix with the number it denotes.

nona-	(9)	octa-	(8)
tri-	(3)	penta-	(5)
quadri-	(4)	bi-	(2)
hepta-	(7)	deca-	(10)
uni-	(1)	hexa-	(6)

Point out that in the original Roman calendar, September was the seventh month, October was the eighth month, and so on. Then in the seventh century B.C., Emperor Numa added January and February, which pushed back all the other months.

COMPUTER
Have students write computer programs that will find the number of diagonals in and the sum of the interior angles of any polygon.

```
(10 INPUT "HOW MANY SIDES";S
 20 LET D = (S-3)*S/2
 30 LET A = (S-2)*180
 40 PRINT "THE POLYGON HAS ";D;"
    DIAGONALS AND THE SUM OF ITS
    INTERIOR ANGLES IS"; A;
    "DEGREES"
 50 END)
```

COMING UP
Talent will take you far, but nothing will help as much as . . .

369

Objective: To practice choosing and using methods and strategies for solving problems

Warm-Up
To prepare students for this lesson, have them solve the following equations.

$36n - 12 = 204$ ($n = 6$)

$\left(\frac{3}{8}\right)n + 7 = 31$ ($n = 64$)

GETTING STARTED

Ask one student to write a problem based on one of the equations above. Then discuss with students the strategies they could use to solve it. Encourage students to use every possible method of solving the problem. Have students write problems for the other equation above and discuss with the class ways of solving it.

TEACHING THE LESSON

These problem-solving pages allow students to choose strategies from those strategies already taught in the textbook. Students also choose the appropriate method for solving each problem. This means students must find an effective approach for each problem and must correctly implement the strategy and method they have chosen. Remind students that they should not stay stuck on a problem; they should try another approach or move on and return later. It might be helpful to have students work these problems in small groups. Encourage students to choose the most efficient method. You may wish to review with students the problem-solving lessons presented so far in this book.

Estimation: pp. 54–55; 136–137

4–Step Plan: pp. 16–17

Using Data from Outside Sources, Including Infobank: pp. 24–25

Using a Graph: pp. 32–33; 248–249

Identifying Extra/Needed Information: pp. 48–49

Choosing the Operation: pp. 62–63; 102–103

Solving Multistep Problems/Making a Plan: pp. 68–69; 270–271

Checking for a Reasonable Answer: pp. 86–87

Using a Table: pp. 96–97

Writing an Equation: pp. 110–111; 288–289

Using a Pictograph: pp. 126–127

Writing a Simpler Problem: pp. 144–145

Interpreting the Quotient and Remainder: pp. 154–155

Choosing/Writing a Sensible Question: pp. 172–173

Using a Formula: pp. 184–185; 222–223

Using a Road Map: pp. 190–191

Writing a Proportion: pp. 204–205

Writing an Organized List: pp. 214–215

Using a Circle Graph: pp. 228–229

Checking That the Solution Answers the Question: pp. 262–263

Guessing and Checking: pp. 290–291

Organizing Information in a Table/Looking for a Pattern: pp. 296–297

Using a Schedule: pp. 302–303

Using a Scattergram: pp. 320–321

Selecting Notation: pp. 338–339

Interpreting a Graph: pp. 344–345

Working Backward: pp. 362–363

| QUESTIONS | TOOLS | SOLUTIONS | CHECKS |

PROBLEM SOLVING
Choosing a Strategy or Method

Write the strategy or method you choose. Then solve.

Strategies and methods will vary.

1. The Washington Monument is 555 feet tall. A statue in Ana's town is 27 feet less than $\frac{1}{3}$ of the Washington Monument's height. How tall is the statue? Writing an Equation; 158 feet

2. Boston's Freedom Trail is a $1\frac{1}{2}$ mile path of landmarks. On one map $\frac{1}{4}$ inch represents the length of the trail. What does 1 inch represent on the map? Writing an Equation; 6 miles

3. Ted had a total of 24 dimes and quarters with a value of $3.75. He had 6 more dimes than quarters. How many dimes did he have? Guessing and Checking; 15 dimes

4. A football team scored 37 points by making some 7-point touchdowns and fewer than five 3-point field goals. How many touchdowns did the team make? Guessing and Checking; 4 touchdowns

5. Cathy works at the mall 4 days each week. The distance from her house to work is 15.2 miles. How many miles does she travel each week going to and from work? Solving Multi-step Problems; 121.6 miles

> Estimation
> Using a Graph
> Choosing the Operation
> Solving Multi-step Problems
> Guessing and Checking
> Making a Table to Find a Pattern
> Writing an Equation
> Interpreting the Quotient and the Remainder
> Using a Formula
> Making an Organized List
> Using a Sample

Use the survey of 200 votes for Exercises 6–9.

STUDENTS' VOTES ON THE TEN MOST USEFUL INVENTIONS

Rank	Invention	Votes	Rank	Invention	Votes
1	Electric light	38	6	Airplane	15
2	Computer	35	7	TV	12
3	Car	30	8	Radio	10
4	Telephone	24	9	Zipper	8
5	Plastic	16	10	Typewriter	6

6. What percent of the students voted for the radio? 5%

7. How many more people voted for the electric light than for TV? 26 more people

370

8. What percent of the students voted for inventions that did not make the top-ten list? **3%**

★9. The town has 1,250 students. What percent of the town's students participated in the survey? **16%**

10. The Cathedral of Saint John the Divine in New York City will be the world's largest cathedral when completed. The ratio of the length to the width is 15:8. The width is 320 feet. What is the length? **600 feet**

11. Each tower of the World Trade Center stands 411.6 meters tall. An architectural model of the towers uses a scale of 4 mm equals 1 m. How tall is the model? **1,646.4 mm**

Use the broken-line graph below for Exercises 12–13.

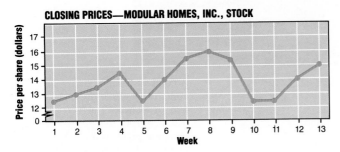

12. During which week did the Modular Homes stock close at its highest price? **week 8**

13. Between which weeks did Modular Homes stock experience the greatest drop in price? **weeks 9 and 10**

Use the circle graph at the right for Exercises 14–16.

FAVORITE EXERCISES — Jumping Rope 5%, 22% Swimming, 40% Jogging, 15% Biking, 18% Walking

14. If a total of 240 people were interviewed, how many prefer biking? **36 people**

15. How many more people prefer jogging than biking and jumping rope? **41 people**

16. Which two exercises have a combined percent that equals jogging's percent? **walking and swimming**

Classwork/Homework, pages H154–H155

ASSIGNMENT GUIDE

Basic: 1–15 o
Average: 2–14 e
Extended: 7–15

Resources
Practice, pp. 154–5   Class/Home, pp. H154–5

Exercise Analysis
1–16 Choose an appropriate strategy or method

FOLLOW-UP ACTIVITIES

CALCULATOR
Have students use calculators to find the square roots of the following *without* using the square root key.

$\sqrt{2,500}$ (50)
$\sqrt{4,096}$ (64)
$\sqrt{10,000}$ (100)
$\sqrt{14,641}$ (121)
$\sqrt{390,625}$ (625)
$\sqrt{1,440,000}$ (1,200)

CALCULATOR
Have students use a calculator to find the following percents.
- 55.3% of 426 (235.578)
- 17.9% of 1,150 (205.85)
- 9.22% of 57 (5.2554)
- 233% of 310 (722.3)
- 7,504.3% of 60 (4,502.58)
- 100.0001% of 7 (7.000007)

COMING UP
One sided figures

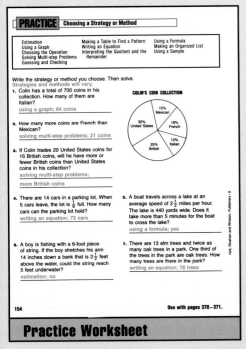

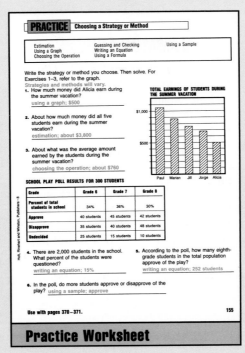

371

Objective: To identify the parts of a circle

Warm-Up
Have students identify each polygon from its verbal description.
- eight sides, all congruent (regular octagon)
- five sides (pentagon)
- four sides, all congruent, one right angle (square)
- three sides, none congruent (scalene triangle)
- four sides, each pair of opposite sides parallel (parallelogram)

GETTING STARTED

Draw a circle on the chalkboard, and mark its center 0. Then draw diameter $\overline{AB}$. Ask how many other line segments that have endpoints on the circle pass through 0. (an infinite number)

Draw radius $\overline{OC}$, and ask how many other line segments have one endpoint at the center and the other on the circle. (an infinite number) Then ask students whether they can determine the relationship between $\overline{AB}$ and $\overline{OC}$. ($\overline{AB}$ is twice as long as $\overline{OC}$.)

TEACHING THE LESSON

Discuss the use of circles in architecture. Have students identify buildings, rooms, and other features that have circular forms. (domes, the Capitol rotunda, spiral staircases, and so on)

Discuss some advantages of circular construction. (In a circular stadium, everyone can see; a circular field maximizes the area per length of fence; a circular hall can have better acoustics.)

Discuss some possible disadvantages. (construction costs, furniture placement)

Circles

The Hirshhorn Museum in Washington, D.C., shown below, is noted for its distinctive circular design.

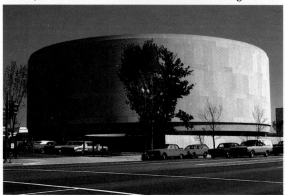

A **circle** is a set of all points in a plane that are the same distance from one point called the **center**.

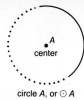

circle A, or $\odot A$

A compass is used to construct a circle or part of a circle. The distance from the compass point to a point on the circle is the **radius** of the circle.

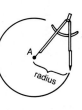

radius

PARTS OF A CIRCLE

Radius: $\overline{AB}$ is a line segment from the center of the circle to any point on the circle.
Chord: $\overline{CD}$ is a line segment whose endpoints are on the circle.
Diameter: $\overline{EF}$ is a chord that passes through the center of the circle and has the length of two radii. $d = 2r$
Arc: $\overgroup{BE}$ is part of the circle.
Central angle: $\angle BAE$ is an angle whose vertex is the center of the circle.

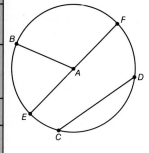

372

COMMON ERRORS

Some students might have difficulty constructing circles. They may find that the beginning points and the endpoints do not meet.

Remediation
For this error, give students additional practice in constructing circles, paying particular attention to how the compass is held and how much pressure is applied. Encourage movement by the knob only. In addition, holding the compass at a 60° angle to the paper rather than perpendicularly might help.

Assign Reteach Master, p. 108.

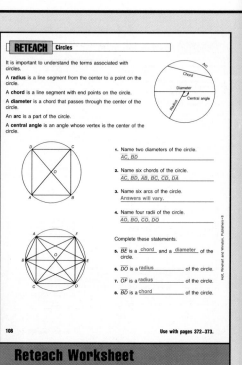

Name each part of the circle.

1. the center **N**

2. the diameter $\overline{MK}$

3. three chords $\overline{LJ};\ \overline{MK};\ \overline{MH}$

4. the longest chord $\overline{MK}$

5. the radii $\overline{MN},\ \overline{HN},\ \overline{NK}$

6. five arcs MH, HJ, JK, KL, LM

7. the central angles
   $\angle MNH;\ \angle HNK;\ \angle MNK$

8. obtuse central angle
   $\angle HNK$

9. acute central angle
   $\angle MNH$

10. intersecting chords
    $\overline{MK}$ and $\overline{LJ}$

11. shortest chord
    $\overline{MH}$

Classify each segment as a *chord*, a *radius*, or a *diameter*. H is the center.

12. $\overline{BE}$ diameter

13. $\overline{AG}$ chord

14. $\overline{HC}$ radius

15. $\overline{DF}$ chord

16. $\overline{BH}$ radius

17. $\overline{HE}$ radius

18. Name two central angles of circle H.
    $\angle BHC$ and $\angle CHE$

For each statement, write *always*, *sometimes*, or *never*.

19. All radii of a circle are the same length. **always**

20. A central angle has its vertex on the circle. **never**

★21. Small circles have measures less than 360° and large circles have measures more than 360°. **never**

22. All points of a circle are the same distance from the center of the circle. **always**

23. Chords are diameters. **sometimes**

24. Some arcs are line segments. **never**

25. Circles are congruent. **sometimes**

26. All circles are regular polygons. **never**

27. The longest chord of any circle is its diameter. **always**

28. A radius of a circle is half the length of the circle's diameter. **always**

Solve. Use the Infobank.

29. Use the information on page 477 to solve. Look at the design of the house pictured. Find the geometric shapes that have been used in this design. Draw a house of your own, using as many geometric shapes as you can. Designs will vary.
    decagon, hexagon, rectangle, square, trapezoid, triangle

Classwork/Homework, page H156

373

ASSIGNMENT GUIDE

Basic: 1–14, 19–29 o

Average: 1–14, 19–29

Extended: 12–29

Resources
Practice, p. 156   Class/Home, p. H156
Reteach, p. 108
Enrich, p. 136

Exercise Analysis

1–18	Name the part of a circle
19–28	Evaluate a statement about circles
29	Data collection and computation

FOLLOW-UP ACTIVITIES

MATH COMMUNICATION
Materials: compasses

Ask students what concentric circles might be. (circles with the same center) Have them draw a set of three concentric circles. Then ask them to give examples of concentric circles found in everyday life. (ripples in water, bull's-eyes, many designs, and so on)

REINFORCEMENT
Materials: compasses, straightedges

Have each student mark at random points A and B and then construct a circle that passes through them. (Students will discover that the center of such a circle must be equally distant from both A and B and that the distance determines the radius of the circle.)

Then have each student mark three nonlinear points—X, Y, and Z—and construct a circle through them. Hint to students that they can use $\overline{XY}$ and $\overline{YZ}$ to help locate the center by finding the intersection of their perpendicular bisectors, which is the center of the circle. Point out that although two points define an infinite number of circles, three points define just one.

COMING UP
Look-alike polygons

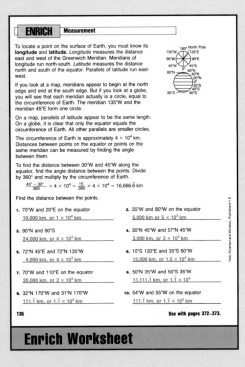

Practice Worksheet

Enrich Worksheet

373

Objective: To identify the corresponding parts of congruent polygons

Warm-Up
Have students identify the measure of the remaining angle of the following figures.
- triangle: 45°, 55° (80°)
- quadrilateral: 55°, 80°, 55° (170°)
- triangle: 45°, 45° (90°)
- pentagon: 120°, 160°, 80°, 70° (110°)
- triangle: 55°, 60° (65°)
- pentagon: 110°, 100°, 105°, 125° (100°)

GETTING STARTED

Materials: pictures of structures made of congruent polygons

Display the pictures. Ask why the architects who designed these structures would have used polygons of the same size and shape. (to obtain symmetry in design, to reproduce a shape motif, to make parts fit together, for economy, and so on) Discuss objects in the classroom that are the same size and shape. (desk tops, windows, light fixtures, and so on)

TEACHING THE LESSON

Emphasize that position does not change the fact that figures are congruent. Figures can "slide," be "flipped," or be "turned" and still be congruent. Some students might have difficulty in identifying corresponding parts, especially when turned. Encourage them to trace figures, cut them out, and match them.

Have students identify whether the three figures in each row are congruent. (yes; no)

Congruent Polygons

Congruent polygons are polygons that have the same size and shape. For example, the dome of the Roundhouse in Baton Rouge, Louisiana, consists of hundreds of congruent hexagons.

The corresponding parts of congruent polygons also are congruent. The slash marks on the sides and the angles of each polygon indicate the corresponding parts that are congruent.

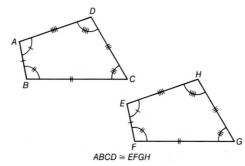
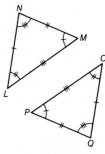

ABCD ≅ EFGH   △LMN ≅ △OPQ

For quadrilaterals *ABCD* and *EFGH*:

Corresponding sides	Corresponding angles
$\overline{AB} \cong \overline{EF}$	$\angle A \cong \angle E$
$\overline{BC} \cong \overline{FG}$	$\angle B \cong \angle F$
$\overline{CD} \cong \overline{GH}$	$\angle C \cong \angle G$
$\overline{DA} \cong \overline{HE}$	$\angle D \cong \angle H$

For congruent triangles *LMN* and *OPQ*:

Corresponding sides	Corresponding angles
$\overline{LM} \cong \overline{OP}$	$\angle L \cong \angle O$
$\overline{MN} \cong \overline{PQ}$	$\angle M \cong \angle P$
$\overline{NL} \cong \overline{QO}$	$\angle N \cong \angle Q$

When naming congruent polygons, be sure to list congruent vertices in the same order. For example,

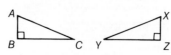

$\triangle LMN \cong \triangle OPQ$ means that $\angle L \cong \angle O$, $\angle M \cong \angle P$, and $\angle N \cong \angle Q$.

374

COMMON ERRORS

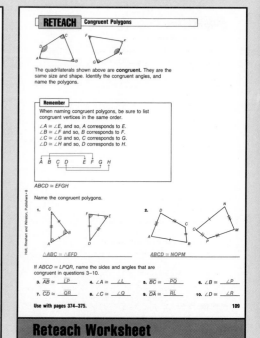

Students who write that $\triangle ABC \cong \triangle XYZ$ do not understand the convention for corresponding parts because $\angle B \not\cong \angle Y$ and $\angle C \not\cong \angle Z$.

Remediation
For this error, have students match pairs of congruent angles before naming the polygon.

Assign Reteach Master, p. 109.

RETEACH | Congruent Polygons

The quadrilaterals shown above are **congruent.** They are the same size and shape. Identify the congruent angles, and name the polygons.

Remember
When naming congruent polygons, be sure to list congruent vertices in the same order.

$\angle A \cong \angle E$, and so, A corresponds to E.
$\angle B \cong \angle F$ and so, B corresponds to F.
$\angle C \cong \angle G$ and so, C corresponds to G.
$\angle D \cong \angle H$ and so, D corresponds to H.

A B C D   E F G H

ABCD ≅ EFGH

Name the congruent polygons.

1. _____   2. _____

△ABC ≅ △EFD   ABCD ≅ NOPM

If *ABCD* ≅ *LPQR*, name the sides and angles that are congruent in questions 3–10.

3. $\overline{AB} = $ _LP_   4. $\angle A = $ _∠L_   5. $\overline{BC} = $ _PQ_   6. $\angle B = $ _∠P_
7. $\overline{CD} = $ _QR_   8. $\angle C = $ _∠Q_   9. $\overline{DA} = $ _RL_   10. $\angle D = $ _∠R_

Use with pages 374–375.   109

Reteach Worksheet

Find the pair of polygons that appears to be congruent.

1.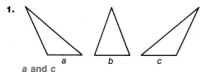

a and c

2.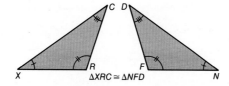

a and b

3.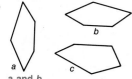

a and b

4.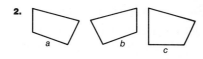

b and c

Use the congruent triangles to answer the following.

5. Name three pairs of congruent angles.
$\angle X \cong \angle N$; $\angle R \cong \angle F$; $\angle C \cong \angle D$
6. Name three pairs of congruent sides.
$\overline{XR} \cong \overline{NF}$; $\overline{RC} \cong \overline{FD}$; $\overline{CX} \cong \overline{DN}$
7. Complete: $\triangle RCX \cong \triangle \blacksquare$ FDN

$\triangle XRC \cong \triangle NFD$

Use the congruent quadrilaterals to answer the following.

8. Name the congruent quadrilaterals.
$ACTR \cong XBDY$
9. Name four pairs of congruent sides.
$\overline{AC} \cong \overline{XB}$; $\overline{CT} \cong \overline{BD}$; $\overline{TR} \cong \overline{DY}$; $\overline{RA} \cong \overline{YX}$

10. Name four pairs of congruent angles.
$\angle A \cong \angle X$; $\angle C \cong \angle B$; $\angle T \cong \angle D$; $\angle R \cong \angle Y$

Use quadrilaterals *CDNR* and *LTYZ* to find the measure of each segment or angle. $CDNR \cong LTYZ$

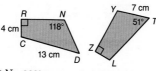

11. $\overline{LT}$ 13 cm **12.** $\angle Y$ 118° **13.** $\overline{ZL}$ 4 cm

14. $\angle N$ 118° **15.** $\overline{DN}$ 7 cm **16.** $\angle L$ 101°

17. $\angle R$ 90° **18.** $\angle D$ 51° **19.** $\angle R + \angle C + \angle D + \angle N$ 360°

Solve.

★20. Quadrilateral *ZABC* has two right angles. Must it be a parallelogram? If possible, draw one figure that is a parallelogram, and one that is not. no

★21. Each diagonal drawn through quadrilateral *PQRS* divides it into two congruent triangles. Is *PQRS* a parallelogram? yes

Classwork/Homework, page H157

375

ASSIGNMENT GUIDE

Basic: 1–13

Average: 1–4, 6–20 e

Extended: 1–9 o, 11–21

Resources
Practice, p. 157   Class/Home, p. H157
Reteach, p. 109
Enrich, p. 137

Exercise Analysis

1–4	Find the congruent polygons
5–7	Name congruent parts of congruent triangles
8–10	Name congruent parts of congruent quadrilaterals
11–19	Find the measure of a corresponding part in congruent quadrilaterals
20–21	Skill applications

FOLLOW-UP ACTIVITIES

PUZZLES AND GAMES
Materials: toothpicks

Have students arrange 3 toothpicks as shown at the left below. Then tell them to make 11 out of those 3. (The solution is shown below at the right.)

PUZZLES AND GAMES
Materials: index cards

Prepare sets of 24 cards. Each set is to be made up of 12 pairs of congruent figures. There is to be a limit of one figure per card. Give each group of students a set of cards, and have them spread out the cards facedown.

For each turn, a player gets to turn up 2 cards. If the figures are congruent, the player gets to keep the pair and can turn up 2 more. If they are not congruent, the cards are turned facedown again and the next player takes his or her turn. The placement of the cards should remain the same so that players can benefit from remembering where the figures are.

The game continues until the last pair is matched. The winner is the player who has the most cards.

COMING UP
Triproofs for triangles

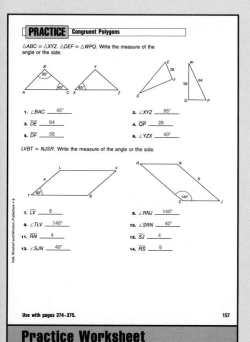

Practice Worksheet

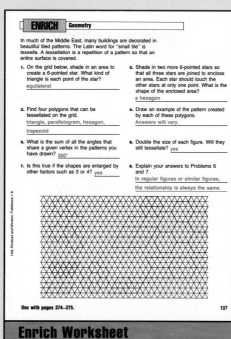

Enrich Worksheet

Objectives: To identify and construct congruent triangles

Warm-Up

Have students draw and name each triangle as you read its description.

- a triangle with all sides equal in length (equilateral)
- a triangle with two congruent sides (isosceles)
- a triangle with no congruent sides (scalene)
- a triangle with all angles equal in measure (equilateral)
- a triangle with an obtuse angle (obtuse)
- a triangle with a right angle (right)
- a triangle with two congruent angles (isosceles)
- a triangle with all acute angles (acute)

GETTING STARTED

Draw a triangle on the chalkboard. Ask: How would you construct a triangle congruent to this one? (One likely answer is by measuring the sides and angles.) Tell students that in this lesson, they will learn the most efficient way to construct and identify congruent triangles.

TEACHING THE LESSON

The three methods given in the text prove congruence because all constructions made according to them produce congruent triangles. To demonstrate this, guide students in using each method to construct congruent triangles. Then have them check their constructions for congruence by measuring with protractors and rulers.

Tell students that angle-angle-side (AAS) also establishes congruence. Have students try to draw pairs of triangles that meet this criteria.

Constructing Congruent Triangles

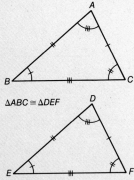

Two triangles are congruent if

- **a.** three pairs of sides are congruent. This is called **side-side-side congruence,** or **SSS.**
  $\overline{AB} \cong \overline{DE}, \overline{BC} \cong \overline{EF}, \overline{CA} \cong \overline{FD}$

- **b.** two pairs of sides and the included pair of angles are congruent. This is called **side-angle-side congruence,** or **SAS.**
  $\overline{AB} \cong \overline{DE}, \overline{BC} \cong \overline{EF}, \angle B \cong \angle E$

- **c.** two pairs of angles and the included pair of sides are congruent. This is called **angle-side-angle congruence,** or **ASA.**
  $\angle C \cong \angle F, \angle B = \angle E, \overline{CB} \cong \overline{FE}$

$\triangle ABC \cong \triangle DEF$

Use the SSS congruence to construct a triangle congruent to $\triangle GHJ$.

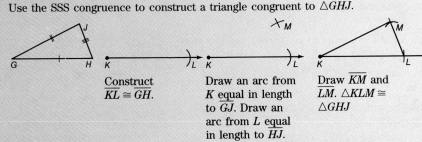

Construct $\overline{KL} \cong \overline{GH}$.

Draw an arc from K equal in length to $\overline{GJ}$. Draw an arc from L equal in length to $\overline{HJ}$.

Draw $\overline{KM}$ and $\overline{LM}$. $\triangle KLM \cong \triangle GHJ$

Use the SAS congruence to construct a triangle congruent to $\triangle DEF$.

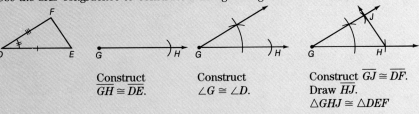

Construct $\overline{GH} \cong \overline{DE}$.

Construct $\angle G \cong \angle D$.

Construct $\overline{GJ} \cong \overline{DF}$. Draw $\overline{HJ}$. $\triangle GHJ \cong \triangle DEF$

Use the ASA congruence to construct a triangle congruent to $\triangle RST$.

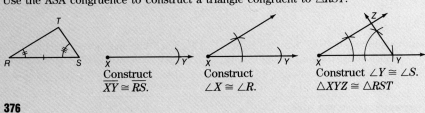

Construct $\overline{XY} \cong \overline{RS}$.

Construct $\angle X \cong \angle R$.

Construct $\angle Y \cong \angle S$. $\triangle XYZ \cong \triangle RST$

376

COMMON ERRORS

Some students might have difficulty in identifying the two congruent triangles in the figure above. They may not see the common side.

Remediation

For this error, have students trace $\triangle ADC$ and $\triangle BDC$ separately before they compare them.

Assign Reteach Master, p. 110.

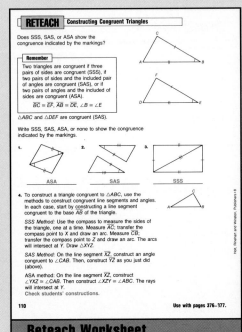

RETEACH | Constructing Congruent Triangles

Does SSS, SAS, or ASA show the congruence indicated by the markings?

Remember
Two triangles are congruent if three pairs of sides are congruent (SSS), if two pairs of sides and the included pair of angles are congruent (SAS), or if two pairs of angles and the included of sides are congruent (ASA).

$\overline{BC} \cong \overline{EF}, \overline{AB} \cong \overline{DE}, \angle B \cong \angle E$

$\triangle ABC$ and $\triangle DEF$ are congruent (SAS).

Write SSS, SAS, ASA, or none to show the congruence indicated by the markings.

1. ASA 2. SAS 3. SSS

4. To construct a triangle congruent to $\triangle ABC$, use the methods to construct congruent line segments and angles. In each case, start by constructing a line segment congruent to the base $\overline{AB}$ of the triangle.

SSS Method: Use the compass to measure the sides of the triangle, one at a time. Measure $\overline{AC}$; transfer the compass point to X and draw an arc. Measure $\overline{CB}$; transfer the compass point to Z and draw an arc. The arcs will intersect at Y. Draw $\triangle XYZ$.

SAS Method: On the line segment $\overline{XZ}$, construct an angle congruent to $\angle CAB$. Then, construct $\overline{YZ}$ as you just did (above).

ASA method: On the line segment $\overline{XZ}$, construct $\angle YXZ \cong \angle CAB$. Then construct $\angle XZY \cong \angle ABC$. The rays will intersect at Y.
Check students' constructions.

110 | Use with pages 376–177.

Reteach Worksheet

Write *SSS*, *SAS*, or *ASA* to show the congruence indicated by the markings.

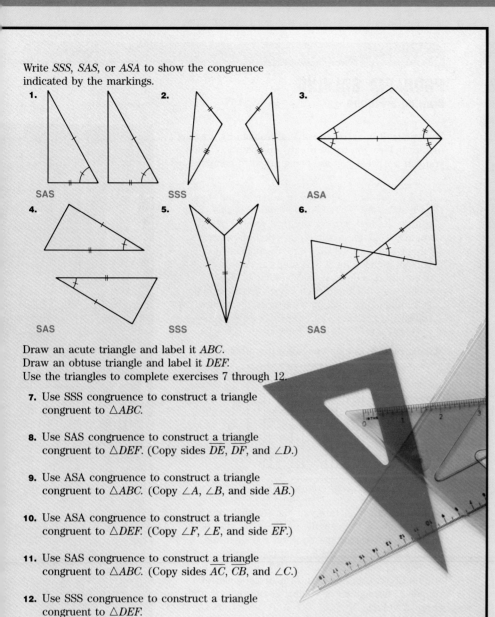

1. SAS
2. SSS
3. ASA
4. SAS
5. SSS
6. SAS

Draw an acute triangle and label it *ABC*.
Draw an obtuse triangle and label it *DEF*.
Use the triangles to complete exercises 7 through 12.

7. Use SSS congruence to construct a triangle congruent to △*ABC*.

8. Use SAS congruence to construct a triangle congruent to △*DEF*. (Copy sides $\overline{DE}$, $\overline{DF}$, and ∠*D*.)

9. Use ASA congruence to construct a triangle congruent to △*ABC*. (Copy ∠*A*, ∠*B*, and side $\overline{AB}$.)

10. Use ASA congruence to construct a triangle congruent to △*DEF*. (Copy ∠*F*, ∠*E*, and side $\overline{EF}$.)

11. Use SAS congruence to construct a triangle congruent to △*ABC*. (Copy sides $\overline{AC}$, $\overline{CB}$, and ∠*C*.)

12. Use SSS congruence to construct a triangle congruent to △*DEF*.

★13. Use the two line segments to construct an isosceles triangle.
Check students' constructions.

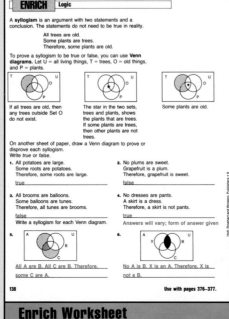

6 cm

3 cm

377

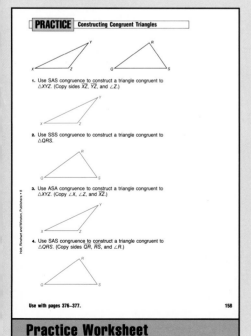

ASSIGNMENT GUIDE

Basic:	1–9
Average:	1–12
Extended:	1–13

Resources
Practice, p. 158   Class/Home, p. H158
Reteach, p. 110
Enrich, p. 138

Exercise Analysis
1–6   Identify how triangles are congruent
7–13   Construct a congruent triangle

FOLLOW-UP ACTIVITIES

PROBLEM SOLVING
Have students use what they have just learned about proving the congruence of triangles to prove why bisecting an angle with a compass works.

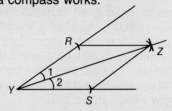

(Because the compass opening used to locate *Z* is the same as that used to draw the arcs locating *R* and *S*, $\overline{YS} \cong \overline{SZ} \cong \overline{ZR} \cong \overline{RY}$. Because $\overline{YZ}$ is congruent to itself, △*ZSY* ≅ △*ZRY* by SSS. Therefore, ∠1 ≅ ∠2.)

REINFORCEMENT
Prepare the following as a handout.

35°   45°   2 cm

Have students use the two angles and the line segment to construct two triangles not congruent to each other.

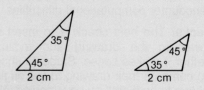

35°
45°
2 cm

45°
35°
2 cm

COMING UP
Problems with math? Unleash the artist in you!

377

Objective: To draw a picture to solve a problem

Warm-Up

To prepare students for this lesson, have them compute the following.

$$3\frac{7}{8} + 2\frac{1}{4} \left(6\frac{1}{8}\right) \qquad 2\frac{3}{5} + 5\frac{4}{5} \left(8\frac{2}{5}\right)$$

$$6\frac{1}{8} + 9\frac{3}{4} \left(15\frac{7}{8}\right) \qquad 12\frac{1}{4} - 7\frac{5}{8} \left(4\frac{5}{8}\right)$$

GETTING STARTED

Have a volunteer leave the classroom while another student draws a geometric figure on a sheet of paper and shows it to the rest of the class. Have the first student return to the room and attempt to draw the same geometric figure on the chalkboard with only the second student's verbal directions as a guide. Discuss any differences between the two figures and the reasons for them.

TEACHING THE LESSON

This lesson is designed to assist students who have difficulty visualizing spatial relationships. Students who experience such difficulty will be helped by drawing a picture of a situation. Explain that drawing a picture or diagram will help a student to determine how things are related.

Questions: Tell students a picture will make evident what it is they are being asked to do. The picture drawn for the introductory problem shows that the distance needed is the sum of the thickness of one full volume and two covers. Without the picture, students would be likely to find the thickness of all three volumes, less the two covers.

Tools: The tool used is the picture itself. Emphasize to students that they should label their pictures, list the measurements, and mark what it is they need to find. They can then analyze the situation by using the labels to refer to the parts. This method is important in preparing students for secondary mathematics.

Solutions: Once students have set up their drawings correctly, they are not likely to encounter computational difficulties.

Checks: The best check is to insert the answer in the drawing and evaluate whether it makes sense. Students should also compare their drawing to the original problem to be sure they have copied information correctly.

| QUESTIONS | TOOLS | SOLUTIONS | CHECKS |

PROBLEM SOLVING
Drawing a Picture

Sometimes it is easier to solve a problem by drawing a picture before you try to do any computation. Then you can see what you are being asked to compute.

> Bookworms are the larvae of a beetle, and they destroy books. Suppose a bookworm begins its trip on the first page of the first volume of a 3-volume work on architecture. The bookworm burrows in a straight line from volume 1 into volume 2 and volume 3. It stops at the last page of the third volume. If each volume is 75 millimeters thick and each cover of each volume is 3 millimeters thick, how far does the bookworm travel?

Make a picture to help you solve the problem.

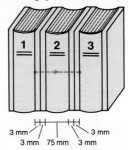

By looking at the picture you can see that the first page of volume 1 is actually on the *right* side of the book (imagine taking the book off the shelf and opening it to the first page). You can also see that the last page of volume 3 is on the *left* side of the book. So, the bookworm burrows through the cover of volume 1, through all of volume 2, and through the cover of volume 3.

$3\,\text{mm} + 3\,\text{mm} + 75\,\text{mm} + 3\,\text{mm} + 3\,\text{mm} = 87\,\text{mm}$

The bookworm travels 87 millimeters.

Write the letter of the drawing you would use to solve each problem.

1. On one wall of an architect's office there are 6 shelves spaced the same distance apart. The bottom of the first is 15 in. from the floor. The bottom of the fourth is 48 in. from the floor. The top of the top shelf is 24 in. below the ceiling. Each shelf is 2 in. thick. How high is the room? **drawing a**

2. The architect's office is on the fourth floor of a building. The fourth floor is 48 ft above the street. The distance between each floor above the fourth is 11 ft. The top floor is 24 ft below the roof. There are 6 floors above street level. How tall is the building? **drawing c**

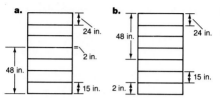
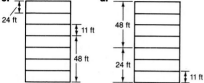

Draw a picture, and solve each problem.

3. The Diagnostic Clinic is an 8-story medical building. Standing outside the building, you see that each story consists of windows 2 meters high. Each window is surrounded on all sides by 1 meter of concrete. What is the height of the building? **25 meters**

4. Fran always sits in a certain seat in the theater. Her favorite seat is located in the fourth row from the front and the twelfth row from the back of the hall. Her seat is 2 seats from the right aisle and 7 seats from the left aisle. How many seats are there in the auditorium? **120 seats**

★5. A 2-volume set of books sits on a library bookshelf. Volume 1 sits to the left of volume 2. The cover of each book is 1.4 mm thick. Each group of 10 pages of these volumes measures 1 mm. Find the distance from the last page of volume 2 to page 60 of volume 1. **8.8 mm**

6. Jo-Jo is delivering three packages to offices in the Empire State Building. He takes the elevator 28 floors to deliver the first package. He takes the elevator another 19 floors to deliver the second package. He then rides the elevator down 13 floors to deliver the last package. He finds that he is now $\frac{1}{3}$ of the way up the building. How many floors does the Empire State Building have? **102 floors**

Classwork/Homework, page H159

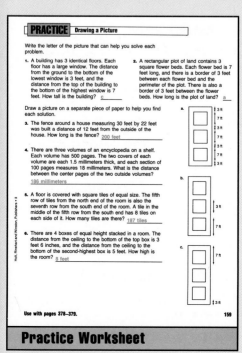

Exercise Analysis
1–2 Choose the correct drawing
3–6 Draw a picture to solve

FOLLOW-UP ACTIVITIES

PROBLEM SOLVING
Copy the information below onto the chalkboard. Have students develop problems from it and challenge each other with the problems. Emphasize that if students get stuck on a problem they should draw a diagram.

- The *campanile* (Leaning Tower) at Pisa, Italy, is 179 feet high and leans more than 16 feet from the perpendicular.
- The Great Pyramid of Cheops was originally 482 feet high but is now only about 450 feet high.
- The terraces in the Hanging Gardens of Babylon were said to rise from a height of about 75 feet to a height of about 300 feet.
- The Eiffel Tower in Paris, France, was originally 984 feet high. A television tower has made it 1,056 feet high.
- The Great Wall of China is about 1,400 miles long. Its height varies from 18 feet to 30 feet.

COMPUTER
Have students make a flowchart to demonstrate the following situation.

The bell rings, signaling the end of the last class of the day. Joan walks to her locker. On Tuesdays and Thursdays, she takes her flute from the locker and goes to band practice. On Mondays and Wednesdays, she swims. Her swim suit and bath towel are stored in her locker. On Fridays, she goes directly home. (Answers will vary.)

COMING UP
One shape, many figures!

Objectives: To identify corresponding parts of similar polygons and use proportions to find the lengths of their sides

Warm-Up
Have students find the missing term in proportions such as the following.
- $\frac{3}{4} = \frac{n}{32}$ ($n = 24$)
- $\frac{17}{n} = \frac{39}{117}$ ($n = 51$)
- $\frac{64}{19} = \frac{256}{n}$ ($n = 76$)

GETTING STARTED

Materials: graph paper, rulers

Have students work in pairs. Have one student draw a simple polygon on graph paper. Have the second student draw the figure at twice the size by doubling the number of squares used for each segment of the first polygon. Then have students cut out the first figure and place it on top of the second figure. Tell them to match each of the angles in the figures and determine whether they are congruent. (yes)

TEACHING THE LESSON

A. Draw the triangles below on the chalkboard. Have students set up ratios of the lengths of the corresponding sides. Then have them use cross products to determine if the dimensions are proportional. (yes)

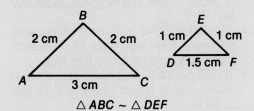

△ ABC ~ △ DEF

$$\frac{1}{2} = \frac{1}{2} = \frac{1.5}{3}$$

B. Caution students not to assume that the areas of similar polygons form a proportion with the ratios of their linear dimensions. Instead, the square of the ratio of corresponding sides is proportional to the ratio of areas.

Checkpoint
The chart lists the common errors students make in identifying corresponding parts of similar polygons.

Correct Answers: 1c, 2d

Remediation
■ For this error, have students trace and cut out the smaller figure and then position it so that each pair of corresponding angles is aligned.

Assign Reteach Master, p. 111.

380

Similar Polygons

A. **Similar polygons** are two polygons that have the same shape.

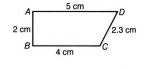

is similar to

$$\triangle ABC \sim \triangle XYZ$$

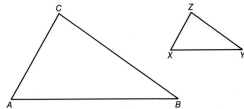

The corresponding angles of similar polygons are congruent.

$$\angle A \cong \angle X$$
$$\angle B \cong \angle Y$$
$$\angle C \cong \angle Z$$

The lengths of the corresponding sides of similar polygons are proportional.

$$\frac{\text{length of } \overline{AB}}{\text{length of } \overline{XY}} = \frac{\text{length of } \overline{BC}}{\text{length of } \overline{YZ}} = \frac{\text{length of } \overline{CA}}{\text{length of } \overline{ZX}}$$

B. In the drawing at the right, $ABCD \sim LMNO$. To find the length of $\overline{LM}$, use a proportion.

$$\frac{5}{600} = \frac{2}{n}$$
$$5n = 1,200$$
$$n = 240 \text{ cm}$$

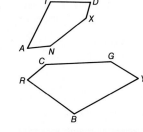

The length of $\overline{LM}$ is 240 cm (2.4 m).

Checkpoint
Write the letter of the correct answer.

Polygon $ANXDT \sim$ polygon $YGCRB$.

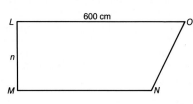

1. The angle that is congruent to $\angle D$ is ■.

a. $\angle A$ **b.** $\angle Y$ **c.** $\angle R$ **d.** $\angle B$

2. Complete the proportion. $\frac{\overline{AT}}{\overline{YB}} = \frac{\overline{NX}}{■}$

a. $\overline{BR}$ **b.** $\overline{YG}$ **c.** $\overline{BY}$ **d.** $\overline{GC}$

380

Math Reasoning, page H226

COMMON ERRORS

Answer Choice	Type of Error
■ 1a, 1b, 1d, 2a, 2b, 2c	Fails to correctly identify the corresponding part

---

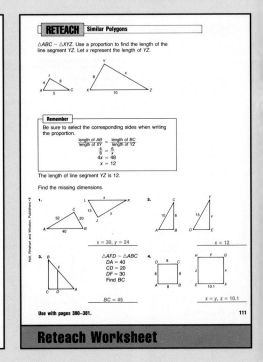

Do the polygons appear similar? Write *yes* or *no*.

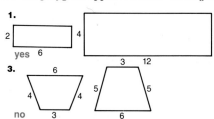

1.
2 [ ] 4
yes 6

2.

6 4 9 6
8 12
yes

3.
6
4 [ ] 4 5 [ ] 5
3 3 12 6
no

4.
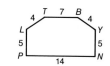
6 3 9 4.5
3 5 4.5 7.5
2 3
yes

Complete.

Quadrilateral *ABCD* ~ quadrilateral *FEHG*.

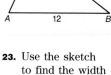

5. ∠*A* ≅ ■ ∠*F*

6. ∠*C* ≅ ■ ∠*H*

7. ∠*D* ≅ ■ ∠*G*

8. ∠*B* ≅ ■ ∠*E*

△*DXN* ~ △*YRC*

9. $\frac{\text{length of } \overline{DX}}{\text{length of } \overline{YR}} = \frac{\text{length of } ■}{\text{length of } ■}$ $\frac{XN}{RC}$ or $\frac{DN}{YC}$

Polygon *VARYCX* ~ polygon *PLTBYN*. Find the length of each segment.

10. $\overline{AV}$ 2.5

11. $\overline{YC}$ 2

12. $\overline{VX}$ 7

13. $\overline{RY}$ 3.5

The polygons in each pair are similar. Find the measure of each side or each angle.

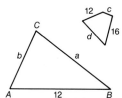

14. *a* = ■ 9

15. *b* = ■ 6

16. *c* = ■ 6

17. *d* = ■ 18

18. ∠*A* = ■ 65°

19. ∠*B* = ■ 37°

20. ∠*C* = ■ 78°

21. ∠*F* = ■ 78°

Solve.

22. To find the height of the Statue of Liberty, Debi put a 2-m stick in the ground. The stick cast a 1.5-m shadow. If the Statue of Liberty casts a 35-m shadow, how high is the statue? 46.6 meters

23. Use the sketch to find the width of the Grand Canyon. 10.5 km

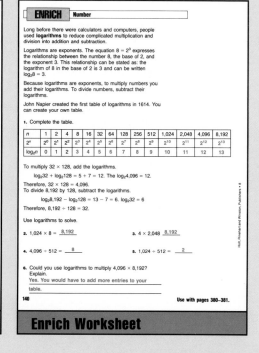
7 km
2 km Grand Canyon
3 km
?

ASSIGNMENT GUIDE

Basic: 1–9, 10–20 e, 22–23

Average: 5–13, 18–23

Extended: 5–23

Resources
Practice, p. 160   Class/Home, p. H160
Reteach, p. 111   Reasoning, p. H226
Enrich, p. 140

Exercise Analysis

1–4   Identify similar polygons
5–9   Name a corresponding part
10–21 Find the measure of a corresponding part
22–23 Skill applications

You may wish to allow students to use calculators for some of these exercises.

FOLLOW-UP ACTIVITIES

 MANIPULATIVES
Materials: construction paper of different colors, scissors, ruler

Cut out the following triangles.
- From red construction paper, △*ABC*, in which $\overline{AB}$ = 4 in., $\overline{BC}$ = 2 in., and $\overline{CA}$ = 3 in.
- From yellow construction paper, △*DEF*, in which $\overline{DE}$ = 6 in., $\overline{EF}$ = 3 in., and $\overline{FD}$ = $4\frac{1}{2}$ in.
- From blue construction paper, △*GHI*, in which $\overline{GH}$ = 10.8 in., $\overline{HI}$ = 5.4 in., and $\overline{IG}$ = 8.1 in.

Lay the triangles on top of one another. △*GHI* is to be on the bottom and △*ABC* on top. Line up vertices *C*, *F*, and *I*.

Have students find each ratio.
- a side of △*ABC* to a side of △*DEF* (2:3)
- a side of △*DEF* to a side of △*GHI* (1:1.8)
- a side of △*GHI* to a side of △*ABC* as a percent (270%)

MANIPULATIVES
Materials: tangrams, rulers

Have students use the tangram to construct a series of similar figures. Have them trace each figure so that they can write ratios comparing the ratio of the *areas*.

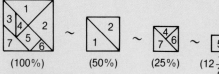
(100%)   (50%)   (25%)   ($12\frac{1}{2}$%)

COMING UP
A time for reflection

381

Objectives: To identify and draw lines of symmetry and reflection

Warm-Up
Draw a series of figures on the chalkboard, and then have volunteers draw lines that divide each figure, if possible, into congruent polygons.

GETTING STARTED

Materials: construction paper cut into the shapes of symmetrical and nonsymmetrical figures

Hand out the figures, and have students determine whether they can fold them into congruent polygons, and if they can, how many different ways they can do it. Point out that although the diagonals of a rectangle divide the rectangle into two congruent triangles, they do not pass this folding test. The triangles are not symmetrical.

TEACHING THE LESSON

A. Point out that circles have an infinite number of lines of symmetry. All of them are diameters. Also point out that regular polygons have exactly as many lines of symmetry as they have sides. Emphasize that the folding test used in Getting Started will always verify a line of symmetry, but remind students that not only must the two resulting polygons be congruent but also that their vertices must line up.

B. Point out that each reflection is not necessarily symmetrical. In the figure below, $\overleftrightarrow{AB}$ is a line of symmetry, but neither $\triangle XYZ$ nor $\triangle X'Y'Z'$ has a line of symmetry.

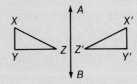

Symmetry and Reflections

The surfaces of many buildings are symmetrical. That is, a line placed in the proper position divides a face of the building into two identical parts. The faces of the Chrysler Building in New York are symmetrical.

A. Some figures have many **lines of symmetry**, while others have none.

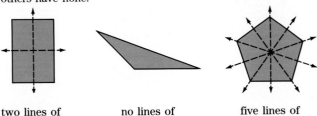

| two lines of symmetry | no lines of symmetry | five lines of symmetry | one line of symmetry |

B. It is also possible to draw the mirror image, or the **reflection,** of a given figure about a line of symmetry. A figure and its reflection are congruent.

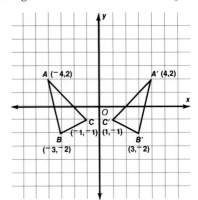

$\triangle A'B'C'$ is the reflection $\triangle ABC$ about the y-axis. The y-axis is the line of symmetry. (Read A' as "A prime.")

Note that the reflection of point $A(^-4,2)$ about the y-axis is $A'(4,^-2)$. Similarly, the reflection of $B(^-3,^-2)$ about the y-axis is $B'(3,^-2)$, and the reflection of $C(^-1,^-1)$ is $C'(1,^-1)$. The reflection of each point has the same y-coordinate, and the x-coordinate of each point differs in sign only.

382

Math Reasoning, page H226

COMMON ERRORS

Some students might translate figures when they mean to reflect them.

Remediation
For this error, have students check their work by folding. Suggest that they draw guidelines perpendicular to the line of symmetry and then place points by counting spaces on either side.

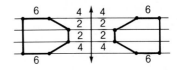

Assign Reteach Master, p. 112.

Trace the following figures. Draw all the lines of symmetry. Write the number of lines of symmetry that each figure has.

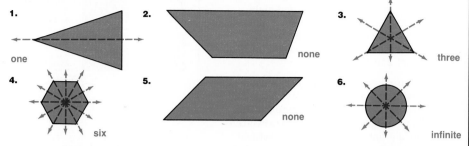

1.

one

2.

3.

three

4.

six

5.

6.

infinite

Find the coordinates of the reflection point about the x-axis.

7. (6,1)
(6,⁻1)

8. (⁻2,3)
(⁻2,⁻3)

9. (0,4)
(0,⁻4)

Plot the reflection in a coordinate plane.

13. Plot the points (4,1), (3,5), and (⁻3,2). Connect the points to form a triangle. Plot its reflection about the x-axis.
(4,⁻1); (3,⁻5); (⁻3,⁻2)

Find the coordinates of the reflection point about the y-axis.

10. (4,2)
(⁻4,2)

11. (2,⁻7)
(⁻2,⁻7)

12. (⁻1,⁻5)
(1,⁻5)

Check students' graphs.

14. Plot the points (⁻6,5), (⁻2,4), (⁻1,⁻3), and (⁻5,6). Connect the points to form a polygon. Plot its reflection about the y-axis.
(6,5); (2,4); (1,⁻3); (5,6)

Solve.

15. If a figure is cut along its line of symmetry, will each piece also have a line of symmetry? Why? Not necessarily; for example, a triangle will not always, but a circle always will.

CHALLENGE

In geometry, it is proved that if two angles of one triangle are congruent to two angles of another triangle, then the two triangles are similar.

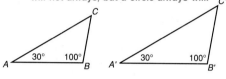

△ABC ∼ △A'B'C'

Find the missing lengths in each pair of similar triangles.

1.

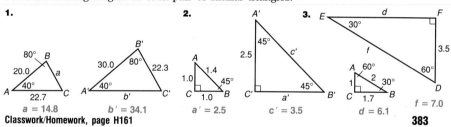

$a = 14.8$

$b' = 34.1$

2.

$a' = 2.5$

$c' = 3.5$

3.

$d = 6.1$

$f = 7.0$

Classwork/Homework, page H161

383

ASSIGNMENT GUIDE

Basic: 1–4, 7–14

Average: 1–14, Chlg

Extended: 1–14, Chlg

Resources
Practice, p. 161   Class/Home, p. H161
Reteach, p. 112   Reasoning, p. H226
Enrich, p. 141

Exercise Analysis

1–6	Draw lines of symmetry
7–12	Name the coordinates of a reflection point
13–14	Draw a figure and its reflection
15	Skill application
16	Data collection and computation

Challenge
These exercises provide practice with similar triangles and indirect measurement.

FOLLOW-UP ACTIVITIES

REINFORCEMENT
Have students identify the capital letters of the alphabet that have more than one line of symmetry. (*H, I, O,* and *X*) Then have them identify the capital letters that remain the same when reflected along a horizontal line of symmetry. (*B, C, D, E, H, I, K, O, X*)

MATH COMMUNICATION
Tell students that *palindromes* are symmetrical words. Then ask them what they think *symmetrical words* might mean. (words that read the same backward and forward)

Give *mom* and *toot* as examples. Explain that lines of symmetry can be drawn through the *o* in *mom* and between the *o*'s in *toot*. Then ask students to place lines of symmetry in such palindromes as "Madam, I'm Adam" (through *I*) and "Able was I ere I saw Elba." (through *r*)

Finally, have students try to devise their own palindromes.

COMING UP
Math is a foreign language; "Translation" forthcoming.

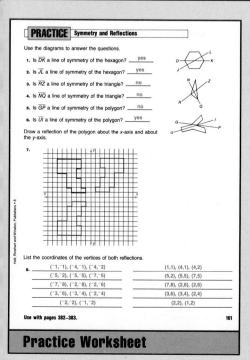

Practice Worksheet

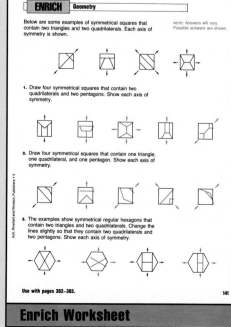

Enrich Worksheet

Objectives: To define and draw translations and rotations

Warm-Up
Have students use capital letters to write palindromes that do not change when they are reflected vertically. (BIB, DEED, and so on)

GETTING STARTED

Materials: construction paper, scissors, plain paper, pencil per pair

Have students work in pairs. Have one student cut a nonsymmetrical geometric figure from the construction paper, place it in a particular orientation on the plain paper, and trace its outline. Direct the other student to look away while the first student performs any combination of slides, flips, or turns of the figure and records what was done to it. Have the second student look at the figure in its new orientation and analyze and describe what was done to the figure to give it its new orientation.

TEACHING THE LESSON

A. Draw the following on the chalkboard, and have students identify which are translations and which are not.

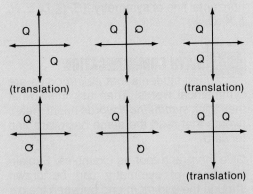

B. To aid students in visualizing rotations, trace △RST on an acetate sheet and stick a compass point through the acetate and the paper at 0 to keep the axes aligned. Then rotate the acetate to show the possible rotations of △RST.

Show that in the exercise above, the figures that were not translations were rotations.

384

Translations and Rotations

A. A 200-year-old house was located at the corner of New Street and Main Street. A high-rise apartment building was planned for that block, and the house was moved to the corner of New Street and Forest Street.

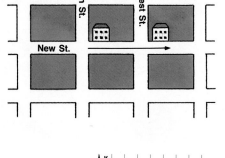

When an entire geometric figure is moved without changing its shape, the movement is called a **transformation.** When a figure is moved, or **translated,** along a line, like the house described above, all parts remain parallel to their former position, and the figure's size and shape do not change.

The diagram shows each point of △ABC moved 3 units down. △A'B'C' is a **translation** of △ABC.

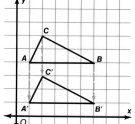

The vertices of △ABC are (1,4), (2,6), and (6,4). The vertices of △A'B'C' are (1,1), (2,3), and (6,1).

B. A **rotation** is another type of transformation or movement. In a rotation, a figure is moved about a point. All the figure's parts keep their original distance from the point and do not change their size or shape.

To rotate △RST around point O along the rotation arrow,

1. use tracing paper to trace △RST, and then draw a dot on the copy at A (the end of the rotation arrow).

2. place the pencil point on O, and turn the paper until the dot is on the tip of the arrowhead.

3. press down on the pencil to outline △RST. This figure, △R'S'T', is the rotation of △RST.

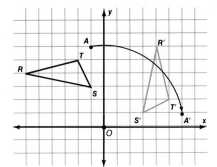

384

COMMON ERRORS

Some students might encounter difficulty in identifying and drawing rotations.

Remediation
For these errors, have students trace the figure to be rotated, use a compass to anchor the tracing paper at the origin, and rotate the tracing paper until the proper rotation is obtained. Students should then mark the new points by pressing hard with their pencils while the tracing paper is still in position.

Assign Reteach Master, p. 113.

384

For each of the following, draw a graph and find the coordinates of the translation.

1. $A(6,5)$; $B(2,3)$
Translate 4 units left.
$A'(2,5)$; $B'(^-2,3)$

2. $C(2,^-3)$; $D(4,1)$; $E(6,^-1)$
Translate 5 units up.
$C'(2,^+2)$; $D'(4,6)$; $E'(6,4)$

3. $F(1,^-4)$; $G(^-5,2)$; $H(^-7,^-2)$;
$J(^-3,^-5)$ $F'(7,^-4)$; $G'(1,2)$; $H'(^-1,^-2)$;
Translate 6 units right. $J'(3,^-5)$
Check students' graphs.

4. $K(^-2,^-1)$; $L(^-5,4)$; $M(^-6,1)$
Translate 5 units right and
4 units down.
$K'(3,^-5)$; $L'(0,0)$; $M'(^-1,^-3)$

Trace each figure, point O, and the rotation arrow.
Then draw the rotation of the given figure about point
O, along the rotation arrow.

5.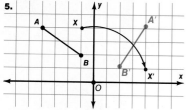

6.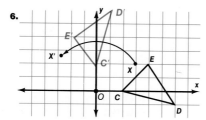

7.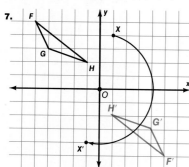

8.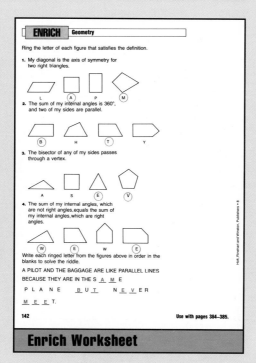

CHALLENGE

You are visiting Washington, D.C. You want to know
the height of the Washington Monument. The easiest
way to find out would be to ask someone, but you
want to figure it out yourself. Devise several ways of
measuring it. **Answers may vary. Sample answer given.
Compare shadow of meter stick to
shadow of monument.**

Classwork/Homework, page H162

385

PRACTICE | Translations and Rotations

Drive the truck along Route 66 by following the instructions
and drawing a new truck for each.

1. Translate the figure 4 units to the right and 5 units down.
2. Rotate the figure around A so that B is at point ($^-10,9$).
3. Translate the figure 4 units to the right and 8 units down.
4. Rotate the figure around point ($^-4,^-1$) so that A is at point ($^-10,^-3$).
5. Translate the figure 11 units to the right and 5 units down.
6. Translate the figure 7 units to the right and 6 units down.

162 | Use with pages 384–385.

Practice Worksheet

ENRICH | Geometry

Ring the letter of each figure that satisfies the definition.

1. My diagonal is the axis of symmetry for two adjacent triangles.

2. The sum of my internal angles is 360°, and two of my sides are parallel.

3. The bisector of any of my sides passes through a vertex.

4. The sum of my internal angles, which are not right angles, equals the sum of my internal angles, which are right angles.

Write each ringed letter from the figures above in order in the blanks to solve the riddle.

A PILOT AND THE BAGGAGE ARE LIKE PARALLEL LINES
BECAUSE THEY ARE IN THE S A M E
P L A N E   B U T   N E V E R
M E E T.

142 | Use with pages 384–385.

Enrich Worksheet

ASSIGNMENT GUIDE

Basic: 1–8
Average: 1–8
Extended: 1–8, Chlg

Resources
Practice, p. 162   Class/Home, p. H162
Reteach, p. 113
Enrich, p. 142

Exercise Analysis
1–4   Translate a figure
5–8   Rotate a figure

Challenge
The key to the solution to this problem is
the use of similar triangles or, more simply,
the proportions between corresponding
parts.

FOLLOW-UP ACTIVITIES

PROBLEM SOLVING
Have students rotate line segment
$\overline{AB}$ in a plane around A. Ask: What
shape does the movement of B describe?
(a circle) Then ask: What shape would be
described if $\overline{AB}$ were lengthened proportionally to its circular movement? (a spiral)

PROBLEM SOLVING
Study the first figure in each row
carefully and then complete the others to
match it.

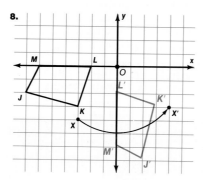

COMING UP
Need some information? You can bank on
our supply.

Warm-Up
Have students compute the following.

37.4 − 15.1 (22.3)   1,852 + 97 (1,949)
25% of 380 (95)   60% of 750 (450)

GETTING STARTED

Ask students where they would find the following information.
- the score of a Sunday afternoon professional basketball game (Monday's newspaper; radio or television on Sunday evening)
- the population of Los Angeles, California, in 1900 (encyclopedia, almanac, 1900 census, specific history books, historical society)
- recipe for bran muffins (cookbook, baker or another person who has made bran muffins)

TEACHING THE LESSON

Tell students that word problems do not always contain all the information needed. Emphasize the importance of being able to find necessary data sources and of being able to obtain the needed information from those sources. The Infobank at the back of this book is a source of easily available information.

Questions: Students sometimes have difficulty with questions that do not contain all needed information. Suggest that students write out the information they have and list the information they need before going to an information source.

Tools: Review the steps in reading various sources of information such as time lines, tables, and graphs. Once students have located the information they need, make sure that they read the information carefully and copy data correctly, using labels or units.

Solutions: Review with students finding the percent of a number.

Checks: Check for accuracy in transferring information from another source. Recheck to be sure the information found is what is actually needed to solve the problem. Students might misread tables such as the one on page 386 by ignoring the fact that the numbers represent thousands. They might also copy information from the wrong column.

| QUESTIONS | TOOLS | SOLUTIONS | CHECKS |

PROBLEM SOLVING
Using Outside Sources Including the Infobank

Some problems do not contain all the information necessary to find the answer. To solve these problems, you will need to use an outside source to find the missing information. Sometimes, the information is found in an Infobank, such as the one on pages 473–478. Otherwise, you can look in an encyclopedia, an almanac, or other outside sources.

> How many more privately owned houses were started in 1983 than in 1981 in the midwestern United States?

To answer this question, you need to know how many houses were started in 1981 and how many were started in 1983 in the midwestern United States. If this information were not given in the table below, you would have to consult an outside source that has the particular information.

NEW, PRIVATELY OWNED HOUSING UNITS STARTED BY REGION: 1981 TO 1983
(negative sign (⁻) indicates decrease)

| Region | Number (in thousands) | | | Percent change | |
	1981	1982	1983	1981–1982	1982–1983
Northeast	117.0	117.0	176.5	0.0	50.9
Midwest	166.0	148.0	214.1	⁻10.8	44.7
South	562.0	591.2	926.8	5.2	56.8
West	240.0	205.8	370.9	⁻14.3	80.2

To answer the question above, you need to compare.

$$\begin{array}{r} 214.1 \text{ thousands of houses started in 1983} \\ - \ 166.0 \text{ thousands of houses started in 1981} \\ \hline 48.1 \text{ thousands more houses started in 1983} \end{array}$$

Notice that to answer the question, you do not need the information about other regions of the country, about 1982, or about the percent change.

386

Would you need to use an outside source to answer each question? Write *yes* or *no*.

1. If 40% of the houses started in the Midwest in 1981 were ranch-style houses, how many midwestern ranch houses were started that year?   yes

2. Stella builds log cabins. She uses 245 logs per cabin. She uses 75% of the logs for the walls. How many logs make up the roof?   no

Solve each problem. Use the Infobank on page 473 and the chart on page 386 to obtain additional information.

3. The Niger River is 2,597 miles long. If Jason traveled 42% of the river's length, how far would he travel?   1,090.74 miles

4. Laura has traveled 3,000 miles along the Amazon River. What percent of the river has she traveled?   74.87%

5. In 1989, Michael Jordan scored 2,633 points in the National Basketball Association (NBA). How many more points did he score in 1987?   408 points

6. What was the average increase in housing starts from 1982 to 1983 for all regions of the United States?   156,575 starts

7. How old was the city of Geneva when Budapest was founded in A.D. 100?   150 years old

8. In 1974, Bob McAdoo scored 2,261 points in the NBA. In 1975, he scored 570 more. How many points did he score in 1975?   2,831 points

9. How many more privately owned houses were started in the Midwest than in the Northeast from 1981 to 1983?   117,600 more houses

10. Ralph is using 2 decks of 52 cards each to build card houses. His biggest house contains 73 cards. How many more cards would he have used if he wanted this house to contain 75% of the cards?
5 more cards

Classwork/Homework, page H163

ASSIGNMENT GUIDE

Basic: 1–4

Average: 3–8

Extended: 3–10

Resources
Practice, p. 163   Class/Home, p. H163
Enrich, p. 143

Exercise Analysis
1–2   Decide whether an outside information source is needed
3–10   Use an outside information source to solve a problem

FOLLOW-UP ACTIVITIES

PROBLEM SOLVING
Have students use the Infobank to solve these problems. If the Infobank does not contain enough information to solve the problem, students should write *cannot answer.*
- What are the five longest rivers in the world? (cannot answer)
- Is the square of the cube root of 729 greater than 4 cubed? (Yes)
- What is the shortest distance from the western coast of Australia to its eastern coast? (cannot answer)
- Was Adrian Dantley's average score per game in 1981 greater than Wilt Chamberlain's average score per game in 1960? (No)

REINFORCEMENT
Materials: daily newspaper

Have students look through a newspaper to find fifteen numerical facts that are listed daily. Examples include temperatures, sports statistics, stock-market prices, television schedules, and so on.

COMING UP
Readin', 'ritin', and 'rithmetic

PRACTICE   Using Outside Sources Including the Infobank

The chart below shows the area and the population of the region of Connacht in the Republic of Ireland and the area and population of the Republic of Ireland itself.

AREA AND POPULATION OF CONNACHT, REPUBLIC OF IRELAND

Counties	Area (square miles)	1966 population	1971 population
Galway	2,293	148,000	149,000
Leitrim	589	31,000	28,000
Mayo	2,084	116,000	110,000
Roscommon	951	56,000	54,000
Sligo	693	51,000	50,000

AREA AND POPULATION OF THE REPUBLIC OF IRELAND

27,137 square miles	2,884,000	2,978,000

Do you need the chart to answer each question? Write *yes* or *no*.

1. At the end of the nineteenth century, 25% of Ireland's population lived in urban areas. In 1971, 52% lived in urban areas. What was the percent of increase?   no

2. If 60% of the population of Sligo was younger than 45 in 1966, how many people in Sligo were older than 45 in 1966?   yes

Solve. Use the chart to obtain additional information.

3. A farm in Leitrim covers 117.8 square miles. What percent of the county does the farm cover?   20%

4. In which county was the percent of decrease in the population the greatest between 1966 and 1971?   Leitrim

5. What was the average population per square mile in Roscommon in 1971? Round to the nearest whole number.   57 people per mi²

6. What percent (to the nearest whole number) of the population of the Republic of Ireland lived in the Connacht region in 1971?   13%

7. Between 1966 and 1971, was the percent of increase in the population of Galway greater or smaller than the percent of increase in the total population of the Republic of Ireland?   smaller

8. If a cartography company had mapped 80% of the Connacht region, how many square miles of the province would it still have to map to complete a map of Connacht?   1,322 mi²

Use with pages 386–387.   163

Practice Worksheet

ENRICH   Problem Solving

You are a photographer under contract to a publishing company, and your work takes you all over the world. Use outside sources to find the additional information you need to solve each problem, and identify the information used to arrive at each solution.

1. You have an assignment to photograph the Paraíba do Sul River. Describe the geometrical figures that are used in the flag of the country you will visit.
Answers will vary; sample: encyclopedia entry for Brazil; circle with a rhombus within a rectangle.

2. What percent of the length of the longest river that passes through the country you will visit is the length of the Paraíba do Sul?
17.5% (Amazon: 4,000 miles; Paraíba do Sul: 700 miles)

3. You are going to take pictures of lemurs in their natural habitat. Will you be on the same side of the equator as you were when you photographed the Paraíba do Sul?
Yes, Madagascar and Brazil are south of the equator.

4. You live in the United States, and the capital of your home state is Topeka. Is the population of your home state greater than the population of the country you will visit to photograph lemurs?
no; 1983 populations: Kansas—2.4 million, Madagascar—9.4 million

5. Is the area of the country through which the Paraíba do Sul flows more than 10 times as great as the combined areas of your home state and the country in which the lemurs live?
yes, Brazil, 3,286,486 mi²; Kansas, 82,264 mi²; Madagascar, 226,444 mi²

6. Calculate the average population per square mile of your home state and of the country you will visit to photograph lemurs. Which is the more densely populated?
Madagascar; information obtained from previous problems

Use with pages 386–387.   143

Enrich Worksheet

Objective: To recognize directional patterns in math

Warm-Up

Write the following on the chalkboard, and have students match the symbols on the right with the words on the left.

1. 25 is more than 15   **a.** $n - 3$
2. 25 more than 15   **b.** $25 > 15$
3. 3 less than a number   **c.** $3 < n$
4. 3 is less than a number **d.** $15 + 25$

(1. b; 2. d; 3. a; 4. c)

GETTING STARTED

Write the following on the chalkboard.

poor dan is in a droop

Have students write this sentence backward to see that it means the same thing, regardless of the direction in which it is read. Explain that this is called a *palindrome*.

Tell students that palindromes can also be words, such as *level*. Have students think of other words that are palindromes and then list them on the chalkboard. (rotor, tat, dad, mom)

TEACHING THE LESSON

Point out that mathematical equations and inequalities are similar to palindromes in that either half can read first or "flipped" around the equation or inequality symbol. Note that in flipping an inequality, the order of the inequality symbol must be reversed. ($6 + 3 < 10; 10 > 6 + 3$) Be sure students realize that the order of the numbers within each half of the equation or inequality *must* remain the same because operations such as subtraction and division are *not* commutative. ($18 \div 3 = 6$ is *not* the same as $6 = 3 \div 18$)

Have students complete the exercises.

MATH COMMUNICATION

When you read English sentences, you begin at the left and read to the right.

Mathematics sentences are equations or inequalities. Equations and inequalities have a left side and a right side.

$$\underset{\text{left} \quad \text{right}}{\underline{7 \cdot 8} = \underline{56}} \qquad \underset{\text{left} \quad \text{right}}{\underline{5 - 2} \neq \underline{8}}$$

You can start reading on the left side or the right side. No matter in which direction the sentence is read, the mathematical statement is equivalent.

Look at this mathematical sentence. It is an equation.

$$7 \cdot 8 = 56$$

Read the left side first: Seven times eight *is equal to* fifty-six.

Read the right side first: Fifty-six *is equal to* seven times eight.

You can start on either side. The equals sign indicates that the two expressions are equivalent.

Look at this mathematical sentence. It is an inequality.

$$5 - 2 \neq 8$$

Read the left side first: Five minus two *is not equal to* eight.

Read the right side first: Eight *is not equal to* five minus two.

You can start on either side. Read either way both statements are true.

Write each in words from left to right and then from right to left. **See Answer Key.**

1. $13 + 5 = 2 \cdot 9$
2. $6 \cdot 9 > 45 - 2$
3. $38 \div 2 < 15 + 6$
4. $x - 6 = 14$
5. $24 \div 3 \geq x - 2$
6. $40 - x \leq \frac{x}{2}$
7. $x + y > 17$
8. $x^2 + y < 5$

388

GROUP PROJECT

The Ideal Recreation Center

The problem: Your community is going to build a recreation center for teenagers. Meet with your classmates, and design the center. Look at the facts and questions below. Then make a scale drawing of the ideal center.

Key Facts

- The community has a limited amount of money to spend on the project. Construction is costly.

- The ground floor of the building must not exceed 1,500 square feet.

- There should be a separate room provided for each activity.

Key Questions

- What kinds of activities will the center accommodate?

- How large should the rooms be?

- Should sports activities take place in the center? If so, which ones and how much space will they require?

- What source of energy should be used to heat the building?

- Should any of the rooms be used for more than one activity?

- Will there be a room reserved for refreshments?

- Should there be a second floor?

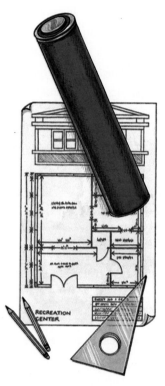

389

ASSIGNMENT GUIDE

Basic:	p. 388, p. 389
Average:	p. 388, p. 389
Extended:	p. 388, p. 389

Objectives: To design a recreation center; to make a scale drawing

USING THE PAGE

Materials: ruler, graph paper, per student

Separate the class into groups of four to seven. Tell students that looking at the Key Facts and the Key Questions in this project will direct their thinking about some factors involved in design and planning.

Have each student write a list of the activities they would like at the center and the type of room needed. Each student should then present his or her list to the group. The group must then decide together which activities and types of rooms they desire. Remind groups that the total floor area of each floor cannot exceed 1,500 square feet, which could be, for example, 50 ft × 30 ft, or 25 ft × 60 ft.

After each group has made its decisions about the center, have each group make a scale drawing of their center. Remind students of the fundamentals of scale drawings: everything is drawn in the same scale, or proportion of the actual size. The scale key gives the relationship between the drawing and the actual objects. Each student in a group should be responsible for converting the actual dimensions of one or more rooms of the center to the dimensions to be used in the scale drawing. Students in the same group can also check each other's work.

Let the class view all the drawings and pick one that they think best uses space for the widest variety of activities.

To extend this cooperative learning activity, tell students that money has been allocated to build another floor on the center. Have groups determine what new activities and new rooms they would add to their centers.

The chart below is designed to help you review the test items by correlating them with the testing objectives that appear in the Chapter Overview.

Item	Objectives
1–4	A
5–7	B
8–10	D
11	C
12	E
13–14	F
15	C
16–17	G
18–20	H
21	I
22	J
23–25	K
26	M
27	G
28–29	B
30	L

Bonus

The bonus question may be used for extra credit, or you may want to assign it to students who complete the test before the rest of the class.

Calculator

You may wish to have students use calculators for the problem-solving portions of the test.

Resources

If you prefer to use this Chapter Test as a review exercise, additional testing materials are available in the Teacher's Resource Book.

CHAPTER TEST

Use the figure to answer Exercises 1–10. (pages 354–357 and 364–365)

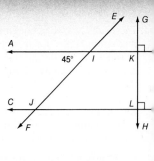

1. Name the lines that intersect at J. $\overleftrightarrow{CD}$ and $\overleftrightarrow{EF}$

2. Name a point on line AB. A, B, I, or K

3. Which line is parallel to $\overleftrightarrow{AB}$? $\overleftrightarrow{CD}$

4. Which line is perpendicular to $\overleftrightarrow{AB}$? $\overleftrightarrow{GH}$

5. Is ∠AIJ an acute angle, an obtuse angle, or a right angle? acute angle

6. Name the supplement of ∠AIJ. ∠KIJ

7. What is the measure of the complement of ∠AIJ? 45°

Find the measure of each angle. (pages 364–365)

8. ∠EIK   45°   9. ∠KIJ   135°   10. ∠IJL   45°

11. Copy $\overline{WX}$ and construct the perpendicular bisector. (pages 364–365) Check students' constructions.

12. Construct a line parallel to $\overleftrightarrow{WX}$. (pages 364–365) Check students' constructions.

Use the figure ABCD to answer Exercises 13–17. The opposite sides are parallel and congruent. (pages 366–369)

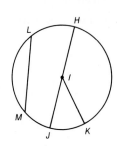

13. Is the triangle ABC scalene, right, or equilateral? scalene

14. What is the measure of ∠CAB?   75°

15. Copy ∠ABC and construct the bisector. Check students' constructions.

16. Name the quadrilateral, ADCB. parallelogram

17. What is the measure of ∠BAD?   95°

Use the circle with center I to answer Exercises 18–20. (pages 372–373)

18. Name a chord. $\overline{LM}$, or $\overline{HJ}$

19. Name a radius. $\overline{IK}$, $\overline{HI}$, or $\overline{IJ}$

20. Name a diameter. $\overline{HJ}$

390

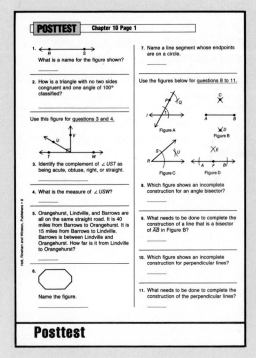

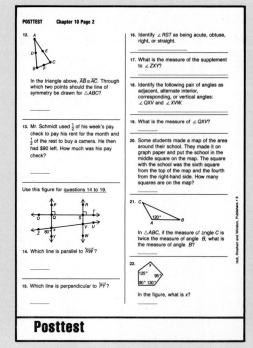

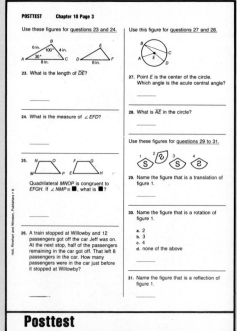

21. Does the diagram show *SSS*, *SAS*, or *ASA* congruence? (pages 374–377) **SAS**

22. Find the length of *x* for the pair of similar triangles. (pages 380–381) **x = 45**

Use the figures for Exercises 23–25. (pages 382–385)

23. Name a translation of Figure *A*. **C**

24. Name a reflection of Figure *A*. **D**

25. Name a rotation of Figure *A*. **B**

Solve. (pages 356–357, 362–363, 368–369, 372–373, and 378–379)

26. A triangle has an exterior angle of 140° and an opposite interior angle of 80°. What are the measures of the other two interior angles? Draw a picture to help you find the answer. **60° and 40°**

27. What is the sum of the measures of the interior angles of a quadrilateral whose opposite sides are parallel and congruent? What is the name of the figure? **360°; parallelogram**

28. If an angle is $\frac{1}{2}$ the measure of its complement, what is the measure of the angle? **30°**

29. If the central angle of a circle is 40°, what is its supplement? **140°**

30. The blueprints for a new arts institute call for $\frac{5}{8}$ of the tower's floors to be galleries and $\frac{1}{4}$ to be administration. Of the remaining floors, $\frac{1}{3}$ will be studios, 3 will be devoted to a performance hall, and 1 will be for maintenance. How many floors will the tower have? **48 floors**

BONUS

Solve.

How many lines of symmetry are there in an isosceles triangle? a square? a regular octagon? a regular pentagon? one; four; eight; five

391

For students who have difficulty with written tests, this test can be given orally.

You may wish to test students, orally or in writing, to see if they can explain the steps used in solving selected items. The following summarizes the procedures for solving key test items.

Ex. 8–10

Finding the measure of an angle in a given figure

To find the measure of an angle in a figure, given the measure of one angle, use the following angle relationship: vertical angles are congruent; alternate interior angles are congruent; corresponding angles are congruent; two angles whose measures have a sum of 180° are supplementary angles.

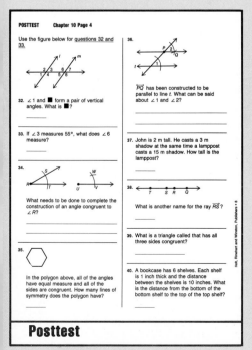

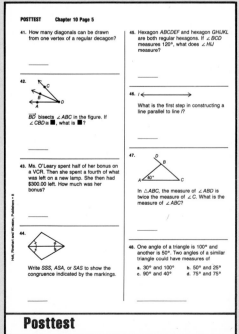

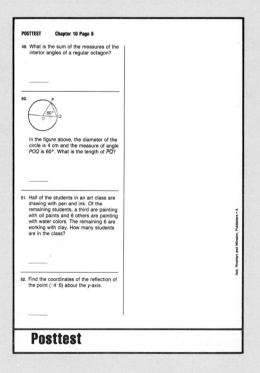

Purpose This Reteaching page provides additional instruction for key concepts in the chapter. It is designed for use by students who have had difficulty with these concepts. It can also be used to provide additional practice for students who require it.

USING THE PAGE

Parallel and perpendicular lines are taught on pages 364–365.

Be sure students understand the definitions of the terms *perpendicular* and *parallel.* Any two lines whose intersection forms a right angle are *perpendicular lines.* When defining *parallel lines,* explain that lines stretch infinitely in either direction and that they must lie in the same plane to be parallel. (Skew lines also do not intersect, but they do not lie in the same plane.) Any line that intersects a pair of parallel lines is a *transversal.* Be sure students understand the angle relationships formed when parallel lines are intersected by a transversal. The congruency of vertical angles should be intuitively obvious. The congruency of corresponding angles and alternate interior angles may not be as obvious to students. Explain that adjacent angles will be supplementary; that is, their measures will have a sum of 180°. Knowing these facts, it is possible to find the measures of all angles created by a transversal if the measure of just one angle is known.

Resources

For other practice and activities related to this chapter, see the Teacher's Resource Book.

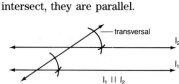

Perpendicular and parallel lines can be constructed with a compass and a straightedge.

A. When two lines in a plane meet to form a right angle, they are perpendicular.

B. When two lines in a plane do not intersect, they are parallel.

C. When parallel lines are intersected by a transversal, special pairs of angles are formed. If $l_1 \| l_2$, the following angle relationships are true:
Vertical angles are congruent.

$\angle 1 \cong \angle 4,\ \angle 2 \cong \angle 3,\ \angle 5 \cong \angle 8,\ \angle 6 \cong \angle 7$

Corresponding angles are congruent.

$\angle 2 \cong \angle 6,\ \angle 1 \cong \angle 5,\ \angle 4 \cong \angle 8,\ \angle 3 \cong \angle 7$

Alternate interior angles are congruent. $\angle 3 \cong \angle 6$, $\angle 4 \cong \angle 5$

Adjacent angles, such as $\angle 1$ and $\angle 2$, and $\angle 6$ and $\angle 8$, are supplementary. Recall that supplementary angles are two angles whose measures have a sum of 180°.

In the given figure, $r \| s$.
If m$\angle 1 = 135°$, find

1. m$\angle 2$ 45°
2. m$\angle 5$ 135°
3. m$\angle 3$ 45°
4. m$\angle 6$ 45°
5. m$\angle 4$ 135°
6. m$\angle 8$ 135°
7. m$\angle 7$ 45°

8. Name a pair of corresponding angles.
$\angle 2$ and $\angle 6$; $\angle 4$ and $\angle 8$; $\angle 1$ and $\angle 5$; $\angle 3$ and $\angle 7$

9. Name a pair of vertical angles.
$\angle 1$ and $\angle 4$; $\angle 2$ and $\angle 3$; $\angle 5$ and $\angle 8$; $\angle 6$ and $\angle 7$

10. Name a pair of alternate interior angles.
$\angle 6$ and $\angle 3$; $\angle 5$ and $\angle 4$

Write *true* or *false.*

11. $\angle 1 \cong \angle 7$ false
12. $\angle 5 \cong \angle 8$ true
13. $\angle 2 \cong \angle 6$ true
14. $\angle 1 \cong \angle 8$ true

392

ENRICHMENT

Constructing Regular Polygons

A regular polygon is a polygon whose sides all have the same length and whose angles all have the same measure. An equilateral triangle is a regular triangle.

To construct a regular triangle, use a compass and a straightedge.

1. Use a straightedge to draw $\overline{AB}$.

2. Open the compass to the length of $\overline{AB}$.

3. With the compass on point A, draw an arc above $\overline{AB}$.

4. With the compass on point B, draw another arc that intersects the first arc. Label the point C.

5. Draw $\overline{AC}$ and $\overline{BC}$.

$\triangle ABC$ is an equilateral or regular triangle.

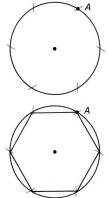

You can also use a compass and a straightedge to construct a regular hexagon.

1. Draw a circle.

2. Open the compass to the length of a radius. With the compass on any point on the circle, draw an arc that intersects the circle. Place the compass on the point where the arc intersects the circle, and draw another arc. Continue around the circle until you have six arcs.

3. Draw chords between the arcs as shown.

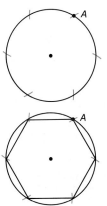

Use only a compass and a straightedge to construct

1. a regular hexagon without drawing a circle.
   (HINT: Use regular triangles.)
   Check students' constructions.

2. a regular dodecagon (twelve-sided figure).
   (HINT: First construct a regular hexagon.)
   Check students' constructions.

393

Purpose This Enrichment page provides an additional challenge for those students whose work throughout the chapter and on the Chapter Test shows a thorough understanding of the material. Alternatively, you may wish to use these exercises as a supplementary lesson for the entire class.

USING THE PAGE

When you present this lesson to students, it will be helpful to construct the polygons on the chalkboard. Explain that a regular hexagon can be arranged from six regular triangles. A regular dodecagon can be constructed in the following manner.

1. Perform Steps 1–3 in constructing a regular hexagon.

2. Construct the perpendicular bisector of one side of the hexagon.

3. Open the compass to the length of a radius. Place the compass on the point where the perpendicular bisector intersects the circle and draw another arc that intersects the circle. Continue around the circle until you have a total of 12 arcs.

4. Draw chords between the arcs.

Resources

For additional Enrichment activities, see the Teacher's Resource Book.

Objectives: To draw with the Logo turtle and to write Logo procedures that use REPEAT and variables

Warm-Up
Have students list the names of all the 3- to 10-sided polygons that they can. (triangle—3, quadrilateral—4, pentagon—5, hexagon—6, heptagon—7, octagon—8, nonagon—9, decagon—10) Discuss the definition of a regular polygon. (a polygon that has all sides equal and all angles equal)

GETTING STARTED

Materials: overhead projector, transparency, felt-tip pen

Trace the design shown below onto a transparency, and project it onto the chalkboard. Elicit from students how they think it was drawn. (Accept all answers.) Trace the outline of one hexagon (shown darker) on the chalkboard. Again elicit from students how they think the design was drawn. (Six hexagons were rotated around a center point.) Have a student trace the other hexagons on the chalkboard.

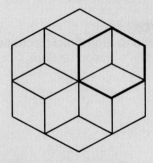

TEACHING THE LESSON

This lesson contains many new concepts for the student who has had little Logo experience. It is recommended that this lesson be taught in three class sessions.

Explain that students may use the commands FORWARD (FD), BACK (BK), RIGHT (RT), and LEFT (LT) to draw a path by using a shape called the *Logo turtle. This text uses the Logo version called Apple Logo. Point out that the Krell and Terrapin Logo versions use a different command to erase. You type PC 6 to begin erasing. To resume drawing, you type PC 1, or the number of the pen color you choose to use. Discuss how to correct mistakes before pressing RETURN or ENTER (check your Logo manual), and how to clear the screen (Apple: CLEARSCREEN or CS; Krell or Terrapin: DRAW; Logowriter: CG or RG). If your monitors have color, give students the color commands and numbers for your version of Logo, and let them discover the colors they generate.*

Explain that any list of commands can be

TECHNOLOGY

A LOGO program is called a **procedure.** Here are some LOGO commands.

FD   This makes the turtle move forward the number of steps shown.

BK   This moves the turtle backward.

RT   This makes the turtle turn to the right the number of degrees shown.

LT   This makes the turtle turn to the left.

PU   This moves the turtle without drawing a line.

PE   This makes the turtle erase as it moves.

PD   This makes the turtle draw again after PU or PE.

REPEAT   This command makes the turtle repeat commands given in the following brackets the number of times shown. For instance, this procedure draws a square.
TO SQUARE
REPEAT 4 [RT 90 FD 50]
END

You can use more than one REPEAT statement in a LOGO procedure. This procedure draws a row of squares.

TO SQUARE ROW
REPEAT 3 [REPEAT 4 [RT 90 FD 50] PU RT 90 FD 50 LT 90 PD]
END

You can also use a variable in a LOGO procedure. This procedure draws squares that have any length sides.

TO SQUARE :SIDE
REPEAT 4 [FD :SIDE RT 90]
END

The variable :SIDE allows you to plug in any length of side. Command the turtle SQUARE 50, and it will draw a square that has sides 50 steps long. Always use a colon (:) when placing a variable.

394

a procedure. To write a procedure, type the word TO and the name of the procedure, and then type the commands and the word END. A procedure name may have no spaces, hyphens, or commas. Words may be separated by periods. Explain that the procedure will be drawn on the screen only when you type its name (without TO). There are simple keyboard commands to define (usually CONTROL-C), change, or correct a procedure. They require that students work on the "flip side" or in the "editor," a Logo mode which uses other keyboard commands to move the cursor (blinking box) to make changes. Consult your Logo manual for these commands, and duplicate or post them.

Explain that a variable allows the user to enter a different value for a command each time the procedure name is typed.

Have students enter and use the SQUARE :SIDE procedure, PENUP (PU), and PEN DOWN (PD), to draw squares of different sizes (and colors).

ASSIGNMENT GUIDE

Basic:	1–3
Average:	1–3
Extended:	1–3

1. The commands below should draw the following figure. They are out of order. Rewrite the procedure in the correct order.

TO CROSS
FD 40 RT 90 FD 20 FD 40 RT 90
LT 90 RT 90 FD 20 FD 40 FD 40
LT 90 FD 40 FD 20 RT 90 RT 90
LT 90 FD 40 FD 40 FD 20 RT 90
RT 90 FD 40
END

Answers will vary.

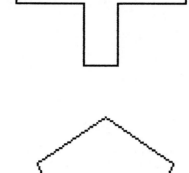

2. Write a procedure to draw this figure. Write it so that the sides can be any length. Use the REPEAT command.

TO PENTAGON :SIDE
REPEAT 5 [FD :SIDE LT 72]
END

3. Write a procedure that will take the turtle out of the maze without hitting any of the walls.

Answers will vary.

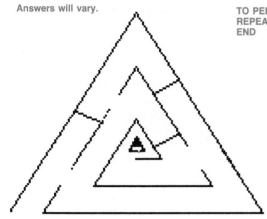

395

FOLLOW-UP ACTIVITIES

COMPUTER
Materials: computer

Explain that Logo procedure names may be used in other Logo procedures. Draw the flower shown below on the chalkboard.

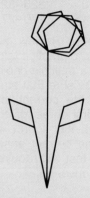

Explain that the first step is to write a procedure that includes the components.

TO FLOWER
LEAVES
BUD
END

The next step is to write the smaller procedures, called *subprocedures*. Explain that once the subprocedures are written, all you have to do is type FLOWER and the computer will locate or "call" each subprocedure in turn to draw the flower.

Have students work in pairs to write and to enter the subprocedures for the flower.

TO FLOWER
LEAVES
BUD
END

TO LEAVES
PU SETXY 0 (–70) PD*
RT 10 FD 60
REPEAT 2 [FD 20 RT 60 FD 20 RT 120]
PU SETXY 0 (–70) PD*
LT 20 FD 60
REPEAT 2 [FD 20 LT 60 FD 20 LT 120]
END

TO BUD
PU SETXY 0 (–70) SETH 0 PD*
FD 130 LT 45
REPEAT 3 [REPEAT 6 [FD 20 RT 60] RT 15]
END

*Logowriter uses SETPOS [0–70] instead of SETXY 0 (–70)

Purpose This Cumulative Review page provides an opportunity to reinforce students' understanding of the concepts and skills taught in previous chapters.

The chart below is designed to aid you in reviewing the material by specifying the pages on which various concepts and skills were taught.

Item	Page
1	316–317
2	316–317
3	316–317
4	314–315
5	340–341
6	334–335
7	298–299
8	300–301
9	206–207
10	326–327
11	270–271

Each Cumulative Review gives students an opportunity to practice taking tests that are written in a multiple-choice, standardized format. Be sure that students understand that if the correct answer is not among the first three given, then they should select the fourth choice—"not given"—as the correct answer. At least one item per test will require students to give this response.

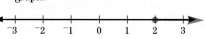

CUMULATIVE REVIEW

Write the letter of the correct answer.

1. What is the mean of 7, 8, 6, 4, 6, 7, 7, 3?

a. 3   **(b.)** 6
c. 7   d. not given

2. What is the median of 234, 6, 3, 12, 96, 7, 9?

(a.) 9   b. 52
c. 96   d. not given

3. What is the mode of 1, 7, 3, 6, 7, 5, 9?

a. 5   b. 6
(c.) 7   d. not given

4. What is the range of 9, 12, 18, 15, 16, 5, 8?

a. 10   **(b.)** 13
c. 15   d. not given

5. There are 7 marbles. If only 2 are striped, what is your probability of picking striped marbles without looking on your first two tries, if you do not return the first marble to the group?

a. $\frac{1}{49}$ **(b.)** $\frac{1}{21}$
c. $\frac{2}{7}$ d. not given

6. What is the probability of tossing an odd number with a 6-sided number cube?

a. $\frac{1}{6}$ b. $\frac{1}{3}$
(c.) $\frac{1}{2}$ d. not given

7. Solve for z: $\frac{2}{3}z + 4 \geq 12$.

(a.) $z \geq 12$ b. $z \geq 24$
c. $z \geq 32$ d. not given

8. Which sentence is shown by the graph?

a. $y < 2$ b. $y > 2$
(c.) $y \geq 2$ d. not given

9. Given a map that has a scale where 1.5 cm equals 50 km, what distance does 4.5 cm represent?

a. 22.5 km   b. 100 km
c. 300 km   **(d.)** not given

10. There are 1,200 students at Montville Junior High School. In a sampling of 100 students, 8 are found to be studying music. How many students can you expect to be studying music in the entire school?

a. 8   **(b.)** 96
c. 800   d. not given

11. XQR's stock opened on Monday at $38\frac{1}{4}$ and closed for the day down $\frac{1}{4}$. On each day during the rest of the week it closed down twice as much as the day before. What was the closing price of XQR on Friday?

(a.) $30\frac{1}{2}$ b. $30\frac{3}{4}$
c. 37   d. not given

396

CHAPTER 11 OVERVIEW

PERIMETER, AREA, VOLUME

SUMMARY

Chapter 11 deals with perimeter, area, and volume. Formulas are presented to find the area of squares, rectangles, parallelograms, triangles, trapezoids, and circles, and to find the surface area and volume of prisms, pyramids, cones, and cylinders.

LESSON SEQUENCE

PROFESSIONAL BACKGROUND

Most perimeter, area, and volume work in the mathematics curriculum aims toward the development and use of formulas. However, without a firm base that supports the learning of these formulas, students cannot go very far in application problems. In a recent National Assessment of Educational Progress, only about 55 percent of 17-year olds who had a year of high school geometry could successfully do routine triangle problems that involved the Pythagorean Rule. Furthermore, less than 20 percent of 17-year olds could find the area of a region made up of two rectangles. Students tended to confuse the formulas and, presumably, the concepts of perimeter and of area.

Research suggests several prerequisites to the learning of formulas or, more precisely, to the reliance on them. Students should be clear about the importance of units in measurements, and be able to compute measurements through the counting of units. They should, for example, be able to compute the volume of a cube from counting unit cubes.

Students should also be able to compute measurements before and after figures have been partitioned and recombined, such as when a parallelogram is derived from a rectangle. This involves conservation of measurement. A comprehensive British study indicated that about 40 percent of 13- and 14-year olds believe that the volume of the cube is not conserved when it is partitioned.

Resources: See Hart; Carpenter et al.; and Bright.

MATERIALS

rulers
graph paper
tacks or pushpins
calculators
string
circular objects
centimeter grid paper
geoboards
posterboard
tape
straws and clay
cylinder-shaped box
small blocks
round balloon
tape measure

VOCABULARY

perimeter (p. 398)
Pythagorean Rule (p. 400)
hypotenuse (p. 400)
legs (p. 400)
sine (p. 402)
cosine (p. 402)
trigonometry (p. 402)
tangent (p. 402)
circumference $C = \pi d$ (p. 404)
area of a circle $A = \pi r^2$ (p. 412)
area of a triangle $A = \frac{1}{2}bh$ (p. 410)
area of a trapezoid $A = \frac{1}{2}(b_1 + b_2)h$ (p. 410)
area of a square $A = s^2$ (p. 408)
area of a rectangle $A = lw$ (p. 408)
area of a parallelogram $A = bh$ (p. 408)
solid figures (p. 416)
polyhedron (p. 416)
edge (p. 416)
base (p. 416)
cone (p. 416)
cylinder (p. 416)
sphere (p. 416)
pyramid (p. 416)
surface area of a prism (p. 418)
surface area of a pyramid (p. 418)
surface area of a cylinder (p. 420)
cubic centimeter (p. 424)
volume of prisms, pyramids (p. 424)
volume of cylinders, cones (p. 426)

ABOUT THE CHAPTER

There is one lesson in this chapter in which students are given the opportunity, in a problem-solving setting, to work cooperatively. In this lesson, students are confronted with a real-life situation through which they are encouraged to develop and apply a variety of strategies.

In Chapter 10, students learn to find the perimeter of polygons and to use the Pythagorean rule. There are lessons on trigonometric ratios, the circumference of a circle, and the area of squares, rectangles, parallelograms, triangles, trapezoids, and circles. Students explore solid figures using models and find the surface area of prisms, pyramids, cylinders, and cones. The chapter ends with lessons on the volume of prisms, pyramids, cylinders, and cones.

Students will use the Pythagorean rule throughout their work in mathematics. Give them ample opportunity to use this formula and apply it to real-life situations. The word *trigonometry* can strike fear in students of any age. Problems can be minimized if the trigonometric ratios are presented in a straightforward way as ratios of the sides of right triangles. Students will be interested to know that both the Pythagorean rule and trigonometry are ancient ways of solving problems about right triangles.

It is important that students understand that pi (3.14159. . .) comes from the ratio of the diameter to the circumference of a circle. It is not just a random number. Give students ample opportunity to discover the number pi for themselves. They should measure the diameter and circumference of a number of circles and then find the ratio of the diameter to the circumference.

Have students estimate area, perimeter, surface area, and volume before computing. Then ask students to carry out the computation and compare the result to their estimate.

Calculators can be used effectively for computations that are cumbersome or difficult. Calculators with memory can be used to find the surface area. The memory can be used to store and then add the areas of the various faces of the figure. You should be familiar with the way each calculator shows numbers too large for the display and with the way each shows decimals which "go off" the display.

The problem-solving lessons in the chapter show students how to identify subgoals and solve multistep problems and to identify hidden assumptions in nonroutine problems. Problem-solving lessons also show students how to draw a picture to solve a problem and how to choose the correct formula.

The Group Project actively involves students in identifying career choices and career plans.

The Enrichment lesson shows students how to find the volume of a sphere. The lesson builds on the chapter and gives students an opportunity to use the calculator.

USING THE CHAPTER OPENER

Each Chapter Opener presents situational problem-solving activities that can be used to explore the skills taught throughout the chapter. The work sheets can be used by individuals, small groups, or the whole class, depending on the needs of the class. The Chapter Opener focuses on a nonalgorithmic approach to mathematics through real-life situations relevant to the children's experiences. Through an interdisciplinary approach, the Chapter Opener helps children explore the relationships between mathematics, other areas of the curriculum, and everyday life while developing different strands of mathematics.

In the Chapter Opener activities, students will explore real-life situations in which perimeter, area, and volume are used. Students will also discuss how these measurements are used in architecture and use this information to help them design buildings of their own.

PROBLEM SOLVING

The lesson Solving Multi-step Problems/Making a Plan addresses those math problems that cannot be solved unless one or more intermediate operations are performed first. The *Mathematics Unlimited* approach to solving these problems is to have students identify the information they need for solving the problem, and then to make a plan that lists the intermediate calculations in the sequence in which they must be performed in order to solve the problem. Be aware that some students may mistakenly believe that multi-step problems contain extra information.

The lesson Using a Picture, focuses on the use of pictures as outside sources to which students will often refer for information in the course of day-to-day problem solving. Students may become confused when attempting to interpret a picture because they are unfamiliar with how to read the picture's scale. The lesson explores how to gather information from a picture, how to organize that information, and how to interpret its scale in order to solve the problem.

Another skill which will be useful to students who are stuck on a problem is taught in the lesson Checking for Hidden Assumptions. *Mathematics Unlimited* stresses a reflective, conceptual approach to problem solving in which students encountering difficulty review the problem to check that they have not assumed conditions that do not apply. This technique is very useful when solving geometry problems, mathematical puzzles, and games.

When solving certain math problems, particularly measurement problems, students will often need to use formulas. Students will have to decide which formula to use to solve a problem, and the choice can sometimes be difficult. The lesson Choosing a Formula focuses on helping students analyze the information given in the problem to find the formula that applies. Students are taught the uses of each formula. They develop an ability to analyze the components of a word problem, perceive a relationship, and apply the problem-solving tool. The lesson lends itself to small-group work, in which students can exchange ideas.

BULLETIN BOARD

"World Records"

Materials: paper to cover bulletin board; lettering; large construction paper; sketches of world-record buildings; push pins; stapler; felt-tip pens

Preparation: Cover bulletin board with paper and arrange display lettering. Cut three large rectangles from construction paper and mount them on the board. Label the sketches of the buildings, and include their measurements. Staple the sketches onto the three paper rectangles.

After pp. 398-399: Have students calculate the perimeter of the hangar and the perimeter of the base of the pyramid. After the class has completed its calculations, write the answers beneath each picture.

After pp. 404-405: Have students calculate the circumference of one tank of the grain elevator. Write the answer beneath that picture.

After pp. 412-413: Have students find the area of the base of the pyramid, of the floor of the hangar, and of one tank of the grain elevator. Write each answer in the appropriate space.

After pp. 426-427: Have students find the volume of the pyramid, of the hangar, and of one tank of the grain elevator. Post the answers.

COMMON ERRORS

Students might make any of several common errors when finding area and volume. The most common error might be to write the units of the answer incorrectly. To remediate this error, explain to students that each unit in a formula must be included in the solution. For example:

$$3 \text{ m} \times 3 \text{ m} \times 1 \text{ m} = 9 \text{ m}^{+3}$$

Another error students might make is to confuse the formula for the surface area of cones and pyramids with the formulas for the volume of them. To remediate this error, explain to students that surface area is found by *adding* the surface areas of the parts. Volume is found by *multiplying* $\frac{1}{3}$ times the height times the base. Have students note that face height is used to find surface area, and the height of the entire solid is used to find volume.

Another error students will make is adding instead of multiplying when they use formulas written in this form: $v = \frac{1}{3}bh$. To remediate this error, have students review the derivation of the various formulas, so that they understand how the desired measure is found without a formula. This will make use of the formula more clear.

SPECIAL NEEDS

Some students need to work with concrete examples to understand the meaning of the formulas for area, perimeter, and volume. Use geoboards or grid paper to develop the formula for the area of a rectangle. Establish the concept of *unit,* and have students determine the number of units it takes to cover the rectangle.

Next introduce the terms *base* and *height,* and develop the formula for the area of a parallelogram. Remind students that the parts of a region can be rearranged without changing the area of the region. Have students prove this by cutting apart and rearranging shapes on grid paper. Provide different-size circles, string, and rulers for your students. Have them measure the circumference and diameter of each circle, charting their results, and using a calculator to find the ratio of $C:d$ in decimal form. Before finding the volume of space figures, have students study each figure carefully to determine its component parts. (For example, a pyramid is formed by one rectangle and four triangles.)

Have advanced students find the volume of irregular geometric solids by drawing a picture and using a calculator.

WORLD RECORDS

Data taken from
1986 Guinness Book of World Records

Largest Hangar
Kelly Air Force Base
San Antonio, Texas

90 ft.
300 ft.
2,000 ft.

Oldest New World Pyramid
La Venta, Mexico
Built by the Olmec people 800 B.C.

108 ft.
420 ft.
420 ft.

Largest Grain Elevator
C-G-F Grain Company
Wichita, Kansas

120 ft.
C G F
3 tanks
123 tanks
Diameter of
1 tank = 30 ft.

MATH LABS

 MATH CONNECTION
(Science)

Have students devise ways to measure the volume of an irregularly-shaped object. (One possibility is to fill a calibrated container to a level that would be enough to cover the object, then place the sphere in the container and read the amount of water displaced by the object.)

Have students solve this problem.

Grace wants to measure the volume of a hard-boiled egg. She has a measuring cup that, she estimates, can hold more than the volume of the egg. However, because the egg is an oval, it will not fit into the measuring cup. Grace also has a cylinder that is large enough to hold the egg. The cylinder's base has a radius of 4 cm; and the cylinder's height is 8 cm. Grace finds that the egg displaces $\frac{1}{8}$ of the volume of the cylinder. How could she determine this? (By filling the cylinder with water, placing the egg in it, and measuring the water that spilled over with the measuring cup.) What is the volume of the egg to the nearest cubic centimeter? (50 cc)

COMPUTER

Have students write a program that will compute the surface area of any triangular or rectangular prism whose base is a regular polygon.

```
10 INPUT "HOW MANY SIDES
   DOES THE BASE HAVE? (3 OR
   4)";S
20 INPUT "WHAT IS THE LENGTH
   OF A SIDE?";L
30 IF S = 3 THEN LET B = SQR(3)/
   2 * L^2
40 IF S = 4 THEN LET B = 2* L^2
50 INPUT "WHAT IS THE
   HEIGHT"; H
60 LET A = S * H * L + B
70 PRINT "THE SURFACE AREA
   IS ";A
80 END
```

CALCULATOR

A calculator should be available for computations involving perimeter, area, and volume exercises. Often, these computations are cumbersome. As students extend their study of perimeter, area, and volume, the number of figures and hence the number of formulas increases. These formulas include area, surface area, and volume. The calculator can aid in obtaining a result from the formulas. The student must understand the principles and choose the correct formula.

Students should use calculators for all problem-solving activities.

Additional Activities: **Drill and Practice:** Develop calculator codes for calculating the volume of prisms, pyramids, cylinders, and cones.

Exploration: Begin with a square. If you double the length of a side, what happens to the area of the square and the volume of the cube? When you double the side length of a regular pentagon, what happens to the area? Investigate the result for a regular *n*-gon.

SUBJECT AREA CONNECTIONS

These Subject Area Connections are useful for reinforcing the concepts presented in this chapter.

p. 405-Science: Students use a list of the approximate diameters of various planets to find the approximate circumference of each.

p. 427-Science: Students measure their vital capacity by blowing up a balloon and finding its circumference, radius, and capacity.

Here are some other activities for presenting these concepts.
- **SOCIAL STUDIES:** Have students identify and discuss the uses of solid figures in buildings and architecture.
- **SOCIAL STUDIES:** Have students research and find the volumes of the five largest Egyptian pyramids.
- **SCIENCE:** Have students research and find the volumes of the capsules (coneshaped) on three U.S. space rockets.

PLAN AHEAD

You will need to prepare cut-out parallelograms for the Teaching the Lesson on T.E. p. 408. You will need posterboard and tape for the activities on T.E. pp. 416–417 and 418–419.

PLANNING CALENDAR
ABBREVIATION KEY

Teacher's Resource Book	Follow-up Activities
MMW—Making Math Work	CALC—Calculator
P—Practice	CMP—Computer
R—Reteach	CNS—Consumer
E—Enrich	P&G—Puzzles and Games
	MNP—Manipulatives
	MC—Math Connection
	MCM—Math Communication
	NS—Number Sense
	PS—Problem Solving
	RFM—Reinforcement

PLANNING CALENDAR

Pages	Lesson Objectives	ASSIGNMENT GUIDE Basic	Average	Extended	Class/ Home	More Practice	Math Reasoning	Follow-up	Reteach	Practice	Enrich
397	Chapter Opener (Use MMW 21,22)	397	397	397							
398,399	To explore and apply perimeter of polygons	398,399	398,399	398,399	H164		H227	RFM P&G	114	164	144
400,401	To explore and use the Pythagorean Rule	400,401	400,401	400,401	H165	H204		CALC CMP	115		145
402,403	To define and use trigonometric ratios	1-14,16-28e	1-29o	2-14e,15-29	H166			PS RFM	116	166	146
404,405	To find the circumference of a circle	1-22	2-30e,31-32	1-21o,23-32	H167		H227	CALC MC	117	167	147
406,407	To make a plan to solve multi-step problems	1-4	2-5	3-6	H168			PS		168	148
408,409	To find the area of squares, rectangles, and parallelograms	1-3,4-22e,24-27	2-22e,24-27	1-23o,24-27	H169	H205		MC MNP	118	169	149
410,411	To find the area of triangles and trapezoids	1-15	1-21o	2-14e,16-21	H170	H205	H227	RFM MNP	119	170	150
412,413	To find the area of a circle	1-19,21-29o,MCR	1-19,20-30e,MCR	1-27o,28-30,MCR	H171		H228	CMP MC	120	171	151
414,415	To use information from a picture to solve problems	p. 414 1-2 p. 415 5-6	p. 414 1-3 p. 415 5-7	p. 414 2-4 p. 415 6-8	H172 H173			PS		172-173	
416,417	To explore solid figures	416,417	416,417	416,417	H174			MC	121	174	152
418,419	To explore and calculate the surface area of prisms and pyramids	418,419	418,419	418,419	H153			PS PS	122	175	153
420,421	To find the surface area of a cylinder or cone	1-5,10-20,22-23	1-6,8-20e,22-24	1-21o,22-25	H176	H205	H228	CALC PS	123	176	154
422,423	To check for hidden assumptions when solving problems	1-6	1-4,6-8e	1-4,5-9o	H177					177	155
424,425	To find the volume of prisms and pyramids	1-4,7-12,15-16, NS	1-13o,15-16,NS	2-12e,13-16,NS	H178	H206	H228	MC NS	124	178	156
426,427	To find the volume of cylinders and cones	1-12,15-16,18-19	4-13,15-16,18-19	4-19	H179			MC	125	179	157
428,429	To choose the correct formula to solve a problem	1-4	2-6	3-8	H180			PS		180	158
430	Calculator: To use geometric formulas	430	430	430							
431	Group Project: To write a questionnaire; to take a survey; to make and interpret a circle graph	431	431	431							

432,433   Chapter Test   435   Enrichment

434   Reteaching   436   Cumulative Review

TESTS

A. To find the perimeter of polygons and the circumference of circles

B. To find the area of squares, rectangles, parallelograms, triangles, trapezoids, and circles

C. To find the length of the side of a right triangle by using the Pythagorean Rule

D. To find the length of a side of a right triangle, using sine, cosine, and tangent ratios

E. To find the surface area of prisms, pyramids, cones, and cylinders

F. To find the volume of prisms, pyramids, cones, and cylinders

G. To identify subgoals and solve multistep problems

H. To use information from a picture to solve problems

I. To choose a formula to solve a problem

FAMILY INVOLVEMENT

Family Involvement for Chapter 11 encourages family members to build and use a surveying transit. Students and their families are encouraged to learn the purpose of a transit—to find the height of objects when only the distance between them is known or the distance between objects when only their height is known. Family members are to assemble a transit from illustrations. Then they are to learn how to use the transit by reading the angle of sight marked by a string hung from it. Family members are to calculate the height of their house, of trees, or of a tall building. If possible, they are to check their calculations by actually measuring the objects they have sighted with the transit. If they are interested in undertaking a more difficult task, family members may attempt to calculate the height of a mountain.

Additional activities might include measuring the perimeter of the house or of the apartment if the family lives in a large building. To extend this activity, have family members calculate the surface area and volume of a room in their home.

STUDENT RESOURCES

Bibliography

Fortman, Janis L. *Creatures of Mystery*. Milwaukee: Raintree Publications, Inc., 1983.

Polis, Richard A., et. al. *Magic Squares and Arrays*. Warrington, Pa.: Fabmath, 1980.

Ripley's Believe It or Not Space Travel and Colonies. New York: Coward, McCann, & Geohegan, Inc., 1982.

Serling, Barbara. *You Can't Eat Peanuts in Church and Other Little Known Laws*. Garden City, New York: Doubleday & Company, Inc., 1975.

Films

Classic Antics in Mathematics. 12 minutes. Color. 1976. Distributed by AIMS Instructional Media, Glendale, Calif.

Mathematics of the Honeycomb. 13 minutes. Color. 1964. Distributed by Moody Institute of Science, Whittier, Calif.

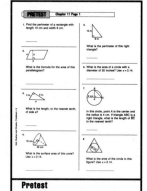

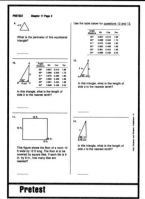

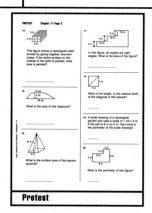

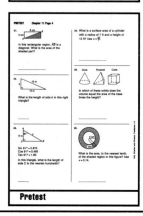

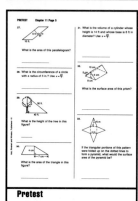

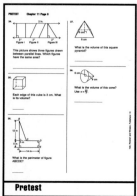

The Pentagon, a five-sided building in Washington, DC., is the largest office building in the world. It covers 29 acres of land and has 3,705,397 square feet of space. Why is it important to know the area or the volume of a building? List all the reasons you can think of.

11 PERIMETER, AREA, VOLUME

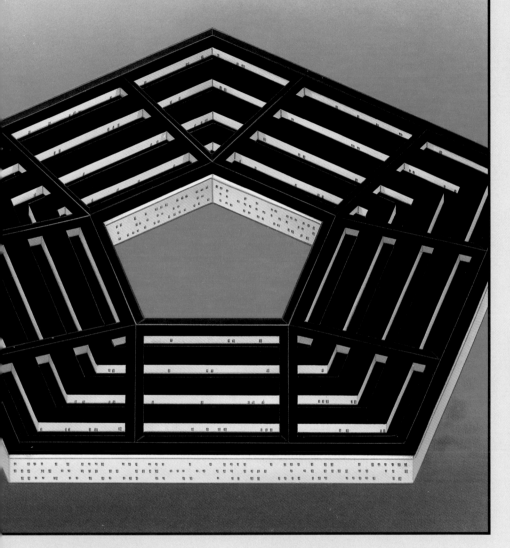

Objectives: To explore problems related to perimeter, area, and volume

Direct students to look at the picture of the Pentagon. The Pentagon, as well as other buildings, was constructed of geometrical shapes. It is easier to find the area, the perimeter, and the volume of buildings of geometrical shapes than it is to find the dimensions of buildings of nongeometrical shapes.

INDIVIDUAL
Geometry
Materials: Making Math Work page 21 per student

Have students complete Making Math Work page 21. Ask them whether the method used on page 21 will work for all buildings. Give them the dimensions of a plot of land on which each student is to construct a building. Tell them that the building code will not allow a building over 100 feet tall. Have each student make a plan for a building to be constructed on this site and explain the rationale behind the plans. Have each student calculate the area, the perimeter, and the volume.

SMALL GROUP
Geometry
Materials: Making Math Work page 22 per student

Have students complete Making Math Work page 22. Then instruct each group to design a classroom. Each group should decide on the dimensions of the items in the room and then leave ample space for people to walk around. Have each group make a scale drawing of the classroom. Remind them to include a key.

WHOLE CLASS
Logic
Discuss the importance of planning a structure on paper before trying to construct it. Ask students how they might go about finding the area, the perimeter, and the volume of an irregularly shaped building. Draw a building of this kind on the chalkboard, and have students speculate about how to figure out its dimensions. Ask students whether they could have predicted the dimensions before they completed the calculations. Discuss how space relationships affect real-life situations.

| MAKING MATH WORK |

Here is a simple way to find the perimeter of a building in your community. Take a step. Measure the length of your stride. (It may be more accurate to take 10 strides and then divide the distance by 10.) Then walk along the length and then the width of the building you have chosen. Answers will vary.

Length of stride: _____

Number of strides: _____

Perimeter of building: _____

To find the area, find the product of the length and the width. Then draw a scale diagram of the building. Answers will vary.

Scale: _____

Diagram:

Area of building: _____

List at least three reasons for finding the perimeter of a building. Then list at least three reasons for finding the area of a building. Compare your reasons with those of your classmates. Answers will vary.

Making Math Work

| MAKING MATH WORK |

Your classroom is probably filled with desks, shelves, chairs, cabinets, and so on. How much room do you have in which to walk around? How could you find the area of walking space in square feet? First, find the area of your classroom. Then find the area that each item in your classroom takes up. Make a scale drawing below. Check students' drawings.

Making Math Work

Objectives: To explore and apply perimeter of polygons

Warm-Up
Have students compute each expression.
- $6 \cdot 2.8$ (16.8)
- $4 \cdot 3\frac{1}{2}$ (14)
- $3.5 + 2.8 + 4.4 + 3.7$ (14.4)
- $4\frac{2}{3} + 3\frac{1}{2} + 4\frac{2}{3} + 3\frac{1}{2}$ ($16\frac{1}{3}$)
- $2 \cdot 3.2 + 2 \cdot 5.8$ (18)

GETTING STARTED

Write the following on the chalkboard.

> perimeter   surface area
> circumference   volume
> area

Have students as a class come up with satisfactory definitions of these terms and name several practical applications involving each.

TEACHING THE LESSON

There are two approaches that you can use in teaching this lesson: (1) have students work individually through the developmental parts and convene in groups of four for Thinking/Working as a Team or (2) have students work through the developmental parts in groups of four and have a class discussion for Thinking/Working as a Team.

A. Make sure that students understand the two rules for arranging the tables. For questions 4 and 5 of Thinking as a Team, have students keep a record of their arrangements. This will make it easier for them to discover a pattern.

B. Lead students to realize that for figures that have several parallel sides, they can find the lengths of missing sides by using the overall length and the overall width of the figure. Ask students what conclusion they can draw about the lengths of sides in a figure that contains all right angles. (The sum of all the horizontal sides at the top of the figure equals the sum of all the horizontal sides at the bottom, and the same fact applies to the vertical sides.)

Discuss with students the several ways in which the problem in Working as a Team can be solved. Students may want to try to assign dimensions to the inner rectangle (as long as the dimensions add to 1,260 ft) to discover whether they will find the same perimeter for the outer rectangle. (Yes, by adding 44 ft—the width of the two runs—to each dimension.) Have them prove this by assigning several sets of dimensions to the inner rectangle. Some students may also be able to

398

Perimeter

A. A restaurant has only small square tables. To seat large groups together the restaurant follows these two rules:

1. Only one person can sit on one side of the table.
2. At least one side of a table must be placed next to the side of another table.

Here are some different ways that six tables can be arranged.

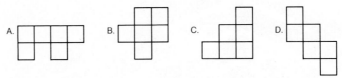

Does each arrangement seat the same size party?   no

How many people can be seated at each arrangement?
A.–14; B.–12; C.–12; D.–14
Which arrangement seats the largest party? the smallest party?   A and D; B and C

The restaurant wants to put crepe paper on the edge of each table where someone will be sitting. If each table is 3 feet on a side, how much crepe paper do they need for the largest party? for the smallest party?   42 ft; 36 ft

Make a different arrangement of six tables. Compare this arrangement with the ones above. Can you seat more people, less people, or the same number as the largest party above? How much crepe paper will be needed for this arrangement?   Answers will vary.

Thinking as a Team

Twelve tables are to be arranged to seat one party. Use tiles or square pieces of paper to show the different arrangements, then compare your arrangements with the other members of the team. Record your results.

1. Show how the tables can be arranged to seat four different-sized parties.   Answers will vary.

398   Math Reasoning, page H227

---

solve the problem by using variables for the dimensions of the rectangle.

$$P_i = 2l + 2w = 2(l + w) = 1{,}260 \text{ ft}$$

So, $l + w = 630$ ft

$$\begin{aligned}
P_o &= 2(l + 44) + 2(w + 44) \\
&= 2l + 88 + 2w + 88 \\
&= 2(l + w) + 176 \\
&= 2 \times 630 + 176 = 1{,}436 \text{ ft}
\end{aligned}$$

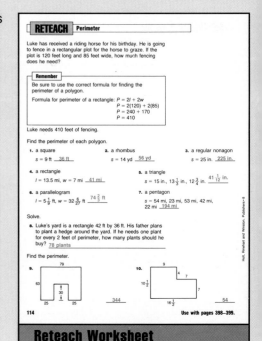

Reteach Worksheet

2. What is the largest party that can be seated? Show how you would arrange the twelve tables. How much crepe paper will be needed? 26 people; answers will vary; 78 ft

3. What is the smallest party that can be seated using all twelve tables? How much crepe paper will be needed? 14 people; 42 ft

4. Try several other numbers of tables and have each member of the team show how the tables can be arranged. Check students' drawings.

5. Which arrangement allows for seating of the largest party? the smallest party? Do you see a pattern? Describe it. Answers will vary. Multiply the number of tables by 2, and then add 2 to get the largest party.

B. The diagrams below show the floor plan of two diffferent restaurants. Each restaurant wants to put molding around the entire perimeter of the floor. How much molding will be needed? $59\frac{3}{4}$ ft, 67 m

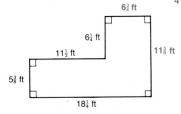
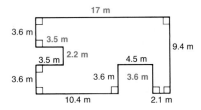

Working as a Team

You are working for the summer at a kennel. Your boss wants you to fence in a rectangular track in a pasture as a dog run. He has marked out the four corners of the interior rectangle and you install a total of 1,260 ft of fencing along the perimeter of this rectangle. The width of the run will be 22 ft. What is the outer perimeter of the run? 1,436 ft

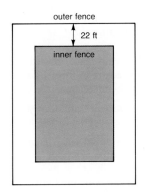

outer fence

22 ft

inner fence

Classwork/Homework, page H164

399

ASSIGNMENT GUIDE

Basic: p. 398, p. 399

Average: p. 398, p. 399

Extended: p. 398, p. 399

Resources
Practice, p. 164   Class/Home, p. H164
Reteach, p. 114   Reasoning, p. H227
Enrich, p. 144

FOLLOW-UP ACTIVITIES

REINFORCEMENT
Draw on graph paper all the possible rectangles that have a perimeter of 24 units. Use only whole numbers. (1 by 11, 2 by 20, 3 by 9, 4 by 8, 5 by 7, and 6 by 6)

PUZZLES AND GAMES
Materials: metric rulers

Have students each draw a square that measures 20 cm by 20 cm. Then have them cut it into two equal pieces that can fit together to form a rectangle that measures 16 cm by 25 cm.

Hint: The cut is not one straight line.

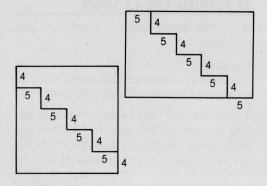

COMING UP
It's Greek to me.

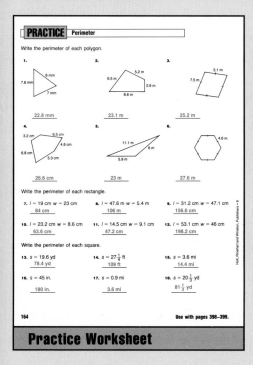
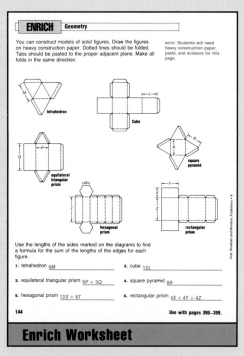

Objectives: To explore and use the Pythagorean Rule

Warm-Up
Have students find each square or square root.

5^2 (25) 8^2 (64) 3^2 (9) 7^2 (49)
14^2 (196) 12^2 (144) 13^2 (169) 6^2 (36)

$\sqrt{81}$ (9) $\sqrt{225}$ (15) $\sqrt{16}$ (4) $\sqrt{1}$ (1)
$\sqrt{400}$ (20) $\sqrt{4}$ (2) $\sqrt{100}$ (10) $\sqrt{121}$ (11)

GETTING STARTED

Materials: string, tacks, cardboard

Tell students that when the ancient Egyptians wanted a square corner for a building or a field, they used a loop of rope knotted into 12 equal segments. They put a stake through one knot 3 segments from one end. Then a man would be positioned three segments to one side of the stake, and another would be positioned four segments to the other side of the stake.

When the two men, called rope stretchers, pulled the rope into a triangle, there was a 90° angle, and the stake was at the vertex. Have students reenact this process by placing a knotted string on a bulletin board and applying tacks to hold the corners. Then have them verify the 90° angle by using a protractor.

TEACHING THE LESSON

Materials: graph paper, centimeter ruler, calculator

Because of the depth of the conceptual development involved, this lesson may be addressed in several class periods.

There are two approaches that you can use in teaching this lesson: (1) have students work individually through the developmental parts and in groups of four for Thinking as a Team or (2) have students work through the developmental parts in groups of four and have a class discussion for Thinking as a Team.

A. Review with students the definitions of leg and hypotenuse, making sure that they understand that those terms apply only to right triangles. Students should draw their triangles on graph paper to ensure they have right angles and should use a centimeter ruler to measure the hypotenuses. Students should be able to see the relationship between Pythagorean triples when they look at the squares of these triples. You may wish to write the rule on the chalkboard after students have discovered it: $a^2 + b^2 = c^2$, where a and b are the lengths of the legs and c is the length of the hypotenuse. Emphasize to students (or have them discover) that this relationship holds true only for right trian-

The Pythagorean Rule

A. In a right triangle the side opposite the right angle is called the **hypotenuse.** The two other sides are called the **legs.** This lesson will explore the relationship among these three sides.

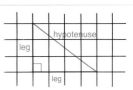

- Using a sheet of graph paper, draw a right triangle with legs of length 3 cm and 4 cm. Measure the length of the hypotenuse. Copy the table and record your measurement.

- Draw another right triangle with legs of length 5 cm and 12 cm and then another right triangle with legs of length 6 cm and 8 cm. Measure the length of each hypotenuse and record your measurements on the table.

leg	leg	hypotenuse
3	4	▦
5	12	▦
6	8	▦

- Using another sheet of graph paper, draw another right triangle with legs of any length, and measure the length of the hypotenuse. Record your measurements on the table.

- Can you find a relationship among the entries in each row of this table? Students may or may not see that $a^2 + b^2 = c^2$.

Thinking as a Team

1. Copy and complete the table at the right by squaring each entry in the table above. Can you find a relationship among the entries in each row of this table? Write a rule to show this relationship? $leg^2 + leg^2 = hypotenuse^2$

$(leg)^2$	$(leg)^2$	$(hypotenuse)^2$
9	16	▦ 25
▦ 25	▦	144 ▦ 169
▦ 36	▦	64 ▦ 100

The rule that shows this relationship is called the Pythagorean Rule. Pythagoras was an ancient Greek mathematician.

2. Do you think that this rule works no matter what the lengths of the legs are? yes

Draw a right triangle with legs of any length. Use a centimeter ruler and a calculator to predict the length of the hypotenuse to the nearest millimeter. Was your prediction correct?

400

gles. After students finish question 2, they should see that the relationship holds for any right triangle. Challenge students to see whether this rule can be used as a test to prove that a given triangle is a right triangle. Tell them to use a calculator to find any three numbers that satisfy the rule (they needn't be whole numbers) and to draw or construct a triangle with sides of those lengths. Have them measure the angles of the triangle, and ask them what they find. (If the lengths of the sides satisfy the rule, the triangle must be a right triangle.)

B. In section B, students discover that the Pythagorean rule can be used not only to find the lengths of the hypotenuses but also to find the lengths of the legs of a right triangle.

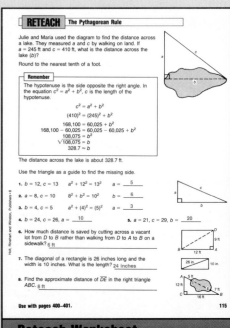

(Continued on p. 401.)

B. Suppose that you know the length of the hypotenuse and the length of one leg of a right triangle. How do you find the length of the other leg? Look at the diagram at right and complete the table below it. You may want to use a calculator. $c^2 \div b^2 = a^2$

6.5 cm
6 cm

C. In this activity you will use the rule you have discovered to help you compare the sizes of square roots.

(leg)²	(leg)²	(hypotenuse)²
■	36	42.25

6.25

Step 1: Draw a right triangle with legs each 1 centimeter long.

- According to the rule that you have written, how many centimeters long is the hypotenuse of this triangle? $\sqrt{2}$ cm

1 cm
1 cm

- Use a ruler to find the length of the hypotenuse to the nearest tenth of a centimeter. **1.4 cm**

Step 2: Draw a 1-cm line perpendicular to the first hypotenuse. Now draw a hypotenuse to make a new right triangle.

1 cm
1 cm
1 cm
1 cm

- What are the lengths of the legs of this triangle?
  $\sqrt{2}$ cm and 1 cm
- What length can you predict for its hypotenuse?
  $\sqrt{3}$ cm
- Use a ruler to find the hypotenuse to the nearest tenth of a centimeter. **1.7 cm**

Step 3: Continue to draw perpendicular lines 1 cm long and hypotenuses to create new right triangles. Measure each hypotenuse and draw new right triangles until you can make a table listing the square roots of the numbers from 1 to 10 to the nearest tenth.

$\sqrt{1} = 1$ $\sqrt{6} \approx 2.4$
$\sqrt{2} \approx 1.4$ $\sqrt{7} \approx 2.6$
$\sqrt{3} \approx 1.7$ $\sqrt{8} \approx 2.8$
$\sqrt{4} = 2$ $\sqrt{9} = 3$
$\sqrt{5} \approx 2.2$ $\sqrt{10} \approx 3.2$

Thinking as a Team

- Use your calculator to compute to the nearest tenth the square roots of the numbers from 1 to 10. How close to correct were your answers to the above problems? How do you explain the discrepancies?

the degree of precision in students' measurements

Classwork/Homework, page H165   More Practice, page H204   **401**

ASSIGNMENT GUIDE

Basic: p. 400, p. 401

Average: p. 400, p. 401

Extended: p. 400, p. 401

Resources
Practice, p. 165   Class/Home, p. H165
Reteach, p. 115   More Practice, p. H204
Enrich, p. 145

C. In Section C, students use the Pythagorean rule to explore square roots and to compare their sizes. Lead them to conclude that the series of triangles will approximate a spiral with successive hypotenuses measuring $\sqrt{2}$ cm, $\sqrt{3}$ cm, $\sqrt{4}$ cm, . . . $\sqrt{10}$ cm in length. After measuring the hypotenuses, students should use their calculators to compute to the nearest tenth the square roots of the numbers 1 to 10. Refer students who need additional practice to More Practice page 488 in the back of the textbook.

FOLLOW-UP ACTIVITIES

CALCULATOR

Have students use calculators to find the missing side of each right triangle.
- $a = 624$ cm; $b = 832$ cm; $c = $ ■ (1,040 cm)
- $a = 936$ in.; $b = $ ■; $c = 1,989$ in. (1,755 in.)
- $a = $ ■; $b = 3,732$ m; $c = 4,043$ m (1,555 m)

COMPUTER

Explain that when the lengths of the sides of a right triangle are whole numbers, the three lengths form a Pythagorean Triple (e.g., 3, 4, 5; 5, 12, 13). There is a special relationship between the numbers in some triples.
- a is an odd number greater than 1
- $b = \frac{(a^2 - 1)}{2}$
- $c = \frac{(a^2 + 1)}{2}$

Write a program to generate the first five Pythagorean Triples.

```
10 PRINT "SIDE A", "SIDE B", SIDE C"
20 FOR A = 3 TO 11 STEP 2
30 LET B = (A^2 − 1)/2
40 LET C = (A^2 + 1)/2
50 PRINT A,B,C
60 NEXT A
70 END
```

COMING UP
A new kind of sign

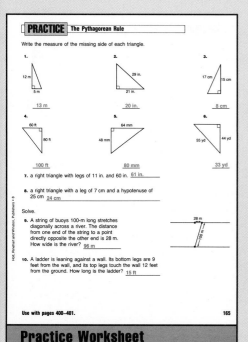

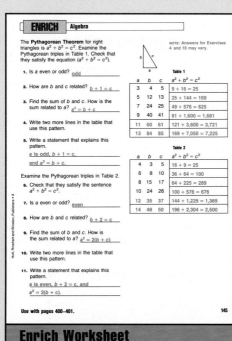

Objectives: To define and use trigonometric ratios

Warm-Up

Have students write each ratio.
- weeks in a year to days in a year (52:365)
- inches in a yard to feet in a yard (36:3)
- number of sides of an octagon to number of sides of a square (8:4)
- number of oranges in a dozen to number of eggs in a dozen (12:12)

GETTING STARTED

Draw these triangles on the chalkboard.

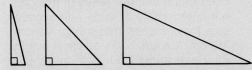

Ask students whether they see a relationship between the top angle and the bottom side. (As one grows, so does the other.)

Then ask whether they see a relationship between the angle on the far right and the bottom side. (As the side grows, the angle gets smaller.)

Explain to the class that there are several relationships among the angles and the sides of a right triangle. Tell them that the study of these relationships and the calculations based on them is called trigonometry.

TEACHING THE LESSON

Draw the right triangle shown below on the chalkboard, and label it as shown.

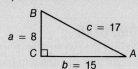

Demonstrate how to find angle A by using each of the three trigonometric ratios. Draw the right triangle below on the chalkboard, label it as shown, and guide the students toward solving for a.

$$\cos \angle B = \frac{a}{c}$$
$$\cos 60° = \frac{a}{18}$$
$$0.5 = \frac{a}{18}$$
$$9 = a$$

Trigonometric Ratios

The word **trigonometry** means "triangle measure." You can use the relationship between the sides and the angles of a right triangle to find missing parts of the triangle.

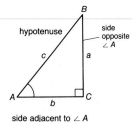

In right triangle ABC, the ratios of sides are given the following special names:

The **sine** of $\angle A = \dfrac{\text{length of side opposite } \angle A}{\text{length of hypotenuse}}$, or $\sin A = \dfrac{a}{c}$.

The **cosine** of $\angle A = \dfrac{\text{length of side adjacent to } \angle A}{\text{length of hypotenuse}}$, or $\cos A = \dfrac{b}{c}$.

The **tangent** of $\angle A = \dfrac{\text{length of side opposite } \angle A}{\text{length of side adjacent to } \angle A}$, or $\tan A = \dfrac{a}{b}$.

In a right triangle, the trigonometric ratios are the same for a certain angle, no matter what the size of the triangle. The trigonometric ratios for some angles measuring 46° through 64° are listed in the table at the right.

You can use one of the three trigonometric ratios to find an unknown side of a right triangle.

Angle Measure	Sin	Cos	Tan
46°	0.719	0.695	1.04
47°	0.731	0.682	1.07
48°	0.743	0.669	1.11
49°	0.755	0.656	1.15
50°	0.766	0.643	1.19
51°	0.777	0.629	1.23
52°	0.788	0.616	1.28
53°	0.799	0.602	1.33
···	···	···	···
60°	0.866	0.500	1.73
61°	0.875	0.485	1.80
62°	0.883	0.469	1.88
63°	0.891	0.454	1.96
64°	0.899	0.438	2.05

Find the length of $\overline{BC}$ (or side a).

To find a to the nearest tenth, use the sine ratio.

$$\sin \angle A = \frac{a}{c}$$
$$\sin 48° = \frac{a}{8}$$
$$0.743 \approx \frac{a}{8}$$
$$5.944 \approx a$$

So, $a \approx 5.9$.

Another example:

Find $\tan B$. Then find the measure of $\angle B$ to the nearest degree.

$$\tan B = \frac{21}{20} = 1.05$$
$$\tan 46° \approx 1.04$$
$$\tan 47° \approx 1.07$$

Since 1.05 is closer to 1.04, $\angle B$ is closer to 46°.

402

COMMON ERRORS

Students often memorize the formulas incorrectly.

Remediation

Help students develop their own mnemonic devices. Because students often remember "sine-cosine-tangent" in order, have them work on remembering the numerators "opposite-adjacent-opposite" in order. Even with this mnemonic, however, students must also remember that for the tangent, the hypotenuse is no longer the denominator.

Assign Reteach Master, p. 116.

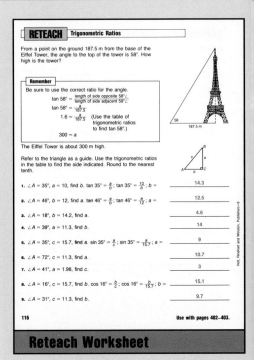

RETEACH Trigonometric Ratios

From a point on the ground 187.5 m from the base of the Eiffel Tower, the angle to the top of the tower is 58°. How high is the tower?

Remember
Be sure to use the correct ratio for the angle.
$$\tan 58° = \frac{\text{length of side opposite } 58° \angle}{\text{length of side adjacent } 58° \angle}$$
$$\tan 58° = \frac{a}{187.5}$$
$$1.6 \approx \frac{a}{187.5} \quad \text{(Use the table of trigonometric ratios to find tan 58°.)}$$
$$300 \approx a$$

The Eiffel Tower is about 300 m high.

Refer to the triangle as a guide. Use the trigonometric ratios in the table to find the side indicated. Round to the nearest tenth.

1. $\angle A = 35°$, $a = 10$, find b. $\tan 35° = \frac{a}{b}$; $\tan 35° = \frac{10}{b}$; $b =$ _____ 14.3

2. $\angle A = 46°$, $b = 12$, find a. $\tan 46° = \frac{a}{b}$; $\tan 46° = \frac{a}{12}$; $a =$ _____ 12.5

3. $\angle A = 18°$, $b = 14.2$, find a. _____ 4.6

4. $\angle A = 39°$, $a = 11.3$, find b. _____ 14

5. $\angle A = 35°$, $c = 15.7$, find a. $\sin 35° = \frac{a}{c}$; $\sin 35° = \frac{a}{15.7}$; $a =$ _____ 9

6. $\angle A = 72°$, $c = 11.3$, find a. _____ 10.7

7. $\angle A = 41°$, $a = 1.98$, find c. _____ 3

8. $\angle A = 16°$, $c = 15.7$, find b. $\cos 16° = \frac{b}{c}$; $\cos 16° = \frac{b}{15.7}$; $b =$ _____ 15.1

9. $\angle A = 31°$, $c = 11.3$, find b. _____ 9.7

116   **Use with pages 402–403.**

Reteach Worksheet

Use the table to find the value.

1. $\tan 45°$ 1.00   **2.** $\tan 30°$ 0.577

3. $\sin 45°$ 0.707   **4.** $\sin 20°$ 0.342

5. $\tan 40°$ 0.839   **6.** $\cos 30°$ 0.866

Use the table to find the measure of $\angle A$.

7. $\tan \angle A = 0.404$ 22°   **8.** $\tan \angle A = 1.000$ 45°

9. $\sin \angle A = 0.358$ 21°   **10.** $\sin \angle A = 0.602$ 37°

11. $\cos \angle A = 0.891$ 27°   **12.** $\cos \angle A = 0.719$ 44°

13. $\tan \angle A = 0.649$ 33°   **14.** $\sin \angle A = 0.515$ 31°

Use the triangles shown and the tables on this page and on page 402 to find each trigonometric ratio to the nearest hundredth. Then find each angle to the nearest degree.

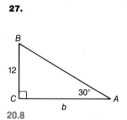

Angle Measure	Sin	Cos	Tan
19°	0.326	0.946	0.344
20°	0.342	0.940	0.364
21°	0.358	0.934	0.384
22°	0.375	0.927	0.404
23°	0.391	0.921	0.424
24°	0.407	0.914	0.445
25°	0.423	0.906	0.466
26°	0.438	0.899	0.488
27°	0.454	0.891	0.510
28°	0.469	0.883	0.532
29°	0.485	0.875	0.554
30°	0.500	0.866	0.577
31°	0.515	0.857	0.601
32°	0.530	0.848	0.625
33°	0.545	0.839	0.649
34°	0.559	0.829	0.675
35°	0.574	0.819	0.700
36°	0.588	0.809	0.727
37°	0.602	0.799	0.754
38°	0.616	0.788	0.781
39°	0.629	0.777	0.810
40°	0.643	0.766	0.839
41°	0.656	0.755	0.869
42°	0.669	0.743	0.900
43°	0.682	0.731	0.933
44°	0.695	0.719	0.966
45°	0.707	0.707	1.00

15. $\sin \angle A$
0.60, 37°
16. $\cos \angle A$
0.80, 37°
17. $\tan \angle A$
0.75, 37°
18. $\sin \angle D$
0.88, 62°
19. $\cos \angle D$
0.47, 62°
20. $\tan \angle D$
1.88, 62°
21. $\sin \angle B$
0.80, 53°
22. $\cos \angle B$
0.60, 53°
23. $\tan \angle B$
1.33, 53°
24. $\sin \angle E$
0.47, 28°
25. $\cos \angle E$
0.88, 28°
26. $\tan \angle E$
0.53, 28°

Use the trigonometric ratios listed in the table to find the side indicated. Round to the nearest tenth.

27.
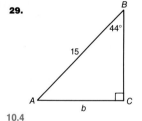
20.8

28.
49.3

29.
10.4

Classwork/Homework, page H166   **403**

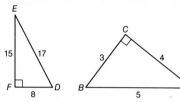

ASSIGNMENT GUIDE

Basic: 1–14, 16–28 e

Average: 1–29 o

Extended: 2–14 e, 15–29

Resources
Practice, p. 166   Class/Home, p. H166
Reteach, p. 116
Enrich, p. 146

Exercise Analysis

1–6	Find a trigonometric ratio, given an angle measure
7–14	Find an angle measure, given a trigonometric ratio
15–26	Find a trigonometric ratio and its angle measure, given side measures
27–29	Find the measure of a side, given one side measure and an angle measure

You might wish to allow students to use calculators for some of these exercises.

FOLLOW-UP ACTIVITIES

PROBLEM SOLVING
Have students solve these problems by drawing models as needed.
- A boy is flying his kite at a 60° angle of elevation. The 300-foot kite string is taut. About how far is the kite above ground? (259.8 ft)
- A jetliner is 10 km from the airport. Its angle of elevation from the airport is 20°. How high is the jet above ground? (3.42 km)

REINFORCEMENT
Have students use trigonometric ratios to find each missing value to the nearest whole number.

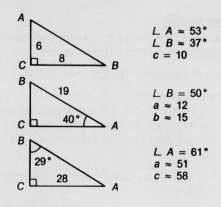

$\angle A \approx 53°$
$\angle B \approx 37°$
$c = 10$

$\angle B = 50°$
$a \approx 12$
$b \approx 15$

$\angle A = 61°$
$a \approx 51$
$c \approx 58$

COMING UP
Circular perimeters

403

Objective: To find the circumference of a circle

Warm-Up
Have students find each product.

2.38 × 4 (9.52)	6.28 × 51 (320.28)
3.17 × 28 (88.76)	27 × 3.24 (87.48)
42 × 5.37 (225.54)	62 × 5.14 (318.68)

GETTING STARTED

Materials: string, 1 or more circular objects (cups, coins, and so on)

Have students use string to measure the distance around the edge of one circular object and to mark the distance on the string. They should then use the same piece of string to measure the diameter of the object. Have them fold the string into lengths equal to the diameter. Elicit approximately how many diameter lengths students found in the circumference of each item. (This ratio should be a little more than 3.) Repeat, using other circular objects.

TEACHING THE LESSON

Stress that either 3.14 or $\frac{22}{7}$ can be used for π, as convenient. Point out that all circumference answers, unless written with π, must be written as approximations because 3.14 is an approximation of π, and an approximation times an exact number is still an approximation.

Another example:

Find the diameter of a circle with $C = 25$ in.

$C = \pi d$
$25 \approx 3.14 \cdot d$
$\frac{25}{3.14} \approx \frac{3.14 \cdot d}{3.14}$
$7.96 \approx d$

You might wish to allow students to use calculators while working through this lesson.

Checkpoint
The chart lists the common errors students make when finding circumferences.

Correct Answers: 1b, 2b

Remediation
■ For these errors, have students review the formulas, and write down the appropriate formula before solving each problem.

☐ For this error, assign Reteach Master, p. 117.

△ For this error, refer students to the examples on p. 142.

Circumference of a Circle

What is the circumference of The Rainbow, a Ferris wheel in Japan, if its diameter is 70.1 m?

The perimeter of a circle is called its **circumference.** The ratio of a circle's circumference (C) to its diameter (d) is the same in every circle. The Greek letter π **(pi)** represents the ratio. $\frac{C}{d} = \pi$

π is a nonterminating, nonrepeating decimal.

$\pi = 3.141592653589793\ldots$

Two common approximations for π are shown below.

$\pi \approx 3.14$ or $\pi \approx \frac{22}{7}$

The ratio can also be written as

$C = \pi d$, or $C = 2\pi r.$ ◀── $d = 2r$

A. To find the circumference of the Ferris wheel, use the formula $C = \pi d$, and use 3.14 for π.

70.1 m

$C = \pi d$
$C \approx 3.14 \cdot 70.1$
$C \approx 220.114$

The circumference of the Ferris wheel, to the nearest hundredth, is 220.11 m.

B. Find the circumference of the circle. Use the formula $C = 2\pi r$, and use $\frac{22}{7}$ for π.

126 ft

$C = 2\pi r$
$C \approx 2 \cdot \frac{22}{7} \cdot 126$
$C \approx 792$

The circumference is approximately 792 ft.

Checkpoint Write the letter of the correct answer.

1. If $d = 49$ in., compute the circumference. Use $\frac{22}{7}$ for π.

  a. 77 in.   **ⓑ** 154 in.

  c. 308 in.   **d.** 1,078 in.

2. If $r = 11.5$ ft, compute the circumference. Use 3.14 for π.

  a. 36.115 ft   **ⓑ** 72.22 ft

  c. 415.265 ft   **d.** 7,222 ft

COMMON ERRORS

Answer Choice	Type of Error
■ 1a	Uses the incorrect formula ($C = \frac{\pi d}{2}$)
■ 1c	Uses the incorrect formula ($C = 2\pi d$)
△ 1d	Fails to complete the multiplication
■ 2a	Uses the incorrect formula ($C = \pi r$)
■ 2c	Uses the incorrect formula ($C = \pi r^{+2}$)
☐ 2d	Omits the decimal point

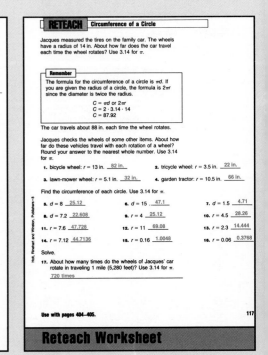

Find the circumference. Use 3.14 for π, and round to the nearest hundredth.

1.

2.8 km
17.58 km

2.

16.4 m
51.50 m

3.

9.3 cm
58.40 cm

Find the circumference. Use $\frac{22}{7}$ for π.

4.

63 mm
198 mm

5.

35.7 cm
224.4 cm

6.

28.14 cm
88.44 cm

Find the circumference. Use 3.14 for π, and round to the nearest hundredth.

7. $r = 11.3$ m
70.96 m

8. $d = 10$ m
31.4 m

9. $d = 84.14$ m
264.20 m

10. $r = 2.6$ cm
16.33 cm

11. $d = 7.3$ m
22.92 m

12. $d = 11.6$ cm
36.42 cm

13. $d = 15.2$ dm
47.73 dm

14. $d = 100$ km
314 km

Find the circumference. Use $\frac{22}{7}$ for π.

15. $r = 49$ ft   308 ft

16. $r = 105$ in.   660 in.

17. $r = 7\frac{1}{2}$ in. $47\frac{1}{7}$ in.

18. $d = 20\frac{1}{2}$ ft $64\frac{3}{7}$ ft

19. $d = 45$ yd
$141\frac{3}{7}$ yd

20. $r = 12\frac{1}{2}$ mi
$78\frac{4}{7}$ mi

21. $r = 28$ yd   176 yd

22. $d = 70$ ft   220 ft

Find the radius or the diameter. Use 3.14 for π, and round to the nearest tenth.

★23. $C = 37.68$ cm
$r = \blacksquare$ 6 cm

★24. $C = 14.13$ cm
$r = \blacksquare$ 2.3 cm

★25. $C = 28.26$ m
$d = \blacksquare$ 9 m

★26. $C = 92.4$ cm
$r = \blacksquare$ 14.7 cm

★27. $C = 39.25$ m
$d = \blacksquare$ 12.5 m

★28. $C = 20.41$ cm
$r = \blacksquare$ 3.3 cm

★29. $C = 150.72$ mm
$r = \blacksquare$ 24 mm

★30. $C = 37.68$ m
$r = \blacksquare$ 6 m

Solve. Round to the nearest hundredth when necessary.

31. The Louisiana Superdome has a diameter of 680 ft. Find the circumference of the Superdome. Use 3.14 for π.   2,135.20 ft

32. The circular entrance to the longest tunnel in the world is 15.5 ft in diameter. Find the circumference of the entrance. Use 3.14 for π.
48.67 ft

Classwork/Homework, page H167   **405**

Objective: To make a plan to solve multistep problems

Warm-Up
To prepare students for this lesson, have them compute the following.

650 ÷ 25 (26)   1,755 ÷ 9 (195)
92 × 50 (4,600)   712 × 32 (22,784)

GETTING STARTED

Ask students about how much time it takes to walk one mile. (about 15 minutes) Then ask them to find that rate of speed in miles per hour. (4 miles per hour) Ask them how many miles they could walk in an 8-hour day. (32 miles) How many miles could they walk in 7 days? (224 miles) Discuss all the steps involved in finding how many miles a person could walk in 1 week.

TEACHING THE LESSON

This lesson addresses problems in which students must perform more than one operation to use known information to find unknown information. As in the introductory problem, this often involves renaming units of length, mass, or time. Emphasize the importance of making a plan when solving such problems. Suggest that students write down the given information, what the question asks, and the information they will need to answer the question. A plan should list each specific step involved in changing the known information to the solution. Be sure students realize there is often more than one way to set up a plan. In solving this problem, students could also use the following steps.
1. Find the number of hours spent walking in 1 week.
2. Find the number of hours spent walking in 82 weeks.
3. Find the number of miles walked in 1 hour.

Questions: Point out that in this problem, there are actually three questions that must be asked.

Tools: The tools students have to work with are the steps in the plan they have formulated. Success depends upon the clarity and completeness of that plan. Be sure students realize that although there may be several ways to arrive at a solution, the best plan is the simplest plan. The plan detailed in the instruction is the simplest one for the introductory problem because each step deals with the same thing—the number of miles walked in ever-smaller units of time. Emphasize that such a clear-cut progression with the same information is always preferable to a more complicated plan. A good strategy would be to begin the

QUESTIONS	TOOLS	SOLUTIONS	CHECKS

PROBLEM SOLVING
Solving Multistep Problems/Making a Plan

A problem may need more than one step in order to be solved. Making a plan can help you solve such problems.

> Beginning on May 4, 1957, David Kwan walked from Singapore to London, a distance of 18,500 miles, in 82 weeks. He walked for 8 hours each day. How fast did he walk?

Needed data: miles walked in 1 week
               miles walked in 1 day

Plan
Step 1: Find the number of miles walked in 1 week.

Step 2: Find the number of miles walked in 1 day.

Step 3: Find the number of miles walked in 1 hour.

Step 1:

$$\text{miles walked in 1 week} = \text{total miles} \div \text{total weeks}$$
$$n = 18,500 \div 82$$
$$n = 226$$
He walked 226 miles per week.

Step 2:

$$\text{miles walked in a day} = \text{miles a week} \div \text{days in a week}$$
$$x = 226 \div 7$$
$$x = 32$$
He walked 32 miles per day.

Step 3:

$$\text{miles walked in 1 hour} = \text{miles a day} \div \text{hours a day}$$
$$y = 32 \div 8$$
$$y = 4$$
He walked 4 miles per hour.

406

question "How fast did he walk?" find the label or units in which the answer will be expressed (miles per hour), and work backward starting with the information you know (he walked 18,500 miles in 82 weeks) setting up the intermediate steps along the way. Writing the plan before beginning the computation is a good idea.

Solutions: Although it is unlikely that students will face computational difficulties, you may want to review division algorithms. You may also wish to allow students to use calculators when solving these problems.

Checks: The first check should be for the reasonableness of the units in the answer. Then the problem should be worked backward with the answer substituted into each step to check for computational errors.

Write the steps you would take to complete each plan.

1. The largest sculpture in the world, carved into Mount Rushmore, shows the faces of four Presidents: Washington, Lincoln, Jefferson, and Theodore Roosevelt. The head of Washington is about 20 yards in height. If the ratio of a man's head to his total height is about 1 to 8, how many feet tall would the complete statue of Washington be?

Step 1: Find the number of ft in Washington's head.

Step 2: Find the number of feet in the statue's height.

2. The first nonstop transpacific airplane flight occurred in 1931. Hugh Herndon and Clyde Pangborn took off from Sabishiro Beach, Japan, dropped their landing gear, and flew to a spot near Wenatchee, Washington. Their average air speed was about 2 miles per minute. The trip was about 4,860 miles long. For how many days were they in the air?

Step 1: Find their speed in miles per hour.

Step 2: Find the number of hours it took them to fly.

Step 3: Find the number of days it took them to fly.

Make a plan for each problem. Solve. See Answer Key.

3. In 1981, President and Mrs. Reagan bought some dishes for the White House. The dishes cost $106,172 for 508 place settings. How much more would the same dishes have cost if they had bought 600 place settings? **$19,228**

4. The peregrine falcon is the fastest-moving animal in the world. It has been electronically timed at 217 mph. How far could it go if it were able to fly at this rate for 2 minutes? (Round your answer to the nearest mile.) **7 mi**

5. The two highest mountains in the world are Mount Everest and Mount Godwin Austen, both in the Himalayas. Their heights are 29,028 feet and 28,741 feet, respectively. If you could put one on top of the other and then place them into the deepest trench in the Pacific Ocean (the Mindanao Deep, which is 37,782 feet in depth), how far would they rise above the ocean's surface? **19,987 ft**

6. The fastest-growing tree ever recorded was an *Albizzia falcata*, which was planted on June 17, 1974, in Sabah, Malaysia. In 13 months, it grew from a seed to a height of 35 feet 3 inches. Assuming that it grew at a steady rate, how tall would it have been in 2 years if it had continued to grow at the same rate? (Round your answer to the nearest foot.) **65 ft**

Classwork/Homework, page H168

OBJECTIVES: To find the area of a square, a rectangle, and a parallelogram

Warm-Up
Have students find each perimeter.

Squares:

side = 4 in. (16 in.)   side = 9 cm (36 cm)
side = 12 m (48 m)   side = 1 cm (4 cm)

Rectangles:

l = 3 m, w = 2 m (10 m)
l = 5 m, w = 3 m (16 m)
l = 9 m, w = 3 m (24 m)
l = 7 m, w = 4 m (22 m)

GETTING STARTED

Materials: 36 paper squares per group

Have students work in groups. Have each group take turns arranging the squares to form as many different rectangles as possible. Each rectangle must be composed of all 36 squares. Have groups keep a list of the dimensions of the rectangles. Ask students to tell you the dimensions of their rectangles. Write the dimensions on the chalkboard. Elicit the fact that rectangles of different dimensions can have the same area. Have students write a formula for the area of a rectangle.

TEACHING THE LESSON

A. Emphasize the fact that because two units are multiplied together, the answer must be expressed in units squared.

B. Extend the lesson by having students find the area of rectangles whose measurements consist of fractions and decimals.

C. Demonstrate why the formula for the area of a parallelogram works by cutting out a paper parallelogram. Then cut off one of its ends, and affix it to the other side to make a rectangle.

Checkpoint
The chart lists the common errors students make when finding areas.

Correct Answers: 1d, 2d

Remediation
■ For this error, have students draw a 3 × 5 rectangle on graph paper. Then have them count the number of squares, the number of rows, and the number of columns to see the relationship.

☐ For these errors, assign Reteach Master, p. 118.

408

Area of Squares, Rectangles, and Parallelograms

The area of a polygon (**A**) is the number of unit squares enclosed by the polygon. A unit square that has a side of 1 cm has an area of 1 square centimeter (1 cm²).

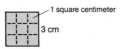

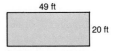

A. To find the area of a square whose side is 3 cm, multiply.

A = side · side, or $A = s^2$.
$A = 3^2 = 3 \cdot 3 = 9$

The area of the square is 9 cm².

B. To find the area of a rectangle whose length is 49 ft and whose width is 20 ft, multiply.

A = length · width, or $A = lw$.
$A = 49 \cdot 20 = 980$

The area of the rectangle is 980 ft².

C. If a parallelogram and a rectangle have equal bases and equal heights, then they are equal in area.

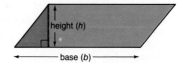

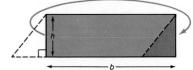

To find the area of a parallelogram whose base is 4.5 cm and whose height is 2.5 cm, multiply.

A = base · height, or $A = bh$.
$A = 4.5 \cdot 2.5 = 11.25$

The area of the parallelogram is 11.25 cm².

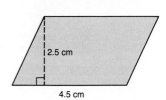

Checkpoint Write the letter of the correct answer.

1. The area of a rectangle whose length is 4.6 m and whose width is 3.9 m is ■.

a. 8.5 m²   **b.** 17 m

c. 17.94 m   **d.** 17.94 m²

2. The area of a parallelogram whose base is 85 mm and whose height is 60 mm is ■.

a. 145 mm²   **b.** 290 mm

c. 5,100 mm   **d.** 5,100 mm²

408

COMMON ERRORS

Answer Choice	Type of Error
■ 1a, 2a	Adds instead of multiplies
☐ 1b, 2b	Finds the perimeter instead of the area
☐ 1c, 2c	Uses the incorrect unit

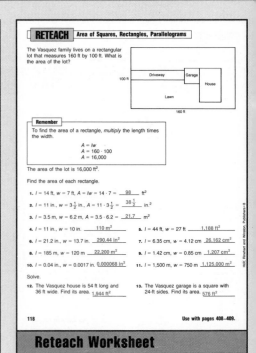

RETEACH Area of Squares, Rectangles, Parallelograms

The Vasquez family lives on a rectangular lot that measures 160 ft by 100 ft. What is the area of the lot?

Remember
To find the area of a rectangle, *multiply* the length times the width.

$A = lw$
$A = 160 \cdot 100$
$A = 16,000$

The area of the lot is 16,000 ft².

Find the area of each rectangle.

1. l = 14 ft, w = 7 ft, $A = lw = 14 \cdot 7 =$ __98__ ft²
2. l = 11 in., $w = 3\frac{1}{2}$ in., $A = 11 \cdot 3\frac{1}{2} =$ __$38\frac{1}{2}$__ in.²
3. l = 3.5 m, w = 6.2 m, $A = 3.5 \cdot 6.2 =$ __21.7__ m²
4. l = 11 in., w = 10 in. __110 m²__
5. l = 44 ft, w = 27 ft __1,188 ft²__
6. l = 21.2 in., w = 13.7 in. __290.44 in²__
7. l = 6.35 cm, w = 4.12 cm __26.162 cm²__
8. l = 185 m, w = 120 m __22,200 m²__
9. l = 1.42 cm, w = 0.85 cm __1.207 cm²__
10. l = 0.04 m, w = 0.0017 in. __0.000068 in²__
11. l = 1,500 m, w = 750 m __1,125,000 m²__

Solve.

12. The Vasquez house is 54 ft long and 36 ft wide. Find its area. __1,944 ft²__
13. The Vasquez garage is a square with 24-ft sides. Find its area. __576 ft²__

118 Use with pages 408–409.

Reteach Worksheet

408

Find the area of the polygon.

1.
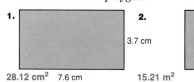
3.7 cm
28.12 cm² 7.6 cm

2.
3.9 m
15.21 m² 3.9 m

3.
12.2 cm 15 cm
211.06 cm² 17.3 cm

Find the area of each square.

4. $s = 14.2$ m
201.64 m²

5. $s = 1.5$ m
2.25 m²

6. $s = 2.5$ cm
6.25 cm²

7. $s = 10$ m
100 m²

Find the area of each rectangle.

8. $l = 18.3$ yd
$w = 8.9$ yd
162.87 yd²

9. $l = 4\frac{1}{2}$ in.
$w = 7$ in.
31.5 in.²

10. $l = 13.1$ in.
$w = 9.3$ in.
121.83 in.²

11. $l = 16$ ft
$w = 5\frac{1}{4}$ ft
84 ft²

12. $l = 4\frac{1}{2}$ mi
$w = 2$ mi
9 mi²

13. $l = 7$ in.
$w = 5\frac{1}{2}$ in.
38.5 in.²

14. $l = 2.5$ ft
$w = 1.5$ ft
3.75 ft²

★15. $l = 20$ ft
$w = 18$ in.
30 ft², or 4,320 in.²

Find the area of each parallelogram.

16. $b = 5.1$ cm
$h = 11.8$ cm
60.18 cm²

17. $b = 9.3$ m
$h = 6$ m
55.8 m²

18. $b = 14.3$ cm
$h = 8$ cm
114.4 cm²

19. $b = 5.75$ m
$h = 18$ m
103.5 m²

20. $b = 52$ cm
$h = 44.6$ cm
2,319.2 cm²

21. $b = 15$ m
$h = 12.4$ m
186 m²

22. $b = 11.8$ m
$h = 9.6$ m
113.28 m²

★23. $b = 8.6$ m
$h = 64$ cm
5.504 m²,
or 55,040 cm²

Solve.

24. Find the area.

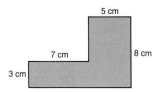
5 cm
7 cm
8 cm
3 cm

61 cm²

25. Find the area of the deck.

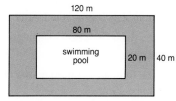
120 m
80 m
swimming pool
20 m 40 m

3,200 m²

26. Bev is installing carpet. If her living room is 7 yd long by 4 yd wide, and her hall is 8 yd long by 2 yd wide, how many square yards of carpet will she need? **44 yd²**

27. Bill is painting a wall that measures 30 ft long by 12 ft high. If a can of paint covers 400 ft² and Bill has one can, will he have enough paint? **yes**

Classwork/Homework, page H169

More Practice, page H205 **409**

ASSIGNMENT GUIDE

Basic: 1–3, 4–22 e, 24–27

Average: 2–22 e, 24–27

Extended: 1–23 o, 24–27

Resources
Practice, p. 169   Class/Home, p. H169
Reteach, p. 118   More Practice, p. H205
Enrich, p. 149

Exercise Analysis

1–3	Find the area of a pictured quadrilateral
4–7	Find the area of a square
8–15	Find the area of a rectangle
16–23	Find the area of a parallelogram
24–27	Skill applications

You might wish to allow students to use calculators for some of these exercises.

FOLLOW-UP ACTIVITIES

MATH CONNECTION (Consumer)
Have students solve this problem.

City Carpet advertised a remnant sale by the roll. The store has labeled each roll according to the number of square yards contained in it. Determine which roll contains enough material to carpet the room shown next to the carpet area on the chart. (Remember: 9 square feet equal 1 square yard.)

Room size	Carpet area	Good deal!	No deal!
15 ft × 20 ft	35 sq yd	(x)	
21 ft × 24 ft	55 sq yd		(x)
12 ft × 12 ft	20 sq yd	(x)	
24 ft × 36 ft	100 sq yd	(x)	
16 ft × 18 ft	30 sq yd		(x)
17 ft × 20 ft	40 sq yd	(x)	

MANIPULATIVES
Materials: graph paper

Have students draw a 35-by-30 rectangle. Tell them that the rectangle represents the floor of an apartment and that each box represents one square foot. Have students draw a floor plan for the apartment and make a list of the rooms and hallways and their areas.

COMING UP
One zoid trap coming up!

409

Objectives: To find the area of a triangle and a trapezoid

Warm-Up
Have students find the area of each.
- rectangle.

  $l = 7$ m, $w = 4$ m (28 m²)
  $l = 9.5$ cm, $w = 3$ cm (28.5 cm²)

- square.

  side = 8 in. (64 in.²)
  side = 1.4 cm (1.96 cm²)

- parallelogram.

  $h = 5$ m, $b = 3$ m (15 m²)
  $h = 6.5$ cm, $b = 5$ cm (32.5 cm²)

GETTING STARTED

Materials: paper, scissors

Draw each kind of triangle on a square sheet of paper. Use the entire sheet.

| Isosceles | Right | Scalene |

Cut out triangles and rearrange the extra pieces to form a second triangle equal to the first. Ask: What part of the square is one triangle? ($\frac{1}{2}$)

TEACHING THE LESSON

A. Emphasize the fact that the height of a triangle is the length of the perpendicular line from the base to the opposite vertex.

Other examples:
- $b = 3\frac{1}{2}$, $h = 5\frac{1}{2}$ ($A = 9\frac{5}{8}$)
- $b = 16$, $h = 4.5$ ($A = 36$)

B. Emphasize that when finding the area of a trapezoid, the bases must be averaged before the result can be multiplied by the height. Caution students not to neglect the parentheses when using this formula.

Point out that the order of the bases does not matter. Either base can be b_1 or b_2.

You might wish to allow students to use calculators while working through this lesson.

Area of Triangles and Trapezoids

A. Find the area of $\triangle ABD$ to the nearest tenth, if the base AD is 6.1 cm and the height is 4.2 cm.

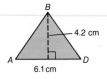

The area of a triangle is $\frac{1}{2}$ the area of a parallelogram that has the same height and base.

Note that parallelogram $ABCD$ at the right has a height of 4.2 cm and a base of 6.1 cm.

Since the formula for the area of a parallelogram is $A = bh$, the formula for the area of a triangle is $A = \frac{1}{2}bh$.

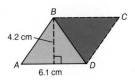

To find the area of $\triangle ABD$, multiply.

$A = \frac{1}{2}$ base · height, or $\boldsymbol{A = \frac{1}{2}bh.}$

$A = \frac{1}{2} \cdot 6.1 \cdot 4.2$

$A = 12.81$

The area of $\triangle ABD$, to the nearest tenth, is 12.8 cm².

B. The area of a trapezoid is $\frac{1}{2}$ the area of a certain parallelogram.

Parallelogram $ABEF$ is formed by two trapezoids equal in area. The area, A, of parallelogram $ABEF = bh$. Since $b = b_1 + b_2$, $A = (b_1 + b_2)h$. The area of trapezoid $ABCD$ is $\frac{1}{2}$ the area of parallelogram $ABEF$.

$A = \frac{1}{2} \cdot$ (base$_1$ + base$_2$) · height, or $\boldsymbol{A = \frac{1}{2}(b_1 + b_2)h.}$

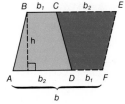

Use the formula to find the area of trapezoid $ABCD$.

$A = \frac{1}{2}(15 + 9) \cdot 12$

$A = \frac{1}{2} \cdot 24 \cdot 12$

$A = 144$

The area of trapezoid $ABCD$ is 144 ft².

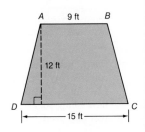

Math Reasoning, page H227

COMMON ERRORS

Students might sometimes forget to multiply the base of a triangle or the sum of the bases of a trapezoid by $\frac{1}{2}$ when finding the area.

Remediation
For this error, have students check that their answer is reasonable by drawing a rectangle on the outside of the triangle or trapezoid and finding its area. If the areas are the same, then the wrong formula was used.

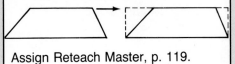

Assign Reteach Master, p. 119.

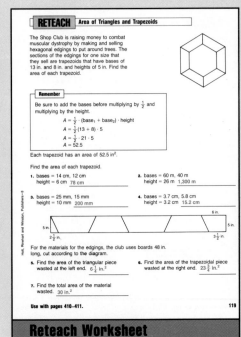

| RETEACH | Area of Triangles and Trapezoids |

The Shop Club is raising money to combat muscular dystrophy by making and selling hexagonal edgings to put around trees. The sections of the edgings for one size that they sell are trapezoids that have bases of 13 in. and 8 in. and heights of 5 in. Find the area of each trapezoid.

Remember
Be sure to add the bases before multiplying by $\frac{1}{2}$ and multiplying by the height.

$A = \frac{1}{2} \cdot$ (base$_1$ + base$_2$) · height
$A = \frac{1}{2}(13 + 8) \cdot 5$
$A = \frac{1}{2} \cdot 21 \cdot 5$
$A = 52.5$

Each trapezoid has an area of 52.5 in².

Find the area of each trapezoid.

1. bases = 14 cm, 12 cm, height = 6 cm 78 cm
2. bases = 60 m, 40 m, height = 26 m 1,300 m
3. bases = 25 mm, 15 mm, height = 10 mm 200 mm
4. bases = 3.7 cm, 5.8 cm, height = 3.2 cm 15.2 cm

For the materials for the edgings, the club uses boards 48 in. long, cut according to the diagram.

5. Find the area of the triangular piece wasted at the left end. 6¼ in.²
6. Find the area of the trapezoidal piece wasted at the right end. 23¾ in.²

7. Find the total area of the material wasted. 30 in.²

Use with pages 410–411.   119

Reteach Worksheet

Find the area of the triangle or the trapezoid. Round to the nearest tenth.

1.
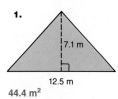
7.1 m
12.5 m
44.4 m²

2.
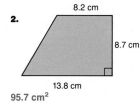
8.2 cm
8.7 cm
13.8 cm
95.7 cm²

3.
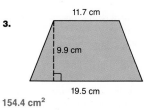
11.7 cm
9.9 cm
19.5 cm
154.4 cm²

Find the area of each triangle. Round to the nearest tenth.

4. base = 18.5 m, height = 5.2 m
48.1 m²

5. base = 13.5 m, height = 11 m
74.3 m²

6. base = 4.3 m, height = 9 m
19.4 m²

7. base = 15.5 cm, height = 3.4 cm
26.4 cm²

8. base = 1.9 km, height = 2.6 km
2.5 km²

9. base = 0.4 km, height = 2.6 km
0.5 km²

Find the area of each trapezoid. Round to the nearest tenth.

10. bases = 6.2 cm, 12.8 cm
height = 5.7 cm
54.2 cm²

11. bases = 6.3 m, 8.5 m
height = 5 m
37 m²

12. bases = 19 m, 6 m
height = 9 m
112.5 m²

13. bases = 63 mm, 82 mm
height = 45 mm
3,262.5 mm²

14. bases = 11 mm, 15 mm
height = 12 mm
156 mm²

15. bases = 4.5 m, 6.25 m
height = 12 m
64.5 m²

Given the area, find the height of the polygon.

★16. triangle, $A = 100$ ft²
base = 20 ft   10 ft

★17. trapezoid, $A = 32$ in.²
bases = 7 in., 9 in.   4 in.

★18. triangle, $A = 20$ yd²
base = 4 yd   10 yd

★19. trapezoid, $A = 100$ mi²
bases = 15 mi, 5 mi   10 mi

Find the area of each composite polygon by adding or subtracting the areas of the parts.

20.
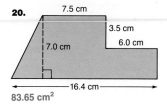
7.5 cm
3.5 cm
7.0 cm
6.0 cm
16.4 cm
83.65 cm²

21.
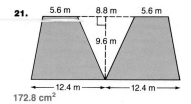
5.6 m   8.8 m   5.6 m
9.6 m
12.4 m   12.4 m
172.8 cm²

Classwork/Homework, page H170   More Practice, page H205   **411**

ASSIGNMENT GUIDE

Basic: 1–15

Average: 1–21 o

Extended: 2–14 e, 16–21

Resources
Practice, p. 170   Class/Home, p. H170
Reteach, p. 119   More Practice, p. H205
Enrich, p. 150   Reasoning, p. H227

Exercise Analysis

1–3   Find the area of a pictured triangle or trapezoid
4–9   Find the area of a triangle
10–15 Find the area of a trapezoid
16–19 Find the height of a triangle or a trapezoid, given the area and base(s)
20–21 Skill applications

You might wish to allow students to use calculators for some of these exercises.

FOLLOW-UP ACTIVITIES

REINFORCEMENT
Listed below are some of the formulas used for perimeter and area. Have students solve for the term indicated.

- $P = 4s$; $s = \blacksquare \left(\frac{P}{4}\right)$
- $P = 2l + 2w$; $w = \blacksquare \left(\frac{P}{2} - l\right)$
- $A = l \cdot w$; $w = \blacksquare \left(\frac{A}{l}\right)$
- $A = \frac{1}{2} bh$; $b = \blacksquare \left(\frac{2A}{h}\right)$

MANIPULATIVES
Materials: geoboards, rubber bands

Have students construct an irregular polygon, and then find its area by using Pick's formula:

b = the number of nails on the boundary
i = the number of nails in the interior

$$A = \frac{b}{2} + i - 1$$

Have them construct and find the area of figures such as those shown below.

$(A = 12)$ $(A = 11\frac{1}{2})$ $(A = 9\frac{1}{2})$

COMING UP
Circular reasoning

411

Objective: To find the area of a circle

Warm-Up

Have students give the diameter of the circle for each radius.

5 cm (10 cm)   3 m (6 m)

9.2 ft (18.4 ft) $3\frac{1}{2}$ m (7 m)

GETTING STARTED

Draw this figure on the chalkboard.

Ask: What is the area of the large square? (d^2) What is the area expressed in terms of r? ($4r^2$)

Tell the class that r^2 is part of the formula for the area of a circle. Have students use the diagram to estimate the formula.

TEACHING THE LESSON

Point out that as the number of wedge-shaped sections increases to infinity, the area of the circle approaches the area of the parallelogram. So, the equal sign can be used.

Have students estimate the area prior to finding it.

Estimate: $r = 30$, $r^2 = 900$, $3 \times r^2 = 2,700$

Mention the extra step needed when the diameter rather than the radius is given.

Point out that the formulas for the areas of all plane figures are derived from that for the area of a parallelogram.

Lead students through a discussion of how to find the radius when the area is given.

$$A = \pi r^2$$
$$\frac{A}{\pi} = r^2$$
$$\sqrt{\frac{A}{\pi}} = r$$

Guide students through the example below.

Find the radius of a circle whose area is 152 cm.

$$\pi r^2 = 152$$
$$r^2 \approx 48$$
$$r \approx 7$$

Area of a Circle

The world's largest working clock has a radius of 29.5 ft. Find the area of the clock face.

The approximate area of a circle can be found by cutting the circle into wedge-shaped sections and then rearranging the pieces to form a figure that has the approximate shape of a parallelogram.

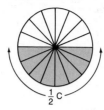 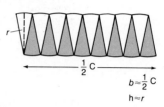

The area of the parallelogram = bh, or

$$A = \frac{1}{2}C \cdot r.$$

To find the formula for the area of a circle, substitute $2\pi r$ for C.

$$A = \frac{1}{2} \cdot 2\pi r \cdot r, \text{ or } \boldsymbol{A = \pi r^2}$$

Use the formula to find the area of the clock face to the nearest tenth. Use 3.14 for π.

$$A = \pi r^2$$
$$A \approx 3.14 \cdot 29.5 \cdot 29.5$$
$$A \approx 2,732.59$$

The area of the clock face, to the nearest tenth, is 2,732.6 ft².

Another example:

Find the area of the circle.

$$A = \pi r^2$$
$$A \approx 3.14 \cdot 6 \cdot 6$$
$$A \approx 113.04$$

Think: If $d = 2r$, then $r = \frac{1}{2}d$.

12 cm

The area is about 113.04 cm².

Math Reasoning, page H228

COMMON ERRORS

Students might confuse d with r^2 because they confuse $2r$ with r^2.

Remediation

For this error, have students review exponents. Have them practice rewriting exponents as products of factors.

Assign Reteach Master, p. 120.

RETEACH   Area of a Circle

The Skateville skating rink's surface forms a circle. Mr. Wilson measures the radius of the rink. The radius is 45.5 m. What is the area of the rink? Round the answer to the nearest tenth. Use 3.14 for π.

Remember

Be sure to use $r \cdot r$ for r^2 in the formula. r^2 is not the same as $r \cdot 2$.

$$A = \pi r^2 \text{ or } \pi \cdot r \cdot r$$
$$A \approx 3.14 \cdot 45.5 \cdot 45.5$$
$$A \approx 6,500.585$$

The area of the rink is about 6,500.6 m².

Find the area of each circle. Use 3.14 for π, and round to the nearest tenth.

1. $r = 5$ in.   78.5 in.²
2. $r = 4.5$ cm   63.6 cm²
3. $r = 2.25$ in.   15.9 in.²
4. $r = 6$ m   113 m²
5. $r = 3.2$ yd   32.2 yd²
6. $r = 17.5$ mi   961.6 mi²
7. $r = 0.25$ m   0.2 m²
8. $r = 8.4$ km   221.6 km²
9. $r = 150$ ft   70,650 ft²
10. $r = 1.35$ cm   5.72 cm²
11. $r = 14.32$ m   643.9 m²
12. $r = 0.85$ in.   2.3 in.²

Solve.

13. The Skateville rink has 6 circles for skaters to practice tricks in. Each circle has a radius of 4.5 m. Find the total area of the practice circles. Round your answer to the nearest tenth. 381.5 m²

14. Pierre says, "I can skate circles around you, Jean!" He skates 8 circles around Jean. Each circle has a radius of 1.875 yd. What is the total area of the circles Pierre skates around Jean? Round your answer to the nearest tenth. 88.3 yd²

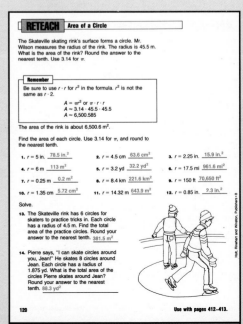

120   Use with pages 412–413.

Reteach Worksheet

Find the area of each circle. Use 3.14 for π, and round to the nearest tenth.

1.
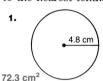
4.8 cm

72.3 cm²

2.
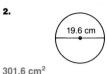
19.6 cm

301.6 cm²

3.

2.9 cm

26.4 cm²

Find the area of each circle. Use $\frac{22}{7}$ for π.

4. $r = 14$ ft 616 ft²	**5.** $r = 280$ in. 246,400 in.²	**6.** $d = 14$ yd 154 yd²	**7.** $d = 84$ in. 5,544 in.²
8. $d = 196$ in. 30,184 in.²	**9.** $d = 91$ in. $6,506\frac{1}{2}$ in.²	**10.** $r = 147$ in. 67,914 in.²	**11.** $r = 119$ in. 44,506 in.²

Find the area of each circle. Use 3.14 for π, and round to the nearest tenth.

12. $r = 6.6$ cm 136.8 cm²	**13.** $d = 8.2$ km 52.8 km²	**14.** $d = 1$ m 0.8 m²	**15.** $r = 2.5$ m 19.6 m²
16. $r = 15.1$ dm 716.0 dm²	**17.** $r = 17.7$ cm 983.7 cm²	**18.** $d = 9$ m 63.6 m²	**19.** $r = 0.5$ m 0.8 m²

Use the given area to find the radius of the circle. Use 3.14 for π.

20. $A = 50.24$ cm² 4 cm	**21.** $A = 78.5$ mm² 5 mm	**22.** $A = 153.86$ m² 7 m	**23.** $A = 113.04$ m² 6 m
24. $A = 254.34$ km² 9 km	**25.** $A = 200.96$ m² 8 m	**26.** $A = 452.16$ km² 12 km	**27.** $A = 907.46$ dm² 17 dm

Find the area of each shaded region. Use 3.14 for π, and round to the nearest tenth.

28.

2.8 cm
2 cm
2.8 cm

4.7 cm²

29.

9.3 m
6.4 m

75.6 m²

30.

12.6 m
30 m

208 m²

MIDCHAPTER REVIEW

Find the missing side of each right triangle. $m\angle C = 90°$.

1. $a = 5$ cm, $b = 12$ cm
$c = 13$ cm

2. $a = 48$ m, $c = 102$ m
$b = 90$ m

3. $b = 32$ km, $c = 40$ km
$a = 24$ km

Use the table on page 403 to find the measure of $\angle A$.

4. $\tan \angle A = 0.445$
$\angle A = 24°$

5. $\sin \angle A = 0.616$
$\angle A = 38°$

6. $\cos \angle A = 0.707$
$\angle A = 45°$

7. $\tan \angle A = 1.000$
$\angle A = 45°$

Classwork/Homework, page H171

413

ASSIGNMENT GUIDE

Basic: 1–19, 21–29 o, MCR

Average: 1–19, 20–30 e, MCR

Extended: 1–27 o, 28–30, MCR

Resources
Practice, p. 171   Class/Home, p. H171
Reteach, p. 120   Reasoning, p. H228
Enrich, p. 151

Exercise Analysis

1–3   Find the area of a pictured circle

4–11   Find the area of a circle, using $\frac{22}{7}$ for π

12–19   Find the area of a circle, using 3.14 for π

20–27   Find the radius, given the area

28–30   Skill applications

You might wish to allow students to use calculators for some of these exercises.

Midchapter Review

These exercises provide an opportunity for you and students to assess their understanding of concepts and skills developed to this point in the chapter.

FOLLOW-UP ACTIVITIES

COMPUTER
Have students write a program to find the circumference and area of circles with the radii of 5, 3, 2.8, and 7.4.

```
10 PRINT "RADIUS", "CIRCUM", "AREA"
20 READ R
30 LET C = 2 * 3.14 * R
40 LET A = 3.14 * R^2
50 PRINT R, C, A
60 GOTO 20
70 DATA 5, 3, 2.8, 7.4
80 END
```

MATH CONNECTION (Consumer)
Ask students whether they have ever wondered how much value coins have per unit of face area. Have students find the area of the face of each coin and then the number of cents per square centimeter. Remind them that 100 mm² = 1 cm².

● penny—$d = 18$ mm (0.39¢ per cm²)
● nickel—$d = 20$ mm (1.59¢ per cm²)
● dime—$d = 17$ mm (4.41¢ per cm²)
● quarter—$d = 2.3$ cm (6.02¢ per cm²)

COMING UP
Pretty as a picture

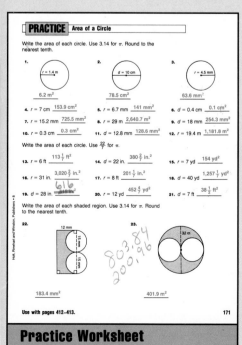

Practice Worksheet

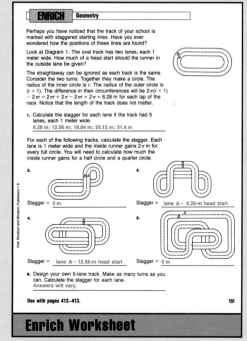

Enrich Worksheet

Warm-Up

Have students complete the following ratios.

- $3:1 = 21:x$ ($x = 7$)
- $4:3 = x:12$ ($x = 16$)
- $8:7 = x:147$ ($x = 168$)
- $9:13 = 117:x$ ($x = 169$)

GETTING STARTED

Display a map of the United States, or ask students to imagine one. Ask students what different kinds of information can be obtained from this map.Answers should vary; if necessary, encourage additional answers such as the following.

- the state in which a particular city is located
- the states that border another state
- the states that have the most cities
- the capital cities of states
- the states that are bordered by the most states
- the states that have the longest shoreline

Point out that the list can go on almost indefinitely. Point out to students that data sources such as maps and architectural blueprints contain vast amounts of information.

TEACHING THE LESSON

To solve these problems, students must be able to look at a picture or chart, judge what kind of information it offers, and quickly determine whether it contains needed information.

Questions: Ask students how they know that these are the measurements for the car. (The instructions tell them.) Tell the class that a picture containing these words is drawn to scale, that is, drawn to a specific fraction of the actual size, normally a small fraction such as $\frac{1}{32}$ or $\frac{1}{64}$.

Tools: Some students may have difficulty in determining which element on the car is identified by a particular measurement. Point out that the line in which the measurement is centered begins at one end of the measured object and ends at the other end. Students may benefit from working in pairs or in small groups; those students who have a better eye for this kind of labeling can help others who do not. Remind students that each measurement on Matt's model is $\frac{1}{2}$ of the corresponding measurement on the actual car.

Solutions: Review with students the method of finding equal ratios.

PROBLEM SOLVING
Using a Picture

To solve certain problems, you may need to find information in a picture.

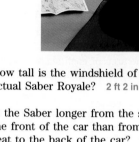

> Matt built a scale model of a Saber Royale. Each 1 inch of the model represents 2 inches of an actual Saber. What is the height of Matt's model?

To answer this problem, you need to know the actual height of a Saber Royale. You can find this information in the picture below.

The height of a Saber Royale is 5 ft 10 in., or 70 in.

To find the height of Matt's model, you multiply the actual height by the scale of Matt's model.

$$1 \text{ inch} = 2 \text{ inches}$$
$$\text{So, } 70 \times \frac{1}{2} = 35.$$

The height of Matt's model is 35 inches.

Use the picture below to solve.

1. How long is the windshield of Matt's model? 11 in.

2. How tall is the windshield of an actual Saber Royale? 2 ft 2 in.

3. What is the diameter of each tire of Matt's model? 19 in.

4. Is the Saber longer from the seat to the front of the car than from the seat to the back of the car? yes

SABER ROYALE

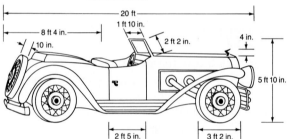

Checks: Students can use addition to check subtraction; they can use subtraction to check addition.

A family tree is a model of a family's history. You can use a family tree to find information about a family.

Brenda Thornton is researching her family history. The chart she made is shown below. How much younger is Brenda's mother than Brenda's Aunt Lily?

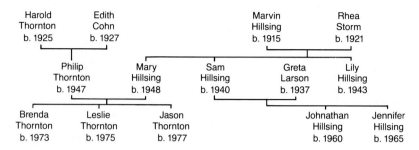

| Harold Thornton b. 1925 | Edith Cohn b. 1927 | | Marvin Hillsing b. 1915 | Rhea Storm b. 1921 |

Philip Thornton b. 1947 — Mary Hillsing b. 1948 — Sam Hillsing b. 1940 — Greta Larson b. 1937 — Lily Hillsing b. 1943

Brenda Thornton b. 1973 — Leslie Thornton b. 1975 — Jason Thornton b. 1977 — Johnathan Hillsing b. 1960 — Jennifer Hillsing b. 1965

To solve this problem, you first have to find on the chart the people mentioned in the problem.

Brenda's mother is listed as Mary Hillsing. Brenda's aunt—her mother's sister—is listed as Lily Hillsing.

Once you have located the people, you can subtract their years of birth to find the difference in their ages.

$$\begin{array}{r} 1948 \text{ Mary Hillsing (Brenda's Mother)} \\ - 1943 \text{ Lily Hillsing (Brenda's Aunt)} \\ \hline 5 \end{array}$$

Brenda's mother is 5 years younger than Brenda's aunt.

Use the family tree to solve.

5. What is the difference in age between Brenda's two grandfathers? **10 years**

6. Greta Larson married Sam Hillsing in 1959. How old was she when she married him? **22 years old**

7. Brenda's birthday is July 27. Leslie's is March 27. How many months older is Brenda? **20 months**

8. Mary Hillsing was married when she was 23 years old. What year was that? **1971**

Classwork/Homework, pages H172–H173

ASSIGNMENT GUIDE

Basic: p. 414 1–2, p. 415 5–6

Average: p. 414 1–3, p. 415 5–7

Extended: p. 414 2–4, p. 415 6–8

Resources
Practice, pp. 172–3   Class/Home, pp. H172–3

Exercise Analysis
p. 414 1–4   Use a picture to solve
p. 415 5–8   Use a family tree to solve

FOLLOW-UP ACTIVITIES

PROBLEM SOLVING
Draw the following picture on the chalkboard. Have students find and list the area of each of the rooms in square feet.

(Living Room: 396   Entrance: 60
Kitchen: 120   Dining Room: 150
Bedroom 1: 150   Bedroom 2: 180)

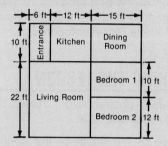

COMING UP
No flab on these figures!

PRACTICE Using a Picture

Read the paragraph. Then use the information in the paragraph and the picture to help you answer each question.

Ramona makes models of buildings for miniature railroad sets. There are 3 popular scales to which models can be built.

Ramona is using this diagram of a freight station to make 3 stations for customers—one for each of the 3 scales described above.

O scale = $\frac{1}{48}$ the size of actual objects.
HO scale is $\frac{1}{87}$ the size of actual objects.
N scale is $\frac{1}{160}$ the size of actual objects.

1. For each of the three scales, what is the perimeter in inches of the rectangular freight-station platform? Round to the nearest inch.
O scale = 26 inches; HO scale = 14 inches; N scale = 8 inches

2. For the N-scale freight station, could a $\frac{3}{4}$-inch-square "freight carton" pass through the large freight entrance? **no**

3. For the O-scale model, what is the height and the length in inches of the freight-station sign?
O scale = $\frac{3}{8}$ in. × 2$\frac{1}{2}$ in.

4. For the HO-scale freight station, would a 3$\frac{3}{4}$-inch dowel be long enough to make the 3 columns at the left? **yes**

5. For the HO scale, what is the height in inches of a tree whose top leaves reach the top of the station sign? (Round to the nearest $\frac{1}{2}$ inch.) 2$\frac{1}{2}$ inches

6. For the O-scale freight station, would a 7-inch dowel be long enough to make the 3 columns at the left? **yes**

172

Use with pages 414–415.

Holt, Rinehart and Winston, Publishers • 8

PRACTICE Using a Picture

Study the time line. Then, answer each question.

1. About how many years are represented on this time line? about 5,457 years

2. About how many years separate the invention of ink and the invention of the newspaper? of ink and the ballpoint pen?
about 4,780 years; about 5,138 years

3. About how many years separate the invention of the first wheeled vehicles and the invention of the bicycle?
about 5,339 years

4. How many years separate the invention of vaccination and the invention of inoculation? 84 years

5. After which year were steam-powered locomotives invented? A.D. 1712

6. About how many years separate the invention of paper and the invention of the newspaper? about 1,490 years

7. Put a check next to the conclusion that you have drawn from this time line.
☐ Without the invention of the hot-air balloon, the satellite could not have been invented.
☐ Without the invention of the piano, there would be no jukebox.
☑ Transistor radios could not have been in use before 1948.
☐ Without the invention of kites, the hot-air balloon could not have been invented.

INVENTIONS
circa 3500 B.C. Wheeled vehicles
circa 3200 B.C. Ink
circa 1000 B.C. Kites that carried people
circa 90 A.D. Paper
1335 A.D. Mechanical clock
1580 A.D. Newspaper
1590 A.D. Microscope
1592 A.D. Thermometer
1608 A.D. Telescope
1712 A.D. Steam Engine
1709 A.D. Piano
1783 A.D. Hot-air balloon
1796 A.D. Vaccination
1839 A.D. Bicycle
1880 A.D. Inoculation
1895 A.D. Radio
1930 A.D. Juke Box
1938 A.D. Ballpoint Pen
1948 A.D. Transistor
1957 A.D. Satellite

Use after pages 414–415.

173

Holt, Rinehart and Winston, Publishers • 8

Objective: To explore solid figures

Warm-Up
Have students find the area of each circle, using 3.14 for π and rounding to the nearest tenth.

$r = 4$ ft $(50.2$ ft$^2)$
$d = 6.2$ in. $(30.2$ in.$^2)$
$r = 1.7$ yd $(9.1$ yd$^2)$
$d = 18.6$ in. $(271.6$ in.$^2)$
$r = 12$ ft $(452.2$ ft$^2)$
$d = 21.2$ yd $(352.8$ yd$^2)$

GETTING STARTED

Ask students whether they can find any 2-dimensional objects in the classroom. Elicit from them that there are no 2-dimensional objects in the room because we live in a 3-dimensional world. Challenge them to explain why even a sheet of paper is 3-dimensional. You may want to discuss how you could show that the paper has thickness (e.g., measure the thickness of several sheets together and then divide). Ask them to name some 2-dimensional representations of 3 dimensions (such as photographs) and discuss the shortcomings of these representations.

TEACHING THE LESSON

Materials: posterboard, rulers, compasses, scissors, tape

Because of the depth of the conceptual development involved, this lesson may be addressed in several class periods. There are two approaches that you can use in teaching this lesson: (1) have students work individually on the developmental parts and in groups of four on Working as a Team or (2) have students work through the developmental parts in groups of four and have a class discussion for Working as a Team.

Have students draw each of the given figures on posterboard. They may first want to draw them to the indicated measurements on graph paper, then cut them out, and then trace them onto thin cardboard. Remind students that a compass can be a helpful tool in drawing triangles to a given size (see page 376). Once students have drawn the figures to size, they should cut them out, fold them as indicated, and tape the edges together. The resulting solid figures should look like those shown in the textbook.

Students should answer question 1 by listing the number of faces, edges, and vertices and by describing the faces and identifying which are congruent or parallel or both congruent and parallel. For question 3, make sure that students realize that al-

Solid Figures

All of the figures pictured so far in this chapter are 2-dimensional figures. **Solid figures** are 3-dimensional. In this lesson you will explore solid figures.

Draw the figures shown below and at the right on posterboard or some other kind of thin cardboard. Use the measurements indicated. You may find it helpful to use a compass to make the triangles.

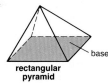

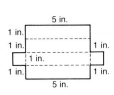
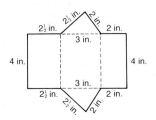
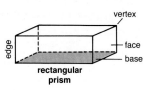

Cut out the figures along the outside lines. Fold them along the broken lines to make the solid figures shown. You can use cellophane tape to fasten the sides together.

rectangular prism

triangular prism

triangular pyramid

rectangular pyramid

Working as a Team

1. Describe the two different kinds of prisms that you have made. Use terms such as *faces, edges, vertices,* and *congruent.*

2. In which ways are rectangular prisms and triangular prisms alike? How are they different?
Check students' answers.

3. A cube is a rectangular prism in which all of the faces are in the shape of congruent squares. On posterboard draw a figure that can be cut out and folded into a cube.

rectangular prism—3 pairs of congruent and parallel rectangular faces; triangular prism—3 rectangular faces and 2 congruent and parallel triangular faces

though all cubes have 6 congruent square faces, not all configurations of 6 congruent squares will fold into cubes. Suggest that they draw their figures on paper first, cut them out, and check to see that they can be folded into cubes. As a challenge you may want to have students come up with all possible configurations of 6 congruent squares and identify which of these can be folded into cubes. For question 4, elicit from students that a hexagonal prism would have two congruent hexagons as parallel faces.

For question 5, have students describe pyramids in the same way that they described prisms. For question 7, elicit from students that a pentagonal pyramid would have a pentagonal base and 5 triangular faces that share 1 vertex.

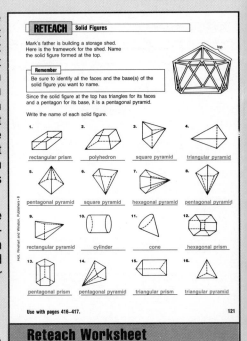

Reteach Worksheet

(Continued on p. 417.)

4. What do you think a hexagonal prism would look like? Make one using straws for edges and clay for vertices.

a prism with 2 congruent and parallel hexagons for bases and 6 rectangles for the remaining faces

5. Describe the two different kinds of pyramids you have made.

rectangular pyramid—1 rectangular base and 4 triangular faces that share a vertex; triangular pyramid—1 triangular base and 3 triangular faces that share a vertex

6. In which ways are rectangular pyramids and triangular pyramids alike? How are they different?
Check students' answers

7. What do you think a pentagonal pyramid would look like? Make one using straws for edges and clay for vertices.   a pyramid with a pentagonal base and 5 triangular faces that share a vertex

All of the solid figures that you have made so far are called **polyhedrons.** All of the faces of a polyhedron have the shape of polygons. A prism is a polyhedron that has at least two congruent faces that are parallel. A pyramid is a polyhedron whose one base is a polygon and whose other faces are triangles that share one vertex.

Working as a Team

1. Can you make a solid figure that is not a polyhedron?   Cylinders, cones, and spheres are solid figures that are not polyhedrons—others are possible.

2. Using poster board, make a cylinder and a cone.

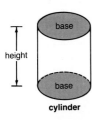
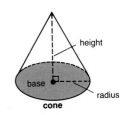

cylinder   **cone**

3. Describe the two kinds of solid figures that you have just made. Are they polyhedrons?
Check students' answers; no.

4. Another kind of solid figure is a sphere. How many examples of spheres can you think of? Share them with the class.   Check students' answers.

5. What can you say about the distance from the center of all points on the surface of a sphere?

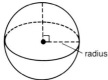

radius

They are all equidistant from the center.

Classwork/Homework, page H174

417

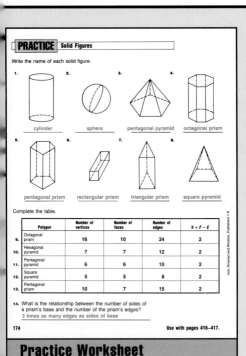
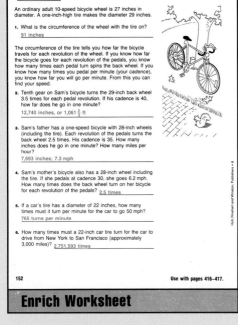

ASSIGNMENT GUIDE

Basic:	p. 416, p. 417
Average:	p. 416, p. 417
Extended:	p. 416, p. 417

Resources
Practice, p. 174   Class/Home, p. H174
Reteach, p. 121
Enrich, p. 152

For question 1 in the second Working as a Team section, have students identify in the classroom solid objects that are not polyhedrons. For question 2, elicit from students that a cylinder consists of one rectangle and two circles and that a cone has one circular base and a slant surface that when it is folded flat, looks like a pizza from which one or two slices are missing. For question 3, students should describe their cylinders and cones in a manner similar to that which they used for prisms and pyramids. For question 5, make sure that students realize that all points on the surface of a sphere are equidistant from the center of the sphere.

FOLLOW-UP ACTIVITIES

MATH CONNECTION (Consumer)
Consumer goods are often packed in geometric containers or are themselves geometric shapes. Have students go to a store or look at home for interesting examples of consumer goods that look like geometric shapes. Have each student make a list of the 10 most interesting examples he or she has found.

COMING UP
Making up the face

417

Objectives: To explore and calculate the surface area of prisms and pyramids

Warm-Up
Have students simplify each.

3(2 + 8) + 5(3 + 4) (65)
2(4 + 1) + 7(3 + 2) + 4(3 + 6) (81)
2(3 × 4) + 3(4 × 5) + 4(5 × 6) (204)
3(1 + 8) + 2(4 × 3) + 5(2 + 3) (76)

GETTING STARTED

Have students look at the prisms and pyramids that they constructed for the previous lesson or at the illustrations on page 416. Ask them to make a table listing the number of vertices *(V)*, faces *(F)*, and edges *(E)* for each prism and pyramid shown. Ask what relationship they can see between the number of vertices, faces, and edges in each solid figure. Guide them to see that $V + F - E = 2$ in each case. This relationship is known as Euler's formula. Challenge students to see whether the formula also holds true for pentagonal prisms and pentagonal pyramids. (It does.)

TEACHING THE LESSON

Materials: posterboard, ruler, scissors

There are two approaches that you can use in teaching this lesson: (1) have students work individually through the developmental parts and convene in groups of four for Thinking as a Team or (2) have students work through the developmental parts in groups of four and have a class discussion for Thinking as a Team.

A. Have students draw the given figure on posterboard. They may first want to draw it on graph paper to the measurements indicated, then cut it out, and then trace it onto thin cardboard. Once students have drawn the figure, they should cut it out, fold it as indicated, and tape the edges together to form a rectangular prism. Make sure that students realize that the surface area of the prism is equal to the sum of the areas of each of its faces.

Students' formulas for a rectangular prism should be of the form $S = 2lw + 2wh + 2hl$. The surface area of a triangular prism is equal to the sum of the areas of the triangles *(bh)* plus the area of each rectangular face.

B. For Section B, students should trace, cut out, and fold together the square pyramid. For question 1, students should realize that the way to find the surface area of any polyhedron is simply to add the areas of each face. For

Surface Area of Prisms and Pyramids

You can discover how to find the **surface area** of a polyhedron.

A. Trace the pattern shown below on posterboard, label it, and cut it out.

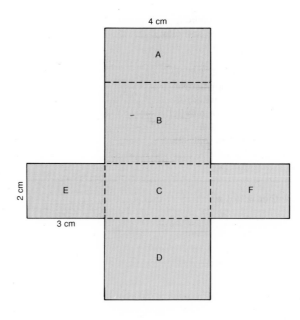

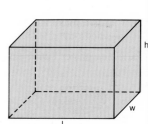

Now fold the pattern along the broken lines and assemble the figure. It should look like the solid figure shown to the right. Use *l*, *w*, or *h* to label the edges of each face.

What is the name of this solid figure?   a rectangular prism

How many faces does this solid figure have? Copy the table. Measure the dimensions of each face, find the area, and write it in the table.   6 faces

What formula did you use to find the area of a face?
$A = l \times w$
Which pairs of faces are congruent?
A and *C*, *B* and *D*, *E* and *F*

418

Surface Area	
Face	**Area in Square Units**
A	$2 \times 4 = 8 \text{ cm}^2$
B	$3 \times 4 = 12 \text{ cm}^2$
C	$2 \times 4 = 8 \text{ cm}^2$
D	$3 \times 4 = 12 \text{ cm}^2$
E	$2 \times 3 = 6 \text{ cm}^2$
F	$2 \times 3 = 6 \text{ cm}^2$

question 2, point out that the pyramid that students put together was a square pyramid and that the formula for the surface area of a rectangular prism is not as simple as that because the formula for the area of the base of a rectangular prism is different and the four triangular faces are not necessarily congruent. Challenge students to find the surface area of a triangular pyramid that you draw on the chalkboard.

As a challenge have students find the surface area of an assortment of packages of food in various shapes. Then have them write ratios for the surface area to the volume. Ask: "For which package is the ratio the least?" Ask why this knowledge is useful. (because this shape maximizes the volume contained by a certain amount of packaging material)

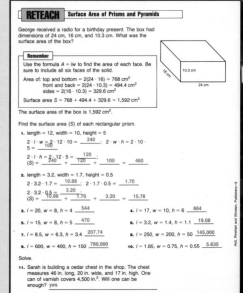

How can you find the combined area of a pair of congruent faces? **Use the formula A = 2lw.**

How can you find the surface area of the entire polyhedron? **Add the areas of the faces**

Thinking as a Team

Replace the dimensions you used to find the prism's surface area with the variables l, w, and h. Try to write a formula for the surface area of a rectangular prism. Use l, w, and h.

1. What formula did you discover?
$A = 2lw + 2wh + 2hl$

2. How would you change the formula to find the surface area of a triangular prism? What formula would you use to find the area of the triangular bases?

The area of each triangular face would be found using the formula $A = \frac{1}{2}bh$ and these areas would be added together.

B. Trace the pattern at the right on posterboard, and cut it out.

Now fold the pattern along the broken lines, and assemble the figure.

* What is the name of this solid figure? **a square pyramid**
* Examine each face and label its dimensions.
* Which pairs of faces are congruent? **All 4 triangular faces are congruent.**
* How can you find the surface area of the entire polyhedron? **Use the formula $A = b^2 + 2bh$**

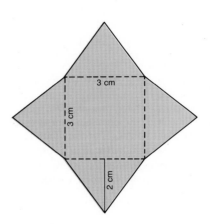

3 cm

3 cm

2 cm

Thinking as a Team

1. Can you use this procedure to find the surface area of other polyhedrons? **yes**

2. Try to write a formula for the surface area of a rectangular pyramid.

$A = lw + lh + wh$ where l = length of base, w = width of base, and h = slant height.

ASSIGNMENT GUIDE

Basic:	p. 418, p. 419
Average:	p. 418, p. 419
Extended:	p. 418, p. 419

Resources
Practice, p. 175   Class/Home, p. H175
Reteach, p. 122
Enrich, p. 153

FOLLOW-UP ACTIVITIES

PROBLEM SOLVING
Ask students whether Euler's formula ($V + F - E = 2$) holds for 2-dimensional figures also. (yes) Ask them what the analogous characteristic of a 2-dimensional figure would be for each characteristic listed. (*V*—vertices, *F*—regions such as interior and exterior, *E*—sides) Have students draw several polygons and apply the formula to see whether it holds true. Then challenge them to see whether it works for any connected network of points and paths. (yes)

PROBLEM SOLVING
Have students solve this problem.
* The Washington Monument is a great obelisk. Its four sides are trapezoids, and its top is a pyramid. The height of each triangular face is 16.8 m. The height of the monument, except for the pyramid, is 152.5 m. Using the diagram below, find its surface area. (approximately 8,680 m²)

10.5 m

16.8 m

COMING UP
Cylinders in the desert

Warm-Up

Have students find the circumference and area of each circle, using 3.14 for π.

- $r = 3$ cm   ($C = 18.84$ cm, $A = 28.26$ cm^2)
- $d = 8$ in. ($C = 25.12$ in., $A = 50.24$ in.^{2})

GETTING STARTED

Materials: cylindrical box

Have students think of situations in which they would have to find the surface area of a cylinder. (when painting a water tower, calculating how much sheet metal has been used for a tin can, and so on)

Cut down and around the box so that it can be flattened. Have students identify congruent figures. In the case of a cylinder, only the top and bottom are congruent.

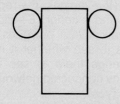

Have students suggest ways to determine the surface area of the cylinder.

TEACHING THE LESSON

A. Prior to working the text example, you may want to work through a simpler example such as a cylinder with a radius of 7 m and a height of 10 m by using $\frac{22}{7}$ for π. ($S = 748$ m^2)

B. Emphasize the fact that the base of the parallelogram formed by the cone is $\frac{1}{2}$ of the cone's circumference.

$$b = \frac{1}{2} \cdot (2\pi r) = \pi r$$

Other examples:

$r = 3$ cm, $l = 7$ cm   ($S \approx 94.2$ cm^2)
$r = 4$ in., $l = 4$ in.   ($S \approx 100.48$ in.^{2})

You might wish to allow students to use calculators while working through this lesson.

Surface Area of Cylinders and Cones

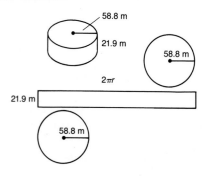

A. One of the largest cylindrical oil tanks in the world is located in Saudi Arabia. The tank is 21.9 m high, and the radius of its circular base is 58.8 m.

Find the surface area of the oil tank.

A cylinder can be cut apart and flattened to form a rectangle and two circles as shown. The area of the rectangle that is formed is called the **lateral area**.

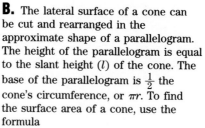

To find the surface area (S) of a cylinder, use the formula

S = lateral area + 2 · area of circular base.

$S = 2\pi rh + 2\pi r^2$
$S \approx 2 \cdot 3.14 \cdot 58.8 \cdot 21.9 + 2 \cdot 3.14 \cdot 58.8 \cdot 58.8$
$S \approx 8{,}086.8816 + 21{,}712.723$
$S \approx 29{,}799.604$

The surface area of the oil tank is about 29,799.6 m^2.

B. The lateral surface of a cone can be cut and rearranged in the approximate shape of a parallelogram. The height of the parallelogram is equal to the slant height (l) of the cone. The base of the parallelogram is $\frac{1}{2}$ the cone's circumference, or πr. To find the surface area of a cone, use the formula

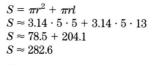

$S = \pi r^2 + \pi rl$
$S \approx 3.14 \cdot 5 \cdot 5 + 3.14 \cdot 5 \cdot 13$
$S \approx 78.5 + 204.1$
$S \approx 282.6$

The surface area of the cone is about 282.6 cm^2.

Math Reasoning, page H228

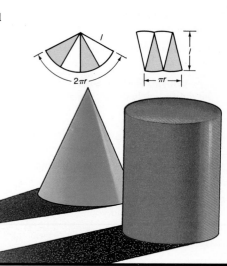

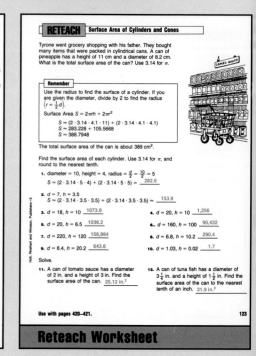

COMMON ERRORS

Students might multiply instead of adding the two terms in the formula for the surface area of a cone.

Remediation
For this error, have students write the intermediate formula S(cone) = S(base) + S(lateral).

Assign Reteach Master, p. 123.

RETEACH   Surface Area of Cylinders and Cones

Tyrone went grocery shopping with his father. They bought many items that were packed in cylindrical cans. A can of pineapple has a height of 11 cm and a diameter of 8.2 cm. What is the total surface area of the can? Use 3.14 for π.

Remember
Use the radius to find the surface of a cylinder. If you are given the diameter, divide by 2 to find the radius $(r = \frac{1}{2} d)$.

Surface Area $S = 2\pi rh + 2\pi r^2$

$S \approx (2 \cdot 3.14 \cdot 4.1 \cdot 11) + (2 \cdot 3.14 \cdot 4.1 \cdot 4.1)$
$S \approx 283.228 + 105.5668$
$S \approx 388.7948$

The total surface area of the can is about 389 cm^2.

Find the surface area of each cylinder. Use 3.14 for π, and round to the nearest tenth.

1. diameter = 10, height = 4, radius = $\frac{d}{2} = \frac{10}{2} = 5$
   $S \approx (2 \cdot 3.14 \cdot 5 \cdot 4) + (2 \cdot 3.14 \cdot 5 \cdot 5) = \underline{282.6}$

2. $d = 7$, $h = 3.5$
   $S \approx (2 \cdot 3.14 \cdot 3.5 \cdot 3.5) + (2 \cdot 3.14 \cdot 3.5 \cdot 3.5) \approx \underline{153.9}$

3. $d = 18$, $h = 10$ $\underline{1073.9}$ 4. $d = 20$, $h = 10$ $\underline{1{,}256}$

5. $d = 20$, $h = 6.5$ $\underline{1036.2}$ 6. $d = 160$, $h = 100$ $\underline{90{,}432}$

7. $d = 220$, $h = 120$ $\underline{158{,}884}$ 8. $d = 6.8$, $h = 10.2$ $\underline{290.4}$

9. $d = 8.4$, $h = 20.2$ $\underline{643.6}$ 10. $d = 1.03$, $h = 0.02$ $\underline{1.7}$

Solve.

11. A can of tomato sauce has a diameter of 2 in. and a height of 3 in. Find the surface area of the can. $\underline{25.12\text{ in.}^2}$

12. A can of tuna fish has a diameter of $3\frac{1}{4}$ in. and a height of $1\frac{1}{2}$ in. Find the surface area of the can to the nearest tenth of an inch. $\underline{31.9\text{ in.}^2}$

Use with pages 420–421.   123

Reteach Worksheet

Find the surface area. Use 3.14 for π, and round to the nearest tenth.

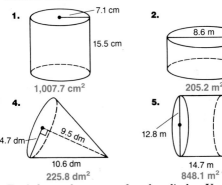

1. 7.1 cm, 15.5 cm
1,007.7 cm²

2. 8.6 m, 3.3 m
205.2 m²

3. 11.3 cm, 10.8 cm, 4.9 cm
249.3 cm²

4. 4.7 dm, 9.5 dm, 10.6 dm
225.8 dm²

5. 12.8 m, 14.7 m
848.1 m²

★6. 12 cm, 3 cm, 5 cm, 8 cm
533.8 cm²

Find the surface area of each cylinder. Use 3.14 for π, and round to the nearest tenth.

7. radius = 12 cm
height = 15 cm
2,034.7 cm²

8. diameter = 14 dm
height = 8 dm
659.4 dm²

9. radius = 60 mm
height = 75 mm
50,868 mm²

10. diameter = 25 cm
height = 5 cm
1,373.8 cm²

11. diameter = 4.8 m
height = 12.3 m
221.6 m²

12. radius = 7.6 dm
height = 11.9 dm
930.7 dm²

13. diameter = 4 dm
height = 2.1 dm
51.5 dm²

14. height = 1 m
radius = 1 m
12.6 m²

15. height = 0.9 m
radius = 0.1 m
0.6 m²

Find the surface area of each cone. Use 3.14 for π, and round to the nearest tenth.

16. radius = 5 cm
slant height = 13 cm
282.6 cm²

17. radius = 6.7 cm
slant height = 9.1 cm
332.4 cm²

18. radius = 11.9 cm
slant height = 18.1 cm
1,121.0 cm²

19. radius = 1.1 m
slant height = 5 m
21.1 m²

20. radius = 21 m
slant height = 8 m
1,912.3 m²

★21. slant height = 400 mm
radius = 300 mm
659,400 mm²

Solve.

22. The cone-shaped front of a space satellite has a diameter of 4.5 m and a slant height of 12.1 m. Find the surface area. 101.4 m²

23. A cylindrical oil tank has a diameter of 34.4 m and a height of 15.7 m. Find the surface area of the oil tank. 3,553.7 m²

★24. A conical mound of sand has a lateral surface area of 2,355 m². If the radius of the base is 10 m, what is the slant height of the mound? 75 m

★25. What is the surface area of the largest cylinder that would fit in your classroom? Answers will vary.

Classwork/Homework, page H176

More Practice, page H205 **421**

ASSIGNMENT GUIDE

Basic: 1–5, 10–20, 22–23

Average: 1–6, 8–20 e, 22–24

Extended: 1–21 o, 22–25

Resources
Practice, p. 176   Class/Home, p. H176
Reteach, p. 123   More Practice, p. H205
Enrich, p. 154   Reasoning, p. H228

Exercise Analysis

1–6   Find the surface area of a pictured cylinder or cone
7–15   Find the surface area of a cylinder
16–21   Find the surface area of a cone
22–24   Skill applications
25   Problem formulation

You might wish to allow students to use calculators for some of these exercises.

FOLLOW-UP ACTIVITIES

CALCULATOR
Have students use calculators to solve this problem.
- A vegetable canning company is planning to print a year's supply of labels for the lateral areas of their cans. The company's per-day production averages 3,700 small cans; 4,900 medium cans; and 3,250 large cans during a 260-day work year. The small can is 4 in. high and has a $2\frac{1}{2}$-in. diameter; the medium can is $4\frac{1}{2}$-in. high and has a $3\frac{1}{4}$-in. diameter; the large can is $6\frac{3}{4}$-in. high and has a 4-in. diameter. About how many square yards of paper must be purchased for the labels? (124,000 yd²)

PROBLEM SOLVING
Have students solve this problem.
- Valerie is building a rocket for her science class. Its main fuselage has a diameter of 6 in. and a height of 18 in. Atop the fuselage is a payload cone that has a slant height of 9 in.

Valerie must buy special material for the outside of the rocket. The material comes in long rolls 18 inches wide and costs $4.59 per foot. About how many linear feet of material will be needed, and what will be the total cost? (2.1 ft, $9.60)

COMING UP
Modeling becomes fashionable.

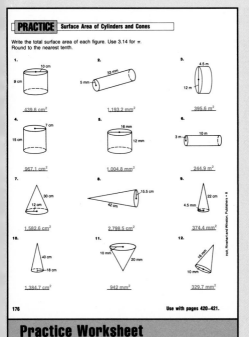

Practice Worksheet

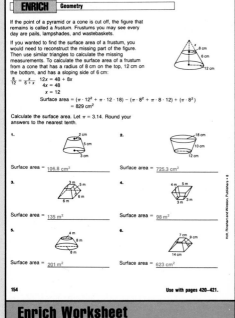

Enrich Worksheet

Objective: To check for hidden assumptions in solving a problem

Warm-Up
Have students draw each of the following.
- a square
- a rhombus
- a quadrilateral
- an equilateral triangle
- an isosceles triangle
- a triangle

Point out that each group of three figures can be represented by a single drawing.

GETTING STARTED

Draw the following shapes on the chalkboard.

Have students write a description of each shape. Ask volunteers to read their descriptions. Point out that the shapes are a pentagon, a hexagon, and an octagon. Tell students that the definition of each of these polygons is nonspecific: any five-sided, six-sided, or eight-sided figure, respectively, qualifies.

TEACHING THE LESSON

Students will often be frustrated by a problem, not because the problem itself is difficult, but because they believe the problem is more complicated than it actually is.

Questions: Emphasize that these questions are tricky and that students should read them carefully, both before starting the problem and once they have found an answer. Have students read carefully to find absolute terms such as *always* and *never*. Students should also look for descriptive terms such as *congruent* or *equilateral*, and so on, when working with geometric forms.

Tools: The second example demonstrates how hidden assumptions occur. Students encounter unusual items that they have assumed do not occur such as a number larger than its squares. Tell students to think about the steps that led to their initial answer for a problem. Have them be as specific as possible in outlining each piece of reasoning that led to the first conclusion. Students will often have to change many steps in their reasoning. Warn students to take care when using shortcuts and rules of thumb. These help in a majority of cases, but exceptions, such as those encountered

---

| QUESTIONS | TOOLS | SOLUTIONS | CHECKS |

PROBLEM SOLVING
Checking for Hidden Assumptions

Sometimes when solving a problem, you assume conditions that do not apply to that problem. If you are stuck on a problem, it is a good idea to check for assumptions you are making that are confusing the problem.

Draw a picture of an equilateral pentagon (one with congruent sides).

> The sketch at the right shows what you usually think of as an equilateral pentagon. But this pentagon has congruent sides *and* congruent angles. Can you draw an equilateral pentagon without five congruent angles?

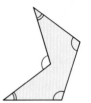

If you are having trouble making the drawing, you should think about the assumptions you are making. A pentagon is a five-sided figure. Any fact other than that may be an assumption. You might be assuming that the pentagon has to be convex. The drawing at the right is a solution to the problem. It is a pentagon with five congruent sides that is not convex.

True or false: x^2 is always greater than x.

Your initial response might be that this is true. For the numbers you try, it is always true.

But the question asks whether this is *always* true. Is the statement true for all numbers? Check for hidden assumptions.

You might be assuming that x is always a whole number. But the symbol x can stand for *any* number. If x is a fraction that is less than 1, x^2 will be *less* than x. The statement which at first seemed obviously true is actually false.

---

in this lesson, often show that students can overgeneralize these rules.

Solutions: This lesson tests logical skills and mastery of mathematical facts. Computation is minimal.

Checks: Students will have to carefully reread the question to examine to see whether the answer they have given is correct. Each step in their reasoning must be checked for hidden assumptions.

Write the letter of each assumption that is correct to make. Then answer the question.

1. True or false: $x + y$ is always greater than $x - y$.
  a. x is greater than y.
  (b.) x and y are real numbers.
  c. x and y are whole numbers.
  false

2. Line A and line B are both perpendicular to the same line C. Must line A and line B be parallel?
  a. Line A intersects line B.
  b. Lines A, B, and C are in one plane.
  (c.) Line A intersects line C.
  false

Solve. Be careful to check for assumptions you might be making in each problem.

3. True or false: $\frac{n}{n}$ always equals 1.
  false; $\frac{0}{0}$ is undefined.

4. True or false: $0 \cdot n$ always equals 0.
  true

5. Line A is perpendicular to line B. Is it possible for line C to be perpendicular to both A and B? If so, how?
  Yes; if line C is in a perpendicular plane

6. Is it possible to start on spot A, walk 10 miles south, then walk 10 miles east, and then walk 10 miles north, and return to spot A?
  yes, from the North Pole

7. A monkey is climbing a 10-foot tree. It climbs 3 feet each hour, and then falls back 2 feet. At this rate, how many hours does it take the monkey to reach the top of the tree? 8 hours

8. Shown below are the floor plans of two houses. Copy each floor plan and try to draw one line, without lifting your pencil, that crosses each wall of each room once and only once. Answers will vary.

no solution

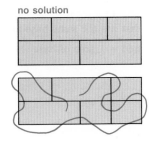

★9. You have a chessboard and 32 dominoes. The chessboard has 64 squares. Each domino can cover 2 squares. You remove 2 opposite corners of the chessboard and take away 1 domino. Is it possible to cover the 62 squares with 31 dominoes? Explain. (HINT: Solve a simpler problem. Try 16 squares and 8 dominoes.)

No; the 2 removed squares are both black or both white. The dominoes must cover an equal number of white and black squares. This is now impossible.

Classwork/Homework, page H177

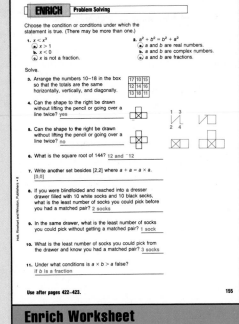

ASSIGNMENT GUIDE

Basic: 1–6
Average: 1–4, 6–8 e
Extended: 1–4, 5–9 o

Resources
Practice, p. 177   Class/Home, p. H177
Enrich, p. 155

Exercise Analysis
1–2   Identify a correct assumption
3–8   Skill applications

FOLLOW-UP ACTIVITIES

PROBLEM SOLVING
Have students write the hidden assumption which might make one think each of the following false statements to be true.

- For all numbers x, $\sqrt[3]{x}$ is irrational. (Assumption: x is not a perfect cube.)
- If two lines are not parallel, they will intersect. (Assumption: The lines are in the same plane.)
- For all numbers x, if the sum of x's digits = multiple of 3, $\frac{x}{3}$ = whole number. (Assumption: x is positive.)
- For all numbers x, (the absolute value of x) − 5 > −5. (Assumption: x does not equal 0.)

MATH CONNECTION (Consumer)
Have students find hidden assumptions in these advertisements that make the offers bargains.

- "Now you can get our new five-gallon carton of whole milk for only $15.00. At this price, you will save more than $3.00 over the single-quart price." (Assumption: You will use all five gallons before the milk spoils.)
- "For only $60.00, you can get a movie pass to the Showplace Theatre, which allows unlimited attendance to all our movies for a month. You'll save $10, $20, even $30 a month over our $5.00 single admission price!" (Assumption: You would normally go to more than 12 movies in a month.)

COMING UP
Voluminous pyramids

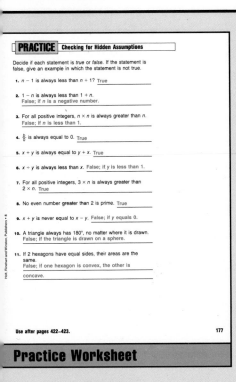

Practice Worksheet

Enrich Worksheet

Objectives: To find the volume of a prism and a pyramid

Warm-Up
Have students simplify each example mentally.

$5 \times 8 \times 6$ (240) 5^3 (125)

3^3 (27) $\frac{1}{3} \times 12 \times 5$ (20)

$2 \times 3 \times 8$ (48) 4^3 (64)

$\frac{1}{2} \times 4 \times 8$ (16) $\frac{1}{4} \times 20 \times 7$ (35)

GETTING STARTED

Materials: 60 small blocks

Use the blocks to demonstrate volume by constructing a $5 \times 4 \times 1$ layer that shows the unit cubes clearly. Ask: How many unit cubes are there? (20) Stack two more $5 \times 4 \times 1$ layers on top of the first to make a $5 \times 4 \times 3$ rectangular prism. Ask: how many unit cubes are there now? (3×20, or 60).

TEACHING THE LESSON

A. Remind students that the base of a prism can be any face. In the example, the base is a rectangle. So, $B = l \cdot w$. Have students rewrite $V = Bh$ for a prism that has a triangular base.

B. Point out that a cube is a special case of a prism in which $l = w = h$. Because $V = Bh$ and $B = l \cdot w$, $V = l \cdot w \cdot h$, that is, l^3, w^3, or h^3.

C. Point out that the height of a pyramid is the length of a perpendicular line segment from the base to the top of the pyramid. It is not the slant height of a side used to find the surface area.

You might wish to allow students to use calculators while working through this lesson.

Volume of Prisms and Pyramids

A. What is the volume of a typical cassette case that is 1.5 cm high, 11 cm long, and 7 cm wide?

The **volume (V)** of a solid figure is the number of unit cubes that can fit inside the figure. A unit cube that measures 1 cm along each edge is called a **cubic centimeter (cm^3)**.

Use this formula to find the volume of a rectangular prism.

V of a prism = area of base · height

$V = Bh$, or $V = lwh$
$V = (11 \cdot 7) \cdot 1.5$
$V = 77 \cdot 1.5$
$V = 115.5$

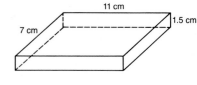

The volume of the cassette case is 115.5 cm^3.

B. Use this formula to find the volume of a cube.

V of a cube = area of base · height

$V = e^3$
$V = 2^3$
$V = 8$

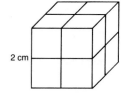

The volume of the cube is 8 cm^3.

C. The volume of a pyramid is equal to $\frac{1}{3}$ the volume of a prism that has the same base and height.

V of a pyramid = $\frac{1}{3}$ area of base · height

$V = \frac{1}{3}Bh$
$V = \frac{1}{3}(6 \cdot 6) \cdot 4$
$V = \frac{1}{3} \cdot 36 \cdot 4$
$V = 48$

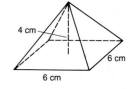

The volume of the pyramid is 48 cm^3.

For additional activities, see **Connecting Math Ideas**, page 472.

424

COMMON ERRORS

Students might sometimes substitute into the formula for volume only one value for the base, thinking that B represents a single linear measurement.

Remediation
For this error, have students review the derivation of the volume formula. Then have them rewrite the formula and replace B with the proper formula for the area of the base. ($l \cdot w$ (rectangle), $\frac{1}{2}bh$ (triangle), and so on)

Assign Reteach Master, p. 124.

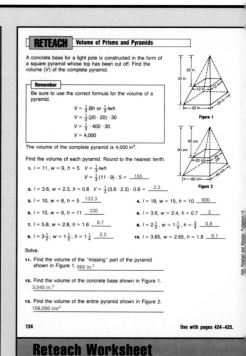

Reteach Worksheet

Find the volume of each polyhedron. Round to the nearest tenth.

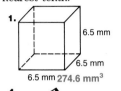

1. 6.5 mm, 6.5 mm, 6.5 mm **274.6 mm³**

2. 6.3 m, 0.5 m, 8 m **25.2 m³**

3. 9.9 cm, 8 cm, 15 cm **396 cm³**

4. 8.8 cm, 15 cm, 15 cm **660 cm³**

★5. 0.8 km, 0.4 km, 0.6 km **0.1 km³**

★6. 14.6 cm, 24 cm, 10.4 cm **1,822.1 cm³**

Find the volume of each polyhedron. Round to the nearest tenth.

7. rectangular prism
length = 5.2 cm, width = 4.4 cm,
height = 4 cm **91.5 cm³**

8. rectangular pyramid
length = 75 m, width = 72 m,
height = 60 m **108,000 m³**

9. cube
edge = 3.5 dm **42.9 dm³**

10. hexagonal prism
Base = 240 m², height = 11 m
2,640 m³

11. rectangular prism
length = 8.1 cm, width = 4.7 cm,
height = 9.2 cm **350.2 cm³**

12. rectangular pyramid
length = 3 m, width = 2.1 m,
height = 3.5 m **7.4 m³**

★13. rectangular pyramid
length = 0.15 km, width = 25 m
height = 10 m **12,500 m³**

★14. triangular prism
height = 15 ft, Base = 8 in.²
1,440 in.³

Solve.

15. The Vehicle Assembly Building where the Apollo rocket was put together is a rectangular prism 716 ft long, 518 ft wide, and 525 ft high. Write the volume in scientific notation. **1.947162 × 10⁸ ft³**

16. The pyramid at Cholula, Mexico, has the greatest volume of any structure built. Its base area is 1,400 ft² and its height is 177 ft. Find its volume. **82,600 ft³**

NUMBER SENSE

Estimate which costs more.

1. 52% of $55 *or* 23% of $85
52% of $55

2. 48% of $950 *or* 127% of $425
127% of $425

Classwork/Homework, page H178

More Practice, page H206   **425**

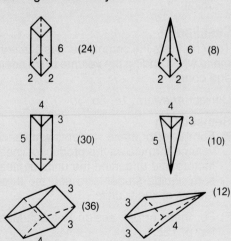

425

Objectives: To find the volume of a cylinder and a cone

Warm-Up

Have students evaluate each expression for $m = 3$, $q = 4$, $t = 2$, and $y = 5$.

$\frac{1}{2} mq$ (6) $\qquad$ ty^2 (50) $\qquad$ tq^2 (32)

ymt^3 (120) $\qquad$ $mqty$ (120) $\qquad$ $\frac{1}{2} qt$ (4)

GETTING STARTED

Ask students to compare the volumes of a prism and a pyramid of the same base and height. (The volume of the pyramid is one third the volume of the prism.) Tell them that this relationship also exists between two other solid figures. Ask them to guess which ones. (cylinder, cone)

TEACHING THE LESSON

A. Before performing the text example, you might wish to guide students through this simpler example.
- Draw a cylinder on the chalkboard with $r = 2$ cm and $h = 5$ cm.

$V = \pi r^2 h$
$V \approx (3.14)(2^2)(5)$
$V \approx (3.14)(4)(5)$
$V \approx 62.80$ cm^3

Emphasize the fact that the cylinder occupies approximately the same space as 63 cubes that have edges of 1 cm. Although this is not a liquid measure, it has a special relationship to one, since 1 cm^3 contains exactly 1 mL.

B. Point out that a cylinder and a prism that have the same area of base and height have the same volume. The same is also true for cones and pyramids.

Checkpoint

The chart lists the common errors students make when finding the volume of cylinders and cones.

Correct Answers: 1c, 2b, 3c

Remediation

■ For this error, have students write each volume formula as the product of linear factors and underline the units of measure. Guide students to see the three factors of linear units.

□ For these errors, assign Reteach Master, p. 125.

△ For this error, refer students to the examples on p. 60.

Volume of Cylinders and Cones

A. A university art class painted the campus water tank to look like a giant soup can. The tank is 120 ft high and has a diameter of 30 ft. Find the volume of the tank.

To find the volume (V) of a cylinder that is 120 ft high and has a diameter of 30 ft, multiply the area of its base by the height of the cylinder.

V of a cylinder = area of base $\cdot$ height; or $V = Bh$

$V = \pi r^2 \cdot h$
$V \approx 3.14 \cdot 15 \cdot 15 \cdot 120$
$V \approx 84{,}780$

The volume of the water tank is 84,780 ft^3.

B. The volume of any cone is equal to $\frac{1}{3}$ the volume of a cylinder that has the same base and height. To find the volume of a cone that is 120 ft high and has a radius of 15 ft, use the formula

Volume of a cone = $\frac{1}{3}$ Base $\cdot$ height, or $V = \frac{1}{3} Bh$.

$V = \frac{1}{3} \pi r^2 \cdot h$
$V \approx \frac{1}{3} \cdot 3.14 \cdot 15 \cdot 15 \cdot 120$
$V \approx 28{,}260$

The volume of the cone is 28,260 ft^3.

Checkpoint Write the letter of the correct answer.

Use 3.14 for π, and round to the nearest tenth.

1. 10 cm, 21.5 cm

The volume of the cylinder is
- **a.** 1,350.2 cm^3.
- **b.** 6,751 cm^2.
- **c.** 6,751 cm^3.
- **d.** 675.1 cm^3.

2. 24 mm, 26 mm, 10 mm

The volume of the cone is
- **a.** 7,536 mm^3.
- **b.** 2,512 mm^3.
- **c.** 502.4 mm^3.
- **d.** 2,721.3 mm^3.

3. 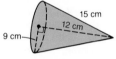 15 cm, 12 cm, 9 cm

The volume of the cone is
- **a.** 226.1 cm^3
- **b.** 3,052.1 cm^3
- **c.** 1,017.4 cm^3.
- **d.** 1,271.7 cm^3.

426 $\qquad$ **Math Reasoning, page H228**

COMMON ERRORS

Answer Choice	Type of Error
□ 1a, 2c, 3a	Confuses 2r with r^2
■ 1b	Uses the incorrect unit
△ 1d	Misplaces the decimal point
□ 2a, 3b	Uses the formula for the cylinder
□ 2d, 3d	Uses the slant height instead of the height

RETEACH | **Volume of Cylinders and Cones**

A standard hockey puck is a cylinder that is 1 inch thick and 3 inches in diameter. Find the volume of a standard hockey puck. Use 3.14 for π.

Remember

Be sure to use the correct formula when calculating the volume of a cylinder.

$V = \pi r^2 \cdot h$
$V = 3.14 \cdot 1.5 \cdot 1.5 \cdot 1$
$V = 7.065$

The volume of a standard hockey puck is about 7.1 in.^{3}.

Complete the table by finding the volume. Use 3.14 for π, and round to the nearest tenth.

	Diameter	Height	Calculation	Volume
1.	10 yd	4 yd	3.14 · 5 · 5 · 4	314 yd^3
2.	6.3 m	3.1 m	3.14 · 3.15 · 3.15 · 3.1	96.6 m^3
3.	2$\frac{1}{2}$ in.	1$\frac{1}{2}$ in.	3.14 · 1$\frac{1}{4}$ · 1$\frac{1}{4}$ · 1$\frac{1}{2}$	7.4 in.^{3}
4.	12 ft	6 ft	3.14 · 6 · 6 · 6	678.2 ft^3
5.	14 km	7 km	3.14 · 7 · 7 · 7	1,077 km^3
6.	150 m	100 m	3.14 · 75 · 75 · 100	1,766,250 m^3
7.	260 cm	120 cm	3.14 · 130 · 130 · 120	6,367,920 cm^3
8.	3.2 yd	1.4 yd	3.14 · 1.6 · 1.6 · 1.4	11.3 yd^3

Solve.

9. Maurice is the shop foreman for the Department of Highways. For a special project, he must oversee the manufacture of manhole covers. Each manhole cover must have a diameter of 71 cm and a thickness of 4.5 cm. What is the volume of the manhole cover? Round your answer to the nearest tenth. Use $V = \frac{1}{3} Bh$. 17,807.3 cm^3

Use with pages 426–427. $\qquad$ 125

Reteach Worksheet

Find the volume. Use 3.14 for π, and round to the nearest tenth.

1.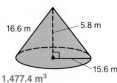

5.0 cm
9.3 cm

730.1 cm³

2.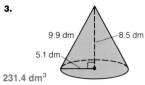

14.2 cm   1.3 cm

205.8 cm³

3.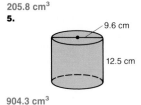

9.9 dm   8.5 dm
5.1 dm

231.4 dm³

4.

16.6 m   5.8 m
15.6 m

1,477.4 m³

5.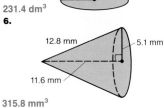

9.6 cm
12.5 cm

904.3 cm³

6.

12.8 mm   5.1 mm
11.6 mm

315.8 mm³

Find the volume. Use 3.14 for π, and round to the nearest tenth.

7. cylinder
radius = 7.6 cm
height = 14 cm
2,539.1 cm³

8. cone
radius = 3.3 m
height = 8.7 m
99.2 m³

9. cylinder
radius = 16.5 cm
height = 25 cm
21,371.6 cm³

10. cone
Base = 116.8 cm²
height = 15 cm
584 cm³

11. cylinder
diameter = 1 m
height = 25 cm
196,250 cm³

12. cone
diameter = 7.2 cm
height = 7.2 cm
97.7 cm³

★13. cylinder
circumference = 12.56 cm
height = 9.1 cm
114.3 cm³

★14. cone
circumference = 6.28 dm
height = 18 dm
18.8 dm³

Find the volume of the shaded portion. Use 3.14 for π, and round to the nearest tenth.

15.

1 cm
8 cm
4 cm
4 cm
102.9 cm³

16.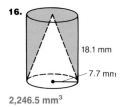

18.1 mm
7.7 mm

2,246.5 mm³

★17.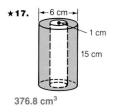

6 cm
1 cm
15 cm

376.8 cm³

Solve. Use 3.14 for π.

18. A large, conical mound of sand has a diameter of 45 ft and a height of 20 ft. Find the volume.
10,597.5 ft³

19. A cylindrical column is 90 ft high and has a diameter of $6\frac{1}{2}$ ft. Find its volume. 2,985.0 ft³

Classwork/Homework, page H179

427

Exercise Analysis

1–6   Find the volume of a pictured cylinder or cone

7–14   Find the volume of a cylinder or cone

15–17   Find the volume of a composite figure

18–19   Skill applications

You might wish to allow students to use calculators for some of these exercises.

FOLLOW-UP ACTIVITIES

MATH CONNECTION (Science)

Materials: spherical balloons, tape measure

Tell students that a person's vital capacity is the amount of air that person's lungs hold. Then have them follow these steps to find their vital capacities.

- Take a deep breath. Blow up the balloon with one breath, expelling as much air as possible from your lungs.
- Use the tape measure to measure the circumference of the balloon.
- Use $C \div 2\pi$ to find r.
- Vital capacity is found by using the formula for the volume of a sphere: $V = \frac{4}{3}\pi r^3$.
- In contrast, the vital capacity of a horse is 30,000 cm.

COMING UP

This formula or that formula? That is the question.

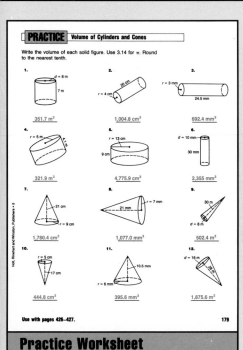

Objective: To choose the correct formula to solve a problem

Warm-Up
To prepare students for this lesson, have them compute the following.

18×13 (234) 7^2 (49)
14^2 (196) 3.14×30 (94.2)

GETTING STARTED

Pick out several items in the classroom (books, a globe, and so on) and ask students which formula they would use to find the perimeter, area, or volume of each. Discuss what the letters in each formula stand for and in what units of measurement the answer might be expressed.

TEACHING THE LESSON

In order to complete this lesson, students should be familiar with the geometric formulas for finding perimeter, area, and volumes. Guide students through each of the steps listed on page 428. Explain that these questions should be asked when solving each problem in this lesson. The first two questions have students analyze the geometric figure they are working with. The third question, by listing the quantity solved for, will pinpoint the formula used. The fourth will assure that all measurements used are consistent.

Questions: Some students may be unable to determine if the question calls for perimeter, area, or volume. Suggest that students figure out beforehand in what units their answer will be expressed. Single units indicate perimeter (or a linear measurement), square units indicate area, and cubic units indicate volume.

Tools: The tools used are the formula and the measurements given to plug into the formula. Students may be unable to match the dimensions given with letters in a formula. It may be helpful to review with students the standard letters used in most geometric formulas (*A, l, w,* and so on) and the meaning of each.

Solutions: Review with students the use of exponents. Emphasize the fact that when two units of measurement are multiplied, the result is expressed in square units and that when three units are multiplied the result is in cubic units.

Checks: Have students make scale drawings of their answers to check that the dimensions are in proportion to each other.

| QUESTIONS | TOOLS | SOLUTIONS | CHECKS |

PROBLEM SOLVING
Choosing a Formula

A formula can help you solve certain kinds of problems.

> Stacy's class is making scale models of famous buildings. The students will place their models on a carpeted rectangular platform 5 feet long and 4 feet wide. How large a carpet is needed for the platform?

To solve the problem, you must choose the correct formula. To choose the correct formula, think about these questions.

- Which geometric figure is described in the problem?
- Which measurements are given in the problem?
- What do you need to solve for?
- In which unit of measurement should the answer be expressed?

The problem describes a rectangle 5 feet long and 4 feet wide. You need to find the area of the rectangle. The area will be expressed in square feet.

Which formula will help you solve this problem?

a. $A = s^2$ **b.** $C = \pi d$ **c.** $A = lw$

Since you are finding the area of a rectangle, $A = lw$ is the formula you would use. After you choose the correct formula, substitute the measurements in the formula. Check to make sure you are using units that are alike, and solve the problem.

$$A = lw$$
$$A = 5 \cdot 4$$
$$A = 20$$

The carpeting must be 20 ft^2.

428

rite the letter of the correct formula.

1. Ralph is making a model of a Greek amphitheater. The radius of the circular stage is $2\frac{1}{4}$ inches. How much flooring is needed for the stage in the model?

  a. $S = r^2 + rl$
  b. $A = \pi r^2$
  c. $A = \frac{1}{2}bh$

2. Lisa is making a model of the Great Pyramid. The base of the pyramid is a square, 6 inches by 6 inches. Each side is a triangle 7 inches high. What is the surface area of the wood Lisa needs to make the model?

  a. $S = \pi r^2 + \pi rl$
  b. $S = s^2 + 4\left(\frac{1}{2}sl\right)$
  c. $A = \frac{1}{2}(b_1 + b_2)h$

veral students are working on a scale model of the ntheon in Rome. For each section of the model, rite the correct formula, and solve.

3. Find the length of side c that forms part of the triangular roof. Side a is 5 inches long, side b is 3 inches long. Angle ACB is a right angle. $a^2 + b^2 = c^2$; 5.831 in.

4. Find the volume of the rectangular porch that measures 10 inches long by 4 inches wide by 6 inches high. $V = lwh$; 240 in.³

5. Find the surface area of the circular column that measures $\frac{1}{2}$ inch in diameter and 6 inches in height. $S = 2\pi rh + 2\pi r^2$; 9.8125 in.²

6. Find the circumference of the base of the dome, the diameter of which is 14 inches. $C = \pi d$; 43.96 in.

7. How large is the light opening in the dome? The opening is a circle that has a 1-inch radius. $A = \pi r^2$; 3.14 in.²

8. Find the volume of the rotunda, a cylindrical space that has a radius of 7 inches and a height of 12 inches. $V = \pi r^2 h$; 1,846.32 in.³

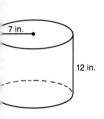
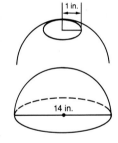
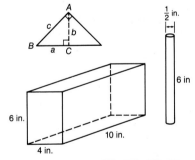

ssework/Homework, page H180

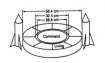

ASSIGNMENT GUIDE

Basic:	1–4
Average:	2–6
Extended:	3–8

Resources
Practice, p. 180 Class/Home, p. H180
Enrich, p. 158

Exercise Analysis

1–2 Choose the correct formula
3–8 Use the correct formula to solve

FOLLOW-UP ACTIVITIES

PROBLEM SOLVING

Write each of the formulas below in one column on the chalkboard. In another column write the information listed next to the formulas. Have students match each formula to its use.

  1. $P = 2l + 2w$ **a.** area of a triangle (8)
  2. $P = 4s$ **b.** Pythagorean rule (3)
  3. $a^2 + b^2 = c^2$ **c.** area of a square (5)
  4. $C = 2\pi r$ **d.** area of a parallelogram (7)
  5. $A = s^2$ **e.** perimeter of a rectangle (1)
  6. $A = lw$ **f.** volume of a cone (17)
  7. $A = bh$ **g.** perimeter of a square (2)
  8. $A = \frac{1}{2}bh$ **h.** area of a rectangle (6)
  9. $A = \frac{1}{2}(b_1 + b_2)h^1$ **i.** surface area of a cylinder (11)
  10. $A = \pi r^2$ **j.** volume of a cube (14)
  11. $S = 2\pi rh + 2\pi r^2$ **k.** circumference of a circle (4)
  12. $S = \pi r^2 + \pi rl$ **l.** area of a trapezoid (9)
  13. $V = lwh$ **m.** volume of a pyramid (15)
  14. $V = e^3$ **n.** surface area of a cone (12)
  15. $V = \frac{1}{3}Bh$ **o.** volume of a cylinder (16)
  16. $V = \pi r^2 h$ **p.** volume of a rectangular prism (13)
  17. $V = \frac{1}{3}\pi r^2 h$ **q.** area of a circle (10)

COMING UP
Fast formulas

11 CALCULATOR/PROJECT

Objective: To use geometric formulas

Warm-Up
Have students use calculators to solve the following exercises.

$3.87 + 42.5 = (46.37)$
$4.26 + 3.52 + 8.11 = (15.89)$
$5.2 + 6.12 + 9.4 + 3.1 = (23.82)$
$2(4.9 + 1.3) = (12.4)$
$2.8^2 + 5.3^2 = (35.93)$

GETTING STARTED

Have students use pencils to draw the following geometric shapes, estimating the lengths given.

rectangle: $l = 4.2$ cm, $w = 2.7$ cm
square: $s = 5$ cm
isosceles triangle: $h = 5.2$ cm, $b = 10.4$ cm
circle: $r = 4$ cm
trapezoid: $b_1 = 5.2$ cm, $b_2 = 6$ cm, $h = 3$ cm
equilateral triangle: $s = 6$ cm
cone: $h = 7$ cm, $r = 4$ cm
cylinder: $h = 8$ cm, $r = 2$ cm
prism: $l = 4.2$ cm, $w = 3$ cm, $h = 2$ cm

TEACHING THE LESSON

Review the geometric formulas with students. Point out that they may need to rewrite a formula to make it easier to compute on calculators. Many calculators have a π key. If there is no such key, explain to students that they can use 3.14 instead.

Some students may have calculators that can square or cube numbers. Have such students practice using these keys to see how they work with other operations keys. Students may have to square or cube numbers before they do other operations.

Point out the benefits of using the fewest keys possible. The calculation takes less time, and there are fewer chances to press an incorrect key. Students should be encouraged to estimate before they perform each operation on their calculators.

NOTE: In Exercises 3–6 the zeros in the answers are not significant digits since the number is a rounded number.

CALCULATOR

A calculator can be very useful when you are working with geometric formulas. Sometimes it is better to rewrite the formula so computation is easier.

Example: Find the perimeter of a rectangle that has a length of 8.2 cm and a width of 4.9 cm.

$P = 2l + 2w = 2 \cdot (l + w)$

Press: [2] [×] [8] [.] [2] [=] [M+] [2] [×] [4] [.] [9] [=] [M+] [RM]

or

Press: [8] [.] [2] [+] [4] [.] [9] [×] [2] [=] The display should show 26.2.

$P = 26.2$ cm

As you can see, the second formula used fewer keys and would work on calculators that do not have a memory. However, on some calculators, you must press " = " after "4.9."

Example: Find the surface area of a sphere with a radius of 5 cm. (Use 3.14 for π.)

$SA = 4\pi r^2$

Press: [4] [×] [3] [.] [1] [4] [×] [5] [×] [5] [=] The display should show 314.

$SA = 314 \text{ cm}^2$

Use a calculator to solve each exercise. Round the answer to the same number of digits as the measurement that is either the *least precise* (Exercises 1–2) or the *least accurate* (Exercises 3–6). See page 197 for the rules on rounding answers.

Find the perimeter.

1. rectangle: $l = 5.3$ in., $w = 2.9$ in. 16.4 in.
2. square: $s = 4.5$ cm 18.0 cm

Find the surface area of each sphere.

3. $r = 6.5$ cm 530 cm^2
4. $r = 12.5$ in. $1{,}960 \text{ in.}^2$

The volume of a sphere equals $\frac{4}{3}\pi r^3$. Find the volume.

5. $r = 7.5$ cm $1{,}800 \text{ cm}^3$
6. $r = 5.9$ in. 860 in.^3

430

GROUP PROJECT

A Graph of the Future

The problem: How much have you thought about your future? Do you have career plans? Do your classmates have career plans? You can find out by taking a survey. Write a questionnaire that asks about career plans. Then make a circle graph to show your findings.

Key Questions

- Do you think that the careers the class members hope to pursue will vary a great deal?

- How will you categorize the career choices for your circle graph?

- Do some of the careers require college training? specialized training?

- Do you think that your class's career choices are similar to those of the other students in your school? your town? the country?

- What conclusions can you draw from looking at the results of your graph?

431

ASSIGNMENT GUIDE

Basic:	p. 430, p. 431
Average:	p. 430, p. 431
Extended:	p. 430, p. 431

Objectives: To write a questionnaire; to take a survey; to make and interpret a circle graph

USING THE PAGE

Have the class form groups of eight to ten. Have the students in each group think about questions to ask in a questionnaire on career plans. Have each person in every group ask a different question of their group and keep a record of the group's responses on a separate sheet of paper. Then have the group members collaborate in collecting the results, writing out the final questionnaire, and making a circle graph based on the survey results. Then have them write the answers to the Key Questions in their notebooks after they have made the circle graphs and discussed their interpretations of the graph within the group.

To extend this activity, each group can poll their members on alternative career paths to pursue if they do not follow their first career choices. Have them plot the second career choice on a circle graph and interpret the alternate careers according to the Key Questions to see if these career categories differ considerably from the first survey results. The survey responses of the entire class to some questions in the first questionnaire also might be collected and graphed.

Purpose: The Chapter Test helps to assess students' understanding of the concepts and skills presented in this chapter.

The chart below is designed to help you review the test items by correlating them with the testing objectives that appear in the Chapter Overview.

Item	Objectives
1–3	A
4–9	B
10–12	C
13–18	E,F
19–21	D
22–25	I
26	G,H

Bonus

The bonus questions may be used for extra credit, or you may want to assign them to students who complete the test before the rest of the class.

Calculator

You may wish to have students use calculators for the problem-solving portions of the test.

Resources

If you prefer to use this Chapter Test as a review exercise, additional testing materials are available in the Teacher's Resource Book.

CHAPTER TEST

Find the perimeter or circumference of each figure. (pages 398–399 and 404–405)

1.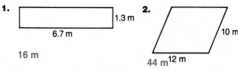
1.3 m
6.7 m
16 m

2.
10 m
44 m 12 m

3.
15 m
94.2 m

Find the area of the figure. Use $\pi = 3.14$. (pages 408–413)

4.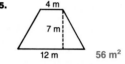
15 cm
7 cm
52.5 cm²

5.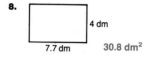
4 m
7 m
12 m
56 m²

6.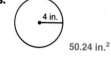
4 in.
50.24 in.²

7.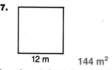
12 m
144 m²

8.
4 dm
7.7 dm
30.8 dm²

9.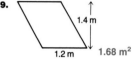
1.4 m
1.2 m
1.68 m²

Use the right triangle ABC to answer Exercises 10–12. (pages 400–401)

10. $b = 4$ cm, $a = 3$ cm, $c = \blacksquare$ cm **5**

11. $b = 15$ m, $a = 36$ m, $c = \blacksquare$ cm **39**

12. $b = 16$ cm, $a = 12$ cm, $c = \blacksquare$ cm **20**

A
c
b
B
a
C

Find the surface area and volume of each figure. Use $3.14 = \pi$. (pages 418–421 and 424–427)

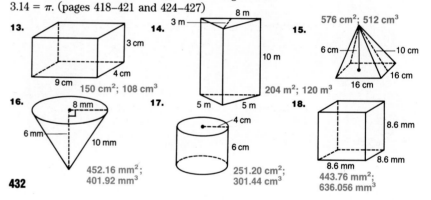

13.
3 cm
4 cm
9 cm
150 cm²; 108 cm³

14.
3 m
8 m
10 m
5 m   5 m
204 m²; 120 m³

15.
576 cm²; 512 cm³
6 cm   10 cm
16 cm

16.
8 mm
6 mm
10 mm
452.16 mm²;
401.92 mm³

17.
4 cm
6 cm
251.20 cm²;
301.44 cm³

18.
8.6 mm
8.6 mm   8.6 mm
443.76 mm²;
636.056 mm³

432

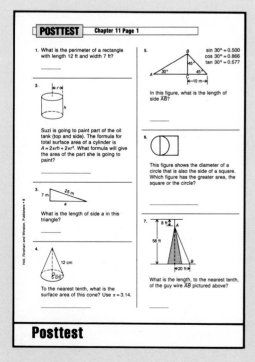
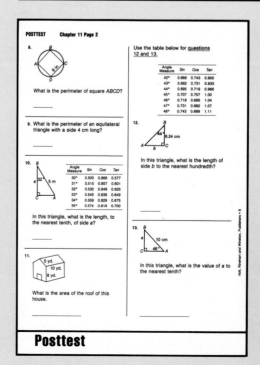
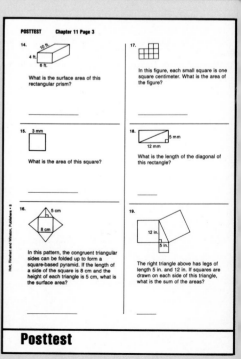

Use the right triangle and the table at the right to solve to the nearest inch. (pages 402–403)

Angle	Sin	Cos	Tan
49°	0.755	0.656	1.15
50°	0.766	0.643	1.19
51°	0.777	0.629	1.23
52°	0.788	0.616	1.28
53°	0.799	0.602	1.33
54°	0.809	0.588	1.38
55°	0.819	0.574	1.43
56°	0.829	0.559	1.48

19. $m\angle B = 49°$, $a = 17$ in., $b = $ ▨ 20 in.

20. $m\angle A = 56°$, $a = 14$ in., $c = $ ▨ 17 in.

21. $m\angle B = 51°$, $c = 4.4$ in., $a = $ ▨ 3 in.

Solve. (pages 422–423, and 428–429)

22. The largest poster made was 311 ft 4 in. long and 141 ft 10 in. wide. What was its area in square inches? **6,358,672 in.²**

23. The largest rope ever made had a radius of 7.48 inches, to the nearest inch. What was its circumference? **47 in.**

24. The tallest load-bearing stone columns measure 69 feet tall. If the base of one column was 5 feet in diameter, what would the surface area of a column be? **1,122.55 ft²**

25. The largest cartoon ever exhibited covered five stories of a university building in 1954. If it was 50 feet by 150 feet, what was its area? **7,500 ft²**

Use the picture to solve. (pages 414–415)

26. Each floor of the building at right is identical. Each side of the building is identical. Find the area of the glass in the building. **8,960 ft²**

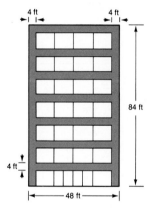

BONUS

Solve.

The largest cherry pie was baked in Charlevoix, Michigan, in 1976. If the pie had a diameter of 14 feet 4 inches and a depth of 24 inches, what was its volume in cubic inches? **557,362.56 in.³**

433

For students who have difficulty with written tests, this test can be given orally.

You may wish to test students, orally or in writing, to see if they can explain the steps used in solving selected items. The following summarizes the procedures for solving key test items.

Ex. 4–9

Finding the area of a two-dimensional figure

To find the area of a rectangle, use the formula $A = lw$.

To find the area of a parallelogram, use the formula $A = bh$.

To find the area of a triangle, use the formula $A = \frac{1}{2}bh$.

To find the area of a trapezoid, use the formula $A = \frac{1}{2}(b_1 + b_2)h$.

To find the area of a circle, use the formula $A = \pi r^2$.

Ex. 13–18

Finding the surface area and volume of solid figures

To find the surface area of a square pyramid, use the formula S = area of base $+ 4$(area of face).

To find the surface area of a cone, use the formula $S = \pi r^2 + \pi rl$, where l = the slant height of the cone.

To find the surface area of a cylinder, use the formula S = lateral area + 2 × area of circular base (the lateral surface area = $2\pi rh$ and the area of the two circular bases = $2\pi r^2$).

To find the volume of a cylinder, use the formula $V = Bh$, or $V = \pi r^2 h$.

To find the volume of a cone, use the formula $V = \frac{1}{3}Bh$, or $V = \frac{1}{3}\pi r^2 h$.

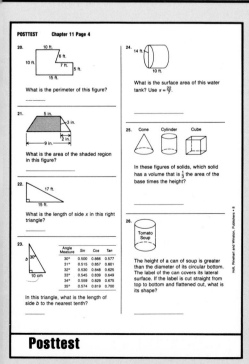

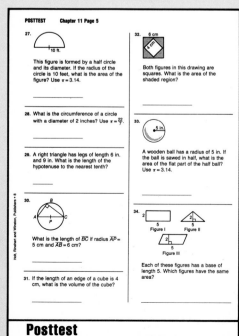

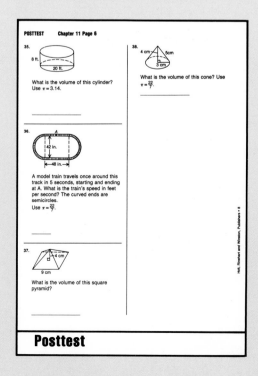

Purpose This Reteaching page provides additional instruction for key concepts in the chapter. It is designed for use by students who have had difficulty with these concepts. It can also be used to provide additional practice for students who require it.

USING THE PAGE

The Pythagorean rule is taught on pages 400–401.

The Pythagorean rule is used to find the lengths of the sides of a right triangle. Emphasize to students that the rule is true only for right triangles. Explain that in the formula $a^2 + b^2 = c^2$, c is the longest side, or the *hypotenuse*—the side opposite the right angle. Watch for students who use the formula only until they find c^2 and present this number as the answer. Have them check their answers by telling them that the sum of the measures of any two sides of a triangle must be greater than the measure of the third side. It may be helpful to list on the chalkboard some whole numbers that satisfy the Pythagorean rule, or sets of "Pythagorean triples" such as 3, 4, 5; 5, 12, 13; 8, 15, 17; 7, 24, 25; 12, 35, 37; or 16, 63, 65. Tell students that any multiples of these sets of triples will also work.

Resources

For other practice and activities related to this chapter, see the Teacher's Resource Book.

RETEACHING

The Pythagorean rule states the relationship among the sides of a right triangle. In a right triangle, if a and b are the legs, and c is the hypotenuse, then $a^2 + b^2 = c^2$.

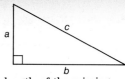

A. To find the length of the hypotenuse, use the formula.

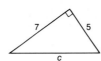

$$a^2 + b^2 = c^2$$
$$5^2 + 7^2 = c^2$$
$$25 + 49 = c^2$$
$$74 = c^2$$
$$8.602 \approx c$$

The hypotenuse is 8.602.

B. To find the length of the missing side, use the formula.

$$a^2 + b^2 = c^2$$
$$5^2 + b^2 = 13^2$$
$$25 + b^2 = 169$$
$$b^2 = 144$$
$$b = 12$$

The missing side is 12.

Find the length of each missing side. Use the tables on pages 82 and 83.

1.

2.
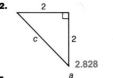

3.
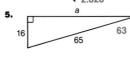

4.

5.
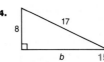

6.
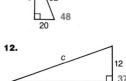

7.

8.

9.

10.

11.

12.
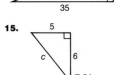

13.

14.

15.

434

ENRICHMENT

Volume of a Sphere

To compute the volume of a basketball or any other sphere, use the formula

$$V = \frac{4}{3}\pi r^3.$$

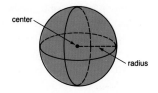

center

radius

Find the volume of a soccer ball that has a 6-inch radius. (Use 3.14 for π.)

$$V = \frac{4}{3}\pi r^3$$

$$V = \frac{4}{3} \cdot 3.14 \cdot 6^3$$

$$V = \frac{4}{3} \cdot 3.14 \cdot 216$$

$$V = 4 \cdot 3.14 \cdot 72$$

$$V = 904.32$$

The volume is 904.32 in.³

Find the volume of each sphere. Use 3.14 for π. Round to the nearest tenth.

1. $r = 9$ in.
3,052.1 in.³

2. $d = 10$ ft
523.3 ft³

3. $d = 24$ m
7,234.6 m³

4. $r = 2$ cm
33.5 cm³

Solve. Use 3.14 for π. Round your answer to the nearest tenth.

5. What is the volume of a beach ball that has a diameter of 2 feet? 4.2 ft³

6. A spherical natural gas tank has a diameter of 32 yards. Find the volume of gas it can contain.
17,148.6 yd³

7. A marble has a diameter of 1.6 cm. Find its volume. 2.1 cm³

8. A hollow rubber ball has an outer diameter of 7 cm. If it has an inner diameter of 6.5 cm, what is the volume of rubber contained in the shell? 35.8 cm³

435

Purpose This Enrichment page provides an additional challenge for those students whose work throughout the chapter and on the Chapter Test shows a thorough understanding of the material. Alternatively, you may wish to use these exercises as a supplementary lesson for the entire class.

USING THE PAGE

Introduce this lesson by telling students that the radius of Earth is about 3.7 times that of the moon, but that the volume of Earth is about 50 times that of the moon. Explain that this is so because the volume of a sphere is proportional to the *cube* of its radius. Thus, if the radius of a sphere is 3.7 times the radius of another, its volume will be 3.7^3 times that of the other ($3.7^3 = 50.653$). If students have difficulty with Exercise 8, explain that the volume of rubber in the ball is equal to the difference between the volume of air in the ball and the volume of the ball itself.

Resources

For additional Enrichment activities, see the Teacher's Resource Book.

Purpose This Cumulative Review page provides an opportunity to reinforce students' understanding of the concepts and skills taught in previous chapters.

The chart below is designed to aid you in reviewing the material by specifying the pages on which various concepts and skills were taught.

Item	Page
1	372–373
2	356–357
3	368–369
4	366–367
5	374–375
6	364–365
7	330–331
8	332–333
9	378–379
10	302–303

Each Cumulative Review gives students an opportunity to practice taking tests that are written in a multiple-choice, standardized format. Be sure that students understand that if the correct answer is not among the first three given, then they should select the fourth choice—"not given"—as the correct answer. At least one item per test will require students to give this response.

CUMULATIVE REVIEW

Write the letter of the correct answer.

1. What kind of line segment is $\overline{CD}$?

a. diameter
(b.) radius
c. chord
d. not given

2. What is the size of the supplement of a 40° angle?

a. 25° b. 50°
(c.) 140° d. not given

3. What kind of polygon is ABCD?

a. square
b. rhombus
(c.) parallelogram
d. not given

4. Classify triangle ABC.

(a.) equilateral
b. scalene
c. right
d. not given

5. Select the congruent triangle.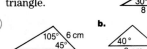

(a.)

b.

c. d. not given

6. Which line segments are perpendicular?

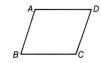

a. $\overline{AB}$ and $\overline{CD}$
(b.) $\overline{AB}$ and $\overline{EF}$
c. $\overline{AB}$ and $\overline{GH}$
d. not given

7. In how many ways could you arrange 5 records on a shelf?

a. 25 b. 60
(c.) 120 d. not given

8. How many combinations could you make from 6 different fruits added to 3 kinds of muffins?

a. 9 b. 20
c. 120 (d.) not given

9. An equilateral triangle has an area of 12 in.². If you bisect each side of the triangle and connect the points, you have another, smaller equilateral triangle. What is the area of this new triangle? Draw a picture to help you solve the problem.

(a.) 3 in.² b. 6 in.²
c. 8 in.² d. not given

10. Dorothy lives in Brooklyn. She has to be in Islip by 1:00 P.M. What is the latest train she can take?

a. 10:23 A.M. (b.) 11:30 A.M.
c. 12:19 P.M. d. not given

Leave			Arrive		
New York	Brooklyn	Jamaica	Bay Shore	Islip	Great River
10:32	10:23	10:51	11:33	11:37	11:41
11:32	11:30	11:51	12:33	12:37	—
12:32	12:19	12:51	1:33	1:37	—
1:32	1:31	1:51	2:33	2:37	2:41
2:40	2:39	3:00	3:47	3:51	3:55
3:23	3:23	3:44	4:33	4:37	

436

EQUATIONS AND INEQUALITIES TWO VARIABLES

SUMMARY

Chapter 12 deals with equations and inequalities in two variables. Included are lessons on solving and graphing equations and inequalities in two variables and recognizing relations and functions from graphs and from sets of ordered pairs.

LESSON SEQUENCE

PROFESSIONAL BACKGROUND

Research with students in the junior-high grades shows that there are large gaps in their skills with graphs. Most can read information from a graph, but few can graph algebraic relationships. In other words, the relationship between an equation and a graph is not a simple matter for the majority of students to understand.

In one study, students between the ages of 13 and 15 were given a problem in which wages appeared as a linear function of hours worked. They were given the equation $w = 2h + 3$, and were asked to compute a few w's for some given h's. Between 40 percent and 50 percent of the students were able to do this. However, only about half of them were able to plot the appropriate points on a graph, and only about half of those students were able to draw the graph of $w = 2h + 3$. Because this was a group which had been fairly successful earlier in the plotting of given points on a graph, it seems reasonable to conclude that the difficulty lies in the algebraic relationship and not in the graphing.

Many students find it difficult to follow the relationship of one variable to another. For these students, provide as much visual support as possible, such as making charts to illustrate how one variable changes as another does.

References: See Driscoll (secondary volume, algebra chapter); Hart; Carpenter et al.; and Rosnick, Peter. 1981. "Some Misconceptions About the Concept of Variable." *The Mathematics Teacher*, 74: 418–420.

MATERIALS

pan balances
scissors
paper clips
calculators
acetate sheet
globe
computer
graph paper
checkerboards and checkers

VOCABULARY

equations in two variables (p. 438)
ordered pair (p. 440)
relations and functions (p. 444)
real number plane (p. 446)
origin (p. 446)
x-axis (p. 446)
y-axis (p. 446)
system of equations (p. 452)
inequalities in two variables (p. 454)

ABOUT THE CHAPTER

This is the fourth chapter in the text to focus on algebra. In fact, most of the work covered in the chapter is an important part of any high school Algebra I course. Students who complete this chapter successfully will certainly be ready for high school algebra next year and may be ready for an accelerated section of the class.

In Chapter 12, students learn to solve equations in two variables by making tables of solutions. Students learn about relations and functions and learn how to graph equations in the real-number plane. Students then learn to graph pairs of equations in two variables. Finally, students learn about inequalities in two variables and about graphing these inequalities in the real-number plane.

It is important that students understand that equations in two variables often have many solutions. Give students ample opportunity to form tables of *x* and *y* values before asking them to solve equations directly.

The function is a fundamental building block of mathematics. A function need not be described by a rule, but it often is. Based upon the definition of a function, give students an opportunity to identify sets of ordered pairs as a function or not a function. Then have students find ordered pairs from a rule and finally identify the rule(s) from sets of ordered pairs.

Even after they grasp this rule, students will have difficulty deciding which portion of the real-number plane to shade. Have students substitute *x* and *y* values from the portion they have chosen in the inequality. If they have chosen correctly, the resulting inequality will be true.

Problem-solving lessons in the chapter show students how to draw pictures and use ordered pairs to solve nonroutine problems and give students an opportunity to choose strategies and methods for solving problems.

The problem-solving project actively involves students in setting up a marathon, including planning the marathon course in and around the area where they live. The project gives students an opportunity to apply problem-solving and other mathematical concepts and skills.

The Enrichment lesson teaches students about graphing parallel lines. The lesson builds carefully on concepts developed in the chapter and gives students more opportunities to work with equations.

USING THE CHAPTER OPENER

Each Chapter Opener presents situational problem-solving activities that can be used to explore the skills taught throughout the chapter. The work sheets can be used by individuals, small groups, or the whole class, depending on the needs of the class. The Chapter Opener focuses on a nonalgorithmic approach to mathematics through real-life situations relevant to the children's experiences. Through an interdisciplinary approach, the Chapter Opener helps children explore the relationships between mathematics, other areas of the curriculum, and everyday life while developing different strands of mathematics.

In the Chapter Opener activities, students will study the use of topographic maps. Students will also learn to use a coordinate grid to enlarge or reduce a map.

PROBLEM SOLVING

Elaborate word problems that involve directions are more easily understood after making a diagram. Some students will have difficulty converting the written facts of a problem into an adequate diagram. The lesson Making a Diagram employs a very direct approach. The problem is reviewed for the important facts which are then expressed as a diagram. Students then use the diagram to solve the problem. This chapter includes two lessons on choosing and using strategies and methods for problem solving. Once students choose a plan of action, they must apply it correctly to solve the problem. Because more than one strategy can often be employed for each problem, the Choosing a Strategy or Method lessons are ideal for work in small groups in which students can brainstorm and share ideas to keep each other from getting stuck.

BULLETIN BOARD

"Mapping"

Materials: paper to cover bulletin board; lettering; construction paper; felt-tip pen; string; push pins; 2 envelopes; index cards

Preparation: Cover bulletin board with paper and attach the title. Draw a pair of coordinate axes in the center of the board. Label all points along each axis clearly. From construction paper, cut a pair of airplanes to serve as markers. Use string and push pins to attach them to the right of the *x*-axis. On index cards, write equations with two variables, one per card. Put the answers on the back of each card and place them in the envelope labeled *Single Flights.* Attach it at the bottom of the board as shown. Each equation shows the flight path of an airplane. Write two equations with two variables on each of several additional cards, put the answers on the back of each card, and place them in the envelope labeled *Twin Flights.* Attach this envelope at the opposite side of the board. These equations show the intersecting flight paths of two airplanes.

After pp. 450-451: Have students select cards from the first envelope and find solutions for the equations with two variables. Tell them to use the solutions to plot the plane's flight path with the string and push pins.

COMMON ERRORS

There are several errors students might make when solving equations in two variables. When given a replacement set (*a,b,c*) for *x*, students might solve the equation for those values, but then neglect to write the answer in ordered pairs, and instead, give the answer as a set of values (*d,e,f*).

To remediate this error, explain to students that the equation is correct only for a certain *x* and a certain *y*. In other words, the specific values of *x* and *y* which make the equation true must be given together in ordered pairs (*x,y*) for the answer to make sense to others.

Another mistake students might make is when given a value for *x*, they might find the correct ordered pair (*x,y*) that solves the equation, but when given a value for *y*; students might write the ordered pair incorrectly as (*y,x*), since *y* was known first.

To remediate this error, explain to students that in each instance, regardless of which value is supplied, *x* comes first and *y* comes second in an ordered pair. Explain that this standard ordering is necessary for ordered pairs to be understood by others.

SPECIAL NEEDS

Equations that have one variable (3*x* = 12) have only one solution, whereas an equation that has two variables (*x* + *y* = 12) may have an infinite number of solutions. This concept will be difficult for some students. A thorough review of inverse properties, solving equations with one variable, and maintaining "balance" in equations is necessary prior to solving equations that have two variables.

Begin with discussion of and practice with ordered pairs. Stress that the *x* variable is always written first in the ordered pair; therefore, (4,2) means *x* = 4, *y* = 2. Have students practice plotting ordered pairs by using a grid numbered 0 to 6 on both the *x* and the *y* axes and number cubes to determine the coordinates.

When solving equations that have two variables, encourage students to assign values to *x* or *y*, solve the equation for the unknown variable, and list the ordered pairs that they have found to be the solutions. Graphing the solutions may be easier for students than computing the solutions because the graph provides a visual stimulus. Encourage them to graph all solutions to find whether or not they make sense.

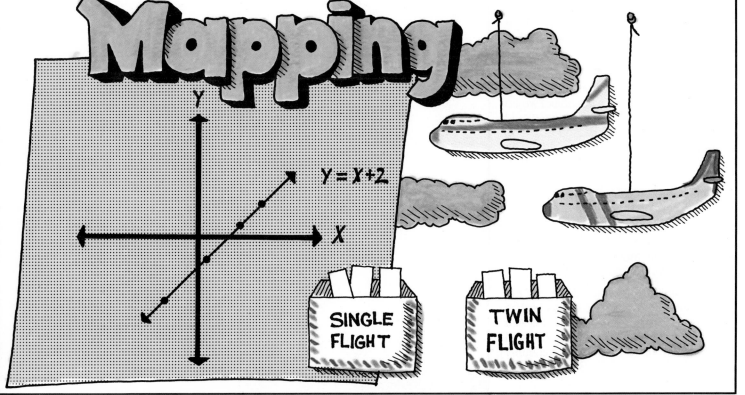

MATH LABS

COMPUTER

Have students write a program that will determine whether a given relation is a function.

```
10 LET X = 1
20 INPUT "ORDERED PAIR ((−99,
   −99) IF NO MORE)"; A(X), B(X)
30 IF A(X) = −99 THEN 60
40 LET X = X + 1
50 GOTO 20
60 FOR G = 1 TO X − 1
70 FOR H = 1 TO X − 1
80 IF A(G) = A(H) THEN 130
90 NEXT H
100 NEXT G
110 PRINT "THE RELATION IS A
    FUNCTION."
120 GOTO 150
130 IF B(G) = B(H) THEN 90
140 PRINT "THE RELATION IS
    NOT A FUNCTION"
150 END
```

MATH CONNECTION
(Science)

Explain that in physics, a location in space can be represented by an equation in two variables, where x is time and y is location. For example, $y = 3$ represents a stationary object at point A on the number line below.

We know that the object is stationary because time (x) is not a factor in the equation. No matter how time changes, the location of the object is always 3.

The equation $y = x + 3$, however, represents a moving object that began moving at A. At $x = 0$, the object would be at A, but at $x = 1$, the object would have moved to point B. And at $x = 2$, the object would have moved on to point C. The rate is the coefficient of x, which in this example is 1 unit/unit of time. If the equation were $y = 2x + 3$, the velocity would be twice as fast, or 2 units/unit of time.

Have students write an equation to describe the motion, and then solve the equation to find each location.

Stan begins his bike ride at school which is 8 miles from his house and he rides directly homeward. He rides at a constant 18 mph. How far is he from home after he's ridden for 25 minutes? ($y = 0.3x − 8 = ^−0.5$; Stan is half a mile from home.)

CALCULATOR

When investigating equations and inequalities in two variables, the calculator can be used to evaluate equations and inequalities for particular values of the variables. This approach helps students understand the relationship between the variables and the process of evaluating equations. This is an important step in understanding the concept of function.

Students should have calculators available for all problem-solving activities.

Additional Activities: **Drill and Practice:** Given the equation $AX + BY + C = 0$, $Y = (−C − AX)/B$, write the calculator code for $A = 3$, $B = 7$, $C = 2$. Find Y for $X = 3, 6, 7, 10$.

Exploration: Given two linear equations $AX + BY = C$ and $DX + EY = F$, write a calculator code to solve the system for given constants A, B, C, D, E, F.

SUBJECT AREA CONNECTIONS

These Subject Area Connections are useful for reinforcing the concepts presented in this chapter.

p. 447-Library Skills: Students research latitude, longitude, prime meridian, equator, and Mercator projection, and relate each to a real number plane. They then locate a list of latitudinal and longitudinal coordinates on a globe.

Here are some other activities for presenting these concepts.
- **LANGUAGE ARTS:** Have students make a crossword puzzle comprised of the vocabulary terms presented in this chapter.
- **SCIENCE:** Have students research the use of real number planes in radar facilities.
- **SOCIAL STUDIES:** Have students locate each student's birthday on a graph by assigning the number of the month as the value for x and assigning the day as the value of y. Have students tell if this graph is a function.

PLAN AHEAD

You will need to prepare a handout for the activity on T.E. p. 445.

PLANNING CALENDAR

Pages	Lesson Objectives	ASSIGNMENT GUIDE			Class/Home	More Practice	Math Reasoning	Follow-up	Reteach	Practice	Enrich
		Basic	Average	Extended							
437	Chapter Opener (Use MMW 23,24)	437	437	437							
438,439	To solve equations in two variables using a replacement set	1-12,13-31o	1-23o,25-37, Chlg	13-37,Chlg	H181			PS MC	126	181	159
440,441	To solve equations in two variables using a table of values	1-9,10-26e, 28-29,AL	1-9,11-27o, 28-31,AL	10-31,AL	H182	H206	H229	CALC PS	127	182	160
442,443	To draw a diagram to solve problems	1-5	1-2, 3-7o	1-7o	H183 H184			PS CALC		183-184	
444,445	To define a relation and a function	1-16,22	3-18,22	7-22,Chlg	H185	H206		PS	128	185	161
446,447	To define the real-number plane	1-18,27-30,MCR	1-9o,11-30,MCR	2-10e,11-30,MCR	H186		H229	MC CMP	129	186	162
448,449	To practice choosing and using methods and strategies for solving problems	1-11,16	1-13,16	1-16	H187 H188					187-188	
450,451	To graph a linear equation	1-12,25-27,31-33	1-21o,25-27,31-33	13-33	H189		H229	MNP PS CMP	130	189	163
452,453	To solve a system of equations by graphing	1-18,AL	7-24,AL	11-28,AL	H190		H230	PS P&G	131	190	164
454,455	To solve inequalities in two variables	1-16,NS1-6	5-16,NS1-6	5-16,NS	H191		H230	NS	132	191	165
456,457	To graph inequalities in two variables	1-18,25-26,Chlg1	7-21,25-28, Chlg1-2	13-24,25-30,Chlg	H192		H230	P&G	133	192	166
458,459	To practice choosing and using methods and strategies for solving problems	1-8,13	2-12e,13	1-13o	H193 H194					193-194	
460	Logical Reasoning: to use *all, some,* and *none* to determine the implications of a set of statements	460	460	460							
461	Group Project: To plan the route for a race; to draw a map to scale	461	461	461							

462,463	Chapter Test
464	Reteaching
465	Enrichment
466,467	Technology
468	Cumulative Review

ABBREVIATION KEY

Teacher's Resource Book	*Follow-up Activities*	MC—Math Connection
MMW—Making Math Work	CALC—Calculator	MCM—Math Communication
P—Practice	CMP—Computer	NS—Number Sense
R—Reteach	P&G—Puzzles and Games	PS—Problem Solving
E—Enrich	MNP—Manipulatives	RFM—Reinforcement

TESTS

A. To write, solve, or then graph the solutions of equations in two variables

B. To graph a pair of equations

C. To write, solve, or then graph the solutions of inequalities in two variables

D. To draw a diagram to solve a problem

FAMILY INVOLVEMENT

Family Involvement for Chapter 12 encourages family members to create figures by graphing a group of equations and inequalities on the same graph. They are given a list of inequalities and shown the pattern that results from graphing inequalities. Family members are then to create simple shapes by graphing several inequalities of their own formulation. As they begin to see the patterns that develop from graphing different equations and inequalities, they are asked to challenge one another to graph even more complex figures.

Additional activities might include finding a map of the city or town so that family members can examine how it has been laid out. Have each member take a piece of graph paper and graph on a coordinate system the locations of the major landmarks in their city or town. Students should bring their graphs to school and compare them.

STUDENT RESOURCES

Bibliography

Carey, Helen H. *How to Use Maps and Globes.* New York: Franklin Watts, 1983.

Daniel, Becky. *Math Thinkercises.* Carthage, IL: Good Apple, Inc., 1988.

Wells, David. *Can You Solve These? Mathematical Problems to Test Your Thinking Powers.* New York: Parkwest Publications, Inc., 1985.

Films

Graphing Inequalities. 9 minutes. Color. 1970. Distributed by Silver Burdett, Summit, N.J.

Possibly So, Pythagoras. 14 minutes. Color. 1963. Distributed by International Film Bureau, Inc., Chicago, Ill.

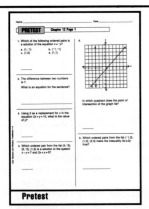

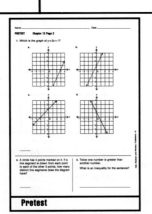

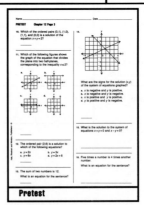

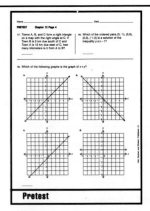

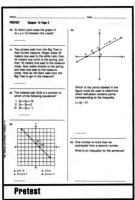

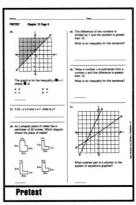

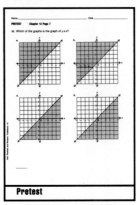

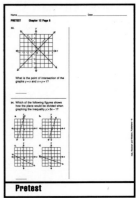

Suppose you wanted to send someone a three-dimensional picture of your geographic area. How would you show distance? How would you show elevation?

12 EQUATIONS AND INEQUALITIES
Two Variables

Objective: To explore problems related to topographic maps

Direct students to look at the topographic map. Tell them that topographic maps are used to show elevation. Each ring on the map connects points of the same elevation. Maps are usually graded in intervals of 50 feet. Such maps are often used by engineers for planning purposes. Topographic maps are also helpful in studying things such as flooding patterns and in planning storm sewers and drains.

INDIVIDUAL
Patterns and Functions
Materials: Making Math Work page 23 per student

Have each student complete Making Math Work page 23. Discuss clues from which the answers to the questions can be found. Be sure students realize the importance of knowing the slope of an area on the map. Ask them how the direction of the river can be found. (It flows from high ground in the northwest to low ground in the southeast.)

SMALL GROUP
Measurement
Materials: Making Math Work page 24 per student

Form the class into groups of three. Have one student sketch on the grid at the top of the page the neighborhood around his or her home. Then have one of the other students reduce the size of the map by copying it onto the smaller grid and another student enlarge the map by copying it onto a larger grid. Explain that grids are often used for enlarging or reducing the size of maps. Suggest that students come up with an approximate scale for each map.

WHOLE CLASS
Logic
Materials: ruler, chalk

With the assistance of the entire class, sketch a topographic map of the area immediately around your school building. First choose a scale for your map, and then decide how large an area you will draw. Plot out the location of buildings and landmarks that you will show on the map. Start with a point on the map as sea level or zero, and work from there to figure out approximate elevations. If students wish, they can try to find a topographic map of the area from the town engineer or from the Army Corps of Engineers and compare it to the map they have drawn.

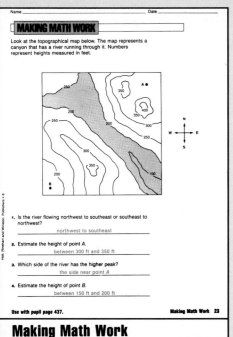

Name _____ Date _____

MAKING MATH WORK

Look at the topographical map below. The map represents a canyon that has a river running through it. Numbers represent heights measured in feet.

1. Is the river flowing northwest to southeast or southeast to northwest?
   northwest to southeast

2. Estimate the height of point A.
   between 300 ft and 350 ft

3. Which side of the river has the higher peak?
   the side near point A

4. Estimate the height of point B.
   between 150 ft and 200 ft

Use with pupil page 437.   Making Math Work **23**

Making Math Work

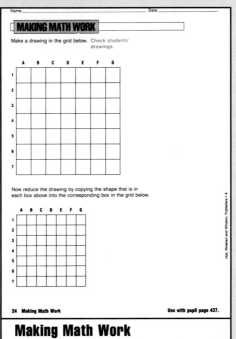

Name _____ Date _____

MAKING MATH WORK

Make a drawing in the grid below. Check students' drawings.

Now reduce the drawing by copying the shape that is in each box above into the corresponding box in the grid below.

24 Making Math Work   Use with pupil page 437.

Making Math Work

Objective: To use a replacement set to solve equations containing two variables

Warm-Up
Have students evaluate each expression for the value indicated.

$3.7h - 0.096$, if $h = 0.08$ (0.2)

$p^2 - \frac{1}{9}$, if $p = \frac{2}{3}$ $\left(\frac{1}{3}\right)$

$\frac{(y-1)}{y^2}$, if $y = 1\frac{1}{2}$ $\left(\frac{2}{9}\right)$

$\frac{2}{k} - k^3$, if $k = 2$ ($^-7$)

GETTING STARTED

Materials: balance, paper, scissors, paper clips per pair of students

Have students work in pairs. Have student A look away while student B writes a simple addition equation such as $4 + 2 = 6$ and makes a pile of paper clips for each number. Student B should then cut out four pieces of paper of equal size. He or she should wrap in paper each set of paper clips that represents an addend and mark one packet x and the other y. Then he or she should place them on the left pan of the balance and place on the right pan the other two pieces of paper and the loose paper clips that represent the sum. Student A must remove either x or y from the left pan and then remove the loose paper clips from the right pan until the balance becomes level. Student A should write the estimated values of both x and y and then unwrap x and y to verify the values.

TEACHING THE LESSON

A. Guide students in completing examples such as those shown below when given a value for one variable. Have them first find y given x and then find x given y. Pay particular attention to writing the solution as an ordered pair.
- $y = 2x + 4$
- $2y - x = 7$

B. Extend the lesson by pointing out that substituting z for 8 in $x + y = 8$ would form an equation in three variables. Ask: How many elements would there be in a solution set for an equation in three variables? for an equation in six variables? (three, six) Then ask whether 1, 2, $^-1$ is a solution for $x - y = z$. (yes)

You might wish to allow students to use calculators to work through this lesson.

Equations in Two Variables

A. Equations such as $3x = y$, $x + y = 8$, and $\frac{y}{x} = 3$ are examples of equations in two variables.

$3x = y$ means one number is 3 times another number.
$x + y = 8$ means the sum of two numbers is 8.
$\frac{y}{x} = 3$ means one number divided by another is 3.

To solve an equation in two variables, choose a replacement value for one variable and then find the value of the other variable that gives a true statement. An equation in two variables usually has many solutions.

Find solutions for $y = 3x$ by using $^-1$, 0, and 2 as replacement values for x. Here are some examples.

If $x = ^-1$,	If $x = 0$,	If $x = 2$,
$y = 3 \cdot ^-1$	$y = 3 \cdot 0$	$y = 3 \cdot 2$
$y = ^-3$	$y = 0$	$y = 6$

A solution is $(^-1, ^-3)$.　　A solution is $(0,0)$.　　A solution is $(2,6)$.

The solutions are usually written as ordered pairs, (x, y). The first number represents the x-value; the second number represents the y-value.

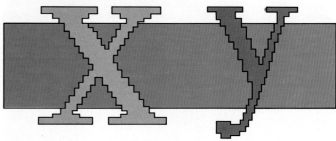

B. You can test an ordered pair in a given equation to determine whether it is a solution to the equation.

Is $(2,6)$ a solution for $\frac{y}{x} = 3$?　　　Is $(^-2,3)$ a solution for $x - 2y = 6$?

Replace y with 6. $\longrightarrow \frac{6}{2} \overset{?}{=} 3$　　Replace x with $^-2$. $\longrightarrow$ $^-2 - 2(3) \overset{?}{=} 6$

Replace x with 2. $\nearrow$ $3 = 3$　　　　Replace y with 3. $\longrightarrow$ $^-8 \neq 6$

So, $(2,6)$ is a solution for $\frac{y}{x} = 3$.　　So, $(^-2,3)$ is *not* a solution for $x - 2y = 6$.

438

COMMON ERRORS

Some students might have difficulty correctly substituting ordered pairs in an equation.

Remediation
For this error, have students match each coordinate alphabetically with its corresponding variable before substituting it into an equation.

$(3,2) \quad\quad 4y + x = 11$

Assign Reteach Master, p. 126.

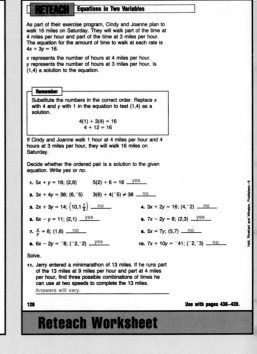

Reteach Worksheet

To solve each equation, use 3 as the replacement value for x. Write each solution as an ordered pair.

1. $x + y = 7$ (3,4)

2. $x - y = 3$ (3,0)

3. $2x + y = 7$ (3,1)

4. $x + y = 12$ (3,9)

5. $x - 2y = 11$ (3,⁻4)

6. $5x - y = 4$ (3,11)

7. $3x + 2y = 13$ (3,2)

8. $x + y = 0$ (3,⁻3)

9. $x - y = 0$ (3,3)

10. $2x - y = 7$ (3,⁻1)

11. $5x + y = 17$ (3,2)

12. $x + 4y = 14$ $\left(3,2\frac{3}{4}\right)$

Use ⁻1, 0, and 2 as replacements for x. Write the solutions for each equation as ordered pairs.

13. $x + y = 4$ (⁻1,5), (0,4), (2,2)

14. $2x + y = 13$ (⁻1,15), (0,13), (2,9)

15. $y - x = 8$ (⁻1,7), (0,8), (2,10)

16. $2y - x = 0$ $\left(-1,-\frac{1}{2}\right)$, (0,0), (2,1)

17. $3x + 2y = 6$ $\left(-1,4\frac{1}{2}\right)$, (0,3), (2,0)

18. $3x - 2y = 6$ $\left(-1,-4\frac{1}{2}\right)$, (0,⁻3), (2,0)

19. $4x + 2y = 8$ (⁻1,6), (0,4), (2,0)

20. $4x - 2y = 8$ (⁻1,⁻6), (0,⁻4), (2,0)

21. $5x - y = 4$ (⁻1,⁻9), (0,⁻4), (2,6)

22. $7x - 3y = 6$ $\left(-1,-4\frac{1}{3}\right)$, (0,⁻2), $\left(2,2\frac{2}{3}\right)$

23. $x + 3y = 9$ $\left(-1,3\frac{1}{3}\right)$, (0,3), $\left(2,2\frac{1}{3}\right)$

24. $2x + 2y = 5$ $\left(-1,3\frac{1}{2}\right)$, $\left(0,2\frac{1}{2}\right)$, $\left(2,\frac{1}{2}\right)$

Decide whether the ordered pair is a solution of $5x + y = 12$. Write *yes* or *no*.

25. (2,2)   yes

26. (7,1)   no

27. (12,0)   no

28. (1,7)   yes

29. (0,12)   yes

30. (3,⁻3)   yes

31. (⁻3,3)   no

32. (4,⁻8)   yes

Write the letter of the equation next to its meaning.

33. The sum of two numbers is 10.   d

34. The difference between two numbers is 6.   c

35. 6 times a number is 3 times another number.   a

36. 2 times a number divided by another number is 12.   e

37. $\frac{1}{4}$ of a number plus 4 times another number is 12.   b

a. $6x = 3y$

b. $\frac{1}{4}x + 4y = 12$

c. $x - y = 6$

d. $x + y = 10$

e. $\frac{2x}{y} = 12$

CHALLENGE   Patterns, Relations, and Functions

If x = the length of one side of a regular polygon, and y = the perimeter of that polygon, which polygon is represented by each of the following equations?

1. $y = 3x$
equilateral triangle

2. $y = 4x$
square

3. $y = 5x$
regular pentagon

4. $y = 6x$
regular hexagon

Classwork/Homework, page H181

439

Exercise Analysis

1–12   Solve, using a one-element replacement set

13–24   Solve, using a three-element replacement set

25–32   Test a given ordered pair

33–37   Match an equation with its description

Challenge

If students encounter difficulty, suggest that they rewrite each equation as a sum. For example, if they rewrite $y = 3x$ as $y = x + x + x$, they can see that the polygon has three sides.

FOLLOW-UP ACTIVITIES

PROBLEM SOLVING

Remind students that the Pythagorean rule states that for any right triangle whose hypotenuse is length c and whose legs are lengths a and b, $a^2 + b^2 = c^2$.

Have students determine which of the following ordered pairs represent possible legs of a right triangle whose hypotenuse length is 5.

5, 1 (no)   4, 3 (yes)
0, 5 (no)   3, 2 (no)

MATH CONNECTION (Consumer)

Tell students that every stereo at Stereo City can be bought on installment after making a down payment of any amount but that the balance plus 18% of that balance must then be paid in 12 monthly payments. Then have them write an equation to represent the payment plan that would be applied to a stereo listing for $540 if p = the final price and d = the down payment. ($p = d + 1.18$ $(540 - d)$)

COMING UP
Free to choose!

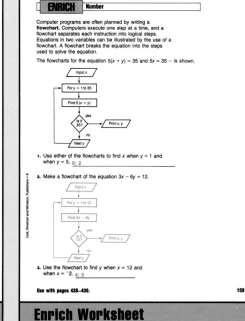

Practice Worksheet

Enrich Worksheet

Objective: To use a table of values to solve equations containing two variables

Warm-Up
Have students use ⁻3 as a replacement value for x to solve each equation.

$y + 3x = 1.8$	$(^-3, 10.8)$
$2x^2 - y = 19$	$(^-3, ^-1)$
$4\frac{y}{x} = ^-4$	$(^-3, 3)$
$x + 6y = \frac{2}{3}$	$\left(^-3, \frac{11}{18}\right)$

GETTING STARTED

Write the equation $x + y = 6$ on the chalkboard. Ask students to use integers, fractions, and rational numbers as replacement values to provide solutions. Then ask how many solutions can be used to solve the equation. (an infinite number) Finally, ask how the solutions might best be displayed. (in table form)

TEACHING THE LESSON

A. Extend the lesson by having students use fractions as replacement values to find additional solutions.
- $\frac{1}{3}$ $\left(y = 6\frac{2}{3}\right)$
- $4\frac{5}{6}$ $\left(y = 2\frac{1}{6}\right)$
- $^-\frac{7}{12}$ $\left(y = 7\frac{7}{12}\right)$

B. Extend the lesson by having students use decimals as replacement values to find additional solutions.
- 0.34 $(y = 4.32)$
- 5.2 $(y = ^-5.4)$
- ⁻1.93 $(y = 8.86)$

You might wish to allow students to use calculators to work through this lesson.

Checkpoint
The chart lists the common errors students make when solving equations containing two variables.

Correct Answers: 1c, 2b

Remediation
■ For these errors, have students rewrite the coefficients to highlight the multiplication. (e.g., $(2 \cdot x) + y = 4$)

☐ For these errors, assign Reteach Master, p. 127.

△ For this error, refer students to the examples on p. 438.

Solving Equations in Two Variables

A. Equations in two variables can be solved if you make a table of values. Choose values for x, and solve the equation for the values of y.

Solve $y = 7 - x$.

x	$y = 7 - x$	y
⁻1	$y = 7 - (^-1)$	8
0	$y = 7 - 0$	7
1	$y = 7 - 1$	6
2	$y = 7 - 2$	5

The ordered pairs $(^-1,8)$, $(0,7)$, $(1,6)$, and $(2,5)$ are solutions to the equation. More solutions are possible.

B. Solve $2x + y = 5$.

x	$2x + y = 5$	y
⁻2	$2(^-2) + y = 5$	9
0	$2(0) + y = 5$	5
2	$2(2) + y = 5$	1
4	$2(4) + y = 5$	⁻3

The ordered pairs $(^-2,9)$, $(0,5)$, and $(2,1)$, and $(4,^-3)$ are four solutions to the equation.

Checkpoint Write the letter of the correct answer.

1. A solution for $y = 4x - 3$ is $x = 1$, $y = $ ■.

   a. 2   b. 7

   ⓒ 1   d. 12

2. A solution for $2x + y = 4$ is the ordered pair ■.

   a. $(4,0)$ ⓑ $(1,2)$

   c. $(2,1)$ d. $(^-2,6)$

Math Reasoning, page H229

COMMON ERRORS

Answer Choice	Type of Error
■ 1a	Adds instead of multiplies
☐ 1b	Adds instead of subtracts
☐ 1d	Multiplies instead of subtracts
■ 2a, 2d	Ignores the coefficient
△ 2c	Transposes the coordinates

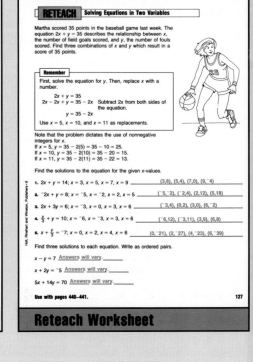

RETEACH Solving Equations in Two Variables

Martha scored 35 points in the baseball game last week. The equation $2x + y = 35$ describes the relationship between x, the number of field goals scored, and y, the number of fouls scored. Find three combinations of x and y which result in a score of 35 points.

Remember
First, solve the equation for y. Then, replace x with a number.

$2x + y = 35$
$2x - 2x + y = 35 - 2x$ Subtract 2x from both sides of the equation.
$y = 35 - 2x$

Use $x = 5$, $x = 10$, and $x = 11$ as replacements.

Note that the problem dictates the use of nonnegative integers for x.
If $x = 5$, $y = 35 - 2(5) = 35 - 10 = 25$.
If $x = 10$, $y = 35 - 2(10) = 35 - 20 = 15$.
If $x = 11$, $y = 35 - 2(11) = 35 - 22 = 13$.

Find the solutions to the equation for the given x-values.

1. $2x + y = 14$; $x = 3$, $x = 5$, $x = 7$, $x = 9$ ___ (3,8), (5,4), (7,0), (9,⁻4)

2. $^-2x + y = 8$; $x = ^-5$, $x = ^-2$, $x = 2$, $x = 5$ ___ (⁻5,⁻2), (⁻2,4), (2,12), (5,18)

3. $2x + 3y = 6$; $x = ^-3$, $x = 0$, $x = 3$, $x = 6$ ___ (⁻3,4), (0,2), (3,0), (6,⁻2)

4. $\frac{x}{3} + y = 10$; $x = ^-6$, $x = ^-3$, $x = 3$, $x = 6$ ___ (⁻6,12), (⁻3,11), (3,9), (6,8)

5. $x + \frac{y}{3} = ^-7$; $x = 0$, $x = 2$, $x = 4$, $x = 6$ ___ (0,⁻21), (2,⁻27), (4,⁻23), (6,⁻39)

Find three solutions to each equation. Write as ordered pairs.

$x - y = 7$ Answers will vary.

$x + 2y = ^-5$ Answers will vary.

$5x + 14y = 70$ Answers will vary.

Use with pages 440–441.   127

Reteach Worksheet

Solve for y using $^-1$ and 2 as replacements for x.

1. $y = x - 4$
$y = ^-5; ^-2$

2. $y = 3 - x$
$y = 4; 1$

3. $y = 2x + 5$
$y = 3; 9$

4. $3x - y = 5$
$y = ^-8; 1$

5. $5x + y = 4$
$y = 9; ^-6$

6. $^-2x + y = 9$
$y = 7; 13$

7. $3x - 2y = 10$
$y = ^-6\frac{1}{2}; ^-2$

8. $5x - y = 20$
$y = ^-25; ^-10$

9. $2x + 5y = 10$
$y = 2\frac{2}{5}; 1\frac{1}{5}$

Make a table of values for each equation. Use $^-1, 0, 1,$ and 2 as the replacement values for x. Check students' tables. See Answer Key.

10. $y = 3x$

11. $y = 3x + 2$

12. $y = 3x - 2$

13. $y = ^-x$

14. $y = 2x - 3$

15. $y = 2 - 3x$

16. $y = 2x + 1$

17. $^-2x + y = ^-1$

18. $3x - 2y = 7$

Find three solutions for each equation. Write as ordered pairs. Other solutions are possible. $(0,2), \left(1, 1\frac{1}{3}\right), \left(2, \frac{2}{3}\right)$

19. $y - x = 10$
$(0,10), (1,11), (2,12)$

20. $x + y = 8$
$(0,8), (1,7), (2,6)$

21. $2x + 3y = 6$

22. $3x + y = 9$
$(0,9), (1,6), (2,3)$

23. $3x - y = 6$
$(0,^-6), (1,^-3), (2,0)$

24. $2x + y = 12$
$(0,12), (1,10), (2,8)$

25. $x - 3y = 6$
$\left(0,^-2\right), \left(1,^-1\frac{2}{3}\right), \left(2,^-1\frac{1}{3}\right)$

26. $3y = x + 1$
$\left(0,\frac{1}{3}\right), \left(1,\frac{2}{3}\right), (2,1)$

27. $y + 3 = 4x$
$(0,^-3), (1,1), (2,5)$

For each equation, write the ordered pair that is *not* a solution.

28. $x = 8y$ $(0,0), (1,1), (8,1), \left(4,\frac{1}{2}\right)$ $(1,1)$

29. $3y + x = 15$ $(0,5), (15,0), (0,15), (9,2)$ $(0,15)$

30. $x + 2y = 7$ $(0,7), (7,0), \left(\frac{1}{2},3\frac{1}{4}\right), \left(0,3\frac{1}{2}\right)$ $(0,7)$

31. $4x - 3y = ^-12$ $(0,4), \left(^-4,^-1\frac{1}{3}\right), (^-3,0), \left(^-4\frac{1}{2},2\right)$ $\left(^-4\frac{1}{2},2\right)$

ANOTHER LOOK

Write and solve an equation for each.

1. The Beatles have sold 1,004 million records and tapes, which is 46 million less than 5 times the number ABBA has sold. How many records and tapes has ABBA sold?
$5a - 46 = 1,004$
$a = 210$
210 million records and tapes

2. In 1976, 80-year-old George Burns became the oldest Academy Award winner. The youngest winner, Shirley Temple, won her Academy Award in 1934 when she was 2 years less than $\frac{1}{10}$ of George's age. How old was Shirley when she won her Academy Award?
$s = \frac{1}{10}(80) - 2$
$s = 6$ More Practice, page H206
6 years old

Classwork/Homework, page H182

441

Exercise Analysis

1–9   Solve, using a two-element replacement set
10–18 Make a table of values, using a four-element replacement set
19–27 Find three solutions for an equation
28–31 Identify the ordered pair that is not a solution

Another Look
This review provides maintenance for writing and solving equations from word problems.

FOLLOW-UP ACTIVITIES

CALCULATOR
Have students use calculators to solve each equation for y, given the replacement value for x.
- $5y - x = 2.4; x = 2.6$ ($y = 1$)
- $2(x + 3) + y = 7; x = 1.5$ ($y = ^-2$)
- $\frac{2y}{3} = \frac{(3x - 6)}{4} + 1; x = 1\frac{1}{3}$ ($y = ^-0.75$)

PROBLEM SOLVING
Have students write equations to represent each number pattern if $x =$ the number and $y =$ its place in the sequence.
- $1, 2, 3, 4, \ldots$ ($x = y$)
- $3, 6, 9, 12, \ldots$ ($x = 3y$)
- $1, 4, 7, 10, \ldots$ ($x = 3(y - 1) + 1$)
- $2, 4, 8, 16, \ldots$ ($x = 2^y$)

COMING UP
Picture that.

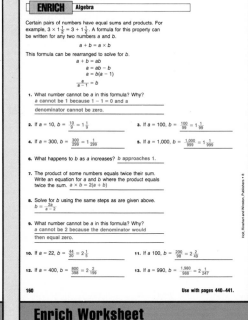

Objective: To make a diagram to solve a problem

Warm-Up
Have students use the Pythagorean rule to find the lengths of the missing sides of the following right triangles:

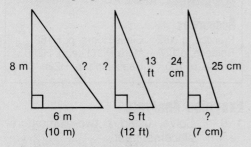

GETTING STARTED

Describe a trip around your school step-by-step to the class. Start at your classroom, with as many twists, turns, and diversions as possible. Have students try to follow your directions in order to understand where the trip you are describing would take them. Make your directions clear, but deliberately make the trip very complicated. Have students guess at the end where the trip takes them. Have students suggest ways to help them keep track of such complicated directions.

TEACHING THE LESSON

Drawing a picture is a good method for helping students organize directions. It is often shorter and clearer than writing the directions longhand. It also enables students to use the rules of geometry to obtain information about physical relationships between places.

Questions: Another question is "How far is the fountain from the first monument Carl saw?" (2 km)

Tools: Students can be given several important hints to help them draw a picture to organize directions.
- Remind students to carefully follow the standard map directions for N-S-E-W directions. This may help save confusion over directions.
- Remind students to carefully label as much information on their drawings as possible. When measured distances cross, be sure the proper section of each line is labeled correctly.
- Tell students to search for geometric figures that can be made in their diagrams. Students can solve for parts of geometric figures to find needed information.
- Tell students that a calculator will help them find some answers.

| QUESTIONS | TOOLS | SOLUTIONS | CHECKS |

PROBLEM SOLVING
Making a Diagram

When solving a problem that involves directions, you may want to draw a diagram.

Carl entered a circular park that measures 6 km in diameter. He entered from the northernmost point of the park. He walked due south for 1 km and stopped at a monument. Then he walked about 2.25 km due east to a food vendor at the edge of the park. From there, he walked due south 2 km to another monument and finally, 2.25 km due west to a fountain. How far is the fountain from the food vendor?

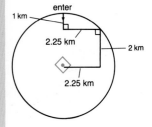

- Draw a picture.
- Use your picture to solve the problem.

The fountain is located in the center of the circle. The distance from the fountain to the food vendor is the radius of the circle. The radius of the circle is 3 km.

The distance between the fountain and the vendor is 3 km.

Write the letter of the correct answer.

1. Becky left a restaurant that was located on Third Street and drove north along Third Street for 2 km. She drove west on Sixth Avenue for 5 km and then south on 11 Street for 2 km. At that point, how far was Becky from the restaurant?

   a. 9 km   **b.** 5 km   c. 14 km

2. Smithtown, Branchville, and Garfield form a right triangle. Branchville is located 12 km due east of Smithtown. Garfield is located 5 km due south of Branchville. Find the distance from Smithtown to Garfield.

   a. 17 km   b. 12.5 km   **c.** 13 km

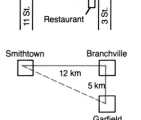

442

Solutions: Review geometric formulas used in the problems. These formulas include the Pythagorean rule, diameter of a circle, and area of a rectangle. The Pythagorean rule is used extensively.

Checks: After drawing a diagram and finding a solution, students should read the problem again, checking the diagram at each step for accuracy.

Draw a picture. Then solve each problem.

3. The shape of a summer camp is like that of a square. It measures 10 km on each side. Warren entered the camp from the center of the south side and walked 2 km due north. He then walked 3 km due east and then 7 km due north. At that point, how far was he from the western border of the camp? **8 kilometers**

4. Albert stood in the center of a circular pool. He took 2 steps toward the edge of the pool and was then 9 m from the edge. If each of Albert's steps measured 1 m, what is the diameter of the pool? **22 meters**

5. Mr. Paxton wants to carpet an L-shape room. The main part of the room measures 5 m by 3 m. The rest of the room measures 4 m by 2 m. The carpet costs $17.95 per square meter. How much will it cost Mr. Paxton to carpet the room? **$412.85**

6. Ralph followed a map made by his friend Sheila. He began his walk at a large rock and walked 11 paces west, 5 paces north, 2 paces east, 13 paces south, 9 paces west, and 8 paces north. If each pace is equal to 1 meter, how far from the rock did Ralph end his walk? **18 meters west of the rock**

7. The state of Colorado has a rectangular shape that measures 578 km by 458 km. The longer sides are the northern and southern borders of the state. A helicopter begins a trip in the northwest corner and flies south until it reaches the southwest corner. It then flies east until it reaches the southeast corner. How far is the helicopter from the northwest corner at this point? Round your answer to the nearest kilometer. You may use a calculator to solve this problem. **737 kilometers**

Classwork/Homework, pages H183-H184

ASSIGNMENT GUIDE

Basic: 1–5

Average: 1–2, 3–7 o

Extended: 1–7 o

Resources
Practice, pp. 183–4   Class/Home pp. H183–4

Exercise Analysis
1–7   Skill applications

FOLLOW-UP ACTIVITIES

PROBLEM SOLVING
Have students solve the following problems.

- A city's blocks are laid in a perfect grid. Tim left his house and walked 5 blocks to the right. Then he turned right and walked 4 blocks. Then he turned left and walked 2 blocks. Then he turned right and walked 1 block. Then he turned right again and walked 10 blocks. Then he turned right and walked 6 blocks. Then he turned right again and walked 3 blocks. How can he return home from this corner? (Turn right and walk 1 block.)

- A bug walked around and around the edge of a metal plate attached vertically to a pole near a street intersection. At regular intervals, the metal plate had a corner and the bug had to make a 135 degree turn to its left. What kind of sign was the bug walking around? (a stop sign)

CALCULATOR
Have students use a calculator with a memory key to find the shortest distance from **A** to **B**.

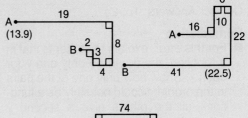

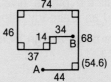

COMING UP
In-laws and their purposes

Objectives: To define a relation and a function

Warm-Up

Have students find the values of y given (⁻1, 0, 2) as the replacement set for x.

- y = 4x + 7 (y = 3, 7, 15)
- y = 5x − 5 (y = ⁻10, ⁻5, 5)
- 3x − 2y = 6 (y = ⁻$\frac{9}{2}$, ⁻3, 0)

GETTING STARTED

Draw the following on the chalkboard.

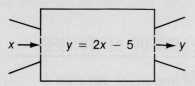

Tell students that the drawing is of a machine that takes any value x, doubles it, subtracts 5, and then outputs the new value as y.

Ask a volunteer to stand in for the machine while others suggest values for x. Use a different rule to repeat the exercise.

TEACHING THE LESSON

A. Extend the lesson by defining *domain* and *range*. The domain is the set of the first coordinates of the ordered pairs in a relation. The range is the set of all second coordinates in the ordered pairs. In the text example of a function, the domain is {2, 3, 4, 8, 9}, and the range is {3, 5, 7, 4, 2}.

B. Explain that to facilitate the finding of values, students can think, "What must be done to x to get y?" In functional notation, this is written as y = f(x) where f is the rule of the function.

Checkpoint

The chart lists the common errors students make when identifying a function.

Correct Answers: 1b, 2a

Remediation

■ For this error, explain to students that in a function, there can be only one y for each x. Show how only one of the pairs in the problem could possibly be a function—all the others give a second y value to an x already listed.

☐ For this error, assign Reteach Master, p. 128.

444

Relations and Functions

A. A relation (R) is a set of ordered pairs (x,y). An example is $R = \{(1,7), (2,4), (3,3), (2,6), (5,1)\}$. A function ($F$) is a relation where each x value has only one y value, for example $F = \{(2,3), (3,5), (4,7), (5,9), (6,11)\}$. If a relation is a function, then for every value of x, there is one and only one value of y.

	Function			Not a function	
x	y		x	y	
2	3	(2,3)	1	4	(1,4)
3	5	(3,5)	2	4	(2,4)
4	7	(4,7)	3	6	(3,6)
8	4	(8,4)	2	6	(2,6)
9	2	(9,2)	5	1	(5,1)

For x = 2, there are two values of y.

B. Sometimes you can use a rule to describe a function. For example, $y = ⁻3x + 2$ is a rule for a function that multiplies every real number by ⁻3 and adds 2. The table of values shows some of the solutions to this equation.

x	y = ⁻3x + 2	y
0	y = ⁻3(0) + 2	2
1	y = ⁻3(1) + 2	⁻1
2	y = ⁻3(2) + 2	⁻4

Some solutions are (0,2), (1,⁻1), and (2,⁻4).
The set {(0,2), (1,⁻1), (2,⁻4)} is a function because for each x-value, there is one and only one value of y.

Checkpoint Write the letter of the correct answer.

1. If (1,3), (2,4), (3,6), (4,5), and (x,y) are ordered pairs of a function, then (x,y) could be ■.

   a. (1,5)   **b.** (6,3)   **c.** (4,2)   **d.** (3,1)

2. If the relation {(x,3), (2,5), (3,7), (4,9)} is a function, then x could be ■.

   a. 1   **b.** 2   **c.** 3   **d.** 4

444

COMMON ERRORS

Answer Choice	Type of Error
■ 1a, 1c, 1d,	Fails to realize that for each x there can only be one, unique y
☐ 2b, 2c, 2d	Finds the function incorrectly

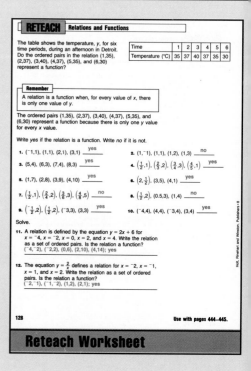

Write *yes* if the relation is a function. Write *no* if it is not.

1. {(0,2), (1,2), (1,4)} no

2. {(0,1), (0,2), (0,3)} no

3. {(1,4), (2,4), (3,4)} yes

4. {(0,0), (1,4), (1, ⁻4)} no

5. {(2,4), (3,4), (3,5), (4,6)} no

6. {(1,1), (2,2), (3,3), (4,4)} yes

7. {(5,6), (⁻2,4), (⁻1,6), (4,3)} yes

8. {(⁻1,3), (⁻2,3), (⁻3,3), (⁻4,3)}yes

9. {(1,2), (1,3), (1,4)} no

10. {(0, ⁻2), (1, ⁻3), (2, ⁻4)}yes

11. {(5,3), (3,5), (4, ⁻2)} yes

12. {(⁻1,3), (⁻2,4), (⁻3,5), (⁻2,6)}no

13. {(1,2), (1,3), (2,1), (2,3)} no

14. {(2,6), (3,6), (5,7), (6,2)} yes

Make a table of values for each equation using $2, 1, 0 ⁻1, ⁻2$, as replacements for x. Is the set of solutions a function? **See Answer Key.**

15. $y = x + 6$ yes

16. $x + y = 1$ yes

17. $y = 3x + 4$ yes

Write the rule if the given relation is a function. Write *no* if it is not a function.

★18. {(0,0), (1,1), (3,3), (4,4)} y = x

★19. {(1,4), (2,5), (0,3), (3,6)} y = x + 3

★20. {(0,0), (1,2), (2,4), (3,6)} y = 2x

★21. {(0,2), (1,1), (0,1), (5, ⁻3)} no

Solve. For Problem 22, use the Infobank.

22. Use the information on page 478 to solve. How many points would you have to eliminate to turn the graphed relation (Graph A) into a graph of a 8 points function?

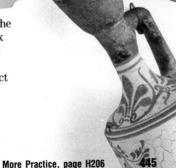

89707

40769

CHALLENGE Patterns, Relations, and Functions

Archeologists often use a system of tags to identify the various artifacts discovered during a dig. If you think about the tags as ordered pairs (x = the tag number; y = the actual artifact), why is it crucial that the ordered pairs be a function? If you let x = the artifact and y = the tag number, what effect would that have on the tag system?

Having more than one artifact per tag number would be confusing; there would be more than one tag number per artifact.

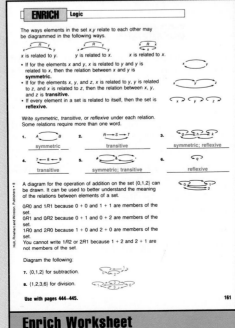

Holt, Rinehart and Winston, Publishers • 8

ASSIGNMENT GUIDE

Basic: 1–16, 22

Average: 3–18, 22

Extended: 7–22, Chlg

Resources
Practice, p. 185   Class/Home, p. H185
Reteach, p. 128   More Practice, p. H206
Enrich, p. 161

Exercise Analysis

1–14 Determine whether a given relation is a function

15–17 Make a table of values for an equation given a replacement set

18–21 Write the rule for a function

22 Data collection and computation

Challenge

This problem requires students to apply the concept of a function to a noncomputational real-life situation.

FOLLOW-UP ACTIVITIES

 **PROBLEM SOLVING**
Have students solve this problem.
• Miguel goes shopping for a memory telephone that can store and also dial his friends' phone numbers. Let *x* = a memory button and *y* = one of his friends' phone numbers. Why must the ordered pairs (*x*, *y*) be a function? (Because if the ordered pairs are not a function, Miguel will not know whom he is calling when he pushes *x*.)

COMING UP

Leaving on a real-number plane

Warm-Up

Have students determine whether each relation is a function.

$\{(2, ^-3, (1, ^-4), (0, ^-5)\}$ (yes)

$\{(\frac{1}{5}, \frac{1}{3}), (\frac{1}{4}, \frac{1}{4}), (\frac{1}{5}, \frac{1}{2})\}$ (no)

$\{(4, ^-4), (3, ^-2), (^-4, 4)\}$ (yes)

GETTING STARTED

Materials: acetate sheet, felt-tip pen

Draw a $^-5$ to $^+5$ number line on the chalkboard, and draw an identical number line on the acetate.

Rotate the acetate number line over the chalkboard so that the acetate number line is perpendicular to the chalkboard number line and intersects it at (0,0). Label any point on the x-axis A and any point on the y-axis B. Ask: What is the y-coordinate of A? (0) What is the x-coordinate of B? (0)

Have students write an ordered pair to describe each point.

TEACHING THE LESSON

A. Explain that ordered pairs are also known as Cartesian coordinates. Tell students that these coordinates were named for French mathematician and philosopher Rene Descartes, who published an essay on the real-number plane in 1637. In that essay, Descartes demonstrated for the first time the relationship between algebraic equations and geometric figures.

B. Have students determine whether each graph is a function. Have a volunteer come to the chalkboard to demonstrate why the nonfunction is not a function.

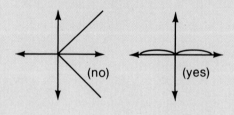

(no)   (yes)

446

The Real-Number Plane

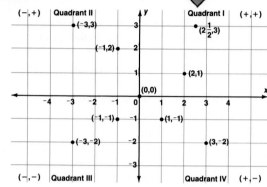

A. You have used whole numbers, integers, rational numbers, and irrational numbers as coordinates of points on the real-number line. You can use ordered pairs of real numbers to represent points on a **real-number plane.** The horizontal **x-axis** and the vertical **y-axis** are perpendicular number lines. They intersect at a point (0,0) called the **origin.** The coordinate axes divide the plane into four quadrants.

In Quadrant I, all ordered pairs are in the form $(^+, ^+)$.

In Quadrant II, all ordered pairs are in the form $(^-, ^+)$.

In Quadrant III, all ordered pairs are in the form $(^-, ^-)$.

In Quadrant IV, all ordered pairs are in the form $(^+, ^-)$.

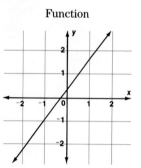

B. Since a function has only one y value for each x value, you can examine the graph to see if it is a graph of a function.

Function   Function   Not a function
For $x = 1$, there are 2 values for y.

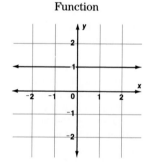
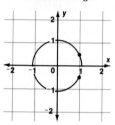

If a vertical line passes through more than one point, the graph is *not* a graph of a function.

446   Math Reasoning, page H229

COMMON ERRORS

Some students might have difficulty determining which coordinate should be plotted along which axis.

Remediation

For this error, emphasize the fact that the first coordinate in an ordered pair is always plotted along the horizontal axis. To help students remember this, point out that if there were only one coordinate, the graph would be a number line, which is customarily horizontal.

Assign Reteach Master, p. 129.

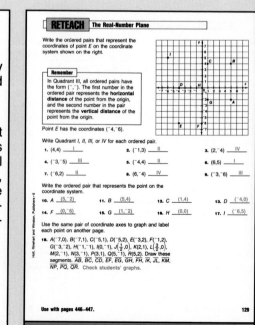

RETEACH The Real-Number Plane

Write the ordered pairs that represent the coordinates of point E on the coordinate system shown on the right.

Remember
In Quadrant III, all ordered pairs have the form $(^-, ^-)$. The first number in the ordered pair represents the **horizontal distance** of the point from the origin, and the second number in the pair represents the **vertical distance** of the point from the origin.

Point E has the coordinates $(^-4, ^-6)$.

Write Quadrant I, II, III, or IV for each ordered pair.

1. (4,4) __I__
2. $(^-1,3)$ __II__
3. $(2,^-4)$ __IV__
4. $(^-3,^-5)$ __III__
5. $(^-4,4)$ __II__
6. (6,5) __I__
7. $(^-6,2)$ __II__
8. $(6,^-4)$ __IV__
9. $(^-3,^-6)$ __III__

Write the ordered pair that represents the point on the coordinate system.

10. A __(5,^-2)__
11. B __(5,4)__
12. C __(1,4)__
13. D __(^-4,0)__
14. F __(0,^-6)__
15. G __(1,^-2)__
16. H __(0,0)__
17. I __(^-6,5)__

Use the same pair of coordinate axes to graph and label each point on another page.

18. $A(^-7,0)$, $B(^-7,1)$, $C(^-5,1)$, $D(^-5,2)$, $E(^-3,2)$, $F(^-1,2)$, $G(^-3,^-2)$, $H(^-1,^-1)$, $I(0,^-1)$, $J(\frac{1}{2},0)$, $K(2,1)$, $L(\frac{3}{2},0)$, $M(2,^-1)$, $N(3,^-1)$, $P(3,1)$, $Q(5,^-1)$, $R(5,2)$. Draw these segments. $\overline{AB}$, $\overline{BC}$, $\overline{CD}$, $\overline{EF}$, $\overline{EG}$, $\overline{GH}$, $\overline{FH}$, $\overline{IK}$, $\overline{JL}$, $\overline{KM}$, $\overline{NP}$, $\overline{PQ}$, $\overline{QR}$. Check students' graphs.

Use with pages 446–447.   129

Reteach Worksheet

Write Quadrant *I, II, III,* or *IV* for each ordered pair.

1. (4,7) I **2.** (2,⁻1) IV **3.** (⁻2,4) II **4.** (⁻1,6) II **5.** (⁻1,⁻3) III

6. (⁻2,⁻5) III **7.** (1,4) I **8.** (3,⁻4) IV **9.** (⁻3,1) II **10.** (5,8) I

Use the same pair of coordinate axes to graph and label each point. Connect the points in alphabetical order. Write *yes* if the figure is a graph of a function. Write *no* if it is not. Check students' graphs. yes

11. *B* (⁻4,⁻7) **12.** *F* (0,1) **13.** *D* (⁻2,⁻3) **14.** *A* (⁻5,⁻9)

15. *E* (⁻1,⁻1) **16.** *G* (1,3) **17.** *C* (⁻3,⁻5) **18.** *H* (2,5)

Draw another pair of axes. Graph and label each point. Connect the points in alphabetical order. Write *yes* if the figure is a graph of a function. Write *no* if it is not. Check students' graphs. no

19. *P* (0,⁻4) **20.** *M* (2,3) **21.** *R* (4,0) **22.** *L* (0,4)

23. *N* (4,0) **24.** *Q* (⁻2,⁻3) **25.** *S* (⁻2,3) **26.** *O* (2,⁻3)

Write *yes* if the graph is a graph of a function. Write *no* if it is not.

27. 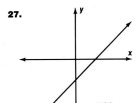 yes

28. 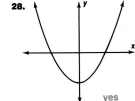 yes

29. 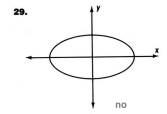 no

Solve. For Problem 30, use the Infobank.

30. Use the information on page 478 to solve. Is the graph of $xy = 1$ a function? In which quadrants would $xy = ⁻1$ be graphed? yes; II and IV

MIDCHAPTER REVIEW

Find three solutions for each equation. Write as ordered pairs. other solutions possible

1. $2x - y = 3$
(2,1), (3,3) ,(4,5)

2. $3y = x + 2$
$(1,1), \left(2,\frac{4}{3}\right), \left(3,\frac{5}{3}\right)$

3. $y + 4 = 2x$
(2,0), (4,4), (6,8)

4. $2x - y = 6$
(6,6), (8,10), (9,12)

ASSIGNMENT GUIDE

Basic: 1–18, 27–30, MCR

Average: 1–9 o, 11–30, MCR

Extended: 2–10 e, 11–30, MCR

Resources
Practice, p. 186   Class/Home, p. H186
Reteach, p. 129   Reasoning, p. H229
Enrich, p. 162

Exercise Analysis
1–10 Identify the quadrant of an ordered pair
11–26 Graph a relation, and then determine whether it is a function
27–29 Determine whether a graph is a graph of a function
30 Data collection and computation

Midchapter Review
This review provides an opportuntiy for you and students to assess their understanding of concepts and skills developed to this point in the chapter.

FOLLOW-UP ACTIVITIES

MATH CONNECTION
(Library skills)
Have students research the following: latitude, longitude, equator, prime meridian, Mercator projection. Then have them relate each to the real-number plane. (Latitude can be represented as the *y*-coordinate; longitude as the *x*-coordinate; the equator as the *x*-axis; the prime meridian as the *y*-axis; and the Mercator projection "flattens out" the globe so that it can be represented as a plane.)

Finally, have students locate each pair of coordinates on a globe.
● 19°24'N, 99°09'W (Mexico City)
● 35°50'N, 14°30'E (Malta)
● 18°58'N, 72°50'E (Bombay)
● 1°17'S, 36°49'E (Nairobi)
● 33°52'S, 151°13'E (Sydney)

COMPUTER
Most computers have a graphics mode that enables them to print designs by plotting points. After familiarizing students with the graphics mode of your computer, have them write programs that will print out a design of their initials.

COMING UP
Picture makes perfect? Preface makes perfect? Presence makes perfect? . . .

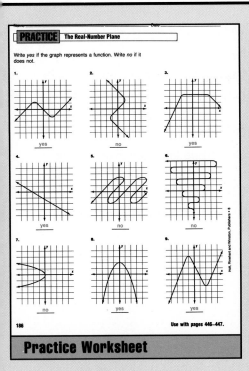

Practice Worksheet

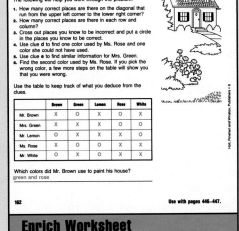

Enrich Worksheet

447

Objective. To practice choosing and using methods and strategies for solving problems

Warm-Up
To prepare students for this lesson, have them solve the following.

$7n + 4 = 67$ (9) $\qquad$ $6p - 8 = 52$ (10)

$\frac{r}{7} - 14 = 6$ (140) $\qquad$ $\frac{z}{16} + 27 = 8$ ($^-$304)

GETTING STARTED

Discuss with students the problem-solving strategies they have been introduced to in *Mathematics Unlimited.* As each strategy is mentioned ask a student to come up with a problem that could be solved using that strategy, and ask another student to solve the problem.

TEACHING THE LESSON

These problem-solving pages allow students to choose strategies from those strategies already taught in the textbook. Students also choose the appropriate method for solving each problem. This means students must find an effective approach for each problem and must correctly implement the strategy and method they have chosen. Remind students that they should not stay stuck on a problem; they should try another approach or move on and return later. It might be helpful to have students work these problems in small groups. Encourage students to choose the most efficient method. You may wish to review with students the problem-solving strategies taught to this point of the book.

448

PROBLEM SOLVING
Choosing a Strategy or Method

Write the strategy or method you choose. Then solve. Strategies and methods will vary.

1. The attendance at a soccer game was 71,500, which is 5,200 more than $\frac{4}{5}$ of the attendance at a football game. How many people attended the football game? Writing an Equation; 82,875 people

2. One container holds a maximum of 500 gallons. This is 150 gallons more than $\frac{2}{3}$ of the capacity of another container. How many gallons does the second container hold? Writing an Equation; 525 gallons

3. One city's new art museum will be rectangular, 160 feet long, and 102 feet wide. What will the area of the building be? Using a Formula; 16,320 feet

4. Brad swam for 45 minutes on Monday. On Tuesday, he swam $1\frac{1}{3}$ times as long. Wednesday, he swam $\frac{2}{3}$ as long as he swam on Monday. How many hours did he swim in all? Solving Multi-step Problems; $2\frac{1}{4}$ hours

6. A circular pool in a museum's courtyard has a diameter of 8 feet. What is the circumference of the pool? Using a Formula; 25.12 feet

8. Michelle spent $0.89 for a soda and $2.75 for a sandwich. She gave the cashier $10.00. How much change did she receive? Solving Multi-step Problems; $6.36

5. Ann has a piece of fabric 5 yards wide and 3 yards long. She needs to cut a piece of $2\frac{1}{2}$ feet by $2\frac{2}{3}$ feet from the fabric. How many square feet of fabric will be left? Solving Multi-step Problems; $128\frac{1}{3}$ square feet

7. Joshua buys a piece of wood that is 75 inches long. How many pieces, each 8 inches long, can he cut from this piece? Interpreting the Quotient; 9 pieces

9. Lucy's car averages 25.8 miles per gallon of gasoline. At this rate, how far can she drive on 8.5 gallons? Choosing the operation; 219.3 miles

Estimation
Using a Table
Choosing the Operation
Solving Multi-step Problems
Guessing and Checking
Making a Table to Find a Pattern
Writing an Equation
Interpreting the Quotient
   and the Remainder
Using a Formula
Making an Organized List
Working Backward

448

Choose a strategy or method and solve.
Strategies and methods will vary.

10. The Martins are planning a trip to Europe. Mrs. Martin wants to buy a road map of France for $7.85, one of Spain for $6.59, one of Italy for $9.35, and one of Greece for $8.25. She has $31.00. Can she buy all the maps? no

11. In a bookstore, Howard sees a world globe for $31.75, a large map of the United States for $15.30, a map of Asia for $12.75, and a road atlas for $9.35. Can he buy all the items with $70.00? yes

12. Tanya is drawing a map of her town. She is using a scale of $\frac{3}{4}$ inch = 6 miles. How many inches would represent a distance of 9 miles? $1\frac{1}{8}$ inches

13. One fruit-punch recipe calls for $1\frac{1}{2}$ quarts apple juice to make 15 servings. How much juice is needed to make 35 servings? $3\frac{1}{2}$ quarts

Use the table for Exercises 14–15.

Some American Colleges and Universities				
Name	**State**	**Year founded**	**Students**	**Teachers**
Beloit	Wisconsin	1846	1,079	97
Bowdoin	Maine	1794	1,371	116
Harvard	Massachusetts	1636	6,537	689
Oberlin	Ohio	1833	2,898	226
Stanford	California	1891	12,341	1,219
Yale	Connecticut	1701	10,448	1,741

14. Which school on the list has the most students? Does that school have the most teachers?
Stanford; no

15. What is average age (number of years since these schools were founded) of these schools?
Answers will depend on current year.

16. From the lesson, choose one problem that you have already solved. Show how the problem can be solved by a different method. Answers will vary.

Classwork/Homework, pages H187–H188

ASSIGNMENT GUIDE

Basic: 1–11, 16

Average: 1–13, 16

Extended: 1–16

Resources
Practice, pp. 187–8   Class/Home, pp. H187–8

Exercise Analysis
1–15   Choose an appropriate strategy or method
16   Use a different method

FOLLOW-UP ACTIVITIES

PROBLEM SOLVING
Direct students to go back over the problems in this lesson and choose four which they could solve using another method. Have them solve the problems with this alternate method and have students share the methods they used for each problem with the class.

CALCULATOR
Write the following problem onto the chalkboard and tell students each letter stands for a different digit. Have students use their calculators to find what digit each letter stands for.

$$\begin{array}{r} A\,B\,C\,D\,E \\ \times\ \ \ \ \ 4 \\ \hline E\,D\,C\,B\,A \end{array}$$

(A = 2; B = 1; C = 9; D = 7; E = 8)

* As a real challenge, ask students to use their calculators to solve the following, which is a multiplication problem followed by an addition problem. Each of the nine digits (no zeros) is used once and only once.

$$\begin{array}{r} A\,B \\ \times\ \ C \\ \hline D\,E \\ +\ F\,G \\ \hline H\,I \end{array}$$

(A = 1; B = 7; C = 4; D = 6; E = 8; F = 2; G = 5; H = 9; I = 3)

COMING UP
Lines on grids

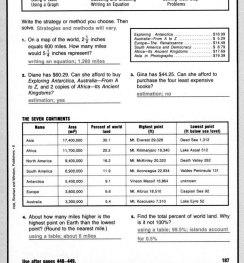

Objective: To graph a linear equation

Warm-Up
Have students identify the quadrant in which each ordered pair is located.

- $(^-12, ^-23)$ (III)
- $(0.5, ^-11.3)$ (IV)
- $(2\frac{1}{2}, 3\frac{1}{3})$ (I)
- $(^-56, 2.298)$ (II)

GETTING STARTED

On the chalkboard, draw a set of axes that show unnumbered marks. Pick a point (a,b) at random, and tell students that it is a solution to a function. Ask: If the rule of the function is $x + k$, how can you find another solution point for the function? (Possible answer: Move one unit to the right and one unit up.)

TEACHING THE LESSON

Explain that the y-coordinate of the point at which a graph crosses the y-axis is called the *y-intercept* and the x-coordinate of the point at which it crosses the x-axis is called the *x-intercept*.

Emphasize the fact that to graph a line, only two points need to be graphed. If these points are plotted and a line is drawn through them, all the other points on this line will also be solutions. Explain that it is often easiest to find the two intercepts. SInce this involves substituting zero, the equations are easy to solve.

Have students find the x- and the y-intercepts for each of the equations in the text. (Top: x-intercept: 2; y-intercept: 4 Bottom: x-intercept: 2; y-intercept: $^-4$)

Graphing Equations in Two Variables

In an earlier lesson, you found ordered-pair solutions to an equation in two variables by using a table of values. The solutions from the table of values can be graphed on the coordinate axes. The graphs in this lesson are straight lines.

To graph $y = 4 - 2x$, list some solutions in a table of values.

x	$y = 4 - 2x$	y	Solutions
0	$y = 4 - 2(0)$	4	$(0,4)$
1	$y = 4 - 2(1)$	2	$(1,2)$
2	$y = 4 - 2(2)$	0	$(2,0)$
3	$y = 4 - 2(3)$	$^-2$	$(3,^-2)$

Graph the solutions. Draw a line through the solutions you have graphed. All the points on the line, such as $(^-1,6)$, $(1.5,1)$, and $(4,^-4)$ are solutions.

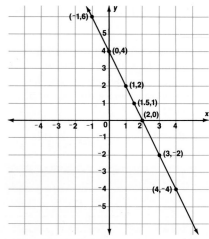

Another example: Graph the equation $2x - y = 4$.

x	y	Solutions
$^-1$	$^-6$	$(^-1,^-6)$
0	$^-4$	$(0,^-4)$
2	0	$(2,0)$
5	6	$(5,6)$

Other points on the line include $(1,^-2)$, $(3,2)$, and $(4,4)$.

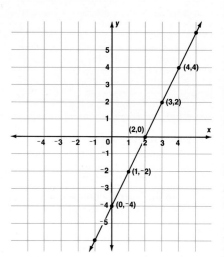

450

Math Reasoning, page H229

COMMON ERRORS

Students sometimes transpose the x- and the y-coordinates in plotting.

Remediation
For this error, have students write the quadrant in which each point should be plotted before actually plotting it. Also, have them label each coordinate, which will serve as a visual reminder during the graphing process.

$x\ y$
$(^-2,3)$

Assign Reteach Master, p. 130.

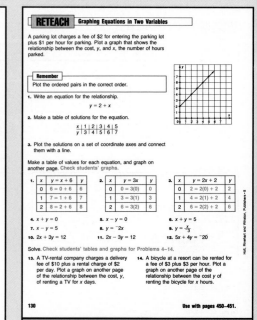

Copy and complete each table of values. Then graph each set of solutions.   Check students' graphs.

1.

x	y = x − 5	y
0	y = 0 − 5	⁻5
1	y = 1 − 5	⁻4
2	y = 2 − 5	⁻3

2.

x	y = 2x + 1	y
0	y = 2(0) + 1	1
1	y = 2(1) + 1	3
2	y = 2(2) + 1	5

3.

x	y = 2x	y
0	y = 2(0)	0
1	y = 2(1)	2
2	y = 2(2)	4

Make a table of values for each equation. Then graph each set of solutions.   Check students' graphs.

4. $2x + y = 14$ **5.** $3x - y = 8$ **6.** $2x + 5y = 10$

7. $3x + 4y = 12$ **8.** $4x - 2y = 8$ **9.** $2x + 3y - 12 = 0$

10. $y = 4x$ **11.** $3y = 4x$ **12.** $y = {}^-3x$

13. $3x = {}^-5y$ **14.** $x + y = 4$ **15.** $y - x = 5$

16. $2x + y = 10$ **17.** $x + 3y = 5$ **18.** $3x - y = 8$

19. $x + y = 7$ **20.** $2x - y = 11$ **21.** $x - y = {}^-4$

22. $2x + 3y + 12 = 0$ ★**23.** $y = \frac{1}{2}x$ ★**24.** $y = \frac{2}{3}x$

For each equation make a table of values that has three values for x. Graph the points and use the graph to find two other points on the line.
Check students' graphs.

25. $x + y = {}^-1$ **26.** $2x - y = 3$ **27.** $x = 3y$

28. $3y - 4 = x$ **29.** $y = x$ **30.** $y - x = 1$

Match each graph with its equation.

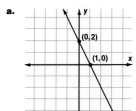 **a.**   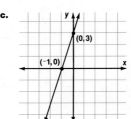 **b.**   **c.**

31. $y = 1 - x$ b   **32.** $y = 2 - 2x$ a   **33.** $y = 3x + 3$ c

Classwork/Homework, page H189   **451**

ASSIGNMENT GUIDE

Basic:	1–12, 25–27, 31–33
Average:	1–21 o, 25–27, 31–33
Extended:	13–33

Resources
Practice, p. 189   Class/Home, p. H189
Reteach, p. 130   Reasoning, p. H229
Enrich, p. 163

Exercise Analysis

1–3	Complete a table of values and then graph
4–24	Make a table of values and then graph
25–30	Graph an equation from three solutions and then use the graph to find two more solutions
31–33	Match a graph with its equation

FOLLOW-UP ACTIVITIES

MANIPULATIVES
Materials: rulers

Have students graph each set of 3 points in a separate number plane. Students can then use a ruler to see if the 3 points are on the same line.

(6,3)(4,1)(−5,−10) (no)
(7,−1)(4,1)(10,−3) (yes)
(0,0)(4,3)(−8,−6) (yes)
(−3,−1)(5,2)(1,0) (no)

PROBLEM SOLVING
Have students determine whether each point is on the graph of the line without actually graphing the line. Have students explain how they found their answers.

(5,3) 3x + 2y = 21 (yes)
(−1,4) 5x = 18 + 2y (no)
(8,14) 4y = 7x (yes)
(−4,−2) 6y = 24 − 3x (no)
(−7,3) 4x = 2 − 10y (yes)
(−13,−8) 2y = 10 + 2x (yes)

COMPUTER
Have students investigate the graphics mode of the computer and learn how to make it plot lines.

COMING UP
Busy intersections

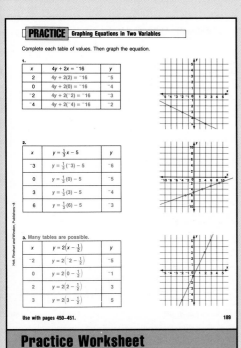

Practice Worksheet

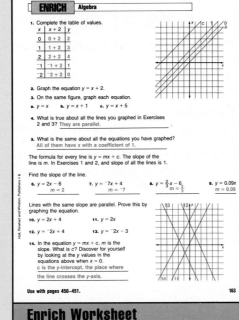

Enrich Worksheet

451

Objective: To solve a system of equations by graphing

Warm-Up
Have students graph the following equations.
- $y = 3x - 2$
- $y = 7 - x$

GETTING STARTED

Have students graph the following two equations in the same coordinate plane.

$y = 2x + 2$
$y = {}^-x + 5$

Ask students what the graph looks like. Ask where the lines intersect. (1,4) Tell the class that today's lesson explains what the point of intersection represents.

TEACHING THE LESSON

Point out that in the first example, the equation has been rewritten to solve for y. The second equation represents a much more convenient way to find and check values.

Advanced students may be interested in using another way to find the solution to a system of equations. Such students should be encouraged to use substitution to solve two equations simultaneously. One of the equations can be solved for a particular variable, and then that solution can be inserted for the variable in the other equation. The second equation will then have only one variable and a unique solution. For example:

Solve $2x + y = 4$ and $3x - y = 11$

$$2x + y = 4 \qquad 3x - y = 11$$
$$y = 4 - 2x \qquad 3x - y = 11$$
$$3x - (4 - 2x) = 11$$
$$5x = 15$$
$$x = 3$$

Then substitute the value for x into either of the original equations to find y.

$$2(3) + y = 4 \qquad 3(3) - y = 11$$
$$y = {}^-2 \qquad\qquad y = {}^-2$$

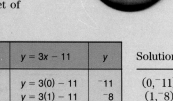

Graphing Pairs of Equations

Look at the pair of equations shown below.

$$2x + y = 4$$
$$3x - y = 11$$

Such a pair of equations is called a **system of equations.** A solution to a system of equations is an ordered pair that is a solution to both equations. You can graph a system of equations to find its solution. Begin by graphing each equation on the same set of axes.

x	$y = 4 - 2x$	y	Solutions
0	$y = 4 - 2(0)$	4	$(0,4)$
1	$y = 4 - 2(1)$	2	$(1,2)$
2	$y = 4 - 2(2)$	0	$(2,0)$

x	$y = 3x - 11$	y	Solutions
0	$y = 3(0) - 11$	$^-11$	$(0,{}^-11)$
1	$y = 3(1) - 11$	$^-8$	$(1,{}^-8)$
2	$y = 3(2) - 11$	$^-5$	$(2,{}^-5)$

The coordinates of the point of intersection $(3,{}^-2)$ are the solution to the system.
Check the solution $(3,{}^-2)$ in each equation.

$$2x + y = 4 \qquad\qquad 3x - y = 11$$
$$2(3) + ({}^-2) \overset{?}{=} 4 \qquad 3(3) - ({}^-2) \overset{?}{=} 11$$
$$6 - 2 \overset{?}{=} 4 \qquad\qquad 9 + 2 \overset{?}{=} 11$$
$$4 = 4 \qquad\qquad\qquad 11 = 11$$

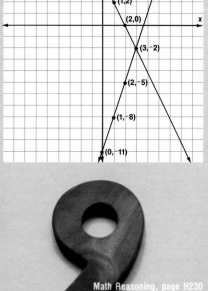

Math Reasoning, page H230

COMMON ERRORS

Some students might transpose the x- and the y-axes, whereas others might graph one or both of the equations incorrectly.

Remediation
For these errors, have students solve the system of equations by graphing, and then check their work by substituting the point of intersection into the original equations.

Assign Reteach Master, p. 131.

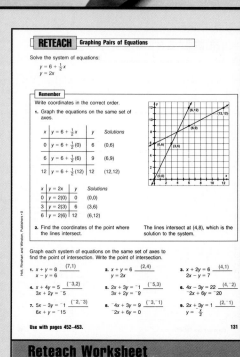

Reteach Worksheet

Graph each system of equations on the same set of axes to find the solution. Check each solution.

1. $x + y = 6$
$x - y = 2$
$(4,2)$

2. $x + y = 8$
$x - y = 4$
$(6,2)$

3. $x + 2y = 15$
$y = 2x$
$(3,6)$

4. $x + 3y = 19$
$x - 3y = 1$
$(10,3)$

5. $3x = 4y + 17$
$2x = {}^-3y$
$(3,{}^-2)$

6. $x + y = 3$
$x - y = 1$
$(2,1)$

7. $2x + y = 6$
$y - x = 3$
$(1,4)$

8. $x + y = 9$
$x - y = 3$
$(6,3)$

9. $x + 2y = 8$
$x - 2y = 4$
$(6,1)$

10. $y + 3x = 8$
$y - 3x = 8$
$(0,8)$

11. $x + 2y = 14$
$3y + x = 18$
$(6,4)$

12. $y = 3x$
$x + y = 8$
$(2,6)$

13. $y = 3x$
$x - y = 2$
$({}^-1,{}^-3)$

14. $x + y = 12$
$x - y = 2$
$(7,5)$

15. $3x + 2y = 9$
$x + y = 3$
$(3,0)$

16. $5x + 2y = 11$
$4x - 3y = 18$
$(3,{}^-2)$

17. $x + y = 12$
$x - y = 4$
$(8,4)$

18. $x + 2y = 8$
$x - 2y = 4$
$(6,1)$

19. $5x + 4y = 27$
$x - 11 = 2y$
$(7,{}^-2)$

20. $2x + y = 12$
$x = 9 - 2y$
$(5,2)$

21. $3x - y = 13$
$2x - 16 = {}^-3y$
$(5,2)$

22. $2x + y = 17$
$5x = 25 + y$
$(6,5)$

23. $x - 2y = 8$
$2y = 3x - 16$
$(4,{}^-2)$

24. $6y = x$
$5y = 2x - 14$
$(12,2)$

Use the system of equations $x + 9y = 12$ and $x - 3y = 6$ to solve.

25. Graph the system of equations to find the solution. In which quadrant is the solution? $\left(7\frac{1}{2}, \frac{1}{2}\right)$
I; check students' graphs.

26. At which point does $x + 9y = 12$ intersect the y-axis? the x-axis?
$\left(0, 1\frac{1}{3}\right)$; $(12,0)$

27. At which point does $x - 3y = 6$ intersect the y-axis? the x-axis?
$(0,{}^-2)$; $(6,0)$

28. Is each equation an equation of a function? yes

ANOTHER LOOK

Compare. Write $>$, $<$, or $=$ for ●.

1. $14.82 ● 14.83$ $<$

2. $31.09 ● 31.092$ $<$

3. $17.7 ● 17.69$ $>$

4. $126.91 ● 128.9$ $<$

5. $7.621 ● 7.66$ $<$

6. $553.9 ● 553.90$ $=$

Classwork/Homework, page H190

453

ASSIGNMENT GUIDE

Basic: 1–18, AL

Average: 7–24, AL

Extended: 11–28, AL

Resources
Practice, p. 190   Class/Home, p. H190
Reteach, p. 131   Reasoning, p. H230
Enrich, p. 164

Exercise Analysis
1–24   Solve a system of equations by graphing
25–28   Skill applications

Another Look
These exercises provide maintenance for comparing of decimals.

FOLLOW-UP ACTIVITIES

PROBLEM SOLVING
Have students solve this problem.
● Interstate highways 10 and 45 meet in Houston. If y = latitude (°N) and x = longitude (°W), the path of Interstate 10 can be described by the line $5y - x = 55$. The path of Interstate 45 can be described by the line $y = 410 - 4x$. At what latitude and longitude is Houston located? (95°W, 30°N)

PUZZLES AND GAMES
Materials: graph paper

Form the class into pairs of players. Have each student draw two coordinate grids on different pieces of graph paper. Both grids should be numbered from ${}^-5$ to ${}^+5$. Then have each player secretly place 3 "battleships" on one of the grids. The battleships should be represented by 3 consecutive horizontal, vertical or diagonal points. Different ships can occupy adjacent points.

In each turn, have the players alternate in calling out the coordinates. If one player calls out the coordinates of another player's ship, that player must tell him or her that there has been a "hit." If a player hits all three points of a ship, he or she has "sunk" the ship. The first player who sinks all the ships of the other player wins.

COMING UP
Not all equations are created equal.

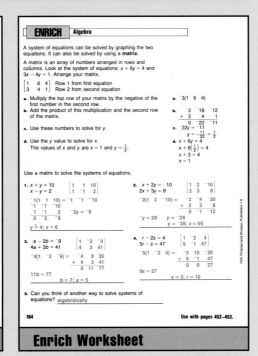

Practice Worksheet

Enrich Worksheet

453

Objective: To solve inequalities in two variables

Warm-Up

Have students solve and graph the following inequalities.

$x > {}^-2$ $y < 4$
$3x \le 12$ $y + 8 \ge 14$

Ask volunteers to describe their graphs.

GETTING STARTED

Review the procedure for solving for y, using the following two-step inequality: $2y - 6 < {}^-12$.

$2y < {}^-6$ (Add 6.)
 $y < {}^-3$ (Divide by 2.)

Then ask students to show how they would solve $2y - x < {}^-12$ for y. (Add x to both sides and then divide both sides by 2 to get $y < \frac{x}{2} - 6$.)

TEACHING THE LESSON

Point out that each graph actually separates the plane into three parts: the points on the line, the points above the line, and the points below the line.

Emphasize the fact that $\ge$ and $\le$ are represented by a solid line that includes the points on the line in the solution set and that $>$ and $<$ are represented by a broken line that does not include the points on the line in the solution set.

Inequalities in Two Variables

Mathematical statements such as $y > x$ and $y \le x$ are inequalities in two variables. These inequalities may be graphed by first graphing the related equation.

To graph $y > x$, first graph $y = x$.

x	$^-1$	0	1
y	$^-1$	0	1

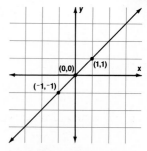

The straight line $y = x$ divides the plane into two half planes. Only the ordered pairs in one half plane make the inequality $y > x$ true.

Choose the test point $(2,1)$ to see whether it makes the inequality true.

$y > x$; $1 > 2$ is false. So, $(2,1)$ is not a solution of $y > x$. The half plane that does not include $(2,1)$ should be shaded. The broken line shows that points on the line $y = x$ are not solutions.

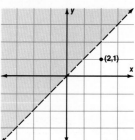

To graph $y \le x$, graph $y = x$ again. You can use the same test point.

$y \le x$; $1 \le 2$ is true. So, the half plane that includes $(2,1)$ should be shaded. The solid line shows that points on the line are solutions.

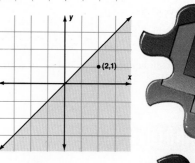

If the inequality does not go through the origin, you can use $(0,0)$ as the test point.

Math Reasoning, page H230

454

COMMON ERRORS

Students might incorrectly substitute the first coordinate (x) of an ordered pair for the variable at the left side (y) of an inequality in $y = mx + b$ form.

Remediation

Remind students that in ordered pairs, the first coordinate is always the one that comes first in the alphabet. Use examples to demonstrate that the position of the variables in an equation or in an inequality does not determine which values are to be substituted for them.

Assign Reteach Master, p. 132.

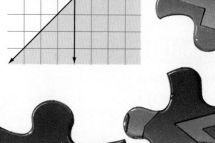

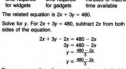

Reteach Worksheet

Write *yes* if the ordered pair is a solution of the inequality. Write *no* if it is not.

1. $y > 2x$; (2,1)   no   **2.** $y < x + 2$; (3,⁻1)   yes

3. $y \geq 2x - 1$; (3,2)   no   **4.** $y \geq x + 2$; (4,3)   no

5. $2x - y \leq 0$; (5,4)   no   **6.** $y < x - 1$; (10,3)   yes

7. $x - y > 4$; (3,2)   no   **8.** $x + y < 6$; (1,2)   yes

9. $3x - y \leq 6$; (4,11)   yes   **10.** $x - 2y < 3$; (4,1)   yes

Match the graph with the inequality.

11. $y \geq \ ^-x$ c   **12.** $y \leq \ ^-x$ a   **13.** $y > \ ^-x$ b

a. 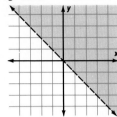   **b.** 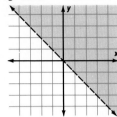   **c.**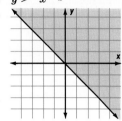

Match the graph with the inequality. Use (0,0) as the test point.

14. $y > x + 1$ b   **15.** $y \geq x + 1$ a   **16.** $y < x + 1$ c

a. 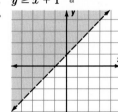   **b.** 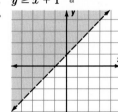   **c.**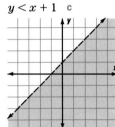

NUMBER SENSE

Compute mentally.

1. $15 + \ ^-6 - 7$ 2   **2.** $12 - 8 - \ ^-6$ 10   **3.** $28 - \ ^-16 + 8$ 52

4. $^-66 - \ ^-21 + 7$ ⁻38   **5.** $18 + 62 - \ ^-10$ 90   **6.** $^-7 + \ ^-8 - \ ^-26$ 11

7. $^-36 - 18 + \ ^-80$ ⁻134   **8.** $9 - 7 + \ ^-6 - \ ^-4$ 0   **9.** $^-5 - \ ^-5 + 10 + \ ^-12$ ⁻2

Classwork/Homework, page H191   **455**

ASSIGNMENT GUIDE

Basic:	1–16, NS 1–6
Average:	5–16, NS 1–6
Extended:	5–16, NS

Resources
Practice, p. 191   Class/Home, p. H191
Reteach, p. 132   Reasoning, p. H230
Enrich, p. 165

Exercise Analysis
1–10   Determine whether an ordered pair is a solution for an inequality
11–16   Match a graph with an inequality

Number Sense
These exercises provide maintenance for evaluating expressions containing integers.

FOLLOW-UP ACTIVITIES

NUMBER SENSE (Mental Math)
Have students mentally compute the intercepts of the dividing line for each inequality. Then have them name the point of intersection of the dividing line with each axis. Also, have them tell whether the dividing line will be broken or solid.

- $y < 3x - 1$
  $((\frac{1}{3},0), (0,^-1),$ broken)
- $y \geq x + 10$
  $((^-10,0), (0,10),$ solid)
- $y \leq 2x - 0.8$
  $((0.4,0), (0,^-0.8),$ solid)
- $y > \frac{3x}{5} + 5$
  $((^-\frac{25}{3},0), (0,5),$ broken)

COMING UP
Often the twain shall meet.

Objective: To graph inequalities containing two variables

Warm-Up

Have students determine whether each ordered pair is a solution for the given inequality.

- $y < 5x - 2$; (2,7) (yes)
- $3y - x > 3$; (3,2) (no)
- $\frac{2y}{3} \leq x - 8$; (0,⁻6) (no)
- $x + 4y \geq 13$; (1,3) (yes)

GETTING STARTED

Materials: checkerboards, checkers

Demonstrate that checkerboards can be used to represent coordinates from ⁻3 to ⁺4 by using checkers to plot points and lines.

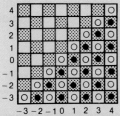

Have students model the inequalities shown below.

$y \leq 1$ $y \geq 1$
$y \leq x - 2$ $x \geq {}^-2$

TEACHING THE LESSON

Extend the lesson by introducing systems of inequalities. Explain that a system of inequalities can be solved just as systems of equations can be solved. Explain, however, that the solution set is not a single point; instead, it is the area in which the shadings overlap.

For example, guide students to find the solution set to $y < {}^-1$ and $x \geq 2$. First, graph the related equations and then use test points to shade them. The solution set is the double-shaded area.

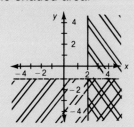

Have students find the solution set for each system of inequalities.

- $y \leq x$ and $y \geq {}^-x$
- $y > x + 1$ and $y < 3$

Graphing Inequalities in Two Variables

You can graph the solutions of an inequality in two variables by first graphing the solutions of its related equation.

Solve.	$y > 5 - 2x$	Solve.	$y \leq 2x + 4$
Write a related equation.	$y = 5 - 2x$	Write a related equation.	$y = 2x + 4$

Make a table of values.   Make a table of values.

x	y = 5 − 2x	y	Solutions
1	$y = 5 - 2(1)$	3	(1,3)
0	$y = 5 - 2(0)$	5	(0,5)
⁻1	$y = 5 - 2(^-1)$	7	(⁻1,7)
⁻2	$y = 5 - 2(^-2)$	9	(⁻2,9)

x	y = 2x + 4	y	Solutions
1	$y = 2(1) + 4$	6	(1,6)
0	$y = 2(0) + 4$	4	(0,4)
⁻1	$y = 2(^-1) + 4$	2	(⁻1,2)
⁻2	$y = 2(^-2) + 4$	0	(⁻2,0)

Graph the solutions on coordinate axes.   Graph the solutions on coordinate axes.

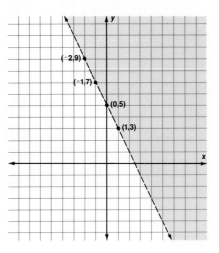

Use a broken line for $>$ or $<$. Choose (0,0) as a test point to see if it makes the inequality true. $y > 5 - 2x$; $0 > 5$ is not true. The half plane that includes (0,0) is not shaded.

Use a solid line for $\geq$ or $\leq$. Choose (0,0) as a test point to see if it makes the inequality true. $y \leq 2x + 4$; $0 \leq 4$ is true. The half plane that includes (0,0) is shaded.

456   **Math Reasoning, page H230**

COMMON ERRORS

When graphing, students often shade the wrong side of the line of the related equation.

Remediation

Have students check to see whether they have shaded the correct side by picking points within the shaded area to determine whether they satisfy the inequality.

Assign Reteach Master, p. 133.

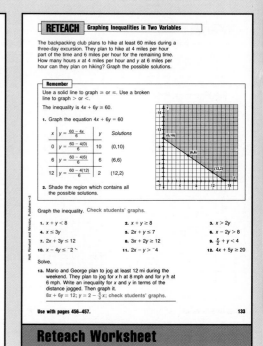

Reteach Worksheet

Make a table of values for each inequality. Then graph the solutions.   **Check students' graphs.**

1. $x + y < 6$
2. $x + 2y > 15$
3. $x + 4y \leq 7$
4. $x \leq 2y + 1$
5. $y \leq 2x$
6. $x - y \geq 2$
7. $y - x < {}^{-}2$
8. $3x - 4y > 6$
9. $x - 2y \geq 4$
10. $y - x < 1$
11. $y \geq 2x + 1$
12. $2x - y \leq 8$
13. $2x + y \leq 5$
14. $3x - y \leq 9$
15. $3x + y < 7$
16. $2x + y \geq 8$
17. $2x - y < 4$
18. $y > 3x$
19. $x + y \leq 12$
20. $x - y > 2$
21. $x \leq {}^{-}2y$
22. $y \leq 4x$
23. $2x + 3y \leq 9$
24. $x + 2y \leq 6$

Write an inequality for each. Then graph it.
Check students' graphs.

25. Twice a number x is less than three added to a number y.
    $2x < y + 3$

26. A number y is more than two added to three times a second number x. $y > 3x + 2$

27. One number minus a second number is more than six. $x - y > 6$

★28. The sum of two numbers minus two is less than zero. $x + y - 2 < 0$

★29. The difference of two numbers divided by seven is less than four.
    $\dfrac{x - y}{7} < 4$

★30. The sum of two numbers divided by three is less than two times their difference. $\dfrac{x + y}{3} < 2(x - y)$

CHALLENGE

Find the volume of each solid. Round to the nearest tenth.

1.
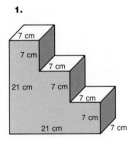
2,058 cm³

2.
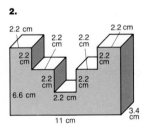
181.0 cm³

3.
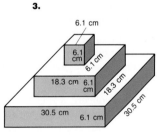
7,944.3 cm³

Classwork/Homework, page H192

457

ASSIGNMENT GUIDE

Basic: 1–18, 25–26, Chlg 1

Average: 7–21, 25–28, Chlg 1–2

Extended: 13–24, 25–30, Chlg

Resources
Practice, p. 192   Class/Home, p. H192
Reteach, p. 133   Reasoning, p. H230
Enrich, p. 166

Exercise Analysis

1–24   Make a table of values for an inequality and then graph it
25–30   Skill applications

Challenge
Suggest to those students who encounter difficulty that they should divide each solid into component solids, each of which would then be a rectangular prism.

FOLLOW-UP ACTIVITIES

PUZZLES AND GAMES
Materials: graph paper

Form the class into pairs, and have each student draw a set of coordinate axes numbered from ⁻10 to ⁺10.

In this Mine Sweep game, each player is to hide a mine at a particular coordinate location. The object is to discover the location of your opponent's mine. To accomplish this, players are to alternate "sweeps."

A sweep consists of a player calling out either a pair of coordinates or an inequality given in $y = mx + b$ form. If a player calls out an ordered pair, the other player merely says "yes" or "no." If a player calls out an inequality, however, the other player has to say whether the mine is on the indicated side of the dividing line.

The first player to find the exact coordinates of the other player's mine wins. If a player gives an incorrect response to another's sweep, he or she automatically loses.

COMING UP
If at first you don't succeed . . .

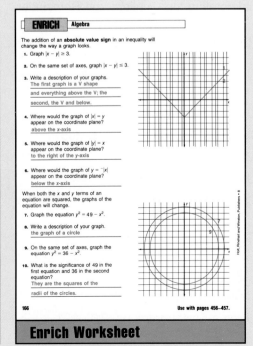

Practice Worksheet

Enrich Worksheet

Objecti . To practice choosing and using methods and strategies for solving
problems

Warm-Up
Have students compute.

$\frac{1}{2} \times \frac{1}{3} \left(\frac{1}{6}\right)$ 14,500 × 4 (58,000)

8 × 7 × 6 × 5 × 4 × 3 × 2 × 1 (40,320)

GETTING STARTED

Have students work in groups. Challenge
the groups to develop the most detailed
description of the school possible. Encourage the students to use as many forms of
description possible. Impose a time-limit
on the class' work. (Students may choose
to draw a map, or make charts listing
rooms, halls, and so on.)

TEACHING THE LESSON

These problem-solving pages allow students to choose strategies from those
strategies already taught in the textbook.
Students also choose the appropriate
method for solving each problem. This
means students must find an effective
approach for each problem and must
correctly implement the strategy and
method they have chosen. Remind students that they should not stay stuck
on a problem; they should try another
approach or move on and return later. It
might be helpful to have students work
these problems in small groups. Encourage students to choose the most efficient
method.

You may wish to review with students the
problem-solving strategies taught to this
point of the book.

Estimation, pp. 54–55, 136–137

4-Step Plan, pp. 16–17

Using Data from Outside Sources, Including the Infobank, pp. 24–25, 386–387

Using a Graph, pp. 32–33, 248–249

Identifying Extra/Needed Information, pp.
48–49

Choosing the Operation, pp. 62–63, 102–
103

Solving Multistep Problems/Making a Plan,
pp. 68–69, 270–271, 406–407

Checking for a Reasonable Answer, pp.
86–87

Using a Table, pp. 96–97

Writing an Equation, pp. 110–111, 288–
289

Using a Pictograph, pp. 126–127

Writing a Simpler Problem, pp. 144–145

458

PROBLEM SOLVING
Choosing a Strategy or Method

Write the strategy or method you
choose. Then solve.   Strategies and
methods will vary.

1. Mark is making a map of his
neighborhood. Starting in front of his
house, he walks 3 blocks east to the
post office. He then turns right and
walks 4 blocks to the library. Turning
right again, he walks 2 blocks, makes
another right, and walks 2 blocks to
the school. At the school, he turns west,
walks 1 block, turns right, and walks 2
blocks. Does he end up at home? How
many blocks does he have to walk to
the library? Drawing a Picture; yes; 7 blocks

2. David is making a physical map of the
area in which he lives. Forests make
up $\frac{1}{3}$ of the map. Mountains make up $\frac{1}{2}$
the remaining land. Of the remaining
area, residential areas make up 40 mi^2,
leaving 27 mi^2 for Lake Gemini. How
many square miles does David's map
cover? Working Backward; 201 mi^2

3. TV station WBBQ broadcasts national
football games. It charges advertisers
$15,750 for 15 seconds of prime time,
$23,625 for 30 seconds, and $55,125 for
90 seconds. How much would 75
seconds of prime time cost? Making a
Table; $47,250

4. A group of 6 people go to a restaurant.
They can only get 2 tables that have 3
chairs each. How many different seating
combinations could there be? Making an
organized List; 20 combinations

5. At a concert, 8 singers will sing solos
and then duets. If each singer sings a
duet with every other singer, how many
duets will be performed? Selecting
Notation; 28 duets

458

Estimation
Drawing a Picture
Choosing the Operation
Solving Multi-step Problems
Guessing and Checking
Making a Table to Find a Pattern
Writing an Equation
Selecting Notation
Making an Organized List
Working Backward

Choose a strategy or method and solve. Strategies and methods will vary.

6. There is a 3-digit number. The sum of all three digits is 16. The first digit equals the sum of the remaining digits. The difference between the second and the third digits is 2. What is the number?
853 or 835

7. Murray has a green tie and an orange tie; a silver shirt and a striped shirt; a pink jacket and a purple jacket. List the different combinations of ties, shirts, and jackets he can wear. See below.

8. Johnny, Ray, and Gene are camping. They have a jar that contains 12 quarts of juice, an empty 8-quart container, and an empty 4-quart container. Describe how they can divide the juice equally among themselves.
Fill the 8-qt jar, then fill the 4-qt jar from it.

9. Acme Car Rental charges $26.50 to rent a car for one day. To rent a car for 2 days costs $40.00. For 3 days, the charge is $53.50, and so on. How much would it cost to rent a car for 6 days? $94.00

10. Sybil's family drove from Seattle, Washington, to Dallas, Texas. After driving 849 mi, they arrived in Salt Lake City, Utah. Driving 1,175 miles farther, they arrived in Oklahoma City, Oklahoma. From there, they drove back 263 mi to get something they left behind. Then, they drove 628 mi to Dallas. How many miles long is the route they took to Dallas? 2,389 miles

11. Sonja took a walk around a right triangular block near her home in San Francisco, California. The perimeter of the block was 540 feet, and the area of the block was 12,150 square feet. If one of the sides of the block adjacent to the right angle was 135 feet long, how long was the longest side of the block? 225 feet

12. There is a 4-digit number. The first digit is 2 greater than the second digit. The fourth digit is 3 greater than the third digit. The second and fourth digits are the same. The sum of the last two digits is 9. What is the number? 8,636

13. Choose one problem that you've already solved in this lesson. Show how you could use another method to solve this problem.
Answers will vary.

green tie, silver shirt, pink jacket
green tie, silver shirt, purple jacket
green tie, striped shirt, pink jacket
green tie, striped shirt, purple jacket
orange tie, silver shirt, pink jacket
orange tie, silver shirt, purple jacket
orange tie, striped shirt, pink jacket
orange tie, striped shirt, purple jacket

Classwork/Homework, pages H193–H194

ASSIGNMENT GUIDE

Basic:	1–8, 13
Average:	2–12 e, 13
Extended:	1–13 o

Resources
Practice, pp. 193–4   Class/Home, pp. H193–4

Exercise Analysis
1–12   Choose an appropriate strategy or method
13   Use a different method

FOLLOW-UP ACTIVITIES

 CALCULATOR
Materials: calculators, pencils, paper

Have students solve the following combinations using their calculators.
- How many combinations are there of 10 things taken 5 at a time? (252)
- How many combinations are there of 15 things taken 7 at a time? (6,435)
- How many combinations are there of 22 things taken 4 at a time? (7,315)
- How many combinations are there of 75 things taken 3 at a time? (67,525)

 CALCULATOR
Materials: calculators, pencils, paper

Have students use their calculators to solve the following problems.

4! + 4! (48)
6! + 9! (363,600)
7! − 3! (5,034)
8! − 6! (39,600)
6! × 3! (4,320)
5! ÷ 4! (5)
3! + 3! ● 6! (<)
8! − 5! ● 3! (>)
3! × 3! ● 9! (<)
10! ÷ 5! ● 2! (>)

COMING UP
Eliminate the illogical!

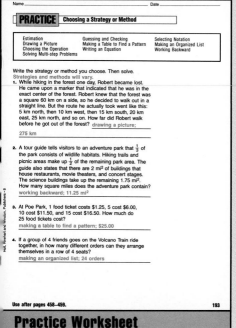

Practice Worksheet

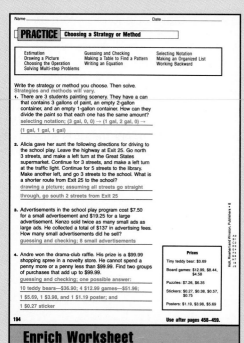

Enrich Worksheet

Objectives: To use *all*, *some*, or *none* to determine the implications of a set of statements

Warm-Up

Write these sentences on the chalkboard and have students write whether $A \subset B$, $B \subset A$, the sets are disjoint, or the sets overlap; for example, some A's are B's and some B's are A's. Remind students that $A \subset B$ means that A is a subset of B.

A. cats   B. dogs (disjoint)
A. fish   B. goldfish ($B \subset A$)
A. spotted dogs B. dogs ($A \subset B$)
A. pets   B. dogs (the sets overlap)

GETTING STARTED

Elicit from students the logical meaning of *some* (at least one), *none* (not one is or all are not), and *all* (not one is not). Then have them describe the relationship between the three sets below by using *all*, *some*, and *none*.

A. goldfish   **B.** dogs   **C.** pets

(no goldfish are dogs, no dogs are goldfish, some dogs are pets, some goldfish are pets, some pets are goldfish, some pets are dogs)

TEACHING THE LESSON

Point out that it is often possible to determine the truth value of one statement if one knows the truth value of another statement which implies that first statement; for example, if one knows that Mr. Smith has two sons and two daughters, one also knows that Mr. Smith has four children.

Remind students that it often helps to draw a Venn diagram when trying to determine whether one statement follows from another. Draw this diagram on the chalkboard to illustrate the example in the lesson.

Point out that the shaded area represents the set of spotted pets that are dogs. Then draw the two diagrams below and ask students which, if either, they think is correct.

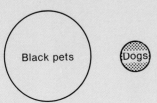

LOGICAL REASONING

You can use several statements to reach a new conclusion. The conclusion is said to be **valid** if it is impossible for the statements to be true and the conclusions to be false. Otherwise the conclusion is said to be **invalid**. Be sure to consider how *all*, *some*, and *none* are used before you reach a conclusion or before you determine whether a given conclusion is valid or invalid. Is the conclusion below valid or invalid?

Statements: Some of the spotted pets are dogs.
              None of the spotted pets are black.
Conclusion: None of the dogs are black.

Think: You know that none of the spotted pets are black. If a dog is spotted, it is not black. But a dog does not have to be spotted. So, the conclusion is *invalid*.

Determine whether the conclusions are *valid* or *invalid*.

Statements	Conclusions
1. ● None of the members of the swim team play polo. ● All the divers are members of the swim team.	**a.** None of the divers play polo. valid **b.** Some of the polo players are divers. invalid
2. ● Some lizards hide under bushes. ● All snakes hide under bushes.	**a.** Some lizards are snakes. invalid **b.** All lizards are snakes. invalid valid
3. ● All elephants are hungry. ● None of the zoo animals are hungry. ● Some of the zoo animals have two legs.	**a.** There are no elephants in the zoo. **b.** No animals with two legs are hungry. invalid
4. ● Some of Angela's pets are rabbits. ● Some of the rabbits have black feet.	**a.** All of Angela's pets have black feet. invalid **b.** None of Angela's pets have black feet. invalid

460

Point out that not enough information is given to determine whether *either* diagram is correct. Though we know from the second statement that *no* spotted dogs are black, we know nothing about whether any unspotted dogs are black. For that reason, the conclusion is invalid. Emphasize that to say that a conclusion is invalid is not to say that it is false, but only that there is not enough information to know whether it is true or false.

GROUP PROJECT

Marathon Map

The problem: The members of the town's Athletic Club are planning a marathon, and your school has been asked to assist them. Your class is going to plan the course. Use the following information to work with your classmates in creating a map of the course. Your marathon map should be drawn to scale.

Key Facts

- A marathon is 26 miles and 385 yards long.

- No part of the course can be covered more than once. The course should pass through as many neighborhoods as possible.

- The course must vary in difficulty.

Key Questions

- Is there a natural route for such a race in your town?

- Can certain roads be closed during the race?

- Do you want to include places along the route where spectators can watch?

- What requirements must be followed in determining where to locate the starting line? the finish line?

- Can the course accommodate a large number of runners?

- Will your map include the locations of
  water stations?
  security personnel?
  timers?
  medical facilities?

461

Objectives: To plan the route for a race; to draw a map to scale

USING THE PAGE

Materials: drawing paper, color pens and pencils per group; world almanacs, runners' magazines, and local road maps

Have students organize into groups of three to six. Tell them to keep the Key Facts and the Key Questions in mind as they plan their marathon route and map. Tell students that their marathon can be run through local streets that they know, or it can be through imaginary streets. Tell groups that each person in the group should be responsible for picking or describing at least one aspect of the course (starting line, water stops, and so on).

Remind groups to draw their route maps to scale and to include a key to the scale on the map. Each person should draw a different part or feature of the group's map. Because the maps will show detail, groups may want to use a scale of more than 1 inch to 1 mile. Have students draw, color, and label landmarks, land formations, buildings, and other structures along the route. Tell them to trace the route in a bright color. Have students consult almanacs and runners' magazines to find the range of winning marathon times for men and women. Have each group predict the times the fastest runners will arrive at each landmark along the route.

To extend this cooperative learning activity, have groups devise different categories of entrants, divided into various groupings by age, experience, and so on. Have them approximate the finish times of the top three winners in each category.

Purpose: The Chapter Test helps to assess students' understanding of the concepts and skills presented in this chapter.

The chart below is designed to help you review the test items by correlating them with the testing objectives that appear in the Chapter Overview.

Item	Objectives
1–10	A
11–14	B
15–17	C
18	D
19	A, B
20–21	C

Bonus

The bonus question may be used for extra credit, or you may want to assign it to students who complete the test before the rest of the class.

Calculator

You may wish to have students use calculators for the problem-solving portions of the test.

Resources

If you prefer to use this Chapter Test as a review exercise, additional testing materials are available in the Teacher's Resource Book.

CHAPTER TEST

Solve. Use 5 as the replacement value for x. Write each solution as an ordered pair. (pages 438–439)

1. $x + y = 7$ (5,2)
2. $2x + y = 13$ (5,3)

3. $x - 2y = 3$ (5,1)
4. $2x + 3y = 1$ (5,⁻3)

5. $5x - y = 0$ (5,25)
6. $3x - 2y = 25$ (5,⁻5)

Prepare a table of values for each equation and graph. (pages 440–441, 450–451)   Check students' graphs.

7. $y = 2x + 1$
8. $x + y = 7$

9. $^-2x + y = ^-1$
10. $2x + y = 16$

Prepare a table of values, and graph each system of equations on the same set of axes. (pages 452–453)   Check students' graphs.

11. $x + y = 6$ $x = 4$
$x - y = 2$ $y = 2$

12. $x + 2y = 14$ $x = 4$
$3y + x = 19$ $y = 5$

13. $x + y = 6$ $x = 3$
$x = 9 - 2y$ $y = 3$

14. $2x + y = 10$ $x = 5$
$x - y = 5$ $y = 0$

Prepare a table of values for each inequality and graph the solutions. (pages 454–457)   Check students' graphs.

15. $x \le 3$
16. $2x - y > 3$
17. $3x + 2y \le 8$

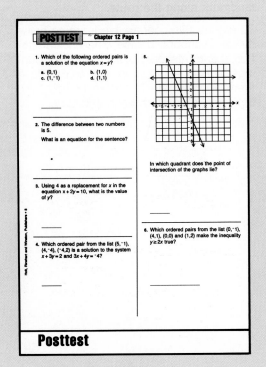

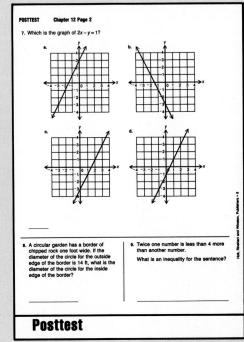

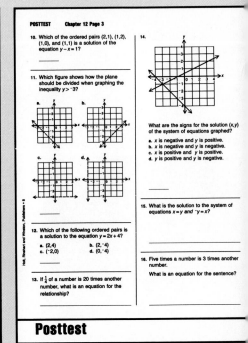

Solve. Draw a picture if necessary.
(pages 442–443 and 452–457)

18. Bob's house is 4 km due south of Town Hall.
His house is 6 km due west of the post office.
The train station is 9 km due east of Town
Hall. How far is the post office from the
train station? **5 km**

19. Write a system of equations. Then solve by
graphing.

3 times one number minus a second number is 14;
twice one number plus a second number is 16.
$3x - y = 14$; $2x + y = 16$; $x = 6$; $y = 4$; check students' graphs.

20. Write and graph this inequality: One number is
greater than three added to twice a second
number. **$x > 2y + 3$; check students' graphs.**

21. Write and graph this inequality: Four times one
number is less than 5 more than $\frac{1}{2}$ a second
number. **$4x < \frac{1}{2}y + 5$; check students' graphs.**

BONUS

Solve.

Graph the equations $x + y = 4$, $x + 2 = y$, and $y = 2x + 4$. Write the points of intersection as ordered pairs.

(0,4); (1,3); (⁻2,0) Check students' graphs.

463

For students who have difficulty with written tests, this test can be given orally.

You may wish to test students, orally or in writing, to see if they can explain the steps used in solving selected items. The following table summarizes the procedures for solving key test items.

Ex. 7–10

Making a table of values for equations, and graphing ordered pairs

To make a table of values, write *x* for the first variable, the equation, and *y* for the second variable across the top of the table. Substitute several values for the first variable under its heading. For each value listed, work across the table to solve the equation and find the value of the other variable that gives a true statement. Reading across the first and third columns of the table gives you a series of ordered pairs.

To graph ordered pairs, start at the origin (0,0). First move right (for positive integers) or left (for negative integers) along the *x*-axis the number of points that is equal to the absolute value of *x*. Then move up (for positive integers) or down (for negative integers) along the *y*-axis the number of points that is equal to the absolute value of *y*. Finally, draw a line through all of the solutions on the graph. All the points on the line are solutions.

Ex. 11–14

Graphing a system of equations on the same set of axes

Make a table of values for each equation and graph the ordered pairs. The coordinates of the point of intersection of the lines formed by the two sets of ordered pairs is the solution to the system.

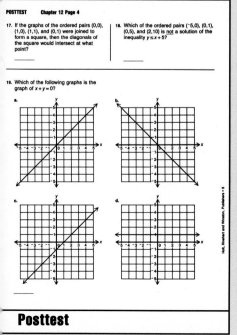

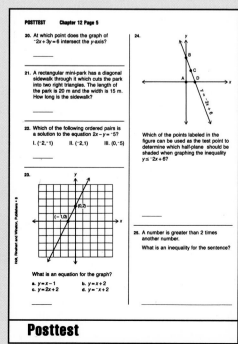

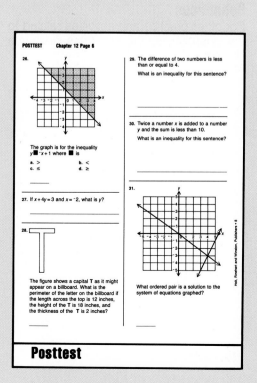

The equation $y = 5 - x$ is an equation in two variables that means that one number is equal to 5 minus another number. The solutions to this equation can be graphed as a line.

First, solve the equation by choosing a replacement value for one variable and then finding the value of the other variable that makes the statement true. Make a table of values.

x	y = 5 − x	y
2	3 = 5 − 2	3
1	4 = 5 − 1	4
7	⁻2 = 5 − 7	⁻2
⁻1	6 = 5 − ⁻1	6
4	1 = 5 − 4	1

(2,3)
(1,4)
(7,⁻2)
(⁻1,6)
(4,1)

The ordered pairs (2,3), (1,4), (7,⁻2), (⁻1,6), and (4,1) are solutions to the equation $y = 5 - x$. Many other solutions are possible.

Next, draw a pair of coordinate axes and graph the solutions from the table of values. Then, draw a line through the solutions that you have graphed.

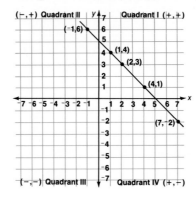

Make a table of values for each equation. Then graph each set of solutions. Check students' graphs.

1. $y = 9 - x$ **2.** $y = 2 - x$ **3.** $y = 6 - x$

4. $y = 14 + 2x$ **5.** $y = 6 - 4x$ **6.** $y = 3x$

7. $x - y = {}^-2$ **8.** $2x = {}^-4y$ **9.** $2x - y = 7$

464

---

urpose This Reteaching page provides additional instruction for key concepts in the chapter. It is designed for use by students who have had difficulty with these concepts. It can also be used to provide additional practice for students who require it.

USING THE PAGE

Graphing a line is taught on pages 450–451.

Emphasize to students that an equation in two variables will graph as a line because there will be not one but a series of solutions, each of which will be an ordered pair (one solution for x and for y). This series of ordered pairs can be plotted on a coordinate plane and connected with a line. Remind students that in solving such equations they must substitute arbitrary values for one variable and solve for the other. Tell students that when choosing values to substitute, they should choose both positive and negative numbers that can be plotted on a small graph. When these values are substituted and the other variable is found, students should then make a list of ordered pairs. Be sure students realize that ordered pairs are of the form (x,y) and that their values should be substituted accordingly. Once they have a set of ordered pairs, students should plot them on a coordinate plane. Review the form of the ordered pairs in each quadrant. The final step in graphing an equation in two variables will be connecting these points with a line. Explain to students that all points on the line are solutions to the equation. Have them choose several intermediate points from the graph on this page and substitute them back into the equation to check that they are true.

Resources

For other practice and activities related to this chapter, see the Teacher's Resource Book.

ENRICHMENT

Graphing Parallel Lines

Graph the system of equations on the same pair of axes.

$y = 2x$
$y = 2x + 4$

x	y = 2x	y
2	y = 2(2)	4
0	y = 2(0)	0
⁻2	y = 2(⁻2)	⁻4

Solutions
(2,4)
(0,0)
(⁻2,⁻4)

x	y = 2x + 4	y
2	y = 2(2) + 4	8
0	y = 2(0) + 4	4
⁻2	y = 2(⁻2) + 4	0

Solutions
(2,8)
(0,4)
(⁻2,0)

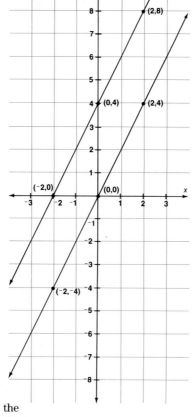

As you can see from the graph at right, the line $y = 2x$ is parallel to the line $y = 2x + 4$.

Graph each system of equations. State whether the lines are *parallel* or *not parallel*. Check students' graphs.

1. $y = 3x$
   $y = 3x - 6$
   parallel
2. $y = 4x + 2$
   $y = 4x + 4$
   parallel
3. $y = 5x + 10$
   $y = 5x + 5$
   parallel
4. $x + y = 7$
   $2x + 2y = 4$
   parallel
5. $y = 2 - 4x$
   $y + 4x = 4$
   parallel
6. $3x - 3y = 6$
   $y = x$
   parallel
7. $y = 4x + 4$
   $y = 3x + 3$
   not parallel
8. $5y - 5x = 5$
   $x = y + 2$
   parallel
9. $7x + 7y = 14$
   $3x + 3y = 6$
   not parallel

465

Purpose This Enrichment page provides an additional challenge for those students whose work throughout the chapter and on the Chapter Test shows a thorough understanding of the material. Alternatively, you may wish to use these exercises as a supplementary lesson for the entire class.

USING THE PAGE

As an extension of this lesson, have students look for patterns in the pairs of equations that graph as parallel lines. Once they spot a pattern, ask them to formulate equations that will graph as a third line that is parallel to each of the given pairs of parallel lines; for example, $y = 2x + 8$ would be parallel to the lines in the introductory problem.

Resources

For additional Enrichment activities, see the Teacher's Resource Book.

Objective: To use the POLY :SIDE :ANGLE procedure to draw regular polygons

Warm-Up

Have students write a Logo procedure that will draw two rectangles, one inside the other. Explain that the procedure must use the REPEAT command, and the rectangles may not share sides.

(Answers will vary; however, here is one possible answer.

```
TO RECTANGLES
REPEAT 2 [FD 40 RT 90 FD 60 RT 90]
PU FD 5 RT 90 FD 5 LT 90 PD
REPEAT 2 [FD 30 RT 90 FD 50 RT 90]
END)
```

Discuss the different answers. Emphasize that students go about solving Logo problems differently.

GETTING STARTED

Elicit from students the size of a turn that would turn you completely around. (360°) Discuss how turning around in place is similar to going completely around the path of a square. (In both, you begin facing forward and end facing forward.) Draw an equilateral triangle on the chalkboard. Elicit from students the size of the turn the turtle needs to make at each corner of the triangle. (120°) If students have difficulty, extend a side at each vertex, and show the external angle the turtle needs to turn. Develop the concept that this angle is greater than 90° and less than 180°. Have students develop a rule to find the amount the turtle must turn at each corner of a regular polygon. (Divide 360° by the number of sides in the shape.)

TEACHING THE LESSON

Write the POLY procedure on the chalkboard. Point out that every time the procedure name POLY is typed, the computer expects two numbers, the first separated from the second by a space. Elicit from students which procedure the turtle is actually following when you type

POLY 60 120

and then press RETURN or ENTER.

(REPEAT 3 [FD 60 RT 120])

Have students explain why division must be used to write the REPEAT command. (to determine how many sides a polygon with a specific angle has) Emphasize that the angles entered for :ANGLE are not the internal angles of that figure. The angles entered are called *external angles*. Draw a hexagon on the chalkboard, and trace the path, using the chalk as if it were the turtle.

TECHNOLOGY

This procedure uses the REPEAT command, two variables, and division to draw a polygon that has any length side and any size angle.

> This variable tells the turtle how long to draw each side.

> This variable tells the turtle the measure of each turn.

TO POLY :SIDE   :ANGLE

> This variable tells the turtle how many sides to draw.

REPEAT 360 / :ANGLE [FD :SIDE RT :ANGLE]

END

HINT: In drawing any polygon, the turtle makes one complete turn of 360°. Therefore, the measure of any single turn the turtle makes divided by 360° will tell the turtle how many sides to draw.

Write the number of sides each of these figures would have if they were drawn by using the POLY procedure.

1. POLY 60 120   3 sides
2. POLY 100 90   4 sides
3. POLY 30 45   8 sides
4. POLY 60 72   5 sides

466

Extend the sides, and show the angle that the turtle must turn. Point out that at each corner, the turtle turns a little bit more, until it turns around completely as it turns the last corner.

Have students explore the POLY procedure, entering first the angles for regular polygons and then any angle. Suggest that they record the values entered and the polygons or designs that result on the screen. After using many values, have students report upon the types of figures created and their values.

ASSIGNMENT GUIDE

Basic:	1–8
Average:	1–8
Extended:	1–8

Use this table for Exercises 5–8.

Measure of each turn	120°	90°	72°	60°	45°	40°
Number of sides		3	4	5	6	8	9

Write POLY procedures to draw each of the following figures. **Lengths of sides will vary.**

5.

POLY 20 72

6.

POLY 20 60

7.

POLY 20 45

8.

POLY 20 40

467

FOLLOW-UP ACTIVITIES

MATH CONNECTION
Materials: pattern (shape) blocks, drawing paper, scissors, glue, computer (optional)

Explain that the work of the artist Escher is known for its shapes that fit together to form a continuous design called a *tessellation*. Have students use from one to three pattern-block shapes to create a continuous design. Then have students trace the blocks on drawing paper, and color all similar shapes the same color. Display the designs and discuss why some shapes tessellate easily. Point out that all corners meet to form a total of 360 degrees.

Have students use the POLY procedure to draw on the computer a tessellating design made of polygons. Have them write a procedure for the design by using the POLY procedure a few times with various input values. Explain that other commands to move the turtle to different positions need to be added.

* Challenge students to make their own Escher-like designs.

Have students write a procedure for the new shape and include it in a tessellation procedure to repeat the pattern on the screen. One such procedure forms an arrow by cutting a triangle out of a square and adding the triangle to the opposite side of the square.

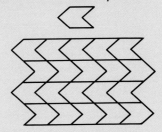

Purpose This Cumulative Review page provides an opportunity to reinforce students' understanding of the concepts and skills taught in previous chapters.

The chart below is designed to aid you in reviewing the material by specifying the pages on which various concepts and skills were taught.

Each Cumulative Review gives students an opportunity to practice taking tests that are written in a multiple-choice, standardized format. Be sure that students understand that if the correct answer is not among the first three given, then they should select the fourth choice—"not given"—as the correct answer. At least one item per test will require students to give this response.

CUMULATIVE REVIEW

Write the letter of the correct answer.

1. What is the length of the hypotenuse in a right triangle that has legs of 5 meters and 12 meters?

  a. $\sqrt{119}$ m   **b.** 13 m
  c. 60 m   **d.** not given

2. What is the circumference? Use 3.14 for π.

  a. 7.85 cm   **b.** 15.7 cm
  c. 19.63 cm   **d.** not given

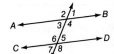

3. Choose the correct ratio for the cosine of $\angle A$.

  a. $\dfrac{a}{c}$ **b.** $\dfrac{a}{b}$
  c. $\dfrac{b}{c}$ **d.** not given

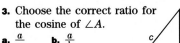

4. Find the area. Use 3.14 for π.

  a. 9.42 m^2
  b. 18.84 m^2
  c. 28.26 m^2
  d. not given

5. Find the surface area.

  a. 60 m^2
  b. 96 m^2
  c. 160 m^2
  d. not given

6. Find the volume.

  a. 15 cm^3
  b. 50 cm^3
  c. 60 cm^3
  d. not given

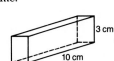

468

7. Which quadrant is ($^-$8,2) in?

  a. Quadrant I   **b.** Quadrant II
  c. Quadrant III   **d.** not given

8. Which is the alternate interior angle for $\angle 3$?

  a. $\angle 1$
  b. $\angle 5$
  c. $\angle 2$
  d. not given

9. The two polygons are similar. What is the measure of side $\overline{AB}$?

  a. 10
  b. 16
  c. 20
  d. not given

10. A triangular prism has a height of 12 cm and a base of 24 cm^2. What is its volume?

  a. 144 cm^3 **b.** 288 cm^3
  c. 576 cm^3 **d.** not given

11. George timed his weekly workout on the school track. According to his scattergram, what would you expect his average running time to be for Week 5?

  a. 90   **b.** 100
  c. 110   **d.** not given

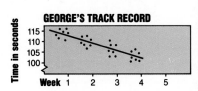

GEORGE'S TRACK RECORD

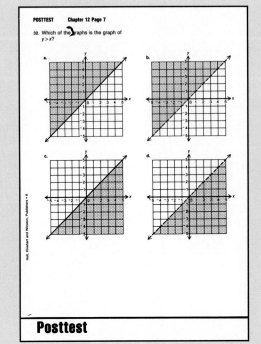

Posttest

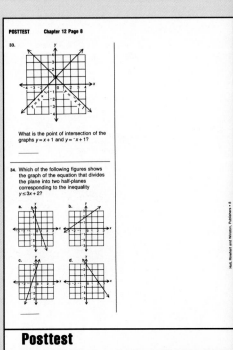

Posttest

Connecting Math Ideas

Page 13   Identifying Relationships

Some problems can be solved by using a logic table.

James, Martin, and Tasha play in the school band. One plays the drum, one plays the trumpet, and one plays the flute. Copy the table and use the clues to find who plays each instrument. Use an X to show that a possibility cannot be true. Use a √ when you are certain that a possibility is true.

Clue 1: James is a senior.
Clue 2: James and the trumpet player practice together after school.
Clue 3: Martin and the flute player are sophomores.

	Drum	Trumpet	Flute
James	√	X	X
Martin	X	√	X
Tasha	X	X	√

Page 39   Exploring Other Number Systems

The example at the right shows an ancient Hindu method of adding the whole numbers 2, 32, 143, and 335.

Sum of ones: $2 + 2 + 3 + 5 =$ 12
Sum of tens: $3 + 4 + 3 =$ 10
Sum of hundreds: $1 + 3 =$ 4
Sum of the sums: 512

Use the ancient Hindu method to find the following sums.
Check students' work.

1. $8 + 16 + 22 + 145$ 191

2. $5 + 22 + 45 + 202$ 274

3. $36 + 123 + 465 + 62$ 686

4. $56 + 732 + 128 + 3 + 19$ 935

Page 75   Extending the Investigation of Number Patterns

This is a famous number sequence called the **Fibonacci sequence.**

$$1, 1, 2, 3, 5, 8, 13, 21, \ldots$$

The **Golden Number,** or Golden Ratio, is 1.618 . . . If you divide any number in the Fibonacci sequence by the previous number, the quotient is an approximation of the Golden Number. For example, $13 \div 8 = 1.625$.

Use a calculator and the Fibonacci sequence to find 5 approximations for the Golden Number.   **Answers will vary. Possible answers:**
$5 \div 3 = 1.\overline{6}$; $21 \div 13 = 1.615$; $34 \div 21 = 1.619$; $55 \div 34 = 1.6176$; $89 \div 55 = 1.6\overline{18}$

Page 85 Extending Scientific Notation

You can add two numbers written in scientific notation if the numbers have the same power of 10.

Example: $4.5 \times 10^3 + 3.2 \times 10^3 = (4.5 + 3.2) \times 10^3$
$$= 7.7 \times 10^3$$

Add. Write the sum in scientific notation.

1. $4.66 \times 10^5 + 1.2 \times 10^5$
    5.86×10^5

2. $2.78 \times 10^2 + 5.01 \times 10^2$
    7.79×10^2

3. $9.23 \times 10^7 + 2 \times 10^7$
    1.123×10^8

Page 109 Solving Application Problems by Solving Linear Equations

A formula can be solved as an equation if you know the values of all but one of the variables.

Example: Use the formula $U = P \div n$ where $U =$ the unit price, $P =$ the total price, and $n =$ the number of units to find the total price of a 305-gram can of soup that has a unit price of $0.002.

$U = P \div n$ ⟵ Replace U with 0.002 and n with 305.
$0.002 = P \div 305$
$0.002 \times 305 = P \div 305 \times 305$
$0.61 = P$ ⟵ The total price is $0.61.

Use the formula $U = P \div n$ to find the missing value of the variable.

1. $U =$ \$0.03 per gram
    $P = \square$
    $n = 68$ grams
    $P = \$2.04$

2. $U =$ \$0.12 per foot
    $P = \square$
    $n = 25$ feet
    $P = \$3.00$

3. $U = \square$
    $P = \$5.62$
    $n = 8$ pounds
    $U = \$0.7025$

Page 147 Drawing Three-Dimensional Figures from Different Perspectives

Look at the cube at the bottom of page 147.

1. What do you know about the shape of each side of the large cube? Each side is a square.

2. Draw what you would see if you looked at the large cube from the top.

3. Suppose you removed one small cube from the large cube. Draw how the small cube would look if it were in the same position as the large cube.

Page 171 Relating Metric Measures

You can find the volume, capacity, and mass of rectangular containers that are not cubes.

Example: length = 4 cm, height = 5 cm, width = 6 cm
Volume = length × width × height
= 4 × 5 × 6
= 120 cm³, capacity = 120 mL, mass = 120 g

Copy and complete the chart for each container of water.

Length	Width	Height	Volume	Capacity	Mass
1. 8 cm	7 cm	2 cm	112 cm³	■ mL112	■ g112
2. 8 m	5 m	3 m	120■ m³	■ kL 120	■ t 120
3. 7 m	5 m	400 cm	140■ m³	■ kL 140	■ t 140

Page 255 Extending Scientific Notation

You can multiply numbers that are written in scientific notation.

Example: $(2.3 \cdot 10^3) \cdot (8.5 \cdot 10^2) = (2.3 \cdot 8.5) \cdot (10^3 \cdot 10^2)$
$$= 19.55 \cdot 10^5$$
$$= 1.955 \cdot 10^6$$

Multiply. Write the product in scientific notation.

1. $(4.2 \cdot 10^3) \cdot (7.1 \cdot 10^4)$ 2.982×10^8 **2.** $(8.2 \cdot 10^3) \cdot (4.5 \cdot 10^5)$ 3.69×10^9

3. $(6 \cdot 10^5) \cdot (4.8 \cdot 10^{-2})$ 2.88×10^4 **4.** $(3.1 \cdot 10^8) \cdot (8.7 \cdot 10^{-3})$ 2.697×10^6

Page 319 Investigating Formats for Presenting Data

The stem-and-leaf plot at the right is a useful way to display data. The numbers on the left are called the stems, and the numbers on the right are called the leaves. The stem and leaf 5 | 2 represents a test score of 52.

Test Scores

```
5 | 2358
6 | 0034688
7 | 0112455788
8 | 00123358899
9 | 13478
```

1. Tell how many test scores are shown in the stem-and-leaf plot. 37

2. What is the median of the test scores? 77

3. Make a stem-and-leaf plot of the data shown for Exercises 1–6 on page 315.

```
2 | 2
3 | 1 2 6 6 7 8 8 9 9
4 | 0 0 1 3 5 6 8
5 | 2
```

Page 325 Investigating Formats for Presenting Data

A box-and-whisker graph is another way to display data. The box-and-whisker graph below displays the data for math class quiz scores.

Example:

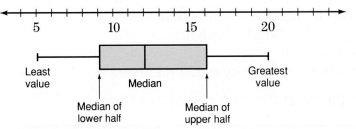

Use the data below for Exercises 1–4.
Weights (in kilograms): 32, 33, 34, 34, 36, 40, 41, 43, 45, 47, 48, 49, 50, 52, 54, 58, 62, 63, 65, 68, 71

1. Find the median of the data. **48**

2. Find the median of the lower half of the data (from 32 to 47). **38**

3. Find the median of the upper half of the data (from 49 to 71). **60**

4. What is the least value? the greatest value? **32; 71**

5. Using the box-and-whisker graph shown above as an example and your answers to Exercises 1–4, make a box-and-whisker graph for the data. **Check students' graphs.**

Page 425 Exploring the Volume of Pyramids and Prisms

Draw these figures using the dimensions given. Then assemble the pyramid and prism.

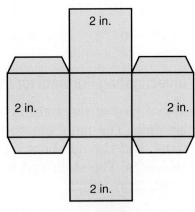

1. Fill the pyramid with sand. Then pour this sand into the prism. Repeat this process until the prism is full.

2. How many times did you pour sand from the pyramid into the prism? **3 times**

3. Write a sentence to tell how the volume of the pyramid compares to the volume of the prism. **The volume of the pyramid is $\frac{1}{3}$ the volume of the prism.**

4. Based on your experiment, write the formulas for the volume of the pyramid and the volume of the prism. **Pyramid: $V = \frac{1}{3}Bh$; prism: $V = Bh$, or $V = lwh$**

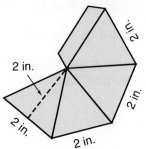

Infobank

APPROXIMATE LENGTH OF PRINCIPAL RIVERS OF THE WORLD

River	Miles	Kilometers
Amazon	3,912	6,296
Mississippi/Missouri	3,880	6,240
Niger	2,600	4,184
Nile	4,180	6,690
Yangtze	3,602	5,797

SPECIFIC GRAVITY OF MINERALS

Mineral	Specific gravity
Barite	4.50
Graphite	2.09–2.23
Magnesite	2.98–3.44
Olivine	3.22–4.39

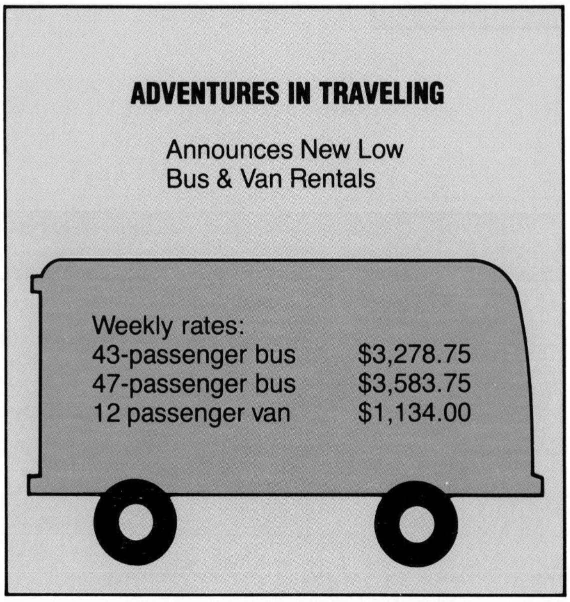

NUTRITIONAL VALUE OF VEGETABLES, FRESH COOKED, PER CUP

	Carbohydrates (grams)	Protein (grams)
Broccoli	7.0	4.8
Cauliflower	5.1	2.9
Celery	4.7	1.2
Corn	31.0	5.3
Green beans	6.8	2.0
Okra	9.6	3.2
Peas	19.4	8.6
Spinach	6.5	5.4

ADVENTURES IN TRAVELING

Announces New Low
Bus & Van Rentals

Weekly rates:
43-passenger bus $3,278.75
47-passenger bus $3,583.75
12 passenger van $1,134.00

CUBES AND CUBE ROOTS

N	N³	∛N̄	N	N³	∛N̄
1	1	1.000	26	17,576	2.962
2	8	1.260	27	19,683	3.000
3	27	1.442	28	21,952	3.037
4	64	1.587	29	24,389	3.072
5	125	1.710	30	27,000	3.107
6	216	1.817	31	29,791	3.141
7	343	1.913	32	32,768	3.175
8	512	2.000	33	35,937	3.208
9	729	2.080	34	39,304	3.240
10	1000	2.154	35	42,875	3.271
11	1331	2.224	36	46,656	3.302
12	1728	2.289	37	50,653	3.332
13	2197	2.351	38	54,872	3.362
14	2744	2.410	39	59,319	3.391
15	3375	2.466	40	64,000	3.420
16	4096	2.520	41	68,921	3.448
17	4913	2.571	42	74,088	3.476
18	5832	2.621	43	79,507	3.503
19	6859	2.668	44	85,184	3.530
20	8000	2.714	45	91,125	3.557
21	9261	2.759	46	97,336	3.583
22	10,648	2.802	47	103,823	3.609
23	12,167	2.844	48	110,592	3.634
24	13,824	2.884	49	117,649	3.659
25	15,625	2.924	50	125,000	3.684

BASKET-WEAVING SUPPLIES

Material	Available sizes	Amount sold
Sea grass	$\frac{3}{16}$ in.	3-lb coil (600 ft)
Flat reed	$\frac{1}{4}$ in., $\frac{3}{8}$ in., $\frac{1}{2}$ in., $\frac{5}{8}$ in.	by the lb
Flat oval reed	$\frac{1}{4}$ in., $\frac{3}{8}$ in.	by the lb
Round reed	$\frac{3}{8}$ in., $\frac{1}{2}$ in., $\frac{5}{8}$ in.	by the lb
Fiber rush	$\frac{3}{32}$ in., $\frac{4}{32}$ in., $\frac{5}{32}$ in., $\frac{6}{32}$ in.	by the lb (250 ft)
White ash or oak	$\frac{5}{8}$ in.	15-strand bundle (6–8 ft)

DISTANCES FROM PERTH TO SYDNEY

Perth–Coolgardie. 537
Perth–Nullarbor. 1,418
Perth–Port Augusta 2,051
Perth–Broken Hill 2,404
Perth–Dubbo. 3,067
Perth–Orange 3,100
Perth–Sydney 3,278

HEIDI'S HEARTY CHICKEN NOODLE SOUP
19 ounces

INGREDIENTS: chicken stock, chicken, enriched egg noodles, mushrooms, carrots, celery, sauterne wine, corn starch, water, salt, sweet peppers, potato starch, yeast extract, hydrolyzed plant protein, monosodium glutamate, natural flavoring, and dehydrated parsley

Nutrition information per serving

Serving size	$9\frac{1}{2}$ oz (269 g)
Servings per container	2
Calories	140
Protein (g)	12
Total carbohydrates (g)	12
simple sugars (g)	1
complex carbohydrates (g)	11
Fat (g)	7
Sodium	1,070 mg/serving

Percentage of U.S. Recommended Daily Allowance (U.S. RDA)

Protein	25%	Riboflavin	10%
Vitamin A	20%	Niacin	20%
Vitamin C	2%	Calcium	2%
Thiamine	6%	Iron	10%

FOUNDING (ESTABLISHMENT) OF FOUR EUROPEAN CITIES

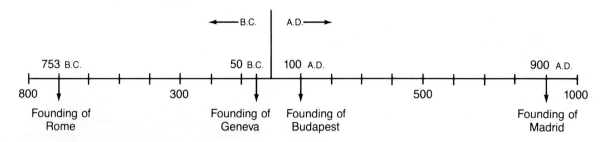

753 B.C.   ← B.C.   A.D. →   50 B.C.   100 A.D.   900 A.D.

800   300   500   1000

Founding of Rome   Founding of Geneva   Founding of Budapest   Founding of Madrid

TELEVISION SYSTEMS OF THE WORLD

Region or country	Number of lines per frame	Number of pictures per second
United Kingdom	405–625	25
North America, South America, Japan	525	30
Europe, Australia, Africa, Eurasia	625	25
France and French dependents	625–819	25

In movies, the illusion of movement is created by projecting a series of still pictures, one after another.

In television, each frame is "drawn" by an electronic scanning spot that races across the screen in straight horizontal lines from top to bottom. When it has finished, it has completed one frame, and returns to the top to begin another. It takes two frames to make one picture. The process is so fast that what we see is moving pictures.

NBA SCORING LEADERS

Year	Scoring champion	Pts	Avg	Year	Scoring champion	Pts	Avg
1950	George Mikan, Minneapolis	1,865	27.4	1970	Jerry West, Los Angeles	2,309	31.2
1951	George Mikan, Minneapolis	1,932	28.4	1971	Lew Alcindor, Milwaukee	2,596	31.7
1952	Paul Arizin, Philadelphia	1,674	25.4	1972	Kareem Abdul-Jabar, Milwaukee	2,822	34.8
1953	Neil Johnston, Philadelphia	1,564	22.3	1973	Nate Archibald, Kansas City-Omaha	2,719	34.0
1954	Neil Johnston, Philadelphia	1,759	24.4	1974	Bob McAdoo, Buffalo	2,261	30.8
1955	Neil Johnston, Philadelphia	1,631	22.7	1975	Bob McAdoo, Buffalo	2,831	34.5
1956	Bob Pettit, St. Louis	1,849	25.7	1976	Bob McAdoo, Buffalo	2,427	31.1
1957	Paul Arizin, Philadelphia	1,817	25.6	1977	Pete Maravich, New Orleans	2,273	31.1
1958	George Yardley, Detroit	2,001	27.8	1978	George Gervin, San Antonio	2,232	27.2
1959	Bob Pettit, St. Louis	2,105	29.2	1979	George Gervin, San Antonio	2,365	29.6
1960	Wilt Chamberlain, Philadelphia	2,707	37.6	1980	George Gervin, San Antonio	2,585	33.1
1961	Wilt Chamberlain, Philadelphia	3,033	38.4	1981	Adrian Dantley, Utah	2,452	30.7
1962	Wilt Chamberlain, Philadelphia	4,029	50.4	1982	George Gervin, San Antonio	2,551	32.3
1963	Wilt Chamberlain, San Francisco	3,586	44.8	1983	Alex English, Denver	2,326	28.4
1964	Wilt Chamberlain, San Francisco	2,948	36.9	1984	Adrian Dantley, Utah	2,418	30.6
1965	Wilt Chamberlain, San Fran., Phila.	2,534	34.7	1985	Bernard King, New York	1,809	32.9
1966	Wilt Chamberlain, Philadelphia	2,649	33.5	1986	Dominique Wilkins, Atlanta	2,366	30.3
1967	Rick Barry, San Francisco	2,775	35.6	1987	Michael Jordan, Chicago	3,041	37.1
1968	Dave Bing, Detroit	2,142	27.1	1988	Michael Jordan, Chicago	2,868	35.0
1969	Elvin Hayes, San Diego	2,327	28.4	1989	Michael Jordan, Chicago	2,633	32.5

ABSTRACT REPRESENTATION OF A HOUSE: GREENVILLE, DELAWARE

AMERICA'S TALLEST BUILDINGS AND MONUMENTS

Structure	Height (ft)
A. Lake Point Towers, Chicago, tallest apartment building	640
B. Peachtree Center Plaza, Atlanta, tallest hotel	754
C. Chrysler Building, New York	1,046
D. Empire State Building, New York	1,250 without mast 1,472 with mast
E. World Trade Center, New York	1,377
F. Sears Tower, Chicago, tallest office building	1,454 without mast 1,559 with mast
G. Statue of Liberty, New York	301 including pedestal
H. Washington Monument, Washington, D.C.	555
I. San Jacinto Column, Texas, tallest monument column	570
J. Gateway Arch, St. Louis, Missouri	630

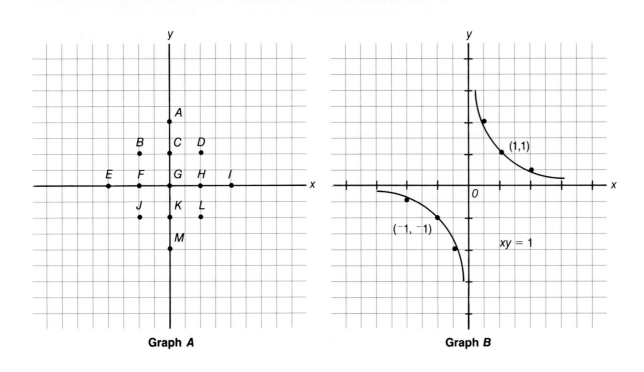

Graph *A*

Graph *B*

ANSWER KEY

Chapter 1, page 19—exercises

6. eight and five hundred forty-three thousandths

7. one and nine millionths

8. four hundred ninety-three ten-thousandths

9. one and one hundred sixty-three hundred-thousandths

10. seven and three thousand five hundred forty-one hundred-thousandths

★23. 26 and 9 thousand 8 hundred 15 ten-thousandths

Chapter 1, page 36—Chapter Test

1. 621 thousand, 472
600,000 + 20,000 + 1,000
+ 400 + 70 + 2

2. 7 billion, 946 million, 310
7,000,000,000 + 900,000,000 +
40,000,000 + 6,000,000 + 300 + 10

3. 40 trillion, 309 thousand, 436
40,000,000,000,000 + 300,000 +
9,000 + 400 + 30 + 6

4. 124 thousandths
0.100 + 0.020 + 0.004

5. 4 and 500092 millionths
4 + 0.5 + 0.00009 + 0.000002

6. 91 and 3906 millionths
91 + 0.003 + 0.0009 + 0.000006

Chapter 1, page 39—Enrichment

1.

2.

3.

XIV

DCLXXXIII

MMMMCCCXLII

Chapter 2, page 69—Problem Solving

1. **Step 2:** Find the total weight of food supplies carried by all club members.

2. **Step 2:** Find the total amount of sales of all large lanterns at $50 each.

3. **Step 1:** Find the number of people who took the raft trip in one day.
Step 2: Find the number of people who rode in one raft on one day. 8 people

4. **Step 1:** Find the total number of people the roller coaster can hold.
Step 2: Find the total number of rides given per day.
Step 3: Find the total number of people that can ride the roller coaster in one day. 4,320 people

5. **Step 1:** Find the total number of passengers checked in in one day.
Step 2: Find the total weight of baggage handled in one day at 30 pounds per passenger. 1,080,000 pounds

6. **Step 1:** Find the total cost of Gail's purchase, including sales tax.
Step 2: Find the total amount of money Gail gave the salesclerk.
Step 3: Find the amount of change. $17.65

7. **Step 1:** Find the cost of one round trip per person.
Step 2: Find the amount of money collected for one round trip.
Step 3: Find the total amount of money collected for 3 round trips. $428.40

8. **Step 1:** Find the total amount of money spent to rent a van for 10 days.
Step 2: Find the total amount of money spent to stay in a hotel for 2 nights.
Step 3: Find the total amount of money spent to stay at a campsite for 8 days.
Step 4: Find the total amount of money spent for food for 10 days.
Step 5: Find the total amount of money spent for the van, the hotel, the campsite, and the food.
Step 6: Find the amount of money remaining in the budget after expenses.
Step 7: Find the amount of money available to spend on other items per day. $31.40

Chapter 3, page 112—Calculator

1. $100 \times 100 = 10,000$

3. $999 \times 999 = 998,001$

5. $1,000 \times 1,000 = 1,000,000$

7. $9,999 \times 9,999 = 99,980,001$

★ 9. $10,000 \times 10,000 = 100,000,000$

★11. $99,999 \times 99,999 = 9,999,800,001$

★13. $100,000 \times 100,000 = 10,000,000,000$

★15. $999,999 \times 999,999 = 999,998,000,001$

★17. $1,000,000 \times 1,000,000 = 1,000,000,000,000$

★19. $9,999,999 \times 9,999,999 = 99,999,980,000,001$

21. $1,000$

23. $98,901$

25. $10 \times 1,000 = 10,000$

27. $99 \times 9,999 = 989,901$

29. $10 \times 10,000 = 100,000$

31. $99 \times 99,999 = 9,899,901$

33. $100 \times 1,000 = 100,000$

35. $999 \times 9,999 = 9,989,001$

37. $100 \times 10,000 = 1,000,000$

39. $999 \times 99,999 = 99,899,001$

★41. $1,000 \times 1,000,000 = 1,000,000,000$

★43. $9,999 \times 9,999,999 = 99,989,990,001$

Chapter 4, page 153—exercises

1. $x = 3\frac{23}{24}$

2. $z = 6\frac{5}{24}$

3. $y = 7\frac{9}{20}$

4. $b = 22\frac{31}{72}$

5. $r = 18$

6. $c = 5\frac{2}{7}$

7. $f = 1\frac{3}{5}$

8. $k = 30\frac{1}{16}$

9. $h = 1\frac{18}{37}$

10. $t = 2\frac{3}{34}$

11. $f = 5\frac{41}{47}$

12. $u = 1\frac{13}{51}$

13. $a = 6\frac{1}{2}$

14. $n = 50$

15. $d = 7$

16. $w = \frac{185}{258}$

Chapter 5, page 169—Challenge

He starts both timers together. As soon as the 3-min timer runs out, he turns it over. When the 5-min timer has run out, 2 min will have passed on the 3-min timer. He then flips over the 3-min timer again and lets those last 2 min run out.

Chapter 5, page 187—Challenge

The boy didn't take into account that his father would have to fly across the international date line and would arrive in New York at 8:00 A.M. the next day. This is easier to understand if you think of it from the point of view of someone who stays behind in New York.

Chapter 9, page 315—exercises

1.

20–24	||
25–29	
30–34		
35–39	|||| |||
40–44	||||	
45–49	||||

7.

25–29.9	||||
30–34.9	|||| |||| |||| ||
35–39.9	|||

12.

10–14	||
15–19	|||| ||
20–24	
25–29		

Chapter 9, page 323—Midchapter Review

3.

5–9	||
10–14	||||
15–19	|||| |||
20–24	||||	

Chapter 9, page 319—exercises

6.

6–7	1
8–9	2
10–11	2
12–13	3
14–15	1
16–17	1

7.

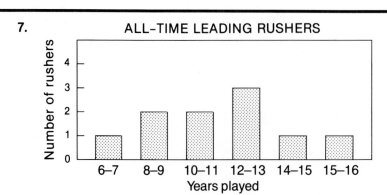

ALL-TIME LEADING RUSHERS

5.

$$\star \lessgtr \begin{smallmatrix} + \\ \checkmark \\ * \end{smallmatrix} \qquad \square \lessgtr \begin{smallmatrix} + \\ \checkmark \\ * \end{smallmatrix} \qquad \triangle \lessgtr \begin{smallmatrix} + \\ \checkmark \\ * \end{smallmatrix} \qquad \bigcirc \lessgtr \begin{smallmatrix} + \\ \checkmark \\ * \end{smallmatrix}$$

Chapter 10, page 388—Reading Math

1. Thirteen plus five is equal to two times nine.
   Two times nine is equal to thirteen plus five.
2. Six times nine is greater than forty-five minus two.
   Forty-five minus two is less than six times nine.
3. Thirty-eight divided by two is less than fifteen plus six.
   Fifteen plus six is greater than thirty-eight divided by two.
4. x minus 6 is equal to fourteen.
   Fourteen is equal to x minus six.
5. Twenty-four divided by three is greater than or equal to x minus two.
   x minus two is less than or equal to twenty-four divided by three.
6. Forty minus x is less than or equal to x divided by two.
   x divided by two is greater than or equal to forty minus x.
7. x plus y is greater than seventeen.
   Seventeen is less than x plus y.
8. x squared plus y is less than five.
   Five is greater than x squared plus y.

Chapter 11, page 407—Problem Solving

3. **Step 1:** Find the cost of one place setting.
   Step 2: Find the number of extra place settings.
   Step 3: Find the difference in price.

4. **Step 1:** Find the speed in miles per minute.
   Step 2: Find the distance for 2 minutes.
   Step 3: Round answer to the nearest mile.

5. **Step 1:** Find the height of the two mountains together.
   Step 2: Find the difference in height between the two mountains and the trench.

6. **Step 1:** Find the tree's growth rate per month.
   Step 2: Find the height for 24 months at that growth rate.
   Step 3: Round answer to the nearest foot.

Chapter 12, page 441—exercises

10.

x	$^-1$	0	1	2
y	$^-3$	0	3	6

11.

x	$^-1$	0	1	2
y	$^-1$	2	5	8

12.

x	$^-1$	0	1	2
y	$^-5$	$^-2$	1	4

13.

x	$^-1$	0	1	2
y	1	0	$^-1$	$^-2$

14.

x	$^-1$	0	1	2
y	$^-5$	$^-3$	$^-1$	1

15.

x	$^-1$	0	1	2
y	5	2	$^-1$	$^-4$

16.

x	$^-1$	0	1	2
y	$^-1$	1	3	5

17.

x	$^-1$	0	1	2
y	$^-3$	$^-1$	1	3

18.

x	$^-1$	0	1	2
y	$^-5$	$^-\frac{7}{2}$	$^-2$	$^-\frac{1}{2}$

Chapter 12, page 445—exercises

15.

x	2	1	0	$^-1$	$^-2$
y	8	7	6	5	4

16.

x	2	1	0	$^-1$	$^-2$
y	9	10	11	12	13

17.

x	2	1	0	$^-1$	$^-2$
y	10	7	4	1	$^-2$

Chapter 12, page 448—Problem Solving

5. **b.** Multiply 3/4 by 1 1/3.
   c. Multiply 3/4 by 2/3.
   d. Add: 3/4 + 12/12 + 6/12 = 2 1/4 hours.

6. **b.** Multiply 15 × 9.
   c. Multiply 2 1/2 by 2 2/3.
   d. Subtract: 135 − 6 2/3 = 128 1/3.

STUDENT HANDBOOK

CLASSWORK HOMEWORK | **Whole-Number Place Value**

Write the number in standard form.

1. 964 trillion, 200 billion, 701 million, 16 thousand
964,200,701,016,000

2. 18 trillion, 322 million, 941 thousand, 1
18,000,322,941,001

3. one million, thirty thousand, six hundred seventy-eight
1,030,678

Write the short word name for each number.

4. 73,079,937   73 million, 79 thousand, 937

5. 9,251,865,804   9 billion, 251 million, 865 thousand, 804

6. 100,200,600,900,700
100 trillion, 200 billion, 600 million, 900 thousand, 700

Write the value of each underlined digit.

7. 43,506,971,384   500 million

8. 621,335,954,628,168   20 trillion

Solve.

9. Hector went to visit his sister Luisa at Yale University. He was impressed with the libraries there. Luisa told him that Yale has more than 8,391,707 books. How would Hector write this number in expanded form?
8,000,000 + 300,000 + 90,000 + 1,000 + 700 + 7

CLASSWORK HOMEWORK | **Comparing and Ordering Whole Numbers**

Write >, <, or =.

1. 674,476 ⊖> 476,674
2. 98,697,996 ⊖< 100,402,140
3. 24,671 ⊖> 24,617
4. 200,020,020 ⊖< 200,020,200
5. 678,675 ⊖= 678,675
6. 111,111,111 ⊖> 11,111,111
7. forty-nine million ⊖< forty-nine billion
8. two hundred twenty trillion ⊖> two hundred two trillion

Write each group of numbers from the greatest to the least.

9. 27,490,179; 22,790,197; 24,790,719; 6,947,791; 24,400,420
27,490,179; 24,790,719; 24,400,420; 22,790,197; 6,947,791

Write each group of numbers from the least to the greatest.

10. 999,999; 55,555; 9,999; 555,555; 55,555,555
9,999; 55,555; 555,555; 999,999; 55,555,555

11. 8,808; 80,880; 88,008; 8,080; 80,808
8,080; 8,808; 80,808; 80,880; 88,008

Solve.

12. In 1980, the estimated population of Australia was 13,548,448. In 1980, the estimated population of the Netherlands was 13,060,115. Which country had a larger estimated population?
Australia

13. In 1980, the estimated population of the Fiji Islands was 588,068. In 1980, the estimated population of Mongolia was 1,594,800. Which country had a larger estimated population?
Mongolia

CLASSWORK HOMEWORK | **Addition and Subtraction**

Write the missing number.

1. 757 + 468 = 468 + _757_
2. 9,003 − 0 = _9,003_
3. 759 + 0 = _759_
4. (15 + 47) + 26 = 15 + (_47_ + 26)
5. 287 − 287 = _0_
6. 217 + 308 = _308_ + 217
7. 94 + (62 + 22) = (94 + 62) + _22_
8. 6,280 + 0 = _6,280_
9. 104 − 0 = _104_
10. 5,091 − 5,091 = _0_
11. 7,462 + 6,186 = _6,186_ + 7,462
12. 80 + 246 = 246 + _80_
13. 41,001 + 0 = _41,001_
14. 175 − 0 = _175_
15. (31 + 91) + 58 = 31 + (_91_ + 58)
16. 9 + 0 = _9_
17. 19,539 − 19,539 = _0_
18. 1,763 − 1,763 = _0_
19. 4,891 + 9,746 = 9,746 + _4,891_
20. 39 + (25 + 10) = (39 + 25) + _10_
21. 615 − 0 = _615_
22. 47 + 86 = _86_ + 47
23. 16 + (37 + 91) = (16 + 37) + _91_
24. 503 − 0 = _503_
25. 601 − 601 = _0_
26. 999 + 0 = _999_
27. 275 + 353 = _353_ + 275
28. (41 + 19) + 15 = _41_ + (19 + 15)
29. 61,580 − 0 = _61,580_
30. 697 − 697 = _0_
31. (15 + 50) + 54 = 15 + (_50_ + 54)
32. 45 − 0 = _45_
33. 6,743 + 0 = _6,743_
34. (27 + 18) + 98 = 27 + (_18_ + 98)
35. 9,132 − 9,132 = _0_
36. 413 + 62 = 62 + _413_
37. 397 − 0 = _397_
38. 9,007 + 0 = _9,007_
39. 452 + 810 = 810 + _452_
40. 550 − 550 = _0_

CLASSWORK HOMEWORK | **Estimation**

The Ecology Club is collecting aluminum cans, glass bottles, and newspapers for recycling. The club will use money from the sale of these items to buy posters, T-shirts, paint, and membership cards. The club has to place an order before it knows exactly how much it will take in from the items.

Here is some information:

• Renting a truck costs about $55 a day.
• Supplies, such as twine, bags, scissors, and gloves, cost $25 per week.
• Within 3 weeks, the club will collect $210–$362.50 worth of cans and bottles.
• Within 3 weeks, the club will collect $372–$672 worth of newspapers.

Answer each question to help the club make choices about which combination of items to order. You may have to go back and revise figures as you work.

> 300 Posters $225
> 100 T-shirts $175
> 8 Gallons of paint $80
> 500 Membership cards $100

1. How much money will the club collect from the sale of cans, bottles, and newspapers after 3 weeks? Should the club underestimate or overestimate the amount? Why?
$582. Underestimate. They may not collect as much as they hope to.

2. How much money should the club plan to spend for renting a truck if the truck is needed for only 2 days to make deliveries to the recycling plant? Should they underestimate or overestimate the amount? Why?
$120; overestimate; better to overestimate expenses

3. How much should the club plan to spend for supplies? Should they underestimate or overestimate the amount? Why?
$100; overestimate; better to overestimate expenses

4. How much money should the club expect to take in from the sale of bottles, cans, and newspapers after paying for the truck and for supplies? $362

5. What is the greatest amount of money the club can expect to earn after expenses? $814.50

6. Which two items should the club order? Explain why.
Posters and paint; these come closest ($305) to the minimum income.

CLASSWORK HOMEWORK — Estimating Sums of Whole Numbers

Write > or <.

1. 4,235 + 7,186 $>$ 11,000
2. 5,134 + 4,389 $<$ 10,000
3. $79.65 + $28.57 $>$ $100
4. $564.39 + $228.88 $<$ $800
5. 51,764 + 9,275 + 23,459 $>$ 80,000
6. 36,297 + 58,498 $<$ 100,000
7. 492,716 + 236,459 $<$ 750,000
8. 789,265 + 976,296 $>$ 1,600,000

Estimate each sum. **Answers will vary. Accept any reasonable estimate.**

9.
```
  5,237
  1,789
  3,465
+ 7,559
```
16,000–18,500

10.
```
  4,369
     87
  9,063
+ 4,527
```
17,000–18,500

11.
```
  $ 9.53
    0.07
    0.39
+  15.18
```
$24–26

12.
```
  3,276,546
     11,327
  2,176,549
+ 1,527,461
```
6,000,000–7,000,000

13.
```
  4,937
  2,175
  5,186
+ 7,559
```
18,000–20,000

14.
```
  2,759
    175
+ 6,108
```
8,000–10,000

15.
```
  $39.88
    0.79
+   1.08
```
$40–42

16.
```
  4,175,268
    895,317
+ 2,105,639
```
7,000,000–7,200,000

Solve. Use the information in the table to answer these questions.

17. On which two days was the total attendance about 25,000?
Tuesday and Wednesday

18. On which two days was the total attendance about 50,000?
Tuesday and Friday

19. On which two days did the total attendance exceed 100,000?
Friday and Saturday, or
Tuesday and Saturday

State Fair	
Day	**Attendance**
Monday	12,654
Tuesday	17,859
Wednesday	7,236
Thursday	9,389
Friday	29,358
Saturday	85,465

Use with pages 10–11.

Student Handbook H5

CLASSWORK HOMEWORK — Estimating Differences of Whole Numbers

Write > or <.

1. 8,165 − 2,089 $>$ 6,000
2. 5,896 − 1,547 $>$ 4,000
3. 6,129 − 387 $<$ 6,000
4. 19,537 − 5,387 $>$ 14,000
5. $48.65 − $19.85 $>$ $20.00
6. $96.37 − $9.55 $>$ $85.00
7. 26,576 − 19,865 $<$ 10,000
8. 82,179 − 19,583 $>$ 60,000
9. 486,925 − 95,467 $<$ 400,000
10. 689,278 − 417,885 $>$ 200,000
11. 5,176,429 − 875,265 $>$ 4,000,000
12. 18,752,469 − 7,895,265 $>$ 10,000,000

Estimate.

13.
```
  4,836
−   978
```
3,900⁻

14.
```
  7,234
− 4,187
```
3,000⁺

15.
```
  $79.56
−  15.89
```
$60⁺

16.
```
  $118.87
−   79.59
```
$40⁻

17.
```
  53,476
−  8,958
```
45,000⁻

18.
```
  81,647
− 25,879
```
60,000⁻

19.
```
  74,529
− 25,287
```
50,000⁻

20.
```
  435,276
−  89,197
```
350,000⁻

Solve.

21. About how many more people attended Thursday than Wednesday?
25,000⁻

22. Did over 25,000 more people attend Friday than attended Thursday?
no

23. About how many more people attended Saturday than Monday?
47,000⁻

24. Did 5,000 more people attend Tuesday than Monday?
no

Date	Attendance
Monday	14,567
Tuesday	18,081
Wednesday	5,869
Thursday	30,287
Friday	54,895
Saturday	61,457

H6 Student Handbook

Use with pages 12–13.

CLASSWORK HOMEWORK — Adding and Subtracting Whole Numbers

Add or subtract. Check your answers by estimating.

1.
```
  4,887,472
+ 1,633,993
```
6,521,465

2.
```
  411,392
  860,128
  341,274
+ 602,835
```
2,215,629

3.
```
  $90,751.04
−  61,562.46
```
$29,188.58

4.
```
  435 billion
+ 125 billion
```
560 billion

5.
```
  $3,839.58
      58.20
     514.36
+    967.26
```
$5,379.40

6.
```
  9,704,152
−    48,345
```
9,655,807

7.
```
  635 trillion
− 558 trillion
```
77 trillion

8.
```
  1,546,360
+    42,350
```
1,588,710

9.
```
  7,933,066
− 4,278,109
```
3,654,957

10.
```
  94 million
+  8 million
```
102 million

11.
```
  394,012
  679,293
    5,653
+ 424,844
```
1,503,802

12.
```
  $9,034,842
−    595,961
```
$8,438,881

13.
```
  237 billion
−  54 billion
```
183 billion

14.
```
  $21,126.75
+      47.05
```
$21,173.80

15.
```
  1,470,422
−   315,683
```
1,154,739

16.
```
  385,807
  583,415
  923,847
+ 782,044
```
2,675,113

17.
```
  625,363
    9,402
  339,930
+ 415,806
```
1,390,501

18.
```
  3,459,408
− 2,234,005
```
1,225,403

19.
```
  857 million
+ 115 million
```
972 million

20.
```
  $84,237.11
+  35,681.25
```
$119,918.36

21.
```
  210 trillion
−  13 trillion
```
197 trillion

22.
```
  $173,820
   976,472
     7,341
+   14,399
```
$1,172,032

23.
```
  6,247,768
+   126,544
```
6,374,312

24.
```
  5,783,504
−    24,064
```
5,759,440

25. 7,014,499 − 227,192 = ____?____ 6,787,307
26. 9,467,977 + 6,285,461 = ____?____ 15,753,438
27. 22,036 + 3,191 + 91,838 = ____?____ 117,065
28. 7,462,023 − 6,386,803 = ____?____ 1,075,220
29. ____?____ − 817,456 = 123,739 941,195
30. 9,624,004 − ____?____ = 9,326,417 297,587

Use with pages 14–15.

Student Handbook H7

CLASSWORK HOMEWORK — Problem Solving: A Four-Step Plan

Use the information in the table. Solve each problem using the four-step plan.

- State the problem in your own words.
- Tell which tools you will use.
- Solve the problem.
- Check your solution.

OLDEST NATIONAL PARKS		
Park	**Year**	**Area (Acres)**
Yellowstone	1872	2,219,785
Kings Canyon	1890	461,901
Sequoia	1890	402,482
Yosemite	1890	761,170

1. How old is Yellowstone National Park?
subtract; answers will vary according to the current year

2. Suppose you could transplant parks. How many Yosemite National Parks
divide; 3 Yosemites

3. How many acres of land were set aside as national parks in 1890?
add; 1,625,553 acres

4. List the four oldest parks in order from smallest to largest.
compare; Sequoia, Kings Canyon, Yosemite, Yellowstone

5. An average acre in Sequoia National Park contains about 50 trees. About how many trees are there in Sequoia National Park?
estimate; multiply;
about 20,124,100 trees

6. An average camper uses 1.5 acres of land during a visit. How many campers can Yosemite accommodate at one time?
estimate; divide;
about 507,447 people

7. The National Park Service manages 68,234,091 acres of federal land. How many Yellowstone National Parks could fit in this area?
divide; 30.7 Yellowstones

8. The summit of Yosemite's highest mountain is 3,960 meters above sea level. The lowest point in Death Valley is 86 meters below sea level. How high above the lowest point is the summit of Yosemite's highest mountain?
add; 4,046 meters

H8 Student Handbook

Use with pages 16–17.

CLASSWORK HOMEWORK — Decimal Place Value

Write the decimal.

1. five hundred ninety-eight thousandths   0.598

2. thirteen thousand, five hundred twenty-two hundred-thousandths   0.13522

3. one millionth   0.000001

4. one thousand one millionths   0.001001

5. one and ninety-eight hundredths   1.98

Write the word name for each number.

6. 0.4786   four thousand, seven hundred eighty-six ten-thousandths

7. 13.925684   thirteen and nine hundred twenty-five thousand, six hundred eighty-four millionths

8. 143.75669   one hundred forty-three and seventy five thousand, six hundred sixty-nine hundred-thousandths

9. 0.46539   forty-six thousand, five hundred thirty-nine hundred-thousandths

10. 5.01   five and one hundredth

Write the value of each underlined digit.

11. 0.92584   5 thousandths

12. 23,809.23809   3 hundredths

13. 57,174.47601   4 tenths

14. 0.602458   4 ten-thousandths

15. 2373.287899   9 millionths

Use with pages 18–19.   Student Handbook   H9

CLASSWORK HOMEWORK — Comparing and Ordering Decimals

Write >, <, or =.

1. 229.783938 ⊙> 229.7839348   2. 0.999999 ⊙< 1

3. 5,674.0123 ⊙< 5,674.123   4. 6.00002 ⊙> 6.000002

5. 323,956.987453 ⊙> 323,956.985753   6. 8.034 ⊙< 80.34

7. 1.019872 ⊙< 1.919872   8. 1.00000 ⊙= 1.00

9. 0.333 ⊙< 0.3333   10. 10.0 ⊙< 100.00000

11. 57.345 ⊙= 57.345   12. 0.99999 ⊙> 0.1

Write each group of decimals from the least to the greatest.

13. 0.656, 0.565, 0.6565, 0.56565, 0.65
0.565, 0.56565, 0.65, 0.656, 0.6565

14. 0.456789, 0.6789, 0.56789, 0.789, 0.89
0.456789, 0.56789, 0.6789, 0.789, 0.89

15. 0.000666, 0.066006, 0.00666, 0.006066, 0.006606
0.000666, 0.006066, 0.006606, 0.00666, 0.066006

16. 0.53298, 0.52398, 0.54398, 0.54298, 0.534
0.52398, 0.53298, 0.534, 0.54298, 0.54398

Write each group of decimals from the greatest to the least.

17. 0.747447, 0.744774, 0.477447, 0.747474, 0.774774
0.774774, 0.747474, 0.747447, 0.744774, 0.477447

18. 0.9286, 0.9386, 0.8386, 0.9376, 0.928
0.9386, 0.9376, 0.9286, 0.928, 0.8386

19. 0.564897, 0.563997, 0.563897, 0.564997, 0.564887
0.564997, 0.564897, 0.564887, 0.563997, 0.563897

20. 0.000003, 0.003, 0.0003, 0.00003, 0.03
0.03, 0.003, 0.0003, 0.00003, 0.000003

H10   Student Handbook   Use with pages 20–21.

CLASSWORK HOMEWORK — Rounding Decimals

Round to the nearest whole number.

1. 0.9111   1   2. 0.1605   0   3. 23.47108   23   4. 55.555   56

5. 7.553   8   6. 0.894   1   7. 15.823   16   8. 83.001   83

Round to the nearest tenth or to the nearest ten cents.

9. 93.451   93.5   10. $0.88 $0.90   11. 0.94738   0.9   12. $1.6302 $1.60

13. 0.387   0.4   14. 14.567   14.6   15. 8.3219   8.3   16. $75.099 $75.10

Round to the nearest hundredth or to the nearest cent.

17. 0.96679   0.97   18. $40.6731 $40.67   19. $0.8263 $0.83   20. 9.14131   9.14

21. $7.5681 $7.57   22. 0.01895   0.02   23. 5.36521   5.37   24. $27.8095 $27.81

Round to the nearest thousandth.

25. 0.87835508   0.878   26. 19.99999   20.000

27. 521.802267   521.802   28. 0.044133   0.044

29. 46.905371   46.905   30. 5.000932   5.001

Round to the nearest ten-thousandth.

31. 402.98434892   402.9843   32. 7,017.53268   7,017.5327

33. 0.5678687   0.5679   34. 70.3295681   70.3296

35. 0.22225   0.2223   36. 5.605987   5.6060

Use with pages 22–23.   Student Handbook   H11

CLASSWORK HOMEWORK — Using Outside Sources Including the Infobank

The chart below shows some famous ocean voyages, the ships that made them, and the distance and duration of the voyages.

Year	From	To	Ship	Distance (Nautical miles)	Duration
1840	Halifax	Liverpool	Brittania	2,610	9 days 21 hours
1854	Liverpool	New York	Baltic	3,037	9 days 17 hours
1928	San Pedro	Honolulu	USS Lexington	2,226	3 days 1 hour
1944	Halifax	Vancouver	St. Roch	7,295	86 days
1950	Japan	San Francisco	USS Boxer	5,000	7 days 19 hours
1962	New York	Capetown	African Comet	6,786	12 days 16 hours

Do you need the Infobank above to solve the problems? Write yes or no.

1. The *Brittania* was the first Cunard liner. Cunard was named after Sir Samuel Cunard, who was born in 1787 and died in 1865. How many years did he live?   no

2. The *St. Roch* was the first vessel to complete the Northwest Passage in one season. How many more miles was its voyage than the voyage of the *Brittania* from Halifax to Liverpool?   yes

Solve. Use the Infobank above for any additional information you need.

3. In 1846, the *Yorkshire* traveled from Liverpool to New York in 16 days. How much less time did the *Baltic* take for the same voyage?   6 days 7 hours

4. The *Yorkshire* covered 3,150 miles on its voyage. How many more miles was this than the *Baltic's* voyage between the same places?   113 miles

5. In 1970 a ship sailed from Capetown to Liverpool via New York, and followed the courses taken by the *African Comet* and the *Baltic*. How many miles was the voyage?   9,823

6. Write the ships in order from the voyage that took the longest amount of time to the voyage that took the shortest amount of time.
St. Roch, African Comet, Brittania, Baltic, Boxer, Lexington

7. Is the order for question 6 the same as the order of the ships according to the distance of the voyages?   no

8. In 1959, Max Conrad flew 5,000 miles solo from Chicago to Rome. It took him 1 day 10 hours. How much longer did it take the *USS Boxer* to cover the same distance?   6 days 9 hours

H12   Student Handbook   Use after pages 24–25.

CLASSWORK HOMEWORK — Estimating Sums and Differences of Decimals

The figure shows the progress of a white-water kayak race.

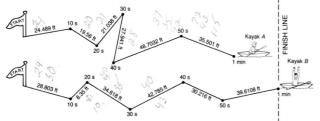

Estimate and write each answer to the nearest whole number.

Note: Answers will vary. Accept any reasonable estimate.

1. How many feet did kayak *A* travel in 40 s?
   90–95 ft

2. How many feet did kayak *B* travel in 40 s?
   110–120 ft

3. Which kayak traveled farther in 40 s?
   kayak *B*

4. How much farther did kayak *A* travel between the 40-s mark and the 50-s mark than between the 50-s mark and the 1-min mark?
   13–14 ft

5. How many feet did kayak *B* travel between the 40-s mark and the 1-min mark?
   69–70 ft

6. How far did kayak *B* travel in the race?
   180–190 ft

7. How many feet did kayak *A* travel between the 40-s mark and the 1-min mark?
   80–85 ft

8. How much farther did kayak *B* travel between the 30-s mark and the 40-s mark than between the 10-s mark and the 20-s mark?
   30–35 ft

9. How far did kayak *A* travel in the race?
   160–180 ft

10. The direct distance from the start to the finish line is 158.307 ft. How far out of the way did kayak *B* travel?
    25–30 ft

Use with pages 26–27. Student Handbook **H13**

CLASSWORK HOMEWORK — Adding Decimals

Add. Check your answer by estimating.

1. 0.6927 + 0.836 = 1.5287
2. 0.1159 + 0.5367 + 0.2863 = 0.9389
3. 5.651 + 89.261 + 87.2426 + 23.1546 = 205.3092
4. $70.11 + 25.62 = $95.73

5. 0.6966 + 0.5125 + 0.3957 = 1.6048
6. 45.4789 + 46.2787 = 91.7576
7. $29.03 + 76.27 + 61.58 + 10.42 = $177.30
8. 0.3978 + 0.302 + 0.9564 + 0.48 = 2.1362

9. $26.87 + 59.47 = $86.34
10. 73.468 + 84.1951 + 6.1828 + 0.254 = 164.0999
11. 71.8132 + 20.746 + 61.9367 = 154.4959
12. 0.605 + 0.8183 = 1.4233

13. 0.143 + 0.9764 + 0.7341 + 0.17 = 2.0235
14. $6,222.03 + 931.91 + 5.15 = $7,159.09
15. 0.3156 + 0.7223 = 1.0379
16. $50.65 + 5.49 + 0.75 = $56.89

17. 63.2108 + 1.367 = 64.5778
18. 8.269 + 4.8265 + 87.923 + 3.7442 = 104.7627
19. 0.4727 + 8.285 + 0.9864 = 9.7441
20. $531.93 + 360.28 + 35.68 + 4.86 = $932.75

21. 3.7575 + 4.7014 + 2.8869 = 11.3458
22. 75.6743 + 0.8 + 4.62 = 81.0943
23. $5,794.84 + 885.72 = $6,680.56
24. 86.3726 + 69.4605 + 64.1016 + 94.2732 = 314.2079

25. 0.9835 + 0.4978   1.4813
26. 0.7452 + 0.6173   1.3625
27. 6.492 + 9.977   16.469
28. 4.394 + 6.5653   10.9593
29. 4.385 + 58.923   63.308
30. 7.4921 + 1.7796   9.2717

H14 Student Handbook Use with pages 28–29.

CLASSWORK HOMEWORK — Subtracting Decimals

Subtract. Check your answer by estimating.

1. 17.5082 − 12.6201 = 4.8881
2. 28.7988 − 14.1648 = 14.6340
3. 9.5102 − 9.3928 = 0.1174
4. $39.28 − 5.58 = $33.70

5. 74.5897 − 30.5261 = 44.0636
6. 87 − 7.613 = 79.387
7. $3.98 − 2.10 = $1.88
8. 67.9105 − 17.0366 = 50.8739

9. 51.5364 − 5.7 = 45.8364
10. 89.4739 − 51.3134 = 38.1605
11. 65.666 − 8.3425 = 57.3235
12. 99.7057 − 70.7603 = 28.9454

13. 3.8203 − 1.676 = 2.1443
14. 6.4977 − 1.8483 = 4.6494
15. 44.8889 − 10.0428 = 34.8461
16. 7.059 − 2.6153 = 4.4437

17. 89.4739 − 51.3134   38.1605
18. 57.5240 − 7   50.5240

What is purple and 5,000 miles long? Subtract. Then copy the puzzle. Write the letter of each problem on the line that has the first two digits of the answer.

A 84.232 − 51.877 = 32.355
E 5 − 2.3614 = 2.6386
G 9.28713 − 7.56349 = 1.72364
P 62.618 − 34.259 = 28.359

T 12.489 − 5.322 = 7.167
O 9.1 − 6.887 = 2.213
F 4.28951 − 3.64728 = 0.64223
N 114.32 − 73.88 = 40.44

R 3.99442 − 1.84357 = 2.15085
H 7.22 − 6.1834 = 1.0366
I 6.43892 − 2.56183 = 3.87709
W 55.410 − 14.882 = 40.528

L 14.927 − 10.333 = 4.594
C 7.52578 − 5.21953 = 2.30625

T	H	E		G	R	A	P	E
71	10	26		17	21	32	28	26

W	A	L	L	O	F	C	H	I	N	A
40	32	45	45	22	06	23	10	38	40	32

Use with pages 30–31. Student Handbook **H15**

CLASSWORK HOMEWORK — Using a Graph

NUMBER OF DEMOCRATIC AND REPUBLICAN SENATORS

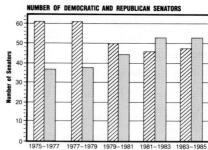

Use the double-bar graph above to answer each question.

1. Which party controlled the Senate during six of the ten years shown in the graph? Democratic party

2. In which years did the Democratic party have the greater number of members in the Senate?
   1975–1977, 1977–1979, 1979–1981

3. In which years did the Republican party have the fewest members in the Senate? 1975–1977

4. In which years did the majority hold the greatest number of seats? How many more seats did the majority party hold during those years? 1975–1977; 24 more seats

5. In which years was the majority the smallest? How many more seats did the majority party hold during those years?
   1983–1985; 6 more seats

H16 Student Handbook Use with pages 32–33.

CLASSWORK HOMEWORK — Multiplication and Division

Complete.

1. $640 \times 36 = 36 \times \underline{\quad?\quad}$ **640**

2. $4 \times (3 + 6) = (4 \times 3) + (4 \times \underline{\quad?\quad})$ **6**

3. $72 \div 1 = \underline{\quad?\quad}$ **72**

4. $5 \times (7 \times 8) = (5 \times 7) \times \underline{\quad?\quad}$ **8**

5. $84 \times 0 = \underline{\quad?\quad}$ **0**

6. $9,029 \times 1 = \underline{\quad?\quad}$ **9,029**

7. $144 \div 6 = 24$
   $6 \times 24 = \underline{\quad?\quad}$ **144**

8. $17 \times 4 = 68$
   $68 \div 17 = \underline{\quad?\quad}$ **4**

9. $95 \times 3 = 3 \times \underline{\quad?\quad}$ **95**

10. $23 \times (6 \times 7) = (23 \times 6) \times \underline{\quad?\quad}$ **7**

11. $16 \times (17 + 8) = (16 \times 17) +$
    $(16 \times \underline{\quad?\quad})$ **8**

12. $49 \times 0 = \underline{\quad?\quad}$ **0**

13. $54 \div 1 = \underline{\quad?\quad}$ **54**

14. $835 \times 1 = \underline{\quad?\quad}$ **835**

15. $720 \div 8 = 90$
    $8 \times 90 = \underline{\quad?\quad}$ **720**

16. $36 \times 4 = 144$
    $144 \div 4 = \underline{\quad?\quad}$ **36**

17. $390 \times 0 = \underline{\quad?\quad}$ **0**

18. $30 \times (2 + 6) = (30 \times 2) +$
    $(30 \times \underline{\quad?\quad})$ **6**

19. $1,864 \div 1 = \underline{\quad?\quad}$ **1,864**

20. $9 \times (42 \times 71) = (9 \times 42) \times \underline{\quad?\quad}$ **71**

21. $55 \times 7 = 7 \times \underline{\quad?\quad}$ **55**

22. $4 \times 1 = \underline{\quad?\quad}$ **4**

23. $546 \div 2 = 273$
    $273 \times 2 = \underline{\quad?\quad}$ **546**

24. $707 \times 3 = 2,121$
    $2,121 \div 707 = \underline{\quad?\quad}$ **3**

25. $85 \times 1 = \underline{\quad?\quad}$ **85**

26. $696 \div 1 = \underline{\quad?\quad}$ **696**

27. $16 \times 94 = 94 \times \underline{\quad?\quad}$ **16**

28. $84 \times (3 \times 2) = (84 \times 3) \times \underline{\quad?\quad}$ **2**

29. $45 \times (46 + 19) = (45 \times 46) +$
    $(45 \times \underline{\quad?\quad})$ **19**

30. $1,561 \times 0 = \underline{\quad?\quad}$ **0**

31. $22 \times 23 = 506$
    $506 \div 23 = \underline{\quad?\quad}$ **22**

32. $7,007 \div 1,001 = 7$
    $1,001 \times 7 = \underline{\quad?\quad}$ **7,007**

Use with pages 42–43. Student Handbook **H17**

CLASSWORK HOMEWORK — Multiplying and Dividing by Multiples of 10

Find the product or quotient.

1. $\frac{4,900}{700}$ **7**

2. 10×500 **5,000**

3. $1,200 \times 30$ **36,000**

4. $290,000 \div 1,000$ **290**

5. $\frac{\$9,000}{600}$ **$15**

6. $15,000 \div 300$ **50**

7. $\frac{5,600}{800}$ **7**

8. $4,000 \times 70$ **280,000**

9. 600×60 **36,000**

10. $\frac{782,000}{100}$ **7,820**

11. $320 \div 80$ **4**

12. $\frac{\$47,500}{100}$ **$475**

13. 70×60 **4,200**

14. 500×30 **15,000**

15. $210,700 \div 700$ **301**

16. 404×100 **40,400**

17. $\frac{6,400}{400}$ **16**

18. $1,500 \times 50$ **75,000**

19. $\frac{84,000}{70}$ **1,200**

20. $9,200 \div 100$ **92**

21. $\frac{9,400,000}{10,000}$ **940**

22. 731×10 **7,310**

23. $100,000 \div 100$ **1,000**

24. $\frac{\$6,300}{70}$ **$90**

25. 450×300 **135,000**

26. $210 \times 7,000$ **1,470,000**

27. 506×30 **15,180**

Solve.

28. The Whatzit Tooyou Opinion Company is asking people if they would like the White House to be painted blue. The company mailed 4,250 questionnaires. Each one contained 100 questions. If every person returns the questionnaire, how many answers will the company receive? **425,000**

H18 Student Handbook Use with pages 44–45.

CLASSWORK HOMEWORK — Estimating Products and Quotients

Write the most reasonable estimate.

1. 34×73 **a. over 2,100** b. under 2,100

2. 8×469 **a. over 3,200** b. under 3,200

3. 18×368 a. over 8,000 **b. under 8,000**

4. 29×468 a. over 15,000 **b. under 15,000**

5. $7\overline{)3,468}$ a. 50 **b. 500** c. 5,000

6. $9\overline{)35,689}$ a. 40 b. 400 **c. 4,000**

7. $5\overline{)423,826}$ a. 800 b. 8,000 **c. 80,000**

Decide how many digits there are in each quotient. Then estimate.

8. $4\overline{)7,354}$ **4** **1,500–2,000**

9. $6\overline{)2,543}$ **3** **400–500**

10. $9\overline{)45,372}$ **4** **5,000–5,100**

11. $53\overline{)4,934}$ **2** **90–100**

12. $28\overline{)13,762}$ **3** **400–500**

Use the data in the chart to estimate.

13. About how many daily papers does Bob deliver
   a. in a week? **300–400**
   b. in a month? **1,200–2,000**
   c. in a year? **15,000–20,000**

Bob's Newspaper Deliveries	
Daily (Mon.–Sat.)	48
Sunday	93

Answers may vary. Accept any reasonable estimate.

14. About how many Sunday papers does Bob deliver
   a. in a month? **360–500**
   b. in a year? **4,500–5,000**

Use with pages 46–47. Student Handbook **H19**

CLASSWORK HOMEWORK — Identifying Extra/Needed Information

Write the letter of the information that is not needed.

1. A radio show host gets paid $2,680 per month. He hosts 2 shows each week, and the average length of each show is $4\frac{1}{2}$ hours. How much does he receive per show?
   a. He gets paid $2,680 per month.
   b. He hosts 2 shows each week.
   c. Each show averages $4\frac{1}{2}$ hours.

2. A radio station charges $3.76 per second of weekday advertising, and $5.26 per second on weekends. Hopscotch, Inc., runs a 30-second ad each weekday. How much does it pay the station each week?
   a. The charge is $3.76 per second.
   b. The weekend charge is $5.26.
   c. Hopscotch runs a 30-second ad each weekday.

Solve.

3. WXYZ Radio has a competition that attracts 630 entries for a $250 prize. Molly gets paid $7.50 per hour for checking the entries, which takes her 2 minutes each. How much does WXYZ pay Molly to check the entries? **$157.50**

4. In one nonleap year, a radio announcer called every 50th number in the local telephone directory. There are 18,150 people listed in the telephone directory. If he dialed one person per day, how many days were there that he did not make a call? **2 days**

5. One radio station has an average of 12 minutes of advertising per hour. The station broadcasts 14 hours per day. How much advertising time can it sell each week? **19 hours 36 minutes**

6. A radio station invites 42 listeners to visit the station. Each listener is given a certificate that costs the station $1.75 and a radio that costs the station $14.63. How much did the station pay for the radios? **$614.46**

7. WXYZ's Twilight Hour show reaches 45,500 listeners, and its Midnight Mood show reaches 8,955 listeners. There are 3,420 people who listen to both shows. How many listeners does WXYZ reach with the two shows? **51,035 listeners**

8. A radio station installs an emergency generator that uses 12 gallons of gasoline per hour. The station decides to store enough gasoline to run for 6 days. Gasoline costs $1.23 per gallon. How much gasoline does the station need? **1,728 gallons**

H20 Student Handbook Use with pages 48–49.

CLASSWORK HOMEWORK · Multiplying Whole Numbers

Multiply.

1. 99,319 × 47 = 4,667,993

2. 85,064 × 226 = 19,224,464

3. 8,613 × 92 = 792,396

4. 58,214 × 7 = 407,498

5. 53,556 × 783 = 41,934,348

6. 42,312 × 21 = 888,552

7. $89,456 × 63 = $5,635,728

8. 287,431 × 120 = 34,491,720

9. 8,016 × 75 = 601,200

10. 42,914 × 716 = 30,726,424

11. 83,382 × 52 = 4,335,864

12. $99.37 × 61 = $6,061.57

13. 5,312 × 3 = 15,936

14. $370.04 × 71 = $26,272.84

15. 7,891 × 729 = 5,752,539

16. 29,907 × 757 = 22,639,599

17. 186,439 × 27 = 5,033,853

18. 5,221 × 974 = 5,085,254

19. 9,491 × 66 = 626,406

20. 3,050 × 6 = 18,300

21. 3 × 407 billion   1,221 billion

22. 7 × 106 million   742 million

23. 8 × 69 million   552 million

24. 8 × 14 trillion   112 trillion

Solve.

25. In 1976, the solar probe *Helios B* reached a speed of 149,125 mph. At this speed, how far would it travel in 12 hours?   1,789,500 miles

26. Earth orbits the sun at about 66,641 mph. About how far does Earth travel in 48 hours?   about 3,198,768 miles

CLASSWORK HOMEWORK · Dividing Whole Numbers

Divide.

1. 310 ÷ 6   51 R4

2. $3,045 ÷ 33 $92 R9

3. 25,965 ÷ 45   577

4. 6,201 ÷ 7   885 R6

5. 391 ÷ 72   5 R31

6. $1,175 ÷ 47 $25

7. 221,044 ÷ 428   516 R196

8. 328 ÷ 5   65 R3

9. 624 ÷ 8   78

10. $42 ÷ 3 $14

11. 3,544 ÷ 4   886

12. 2,111 ÷ 18   117 R5

13. $\frac{1,856}{7}$ 265 R1

14. $\frac{7,875}{9}$ 875

15. $\frac{217}{3}$ 72 R1

16. $\frac{391}{72}$ 5 R31

17. $\frac{\$998}{74}$ $13 R36

18. $\frac{6,177}{71}$ 87

19. $\frac{535}{15}$ 35 R10

20. $\frac{21,859}{54}$ 404 R43

21. $\frac{295}{4}$ 73 R3

22. 72)28,990   402 R46

23. 469)418,718   892 R370

24. 8)416   52

25. 783)749,331   957

26. 35)14,168   404 R28

27. 16)4,736   296

Solve.

28. The Crunchy Breakfast Cereal Company decided to introduce its new cereal by sending an equal number of sample boxes to homes in 72 neighborhoods throughout the state. The company sent out 13,536 sample boxes. How many homes in each neighborhood received a sample?   188 homes

CLASSWORK HOMEWORK · Estimation

Write the letter of the answer that describes the correct way to estimate to solve the problem.

1. Charlotte is sending a boat anchor by freight. The anchor weighs 96 pounds, and Charlotte believes that the freight charges are $1.42 per pound. How much money should she take to the freight office to be sure that she has enough?
  a. Overestimate the weight, and underestimate the charges.
  (b.) Overestimate both the weight and the charges.
  c. Underestimate both the weight and the charges.

2. Ralph wants to photograph the end of a boat race. The race is 138 miles long, and the fastest boat is expected to average 87 miles per hour. How long after the start of the race should Ralph arrive at the finish line?
  a. Overestimate the miles, and underestimate the speed.
  b. Overestimate both the miles and the speed.
  (c.) Underestimate the miles, and overestimate the speed.

Solve by estimation.

3. A race starts at 12:15 P.M. Judith's boat is docked 27 miles from the starting line, and can travel at an average speed of 11 miles per hour. If Judith leaves at 10:00 A.M., will she arrive at the race before it begins?   no

4. A ferry charges $5.85 for each car it carries, and $1.55 for each person in the car. Marco and 3 friends are riding in a car and want to take the ferry. They have $12.50 among them. Is it enough for the ferry ride?   yes

5. Overnight docking at a marina costs $23.20. The price is reduced by $1.95 for each member of the boat's crew who eats at the Marina café. To the nearest dollar, about how much does it cost Jacob to dock 3 members of his crew eat at the café?   about $17

6. The captain of a fishing boat needs to buy 42 feet of wood to make repairs to the deck. The wood costs $4.83 per foot. To the nearest $10, how much will the captain pay for the wood to repair the deck?   about $200

7. Thelma is organizing a fishing contest at the lake near her house. The prize for catching the largest fish is $50. The entry fee for the first 12 people to enter is $3.80, and all other contestants pay $4.15. If 20 people enter the contest, how much (to the nearest $10) will Thelma have left after paying the prize money?   about $30

CLASSWORK HOMEWORK · Decimals and Powers of 10

Compute.

1. 0.006 × 100   0.6

2. 32.58 ÷ 10   3.258

3. 22.88 × 1,000   22,880

4. 30.8 × 10   308

5. 0.007 × 100   0.7

6. 1.6 ÷ 10   0.16

7. 0.5 ÷ 1,000   0.0005

8. 476.7 ÷ 10   47.67

9. 0.004 × 1,000   4

10. 0.077 × 10   0.77

11. 10.2761 × 10   102.761

12. 98.95 ÷ 100   0.9895

13. 52.04 ÷ 1,000   0.05204

14. 0.25 × 100   25

15. 2.316 × 10   23.16

16. 0.74 ÷ 10   0.074

17. 189.7 ÷ 1,000   0.1897

18. 5.778 × 100   577.8

19. 5.316 × 100   531.6

20. 16.64 × 10   166.4

21. 0.06 ÷ 1,000   0.00006

22. 68.96 ÷ 10   6.896

23. 0.85 ÷ 1,000   0.00085

24. 32.14 × 100   3,214

25. 38.652 × 10   386.52

26. 21.5 ÷ 10   2.15

27. 0.38 ÷ 100   0.0038

28. 619.5 ÷ 1,000   0.6195

29. 0.01116 × 100   1.116

30. 0.59 × 10   5.9

31. 78.64 ÷ 10   7.864

32. 2,041 ÷ 1,000   2.041

33. 71.3 × 100   7.130

34. 0.2413 × 1,000   241.3

35. 799.8 ÷ 10   79.98

36. 645.8 ÷ 100   6.458

37. 7.8 × 10   78

38. 4.004 × 100   400.4

CLASSWORK HOMEWORK — Estimating Products of Decimals

Use the numbers in the box to answer the questions.

1. Which decimals are close to but greater than 1? 1.109, 1.038 – 1.109

2. Which decimals are close to but less than 1? 0.98, 0.900, 0.897, 0.9001

3. Which decimals are close to but greater than one half? 0.51

4. Which decimals are close to but less than one half? 0.499, 0.49, 0.498, 0.48236

0.499	1.038–1.109
0.0099	0.98, 0.900, 0.897
0.48236	0.51
1.109	0.9001
0.49	0.499, 0.48236

Estimate to find the most sensible answer.

5. 3.17 × 17.15   a. 5.44   (b.) 54.37   c. 543.66

6. 0.624 × 0.482   (a.) 0.30   b. 3.01   c. 30.08

7. 3.009 × 2.156   (a.) 6.49   b. 64.87   c. 648.74

8. 0.98 × 4.86   a. 0.47628   (b.) 4.76   c. 47.62

9. 3.68 × 0.512   a. 0.1884   (b.) 1.884   c. 18.84

10. 7.38 × 4.15   a. 3.063   (b.) 30.62   c. 306.3

Estimate. Adjust by writing + or – where possible.

11. 4.28 × 5.76   24
12. 1.34 × 7.8   8
13. 0.98 × 12.5   12.5⁻

14. 0.489 × 2.4   1⁺
15. 3.56 × 1.12   3.5⁺
16. 0.503 × 4.31   2⁺

17. 3.45 × 1.1123   3.5⁺
18. 12.4 × 5.78   72
19. 0.894 × 3.44   3

Solve.

20. The typical American eats 96.3 pounds of beef each year. If the average price of beef is $2.42 per pound, about how much is spent on beef by each American? $200–$240

21. The typical American eats about 73.5 pounds of hamburger each year. If the average price of hamburger is $1.19, about how much is spent on hamburger? $74–$90

Use with pages 58–59.   Student Handbook **H25**

CLASSWORK HOMEWORK — Multiplying Decimals

Multiply. Round the product to the nearest cent where necessary.

1. $3.71 × 0.06 = $0.22

2. 0.739 × 0.008 = 0.005912

3. 26.342 × 0.697 = 18.360374

4. 0.781 × 29.6 = 23.1176

5. 6.186 × 3.05 = 18.8673

6. $33.56 × 68.5 = $2,298.86

7. 4.059 × 4.13 = 16.76367

8. 0.0213 × 0.71 = 0.015123

9. 55.36875 × 1.03 = 57.0298125

10. 4.302 × 0.009 = 0.038718

11. 20.9413 × 0.03 = 0.628239

12. $2.97 × 3.3 = $9.80

13. 0.010 × 0.02 = 0.0002

14. 226.479 × 2.31 = 523.16649

15. $7.98 × 2.6 = $20.75

16. 6.91532 × 1.78 = 12.309269

17. 3.9 × 6.1   23.79
18. 0.698 × 3.07   2.14286

19. 0.02 × 0.048   0.00096
20. 0.0213 × 0.71   0.015123

21. 1.8 × 5.8 × 7.4   77.256
22. 3.743 × 15   56.145

Solve. Round to the nearest cent if necessary.

23. Tracy wants to sell a gold bracelet she never wears. She wants to buy a video cassette recorder that costs $270. Her bracelet contains 0.78 ounces. If the jeweler will pay $380.35 per ounce for her bracelet, how much money will Tracy have left after she buys the video cassette recorder? $26.67

H26   Student Handbook   Use with pages 60–61.

CLASSWORK HOMEWORK — Choosing the Operation

Write the letter of the operation you would use to solve each problem.

1. The distance from San Antonio, Texas to Dallas, Texas is 250 miles. The distance from San Antonio to Corpus Christi , Texas is 153 miles. What is the distance from Dallas to Corpus Christi via San Antonio?
   (a.) addition
   b. subtraction
   c. multiplication

2. The Mississippi–Missouri River System is 3,740 miles long. The Missouri river is 2,683 miles long. How long is the Mississippi after the Missouri meets it?
   a. addition
   (b.) subtraction
   c. multiplication

Solve.

3. Mount Washington in New Hampshire is 2,096 yards high. How many feet is the mountain? (There are 3 feet to a yard.) 6,288 feet

4. Big Elk Peak in Idaho is 9,478 feet tall. How many feet have you traveled if you went to the top and came down? 18,956 feet

5. The distance from Milwaukee, Wisconsin to Chicago, Illinois is 87 miles. Julia drives from one city to the other 8 times per week. How much is her total mileage? 696 miles

6. The Republic of Andorra lies between France and Spain. The border it shares with France is 37.3 miles, and the border it shares with Spain is 40.4 miles. How long is Andorra's border? 77.7 miles

7. The border of China is 17,445 miles long. Its border with Mongolia is 2,904 miles long. Its border with the Soviet Union is 4,673 miles long, and its border with all other countries is 5,822 miles long. How long is China's coastline? 4,046 miles

8. The highest point in Alabama is 2,400 feet high. The lowest point is 500 feet high. How much higher is the highest point than the lowest point? 1,900 feet

9. The Gobi desert is 500,000 square miles, and the Kalahari desert is 225,000 square miles. The Sahara desert is 2,775,000 square miles larger than the two other deserts combined. How many square miles is the Sahara? 3,500,000 square miles

10. The world's largest island, Greenland, is 2.75 times larger than the world's second largest island, New Guinea. New Guinea covers 306,000 square miles. How many square miles does Greenland cover? 841,500 square miles

Use after pages 62–63.   Student Handbook **H27**

CLASSWORK HOMEWORK — Dividing Decimals by Whole Numbers

Divide. Round the quotient to the nearest thousandth or to the nearest cent where necessary.

1. 620.1 ÷ 8   77.513
2. 1,863.36 ÷ 288   6.47
3. 8.33 ÷ 2   4.165

4. $\frac{749.331}{783}$ 0.957
5. $\frac{14.4}{36}$ 0.4
6. $\frac{1.819}{4}$ 0.455

7. $196.32 ÷ 64 $3.07
8. 0.1293 ÷ 5   0.026
9. 38.35 ÷ 65   0.59

10. 5.351 ÷ 7   0.764
11. 14.88 ÷ 62   0.24
12. 2.984 ÷ 2   1.492

13. 58.6219 ÷ 328   0.179
14. 6.177 ÷ 71   0.087
15. 206.6 ÷ 4   51.65

16. $\frac{31.80}{32}$ 0.994
17. $\frac{3.835}{65}$ 0.059
18. $\frac{841.2}{6}$ 140.2

19. 215)$241.7893 $1.12
20. 47)117.5   2.5
21. 673)58.2614   0.087

22. 22)1.122   0.051
23. 318)$418.71 $1.32
24. 7)535.1   76.443

25. 4)84.12   21.03
26. 55)2.530   0.046
27. 151)23.426   0.155

H28   Student Handbook   Use with pages 64–65.

CLASSWORK HOMEWORK | **Dividing Decimals by Decimals**

Divide. Round your answer to the nearest thousandth or to the nearest cent where necessary.

1. $\frac{1.352}{0.8}$ 1.69

2. $0.016 \div 0.04$ 0.4

3. $\frac{0.624}{0.078}$ 8

4. $\frac{\$6.45}{8.6}$ $0.75

5. $\frac{428}{6.4}$ 66.875

6. $7.5 \div 0.15$ 50

7. $5.632 \div 3.2607$ 1.727

8. $\$1.40 \div 2.818$ $0.50

9. $\frac{4.346}{0.2173}$ 20

10. $\frac{0.87571}{9.218}$ 0.095

11. $8,564 \div 32.54$ 263.184

12. $\frac{6.7}{2.264}$ 2.959

13. $7.4\overline{)3,500.8}$ 473.081

14. $0.87\overline{)0.00435}$ 0.005

15. $0.004\overline{)0.00372}$ 0.93

16. $2.818\overline{)1,409}$ 500

17. $5.8\overline{)\$15.95}$ $ 2.75

18. $8.04\overline{)0.602}$ 0.075

Solve.

19. Mandy is trying to create a liquid that will not evaporate. Her beaker contains 47.5 mL of solution. She wants to put an equal amount of the solution into test tubes by using an eyedropper that holds 0.98 mL. How many times can she fill the eyedropper completely?

48 times

Use with pages 66–67.

Student Handbook **H29**

CLASSWORK HOMEWORK | **Solving Multi-step Problems/Making a Plan**

Complete the plan for each problem by writing the missing steps.

1. The purchasing committee for the Student Council Bookstore is ordering supplies. Notebook paper is shipped in boxes of 24 packages each. The committee orders 30 boxes of paper. If the cost of the paper is $0.22 per package, find the total cost of the order.

   Step 1: Find the cost of a box of paper.

   Step 2: ___?___ Find the cost of 30 boxes of paper.

2. The bookstore sold 321 packages of notebook paper during the first month of the school year. The store paid $0.22 for each package of paper. It sells each package of paper for $0.30. How much profit did the bookstore make on the paper?

   Step 1: Find the amount received for the paper.

   Step 2: ___?___ Find the cost of the paper.

   Step 3: ___?___ Find the profit by subtracting the cost from the amount received.

Make a plan for each problem. Solve.

3. A package holds 24 pencils. Pencils are shipped in boxes of 10 packages each. If each pencil costs $0.12 and the bookstore purchasing committee orders 15 boxes of pencils, what is the cost of the order? $432

4. The bookstore sold 4 boxes of pencils last month. Each box has 10 packages of pencils, and each package contains 24 pencils. If the pencils sell for $0.15 each and cost $0.12 each, how much profit did the bookstore make on the pencils? $28.80

5. The bookstore also sells graph paper at $0.03 per sheet. The store buys the graph paper in packs of 200 sheets each. If each pack costs $4.58, how much profit was made from selling 2 packs of graph paper? $2.84

6. The bookstore started the year with a cash balance of $37.62. If the receipts for September were $321.72 and the expenditures were $325.18, what was the balance at the end of September? $34.16

H30 Student Handbook

Use with pages 68–69.

CLASSWORK HOMEWORK | **Divisibility**

Write *yes* or *no*.

Is the number divisible by 2?

1. 8,356 yes
2. 53,775 no
3. 437 no
4. 29 no

5. 1,274 yes
6. 322 yes
7. 2,180 yes
8. 33,455 no

Is the number divisible by 3?

9. 243 yes
10. 1,200 yes
11. 6,801 yes
12. 11 no

13. 15 yes
14. 25,006 no
15. 421 no
16. 100,005 yes

Is the number divisible by 4?

17. 76,521 no
18. 390,062 no
19. 973 no
20. 48 yes

21. 886 no
22. 567 no
23. 2,004 yes
24. 6,935 no

Is the number divisible by 5?

25. 13 no
26. 95,215 yes
27. 3,750 yes
28. 102,211 no

29. 26 no
30. 500,909 no
31. 638 no
32. 773 no

Is the number divisible by 6?

33. 672 yes
34. 34 no
35. 611 no
36. 48,928 no

37. 199 no
38. 47,068 no
39. 21 no
40. 5,940 yes

Is the number divisible by 9?

41. 155 no
42. 81 yes
43. 77 no
44. 5,001 no

45. 563 no
46. 4,292 no
47. 6,885 yes
48. 19 no

Is the number divisible by 10?

49. 300 yes
50. 400,000 yes
51. 6,020 yes
52. 909 no

53. 25,005 no
54. 170 yes
55. 898 no
56. 50,000 yes

Use with pages 80–81.

Student Handbook **H31**

CLASSWORK HOMEWORK | **Power and Roots**

Write as a product of factors and evaluate.

1. 4^3 $4 \times 4 \times 4 = 64$
2. 3^4 $3 \times 3 \times 3 \times 3 = 81$
3. 2^5 $2 \times 2 \times 2 \times 2 \times 2 = 32$

4. 10^3 $10 \times 10 \times 10 = 1,000$
5. 8^2 $8 \times 8 = 64$
6. 5^5 $5 \times 5 \times 5 \times 5 \times 5 = 3,125$

Rewrite and evaluate each. Use exponents.

7. $8 \times 8 \times 8$
   $8^3 = 512$

8. $2 \times 2 \times 2$
   $2^3 = 8$

9. 11×11
   $11^2 = 121$

10. $4 \times 4 \times 4 \times 4 \times 4$
    $4^5 = 1,024$

11. $5 \times 5 \times 10 \times 10$
    $5^2 \times 10^2 = 2,500$

12. $7 \times 7 \times 7 \times 7$
    $7^4 = 2,401$

Find the square root. Use this table.

13. $\sqrt{16}$ 4
14. $\sqrt{49}$ 7
15. $\sqrt{144}$ 12
16. $\sqrt{361}$ 19
17. $\sqrt{21}$ 4.583
18. $\sqrt{14}$ 3.742
19. $\sqrt{256}$ 16
20. $\sqrt{484}$ 22
21. $\sqrt{39}$ 6.245
22. $\sqrt{576}$ 24
23. $\sqrt{22}$ 4.690
24. $\sqrt{43}$ 6.557
25. $\sqrt{625}$ 25
26. $\sqrt{1,024}$ 32
27. $\sqrt{47}$ 6.856
28. $\sqrt{33}$ 5.745
29. $\sqrt{2,116}$ 46
30. $\sqrt{50}$ 7.071
31. $\sqrt{28}$ 5.292
32. $\sqrt{34}$ 5.831

n	n^2	$\sqrt{n}$	n	n^2	$\sqrt{n}$
1	1	1.000	26	676	5.099
2	4	1.414	27	729	5.196
3	9	1.732	28	784	5.292
4	16	2.000	29	841	5.385
5	25	2.236	30	900	5.477
6	36	2.449	31	961	5.568
7	49	2.646	32	1,024	5.657
8	64	2.828	33	1,089	5.745
9	81	3.000	34	1,156	5.831
10	100	3.162	35	1,225	5.916
11	121	3.317	36	1,296	6.000
12	144	3.464	37	1,369	6.083
13	169	3.606	38	1,444	6.164
14	196	3.742	39	1,521	6.245
15	225	3.873	40	1,600	6.325
16	256	4.000	41	1,681	6.403
17	289	4.123	42	1,764	6.481
18	324	4.243	43	1,849	6.557
19	361	4.359	44	1,936	6.633
20	400	4.472	45	2,025	6.708
21	441	4.583	46	2,116	6.782
22	484	4.690	47	2,209	6.856
23	529	4.796	48	2,304	6.928
24	576	4.899	49	2,401	7.000
25	625	5.000	50	2,500	7.071

Solve. Use the table of square roots. Round to the nearest tenth.

33. The area of a square carpet is 42 m². What is the length of each side? 6.5 m

34. The area of a square garden is 27 m². What is the length of each side? 5.2 m

H32 Student Handbook

Use with pages 82–83.

CLASSWORK HOMEWORK — Scientific Notation

Write in scientific notation.

1. 400 4×10^2
2. 800 8×10^2
3. 1,100 1.1×10^3
4. 2,000 2×10^3
5. 6,500 6.5×10^3
6. 8,300 8.3×10^3
7. 9,800 9.8×10^3
8. 33,000 3.3×10^4
9. 41,000 4.1×10^4
10. 76,000 7.6×10^4
11. 59,350 5.935×10^4
12. 304,685 3.04685×10^5
13. 680,000 6.8×10^5
14. 93,215,000 9.3215×10^7
15. 8,499,315 8.499315×10^6
16. 54,975,000 5.4975×10^7
17. 1,110,000 1.11×10^6
18. 476,000,000 4.76×10^8
19. 888,888 8.88888×10^5
20. 6,981 6.981×10^3
21. 33,450 3.345×10^4

Express in standard form.

22. 6×10^2 600
23. 5×10^4 50,000
24. 3.7×10^3 3,700
25. 8.9×10^4 89,000
26. 4.4×10^5 440,000
27. 1.1×10^2 110
28. 3.56×10^5 356,000
29. 7.38×10^7 73,800,000
30. 4.07×10^6 4,070,000
31. 5.289×10^8 528,900,000
32. 6.12345×10^{10} 61,234,500,000
33. 9.751×10^9 9,751,000,000

Solve.

34. The longest biography in publishing history is that of Sir Winston Churchill. The book contains about 7,620,000 words. Express this number in scientific notation.

7.62×10^6

35. The Library of Congress in Washington, D.C., is one of the world's largest libraries. It contains over 80,798,000 items, including books, maps, and other documents. Express this number in scientific notation.

8.0798×10^7

CLASSWORK HOMEWORK — Checking for a Reasonable Answer

Read each problem. Without computing the exact answer, write the letter of the most reasonable answer.

1. Alan ordered 45 windows for a house he was building. The bill came to $1,647. What was the price of each window?
   a. $3.60
   b. $36
   c. $72

2. A brick weighs 2.3 kilograms. Sheila is calculating the weight of a stack of 37 bricks. What is the closest answer?
   a. 85 kilograms
   b. 95 kilograms
   c. 120 kilograms

3. There are 144 nails in a box. If Rosa has 3,000 nails, about how many boxes does she have?
   a. about 12
   b. about 15
   c. about 20

4. Katsiko is estimating quantities of supplies he needs from a building plan. He has to find the cube root of 64,000. What is the answer?
   a. 400
   b. 40
   c. 4,000

5. A hardware company designed a new lock for private garages. In the first month of sale, 3,258 locks were sold for $17.25 each. What was the total amount paid?
   a. $5,500
   b. $55,000
   c. $550,000

6. Antonio is deciding how many lamps he will need for an apartment complex. Each apartment has 13 lamps, and there are 87 apartments in the complex. How many lamps does he need?
   a. 1,100
   b. 1,500
   c. 950

7. The Verrazano Narrows bridge in New York is 1,300,000 millimeters long. The Delaware River bridge is 500,000 millimeters long. What is the sum of the lengths in meters?
   a. 18×10^3 meters
   b. 1.8×10^2 meters
   c. 1.8×10^3 meters

8. A building supply catalog has 9,346 items listed in it. The catalog is 124 pages long. About how many items are there per page?
   a. about 95
   b. about 125
   c. about 75

CLASSWORK HOMEWORK — Factors, Primes, and Composites

Write all the factors of the number.

1. 63 1, 3, 7, 9, 21, 63
2. 33 1, 3, 11, 33
3. 91 1, 7, 13, 91
4. 12 1, 2, 3, 4, 6, 12
5. 16 1, 2, 4, 8, 16
6. 119 1, 7, 17, 119
7. 9 1, 3, 9
8. 17 1, 17
9. 57 1, 3, 19, 57
10. 20 1, 2, 4, 5, 10, 20
11. 125 1, 5, 25, 125
12. 35 1, 5, 7, 35
13. 39 1, 3, 13, 39
14. 74 1, 2, 37, 74
15. 7 1, 7
16. 26 1, 2, 13, 26
17. 52 1, 2, 4, 13, 26, 52
18. 66 1, 2, 3, 6, 11, 22, 33, 66

Write prime or composite.

19. 109 prime
20. 17 prime
21. 18 composite
22. 29 prime
23. 79 prime
24. 52 composite
25. 72 composite
26. 19 prime
27. 39 composite
28. 96 composite
29. 91 composite
30. 59 prime
31. 47 prime
32. 144 composite
33. 2 prime
34. 71 prime
35. 57 composite
36. 36 composite
37. 13 prime
38. 189 composite
39. 300 composite
40. 3 prime

CLASSWORK HOMEWORK — Prime Factorization

Write the prime factorization of each number using exponents.

1. 950 $2 \times 5^2 \times 19$
2. 104 $2^3 \times 13$
3. 192 $2^6 \times 3$
4. 84 $2^2 \times 3 \times 7$
5. 81 3^4
6. 448 $2^6 \times 7$
7. 196 $2^2 \times 7^2$
8. 414 $2 \times 3^2 \times 23$
9. 222 $2 \times 3 \times 37$
10. 670 $2 \times 5 \times 67$

Draw a factor tree for each number. Then write the prime factorization with and without exponents.

11. 720
$2 \times 2 \times 2 \times 2 \times 3 \times 3 \times 5$
$2^4 \times 3^2 \times 5$

12. 279
$3 \times 3 \times 31$
$3^2 \times 31$

13. 2310
$2 \times 3 \times 5 \times 7 \times 11$
$2 \times 3 \times 5 \times 7 \times 11$

Write the number for each prime factorization.

14. $2^2 \times 3^2 \times 11$ 396
15. $2 \times 3 \times 7^2$ 294
16. $2^4 \times 3 \times 5^2$ 1,200
17. $2^2 \times 3 \times 13$ 156
18. $3^2 \times 5^2$ 225
19. $2^3 \times 3^2$ 72
20. $2^2 \times 5^2$ 100
21. $2^3 \times 3^2 \times 11$ 792
22. $2 \times 3 \times 5^2$ 150
23. $11 \times 13 \times 5^2$ 3,575
24. $5 \times 7 \times 11$ 385
25. $2 \times 3 \times 11^2$ 726

Greatest Common Factor (GCF)

Write the GCF. Find it by listing the factors.

1. 16, 24 8	**2.** 15, 35 5	**3.** 24, 72 24
4. 42, 105 21	**5.** 63, 81 9	**6.** 24, 49 1
7. 18, 27, 45 9	**8.** 35, 84 7	**9.** 12, 20, 28 4
10. 24, 36, 60 12	**11.** 26, 208 26	**12.** 88, 121 11

Write the GCF. Find it by using prime factorization.

13. 60, 140 20	**14.** 96, 128 32	**15.** 40, 64 8
16. 64, 96, 112 16	**17.** 81, 108 27	**18.** 34, 51 17
19. 72, 180 36	**20.** 15, 80 5	**21.** 21, 56 7
22. 25, 225 25	**23.** 60, 84, 114 6	**24.** 552, 648 24
25. 39, 65, 91 13	**26.** 115, 138, 184 23	**27.** 133, 152 19

Least Common Multiple

List the first five nonzero multiples of each number.

1. 4	4, 8, 12, 16, 20	**2.** 30	30, 60, 90, 120, 150
3. 13	13, 26, 39, 52, 65	**4.** 8	8, 16, 24, 32, 40
5. 50	50, 100, 150, 200, 250	**6.** 17	17, 34, 51, 68, 85
7. 70	70, 140, 210, 280, 350	**8.** 19	19, 38, 57, 76, 95
9. 15	15, 30, 45, 60, 75	**10.** 60	60, 120, 180, 240, 300

Write the LCM. Find it by listing multiples.

11. 8, 6 24	**12.** 12, 48, 72 144	**13.** 5, 37 185
14. 14, 35 70	**15.** 12, 18 36	**16.** 8, 24 24
17. 23, 5 115	**18.** 3, 7 21	**19.** 10, 40, 50 200

Write the LCM. Find it by using prime factorization.

20. 12, 28, 45 1,260	**21.** 14, 52 364	**22.** 32, 48 96
23. 60, 90 180	**24.** 21, 70 210	**25.** 22, 35 770
26. 12, 36, 48 144	**27.** 36, 72 72	**28.** 8, 24 24

Using a Table

UTILITY RATES

Electric	
service charge	$7.65 per month
first 300 Kwh	7.918¢ per Kwh
next 700 Kwh	4.87¢ per Kwh
over 1,000 Kwh	4.168¢ per Kwh

Gas	
service charge	$7.80 per month
first 6,000 cu ft	$7.06 per 1,000 cu ft
over 6,000 cu ft	$6.39 per 1,000 cu ft

Water	
service charge	$18.27 per quarter
first 6,000 cu ft	$1.266 per 100 cu ft
over 6,000 cu ft	$1.005 per 100 cu ft

Kwh = Kilowatt hours
Cu ft = cubic feet

Use the rate tables above to solve. Note that the service charge must be paid even if no gas, electricity, or water is used.

1. The Alvarez family will be out of town for 3 months (1 quarter). How much will it cost to maintain service for all three utilities for this period? $64.62

2. The Williams' largest gas bill was last January when they used 19,200 cubic feet of gas. How much was the bill? $134.51

3. The Williams family used 6,700 cubic feet of gas this month. How much will they have to pay for the gas? $54.63

4. A family used 1,270 Kwh of electricity last month. How much did they pay for the electricity? $76.75

5. In December of last year, the DeAngelis family used 2,450 Kw hours of electricity. Calculate the electric bill. $125.93

6. The Washington's water bill this quarter is based on their using 2,000 cubic feet of water. Calculate the water bill. $43.59

7. If one cubic foot of water is about 7.5 gallons, how many gallons of water did the Washington family use during the quarter? 15,000

8. The Washington family has a swimming pool that holds 1,800 cubic feet of water. If the family had filled the pool during the quarter, how much more would their bill have been? $22.79

Using a Table

The table below shows the long-distance rates charged by a phone company for direct-dial calls.

Distance to Called Place (Airline Miles)	Weekday Full Rate 8 AM–9 PM		Evening 35% Discount 9 PM–11 PM		Night 11 PM–8 AM & Weekend 60% Discount	
	initial 1 min	each addl min	initial 1 min	each addl min	initial 1 min	each addl min
1–16 miles	$0.23	$0.15	$0.14	$0.10	$0.09	$0.06
17–30 miles	.33	.21	.21	.14	.13	.09
31–55 miles	.43	.28	.27	.19	.17	.12
56–100 miles	.53	.34	.34	.23	.21	.14
101–172 miles	.62	.40	.40	.26	.24	.16
173–244 miles	.69	.45	.44	.30	.27	.18
245–316 miles	.75	.49	.48	.32	.30	.20

Use the rate table to solve.

1. Linda called Inez at 12 noon on Wednesday. Inez lives 90 miles away. How much did the call cost if Linda and Inez talked for 12 minutes? $4.27

2. How much would Linda have saved if she had made a call of the same length to Inez at 9:30 P.M. on Wednesday? $1.40

3. How much would Linda have saved if she had made a call of the same length to Inez at 11:30 P.M.? $2.52

4. Ben lives in Indianapolis, 294 miles from his aunt. At 8:00 P.M. on Saturday, Ben called his aunt and talked for 17 minutes. How much did the call cost? $3.50

5. The EZ Company does business with a bank 40 miles away. The president of EZ makes a 5-minute call to the bank at 10:00 A.M. on Friday. How much does the call cost? $1.55

6. The EZ Company makes 25 weekly calls to an insurance company, 185 miles away. The calls last an average of 15 minutes each and occur between 9:30 A.M. and 4:30 A.M. on weekdays. How much does the company pay per week for the 25 calls? $174.75

7. If the EZ Company could call the insurance company at 7:30 A.M., how much would it save each week on the 25 phone calls? $105.00

CLASSWORK HOMEWORK — Order of Operations

Simplify.

1. $6 + 9 \cdot 3$ 33
2. $12 - 8 + 7$ 11
3. $16 + 32 \div 4$ 24
4. $24 - (17 - 5)$ 12
5. $6 + 10^2$ 106
6. $31 - 7 \cdot (14 - 10)$ 3
7. $(15 - 6)^2$ 81
8. $70 - 3 \cdot (15 - 2)$ 31
9. $(8^2 + (13 - 4)^2) \div 5$ 29
10. $7 + 9^2$ 88
11. $18 \div 6 + 11$ 14
12. $300 - 36 \cdot 8$ 12
13. $17 + (3 + 2)^3$ 142
14. $4 \cdot 16 + 8 - 9 \div 3$ 69
15. $64 \div 4 + 4$ 20

Rewrite using parentheses to make each answer true.

16. $21 \div (3 + 4) = 3$
17. $(9 + 3) \div (2 + 10) = 1$
18. $(9 - 2) \cdot 3 = 21$
19. $3.8 + (4.4 \div 2) = 6$
20. $30 \div (5 + 10) = 2$
21. $(2.4 - 0.4) \cdot 6 = 12$
22. $30 \div (5 + 1) = 5$
23. $(4 + 2) \cdot 6 = 36$
24. $40 \div 4 - (2 + 8) = 0$

Simplify each expression. Then write the letter of the expression on the line or lines above its simplified form.

H. $(264 \div 3) + 2 \cdot 17 + (196 - 70)$ 248
I. $(840 \div 5) \div (104 \div 26)$ 42
T. $333 \div 9 + 74 \cdot (9 - 5) \div 8 + 17$ 91
N. $145 - 28 \cdot 2 - (12 \cdot 5) \div 3 - 21$ 48
L. $(44 + 31) \div (2 \cdot 17 - 9) + 6 - 2$ 7
O. $68 - (32 + 17) + (90 \cdot 6)$ 559
C. $56 - (21 \cdot 4 - 38) + 5^2$ 35
K. $(4 + 5)^2 \cdot 4 + 130 - 7$ 447
G. $500 \div 5^2 \cdot 10 + (77 - 75)^2 + 9$ 59
S. $16 + 8^2 \div 32 \cdot (3 + 7)^2 - 216$ 0

Where did Sir Galahad study?

$$\frac{K}{447} \; \frac{N}{48} \; \frac{I}{42} \; \frac{G}{59} \; \frac{H}{248} \; \frac{T}{91} \; \frac{S}{0} \; \frac{C}{35} \; \frac{H}{248} \; \frac{O}{559} \; \frac{O}{559} \; \frac{L}{7}$$

CLASSWORK HOMEWORK — Equations

Write *T* for true if the replacement value is a solution. Write *F* for false if it is not.

1. $a + 8 = 9$, if $a = 2$ F
2. $3 \times b = 18$, if $b = 6$ T
3. $\frac{15}{b} = 3.25$, if $b = 4$ F
4. $c - 8 = 3$, if $c = 12$ F
5. $5.6 + c = 7$, if $c = 1.4$ T
6. $\frac{a}{6} = 1$, if $a = 6$ T
7. $3d = 24$, if $d = 9$ F
8. $9 + d = 12$, if $d = 4$ F
9. $7.2 - a = 5.2$, if $a = 2$ T
10. $a - 7 = 3$, if $a = 10$ T
11. $\frac{c}{4} = 2$, if $c = 12$ F
12. $3c = 15$, if $c = 5$ T

Find the solution. Use the replacement set {0, 1, 2, . . .}

13. $x + 3.6 = 7.6$ $x = 4$
14. $36 = m - 27$ $m = 63$
15. $g + 49 = 51$ $g = 2$
16. $105 = z + 47$ $z = 58$
17. $7 + e = 18$ $e = 11$
18. $\frac{99}{a} = 3$ $a = 33$
19. $96 - x = 18$ $x = 78$
20. $19d = 171$ $d = 9$
21. $14 - v = 14$ $v = 0$
22. $\frac{f}{6} = 6$ $f = 36$
23. $39 = 13a$ $a = 3$
24. $10.6f = 53$ $f = 5$
25. $103 = 71 + b$ $b = 32$
26. $s - 106 = 34$ $s = 140$
27. $446 = 307 + n$ $n = 139$
28. $4.4 = \frac{17.6}{x}$ $x = 4$
29. $\frac{308}{b} = 77$ $b = 4$
30. $95 + z = 107$ $z = 12$
31. $27a = 324$ $a = 12$
32. $136 = r + 27$ $r = 109$
33. $11 = \frac{121}{r}$ $r = 11$
34. $c + 26 = 95$ $c = 69$
35. $147 = 49w$ $w = 3$
36. $c - 3 = 115$ $c = 118$

CLASSWORK HOMEWORK — Choosing the Operation

Write the operation you would use to solve each problem.

1. The tallest tree in the world is the Howard Libby redwood tree, 366 feet tall. The tallest spruce tree is a 126-foot blue spruce in Colorado. How many times taller is the redwood than the spruce?
   a. add   b. subtract   c. multiply   **d. divide**

2. White pine trees average 100 feet in height. Scotch pine trees average 30 feet less in height. About how tall are most scotch pines?
   a. add   **b. subtract**   c. multiply   d. divide

Solve.

3. The diameter of a mature chestnut oak is about 2.5 feet. The diameter of a mature sequoia is about 20 feet. About how many times greater is the diameter of the sequoia than the oak? about 8

4. The General Sherman sequoia tree is 272 feet high. Its lowest branch is 130 feet high. How many feet of the tree contain branches? 142 feet

5. The fastest-growing tree is a type of silk tree which has grown as fast as 2.7 feet in one month. How tall might a tree like this grow in $\frac{1}{2}$ a year? 16.2 feet

6. The wood of a black ironwood tree weighs up to 93 pounds per cubic foot. The wood of the lightest balsa wood tree is 37.2 times lighter. What is the balsa wood's weight per cubic foot? 2.5 pounds

7. The northernmost tree, a Sitka spruce, took 98 years to grow 28 cm. About how many years did it take to grow one cm? 3.5 years

8. The tallest recorded apple tree was 70 feet high. The tallest known shellbark hickory tree was 1.5 times taller. How tall was the hickory? 105 feet

CLASSWORK HOMEWORK — Solving Equations (+ and −)

Solve.

1. $x - 14 = 99$ $x = 113$
2. $186 + c = 747$ $c = 561$
3. $z + 14 = 63$ $z = 49$
4. $83 - n = 65$ $n = 18$
5. $2.7 + c = 9.4$ $c = 6.7$
6. $m - 3 = 12.9$ $m = 15.9$
7. $a + 108 = 306$ $a = 198$
8. $25.6 + r = 74.4$ $r = 48.8$
9. $s - 214 = 36$ $s = 250$
10. $99 - n = 46$ $n = 53$
11. $11.7 + t = 109.8$ $t = 98.1$
12. $v + 175 = 203.2$ $v = 28.2$
13. $36 - s = 14$ $s = 22$
14. $b - 83 = 207.2$ $b = 290.2$
15. $f - 13 = 221$ $f = 234$
16. $154 - g = 78$ $g = 76$
17. $b + 7.2 + 2.1 = 11.4$ $b = 2.1$
18. $19 + z = 101$ $z = 82$
19. $14.5 + r = 22.7$ $r = 8.2$
20. $w + 22 = 104.8$ $w = 82.8$
21. $a - 18.3 = 24.1$ $a = 42.4$
22. $11.7 - b = 4.2$ $b = 7.5$
23. $z - 27.2 = 36.1$ $z = 63.3$
24. $204 + c = 807$ $c = 603$
25. $59.6 + m = 83.2$ $m = 23.6$
26. $n + 3.5 = 10.2$ $n = 6.7$
27. $201 - s = 174$ $s = 27$
28. $t - 114.3 = 236.1$ $t = 350.4$
29. $b + 19 = 30$ $b = 11$
30. $25.3 + v = 108$ $v = 82.7$
31. $19.2 + a = 19.2$ $a = 0$
32. $c - 7 - 2 = 9$ $c = 18$
33. $22 + t = 121$ $t = 99$
34. $336 + b = 407$ $b = 71$

Write the equation.

35. The sum of 18 and a number, x, is 36. $x + 18 = 36$
36. A number, r, decreased by 6 is 136.2. $r - 6 = 136.2$
37. 49 decreased by a number, z, is 11. $49 - z = 11$
38. The sum of a number, b, and 207 is 404. $b + 207 = 404$

CLASSWORK HOMEWORK — Solving Equations (× and ÷)

Solve.

1. $7z = 84$ $z = 12$
2. $\frac{r}{3} = 38$ $r = 114$
3. $\frac{c}{30} = 0.5$ $c = 15$
4. $\frac{m}{15} = 6$ $m = 90$
5. $202n = 404$ $n = 2$
6. $6n = 96$ $n = 16$
7. $\frac{r}{0.4} = 50$ $r = 20$
8. $\frac{t}{5} = 3.5$ $t = 17.5$
9. $19m = 228$ $m = 12$
10. $\frac{a}{80} = 7$ $a = 560$
11. $36b = 540$ $b = 15$
12. $\frac{m}{0.1} = 6$ $m = 0.6$
13. $45n = 315$ $n = 7$
14. $\frac{x}{15} = 2.5$ $x = 37.5$
15. $\frac{r}{9} = 0.3$ $r = 2.7$
16. $7s = 182$ $s = 26$
17. $23a = 184$ $a = 8$
18. $5.5c = 335.5$ $c = 61$
19. $\frac{w}{3.2} = 8.5$ $w = 27.2$
20. $\frac{m}{21} = 5.8$ $m = 121.8$
21. $\frac{y}{5} = 0.016$ $y = 0.08$
22. $1.05n = 60.27$ $n = 57.4$
23. $6.2m = 80.6$ $m = 13$
24. $\frac{e}{5} = 1.4$ $e = 7$
25. $\frac{s}{12} = 0.8$ $s = 9.6$
26. $78k = 81.12$ $k = 1.04$

Write the equation and solve.

27. If 72 is 8 times a number, a, what is the number? $8a = 72$; $a = 9$
28. A number, c, divided by 0.4 is 10. What is c? $c \div 0.4 = 10$; $c = 4$
29. A number, j, times 4.8 is 33.6. What is j? $4.8j = 33.6$; $j = 7$
30. A number, t, divided by 4.2 is 1.9. What is t? $\frac{t}{4.2} = 1.9$; $t = 7.98$

CLASSWORK HOMEWORK — Solving Two-Step Equations

Solve.

1. $5z + 7 = 32$ $z = 5$
2. $\frac{s}{3} + 3 = 5$ $s = 6$
3. $\frac{a}{8} - 3 = 9$ $a = 96$
4. $4w - 6 = 14$ $w = 5$
5. $\frac{b}{4} + 13 = 17$ $b = 16$
6. $9c + 12 = 21$ $c = 1$
7. $10h - 34 = 66$ $h = 10$
8. $\frac{x}{10} + 8 = 13$ $x = 50$
9. $\frac{m}{6} - 6 = 0$ $m = 36$
10. $16n - 28 = 4$ $n = 2$
11. $5k - 2 = 43$ $k = 9$
12. $\frac{z}{3} + 4 = 13$ $z = 27$
13. $4v - 22 = 22$ $v = 11$
14. $4y - 8 = 20$ $y = 7$
15. $\frac{c}{5} + 7 = 12$ $c = 25$
16. $\frac{d}{4} + 3 = 33$ $d = 120$
17. $3r + 15 = 75$ $r = 20$
18. $\frac{b}{3} + 17 = 48$ $b = 93$
19. $8t - 14 = 82$ $t = 12$
20. $5x + 6 = 41$ $x = 7$
21. $\frac{v}{2} - 4 = 26$ $v = 60$
22. $\frac{p}{2} - 5 = 9$ $p = 28$
23. $0.5j + 2 = 6$ $j = 8$
24. $4y + 15 = 67$ $y = 13$

Write a two-step equation and solve.

25. The sum of 9 and $\frac{1}{3}$ of a number, x, is 13. What is the number? $\frac{1}{3}x + 9 = 13$ $x = 12$
26. The sum of 7 and three times a number, a, is 16. What is the number? $3a + 7 = 16$ $a = 3$
27. The sum of 8 and $\frac{1}{4}$ of a number, b, is 10. What is the number? $\frac{1}{4}b + 8 = 10$ $b = 8$
28. The sum of 11 and four times a number, c, is 55. What is the number? $4c + 11 = 55$ $c = 11$

CLASSWORK HOMEWORK — Writing an Equation

Write the letter of the correct equation.

1. The Mark 2 model of the Trans computer costs $785. This is $45 less than 1.5 times the cost of the Mark 1 model. How much does the Mark 1 model cost?
   a. $1.5n - 45 = 785$
   b. $1.5n = 785 - 45$
   c. $n + 45 = 785 - 1.5$

2. The Mark 1 model has a memory storage of 32K. The memory of the Mark 2 model is 10K more than 5 times the memory of the Mark 1. How many K's is the Mark 2's memory?
   a. $n + 10 = 32 \times 5$
   b. $\frac{n}{5} = 32 + 10$
   c. $n - 10 = 32 \times 5$

Write an equation, and solve.

3. The Gant printer can print 600 characters per minute. The Nole printer can print 20 characters per minute more than 1.8 times the characters per minute of the Gant printer. How many characters per minute can the Nole printer print? $10n = 4 \times 7.80 - 6$ 1,100 characters

4. The weight of a hard disk unit of a computer is 0.5 times the total weight of the printer and the terminal. The hard disk unit weighs 14.85 kilograms, and the terminal weighs 10.6 kilograms. How many kilograms does the printer weigh? $0.5 (n + 10.6) = 14.85$ 19.1 kg

5. A pack of 10 soft disks costs $6 less than 4 printer ribbons. Each printer ribbon costs $7.80. What is the cost of each soft disk? $10n + 6 = 4 \times 7.80$ $2.52

6. Max has $65.00. He buys 5 copies of a computer manual, and his change is $2.75. How much does each copy of the manual cost? $5n = 65 - 2.75$ $12.45

7. The total memory of two computers is 192K. The second computer has double the memory of the first computer. How much memory does the second computer have? $3n = 192$, $n = 64$ 128K

8. Katrine has programmed a computer so that any number she enters will be squared and then the square will be doubled. If she enters the number 1.2 what will the computer show? $n = 2(1.2^2)$ 2.88

CLASSWORK HOMEWORK — Equivalent Fractions

Write two equivalent fractions for each.   Answers will vary.

1. $\frac{7}{11}$ $\frac{14}{22}$; $\frac{28}{44}$
2. $\frac{2}{3}$ $\frac{4}{6}$; $\frac{8}{12}$
3. $\frac{2}{5}$ $\frac{4}{10}$; $\frac{8}{20}$
4. $\frac{1}{3}$ $\frac{2}{6}$; $\frac{4}{12}$

Write the fraction in simplest form.

5. $\frac{56}{72}$ $\frac{7}{9}$
6. $\frac{26}{28}$ $\frac{13}{14}$
7. $\frac{40}{110}$ $\frac{4}{11}$
8. $\frac{9}{54}$ $\frac{1}{6}$
9. $\frac{48}{64}$ $\frac{3}{4}$
10. $\frac{28}{35}$ $\frac{4}{5}$
11. $\frac{18}{24}$ $\frac{3}{4}$
12. $\frac{24}{48}$ $\frac{1}{2}$
13. $\frac{51}{68}$ $\frac{3}{4}$
14. $\frac{24}{84}$ $\frac{2}{7}$
15. $\frac{45}{99}$ $\frac{5}{11}$
16. $\frac{12}{48}$ $\frac{1}{4}$

Find the missing term.

17. $\frac{40}{52} = \frac{d}{13}$ $d = 10$
18. $\frac{60}{75} = \frac{u}{15}$ $u = 12$
19. $\frac{2}{3} = \frac{34}{t}$ $t = 51$
20. $\frac{63}{75} = \frac{21}{w}$ $w = 25$
21. $\frac{16}{18} = \frac{48}{p}$ $p = 54$
22. $\frac{24}{64} = \frac{s}{16}$ $s = 6$
23. $\frac{18}{99} = \frac{6}{r}$ $r = 33$
24. $\frac{75}{125} = \frac{3}{k}$ $k = 5$
25. $\frac{21}{28} = \frac{a}{4}$ $a = 3$
26. $\frac{44}{121} = \frac{j}{11}$ $j = 4$
27. $\frac{6}{7} = \frac{54}{h}$ $h = 63$
28. $\frac{24}{42} = \frac{t}{7}$ $f = 4$

Solve.

29. The Benny Button Company supplies 105 clothing manufacturers with an equal number of buttons each month. The Benny Brass Button is their best-selling button, and 45 companies order only Benny Brass Buttons. If the Benny Button Company ships 315 cases of buttons per month, how many cases are there of Benny Brass Buttons? 135 cases

30. The Benny Button Company ships 63 cases of buttons by truck each month, 140 cases of buttons by train, and 112 cases by air. What is the fraction of buttons shipped by truck, train, and air in simplest form? truck $\frac{1}{5}$; train $\frac{4}{9}$; air $\frac{16}{45}$

CLASSWORK HOMEWORK | Mixed Numbers

Write each mixed number as a fraction.

1. $5\frac{5}{12}$ $\frac{65}{12}$
2. $7\frac{9}{16}$ $\frac{121}{16}$
3. $6\frac{2}{9}$ $\frac{56}{9}$
4. $14\frac{2}{3}$ $\frac{44}{3}$
5. $146\frac{3}{8}$ $\frac{1,171}{8}$

Write each fraction as a whole number or a mixed number in simplest form.

6. $\frac{374}{22}$ 17
7. $\frac{30}{14}$ $2\frac{1}{7}$
8. $\frac{222}{35}$ $6\frac{12}{35}$
9. $\frac{100}{7}$ $14\frac{2}{7}$
10. $\frac{216}{44}$ $4\frac{10}{11}$

For each number on the left, find its equivalent on the right. Use a straightedge to sight along an imaginary line connecting the dots next to the two numbers. The line will pass through a number and a letter. Use the number and corresponding letter to answer the riddle. Do not write in this book.

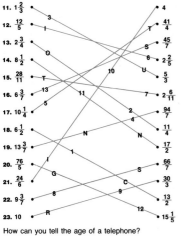

11. $1\frac{2}{3}$
12. $\frac{12}{5}$
13. $2\frac{3}{4}$
14. $8\frac{1}{2}$
15. $\frac{28}{11}$
16. $6\frac{3}{7}$
17. $10\frac{1}{4}$
18. $6\frac{1}{2}$
19. $13\frac{3}{7}$
20. $\frac{76}{5}$
21. $\frac{24}{6}$
22. $9\frac{3}{7}$
23. 10

• 4
• $\frac{41}{4}$
• $\frac{45}{7}$
• $2\frac{2}{5}$
• $\frac{5}{3}$
• $2\frac{6}{11}$
• $\frac{94}{7}$
• $\frac{11}{4}$
• $\frac{17}{2}$
• $\frac{66}{7}$
• $\frac{30}{3}$
• $\frac{13}{2}$
• $15\frac{1}{5}$

How can you tell the age of a telephone?

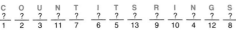

C O U N T   I T S   R I N G S
? ? ? ? ? ? ? ? ? ? ? ? ?
1 2 3 11 7 6 5 13 9 10 4 12 8

Use with pages 122–123. | Student Handbook **H49**

CLASSWORK HOMEWORK | Comparing Fractions and Mixed Numbers

Compare. Write >, <, or =. Use the LCD.

1. $\frac{12}{19}$ ⊙> $\frac{23}{40}$
2. $\frac{1}{6}$ ⊙< $\frac{2}{8}$
3. $6\frac{3}{7}$ ⊙< $6\frac{4}{7}$
4. $\frac{18}{4}$ ⊙> $\frac{30}{7}$

5. $\frac{4}{7}$ ⊙> $\frac{3}{7}$
6. $\frac{22}{7}$ ⊙> $\frac{68}{28}$
7. $\frac{19}{54}$ ⊙> $\frac{7}{21}$
8. $2\frac{3}{8}$ ⊙> $2\frac{4}{11}$

9. $1\frac{2}{11}$ ⊙> $1\frac{4}{7}$
10. $\frac{6}{11}$ ⊙= $\frac{66}{121}$
11. $\frac{41}{23}$ ⊙> $\frac{29}{16}$
12. $2\frac{2}{3}$ ⊙> $2\frac{5}{9}$

13. $\frac{5}{9}$ ⊙< $\frac{14}{25}$
14. $\frac{12}{17}$ ⊙< $\frac{25}{33}$
15. $7\frac{8}{19}$ ⊙= $7\frac{24}{57}$
16. $\frac{18}{11}$ ⊙> $\frac{5}{6}$

17. $\frac{6}{9}$ ⊙> $\frac{4}{9}$
18. $\frac{13}{9}$ ⊙< $\frac{7}{4}$
19. $6\frac{5}{9}$ ⊙> $6\frac{5}{3}$...

19. $6\frac{5}{9}$ ⊙> $6\frac{3}{5}$
20. $4\frac{42}{55}$ ⊙> $4\frac{5}{7}$

21. $\frac{16}{91}$ ⊙< $\frac{9}{50}$
22. $3\frac{6}{15}$ ⊙< $3\frac{2}{3}$
23. $\frac{42}{8}$ ⊙> $\frac{85}{17}$
24. $\frac{6}{11}$ ⊙> $\frac{12}{23}$

Write the numbers in order from the least to the greatest.

25. $\frac{3}{8}, \frac{6}{8}, \frac{1}{4}, \frac{5}{4}$ $\frac{1}{4}, \frac{3}{8}, \frac{6}{8}, \frac{5}{4}$

26. $\frac{3}{10}, \frac{2}{3}, \frac{3}{8}, \frac{1}{2}$ $\frac{3}{10}, \frac{3}{8}, \frac{1}{2}, \frac{2}{3}$

27. $5\frac{3}{5}, 5\frac{3}{8}, 5\frac{2}{10}, 4\frac{1}{4}$ $4\frac{1}{4}, 5\frac{2}{10}, 5\frac{3}{8}, 5\frac{3}{5}$

28. $\frac{15}{6}, 2\frac{1}{7}, 3\frac{1}{4}, \frac{50}{14}$ $2\frac{1}{7}, \frac{15}{6}, 3\frac{1}{4}, \frac{50}{14}$

Solve.

29. Marie drank $1\frac{2}{3}$ cups of juice. Roger drank $1\frac{3}{5}$ cups of juice. Who drank more juice? Marie

30. Lila has two different recipes for banana bread. Recipe A uses $3\frac{3}{4}$ cups of bananas. Recipe B uses $3\frac{7}{8}$ cups of bananas. Which recipe uses less? Recipe A

H50 Student Handbook | **Use with pages 124–125.**

CLASSWORK HOMEWORK | Using a Pictograph

PIZZA PALACE SALES

Monday	🍕🍕🍕🍕🍕
Tuesday	🍕🍕🍕🍕🍕🍕
Wednesday	🍕🍕🍕🍕🍕
Thursday	🍕🍕🍕🍕🍕🍕
Friday	🍕🍕🍕🍕🍕🍕🍕🍕
Saturday	🍕🍕🍕🍕🍕🍕🍕
Sunday	🍕🍕🍕🍕🍕🍕

🍕 = 50 pizzas

The pictograph above shows the average sales of pizzas for various days of the week. Use the pictograph to solve.

1. On which day are the most pizzas sold? Friday

2. On which days are the least pizzas sold?
Monday and Wednesday

3. How many more pizzas are normally sold on Thursday than on Sunday? 75

4. What is the average number of pizzas sold per week?
2,450

5. How many more pizzas does the Palace normally sell during the week (Monday through Friday) than on weekends? 1,050

6. When there is a Friday night football game, the Pizza Palace sales are usually 1.6 times the normal Friday sales. About how many are sold on a football Friday? 680

7. During a holiday weekend the sales on Friday, Saturday, and Sunday are usually 1.5 times the usual sales. Calculate the sales for each of these three days during the holiday weekend. (Round to the nearest whole number.) Friday 638; Saturday 563; Sunday 488

8. If the average profit on a pizza is $2.63, how much profit does the Pizza Palace earn on the sales of pizzas during an average week? $6,443.50

Use after pages 126–127. | Student Handbook **H51**

CLASSWORK HOMEWORK | Estimating Sums and Differences

Write > or <.

1. $1\frac{1}{9} + 2\frac{3}{8}$ ⊙> 3
2. $2\frac{4}{5} + 1\frac{7}{8}$ ⊙< 5
3. $4\frac{8}{9} + 3\frac{6}{7}$ ⊙< 9
4. $7\frac{8}{11} + 6\frac{7}{9}$ ⊙> 13
5. $6\frac{1}{7} + 5\frac{3}{19}$ ⊙> 11
6. $8\frac{1}{7} + 13\frac{2}{21}$ ⊙< 22
7. $4\frac{7}{9} + 2\frac{6}{16}$ ⊙> 7
8. $4\frac{5}{6} + 1\frac{9}{11}$ ⊙< 7
9. $14\frac{5}{6} + 9\frac{8}{9}$ ⊙> 23
10. $\frac{4}{7} + \frac{5}{9}$ ⊙> 1
11. $2\frac{6}{11} + 3\frac{5}{8}$ ⊙> 6
12. $6\frac{3}{17} + 2\frac{2}{19}$ ⊙< 9
13. $14\frac{8}{11} + 1\frac{3}{4}$ ⊙> 16
14. $3\frac{9}{10} + 1\frac{5}{7}$ ⊙> 5
15. $7\frac{2}{3} + 6\frac{5}{7}$ ⊙> 14
16. $4 - 2\frac{1}{8}$ ⊙< 2
17. $3\frac{1}{5} - 1\frac{7}{8}$ ⊙> 1
18. $8\frac{7}{8} - 5\frac{1}{5}$ ⊙> 3
19. $9\frac{7}{8} - 2\frac{1}{15}$ ⊙> 7
20. $5\frac{4}{7} - 1\frac{3}{11}$ ⊙> 4
21. $12\frac{3}{5} - 5\frac{9}{10}$ ⊙> 6
22. $6\frac{2}{11} - 1\frac{5}{7}$ ⊙> 3
23. $15\frac{7}{8} - 3\frac{2}{19}$ ⊙> 12
24. $20\frac{7}{8} - 10\frac{3}{7}$ ⊙> 10

Solve.

25. Do the apples and oranges weigh more than 8 pounds altogether?
no

26. Do the bananas and berries weigh more than 4 pounds altogether?
yes

27. Which two bags of fruit weigh about 5 pounds?
berries and oranges or apples and pears

28. Is the total weight of all five bags of fruit more than 12 pounds?
yes

H52 Student Handbook | **Use with pages 128–129.**

CLASSWORK HOMEWORK — Adding Fractions and Mixed Numbers

Add. Write the answer in simplest form.

1. $\dfrac{3}{8} + \dfrac{1}{8} + \dfrac{3}{8} = \dfrac{7}{8}$
2. $5\dfrac{2}{5} + 4\dfrac{1}{5} = 9\dfrac{3}{5}$
3. $\dfrac{3}{5} + \dfrac{1}{5} + \dfrac{4}{5}$
4. $3\dfrac{1}{4} + 4\dfrac{1}{2} = 7\dfrac{3}{4}$
5. $\dfrac{1}{6} + \dfrac{1}{4} = \dfrac{5}{12}$

6. $\dfrac{1}{6} + \dfrac{1}{2} = \dfrac{2}{3}$
7. $\dfrac{8}{9} + \dfrac{5}{9} = 1\dfrac{4}{9}$
8. $3\dfrac{2}{3} + 7\dfrac{2}{3} = 11\dfrac{1}{3}$
9. $\dfrac{4}{10} + \dfrac{3}{10} + \dfrac{1}{10} + \dfrac{4}{5}$
10. $2\dfrac{3}{6} + 1\dfrac{1}{6} = 3\dfrac{2}{3}$

11. $7\dfrac{2}{5} + 8\dfrac{1}{5} = 15\dfrac{3}{5}$
12. $\dfrac{1}{8} + \dfrac{3}{16} + \dfrac{1}{2} = \dfrac{13}{16}$
13. $\dfrac{1}{3} + \dfrac{2}{5} = \dfrac{11}{15}$
14. $2\dfrac{3}{12} + 7\dfrac{3}{4} = 10$
15. $9\dfrac{1}{10} + 10\dfrac{1}{6} = 19\dfrac{4}{15}$

16. $4\dfrac{2}{3} + 3\dfrac{8}{9} = 8\dfrac{5}{9}$
17. $\dfrac{2}{3} + \dfrac{5}{8} + \dfrac{5}{6} = 2\dfrac{1}{8}$
18. $3\dfrac{1}{2} + 5\dfrac{1}{6} = 8\dfrac{2}{3}$
19. $\dfrac{5}{9} + \dfrac{2}{3} = 1\dfrac{2}{9}$
20. $\dfrac{5}{12} + \dfrac{1}{4} + \dfrac{2}{3} = 1\dfrac{1}{3}$

21. $\dfrac{1}{6} + \dfrac{2}{3} + \dfrac{5}{12}$ — $1\dfrac{1}{4}$
22. $5\dfrac{1}{4} + 3\dfrac{3}{8} + 4\dfrac{5}{8}$ — $13\dfrac{1}{4}$
23. $\dfrac{1}{7} + \dfrac{3}{7} + \dfrac{2}{7}$ — $\dfrac{6}{7}$
24. $5\dfrac{1}{9} + 7\dfrac{4}{9} + 3\dfrac{8}{9}$ — $16\dfrac{4}{9}$

Solve.

25. Viola made a fruit mix with $1\dfrac{1}{2}$ cup raisins, $1\dfrac{1}{3}$ cup dried apples, and $1\dfrac{1}{4}$ cup dried apricots. How much fruit did she use in all? $4\dfrac{1}{12}$ cups

26. Marc used two pieces of wood that were $15\dfrac{5}{8}$ in. long and $17\dfrac{3}{4}$ in. long. What was the total length of the wood used? $33\dfrac{3}{8}$ in.

CLASSWORK HOMEWORK — Subtracting Fractions and Mixed Numbers

Subtract. Write the answer in simplest form.

1. $\dfrac{5}{6} - \dfrac{1}{3}$
2. $17\dfrac{4}{5} - 10\dfrac{7}{10} = 7\dfrac{1}{10}$
3. $12\dfrac{5}{8} - 9\dfrac{1}{4} = 3\dfrac{3}{8}$
4. $\dfrac{3}{5} - \dfrac{2}{5} = \dfrac{1}{5}$
5. $9\dfrac{1}{2} - 3\dfrac{1}{8} = 6\dfrac{3}{8}$

6. $11\dfrac{1}{2} - 1\dfrac{3}{7} = 10\dfrac{1}{14}$
7. $\dfrac{9}{10} - \dfrac{3}{10} = \dfrac{3}{5}$
8. $18\dfrac{1}{3} - 10\dfrac{2}{6} = 8\dfrac{1}{6}$
9. $\dfrac{2}{9} - \dfrac{1}{6} = \dfrac{1}{18}$
10. $15\dfrac{1}{3} - 14\dfrac{1}{6} = 1\dfrac{1}{6}$

11. $\dfrac{4}{5} - \dfrac{7}{10} = \dfrac{1}{10}$
12. $10\dfrac{1}{3} - 10\dfrac{1}{9} = \dfrac{2}{9}$
13. $9\dfrac{1}{2} - 5\dfrac{1}{3} = 4\dfrac{1}{6}$
14. $\dfrac{3}{4} - \dfrac{1}{3} = \dfrac{5}{12}$
15. $10\dfrac{1}{2} - 4\dfrac{3}{8} = 6\dfrac{1}{8}$

16. $20\dfrac{5}{6} - 16\dfrac{1}{2} = 4\dfrac{1}{3}$
17. $3\dfrac{1}{2} - 2\dfrac{1}{4} = 1\dfrac{1}{4}$
18. $\dfrac{3}{5} - \dfrac{3}{10} = \dfrac{3}{10}$
19. $18\dfrac{1}{4} - 13\dfrac{1}{6} = 5\dfrac{1}{12}$
20. $18\dfrac{4}{7} - 5\dfrac{1}{2} = 13\dfrac{1}{14}$

21. $19\dfrac{1}{2} - 14\dfrac{1}{3} = 5\dfrac{1}{6}$
22. $\dfrac{5}{6} - \dfrac{4}{9} = \dfrac{7}{18}$
23. $8\dfrac{9}{10} - 5\dfrac{5}{6} = 3\dfrac{1}{15}$
24. $4\dfrac{8}{9} - 1\dfrac{1}{2} = 3\dfrac{7}{18}$
25. $19\dfrac{7}{8} - 11\dfrac{1}{2} = 8\dfrac{3}{8}$

26. $\dfrac{4}{5} - \dfrac{1}{2}$ — $\dfrac{3}{10}$
27. $8\dfrac{4}{5} - 2\dfrac{1}{4}$ — $6\dfrac{11}{20}$
28. $12\dfrac{8}{9} - 7\dfrac{5}{9}$ — $5\dfrac{1}{3}$
29. $22\dfrac{5}{7} - 6\dfrac{2}{3}$ — $16\dfrac{1}{21}$

Solve.

30. Peter picked $4\dfrac{1}{2}$ pounds of strawberries and ate $\dfrac{1}{3}$ pound. Ellen picked $4\dfrac{1}{4}$ pounds of strawberries and ate $\dfrac{1}{6}$ pound. Who has more left and how much? Peter; $\dfrac{1}{12}$ pound

CLASSWORK HOMEWORK — Subtracting Mixed Numbers with Renaming

Subtract. Write the answer in simplest form.

1. $16\dfrac{1}{5} - 15\dfrac{1}{2} = \dfrac{7}{10}$
2. $19\dfrac{1}{2} - 14\dfrac{1}{3} = 5\dfrac{1}{6}$
3. $17\dfrac{4}{5} - 10\dfrac{7}{10} = 7\dfrac{1}{10}$
4. $16 - 7\dfrac{3}{5} = 8\dfrac{2}{5}$
5. $8\dfrac{4}{5} - 2\dfrac{1}{4} = 6\dfrac{11}{20}$

6. $16\dfrac{2}{5} - 5\dfrac{4}{5} = 10\dfrac{3}{5}$
7. $9 - 2\dfrac{1}{5} = 6\dfrac{4}{5}$
8. $16\dfrac{3}{4} - 5\dfrac{4}{5} = 10\dfrac{19}{20}$
9. $12\dfrac{5}{8} - 9\dfrac{1}{4} = 3\dfrac{3}{8}$
10. $9\dfrac{1}{2} - 3\dfrac{3}{8} = 6\dfrac{1}{8}$

11. $12\dfrac{1}{6} - 10\dfrac{5}{9} = 1\dfrac{11}{18}$
12. $19 - 2\dfrac{1}{2} = 16\dfrac{1}{2}$
13. $15\dfrac{1}{3} - 14\dfrac{1}{6} = 1\dfrac{1}{6}$
14. $5 - 2\dfrac{7}{9} = 2\dfrac{2}{9}$
15. $18\dfrac{1}{3} - 10\dfrac{2}{3} = 7\dfrac{2}{3}$

16. $13\dfrac{1}{2} - 3\dfrac{3}{5} = 9\dfrac{9}{10}$
17. $4\dfrac{8}{9} - 1\dfrac{1}{9} = 3\dfrac{7}{9}$
18. $10\dfrac{1}{4} - 3\dfrac{2}{3} = 6\dfrac{7}{12}$
19. $18\dfrac{4}{7} - 5\dfrac{1}{2} = 13\dfrac{1}{14}$
20. $10\dfrac{1}{3} - 10\dfrac{1}{9} = \dfrac{2}{9}$

21. $5 - 3\dfrac{2}{3} = 1\dfrac{1}{3}$
22. $3\dfrac{1}{4} - 2\dfrac{1}{4} = 1$
23. $14 - 1\dfrac{5}{6} = 12\dfrac{1}{6}$
24. $9\dfrac{3}{4} - 5\dfrac{1}{3} = 4\dfrac{5}{12}$
25. $19\dfrac{7}{8} - 11\dfrac{1}{2} = 8\dfrac{3}{8}$

26. $12\dfrac{1}{9} - 11\dfrac{1}{2}$ — $\dfrac{11}{18}$
27. $10\dfrac{1}{2} - 4\dfrac{3}{7}$ — $6\dfrac{1}{14}$
28. $11\dfrac{3}{4} - 2\dfrac{9}{10}$ — $8\dfrac{17}{20}$
29. $20 - 2\dfrac{3}{10}$ — $17\dfrac{7}{10}$
30. $11\dfrac{4}{7} - 1\dfrac{3}{7}$ — $10\dfrac{1}{7}$
31. $10\dfrac{2}{3} - 9\dfrac{1}{6}$ — $1\dfrac{1}{2}$
32. $18\dfrac{1}{4} - 13\dfrac{1}{6}$ — $5\dfrac{1}{12}$
33. $13 - 6\dfrac{8}{9}$ — $6\dfrac{1}{9}$
34. $10\dfrac{2}{6} - 7\dfrac{3}{6}$ — $2\dfrac{5}{6}$
35. $10\dfrac{3}{4} - 2\dfrac{1}{3}$ — $8\dfrac{5}{12}$

CLASSWORK HOMEWORK — Estimation

Use estimation to solve.

1. Cindy is building a workbench. She has to hammer a nail through two pieces of wood, each $\dfrac{9}{16}$ inches thick, into the top of a support. If she wants the nail to go at least $\dfrac{3}{4}$ inch into the support, can she use a $1\dfrac{3}{4}$-inch nail? no

2. One part of the workbench is made from 3 pieces of wood each measuring $7\dfrac{3}{8}$ inches by 7 inches. Can Cindy cut the pieces from a board measuring $7\dfrac{1}{4}$ inches by 24 inches? yes

3. It took Cindy $1\dfrac{1}{4}$ hours to buy the wood, $2\dfrac{3}{4}$ hours to build the bench, $1\dfrac{1}{2}$ hours to paint it, and $\dfrac{1}{4}$ hour to set it up in the garage. Did she spend more than 5 hours on the project? yes

4. Otto needs five strips of wood, measuring $4\dfrac{3}{8}$ inches, $7\dfrac{1}{2}$ inches, $9\dfrac{3}{4}$ inches, $6\dfrac{1}{8}$ inches, and $8\dfrac{5}{8}$ inches long. Can he cut the strips from a one-yard length of wood strip? no

5. George has a board of wood 6 feet long. From it, he cuts 2 pieces that are each $18\dfrac{1}{8}$ inches long, a piece $15\dfrac{1}{4}$ inches long, and a piece $7\dfrac{5}{8}$ inches long. About how long, to the nearest inch, is the piece of wood that he has left over? about 13 inches, or 1 foot 1 inch

6. Gayle, Mario, and Geoff are building a cabinet. Gayle cuts a piece of wood $25\dfrac{3}{4}$ inches long, Mario cuts a piece $25\dfrac{7}{16}$ inches long, and Geoff cuts 2 pieces that are each $12\dfrac{15}{16}$ inches long. Who cut the most wood? Geoff

CLASSWORK HOMEWORK — Multiplying Fractions

Multiply. Write the answer in simplest form.

1. $\frac{2}{3} \times \frac{9}{10}$ $\frac{3}{5}$ 2. $\frac{1}{6} \times \frac{1}{9} \times \frac{3}{4}$ $\frac{1}{72}$ 3. $\frac{2}{3} \times \frac{5}{6} \times \frac{3}{8}$ $\frac{5}{24}$

4. $\frac{1}{6} \times \frac{1}{9}$ $\frac{1}{54}$ 5. $\frac{1}{9} \times \frac{9}{10}$ $\frac{1}{10}$ 6. $\frac{1}{4} \times \frac{2}{3}$ $\frac{1}{6}$

7. $\frac{1}{2} \times \frac{5}{8} \times \frac{4}{5}$ $\frac{1}{4}$ 8. $\frac{1}{7} \times \frac{1}{5}$ $\frac{1}{35}$ 9. $\frac{4}{5} \times \frac{5}{7}$ $\frac{4}{7}$

10. $\frac{2}{5} \times \frac{1}{2}$ $\frac{1}{5}$ 11. $\frac{2}{3} \times \frac{1}{2}$ $\frac{1}{3}$ 12. $\frac{2}{3} \times \frac{3}{4} \times \frac{7}{8}$ $\frac{7}{48}$

13. $\frac{6}{7} \times \frac{1}{6}$ $\frac{1}{7}$ 14. $\frac{3}{8} \times \frac{2}{8}$ $\frac{3}{32}$ 15. $\frac{3}{4} \times \frac{4}{9} \times \frac{1}{2}$ $\frac{1}{6}$

16. $\frac{7}{8} \times \frac{3}{4} \times \frac{3}{10}$ $\frac{63}{640}$ 17. $\frac{1}{8} \times \frac{2}{3}$ $\frac{1}{12}$ 18. $\frac{3}{4} \times \frac{7}{9}$ $\frac{7}{12}$

19. $\frac{1}{6} \times \frac{1}{3}$ $\frac{1}{18}$ 20. $\frac{2}{7} \times \frac{6}{7}$ $\frac{12}{49}$ 21. $\frac{2}{5} \times \frac{1}{2} \times \frac{1}{7}$ $\frac{1}{35}$

22. $\frac{3}{10} \times \frac{5}{9}$ $\frac{1}{6}$ 23. $\frac{5}{6} \times \frac{3}{8}$ $\frac{5}{16}$ 24. $\frac{1}{8} \times \frac{1}{4}$ $\frac{1}{32}$

25. $\frac{12}{17} \times \frac{1}{2}$ $\frac{6}{17}$ 26. $\frac{6}{7} \times \frac{1}{5}$ $\frac{6}{35}$ 27. $\frac{9}{10} \times \frac{2}{3}$ $\frac{3}{5}$

28. $\frac{5}{6} \times \frac{2}{15}$ $\frac{1}{9}$ 29. $\frac{3}{7} \times \frac{14}{15}$ $\frac{2}{5}$ 30. $\frac{2}{9} \times \frac{3}{5}$ $\frac{2}{15}$

Solve.

31. Larry had $\frac{3}{4}$ can of shellac. He used $\frac{2}{3}$ of it. What part of the can of shellac did Larry use?
$\frac{1}{2}$ can

32. Helen had $\frac{2}{3}$ of a box of pipe cleaners. She used $\frac{5}{6}$ of them to make a mobile. What part of the box of pipe cleaners did she use?
$\frac{5}{9}$ box

CLASSWORK HOMEWORK — Estimating Products and Quotients

Write > or <.

1. $2\frac{1}{8} \times 1\frac{1}{9}$ ⊙ > 2   2. $3\frac{2}{7} \times 2\frac{1}{6}$ ⊙ < 12

3. $4\frac{1}{7} \times 2$ ⊙ > 8   4. $5\frac{2}{3} \times 4\frac{3}{4}$ ⊙ < 30

5. $3\frac{4}{9} \times 5$ ⊙ < 20   6. $2\frac{3}{4} \times 2\frac{7}{8}$ ⊙ < 9

7. $6 \times 5\frac{7}{11}$ ⊙ > 30   8. $\frac{7}{8} \times 5$ ⊙ < 5

9. $8\frac{1}{9} \times 2\frac{1}{5}$ ⊙ > 16   10. $3\frac{1}{7} \times 12\frac{8}{9}$ ⊙ > 36

11. $4\frac{4}{8} \times 2$ ⊙ > 8   12. $14\frac{7}{8} \times 2\frac{9}{11}$ ⊙ < 45

13. $\frac{4}{5} \div \frac{1}{9}$ ⊙ > 1   14. $\frac{1}{9} \div \frac{4}{5}$ ⊙ < 1

15. $1\frac{1}{2} \div 2$ ⊙ < 1   16. $2\frac{1}{4} \div 1\frac{7}{8}$ ⊙ > 1

17. $7\frac{3}{4} \div 8\frac{1}{9}$ ⊙ < 1   18. $5\frac{1}{3} \div 2\frac{7}{8}$ ⊙ > 1

Estimate. Answers will vary. Accept any reasonable estimates.

19. $15\frac{1}{7} \div 4\frac{11}{12}$ 3–4   20. $6\frac{1}{7} \div 1\frac{8}{9}$ 3–4

21. $5\frac{1}{8} \div \frac{9}{10}$ 5–6   22. $28\frac{7}{8} \div 8\frac{1}{4}$ 3–4

23. $10\frac{2}{3} \div 4\frac{1}{7}$ 2–3   24. $6\frac{1}{7} \div 1\frac{3}{4}$ 3–4

25. $5\frac{7}{8} \div 2\frac{9}{11}$ 2–3   26. $8\frac{1}{11} \times 7\frac{2}{19}$ 56–60

27. $3\frac{8}{9} \times 7\frac{10}{13}$ 28–32   28. $14\frac{1}{6} \times 2\frac{1}{15}$ 28–30

29. $1\frac{1}{9} \times 5\frac{1}{8}$ 5–6   30. $\frac{9}{10} \times 5\frac{4}{5}$ 5–6

CLASSWORK HOMEWORK — Multiplying Mixed Numbers

Multiply. Write the answer in simplest form.

1. $4\frac{1}{5} \times 1\frac{3}{7}$ 6   2. $\frac{3}{4} \times 2\frac{8}{9} \times \frac{9}{10}$ $1\frac{19}{20}$

3. $\frac{2}{5} \times 85$ 34   4. $6\frac{9}{10} \times 1\frac{1}{3} \times 2\frac{1}{3}$ $21\frac{7}{15}$

5. $8\frac{1}{5} \times 5\frac{5}{6}$ $47\frac{5}{6}$ 6. $2\frac{1}{2} \times 8\frac{7}{10} \times 2\frac{3}{8}$ $51\frac{21}{32}$

7. $10\frac{1}{2} \times 8\frac{5}{7} \times 5\frac{1}{6}$ $472\frac{3}{4}$ 8. $10 \times \frac{2}{5} \times \frac{1}{3}$ $1\frac{1}{3}$

9. $4\frac{1}{6} \times 2\frac{1}{5}$ $9\frac{1}{6}$ 10. $2\frac{2}{7} \times 8\frac{3}{4} \times 32\frac{5}{8}$ $652\frac{1}{2}$

11. $6\frac{5}{8} \times 1\frac{3}{5}$ $10\frac{3}{5}$ 12. $48 \times \frac{2}{3}$ 32

13. $10\frac{5}{6} \times 6\frac{2}{5}$ $69\frac{1}{3}$ 14. $36 \times \frac{2}{9}$ 8

15. $70 \times \frac{4}{5} \times 2\frac{2}{3}$ $149\frac{1}{3}$ 16. $\frac{4}{9} \times 27$ 12

Complete each problem. Then find the fraction below that is the same as the fraction in your answer. Write the matching code letters to solve the riddle.(You won't use all letters.)

17. $8\frac{3}{7} \times 5\frac{5}{6}$ $49\frac{1}{6}$ [A]   18. $10\frac{3}{10} \times 2\frac{1}{2}$ $25\frac{3}{4}$ [S]

19. $1\frac{1}{8} \times 2\frac{7}{9}$ $3\frac{1}{8}$ [T]   20. $4\frac{2}{3} \times 3\frac{5}{6}$ $17\frac{8}{9}$ [E]

21. $1\frac{1}{3} \times 3\frac{3}{5}$ $4\frac{2}{5}$ [P]   22. $9\frac{1}{10} \times 3\frac{3}{7}$ $31\frac{1}{5}$ [G]

23. $7\frac{4}{5} \times 2\frac{1}{6}$ $16\frac{9}{10}$ [A]   24. $2\frac{3}{10} \times 5\frac{5}{6}$ $13\frac{5}{12}$ [R]

25. $6\frac{1}{4} \times 4\frac{4}{7}$ $28\frac{4}{7}$ [R]   26. $7\frac{1}{3} \times 8\frac{1}{2}$ $62\frac{1}{3}$ [F]

27. $6\frac{3}{8} \times 6\frac{3}{8}$ $40\frac{3}{8}$ [H]   28. $5\frac{7}{9} \times 3\frac{1}{2}$ $20\frac{2}{9}$ [Y]

$\underset{?}{H}$ $\underset{?}{A}$ $\underset{?}{R}$ $\underset{?}{E}$ $\underset{?}{S}$ $\underset{?}{P}$ $\underset{?}{R}$ $\underset{?}{A}$ $\underset{?}{Y}$

$\frac{3}{8}$ $\frac{9}{10}$ $\frac{4}{7}$ $\frac{8}{9}$ $\frac{3}{4}$ $\frac{2}{5}$ $\frac{5}{12}$ $\frac{1}{6}$ $\frac{2}{9}$

CLASSWORK HOMEWORK — Writing a Simpler Problem

Write the letter of the better plan for simplifying each problem.

1. It took 11 carpenters $4\frac{1}{2}$ hours to cut 1,260 dowels. How long would it take one carpenter working at the same speed to cut 196 dowels?

a. step 1: $200 \times 10 = 2,000$
   step 2: $2,000 \div 5 = 400$
   step 3: $1,200 \div 400 = 3$

b. step 1: $1,250 \div 5 = 250$
   step 2: $250 \div 10 = 25$
   step 3: $200 \div 25 = 8$

2. A fence painter uses $8\frac{3}{4}$ gallons of paint for every 210 feet of fence. How much paint would he use to paint 752 feet of fence?

a. step 1: $200 \div 10 = 20$
   step 2: $800 \div 20 = 40$

b. step 1: $750 + 200 = 950$
   step 2: $950 \div 10 = 95$

Solve. Simplify the problem if you need to.

3. A bricklayer uses 1,785 bricks to build 15 fireplaces. If he builds 6 fireplaces in 2 days, how many bricks does he use per day? 357 bricks

4. Phillip has three boxes of nails. The boxes contain 126 nails, 240 nails, and 342 nails. If he uses $\frac{5}{6}$ of the nails, how many nails will he have left? 118 nails

5. Louise needs 164 feet of board for a client's wooden floor. The wood costs $3.40 per foot, and Louise wants to make $1.25 for every foot of board that she installs. How much does she charge the client for installing the floor? $762.60

6. Roger uses $7\frac{1}{4}$ cans of putty to set 29 windows. He expects to set 210 windows this week. How much putty will he use?
$52\frac{1}{2}$ cans

7. Dawson Construction built 53 houses each year from 1971 to 1980. From 1981 to 1985, it built 76 houses each year. How many houses did Dawson Construction build from 1971 to 1985?
910 houses

8. Jance Buildings constructed 140 houses from 1978 to 1982. If construction was increased by $\frac{1}{5}$, how many houses would Jance build from 1983 to 1987?
168 houses

CLASSWORK HOMEWORK | Dividing Fractions

Divide. Write the answer in simplest form.

1. $\frac{3}{5} \div \frac{9}{10}$ $\frac{2}{3}$
2. $\frac{1}{10} \div \frac{9}{10}$ $\frac{1}{9}$
3. $\frac{19}{81} \div \frac{1}{3}$ $\frac{19}{27}$
4. $\frac{7}{27} \div \frac{4}{9}$ $\frac{7}{12}$
5. $\frac{1}{6} \div \frac{1}{4}$ $\frac{2}{3}$
6. $\frac{1}{10} \div \frac{1}{3}$ $\frac{3}{10}$
7. $\frac{4}{7} \div \frac{4}{5}$ $\frac{5}{7}$
8. $\frac{3}{8} \div \frac{3}{5}$ $\frac{5}{8}$
9. $\frac{1}{3} \div \frac{1}{2}$ $\frac{2}{3}$
10. $\frac{3}{22} \div \frac{2}{11}$ $\frac{3}{4}$
11. $\frac{1}{7} \div \frac{1}{6}$ $\frac{6}{7}$
12. $\frac{1}{2} \div \frac{3}{4}$ $\frac{2}{3}$
13. $\frac{1}{12} \div \frac{2}{3}$ $\frac{1}{8}$
14. $\frac{2}{15} \div \frac{4}{5}$ $\frac{1}{6}$
15. $\frac{7}{12} \div \frac{7}{9}$ $\frac{3}{4}$
16. $\frac{4}{9} \div \frac{1}{2}$ $\frac{8}{9}$
17. $\frac{1}{5} \div \frac{3}{5}$ $\frac{1}{3}$
18. $\frac{1}{8} \div \frac{1}{3}$ $\frac{3}{8}$
19. $\frac{1}{15} \div \frac{3}{5}$ $\frac{1}{9}$
20. $\frac{2}{3} \div \frac{4}{5}$ $\frac{5}{6}$
21. $\frac{5}{28} \div \frac{1}{4}$ $\frac{5}{7}$
22. $\frac{2}{27} \div \frac{1}{3}$ $\frac{2}{9}$
23. $\frac{3}{50} \div \frac{1}{10}$ $\frac{3}{5}$
24. $\frac{8}{27} \div \frac{1}{3}$ $\frac{8}{9}$
25. $\frac{3}{8} \div \frac{3}{4}$ $\frac{1}{2}$
26. $\frac{70}{99} \div \frac{7}{9}$ $\frac{10}{11}$
27. $\frac{3}{10} \div \frac{9}{10}$ $\frac{1}{3}$
28. $\frac{3}{10} \div \frac{2}{5}$ $\frac{3}{4}$
29. $\frac{7}{72} \div \frac{1}{6}$ $\frac{7}{12}$
30. $\frac{10}{21} \div \frac{6}{7}$ $\frac{5}{9}$

CLASSWORK HOMEWORK | Dividing Mixed Numbers

Divide. Write the answer in simplest form.

1. $3\frac{1}{2} \div 1\frac{7}{8}$ $1\frac{13}{15}$
2. $1\frac{3}{4} \div 4\frac{1}{2}$ $\frac{7}{18}$
3. $1\frac{1}{5} \div 1\frac{1}{2}$ $\frac{4}{5}$
4. $4\frac{1}{3} \div 2\frac{1}{2}$ $1\frac{11}{15}$
5. $3\frac{1}{6} \div 2$ $1\frac{7}{12}$
6. $7\frac{1}{3} \div \frac{1}{3}$ 22
7. $7\frac{1}{2} \div 2\frac{7}{9}$ $2\frac{7}{10}$
8. $3\frac{1}{2} \div 3$ $1\frac{1}{6}$
9. $9\frac{1}{5} \div 2$ $4\frac{3}{5}$
10. $3\frac{1}{3} \div 1\frac{5}{9}$ $2\frac{1}{7}$
11. $\frac{9}{10} \div 9\frac{3}{4}$ $\frac{6}{65}$
12. $4\frac{2}{3} \div 2\frac{2}{3}$ $1\frac{3}{4}$
13. $4\frac{5}{8} \div \frac{7}{8}$ $5\frac{2}{7}$
14. $8\frac{1}{3} \div 4$ $2\frac{1}{12}$
15. $8\frac{1}{4} \div \frac{3}{4}$ 11
16. $1\frac{1}{2} \div 1\frac{1}{2}$ 1
17. $1\frac{2}{7} \div 1\frac{1}{5}$ $1\frac{1}{14}$
18. $3\frac{1}{5} \div 4\frac{4}{7}$ $\frac{7}{10}$
19. $4\frac{1}{4} \div 3$ $1\frac{5}{12}$
20. $\frac{1}{6} \div 10\frac{3}{4}$ $\frac{2}{129}$
21. $9\frac{2}{7} \div 1\frac{5}{7}$ $5\frac{5}{12}$
22. $6\frac{2}{5} \div \frac{7}{10}$ $9\frac{1}{7}$
23. $6\frac{1}{6} \div \frac{2}{3}$ $9\frac{1}{4}$
24. $9\frac{1}{3} \div 1\frac{1}{3}$ 7
25. $4\frac{2}{7} \div 1\frac{1}{2}$ $2\frac{6}{7}$
26. $10\frac{3}{4} \div 2$ $5\frac{3}{8}$
27. $6\frac{1}{2} \div 1\frac{1}{6}$ $5\frac{4}{7}$
28. $4\frac{1}{3} \div 1\frac{5}{8}$ $2\frac{2}{3}$
29. $2\frac{1}{4} \div 6\frac{3}{4}$ $\frac{1}{3}$
30. $7\frac{1}{10} \div \frac{3}{8}$ $18\frac{14}{15}$

CLASSWORK HOMEWORK | Decimals and Fractions

Write a decimal for each fraction or mixed number. Use a bar to show repeating decimals.

1. $\frac{18}{25}$ 0.72
2. $\frac{7}{20}$ 0.35
3. $2\frac{7}{22}$ $2.3\overline{18}$
4. $4\frac{6}{25}$ 4.24
5. $\frac{29}{50}$ 0.58
6. $12\frac{80}{91}$ $12.8\overline{79120}$
7. $\frac{5}{24}$ $0.208\overline{3}$
8. $7\frac{86}{90}$ $7.9\overline{5}$
9. $\frac{27}{40}$ 0.675

Write a fraction or mixed number, in simplest form, for each decimal.

10. $0.\overline{2}$ $\frac{2}{9}$
11. 4.8125 $4\frac{13}{16}$
12. 9.3 $9\frac{3}{10}$
13. 0.765 $\frac{153}{200}$
14. $3.\overline{3}$ $3\frac{1}{3}$
15. $9.\overline{5}$ $9\frac{5}{9}$
16. 13.96 $13\frac{24}{25}$
17. 0.125 $\frac{1}{8}$
18. $4.\overline{8}$ $4\frac{8}{9}$

Compare. Write $<$, $>$, or $=$.

19. 0.34 $\bigcirc >$ $\frac{1}{3}$
20. 0.125 $\bigcirc =$ $\frac{1}{8}$
21. 0.55 $\bigcirc <$ $\frac{12}{20}$
22. $\frac{5}{7}$ $\bigcirc >$ 0.714281
23. $\frac{8}{9}$ $\bigcirc <$ 0.89
24. 0.756 $\bigcirc <$ $\frac{19}{25}$

Solve.

25. There are 100 beads on Julie's necklace. Of these, 0.45 are blue. What fraction of the beads are blue? $\frac{9}{20}$

26. Out of 1,000 tickets for the crafts fair, all but 150 were sold. What part of the tickets were sold? Write the answer as a decimal and as a fraction in simplest form. $0.85; \frac{17}{20}$

CLASSWORK HOMEWORK | Solving Equations with Fractions

Solve. Write the answer in simplest form.

1. $x + 2\frac{1}{3} = 7$ $x = 4\frac{2}{3}$
2. $n - 4\frac{3}{5} = 12\frac{1}{3}$ $n = 16\frac{14}{15}$
3. $\frac{1}{9}a + 3\frac{2}{3} = 4\frac{1}{2}$ $a = 7\frac{1}{2}$
4. $1\frac{3}{4}b - 13 = 2\frac{1}{4}$ $b = 8\frac{5}{7}$
5. $3\frac{1}{3}w + \frac{2}{3} = 20\frac{1}{2}$ $w = 5\frac{19}{20}$
6. $3\frac{3}{10}r \div 2\frac{1}{3} = 1\frac{5}{6}$ $r = 1\frac{8}{27}$
7. $\frac{1}{2}g + \frac{4}{3} = 7$ $g = 11\frac{1}{3}$
8. $\frac{4}{9}s - 2 = 14$ $s = 36$

Copy and solve each equation. To unscramble the limerick, write the words from each box in the order given.

$3X \div 5 = 9$ $X = \underline{\ ?\ }$ 15 WHEN HE ROSE	$\frac{5}{3}X = 15$ $X = \underline{\ ?\ }$ 9 EXCEEDINGLY NEAT	$2X \div 3 = 14$ $X = \underline{\ ?\ }$ 21 WHO WAS SO
$5\frac{1}{4}X = 42$ $X = \underline{\ ?\ }$ 8 ON HIS HEAD	$3\frac{2}{3}X = 44$ $X = \underline{\ ?\ }$ 12 THERE WAS A	$1\frac{3}{5}X = 32$ $X = \underline{\ ?\ }$ 20 HIS FEET
$\frac{5}{12}X + 1 = 21$ $X = \underline{\ ?\ }$ 48 OUT OF BED	$7X - 3 = 39$ $X = \underline{\ ?\ }$ 6 DID DIRTY	$\frac{8}{9}X = 2\frac{2}{3}$ $X = \underline{\ ?\ }$ 3 HE STOOD
$3\frac{3}{7}X - 5 = 19$ $X = \underline{\ ?\ }$ 7 FROM CRETE	$\frac{X}{23} + 13 = 14$ $X = \underline{\ ?\ }$ 23 YOUNG FELLOW	$5X - 2\frac{3}{7} = 7\frac{4}{7}$ $X = \underline{\ ?\ }$ 2 AND NEVER

12, 23, 7   THERE WAS A YOUNG FELLOW FROM CRETE
21, 9   WHO WAS SO EXCEEDINGLY NEAT
15, 48   WHEN HE ROSE OUT OF BED
3, 8   HE STOOD ON HIS HEAD
2, 6, 20   AND NEVER DID DIRTY HIS FEET

CLASSWORK HOMEWORK | Interpreting the Quotient and the Remainder

Write the letter of the correct answer.

1. Albert wants to put 250 eggs in cartons that hold a dozen eggs each. How many cartons will he need?

   a. 20 cartons
   b. $20\frac{5}{6}$ cartons
   c. 21 cartons

2. Hassan is reading a 4-volume set of cookbooks. Each book has 250 pages. He is now on page 437. How many pages of the second book has he finished?

   a. 187 pages
   b. 63 pages
   c. $\frac{187}{250}$ book

Solve.

3. Chef Salim prepares 35 tea sandwiches in 2 minutes. After 7 minutes and 45 seconds, how many whole sandwiches has she prepared if she makes them at her regular speed? 135 sandwiches

4. It takes Ruth 2 minutes to chop 3 pounds of celery into small pieces. How long will it take her to chop $5\frac{1}{2}$ pounds? 3 minutes 40 seconds

5. Talal's kitchen floor measures 110 feet square. He wants to cover the floor with tiles that measure $7\frac{1}{2}$ feet square each. How many tiles will he need? 15 tiles

6. Sadako's new restaurant has 8 rooms. To paint the rooms, he needs 10 gallons of paint. He has already used $3\frac{1}{4}$ gallons of paint. How many rooms has he completed painting if he is painting 1 at a time? 2 rooms

7. Betty is selling her old paperback cookbooks at 3 for $3.50. A customer wants only one book. What is the price she should charge if she does not want to lose money? $1.17

8. A grocery chain sells melons at 3 for $4.00. The computer that it uses to calculate prices drops all fractions of a cent. How much does one melon cost? $1.33

9. In making loaves of whole wheat bread, a baker uses $2\frac{1}{2}$ pounds of flour to make 5 loaves. The baker purchases flour in 50-pound bags. How many loaves have been made if $22\frac{1}{4}$ pounds of flour have been used so far? 44 loaves

10. The bakery ships loaves of bread in boxes that hold 2 dozen loaves each. If the bakery ships 372 loaves to a restaurant, how many boxes of bread are delivered to the restaurant? 16 boxes

Use after pages 154–155.   Student Handbook **H65**

CLASSWORK HOMEWORK | Metric Units of Length

kilometer (km)	hectometer (hm)	dekameter (dm)	meter (m)	decimeter (dm)	centimeter (cm)	millimeter (mm)
1,000 m	100 m	10 m	1 m	0.1 m	0.01 m	0.001 m

Write the unit used to measure

1. the thickness of a phone book. centimeter
2. the width of an ocean. kilometer
3. the thickness of a quarter. millimeter
4. the length of a swimming pool. meter

Complete. Use the chart to help you.

5. 9,100 cm = __?__ m 91
6. 49 cm = __?__ m 0.49
7. 25,000 mm __?__ m 25
8. 27 m = __?__ mm 27,000
9. 16 km = __?__ m 16,000
10. 4.33 m = __?__ cm 433
11. 855 cm = __?__ m 8.55
12. 58,000 m = __?__ km 58
13. 3.779 km = __?__ m 3,779
14. 71 m = __?__ cm 7,100
15. 0.53 m = __?__ cm 53
16. 5.28 m = __?__ cm 528
17. 10,000 cm = __?__ m 100
18. 570 m = __?__ km 0.57
19. 5 m = __?__ cm 500
20. 6,528 m = __?__ km 6.528
21. 3.848 m = __?__ mm 3,848
22. 16 km = __?__ m 16,000
23. 923 mm = __?__ m 0.923
24. 100 m = __?__ cm 10,000
25. 4,300 m = __?__ km 4.3
26. 5,062 m = __?__ km 5.062
27. 10 km = __?__ m 10,000
28. 741 cm = __?__ m 7.41
29. 8.4 m = __?__ m 8,400
30. 9.790 m = __?__ mm 9,790
31. 9,000 cm = __?__ m 90
32. 1,800 cm = __?__ m 18

H66 Student Handbook   Use with pages 166–167.

CLASSWORK HOMEWORK | Metric Units of Capacity and Mass

kilogram (kg)	gram (g)	milligram (mg)
1,000 g	1,000 mg	0.001 g

kiloliter (kL)	liter (L)	milliliter (mL)
1,000 L	1,000 mL	0.001 L

Write the unit used to measure

1. a raindrop. milliliter
2. the mass of a person. kilogram
3. the capacity of a milk pitcher. liter
4. the mass of an orange. gram

Complete. Use the charts to help you.

5. 15,000 mL = __?__ L 15
6. 62 kL = __?__ L 62,000
7. 0.378 L = __?__ mL 378
8. 6,622 mL = __?__ L 6.622
9. 39,000 g = __?__ kg 39
10. 513 g = __?__ mg 513,000
11. 918 g = __?__ kg 0.918
12. 1,785 mg = __?__ g 1.785
13. 3,186 mL = __?__ L 3.186
14. 642 L = __?__ kL 0.642
15. 47 kg = __?__ g 47,000
16. 65 g = __?__ kg 0.065
17. 49.992 kg = __?__ g 49,992
18. 5.828 L = __?__ mL 5,828
19. 50 kL = __?__ L 50,000
20. 313.103 kg = __?__ g 313,103
21. 500 mg = __?__ g 0.5
22. 8,906 g = __?__ kg 8.906
23. 23 L = __?__ mL 23,000
24. 80.044 g = __?__ mg 80,044

Solve.

25. Phyllis has a piece of cheese with a mass of 258 g. Irene has a piece of cheese with a mass of 0.3 kg. Whose piece of cheese has the greater mass? Irene's

26. Brian drank 575 mL of juice. Robert drank 0.55 L of juice. Who drank more juice? Brian

Use with pages 168–169.   Student Handbook **H67**

CLASSWORK HOMEWORK | Relating Metric Measures

Copy and complete the chart.

	Length	Width	Height	Volume		Capacity		Mass	
1.	12 cm	8 cm	10 cm	960	cm³	960	mL	960	g
2.	40 mm	20 mm	111 mm	88.8	cm³	88.8	mL	88.8	g
3.	6 m	2 m	90 cm	10.8	m³	10.8	kL	10.8	t
4.	30 m	14 m	8 m	3,360	m³	3,360,000	L	3,360	t
5.	50 cm	25 cm	60 cm	75,000	cm³	75	L	75	kg
6.	650 mm	10 cm	2 m	130,000	cm³	130,000	mL	130,000	g
7.	50 m	35 m	75 mm	131.25	m³	131.25	kL	131.25	t
8.	65 cm	40 cm	3 m	780,000	cm³	780,000	mL	780,000	g
9.	15 m	6 m	9 m	810	m³	810	kL	810	t
10.	8 cm	7 cm	12 cm	672	cm³	672	mL	672	g

Solve.

11. An empty container has a mass of 240 grams. When filled with water, the container and the water have a total mass of 875 grams. How many milliliters of water are there in the container? 635 mL

12. The inside dimensions of a fish tank are 50 cm by 25 cm by 30 cm. Find the mass of water in the tank when it is full. Express your answer in kilograms. 37.5 kg

13. The volume of a juice carton is 960 cm³. How many liters of juice does it hold? 0.96 L

14. A gas station pumps 2,000 L of gas each day. How long does it take the station to use up a 14-kL delivery? 7 days (1 week)

H68 Student Handbook   Use with pages 170–171.

CLASSWORK HOMEWORK | Choosing/Writing a Sensible Question

Steve and Leiko opened a frozen yogurt parlor across the street from the Mason Junior High and High School. The shop sells 15 flavors of homemade, wholesome, all-natural frozen yogurt with no preservatives. After the first few weeks of business, Steve and Leiko have some decisions to make.

NOTE: Answers will vary for all problems. Sample answers are given.

Read each statement, and write a question that Steve and Leiko should answer before making a decision.

1. Business has been very good in the first few weeks. Some friends say that the prices are too low and should be raised.
   Would raising prices cut the number of sales per week?

2. Some kids suggested that the store add at least 3 or 4 tables and have even more flavors.
   How much will additional tables and chairs cost?

3. As business increases, Steve and Leiko find it hard to make enough frozen yogurt. They want to hire someone to help them.
   How much should we pay the person per hour? Is it a full-time job?

4. The cost of the ingredients for making frozen yogurt is increasing. The landlord wants to raise the rent.
   By what percent should we increase prices in order to meet expenses?

5. The yearbook staff of the school asks them to buy an ad. Other salespersons from the town newspapers and several magazines also solicit their business.
   Which publication has the largest audience?

6. One of their customers told her mother how good their frozen yogurt was. Her mother wants Steve to cater a party for her friends.
   How many people will be at the party?

7. Leiko wants to print a newsletter on a regular basis to inform customers about health and nutrition.
   How much time per week will it take to write the newsletter?

8. The kids want the owners to install a public telephone, a juke box, and video game machines.
   Will these items increase business or simply become nuisances?

CLASSWORK HOMEWORK | Customary Units of Length

12 inches (in.) = 1 foot (ft)
36 in. = 3 ft = 1 yard (yd)
5,280 ft = 1,760 yd = 1 mile (mi)

Write the unit used to measure

1. the height of a refrigerator. foot
2. a tennis court. yard or foot
3. the distance to the moon. mile
4. the width of a shelf. inch

What is the middle of India? Find the equivalent on the right for each measurement on the left. Write the letters of your answers horizontally on a separate sheet of paper. Then read across to answer the riddle. THE LETTER D

5. $\frac{1}{4}$ ft　T
6. 1,104 in.　H
7. 84 ft　E
8. 32 in.　L
9. 92 yd　E
10. $\frac{3}{4}$ mi　T
11. $20\frac{1}{3}$ yd　T
12. 63 ft　E
13. 129 in.　R
14. 440 yd　D

H. 92 ft
L. $2\frac{2}{3}$ ft
T. 61 ft
D. $\frac{1}{4}$ mi
T. 3 in.
E. 276 ft
E. 28 yd
T. 3,960 ft
R. $10\frac{3}{4}$ ft
E. 21 yd

CLASSWORK HOMEWORK | Customary Units of Capacity and Weight

8 fluid ounces (fl oz) = 1 cup (c)
2 c = 1 pint (pt)
2 pt = 1 quart (qt)
4 qt = 1 gallon (gal)

16 ounces (oz) = 1 pound (lb)
2,000 lb = 1 ton (T)

Write the unit used to measure

1. the weight of an airplane. ton
2. the amount of juice in a glass. fl oz
3. the capacity of a swimming pool. gallon
4. the weight of a marble. ounce

Complete. Use the charts to help you.

5. 22 c = ___?___ pt　11
6. $4\frac{3}{4}$ lb = ___?___ oz　76
7. 159 lb = ___?___ oz　2,544
8. 55,000 lb = ___?___ T　$27\frac{1}{2}$
9. 148 qt = ___?___ gal　37
10. 43 pt = ___?___ qt ___?___ pt　21　1
11. 192 oz = ___?___ lb　12
12. 300 oz = ___?___ lb　$18\frac{3}{4}$
13. 32,000 lb = ___?___ T　16
14. 14 c = ___?___ fl oz　112
15. $40\frac{1}{10}$ T = ___?___ lb　80,200
16. 7 qt 3 pt = ___?___ pt　17
17. $23\frac{1}{4}$ gal = ___?___ qt　93
18. 21 c = ___?___ pt　$10\frac{1}{2}$
19. 7 T = ___?___ lb　14,000
20. 240 fl oz = ___?___ c　30
21. 12 qt 3 pt = ___?___ pt　27
22. 29 pt = ___?___ qt　$14\frac{1}{2}$

Solve.

23. A large apple weighs 7 ounces. If Peter and John each eat an apple a day, how many pounds of apples do they eat in 2 weeks? $12\frac{1}{4}$ lb

24. A recipe for soup uses 1 quart beef broth, 1 pint tomato juice, and 1 cup of milk. How many 1-cup servings will it make? 7 c

---

CLASSWORK HOMEWORK | Choosing a Strategy or Method

Estimation	Choosing the Operation	Using a Table
Using a Graph	Solving Multi-step Problems	Writing an Equation
Identifying Extra/Needed Information	Checking for a Reasonable Answer	Interpreting the Quotient and the Remainder

Write the strategy or method you choose. Then solve. Strategies and methods will vary.

1. To start her company, Maria needs $160,000. Each of 5 investors is paying $15,000, and 4 others are paying $17,000 each. Maria has to invest the rest herself. How much money will she need?
   solving multi-step problems; $17,000

2. A manufacturer in Boston pays Carlos $0.37 per mile one way to deliver its product in Atlanta, 1037 miles away. On the return trip, Carlos is paid $0.24 per mile to deliver another product in Boston. How much money does Carlos make after 7 round-trips? solving multi-step problems; $4,427.99

3. The Johnsons are getting ready to move to New York. They can pack 12 books in each box. If they have 546 books, how many boxes will they need for books?
   interpreting the quotient and remainder; 46 boxes

4. Mrs. Lee wants to buy a new car. She sees one for $10,750. The car has 4 options, costing $389, $429, $318, and $211. With all the options, about how much will the car cost?
   estimation; about $12,100

Use the graph at the right for Exercises 5–8.

5. By which year has California's population surpassed New York's? 1970

6. About how many people lived in California in 1980? about 24 million

7. Which state had the biggest increase in population? When and how much was it? California, from 1950 to 1960; about 5 million

8. About how many more people lived in California than in New York in 1970? about 2 million more people

APPROXIMATE POPULATION BY STATE AND YEAR

Millions of People: 25.0, 20.0, 15.0, 10.0, 5.0 — years 1950, 1960, 1970, 1980 — CA, NY

CLASSWORK HOMEWORK | Choosing a Strategy or Method

Estimation	Choosing the Operation	Writing an Equation
Using a Graph	Solving Multi-step Problems	Interpreting the Quotient
Identifying Extra/Needed	Checking for a Reasonable Answer	and the Remainder
Information	Using a Table	

Write the strategy or method you choose. Then solve.
Strategies and methods will vary.

1. Roberto wants to buy a $43 gift for his father. He finished one odd job in 4 hours at $3.75 an hour. He is now working at a job which pays $4.00 an hour. How many hours does he have to work to earn the money he needs?
solving multi-step problems; 7 hours

2. Andrea had $20.00. She bought 4 paper pads at $1.19 each, 3 notebooks at $1.89 each, and a book at $4.95. Now she wants to use the remaining money to buy as many pens at $0.79 each as possible. How many pens can she buy?
solving multi-step problems; 5 pens

3. In 1950, there were about 48.4 million $50-bills in the United States. About how much money did these bills amount to?
estimation; about $2,500,000,000

4. An armored truck traveled at 42 miles per hour for a quarter of a mile. If the truck traveled at the same speed for 5.8 hours, about how far did it go?
estimation; about 240 miles

5. It takes Una 15 minutes to walk to school. This is 10 minutes more than $\frac{1}{2}$ the time it takes Lin to walk to school. How long does it take Lin? writing an
equation; 10 minutes

6. Oscar drove 4 hours at 55 mph, and then drove 45 miles at 50 mph. Then he drove for $2\frac{1}{2}$ hours at 52 mph. How far did he go? solving multi-step
problems; 395 miles

7. Last year, 78 students had perfect attendance records. That was $\frac{2}{3}$ the number of students that had perfect records this year. How many had perfect records this year?
writing an equation; 171 students

8. In the last 4 months, Jeremy has rented 18 videos. This is 4 more than twice the number of videos he rented during the previous 4 months. How many videos has Jeremy rented in the last 8 months?
writing an equation; 25 videos

9. The gas tank in Art's truck holds 12 gallons. The truck gets 18 miles per gallon. If Art fills the tank just before leaving on a 678-mile trip, how many more times will he have to fill the tank during the trip? interpreting the
quotient and remainder; 4 times

10. Rachel bought 16 rose bushes for $5.95 each. She also bought 8 gardenias for $3.98 each and 7 jasmine plants for $2.65 each. She gave the clerk eight $20-bills. How much change did she receive? solving
multi-step problems; $14.41

CLASSWORK HOMEWORK | Precision and Greatest Possible Error

Two measures for a length are given. Write the more precise measure.

1. 42 cm; 422 mm   422 mm
2. $3\frac{1}{2}$ in.; $3\frac{3}{4}$ in. $3\frac{3}{4}$ in.
3. 37 in.; 3 ft.   37 in.
4. 2,120 m; 2 km   2,120 m
5. 2 mi; 3,522 yd   3,522 yd
6. 8 cm; 83 mm   83 mm
7. 4.2 m; 423 cm   423 cm
8. 12 m; 1,206 mm   1,206 mm
9. 7 ft; 82 in.   82 in.
10. 7 km or 700 m   700 m
11. 15 km or 15,000 m   15,000 m
12. 6 g or 6,012 mg   6,012 mg
13. 6 ft or 73 in.   73 in.
14. 1 ft or 14 in.   14 in.
15. 500 mm or 50 cm   500 mm
16. 3,300 m or 3 km   3,300 m
17. 2 yd or 71 in.   71 in.
18. 10 m or 100 cm   100 cm

Find the greatest possible error of measurement.

19. 435 mm   0.5 mm
20. 3,840 cm   0.5 cm
21. 367 cm   0.5 cm
22. 76 mm   0.5 mm
23. 8,845 m   0.5 m
24. 7,355 km   0.5 km
25. 295 km   0.5 km
26. 26 cm   0.5 cm
27. 22 mm   0.5 mm
28. 617 km   0.5 km
29. 3 m   0.5 m
30. 549 mm   0.5 mm
31. 600 cm   0.5 cm
32. 5 cm   0.5 cm
33. 4 km   0.5 km
34. 78,125 km   0.5 km
35. 4.17 dm   0.005 dm
36. 9.85 m   0.005 m

CLASSWORK HOMEWORK | Time and Elapsed Time

| 60 seconds (s) = 1 minute (min) |
| 60 min = 1 hour (h) |
| 24 h = 1 day (d) |

Find the time.

1. 3 h 13 min before 6:45 A.M.   3:32 A.M.

2. 6 h 27 min after 3:10 P.M.   9:37 P.M.

Find the elapsed time between

3. 1 P.M. and 11 A.M.   22 h

4. 12:37 A.M. and 3 P.M.   14 h 23 min

5. 3:15 A.M. and 3:02 P.M.   11 h 47 min

Write the missing number.

6. $3\frac{1}{2}$ h = _210_ min

7. 18 h = _$\frac{3}{4}$_ d

8. $2\frac{1}{2}$ min = _150_ s

9. 360 s = _6_ min

This is a typical weekday for Rocky Rhodes.

Wake up	7:05	Work	9:10–12:30	Bus home	5:40–6:10	Television	7:30–8:30
Breakfast	30 min	Lunch	40 min	Nap	20 min	Extra office work	8:30–9:30
Bus to office	8:20–9:00	Work	1:30–5:30	Supper	50 min	Go to bed	11:15

10. How much time does Rocky spend sleeping? _490_ minutes.

11. How much time does he spend eating? _2_ hours _0_ minutes

12. How much time at home does he spend that is unaccounted for on this table?
_2_ hours _40_ minutes

13. How much time does he spend doing office work? _500_ minutes

CLASSWORK HOMEWORK | Using a Formula ($d = rt$)

Write the letter of the correct answer to each problem.

1. In 1.3 hours, a pilot flew a twin-engine propeller plane 403 miles. What was the average speed of the aircraft?
a. 310 mph   b. 313 mph   c. 303 mph

2. Captain Roberts piloted a 727 jet 3,200 miles across the United States at an average speed of 510 miles per hour. How long did the flight take?
a. 6.25 hours   b. 6.27 hours   c. 6.30 hours

Solve.

3. Lin flew from San Francisco, California, to Phoenix, Arizona, in 1 hour 30 minutes. The plane flew at an average speed of 406 miles per hour. About how far is Phoenix from San Francisco?   609 miles

4. New York City is located between Washington, D.C., and Boston, Massachusetts. New York is 227 miles from Washington and 185 miles from Boston. How far is Boston from Washington by way of New York?
412 miles

5. Leslie takes a train from Pittsburgh, Pennsylvania, to Philadelphia, a distance of 260 miles. What is the train's average speed if Leslie reaches Philadelphia in 4 hours 20 minutes?
60 mph

6. A test pilot flew a jet at the rate of 1,855 miles per hour for 0.6 of an hour. Then the pilot flew the plane for 0.8 of an hour at 1,900 miles per hour. How far did the plane travel during its test flight?   2,633 miles

7. Juaquin flew from San Diego, California, to Denver, Colorado. The trip took $2\frac{3}{4}$ hours, and the plane traveled at an average speed of 466 miles per hour. About how far is it from San Diego to Denver?   about $1281\frac{1}{2}$ miles

8. At 9:00 A.M., Seigi and Roberta took separate flights from Boston to Miami, Florida, a distance of 1,236 miles. Seigi's plane flew at 620 mph for 550 miles and then flew the rest of the way at 505 mph. Roberta's plane averaged 570 mph but stopped for 1 hour in Charleston, South Carolina. About how much earlier than Roberta did Seigi arrive in Miami?   about 1 hour

9. In 1927, Charles Lindbergh flew 3,600 miles from New York City to Paris, France. The trip took $33\frac{1}{2}$ hours. What was Lindbergh's average rate of speed?
about $107\frac{1}{2}$ mph

10. In 1903, the Wright Brothers flew 120 feet in 12 seconds in one of the first plane flights. What was their plane's average rate of speed?
10 feet per second

Classwork/Homework

CLASSWORK HOMEWORK | Time Zones

Use the time-zone map on page 186 of your textbook to answer the following questions.

It is 6:00 P.M. Wednesday in Washington, D.C. Write the time in each city.

1. Houston 5:00 P.M. Wednesday

2. Vancouver 3:00 P.M. Wednesday

3. Hong Kong 7:00 A.M. Thursday

4. Algiers 11:00 P.M. Wednesday

5. Philadelphia 6:00 P.M. Wednesday

6. Oslo 12:00 A.M. Thursday

7. Honolulu 1:00 P.M. Wednesday

8. Athens 1:00 A.M. Thursday

It is 7:45 A.M. Monday in Paris. Write the time in each city.

9. Seattle 10:45 P.M. Sunday

10. Nairobi 9:45 A.M. Monday

11. Sydney 4:45 P.M. Monday

12. Denver 11:45 P.M. Sunday

13. Miami 1:45 A.M. Monday

14. Madrid 7:45 A.M. Monday

15. Tokyo 3:45 P.M. Monday

16. Oslo 7:45 A.M. Monday

It is 3:20 P.M. Friday in Tokyo. Write the time in each city.

17. Athens 8:20 A.M. Friday

18. Vancouver 10:20 P.M. Thursday

19. Honolulu 8:20 P.M. Thursday

20. Paris 7:20 A.M. Friday

21. Montreal 1:20 A.M. Friday

22. Los Angeles 10:20 P.M. Thursday

23. Houston 12:20 A.M. Friday

24. Miami 1:20 A.M. Friday

Use with pages 186–187.   Student Handbook **H77**

CLASSWORK HOMEWORK | Temperature

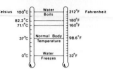

Write the letter of the best estimate.

1. the freezing point of water   a. 32°C   (b.) 0°C   c. 100°C

2. a warm day   a. 45°F   (b.) 80°F   c. 197°F

3. inside a refrigerator   (a.) 2°C   b. 45°C   c. 66°C

4. inside a freezer   a. 50°F   b. 69°F   (c.) 20°F

Find the temperature.

5. 36°F, rose 14°   50°F

6. 17°C, dropped 13°   4°C

7. ⁻5.5°C, rose 26°   20.5°C

8. ⁻12°F, dropped 6°   ⁻18°F

9. 78°F, rose 6°   84°F

10. 9.5°C, dropped 1.7°   7.8°C

11. 112.4°C, rose 42.3°   154.7°C

12. 100°F, dropped 64°   36°F

13. ⁻16°F, rose 124°   108°F

14. 2.7°C, dropped 18°   ⁻15.3°C

Find the change in temperature.

15. ⁻12°F to ⁻27°F   ⁻15°F

16. ⁻30.7°C to ⁻45.3°C   ⁻14.6°C

17. 100°F to 167°F   67°F

18. 70°C to 98°C   28°C

19. 32°F to 6°F   ⁻26°F

20. ⁻14.6°C to ⁻22.8°C   ⁻8.2°C

21. ⁻5°F to 6°F   11°F

22. 75°C to 98°C   23°C

23. 68°F to 202°F   134°F

24. 27.3°C to 98.4°C   71.1°C

25. 14°F to ⁻16°F   ⁻30°F

26. 6°C to ⁻1°C   ⁻7°C

H78 Student Handbook   Use with pages 188–189.

CLASSWORK HOMEWORK | Using a Road Map

Solve. Use the road map to answer each question.

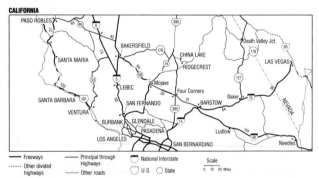

CALIFORNIA

— Freeways
····· Other divided highways
— Principal through Highways
— Other roads
National Interstate
U.S.   State
Scale
0 10 20 Miles

1. Martin drives from Las Vegas, Nevada, to Ludlow, California, via Barstow, California. What are the numbers of the highways he will drive on? 15, 40

2. About how far along the freeways is it from Las Vegas, Nevada, to Needles, California (on Route 40 near Arizona)? 298 miles

3. Samuel drives on Route 58 from Bakersfield to Barstow. His car travels 20 miles per gallon. If he has 6 gallons of gas in his tank, can he complete his trip without buying more gas? no

4. Muriel's mother begins her trip from San Fernando to Paso Robles on Route 5. Muriel's father drives from Ventura to Paso Robles. Does one of them drive farther? Who and by how much?
Yes; Muriel's mother drives about 25 more miles.

5. Naomi's car travels 25 miles per gallon. If gas costs her $1.05 per gallon, about how much will she have to spend on gas to make the longer trip described in Problem 4? $7.77

6. Lebec is halfway between Bakersfield and San Fernando. Mojave is directly east of Lebec. Armand wants to drive on the freeway from Mojave to Lebec. Would it be quicker for him to go through Bakersfield or through San Fernando?
through Bakersfield

Use after pages 190–191.   Student Handbook **H79**

CLASSWORK HOMEWORK | Ratios and Rates

Write each ratio in fraction form. Simplify where necessary.

1. 5 to 3 $\frac{5}{3}$

2. 1:14 $\frac{1}{14}$

3. 1.5 to 4.5 $\frac{1}{3}$

4. 6:6 $\frac{1}{1}$

5. 24.8:13.4 $\frac{12.4}{6.7}$

6. 101.9 to 98.6 $\frac{101.9}{98.6}$

7. 3:5 $\frac{3}{5}$

8. 1,295 to 1,187 $\frac{1,295}{1,187}$

9. 12:19 $\frac{12}{19}$

10. 10 to 100 $\frac{1}{10}$

11. 25 to 63 $\frac{25}{63}$

12. 3:20 $\frac{3}{20}$

13. 15 to 10 $\frac{3}{2}$

14. 13:80 $\frac{13}{80}$

15. 65 to 200 $\frac{13}{40}$

16. 2:1 $\frac{2}{1}$

17. 136 to 358 $\frac{68}{179}$

18. 746:746 $\frac{1}{1}$

19. 5:450 $\frac{1}{90}$

20. 28 to 29 $\frac{28}{29}$

21. 8 to 64 $\frac{1}{8}$

22. 100 to 200 $\frac{1}{2}$

23. 4.1:1.6 $\frac{4.1}{1.6}$

24. 10:15 $\frac{2}{3}$

25. 61:33 $\frac{61}{33}$

26. 4.2 to 1.4 $\frac{3}{1}$

27. 3:11 $\frac{3}{11}$

28. 5 motorcycles to 4 bicycles $\frac{5}{4}$

29. 28 cars to 8 motorcycles $\frac{7}{2}$

30. 2 bikers to 30 motorists $\frac{1}{15}$

31. 400 miles in 5 hours $\frac{80}{1}$

Write the unit rate.

32. $3,600 for 3 motorcycles $1,200 per motorcycle

33. 16 riders for 16 motorcycles   1 rider per motorcycle

34. 175 miles in 3.5 hours   50 miles per hour

35. 212.5 miles on 2.5 gallons of gas   85 miles per gallon

H80 Student Handbook   Use with pages 200–201.

CLASSWORK HOMEWORK — Proportions

Write the value of *x* in each proportion.

1. $\frac{3}{1} = \frac{45}{x}$ x = 15
2. $\frac{12}{7} = \frac{48}{x}$ x = 28
3. $\frac{65}{x} = \frac{20}{4}$ x = 13
4. $\frac{x}{63} = \frac{21}{49}$ x = 27
5. $\frac{32}{96} = \frac{x}{12}$ x = 4
6. $\frac{69}{57} = \frac{23}{x}$ x = 19
7. $\frac{10}{1} = \frac{x}{19}$ x = 190
8. $\frac{14}{x} = \frac{70}{85}$ x = 17
9. $\frac{x}{68} = \frac{1}{17}$ x = 4
10. $\frac{28}{12} = \frac{x}{21}$ x = 49
11. $\frac{84}{18} = \frac{x}{12}$ x = 56
12. $\frac{3}{10} = \frac{27}{x}$ x = 90
13. $\frac{28}{6} = \frac{x}{15}$ x = 70
14. $\frac{144}{24} = \frac{x}{14}$ x = 84
15. $\frac{9}{x} = \frac{15}{70}$ x = 42
16. $\frac{21}{11} = \frac{84}{x}$ x = 44
17. $\frac{48}{16} = \frac{78}{x}$ x = 26
18. $\frac{x}{42} = \frac{15}{18}$ x = 35
19. $\frac{54}{81} = \frac{x}{36}$ x = 24
20. $\frac{32}{100} = \frac{x}{25}$ x = 8
21. $\frac{8}{10} = \frac{44}{x}$ x = 55
22. $\frac{x}{28} = \frac{39}{12}$ x = 91
23. $\frac{35}{x} = \frac{80}{32}$ x = 14
24. $\frac{4}{27} = \frac{x}{81}$ x = 12
25. $\frac{x}{16} = \frac{21}{84}$ x = 4
26. $\frac{180}{70} = \frac{18}{x}$ x = 7
27. $\frac{8}{36} = \frac{10}{x}$ x = 45
28. $\frac{13}{28} = \frac{x}{56}$ x = 26
29. $\frac{72}{x} = \frac{48}{36}$ x = 54
30. $\frac{x}{48} = \frac{12}{64}$ x = 9

CLASSWORK HOMEWORK — Writing a Proportion

Write the letter of the correct proportion.

1. Choan wants to change the engine in her car. The current engine is 250 cubic centimeters and has a 14-inch fan belt. The new engine is 350 cubic centimeters and has a proportionally larger fan belt. What size fan belt will Choan need for her new engine?

   a. $\frac{14}{250} = \frac{n}{350}$ b. $\frac{350}{14} = \frac{n}{250}$ c. $\frac{350}{1} = \frac{250}{n}$

2. After Choan bought the new engine, she put a larger gas tank into her car. Her old gas tank held 15 gallons, and she could drive 360 miles on a full tank. Now she can drive 465 miles on a full tank of gas. What size gas tank did she install?

   a. $\frac{1}{15} = \frac{n}{465}$ b. $\frac{360}{465} = \frac{n}{15}$ c. $\frac{15}{360} = \frac{n}{465}$

Solve.

3. A city is planning to build a parking lot for fans who drive to football games and hockey matches. For every 12 parking spaces reserved for hockey fans, football fans will have 30. How many spaces will football fans have if hockey fans have 2,000?
   $\frac{12}{30} = \frac{2,000}{n}$; n = 5,000

4. A group of 16 fans attending a football game brought along a number of jugs of apple juice. If they brought 10 quarts of juice, how many $2\frac{1}{2}$-quart jugs were needed to carry the juice? 4

5. For every 5 people who bought $9.75 tickets to the football game, 3 people bought $14.50 tickets. If each of 35 people bought a $9.75 ticket, how many people bought the more expensive ticket?
   $\frac{3}{5} = \frac{n}{35}$; n = 21

6. After entering the stadium, all the fans wanted souvenirs. For every 2 people who bought programs, 7 people bought football jerseys. If 42 people bought jerseys, how many people bought programs?
   $\frac{2}{7} = \frac{n}{42}$; n = 12

7. Lucy goes to the stands to buy snacks for her friends. She has been asked to buy peanuts for 11 people. A bag of peanuts costs $0.89, and 2 bags sell for $1.60. Lucy collected $8.50 to spend for peanuts. Will she be able to buy a bag for each person? no

8. The average price of a ticket to a football game is $12.00. The stadium owners make an 8% profit on each ticket. By how much would they have to raise the average ticket price to make a profit of 11%?
   $\frac{12}{8} = \frac{n}{11}$; n = 16.50; $16.50 − $12.00 = $4.50

CLASSWORK HOMEWORK — Scale Drawings

Use the diagram and scale of this modern metal sculpture to answer the questions.

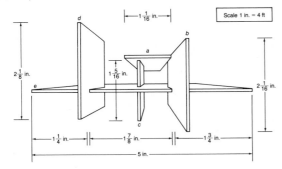

Scale 1 in. = 4 ft

1. How wide is *a*? 4 ft 3 in.
2. How long is *b*? 8 ft 3 in.
3. How far is *b* from the right edge of *e*? 7 ft
4. How long is *c*? 5 ft 3 in.

Use a scale of 1 in.: $3\frac{1}{2}$ ft to find your answer.

5. How long is *d*? 7 ft 5$\frac{1}{4}$ in.
6. How far is *d* from the left edge of *e*? 4 ft 4$\frac{1}{2}$ in.
7. How wide is the entire sculpture? 20 ft

CLASSWORK HOMEWORK — The Meaning of Percent

Write each ratio as a percent.

1. 3 to 5 60%
2. $\frac{14}{100}$ 14%
3. $\frac{6}{20}$ 30%
4. 1:4 25%
5. 9 to 10 90%
6. $\frac{35}{100}$ 35%
7. 7:25 28%
8. 6 to 50 12%
9. $\frac{17}{20}$ 85%
10. 38:50 76%
11. 6 to 25 24%
12. $\frac{98}{100}$ 98%
13. 9:25 36%
14. 1 to 2 50%
15. $\frac{3}{4}$ 75%
16. 8 to 10 80%
17. 13:20 65%
18. $\frac{66}{100}$ 66%
19. 49 to 50 98%
20. 7 per 100 7%
21. $\frac{8}{50}$ 16%
22. 1:25 4%
23. 2:5 40%
24. $\frac{38}{100}$ 38%
25. 3:20 15%
26. 1 to 10 10%
27. $\frac{4}{5}$ 80%
28. 17:20 85%
29. $\frac{62}{100}$ 62%
30. 1:50 2%
31. 3 to 100 3%
32. 1 to 5 20%
33. $\frac{3}{25}$ 12%
34. 47 per 50 94%
35. 16 of 25 64%
36. 8 tulips of 10 flowers 80%
37. 53 daisies per 100 seeds 53%
38. 1 rose of 5 flowers 20%
39. 14 mums of 20 flowers 70%

CLASSWORK HOMEWORK — Percents and Decimals

Write as a decimal.

1. 91% 0.91
2. 59.3% 0.593
3. 360% 3.6
4. 761% 7.61
5. 0.48% 0.0048
6. 0.03% 0.0003
7. 7% 0.07
8. 6% 0.06
9. 23.5% 0.235
10. 84% 0.84
11. 3,001% 30.01
12. 0.9% 0.009
13. 0.8% 0.008
14. 7,613% 76.13
15. 66.02% 0.6602
16. 25.82% 0.2582
17. 100% 1.0
18. 400% 4.0

Write as a percent.

19. 0.005 0.5%
20. 0.872 87.2%
21. 3.678 367.8%
22. 9.2 920%
23. 0.4 40%
24. 4.30 430%
25. 0.929 92.9%
26. 0.15 15%
27. 0.1258 12.58%
28. 0.08 8%
29. 0.125 12.5%
30. 0.0003 0.03%
31. 0.67 67%
32. 0.0017 0.17%
33. 0.4028 40.28%
34. 0.6954 69.54%
35. 0.03 3%
36. 2.7833 278.33%

Use with pages 210–211.

Student Handbook **H85**

CLASSWORK HOMEWORK — Percents and Fractions

Write as a fraction or as a mixed number in simplest form.

1. 125% $1\frac{1}{4}$
2. $66\frac{2}{3}$% $\frac{2}{3}$
3. 95% $\frac{19}{20}$
4. $37\frac{1}{2}$% $\frac{3}{8}$
5. 240% $2\frac{2}{5}$
6. 90% $\frac{9}{10}$
7. 84% $\frac{21}{25}$
8. $133\frac{1}{3}$% $1\frac{1}{3}$
9. $17\frac{1}{2}$% $\frac{7}{40}$
10. $6\frac{4}{5}$% $\frac{17}{250}$
11. $5\frac{2}{3}$% $\frac{17}{300}$
12. $9\frac{1}{5}$% $\frac{23}{250}$
13. $27\frac{1}{4}$% $\frac{109}{400}$
14. $28\frac{1}{4}$% $\frac{113}{400}$
15. $23\frac{1}{8}$% $\frac{37}{160}$
16. $55\frac{5}{9}$% $\frac{5}{9}$

Write as a percent.

17. $\frac{5}{12}$ $41\frac{2}{3}$%
18. $1\frac{7}{8}$ 187.5%
19. $\frac{5}{16}$ 31.25%
20. $2\frac{17}{40}$ 242.5%
21. $\frac{36}{8}$ 450%
22. $\frac{165}{100}$ 165%
23. $3\frac{8}{100}$ 308%
24. $\frac{2}{6}$ $33\frac{1}{3}$%
25. $\frac{7}{18}$ $38\frac{8}{9}$%
26. $\frac{3}{20}$ 15%
27. $\frac{3}{11}$ $27\frac{3}{16}$%
28. $\frac{9}{16}$ $56\frac{1}{4}$%
29. $\frac{14}{15}$ $93\frac{1}{3}$%
30. $\frac{1}{7}$ $14\frac{2}{7}$%

H86 Student Handbook

Use with pages 212–213.

CLASSWORK HOMEWORK — Making an Organized List/Acting It Out

Solve by making an organized list.

1. At a cast party after a play, the leading actor wants to introduce her family to the director of the play. Her family includes her mother, father, husband, and daughter. How many possible ways can she introduce the family to the director if she always introduces her husband first? 6

2. The actor is starring in a play made up of 6 scenes that can be performed in any order. The scenes are entitled "Rebox," "Chromus," "Instant," "Chorale," "Allegro," and "Exit." This week the actors will begin each performance with "Chromus," followed by "Exit." From how many combinations can they choose the order of the remaining scenes? 24

3. The director holds auditions for a new play. Out of 200 actors, 6 have been chosen to perform in groups of 4 actors each. In how many combinations can the director use the 6 actors? 15

4. The producer has received manuscripts of new plays from playwrights. There is a stack of 6 plays to be read, and the producer has decided to read 5 of the plays during the next 2 days. The titles are *Quantity, The Next Bus, Walk North, Special, Concert Etude,* and *Pick a Number.* How many different combinations of 5 plays can the producer read? 6

5. The set designer is working on staging for a new play. He will use 3 panels of solid colors for each of 5 scenes. He can choose from 6 colors: orange, grey, calliope red, black, yellow, and pale blue. How many combinations of 3 colors are possible? 20

Use after pages 214–215.

Student Handbook **H87**

CLASSWORK HOMEWORK — Making an Organized List/Acting It Out

Solve by making an organized list.

6. Venezuela won 3 medals in the 1984 Summer Olympics. Each medal was either gold, silver, or bronze. How many possible combinations of the 3 medals could the Venezuelans have won? 27

7. The South Korean team won 19 medals in all, winning the same number of gold medals as silver medals. In how many different ways could it have won gold, silver and bronze medals? 10

8. The South Koreans won one more bronze medal than silver or gold medals. Which combination of those you counted for problem 2 is the one that the South Koreans actually won? 6-6-7

9. Ms. Casey has 3 forwards, 2 centers, and 3 guards on her basketball team. She sends 2 forwards, one center, and 2 guards to play at one time. How many different team combinations can she send into the game? 18

10. A relay team has 4 runners. How many ways can the order of the runners be arranged? 24

11. How many ways can a 4-person relay team be arranged if one runner must always run in the second or third position? 12

12. A round-robin format is often used in the Olympics. In this format, each team plays the other teams in the same division once. How many games would be played in a round robin with six teams? 15

13. Hans planned to watch Olympic games all day. In the morning he could have watched either wrestling or the high jump. In the afternoon he could have watched either the high jump, 100-meter run, or hurdles. In the evening, he could have watched wrestling, volley ball, or basketball. He did not want to watch any sport twice. How many ways could he have combined his sports viewing? 12

H88 Student Handbook

Use after pages 214–215.

CLASSWORK HOMEWORK | **Finding the Percent of a Number**

Write the percent of the number.

1. 6% of 900 — 54
2. 20% of 20.5 — 4.1
3. 30% of 70 — 21
4. 150% of 17 — 25.5
5. 325% of 4 — 13
6. 12% of 50 — 6
7. $133\frac{1}{3}$% of 330 — 440
8. 0.1% of 0.1 — 0.0001
9. 0.5% of 98 — 0.49
10. 20% of 16 — 3.2
11. 75% of 4,004 — 3,003
12. 225% of 50 — 112.5
13. 22% of 100 — 22
14. 88% of 10 — 8.8
15. 17.5% of 20 — 3.5
16. $66\frac{2}{3}$% of 3 — 2
17. $8\frac{1}{2}$% of 80 — 6.8
18. $37\frac{1}{2}$% of 240 — 90
19. 3.5% of 600 — 21
20. 100% of 17 — 17
21. 15% of 120 — 18
22. 1% of 5 — 0.05
23. 1% of 1 — 0.01
24. 6% of 120 — 7.2
25. 0.3% of 400 — 1.2
26. 25% of 1,300 — 325
27. 60.7% of 5,000 — 3,035
28. 50% of 8 — 4
29. 8.25% of 200 — 16.5
30. 12.5% of 80 — 10
31. 90% of 2 — 1.8
32. 60% of $75 — $45
33. 350% of 16 — 56
34. 40% of $150.00 — $60.00
35. 25% of 212 — 53
36. $26\frac{1}{2}$% of $720 — $190.80

CLASSWORK HOMEWORK | **Finding What Percent**

Write the percent.

1. What percent of 18 is 6? — $33\frac{1}{3}$%
2. 0.4 is what percent of 10? — 4%
3. 6.7 is what percent of 80? — 8.375%
4. What percent of 72 is 6? — $8\frac{1}{3}$%
5. What percent of 9 is 7.5? — $83\frac{1}{3}$%
6. 36 is what percent of 48? — 75%
7. 0.9 is what percent of 0.2? — 450%
8. What percent of 25 is 26? — 104%
9. What percent of 40 is 0.8? — 2%
10. 450 is what percent of 270? — $166\frac{2}{3}$%
11. 2.9 is what percent of 1.6? — 181.25%
12. What percent of 8 is 2.8? — 35%
13. What percent of 7.5 is 15? — 200%
14. 1.95 is what percent of 300? — 0.65%
15. 67 is what percent of 268? — 25%
16. What percent of 20 is 61? — 305%
17. What percent of 96 is 60? — 62.5%
18. 96.2 is what percent of 769.6? — 12.5%
19. 18 is what percent to 100? — 18%
20. What percent of 80.4 is 0.201? — 0.25%
21. What percent of 25 is 4.6? — 18.4%
22. 650 is what percent of 1,000? — 65%
23. 5.1 is what percent of 30? — 17%
24. What percent of 0.25 is 0.5? — 200%
25. What percent of 300 is 975? — 325%
26. 33 is what percent of 1? — 3,300%
27. 92 is what percent of 460? — 20%
28. What percent of 13.2 is 66? — 500%
29. What percent of 9,000 is 63? — 0.7%
30. 13.68 is what percent of 72? — 19%
31. 0.03 is what percent of 10? — 0.3%
32. What percent of 20 is 0.8? — 4%
33. What percent of 0.1 is 9.9? — 9,900%
34. 0.45 is what percent of 150? — 0.3%
35. 4.3 is what percent of 50? — 8.6%
36. What percent of 36 is 2.7? — 7.5%

CLASSWORK HOMEWORK | **Finding the Total Number**

Write the number.

1. 75% of what number is 21? — 28
2. 8.99 is 29% of what number? — 31
3. 42 is 12% of what number? — 350
4. 6.2% of what number is 3.1? — 50
5. 66 is $66\frac{2}{3}$% of what number? — 99
6. 15.39 is 27% of what number? — 57
7. 1.8 is 25% of what number? — 7.2
8. $83\frac{1}{3}$% of what number is 30? — 36
9. 4% of what number is 6? — 150
10. 32 is 20% of what number? — 160
11. 9.8 is 2% of what number? — 490
12. 40% of what number is 16.6? — 41.5
13. 72 is $37\frac{1}{2}$% of what number? — 192
14. 68% of what number is 65.28? — 96
15. 5.5 is 500% of what number? — 1.1
16. 25% of what number is 0.88? — 3.52
17. 20% of what number is 2.4? — 12
18. 10.63 is 69% of what number? — 15.4
19. 36% of what number is 64.8? — 180
20. 34% of what number is 207.06? — 609
21. $33\frac{1}{3}$% of what number is 75? — 225
22. 9.43 is 85% of what number? — 11.09
23. 28.47 is 3% of what number? — 949
24. 97.5% of what number is 7.8? — 8
25. 93.75 is $12\frac{1}{2}$% of what number? — 750
26. 61.6 is 112% of what number? — 55
27. 8.84 is 10% of what number? — 88.4
28. 230% of what number is 2.3? — 1
29. 25% of what number is 40? — 160
30. 28% of what number is 7? — 25
31. 87 is 116% of what number? — 75
32. 45 is 75% of what number? — 60
33. 68% of what number is 17? — 25
34. 10.08 is 21% of what number? — 48
35. 96.2% of what number is 211.64? — 220
36. 332% of what number is 8.3? — 2.5

CLASSWORK HOMEWORK | **Using a Formula (I = prt)**

Write the letter of the correct form of the interest formula.

1. Jo Ann Vance wants to deposit some of her $27,500 game-show winnings in a special bank account. She wants to earn $3,000 in interest in 3 years. How much of the $27,500 should she deposit in an account that pays 12.5% interest per year?

   a. I = prt　b. p = I ÷ rt
   c. p = Irt　d. r = pt ÷ I

2. Neil Green will borrow $2,800 to buy a trailer to carry the sailboat he won on *Shop Around*. The store will charge him interest at 17.5% per year for 3 years. How much interest will he have to pay?

   a. I = pr − t　b. I = prt
   c. p = Irt　d. r = pt ÷ I

Solve. Round to the nearest cent.

3. Al Lynch put the $6,575 he earned by playing *Name That Movie* in an account that pays $5\frac{3}{4}$% annual interest. He kept that amount in his account for $2\frac{1}{2}$ years. How much interest did he earn? $945.16

4. Marla Blanc Productions borrows $45,500 to make a pilot for a game show. The bank's rate is $16\frac{3}{4}$%, and the loan must be repaid in 1.5 years. What amount of money will the company pay the bank? $56,931.88

5. Alexandra Livi wants to use interest from her $15,842 winnings on *What's the Word* to pay for her room and board at college. She needs to receive $1,200 per year. The bank pays an annual interest rate of $7\frac{3}{4}$%. How much of the $15,842 does she have to put in the bank to earn the necessary interest? $15,483.87

6. Arnold Hooper charged $642.59 worth of clothes to wear as a contestant on *Fast Tracks*. Arnold won $750 on the show. The credit-card company charges an annual interest rate of 19.5%, and Arnold paid off the money after $1\frac{1}{2}$ years. Did his winnings pay for his clothing expenses? no

7. Ellen Holmes needs a car to pull the trailer she won on *Guess Who*. She wants a car in the $7,500 to $9,000 price range, and she wants to be able to pay off the principal at the lowest possible interest rate. Look at the chart at the right. Which car should Ellen Holmes purchase? Tiger

	Tiger	Zephyr	Prairie
Price	$7,999	$8,325	$7,595
Down payment	$1,999	$1,250	$2,595
Principal	$6,000	$7,075	$5,000
Interest	$4,320	$4,245	$2,312.50
Payment period (years)	4	3	$2\frac{1}{2}$

CLASSWORK HOMEWORK — Percent Using Proportions

Use a proportion to solve each problem.

1. 125 is 250% of what number? 50
2. 75.25 is what percent of 25? 301%
3. What number is 4% of 0.5395? 0.02158
4. What number is 1% of 62? 0.62
5. 4,541.6 is 5.6% of what number? 81,100
6. 0.0755 is what percent of 0.539? 14%
7. What number is 24% of 886? 212.64
8. 18.92 is what percent of 22? 86%
9. 217.25 is 79% of what number? 275
10. What number is 80% of 189.89? 151.912

Four people traveled across the Isthmus of Idic from west to east. Use the diagram of the isthmus to answer the questions.

11. Carole wanted to exercise as much as possible; so, she took no bridges or tunnels during her trip. How many meters did she climb altogether? 2,500 m

12. Michael traveled all the bridges, but no tunnels. His route involved climbing 1,500 meters. What percent of Carole's climb is this? 60%

13. Dorothy wanted to walk as little as possible. Her climb was only 80% of Michael's climb. How many meters did she climb? 1,200 m

14. Dorothy's climb was 75% of Peter's climb. Peter took a scenic route. How many meters did Peter climb? 1,600 m

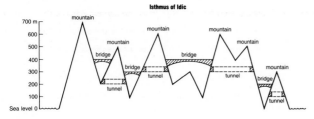

Isthmus of Idic

CLASSWORK HOMEWORK — Percent of Increase and Decrease

Write the percent of increase or decrease.

1. Original value: 400
   Decrease: 68 — 17%
2. Decrease: 0.01
   Original value: 0.5 — 2%
3. Original price: $24
   Decrease: $6 — 25%
4. Original value: 50
   New value: 18.5 — 63%
5. Increase: 157.5
   Original value: 1,500 — $10\frac{1}{2}$%
6. Original value: 400
   Increase: 44 — 11%
7. Original value: 36
   Increase: 4 — 11.1%
8. Decrease: $9.90
   Original price: $36 — 27.5%
9. Original value: 660
   Decrease: 220 — $33\frac{1}{3}$%
10. Original value: 200
   New value: 30.4 — 84.8%
11. Original value: 14
   New value: 35 — 150%
12. Original value: 79
   Increase: 197.5 — 250%
13. Original value: 2
   Increase: 0.4 — 20%
14. Increase: $0.22
   Original price: $55 — 0.4%
15. Original value: 19
   New value: 15.2 — 20%
16. Original price: $4.00
   Increase: $7.00 — 175%
17. Increase: 37
   Original value: 7.4 — 500%
18. Original price: $136.00
   New price: $68.00 — 50%

CLASSWORK HOMEWORK — Using a Circle Graph

ADVERTISEMENT EXPENDITURES—1986
Bubble Soap, Inc.

Network radio 0.2% · Magazines 4.9% · Newspapers 1.4% · Network TV 64.1% · Local TV 29.4%

Total Expenditures = $726,100,000

ADVERTISEMENT EXPENDITURES—1986
Yum-Yum Food, Inc.

Newspapers 1.4% · Local radio 1.2% · Outdoor print 6.6% · Local TV 8.4% · Network TV 51.6% · Magazines 30.8%

Total Expenditures = $271,000,000

Copy each question that can be answered by using the circle graphs above. Then answer the questions. Students should copy and answer questions 1 and 3.

1. How much money was spent by both companies on TV advertisements in 1986? $841,503,500

2. What percent of the two companies' earnings for 1986 was spent on advertising?

3. Which company spent more on magazine ads in 1986? Yum-Yum Food, Inc.

4. How much did producing a TV commercial cost in 1986?

Solve.

5. How much money did Bubble Soap, Inc., spend on newspaper and magazine ads? $45,744,300

6. How much money did Yum-Yum Food, Inc., spend on TV ads? $162,600,000

7. How much money did Yum-Yum Food, Inc., spend on print advertisements? $105,148,000

8. Which company spent more money on magazine ads? Yum-Yum Food, Inc.

9. After 1986, the managers of Bubble Soap, Inc., plan to spend the same proportion of the budget on newspaper ads and on magazine ads as they spent in 1986. They increase the percent spent on newspaper ads to 3.5% of the total advertising budget. What percent of their ad budget will they spend on magazines? 2.8%

10. Which of the following conclusions can you draw from the circle graphs? d
   a. Both companies spend the same amount of money on newspaper ads.
   b. Each company spends more than $\frac{3}{4}$ of its ad budget on TV ads.
   c. More people read magazines than newspapers.
   d. Each company spends at least $\frac{3}{5}$ of its ad budget on TV ads.

CLASSWORK HOMEWORK — The Meaning of Integers

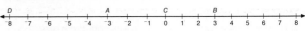

Use the number line to answer each problem.

1. What is the position of point A? ⁻3

2. What is the position of point B? 3

3. If point E is added to the number line at ⁻6, between which two points is E located? between D and A

Write the opposite of each integer.

4. ⁻21   21
5. 618   ⁻618
6. 8   ⁻8
7. 0   0

Write the absolute value for each number.

8. |9| 9
9. |⁻39| 39
10. |⁻94| 94
11. |189| 189

Write the numbers from the least to the greatest.

12. 55, ⁻64, ⁻54, 64   ⁻65, ⁻54, 55, 64
13. 49, ⁻101, ⁻5, 17, ⁻618   ⁻618, ⁻101, ⁻5, 17, 49

Write the numbers from the greatest to the least.

14. ⁻188, ⁻190, ⁻100, 100   100, ⁻100, ⁻188, ⁻190
15. 12, ⁻4, ⁻16, 3, 9   12, 9, 3, ⁻4, ⁻16

Compare. Write >, <, or =.

16. ⁻9 < 0
17. 5 > ⁻2
18. ⁻8 < ⁻4
19. 250 > ⁻250
20. ⁻95 > ⁻103
21. 39 > ⁻56

CLASSWORK HOMEWORK — Properties of Integers

Use the properties to find the missing integer.

1. 757 + 468 = 468 + ___?___ [757]
2. -6 × -2 = -2 × ___?___ [-6]
3. -1(-3 × 5) = (-1 × -3) × ___?___ [5]
4. 1 × 379 = ___?___ [379]
5. -94 + (62 + 22) = (-94 + 62) + ___?___ [22]
6. -105 + 0 = ___?___ [-105]
7. 3(-9 + 1) = (3 × -9) + (3 × ___?___) [1]
8. 137 + (-16 + 8) = (137 + -16) + ___?___ [8]
9. 26 × 0 = ___?___ [0]
10. 2(14 × 6) = (2 × 14) × ___?___ [6]
11. -186 × 1 = ___?___ [-186]
12. -15 + -13 = -13 + ___?___ [-15]
13. 96 + 0 = ___?___ [96]
14. -66(2 + 49) = (-66 × 2) + (-66 × ___?___) [49]
15. 4(-66 × 12) = (4 × -66) × ___?___ [12]
16. 503 + (-1 + -17) = (503 + -1) + ___?___ [-1]
17. 75(-2 + -4) = (75 × -2) + (75 × ___?___) [-4]
18. -38 + 16 = 16 + ___?___ [-38]
19. 367 × 12 = 12 × ___?___ [367]
20. -942 × 0 = ___?___ [0]
21. 66 + (32 + 109) = (66 + 32) + ___?___ [109]
22. -43 × 44 = 44 × ___?___ [-43]
23. 16 + -34 = -34 + ___?___ [16]
24. -7(-9 × -6) = (-7 × -9) × ___?___ [-6]
25. -632 × 471 = 471 × ___?___ [-632]
26. 0 + -55 = ___?___ [-55]
27. 15 + (-6 + 4) = (15 + -6) + ___?___ [4]
28. -90 + -80 = -80 + ___?___ [-90]
29. -7(-3 + -6) = (-7 × -3) + (-7 × ___?___) [-6]
30. 6(9 + 5) = (6 × 9) + (6 × ___?___) [5]
31. 300 + -4 = -4 + ___?___ [300]
32. -7 × -12 = -12 × ___?___ [-7]

Name the properties. Write C for Commutative, A for Associative, D for Distributive, I for Identity, and Z for Zero Property.

33. -3(6 × -9) = (-3 × 6) × -9   A
34. -25 × 0 = 0   Z
35. -19 + 0 = -19   I
36. (18 + -7) + 5 = 18 + (-7 + 5)   A
37. -5 + 7 = 7 + -5   C
38. 15(-3 + 17) = (15 × -3) + (15 × 17)   D

CLASSWORK HOMEWORK — Subtracting Integers

Add.

1. 11 + 5 = 16
2. 2,931 + -685 = 2,246
3. 458 + -393 = 65
4. -62 + -71 = -133
5. 674 + -39 + 102 = 737
6. -603 + 906 = 303
7. 815 + 281 = 1,096
8. 9 + -12 = -3
9. -763 + 54 = -709
10. (36 + -27) + 446 = 455
11. -698 + (-32 + 250) = -480
12. -8,815 + -9,776 = -18,591
13. -310 + -908 = -1,218
14. (358 + 1,024) + -761 = 621
15. 562 + -593 = -31
16. -176 + -229 = -405
17. 103 + -702 = -599
18. -894 + -979 = -1,873
19. -84 + -22 = -106
20. 94 + -87 = 7
21. (-95 + 521) + -299 = 127
22. -838 + -719 = -1,557
23. -1,432 + 1,098 = -334
24. 239 + -184 + -313 = -258
25. -51 + -98 = -149
26. 952 + -398 = 554
27. -54 + 235 = 181
28. -453 + -198 + -352 = -1,003
29. -12 + -15 + -34 = -61
30. 1,234 + -5,309 = -4,075
31. -17 + (-12 + -9) = -38
32. (0 + -5) + -3 = -8
33. -117 + (153 + -321) = -285
34. (-16 + 13) + -20 = -23

Solve.

35. The temperature at 4:00 A.M. was -6°C. Since then it has risen 12 degrees. What is the temperature now?   6°C
36. The temperature at 7:00 P.M. was 9°C. Since then it has fallen 12 degrees. What is the temperature now?   -3°C

CLASSWORK HOMEWORK — Adding Integers

Subtract.

1. -98 − 51 = -149
2. 9,900 − 972 = 8,928
3. 94 − -46 = 140
4. 663 − 248 = 415
5. -6,731 − 3,003 = -9,734
6. -18 − -30 = 12
7. -247 − -338 = 91
8. -715 − -582 = -133
9. 262 − 243 = 19
10. -80 − -96 = 16
11. 5 − 9 = -4
12. -665 − 99 = -764
13. 104 − -243 = 347
14. 95 − -35 = 130
15. -679 − 308 = -987
16. 975 − 976 = -1
17. 29 − 100 = -71
18. -71 − 490 = -561
19. -26 − -24 = -2
20. -11 − 94 = -105
21. 208 − 724 = -516
22. -24 − 21 = -45
23. -466 − -235 = -231
24. 67 − 3 = 64
25. -7,272 − -2,931 = -4,341
26. -406 − -790 = 384
27. -3 − 17 = -20
28. 685 − 832 = -147
29. 6,827 − -8,354 = 15,181
30. -1,653 − -9,679 = 8,026
31. 396 − -2,021 = 2,417
32. -29 − 201 = -230
33. -777 − -801 = 24
34. 366 − -14 = 380

Solve.

35. In the morning, the temperature was 14°C. It is now 26°C. How much did the temperature change?   12°C
36. The temperature at 3:00 P.M. was 11°C. At 10:00 P.M., the temperature was -2°C. How much did the temperature change?   13°C

CLASSWORK HOMEWORK — Using Graphs

AMOUNT OF OFFICE FURNITURE SOLD BY MONTH

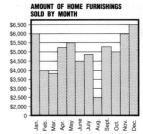

AMOUNT OF HOME FURNISHINGS SOLD BY MONTH

Can you use the line graph or the bar graph to answer each question? Write yes or no.

1. In which month did the office-furniture division sell the most?   yes
2. How much did the home-furnishings division sell on Labor Day weekend?   no
3. Did the office-furniture division sell more in June than in October?   yes
4. Did the company make a profit in August?   no

Use the line graph to answer each question.

5. In which three months is the most office furniture sold?   September, October, November
6. In which two months were sales the closest?   February and March
7. Which month shows the greatest increase in sales over the previous month?   September
8. Were sales higher or lower for the period from January to April than for the period from May to August?   higher

Use the bar graph to answer each question.

9. Which month shows the greatest decrease from the previous month?   August
10. What is the difference in sales between the highest-selling and the lowest-selling months? $4,000

Use both graphs to answer each question.

11. Which division shows higher sales?   the office-furniture division
12. In which month did the home-furnishings division sell more than the office-furniture division?   December

CLASSWORK HOMEWORK · Multiplying Integers

Multiply.

1. ⁻823 · 5   ⁻4,115
2. (⁻17 · 15) · 3   ⁻765
3. ⁻10 · (⁻2 · 18)   360
4. ⁻988 · 30   ⁻29,640
5. (11 · ⁻4) · ⁻10   440
6. ⁻13 · ⁻12   156
7. 12 · ⁻15   ⁻180
8. ⁻13 · 63   ⁻819
9. ⁻40 · ⁻18   720
10. 13 · (⁻7 · ⁻9)   819
11. ⁻12 × ⁻18   216
12. 18 × 8   144
13. 36 × 297   10,692
14. (⁻17 × 17) × 5   ⁻1,445
15. 19 × 10   190
16. ⁻23 × ⁻14   322
17. 19 × ⁻15   ⁻285
18. ⁻792 × 12   ⁻9,504
19. ⁻5 × (6 × ⁻25)   750
20. 1,111 × ⁻6,962   ⁻7,734,782
21. ⁻147 × ⁻579   85,113
22. ⁻10 × ⁻16   160
23. 17 × 14   238
24. 92 × ⁻29   ⁻2,668
25. (⁻63 × 20) × 8   ⁻10,080
26. ⁻66 × ⁻88   5,808
27. ⁻16 × 11   ⁻176
28. ⁻94 × 20   ⁻1,880
29. 500 × 18   9,000
30. (⁻4 × 14) × ⁻11   616
31. ⁻72 × 66   ⁻4,752
31. 6 × ⁻323   ⁻1,938
33. ⁻13 × (⁻2 × 24)   624
34. 202 × 76   15,352

Solve.

35. Ricardo descended to a depth of 24 feet below sea level. His friend Martin descended 3 times as far. Write as an integer the depth of Martin's descent.   ⁻72 ft

36. To finance their treasure hunt, the Diving Dolphins borrowed money from 5 friends. They now owe each friend $150. How much do the Dolphins owe in all? $750

CLASSWORK HOMEWORK · Dividing Integers

Divide.

1. ⁻672 ÷ 96   ⁻7
2. 56 ÷ ⁻8   ⁻7
3. ⁻360 ÷ 60   ⁻6
4. ⁻1 ÷ ⁻1   1
5. ⁻2,772 ÷ ⁻63   44
6. 110 ÷ 2   55
7. ⁻222 ÷ 37   ⁻6
8. ⁻891 ÷ ⁻99   9
9. 3,600 ÷ 48   75
10. 132 ÷ ⁻12   ⁻11
11. ⁻656 ÷ ⁻82   8
12. 594 ÷ ⁻11   ⁻54
13. 4,620 ÷ ⁻60   ⁻77
14. ⁻6,144 ÷ ⁻768   8
15. ⁻195 ÷ ⁻5   39
16. ⁻1,328 ÷ ⁻83   16
17. ⁻1,034 ÷ ⁻22   47
18. ⁻7,221 ÷ 87   ⁻83
19. ⁻72 ÷ ⁻9   8
20. ⁻294 ÷ ⁻7   42
21. ⁻1,411 ÷ ⁻17   83
22. 18 ÷ 3   6
23. ⁻844 ÷ 4   ⁻211
24. ⁻592 ÷ 37   ⁻16
25. 4,081 ÷ 53   77
26. ⁻144 ÷ 2   ⁻72
27. ⁻444 ÷ ⁻74   6
28. ⁻183 ÷ ⁻61   3

Solve.

29. Wrectronics, Inc., manufactures household robots. Because of a newspaper story which reported that the robots' arms fell off after 6 months of normal use, Wrectronics stock dropped 20 points during a 5-day period. What was the average daily change in the stock price?   ⁻4 points

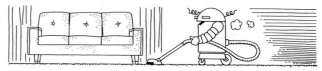

CLASSWORK HOMEWORK · Integers as Exponents

Write each number with a negative exponent.

1. $\frac{1}{5^2}$ 5^{-2}
2. $\frac{1}{2^4}$ 2^{-4}
3. $\frac{1}{125}$ 5^{-3}
4. $\frac{1}{64}$ 8^{-2}
5. $\frac{1}{10}$ 10^{-1}
6. $\frac{1}{8}$ 2^{-3}
7. $\frac{1}{17^2}$ 17^{-2}
8. $\frac{1}{6^5}$ 6^{-5}

Write each number in scientific notation.

9. 540.89 5.4089×10^2
10. 1.3467 1.3467×10^0
11. 0.00101 1.01×10^{-3}
12. 10,000 1×10^4

Write each number in standard form.

13. 3.076×10^{-2} 0.03076
14. 1×10^5 100,000
15. 5.0154×10^2 501.54
16. 4.49×10^{-1} 0.449

Write the missing exponent for each problem below. Then use the exponents to find the first eight plays of the Mud Bowl. An exponent of 5 means the Muskrats moved forward 5 yards. An exponent of ⁻5 means the Muskrats moved back 5 yards. The Muskrats started from their own 40-yard line. Look at the field to help answer the last question.

17. $\frac{1}{6^3} = 6^{\underline{?}}$ ⁻3
18. $0.000273 = 2.73 \times 10^{\underline{?}}$ ⁻4
19. $5^{-2} \div 5^{-17} = 5^{\underline{?}}$ 15
20. $24,980 = 2.4980 \times 10^{\underline{?}}$ 4
21. $\frac{1}{12^5} = 12^{\underline{?}}$ ⁻5
22. $31^{23} \times 31^{12} = 31^{\underline{?}}$ 35
23. $17^{10} \times 17^4 = 17^{\underline{?}}$ 14
24. $7^{-2} \times 7^{-8} = 7^{\underline{?}}$ ⁻10

25. Did the Muskrats score a touchdown?   no

```
            MUSKRATS
   G                      G
  10                     10
  20                     20
  30                     30
  40                     40  ← START
  50                     50
  40                     40
  30                     30
  20                     20
  10                     10
   G                      G
            MUD HOGS
```

CLASSWORK HOMEWORK · Choosing a Strategy or Method

Estimation	Checking for a Reasonable Answer	Writing an Equation
Using a Graph	Writing an Equation	Using a Road Map
Choosing the Operation	Interpreting the Quotient and the	Making an Organized List
Solving Multi-step Problems	Remainder	Using a Formula

Write the strategy or method you choose. Then solve.
Strategies and methods will vary.

1. A company has 17 trucks that can carry 2,532 bricks each. It also has a truck that can carry 4,697 bricks. What is the average number of bricks per truck for all 18 trucks?   choosing the operation; 2,652 bricks

2. Ross borrowed $2,100 to buy a boat. He paid $504 interest over 2 years. What was the rate of interest?   using a formula; 0.12 per year or 12% per year

3. Eduardo has $26.15 to buy nautical flags. He wants 3 flags that cost $5.88, $12.95, and $17.50. Does he have enough money for the flags?   estimation; no

4. The winning boat in a race across a lake $2\frac{3}{4}$ miles wide finished the course in $1\frac{1}{2}$ minutes. What was its average speed?   using a formula; 110 miles per hour or $1\frac{5}{6}$ miles per minute

5. Patrick is buying life jackets. He can choose from seat cushions and wearable life jackets. He can also choose red, green, or gold. How many different combinations are available to Patrick?   making an organized list; 6 combinations

6. Metrobuild constructed 1,200 houses in 1989. Of these, 84% sold for more than $100,000 and 12% sold for more than $225,000. The remaining houses were unsold. How many houses did Metrobuild sell in 1989?   solving multi-step problems; 1,152 houses

7. Marian auctions used window frames in lots of 20. How many lots can she auction from a group of 956 frames?   interpreting the quotient and remainder; 47 lots

CLASSWORK HOMEWORK — Choosing a Strategy or Method

Estimation	Checking for a Reasonable Answer	Using a Formula
Using a Graph	Writing an Equation	Using a Road Map
Choosing the Operation	Interpreting the Quotient and the	Making an Organized List
Solving Multi-step Problems	Remainder	

Write the strategy or method you choose. Then solve.
Strategies and methods will vary.

1. A powerboat was driven for 3 hours 45 minutes at an average speed of 44 miles per hour. How far did it travel?
using a formula; 165 miles

2. Danielle wants to buy several boat models. The barge costs $8.69. The schooner costs $18.98. The clipper costs $12.25. Can Danielle buy one of each model with $40.00?
estimation; yes

3. A supplier sells roofing shingles in boxes of 24. Martin needs 225 shingles for a repair job. How many boxes does he need to buy?
interpreting the quotient and
remainder; 10 boxes

4. In 1989, a construction company used an average of $35\frac{1}{4}$ tons of cement each month. In January of 1990, it used $30\frac{3}{8}$ tons. What is the average weight of cement used per month for the 13 months?
choosing the operation; $34\frac{7}{8}$ tons

5. Which two major routes would you travel from Austin to Owatonna, and how far would you travel?
using a road map; Routes 90 and 35;
48 miles

6. If you used the direct route and cycled at an average speed of $10\frac{1}{3}$ miles per hour, how long would it take to travel
using a road map; 3 hours

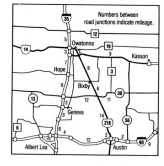
Numbers between road junctions indicate mileage.

Use after pages 256–257.

Student Handbook **H105**

CLASSWORK HOMEWORK — Rational Numbers

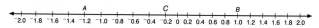

Use the number line to answer each problem.

1. What is the position of point A? ⁻1.2

2. What is the position of point B? 1.0

3. If point E is added to the number line at 0.6, between which two points is E located? between C and B

Write >, <, or = .

4. $\frac{7}{9}$ ⊘ $\frac{⁻1}{2}$ (>)

5. 0.1 ⊘ ⁻6   (>)

6. ⁻0.73 ⊘ ⁻0.69   (<)

7. ⁻0.05 ⊘ ⁻0.05   (=)

8. $\frac{⁻7}{8}$ ⊘ $\frac{⁻2}{9}$ (<)

9. $\frac{3}{5}$ ⊘ ⁻0.07   (>)

Write the numbers from the least to the greatest.

10. ⁻9, $\frac{5}{6}$, ⁻$1\frac{1}{3}$ ⁻9, ⁻$1\frac{1}{3}$, $\frac{5}{6}$

11. 0.03, 7.75, ⁻0.03, ⁻4.14
⁻4.14, ⁻0.03, 0.03, 7.75

12. ⁻4.4, $\frac{1}{2}$, 0.62, ⁻$10\frac{1}{3}$, $\frac{3}{5}$
⁻$10\frac{1}{3}$, ⁻4.4, $\frac{1}{2}$, $\frac{3}{5}$, 0.62

Write the numbers from the greatest to the least.

13. 0.05, ⁻0.8, 0.82   0.82, 0.05, ⁻0.8

14. $\frac{2}{5}$, $6\frac{2}{5}$, ⁻$2\frac{1}{6}$, ⁻$5\frac{1}{6}$
$6\frac{2}{5}$, $\frac{2}{5}$, ⁻$2\frac{1}{6}$, ⁻$5\frac{1}{6}$

15. ⁻5.82, ⁻$5\frac{1}{4}$, $1\frac{1}{2}$, 1.7, ⁻1.6
1.7, $1\frac{1}{2}$, ⁻1.6, ⁻$5\frac{1}{4}$, ⁻5.82

H106 Student Handbook

Use with pages 258–259.

CLASSWORK HOMEWORK — Adding and Subtracting Rational Numbers

Add or subtract. Simplify where necessary.

1. $16 - \frac{⁻4}{7}$ $16\frac{4}{7}$

2. ⁻0.07 + ⁻9.42   ⁻9.49

3. ⁻2.3 − ⁻0.9   ⁻1.4

4. $\frac{1}{6} + ⁻4\frac{3}{4}$ ⁻$4\frac{7}{12}$

5. $5 - \frac{1}{2}$ $4\frac{1}{2}$

6. 0.02 + ⁻8   ⁻7.98

7. $\frac{⁻5}{6} - ⁻10$ $9\frac{1}{6}$

8. ⁻$5\frac{7}{10} + ⁻14\frac{1}{6}$ ⁻$19\frac{13}{15}$

9. 2.04 − ⁻0.4   2.44

10. ⁻6.98 + 11.3   4.32

11. $\frac{⁻7}{10} - 12\frac{1}{3}$ ⁻$13\frac{1}{30}$

12. $6\frac{1}{6} + \frac{7}{9}$ $6\frac{17}{18}$

13. ⁻0.6 − 0.4   ⁻1

14. 14.55 + 3.9   18.45

15. $\frac{1}{8} - ⁻8$ $8\frac{1}{8}$

16. ⁻$12\frac{1}{10} + ⁻2\frac{8}{9}$ ⁻$14\frac{89}{90}$

17. 6.6 − 9.16   ⁻2.56

18. ⁻0.1 + ⁻0.03   ⁻0.13

19. ⁻$3 - \frac{3}{10}$ ⁻$3\frac{3}{10}$

20. $9\frac{3}{5} + ⁻4\frac{7}{9}$ $4\frac{9}{9}$

21. ⁻0.21 − ⁻2.5   2.29

22. 0.61 + ⁻0.94   ⁻0.33

23. $20\frac{2}{3} - ⁻16\frac{2}{3}$ $37\frac{1}{3}$

24. ⁻$5\frac{3}{5} + \frac{7}{10}$ ⁻$4\frac{9}{10}$

25. 0.16 − 0.5   ⁻0.34

26. ⁻8.98 + 9   0.02

27. ⁻$6\frac{1}{6} - 6\frac{2}{9}$ ⁻$12\frac{7}{18}$

28. $15\frac{1}{10} + 12\frac{3}{4}$ $27\frac{17}{20}$

29. ⁻6.7 − ⁻9.1   2.4

30. 0.02 + 19.8   19.82

31. $15\frac{1}{2} - \frac{7}{10}$ $14\frac{4}{5}$

32. ⁻$\frac{1}{7} + 2\frac{1}{6}$ $2\frac{1}{42}$

33. 0.69 − 1   ⁻0.31

34. ⁻5.79 + ⁻19.5   ⁻25.29

Use with pages 260–261.

Student Handbook **H107**

CLASSWORK HOMEWORK — Check That the Solution Answers the Question

Write the letter of the correct answer.

1. A mine shaft is ⁻730 feet deep. Every ⁻20 feet, a sample of the rock was taken. Were more than 35 samples taken from the mine shaft?
a. one
(b.) yes
c. 36

2. One sample 6.8×10^{-1} meters long contains an average of one trace of gold every 1.6×10^{-2} meters. Are there at least 50 traces of gold in the sample?
(a.) no
b. ten fewer
c. yes

Solve.

3. A geologist has 3 samples of gold, labeled A, B, and C. A measures 5.75×10^{-3} meters long, B measures 9.9×10^{-4} meters long, and C measures 1.86×10^{-2} meters long. Is the order from the smallest to the greatest A, C, B? no

4. A miner is working in a shaft at a depth of ⁻981 feet. Every hour, he digs ⁻5 feet deeper. Will he reach the ⁻1,000-foot level if he digs for 4 hours? yes

5. A mechanical hoist is positioned 55 feet above a mine shaft, and a wire is run from the hoist to the ⁻465-foot level. Will 525 feet of wire be enough to reach that level? yes

6. In 1983, a geological exploration drilled to a depth of ⁻39,370 feet. If the drill hole was extended by 30 feet per day, would a depth of ⁻40,000 feet be reached in less than 3 weeks? no

7. A team of miners runs a telephone cable from a station that is at a level of ⁻1,000 feet in a tunnel 250 feet from the mine shaft. The cable runs up the shaft and then to an office $\frac{1}{3}$ mile away. Did they use fewer than 3,000 feet of cable? no

8. A bucket is lowered from the top of a 55-foot hoist. If it takes 3 minutes to reach ⁻890 feet, is it descending faster or slower than 3.5 miles per hour?
faster

H108 Student Handbook

Use with pages 262–263.

CLASSWORK HOMEWORK — Multiplying and Dividing Rational Numbers

Multiply or divide. Simplify when necessary.

1. $^-0.2 \cdot 0.81$ $^-0.162$
2. $^-6.16 \div 0.7$ $^-8.8$
3. $^-\frac{2}{9} \cdot ^-\frac{3}{4}$ $\frac{1}{6}$
4. $1\frac{1}{3} \div 1\frac{1}{4}$ $1\frac{1}{15}$
5. $^-0.8 \cdot ^-0.6$ 0.48
6. $2.37 \div 0.1$ 23.7
7. $9\frac{1}{10} \cdot 8\frac{3}{7}$ $76\frac{7}{10}$
8. $^-\frac{1}{3} \div \frac{3}{7}$ $^-\frac{7}{9}$
9. $9.1 \cdot ^-0.45$ $^-4.095$
10. $0.99 \div 0.05$ 19.8
11. $\frac{2}{3} \cdot ^-10\frac{1}{2}$ $^-7$
12. $\frac{2}{7} \div ^-1$ $^-\frac{2}{7}$
13. $1.34 \cdot 0.07$ 0.0938
14. $5.52 \div ^-6$ $^-0.92$
15. $^-\frac{2}{3} \cdot ^-3$ 2
16. $^-16 \div \frac{5}{7}$ $^-22\frac{2}{5}$
17. $^-0.13 \cdot ^-3.9$ 0.507
18. $0.06 \div 0.3$ 0.2
19. $\frac{3}{4} \cdot ^-\frac{2}{9}$ $^-\frac{1}{6}$
20. $6\frac{1}{2} \div 1\frac{4}{9}$ $4\frac{1}{2}$
21. $^-9.5 \cdot 12.7$ $^-120.65$
22. $^-8.4 \div ^-4.2$ 2
23. $^-9 \cdot \frac{2}{7}$ $^-2\frac{4}{7}$
24. $9\frac{3}{7} \div 1\frac{1}{3}$ $7\frac{1}{14}$
25. $^-0.05 \cdot ^-16$ 0.8
26. $1.4 \div ^-7$ $^-0.2$
27. $^-\frac{3}{4} \cdot 10\frac{2}{3}$ $^-8$
28. $^-\frac{1}{4} \div ^-1$ $\frac{1}{4}$
29. $^-0.05 \cdot 1.7$ $^-0.085$
30. $2.79 \div 3.1$ 0.9
31. $9\frac{3}{4} \cdot 2\frac{2}{3}$ 26
32. $9\frac{1}{10} \div ^-\frac{7}{9}$ $^-11\frac{7}{10}$

33. Ahmed has a summer job finishing tables for a furniture maker. He can finish $2\frac{1}{3}$ tables per week (7 days). The furniture maker received an order for 13 tables that must be done in five weeks and one day. Will Ahmed be able to finish them all on time? If not, how many will the furniture maker have to finish himself?

no; 1 table

Use with pages 264–265.   Student Handbook **H109**

CLASSWORK HOMEWORK — Real Numbers

Write *R* if the number is rational and *I* if the number is irrational.

1. $41.373737\ldots$ *R*
2. $6.246247248\ldots$ *I*
3. $17.59086732\ldots$ *I*
4. 8.21679 *R*
5. $6.21508462150846\ldots$ *R*
6. $3.141592653\ldots$ *I*
7. 56.3902064198 *R*
8. $7.23852385\ldots$ *R*
9. 458.37928046 *R*
10. $38.221222223\ldots$ *I*
11. $27.10429638\ldots$ *I*
12. $12.240240240\ldots$ *R*
13. 5.413709 *R*
14. $0.001001\ldots$ *R*
15. $32.7333\ldots$ *R*
16. $4.2358132134\ldots$ *I*

Estimate the square root to the nearest tenth. Estimates may vary.

17. $\sqrt{15}$ 3.9
18. $\sqrt{64}$ 8
19. $\sqrt{45}$ 6.7
20. $\sqrt{36}$ 6
21. $\sqrt{121}$ 11
22. $\sqrt{20}$ 4.5
23. $\sqrt{2}$ 1.4
24. $\sqrt{196}$ 14
25. $\sqrt{49}$ 7
26. $\sqrt{100}$ 10
27. $\sqrt{44}$ 6.6
28. $\sqrt{16}$ 4
29. $\sqrt{33}$ 5.7
30. $\sqrt{47}$ 6.9
31. $\sqrt{81}$ 9
32. $\sqrt{38}$ 6.2

H110   Student Handbook

CLASSWORK HOMEWORK — Graphing Real Numbers

I.

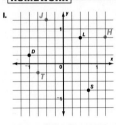
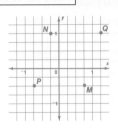

Copy graph I. Then use the graph to answer Problems 1 through 6.

1. What are the coordinates of point *D*? $(^-1, 0.25)$
2. What are the coordinates of point *S*? $(0.75, ^-0.75)$
3. What are the coordinates of point *L*? $(0.5, 0.75)$
4. Graph point *H* at $(1.25, 0.75)$.
5. Graph point *T* at $(^-0.75, ^-0.25)$.
6. Graph point *J* at $(^-0.5, 1.25)$.

Draw a real-number plane for Problems 7 through 12.

7. Graph point *M* at $(0.75, ^-0.5)$.
8. Graph point *N* at $(^-0.25, 1)$.
9. Graph point *P* at $(^-0.75, ^-0.5)$.
10. Graph point *Q* at $(1.25, 1)$.
11. In which quadrant would $(^-4.5, 6.2)$ be? II
12. In which quadrant would $(3.1415, ^-4.6)$ be? IV

Use with pages 268–269.   Student Handbook **H111**

CLASSWORK HOMEWORK — Solving Multistep Problems/Making a Plan

Each problem can be solved in four steps. Complete the plan for solving each problem by writing the three missing steps. Solve.

1. An antenna 20.6 meters high is erected at the top of a mine shaft. From the top of the antenna, 0.4 kilometers of wire are run down the shaft. The wire is 50 meters too short to reach the station level. How deep is the station level?

   Step 1: Convert 0.4 kilometers to meters.

   Step 2: ? Subtract 20.6 meters from 400 meters.

   Step 3: ? Change 379.4 to $^-379.4$.

   Step 4: ? Add $^-50$ to $^-379.4 = ^-429.4$ meters.

2. Samples are taken at regular distances in a mine. Sample 24 is taken at a depth of $^-1.2$ kilometers. How many meters below the sample 24 will the sample 30 be taken?

   Step 1: Convert $^-1.2$ kilometers to meters

   Step 2: ? Divide $^-1,200$ meters by 24.

   Step 3: ? Subtract 24 from 30.

   Step 4: ?
   Multiply $^-50$ by $6 = ^-300$ meters.

Make a plan, and solve.

3. A mine is 3^4 kilometers from a town. The road is marked so that there are 3^2 equal sections, and each section is divided into 90 subsections. How many meters long is each subsection?
   100 meters

4. A bucket is hoisted up from a depth of $^-840$ meters inside a mine. It moves at a rate of 125 centimeters per second. How many meters below the surface is the bucket after 3 minutes?
   $^-615$ meters

5. A mining company takes out a 2-year loan to buy a bulldozer that costs $125,000. The interest rate on the loan is 15%, and the company pays $30,000 down. What is the total price the company will pay? $153,500

6. A miner walked 550 yards from his car to a shaft that is $^-1,490$ feet deep. He descended to a point $\frac{4}{5}$ the depth of the shaft, took a sample, then traveled up the shaft, and returned to his car. How many feet did he travel? 5,684 feet

7. An ore zone begins at a depth of $^-214$ meters and ends at a depth of $^-307$ meters. A silver vein running through the zone is $\frac{1}{150}$ of the width of the zone. How many centimeters wide is the vein? 62 cm

8. A geologist labels samples according to the depth from which they were taken. Write these samples in order from the least to the greatest depth: (A) $^-2.4$ meters; (B) $^-1.1$ kilometers; (C) $^-0.8$ meters; (D) $^-810$ centimeters; (E) $^-980$ meters. C, A, D, E, B

H112   Student Handbook   Use after pages 270–271.

CLASSWORK HOMEWORK | Algebraic Expressions

Write each as an algebraic expression.

1. b increased by 14 $b + 14$
2. the product of 7 and c $7c$
3. g divided by 2 $\frac{g}{2}$
4. r decreased by 10 $r - 10$
5. the product of a and $^-6$ ^-6a
6. z divided by $^-1$ $\frac{z}{^-1}$ or ^-z
7. 12 subtracted from q $q - 12$
8. 16 times p $16p$
9. 8 more than t $t + 8$
10. 18 divided by n $\frac{18}{n}$
11. the difference of y and 4 $y - 4$
12. s increased by 11 $s + 11$
13. 32 less than k $k - 32$
14. j added to 26 $26 + j$
15. h divided by 9 $\frac{h}{9}$
16. the product of 18 and b $18b$

Evaluate each expression if the variable equals 1, 2, 3, 4, and 5.

17. $18 - s$ 17, 16, 15, 14, 13
18. $5s$ 5, 10, 15, 20, 25
19. $\frac{s}{4}$ $\frac{1}{4}, \frac{1}{2}, \frac{3}{4}, 1, 1\frac{1}{4}$
20. $9 + s$ 10, 11, 12, 13, 14

Evaluate each expression if the variable equals $^-1$, 0, 1, 2, and 3.

21. $k - 3$ $^-4, ^-3, ^-2, ^-1, 0$
22. $14 + k$ 13, 14, 15, 16, 17
23. $5(k - 1)$ $^-10, ^-5, 0, 5, 10$
24. $k \div 3$ $^-\frac{1}{3}, 0, \frac{1}{3}, \frac{2}{3}, 1$

Write the letter of the correct algebraic expression.

25. Maria has many records. Fred has 5 times that amount.
   a. $5r$ **b.** $5 - r$ **c.** $r + 5$

26. Paul had some tapes. He divided them equally among 4 friends.
   a. $\frac{4}{t}$ **b.** $4t$ **c.** $\frac{t}{4}$

27. Setsuko had 12 record albums. She bought a few more.
   a. $12a$ **b.** $12 + a$ **c.** $a - 12$

Use with pages 280–281.   Student Handbook **H113**

CLASSWORK HOMEWORK | Solving One-Step Equations

Solve.

1. $n + 9\frac{1}{4} = 13\frac{3}{8}$ $n = 4\frac{1}{8}$
2. $r + 759 = 529$ $r = ^-230$
3. $\frac{1}{7}c = 6$ $c = 42$
4. $\frac{1}{23}w = 15$ $w = 345$
5. $0.5w = 1.415$ $w = 2.83$
6. $^-71.3n = 63.457$ $n = ^-0.89$
7. $d + 0.069 = 0.139$ $d = 0.07$
8. $0.004 - n = ^-0.636$ $n = 0.64$
9. $4t = ^-28$ $t = ^-7$
10. $n - \frac{5}{12} = \frac{7}{12}$ $n = 1$
11. $z - \frac{1}{3} = \frac{4}{15}$ $z = \frac{3}{5}$
12. $4\frac{1}{2} + b = ^-1\frac{2}{5}$ $b = ^-5\frac{9}{10}$
13. $10\frac{1}{2}n = 6\frac{9}{16}$ $n = \frac{5}{8}$
14. $n - \frac{2}{7} = \frac{3}{14}$ $n = \frac{1}{2}$
15. $a - 733 = 129$ $a = 862$
16. $^-0.55h = 4.40$ $h = ^-8$
17. $n - 0.41 = 0.09$ $n = 0.5$
18. $25 - p = 7$ $p = 18$
19. $c + \frac{3}{10} = \frac{31}{70}$ $c = \frac{1}{7}$
20. $w + 6\frac{1}{2} = 10\frac{1}{6}$ $w = 3\frac{2}{3}$
21. $12.4d = 111.6$ $d = 9$
22. $94.2 - w = 19.65$ $w = 74.55$
23. $b - 93 = ^-12$ $b = 81$
24. $\frac{3}{8}m = ^-\frac{27}{80}$ $m = ^-\frac{9}{10}$
25. $211 + z = 657$ $z = 446$
26. $^-203 - z = 420$ $z = ^-623$
27. $^-16 - t = 40$ $t = ^-56$
28. $6.174 + n = 5.324$ $n = ^-0.85$
29. $^-\frac{1}{9}r = 9$ $r = ^-81$
30. $6.4n = 352.64$ $n = 55.1$

31. The state in which Melissa and Edward live requires a nickel deposit on all soft-drink containers. Edward and Melissa collect containers to cash in for the deposit. After one week, Melissa had 75 containers, which was $1\frac{1}{2}$ times as many as Edward had collected. The number of containers Melissa collected is given by the equation $1\frac{1}{2}n = 75$. How many bottles and cans did Edward collect?   **50 bottles and cans**

H114 Student Handbook   Use with pages 282–283.

CLASSWORK HOMEWORK | Solving Two-Step Equations

Solve.

1. $2n + 17 = 47$ $n = 15$
2. $\frac{1}{6}w + 76\frac{5}{8} = 54\frac{5}{8}$ $w = ^-132$
3. $36.2 - 3b = 85.1$ $b = ^-16.3$
4. $1.75y - 99.9 = 75.1$ $y = 100$
5. $\frac{1}{2}m + 89 = 114$ $m = 50$
6. $3e - 1 = ^-2$ $e = ^-\frac{1}{3}$
7. $1.25a + 13 = 38$ $a = 20$
8. $7 - 0.6p = 6.88$ $p = 0.2$
9. $100c + 16 = 46$ $c = 0.3$
10. $\frac{1}{5}a - 42.3 = 105.1$ $a = 737$
11. $3.875z + 1.25 = 40$ $z = 10$
12. $19\frac{1}{8} + 3n = 22\frac{5}{16}$ $n = 1\frac{1}{16}$
13. $750 - \frac{1}{2}s = 700$ $s = 100$
14. $26b + 14 = ^-25$ $b = ^-1.5$
15. $10r + 0.4 = 2$ $r = 0.16$
16. $10.75 - 350z = 5.5$ $z = 0.015$
17. $97 - 500t = 72$ $t = 0.05$
18. $6v - 27\frac{3}{8} = ^-34\frac{7}{8}$ $v = ^-1\frac{1}{4}$
19. $^-909 + 0.17b = ^-926$ $b = ^-100$
20. $24\frac{3}{8} - \frac{1}{5}c = 4\frac{3}{8}$ $c = 100$
21. $3h + 75 = 150$ $h = 25$
22. $3f - 15 = ^-48$ $f = ^-11$
23. $88\frac{1}{3} - 4s = ^-88\frac{1}{3}$ $s = 44\frac{1}{6}$
24. $97.6 - 2.3q = 99.9$ $g = ^-1$
25. $^-0.709t + 141.8 = 0$ $t = 200$
26. $\frac{1}{16}j - 40 = 10$ $j = 800$

Solve.

27. Fred gave his duplicate baseball cards to his cousin Karl. Duplicates were $\frac{1}{4}$ of Fred's collection. Karl already had 18 cards and now he has 34. The equation representing the size of Karl's collection is $\frac{1}{4}y + 18 = 34$. How many cards did Fred have to begin with?   **64 cards**

Use with pages 284–285.   Student Handbook **H115**

CLASSWORK HOMEWORK | Word Problems from Equations

Write the letter of the equation that describes the problem.

1. A number increased by 9 is $^-13$.
   a. $b + ^-13 = 9$ **b.** $b - 9 = ^-13$ **c.** $b + 9 = ^-13$

2. The product of a number and 6, when increased by 8, is 16.
   a. $6y + 8 = 16$ **b.** $y(6 + 8) = 16$ **c.** $8(y + 6) = 16$

3. A number divided by $^-4$ and then decreased by 12 is 96.
   a. $^-4m - 12 = 96$ **b.** $\frac{1}{4}(m - 12) = 96$
   c. $\frac{m}{^-4} - 12 = 96$

4. Mike scored 38 points in one basketball game, four less than twice the school record.
   a. $\frac{x}{2} + 38 = 4$ **b.** $2x - 4 = 38$ **c.** $4 + 2x = 38$

5. The Gonzales family drove 750 miles during their vacation. They drove the same number of miles per day for 5 days, and 150 miles the sixth day.
   a. $\frac{7}{570}x = 150$ **b.** $5x - 150 = 750$
   c. $5x + 150 = 750$

6. Susan, Paul, and Eva ran the same distance together, and then Eva ran $1\frac{1}{2}$ miles more alone. The 3 ran a total of 12 miles.
   a. $3x + 1\frac{1}{2} = 12$ **b.** $1\frac{1}{2}x + 3 = 12$
   c. $12x - 3 = 1\frac{1}{2}$

Write a word problem for each equation and solve.

7. $^-2g + 9 = ^-11$ Word problems will vary; $g = 10$.

8. $\frac{1}{3}n - 8 = 10$ Word problems will vary; $n = 54$.

9. $5y + 20 = 35$ Word problems will vary; $y = 3$.

H116 Student Handbook   Use with pages 286–287.

CLASSWORK HOMEWORK | Writing an Equation

Write the letter of the correct equation.

1. The Science Club arranged a trip to the Smithsonian. Only $\frac{2}{3}$ of the members were able to attend, which left one seat empty on the 25-passenger bus. How many members does the Science Club have?

   a. $1 + n = \frac{2}{3} \times 25$

   b. $\frac{2}{3} \times 25 = n + 1$

   c. $\frac{2}{3}n = 25 - 1$ ✓

2. This year, the Nature Club made 3 exhibits per month for its annual fair. This year's fair has twice as many exhibits as last year's. How many exhibits were there in last year's fair?

   a. $n = 2 \times 3$

   b. $2n = 12 \times 3$ ✓

   c. $12 \times 3n = 2$

Write an equation, and solve.

3. The Singing Club charged each of its 20 members $2.60 to hire a hall for a performance. The hall owner gave the club $4.50 change. How much did the club pay to hire the hall?

   $n + \$4.50 = 20 \times \$2.60 ; \$47.50$

4. The Singing Club keeps sheet music in files. Each file holds 12 sheets. Of all the club's music, $\frac{2}{3}$ fit into 3 files. how many sheets of music does the club have?

   $\frac{2}{3}n = 3 \times 12 ; $ 54 sheets

5. The Tennis Club has 5 new members. Each buys a racket and a tube of balls. If 6 rackets cost $186.00 and 6 tubes of balls cost $27.00, how much do the 5 people pay for rackets and balls?

   $n = \frac{5}{6}(186 + 27) ; \$177.50$

6. The Art Club visits a mansion that has 3 flights of stairs. The first flight is 29 steps long. The second flight is 4 steps longer than the third flight. There are 67 steps altogether. How many steps are there in the third flight?

   $2n + 4 = 67 - 29; $ 17

7. The Art Club held a show for 2 days. A total of 269 people attended the show. On the second day, 15 more people attended than had come to the show the first day. How many people attended on the first day?

   $2n + 15 = 269; $ 127 people

8. The Acting Club's two-act play begins at 3:20 P.M. The first act is twice as long as the second act, and there is a 15-minute break between acts. The play ends at 4:50 P.M. How long is Act I?

   $n + \frac{n}{2} + 15 = 90; $ 50 minutes

CLASSWORK HOMEWORK | Guessing and Checking

Use the guess-and-check method to solve.

1. Find a 2-digit number less than 20. When the product of its digits is squared, the square is 2 greater than the original number. 14

2. Find a 2-digit number for which the square root of the sum of the digits is the cube root of the original number. 27

3. The number 10 can be squared, and the sum of the digits of the square equals the sum of the digits of the original number $(1 + 0 = 1 + 0 + 0)$. Find another 2-digit number between 10 and 20 that is like that. 19

4. If you double the number 117, the sum of the digits will be the same as the sum of the digits of the original number. Find a number between 120 and 140 that is like that. 126

5. Find a 2-digit number less than 25 for which the sum of its digits is the same as the product of its digits. 22

6. Find a 2-digit number less than 20 for which the sum of its digits is half the original number. 18

7. Find a 2-digit number less than 50 for which the product of its digits is half the original number. 36

8. There are three numbers between 2 and 100 that, when squared, create numbers whose digits can be reversed without changing the squares. The highest of the three numbers is 26 $(26^2 = 676)$, and the lowest is 11 $(11^2 = 121)$. Find the third number. 22

CLASSWORK HOMEWORK | Guessing and Checking

Use the guess-and-check method to solve.

9. Find a 2-digit number less than 20 for which the product of the digits equals half the sum of the digits. 11

10. A 2-digit number between 20 and 30 has 5 factors less than the number itself. When added together, the factors equal the number. What is the number? 28

11. When a certain single-digit number is multiplied by 4, the sum of the digits of the product equals the original number. What is the single-digit number? 9

12. Find a number between 30 and 40 that is the product of two single-digit prime numbers. The sum of its digits is a cube. 35

13. Find a 2-digit number less than 20 for which the product of its digits is $\frac{1}{3}$ of the original number. 15

14. The sum of the digits of the number 180 equals the sum of the digits of half the number $(1 + 8 + 0 = 9 + 0)$. Find a number between 190 and 200 that is like that. 198

15. If you double the number 306, the sum of the digits equals the sum of the digits of the original number. $(3 + 0 + 6 = 6 + 1 + 2)$. Find another number between 300 and 320 that is like that. 315

16. The square of the number 3 is equal to the sum of the digits of the cube of the number 3. Find another single-digit number (other than the number 1) that is like that. 6

CLASSWORK HOMEWORK | Inequalities

Use the real numbers as the replacement set. Write the letter of the solution set of the inequality.

1. $4y < 4$ f

2. $3 + y \geq 1$ m

3. $\frac{5}{y} = 5$ e

4. $y - 1 > 8$ r

5. $\frac{1}{2}y \leq {}^-3$ o

6. $2y > 8$ k

7. $y - 2 \geq 2$ c

8. $\frac{1}{8}y \geq 2$ g

9. ${}^-1 + y > 1$ l

10. $\frac{1}{3}y > 15$ j

11. $3y = 0$ h

12. $y + 2 > {}^-8$ b

13. $y - 4 \leq 5$ i

14. $y + 1 = {}^-4$ d

15. $y - 2 > {}^-96$ n

16. $\frac{1}{4}y \geq {}^-4$ q

17. $5y \geq 95$ a

18. $3y < {}^-9$ p

a. $y = \{19,20,21, \ldots\}$

b. $y = \{{}^-9, {}^-8, {}^-7, \ldots\}$

c. $y = \{4,5,6,7 \ldots\}$

d. $y = \{{}^-5\}$

e. $y = \{1\}$

f. $y = \{\ldots {}^-2, {}^-1,0\}$

g. $y = \{16,17,18, \ldots\}$

h. $y = \{0\}$

i. $y = \{\ldots 7,8,9\}$

j. $y = \{46,47,48, \ldots\}$

k. $y = \{5,6,7, \ldots\}$

l. $y = \{3,4,5, \ldots\}$

m. $y = \{{}^-2, {}^-1,0, \ldots\}$

n. $y = \{{}^-93, {}^-92, {}^-91, \ldots\}$

o. $y = \{\ldots {}^-8, {}^-7, {}^-6\}$

p. $y = \{\ldots {}^-6, {}^-5, {}^-4\}$

q. $y = \{\ldots {}^-16, {}^-15, {}^-14, \ldots\}$

r. $y = \{10, 11, 12, \ldots\}$

CLASSWORK HOMEWORK — Solving One-Step Inequalities

Solve.

1. $4y > 24$ $y > 6$

2. $9\frac{1}{4} + b < 1\frac{1}{4}$ $b < {}^-9$

3. $p - 7 \leq {}^-1$ $p \leq 6$

4. $s \div 8 \geq 0$ $s \geq 0$

5. $\frac{r}{2} > {}^-\frac{3}{7}$ $r > {}^-\frac{6}{7}$

6. $c + 47.2 < 50$ $c < 2.8$

7. $^-4 + m \leq 5$ $m \leq 9$

8. $d + 0.51 > 0.39$ $d > {}^-0.12$

9. $0.9s \neq 90$ $s \neq 100$

10. $^-83.2 + y > {}^-100$ $y > {}^-16.8$

11. $w - 14 > {}^-6$ $w > 8$

12. $16z < 12$ $z < \frac{3}{4}$

13. $\frac{t}{5} \geq 17$ $t \geq 85$

14. $m + 4 \leq 6$ $m \leq 2$

Solve. Then find the group in which each answer appears to solve the riddle in Problem 19.

E

15. $4n + 7 > 23$ $n > \underline{}$ 4

$18g \leq 36$ $g \leq \underline{}$ 2

$\frac{1}{5}a < 1.2$ $a < \underline{}$ 6

$3h - 2 \geq 7.6$ $h \geq \underline{}$ 3.2

C

16. $f + 44.2 < 34.2$ $f < \underline{}$ $^-10$

$v - 37 > {}^-45$ $v > \underline{}$ $^-8$

$8x + 9 \leq {}^-63$ $x \leq \underline{}$ $^-9$

$\frac{1}{3}u > {}^-3$ $u > \underline{}$ $^-9$

F

17. $i - 22 > 33$ $i > \underline{}$ 55

$3z - 161 \leq {}^-2$ $a \leq \underline{}$ 53

$9r - 7 \leq 506$ $r \leq \underline{}$ 57

$0.8 + \frac{1}{4}h < 14.8$ $h < \underline{}$ 56

N

18. $a + 13.6 < 30.8$ $a < \underline{}$ 17.2

$4b + 16 \geq 89$ $b \geq \underline{}$ $18\frac{1}{4}$

$\frac{1}{5}c - 3 < 0$ $c < \underline{}$ 15

$2z - 6\frac{3}{4} < 21\frac{1}{4}$ $z < \underline{}$ 14

19. What goes all around and never moves?

A $\underline{}$ $\underline{}$ $\underline{}$ $\underline{}$ $\underline{}$
   F   E   N   C   E
   ≤ 57 ≥ 3.2 < 15 $\leq {}^-7$ ≤ 2

CLASSWORK HOMEWORK — Making a Table to Find a Pattern

Solve by making a table to find the pattern.

1. Jake is at a camera store. He has chosen a camera but is not sure how many rolls of film to buy. If he buys 1 roll of film, the total bill will be $64.95. If he buys 2 rolls of film, the total bill will be $67.40. How much will the total bill be if Jake buys the camera and 6 rolls of film? $77.20

2. If Jake has $74.00, how many rolls of film can he buy when he buys the camera? 4 rolls of film

3. A film-processing company has a special price rate for printing up to 6 copies from a negative. One print costs $0.45; 2 prints cost $0.85; 3 prints cost $1.20; and 4 prints cost $1.50. If the price rate is constant how much will 6 prints cost? $1.95

Copy and complete the table. Then solve.

4. Nina performed faster and faster as she carried out her summer project, taking photographs of animals in the park. Each day, she took 3 more photographs than she had taken on the previous day. On the first day of her project, she took 6 photographs. How many photographs had she taken by the end of the day 15? 405 photographs

Day	1	2	3	4	5	6	7	8	9	10	11	12	13	14	15
Photos that day	6	9	12	15	18	21	24	27	30	33	36	39	42	45	48
Total photos to date	6	15	27	42	60	81	105	132	162	195	231	270	312	357	405

5. How many photographs did Nina take on the day 11 of her project? 36 photographs

6. If Nina needed only 300 photographs, on which day could she have finished her project? day 13

CLASSWORK HOMEWORK — Making a Table to Find a Pattern

Solve by making a table to find the pattern.

1. Blanca has joined a junior tennis club. She paid a membership fee and pays a set amount per hour each time she uses a tennis court. After her first visit, she had paid a total of $58.25; after her second visit, she had paid a total of $61.50. How much will Blanca have paid after she has gone to the tennis club 7 times? $77.75

2. How much does membership to the tennis club cost? $55.00

3. If Blanca introduces new members to the club, the amount she pays for using a court is reduced. If she introduces one new member, she will pay $2.85 per hour. If she introduces 2 new members, she will pay $2.45 per hour. What will be Blanca's cost for each visit if she introduces 5 new members? $1.25

Copy and complete the table. Then solve.

4. The Health Club closes at 8.55 P.M. One night, between 8.15 P.M. and 8.20 P.M., 3 people left the club. Every 5 minutes thereafter, twice as many people leave the club as had left during the previous 5 minutes. If there were 375 people in the club that night, when was the club empty? 8.50 P.M.

Time	8:20 P.M.	8:25 P.M.	8:30 P.M.	8:35 P.M.	8:40 P.M.	8:45 P.M.	8:50 P.M.	8:55 P.M.
Members who left	3	6	12	24	48	96	192	384
Total members who have left	3	9	21	45	93	189	381	765

5. If there were 375 people in the club, at what time was the club about half-full? 8:45 P.M.

6. If there had been 750 people in the club, would the club have been empty by 8:55 P.M.? yes

CLASSWORK HOMEWORK — Solving Two-Step Inequalities

Solve.

1. $\frac{1}{8}y + 4 > 12$ $y > 64$

2. $5t + 9 < {}^-31$ $t < {}^-8$

3. $5g - 10 \geq {}^-25$ $g \geq {}^-3$

4. $400d - 6 > 34$ $d > 0.1$

5. $\frac{1}{2}s + 4 > {}^-6$ $s > {}^-20$

6. $\frac{1}{5}a + 11 > 21$ $a > 50$

7. $83.2t + 10 > 51.6$ $t > \frac{1}{2}$

8. $2v + 4 \geq {}^-1$ $v \geq {}^-2\frac{1}{2}$

9. $\frac{5}{6}w + 9 \leq 0$ $w \leq {}^-10\frac{4}{5}$

10. $14c + 8 < 22$ $c < 1$

11. $114u + 0.7 < 69.1$ $u < 0.6$

12. $\frac{3}{7}s + 10 < {}^-20$ $s < {}^-70$

13. $\frac{1}{6}m - 4 \geq {}^-4$ $m \geq 0$

14. $56r - 2 > 166$ $r > 3$

15. $15r + 6 > {}^-24$ $r > {}^-2$

16. $0.8t + 0.2 \leq 16.2$ $t \leq 20$

17. $\frac{11}{15}v - \frac{14}{15} > {}^-\frac{3}{10}$ $v > \frac{19}{22}$

18. $\frac{1}{9}a + 4 < 12$ $a < 72$

19. $\frac{3}{4}p + 16.2 < {}^-58.8$ $p < {}^-100$

20. $150b + 3 < 63$ $b < 0.4$

21. $700n - 500 < 200$ $n < 1$

22. $\frac{4}{5}c - 5\frac{1}{3} \leq {}^-6\frac{14}{15}$ $c \leq {}^-2$

Write an inequality and solve. Use x for the variable.

23. Bruce has to collect at least 100 signatures to get his name on the ballot for student-body elections. He already has 25 signatures, but he must hurry; so, two friends agree to help him. How many signatures each must Bruce and his two friends collect for Bruce to get his name on the ballot? $3x + 25 \geq 100; x \geq 25$

24. Each candidate for student-body office gives a speech in a special assembly. This year there are 15 candidates. The assembly must be no longer than 55 minutes, and the school principal needs 10 minutes to speak. What is the longest that each speech can be? $15x + 10 \leq 55; x \leq 3$ min

CLASSWORK/HOMEWORK — Graphing Equations and Inequalities

Solve and graph the equation or inequality.

1. $x + 4 < {}^-2$ $x < {}^-6$

2. $2a + 3 = {}^-3$ $a = {}^-3$

3. $\frac{1}{2}h \le {}^-7$ $h \le {}^-14$

4. $7m > {}^-14$ $m > {}^-2$

5. $\frac{1}{5}y - 3 = {}^-2$ $y = 5$

6. $8b - 4 = {}^-4$ $b = 0$

7. $\frac{1}{6}v - 1 \le 0$ $v \le 6$

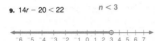

8. $n + 6 > 8$ $n > 2$

9. $14r - 20 < 22$ $n < 3$

10. $z - 6 \ge 6$ $z \ge 12$

Use with pages 300–301.

Student Handbook **H125**

CLASSWORK/HOMEWORK — Using a Schedule

Bethania travels frequently between Burlington, Boston, and Bangor. In order to fly between Burlington and Bangor, she has to change planes in Boston, which takes 15 minutes.

BURLINGTON		FLIGHT	FREQ
To Albany			
	6:55 A.M.	311	×167
6:15 A.M.	7:00 A.M.	351	1
6:20 A.M.	8:50 A.M.	660	6
7:40 A.M.	12:30 P.M.	314	×6
11:10 A.M.	6:40 P.M.	316	×6
5:21 P.M.			
To Binghamton			
6:20 A.M.	7:20 A.M.	100	×67
7:00 A.M.	9:35 A.M.	392	7
2:20 P.M.	3:50 P.M.	392	7
2:55 P.M.	5:20 P.M.	374	×6
3:10 P.M.	4:10 P.M.	102	×6
To Boston			
6:05 A.M.	7:15 A.M.	220	7
7:00 A.M.	8:00 A.M.	122	×67
7:00 A.M.	8:10 A.M.	270	7
8:00 A.M.	9:00 A.M.	722	6
8:15 A.M.	11:00 A.M.	224	×67
10:00 A.M.	11:00 A.M.	124	×67
1:00 P.M.	1:55 P.M.	363	×6
2:30 P.M.	3:40 P.M.	222	7
4:00 P.M.	4:55 P.M.	128	67
4:50 P.M.	4:55 P.M.	365	×67
5:30 P.M.	6:40 P.M.	226	×67
From Boston			
8:45 A.M.	9:40 A.M.	372	×67
8:45 A.M.	9:55 A.M.	272	7
10:15 A.M.	10:30 A.M.	723	6
10:00 A.M.	11:05 A.M.	225	×67
12:00 P.M.	1:00 P.M.	125	×67
2:15 P.M.	3:10 P.M.	364	×6
7:30 P.M.	8:40 P.M.	227	×67
9:30 P.M.	10:40 P.M.	230	×6

FREQUENCY SYMBOLS			
X–Except	2–Tuesday	4–Thursday	6–Saturday
1–Monday	3–Wednesday	5–Friday	7–Sunday
D–Daily			

BOSTON					
	To Bangor	Fl.	**From Bangor**		Fl.
Weekdays	8:10 A.M. 10:00 A.M.	400	7:45 A.M. 9:50 A.M.		406
	9:00 A.M. 11:00 A.M.	391	9:00 A.M. 11:25 A.M.		408
	10:15 A.M. 12:10 P.M.	407	11:00 A.M. 12:55 A.M.		392
	12:05 P.M. 2:00 P.M.	409	2:10 P.M. 4:15 P.M.		510
	3:40 P.M. 5:30 P.M.	505	4:25 P.M. 6:30 P.M.		519
	5:10 P.M. 7:05 P.M.	511			
Weekends	9:30 A.M. 11:25 A.M.	575	9:10 A.M. 11:00 A.M.		703
	2:15 P.M. 4:05 P.M.	580	3:25 P.M. 5:20 P.M.		584

Use the schedules to solve.

1. How many flights from Burlington to Binghamton are there on Saturday?
   none

2. When is the earliest Saturday flight from Burlington to Albany? 7:40 A.M.

3. If Bethania takes Flight 270 from Burlington, which flight will she take from Boston to Bangor? flight 575

4. Bethania takes Flight 222 to Boston from Burlington. How long will she have to wait for a flight to Bangor? $16\frac{1}{2}$ hours

5. If Bethania leaves Bangor at 7:45 A.M. on a Tuesday and the flight lands 5 minutes early, what is the earliest flight she can take to Burlington? flight 225

6. From Burlington, Bethania needs to fly to Boston and back to drop a package at the airline terminal. Which weekday flight would involve the least amount of waiting before boarding the return flight? flight 363

7. Bethania leaves Burlington at 7:00 A.M. on a Friday. When will she arrive in Bangor if the flights are on schedule? 11:00 A.M.

8. If Bethania wants to travel from Bangor to Burlington on a Saturday, which flights would carry her there the fastest? flight 584 and flight 129

H126 Student Handbook

Use after pages 302–303.

CLASSWORK/HOMEWORK — Arranging Data

The average scores for Masters Bowling Tournament champions from 1973 to 1984 were 218, 234, 213, 220, 218, 200, 202, 206, 218, 205, 212, 212.

1. Make a frequency table. Start with 200, and use intervals that have a width of 5. Complete the average score, tally, frequency, and relative frequency for each interval.

Average score	Tally	Frequency	Relative frequency
200–204	//	2	16.7%
205–209	//	2	16.7%
210–214	///	3	25%
215–219	///	3	25%
220–224	/	1	8.3%
225–229		0	0%
230–234	/	1	8.3%

2. What is the range for the set of data? 34

3. In how many years was the average 205–209? 2

4. For what percent of the years was the average 215–219? 25%

From 1969 to 1983, the amounts for the Professional Golf Association's leading money winners were as follows: $175,223; $157,037; $244,490; $320,542; $308,362; $353,201; $323,149; $266,438; $310,653; $362,429; $462,636; $530,808; $375,699; $446,462; $426,668.

Winnings	Tally	Frequency	Relative frequency
$100,000–$149,999		0	0%
$150,000–$199,999	//	2	13.3%
$200,000–$249,999	/	1	6.7%
$250,000–$299,999	/	1	6.7%
$300,000–$349,999	////	4	26.7%
$350,000–$399,999	///	3	20%
$400,000–$449,999	//	2	13.3%
$450,000–$499,999	/	1	6.7%
$500,000–$549,999	/	1	6.7%

5. Make a frequency table. Start with $100,000 and use intervals that have a width of $50,000. (The first is $100,000–$149,999.) Complete the average score, tally, frequency, and relative frequency for each interval.

6. What is the range for this set of data? $373,771

7. For what percent of the years were the winnings $100,000–$249,999? 20%

8. For what percent of the years were the winnings $350,000 or more? Round to the nearest tens place value. 46.7%

Use with pages 314–315.

Student Handbook **H127**

CLASSWORK/HOMEWORK — Median, Mode, and Mean

Write the median of each set of numbers.

1. 10, 11, 17, 14, 2   11

2. 8.9, 2.53, 11.04, 2.1, 3.57   3.57

3. $27, $54, $31, $57, $22 $31

4. 32, 158, 143, 32   87.5

5. 9.3, 1.6, 8.2, 4.7   6.45

6. 0.2, 0.03, 0.15, 0.06, 0.21   0.15

Write the mode(s) of each set of numbers.

7. 18, 16.26, 16.26, 5, 10.35   16.26

8. 11.4, 14, 17, 14, 13   14

9. 6, 9, 5, 3, 6, 9, 1, 4   6; 9

10. $2.50, $3.75, $2.25, $2.50 $2.50

11. 2.9, 17, 2.9, 6.24, 9.89   2.9

12. 30, 90, 60, 40, 90   90

Write the mean of each set of numbers. Round to the nearest hundredths place value.

13. 8.5, 14, 13.8, 7.92, 13.63   11.57

14. 3.7, 11.2, 15   9.97

15. 19.5, 7, 20.5   15.67

16. 16, 41, 176, 14   61.75

17. 88, 56, 91, 77, 32   68.80

18. $1.25, $3.20, $5.40, $3.70 $3.39

Write the missing number.

19. mean = 7.8   5, 8, __?__, 12, 3   11

20. mean = 15.75   13.8, 14.2, 19.6, __?__   15.4

21. mean = 12   9, 12, 15, 21, 4, __?__   11

22. mean = 36   24.5, 28, 48, 37, __?__   42.5

23. mean = 28.5 km   __?__, 22 km, 45 km   18.5 km

24. mean = 69.25%   97%, 32%, __?__, 84%   64%

Solve.

25. Pat's scores on her last five mathematics tests were 89, 95, 78, 94, and 99. What was her average score? If Pat takes one more test this year, what is the highest average she can achieve? 91; 92.5

26. An absentminded teacher lost a test paper from one of his students. He remembered that the mean score for the class of 25 was 83, and that the sum of the other 24 scores was 1,980. What was the grade on the lost paper? 95

H128 Student Handbook

Use with pages 316–317.

The table shows the number of each dish served in a Chinese restaurant on two different days.

DISHES SERVED

Dish	Monday	Tuesday
Beef with broccoli	43	40
Chow mein	59	41
Fried rice	62	45
Lo mein	51	42
Pepper steak	49	38
Daily special	44	72

1. Construct a horizontal double-bar graph to reflect these figures.

2. On which day was the greater number of meals served? Monday

3. Which dish had the greatest change in popularity? Daily special

This histogram shows the range of lunch bills in the restaurant one day.

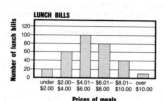

LUNCH BILLS

4. Into which price range did most of the bills fall? $4.01–$6

5. Into which price range did the fewest bills fall? over $10

6. How many customers paid between $8.01–$10? 40

7. What is the total number of bills shown? 310

The Off-Center Art Center held a show of sculptures made by local artists. All the money made by selling the works was donated to the neighborhood Free Studio. The scattergram below shows the heights and the prices of the sculptures in the show.

Can you use the scattergram to answer each question? Write *yes* or *no*.

1. How many sculptures were sold? no
2. How many sculptures were shown? yes

Use the scattergram to answer each question.

3. Were most sculptures priced at more than $150 or less than $150? more
4. Was the tallest sculpture the highest priced? no

5. How many of the sculptures were more than 4 feet 6 inches tall? 10 sculptures
6. How many sculptures were priced at less than $80? 7 sculptures

7. What percent of the sculptures were priced at more than $225? 30%
8. Was any piece of sculpture less than 4 feet tall priced at more than $200? yes

Does the scattergram support each statement? Write *yes* or *no*.

9. In general, the larger sculptures were the most expensive. yes
10. Sculptures that were the same height were generally the same price. no

11. The sculptures priced at less than $70 were not good work. no
12. The cost of materials probably has something to do with the price. yes

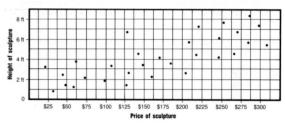

1. Make a broken-line graph to show the following statistics on silver production.

1925	66.16 million ounces
1930	50.75 million ounces
1935	45.92 million ounces
1940	69.59 million ounces
1945	29.06 million ounces
1950	42.31 million ounces
1955	36.47 million ounces
1960	36.00 million ounces

SILVER PRODUCTION

2. Which year had the greatest increase in silver production over the year before? 1940

3. Make a double broken-line graph of the average temperatures each month in these two cities.

Month	Chicago	New Orleans
Jan.	26	55
Feb.	28	57
Mar.	36	61
Apr.	49	68
May	60	74
June	71	80
July	76	82
Aug.	74	82
Sept.	66	78
Oct.	55	70
Nov.	40	60
Dec.	29	55

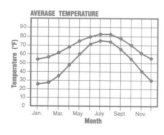

AVERAGE TEMPERATURE

4. For which city is the variation in temperature greater? Chicago

5. Which month shows the least difference between the two lines on the graph? July

1. Use a compass and a protractor to construct a circle graph that shows the number of pages each person contributed to the Chess Club's newsletter. Use the first letter of each person's name to represent his or her contribution. Mark each part of the graph with the percent that it represents.

Andre	4	Eva	2
Beth	4	Franco	8
Carlos	4	Gordon	6
Dionne	2	Helga	2

2. What is the measure of the central angle of the part that represents Carlos's contribution? 45

3. What fraction of the total did Gordon contribute? $\frac{3}{16}$

4. What fraction of the total did Andre contribute? $\frac{1}{8}$

5. What fraction of the total did Andre, Dionne, and Beth contribute together? $\frac{5}{16}$

6. What is the ratio of Gordon's contribution compared to Eva's? 3:1

Selecting an Appropriate Format • Tell which type of graph would best display the data. Answers may vary.

7. the monthly temperatures of a city for a year broken-line graph
8. the lengths of the eight longest rivers in the world bar graph

9. the percent of space used for clothing, sporting goods, kitchen appliances, and furniture circle graph
10. the frequency of weights between 100–110 lbs, 110–120 lbs, 120–130 lbs, and 130–140 lbs histogram

11. the percent of a garden used for azaleas, petunias, roses, and geraniums circle graph
12. the monthly precipitation in 2 different cities for 12 months double broken-line graph

Tweed Polls, Inc., conducted a poll to ask residents of Ringford (population 16,000) their opinions about the choice of a raccoon as the new town mascot. Three groups of 250 people each were questioned. The table below shows their responses.

Age group	15–25	26–45	Older than 45
Percent of the town population	25%	40%	20%
Approve	115	90	120
Disapprove	100	105	80
Undecided	35	55	50

Assume that the poll is representative of the opinions of all Ringford residents in the age groups sampled. Use the table to solve.

1. Which age group voiced the greatest difference of opinion between approval and disapproval? Older than 45

2. What percent of the 26–45 age group was undecided? 22%

3. In which age group did 40% of the people disapprove? 15–25

4. How many Ringford residents are more than 45 years old? 3,200 residents

5. How many Ringford residents in the 15–25 age group disapproved? 1,600 residents

6. How many Ringford residents in the 26–45 age group approved? 2,304 residents

7. What percent of all Ringford residents 15 years of age and older disapproved? 38%

8. How many residents of Ringford are less than 15 years of age? 2,400 residents

9. If 80% of the undecideds in the older-than-45 age group had disapproved and 20% had approved, would the majority of the age group have disapproved? no

10. Do the majority of residents of Ringford who are 15 years of age and older approve or disapprove? approve

To find out whether passengers would use a new service, Airways North conducted a poll. The results are shown below.

Age	20–40	20–40	Older than 40	Older than 40
Career	Self-employed	Executives	Self-employed	Executives
Percent of total first-class passengers	20%	28%	12%	24%
Will use the service	150	210	175	270
Will not use the service	200	240	215	170
Undecided	150	50	110	60

A total of 8,260 passengers fly first class between New York and Rome each month. Based on the assumption that the passengers in the poll represent all of Airways North's first-class passengers, solve.

1. What percent of self-employed passengers questioned said they would use the new service? 32.5%

2. Suppose that Airways North had questioned only executives older than 40, and the results showed that 60% of those polled would use the new service. Would this poll be a good indicator of the total population of passengers? Explain your answer. No; the sample would be biased.

3. To the nearest person, how many passengers are likely to use the service? 3,325 passengers

4. If Airways North reduced the fare paid by executives by 10%, they expect that 75% of the undecided executives would use the new service. The airline, however, would have to book at least 3,100 passengers per month to make a profit. Can they obtain that number of passengers if they reduce the fare for executives? yes

5. To make a profit, Airways North needs at least 2,750 passengers to use its new service each month. Using only the categories represented in the poll, should the new service be started? yes

6. How many passengers will the airline have if it reduces the fare?

not enough information

You are going to toss a penny and spin the spinner at the right.

1. Draw a tree diagram to show the possible outcomes.

2. Write the possible outcomes.

   H10, H20, H30, H40, T10, T20, T30, T40

3. How many possible outcomes are there? 8

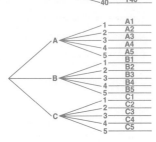

4. Is the number of possible outcomes equal to 2 · 4? yes

Gym lockers are identified by the use of a letter (A, B, or C) and a number (1, 2, 3, 4, 5).

5. Draw a tree diagram to show the sample space.

6. Write the possible outcomes.

   A1, A2, A3, A4, A5, B1, B2, B3, B4, B5, C1, C2, C3, C4, C5

7. How many possible outcomes are there? 15

8. Write a multiplication sentence for the number of possible outcomes.

   3 · 5 = 15

Solve.

9. Edgar is going to the sporting-goods store. He can take the bus, ride his bicycle, or walk. He can use Elm Street, Maple Boulevard, or Oak Avenue. How many different ways can Edgar get to the sporting-goods store?

   9 ways

10. A football stadium seats 25,000. Tickets are identified using a letter of the alphabet (A to Z) followed by a 3-digit number (0 to 9 in each place). Which is greater—the number of seats or the number of tickets? how much greater?

   number of tickets; 1,000

Write the number of permutations.

1. $_7P_2$ 42
2. $_5P_4$ 120
3. $_9P_6$ 60,480
4. $_8P_3$ 336
5. $_{10}P_2$ 90
6. $_6P_3$ 120
7. $_{12}P_5$ 95,040
8. $_{20}P_4$ 116,280
9. $_{15}P_6$ 3,603,600
10. $_{17}P_3$ 4,080
11. $_{100}P_2$ 9,900
12. $_{40}P_5$ 78,960,960

13. Evaluate 10! 3,628,800

Find the factorial.

14. 3! + 3! 12
15. 8! ÷ 5! 336
16. 4 × 4! 96
17. 2! × 7! 10,080
18. 9! + 6! 363,600
19. 21! ÷ 18! 7,980
20. 3 × 5! 360
21. 7! ÷ 4 1,260
22. 10! ÷ 5! 30,240

Write *true* or *false*.

23. 9 × 8! = 9! true
24. 64! ÷ 63! = 64 true
25. 3! + 5! = 8! false
26. 47! ÷ 47 = 46! true
27. 5! × 4! = 20! false
28. 10! ÷ 7! = 720 true

Solve.

29. Peter Possible has 25 different books on his shelf. In how many ways can he pick 3 books? 13,800 ways

30. Mary Maybe has 16 different bottles of perfume. In how many ways can she arrange them 5 at a time? 524,160 ways

31. In how many different ways can 8 people line up in front of a movie box office? 40,320 ways

32. In how many ways can 7 photographs be hung in a horizontal line? 5,040 ways

CLASSWORK HOMEWORK | Numbers of Permutations and Combinations

Write the number of combinations.

1. $_5C_2$ 10

2. $_7C_4$ 35

3. $_4C_3$ 4

4. $_8C_5$ 56

5. $_6C_3$ 20

6. $_9C_5$ 126

7. $_7C_3$ 35

8. $_8C_7$ 8

9. $_{10}C_5$ 252

10. $_{11}C_8$ 165

11. $_{12}C_7$ 792

12. $_{14}C_{13}$ 14

Write *permutation* or *combination*.

13. In how many ways can you arrange 5 letters 3 at a time? — permutation

14. How many committees of 4 students can be made from 16 students? — combination

15. How many bunches of 5 flowers can be made from 14 flowers? — combination

16. In how many ways can 5 students be seated in 5 chairs? — permutation

17. How many different 4-digit numbers can be made from the digits 1, 2, 6, 8, 9? — permutation

18. How many teams of 8 players can be formed from 20 players? — combination

19. Write the $_5C_2$ combinations of the set A, B, C, D, E.
AB, AC, AD, AE, BC, BD, BE, CD, CE, DE

Solve.

20. Richard has a penny, a nickel, a dime, a quarter, and a half-dollar. How many different amounts can he leave as a tip if he wants to use exactly two coins?
10 amounts

21. Julie has 9 books. In how many different ways can she choose 3 books to read? 84 ways

22. The Golden Happiness Store sells 7 different brands of persimmon juice. In how many different ways can Keiji buy 2 brands? 21 ways

23. There are 10 people waiting to play tennis. How many different pairs can be selected for playing singles? 45 pairs

Use with pages 332–333.   Student Handbook **H137**

CLASSWORK HOMEWORK | Probability

The following symbols are written on a set of cards.

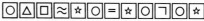

The cards are shuffled and placed facedown in a stack. After a card is drawn from the stack at random, it is returned to the stack and the cards are shuffled and placed facedown again.

1. What is the probability of drawing a ≈ ? (Express as a fraction.) $\frac{1}{12}$

2. What is the probability of drawing a ◯ ? (Express as a percentage to the nearest tenth.) $33.\bar{3}$

3. What is the probability of drawing any of the following symbols: ☆ , ◯ , = ? (Express as a ratio.) 2:3

4. Drawing a Z has a probability of zero. What is the term for such an event? impossible

5. Drawing a symbol has the probability of one. What term applies to this event? certain

Write the fraction for each probability.

6. P(△) $\frac{1}{12}$

7. P(not ⌐) $\frac{11}{12}$

8. P(= or ☆) $\frac{1}{3}$

9. P( ) 0

10. P(◯ or not ◯) 1

11. P(□ or ◠) $\frac{1}{12}$

Solve.

12. You toss a number cube numbered 1 to 6. If it lands on a 1 or a 6, you win. What is the probability that you will win? $\frac{1}{3}$

13. A spinner has 8 equal sections, numbered 1, 3, 4, 5, 5, 6, 7, 7. What is the probability that you will spin an even number? $\frac{1}{4}$

14. Using the same spinner as above, what is the probability you will spin a prime number greater than 2? $\frac{5}{8}$

H138 Student Handbook   Use with pages 334–335.

CLASSWORK HOMEWORK | Independent Events

A coin is tossed and the spinner at the right is spun. Write each probability as a fraction.

blue purple
red   green
yellow

1. P(green, heads) $\frac{1}{10}$

2. P(not red, tails) $\frac{2}{5}$

3. P(blue, tails) $\frac{1}{10}$

4. P(orange, heads) 0

5. P(yellow, heads) $\frac{1}{10}$

6. P(not purple, heads) $\frac{2}{5}$

A number cube with faces 1, 2, 3, 4, 5, 6 is rolled three times. Answer the following questions about these events and express your answers as fractions.

7. What is the probability an even number will come up each time? $\frac{1}{8}$

8. What is the probability a number less than 5 will come up each time? $\frac{8}{27}$

9. What is the probability that all three rolls will be different? $\frac{5}{9}$

10. What is the probability that the sum of the three rolls will be 20? 0

Three coins are tossed. Answer the following questions about these events and express your answers as fractions.

11. What is the probability that all heads show? $\frac{1}{8}$

12. What is the probability that no heads show? $\frac{1}{8}$

13. What is the probability of getting heads only on the middle toss? $\frac{1}{8}$

14. What is the probability of getting exactly two heads or exactly two tails? (HINT: Consider favorable outcomes and total number of outcomes.) $\frac{1}{2}$

Use with pages 336–337.   Student Handbook **H139**

CLASSWORK HOMEWORK | Selecting Notation

Write the letter of the correct answer.

1. There are 6 debating teams in a league. Each team has to debate 3 other teams. How many debates have to be held? Each dot represents a team, and each line segment represents a debate held.

a.   **b.**   **c.**   **d.**

6 debates   15 debates   9 debates   8 debates

2. How many combinations of quarts and pints can you use to make 2 gallons? The first number of the ordered pair represents the number of quarts, and the second number represents the number of pints.

a. (1,6) (2,4) (3,2) (2,2)

b. (6,4) (4,8) (2,12)

c. (7,2) (6,4) (5,6) (4,8) (3,10) (2,12) (1,14)

Solve.

3. There are 5 members of a chess club. Can a tournament be arranged so that each member plays 3 other members one game each? no

4. If there are 8 members of a chess club, how many games would be played if each member played 3 other members one game each? 12

5. Darlene has a container that holds 5 lb flour and a container that holds 2 lb flour. She needs 1 lb of flour for a recipe. How can she use the containers to measure out 1 lb? Use ordered pairs. (5,0) (3,2) (3,0) (1,2) (1,0)

6. How many combinations of quarters and dimes can you use to equal $1.80? 3

H140 Student Handbook   Use with pages 338–339.

519

CLASSWORK HOMEWORK | Dependent Event

Pick a card. Do not replace it. Pick a second card. Write each probability as a fraction.

| B | A | S | E |

| B | A | L | L |

1. P(B, then A) $\frac{1}{14}$　　2. P(B, then E) $\frac{1}{28}$　　3. P(S, then E) $\frac{1}{56}$

4. P(A, then A) $\frac{1}{28}$　　5. P(A, then not A) $\frac{3}{14}$　　6. P(S, then S) 0

The numbers 1 through 10 are written on pieces of paper. The papers are put into a hat and drawn out one by one. Answer the following questions about these events and express your answers as fractions.

7. What is the probability that the first two numbers are even? $\frac{2}{9}$

8. What is the probability that the first two numbers are multiples of 3? $\frac{1}{15}$

9. What is the probability that the first two numbers are 1 and 2, in that order? $\frac{1}{90}$

10. What is the probability that the first three numbers are all different? 1

Five kittens and four puppies are in a kennel together. One animal at a time goes through the pet door. Answer the following questions about these events and express your answers as fractions.

11. What is the probability that the first pet through the door will be a puppy? $\frac{4}{9}$

12. What is the probability that the first two will be puppies? $\frac{1}{6}$

13. What is the probability that the first two will be kittens? $\frac{5}{18}$

14. What is the probability that the first three will be puppies? $\frac{1}{21}$

15. What is the probability that the first three animals will be different? 0

Use with pages 340–341.　　Student Handbook **H141**

CLASSWORK HOMEWORK | Prediction

Mrs. Andersen's hens produced 630 white eggs and 210 brown eggs last week. Make your way from the front door of the chicken coop, around the nests and roosts, to the back door by answering the questions. Each answer will tell you which area of the coop to move to next. Copy the floor plan of the chicken coop. On your paper, draw a line from area to area to show your progress.

1. If 100 eggs are produced one day, how many would you predict will be brown? 25

2. If 104 eggs are produced, predict how many will be brown. 26

3. If 28 eggs are produced, predict how many will be white. 21

4. If 5 brown eggs are produced, predict how many white eggs will be produced. 15

5. If 12 eggs are produced, predict how many will be white. 9

6. How many white eggs are produced for every brown egg? 3

7. If 16 eggs are produced, predict how many will not be white. 4

8. If 33 white eggs are produced, how many brown eggs are likely to be produced? 11

9. How many eggs should be produced to get 9 that are white? 12

10. How many white eggs would you expect if 8 eggs are produced? 6

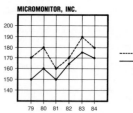
Chicken Coop

H142　Student Handbook　　Use with pages 342–343.

CLASSWORK HOMEWORK | Interpreting a Graph

The graphs below show the steel production of the United States and Japan between the years 1945 and 1970.

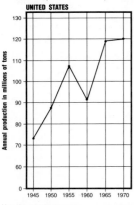

Use the graphs to solve.

1. Which country produced the most steel in 1970? the United States

2. Which country increased its steel production by the greatest tonnage between 1960 and 1965? the United States

3. Which country increased its steel production by the greatest tonnage between 1955 and 1965? Japan

4. In which years did Japan's steel production drop? none

5. By about how much did Japan's steel production increase in 1960 beyond its production in 1955? about twice

6. Did the rate of steel production in the United States double between 1945 and 1970? no

7. How did Japan's 1970 steel production compare with that of the United States in 1960? It was the same.

8. Which country would you expect to have produced more steel in 1980 if both followed the trends plotted in the graphs? Japan

Use after pages 344–345.　　Student Handbook **H143**

CLASSWORK HOMEWORK | Interpreting a Graph

Dobbs Industries started two new companies, Waveform, Inc., and Micromonitor, Inc. Dobbs invested the same amount of money in each company, but did not invest any further amounts after the two companies started operations in January 1979. The graphs below show the performance of each company from 1979 to 1984.

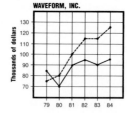

- - - - - Total Income
——— Total Expenses

1. Which company made the most profit in 1983? Waveform, Inc.

2. In which year did both companies make the same amount of profit? 1981

3. Which company performed better between the years 1979 and 1981? Micromonitor, Inc.

4. If Dobbs Industries had invested $50,000 in each company, in which year would the accumulated profits of Waveform, Inc., have been enough to repay Dobbs' investment in Waveform? 1983

5. In which year could Micromonitor, Inc., repay Dobbs' investment in Micromonitor? 1981

6. If Dobbs Industries expected yearly interest of 5% on its investment, in which year could Micromonitor repay Dobbs Industries? 1983

H144　Student Handbook　　Use after pages 344–345.

CLASSWORK HOMEWORK Basic Ideas

Draw each of the following.

1. line AB

2. ray DG

3. line segment SV

4. point R on line EF

5. $\overline{AE}$ with midpoint T

6. $\overleftrightarrow{SU}$

7. $\overleftrightarrow{MN}$

8. $\overleftrightarrow{RT}$ and $\overleftrightarrow{CN}$ intersecting at S

9. parallel line segments GK and QZ

10. $\overline{HJ}$ congruent to $\overline{IL}$

Use with pages 354–355.

Student Handbook **H145**

CLASSWORK HOMEWORK Angles and Angle Measure

Classify each angle by writing *acute, right, obtuse,* or *straight.*

1. ∠ABC	obtuse	**2.** an angle of 27°	acute
3. ∠CBD	acute	**4.** an angle of 180°	straight
5. ∠ABD	straight	**6.** an angle of 165°	obtuse
7. ∠DBE	right	**8.** an angle of 42°	acute
9. ∠CBE	obtuse	**10.** an angle of 90°	right
11. ∠ABE	right	**12.** an angle of 98°	obtuse

13. Which two angles are complementary? ∠H and ∠I

14. Which two angles are supplementary? ∠F and ∠G

Use a protractor to measure the angles.

15. **16.** **17.**

45°   30°   125°

H146 Student Handbook

Use with pages 356–357.

CLASSWORK HOMEWORK Congruent Line Segments and Angles

Use a compass and a straightedge to construct a line segment that is congruent to each line segment below.

1. A———B   A———B

2. C————D   C————D

3. E——F   E——F

4. G————————H   G————————H

5. I—————J   I—————J

Use a compass and a straightedge to construct an angle that is congruent to each angle below.

6.

7.

8.

9.

10.

Use with pages 358–359.

Student Handbook **H147**

CLASSWORK HOMEWORK Bisecting Line Segments and Angles

Copy each line segment. Then use a compass and a straightedge to construct the bisector of each line segment.

1.   **2.**

3.   **4.**

5.   **6.**

Copy each angle. Then construct the bisector of each angle.

7.   **8.**

9.   **10.**

11.   **12.**

H148 Student Handbook

Use with pages 360–361.

CLASSWORK HOMEWORK | Working Backward

Work backward. Write the letter of the correct answer.

1. Alex is painting a house. He uses $\frac{1}{3}$ of the paint he bought on the dining room. He uses twice as much on the living room as on the kitchen, where he uses $1\frac{1}{2}$ gallons. He has $1\frac{1}{2}$ gallons of paint left. How much paint did Alex buy?

   a. 12 gallons
   b. 16 gallons
   c. 9 gallons (circled)

2. Naomi is cleaning out a storeroom at the paint shop. She puts $\frac{1}{2}$ the paint on display in the shop and takes $\frac{1}{2}$ of what is left to the basement. Although she takes $\frac{3}{4}$ of the remaining paint home, there are still 7 gallons left in the storeroom. How much paint was in the storeroom before she cleaned it?

   a. 168 gallons
   b. 112 gallons (circled)
   c. 56 gallons

Solve.

3. It took Nancy and Ramon 3 weeks to paint a house in their spare time. During the second week, they used $3\frac{1}{2}$ fewer gallons of paint than they used in the first week. In the third week, they used 13 gallons, which was twice as many as the number of gallons used in the second week. How much paint did they use?

   $29\frac{1}{2}$ gallons

4. Toku follows a budget to buy supplies to paint his room. He spends $\frac{1}{2}$ of his budget on a roller, a tray, and tape. He spends $12.27 on paint, and of the remaining money, he spends $\frac{2}{3}$ on a trim brush, which costs $3.82. How much money has he budgeted? $36.00

5. Susan wants to use blue, yellow, green, and pink paint to decorate her house. She needs 3 times as much blue paint as yellow paint and $\frac{1}{2}$ as much yellow paint as green paint. She needs $3\frac{1}{4}$ gallons of pink paint, which is $\frac{3}{4}$ of a gallon more than the green paint she needs. How much paint does Susan need in all?

   $10\frac{3}{4}$ gallons

6. Colleen's family plans to paint the windows of their house. Her father will paint twice as many windows as her mother, and Colleen and her 2 brothers will paint an equal number of the rest of the windows. Colleen decides to do her own share and her mother's share and paints 7 windows, which is one less than her father's share. How many windows are there? 21 windows

---

CLASSWORK HOMEWORK | Working Backward

Work backward. Write the letter of the correct answer.

1. In the first act of a play, all the actors were onstage. The second act opened with $\frac{1}{2}$ the actors onstage, and then 5 actors left. After that, $\frac{1}{2}$ the remaining actors left, and 4 actors remained onstage. How many actors were onstage in the first act?

   a. 36
   b. 26 (circled)
   c. 28

Solve.

2. Sam bought 8 of his friends tickets for a play. Each ticket cost $8.70. He also bought 2 books of plays, each costing $4.45. He spent exactly $\frac{1}{2}$ the money he had left for a record that cost $6.20. How much money did Sam originally have?

   a. $90.90 (circled)
   b. $84.70
   c. $67.10

3. In one scene of a play, 23 lines were spoken by the lead actor. The rest of the lines were spoken by Roger and Francis. Francis spoke twice as many lines as Roger, who had 9 lines. How many lines were spoken in the scene? 50 lines

4. Rufus is in charge of lighting a play. Half the lights he uses are white. Of the remaining lights, $\frac{1}{3}$ have red filters, and 4 have blue filters. The 10 lights left have yellow filters. How many lights does Rufus use for the play? 42 lights

5. Sally took money from her bank account to go out of town for an audition. She spent $54.00 for a round-trip bus ticket and $\frac{1}{2}$ of the remaining money for her hotel bill. She spent $7.90 for food and arrived home with $15.10. How much money did Sally take from her bank account? $100.00

6. Act I of a play lasts $\frac{2}{3}$ the time of the whole play. There is a 15-minute intermission. In Act II, Jack's speech takes up $\frac{1}{2}$ the time, and the rest is divided equally between speeches made by Rosa and Zoe. Zoe talks for 6 minutes, and the play ends at 8:17 P.M. When did the play begin? 6:50 P.M.

7. At intermission, Xavier sold refreshments. Of the items he had, $\frac{1}{5}$ were granola bars and $\frac{1}{2}$ the remaining items were containers of popcorn. The rest were divided equally among apples, rice cakes, and containers of yogurt. Xavier sold the 8 apples he had. How many items did he originally have?

   60 items

8. Information about a play took up $\frac{1}{3}$ of the pages in the program. Information about the actors took up $\frac{1}{4}$ of the remaining pages. Information about the director, the producer, and the designer took up 2 pages, the same number of pages devoted to the actors. How many pages were there in the program?

   12 pages

CLASSWORK HOMEWORK | Perpendicular and Parallel Lines

In the given figure, $\overleftrightarrow{a} \parallel \overleftrightarrow{b}$. Write *vertical*, *adjacent*, *corresponding*, or *alternate interior* to identify each pair of angles.

1. ∠2 and ∠7   vertical
2. ∠5 and ∠6   adjacent
3. ∠1 and ∠8   corresponding
4. ∠2 and ∠3   alternate interior

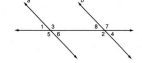

Using the same figure, write *congruent* or *supplementary* to name each pair of angles.

5. ∠2 and ∠3   congruent
6. ∠2 and ∠8   supplementary
7. ∠5 and ∠8   supplementary
8. ∠6 and ∠7   supplementary
9. ∠2 and ∠7   congruent
10. ∠1 and ∠6   congruent
11. ∠3 and ∠4   supplementary
12. ∠4 and ∠5   supplementary

In the figure at right, $\overline{MN} \parallel \overline{OP}$. Write *true* if the angles are congruent and *false* if they are not congruent.

13. ∠QRP ≅ ∠MQR   true
14. ∠SQN ≅ ∠ORT   true
15. ∠MQS ≅ ∠ORT   false
16. ∠ORT ≅ ∠QRO   false

Use the figure at right to find the measure of each angle. In the figure, $\overleftrightarrow{c} \parallel \overleftrightarrow{d}$ and m∠5 = 155°.

17. m∠1   25°
18. m∠4   25°
19. m∠7   155°
20. m∠6   25°

Solve.

21. Draw a line. Construct a line parallel to it. Then construct a line that is perpendicular to the parallel lines.

CLASSWORK HOMEWORK | Classifying Triangles

Write *acute*, *obtuse*, or *right*; and *equilateral*, *scalene*, or *isosceles* to classify each triangle.

1.    scalene   acute
2.    isosceles   obtuse
3.    scalene   acute

Write the measure of the third angle of each triangle.

4. 70°
5. 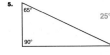 25°
6. 60°
7. 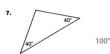 100°

8. triangle with two angles of 42°   96°
9. triangle with an angle of 60° and one of 110°   10°

CLASSWORK HOMEWORK | Polygons

Write the name of the polygon. Then write *regular* or *irregular* for each.

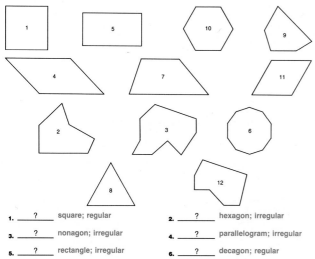

1. ___?___ square; regular
2. ___?___ hexagon; irregular
3. ___?___ nonagon; irregular
4. ___?___ parallelogram; irregular
5. ___?___ rectangle; irregular
6. ___?___ decagon; regular
7. ___?___ trapezoid; irregular
8. ___?___ triangle; regular
9. ___?___ pentagon; irregular
10. ___?___ hexagon; regular
11. ___?___ rhombus; irregular
12. ___?___ heptagon; irregular

13. What is the sum of the interior angles of a polygon with six sides? 720°

14. What is the sum of the interior angles of a polygon with nine sides? 1,260°

Use with pages 368–369. | Student Handbook **H153**

CLASSWORK HOMEWORK | Choosing a Strategy or Method

Estimation	Making a Table to Find a Pattern	Using a Formula
Using a Graph	Writing an Equation	Making an Organized List
Choosing the Operation	Interpreting the Quotient and the	Using a Sample
Solving Multi-step Problems	Remainder	
Guessing and Checking		

Write the strategy or method you choose. Then solve.
Strategies and methods will vary.

1. Colin has a total of 700 coins in his collection. How many of them are Italian?
   using a graph; 84 coins

2. How many more coins are French than Mexican?
   solving multi-step problems; 21 coins

3. If Colin trades 20 United States coins for 16 British coins, will he have more or fewer British coins than United States coins in his collection?
   solving multi-step problems;
   more British coins

COLIN'S COIN COLLECTION
- 15% Mexican
- 30% United States
- 18% French
- 12% Italian
- 25% British

4. There are 14 cars in a parking lot. When 5 cars leave, the lot is $\frac{1}{8}$ full. How many cars can the parking lot hold?
   writing an equation; 72 cars

5. A boat travels across a lake at an average speed of $2\frac{1}{2}$ miles per hour. The lake is 440 yards wide. Does it take more than 5 minutes for the boat to cross the lake?
   using a formula; yes

6. A boy is fishing with a 6-foot piece of string. If the boy stretches his arm 14 inches down a bank that is $2\frac{1}{2}$ feet above the water, could the string reach 5 feet underwater?
   estimation; no

7. There are 13 elm trees and twice as many oak trees in a park. One third of the trees in the park are oak trees. How many trees are there in the park?
   writing an equation; 78 trees

H154 Student Handbook | Use after pages 370–371.

CLASSWORK HOMEWORK | Choosing a Strategy or Method

Estimation	Guessing and Checking	Using a Sample
Using a Graph	Writing an Equation	
Choosing the Operation	Using a Formula	

Write the strategy or method you choose. Then solve. For Exercises 1–3, refer to the graph.
Strategies and methods will vary.

1. How much money did Alicia earn during the summer vacation?
   using a graph; $500

2. About how much money did all five students earn during the summer vacation?
   estimation; about $3,800

3. About what was the average amount earned by the students during the summer vacation?
   choosing the operation; about $760

TOTAL EARNINGS OF STUDENTS DURING THE SUMMER VACATION

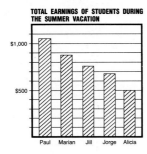

Paul   Marian   Jill   Jorge   Alicia

SCHOOL PLAY POLL RESULTS FOR 300 STUDENTS

Grade	Grade 6	Grade 7	Grade 8
Percent of total students in school	34%	36%	30%
Approve	40 students	45 students	42 students
Disapprove	35 students	40 students	48 students
Undecided	25 students	15 students	10 students

4. There are 2,000 students in the school. What percent of the students were questioned?
   writing an equation; 15%

5. According to the poll, how many eighth-grade students in the total population approve of the play?
   writing an equation; 252 students

6. In the poll, do more students approve or disapprove of the play? using a sample; approve

Use after pages 370–371. | Student Handbook **H155**

CLASSWORK HOMEWORK | Circles

Use circle A to answer questions 1–6.

1. Name the center of the circle. A
2. Name a radius of the circle. $\overline{AB}$ or $\overline{AC}$ or $\overline{AE}$
3. Name a chord. $\overline{CD}$
4. Name a diameter of the circle. $\overline{BE}$
5. Name a central angle. ∠EAC or ∠CAB
6. Name an arc. $\overarc{BC}$ or $\overarc{BD}$ or $\overarc{BE}$ or $\overarc{CD}$ or $\overarc{CE}$ or $\overarc{DE}$

Circle A

Use circle P to answer questions 7–12.

7. Name a diameter of the circle. $\overline{RS}$
8. Name two radii of the circle. Two of: $\overline{AP}$, $\overline{PR}$, $\overline{PS}$, $\overline{PW}$
9. Name two arcs.
   Two of: $\overarc{AN}$, $\overarc{AS}$, $\overarc{AW}$, $\overarc{AR}$, $\overarc{NS}$, $\overarc{NW}$, $\overarc{NR}$, $\overarc{SW}$, $\overarc{SR}$, $\overarc{WR}$
10. Name a chord. $\overline{AN}$ or $\overline{SW}$
11. Name two central angles.
    Two of: ∠APR, ∠APW, ∠APS, ∠RPW, ∠WPS
12. Name the center of the circle. P

Circle P

13. If a circle has a radius of 4 inches, what is its diameter?
    8 in.

14. If a circle has a diameter of 19 cm, what is its radius?
    9.5 cm

H156 Student Handbook | Use with pages 372–373.

△ABC ≅ △XYZ. △DEF ≅ △WPQ. Write the measure of the angle or the side.

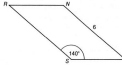

1. ∠BAC   45°
2. ∠XYZ   95°
3. $\overline{DE}$ 64
4. $\overline{QP}$ 28
5. $\overline{DF}$ 56
6. ∠YZX   40°

LVBT ≅ NJSR. Write the measure of the angle or the side.

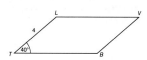

7. $\overline{LV}$ 6
8. ∠RNJ   140°
9. ∠TLV   140°
10. ∠SRN   40°
11. $\overline{RN}$ 4
12. $\overline{SJ}$ 4
13. ∠SJN   40°
14. $\overline{RS}$ 6

1. Use SAS congruence to construct a triangle congruent to △XYZ. (Copy sides $\overline{XZ}$, $\overline{YZ}$, and ∠Z.)

2. Use SSS congruence to construct a triangle congruent to △QRS.

3. Use ASA congruence to construct a triangle congruent to △XYZ. (Copy ∠X, ∠Z, and $\overline{XZ}$.)

4. Use SAS congruence to construct a triangle congruent to △QRS. (Copy sides $\overline{QR}$, $\overline{RS}$, and ∠R.)

Write the letter of the picture that can help you solve each problem.

1. A building has 3 identical floors. Each floor has a large window. The distance from the ground to the bottom of the lowest window is 3 feet, and the distance from the top of the building to the bottom of the highest window is 7 feet. How tall is the building? c

2. A rectangular plot of land contains 3 square flower beds. Each flower bed is 7 feet long, and there is a border of 3 feet between each flower bed and the perimeter of the plot. There is also a border of 3 feet between the flower beds. How long is the plot of land? a

Draw a picture on a separate piece of paper to help you find each solution.

3. The fence around a house measuring 30 feet by 22 feet was built a distance of 12 feet from the outside of the house. How long is the fence? 200 feet

4. There are three volumes of an encyclopedia on a shelf. Each volume has 500 pages. The two covers of each volume are each 1.5 millimeters thick, and each section of 100 pages measures 18 millimeters. What is the distance between the center pages of the two outside volumes?
186 millimeters

5. A floor is covered with square tiles of equal size. The fifth row of tiles from the north end of the room is also the seventh row from the south end of the room. A tile in the middle of the fifth row from the south end has 8 tiles on each side of it. How many tiles are there? 187 tiles

6. There are 4 boxes of equal height stacked in a room. The distance from the ceiling to the bottom of the top box is 3 feet 6 inches, and the distance from the ceiling to the bottom of the second-highest box is 5 feet. How high is the room? 8 feet

a.

b.

c.

△LDR ~ △KCG. Write the measure of the angle or the side.

1. ∠CKG   49°
2. $\overline{CK}$ 15
3. ∠CGK   72°
4. $\overline{KG}$ $13\frac{1}{2}$

Polygon AZETMHS ~ polygon JBFIPQN. Write the measure of the angle or the side.

5. ∠JBF   117°
6. $\overline{FI}$ $4\frac{1}{4}$
7. $\overline{PI}$ 3
8. ∠NJB   148°
9. ∠FIP   119°
10. $\overline{BF}$ 3
11. ∠BFI   136°
12. $\overline{QP}$ $4\frac{3}{4}$
13. $\overline{NQ}$ $4\frac{1}{2}$
14. ∠QNJ   90°
15. ∠QPI   137°
16. $\overline{NJ}$ 2

524

Symmetry and Reflections

Use the diagrams to answer the questions.

1. Is $\overline{DK}$ a line of symmetry of the hexagon? yes

2. Is $\overline{JL}$ a line of symmetry of the hexagon? yes

3. Is $\overline{RZ}$ a line of symmetry of the triangle? no

4. Is $\overline{NQ}$ a line of symmetry of the triangle? no

5. Is $\overline{GP}$ a line of symmetry of the polygon? no

6. Is $\overline{UI}$ a line of symmetry of the polygon? yes

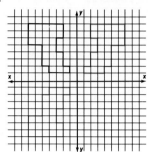

Copy the polygon on a real-number plane. Then draw a reflection of the polygon about the *x*-axis and about the *y*-axis.

7.

8. List the coordinates of the vertices of both reflections.

($^-$1,$^-$1), ($^-$4,$^-$1), ($^-$4,$^-$2)   (1,1), (4,1), (4,2)

($^-$5,$^-$2), ($^-$5,$^-$5), ($^-$7,$^-$5)   (5,2), (5,5), (7,5)

($^-$7,$^-$8), ($^-$2,$^-$8), ($^-$2,$^-$6)   (7,8), (2,8), (2,6)

($^-$3,$^-$6), ($^-$3,$^-$4), ($^-$2,$^-$4)   (3,6), (3,4), (2,4)

($^-$2,$^-$2), ($^-$1,$^-$2)   (2,2), (1,2)

Translations and Rotations

Copy the truck on a real-number plane. Then drive the truck along Route 66 by following the instructions and drawing a new truck for each.

1. Translate the figure 4 units to the right and 5 units down.

2. Rotate the figure around *A* so that *B* is at point ($^-$10,9).

3. Translate the figure 4 units to the right and 8 units down.

4. Rotate the figure around point ($^-$4,$^-$1) so that *A* is at point ($^-$10,$^-$3).

5. Translate the figure 11 units to the right and 5 units down.

6. Translate the figure 7 units to the right and 6 units down.

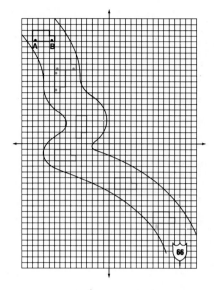

Using Outside Sources Including the Infobank

The chart below shows the area and the population of the region of Connacht in the Republic of Ireland and the area and population of the Republic of Ireland itself.

AREA AND POPULATION OF CONNACHT, REPUBLIC OF IRELAND

Counties	Area (square miles)	1966 population	1971 population
Galway	2,293	148,000	149,000
Leitrim	589	31,000	28,000
Mayo	2,084	116,000	110,000
Roscommon	951	56,000	54,000
Sligo	693	51,000	50,000

AREA AND POPULATION OF THE REPUBLIC OF IRELAND

27,137 square miles	2,884,000	2,978,000

Do you need the chart to answer each question? Write *yes* or *no*.

1. At the end of the nineteenth century, 25% of Ireland's population lived in urban areas. In 1971, 52% lived in urban areas. What was the percent of increase? no

2. If 60% of the population of Sligo was younger than 45 in 1966, how many people in Sligo were older than 45 in 1966? yes

Solve. Use the chart to obtain additional information.

3. A farm in Leitrim covers 117.8 square miles. What percent of the county does the farm cover? 20%

4. In which county was the percent of decrease in the population the greatest between 1966 and 1971? Leitrim

5. What was the average population per square mile in Roscommon in 1971? Round to the nearest whole number. 57 people per mi²

6. What percent (to the nearest whole number) of the population of the Republic of Ireland lived in the Connacht region in 1971? 13%

7. Between 1966 and 1971, was the percent of increase in the population of Galway greater or smaller than the percent of increase in the total population of the Republic of Ireland? smaller

8. If a cartography company had mapped 80% of the Connacht region, how many square miles of the province would it still have to map to complete a map of Connacht? 1,322 mi²

Perimeter

Write the perimeter of each polygon.

1.
8 mm
7.8 mm
7 mm
22.8 mm

2.
5.2 m
6.5 m
2.8 m
8.6 m
23.1 m

3.
5.1 m
7.5 m
25.2 m

4.
3.2 cm
6.5 cm
4.8 cm
6.8 cm
5.3 cm
26.6 cm

5.
11.1 m
6 m
5.9 m
23 m

6.
4.6 m
27.6 m

Write the perimeter of each rectangle.

7. l = 19 cm w = 23 cm 84 cm

8. l = 47.6 m w = 5.4 m 106 m

9. l = 31.2 cm w = 47.1 cm 156.6 cm

10. l = 23.2 cm w = 8.6 cm 63.6 cm

11. l = 14.5 cm w = 9.1 cm 47.2 cm

12. l = 53.1 cm w = 46 cm 198.2 cm

Write the perimeter of each square.

13. s = 19.6 yd 78.4 yd

14. s = $27\frac{1}{4}$ ft 109 ft

15. s = 3.6 mi 14.4 mi

16. s = 45 in. 180 in.

17. s = 0.9 mi 3.6 mi

18. s = $20\frac{1}{3}$ yd $81\frac{1}{3}$ yd

CLASSWORK HOMEWORK The Pythagorean Rule

Write the measure of the missing side of each triangle.

1.
12 m, 5 m
13 m

2.
29 in., 21 in.
20 in.

3.
17 cm, 15 cm
8 cm

4. 60 ft, 80 ft
100 ft

5. 64 mm, 48 mm
80 mm

6. 55 yd, 44 yd
33 yd

7. a right triangle with legs of 11 in. and 60 in. 61 in.

8. a right triangle with a leg of 7 cm and a hypotenuse of 25 cm 24 cm

Solve.

9. A string of buoys 100-m long stretches diagonally across a river. The distance from one end of the string to a point directly opposite the other end is 28 m. How wide is the river? 96 m

28 m, 100 m

10. A ladder is leaning against a wall. Its bottom legs are 9 feet from the wall, and its top legs touch the wall 12 feet from the ground. How long is the ladder? 15 ft

CLASSWORK HOMEWORK Trigonometric Ratios

Use the table of trigonometric ratios on pages 402–403 of your text to find the value.

1. tan 44° 0.966
2. tan 32° 0.625
3. sin 19° 0.326
4. sin 24° 0.407
5. cos 31° 0.857
6. tan 36° 0.727
7. cos 20° 0.940
8. cos 37° 0.799
9. sin 31° 0.515
10. tan ∠A = 0.625 ∠A = __?__ 32°
11. sin ∠A = 0.454 ∠A = __?__ 27°
12. cos ∠A = 0.707 ∠A = __?__ 45°
13. cos ∠A = 0.940 ∠A = __?__ 20°
14. sin ∠A = 0.407 ∠A = __?__ 24°
15. tan ∠A = 0.675 ∠A = __?__ 34°

Write the measure of side x. Use the tables of trigonometric ratios on pages 402 and 403 of your text. Round to the nearest tenth.

16.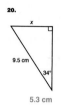
39°, 8 m, x
6.5 m

17.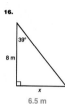
x, 26°, 88 cm
97.9 cm

18.
53°, 7.5 ft, x
9.4 ft

19.
x, 53°, 5.9 in.
9.8 in.

20.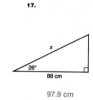
x, 9.5 cm, 34°
5.3 cm

21.
x, 64°, 3.5 m
7.2 m

CLASSWORK HOMEWORK Circumference of a Circle

Write the circumference of each circle. Use 3.14 for π and round to the nearest tenth.

1. d = 27 mm
84.8 mm

2. r = 40 cm
251.2 cm

3. r = 8.6 m
54.0 m

4. d = 15 cm
47.1 cm

5. r = 9 km
56.5 km

6. d = 35 cm
109.9 cm

7. r = 210 m
1,318.8 m

8. d = 50 mm
157 mm

Write the circumference of each circle. Use $\frac{22}{7}$ for π.

9. r = 20 ft
$125\frac{5}{7}$ ft

10. d = $11\frac{1}{4}$ in.
$35\frac{5}{14}$ in.

11. d = 21 mi
66 mi

12. r = $1\frac{3}{4}$
11 yd

13. r = 6 yd
$37\frac{5}{7}$ yd

14. r = 50 in.
$314\frac{2}{7}$ in.

15. d = 14 ft
44 ft

16. d = 17 mi
$53\frac{3}{7}$ mi

Complete. Use 3.14 for π. Round to the nearest tenth.

17. C = 42.6 cm   d = __?__ 13.6 cm
18. C = 53.38 m   r = __?__ 8.5 m
19. C = 62.8 mm   d = __?__ 20 mm
20. C = 69.08 cm   r = __?__ 11 cm

Solve. Use 3.14 for π.

21. The radius of Sylvia's bicycle wheel is 31 centimeters. To the nearest tenth, how far does the wheel travel in 1 revolution? 194.7 cm

22. If Sylvia rides 10 kilometers, how many revolutions will the wheel make? Round to the nearest whole number.
5,136 revolutions

CLASSWORK HOMEWORK Solving Multistep Problems/Making a Plan

Write the missing steps. Then solve.

1. The author of a gardening book suggests that a gardener use $\frac{1}{3}$ lb of fertilizer per month for every 10-ft row of plants. Richard's garden has three 12-ft rows and eight 10-ft rows. Will a 5-lb bag of fertilizer be enough for one month?

Step 1: Find the number of feet of rows in the garden. 116 ft

Step 2: __?__ Find the number of pounds of fertilizer needed for a 1-ft row $\frac{1}{30}$ lb

Step 3: __?__ Find the number of pounds of fertilizer needed for the whole garden. About 3.5 lb; a 5-lb bag is enough.

2. Richard read that each foot of each row of snap-bean plants will produce $\frac{1}{2}$ lb of snap beans. Richard has room for 40 ft of bean plants. How much money can Richard expect to earn if he sells $\frac{1}{4}$ of his crop at $1.25 a pound?

Step 1: __?__ Find the number of pounds of beans 40 ft of plants will produce. 20 lb

Step 2: __?__ Find the number of pounds Richard will sell. 5 lb

Step 3: __?__ Find the amount of money Richard will earn. $6.25

Solve.

3. Young parsnip plants should be thinned so that they grow 4.5 in. apart from one another. Richard will plant two 12-ft rows of parsnips. How many plants will fit in this space? 64 plants

4. Richard is going to buy some young pepper plants at $2.29 per flat. (There are 4 plants to a flat.) He is going to plant the pepper plants $1\frac{1}{2}$ ft apart from one another in two 12-ft rows. How many flats will he need to buy, and how much will he pay for them?
He will have to purchase 4 flats; $9.16.

5. When a blueberry bush is between three and five years old, it will yield from 6 to 16 pints of blueberries. Richard plants 2 one-year-old blueberry bushes. What is the greatest amount of money he can earn from selling blueberries the next season at $1.69 per pint?
He will not earn anything—the plants will be too young.

6. A 10-ft row of cucumber plants yields 25 lb of cucumbers. A 15-ft row of turnip plants yields 15 lb. Cucumbers sell for $0.69/lb; turnips for $1.79/lb. Which crop will be more profitable when planted in two 12-ft rows?
The turnip crop will be more profitable.

CLASSWORK/HOMEWORK Area of Squares, Rectangles and Parallelograms

Write the area of each square.

1. $s = 14\frac{1}{2}$ ft $\quad$ 2. $s = 6$ yd $\quad$ 3. $s = 19$ mi $\quad$ 4. $s = 32$ in.

$210\frac{1}{4}$ ft^2 $\qquad$ 36 yd^2 $\qquad$ 361 mi^2 $\qquad$ 1,024 in.^{2}

5. $s = 25$ mi $\quad$ 6. $s = 6\frac{3}{4}$ in. $\quad$ 7. $s = 40$ yd $\quad$ 8. $s = 1$ ft

625 mi^2 $\qquad$ $45\frac{9}{16}$ in.^{2} $\qquad$ 1,600 yd^2 $\qquad$ 1 ft^2

Write the area of each rectangle.

9. $l = 50$ m, $w = 35$ m $\quad$ 1,750 m^2 $\quad$ 10. $l = 14.5$ cm, $w = 2.7$ cm $\quad$ 39.15 cm^2

11. $l = 0.4$ m, $w = 5.2$ m $\quad$ 2.08 m^2 $\quad$ 12. $l = 4$ mm, $w = 8$ mm $\quad$ 32 mm^2

13. $l = 81$ cm, $w = 99$ cm $\quad$ 8,019 cm^2 $\quad$ 14. $l = 8$ cm, $w = 1$ cm $\quad$ 8 cm^2

15. $l = 16.2$ m, $w = 2.8$ m $\quad$ 45.36 m^2 $\quad$ 16. $l = 0.6$ m, $w = 10$ m $\quad$ 6 m^2

Write the area of each parallelogram.

17. $b = 74$ in., $h = 6$ in $\quad$ 444 in.^{2} $\quad$ 18. $b = 46$ ft, $h = 33$ ft $\quad$ 1,518 ft^2

19. $b = 43$ ft, $h = 8$ ft $\quad$ 344 ft^2 $\quad$ 20. $b = 18$ in., $h = 17\frac{1}{2}$ in. $\quad$ 315 in.^{2}

21. $b = 5\frac{1}{2}$ mi, $h = \frac{3}{4}$ mi $\quad$ $4\frac{1}{8}$ mi^2 $\quad$ 22. $b = 7$ yd, $h = 33$ yd $\quad$ 231 yd^2

23. $b = 200$ in., $h = 47\frac{1}{2}$ in. $\quad$ 9,500 in.^{2} $\quad$ 24. $b = 22$ ft, $h = 15$ ft $\quad$ 330 ft^2

Solve.

25. How many 1-cm^2 tiles will Joseph need to cover a rectangular tabletop that is 55 cm long and 33 cm wide? 1,815 tiles

26. Rosetta used 9 m^2 of carpeting in her foyer. The room is rectangular, with a length of 3.6 m. What is the width of the foyer? 2.5 m

CLASSWORK/HOMEWORK Area of Triangles and Trapezoids

Write the area of each triangle.

1. 42 yd, 54 yd $\quad$ 2. 15.5 mm, 17.7 mm $\quad$ 3. 54 in., 58 in.

1,134 yd^2 $\qquad$ 137.175 mm^2 $\qquad$ 1,566 in.^{2}

4. $b = 13.1$ m, $h = 5.5$ m $\quad$ 36.025 m^2 $\quad$ 5. $b = 89$ km, $h = 29$ km $\quad$ 1,290.5 km^2

6. $b = 56$ ft, $h = 6$ ft $\quad$ 168 ft^2 $\quad$ 7. $b = 6.8$ cm, $h = 14.7$ cm $\quad$ 49.98 cm^2

Write the area of each trapezoid.

8. 11 cm, 9 cm, 4 cm $\quad$ 9. 2 in., 3 in., 8 in. $\quad$ 10. 7.9 mm, 17.9 mm, 13.9 mm

67.5 cm^2 $\qquad$ 11 in.^{2} $\qquad$ 195.11 mm^2

11. $b_1 = 27$ ft, $b_2 = 4$ ft, $h = 64$ ft $\quad$ 992 ft^2

12. $b_1 = 0.6$ mm, $b_2 = 0.2$ mm, $h = 0.4$ mm $\quad$ 0.16 mm^2

Write the area of each polygon by adding the areas of the parts.

13. 14 in., 11 in., 9 in., 10 in., 24 in., 7 in., 18 in., 10 in.

255 in.^{2}

14. 17 m, 12 m, 6 m, 15 m, 4 m, 15 m, 16 m, 11 m

235.5 m^2

CLASSWORK/HOMEWORK Area of a Circle

Write the area of each circle. Use 3.14 for π. Round to the nearest tenth.

1. $r = 1.4$ m $\quad$ 2. $d = 10$ cm $\quad$ 3. $r = 4.5$ mm

6.2 m^2 $\qquad$ 78.5 cm^2 $\qquad$ 63.6 mm^2

4. $r = 7$ cm $\quad$ 153.9 cm^2 $\quad$ 5. $r = 6.7$ mm $\quad$ 141 mm^2 $\quad$ 6. $d = 0.4$ cm $\quad$ 0.1 cm^2

7. $r = 15.2$ mm $\quad$ 725.5 mm^2 $\quad$ 8. $r = 29$ m $\quad$ 2,640.7 m^2 $\quad$ 9. $d = 18$ mm $\quad$ 254.3 mm^2

10. $r = 0.3$ cm $\quad$ 0.3 cm^2 $\quad$ 11. $d = 12.8$ mm $\quad$ 128.6 mm^2 $\quad$ 12. $r = 19.4$ m $\quad$ 1,181.8 m^2

Write the area of each circle. Use $\frac{22}{7}$ for π.

13. $r = 6$ ft $\quad$ $113\frac{1}{7}$ ft^2 $\quad$ 14. $d = 22$ in. $\quad$ $380\frac{2}{7}$ in.^{2} $\quad$ 15. $r = 7$ yd $\quad$ 154 yd^2

16. $r = 31$ in. $\quad$ $3,020\frac{2}{7}$ in.^{2} $\quad$ 17. $r = 8$ ft $\quad$ $201\frac{1}{7}$ in.^{2} $\quad$ 18. $d = 40$ yd $\quad$ $1,257\frac{1}{7}$ yd^2

19. $d = 28$ in. $\quad$ 615 in.^{2} $\quad$ 20. $r = 12$ yd $\quad$ $452\frac{4}{7}$ yd^2 $\quad$ 21. $d = 7$ ft $\quad$ $38\frac{1}{2}$ ft^2

Write the area of each shaded region. Use 3.14 for π. Round to the nearest tenth.

22. 12 mm, 15 mm, 15 mm

183.4 mm^2

23. 32 m

401.9 m^2

CLASSWORK/HOMEWORK Using a Picture

Read the paragraph. Then use the information in the paragraph and the picture to help you answer each question.

Ramona makes models of buildings for miniature railroad sets. There are 3 popular scales to which models can be built.

Ramona is using this diagram of a freight station to make 3 stations for customers— one for each of the 3 scales described above.

O scale is $\frac{1}{48}$ the size of actual objects. HO scale is $\frac{1}{87}$ the size of actual objects. N scale is $\frac{1}{160}$ the size of actual objects.

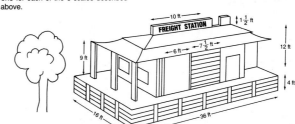
FREIGHT STATION — 10 ft, $1\frac{1}{2}$ ft, 12 ft, 9 ft, 6 ft, $7\frac{1}{2}$ ft, 4 ft, 16 ft, 36 ft

1. For each of the three scales, what is the perimeter in inches of the rectangular freight-station platform? Round to the nearest inch.
O scale = 26 inches; HO scale = 14 inches; N scale = 8 inches

2. For the N-scale freight station, could a $\frac{3}{4}$-inch-square "freight carton" pass through the large freight entrance? no

3. For the O-scale model, what is the height and the length in inches of the freight-station sign?
O scale = $\frac{3}{8}$ in. $\times$ $2\frac{1}{2}$ in.

4. For the HO-scale freight station, would a $3\frac{3}{4}$-inch dowel be long enough to make the 3 columns at the left? yes

5. For the HO scale, what is the height in inches of a tree whose top leaves reach the top of the station sign? (Round to the nearest $\frac{1}{2}$ inch.) $2\frac{1}{2}$ inches

6. For the O-scale freight station, would a 7-inch dowel be long enough to make the 3 columns at the left? yes

CLASSWORK HOMEWORK | Using a Picture

Study the time line. Then, answer each question.

1. About how many years are represented on this time line? about 5,457 years

2. About how many years separate the invention of ink and the invention of the newspaper? of ink and the ballpoint pen?
   about 4,780 years; about 5,138 years

3. About how many years separate the invention of the first wheeled vehicles and the invention of the bicycle?
   about 5,339 years

4. How many years separate the invention of vaccination and the invention of inoculation? 84 years

5. After which year were steam-powered locomotives invented? A.D. 1712

6. About how many years separate the invention of paper and the invention of the newspaper? about 1,490 years

7. Which conclusion can you draw from this time line? c

   a. Without the invention of the hot-air balloon, the satellite could not have been invented.

   b. Without the invention of the piano, there would be no jukebox.

   c. Transistor radios could not have been in use before 1948.

   d. Without the invention of kites, the hot-air balloon could not have been invented.

INVENTIONS

- circa 3500 B.C. Wheeled vehicles
- circa 3200 B.C. Ink
- circa 1000 B.C. Kites that carried people
- circa 90 A.D. Paper
- 1335 A.D. Mechanical clock
- 1580 A.D. Newspaper
- 1590 A.D. Microscope
- 1592 A.D. Thermometer
- 1608 A.D. Telescope
- 1709 A.D. Piano
- 1712 A.D. Steam Engine
- 1783 A.D. Hot-air balloon
- 1796 A.D. Vaccination
- 1839 A.D. Bicycle
- 1880 A.D. Inoculation
- 1895 A.D. Radio
- 1930 A.D. Juke Box
- 1938 A.D. Ballpoint Pen
- 1948 A.D. Transistor
- 1957 A.D. Satellite

Use after pages 414–415.   Student Handbook H173

CLASSWORK HOMEWORK | Solid Figures

Write the name of each solid figure.

1. cylinder
2. sphere
3. pentagonal pyramid
4. octagonal prism

5. pentagonal prism
6. 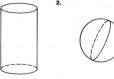 rectangular prism
7. triangular prism
8. square pyramid

Copy and complete the table.

	Polygon	Number of vertices	Number of faces	Number of edges	V + F − E
9.	Octagonal prism	16	10	24	2
10.	Hexagonal pyramid	7	7	12	2
11.	Pentagonal pyramid	6	6	10	2
12.	Square pyramid	5	5	8	2
13.	Pentagonal prism	10	7	15	2

14. What is the relationship between the number of sides of a prism's base and the number of the prism's edges?
    3 times as many edges as sides of base

H174   Student Handbook   Use with pages 416–417.

CLASSWORK HOMEWORK | Surface Area of Prisms and Pyramids

Write the total surface area of each prism. Round to the nearest tenth.

1. 2,528 in.²
2. 301.5 cm²
3. 1,584.4 mm²
4. 16.9 m²
5. 1,224 in.²
6. 1,116 in.²

Write the total surface area of each pyramid. Round to the nearest tenth.

7. 576 in.²
8. 1,440 m²
9. 1,540 ft²
10. 744 yd²
11. 30,000 ft²
12. 95.3 km²

Use with pages 418–419.   Student Handbook H175

CLASSWORK HOMEWORK | Surface Area of Cylinders and Cones

Write the total surface area of each figure. Use 3.14 for π. Round to the nearest tenth.

1. 439.6 cm²
2. 1,193.2 mm²
3. 395.6 m²
4. 967.1 cm²
5. 1,004.8 mm²
6. 244.9 m²
7. 1,582.6 cm²
8. 2,798.5 cm²
9. 374.4 mm²
10. 1,384.7 cm²
11. 942 mm²
12. 329.7 mm²

H176   Student Handbook   Use with pages 420–421.

CLASSWORK HOMEWORK — Checking for Hidden Assumptions

Decide if each statement is *true* or *false*. If the statement is false, give an example in which the statement is not true.

1. $n - 1$ is always less than $n + 1$? True

2. $1 - n$ is always less than $1 + n$.
False; if n is a negative number.

3. For all positive numbers, $n \times n$ is always greater than n.
False; if n is less than 1.

4. $\frac{b}{0}$ is always equal to 0. True

5. $x + y$ is always equal to $y + x$. True

6. $x \div y$ is always less than x. False; if y is less than 1.

7. For all positive integers, $3 \times n$ is always greater than $2 \times n$. True

8. No even number greater than 2 is prime. True

9. $x + y$ is never equal to $x - y$. False; if y equals 0.

10. The sum of the measures of the angles of a triangle always equals $180°$. True

11. If 2 hexagons have equal sides, their areas are the same.
False; if one hexagon is convex, the other is concave.

CLASSWORK HOMEWORK — Volume of Prisms and Pyramids

Write the volume of each solid figure. Round to the nearest tenth.

1.
15 mm, 12 mm, 10.4 mm, 12 mm
936 mm³

2.
5.5 m, 3.3 m, 3 m
54.5 m³

3.
50 mm, 50 mm, 28 mm
35,000 mm³

4.
8 cm, 8 cm, 8 cm
512 cm³

5.
6 mm, 7.5 mm, 28 mm
1,260 mm³

6.
2.2 cm, 7.7 cm, 4.4 cm
37.3 cm³

7.
18 ft, 10 ft, 20 ft, 14 ft
3,200 ft³

8.
28 cm, 12 cm, 12 cm, 20 cm
1,152 cm³

9.
25 mm, 50 mm, 50 mm
20,833.3 mm³

Solve.

10. Which has the greater volume: a 6-cm cube or a prism with a 3-cm square base and height of 12 cm? How many times as great?
Cube is twice as great.

11. The Great Pyramid of Cheops has a square base 230 meters along each side, and a height of 150 meters. Find the volume. 2,645,000 m³

CLASSWORK HOMEWORK — Volume of Cylinders and Cones

Write the volume of each solid figure. Use 3.14 for π. Round to the nearest tenth.

1.
$d = 8$ m, 7 m
351.7 m³

2.
20 cm, $r = 4$ cm
1,004.8 cm³

3.
$r = 3$ mm, 24.5 mm
692.4 mm³

4.
$r = 5$ m, 4.1 m
321.9 m³

5.
$r = 13$ cm, 9 cm
4,775.9 cm³

6.
$d = 10$ mm, 30 mm
2,355 mm³

7.
21 cm, $r = 9$ cm
1,780.4 cm³

8.
$r = 7$ mm, 21 mm
1,077.0 mm³

9.
30 m, $d = 8$ m
502.4 m³

10.
$r = 5$ cm, 17 cm
444.8 cm³

11.
10.5 mm, $r = 6$ mm
395.6 mm³

12.
$d = 16$ m, 28 m
1,875.6 m³

CLASSWORK HOMEWORK — Choosing a Formula

Write the letter of the formula that you would use to solve each problem.

1. James is making a model of a spaceship. The bottom of the command and living areas is circular and measures 58.4 cm in diameter. James wants to put tape around the perimeter of this area. He has a 144 cm length of tape. Is it long enough?
a. $C = \pi d$　**b.** $A = \pi r^2$
c. $S = 2\pi rh + 2\pi r^2$　**d.** $A = s^2$

2. The command section of the ship is a cylinder with a radius of 14.3 cm and a height of 12.4 cm. How many square inches of foil does James need to cover the inside of the command section?
a. $V = r^2 h$　**b.** $V = lwh$
c. $S = 2\pi rh + 2\pi r^2$　**d.** $A = \frac{1}{2}bh$

Write the formula, then solve. Round to the nearest tenth of a centimeter.

1. The landing pad for the spaceship will be made of balsa wood. It is a rectangular prism 98.2 cm long, 88.6 cm wide, and 2.4 cm high. If Angie decides to fill it with sand, how many cubic centimeters of sand will she need?
$V = lwh$　20,881.2

2. The tail fins for the fuel tanks are each triangles with a base 1.8 cm wide and a height of 3.4 cm. How long is the slanted side of each fin?
$a^2 + b^2 = c^2$　3.9 cm

3. Ramon is making conical caps for the fuel tanks. The radius of the tanks is 2.8 cm and the height of the caps is to be 3.5 cm. The main part of each tank is a cylinder 20.32 cm high. How much material will Ramon need in order to make both fuel tanks?
$S = 2(\pi rl + \pi r^2 + 2\pi rh) + 6\left(\frac{1}{2}bh\right)$
861.4 cm²

4. Angie will paint the curved walls of the living module. The diameter of the module's outside wall is 58.4 cm. The diameter of the module's inside wall is 32.4 cm. The height of the module is 12.4 cm. How many cm² is the area Angie will paint?
$S = 2\pi rh + 2\pi r^2$　3,535.16

5. Is a sheet of tin 3.4 cm by 5.4 cm large enough to make 6 tail fins?
$A = lw.$　yes

58.4 cm, 32.4 cm, 28.6 cm
Command
Living

CLASSWORK HOMEWORK | Equations in Two Variables

Write the letter of the ordered pair that satisfies the equation.

1. $y = 3x - 5$ **a.** (9,23)   **b.** (10,20)   **c.** (11,28)

2. $y = 4(x + 4)$ **a.** (7,40)   **b.** (4,32)   **c.** (12,34)

3. $y = 9x + 12$ **a.** (⁻2,⁻6)   **b.** (3,38)   **c.** (0,9)

4. $8y = 8x + 16$ **a.** (3,17)   **b.** (7,9)   **c.** (13,16)

5. $2y + 3x = 10$ **a.** (⁻4,6)   **b.** (10,12)   **c.** (8,⁻7)

6. $\frac{1}{6}y = x + 1$ **a.** (5,32)   **b.** (3,24)   **c.** (9,70)

7. $y = \frac{1}{2}x - 4$ **a.** (6,⁻1)   **b.** (12,3)   **c.** (14,11)

8. $x + y = ⁻3$ **a.** (9,6)   **b.** (3,⁻6)   **c.** (17,20)

9. $7y + x = 14$ **a.** (7,1)   **b.** (12,7)   **c.** (0,6)

10. $⁻4y + 3x = ⁻7$ **a.** (1,⁻1)   **b.** (4,2)   **c.** (3,4)

11. $x - \frac{1}{2}y = 15$ **a.** (27,26)   **b.** (28,27)   **c.** (29,28)

12. $7y - 0 = x$ **a.** (3,13)   **b.** (14,2)   **c.** (⁻21,⁻3)

13. $y = ⁻6x + 10$ **a.** (4,⁻14)   **b.** (⁻4,14)   **c.** (2,⁻14)

14. $10(x - 2) = y$ **a.** (4,24)   **b.** (4,2)   **c.** (2,0)

15. $4y - 27 = x$ **a.** (⁻11,4)   **b.** (7,5)   **c.** (⁻11,⁻4)

16. $x = 13 - \frac{1}{2}y$ **a.** (⁻1,28)   **b.** (1,⁻28)   **c.** (⁻1,14)

17. $\frac{1}{2}y = 3x - 7$ **a.** (⁻5,⁻16)   **b.** (5,16)   **c.** (4,12)

Use ⁻2, 0, 1 as replacements for x. Write the solutions for each equation as ordered pairs.

18. $x + y = 5$
(⁻2,7) (0,5) (1,4)

19. $2x + 3y = 8$
(⁻2,4) $\left(0, 2\frac{2}{3}\right)$ (1,2)

20. $2y - x = 10$
(⁻2,4) (0,5) $\left(1, 5\frac{1}{2}\right)$

CLASSWORK HOMEWORK | Solving Equations in Two Variables

Copy and complete each table of values. Write the ordered pairs that are the solutions.

1. $y = 2x - 1$

x	2x − 1	y
⁻2	2(⁻2) − 1	⁻5
⁻1	2(⁻1) − 1	⁻3
0	2(0) − 1	⁻1
1	2(1) − 1	1
2	2(2) − 1	3

(⁻2,⁻5) (⁻1,⁻3) (0,⁻1) (1,1) (2,3)

2. $y = 3x - 4$

x	3x − 4	y
0	3(0) − 4	⁻4
1	3(1) − 4	⁻1
2	3(2) − 4	2
3	3(3) − 4	5
4	3(4) − 4	8

(0,⁻4) (1,⁻1) (2,2) (3,5) (4,8)

3. $y = x + 5$

x	x + 5	y
⁻4	⁻4 + 5	1
⁻3	⁻3 + 5	2
⁻2	⁻2 + 5	3
⁻1	⁻1 + 5	4
0	0 + 5	5

(⁻4,1) (⁻3,2) (⁻2,3) (⁻1,4) (0,5)

4. $y = 2 - x$

x	2 − x	y
⁻10	2 − (⁻10)	12
⁻5	2 − (⁻5)	7
0	2 − 0	2
5	2 − 5	⁻3
10	2 − 10	⁻8

(⁻10,12) (⁻5,7) (0,2) (5,⁻3) (10,⁻8)

5. $⁻3x + y = 3$

x	⁻3x + y = 3	y
⁻3	⁻3(⁻3) + y = 3	⁻6
⁻1	⁻3(⁻1) + y = 3	0
0	⁻3(0) + y = 3	3
2	⁻3(2) + y = 3	9
4	⁻3(4) + y = 3	15

(⁻3,⁻6) (⁻1,0) (0,3) (2,9) (4,15)

6. $2x + 3y = 1$

x	2x + 3y = 1	y
⁻7	2(⁻7) + 3y = 1	5
⁻5	2(⁻5) + 3y = 1	$3\frac{2}{3}$
1	2(1) + 3y = 1	$⁻\frac{1}{3}$
8	2(8) + 3y = 1	⁻5
11	2(11) + 3y = 1	⁻7

(⁻7,5) $\left(⁻5, 3\frac{2}{3}\right)$ $\left(1, ⁻\frac{1}{3}\right)$ (8,⁻5) (11,⁻7)

CLASSWORK HOMEWORK | Making a Diagram

On a separate sheet of paper, draw a diagram and solve. Write your number in the space provided. Round to the nearest whole number.

1. Here is a scavenger hunt clue: Enter the 24 ft by 36 ft rectangular plaza in the Ashworth Park on the east border. (There are two entrances directly in the middle of the short sides of the plaza.) Walk due west 18 ft, straight north 6 ft, and then due west 6 ft where you will find a piece of purple string. If you use the shortest route, how far away is the string from the western entrance? **13 ft**

2. A clue in a scavenger hunt is to Go 10 miles west, $2\frac{1}{2}$ miles due north, 10 miles due east, and $2\frac{1}{2}$ miles due south. Take one red button from the pile hidden in an opening in a large elm tree. Roger wants to figure out how long it would take him to get to the elm tree if he drives 35 mph. How long would it take him? **0 minutes**

3. Roger was directed to go 3 blocks north along 8th Road turn right and go 6 blocks due east along 6th Avenue to 14th Road. The blocks along 8th Road are 276 ft long, which is 3 times as long as the blocks along 6th Avenue. If a long diagonal were drawn from Roger's starting point to his stopping point, how long would it be? **995 ft**

4. A scavenger hunt clue sends Chris to a rectangular yard with a perimeter of 126 ft. Chris walks along the entire south border due west, a distance of 25 ft. He must find a marker on a bush in the middle of the west border. How many feet does he have to walk before he should start looking for the bush? **19 ft**

5. Brian enters an L-shape hotel lobby to search for a clue. The larger part of the lobby is 120 ft square; the smaller part is 40 ft by 40 ft. Roger can walk in a straight path from the northwest corner of the larger part to the southeast corner of the smaller part. How many feet long is that path? **200 ft**

6. At the end of the scavenger hunt, all the hunters must meet at the center of circular park. From a point 400 yards due west of the center of the park, Bruce walks 300 yards north. From that point, he walks diagonally toward the center of the park for 300 yards. He is now at the perimeter of the park. How many square yards is the park? **125,600**

CLASSWORK HOMEWORK | Making a Diagram

On a separate sheet of paper, draw a diagram and solve. Round decimal answers to the nearest tenth.

1. Candice Smythe, detective, is searching for buried treasure. Directions for finding the treasure say that it is in a rectangular area $2\frac{1}{2}$ mi by $5\frac{1}{2}$ mi. The treasure is in the middle of a straight path that runs northeast by southwest. About how many miles does Candice have to travel from the northeast corner before she starts digging? **about 3 mi**

2. A missing zebra was reported to be in the northwest corner of a rectangular area 65 ft by 65 ft. The runaway animal went on a straight path from the southeast corner to the southwest corner, from the southwest corner to the northeast corner, and then from the northeast corner to the northwest corner. How many feet did it travel? **222 ft**

3. Candice is 2 ft into a 201 ft² circular area when her assistant, Nedda Lovelace, calls her. Nedda says she is in the center of the area and is sinking in quicksand. About how many feet apart are they? **6 ft**

4. To find a missing circus elephant, Candice follows a trail of peanuts that starts at the elephant's cage. She follows the trail north 400 ft along Jones Street, then due east 800 ft on Claremont Avenue, and then due south 400 ft on Simmons Street. At that point, how far was Candice from the elephant's cage? **800 ft**

5. Candice must find a needle (a gold and emerald one) in a haystack. The haystack is in a square field with sides 3 mi long. Directions for finding the haystack are as follows: Start at the northeast corner. Travel south along the eastern border $1\frac{1}{2}$ mi. Then go due west 1 mi, and then go $\frac{3}{4}$ mi north. The haystack will be there. Candice wants to start at the northeast corner and take the shortest path to the haystack. How long is the shortest path? **$1\frac{1}{4}$ mi**

6. Candice led the police to a counterfeiters' hideout even though she had been taken there blindfolded and in a roundabout way. She had memorized the following directions: Start at my office building. Walk 25 paces due west, 15 paces due south, 10 paces north, 17 paces east, 5 paces north, 8 paces east, then 20 paces north. How many paces from Candice's office building was the counterfeiters' hideout? **20 paces**

Relations and Functions

CLASSWORK HOMEWORK

Copy and complete each table. Is the set of solutions a function? Write *yes* or *no.*

1. $y = {}^-4x + 10$

x	$^-4x + 10$	y
7	$^-4(7) + 10$	$^-18$
4	$^-4(4) + 10$	$^-6$
$^-1$	$^-4(^-1) + 10$	14
0	$^-4(0) + 10$	10
$\frac{1}{2}$	$^-4(\frac{1}{2}) + 10$	8

yes

2. $y = 12 - 3x$

x	$12 - 3x$	y
12	$12 - 3(12)$	$^-24$
$\frac{1}{3}$	$12 - 3(\frac{1}{3})$	11
0	$12 - 3(0)$	12
7	$12 - 3(7)$	$^-9$
$^-5$	$12 - 3(^-5)$	27

yes

Is the set of ordered pairs a function? Write *yes* or *no.*

3. $\left(1, \frac{1}{2}\right)$ $\left(3, \frac{3}{2}\right)$ (4,2) (0,0)   yes

4. (17,16) (10,11) (10,15) (17,17)   no

5. (3,5) (4,7) $\left(13, \frac{1}{2}\right)$ (2,5)   yes

6. (0,6) (4,7) (5,6) $\left(9, \frac{4}{10}\right)$ yes

7. $(^-1,2)$ (3,5) $(^-1,4)$ (4,7)   no

8. (0,5) (3,5) (7,5) (9,5) (13,5)   yes

9. $(^-1,6)$ $(^-2,4)$ (0,0) (1,0) (3,4)   yes

10. (4,9) (5,15) (3,10) (4,8) (6,13)   no

Solve.

11. Bob Avis has been keeping track of the number of times his pet parakeet tweets per minute and of the room temperature. The table at the right shows his findings. Can you find the rule (let *t* represent temperatures and *w* represent tweets)?   yes; $w = t - 10$

Temperature (°F)	50	51	52	53	54
Tweets per minute	40	41	42	43	44

Use with pages 444–445.   Student Handbook **H185**

The Real-Number Plane

CLASSWORK HOMEWORK

Write *yes* if the graph represents a function. Write *no* if it does not.

1.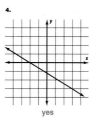
yes

2.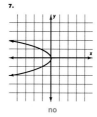
no

3.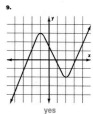
yes

4.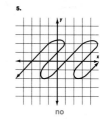
yes

5.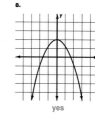
no

6.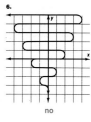
no

7.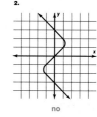
no

8.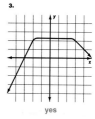
yes

9.
yes

H186 Student Handbook   Use with pages 446–447.

Choosing a Strategy or Method

CLASSWORK HOMEWORK

Estimation	Choosing the Operation	Using a Formula
Using a Table	Guessing and Checking	Solving Multi-step
Using a Graph	Writing an Equation	Problems

Write the strategy or method you choose. Then solve. Strategies and methods will vary.

1. On a map of the world, $2\frac{1}{2}$ inches equals 600 miles. How many miles would $5\frac{1}{4}$ inches represent?
writing an equation; 1,260 miles

Exploring Antarctica	$18.99
Australia—From A to Z	$ 5.29
Europe—The Renaissance	$14.49
South America and Democracy	$ 8.79
Africa—Its Ancient Kingdoms	$17.69
Asia in Photographs	$19.39

2. Diane has $60.29. Can she afford to buy *Exploring Antarctica*, *Australia—From A to Z*, and 2 copies of *Africa—Its Ancient Kingdoms*?
estimation; yes

3. Gina has $44.25. Can she afford to purchase the four least expensive books?
estimation; no

THE SEVEN CONTINENTS

Name	Area (mi²)	Percent of world land	Highest point (ft)	Lowest point (ft below sea level)
Asia	17,400,000	30.1	Mt. Everest 29,028	Dead Sea 1312
Africa	11,700,000	20.2	Mt. Kilimanjaro 19,340	Lake Assal 512
North America	9,400,000	16.2	Mt. McKinley 20,320	Death Valley 282
South America	6,900,000	11.9	Mt. Aconcagua 22,834	Valdes Peninsula 131
Antarctica	5,400,000	9.1	Vinson Massif 16,864	unknown
Europe	3,800,000	6.6	Mt. Albrus 18,510	Caspian Sea 92
Australia	3,300,000	5.4	Mt. Kosciusko 7,310	Lake Eyre 52

4. About how many miles higher is the highest point on Earth than the lowest point? (Round to the nearest mile.)
using a table; about 6 miles

5. Find the total percent of world land. Why is it not 100%?
using a table; 99.5%; islands account for 0.5%

Use after pages 448–449.   Student Handbook **H187**

Choosing a Strategy or Method

CLASSWORK HOMEWORK

Estimation	Writing an Equation	Drawing a Picture
Using a Table	Solving Multi-step Problems	Using a Formula
Choosing the Operation	Working Backward	

Write the strategy or method you choose. Then solve. Strategies and methods will vary.

1. The Kalahari Desert has an area of about 225,000 mi², which is 150,000 fewer square miles than $\frac{3}{4}$ of the area of the Gobi Desert. What is the area of the Gobi Desert?
writing an equation; 500,000 mi²

2. Lake Michigan has an area of 22,300 mi², which is 14,372 mi² greater than $\frac{4}{5}$ of the area of Lake Erie. What is the area of Lake Erie?
writing an equation; 9,910 mi²

3. Museum workers want to build a circular platform with a diameter of 12 feet. They will cover the platform edge with a strip of lace. How much lace will the workers need? Use 3.14 for π.
using a formula; 37.68 feet

4. Artists want to use 6-in. square tiles to make a mosaic of famous volcanoes. The wall to be covered is 10 ft by 15 ft. How many tiles will they need?
solving multi-step problems; 600 tiles

5. The area of the Caspian Sea is 111,544 square miles greater than the area of Lake Superior. The area of Lake Superior is 9,400 square miles greater than the area of the Caspian Sea. The area of the Caspian Sea is 143,244 square miles. What is the area of Lake Michigan?
working backward; 22,300 square miles

6. An exhibit will show a comparison between the height of the Sears Tower and the height of Mount Everest. Mount Everest is 29,028 ft tall. The Sears Tower is 1,454 ft tall. The scale of the exhibit is 10 in. = 1 mi. About how many inches taller than the model of the Sears Tower will the model of Mount Everest be?
solving multi-step problems; about 52 in.

H188 Student Handbook   Use after pages 448–449.

531

Copy and complete each table of values. Then graph the equation.

1.

x	4y + 2x = ⁻16	y
2	4y + 2(2) = ⁻16	⁻5
0	4y + 2(0) = ⁻16	⁻4
⁻2	4y + 2(⁻2) = ⁻16	⁻3
⁻4	4y + 2(⁻4) = ⁻16	⁻2

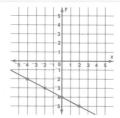

2.

x	y = ⅓x − 5	y
⁻3	y = ⅓(⁻3) − 5	⁻6
0	y = ⅓(0) − 5	⁻5
3	y = ⅓(3) − 5	⁻4
6	y = ⅓(6) − 5	⁻3

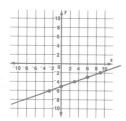

3. Many tables are possible.

x	y = 2(x − ½)	y
⁻2	y = 2(⁻2 − ½)	⁻5
0	y = 2(0 − ½)	⁻1
2	y = 2(2 − ½)	3
3	y = 2(3 − ½)	5

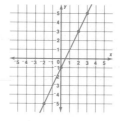

Use with pages 450–451.

Copy and complete the table of values for each equation. Then solve the system of equations by graphing. Check each solution.

1. x + y = 5
x − y = 1

x	x + y = 5	y
⁻1	⁻1 + y = 5	6
0	0 + y = 5	5
1	1 + y = 5	4
2	2 + y = 5	3

x	x − y = 1	y
0	0 − y = 1	⁻1
1	1 − y = 1	0
2	2 − y = 1	1
3	3 − y = 1	2

(3,2)

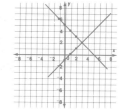

2. y = 2x − 1
y = 3x

x	y = 2x − 1	y
⁻1	y = 2(⁻1) − 1	⁻3
0	y = 2(0) − 1	⁻1
1	y = 2(1) − 1	1
2	y = 2(2) − 1	3

x	y = 3x	y
⁻1	y = 3(⁻1)	⁻3
0	y = 3(0)	0
1	y = 3(1)	3
2	y = 3(2)	6

(⁻1,⁻3)

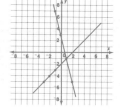

3. 4x + y = 3
y − x = ⁻2

x	4x + y = 3	y
⁻1	4(⁻1) + y = 3	7
0	4(0) + y = 3	3
1	4(1) + y = 3	⁻1
2	4(2) + y = 3	⁻5

x	y − x = ⁻2	y
⁻3	y − (⁻3) = ⁻2	⁻5
⁻2	y − (⁻2) = ⁻2	⁻4
⁻1	y − (⁻1) = ⁻2	⁻3
0	y − (0) = ⁻2	⁻2

(1,⁻1)

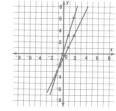

Use with pages 452–453.

Copy and complete each table of values. Then graph the inequality.

1. x − y ≥ 3

x	x − y = 3	y
⁻2	⁻2 − y = 3	⁻5
⁻1	⁻1 − y = 3	⁻4
0	0 − y = 3	⁻3
1	1 − y = 3	⁻2
2	2 − y = 3	⁻1

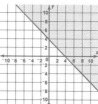

2. x + y ≥ 4

x	x + y = 4	y
⁻4	⁻4 + y = 4	8
⁻2	⁻2 + y = 4	6
0	0 + y = 4	4
1	1 + y = 4	3
3	3 + y = 4	1

3. 3y − x < 0

x	3y − x = 0	y
⁻9	3y − (⁻9) = 0	⁻3
⁻6	3y − (⁻6) = 0	⁻2
0	3y − (0) = 0	0
3	3y − (3) = 0	1
9	3y − (9) = 0	3

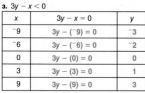

Use with pages 454–455.

Copy and complete each table of values. Graph the inequality.

1. ⁻y > 4 + ½x

x	⁻y = 4 + ½x	y
⁻4	⁻y = 4 + ½(⁻4)	2
⁻2	⁻y = 4 + ½(⁻2)	⁻3
0	⁻y = 4 + ½(0)	⁻4

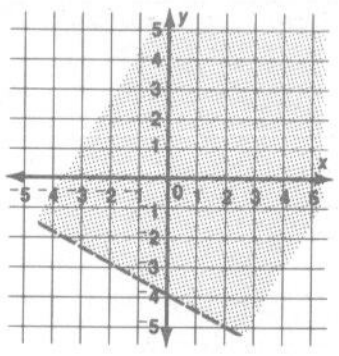

2. 24 + 12y ≤ 4x

x	24 + 12y = 4x	y
⁻1	24 + 12y = 4(⁻1)	⁻2⅓
0	24 + 12y = 4(0)	⁻2
3	24 + 12y = 4(3)	⁻1

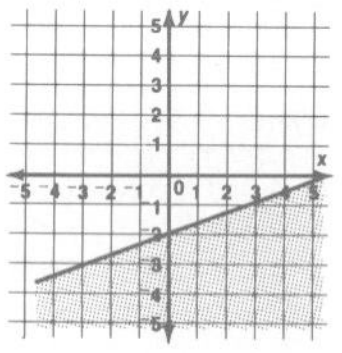

3. 3x − y > 5   Many tables are possible.

x	3x − y = 5	y
0	3(0) − y = 5	⁻5
1	3(1) − y = 5	⁻2
2	3(2) − y = 5	1
3	3(3) − y = 5	4

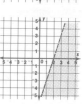

Solve.

4. The citizens of Planesville are planning a park for their town. Two of the boundaries of the park will be portions of the positive x and y axes. The park will include all the points that are solutions to both the inequalities x + 2y ≤ 6 and 3x + 2y ≤ 10. Graph the inequalities; then shade the area of the park.

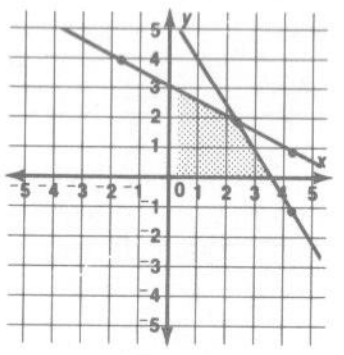

Use with pages 456–457.

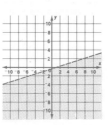
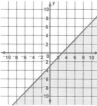

CLASSWORK HOMEWORK | Choosing a Strategy or Method

Estimation	Guessing and Checking	Selecting Notation
Drawing a Picture	Making a Table to Find a Pattern	Making an Organized List
Choosing the Operation	Writing an Equation	Working Backward
Solving Multi-step Problems		

Write the strategy or method you choose. Then solve.
Strategies and methods will vary.

1. While hiking in the forest one day, Robert became lost. He came upon a marker that indicated that he was in the exact center of the forest. Robert knew that the forest was a square 60 km on a side, so he decided to walk out in a straight line. But the route he actually took went like this: 5 km north, then 10 km west, then 15 km south, 20 km east, 25 km north, and so on. How far did Robert walk before he got out of the forest? drawing a picture;

   275 km

2. A tour guide tells visitors to an adventure park that $\frac{1}{3}$ of the park consists of wildlife habitats. Hiking trails and picnic areas make up $\frac{1}{2}$ of the remaining park area. The guide also states that there are 2 mi^2 of buildings that house restaurants, movie theaters, and concert stages. The science buildings take up the remaining 1.75 mi^2. How many square miles does the adventure park contain? working backward; 11.25 mi^2

3. At Poe Park, 1 food ticket costs $1.25, 5 cost $6.00, 10 cost $11.50, and 15 cost $16.50. How much do 25 food tickets cost? making a table to find a pattern; $25.00

4. If a group of 4 friends goes on the Volcano Train ride together, in how many different orders can they arrange themselves in a row of 4 seats? making an organized list; 24 orders

---

CLASSWORK HOMEWORK | Choosing a Strategy or Method

Estimation	Guessing and Checking	Selecting Notation
Drawing a Picture	Making a Table to Find a Pattern	Making an Organized List
Choosing the Operation	Writing an Equation	Working Backward
Solving Multi-step Problems		

Write the strategy or method you choose. Then solve.
Strategies and methods will vary.

1. There are 3 students painting scenery. They have a can that contains 3 gallons of paint, an empty 2-gallon container, and an empty 1-gallon container. How can they divide the paint so that each one has the same amount? selecting notation; (3 gal, 0, 0) → (1 gal, 2 gal, 0) →

   (1 gal, 1 gal, 1 gal)

2. Alicia gave her aunt the following directions for driving to the school play. Leave the highway at Exit 25. Go north 3 streets, and make a left turn at the Great States supermarket. Continue for 3 streets, and make a left turn at the traffic light. Continue for 5 streets to the library. Make another left, and go 3 streets to the school. What is a shorter route from Exit 25 to the school? drawing a picture; assuming all streets go straight

   through, go south 2 streets from Exit 25

3. Advertisements in the school play program cost $7.50 for a small advertisement and $19.25 for a large advertisement. Kenzo sold twice as many small ads as large ads. He collected a total of $137 in advertising fees. How many small advertisements did he sell? guessing and checking; 8 small advertisements

4. Andre won the drama-club raffle. His prize is a $99.99 shopping spree in a novelty store. He cannot spend a penny more or a penny less than $99.99. Find two groups of purchases that add up to $99.99.
   guessing and checking; one possible answer:

   10 teddy bears—$36.90; 4 $12.99 games—$51.96;

   1 $5.69, 1 $3.98, and 1 $1.19 poster; and

   1 $0.27 sticker

Prices
Tiny teddy bear: $3.69
Board games: $12.99, $8.44, $4.58
Puzzles: $7.26, $6.35
Stickers: $0.27, $0.38, $0.57, $0.75
Posters: $1.19, $3.98, $5.69

MORE PRACTICE

Chapter 1, page 3

Write each in standard form.

1. 8 million, 300 thousand, 387
8,300,387
2. 42 million, 96 thousand, 400
42,096,400
3. 208 billion, 39 thousand, 18
208,000,039,018
4. 324 trillion, 82 million, 402
324,000,082,000,402

Write the short word name.

5. 8,450,000
8 million, 450 thousand
6. 32,001,062
32 million, 1 thousand, 62
7. 49,000,000,483
49 billion, 483
8. 40,002,000
40 million, 2 thousand
9. 526,000,800,400
526 billion, 800 thousand, 400
10. 13,040,000,083
13 billion, 40 million, 83

Write the place and the value of the underlined digit.

11. 9,724,862
hundreds; 800
12. 189,356,482
ten millions; 80 million
13. 9,068,342,184
hundred thousands; 300 thousand
14. Write 8,400,560 in expanded form.
8,000,000 + 400,000 + 500 + 60

Chapter 1, page 5

Compare. Write >, <, or = for ●.

1. 74,286 ● 76,286   <
2. 121,845 ● 112,854   >
3. 29,684 ● 28,795   >
4. 412,777 ● 422,777   <
5. 54,012 ● 54,102   <
6. 40,465,100 ● 40,465,100   =
7. 84,533,334 ● 84,353,334   >

Order the numbers from the least to the greatest.

8. 965; 9,650; 960; 9,656
960; 965; 9,650; 9,656
9. 332; 322; 3,323; 3,233
322; 332; 3,233; 3,323
10. 6,895; 6,985; 6,859; 6,589; 6,588
6,588; 6,589; 6,859; 6,895; 6,985

Chapter 1, page 29

Add.

1. 0.73
 + 0.43
 1.16
2. 3.84
 + 5.96
 9.80
3. 82.473
 + 29.248
 111.721
4. $19,801.46
 + 8,796.82
 $28,598.28
5. 0.492 + 8.978 + 4.527   13.997
6. 15,141.9 + 7.23 + 5,848.9 + 87.6
21,085.63
7. 45 + 856.9 + 833.86
1,735.76
8. $468.04 + $8.25 + $0.68 + $2.95
$479.92

Chapter 1, page 31

Subtract.

1. 87.6
 − 26.2
 61.4
2. 84.52
 − 32.38
 52.14
3. 754.58
 − 237.96
 516.62
4. 8.4391
 − 5.7846
 2.6545
5. 0.876
 − 0.59
 0.286
6. 0.8071
 − 0.694
 0.1131
7. 0.87
 − 0.495
 0.375
8. 0.8009
 − 0.437
 0.3639
9. 0.325
 − 0.253
 0.072
10. 1.697
 − 0.379
 1.318
11. 9.159
 − 7.395
 1.764
12. 40.59
 − 3.599
 36.991
13. 896.248 − 7.9063
888.3417
14. $926 − $427.32
$498.68
15. 5.0732 − 0.96438
4.10882

Chapter 2, page 61

Multiply.

1. 4.5
 × 7
 31.5
2. 18.76
 × 0.9
 16.884
3. 407.26
 × 0.5
 203.63
4. 0.2046
 × 7
 1.4322
5. 0.872
 × 0.48
 0.41856
6. 9.63
 × 82
 789.66
7. 567.43
 × 8.2
 4,652.926
8. 0.0025
 × 48
 0.12
9. 5.12
 × 0.3
 1.536
10. 9.25
 × 35.2
 325.6
11. 35.12
 × 12.2
 428.464
12. 465.32
 × 32.6
 15,169.432
13. 0.899 × 863.04
755.87296
14. 5,287.6 × 0.00487
25.750612
15. 4.7 × 8 × 0.83 × 9.5
296.476
16. 0.187 × 63,412.1 × 7.2
85,378.05144

Chapter 2, page 67

Divide.

1. 0.9)8.1   9
2. 0.8)0.00264   0.0033
3. 7)1.68   0.24
4. 3.6)72.12   20.0333
5. 2.7)91.8   34
6. 0.6)0.024   0.04
7. 0.008)0.048   6
8. 23)29.9   1.3
9. 2.8)169.12   60.4
10. 8.6)144.48   16.8
11. 0.72)169.20   235
12. 7)3.57   0.51
13. 8.5)49.98   5.88
14. 3.4 ÷ 0.84   4.047619
15. 3.81 ÷ 0.104   36.634615
16. 0.7)274.1   391.57143

Chapter 3, page 93

List the factors to find the GCF.

1. 28, 88   4
2. 24, 72   24
3. 18, 90   18
4. 6, 15   3
5. 63, 18   9
6. 40, 56   8
7. 12, 21   3
8. 24, 42   6
9. 16, 24, 32   8
10. 6, 100, 48   2

Use the prime factorization to find the GCF.

11. 25, 41   1
12. 12, 48   12
13. 64, 46   2
14. 15, 54   3
15. 180, 45, 90   45
16. 4, 17, 97   1

Chapter 3, page 105

Solve each equation.

1. $y − 15 = 72$ $y = 87$
2. $x − 34 = 89$ $x = 123$
3. $j − 5.4 = 8.7$ $j = 14.1$
4. $18 − x = 4$ $x = 14$
5. $a − 10.3 = 17.9$ $a = 28.2$
6. $7 + y = 32$ $y = 25$
7. $x + 114 = 257$ $x = 143$
8. $64 = 89 − b$ $b = 25$
9. $x − 4.7 = 2.1$ $x = 6.8$
10. $14 + m = 96$ $m = 82$
11. $y − 11.2 = 83$ $y = 94.2$
12. $z + 8.9 = 21$ $z = 12.1$
13. $x + 24.7 = 32.1$ $x = 7.4$
14. $10 + s = 16$ $s = 6$
15. $r − 43.7 = 91.2$ $r = 134.9$

Chapter 3, page 107

Solve each equation.

1. $3x = 27$ $x = 9$
2. $4y = 120$ $y = 30$
3. $3.5m = 182$ $m = 52$
4. $9t = 423$ $t = 47$
5. $2.8y = 8.4$ $y = 3$
6. $0.6x = 84.6$ $x = 141$
7. $24a = 312$ $a = 13$
8. $8m = 192$ $m = 24$
9. $16r = 304$ $r = 19$
10. $\frac{x}{2.5} = 12$ $x = 30$
11. $\frac{w}{7} = 15$ $w = 105$
12. $\frac{x}{32} = 4$ $x = 128$
13. $\frac{m}{19} = 38$ $m = 722$
14. $\frac{x}{0.5} = 14$ $x = 7$
15. $\frac{t}{4} = 197$ $t = 788$
16. $\frac{x}{10} = 0.5$ $x = 5$
17. $\frac{y}{6} = 3.2$ $y = 19.2$
18. $\frac{a}{2.2} = 20$ $a = 44$
19. $\frac{z}{28} = 4$ $z = 112$
20. $\frac{p}{14} = 9$ $p = 126$
21. $\frac{r}{54} = 6$ $r = 324$

Chapter 3, page 109

Solve.

1. $8m − 15 = 9$ $m = 3$
2. $8d − 32 = 16$ $d = 6$
3. $\frac{x}{3} + 4 = 20$ $x = 48$
4. $\frac{x}{5} − 9 = 15$ $x = 120$
5. $\frac{y}{2} − 8 = 17$ $y = 50$
6. $3x + 4 = 79$ $x = 25$
7. $4x + 8 = 32$ $x = 6$
8. $\frac{x}{8} + 12 = 16$ $x = 32$
9. $\frac{y}{9} − 9 = 15$ $y = 96$
10. $7x − 3 = 32$ $x = 5$
11. $\frac{x}{5} − 4 = 7$ $x = 55$
12. $9x − 4 = 50$ $x = 6$
13. $0.5x + 4 = 9.5$ $x = 11$
14. $26.1 + 6x = 40.5$ $x = 2.4$
15. $2x − 46 = 80$ $x = 63$

Chapter 4, page 133

Subtract. Write the answer in simplest form.

1. $\frac{7}{9} − \frac{4}{9}$ $\frac{1}{3}$
2. $\frac{9}{11} − \frac{5}{11}$ $\frac{4}{11}$
3. $\frac{2}{3} − \frac{1}{3}$ $\frac{1}{3}$
4. $\frac{14}{15} − \frac{8}{15}$ $\frac{2}{5}$
5. $\frac{3}{4} − \frac{5}{8}$ $\frac{1}{8}$
6. $\frac{4}{5} − \frac{3}{10}$ $\frac{1}{2}$
7. $\frac{21}{24} − \frac{4}{6}$ $\frac{5}{24}$
8. $\frac{1}{2} − \frac{1}{3}$ $\frac{1}{6}$
9. $\frac{7}{9} − \frac{2}{3}$ $\frac{1}{9}$
10. $\frac{2}{3} − \frac{3}{11}$ $\frac{13}{33}$
11. $\frac{3}{4} − \frac{1}{5}$ $\frac{11}{20}$
12. $\frac{3}{5} − \frac{2}{7}$ $\frac{11}{35}$
13. $4\frac{7}{10} + 2\frac{1}{8}$ $2\frac{23}{40}$
14. $8\frac{19}{24} − 2\frac{8}{36}$ $6\frac{41}{72}$
15. $18\frac{1}{2} − 8\frac{1}{4}$ $10\frac{1}{4}$

Chapter 4, page 143

Multiply. Write the answer in simplest form.

1. $3\frac{4}{5} × 2\frac{1}{3}$ $8\frac{13}{15}$
2. $6\frac{3}{4} × 4\frac{1}{3}$ $29\frac{1}{4}$
3. $8\frac{5}{9} × 7\frac{3}{7}$ $63\frac{5}{9}$
4. $2\frac{1}{2} × 3\frac{1}{3}$ $8\frac{1}{3}$
5. $2\frac{1}{2} × 4\frac{3}{8}$ $10\frac{15}{16}$
6. $10\frac{3}{4} × 7\frac{2}{3}$ $82\frac{5}{12}$
7. $5\frac{7}{9} × 13\frac{1}{2}$ 78
8. $4\frac{4}{5} × 3\frac{1}{8}$ 15
9. $4\frac{1}{4} × 3\frac{2}{3}$ $15\frac{7}{12}$
10. $18 × 7\frac{2}{3}$ 138
11. $2\frac{5}{6} × 12$ 34
12. $48 × 2\frac{1}{2}$ 120
13. $1\frac{1}{3} × \frac{3}{4} × 4\frac{1}{2}$ $4\frac{1}{2}$
14. $8\frac{1}{8} × 4\frac{4}{5} × 6\frac{1}{2}$ $257\frac{2}{5}$
15. $3\frac{1}{2} × 1\frac{1}{4} × 2\frac{1}{3}$ $10\frac{5}{24}$
16. $6\frac{1}{2} × 4\frac{2}{3} × 15$ 455

Chapter 4, page 149

Divide. Write the answer in simplest form.

1. $4\frac{2}{3} \div 1\frac{1}{3}$ $3\frac{1}{2}$
2. $6\frac{1}{4} \div 2\frac{3}{4}$ $2\frac{3}{11}$
3. $5\frac{7}{8} \div 3\frac{1}{8}$ $1\frac{22}{25}$
4. $2\frac{1}{5} \div 1\frac{1}{2}$ $1\frac{4}{7}$

5. $7 \div 3\frac{1}{2}$ 2
6. $20 \div 3\frac{1}{3}$ 6
7. $18 \div 2\frac{5}{9}$ $7\frac{1}{23}$
8. $2 \div 1\frac{1}{4}$ $1\frac{3}{5}$

9. $4 \div 1\frac{3}{4}$ $2\frac{2}{7}$
10. $9 \div 2\frac{2}{3}$ $3\frac{3}{8}$
11. $8 \div \frac{2}{3}$ 12
12. $7\frac{5}{9} \div \frac{1}{2}$ $15\frac{1}{9}$

13. $6\frac{2}{3} \div \frac{1}{6}$ 40
14. $12\frac{1}{2} \div 2\frac{5}{9}$ $4\frac{41}{46}$
15. $6 \div 3\frac{4}{7}$ $1\frac{17}{25}$
16. $10\frac{1}{6} \div 2\frac{2}{3}$ $3\frac{13}{16}$

Chapter 4, page 151

Write a fraction or a mixed number in simplest form for each decimal.

1. 0.75 $\frac{3}{4}$
2. 0.6 $\frac{3}{5}$
3. 0.45 $\frac{9}{20}$
4. 4.25 $4\frac{1}{4}$
5. 5.64 $5\frac{16}{25}$

Write a decimal for each fraction or mixed number. Use a bar to show repeating decimals.

6. $\frac{3}{4}$ 0.75
7. $\frac{7}{20}$ 0.35
8. $\frac{11}{66}$ $0.1\overline{6}$
9. $\frac{15}{36}$ $0.41\overline{6}$
10. $\frac{1}{6}$ $0.1\overline{6}$

11. $\frac{13}{15}$ $0.8\overline{6}$
12. $\frac{5}{9}$ $0.\overline{5}$
13. $1\frac{1}{2}$ 1.5
14. $\frac{13}{5}$ 2.6
15. $2\frac{1}{3}$ $2.\overline{3}$

Chapter 5, page 171

Copy and complete the chart for each container of water.

Length	Width	Height	Volume	Capacity	Mass
6 cm	5 cm	3 cm	1. ■ cm³	2. ■ mL	3. ■ g
9 m	6 m	4 m	4. ■ m³	5. ■ kL	6. ■ t
40 mm	50 mm	30 mm	7. ■ cm³	8. ■ mL	9. ■ g
30 dm	8 dm	3 dm	10. ■ m³	11. ■ kL	12. ■ t
120 cm	50 cm	60 cm	13. ■ m³	14. ■ kL	15. ■ t
55 mm	21 mm	33 mm	16. ■ mm³	17. ■ mL	18. ■ g

1. 90 2. 90 3. 90 4. 216 5. 216 6. 216 7. 60 8. 60 9. 60
10. 0.72 11. 0.72 12. 0.72 13. 0.36 14. 0.36 15. 0.36 16. 38,115 17. 38.115 18. 38.115

Chapter 5, page 175

Complete.

1. 12 ft = ■ in. 144
2. 5 mi = ■ yd 8,800
3. 14 yd = ■ ft 42
4. 96 in. = ■ ft 8
5. 57 ft = ■ yd 19
6. 21,120 ft = ■ mi 4
7. $8\frac{1}{2}$ ft = ■ in. 102
8. $8\frac{2}{3}$ yd = ■ ft 26
9. $2\frac{3}{5}$ mi = ■ ft 13,728
10. 90 in. = ■ ft $7\frac{1}{2}$
11. 30 in. = ■ yd $\frac{5}{6}$
12. 14 ft = ■ yd $4\frac{2}{3}$
13. 63 in. = ■ ft $5\frac{1}{4}$
14. 1,320 yd = ■ mi $\frac{3}{4}$
15. $3\frac{1}{2}$ mi = ■ ft 18,480
16. 4,224 yd = ■ mi $2\frac{2}{5}$
17. 9,240 ft = ■ mi $1\frac{3}{4}$
18. 414 in. = ■ yd $11\frac{1}{2}$
19. 66 in. = ■ yd $1\frac{5}{6}$
20. $1\frac{1}{6}$ mi = ■ ft 6,160
21. 306 in. = ■ yd $8\frac{1}{2}$

Chapter 5, page 177

Complete.

1. 5 qt = ■ pt 10
2. 15 gal = ■ qt 60
3. 7 lb = ■ oz 112
4. 64 fl oz = ■ c 8
5. 128 oz = ■ lb 8
6. 15 qt = ■ gal $3\frac{3}{4}$
7. $5\frac{1}{2}$ gal = ■ qt 22
8. $3\frac{1}{4}$ c = ■ fl oz 26
9. $7\frac{1}{2}$ lb = ■ oz 120
10. 15,000 lb = ■ T $7\frac{1}{2}$
11. 7 gal 2 qt = ■ qt 30
12. 94 oz = ■ lb ■ oz 5 14
13. 56 fl oz = ■ pt $3\frac{1}{2}$
14. $1\frac{1}{2}$ qt = ■ fl oz 48
15. 16 fl oz = ■ gal $\frac{1}{8}$
16. 7 c = ■ qt $1\frac{3}{4}$
17. $7\frac{1}{2}$ gal = ■ pt 60
18. $3\frac{1}{2}$ qt = ■ fl oz 112

Chapter 5, page 181

Find the greatest possible error in measurement.

1. 13 m ± 0.5 m
2. 18 cm ±0.5 cm
3. 48 mm ±0.5 mm
4. 12 km ±0.5 km
5. 300 cm ±0.5 cm
6. 40 mm ±0.5 mm
7. 325 cm ±0.5 cm
8. 875 km ±0.5 km
9. 48.2 km ±0.05 km
10. 76.4 mm ±0.05 mm
11. 9.6 m ±0.05 m
12. 48.5 mm ±0.05 mm
13. 17.25 km ± 0.005 km
14. 18.75 m ±0.005 m
15. 4.75 cm ±0.005 cm
16. 18.645 km ±0.0005 km

Chapter 6, page 213

Copy and write the missing fraction or percent.

1. $65\% = ■$ $\frac{13}{20}$
2. $■\% = \frac{1}{9}$ $11\frac{1}{9}\%$
3. $88\% = ■$ $\frac{22}{25}$
4. $■\% = \frac{5}{6}$ $83\frac{1}{3}\%$
5. $96\% = ■$ $\frac{24}{25}$
6. $■\% = \frac{99}{22}$ 450%
7. $27\% = ■$ $\frac{27}{100}$
8. $■\% = 18.2$ $1,820\%$
9. $49\% = ■$ $\frac{49}{100}$
10. $■ = 62\frac{1}{2}\%$ $\frac{5}{8}$
11. $\frac{15}{18} = ■\%$ $83\frac{1}{3}\%$
12. $■\% = 59.6$ $5,960\%$
13. $92\% = ■$ $\frac{23}{25}$
14. $■ = 40\%$ $\frac{2}{5}$
15. $37\frac{1}{2}\% = ■$ $\frac{3}{8}$

Chapter 6, page 225

Use a proportion to solve each problem.

1. Find 22% of 65. 14.3
2. What percent of 25 is 22? 88%
3. 6.4 is what percent of 40? 16%
4. Find 36% of 21. 7.56
5. What number is 13% of 250? 32.5
6. 225 is what percent of 500? 45%
7. Find 12% of 91. 10.92
8. 13 is what percent of 52? 25%
9. What is 125% of 40? 50
10. What is 25% of 116? 29
11. 35 is what percent of 700? 5%
12. Find 9% of 429. 38.61

Chapter 7, pages 251 and 253

Find the product.

1. $5 \cdot {}^-5$ -25
2. $^-5 \cdot 10$ -50
3. $^-15 \cdot {}^-4$ 60
4. $^-7 \cdot {}^-6$ 42
5. $^-22 \cdot {}^-13$ 286
6. $^-19 \cdot 27$ -513
7. $36 \cdot {}^-14$ -504
8. $^-52 \cdot {}^-4$ 208
9. $^-4 \cdot (8 \cdot 9)$ -288
10. $(^-4 \cdot {}^-8) \cdot 9$ 288
11. $(^-15 \cdot {}^-7) \cdot {}^-15$ $-1,575$
12. $16 \cdot (5 \cdot {}^-21)$ $-1,680$

Divide.

13. $^-24 \div {}^-6$ 4
14. $^-169 \div {}^-13$ 13
15. $^-225 \div 45$ -5
16. $625 \div {}^-125$ -5
17. $^-82 \div 2$ -41
18. $576 \div 24$ 24
19. $^-488 \div {}^-8$ 61
20. $1,024 \div {}^-32$ -32

Evaluate.

21. $(^-9 \cdot 21) + (^-8 \cdot {}^-7)$ -133
22. $\frac{14 \cdot (^-2 - 30)}{^-7 + 14}$ -64

Chapter 7, page 261

Compute. Write the answer in simplest form.

1. $\frac{1}{4} + \frac{3}{4}$ 1
2. $\frac{3}{8} - \frac{1}{8}$ $\frac{1}{4}$
3. $\frac{1}{2} - \frac{1}{2}$ 1
4. $\frac{-2}{3} + \frac{-1}{3}$ -1
5. $\frac{2}{9} - \frac{2}{18}$ $\frac{1}{9}$
6. $\frac{6}{7} + 4$ $4\frac{6}{7}$
7. $\frac{-4}{5} + \frac{3}{7}$ $-\frac{1}{35}$
8. $\frac{9}{14} - 7$ $-6\frac{5}{14}$
9. $^-24 + {}^-4\frac{1}{3}$ $-28\frac{1}{3}$
10. $\frac{-4}{7} + \frac{-2}{9}$ $-\frac{50}{63}$
11. $\frac{10}{15} - \frac{41}{45}$ $-\frac{1}{45}$... $\frac{26}{45}$
12. $^-1\frac{7}{8} - {}^-12$ $10\frac{1}{8}$
13. $16.35 + {}^-16.35$ 0
14. $0.56 - {}^-1.48$ 2.04
15. $^-4.63 - {}^-4.63$ 0
16. $^-12.1 + {}^-15.64$ -27.74
17. $31.3 + {}^-3.41$ 27.89
18. $^-264 - 8.65$ -272.65

Chapter 7, page 265

Compute. Write the answer in simplest form.

1. $\frac{1}{4} \div \frac{-1}{12}$ -3
2. $\frac{-2}{3} \cdot \frac{-1}{2}$ $\frac{1}{3}$
3. $\frac{-1}{2} \div \frac{-9}{4}$ $1\frac{1}{3}$
4. $\frac{3}{4} \cdot \frac{-8}{9}$ $-\frac{2}{3}$
5. $\frac{-7}{8} \cdot {}^-4$ $3\frac{1}{2}$
6. $1\frac{2}{3} \div {}^-1\frac{2}{3}$ -1
7. $\frac{-3}{5} \cdot \frac{9}{15}$ $-\frac{9}{25}$
8. $\frac{-12}{13} \div \frac{-1}{2}$ $1\frac{11}{13}$
9. $\frac{-7}{9} \cdot \frac{9}{11}$ $-\frac{7}{11}$
10. $^-1\frac{2}{3} \div {}^-3\frac{5}{9}$ (answer)
11. $\frac{15}{19} \div \frac{-2}{3}$ $-1\frac{7}{38}$
12. $^-2\frac{6}{7} \cdot {}^-5$ $14\frac{2}{7}$
13. $^-25 \div {}^-1.25$ 20
14. $^-6.7 \cdot 5.62$ -37.654
15. $12.9 \div {}^-12.9$ -1
16. $^-4.16 \cdot 2.33$ -9.6928
17. $229.9 \div {}^-22.99$ -10
18. $^-15.9 \cdot {}^-8.14$ 129.426

Chapter 7, page 267

If the number is rational, write it as a repeating or a terminating decimal. If it is irrational, estimate it to the nearest whole number.

1. $\sqrt{25}$ 5
2. $\frac{-4}{5}$ -0.8
3. $\sqrt{10}$ 3
4. $\frac{-10}{5}$ -2
5. $1\frac{2}{5}$ 1.4
6. $\frac{-6}{11}$ $-0.\overline{54}$
7. $\sqrt{5}$ 2
8. $3\frac{2}{9}$ 3.2
9. $\sqrt{26}$ 5
10. $\frac{-9}{2}$ -4.5
11. $\sqrt{99}$ 10
12. $^-1\frac{1}{2}$ -1.5
13. $\frac{-9}{17}$ -1
14. $2\frac{4}{9}$ 2.4
15. $\sqrt{45}$ 7
16. $^-6\frac{8}{9}$ $-6.\overline{8}$
17. $\sqrt{19}$ 4
18. $\frac{11}{4}$ 2.75
19. $\sqrt{81}$ 9
20. $\frac{-21}{8}$ -2.625
21. $\sqrt{144}$ 12
22. $\frac{-3}{8}$ -0.375
23. $\sqrt{65}$ 8
24. $\frac{-8}{23}$ 0
25. $\sqrt{1}$ 1

Chapter 8, page 285

Solve.

1. $2x + 6 = 28$ $x = 11$
2. $9y - 15 = 21$ $y = 4$
3. $4m + 6 = 34$ $m = 7$
4. $9t - 9 = 36$ $t = 5$
5. $\frac{1}{4}w + 5 = 25$ $w = 80$
6. $7g - 13 = 29$ $g = 6$
7. $\frac{c}{0.5} + 6 = 31$ $c = 12.5$
8. $5c - \frac{1}{2} = 9\frac{1}{2}$ $e = 2$
9. $\frac{p}{3} + 10 = 16$ $p = 18$
10. $\frac{d}{2} + 13 = 25$ $d = 24$
11. $\frac{z}{6} - 4 = 2$ $z = 36$
12. $\frac{a}{9} - 4 = 4$ $a = 72$
13. $0.25b - 11 = 4$ $b = 60$
14. $0.05r + 5.75 = 10$ $r = 85$
15. $\frac{r}{12} - 1.25 = 3$ $r = 51$
16. $\frac{f}{6} + 16 = 8$ $f = 48$
17. $\frac{-h}{3} + 15 = 9$ $h = 18$
18. $\frac{v}{8} - 2 = {}^-9$ $v = 56$
19. $\frac{1}{8}j + 5 = 10$ $j = 40$
20. $1\frac{1}{4}l - 20 = 105$ $l = 100$
21. $\frac{-d}{3} - 16 = {}^-24$ $d = 24$

Chapter 8, page 295

Solve and graph the inequality. **Check students' graphs.**

1. $m + 6 < 10$ $m < 4$
2. $o + 10 > 19$ $o > 9$
3. $x - 9 \le 4$ $x \le 13$
4. $z - 2 \ge 14$ $z \ge 16$
5. $8d > 72$ $d > 9$
6. $\frac{b}{7} > 3$ $b > 21$
7. $\frac{a}{8} \ge 4$ $a \ge 32$
8. $7q > 56$ $q > 8$
9. $0.25g < 25$ $g < 100$
10. $1.6s > 3.2$ $s > 2$
11. $j + \frac{1}{4} \ne 2$ $j \ne 1\frac{3}{4}$
12. $\frac{y}{1.5} < 8$ $y < 12$
13. $f - 9 \ne {}^-5$ $f \ne 4$
14. $\frac{x}{\frac{1}{2}} \ge 4$ $x \ge 2$
15. $p - 18 < {}^-9$ $p < 9$
16. $\frac{n}{\frac{1}{3}} \le \frac{2}{3}$ $n \le \frac{2}{9}$
17. $\frac{y}{8} < 4$ $y < 32$
18. $\frac{-z}{7} > 4$ $z > 28$
19. $\frac{-r}{11} \ne 2$ $r \ne 22$
20. $\frac{1}{10}t < {}^-40$ $t < {}^-400$

Chapter 8, page 299

Solve.

1. $3x + 2 < 5$ $x < 1$
2. $7z - 4 \ge 2$ $z \ge \frac{6}{7}$
3. $8q + 12 \ne 19$ $q \ne \frac{7}{8}$
4. $14r - 70 \le 28$ $r \le 7$
5. $\frac{f}{10} - 8 > 12$ $f > 200$
6. $\frac{d}{3} + 17 \ne 26$ $d \ne 27$
7. $\frac{m}{12} - 42 \ne 6$ $m \ne 576$
8. $\frac{k}{8} + 36 > 9$ $k > {}^-216$
9. $6.1n + 4 \ne 16.2$ $n \ne 2$
10. $7.6c - 8.4 > 15.92$ $c > 3.2$
11. $\frac{p}{9.1} - 7 < 16.8$ $p < 216.58$
12. $\frac{j}{76} + 18.2 \le 5.4$ $j \ge {}^-97.28$
13. $4e + \frac{3}{4} \ne 12\frac{1}{2}$ $e \ne 2\frac{15}{16}$
14. $\frac{2}{3}y - 8 \le 6$ $y \le 21$
15. $\frac{t}{12} - \frac{4}{7} > \frac{13}{14}$ $t > 21$
16. $\frac{s}{5} + \frac{9}{11} > \frac{17}{33}$ $s > {}^-1\frac{17}{33}$
17. $16u - {}^-4 > {}^-92$ $u > {}^-6$
18. $5v + 6 \le {}^-17$ $v \le {}^-4\frac{3}{5}$
19. $\frac{-q}{2} - 10 \ne {}^-10$ $q \ne 0$
20. $\frac{g}{7} + {}^-3 > {}^-14$ $g > {}^-77$

Chapter 9, page 317

For each set of data find the median, mode, and mean.

Set of data	Median	Mode	Mean
21, 23, 49, 18, 7, 21, 8	**1.** ■ 21	**2.** ■ 21	**3.** ■ 21
37.2, 41.8, 29, 37.2, 46, 28.5	**4.** ■ 37.2	**5.** ■ 37.2	**6.** ■ 36.616
$3\frac{1}{4}, 1\frac{1}{2}, 5\frac{2}{5}, 3\frac{1}{8}, \frac{9}{10}, \frac{5}{8}, 1\frac{3}{8}$	**7.** ■ $1\frac{1}{2}$	**8.** ■ none	**9.** ■ $2\frac{87}{280}$
2,192; 4,617; 3,147; 5,908	**10.** ■ 3,882	**11.** ■ none	**12.** ■ 3,966

Chapter 9, page 333

Find the number of permutations or combinations.

1. $_4P_2$ 12
2. $_5P_2$ 20
3. $_5P_3$ 60
4. $_7P_3$ 210
5. $_4P_3$ 24
6. $_4C_3$ 4
7. $_6C_3$ 20
8. $_6P_4$ 360
9. $_7C_3$ 35
10. $_7C_5$ 21
11. $_{12}P_5$ 95,040
12. $_{10}C_5$ 252
13. $_{14}C_6$ 3,003
14. $_{20}P_5$ 1,860,480
15. $_{11}C_9$ 55
16. $_{15}C_{10}$ 3,003

Solve.

17. How many numbers greater than 90,000 can be formed using each of the digits 5, 6, 7, 8, and 9 only once? 24

Chapter 11, page 401

For each right triangle, find the missing side, rounded to the nearest tenth. (HINT: Sketch the triangle.) m∠C = 90°.

1. $a = 4$ cm, $b = 6.5$ cm 7.6 cm
2. $a = 2.2$ m, $b = 3.5$ m 4.1 m
3. $a = 4$ km, $b = 4$ km 5.7 km
4. $a = 9.3$ mm, $b = 8.6$ mm 12.7 mm
5. $a = 7$ cm, $c = 10.6$ cm 8 cm
6. $b = 2$ m, $c = 7.2$ m 6.9 m
7. $a = 10$ in., $b = 12$ in. 15.6 in.
8. $a = 5$ m, $c = 13$ m 12 m
9. $b = 2$ m, $c = \sqrt{5}$ m 1 m
10. $b = 2$ mm, $c = 3$ mm 2.2 mm

Chapter 11, page 409

Find the area of each square.

1. $s = 6$ cm 36 cm²
2. $s = 14$ m 196 m²
3. $s = 7.5$ km 56.25 km²
4. $s = 12.8$ dm 163.84 dm²

Find the area of each rectangle.

5. $l = 7$ m $w = 5$ m 35 m²
6. $l = 8.2$ cm $w = 4.5$ cm 36.9 cm²
7. $l = 14.7$ mm $w = 12.9$ mm 189.33 mm²

Find the area of each parallelogram.

8. $l = 9$ dm $w = 4$ dm 36 dm²
9. $l = 22$ m $w = 7.1$ m 156.2 m²
10. $l = 23.2$ dam $w = 5.7$ dam 132.24 dam²

Chapter 11, page 411

Find the area of each triangle.

1. $b = 6$ m $h = 12$ m 36 m²
2. $b = 7$ cm $h = 6$ cm 21 cm²
3. $b = 11.9$ cm $h = 3$ cm 17.85 cm²
4. $b = 14$ km $h = 7.3$ km 51.1 km²
5. $b = 6.9$ m $h = 6.9$ m 23.805 m²
6. $b = 31.8$ dm $h = 28.4$ dm 451.56 dm²

Find the area of each trapezoid.

7. $b_1 = 9$ cm $b_2 = 12$ cm $h = 4$ cm 42 cm²
8. $b_1 = 15.6$ m $b_2 = 7$ m $h = 8$ m 90.4 m²
9. $b_1 = 71$ mm $b_2 = 42.8$ mm $h = 66.9$ mm 3,806.61 mm²

Chapter 11, page 421

Find the surface area of each cylinder. Use 3.14 for π, and round to the nearest tenth.

1. radius = 4 cm height = 6 cm 251.2 cm²
2. radius = 12 m height = 7 m 1,431.8 m²
3. diameter = 28 mm height = 106 mm 10,550.4 mm²
4. radius = 9.2 m height = 17 m 1,513.7 m²
5. diameter = 11.5 cm height = 15.2 cm 756.5 cm²
6. diameter = 6.7 dm height = 6.7 dm 211.4 dm²

Find the surface area of each cone. Use 3.14 for π, and round to the nearest tenth.

7. radius = 9 km slant height = 2 km 310.9 km²
8. radius = 7.5 m slant height = 12 m 459.2 m²
9. diameter = 37.8 mm slant height = 105.2 mm 7,364.8 mm²

Chapter 11, page 425

Find the volume of each rectangular prism. Round to the nearest tenth.

1. $\ell = 12$ cm, $w = 17$ cm, $h = 14$ cm 2,856 cm³
2. $\ell = 9.9$ m, $w = 21$ m, $h = 4.7$ m 977.1 m³

Find the volume of each hexagonal prism. Round to the nearest tenth.

3. $B = 142$ km², $h = 7$ km 994 km³
4. $B = 26.7$ m², $h = 31.4$ m 838.4 m³

Find the volume of each pyramid. Round to the nearest tenth.

5. $B = 40$ cm², $h = 15$ cm 200 cm³
6. $h = 6.6$ mm, $B = 21.4$ mm² 47.1 mm³

Chapter 12, page 441

Solve for y, using ⁻3 and 4 as replacements for x.

1. $y = x - 5$ $y = {}^-8$; ⁻1
2. $y = 7 + x$ $y = 4$; 11
3. $y = 9x + 2$ $y = {}^-25$; 38
4. $^-x + y = 17$ $y = 14$; 21
5. $y - 3x = 4$ $y = {}^-5$; 16
6. $5x - 2y = 7$ $y = {}^-11$; $6\frac{1}{2}$

Make a table of values for each equation. Use ⁻2, ⁻1, 0, and 3 as replacement values for x.

7. $y = 7x$

x	⁻2	⁻1	0	3
y	⁻14	⁻7	0	21

8. $y = 4x - 2y$

| x | | ⁻10 | ⁻6 | ⁻2 | 10 |

9. $6x + 3y = 9$

x	⁻2	⁻1	0	3
y	7	5	3	⁻3

For each equation, write the ordered pair that is *not* a solution.

10. $x + y = 8$ (0,8), (3,5), (2,9), (7,1) (2,9)
11. $7x - 2y = 15$ $\left(2, \frac{-1}{2}\right)$, (5,10), $\left(4,6\frac{1}{2}\right)$, $\left(0, 7\frac{1}{2}\right)$ $\left(0, 7\frac{1}{2}\right)$

Chapter 12, page 445

Write *yes* if the relation is a function and *no* if it is not a function.

1. {(2,4), (3,5), (4,6), (5,7)} yes
2. {(7,13), (8,15), (9,17), (10,19)} yes
3. {(1,7), (1,8), (2,9), (3,10)} no
4. {(1,11), (3,11), (5,11), (7,11)} yes
5. {(0,9), (⁻1,18), (1,27), (0,36)} no
6. {(⁻2,⁻3), (⁻4,⁻5), (⁻6,⁻7), (⁻8,⁻9)} yes

MATH REASONING

Chapter 1

Logical Reasoning, pages 6–7

Using the Commutative and Associative Properties, regroup the numbers to find the sum by using mental math. Then find the sum.

1. $12 + 13 + 17 + 8$
$12 + 8 + 13 + 17 =$
$20 + 30 = 50$

2. $25 + 99 + 75 + 1$
$25 + 75 + 99 + 1 =$
$100 + 100 = 200$

3. $85 + 22 + 10 + 15$
$85 + 15 + 22 + 10 =$
$100 + 32 = 132$

Logical Reasoning, page 8

After more than two months of climbing, Sir Edmund Hillary and Tenzing Norgay became the first men to climb Mount Everest, the highest mountain in the world. The precise height of Mount Everest has been the subject of considerable debate. At various times in the past, it has been set at 29,002 ft by the British Government, 29,028 ft by the Indian Government, and 29,141 ft by wide, though unofficial, public usage. If you were reporting the approximate height of Mount Everest, what would you say it is?   Answers will vary.
Encourage students to explain their answers.

Challenge, pages 22–23

Find the 4-digit number that satisfies all of these conditions.

- The number is less than 100 and greater than 90.
- If the number is rounded to the nearest whole number, the result is 94.
- The number's tenths digit is 2 less than its hundredths digit.
- If the number is rounded to the nearest tenth, the result is 93.6.
93.57

Math Reasoning   Student Handbook   **H207**

Chapter 1

Logical Reasoning, pages 26–27

Copy the star and the circled numbers on your paper. Write numbers in the blank circles so that each straight line has a sum of 4.0.

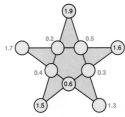

Logical Reasoning, pages 28–29

Suppose that the ⑥ key does not work on your calculator. Show how you might use the calculator to do these addition problems.
Possible answers are given.

1. $355.9 + 34.6$ $355.9 + 34.2 + 0.4$

2. $1,624 + 126.4 + 821.64$ $1,324 + 300 + 123.4 + 3 + 821.34 + 0.3$

3. 36×37 $35 \times 37 + 37$

4. $1,496 - 395$ $1,497 - 395 - 1$

Challenge, pages 30–31

Place plus or minus signs and decimal points between the digits, as necessary, to make the statements true.

Example: $4\ 2\ 1\ 7\ 6\ 3 = 21.83$

$4.2 + 17.63 = 21.83$

1. $7\ 5\ 8\ 4\ 9\ 3 = 3.54$
$7 + 5.84 - 9.3 = 3.54$

2. $2\ 1\ 5\ 0\ 7\ 5 = 17.2$
$21.5 + 0.7 - 5 = 17.2$

3. $6\ 3\ 8\ 2\ 7\ 9 = 50.3$
$6 + 38 - 2.7 + 9 = 50.3$

H208   Student Handbook   **Math Reasoning**

Chapter 2

Challenge, pages 52–53

"Messy Margie" created a puzzle square using operation signs that became unreadable inkblots. Can you help her fill in the correct signs? Copy the puzzle on your paper. Insert $+$, $-$, $\times$, or $\div$ in place of each inkblot to make the problems in each row and column correct.

8	●	3	●	2	=	12
●		●		●		●
5	●	2	●	9	=	12
●		●		●		●
9	●	2	●	6	=	12
=		=		=		=
12	●	12	●	12	=	36

$\times$; $\div$

$-$; $\times$; $\times$; $+$

$-$; $+$

$+$; $\times$; $-$; $+$

$\times$; $-$

$+$; $+$

Logical Reasoning, pages 56–57

second year; $3.78

During the first year that Brenda had her savings account, she received interest that equaled $0.0565 \times \$1,000$. The following year, the interest was $0.0548 \times \$1,100$. In which year did she receive more interest? What was the difference in the amounts of interest?

Logical Reasoning, pages 60–61

Look for a pattern as you complete Exercises 1–3. Use the pattern to complete Exercises 4–5.

1. $9 \times 8 = $ ■ 72

2. $9 \times 8.8 = $ ■ 79.2

3. $9 \times 88.8 = $ ■ 799.2

4. $9 \times 888.8 = $ ■ 7,999.2

5. $9 \times 8,888.8 = $ ■ 79,999.2

Math Reasoning   Student Handbook   **H209**

Chapter 2

Logical Reasoning, pages 62–63

Bob wants to rent some camping equipment for a nine-day period. The equipment rental fee is $17.65 per day.

1. If Bob rents the equipment at this rate, how much will it cost for nine days? $158.85

2. Suppose he can pay a weekly rate of $110 and the daily rate for each additional day. Should he do this? Explain the reason for your answer.
Yes; the cost is $145.30. He will save $13.55.

Challenge, pages 64–65

Use the digits 1, 2, 3, 4, and 5 to complete the division problem.

```
              ■.■■        1.52
      34■■ ) 5 1 . 6 8
          -  ■■            3 4
          ─────
             1 7
```

Challenge, pages 66–67

Place multiplication or division signs and decimal points between the digits to make the statement true. Exercise 1 is done for you.

1. $3\ 2\ 1\ 6\ 2\ 2 = 4.4$
$32 \div 16 \times 2.2 = 4.4$

2. $3\ 8\ 0\ 5\ 2 = 3.8$
$3.8 \times 0.5 \times 2 = 3.8$

3. $5\ 1\ 2\ 6\ 1 = 1$
$5 \times 1.2 \div 6 \times 1 = 1$

H210   Student Handbook   **Math Reasoning**

Chapter 3

Challenge, pages 82–83

Write the square roots and cube roots. Then use the code to discover Jennifer's goal. Use the square root table on page 83 and the cube root table on page 474. TO BECOME A DOCTOR

$\sqrt{81}$ $\sqrt[3]{27}$ 9; 3

$\sqrt{49}$ $\sqrt[3]{64}$ $\sqrt[3]{512}$ $\sqrt{9}$ $\sqrt[3]{125}$ $\sqrt{16}$ 7; 4; 8; 3; 5; 4

$\sqrt{196}$ $\sqrt{121}$ $\sqrt[3]{27}$ $\sqrt{64}$ $\sqrt[3]{729}$ $\sqrt{9}$ $\sqrt[3]{216}$ 14; 11; 3; 8; 9; 3; 6

3 = O 4 = E
5 = M 6 = R
7 = B 8 = C
9 = T 11 = D
14 = A

Logical Reasoning, pages 88–89

The mathematician Christian Goldbach (1690–1764) stated that every even number greater than 2 can be expressed as the sum of two prime numbers.

12 = 5 + 7 8 = 5 + 3

Show how each even number can be expressed as the sum of two prime numbers. Answers may vary. Possible answers are given.

1. 10 3 + 7
2. 16 13 + 3
3. 20 13 + 7
4. 32 29 + 3
5. 50 47 + 3

Logical Reasoning, pages 94–95

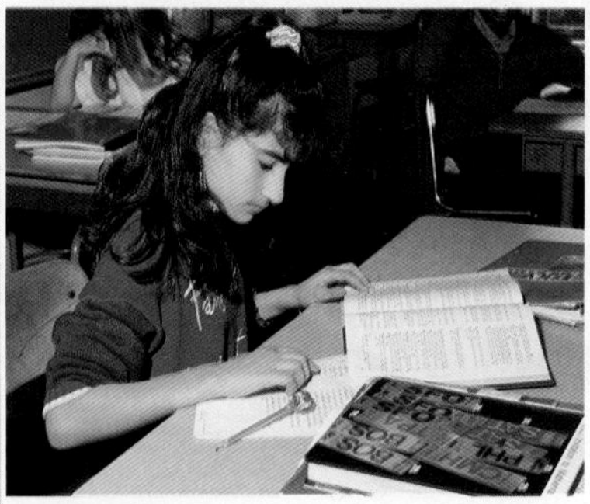

Solve.

1. Which is greater—the greatest common factor of 16 and 55 or the greatest common factor of 22 and 42? GCF of 22 and 42
2. The GCF of two numbers is 8. The LCM of the numbers is 48. Both of the numbers are less than 30. What are the numbers? 16 and 24

Chapter 3

Logical Reasoning, pages 98–99

The number 4 can be expressed by $4 = 4 \times (4 - 4) + 4$ using four 4's and the rules for order of operations.
Answers may vary. Possible answers are given.

1. Express the number 1 using four 4's. $1 = (4 + 4) \div (4 + 4)$
2. Express the number 2 using four 4's. $2 = (4 \times 4) \div (4 + 4)$
3. Express the number 5 using five 5's. $5 = 5 \times 5 \times 5 \div (5 \times 5)$
4. Express the number 6 using five 6's. $6 = 6 \div 6 \times 6 \times 6 \div 6$

Visual Thinking, pages 106–107

The key to a code is at the right. Numbers are represented by the shapes of the lines they are within. For example, the number 3 is represented as └.

1	2	3
4	5	6
7	8	9

Solve the following problems. Write each answer in code and as a number.

1. ┌×□=⊐□ 9 × 5 = 4 5
2. ⊓┌⊔÷⊐=⊔⊔└ 8 9 2 ÷ 4 = 2 2 3
3. ┘⊐⊐÷┘⊔=┘□ 1 4 4 ÷ 1 2 = 1 2
4. ⊏□┘┘−⊓└⊓=□⊏┐└ 6 5 1 1 − 8 3 8 = 5 6 7 3

Visual Thinking, pages 110–111

Three small coin bags contain two coins each. One bag contains two dimes, another two nickels, and the third contains a nickel and a dime. Each bag is labeled 20¢, 10¢, or 15¢, but each is mislabeled. If you can remove only one coin, from which bag would you remove a coin to determine how all three bags should be labeled? Explain your answer.

Remove a coin from the bag labeled 15¢. If you remove a nickel, the bag should be labeled 10¢. Then the 20¢ label should say 15¢ and the 10¢ label should say 20¢. If you remove a dime, the bag should be labeled 20¢. The 20¢ label should say 10¢ and the 10¢ label should say 15¢.

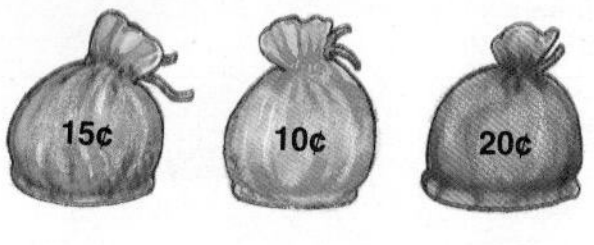
15¢
10¢
20¢

Chapter 4

Visual Thinking, pages 120–121

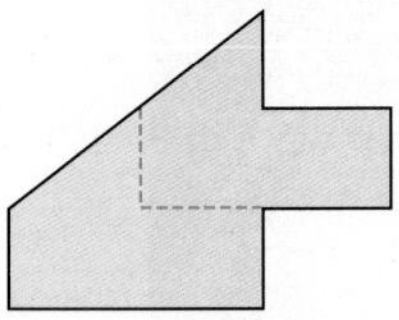

Copy this figure on your paper. Then divide the figure into two equal pieces by drawing two straight lines.

Challenge, pages 130–131

Eduardo needs to draw a line that is 6 in. long, but he does not have a ruler. He does have some sheets of notebook paper that are each $8\frac{1}{2}$ in. wide and 11 in. long. Describe how the notebook paper can be used to measure 6 in. He can add the measure of two papers widths (17 in.). Then he can subtract the measure of one paper's length (11 in.). The difference will be exactly 6 in.

Challenge, pages 142–143

Copy the magic square on your paper. Complete the square so that the product of the numbers in each row, each column, and each diagonal is equal to 1.

2	4	$\frac{1}{8}$
$\frac{1}{16}$	1	16
8	$\frac{1}{4}$	$\frac{1}{2}$

Chapter 4

Logical Reasoning, pages 148–149

Liechtenstein is the leading exporter of false teeth in the world. Assume that the manufacturers shipped out $36\frac{1}{2}$ million sets of teeth in a year. During that period, they averaged one defect in every 100 sets of teeth that were shipped. If shipments were sent out every day of the year, about how many sets of teeth with a defect would have been shipped on an average day? about 1,000 sets

Visual Thinking, pages 150–151

Trace or copy the points on your paper. Draw a horizontal or vertical straight line between the points that are equivalent quantities. You will end up spelling a good name for a European race car driver. OTTO

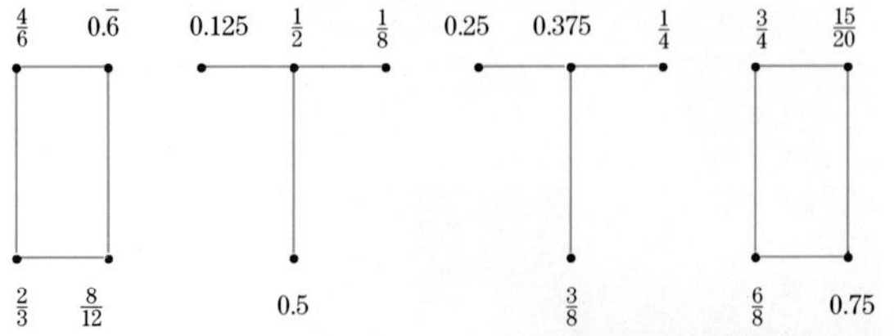
$\frac{4}{6}$
$0.\overline{6}$
0.125
$\frac{1}{2}$
$\frac{1}{8}$
0.25
0.375
$\frac{1}{4}$
$\frac{3}{4}$
$\frac{15}{20}$
$\frac{2}{3}$
$\frac{8}{12}$
0.5
$\frac{3}{8}$
$\frac{6}{8}$
0.75

Challenge, pages 152–153

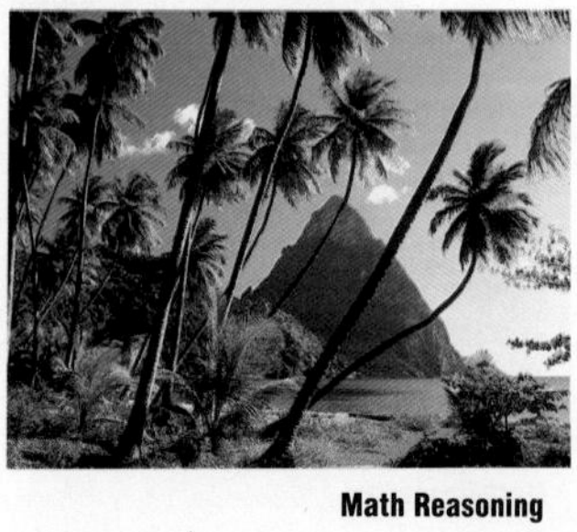

On the small imaginary island of Nore, the residents were Bores and Snorers. Four-tenths of the Bores were Snorers. One-tenth of the Snorers were Bores. Six Bores were not Snorers. How many Snorers were there? 40 Snorers

Chapter 5

Visual Thinking, pages 166–167

A treasure-hunting expedition will launch a robotic submersible at Point A. Its intended search pattern follows.

- travel east for 100 m
- travel south for 10 m
- travel west for 0.2 km
- travel east for $\frac{1}{100}$ km

Then it will surface. Ignoring any effects of ocean currents, how far should the submersible be from Point A when it surfaces?

It should be at Point A.

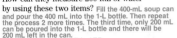
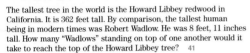

Challenge, pages 168–169

The Martin family has gone camping. In their provisions is a package of freeze-dried spaghetti that they want to prepare for dinner. It requires 200 mL of water. The problem is that the Martins forgot to bring their measuring utensils. They do, however, have a 1-L soft-drink bottle and an empty 400-mL soup can. How can they measure 200 mL of water by using these two items? Fill the 400-mL soup can and pour the 400 mL into the 1-L bottle. Then repeat the process 2 more times. The third time, only 200 mL can be poured into the 1-L bottle and there will be 200 mL left in the can.

Challenge, pages 174–175

The tallest tree in the world is the Howard Libbey redwood in California. It is 362 feet tall. By comparison, the tallest human being in modern times was Robert Wadlow. He was 8 feet, 11 inches tall. How many "Wadlows" standing on top of one another would it take to reach the top of the Howard Libbey tree? 41

Chapter 5

Visual Thinking, pages 182–183

Use a clock to help you answer these questions.

1. What time is it when the number of hours after noon is 2 more than the number of hours before midnight? 7 P.M.

2. What time is it when the number of hours after noon is 4 less than the number of hours before midnight? 4 P.M.

Logical Reasoning, pages 186–187

Grace has 20 minutes to get to the airport before her plane departs. The airport is 20 miles away from her home. She drives at a speed of 30 miles per hour for the first 10 miles. Will she get to the airport before her plane leaves? No; at 30 miles per hour she can travel 10 miles in 20 minutes. She will be 10 miles from the airport when the plane leaves.

Challenge, pages 188–189

This table shows the relationship between temperatures in degrees Celsius (°C) and degrees Fahrenheit (°F).

°C	5	10	15	20	25	30	32.5
°F	41	50	59	68	■	■	■

    77   86   90.5

1. Copy and complete the table.

2. This rule can be used to convert °C to °F. Use the table above to complete the rule.

$$°F = 1.8 \times °C + \blacksquare$$
                 32

Chapter 6

Challenge, pages 200–201

There are red, blue, and green marbles in a bag. The ratio of the number of blue marbles to the number of green marbles is 2 : 3. The ratio of the number of red marbles to the number of blue marbles is 6 : 5. The ratio of the number of red marbles to the number of green marbles is 4 : 5. There are fewer than 40 marbles in the bag. Find the total number of marbles in the bag. 37 marbles

Challenge, pages 210–211

1. When the percent for the fraction $\frac{1}{5}$ is known, what is a shortcut for finding the percent for $\frac{3}{5}$? Show that your answer is correct.
Multiply the percent by 3. $\frac{1}{5} = 20\%$, $\frac{3}{5} = 3 \times 20\% = 60\%$

2. When the fraction $\frac{a}{b}$ is expressed as a percent, the percent is greater than 100. How does the value of a compare with value of b? $a > b$

Visual Thinking, pages 212–213

Use the figure to answer the questions.

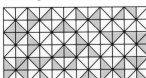

1. What percent of the figure is shaded? $33\frac{1}{3}\%$

2. How many more triangles would have to be shaded in order for 50% of the figure to be shaded? 24

3. How many triangles would have to have the shading removed in order for 25% of the figure to be shaded? 12

Chapter 6

Logical Reasoning, pages 216–217

Bob wants to borrow $250 from his brother Karl. Karl is willing to loan Bob the money if Bob repays the money in 5 equal monthly payments. Bob wants to repay the money by paying 20% of the outstanding balance each month until the debt is paid.

1. How much would Bob pay each month according to Karl's payment schedule? $50

2. How much would Bob pay the first month according to his own schedule? $50

3. At the end of 3 months, how much would Bob still owe if he uses his own payment schedule? $128

4. Using his own payment schedule, will Bob ever pay off the loan? No; he will continue to pay just 20% of the balance. The 20% decreases each time.

Challenge, pages 220–221

Jessica sold 40% of her baseball cards. Then she gave away 25% of the cards she had left. Now she has 18 cards. How many did she have before she began selling them and giving them away? 40 cards

Visual Thinking, pages 226–227

Show how you can decrease the number of small, identical squares in the figure by 30% by removing 5 of the 24 sticks.

Answers can vary. Possible answer is shown.

Chapter 7

Logical Reasoning, pages 240–241

Solve.

1. If t is a positive number, is ^-t positive or negative?
negative

2. If ^-t is a positive number, is t positive or negative?
negative

3. If t is a negative number, is ^-t positive or negative?
positive

4. If ^-t is a negative number, is t positive or negative?
positive

5. If ^-t is a positive number, is $^-(^-t)$ positive or negative?
negative

6. If ^-t is a negative number, is $^-(^-t)$ positive or negative?
positive

Challenge, pages 244–245

Find the values for the variables in the magic square. The sum of each row, each column, and each diagonal should be the same.

$^-3$	t	$^-5$
x	$^-2$	b
s	a	$^-1$

$t = 2$

$x = {}^-4, b = 0$

$s = 1, a = {}^-6$

Challenge, pages 252–253

Solve.

1. $(^-4 \times 6 + 18 - {}^-11) \times (^-2 - {}^-13)$ 55

2. $(^-9 \times {}^-8) \div (4 \times {}^-2)$ $^-9$

3. $12 - {}^-8 \times 2 + 20 \div {}^-4 + {}^-9$ 14

Chapter 7

Challenge, pages 258–259

John, Penny, and Julian played a game. They each picked a rational number in the form of a fraction. The person who picked the number that was not the least and not the greatest was the winner. Here are the numbers they picked.

John: $^-\frac{73}{58}$ Penny: $^-\frac{50}{33}$ Julian: $^-\frac{91}{72}$

Use a calculator to determine the winner of the game.
Julian was the winner.

Logical Reasoning, pages 264–265

Jean tells Mary that she has 2 rational numbers in mind. One of these, she says, is 5 times as large as the other, and their sum is $\frac{3}{4}$. What are the two rational numbers?
$\frac{1}{8}$ and $\frac{5}{8}$

Challenge, pages 268–269

On graph paper, draw a real-number plane. Graph each pair of points and connect them with a straight line. When you finish, you will discover the names of Sue's best friends. Kim, Joy

1. $(^-9,1), (^-9,5)$ **2.** $(^-9,3), (^-7,5)$ **3.** $(^-9,3), (^-7,1)$

4. $(^-5,1), (^-5,5)$ **5.** $(^-3,1), (^-3,5)$ **6.** $(^-3,5), (^-1,3)$

7. $(^-1,3), (1,5)$ **8.** $(1,5), (1,1)$ **9.** $(^-9,{}^-3), (^-7,{}^-3)$

10. $(^-8,{}^-3), (^-8,{}^-7)$ **11.** $(^-8,{}^-7), (^-10,{}^-7)$ **12.** $(^-10,{}^-7), (^-10,{}^-6)$

13. $(^-5,{}^-3), (^-5,{}^-7)$ **14.** $(^-5,{}^-3), (^-3,{}^-3)$ **15.** $(^-3,{}^-3), (^-3,{}^-7)$

16. $(^-1,{}^-3), (1,{}^-5)$ **17.** $(1,{}^-5), (3,{}^-3)$ **18.** $(1,{}^-5), (1,{}^-7)$

Chapter 8

Challenge, pages 280–281

Evaluate each expression for $n = 3$ in this magic square. What is the sum of each row, each column, and each diagonal? 30

4	18	8
$7 - n$	$6n$	$n + 5$
14	10	6
$n + 11$	$n + 7$	$2n$
12	2	16
$4n$	$n - 1$	$19 - n$

Logical Reasoning, pages 282–283

1. If $3x = 6$, then $6x = \blacksquare$. 12

2. If $8t = 12$, then $4t = \blacksquare$. 6

3. If $x + 5 = 9$, then $2x + 10 = \blacksquare$. 18

4. If $b - 3 = 15$, then $3b - 9 = \blacksquare$. 45

5. If $\frac{n}{3} = 10$, then $\frac{n}{6} = \blacksquare$. 5

6. If $\frac{p}{4} = {}^-8$, then $\frac{p}{2} = \blacksquare$. $^-16$

Logical Reasoning, pages 284–285

Find a pattern. Use the pattern to find the value of each variable.

1. $1 \times 8 + n = 9$ 1

2. $12 \times 8 + x = 98$ 2

3. $123 \times 8 + p = 987$ 3

4. $1,234 \times 8 + s = 9,876$ 4

5. $12,345 \times 8 + t = 98,765$ 5

6. $y \times 8 + w = 987,654$ 123,456; 6

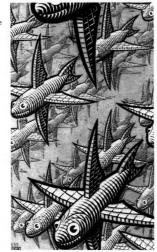

Chapter 8

Challenge, pages 292–293

Tim gave his friend this problem.

I am thinking of five different whole numbers that have a sum less than 16. The sum of the squares of these whole numbers is less than 56. Find

1. the numbers that solve the problem. 1, 2, 3, 4, 5

2. the sum of the numbers. 15

3. the sum of the squares of the numbers. 55

Logical Reasoning, pages 294–295

Complete. Write $<$ or $>$.

1. If $a < 5$, then $a + 6 \bullet 5 + 6$. $<$

2. If $c > 10$, then $c - 6 \bullet 10 - 6$. $>$

3. If $a < b$ and $b < c$, then $a \bullet c$. $<$

4. If $r > s$ and $s > t$, then $r \bullet t$. $>$

Visual Thinking, pages 300–301

The graph shows the solution of an inequality.

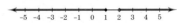

$-5 \quad -4 \quad -3 \quad -2 \quad -1 \quad 0 \quad 1 \quad 2 \quad 3 \quad 4 \quad 5$

1. What numbers are solutions of the inequality?
all numbers less than or equal to 1 and greater than 2

2. What numbers are not solutions of the inequality?
all numbers less than or equal to 2 and greater than 1

Chapter 9

Logical Reasoning, pages 316–317

The mean of 5 one-digit numbers is 4.8.

The median of the 5 numbers is 5.

The mode of the 5 numbers is 2.

What are the numbers? 2, 2, 5, 7, 8 or 2, 2, 5, 6, 9

Visual Thinking, pages 322–323

A driver is sitting in a car at a stoplight, waiting for the light to turn green. The light turns green and the driver accelerates the car. Which of the following graphs fits the situation? b

a. **b.** **c.**

Challenge, pages 328–329

The license plates in a certain state have 2 letters and a 4-digit number.

1. How many different license plates can be made if any letter can be used and any of the digits 0 to 9 can be used?
   6,760,000
2. How many different license plates can be made if the four-digit number has to be an odd number?
   3,380,000

Chapter 9

Challenge, pages 332–333

You and 7 friends are at a restaurant. You are going to sit together at a table that seats 8.

1. In how many ways can your group be seated?
   40,320 ways
2. Suppose that it takes 10 seconds to change the seating order. How many seconds would it take to sit in all the possible seating arrangements?
   403,200 seconds
3. How many days would it take to sit in all the possible seating arrangements?
   $4\frac{2}{3}$ days

Logical Reasoning, pages 334–335

Jason types 3 letters and addresses 3 envelopes. Before he places the letters in the envelopes, he accidentally drops all of them on the floor. He picks up the letters and envelopes and without looking, inserts each letter into an envelope. What is the probability that each letter was inserted into the correct envelope? $\frac{1}{6}$

Challenge, pages 336–337

A cube with sides numbered 1 to 6 is tossed 6 times. The number 5 is rolled on the first toss. What is the probability of getting the number 5 on the next 5 tosses? $\frac{1}{7,776}$

Chapter 10

Logical Reasoning, pages 356–357

A reflex angle is an angle with a measure between 180° and 360°.

1. What degree measure would you use on a protractor to draw a reflex angle of 200°?
   160°
2. Draw a reflex angle of 320°.

Reflex angle

320°

Challenge, pages 360–361

Use a protractor to draw angles of 30° and 45°. Then use the angles you drew, a compass, and a straightedge to construct the following angles. Possible angle choices are given.

1. 60°   2. 90°   3. 75°   4. 120°
   30° + 30°   45° + 45°   45° + 30°   45° + 45° + 30°

Visual Thinking, pages 366–367

How many triangles are in this figure?
14

Chapter 10

Challenge, pages 368–369

Use polygons to solve the following problems.

1. Each of 5 persons talked to the other 4 by telephone. How many calls were made?
   10 calls
2. Each of 8 persons talked to the other 7 by telephone. How many calls were made?
   28 calls

Visual Thinking, pages 380–381

Make four copies of this trapezoid. Then show how you can use the four congruent trapezoids to make a larger similar trapezoid.

Visual Thinking, pages 382–383

Trace each of the figures. Then write the word that results when the figure is reflected over the given line.

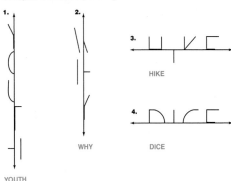

1.

2.

3. HIKE

4. DICE

WHY   DICE

YOUTH

543

Chapter 11

Visual Thinking, pages 398–399

Use graph paper to draw six different polygons, each having a perimeter of 12 units. Make sure that the length of each side is a whole number. One polygon is drawn for you.
Possible answers are given.

Challenge, pages 404–405

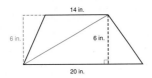

The diameter of each wheel on Robbie's bicycle is 28 inches.

1. How many feet will Robbie ride if each wheel makes 100 revolutions? Use $\frac{22}{7}$ for π. $733\frac{1}{3}$ ft

2. How many revolutions will each wheel make if Robbie rides his bicycle 1 mile?
720 revolutions

Visual Thinking, pages 410–411

You have seen that the area of a trapezoid can be $\frac{1}{2}$ the area of a certain parallelogram. Copy the trapezoid at the right. Show how the area of the trapezoid can be the sum of the areas of two triangles. Then find the area of the trapezoid.

$A = \frac{1}{2} \cdot 6 \cdot 20 + \frac{1}{2} \cdot 6 \cdot 14$
$= 60 + 42$
$= 102 \text{ in.}^2$

Chapter 11

Challenge, pages 412–413

 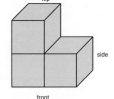

1. A circle has a radius of 7 in. The area of a rectangle that has a length of 14 in. is the same as the area of the circle. Find the width of the rectangle. Use $\frac{22}{7}$ for π.   11 in.

2. Compare the area of a circle having a diameter of 14 in. with the area of a square with sides of 14 in. Use $\frac{22}{7}$ for π.
The area of the square is 42 in.^{2} larger.

Visual Thinking, pages 426–427

Draw a picture of how this solid figure would look from

1. the top.
2. the side.
3. the front.

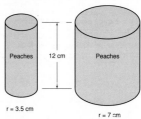

Logical Reasoning, pages 426–427

These two cans of peaches have the same unit price (price per ounce). The small can costs $1.28. What is the cost of the large can? $5.12

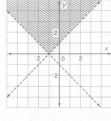

Chapter 12

Logical Reasoning, pages 440–441

Look for a pattern in the ordered pairs. Then complete the equation for the table of values.

1. $y = \blacksquare$
$2x$

x	y
3	6
2	4
1	2
0	0
⁻1	⁻2
⁻2	⁻4

2. $y = \blacksquare + \blacksquare$
$x, 4$

x	y
3	7
2	6
1	5
0	4
⁻1	3
⁻2	2

3. $y = \blacksquare - 3$
$2x$

x	y
3	3
2	1
1	⁻1
0	⁻3
⁻1	⁻5
⁻2	⁻7

Visual Thinking, pages 446–447

Without graphing any points, describe the graph of each relation.

1. all the points that have the same x coordinate
the y-axis or a line parallel to y-axis
2. all the points that have the same y coordinate
the x-axis or a line parallel to x-axis
3. all the points that have 0 as the x coordinate
the y-axis
4. all the points that have 0 as the y coordinate
the x-axis

Challenge, pages 450–451

1. Graph the equation $x + y = 6$ using 6, 3, 0, and ⁻3 as replacements for x.
(6,0), (3,3), (0,6), (⁻3,9)
Check students' graphs.

2. On the same set of axes, graph the equation $x - y = 6$. Use the same values for x that you used for $x + y = 6$.
(6,0), (3, ⁻3), (0, ⁻6), (⁻3, ⁻9)

3. How do the y values found for $x + y = 6$ compare to the y values found for $x - y = 6$?
They are opposites.

4. Where do the equations $x + y = 6$ and $x - y = 6$ intersect? Describe the relationship between the graphs of the equations. at (6,0); one is a reflection of the other.

Chapter 12

Challenge, pages 452–453

Graph each system of equations. Tell how many solutions there are for each system.
Check students' graphs.

1. $y = x + 2$
$2y = 2x + 4$
same line; infinite number of solutions

2. $y = x + 10$
$y = x - 1$
parallel lines; no solutions

Logical Reasoning, pages 454–455

What two numbers are not on the graph described by these clues?
5 and ⁻5
Clue 1: $|x| > 5$ **Clue 2:** $|x| < 5$

Challenge, pages 456–457

Graph the system of inequalities on the same coordinate axes to find the solution. Describe the solution of the system.
The solution is all the points that the graphs of the inequalities have in common.
$y > x + 1$
$y > ⁻x - 1$

TABLE OF MEASURES

TIME

1 minute (min) = 60 seconds (s)
1 hour (h) = 60 minutes
1 day (d) = 24 hours
1 week (wk) = 7 days
1 year (y) = 12 months (mo)
1 year = 52 weeks
1 year = 365 days
1 century = 100 years

METRIC UNITS

LENGTH

1 millimeter (mm) = 0.001 meter (m)
1 centimeter (cm) = 0.01 meter
1 decimeter (dm) = 0.1 meter
1 dekameter (dam) = 10 meters
1 hectometer (hm) = 100 meters
1 kilometer (km) = 1,000 meters

MASS

1 milligram (mg) = 0.001 gram (g)
1 centigram (cg) = 0.01 gram
1 decigram (dg) = 0.1 gram
1 dekagram (dek) = 10 grams
1 hectogram (hg) = 100 grams
1 kilogram (kg) = 1,000 grams
1 metric ton (t) = 1,000 kilograms

CAPACITY

1 milliliter (mL) = 0.001 liter (L)
1 centiliter (cL) = 0.01 liter
1 deciliter (dL) = 0.1 liter
1 dekaliter (daL) = 10 liters
1 hectoliter (hL) = 100 liters
1 kiloliter (kL) = 1,000 liters

VOLUME/CAPACITY/ MASS FOR WATER

1 cubic centimeter (cm^3) $\rightarrow$ 1 milliliter $\rightarrow$ 1 gram
1,000 cubic centimeters $\rightarrow$ 1 liter $\rightarrow$ 1 kilogram

TEMPERATURE

0° Celsius (C) . . . . Water freezes
100° Celsius (C) . . . . Water boils

CUSTOMARY UNITS

LENGTH

1 foot (ft) = 12 inches (in.)
1 yard (yd) = 36 inches
1 yard = 3 feet
1 mile (mi) = 5,280 feet
1 mile = 1,760 yards

WEIGHT

1 pound (lb) = 16 ounces (oz)
1 ton (T) = 2,000 pounds

CAPACITY

1 cup (c) = 8 fluid ounces (fl oz)
1 pint (pt) = 2 cups
1 quart (qt) = 2 pints
1 quart = 4 cups
1 gallon (gal) = 4 quarts

TEMPERATURE

32° Fahrenheit (F) . . . . Water freezes
212° Fahrenheit (F) . . . . Water boils

FORMULAS

PERIMETER	Polygon	$P = $ sum of the sides
	Rectangle	$P = 2l + 2w$
	Square	$P = 4s$
CIRCUMFERENCE	Circle	$C = 2\pi r$, or $C = \pi d$
AREA	Circle	$A = \pi r^2$
	Parallelogram	$A = bh$
	Rectangle	$A = lw$
	Square	$A = s^2$
	Trapezoid	$A = \frac{1}{2}(b_1 + b_2)h$
	Triangle	$A = \frac{1}{2}bh$
SURFACE AREA	Cone	$S = \pi r^2 + \pi rl$
	Cylinder	$S = 2\pi rh + 2\pi r^2$
	Rectangular prism	$S = 2lw + 2lh + 2wh$
	Square pyramid	$S = s^2 + 4\left(\frac{1}{2}bh\right)$
VOLUME	Cone	$V = \frac{1}{3}Bh$, or $V = \frac{1}{3}\pi r^2 h$
	Cube	$V = e^3$
	Cylinder	$V = Bh$, or $V = \pi r^2 h$
	Rectangular prism	$V = lwh$
	Square pyramid	$V = \frac{1}{3}Bh$
	Triangular prism	$V = \frac{1}{2}Bh$
OTHER	Diameter	$d = 2r$
	Pythagorean rule	$c^2 = a^2 + b^2$
TRIGONOMETRIC RATIOS	sine of $\angle A$	$\sin A = \frac{a}{c}$
	cosine of $\angle A$	$\cos A = \frac{b}{c}$
	tangent of $\angle A$	$\tan A = \frac{a}{b}$
CONSUMER	Distance traveled	$d = rt$
	Interest (simple)	$I = prt$

SYMBOLS

$<$	is less than	$^-4$	negative 4	$m\angle A$	measure of $\angle A$
$>$	is greater than	$|^-5|$	absolute value of negative 5	$\triangle ABC$	triangle ABC
$\leq$	is less than or equal to			$\perp$	is perpendicular to
$\geq$	is greater than or equal to	5^{-4}	5 to the negative fourth power	$\parallel$	is parallel to
$\neq$	is not equal to			$\cong$	is congruent to
$\approx$	is approximately equal to	$\%$	percent	$\leftrightarrow$	corresponds to
$2 \cdot 3$	2 times 3	$3:5$	the ratio 3 to 5	$\sim$	is similar to
$4 \div 2$	4 divided by 2	$\$4/h$	the rate \$4 per hour	π	pi (about 3.14)
5^4	5 to the fourth power	@	at a certain amount each	$(5,3)$	the ordered pair 5,3
$0.\overline{36}$	$0.363636\ldots$	$^\circ$	degree	$P(5)$	the probability of the outcome 5
$\sqrt{}$	square root	$\cdot A$	point A		
$\sqrt[3]{}$	cube root	$\overleftrightarrow{AB}$	line AB	$3!$	$3 \cdot 2 \cdot 1$
		$\overrightarrow{AB}$	ray AB	$_7P_4$	$7 \cdot 6 \cdot 5 \cdot 4$
		$\overline{AB}$	line segment AB	$_5C_2$	$\frac{5 \cdot 4}{2 \cdot 1}$
		$\angle ABC$	angle ABC		

GLOSSARY

Absolute value of a number An integer's distance from zero. The distance is never negative.

Examples: $|{}^-4| = 4$

$\qquad |4| = 4$

Acute angle An angle whose measure is less than 90°.

Adjacent angles Two angles that have a common vertex, a common ray, and no common interior points.

Example: $\angle WXY$ and $\angle YXZ$ are adjacent angles.

Alternate interior angles In the figure below, $\angle j$ and $\angle m$ are alternate interior angles, and so are $\angle k$ and $\angle l$.

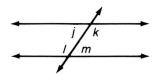

Angle Two rays that have a common endpoint. The endpoint is called the vertex of the angle.

Arc Part of a circle.

Associative Property of Addition The grouping of the addends does not change the sum. For any numbers a, b, and c, $a + (b + c) = (a + b) + c$.

Associative Property of Multiplication The grouping of the factors does not change the product. For all numbers a, b, and c, $(a \times b) \times c = a \times (b \times c)$.

BASIC A computer-programming language.

Basic counting principle If a first event has x outcomes and a second event has y outcomes, then the first event followed by the second event has $x \cdot y$ outcomes.

Binary A base-two system of numeration.

Bisect To divide into two congruent parts.

Bit Binary digit, 0 or 1.

Byte String of bits whose length is the smallest accessible unit in computer memory.

Central angle An angle whose vertex is at the center of a circle.

Chord A line segment whose endpoints are on a circle.

Circumference The perimeter of a circle.

Common factor A factor of two or more numbers. Example: 6 is a common factor of 12 and 18.

Common multiple A multiple of two or more numbers.

Example: 15 is a common multiple of 3 and 5.

Commutative Property of Addition The order of the addends does not change the sum. For any numbers a and b, $a + b = b + a$.

Commutative Property of Multiplication The order of the factors does not change the products. For any numbers a and b, $a \times b = b \times a$.

Complementary angles Two angles whose measures have a sum of 90°.

Complex fraction A fraction in which the numerator or denominator or both have a fraction or a mixed number as a term.

Example: $\dfrac{{}^-\frac{1}{4}}{3\frac{2}{3}}$

Composite number A number greater than 1 that has more than two factors.

Example: 12 is a composite number.
$\qquad$ Factors: 1, 2, 3, 4, 6, 12

Congruent figures Figures that have the same size and shape.

Coordinates Numbers matched with points on a line. Number pairs matched with points on a plane.

Corresponding angles In the figure below, pairs of corresponding angles are $\angle p$ and $\angle t$, $\angle q$ and $\angle u$, $\angle r$ and $\angle v$, $\angle s$ and $\angle w$.

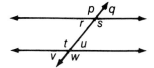

Corresponding parts In the triangles below, pairs of corresponding angles are $\angle U$ and $\angle X$, $\angle V$ and $\angle Z$, $\angle W$ and $\angle Y$. The corresponding sides are $\overline{ZY}$ and $\overline{VW}$, $\overline{VU}$ and $\overline{ZX}$, $\overline{UW}$ and $\overline{XY}$.

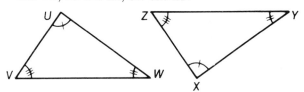

Cosine A trigonometric ratio, $\cos \angle A =$ $\dfrac{\text{length of side adjacent } \angle A}{\text{length of hypotenuse}}$, or $\dfrac{b}{c}$.

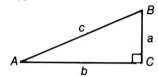

Cross products In the equation $\dfrac{w}{x} = \dfrac{y}{z}$, the products wz and xy are called cross products. Two ratios $\dfrac{w}{x}$ and $\dfrac{y}{z}$ are equal if, and only if, the product of the means $(x \cdot y)$ equals the product of the extremes $(w \cdot z)$.

Data A collection of facts that have not been processed into information.

Dependent events Events such that the outcome of the first event affects the probabilities of the outcome of the second event.

Diagonal A line segment other than a side that joins two vertices of a polygon.

Diameter A chord that passes through the center of a circle and has the length of two radii.

Discount Amount deducted from the marked price.

Distributive Property of Multiplication To multiply a sum by a number, you can multiply each addend by the number and then add the products. For any numbers a, b, and c, $a \times (b + c) = (a \times b) + (a \times c)$.

Endpoint A point at an end of a line segment or a ray.

Equally likely outcomes Outcomes that have the same chance of occurring.

Equation A number sentence that shows equality.

Examples: $5 + 6 = 11$, $4 + x = 31$

Equivalent fractions Fractions that name the same number, but use different terms.

Expanded form A representation of a number as a sum of multiples of powers of 10.

Exponent An exponent shows how many times a number or base is used as a factor.

Example: $8^4 = 8 \times 8 \times 8 \times 8$: 4 is the exponent.

Expression (algebraic) Symbols or the combination of symbols, such as numerals, letters, operation symbols, and parentheses, used to name a number.

Extremes In a proportion, the first and fourth terms are the extremes.

Example: $\dfrac{3}{4} = \dfrac{9}{12}$
3 and 12 are the extremes.

Factorial If $x > 0$, then x factorial is written $x!$ and means to multiply all the consecutive numbers from x to 1.

Example: $7! = 7 \times 6 \times 5 \times 4 \times 3 \times 2 \times 1 = 5,040$

FOR/NEXT A two-part BASIC command that makes a computer count and loop.

Fraction The quotient of two whole numbers; $x \div y = \dfrac{x}{y}$, $y \neq 0$. In the fraction $\dfrac{x}{y}$, x is called the *numerator* and y is called the *denominator*.

Frequency The number of times an item appears in a list of data.

GOTO A BASIC command that makes a computer go to the line number that follows.

Graph of an equation A picture of all solutions to an equation.

Greatest common factor The largest common factor of two or more numbers.

Example: For 12 and 20, 4 is the greatest common factor.

Greatest possible error One half the smallest unit of measurement used.

Histogram A bar graph that shows the frequencies of intervals of data.

HOME A BASIC command that tells a computer to move the cursor to the start of the first line on a CRT screen.

Hypotenuse In a right triangle, the side opposite the right angle.

IF/THEN A BASIC command that tells a computer to make a decision.

Example: IF N < 7 THEN 40 tells a computer to go to line 40 if the number in storage place N is less than 7; otherwise it is to go to the next line.

Independent events Events in which the outcome of the second event does not depend on the outcome of the first event.

Inequality A number sentence that uses a symbol such as $>$, $<$, $\leq$, $\geq$, or $\neq$.

Example: $x - 7 < 8$, $x + 14 > 21$, $6x \neq 18$

Infinite Continues without end; endless.

INPUT A BASIC command that tells a computer to wait for input and then to store the input in its memory.

INT In a BASIC computer program, INT(X) makes a computer cut off all the digits of the number X to the right of the decimal point.

Integers The whole-numbers and their opposites.

Examples: 0, 1, ⁻1, 2, ⁻2

Interest Payment for use of money.

Intersecting lines Lines that meet at one common point.

Inverse operations Operations that undo each other. Addition and subtraction as well as multiplication and division are inverse operations.

Example: $17 + 31 = 48$ and $48 - 31 = 17$
$36 \div 9 = 4$ and $4 \times 9 = 36$

Irrational number A number that cannot be written as a terminating or repeating decimal.

Examples: 0.161661666 . . .

Least Common Denominator (LCD) The least common multiple of the denominators of two or more fractions.

Least Common Multiple The smallest nonzero common multiple of two or more numbers.

Example: For 8 and 12, 24 is the least common multiple.

Legs of a right triangle The perpendicular sides of a right triangle.

LET A BASIC command that tells a computer to store information in its memory.

Line A straight path of points that continues infinitely in two directions.

Line segment Part of a line with two endpoints.

Loop A command that causes a computer to go back to an earlier step in the program and repeat it.

Mean The sum of the numbers divided by the number of addends.

Example: The mean for 22, 33, 19, 8 is 20.5.

Means In a proportion, the second and third terms are the means.

Example: $\dfrac{2}{3} = \dfrac{8}{12}$
3 and 8 are the means.

Median When a set of numbers are arranged in order, the middle number or the average of the middle two numbers.

Examples: The median for 56, 73, 77, 84, 94 is 77.
The median for 38, 42, 48, 51 is 45.

Midpoint A point that separates a line segment into two congruent segments.

Mixed number The sum of a whole number and a fraction.

Mode The number occurring most often in a set of data.

Multiple Any product that has the number as a factor.

NEW A command that tells some computers to erase any programs or information stored in their memories.

Obtuse angle An angle whose measure is greater than 90° and less than 180°.

Opposite A number that is an equal distance from zero as another number, but in the opposite direction.

Example: $8 + {}^-8 = 0$
8 is the opposite of $^-8$.
$^-8$ is the opposite of 8.

Ordered pair A pair of numbers (x,y) arranged in order so that x is first and y is second, usually used to describe a location in a coordinate plane.

Order of operations When there is more than one operation used; first multiply as indicated by exponents; second, multiply and divide from left to right in order; third, add and subtract from left to right in order, and; fourth, if parentheses are used, simplify within the parentheses first, using the first three rules.

Origin The point assigned to 0 on the number line or the point where the x- and y-axes intersect.

Outcome Any possible result in a probability experiment.

Parallel lines Two or more lines in a plane that do not intersect.

Parallelogram A quadrilateral in which each pair of opposite sides is parallel and congruent.

Percent Ratio of a number to 100, using the % sign.

Example: 13% means 13 of 100.

Permutation An ordered arrangement of some or all of the elements in a set. For example, there are 6 permutations of 2 letters from the 3 letters X, Y, and Z. The permutations are XY, XZ, YX, YZ, ZX, and ZY.

Perpendicular bisector A line that bisects a segment and is perpendicular to it.

Perpendicular lines Two lines that intersect to form right angles.

Pi (π) The number that is the ratio of the circumference of any circle to the length of a diameter of that circle. Approximations for π are 3.14 and $\dfrac{22}{7}$.

Plane A flat surface that continues infinitely in all directions.

Polygon A closed plane figure made up of three or more line segments joined at their endpoints.

Polyhedron A solid whose faces are polygons.

Power of a number A number found by multiplying another number by itself one or more times.

Example: 64 is a power of 4 because $64 = 4 \times 4 \times 4$.

Prime factorization A factorization in which all factors are prime numbers.

Example: $40 = 2 \times 2 \times 2 \times 5$

Prime number Any whole number greater than 1, whose only factors are itself and 1.

Principal The amount of money borrowed or saved on which interest is paid.

Prism A polyhedron that has two congruent bases in parallel planes and whose other faces are parallelograms.

Probability The number of favorable outcomes divided by the number of all possible outcomes. A number from 0 to 1.

Program Step-by-step instruction that directs the computer to perform operations.

Property of One The product of a number multiplied by 1, and the quotient of a number divided by 1 are the number itself. For any number a, $a \times 1 = a$, $a \div 1 = a$.

Proportion An equation that shows two equal ratios.

Example: $\dfrac{5}{10} = \dfrac{1}{2}$

Pythagorean Rule In any right triangle, the sum of the squares of the lengths of the legs is equal to the square of the length of the hypotenuse. $a^2 + b^2 = c^2$.

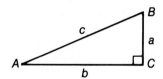

Quadrants The x-axis and y-axis divide the real-number plane into four parts called quadrants.

Quadrilateral A polygon that has four sides.

Radius A line segment from a point on a circle to the center of the circle.

RAM The part of the memory of a computer where the user can store information and programs. *RAM* stands for "Random Access Memory." This part of the memory is erased when NEW is entered.

Range The difference between the largest and the smallest number in a set of data.

Rate A ratio that compares different kinds of units.

Ratio Comparison of two numbers by division.

Rational number A number that can be written as the ratio of two integers, where the denominator is not zero.

Ray A part of a line that has one endpoint and continues infinitely in one direction.

Real numbers The set of rational and irrational numbers, whole numbers, and integers.

Reciprocals Two numbers whose product is 1.

Example: $\dfrac{7}{8}$ and $\dfrac{8}{7}$ are reciprocals of each other, because $\dfrac{7}{8} \times \dfrac{8}{7} = 1$.

Reflection A motion in which a geometric figure is flipped about a line.

Regular polygon A polygon with congruent sides and congruent angles.

Relatively prime Two numbers whose only common factor is 1.

Example: 4 and 9 are relatively prime.

Repeating decimal A decimal in which one or more digits repeat endlessly.

Examples: $0.\overline{6}$ and $0.\overline{18}$

Right angle An angle that measures 90°.

Rotation A motion in which a geometric figure is turned about a fixed point.

Sample A segment of a population selected for study to predict characteristics of the whole.

Sample space A set of possible outcomes of an experiment.

Example: If a coin is flipped, the sample space is (H, T)

Scattergram A graph of ordered pairs of points showing positive, negative or no correlation between two sets of data.

Scientific notation Expressing a number as a product of two factors. One factor is a power of 10. The other factor is greater than or equal to 1 and less than 10.

Example: 4.72×10^5 is scientific notation for 472,000.

Significant digits The digits used in a measurement that tell the number of times the unit is contained in the measurement.

Similar polygons Two polygons that have the same shape, but not necessarily the same size.

Simplest form A fraction is in simplest form when its numerator and denominator are relatively prime.

Sine A trigonometric ratio. sin $\angle A$ =

$\dfrac{\text{length of side opposite } \angle A}{\text{length of hypotenuse}}$, or $\dfrac{a}{c}$.

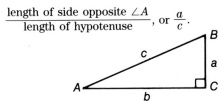

Skew lines Lines in space that are not parallel and do not intersect.

Slant height The distance along a face of a pyramid or a cone from the vertex to the base.

Solution A replacement of a variable that makes a number sentence true.

Example: $3x - 12 = 9$ 7 is the solution.

         $x > 17$ 18, 19, 20, 21, . . . are solutions.

Square root A number when multiplied by itself gives the original number.

Example: 6 is the square root of 36.

Straight angle An angle whose measure is 180°.

String variables In BASIC, locations in a computer that store data of any kind. A letter and the $ symbol form string variables. $A\$$, $B\$$, etc.

Supplementary angles Two angles whose measures have a sum of 180°.

Symmetry The correspondence of parts on opposite sides of a point, line, or plane.

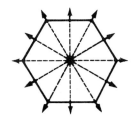

Tangent A trigonometric ratio. tan $\angle A$ =

$\dfrac{\text{length of side opposite } \angle A}{\text{length of side adjacent to } \angle A}$

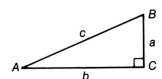

Terminating decimal A decimal that does not repeat.

Example: 0.25

Translation A translation moves a geometric figure along a line to a new position.

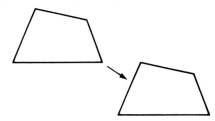

Transversal A line intersecting two or more lines at a different point on each line. $\overleftrightarrow{CD}$ is a transversal.

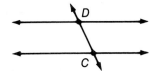

Tree diagram A diagram used to find the total number of outcomes in a probability experiment.

Unit price The ratio of the total price to the number of units.

Variable A letter or other symbol that may represent a number.

Vertex A point common to two rays of an angle, two sides of a polygon, or two edges of a solid figure.

Vertical angles Congruent angles formed by two intersecting lines. $\angle 3$ and $\angle 4$ form a pair of vertical angles.

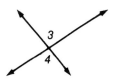

Whole number Any of these numbers: 0, 1, 2, 3, 4, 5, 6, . . .

Zero Property for Addition and Subtraction The sum or difference when zero is added to or subtracted from a number is the number. For any number a, $a + 0 = a$ and $a - 0 = a$.

Zero Property for Multiplication The product of a number and 0 is 0. For any number a, $a \times 0 = 0$.

Index